Handy A-Z GB BRITAIN

CONTENTS

Reference and Tourist Information...................... 2-3

Road Maps at approx. 5 miles to 1" (1:307,865)..... 4-169

Outer Hebrides at 9.72 miles to 1" (1:615,730)....... 170-171

Northern Isles at 9.72 miles to 1" (1:615,730)........ 172-173

Channel Tunnel Map...................................... 174

Mileage Chart... 175

Route Planning Maps..................................... 176-179

Index to Towns, Villages & Hamlets..................... 180-256

Geographers' A-Z Map Company Ltd.

Fairfield Road, Borough Green, Sevenoaks, Kent TN15 8PP
Telephone : 01732 781000 (Enquiries & Trade Sales)
01732 783422 (Retail Sales)

Edition 21 2013   Copyright © Geographers' A-Z Map Company Ltd.
An AtoZ publication

REFERENCE	Légende	Zeichenerklärung
MOTORWAY — M1	Autoroute — M1	Autobahn — M1
MOTORWAY UNDER CONSTRUCTION	Autoroute en construction	Autobahn im Bau
MOTORWAY PROPOSED	Autoroute prévue	Geplante Autobahn
MOTORWAY JUNCTIONS WITH NUMBERS — Unlimited interchange 4 / Limited interchange 5	Echangeur numéroté — Echangeur non limité 4 / Echangeur limité 5	Autobahnanschlußstelle mit Nummer — Unbeschränkter Fahrtrichtungswechsel 4 / Beschränkter Fahrtrichtungswechsel 5
MOTORWAY SERVICE AREA — HESTON — with access from one carriageway only	Aire de services d'autoroute — HESTON — à sens unique	Rastplatz oder Raststätte — HESTON — Einbahn
MAJOR ROAD SERVICE AREAS — with 24 hour Facilities — Primary Route LEEMING — Class A Road OLDBURY	Aire de services de route prioriataire — Ouverte 24h sur 24 — Route à grande circulation LEEMING — Route de type A OLDBURY	Raststätte — Durchgehend geöffnet — Hauptverkehrsstraße LEEMING — A-Straße OLDBURY
TRUCKSTOP (Selected) — T	Choix d'aire pour poids lourds — T	Auswahl von Fernfahrerrastplatz — T
PRIMARY ROUTE — A41	Route à grande circulation — A41	Hauptverkehrsstraße — A41
PRIMARY ROUTE JUNCTION WITH NUMBER — 5	Echangeur numéroté — 5	Hauptverkehrsstraßenkreuzung mit Nummer — 5
PRIMARY ROUTE DESTINATION — **DOVER**	Route prioritaire, direction — **DOVER**	Hauptverkehrsstraße Richtung — **DOVER**
DUAL CARRIAGEWAYS (A & B Roads)	Route à deux chaussées séparées (route A & B)	Zweispurige Schnellstraße (A- und B-Straßen)
CLASS A ROAD — A129	Route de type A — A129	A-Straße — A129
CLASS B ROAD — B177	Route de type B — B177	B-Straße — B177
NARROW MAJOR ROAD (Passing Places)	Route prioritaire étroite (possibilité de dépassement)	Schmale Hauptverkehrsstraße (mit Überholmöglichkeit)
MAJOR ROADS UNDER CONSTRUCTION	Route prioritaire en construction	Hauptverkehrsstraße im Bau
MAJOR ROADS PROPOSED	Route prioritaire prévue	Geplante Hauptverkehrsstraße
GRADIENT 1:5(20%) & STEEPER (Ascent in direction of arrow)	Pente égale ou supérieure à 20% (dans le sens de la montée)	20% Steigung und steiler (in Pfeilrichtung)
TOLL	Péage	Gebührenpflichtig
MILEAGE BETWEEN MARKERS — 8	Distance en milles entre les flèches — 8	Strecke zwischen Markierungen in Meilen — 8
RAILWAY AND STATION	Voie ferrée et gare	Eisenbahnlinie und Bahnhof
LEVEL CROSSING AND TUNNEL	Passage à niveau et tunnel	Bahnübergang und Tunnel
RIVER OR CANAL	Rivière ou canal	Fluß oder Kanal
COUNTY OR UNITARY AUTHORITY BOUNDARY	Limite des comté ou de division administrative	Grafschafts- oder Verwaltungsbezirksgrenze
NATIONAL BOUNDARY	Frontière nationale	Landesgrenze
BUILT-UP AREA	Agglomération	Geschlossene Ortschaft
VILLAGE OR HAMLET	Village ou hameau	Dorf oder Weiler
WOODED AREA	Zone boisée	Waldgebiet
SPOT HEIGHT IN FEET · 813	Altitude (en pieds) · 813	Höhe in Fuß · 813
HEIGHT ABOVE SEA LEVEL — 400'-1,000' 122m-305m / 1,000'-1,400' 305m-427m / 1,400'-2,000' 427m-610m / 2,000'+ 610m+	Altitude par rapport au niveau de la mer — 400'-1,000' 122m-305m / 1,000'-1,400' 305m-427m / 1,400'-2,000' 427m-610m / 2,000'+ 610m+	Höhe über Meeresspiegel — 400'-1,000' 122m-305m / 1,000'-1,400' 305m-427m / 1,400'-2,000' 427m-610m / 2,000'+ 610m+
NATIONAL GRID REFERENCE (Kilometres) ¹00	Coordonnées géographiques nationales (Kilometres) ¹00	Nationale geographische Koordinaten (Kilometer) ¹00
PAGE CONTINUATION — 48	Suite à la page indiquée — 48	Seitenfortsetzung — 48

```
0   1   2   3   4   5            10                    15                    20 Miles
0   1   2   3   4   5          10         15         20         25         30 Kilometres
```

Tourist Information		Information		Touristeninformationen	
AIRPORT	⊕	Aéroport	⊕	Flughafen	⊕
AIRFIELD	+	Terrain d' aviation	+	Flugplatz	+
HELIPORT	✈	Héliport	✈	Hubschrauberlandeplatz	✈
BATTLE SITE AND DATE	⚔ 1066	Champ de bataille et date	⚔ 1066	Schlachtfeld und Datum	⚔ 1066
CASTLE (Open to Public)	🏰	Château (ouvert au public)	🏰	Schloss / Burg (für die Öffentlichkeit zugänglich)	🏰
CASTLE WITH GARDEN (Open to Public)	🏰	Château avec parc (ouvert au public)	🏰	Schloß mit Garten (für die Öffentlichkeit zugänglich)	🏰
CATHEDRAL, ABBEY, CHURCH, FRIARY, PRIORY	✝	Cathédrale, abbaye, église, monastere, prieuré	✝	Kathedrale, Abtei, Kirche, Mönchskloster, Kloster	✝
COUNTRY PARK	⛺	Parc régonal	⛺	Landschaftspark	⛺
FERRY (Vehicular, sea) (Vehicular, river) (Foot only)	⛴ ⛴ 👥	Bac (véhicules, mer) (véhicules, rivière) (Piétons)	⛴ ⛴ 👥	Fähre (Autos, meer) (Autos, fluß) (nur für Personen)	⛴ ⛴ 👥
GARDEN (Open to Public)	✿	Jardin (ouvert au public)	✿	Garten (für die Öffentlichkeit zugänglich)	✿
GOLF COURSE (9 Hole) (18 Hole)	🏌 🏌	Terrain de golf (9 trous) (18 trous)	🏌 🏌	Golfplatz (9 Löcher) (18 Löcher)	🏌 🏌
HISTORIC BUILDING (Open to Public)	🏛	Monument historique (ouvert au public)	🏛	Historisches Gebäude (für die Öffentlichkeit zugänglich)	🏛
HISTORIC BUILDING WITH GARDEN (Open to Public)	🏛	Monument historique avec jardin (ouvert au public)	🏛	Historisches Gebäude mit Garten (für die Öffentlichkeit zugänglich)	🏛
HORSE RACECOURSE	🏇	Hippodrome	🏇	Pferderennbahn	🏇
LIGHTHOUSE	🗼	Phare	🗼	Leuchtturm	🗼
MOTOR RACING CIRCUIT	🏎	Circuit automobile	🏎	Automobilrennbahn	🏎
MUSEUM, ART GALLERY	🖼	Musée	🖼	Museum, Galerie	🖼
NATIONAL PARK	——	Parc national	——	Nationalpark	——
NATIONAL TRUST PROPERTY (Open) (Restricted Opening) (National Trust for Scotland)	NT NT NTS NTS	National Trust Property (ouvert) (heures d'ouverture) (National Trust for Scotland)	NT NT NTS NTS	National Trust-Eigentum (geöffnet) (beschränkte Öffnungszeit) (National Trust for Scotland)	NT NT NTS NTS
NATURE RESERVE OR BIRD SANCTUARY	🐦	Réserve naturelle botanique ou ornithologique	🐦	Natur- oder Vogelschutzgebiet	🐦
NATURE TRAIL OR FOREST WALK	🍃	Chemin forestier, piste verte	🍃	Naturpfad oder Waldweg	🍃
PLACE OF INTEREST	Monument •	Site, curiosité	Monument •	Sehenswürdigkeit	Monument •
PICNIC SITE	⛱	Lieu pour pique-nique	⛱	Picknickplatz	⛱
RAILWAY, STEAM OR NARROW GAUGE	🚂	Chemin de fer, à vapeur ou à voie étroite	🚂	Eisenbahn, Dampf- oder Schmalspurbahn	🚂
THEME PARK	🎢	Centre de loisir	🎢	Vergnügungspark	🎢
TOURIST INFORMATION CENTRE	ℹ	Syndicat d'initiative	ℹ	Information	ℹ
VIEWPOINT (360 degrees) (180 degrees)	☀ ☀	Vue panoramique (360 degrés) (180 degrés)	☀ ☀	Aussichtspunkt (360 Grade) (180 Grade)	☀ ☀
VISITOR INFORMATION CENTRE	V	Centre d'information touristique	V	Besucherzentrum	V
WILDLIFE PARK	🦌	Réserve de faune	🦌	Wildpark	🦌
WINDMILL	🏚	Moulin à vent	🏚	Windmühle	🏚
ZOO OR SAFARI PARK	🐘	Parc ou réserve zoologique	🐘	Zoo oder Safari-Park	🐘

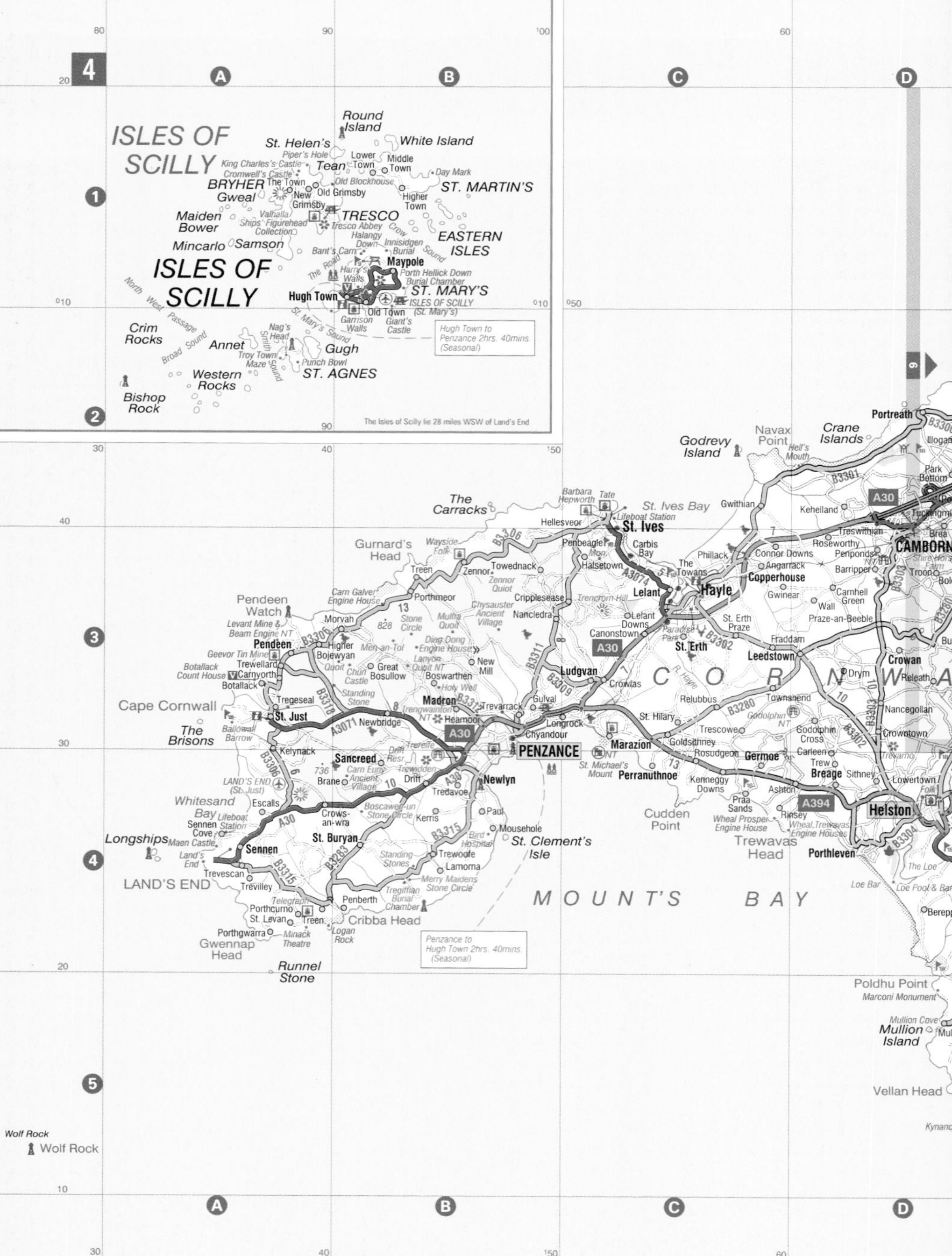

4
ISLES OF SCILLY
Round Island
St. Helen's
White Island
Piper's Hole
King Charles's Castle
Tean
Lower Town
Middle Town
Cromwell's Castle
Day Mark
BRYHER
The Town
Old Blockhouse
ST. MARTIN'S
Gweal
New Grimsby
Old Grimsby
Higher Town
Maiden Bower
Valhalla Ships' Figurehead Collection
TRESCO
Tresco Abbey
Crow Sound
EASTERN ISLES
Mincarlo
Samson
Halangy Down
Innisidgen Burial
Bant's Carn
Maypole
ISLES OF SCILLY
North West Passage
The Road
Harry's Walls
Porth Hellick Down Burial Chamber
Hugh Town
ST. MARY'S
ISLES OF SCILLY (St. Mary's)
Old Town
Garrison Walls
Giant's Castle
Crim Rocks
St. Mary's Sound
Nag's Head
Hugh Town to Penzance 2hrs. 40mins. (Seasonal)
Broad Sound
Annet
Gugh
Smith Sound
Troy Town Maze
Punch Bowl
Western Rocks
ST. AGNES
Bishop Rock
The Isles of Scilly lie 28 miles WSW of Land's End
6
Portreath
Navax Point
Crane Islands
Godrevy Island
Hell's Mouth
Illogan
Park Bottom
A30
The Carracks
Barbara Hepworth
Tate
St. Ives Bay
Gwithian
Kehelland
Lifeboat Station
Hellesveor
St. Ives
Treswithian
CAMBORNE
Gurnard's Head
Wayside Folk
B3306
Penbeagle
Carbis Bay
Roseworthy
Connor Downs
Penponds
Phillack
Treen
Zennor
Towednack
Halsetown
The Towans
Angarrack
Barripper
Troon
Zennor Quoit
A3074
Copperhouse
Carn Galver Engine House
Porthmeor
Lelant
Hayle
Gwinear
Carnhell Green
Pendeen Watch
Chysauster Ancient Village
Cripplesease
Trencrom Hill
Wall
Mulfra Quoit
Nancledra
Lelant Downs
Praze-an-Beeble
Levant Mine & Beam Engine NT
Morvah
Stone Circle
Canonstown
Paradise Park
St. Erth Praze
Pendeen
Higher Bojewyan
Men-an-Tol
Ding Dong Engine House
B3302
Fraddam
Geevor Tin Mine
Lanyon Quoit NT
New Mill
A30
St. Erth
Leedstown
Crowan
Botallack Count House
Trewellard
Carnyorth
Chûn Castle
Great Bosullow
Boswarthen
Ludgvan
B3311
CORNWALL
Drym
Releath
Botallack
Standing Stone
Holy Well
Crowlas
Cape Cornwall
Tregeseal
B3318
Madron
Trengwainton NT
Relubbus
Townshend
Nancegollan
St. Just
Newbridge
Heamoor
Trevarrack
Gulval
St. Hilary
B3280
Godolphin NT
The Brisons
Ballowall Barrow
A3071
Longrock
Trescowe
Godolphin Cross
Crowntown
Chyandour
Goldsithney
Kelynack
Drift Resr
PENZANCE
Marazion
Rosudgeon
Germoe
Carleen
Sancreed
Carn Euny Ancient Village
St. Michael's Mount NT
Perranuthnoe
Trew
LAND'S END (St. Just)
Brane
Trewidden
Drift
Newlyn
Breage
Sithney
Lowertown
Tredavoe
Kenneggy Downs
Ashton
Whitesand Bay
Escalls
Boscawen-un Stone Circle
Cudden Point
Praa Sands
A394
Helston
Crows-an-wra
Kerris
Paul
Rinsey
Lifeboat Station
Wheal Prosper Engine House
Wheal Trewavas Engine Houses
Sennen Cove
Maen Castle
St. Buryan
B3315
Mousehole
Longships
Bird Hospital
St. Clement's Isle
Trewavas Head
Sennen
Trewoofe
Porthleven
Land's End
Standing Stones
Lamorna
The Loe
Trevescan
Merry Maidens Stone Circle
LAND'S END
Trevilley
B3283
Loe Bar
Loe Pool
Telegraph
Penberth
Tregiffian Burial Chamber
MOUNT'S BAY
Porthcurno
St. Levan
Treen
Cribba Head
Logan Rock
Porthgwarra
Minack Theatre
Gwennap Head
Penzance to Hugh Town 2hrs. 40mins. (Seasonal)
Runnel Stone
Poldhu Point
Marconi Monument
Mullion Cove
Mullion Island
Vellan Head
Wolf Rock
Wolf Rock
A
B
C
D
1
2
3
4
5

Watergate Bay
Tregurrian
NEWQUAY CORNWALL
Vale of Mawgan
Gluvian
A39
St. Wenn
B3274
Tregonetha
Demelza
Retire
Lamorick
Lanivet
Tregullon
Towan Head
Huer's Hut
NEWQUAY
Newquay Bay
St. Columb Minor
Porth
A3059
Trebarber
St. Columb Major
703
744
Belowda
Trekenning
Trebudannon
Port Resr.
Colan
Mountjoy
A392
Black Cross
Screech Owl Sanctuary
Ruthvoes
Trevarren
A30
Goss Moor
Roche
Victoria
A391
Bilberry
Lockengate
Sweetshouse
Trebyan
Lanhydrock
Bokiddick
Maudlin
5
Fistral Bay
Kelsey Head
Pentire
West Pentire
Crantock
Trencreek
Blue Reef Aquarium
6
Holywell Bay
Holywell
Quintrell Downs
Penhale Point
Holywell Bay Fun Park
Penhale Camp
Cubert
DairyLand Farm World
Kestle Mill
NT Trerice
A3075
A3058
St. Columb Road
Indian Queens
Fraddon
Enniscaven
St. Dennis
Roche Rock
B3274
Hensbarrow Downs
1025
Bugle
Rosevean
Rescorla
Stenalees
Lanlivery
A390
Luxulyan
Hidden Valley
Penpillick
Ligger or Perran Bay
Mount
St. Piran's Oratory
Rejerrah
St. Newlyn East
Lappa Valley Steam Railway
A3076
St. Enoder
Penhale
Summercourt
B3275
Hendra
Whitemoor
Treviscoe
B3279
Nanpean
Carthew
Penwithick
Trethurgy
Eden Project
Tywardreath Highway
Perranzabuloe
Rose
St. Piran's Round
Perranporth
Bolingey
Goonhavern
Chapel Town
Mitchell
Brighton
Menna
Trethosa
Goonabarn
Foxhole
China Clay Country Park
A391
St. Blazey
Tregrehan Mills
St. Blazey Gate
Tywardreath
Par
A3082
Bawden Rocks
Carnkief
Newlyn Downs
490
Carland Cross
Trendeal
Carpalla
High Street
A3058
St. AUSTELL
St. Stephen
Trewoon
Boscoppa
Holmbush
Polkerris
St. Agnes Head
Lifeboat Station
Trevellas
B3285
Zelah
Trelassick
New Mills
Coombe
St. Mewan
Tregorrick
Charlestown
Carlyon Bay
Menabilly
St. Agnes
Perranzabuloe
Penhallow
Cyder Farm
Callestick
St. Allen
Trispen
Tregear
Ladock
Downderry
Polgooth
London Apprentice
Higher Porthpean
St. Austell Bay
Wheal Coates Engine House
Mithian
Goonbell
Goonvrea
Coldharbour
A3075
Allet
St. Erme
Grampound Road
A390
Sticker
Hewas Water
Tortoise Garden
B3273
Daymark NT
Mount Hawke
B3277
A30
B3284
Shortlanesend
Idless
Probus
Trewithen
Grampound
Rescorla
Trenarren
Black Head
7
35mins. (Seasonal)
Three Burrows
A390
Kenwyn
Tresillian
Creed
Lost Gardens of Heligan
Pentewan
St. Ewe
Tregiskey
Mawla
Blackwater
Rly. Cornwall Cathedral
Mevagissey Bay
2
Cambrose
Greenbottom
Chacewater
Roseland House
Threemilestone
Highertown
Boswyn
TRURO
A390
Merther
A3078
Polmassick
Polmassick Vineyard
Kestle
Tregony
Mevagissey
Portmellon
World of Model Railways
Scorrier
Wheal Busy Engine House
Hugus
Skinner's Brewery
St. Clement
Trevarrick
Gorran High Lanes
Chapel Point
Mount Ambrose
St. Day
A3047
Kea
Malpas
Rescassa
Gorran Churchtown
REDRUTH
Carharrack
Twelveheads
A39
Old Kea
St. Michael Penkevil
Lamorran
Ruan Lanihorne
St. Michael Caerhays
Caerhays Castle
Boswinger
Gorran Haven
Carn Brea Village
Gwennap Pit
Bissoe
Carnon Downs
Playing Place
Coombe
Veryan Green
Portholland
Cusgarne
Gwennap
Penelewey
Ruan High Lanes
Melinsey Mill
Trist House
Veryan Bay
Penare
Cliff Castle
Lanner
Perranwell
Penpol
Trelissick NT
Trelissick
Philleigh
Veryan
Portloe
Dodman Point
Burncoose Nurseries
Devoran
Feock
Treworthal
Carne
Four Lanes
Penhalvean
Perranarworthal
Harcourt
Gerrans Bay
Gull Rock
Ponsanooth
Mylor Bridge
Lanterns
Carrick Roads
St. Just in Roseland
Trewithian
Nare Head
828
Stithians
Stithians Lake
Stithians Reservoir
A393
B3292
Mylor Churchtown
St. Gluvias
St. Just
A3078
Gerrans
Portscatho
3
Penmarth
Carnkie
Rame
Penryn
Flushing
Greeb Point
Porkellis
Longdowns
Mabe Burnthouse
A39
FALMOUTH
St. Mawes
St. Anthony
Bohortha
A394
Budock Water
Trenear
Treverva
Pendennis
Pendennis Point
St. Anthony Battery
Zone Point
Wendron
Seworgan
Penjerrick
Maenporth
Falmouth Bay
6
Brill
Potager
Constantine
Carlidnack
Mawnan Smith
Carwinion
Rosemullion Head
Trewennack
Glendurgan
Porth Navas
Trebah
Mawnan
Gweek
Seal Sanctuary
Helford
Helford River
Bosahan
St. Anthony-in-Meneage
Culdrose
Mawgan
Halliggye Fogou
Gillan
Nare Point
4
Manaccan
Garras
St. Martin
B3293
Roskorwell
Porthallow
Newtown-in-St. Martin
Tregarne
White Cross
Cross Lanes
Tregowris
Giant Quoits
Porthoustock
Manacle Point
Traboe
Lanarth
369
St. Keverne
The Manacles
Cury
Bonython Estate
Goonhilly Downs
Roskilly's Organic Farm
Mullion
Raised Beach
B3294
Trelan
B3296
Penhale
Ponsongath
Coverack
Gwenter
Cove
Ruan Major
Kuggar
A3083
Poltesco
St. Ruan
Ruan Minor
Black Head
5
Cadgwith
TOLL
Devil's Frying Pan
Lizard
Hot Point
Lizard
LIZARD POINT
E
F
G
H
70
80
90
200
60
50
40
30
20
10

Padstow
Wadebridge
NEWQUAY
St. Columb Major
St. Austell
TRURO
REDRUTH
CAMBORNE
FALMOUTH
Penryn
Helston
Perranporth
St. Agnes
Mevagissey
St. Mawes
TREVOSE HEAD
Trevone
Rock
St. Minver
Port Isaac
Polzeath
Pentire Point
Padstow Bay
Constantine Bay
Watergate Bay
Fistral Bay
Crantock
Kelsey Head
Holywell Bay
Penhale Point
Ligger or Perran Bay
Bawden Rocks
St. Agnes Head
Portreath
Crane Islands
Indian Queens
St. Dennis
Roche
Bugle
Probus
Grampound
Tregony
Veryan
Portscatho
Gerrans Bay
Nare Head
Gull Rock
Veryan Bay
Dodman Point
Zone Point
Pendennis Point
Falmouth Bay
Rosemullion Head
Carrick Roads
Chacewater
Stithians
Perranarworthal
Devoran
Constantine
Gweek
Mawnan
Crowan
Breage
Wendron
Goonhavern
St. Newlyn East
Mitchell
Ladock
Tresillian
Summercourt
Fraddon
A30
A39
A390
A392
A3059
A3058
A3075
A3076
A3078
A389
A393
A394
B3276
B3274
B3275
B3285
B3284
B3277
B3300
B3301
B3297
B3303
B3280
B3287
B3289
B3314
B3267
B3273
70
80
90
200
60
50
A
B
C
D
1
2
3
4
5

Treligga
Delabole
Rockhead
Slate Quarry
Trevia
Camelford
Tregoodwell
Crowdy Resr.
St. Clether
Holy Well
St. Clether
Laneast
Pipers Pool
Launceston
Tregadillett
Lifton
Tinhay
Dippertown
Westdowns
Pengelly
Valley
Trewalder Truck
Pencarrow
Charlotte Dymond Monument
Bowithick
Trewen
R. Inny
South Petherwin
Daw's House
Lawrence House
Lawhitton
Marystow
Helstone
Tresinney
Treween
Polyphant
Tregada
Meadwell
Kelly
Chillaton
St. Teath
Hut Circles
Rough Tor
Altarnun
Wesley Cottage
Tredaule
Fivelanes
Lewannick
Trewarlett
Bradstone
Abbot
Pendoggett
Treveighan
Stone Circle
Brown Willy
Michaelstow
Fentonadle
Trevadlock
Congdon's Shop
Illand
Newtown
Lezant
Trekenner
Dunterton
Hotel Endsleigh
Chado
Trelill
St. Breward
King Arthur's Hall
Garrow Tor
Codda
B O D M I N
Treburley
Trebullett
Rezare
Coad's Green
Bealsmill
Sydenham Damerel
Rushf
St. Tudy
Row
Lank
De Lank R.
Daphne Du Maurier's Smugglers
Bolventor
Jamaica Inn
Trebartha
North Hill
Tutwell
St. Kew Highway
Wenfordbridge
Stripple Stones
M O O R
River
Middlewood
Venterdon
Penpont
Jubilee Rock
Dozmary Pool
Kilmar Tor
Bathpool
Bray Shop
Stoke Climsland
Horsebridge
Blisland
Colliford Lake
Henwood
Rilla Mill
Old Mill
Luckett
Latchley
St. Mabyn
Old Mill Herbary
Waterloo
Temple
Brown Gelly Barrows
Fowey
Cheesewring
Linkinhorne
Plushabridge
South Hill
Downgate
Chilsworthy
Croanford
Hellandbridge
Colliford Lake
The Hurlers
Minions
Upton
Upton Cross
Kelly Bray
Kit Hill
St. Ann's Chapel
Gunnis
Pencarrow
Helland
Maidenwell
Danger Area
Millpool
Siblyback Lake
Heritage Centre
Caradon Hill
Caradon Town
Golberdon
Washaway
Churchyard Cross
Bury Castle
Downgate
Darite
Haye
Trevigro
Callington
Albaston
Drakewalls
Metherell
Harrowbarrow
Cotehele Quay
Morwellham
C O R N W A L L
Bodmin
Berry Tower
Cardinham
Warleggan
Fawton
St. Neot
Redgate
Common Moor
Golitha Falls
King Doniert's Stone
Trethevy Quoit
Tremar
St. Cleer
Well
Pensilva
Ken-Caro
Gang
Frogwell
Dupath Well
Cotehele
Calstock
Lanhydrock
St. Lawrence
Mount
St. Neot Holy Well
Carnglaze Caverns
St. Ive
Keason
Parkfield
Cadson Bury Fort
St. Dominick
Bere Alston
Tredinnick
Ley
Pinsla
Liskeard
Merrymeet
Quethiock
St. Mellion
Cotts
Tamar Heritage
Tregullon
Lanivet
Doublebois
Dobwalls
Pengover Green
Pillaton
Cutmadoc
West Taphouse
Trevelmond
Trehunist
Blunts
Ellbridge
Cargreen
Trebyan
Middle Taphouse
East Taphouse
St. Pinnock
Lamellion
Menheniot
Cuttivett
Maudlin
Restormel
Magnificent Music Machines
Hatt
Botus Fleming
Landulph
Bokiddick
Sweetshouse
Bodrane
St. Keyne
Tideford Cross
Landrake
Lockengate
Polscoe
Herodsfoot
Trewidland
Budge's Shop
Saltash
Carkeel
Couch's Mill
Tideford
Trematon
Lostwithiel
Lanlivery
Porfell
Port Eliot
St. Erney
Burraton
Washaway
Duloe
Widegates
Trerulefoot
Markwell
Trehan
Royal Albert Bridge
Rescorla
Luxulyan
Milltown
Bocaddon
St. Germans
Stephens
Hidden Valley
St. Winnow
Tredinnick
Hessenford
Antony Woodland
Penwithick
Penpillick
Lerryn
Lanreath
Sandplace
Morval
Polbathic
Antony NT
Wilcove
Trethurgy
Eden Project
Tywardreath Highway
Golant
Muchlarnick
Narkurs
Maryfield
Devonp
St. Blazey
Castle Dore
St. Veep
Penpoll
Pelynt
St. Martin
Seaton
St. Winnolls
Sheviock
Tregrehan Mills
St. Blazey Gate
Tywardreath
Lanteglos Highway
Plaidy
Monkey Sanctuary
Crafthole
Antony
Torpoint
Par
Fowey
Trenewan
East Looe
Downderry
Portwrinkle
St. John
Cremy
Holmbush
Carlyon Bay
Polkerris
Bodinnick
Porthallow
West Looe
Looe
Looe Bay
Grotto
Freathy
Millbrook
Charlestown
Menabilly
Readymoney
Lansallos
Model Village
Tregonhawke
Higher Porthpean
St. Catherine's
Polruan
Polperro
Smuggling & Fishing
Talland Bay
St. George's or Looe Island
Whitsand Bay
Kingsan
Cawsa
St. Austell Bay
Daymark NT
Gribbin Head
Pencarrow Head
Rame
Trenarren
Penlee Point
Rame Head
Black Head
35mins. (Seasonal)
Mevagissey
Bay
World of Railways
Chapel Point
Eddystone Rocks
A30
A39
A38
A390
A388
A387
A374
A3082
B3266
B3267
B3314
B3257
B3254
B3362
B3251
B3268
B3269
B3359
B3253
B3252
B3247
B3249
E
F
G
H
1
2
3
4
5
7
8
10
20
30
40
50

8
7
11
A
B
C
D
1
2
3
4
5
DARTMOOR
DARTMOOR NATIONAL PARK
DARTMOOR FOREST
DEVON
PLYMOUTH
TAVISTOCK
SALTASH
Lifton
Tinhay
Dippertown
Lydford
Lydford Gorge NT
Coryton
Marystow
Liddaton
Lawhitton
Chillaton
Meadwell
Kelly
North Brentor
Black Down
Wheal Betsy NT
Brentor
Milton Abbot
Mary Tavy
Horndon
Cudlipptown
Peter Tavy
Dunterton
B3362
Hotel Endsleigh
Chaddlehanger
Rezare
Bealsmill
Lamerton
Sydenham Damerel
Rushford
Tutwell
Venterdon
Horsebridge
Stoke Climsland
Old Mill
Luckett
Latchley
Downgate
Chilsworthy
Kit Hill
Gunnislake
St. Ann's Chapel
Albaston
Drakewalls
Bray
Harrowbarrow
Dupath Well
Metherell
Cotehele
Calstock
St. Dominick
Bere Alston
St. Mellion
Pillaton
Cotts
Tamar Belle Heritage Centre
Ellbridge
Cargreen
Bere Ferrers
Cuttivett
Hatt
Botus Fleming
Landulph
Landrake
A38
Carkeel
Tideford
Trematon
St. Erney
Saltash
Burraton
Trehan
Markwell
St. Germans
Sheviock
Crafthole
Antony
Torpoint
St. John
Cremyll
Millbrook
Whitsand Bay
Freathy
Tregonhawke
Kingsand
Cawsand
Rame
Rame Head
Penlee Point
Plymouth Breakwater
Drake's Island
The Sound
The Hoe
Turnchapel
Plymstock
Hooe
Goosewell
Staddiscombe
Down Thomas
Heybrook Bay
Marine Centre
Wembury
Wembury Bay
Knighton
Newton Ferrers
Bridgend
Noss Mayo
Great Mew Stone
Netton
Stoke Point
Plymouth to: Roscoff 6hrs. (Seasonal) Santander 20hrs. (Seasonal)
Eddystone Rocks
Devonport
Ford
Maryfield
Wilcove
Antony Woodland
St. Budeaux
Pennycross
Ham
Ernesettle
Whitleigh
Tamerton Foliot
Roborough
Estover
Eggbuckland
Leigham
Woodford
Higher Compton
Plym Valley
Saltram NT
Plympton
Hemerdon
Underwood
Elburton
Brixton
Yealmpton
Torr
Dunstone
Ford
Luson
Holbeton
Battisborough Cross
Mothecombe
Merrivale
Merrivale Prehistoric Settlement
Rundlestone
Princetown
Dartmoor Prison
Two Bridges
High Moorland (Dartmoor Nat. Pk.)
Middlemoor
Whitchurch
Sampford Spiney
Grenofen
Horrabridge
Walkhampton
Buckland Monachorum
The Garden House
Paperweight
Buckland Abbey NT
Crapstone
Milton Combe
Yelverton
Dousland
Burrator Resr.
Sheepstor
Meavy
Upper Plym Valley Prehistoric Sites
Clearbrook
Shaugh Prior
Wotter
Bickleigh
Woolwell
Lee Moor
Shell Top
Lutton
Cornwood
Moor Cross
Sparkwell
Lee Mill
Ivybridge
Harford
Ugborough Beacon
Cheston
Lukesland
Bittaford
Ugborough
Penquit
Ermington
Modbury
East Leigh
Brownston
Great Torr
Kingston
St. Ann's Chapel
Ringmore
Bigbury
Challaborough
Bigbury-on-Sea
Burgh Island
Bigbury Bay
Bantham
East Buckland
West Buckland
Thurlestone
South Huish
Galmpton
Outer Hope
Bolt Tail
Inner Hope
Malborough
Bolberry
Collaton
Rew
Salcombe
Batson
East Portlemouth
Rickham
Overbeck's NT
Bolt Head
Prawle Point
Fernworthy Resr.
Grey Wethers Stone Circles
Sittaford Tor
Cut Hill
Tavy Cleave
Cocks Hill
Rough Tor
Great Mis Tor
Postbridge
Bellever
Crockern Tor
Dartmeet
Hexworthy
Whiteworks
Cater's Beam
William Crossing Memorial
Ryder's Hill
Avon Dam Resr.
Stall Moor Stone Row
Rider's Rings Enclosures
Butterdon Stone Row
Didworthy
Lettaford
North Bovey
Miniature Pony Centre
Grimspound
Hameldown Tor
Manaton
Water
Bowerman's Nose
Hound Tor Medieval Village
Granite Tramway
Haytor Rocks
Bonehill
Church House NT
Widecombe in the Moor
Higher Dunstone
Ponsworthy
Leusdon
Buckland in the Moor
Ten Commandments Stone
Poundsgate
Venford Resr.
Ashburton
Holne
River Dart Adventures
Michelcombe
Scorriton
Combe
Hembury Castle
Buckfast
Abbey
Valiant Soldier
Buckfastleigh
Butterflies & Otters
Higher Dean
Lower Dean
Dean Prior
Pennywell Farm Centre
Harbourneford
Rattery
Culverlane
Lutton
Aish
Hillside
South Brent
Avonwick
Diptford
North Huish
Curtisknowle
Lupridge
Boreston
Moreleigh
Woodleigh
Ashford
Aveton Gifford
Loddiswell
Venn
Churchstow
Ledstone
Goveton
Buckland-tout-Saints
Kingsbridge
Dodbrooke
West Alvington
Upton
South Milton
Woolston
West Charleton
A386
A388
A390
A374
A379
A3121
A381
A385
A38
B3357
B3212
B3387
B3257
B3413
B3432
B3373
B3416
B3417
B3213
B3196
B3186
B3392
B3247
DANGER AREA

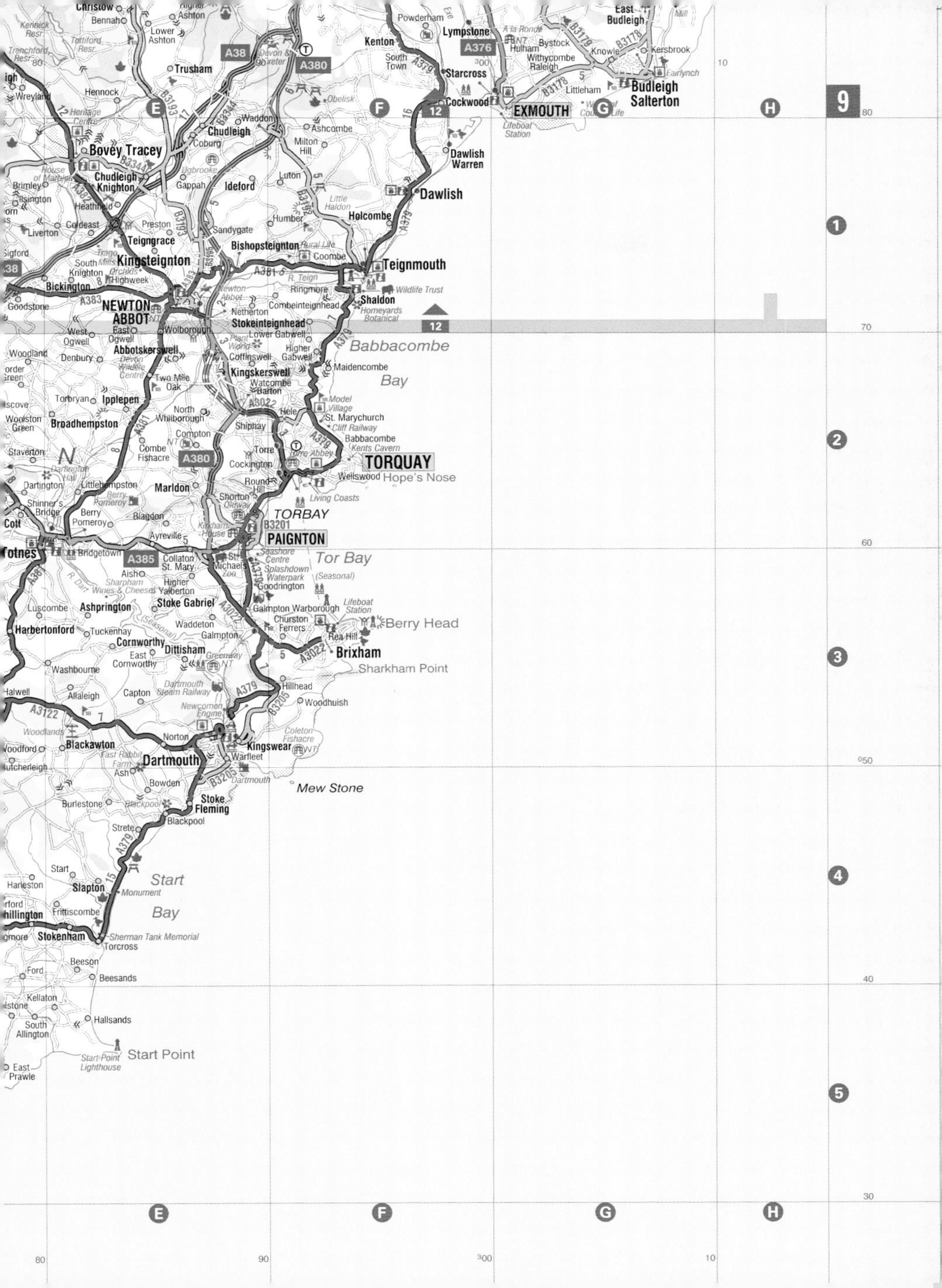

9
Exmouth
Budleigh Salterton
Dawlish
Teignmouth
Kingsteignton
Newton Abbot
Bovey Tracey
Chudleigh
Kingskerswell
Babbacombe Bay
Torquay
Hope's Nose
Torbay
Paignton
Tor Bay
Berry Head
Brixham
Sharkham Point
Totnes
Dartmouth
Kingswear
Mew Stone
Stoke Fleming
Start Bay
Slapton
Stokenham
Torcross
Start Point
A38
A380
A381
A383
A385
A379
A3022
A3122
A376
B3205

10
A
B
18
C
D
Hartland Quay
Stoke
Hartland
Velly
Clovelly Donkeys
Higher Clovelly
Natcott
Buck's Mills
Buck's Cross
Docton Mill
Milford
Philham
Milky Way Adventure Park
Elmscott
Edistone
Welsford
A39
Woolfardisworthy or Woolsery
South Hole
Alminstone Cross
Knaps Longpeak
Welcombe
R. Torridge
Mead
Meddon
Ashmansworthy
Gooseham
Woolley
Morwenstow
East Youlstone
Dinworthy
West Putford
Hawker's Hut
Eastcott
Gnome Reserve & Wild Flower Garden
Higher Sharpnose Point
Shop
West Youlstone
Bradworthy
Woodford
Upper Tamar Lake
Lower Sharpnose Point
Tamar Lakes
Alfardisworthy
Coombe
Kilkhampton
Sutcombe
Thurdon
Lower Tamar Lake
Stibb
Soldon Cross
B3254
Dexbeer
A388
Bude Bay
Poughill
Bush
Holsworthy Beacon
Stratton 1643
Hersham
Flexbury
Stratton
Grimscott
Lana
Bude
A3072
Launcells
Pancrasweek
Chilsworthy
Lynstone
Red Post
Holsworthy
A3073
Hobbacott Inclined Plane
Upton
Bridgerule
Derril
Derriton
Staddon
Marhamchurch
Pyworthy
Chasty
Whimble
A39
Widemouth Bay
Titson
Box's Shop
Leworthy
Coppathorne
Dizzard Point
Bangors
R. Deer
Clawton
Dizzard
Poundstock
Treskinnick Cross
Whitstone
Tregole
Penhallam Manor
Week St. Mary
Crackington Haven
St. Gennys
Trewint
Street
Moortown
Cambeak
Wainhouse Corner
Week Green
North Tamerton
Tetcott
Lana
Jacobstow
Sweets
CORNWALL
High Cliff
Higher Whiteleigh
Luffincott
Trespsarrett Posts
West Curry
Fire Beacon Point
Trengune
South Wheatley
Chapmans Well
Witchcraft
Beeny
B3263
Langdon
Maxworthy
Northcott
Trespsarrett
Canworthy Water
Bennacott
Boyton
Marshgate
Hele
West Panson
Boscastle
Brazacott
Lesnewth
Otterham
Trelash
Warbstow
Rocky Valley
Trevalga
North Petherwin
Tamar Otter & Wildlife Centre
Langdon Cross
St. Giles on the Heath
Tintagel Head
Bossiney
Tremaine
Halls
Halgabron
B3262
Petherwin Gate
Tintagel
Splatt
Tintagel
Hallworthy
Treneglos
Ladycross
Werrington
Old Post Office NT
Tresmeer
Yeolmbridge
Gull Rock
Treknow
Trewarmett
Davidstow
Tregeare
Egloskerry
Langore
B3263
B3266
A39
Trewassa
Tremail
Cold Northcott
Badgall
Launceston Steam Railway
St. Stephens
Dutson
Trebarwith
Slaughterbridge
Trevivian
A395
Liftondown
Treligga
Rockhead
Tretrew
St. Clether Holy Well
Hidden Valley
Newport
Delabole
North Cornwall
Crowdy Resr.
Pipers Pool
Launceston
Slate Quarry
Trevia
Tregoodwell
St. Clether
Laneast
Tregadillett
Pengelly
Camelford
Westdowns
Valley Truckle
Bowithick
Trewen
R. Inny
Trethorne Farm
Daw's House
Lawrence House
Lawhitton
Port Isaac Bay
Trewalder
Pencarrow
Charlotte Dymond Monument
South Petherwin
Port Gaverne
Helstone
Tresinney
Treween
Polyphant
Tregada
Port Quin
Port Isaac
St. Teath
Hut Circles
Rough Tor
Altarnun
Tredaule
A30
Lewannick
Lifeboat Station
Trewetha
Wesley Cottage
Fivelanes
Trewarlett
Long Cross Victorian Gardens
Tregeare Rounds
1377 Brown Willy
B3257
B3267
Pendoggett
Treveighan
Stone Circle
Stone Circle
Trelights
Michaelstow
1209
Lezant
Porteath Bee Centre
B3314
St. Endellion
Trelill
Fentonadle
Tregadlock
Congdon's Shop
Illand
Trekenner
St. Breward
King Arthur's Hall
Garrow Tor
Codda
1082
Newtown
Trebullett
Treburley
St. Minver
St. Kew
St. Tudy
Row
BODMIN
Daphne Du Maurier's Smugglers
Bolventor
Jamaica Inn
Trebartha
Coad's Green
North Hill
Lower Amble
Chapel Amble
Lank
Stripple Stones
MOOR
Middlewood
A388
St. Kew Highway
Wenfordbridge
Penpont
1280 Kilmar Tor
Henwood
Bathpool
Bray Shop
Jubilee Rock
Colliford Lake
Dozmary Pool
Bodieve
Blisland
Waterloo
Temple
Cheesewring
Rilla Mill
Linkinhorne
Trevanson
Wadebridge
St. Mabyn
Old Mill Herbary
1109 Brown Gelly Barrows
The Hurlers
Upton
Upton Cross
Plushabridge
South Hill
St. Breock
Egloshayle
Croanford
Hellandbridge
Colliford Lake
Minions
Royal Cornwall Showground
Culverhouse
Pencarrow
1216 Caradon Hill
Caradon Town
Kelly Bray
Sladesbridge
A389
A30
Maidenwell
Siblyback Lake
Heritage Centre
Golberdon
Pawton Quoit
Helland
DANGER AREA
Downgate
Burlawn
Washaway
Millpool
7
Darite
Pensilva
Trevigro
Callington
Polbrock
Churchyard Cross
Bury Castle
Warleggan
Redgate
Common Moor
Trethevy Quoit
Ken-Caro
St. Breock Downs Monolith
Camel Valley Vineyard
Bodmin
Cardinham
Fawton
St. Neot
King Doniert's Stone
Golitha Falls
Frogwell
Nanstallon
Bodmin
Berry Tower
Mount
St. Neot Holy Well
924
Tremar
St. Cleer
Keason
Ruthernbridge
Bodmin & Wenford
Tredinnick
Ley
Carnglaze Caverns
St. Ive
Parkfield
Cadson Bury Fort
A390
B3254
B3257
B3362
B3266
B3267
B3314
B3248
B3237

11
12
Great Torrington
South Molton
George Nympton
Bishop's Nympton
Umberleigh
Atherington
High Bickington
Chittlehamholt
King's Nympton
Romansleigh
Burrington
Chulmleigh
Chawleigh
Eggesford
Wembworthy
Winkleigh
Lapford
Morchard Bishop
Copplestone
Bow
North Tawton
Zeal Monachorum
Sampford Courtenay
Exbourne
Jacobstowe
Hatherleigh
Highampton
Black Torrington
Sheepwash
Meeth
Merton
Dolton
Beaford
Petrockstowe
Shebbear
Langtree
Bulkworthy
Buckland Brewer
Littleham
Weare Giffard
St. Giles in the Wood
Halwill Junction
Northlew
Folly Gate
Okehampton
Sticklepath
South Zeal
Belstone
Throwleigh
Drewsteignton
Chagford
Moretonhampstead
North Bovey
Lustleigh
Bratton Clovelly
Lydford
Mary Tavy
Peter Tavy
Lamerton
Milton Abbot
Sydenham Damerel
Stowford
TAVISTOCK
Princetown
Two Bridges
Postbridge
Widecombe in the Moor
Haytor Vale
Ashburton
Buckfast
Gunnislake
Calstock
Bere Alston
Buckland Monachorum
Horrabridge
Yelverton
Dousland
Walkhampton
Chilsworthy
DARTMOOR
NATIONAL DARTMOOR PARK
FOREST
D E V O N
A30
A386
A377
A3124
A3072
A3079
A382
A390
A38
B3227
B3217
B3220
B3216
B3215
B3260
B3212
B3357
B3387
B3206

12
A
B
C
D
20
South Molton
Bish Mill
Newtown
Cross Side
East Knowstone
Oldways End
Exebridge
Petton
Bathealton
Shillingford
Clayhanger
Stawley
Chipley
Langford Budville
Bishop's Nympton
Ash Mill
Knowstone
Roachill
Oakfordbridge
Bampton
Kittisford
Runnington
Alswear
Mariansleigh
Rose Ash
A361
Oakford
Appley
Cothay Manor
Thorne St. Margaret
Tone
Romansleigh
Ashbrittle
Greenham
Holywell Lake
Huntsham
Meshaw
Creacombe
Stoodleigh Beacon
Cove
Staple Cross
Hockworthy
Stoodleigh
Venhay
Rackenford
Ford Barton
Holcombe Rogus
Sampford Arundel
Fair Oak
Westleigh
Bradford Barton
Queen Dart
Mogworthy
Week
Lutworthy
North Coombe
Loxbeare
Washfield
Chevithorne
Uplowman
Whitnage
Burlescombe
Nicholashayne
Knightshayes Court NT
Ayshford
Witheridge
Nomansland
Templeton
Lurley
Calverleigh
Bolham
Chettiscombe
A361
Halberton
Sampford Peverell
Appledore
Prescott
East Worlington
Drayford
Cheldon
West Worlington
Thelbridge Barton
Withleigh
B3137
Cowleymoor
TIVERTON
Uffculme
Northcott
Culmstock
Chawleigh
Mid Devon
Cotteylands
TIVERTON
M5
Craddock
Washford Pyne
Pennymoor
Cruwys Morchard
Ash Thomas
Smithincott
Ashill
Filleigh
Littleborough
Puddington
Way Village
Willand
Stenhill
Black Dog
East Butterleigh
Diggerland
Blackborough
A377
Lapford
Eastington
Poughill
Kentisbeare
Brownstone
Upham
Devon Railway Cen.
Butterleigh
CULLOMPTON
Stoneyford
Saint Hill
Nymet Rowland
Lapford Cross
Woolfardisworthy
Morchard Bishop
Kennerleigh
Hayne
Cadeleigh
Bickleigh
Cullompton
Oldborough
Stockleigh English
Cheriton Fitzpaine
Colebrook
Dulford
Kerswell
Weeke
Cadbury Castle
East Village
857
Broadhembury
East Leigh
Down St. Mary
Fursdon
Mutterton
Zeal Monachorum
Chilton
Cadbury
Chitterley
Bradninch
Westcott
Colliton
A3072
Newbuildings
West Sandford
Upton Hellions
Stockleigh Pomeroy
Silverton
Norman's Green
Burston
Copplestone
Elston
Uppincott
Up Exe
Hele
Langford
Plymtree
Luton
Bow
Coleford
A377
Sandford
Thorverton
Ellerhayes
Lower Tale
Upton
Payhembury
Knowle
Shobrooke
Efford
Clyst Hydon
Higher Tale
Lower Cheriton
Higher Cheriton
Nymet Tracey
Penstone
Crediton
Shute
Nether Exe
Killerton NT
Budlake
Colestocks
Colebrooke
Wyke
Rewe
Budlake Old Post Office
Clyst St. Lawrence
Talaton
Fordton
Sweetham
Brampford Speke
Westwood
Feniton
Hillerton
Uton
Hookway
Smallbrook
Upton Pyne
Stoke Canon
Huxham
Escot
Yeoford
Venny Tedburn
Newton St. Cyres
Broadclyst
Whimple
Fairmile
Woodland Head
Oldridge
Poltimore
Marker's Cott. NT
Hand and Pen
Talaford
Hittisleigh Barton
Cowley
Dog Village
Cranbrook
B3174
Tedburn St. Mary
Pinhoe
Rockbeare
A30
Ottery St. Mary
Hittisleigh
A30
A377
Pennsylvania
Clyst Honiton
Allercombe
West Hill
Pathfinder Village
Exwick
Whipton
EXETER INTERNATIONAL
Broad Oak
Wiggaton
Cheriton Bishop
Cheriton Cross
Whitestone
EXETER
Heavitree
Sowton
Marsh Green
Fluxton
Crockernwell
Wheatley
EXETER
Clyst St. Mary
Aylesbeare
Metcombe
Coombe
A30
Longdown
St. Thomas
Farringdon
Venn Ottery
Tipton St. John
Drewsteignton
B3212
Southerton
Harpford
Culver
Ide
Alphington
Devon County Showground
Crealy
Bowd
Easton
Dunsford
Lower Wear
Topsham
Clyst St. George
Woodbury Salterton
Burrow
Newton Poppleford
B3193
Shillingford St. George
M5
Exminster
Woodbury
Hawkerland
DANGER AREA
Colaton Raleigh
Bridford
Dunchideock
Ebford
Clapham
Doddiscombsleigh
Exton
Woodbury Castle
Stowford
Sloncombe
Moretonhampstead
Kennford
Kenn
Bicton Park
Woodmanton
Yettington
Otterton
Christow
Higher Ashton
Bennah
East Budleigh
North Bovey
Lower Ashton
Powderham
A376
Kennick Resr.
Tottiford Resr.
Lympstone
Kenton
Bystock
Withycombe Raleigh
Knowle
Kersbrook
A38
A380
South Town
Trusham
Starcross
Lustleigh
Trenchford Resr.
Manaton
Wreyland
Hennock
Obelisk
Cockwood
EXMOUTH
Littleham
Budleigh Salterton
Grimspound
Water
Becky Falls
Hound Tor
Waddon
World of Country Life
Chudleigh
Ashcombe
Lifeboat Station
Coburg
Milton Hill
Bovey Tracey
Dawlish Warren
Bonehill
Haytor Rocks
Chudleigh Knighton
Luton
Ideford
Dawlish
Gappah
Haytor Vale
Brimley
Ilsington
Heathfield
Little Haldon
Humber
Holcombe
Lewthorn Cross
Liverton
Coldeast
Preston
Sandygate
Teigngrace
Bishopsteignton
Buckland in the Moor
Sigford
Coombe
Teignmouth
Leusdon
Kingsteignton
South Knighton
Highweek
A38
Caton
Bickington
R. Teign
Ringmore
Wildlife Trust
Shaldon
Combeinteignhead
Goodstone
NEWTON ABBOT
Netherton
Homeyards Botanical
Ashburton
Stokeinteignhead
Wolborough
Lower Gabwell
Holne
East Ogwell
West Ogwell
Abbotskerswell
Higher Gabwell
Woodland
Denbury
Coffinswell
Maidencombe
Forder Green
Kingskerswell
Babbacombe
Buckfast
Two Mile Oak
Ipplepen
A380
Torbryan
Landscove
Bay
300
10

Fitzwarren
Oake
East Nynehead
Hillfarrance
Rumwell
TAUNTON
Ruishton
Henlade
Thornfalcon
Haydon
Lillesdon
Newport
Wellington
Bradford-on-Tone
Trull
Staplehay
Shoreditch
Stoke St. Mary
Orchard Portman
Thurlbear
West Hatch
Meare Green
Wrantage
Curry Mallet
Fivehead
Swell
Isle Abbotts
Isle Brewers
Drayton
Muchelney
Muchelney Ham
Midelney
Thorney
Long Load
Milton
Sutton
Knole
Northover
Ilchester
Limington
Poole
Ham
West Buckland
TAUNTON DEANE
Rockwell Green
Pitminster
Fulwood
Corfe
Howleigh
Angersleigh
Lowton
Sellick's Green
Blagdon Hill
Staple Fitzpaine
Curland
Bickenhall
Hatch Beauchamp
Hatch Green
Beercrocombe
Slough Green
Stewley
Merryfield
Puckington
Westport
Hambridge
Stembridge
West Lambrook
New Cross
East Lambrook
Mid Lambrook
Kingsbury Episcopi
Stapleton
Ash
Coat
Martock
Hurst
Tintinhull
Chilthorne Domer
Stoke sub Hamdon
Montacute
Preston Plucknett
Barrington
Shepton Beauchamp
South Petherton
Bower Hinton
Ilton
Ilford
Rapps
Stocklinch
Hurcott
Moor
Ashill
Windmill Hill
Broadway
Horton Cross
Horton
SOMERSET
BLACK DOWN HILLS
Staple Hill
Curland Common
Culm Davy
Clayhidon
Rosemary Lane
Churchstanton
Otterford
Blackwater
Blindmoor
Birchwood
Buckland St. Mary
Hare
Ham
Millhayes
Stapley
Hemyock
Royston Water
Churchinford
Bishopswood
Street Ash
Newtown
Beetham
Combe St. Nicholas
Bolham Water
Madford
Dunkeswell Abbey
Smeatharpe
Marsh
Northay
Wadeford
Whitestaunton
Howley
Cuttiford's Door
Crimchard
Donyatt
Winterhay Green
Whitelackington
Ilminster
Seavington St. Mary
Seavington St. Michael
Over Stratton
Lopen
Wigborough
Norton sub Hamdon
East Stoke
Odcombe
Brympton D'Evercy
West Coker
Chiselborough
West Chinnock
Middle Chinnock
East Chinnock
Hardington Moor
North Coker
Sea
Dowlish Wake
Kingstone
Allowenshay
Dinnington
Merriott
Peasmarsh
Knowle St. Giles
Cricket Malherbie
Chillington
Hinton St. George
Broadshard
Lower Severalls
Haselbury Plucknett
Hardington Mandeville
Sutton Bingham
Pendomer
Hornsbury
Chaffcombe
Lydmarsh
Cudworth
Crewkerne
Roundham
Heritage Centre
North Perrott
Hardington Marsh
Higher Halstock Leigh
Newcott
Yarcombe
Crawley
Wambrook
Chard
Purtington
Hewish
Lakes & Gdns.
Cricket St. Thomas
Woolminstone
Misterton
South Perrott
Dunkeswell
Upottery
Luppitt
Rawridge
Beacon
Street
Forton
Whatley
Winsham
Wayford
Clapton
Seaborough
Mosterton
Weston
Chedington
Corscombe
East Chelborough
West Chelborough
Burridge
Tatworth
Holy City
Stockland
Furley
Chardstock
South Chard
Perry Street
Chard Junction
Bridge
Forde Abbey
Horn Ash
Laymore
Drimpton
Greenham
Littlewindsor
Dibberford
Benville
Wick
Monkton
Millhayes
Birchill
Tytherleigh
Holditch
Lower Holditch
Wadbrook
Hewood
Thorncombe
Blackdown
Hursey
Burstock
Broadwindsor
Newtown
Combe Raleigh
Awliscombe
Cotleigh
Heathstock
Membury
Alston
Churchill
South Common
Turfmoor
Smallridge
Pilsdon Pen
Stoke Abbott
Beaminster
Toller Whelme
Hooke
Weston
Honiton
Offwell
Wilmington
Widworthy
Dalwood
Loughwood Meeting House NT
Weycroft
Hawkchurch
Birdsmoorgate
Marshalsea
Bettiscombe
Pilsdon
Blackney
North Bowood
South Bowood
Mapperton
North Poorton
South Poorton
Gittisham
Kilmington
Shute
Shute Barton NT
Axminster
Abbey Gate
Raymond's Hill
Blackpool Corner
Coney's Castle
Marshwood
Lambert's Castle
Fishpond Bottom
Monkwood
Netherbury
Waytown
Oxbridge
Melplash
Loscombe
West Milton
Powerstock
DORSET
Church Green
Farway
Northleigh
Seaton Junction
Hampton
Whitford
Maidenhayne
Monkton Wyld
Wootton Fitzpaine
Whitchurch Canonicorum
Marshwood Vale
Filford
Broadoak
Salwayash
Dottery
Wooth
Pymore
Nettlecombe
Mangerton Mill
Woodbridge
Harcombe Bottom
Penn
Catherston Leweston
Ryall
Moorbath
Morcombelake
North Chideock
Loders
Uploders
Eggardon Hill
Broad Down
Colyton
Musbury
Prescott Pinetum
Yawl
Uplyme
Charmouth
Symondsbury
Bradpole
Askerswell
Southleigh
Motoring Memories
Colyford
Combpyne
Lyme Regis
Heritage Coast
Golden Cap
Chideock
Antrim Monument
Seatown
Watton
Lower Eype
Bridport
Walditch
Bothenhampton
Shipton Gorge
Chilcombe
Litton Cheney
Blackbury Camp
Sidford
Harcombe
Seaton
Tramway
Axmouth
Rousdon
Dowlands
Lifeboat Station
Marine Aquarium
LYME BAY
West Bay
Palmers Brewery
Burton Bradstock
Puncknowle
The Donkey Sanctuary
Quarry Caves
Pecorama
Beer
Seaton Bay
Vicarage
Weston
Sid
Salcombe Regis
Branscombe
Old Bakery
Beer Head
SIDMOUTH
Swyre
West Bexington
M5
A30
A35
A303
A358
A356
A37
A3088
A375
A373
A3052
A3066
B3170
B3168
B3165
B3167
B3162
B3164
B3163
B3161
B3261
B3172
B3174
B3157
B3151
13
14
21
E
F
G
H
1
2
3
4
5
80
70
20
30
40
350

14
Sutton
Knole
Podimore
Northover
Bridgehampton
West Camel
Queen Camel
Sutton Montis
Cadbury
Charlton Horethorne
North Cheriton
Horsington
Weston
Kington Magna
Upper Nyland
Lower Nyland
West Stour
East Stour
Stour Provost
Sherborne Causeway
Ilchester
Yeovilton
Chilton Cantelo
Marston Magna
Corton Denham
Rimpton
Stowell
Abbas Combe
Templecombe
Henstridge Ash
Henstridge Marsh
Henstridge Bowden
Henstridge
Fifehead Magdalen
Stour Row
Todber
Guy's Marsh
Limington
Draycott
Tintinhull
Adber
Sandford Orcas
Milborne Wick
Poyntington
Milborne Port
Pillwell
Marnhull
Moorside
Twyford
Margaret Marsh
East Orchard
Bedchester
West Orchard
Sutton Waldron
Farrington
Hammoon
Iwerne Minster
Martock
Hurst
Stoke sub Hamdon
East Stoke
Chilthorne Domer
Montacute
Yeovil Marsh
Mudford
Trent
Over Compton
Nether Compton
Stallen
Oborne
Goathill
Purse Caundle
Stalbridge Weston
Stalbridge
Walton Elm
Hinton St. Mary
Manston
Norton sub Hamdon
Odcombe
Brympton D'Evercy
Preston Plucknett
YEOVIL
Sherborne
Haydon
North Wootton
Alweston
Bishop's Caundle
Stourton Caundle
Sturminster Newton
Lydlinch
Chiselborough
West Chinnock
West Coker
Barwick
Bradford Abbas
Thornford
Folke
Longburton
BLACKMOOR VALE
Newton
Broad Oak
Child Okeford
Iwerne Courtney or Shroton
Middle Chinnock
East Chinnock
Hardington Moor
North Coker
East Coker
Stoford
Beer Hackett
Lillington
Knighton
Bishop's Down
Boys Hill
Woodbridge
Holwell
Crouch Hill
Packers Hill
King's Stag
Puxey
Fifehead Neville
Okeford Fitzpaine
Hanford
Shillingstone
Haselbury Plucknett
Hardington Mandeville
Sutton Bingham
Ryme Intrinseca
Yetminster
Sandhills
Pulham
Kingston
Woodrow
Hazelbury Bryan
Fifehead St. Quintin
Belchalwell
Belchalwell Street
North Perrott
Pendomer
Closworth
Hardington Marsh
Higher Halstock Leigh
Halstock
Melbury Osmond
Chetnole
Leigh
Totnell
Glanvilles Wootton
Pidney
Droop
Wonston
Ibberton
Durweston
Turnworth
South Perrott
Weston
East Chelborough
Melbury Sampford
Melbury Bubb
Hermitage
Middlemarsh
Duntish
Westfields
Woolland
Stoke Wake
Bryanston
Chedington
Corscombe
West Chelborough
Evershot
Hilfield
Lyon's Gate
Buckland Newton
Sharnhill Green
Mappowder
Bulbarrow Hill
Higher Ansty
Winterborne Houghton
Winterborne Stickland
Dibberford
Holywell
Batcombe
Minterne Magna
Minterne Parva
Henley
Lower Ansty
Melcombe Bingham
Hilton
Thornicombe
Broadwindsor
Newtown
Benville
Uphall
Rampisham
Frome St. Quintin
Up Cerne
Cerne Giant
Alton Pancras
Plush
Higher Melcombe
Bingham's Melcombe
Winterborne Clenston
Higher Whatcombe
Stoke Abbott
Beaminster
Toller Whelme
Higher Wraxall
Lower Wraxall
Up Sydling
Cerne Abbas
Piddletrenthide
Milton Abbas
Lower Whatcombe
Mapperton
Hooke
Higher Kingcombe
Cattistock
Sydling St. Nicholas
Cheselbourne
Netherbury
North Poorton
Lower Kingcombe
Nether Cerne
White Lackington
Dewlish
Milborne St. Andrew
Winterborne Whitechurch
Waytown
Loscombe
South Poorton
Toller Porcorum
Chilfrome
Maiden Newton
Winterborne Kingston
Oxbridge
West Milton
Powerstock
Toller Fratrum
Godmanstone
Piddlehinton
Salwayash
Mangerton Mill
Nettlecombe
Cruxton
Notton
Wynford Eagle
Forston
Charlton Down
Wooth
Pymoor
Loders
Eggardon Hill
West Compton
Frampton
Grimstone
Puddletown
Burleston
Tolpuddle
Turners Puddle
Bere Regis
Bradpole
Uploders
Hardy's Cottage NT
Athelhampton
Affpuddle
Briantspuddle
Bridport
Walditch
Bothenhampton
Askerswell
Compton Valence
Muckleford
Stratton
Bradford Peverell
Charminster
Burton
Stinsford
Higher Bockhampton
Ilsington
Tincleton
Pallington
Palmers Brewery
West Bay
Shipton Gorge
Chilcombe
Litton Cheney
Kingston Russell
Winterbourne Abbas
Nine Stones
Poundbury
Kingston Maurward
Lower Bockhampton
Woodsford
Clouds Hill
Burton Bradstock
Long Bredy
Black Down
Poor Lot Barrows
Winterbourne Steepleton
DORCHESTER
Max Gate
West Stafford
Moreton
Bovington Camp
Puncknowle
Littlebredy
Winterborne St. Martin (Martinstown)
Maiden Castle
Winterborne Monkton
Maumbury Rings
Whitcombe
Crossways
Monkey World
Tank
Swyre
Kingston Russell Stone Circle
Hardy Monument NT
Winterborne Herringston
West Knighton
Mill House Cider & Clocks
East Burton
Stokeford
West Bexington
Portesham
Friar Waddon
Broadmayne
Warmwell
Owermoigne
Blacknoll
Wool
East Stoke
Abbotsbury
Subtropical
Chapel
Children's Farm
Swannery
Elworth
Coryates
Upwey
Shilvinghampton
Rodden
Broadwey
Bincombe
White Horse
Sutton Poyntz
Littlemoor
Osmington
Poxwell
Galton
East Knighton
Winfrith Newburgh
Coombe Keynes
Shaggs
Nottington
Upton
Holworth
Chaldon Herring or East Chaldon
Preston
Roman Temple
TOLL
West Chaldon
Chaldon Down
Langton Herring
Buckland Ripers
Overcombe
Weymouth Bay
Osmington Mills
Ringstead Bay
West Lulworth
Lulworth
Lulworth Camp
East Lulworth
Chesil Beach
Fleet
Chickerell
Radipole
Melcombe Regis
Sea Life
Heritage Centre
Durdle Door
Lulworth Cove
Worbarrow Bay
Westham
WEYMOUTH
Charlestown
DANGER AREA
Nothe Fort
Wyke Regis
Rodwell
Sandsfoot Castle
Portland Harbour
Weymouth to:
Guernsey 2hrs. 30 mins. (Fast Ferry)
Jersey 4hrs. (Fast Ferry)
St. Malo 5hrs. 30mins. (Fast Ferry)
Chesil Beach
Portland
Castletown
Fortuneswell
Chiswell
West Bay
Grove
Tout Quarry Sculpture Park
Easton
ISLE OF PORTLAND
Weston
Rufus
Southwell
Portland
BILL OF PORTLAND
Portland Bill Lighthouse
D
O
R
S
E
E N
A303
A37
A3088
A359
A30
A357
A3030
A352
A356
A3066
B3163
A35
A354
A353
A31
B3157
B3159
B3143
B3146
B3092
B3081
B3091
B3390
B3071
B3070
B3162
B3151
B3148
B3145
A350
22
13
A B C D
1 2 3 4 5
350 60 70 80

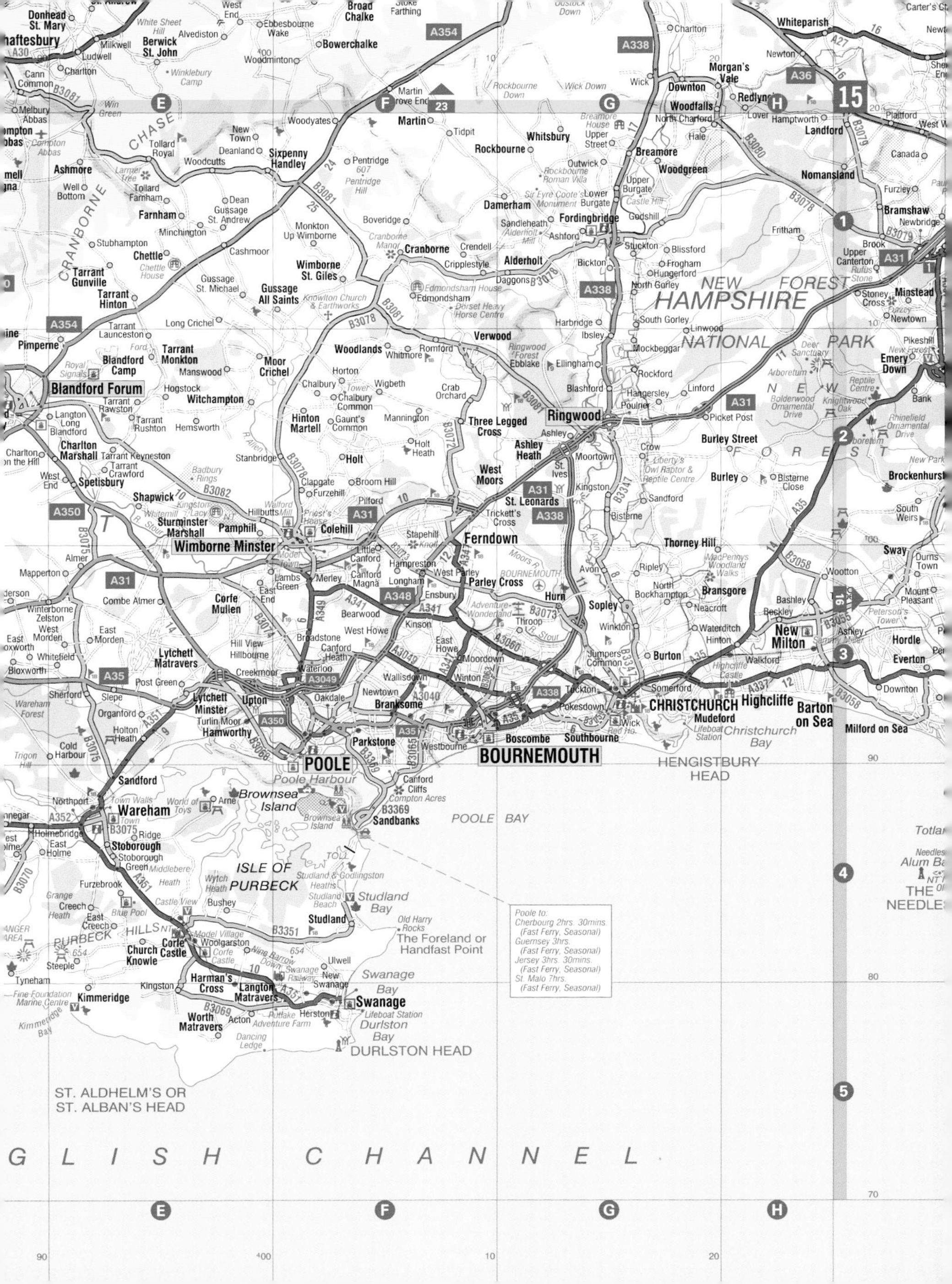

15
NEW FOREST
HAMPSHIRE
NATIONAL PARK
CRANBORNE CHASE
ISLE OF PURBECK
POOLE
BOURNEMOUTH
CHRISTCHURCH
Wimborne Minster
Blandford Forum
Ringwood
Wareham
Swanage
Poole Harbour
Brownsea Island
POOLE BAY
HENGISTBURY HEAD
DURLSTON HEAD
ST. ALDHELM'S OR ST. ALBAN'S HEAD
THE NEEDLES
Christchurch Bay
Studland Bay
Swanage Bay
Durlston Bay
The Foreland or Handfast Point
GLISH CHANNEL
Poole to:
Cherbourg 2hrs. 30mins. (Fast Ferry, Seasonal)
Guernsey 3hrs. (Fast Ferry, Seasonal)
Jersey 3hrs. 30mins. (Fast Ferry, Seasonal)
St. Malo 7hrs. (Fast Ferry, Seasonal)
A354
A338
A36
A31
A35
A350
A348
A341
A3049
A352
A351
A337
E
F
G
H

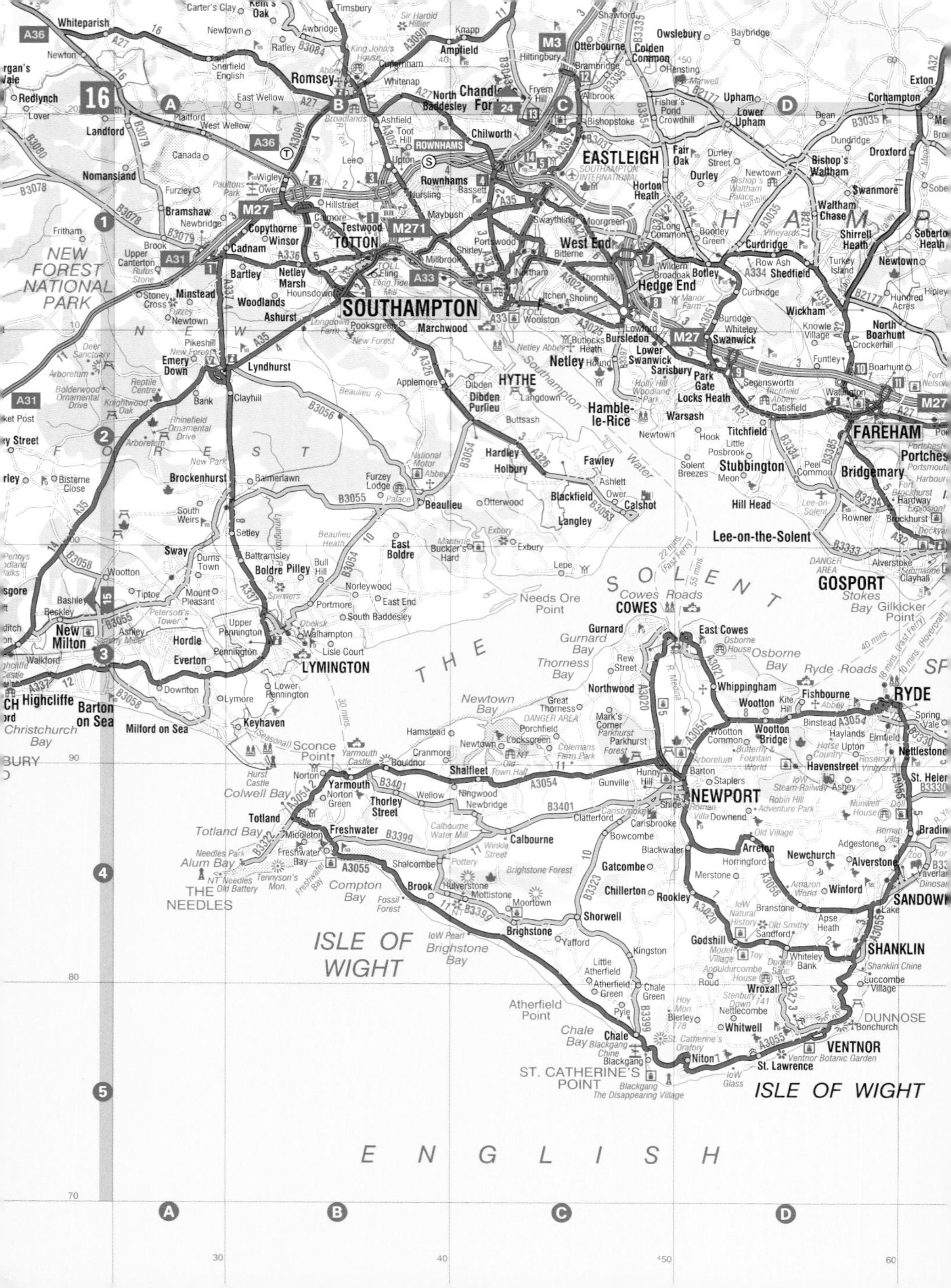
16
A
B
C
D
1
2
3
4
5
Whiteparish
Romsey
Chandler's Ford
Otterbourne
Owslebury
Colden Common
Bishopstoke
EASTLEIGH
SOUTHAMPTON INTERNATIONAL
Upham
Lower Upham
Corhampton
Exton
Droxford
Bishop's Waltham
Swanmore
Waltham Chase
Shirrell Heath
Redlynch
Landford
Nomansland
Bramshaw
Cadnam
Copythorne
Totton
Testwood
Rownhams
Nursling
Chilworth
North Baddesley
Ampfield
West End
Hedge End
Botley
Curdridge
Shedfield
Wickham
North Boarhunt
NEW FOREST NATIONAL PARK
Minstead
Bartley
Netley Marsh
Woodlands
Ashurst
SOUTHAMPTON
Marchwood
Woolston
Sholing
Bursledon
Lower Swanwick
Swanwick
Sarisbury
Park Gate
Locks Heath
Netley
HYTHE
Dibden
Dibden Purlieu
Applemore
Emery Down
Lyndhurst
Bank
Clayhill
Hamble-le-Rice
Warsash
Titchfield
Stubbington
FAREHAM
Portchester
Bridgemary
Lee-on-the-Solent
GOSPORT
Stokes Bay
Gilkicker Point
Hardley
Holbury
Fawley
Blackfield
Calshot
Langley
Brockenhurst
Beaulieu
Exbury
Lepe
Southampton Water
East Boldre
Sway
Boldre
Pilley
Bashley
New Milton
Hordle
Everton
LYMINGTON
Pennington
Walhampton
Highcliffe
Barton on Sea
Milford on Sea
Keyhaven
Christchurch Bay
Hurst Castle
THE SOLENT
Cowes Roads
COWES
East Cowes
Osborne Bay
Ryde Roads
RYDE
Gurnard
Gurnard Bay
Thorness Bay
Northwood
Whippingham
Wootton
Wootton Bridge
Fishbourne
Binstead
Newtown Bay
Newtown
Shalfleet
Yarmouth
Norton
Colwell Bay
Totland
Totland Bay
Freshwater
Alum Bay
THE NEEDLES
Compton Bay
Brook
Brighstone
Brighstone Bay
Calbourne
Shorwell
Gatcombe
Chillerton
Rookley
NEWPORT
Carisbrooke
Havenstreet
Ashey
Nettlestone
St. Helens
Brading
Newchurch
Arreton
Alverstone
SANDOWN
Lake
SHANKLIN
Godshill
Wroxall
Whitwell
Niton
Chale
Chale Bay
Atherfield Point
St. Lawrence
VENTNOR
Bonchurch
DUNNOSE
ST. CATHERINE'S POINT
ISLE OF WIGHT
ENGLISH
M3
M27
M271
A36
A31
A35
A33
A337
A3054
A3055
A3020
B3055
B3054
20
10
90
80
70
30
40
450
50
60

Lower Bordean
Stroud
PETERSFIELD
A272
Fyning
Chithurst
Rogate
Durford Bridge
B2199
Woolbeding
Easebourne
Lodsworth
River
Upperton
Petworth House & Park
Petworth
A272
Stroud Green
Riplington
Langrish
Ramsdean
Weston
East Meon
Habin
Nyewood
Trotton
Iping
Stedham
Midhurst
Cowdray Ho.
Castle (Ruin)
Tillington
Bedham
SOUTH
DOWNS
NATIONAL
PARK
Dumpford
Minsted
West Lavington
South Ambersham
Selham
Byworth
17
Coldwaltham
Codmore
Butser Hill
Coombe
War Down
Buriton
Nursted
West Harting
25
East Harting
Elsted
Elsted Marsh
Cocking Causeway
Coultershaw Bridge
Beam Pump
Fittleworth
Coates
Pulborough
Stopham
Hill Fort
A3
Queen Elizabeth
South Harting
Treyford
Didling
Bepton
Heyshott
Hoyle
Graffham
Upper Norwood
Duncton
Lower Horncroft
Hardham
Chidden
Hambledon Cricket Club Memorial
Clanfield
Uppark
Devil's Jumps Barrows
Cocking
Butser Ancient Farm
Chalton
North Marden
East Marden
Bevis's Thumb
Compton
East Lavington
Barlavington
Sutton
Bignor
Bignor Roman Villa
West Burton
Watersfield
Hambledon
Catherington
Blendworth
West Marden
Up Marden
Chilgrove
Singleton
Charlton
Upwaltham
Amberley
HORNDEAN
Anthill Common
FOREST
Finchdean
Forestside
West Dean
Weald & Downland Open Air Museum
East Dean
Stane Street
Bury
Houghton
Lovedean
Cowplain
Denmead
Soake
Anmore
Furzeley Corner
Deanlane End
Rowland's Castle
Stansted Park
Stoughton
Walderton
Lordington
Goodwood
The Trundle
S O U T H   D O W N S
W E S T
S U S S E X
BERE
A3(M)
Durrants
WATERLOOVILLE
Southwick
Stakes
Leigh Park
Aldsworth
Funtington
Woodend
West Stoke
Mid Lavant
Goodwood House
East Lavant
Waterbeach
Halnaker
Boxgrove
Eartham
Slindon
Madehurst
North Stoke
South Stoke
Offham
Arundel Park
Wetland Centre
Arundel
A27
Purbrook
HAVANT
New Brighton
Westbourne
Woodmancote
A27
West Ashling
East Ashling
Sennicotts
Westerton
Westhampnett
Tangmere
Military Aviation
Norton
Nyton
Fontwell
Fontwell Park
Binstead
Tortington
Crossbush
Warningcamp
Wymering
Drayton
Cosham
Bedhampton
Warblington
Emsworth
Hermitage
Southbourne
Breach
Hambrook
Summersdale
CHICHESTER
Aldingbourne
Westergate
Walberton
Eastergate
Lyminster
Poling
Farlington
Langstone
A259
Prinsted
Nutbourne
Broadbridge
Fishbourne
Oving
Woodgate
Barnham
Ford
Wick
M275
A27
Northney
North Hayling
Stoke
Chidham
West Thorney
Bosham
Apuldram
Planetarium
Runcton
Merston
Colworth
Lidsey
Yapton
Climping
Rustington
Hilsea
North End
Langstone Harbour
Tye
Thorney Island
Donnington
Hunston
North Mundham
Elbridge
North Bersted
Shripney
Bilsham
Flansham
Fleet
Landport
Fratton
PORTSEA ISLAND
Milton
Beam Engine
Rylc. Marines
Eastney
SOUTH HAYLING
Chichester Harbour
West Itchenor
Birdham
Shipton Green
Rookwood
Falconry Centre
Lagness
South Mundham
A259
South Bersted
Felpham
Middleton-on-Sea
Ancton
Atherington
LITTLEHAMPTON
Harbour Park
West Town
Lifeboat Station
West Wittering
Somerley
Highleigh
Street End
Nyetimber
Aldwick
BOGNOR REGIS
PORTSMOUTH
HAYLING ISLAND
Hayling Bay
Almodington
Earnley Butterflies
Earnley
Sidlesham
Pagham
Pagham Harbour
East Wittering
Bracklesham
Norton
Church Norton
Horse Sand Fort
HEAD
No Man's Land Fort
Bracklesham Bay
East Beach
Selsey
Lifeboat
Lifeboat Station
SELSEY BILL
Portsmouth to:
Bilbao 24hrs.
Caen 3hrs. 45mins. (Fast Ferry, Seasonal)
Caen 6hrs. (Seasonal)
Cherbourg 4hrs. 30mins. (Seasonal)
Cherbourg 3hrs. (Fast Ferry, Seasonal)
Guernsey 7hrs.
Jersey 9hrs.
Le Havre 5hrs. 30mins.
St. Malo 9hrs.
Santander 24hrs.
Seaview
St. Helen's Fort
Bembridge Point
Bembridge
FORELAND
Lane End
Lifeboat Station
Whitecliff Bay
Culver Cliff
Nab Tower
C H A N N E L
E
F
G
H
1
2
3
4
5
70
80
90
500

B R I S T O L

North West
Point
LUNDY

*Lundy
Marine
Conservation
Zone*

Lundy to
Bideford 2hrs. (Seasonal)
Ilfracombe 2hrs.
(Seasonal)

South West
Point

Rat Island

BARNSTAPLE

OR

HARTLAND POINT   Windbury
Point   *BIDEFORD BAY*

Titchberry
Hartland   Clovelly
Abbey   Charlotte Lavender   Court   **Clovelly**
Clovelly
Donkeys
Hartland   Velly   **Hartland**   Higher
Quay   Clovelly   **Buck's Mills**
Stoke   B3248   Natcott
Docton Mill   Buck's
Milford   Phillham   710   Milky Way   Cross
Elmscott   Edistone   Welsford   Adventure Park
24   **A39**
Woolfardisworthy
or **Woolsery**
South Hole   Parkh
Almshouse   Ash
10   Cross
Knaps
Longpeak   Welcombe   771   *Torridge*
Mead   Ashmansworthy
Meddon
Gooseham   Woolley
East   West Putford
Morwenstow   Shop   Eastcott   Youlstone   Dinworthy
Hawker's Hut   West   Gnome Reserve &
Higher Sharpnose   Woodford   Youlstone   Wild Flower Garden
Point   **Bradworthy**
CORNWALL   Upper
Lower Sharpnose   Tamar
Point   Alfardisworthy   Lakes
Coombe   **Kilkhampton**   Thurdon   **Sutcombe**   Venr
Lower
Stibb   B3254   Tamar Lake   Soldon
Cross
A39   **10**   *Weldon*
A39   **C**   Dexbeer   **D**
Poughill   Holsworthy
Bude   Stratton   Bush   Grimscott   Lana   Beacon
Flexbury   Stratton   **Stratton**   Chilsworthy

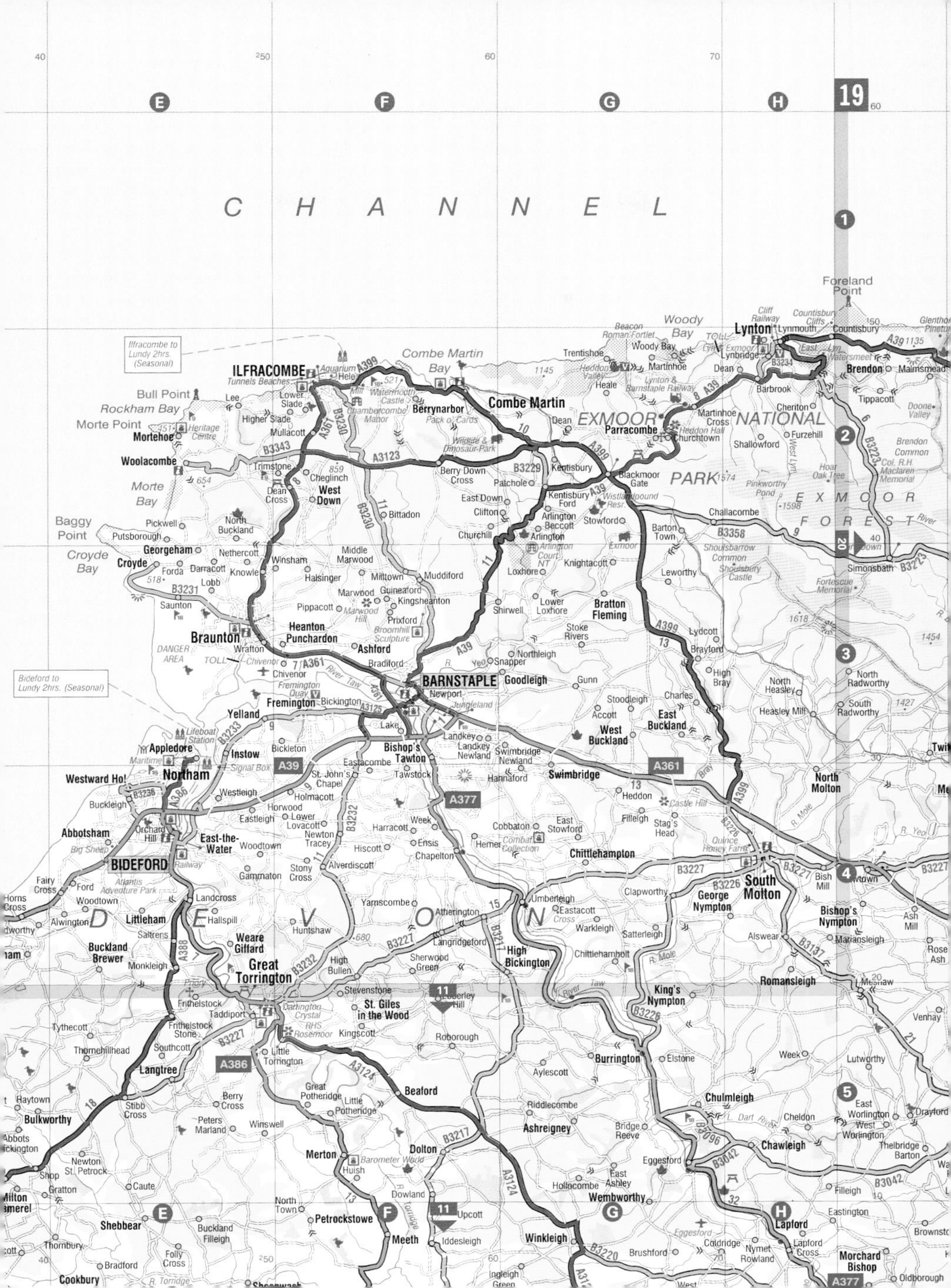

40
250
60
70
E
F
G
H
C H A N N E L
1
2
3
4
5
Foreland Point
Ilfracombe to Lundy 2hrs. (Seasonal)
Bideford to Lundy 2hrs. (Seasonal)
ILFRACOMBE
Tunnels Beaches
Aquarium
Hele
Combe Martin Bay
Lee
Lower Slade
Bull Point
Rockham Bay
Morte Point
Mortehoe
Heritage Centre
Higher Slade
Mullacott
Chambercombe Manor
Watermouth Castle
Berrynarbor
Pack o' Cards
Combe Martin
Wildlife & Dinosaur Park
Woolacombe
Morte Bay
Trimstone
Cheglinch
West Down
Dean Cross
Berry Down Cross
Patchole
Kentisbury
Kentisbury Ford
Blackmoor Gate
Baggy Point
Putsborough
Pickwell
North Buckland
Croyde Bay
Croyde
Georgeham
Nethercott
Darracott
Forda
Knowle
Lobb
Saunton
Braunton
Wrafton
Chivenor
DANGER AREA
TOLL
Heanton Punchardon
Ashford
Bradiford
Winsham
Halsinger
Middle Marwood
Milltown
Muddiford
Marwood
Guineaford
Kingsheanton
Pippacott
Marwood Hill
Prixford
Broomhill Sculpture
Bittadon
East Down
Clifton
Churchill
Arlington
Arlington Beccott
Arlington Court NT
Loxhore
Stowford
Knightacott
Shirwell
Lower Loxhore
Bratton Fleming
Stoke Rivers
Northleigh
Snapper
Goodleigh
BARNSTAPLE
Newport
Jungleland
Fremington
Fremington Quay
Bickington
Lake
River Taw
Yelland
Lifeboat Station
Instow
Bickleton
Appledore
Maritime
Northam
Signal Box
Westward Ho!
Buckleigh
Abbotsham
Big Sheep
Orchard Hill
East-the-Water
Westleigh
Eastleigh
Horwood
Lower Lovacott
Holmacott
Newton Tracey
St. John's Chapel
Eastacombe
Bishop's Tawton
Tawstock
Landkey
Landkey Newland
Swimbridge Newland
Hannaford
Swimbridge
BIDEFORD
Atlantis Adventure Park
Woodtown
Stony Cross
Gammaton
Alverdiscott
Harracott
Hiscott
Week
Ensis
Chapelton
Herner
Cobbaton
Combat Collection
East Stowford
Chittlehampton
Fairy Cross
Ford
Horns Cross
Alwington
Littleham
Landcross
Hallspill
Saltrens
Weare Giffard
Huntshaw
Yarnscombe
Atherington
Umberleigh
Eastacott Cross
Warkleigh
Clapworthy
Satterleigh
Buckland Brewer
Monkleigh
Great Torrington
High Bullen
Langridgeford
Sherwood Green
High Bickington
Chittlehamholt
Priory
Frithelstock
Taddiport
Dartington Crystal
RHS Rosemoor
Stevenstone
St. Giles in the Wood
Kingscott
Roborough
Tythecott
Frithelstock Stone
Southcott
Thornehillhead
Little Torrington
Langtree
Great Potheridge
Little Potheridge
Beaford
Haytown
Stibb Cross
Berry Cross
Bulkworthy
Peters Marland
Winswell
Abbots Bickington
Newton St. Petrock
Shop
Gratton
Caute
Merton
Huish
Barometer World
Dolton
Dowland
North Town
Petrockstowe
Meeth
Iddesleigh
Upcott
Shebbear
Buckland Filleigh
Thornbury
Folly Cross
Bradford
Cookbury
R. Torridge
Ingleigh Green
Milton Damerel
Trentishoe
Heddon Valley
Heale
Woody Bay
Beacon Roman Fortlet
Martinhoe
Lynton & Barnstaple Railway
Martinhoe Cross
Dean
Lynton
Lynmouth
Lynbridge
Cliff Railway
Countisbury Cliffs
Countisbury
Watersmeet
East Lyn
Brendon
Malmsmead
Glenthorne Pinetum
Barbrook
Tippacott
Doone Valley
Cheriton
Furzehill
Parracombe
Churchtown
Heddon Hall
EXMOOR NATIONAL PARK
Shallowford
West Lyn
Brendon Common
Hoar Oak Tree
Col. R.H Maclaren Memorial
Pinkworthy Pond
Wistlandpound Resr
EXMOOR FOREST
Challacombe
Barton Town
Shoulsbarrow Common
Shoulsbury Castle
Simonsbath
Leworthy
Fortescue Memorial
Lydcott
Brayford
High Bray
North Heasley
North Radworthy
Heasley Mill
South Radworthy
Gunn
Stoodleigh
Accott
Charles
East Buckland
West Buckland
North Molton
Heddon
Castle Hill
Filleigh
Stag's Head
Quince Honey Farm
South Molton
Bish Mill
George Nympton
Bishop's Nympton
Ash Mill
Alswear
Mariansleigh
Rose Ash
King's Nympton
Romansleigh
Meshaw
Venhay
Burrington
Elstone
Week
Lutworthy
Aylescott
Riddlecombe
Ashreigney
Chulmleigh
Bridge Reeve
Cheldon
East Worlington
West Worlington
Drayford
Chawleigh
Thelbridge Barton
Eggesford
East Ashley
Hollocombe
Wembworthy
Filleigh
Lapford
Eastington
Coldridge
Nymet Rowland
Lapford Cross
Brushford
Winkleigh
Morchard Bishop
Brownston
Oldborough
River Taw
R. Mole
L. Dart River
D E V O N
A39
A361
A377
A386
A388
A399
A3123
A3124
A3125
B3230
B3231
B3232
B3233
B3236
B3343
B3229
B3358
B3227
B3226
B3217
B3137
B3096
B3042
B3220
B3223
B3234

20
BRISTOL CHANNEL
EXMOOR NATIONAL PARK
EXMOOR FOREST
BRENDON HILLS
DEVON
Lynton
Lynmouth
Countisbury
Foreland Point
Brendon
Porlock
Porlock Bay
MINEHEAD
Dunster
Watchet
Blue Anchor Bay
Simonsbath
Exford
Winsford
Dulverton
Wiveliscombe
South Molton
North Molton
Bampton
Tiverton
Cullompton
Withypool
Luccombe
Wootton Courtenay
Dunkery Beacon
Timberscombe
Carhampton
Williton
Washford
Stogumber
Brompton Regis
Brompton Ralph
Molland
Twitchen
Knowstone
Witheridge
Rackenford
Templeton
Chawleigh
Lapford
Morchard Bishop
Puddington
Poughill
Cadeleigh
Halberton
Sampford Peverell
Uffculme
Willand
Kentisbeare
Holcombe Rogus
Milverton
Tolland
Skilgate
Exebridge
East Anstey
Brushford
Romansleigh
Bishop's Nympton
Meshaw

Flat Holm
Sand Bay
Bourton
A370
BRISTOL INTERNATIONAL
21
A38
Kewstoke
St. George's
M5
Hewish
West Hewish
Puxton
Congresbury
Redhill
NORTH SOMERSET
Wrington
Weston Bay
Milton
Worle
West Wick
Lower Langford
Cowslip Green
Butcombe
Regil
SeaQuarium
Steep Holm
E
F
G
H
WESTON-SUPER-MARE
33
A370
A371
Stonebridge
Banwell
A368
Churchill
Sandford
Rickford
Blagdon
Nempnett Thrubwell
Ubley
Brean Down Fort
Brean Down
Uphill
Hutton
Locking
Knightcott
Upper Langford
Burrington
A38
Oldmixon
Bleadon
Bleadon Hill
Christon
Winscombe
Rowberrow
Shipham
Sidcot
MENDIP
Compton Martin
Brean
Loxton
Barton
Compton Bishop
Charterhouse
Brean Leisure Park
Lympsham
Eastertown
Lower Weare
Cross
Axbridge
A371
Cheddar
Animal Farm Adventure Park
Wick
Edingworth
Biddisham
Cheddar Resr.
Cheddar Gorge
Mendip Forest
HILLS
BRIDGWATER
BAY
SEDGEMOOR
Badgworth
Weare
Tarnock
King John's Hunting Lodge
Brinscombe
Bradley Cross
DANGER AREA
B3140
East Brent
Rooks Bridge
A38
Stone Allerton
Alston Sutton
Clewer
Nyland Hill
Berrow
Brent Knoll
M5
Chapel Allerton
Ashton
Draycott
Priddy
Priddy Nine Barrows
Battleborough
Edithmead
Middle Stoughton
Crickham
Rodney Stoke
Ebbor Gorge
BURNHAM-ON-SEA
Vole
Northwick
West Stoughton
Cocklake
Westbury-sub-Mendip
Wookey Hole
Highbridge
B3140
22
Mark
Blackford
Wedmore
R. Axe
Easton
Alstone
B3139
Mark Causeway
Yarrow
Westham
Sand
Theale
Wookey
Haybridge
Stolford
Steart
Bason Bridge
Heath House
Bagley
Panborough
Henton
Huntspill
East Huntspill
Mudgley
Bleadney
Lilstock
Knighton
Wick
Secret World
Yarley
B3139
Burcott
East Quantoxhead
Kilton
Burton
Shurton
Stockland Bristol
West Huntspill
B3151
Castle
Coxley
Stogursey
Otterhampton
Stretcholt
Upper Godney
Polsham
Kilve
Stringston
Pawlett
B3141
Lower Godney
Southway
Launcherley
Combwich
Burtle
Westhay
A39
Holford
Coultings
Coleridge Cottage NT
Dunball
Puriton
Woolavington
Meare
Fish House
Oxenpill
Stileway
Dodington
Fiddington
Rodway
Chilton Trinity
A39
Cossington
Chilton Polden
B3151
Edington
22
Glastonbury Abbey Tor
Norwood Park
QUANTOCK
Nether Stowey
Over Stowey
Walled
Cannington
23
Bawdrip
Catcott
Glastonbury
Edgarley
Alfoxton
Horsey
Stawell
Shapwick
Northover
A361
Havyatt
Bradley Green
Wembdon
Ashcott
A39
Walton
Street
Aley
Charlynch
Spaxton
Four Forks
Sydenham
Chedzoy
BRIDGWATER
Sutton Mallet
Moorlinch
Greinton
Court Barn NT
Crowcombe
Plainsfield
Northfield
Durleigh Resr.
Pedwell
Triscombe
Aisholt
Pightley
Durleigh
Hamp
Sedgemoor 1685
Bussex
POLDEN
Shoe
Overleigh
Butleigh Wootton
Baltonsborough
Enmore
A372
12
BRIDGWATER
Wills Neck
Merridge
Goathurst
Westonzoyland
King's Sedge Moor
HILLS
Butleigh
West Bagborough
Courtway
Huntworth
A361
Greylake
Seven Ash
Heathfield
Huntstile
Pumping Station
M
E
R
S
E
T
Terhill
North Petherton
M5
24
Middlezoy
Henley
Compton Dundon
Barton St. David
Lydeard
Lawrence
East Combe
Fyne Court
Broomfield
Thorngrove
High Ham
Dundon
Combe Florey
Cothelstone
Northmoor Green or Moorland
Othery
Beer
Kingweston
North Newton
Pathe
Littleton
Shearston
Thurloxton
Maunsel Lock Canal Centre
King Alfred's Monument
22
Stembridge
Hurcott
Keinton Mandeville
Kingston St. Mary
Adsborough
Burrow Mump
Burrowbridge
Ash Priors
Bishops Lydeard
Fulford
Hestercombe
West Monkton
Hedging
Bankland
Athelney
Stathe
Aller
Bowdens
Low Ham
Westcombe
Somerton
West Somerset Railway
A358
Upper Cheddon
West Newton
A361
DANGER AREA
Wearne
Pitney
Charlton Mackrell
Charlton Adam
TAUNTON
DEANE
Nailsbourne
Cheddon Fitzpaine
Monkton Heathfield
Durston
West Lyng
East Lyng
Willows & Wetlands
Woodhill
Oath
A372
Pict's Hill
B3153
Midney
Preston Bowyer
Cotford St. Luke
Staplegrove
A3259
Creech Heathfield
R. Tone
Meare Green
Stoke St. Gregory
Langport
Wick
Portfield
1645 Langport
Upton
South Hill
Kingsdon
Lytes Cary NT Manor
Heathfield
Langford
Bathpool
Charlton
Huish Episcopi
Pibsbury
A372
B3227
Hillcommon
Norton Fitzwarren
Bishop's Hull
Creech St. Michael
Knapp
North Curry
Hunham
Curry Rivel
A378
Priest's House
Long Sutton
Catsgore
4
Oake
Lambrook
Ruishton
Ham
Helland
West Sedge Moor
Monument
Drayton
Muchelney
Knole
Northover
Hillfarrance
A3065
25
Henlade
Thornfalcon
Newport
Abbey
R. Yeo
East Nynehead
Rumwell
Galmington
TAUNTON
Haydon
A358
Lillesdon
15
Swell
Isle
Midelney
Muchelney Ham
Long Load
A303
Ilchester
Wellington
Bradford-on-Tone
A38
Sheppy's Cider
Trull
Shoreditch
Stoke St. Mary
Wrantage
A378
Meare Green
Curry Mallet
Fivehead
Thorney
Town Tree Nature
Milton
Limington
Poole
Ham
West Buckland
TAUNTON DEANE
Staplehay
M5
Orchard Portman
Thurlbear
West Hatch
Beercrocombe
Isle Abbotts
Isle Brewers
Hambridge
Lock-up
Kingsbury Episcopi
Stapleton
Rockwell Green
Chelston
Fulwood
Pitminster
Corfe
B3170
Slough Green
Hatch Beauchamp
Stembridge
Coat
Ash
Tintinhull NT
A37
Westport
Burrow Hill Cider
West Lambrook
New Cross
East Lambrook
Martock
Treasurer's House NT
Tintinhull
A3088
Ford Street
Angersleigh
Howleigh
Sellick's Green
Staple Fitzpaine
13
Merryfield
Stewley
Puckington
Barrington NT
Manor
Mid Lambrook
Hurst
Stoke sub Hamdon
Chilthorne Domer
Montacute House NT
Lowton
Blagdon Hill
Curland
Bickenhall
Ilton
Ilford
Rapps
Barrington Court
Shepton Beauchamp
South Petherton
Bower Hinton
Priory NT
East Stoke
Montacute
Preston Plucknett
Wrangway
918
BLACK DOWN HILLS
1034 Staple Hill
Curland Common
Windmill Hill
Ashill
A358
Stocklinch
Hurcott
Moor
Over Stratton
A303
Norton sub Hamdon
Odcombe
Culm Davy
Clayhidon
Rosemary Lane
Churchstanton
Otterford
Blackwater
Broadway
Horton Cross
Horton
Winterhay Green
Whitelackington
Seavington St. Mary
Seavington St. Michael
Lopen
Wigborough
Chiselborough
Brympton D'Evercy
West Coker
Millhayes
Stapley
Blindmoor
Birchwood
Buckland St. Mary
Hare
Donyatt
Ilminster
Allowenshay
Merriott
A356
West Chinnock
Hemyock
Royston Water
Bishopswood
Ham
A303
Sea
Kingstone
Dowlish Wake
Dinnington
Middle Chinnock
East Chinnock
Hardington Moor
Bolham Water
Churchinford
Street Ash
Newtown
Beetham
Combe St. Nicholas
Nimmer
Peasmarsh
Knowle St. Giles
Cricket Malherbie
Perry's Cider
Hinton St. George
Lower Severalls
A30
Haselbury Plucknett
Hardington Mandeville
Sutton Bingham
Madford
Dunkeswell Abbey
Abbey
Smeatharpe
Marsh
Whitestaunton
Northay
Wadeford
Cuttiford's Door
Hornsbury
Chaffcombe
Cudworth
Chillington
Broadshard
Crewkerne
A3066
North Perrott
Hardington Marsh
E
F
G
H
A303
Newcott
Howley
Crimchard
13
Lakes & Gdns.
Purtington
Roundham
Heritage Centre
Higher Halstock Leigh
Dunkeswell
Yarcombe
A30
Chard
Wambrook
Cricket St. Thomas
Hewish
B3165
Misterton
South Perrott
Upottery
Crawley
Street
Winsham
Wayford
Clapton
Luppitt
Rawridge
A30
Forton
Whatley
Seaborough
Chelborough

22
BATH
BATH & N.E. SOMERSET
SOMERSET
MENDIP HILLS
BLACKMOOR VALE
DORSET
Chew Magna
Pensford
Compton Dando
Corston
Newton St. Loe
Twerton
Southdown
Farleigh Wick
Great Chalfield
Bradford Leigh
Bradford-on-Avon
Winsley
Freshford
Westwood
Trowle Common
Upper Studley
TROWBRIDGE
Wrington
Redhill
Lower Langford
Upper Langford
Rickford
Burrington
Blagdon
Ubley
Regil
Butcombe
Chew Stoke
West Town
Nempnett Thrubwell
Bishop Sutton
Stowey
Clutton
High Littleton
Timsbury
Farmborough
Priston
Marksbury
Chelwood
Hunstrete
Stanton Drew
Stanton Wick
Inglesbatch
Stanton Prior
Englishcombe
Wilmington
Odd Down
Monkton Combe
Combe Down
Claverton
Limpley Stoke
Midford
Combe Hay
Twinhoe
Wellow
Hinton Charterhouse
Dunkerton
Tunley
Carlingcott
Peasedown St. John
Shoscombe
Meadgate
Camerton
Radford
Paulton
Clandown
Welton
Radstock
Foxcote
Norton St. Philip
Farleigh Hungerford
Tellisford
Wingfield
Southwick
North Bradley
Hawkeridge
Rode
Woolverton
Faulkland
Laverton
Hemington
Hardington
Lullington
Beckington
Rudge
Buckland Dinham
Standerwick
Dilton Marsh
Oldford
Berkley
Great Elm
Mells
Vobster
Whatley
FROME
Chantry
Keyford
Chapmanslade
Upton Scudamore
Corsley
Lane End
Corsley Heath
Nunney
Tytherington
West Woodlands
Trudoxhill
Longhedge
East Woodlands
Longleat House
Safari & Adventure Park
Crockerton
Horningsham
Newbury
Gare Hill
Pottle Street
Hill Deverill
Brixton Deverill
Maiden Bradley
Kingston Deverill
Kilmington
Norton Ferris
White Sheet Hill
Stourhead NT
Stourton
Bonham
Gasper
Zeals
Mere
West Knoyle
Burton
Wolverton
Penselwood
Bourton
Barrow Street
Huntingford
Milton on Stour
Gillingham
Sedgehill
Wyke
Ham Common
Elm Hill
Motcombe
Cheddar
Charterhouse
Compton Martin
West Harptree
East Harptree
Coley
Sherborne
Litton
Ford
Smitham Hill
Greendown
Hinton Blewett
Temple Cloud
Cameley
North Widcombe
South Widcombe
Hallatrow
Farrington Gurney
Midsomer Norton
Clapton
Ston Easton
Chewton Mendip
Chilcompton
Bathway
Emborough
East End
Downside
Stratton-on-the-Fosse
Lipyeate
Charlton
Kilmersdon
Haydon
Holcombe
Highbury
Coleford
Leigh-upon-Mendip
Gurney Slade
Binegar
Nettlebridge
Ashwick
Oakhill
Stoke St. Michael
Little Elm
Downhead
West Horrington
East Horrington
Maesbury Castle
Bradley Cross
Draycott
Rodney Stoke
Priddy
Priddy Nine Barrows
Green Ore
Westbury-sub-Mendip
Easton
Wookey Hole
Ebbor Gorge
Walcombe
Haybridge
Theale
Panborough
Wookey
Henton
Bleadney
Yarley
Burcott
Dulcote
Wells
Dinder
Croscombe
Bowlish
Shepton Mallet
Downside
Waterlip
Chelynch
Dean
Doulting
Leighton
Holwell
Cloford
East Cranmore
West Cranmore
Weston Town
Wanstrow
Witham Friary
Upton Noble
Bruton Forest
Upper Godney
Polsham
Castle
Coxley
Lower Godney
Southway
Launcherley
North Wootton
Worminster
West Compton
East Compton
Meare
Stileway
Glastonbury
Northover
Norwood Park
Edgarley
Havyatt
West Pennard
Sticklinch
Pilton
Pylle
Street on the Fosse
East Pennard
Prestleigh
Evercreech
Westcombe
Stoney Stratton
Batcombe
Chesterblade
Higher Alham
Milton Clevedon
Lamyatt
North Brewham
South Brewham
Street
Walton
Overleigh
Butleigh Wootton
Baltonsborough
West Bradley
Parbrook
Huxham Green
Wraxall
Ditcheat
Lottisham
Ham Street
Alhampton
Wyke Champflower
Bruton
Hardway
Redlynch
Butleigh
Southwood
Hornblotton Green
Sutton
Clanville
Ansford
Castle Cary
Pitcombe
Cole
Compton Dundon
Dundon
Barton St. David
Lydford Fair Place
Alford
East Lydford
West Lydford
Dimmer
Kingweston
Stoney Stoke
Shepton Montague
Barrow
Charlton Musgrove
Bratton Seymour
Wincanton
Bayford
Leigh Common
Stoke Trister
Cucklington
Littleton
Hurcott
Keinton Mandeville
Lovington
North Barrow
South Barrow
Foddington
Galhampton
Yarlington
Babcary
Somerton
Westcombe
Pitney
Charlton Mackrell
Charlton Adam
Midney
Upton
Kingsdon
South Hill
North Cadbury
Woolston
Sparkford
Downhead
Blackford
Holton
Maperton
Lattiford
South Cheriton
North Cheriton
Compton Pauncefoot
South Cadbury
Weston Bampfylde
Queen Camel
West Camel
Sutton Montis
Long Sutton
Catsgore
Knole
Podimore
Northover
Bridgehampton
Yeovilton
Ilchester
Chilton Cantelo
Limington
Draycott
Marston Magna
Rimpton
Corton Denham
Charlton Horethorne
Stowell
Abbas Combe
Horsington
Templecombe
Yenston
Henstridge Ash
Henstridge Marsh
Henstridge
Buckhorn Weston
Kington Magna
Upper Nyland
Lower Nyland
West Stour
East Stour
Stour Provost
Stour Row
Fifehead Magdalen
Sherborne Causeway
Guy's Marsh
Todber
Long Load
Milton
Stapleton
Ash
Tintinhull
Mudford
Adber
Sandford Orcas
Milborne Wick
Henstridge Bowden
Poyntington
Milborne Port
Oborne
Chilthorne Domer
Yeovil Marsh
Stoke sub Hamdon
Montacute
Norton sub Hamdon
Odcombe
Preston Plucknett
Brympton D'Evercy
YEOVIL
Trent
Over Compton
Nether Compton
Stallen
Sherborne
Sherborne Castle
Goathill
Purse Caundle
Stalbridge Weston
Stalbridge
Marnhull
Walton Elm
Moorside
Margaret Marsh
East Orchard
Bedchester
West Orchard
Hinton St. Mary
Manston
Sutton Waldron
Farrington
Hammoon
Iwerne Minster
Chiselborough
West Chinnock
West Coker
East Coker
North Coker
Barwick
Stoford
Bradford Abbas
Thornford
Haydon
North Wootton
Alweston
Folke
Bishop's Caundle
Stourton Caundle
Lydlinch
Sturminster Newton
Child Okeford
Iwerne Courtney or Shroton
Fiddleford
Middle Chinnock
East Chinnock
Hardington Moor
Haselbury Plucknett
Hardington Mandeville
Sutton Bingham
Pendomer
Beer Hackett
Lillington
Knighton
Ryme Intrinseca
Yetminster
Longburton
Bishop's Down
Boys Hill
Holwell
Woodbridge
Packers Hill
Crouch Hill
King's Stag
Kingston
Puxey
Newton
Broad Oak
Fifehead Neville
Okeford Fitzpaine
Hanford
Shillingstone
North Perrott
Hardington Marsh
Closworth
Leigh
Chetnole
Totnell
Sandhills
Glanvilles Wootton
Pulham
Woodrow
Hazelbury Bryan
Pidney
Fifehead St. Quintin
Belchalwell
Belchalwell Street
Durweston
Higher Halstock Leigh
Halstock
Melbury Osmond
South Perrott
Hermitage
Middlemarsh
Wonston
Droop
Ibberton
Turnworth
Woolland
Stoke
Westfields
East Chelborough
Melbury Sampford
Weston
A4
A36
A37
A38
A39
A303
A350
A357
A359
A361
A362
A363
A366
A367
A368
A371
A372
A3030
A3088
A3098
B3081
B3092
B3114
B3135
B3139
B3151
B3153
B3355
B3356
34
14
21

23
MELKSHAM
Bromham
St. Edith's Marsh
Roundway Hill
Bishops Cannings
Horton
Allington
964 Tan Hill
Stanton St. Bernard
White Horse
Alton Priors
Alton Barnes
Huish
West Stowell
Oare
Wootton Rivers
Great Bedwyn
Durley
Stibb Green
Crofton Beam Engines
Kennet & Avon Canal
Bowerhill
Sells Green
Rowde
Roundway
Dunkirk
Coate
All Cannings
Honey Street
Wilcot
Pewsey
New Mill
Ram Alley
Burbage
Eastcourt
Wilton
Marten
Semington
Seend Cleeve
DEVIZES
Wiltshire Heritage
Nursteed
Broadleas
Woodborough
VALE OF PEWSEY
Milton Lilbourne
Easton Royal
West Grafton
Grafton
Poulshot
Stert
Beechingstoke
Gores
Bottlesford
Sharcott
Southcott
Manningford Bruce
Wexcombe
Great Hinton
Potterne
Patney
Wedhampton
Marden
Hilcott
Easton Hill
Tidcombe
Ashton Common
Keevil
Bulkington
Worton
Potterne Wick
Urchfont
Chirton
Wilsford
North Newton
Manningford Bohune
White Horse
Pewsey Hill
781
A350
Steeple Ashton
Marston
Conock
Charlton
Rushall
Pewsey Down
Aughton
Brunton
West Ashton
Eastcott
DANGER AREA
Easterton
Littleton Pannell
Market Lavington
Upavon
Lower Everleigh
Collingbourne Kingston
Dunge
Great Cheverell
East Coulston
Sunton
Cadley
Edington
Erlestoke
Little Cheverell
West Lavington
West Chisenbury
East Chisenbury
East Everleigh
Everleigh
Collingbourne Ducis
Upper Chute
Bratton
Stradbrook
Bratton Camp
White Horse
Heritage Centre
Littleton Down
Compton Down
Compton
Enford
Littlecott
Longstreet
Ludgershall
Westbury
WILTSHIRE
Black Heath
DANGER AREA
Fifield
Coombe
Haxton Down
735
Fittleton
Enford Down
Netheravon
North Tidworth
Tidworth
Great Shoddesden
Summer Down
West Lavington Down
Imber
Tilshead
West Down
Orcheston Down
Dovecote
Figheldean
Tidworth Camp
South Tidworth
Perham Down
Little Shoddesden
DANGER AREA
Ablington
DANGER AREA
SALISBURY
Fyfield
Kimpton
Thruxton
WARMINSTER
Dewey
Boreham
619
DANGER AREA
Orcheston
DANGER AREA
Knighton Down
482
Brigmerston
Milston
Durrington
Shipton Bellinger
Beacon Hill
Amport
Quarley
Chitterne
Elston
Maddington
Larkhill
Norton Bavant
Heytesbury
B390
Shrewton
Woodhenge
Bulford
Bulford Camp
Grateley
Stonehenge
Countess
Charlie's Farm
Cholderton
PLAIN
Sutton Veny
Knook
Tytherington
Corton
Upton Lovell
Codford St. Peter
Codford St. Mary
Winterbourne Stoke
West Amesbury
Amesbury
Newton Toney or Newton Tony
Boyton
Sherrington
Fisherton de la Mere
Deptford
Berwick St. James
Wilsford
Boscombe Down
Allington
Boscombe
Stockton
Bapton
Wylye
Steeple Langford
Over Street
Stapleford
Lake
Great Durnford
Upper Woodford
DANGER AREA
Over Wallop
Idmiston
Great Ridge
Hanging Langford
Little Langford
Heale
Netton
Middle Woodford
Salterton
Porton
Lopcombe Corner
Pertwood
Great Wishford
Stoford
Lower Woodford
Gomeldon
Chicklade
South Newton
Winterbourne Dauntsey
Winterbourne Gunner
Middle Winterslow
East Winterslow
Hindon
Berwick St. Leonard
Farmer Giles Farmstead
Teffont Magna
Philipps House
Little Clarendon
Grovely Wood
Chilhampton
Hurdcott
Winterbourne Earls
Figsbury Ring
Firsdown
The Common
Whiteshoot Hill
Fonthill Bishop
Chilmark
Ridge
Dinton
Baverstock
Fugglestone St. Peter
Ditchampton
Ugford
Stratford sub Castle
Old Sarum
Bishopdown
Laverstock
West Winterslow
Fonthill Gifford
Teffont Evias
Lower Chicksgrove
Compton Chamberlayne
Barford St. Martin
Burcombe
Wilton
Quidhampton
Bemerton
SALISBURY
Petersfinger
Pitton
Farley
West Tytherley
Tisbury
East Hatch
Upper Chicksgrove
Sutton Mandeville
Fovant
Wilton House
Netherhampton
West Harnham
East Harnham
Britford
Newtown
Pythouse Kitchen
Badges
Salisbury
East Grimstead
West Dean
Semley
Old Wardour
Swallowcliffe
Chiselbury Hillfort
Alderbury
Bodenham
Whaddon
Ansty
Bishopstone
Stratford Tony
Coombe Bissett
Odstock
Homington
West Grimstead
Dean Hill
East Dean
St. Bartholomew's Hill
Donhead St. Andrew
Fifield Bavant
Broad Chalke
Stoke Farthing
Croucheston
Nunton
Odstock Down
The Pepperbox
Carter's Clay
Donhead St. Mary
West End
Ebbesbourne Wake
White Sheet Hill
Alvediston
Charlton
Whiteparish
Shaftesbury
Milkwell
Berwick St. John
Bowerchalke
Ludwell
Woodminton
Newton
Cann Common
Charlton
Winklebury Camp
Rockbourne Down
Wick Down
Wick
Morgan's Vale
Downton
Redlynch
Martin Drove End
Woodfalls
Hamptworth
Plaitford
Melbury Abbas
Win Green
Woodyates
Martin
Breamore House
North Charford
Lover
Landford
Compton Abbas
CHASE
Tidpit
New Town
Whitsbury
Upper Street
Hale
Tollard Royal
Deanland
Sixpenny Handley
Rockbourne
Breamore
Canada
Ashmore
Woodcutts
Pentridge
607
Outwick
Woodgreen
Nomansland
Larmer Tree
Pentridge Hill
Rockbourne Roman Villa
Upper Burgate
Furzley
Well Bottom
Tollard Farnham
Dean
Sir Eyre Coote's Monument
Lower Burgate
Castle Hill
NEW
Bramshaw
Gussage St. Andrew
Damerham
Newbridge
Farnham
Minchington
Boveridge
Sandleheath
Fordingbridge
Godshill
FOREST
Alderholt Mill
Ashford
Fritham
CRANBORNE
Monkton Up Wimborne
Cranborne Manor
Brook
Stubhampton
Cashmoor
Cranborne
Crendell
Stuckton
Blissford
Upper Canterton
Chettle
Chettle House
Cripplestyle
Alderholt
Bickton
Frogham
Rufus Stone
Tarrant Gunville
Gussage St. Michael
Wimborne St. Giles
Daggons
Hungerford
North Gorley
NEW FOREST
Minstead
Tarrant Hinton
Gussage All Saints
Knowlton Church & Earthworks
Edmondsham House
Edmondsham
HAMPSHIRE
Stoney Cross
Furzey Gardens
Dorset Heavy Horse Centre
South Gorley
Newtown
Tarrant Launceston
Long Crichel
Harbridge
Linwood
Pimperne
Tarrant Monkton
Verwood
Ibsley
NATIONAL PARK
Pikeshill
Ringwood Forest
Deer Sanctuary
New Forest
Woodlands
Whitmore
Ebblake
Mockbeggar
Blandford Camp
Manswood
Moor Crichel
Ellingham
Emery Down
Royal Signals
Horton
Rockford
Arboretum
Reptile Centre
Blandford Forum
Hogstock
Chalbury
Wigbeth
Tower
Crab Orchard
Blashford
Linford
Bolderwood Ornamental Drive
Knightwood Oak
Witchampton
Chalbury Common
Hangersley
Poulner
Bank
Tarrant Rawston

24
A
B
C
D
36
1
2
3
4
5
23
16
WILTSHIRE
H
A
M
P
S
H
I
R
E
NEW FOREST NATIONAL PARK
NEW FOREST
Great Bedwyn
Durley
Ram Alley
Stibb Green
Crofton
Burbage
Easton Royal
Grafton
East Grafton
Wilton
Marten
Shalbourne
Ham
Rivar
Oxenwood
Wexcombe
Tidcombe
Fosbury
Haydown Hill 860
Lower Green
Inkpen
Upper Green
West Woodhay
Combe Gibbet
Buttermere
Combe
Walbury Hill 947
East Woodhay
North End
Ball Hill
Broad Laying
Woolton Hill
East End
Highclere
Pound Street
Enborne Row
Newtown
Burghclere
Sandham Memorial Chapel
Whitway
Old Burghclere
Highclere Castle
Beacon Hill
Sydmonton
Watership Down
Kingsclere
Ecchinswell
Crookham
Headley
Plastow Green
Ashford Hill
Aldermaston Soke
Heath End
Baughurst
Tadley
Fair Oak
Wolverton Common
Pamber Green
Towns End
West Heath
Wolverton
Ramsdell
Charter Alley
Monk Sherborne
Hannington
Ibworth
North Oakley
Upper Wootton
Wootton St. Lawrence
Winklebury
Worting
Newfound
BASINGSTOKE
Oakley
East Oakley
Kempshott
Deane
Ashe
Quidhampton
Overton
Southington
Laverstoke
Pardown
Steventon
Hatch Warren
North Waltham
Dummer
Popham
Micheldever Station
Woodmancott
Preston Candover
Chilton Candover
Brown Candover
Northington
Swarraton
Grange
Abbotstone
Old Alresford
New Alresford
Bighton
Gundleton
Bishops Sutton
Itchen Stoke
Ovington
Tichborne
Cheriton
Cheriton 1644
New Cheriton
Hinton Ampner
Kilmeston
Beauworth
Lane End
Linkenholt
Little Down
Vernham Street
Faccombe
Netherton
Ashmansworth
Crux Easton
Vernham Dean
Upton
Woodcott
Litchfield
Dunley
Wadwick
Binley
Egbury
Aughton
Collingbourne Kingston
Brunton
Sunton
Cadley
Collingbourne Ducis
East Everleigh
Ludgershall
Upper Chute
Chute Standen
Lower Chute
Tangley
Hurstbourne Tarrant
Ibthorpe
Bourne
Doles Wood
Stoke
Wildhern
Swampton
St. Mary Bourne
Cole Henley
Freefolk Priors
Whitchurch
Silk Mill
Tufton
Hurstbourne Priors
North Tidworth
Tidworth
Tidworth Camp
South Tidworth
Great Shoddesden
Perham Down
Little Shoddesden
Appleshaw
Ragged Appleshaw
Duck Street
Clanville
Hatherden
Upper Enham
Little London
Smannell
Enham-Alamein
East Anton
Penton Mewsey
Charlton
Picket Piece
Finkley Down Farm
Weyhill
Fyfield
Kimpton
Thruxton
Shipton Bellinger
Andover
ANDOVER
Andover Down
East Aston
Deadman's Plague
Middleton
Longparish
Forton
Monxton
Amport
Quarley
Abbots Ann
Anna Valley
Upper Clatford
Harewood Forest
Goodworth Clatford
Grateley
Cholderton
Newton Toney or Newton Tony
Palestine
Allington
Bransbury
Lower Bullington
Upper Bullington
Newton Stacey
Barton Stacey
Egypt
Hunton
SUTTON SCOTNEY
Sutton Scotney
Wonston
Stoke Charity
Micheldever
West Stratton
East Stratton
Micheldever Wood
Wherwell
Chilbolton
Fullerton
DANGER AREA
Middle Wallop
Army Flying
Over Wallop
Middle Wallop
Danebury Hill Fort
Leckford
Longstock
Nether Wallop
Lopcombe Corner
South Wonston
Crawley
WINCHESTER
Stockbridge
Woolbury
New Art Centre
Middle Winterslow
East Winterslow
The Common
West Winterslow
Firsdown
Pitton
Whiteshoot Hill
Broughton
Houghton Lodge
Houghton
Little Somborne
Up Somborne
Worthy Down
Kings Worthy
Abbots Worthy
Martyr Worthy
Itchen Abbas
Chilland
Avington
Easton
Flowerdown Barrows
Littleton
Headbourne Worthy
Dean
Sparsholt
Weeke
Fulflood
Giles's Hill
Horsebridge
Ashley
King's Somborne
Farley
West Tytherley
East Tytherley
Farley Mount 584
Horse Monument
Brook
East Grimstead
West Dean
West Grimstead
Dean Hill
East Dean
The Pepperbox
Lockerley
Mottisfont
Pitt
Stanmore
St. Cross
Chilcomb
Standon
Oliver's Battery
Compton
Twyford
Morestead
Longwood Warren
Michelmersh
Braishfield
Hursley
Sir Harold Hillier
Dunbridge
Carter's Clay
Kent's Oak
Newtown
Timsbury
Awbridge
Whiteparish
Ratley
Knapp
Ampfield
Shawford
Owslebury
Baybridge
Newton
Sherfield English
Romsey
King John's House
Abbey
Cupernham
Whitenap
Hiltingbury
Otterbourne
Brambridge
Colden Common
Hensting
Marwell
Fisher's Pond
Upham
Lower Upham
Crowdhill
Redlynch
Lover
Hamptworth
Landford
Plaitford
West Wellow
East Wellow
Broadlands
North Baddesley
Chandler's Ford
Fryern Hill
Allbrook
Bishopstoke
Ashfield
Toot Hill
ROWNHAMS
Chilworth
Lee
Upton
Rownhams
Nursling
Bassett
EASTLEIGH
SOUTHAMPTON INTERNATIONAL
Fair Oak
Durley Street
Durley
Horton Heath
Bishop's Waltham
Bishop's Waltham Palace
Dean
Dundridge
Droxford
Swanmore
Waltham Chase
Corhampton
Exton
Canada
Nomansland
Furzley
Wigley
Ower
Paultons Park
Hillstreet
Bramshaw
Newbridge
Copythorne
Winsor
Cadnam
Calmore
Testwood
TOTTON
Maybush
Swaythling
Moorgreen
West End
Bitterne
Long Common
Boorley Green
Curdridge
Vineyards
Shirrell Heath
Newtown
Row Ash
Shedfield
Turkey Island
Soberton Heath
Fritham
Brook
Upper Canterton
Rufus Stone
Bartley
Netley Marsh
Eling
Eling Tide Mill
Millbrook
Shirley
Portswood
Northam
Thornhill
Wildern
Broadoak
Botley
Hedge End
Manor Farm
Curbridge
Wickham
Hundred Acres
Hipley
Stoney Cross
Minstead
Woodlands
Hounsdown
SOUTHAMPTON
Itchen
Sholing
Woolston
Ashurst
Longdown
Pooksgreen
Marchwood
New Forest
Lowford
Bursledon
Burridge
Whiteley
Swanwick
Lower Swanwick
Sarisbury
Knowle Village
North Boarhunt
Crockerhill
Funtley
Boarhunt
Pikeshill
Emery Down
Deer Sanctuary
Arboretum
Lyndhurst
Netley Abbey
Netley
Butlocks Heath
Hound
Park Gate
Locks Heath
Segensworth
Titchfield Abbey
Catisfield
Wallington
Fort Nelson
Reptile Centre
Bolderwood Ornamental Drive
Knightwood Oak
Bank
Clayhill
Beaulieu R.
Appiemore
Dibden
Dibden Purlieu
HYTHE
Langdown
Hamble
Southampton Water
A31
A34
A339
B3051
A340
A338
A343
B3048
A303
A3093
B3402
B3400
M3
A30
B3420
A3057
A272
B3049
A33
B3047
B3046
A3090
B3404
A31
B3084
A36
A27
A3090
B3043
B3335
B3354
B2177
B3035
A32
A335
A35
M27
M271
B3079
B3078
B3080
A336
A337
A3024
A3025
B3397
A3051
A326
B3056
A334
A3026
A342
A346
B3037
B3342

25
Mortimer
Swallowfield
Crowthorne
Windlesham
Addlestone
Silchester
Finchampstead
Bagshot
Eversley
Sandhurst
Lightwater
Chobham
Woodham
Owlsmoor
CAMBERLEY
Yateley
Frogmore
Blackwater
Bramley
Stratfield Turgis
Cricket Hill
Horsell
Sherfield on Loddon
Mattingley
Hawley
Frimley
Bisley
Knaphill
WOKING
Rotherwick
Hartley Wintney
Fox Lane
Frimley Green
Deepcut
Brookwood
Mayford
FLEET
M3
Phoenix Green
Mytchett
Pirbright
Newnham
Hook
Cove
FARNBOROUGH
Send
Old Basing
Fleet
Ash Vale
Worplesdon
Sutton Green
North Warnborough
Crookham Village
Church Crookham
ALDERSHOT
Jacobswell
West Clandon
Greywell
Odiham
Wood Street
Normandy
Cliddesden
Ash
Flexford
SURREY
Onslow Village
Crondall
Upton Grey
Long Sutton
Tongham
A31
Puttenham
GUILDFORD
Chilworth
South Warnborough
FARNHAM
Compton
Shalford
Farleigh Wallop
Ellisfield
Shackleford
Wonersh
NORTH DOWNS
Lower Froyle
Bentley
Peper Harow
Tilford
Elstead
GODALMING
Upper Froyle
Millbridge
Milford
Bradley
Holybourne
Frensham
Alton
Binsted
Rushmoor
Thursley
Witley
Hascombe
Bentworth
Beech
Kingsley
Churt
Wormley
Hambledon
Medstead
Chawton
East Worldham
Beacon Hill
Dunsfold
Upper Farringdon
Lindford
Arford
Headley
Headley Down
Hindhead
Chiddingfold
Four Marks
Bordon
Grayshott
Grayswood
Whitehill
Bramshott
Selborne
Haslemere
Ropley
East Tisted
Greatham
Linchmere
Ifold
Plaistow
Liphook
Hawkley
Liss Forest
Fernhurst
Northchapel
Liss
Rake
Hill Brow
Milland
Kirdford
Steep
Sheet
Stroud
West Meon
PETERSFIELD
Rogate
Easebourne
Lodsworth
Petworth
East Meon
Trotton
Stedham
Midhurst
SOUTH DOWNS NATIONAL PARK
Buriton
Minsted
Tillington
West Lavington
Cocking Causeway
Byworth
Pulborough
Fittleworth
Stopham
Clanfield
Treyford
Heyshott
Graffham
Duncton
Cocking
WEST SUSSEX
SOUTH DOWNS
Coldwaltham
Watersfield
Hambledon
Chilgrove
Sutton
HORNDEAN
Forestside
Singleton
Amberley
West Dean
Bury
Houghton
Denmead
Cowplain
Rowland's Castle
WATERLOOVILLE
A3(M)
Mid Lavant
East Lavant
Slindon
Arundel
Purbrook
HAVANT
Westbourne
East Ashling
Boxgrove
Fontwell
A27

26
GUILDFORD
Worplesdon
Fox Corner
Pitch Place
Sutton Green
Burntcommon
Send
Jacobswell
West Clandon
East Clandon
West Horsley
East Horsley
Little Bookham
Great Bookham
Effingham
Mickleham
Westhumble
Polesden Lacey NT
Box Hill
Lower Kingswood
Kingswood
Margery
Ash Vale
Army Medical Services
DANGER AREA
Willey Green
Fairlands
Stoughton
Wyke
Normandy
Wood Street Village
Burpham
Clandon Park NT
Merrow
Newlands Corner
Hatchlands Park
Ranmore Common
Denbies Wine Estate
Buckland
Betchworth
Brockham
REIGATE
Flexford
Onslow Village
Silent Pool
Sherbourne Farm
Gomshall
Westcott
DORKING
Strood Green
Gadbrook
Doversgreen
Badshot Lea
Tongham
Wanborough
Puttenham
Artington
Littleton
Compton
Shalford Mill
Chilworth
Shalford
Albury
Shere
Abinger Hammer
Wotton
North Holmwood
Stonebridge
Leigh
Salfords
FARNHAM
Runfold
Seale
The Sands
Hog's Back
Loseley Park
Peasmarsh
Blackheath
Brook
Friday Street
Sutton Abinger
Dawesgreen
Sidlow
Waverley
Shackleford
Farncombe
Tower
Wonersh
Farley Green
Peaslake
Abinger Common
South Holmwood
Blackbrook
Nalderswood
Peper Harow
Hurtmore
Bramley
Catteshall
Eashing
GODALMING
Shamley Green
Holmbury St. Mary
Hurtwood Common
Coldharbour
Leith Hill Tower NT
Norwood Hill
Parkgate
Meath Green
Tilford
Rural Life Centre
Millbridge
Little Pond
Elstead
Busbridge
Thorncombe Street
Winkworth Arboretum
Grafham
Beare Green
Hookwood
Milford
Busbridge Lakes
Tuesley
Hydestile
Rowly
Forest Green
Newdigate
Cudworth
LONDON GATWICK
Rushmoor
Thursley
Wheelerstreet
Witley
Hascombe
Ewhurst
Capel
Ockley
Clark's Green
Charlwood
Lowfield Heath
Russ Hill
Langley Green
Millais Gardens
Churt
Bowlhead Green
Brook
Wormley
Sandhills
Hambledon
Oakhurst Cottage
Loxhill
Cranleigh
Ewhurst Green
Mayes Green
Walliswood
Hannah Peschar Sculpture
Ifieldwood
Ifield
CRAWLEY
Beacon Hill
Devil's Punch Bowl
Hindhead
Gibbet Hill
Vachery Pond
Dunsfold
Alfold Crossways
Oakwoodhill
Kingsfold
Rusper
Lambs Green
Gossops Green
Grayshott
Chiddingfold
Grayswood
Highstreet Green
Alfold
Alfold Bars
Ellen's Green
Cox Green
Rudgwick
Rowhook
Warnham
Faygate
Holmbush Farm World
Pease Pottage
Broadfield
Shottermill
Haslemere
Ramster
Educational
Bucks Green
Loxwood
Tisman's Common
Strood Green
Broadbridge Heath
Roffey
Colgate
Tilgate Row
Hammer
Camelsdale
Linchmere
Anstead Brook
Ramsnest Common
Fisherstreet
Plaistow
Ifold
Park Street
Slinfold
The Haven
HORSHAM
ST. LEONARDS FOREST
Liphook
Kingsley Green
Black Down
Roundhurst
The Lake
Doomsday Green
Hollycombe
Fernhurst
Northchapel
Ebernoe
Roundstreet Common
Five Oaks
Itchingfield
Tower Hill
Denne Park
Mannings Heath
Plummers Plain
Ashfold Crossways
Lurgashall Winery
Dial Green
Lurgashall
Southwater Street
Monk's Gate
Lower Beeding
Slaugham
Woodmansgreen
Newpound Common
Kirdford
Barns Green
Redford
Henley
Lickfold
Balls Cross
Fishers Farm Park
Billingshurst
Southwater
Nuthurst
Warninglid
Bexleyhill
Wisborough Green
Parbrook
Copsale
Crabtree
Brooks Green
Maplehurst
Woolbeding
Lodsworth
Petworth House & Park
Strood Green
Adversane
Dragons Green
Easebourne
Coneyhurst Common
Coolham
Bolney
Stedham
River
Upperton
Petworth
Bedham
North Heath
Shipley
Whitehall
Cowfold
Midhurst
Cowdray Ho. (Ruin)
West Lavington
Tillington
Selham
Gay Street
Broadford Bridge
Brooner's Corner
Knepp Castle
Littleworth
Kent Street
Hickstead
Twineham
Cocking Causeway
South Ambersham
Coultershaw Bridge
Byworth
Little Bognor
Codmore Hill
West Grinstead
Wineham
Hickstead All England Jumping Course
Beam Pump
Fittleworth
Coates
Pulborough
Nutbourne
Vineyards
Dial Post
Partridge Green
Shermanbury
Sayers Common
Heyshott
Hoyle
Upper Norwood
Stopham
Lower Horncroft
Hardham
Marehill
West Chiltington
Spear Hill
Cocking
Graffham
Duncton
Wiggonholt
West Chiltington Common
Thakeham
Bines Green
Henfield
Blackstone
Albourne
East Lavington
Barlavington
Coldwaltham
Warminghurst
Ashington
Sutton
Watersfield
Greatham
Parham
Hole Street
Ashurst
Woodmancote
SOUTH
Bignor
Bignor Roman Villa
West Burton
Amberley
Cootham
Rackham
Storrington
Heath Common
Rock
Wiston
Oreham Common
Singleton
Charlton
Upwaltham
Bury
Sullington
Washington
Small Dole
Poynings
Devil's Dyke
East Dean
Weald & Downland Open Air
Stane Street
Houghton
Kithurst Hill 700
Chanctonbury Ring
Bramber
Edburton
West Dean
Goodwood
SOUTH DOWNS NATIONAL PARK
Steyning
Upper Beeding
Fulking
The Trundle
Cass Sculpture Foundation
Madehurst
North Stoke
South Stoke
Bramber St. Mary's
Mid Lavant
Goodwood Motor Circuit
Eartham
Arundel Park
Wetland Centre
Offham
Burpham
Wepham
549 Harrow Hill
North End
Findon
Cissbury Ring
Botolphs
Coombes Farm
Coombes
East Lavant
Waterbeach
Halnaker
Boxgrove
Slindon
Fontwell
Arundel
Warningcamp
Findon Valley
Upper Cokeham
Lancing College Chapel
Mile Oak
Westerton
Westhampnett
Summersdale
Tangmere
Military Aviation
Norton
Nyton
Fontwell Park
Binstead
Crossbush
Patching
Clapham
High Salvington
North Lancing
SOUTHWICK
Kingston by Sea
Aldingbourne
Walberton
Eastergate
Tortington
Poling Corner
Angmering
Westergate
Lyminster
Poling
Hill Fort Highdown
Durrington
Sompting
Lancing
Ford
Oving
Woodgate
Barnham
Colworth
Wick
Hangleton
South Lancing
SHOREHAM-BY-SEA
Portslade-by-Sea
Runcton
Merston
Lidsey
Yapton
Rustington
Open Late 2012
Climping
East Preston
Kingston
Ferring
Church
Elbridge
North Bersted
Shripney
Bilsham
Flansham
Hunston
North Mundham
LITTLEHAMPTON
Angmering-on-Sea
Goring-by-Sea
West Worthing
WORTHING
South Bersted
Ancton
Atherington
Harbour Park
Lagness
Mundham
Middleton-on-Sea
Street End
Felpham
Nyetimber
Aldwick
Pagham
BOGNOR REGIS
Sidlesham
Pagham Harbour
ENGLISH
SURREY
WEST SUSSEX
NORTH DOWNS
SOUTH DOWNS
A3
A31
A24
A29
A272
A283
A27
A259
A280
A264
A23
M25
A217
A286
A285
A281
B2130
B2127
B2128
B2133
B2139
B2135
B2116
B2132
B2233
B2140
B2166
B2145

27
CATERHAM
SEVENOAKS
Westerham
Oxted
Limpsfield
Godstone
REDHILL
Bletchingley
M25
M23
A22
A21
A26
A228
Plaxtol
Mereworth
Wateringbury
Hildenborough
TONBRIDGE
Hadlow
East Peckham
Paddock Wood
Edenbridge
Lingfield
HORLEY
Penshurst
Southborough
Pembury
Matfield
Copthorne
Felbridge
EAST GRINSTEAD
Forest Row
Hartfield
Groombridge
ROYAL TUNBRIDGE WELLS
Frant
Lamberhurst
Crawley Down
Turners Hill
West Hoathly
Sharpthorne
Balcombe
Ardingly
ASHDOWN FOREST
CROWBOROUGH
Rotherfield
Mark Cross
Wadhurst
Ticehurst
Stonegate
Mayfield
HAYWARDS HEATH
Cuckfield
Lindfield
Danehill
Nutley
Maresfield
Uckfield
Buxted
Heathfield
Burwash
BURGESS HILL
Hurstpierpoint
Hassocks
Ditchling
Newick
Framfield
Horam
Herstmonceux
Halland
Laughton
Ringmer
LEWES
Glynde
HAILSHAM
Polegate
Pevensey
Pevensey Bay
BRIGHTON
Rottingdean
Woodingdean
Saltdean
Peacehaven
NEWHAVEN
SEAFORD
Willingdon
EASTBOURNE
Langney Point
KENT
HIGH WEALD
EAST SUSSEX
SOUTH DOWNS
CHANNEL
Newhaven to: Dieppe 4hrs.

28
Mereworth
Bearsted
Harrietsham
Lenham
NORTH
Leeds
Teston
Barming
Wateringbury
Nettlestead
East Farleigh
Loose
Otham
Langley
Broomfield
M20
Charing Heath
Lenham Heath
Charing
Challock
Coxheath
Boughton Monchelsea
Chart Sutton
Linton
Yalding
Hadlow
Sutton Valence
Ulcombe
Egerton
Boughton Lees
Westwell
East Peckham
Golden Green
Collier Street
Paddock Wood
Marden
Staplehurst
Headcorn
Pluckley
Hothfield
ASHFORD
Pembury
Matfield
Brenchley
Horsmonden
Frittenden
Smarden
Great Chart
Bethersden
Kingsnorth
ROYAL TUNBRIDGE WELLS
Goudhurst
Cranbrook
Sissinghurst
Biddenden
High Halden
Shadoxhurst
Lamberhurst
Kilndown
Hartley
St. Michaels
Tenterden
Woodchurch
Hamstreet
HIGH WEALD
Wadhurst
Cousley Wood
Sparrow's Green
Durgates
Flimwell
Hawkhurst
Benenden
Rolvenden
Rolvenden Layne
Appledore
Appledore Heath
Ticehurst
Stonegate
Sandhurst
Wittersham
Isle of Oxney
Hurst Green
Etchingham
Newenden
Bodiam
Northiam
Beckley
Peasmarsh
Iden
Brookland
Burwash
Robertsbridge
EAST SUSSEX
Playden
Rye
WALLAND MARSH
Broad Oak
Udimore
Camber
Rye Harbour
Battle
Whatlington
Sedlescombe
Brede
Winchelsea
Icklesham
Rye Bay
Westfield
Three Oaks
Pett
Fairlight
Herstmonceux
Windmill Hill
Ninfield
Crowhurst
Baldslow
HASTINGS
St. Leonards
BEXHILL
Hooe
Cooden
Pevensey
Pevensey Bay
ENGLIS
Langney Point
EASTBOURNE
A
B
C
D
70
80
90
600

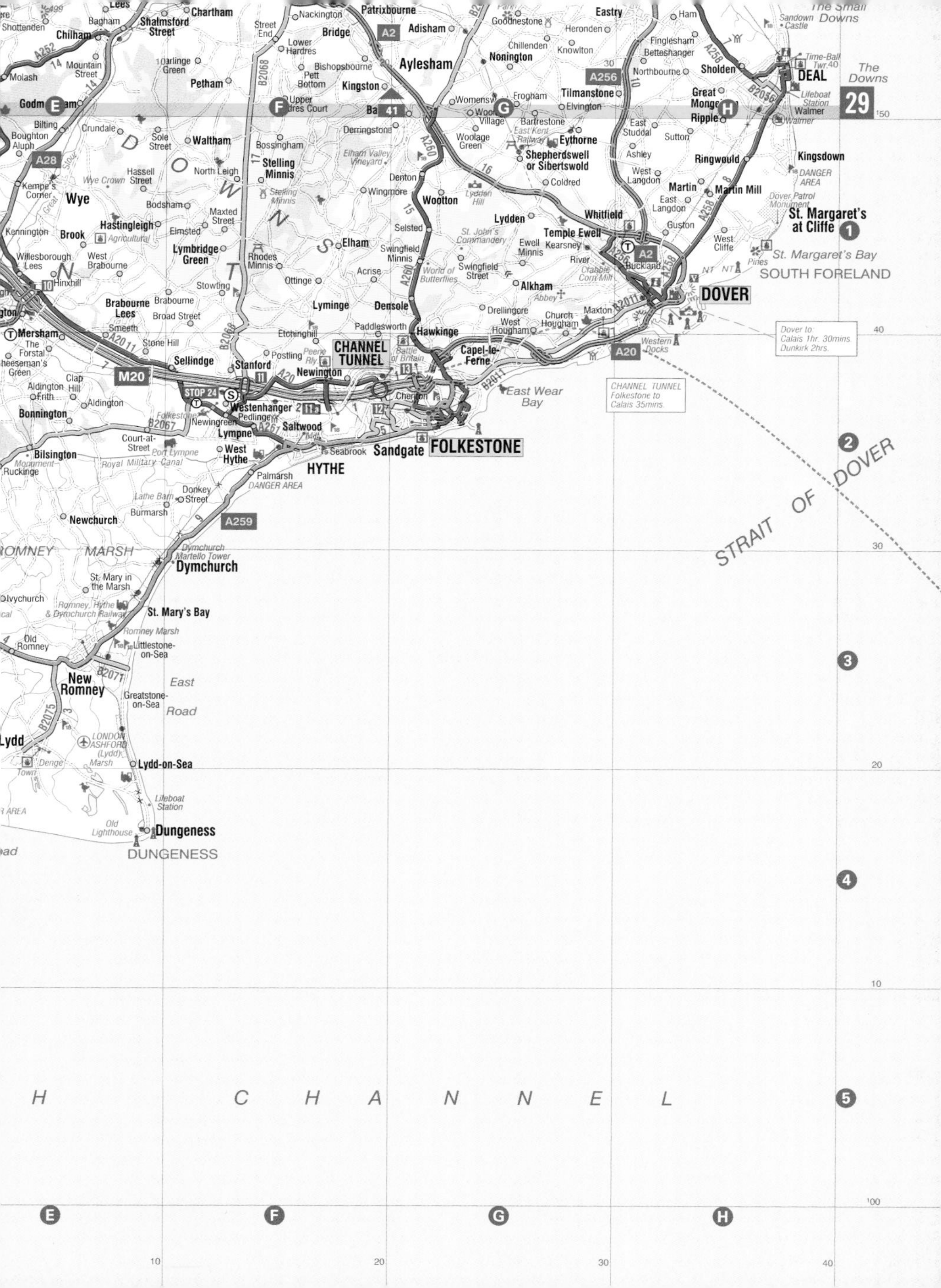

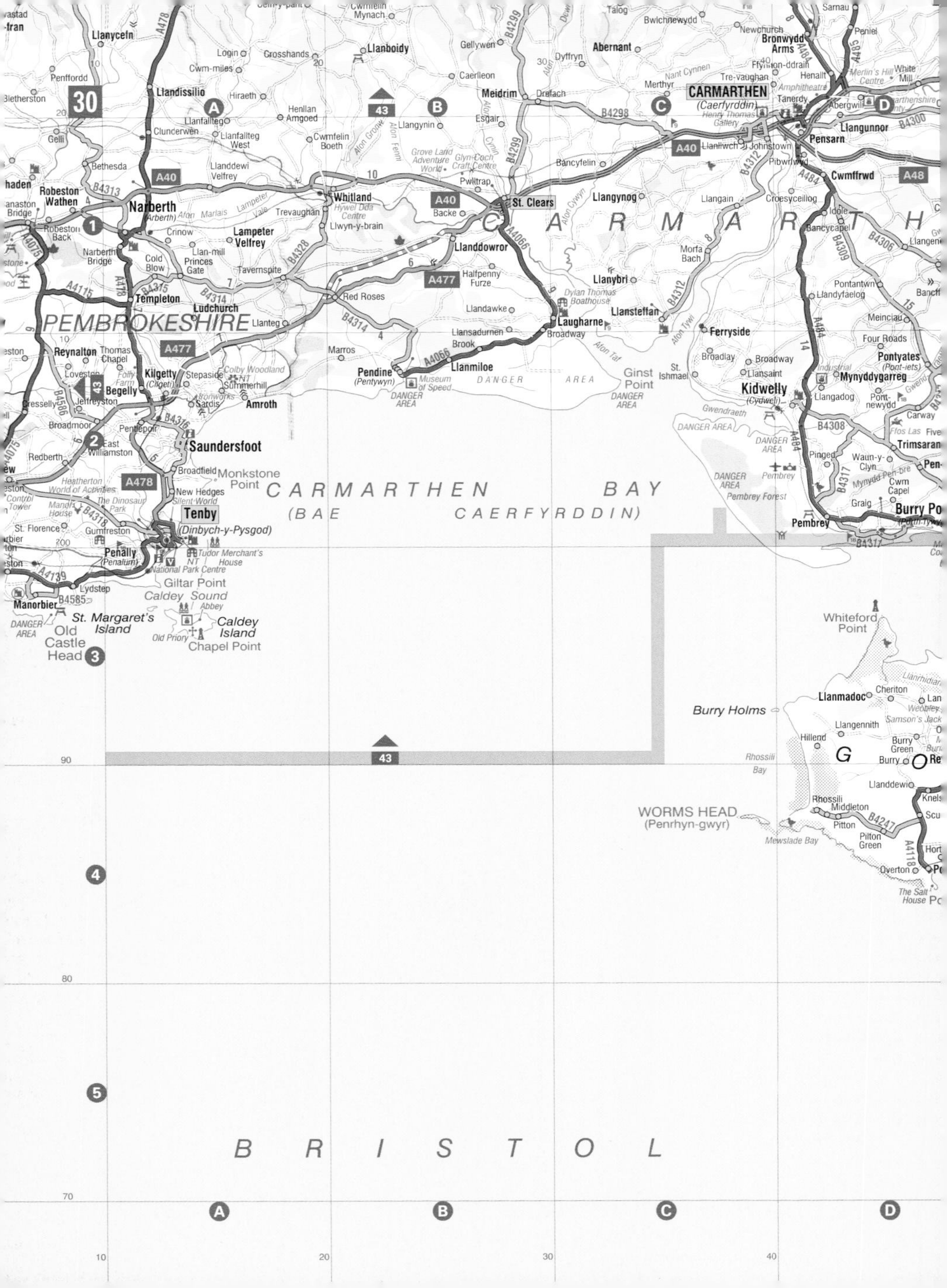

30
43
PEMBROKESHIRE
CARMARTHEN
(Caerfyrddin)
C A R M A R T H
CARMARTHEN BAY
(BAE CAERFYRDDIN)
B R I S T O L
Narberth
Whitland
St. Clears
Tenby
(Dinbych-y-Pysgod)
Saundersfoot
Kidwelly
Laugharne
Pendine
Amroth
Kilgetty
Templeton
Llanboidy
Meidrim
Llansteffan
Ferryside
Pembrey
Burry Port
Caldey Island
Worms Head
(Penrhyn-gwyr)
Burry Holms
Whiteford Point
Llanmadoc
Rhossili
Manorbier
Penally
Old Castle Head
St. Margaret's Island
Giltar Point
Monkstone Point
A40
A477
A478
A4066
A484
A48
A B C D
10 20 30 40
90 80 70

31
POWYS
BLACK MOUNTAIN
FFOREST FAWR
BRECON BEACONS NATIONAL PARK
NEATH
PORT TALBOT
AFAN FOREST PARK
SWANSEA
CARMARTHENSHIRE
CHANNEL
Swansea Bay
(Bae Abertawe)
Llandeilo
Ffairfach
Rhosmaen
Pen-y-banc
Felingwmuchaf
Felingwmisaf
Llanfihangel-uwch-Gwili
Nantgaredig
Pont-ar-gothi
Court Henry
Broad Oak
Llangathen
Cilsan
Dryslwyn
Llanarthne
Golden Grove
Dinefwr Park
Gelli Aur Arboretum
Paxton's Tower
National Botanic Garden of Wales
Carreg Cennen
Trapp
Temple Bar
Pant-y-llyn
Llandyfan
Carmel
Maesybont
Pentre Gwenlais
Llanddarog
Porthyrhyd
Llandybie
Cae'r-bryn
Gorslas
Cefneithin
Drefach
Cross Hands
Pen-y-groes
Saron
Tir-y-dail
Ammanford
(Rhydaman)
Glanaman
Garnant
Pontamman
Betws
Pantyffynnon
Tycroes
Capel Hendre
Cwmgwili
Penybanc
Tumble
(Y Tymbl)
Pontyberem
Capel Seion
Cwm-mawr
Crwbin
Pont-Henri
Llannon
Pont Abraham
Llwyn-Teg
Sylen
Cynheidre
Horeb
Sardis
Fforest
Pontarddulais
Hendy
Pentrebach
Garnswllt
Cwmcerdinen
Mynydd y Gwair
Mynydd Garn-fach
Upper Lliw Resr.
Lower Lliw Resr.
Tyn-y-cwm
Felindre
Cwm Dulais
Llwyncelyn
Cynghordy
Craig-cefn-parc
Fagwyr
Clydach
Pontardawe
Trebanos
Alltwen
Rhos
Gellinudd
Cilybebyll
Ynysmeudwy
Llangiwg
Rhyd-y-fro
Cilmaengwyn
Godre'r-graig
Ystalyfera
Glan-rhyd
Cwm-twrch Isaf
Gurnos
Ystradgynlais
Cwmgiedd
Abercraf
Caehopkin
Cae'r-bont
Penrhos
Coelbren
Onllwyn
Dyffryn Cellwen
Seven Sisters
(Blaendulais)
Glyn-neath
Morfa Glas
Pentreclwydau
Blaengwrach
Cwmgwrach
Crynant
Resolven
(Resolfen)
Melincourt
Abergarwed
Clyne
(Y Clun)
Glyncorrwg
Aberdulais
Cilfrew
Cadoxton-Juxta-Neath
Bryn-coch
Tonna
(Tonnau)
Neath Abbey
Rhydding
NEATH
(Castell-nedd)
Cimla
Tonmawr
Abercregan
Cymmer
(Cymer)
Abergwynfi
Croeserw
Caerau
Cynonville
Duffryn
Dyffryn
Nantyffyllon
Pontycymer
MAESTEG
Cwmfelin
Llangynwyd
Coytrahen
Tondu
Aberkenfig
Cefn Cribwr
Kenfig Hill
Pyle
North Cornelly
South Cornelly
Kenfig
Mawdlam
Sker Point
Nottage
PORTHCAWL
Newton
Laleston
Pen-y-fai
Cefn Glas
Newcastle
Tythegston
Merthyr Mawr
Candleston
Ogmore
St. Bride's Major
Ogmore-by-Sea
Southerndown
Tusker Rock
Margam
Groes
Eglwys Nunydd Resr.
Margam Stones
Taibach
Goytre
PORT TALBOT
Aberavon
(Aberafan)
Sandfields
Baglan
Cwmafan
Corlannau
Bryn
Brynbryddan
Pwll-y-glaw
Pontrhydyfen
Efail-fach
Briton Ferry
(Llansawel)
Ynysmaerdy
Pencaerau
Skewen
Pentre-dwr
Llandarcy
Jersey Marine
Port Tennant
Birchgrove
Llansamlet
Glais
Ynystawe
Ynysforgan
Pant-lasau
Morriston
Llangyfelach
Penllergaer
Tircoed
Pontlliw
Swansea West
Gorseinon
Penyrheol
Grovesend
Bynea
Llwynhendy
Pemberton
Bryn
Llangennech
Allt
Felinfoel
Dafen
Furnace
Sandy
Pwll
Cefncaeau
LLANELLI
National Wetland Centre Wales
Loughor
Ysbitty
Garden Village
Cadle
Port Mead
Fforest-fach
Landore
Winsh-wen
Bon-y-maen
Mayhill
Townhill
Waunarlwydd
Gowerton
Pen-clawdd
Crofty
Llanmorlais
Three Crosses
Blue Anchor
Dunvant
Killay
Sketty
Upper Killay
Lower Sketty
Brynmill
St. Thomas
SWANSEA
(Abertawe)
Swansea Centre
Dylan Thomas Centre
National Waterfront
Egypt Centre
Mayals
Black Pill
West Cross
Norton
Oystermouth
Newton
Langland
Mumbles
(Mwmbwls)
Mumbles Head
Northway
Murton
Bishopston
Kittle
Caswell
Southgate
Pwlldu Head
Pennard
Parkmill
Lunnon
Ilston
Sandylane
Penmaen
Nicholaston
Penrice
Oxwich
Oxwich Bay
Oxwich Green
Slade
Port-Eynon
Little Reynoldston
Llethrid
Llanrhidian
Cilifor Top
Parc le Breos Burial Chamber
Penmaen Burrows Chambered Tomb
River Loughor
(Afon Llwchwr)
Upper Brynamman
Brynamman
Lower Brynamman
Rhosaman
Black Mountain Centre
Gwaun-Cae-Gurwen
Cwmgors
Tairgwaith
Cwm-twrch Uchaf
Cefn-bryn-brain
Cwmllynfell
Ystradowen
Pen Rhiwfawr
Twynllanan
Pontarllechau
Llanddeusant
Capel Gwynfe
Neuadd
Trichrug
Y Garn Goch Hill Forts
Source of R. Usk
Afon Sawdde
Llyn y Fan Fach
Fan Fach
Glas Fynydd Forest
Moel Feity
Llyn y Fan-Fawr
Cray Resr.
Gareg Las
Foel Fraith
Bylchau Rhos-faen
Cefn Carn-Fadog
Carreg-lem
Castell-y-geifr
National Showcaves Centre for Wales
Craig-y-nos
Glyntawe
Penwyllt
Pen-y-cae
Ynyswen
Henrhyd Waterfall
Fan-Gihirych
Afon Pyrddin Waterfalls
Melincourt Waterfall
Mynydd Marchywel
Cefn Coed Colliery
Mynydd Margam
Moel Ton-mawr
Mynydd Caerau
Mynydd Baedon
Garw Fechan Woodland Park
Afon Afan
Afon Forest Park
South Wales Miners
Kenfig
Cribwr Ironworks
M4
A40
A48
A483
A4138
A474
A465
A4067
A4069
A4221
A4109
A476
A484
A4240
A4118
B4297
B4300
B4310
B4556
B4317
B4306
B4309
B4308
B4620
B4295
B4296
B4271
B4436
B4593
B4290
B4287
B4282
B4242
B4434
B4283
B4281
B4524
A4106
A4229
A4063

32
POWYS
NEATH
PORT TALBOT
RHONDDA
CYNON
TAFF
MERTHYR TYDFIL
BRIDGEND
THE VALE OF GLAMORGAN
BRISTOL CHAN
Ystalyfera
Ystradgynlais
Abercraf
Cwmllynfell
Rhosaman
Lower Brynamman
Coelbren
Seven Sisters
(Blaendulais)
Glyn-neath
Pontneddfechan
Ystradfellte
Penderyn
Hirwaun
Cefn-coed-y-cymmer
MERTHYR TYDFIL
(Merthyr Tudful)
RHYMNEY
(Rhymni)
Pontlottyn
Crynant
Blaengwrach
Resolven
(Resolfen)
Cilfrew
Clyne
(Y Clun)
Tonna
(Tonnau)
NEATH
(Castell-nedd)
Briton Ferry
(Llansawel)
Baglan
Cwmafan
Aberavon
(Aberafan)
PORT TALBOT
Margam
Pyle
North Cornelly
South Cornelly
Kenfig
Sker Point
Nottage
PORTHCAWL
Newton
Merthyr Mawr
Ogmore
Ogmore-by-Sea
St. Bride's Major
Southerndown
Tusker Rock
Wick
Broughton
Monknash
Marcross
St. Donat's
(Sain Dunwyd)
Llantwit Major
(Llanilltud Fawr)
Nash Point
Boverton
St. Athan
(Sain Tathan)
Gileston
West Aberthaw
Breaksea Point
Fonmon
Rhoose
(Y Rhws)
Porthkerry
(Porthceri)
Penmark
(Pen-marc)
Llancarfan
Bonvilston
(Tresimwn)
Wenvoe
Dyffryn
St. Nicholas
Peterston-super-Ely
Cowbridge
(Y Bont-Faen)
Llanblethian
(Llanfleiddan)
Colwinston
(Tregolwyn)
Llandow
(Llandw)
Sigingstone
(Tresigin)
Flemingston
Llanmaes
Ewenny
Corntown
Treoes
Llangan
Penllyn
Ystradowen
Welsh St. Donats
Aberthin
Pendoylan
BRIDGEND
(Pen-y-Bont Ar Ogwr)
Pencoed
Coychurch
Laleston
(Trelales)
Newcastle
Tythegston
Pen-y-fai
Cefn Cribwr
Kenfig Hill
Aberkenfig
Sarn
Tondu
Brynmenyn
Bryncethin
Llangeinor
Blackmill
Bettws
Pontycymer
Nantyffyllon
MAESTEG
Garth
Caerau
Cymmer
(Cymer)
Croeserw
Blaengwynfi
Abergwynfi
Blaengarw
Nant-y-moel
Ogmore Vale
Price Town
Treorchy
(Treorci)
Treherbert
Tynewydd
Blaenrhondda
Cwmparc
Ton-Pentre
Ystrad
Pentre
Ferndale
Maerdy
Tonypandy
Llwynypia
Porth
Ynyshir
Trealaw
Penygraig
Gilfach Goch
Evanstown
Tonyrefail
PONTYPRIDD
Treforest
Church Village
Beddau
Llantrisant
Talbot Green
Pontyclun
Llanharan
Llanharry
Brynna
Creigiau
Abercynon
Ynysybwl
Cilfynydd
MOUNTAIN ASH
(Aberpennar)
Abercwmboi
Aberaman
ABERDARE
(Aberdar)
Cwmbach
Abernant
Robertstown
Trecynon
Aberfan
Merthyr Vale
(Ynysowen)
Troedyrhiw
Bedlinog
Treharris
Nelson
Pentrebach
Dowlais
Trefechan
Vaynor
Pontsticill
A465
A470
A4060
A4059
A4061
A4063
A4107
A4109
A4067
A4221
A4233
A4093
A4119
A473
A48
A4106
A4229
A4232
A4226
A4050
B4242
B4434
B4280
B4281
B4282
B4265
B4524
B4270
B4278
B4287
M4
CARDIFF WEST
SARN PARK
CARDIFF INTERNATIONAL
46
20
31
A
B
C
D
1
2
3
4
5
80
70
60
90
300
10

ABERGAVENNY
(Y Fenni)
MONMOUTH
(Trefynwy)
33
BLAENAU
GWENT
MONMOUTHSHIRE
TORFAEN
EBBW VALE
(Glyn Ebwy)
Brynmawr
Beaufort
Nantyglo
Blaenavon
Blaina
Govilon
Clydach
Abertillery
(Abertyleri)
Abersychan
New Tredegar
Raglan
Usk
(Brynbuga)
PONTYPOOL
(Pontypŵl)
CWMBRAN
Newbridge
(Cefn Bychan)
Oakdale
Blackwood
(Coed Duon)
Crumlin
Abercarn
Bargoed
Hengoed
Tintern
Devauden
St. Arvans
Caerleon
(Caerllion)
Risca
Bedwas
Machen
CAERPHILLY
(Caerffili)
NEWPORT
(Casnewydd)
Caldicot
Caerwent
Magor
(Magwyr)
Undy
Rogiet
Portskewett
Second
Severn
Crossing
CARDIFF
(Caerdydd)
Penarth
Dinas
Powys
BARRY
(Barri)
Sully
Lavernock
Point
Sully
Island
Flat Holm
Steep Holm
SEVERN
THE
OF
MOUTH
N E L
Portishead
Point
Portishead
Avonmouth
Portbury
CLEVEDON
Nailsea
NORTH
SOMERSET
Yatton
Congresbury
Backwell
Wrington
Lower
Langford
Sand Point
Sand
Bay
Kewstoke
St. George's
Weston Bay
WESTON-SUPER-MARE
Banwell
Sandford
Churchill
Winscombe
Shipham
Blagdon
Bleadon
Uphill
Locking
Hutton
M4
M48
M5
A40
A449
A4042
A48
A370
A371
A368
A38
A403
A465
A470
A48(M)

34
MONMOUTH
(Trefynwy)
A40
Upper Lydbrook
Hillersland
Christchurch
Staunton
Berry Hill
Cinderford
Littledean
Westbury-on-Severn
Chaxhill
Farley's End
Quedgeley
Whaddon
Brookthorpe
M5
Wyesham
Kymin
Coleford
Broadwell
Coalway
Ruspidge
Upper Soudley
Soudley
48
Newnham
Arlingham
Rodley
Epney
Hardwicke
Upper Framilode
Colethrop
Haresfield
Harescombe
Edge
Jingle Street
Penallt
Redbrook
Mitchel Troy
Mitchel Troy Common
A40
Cwmcarvan
Newland
Clearwell
Milkwall
Parkend
Ellwood
FOREST OF DEAN
Two Bridges
Yorkley
Viney Hill
A48
Awre
Fretherne
Saul
Moreton Valence
Whitminster
Standish
Pitchcombe
Whiteshill
The North
Whitebrook
Stowe
Bream's Meend
Pillowell
Whitecroft
Blakeney
Etloe
Frampton on Severn
Church End
Nupend
Randwick
Callowell
Stonehouse
Ebley
OLDBURY
Llangovan
Trelleck
Cotland
Llandogo
Lower Meend
St. Briavels
Bream
Allaston
Primrose Hill
Lydney
Purton
SEVERN
Claypits
Eastington
Middle Street
King's Stanley
Leonard Stanley
Dudbridge
Rodborough
Selsley
Thrupp
Brimscombe
Llanishen
Parkhouse
Catbrook
Coldharbour
Hewelsfield
Aylburton Common
Aylburton
Sharpness
Halmore
Brookend
Newtown
Cambridge
Slimbridge
Moorend
Gossington
Frocester
Middleyard
Woodchester
Trelleck Grange
Tintern
Brockweir
Netherend
Alvington
Wanswell
Breadstone
Coaley
Lower Cam
Nympsfield
Inchbrook
Amberley
Devauden
Chapel Hill
Woolaston
48
Hook Street
Berkeley
The Quarry
Cam
Ashmead Green
Far Green
Dursley
Forest Green
Worley
Box
A48
Stroat
RIVER
Ham
Newport
Stinchcombe
Uley
Horsley
B4058
Nailsworth
St. Arvans
Boughspring
Wibdon
Itton Common
Woodcroft
Cross Hill
Tidenham
Bevington
Woodford
M5
Forthay
Millend
Pitt Court
North Nibley
Southend
A4135
Tiltups End
Kingscote
Shirenewton
Crossway Green
Mynydd-bach
Mounton
Pwllmeyric
Tutshill
Sedbury
CHEPSTOW
(Cas-gwent)
Shepperdine
Hill
Stone
MICHAELWOOD
Tidal Reservoir
Rockhampton
Tortworth
Bradley
Holywell
Coombe
Ozleworth
Newington Bagpath
Beverston
Newton Green
Mathern
Beachley
Oldbury-on-Severn
Lower Morton
Falfield
Whitfield
Charfield
Wotton-under-Edge
Kingswood
Wortley
Tresham
Leighterton
M48
Caerwent
Crick
Severn Bridge
Littleton-upon-Severn
Kington
Morton
Cromhall
Alderley
Westonbirt National Arboretum
Caldicot
Leechpool
Portskewett
SEVERN VIEW
Aust
Elberton
Thornbury
Milbury Heath
Cromhall Common
West End
Wickwar
Hillesley
Lower Kilcott
Upper Kilcott
Oldbury on the Hill
Knockdown
Rogiet
The Pill
Sudbrook
Severn Tunnel
Ingst
M48
Olveston
Old Down
Alveston
Tytherington
SOUTH
Bagstone
Hawkesbury
Hawkesbury Upton
A433
Didmarton
Sopworth
M4
DANGER AREA
Redwick
Northwick
Tockington
Rudgeway
Itchington
Earthcott Green
GLOUCESTERSHIRE
Second Severn Crossing
Severn Beach
Pilning
Almondsbury
M4
Rangeworthy
Bury Hill
Horton
Dunkirk
Little Badminton
Sherston
Latteridge
B4059
Engine Common
Gaunt's Earthcott
Little Sodbury
Luckington
Alderton
A403
M49
Easter Compton
Over
Patchway
Iron Acton
Frampton Cotterell
Goose Green
Yate
Old Sodbury
Badminton
A46
Compton Greenfield
Bradley Stoke
Winterbourne
Mayshill
A432
Chipping Sodbury
Acton Turville
Littleton Drew
Hallen
M5
Cribbs Causeway
Stoke Gifford
Harry Stoke
Coalpit Heath
Westerleigh
Dodington
Wapley
Codrington
B4040
Grittleton
Portishead Point
Avonmouth
Filton
Henbury
Kendleshire
Henfield
Tormarton
Burton
M4
Portishead
Sheepway
Shirehampton
Westbury on Trym
A4174
M32
Hambrook
Downend
MANGOTSFIELD
M4
Nettleton
West Kington
Castle Combe
Easton-in-Gordano
Sea Mills
Horfield
Broomhill
Staple Hill
Hinton
Pucklechurch
Dyrham Park
Yatton Keynell
GORDANO
North Weston
Portbury
Pill
Ham Green
A4
Stapleton
Fishponds
Shortwood
Siston
Abson
Dyrham
West Littleton
North Wraxall
West Yatton
Clapton-in-Gordano
Lower Failand
Abbots Leigh
Redland
Clay Hill
Soundwell
A4174
Warmley
Upper Wraxall
Ford
A420
M5
Stone-edge-Batch
Wraxall
Clifton
BRISTOL
Kingswood
Bridgeyate
Doynton
Pennsylvania
Wick
A420
Marshfield
Slaughterford
Giddeahall
Biddestone
Nailsea
Failand
Long Ashton
Cornham
Hanham
Hanham Green
A4
Oldland
Beach
Tadwick
Cold Ashton
Thickwood
Corsham
A4
West End
Farleigh
Yanley
Bedminster
Knowle
Brislington
Willsbridge
Upton Cheyney
St. Catherine
Colerne
Rudloe
Chelvey
Backwell
Flax Bourton
Headley Park
Bishopsworth
Bitton
North Stoke
Langridge
Lansdown
A46
Ditteridge
Moor Green
West Town
Brockley
Barrow Gurney
Barrow Common
Dundry
East Dundry
A4174
Stockwood
Queen Charlton
KEYNSHAM
Swineford
Saltford
Woolley
Swainswick
Batheaston
Box
Ashley
Kingsdown
Wadswick
Cleeve
Lulsgate Bottom
Upper Town
Whitchurch
A37
Chewton Keynsham
Kelston
Weston
Charlcombe
Larkhall
Bathampton
Bathford
Monkton Farleigh
South Wraxall
Atworth
Felton
Winford
North Wick
Norton Malreward
Norton Hawkfield
Woollard
Burnett
Compton Dando
Publow
Pensford
Corston
Newton St. Loe
A4
Twerton
BATH
Claverton
Farleigh Wick
BRISTOL INTERNATIONAL
A38
Redhill
Chew Magna
Stanton Drew
BATH &
Stanton Prior
Englishcombe
Southdown
Combe Down
A36
Great Chalfield
Bradford Leigh
Congresbury
Wrington
Regil
Chew Stoke
Stanton Wick
Chelwood
Hunstrete
Marksbury
Wilmington
Odd Down
Monkton Combe
Limpley Stoke
Bradford-on-Avon
Woolley Green
Lower Langford
Cowslip Green
Butcombe
West Town
N.E. SOMERSET
Inglesbatch
Southstoke
Turleigh
Winsley
Nempnett Thrubwell
Bishop Sutton
Stowey
Clutton
Farmborough
Priston
Midford
Freshford
Rickford
Blagdon
Burrington
Upper Langford
Ubley
Chew Valley Lake
North Widcombe
Cameley
A37
High Littleton
Timsbury
Meadgate
Tunley
Dunkerton
Carlingcott
Combe Hay
Wellow
Hinton Charterhouse
Westwood
Trowle Common
Upper Studley
Farleigh Hungerford
South Widcombe
Temple Cloud
Hinton Blewett
Hallatrow
Radford
Camerton
Peasedown St. John
Compton Martin
Paulton
A368
22

Birdlip
Great Witcombe
Cowley
Coberley
Colesbourne
Cranham
Yanworth
Northleach
Sherborne
Great Barrington
Taynton
Windrush
Little Barrington
Eastington
Mill End
Chedworth Roman Villa
Brimpsfield
Elkstone
Lodge Park
Burford
Fulbrook
Caudle Green
Syde
Chedworth
Pancakehill
Fossebridge
Coln St. Dennis
Calcot
Aldsworth
Westwell
Signet
Sheepscombe
Whiteway
Winstone
Rendcomb
Miserden
The Camp
Woodmancote
Calmsden
Coln Rogers
Winson
Ablington
Holwell
Shilton
Cotswold Wildlife Park
Througham
Duntisbourne Abbots
North Cerney
Sudgrove
Edgeworth
Duntisbourne Leer
Bagendon
Perrott's Brook
Arlington
Bibury
Hatherop
Eastleach Turville
Eastleach Martin
Bisley
Duntisbourne Rouse
Waterlane
Daglingworth
Coln St. Aldwyns
Barnsley
Filkins
Kencot
Alvescot
Broadwell
Bussage
Bournes Green
Far Oakridge
Chalford
Oakridge
Sapperton
Frampton Mansell
Stratton
Baunton
Abbey Home Farm
Quenington
Fyfield
Broughton Poggs
Southrop
Langford
CIRENCESTER
Ampney Crucis
Ampney St. Mary
Little Faringdon
Little Clanfield
Hyde
Minchinhampton
Aston Down
Coates
Preston
Harnhill
Ampney St. Peter
Poulton
Milton End
Fairford
Horcott
Grafton
Hampton Fields
Tarlton
Chesterton
Siddington
Driffield
Meysey Hampton
Marston Hill
Whelford
Lechlade on Thames
Kelmscott
Kelmscott Manor
Eaton Hastings
Avening
Cherington
Rodmarton
Kemble
Ewen
South Cerney
Down Ampney
Fairford
Marston Meysey
Kempsford
Upper Inglesham
Buscot
Buscot Park
Faringdon
Poole Keynes
Somerford Keynes
Shorncote
Cotswold Water Park
Cerney Wick
Latton
Castle Eaton
Hannington Wick
Tetbury Upton
Culkerton
Ashley
North End
Ashton Keynes
Cricklade
Chelworth
Oaksey
Chelworth Upper Green
Hannington
Coleshill
Great Coxwell
Tetbury
Chedglow
Crudwell
Eastcourt
Leigh
Chelworth Lower Green
Hampton
Highworth
Little Coxwell
Long Newton
Broad Blunsdon
Longcot
Hankerton
Minety
Upper Minety
Purton Stoke
Blunsdon St. Andrew
Stanton Fitzwarren
Sevenhampton
Watchfield
Shipton Moyne
Perry Green
Brokenborough
Charlton
Kingsdown
South Marston
Roves Farm
Shrivenham
Easton Grey
Garsdon
Widham
Purton
Haydon Wick
Penhill
Woolstone
Milbourne
Malmesbury
Lea
Restrop
Lydiard Millicent
Nine Elms
Stratton St. Margaret
Compton Beauchamp
Bourton
Foxley
Cleverton
The Common
Little Somerford
Hook
Lydiard House
Even Swindon
Covingham
Walcot
Idstone
Ashbury
Norton
Corston
Rodbourne
Brinkworth
Callow Hill
SWINDON
Okus
Coate
Horpit
Bishopstone
Great Somerford
Dauntsey Green
Grittenham
Hinton Parva
Ashdown House
Startley
Dauntsey
Tockenham Wick
Woodshaw
Royal Wootton Bassett
North Wroughton
Wroughton
Wanborough
Liddington
Hullavington
Lower Stanton St. Quintin
Lower Seagry
Dauntsey Lock
Hodson
Badbury
Stanton St. Quintin
Upper Seagry
Elcombe
Tockenham
Overtown
Chiseldon
Bradenstoke
Lyneham
Church End
White Horse
Baydon
Sutton Benger
Christian Malford
Broad Town
Uffcott
Draycot Foliat
Upper Upham
Kington St. Michael
Bushton
Preston
Goatacre
Clyffe Pypard
Kington Langley
Foxham
Charlcutt
Broad Hinton
Barbury Castle (Fort)
Woodsend
Aldbourne
Hardenhuish
East Tytherton
Hilmarton
Clevancy
Winterbourne Bassett
Hackpen White Horse
Marlborough Downs
Ogbourne St. George
Langley Burrell
West Tytherton
WILTSHIRE
Preston
CHIPPENHAM
Bremhill
Hackpen Hill
Ogbourne St. Andrew
Berwick Bassett
Winterbourne Monkton
Rockley
Ramsbury
Rowden Hill
Studley
Heritage Centre
Compton Bassett
Yatesbury
Windmill Hill
Ogbourne Maizey
Knighton
Easton
Corsham Court
Derry Hill
Calne
Cherhill
Great Barn
Stone Circle
Axford
Quemerford
Alexander Keiller
Avebury
Devil's Den
Marlborough
Mildenhall
Stitchcombe
Notton
Reybridge
Bowood House
Sandy Lane
Monument
White Horse
Calstone Wellington
Avebury Trusloe
West Kennett
Fyfield
Lacock
Blackland
Beckhampton
Manton
Preshute
St. Margaret's
Froxfield
Gastard
East Kennett
West Overton
Lockeridge
Lacock Abbey
Bowden Hill
Chittoe
Stockley
Morgan's Hill
Silbury Hill
West Kennett Long Barrow
The Sanctuary
Heddington
Cadley
Savernake Forest
Chisbury
Beanacre
Westbrook
Roundway Down
Clench Common
Sandridge
Netherstreet
St. Edith's Marsh
Bourton
Tan Hill
Shaw
Bromham
Bishops Cannings
White Horse
Huish
Wootton Rivers
Great Bedwyn
Durley
MELKSHAM
Allington
Horton
Stanton St. Bernard
Alton Priors
West Stowell
Oare
Bowerhill
Sells Green
Rowde
Roundway
Alton Barnes
New Mill
Ram Alley
Stibb Green
Crofton
Kennet & Avon Canal
Coate
All Cannings
Honey Street
Burbage
Seend Cleeve
Semington
DEVIZES
Seend
Wilcot
Pewsey
Eastcourt
Wilton
Nursteed
Woodborough
Milton Lilbourne
Easton Royal
West Grafton
East Grafton
Marten
Poulshot
Stert
Etchilhampton
VALE OF PEWSEY
Southcott
Great Hinton
Potterne
Patney
Gores
Bottlesford
Hilcott
Manningford Bruce
Easton Hill
Wexcombe
Ashton Common
Bulkington
Worton
Wedhampton
Marden
Tidcombe
Keevil
Potterne Wick
Urchfont
Chirton
Wilsford
North Newnton
Manningford Bohune
White Horse
Pewsey Hill
Steeple
Marston
Conock
Charlton
Pewsey Down
A417
A435
A40
A429
B4425
A419
A433
A361
B4070
B4020
A4095
A420
B4019
B4000
B4508
B4507
B4040
B4042
B4696
B4553
B4534
A4311
B4006
B4587
B4289
A4312
B4005
A4259
A3102
M4
B4069
B4122
A350
A346
B4192
B4003
A4
A345
A342
A3102
A365
B4528
A360
A338
B3087
B3098
A361
B3353
B4528

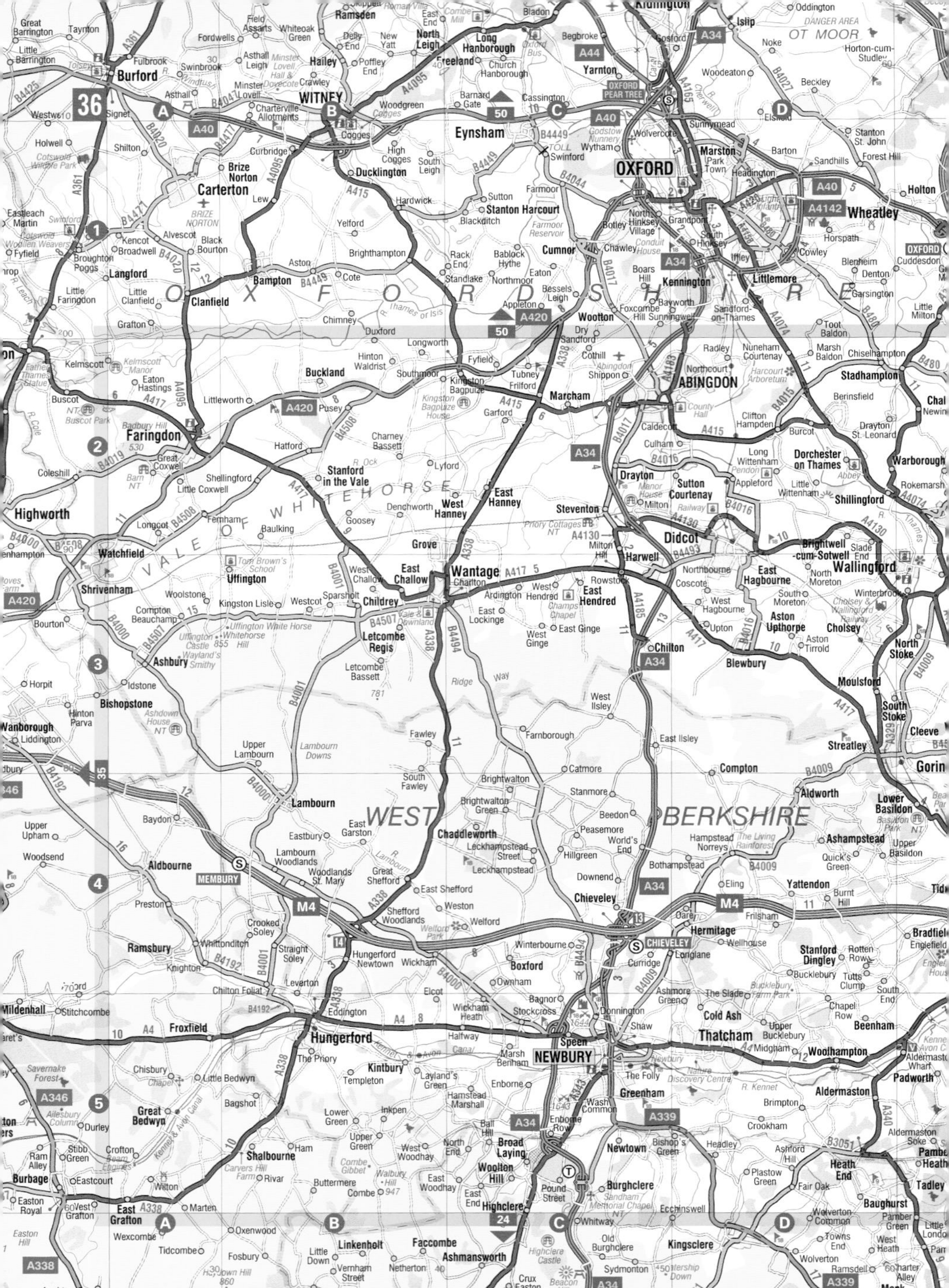

36
OXFORD
OXFORDSHIRE
VALE OF WHITEHORSE
WEST BERKSHIRE
Burford
Witney
Carterton
Eynsham
Wheatley
Abingdon
Faringdon
Highworth
Wantage
Didcot
Wallingford
Hungerford
NEWBURY
Thatcham
Lambourn
M4
A34
A40
A420
A338
35
50
24

AYLESBURY
BUCKINGHAMSHIRE
CHILTERN
HIGH WYCOMBE
BEACONSFIELD
AMERSHAM
CHESHAM
BERKHAMSTED
CHORLEYWOOD
MARLOW
MAIDENHEAD
SLOUGH
WINDSOR
HENLEY-ON-THAMES
READING
WOKINGHAM
BRACKNELL
CAMBERLEY
WOKING
Thame
Tring
Wendover
Princes Risborough
Great Missenden
Watlington
Stokenchurch
Gerrards Cross
Eton
Egham
Crowthorne
Sandhurst
Yateley
Bagshot
Sunninghill
Twyford
Pangbourne
Long Crendon
Haddenham
Chinnor
37
51
25
38

38
The Lee
Lee Clump
Chartridge
Ballinger Common
South Heath
AYLESBURY
Lye Green
Whelpley Hill
Bovingdon
HEMPSTEAD
Kings Langley
Bedmond
Chiswell Green
London Colney
Brookmans Park
Park Street
Frogmore
Botley
Chipperfield
Flaunden
Belsize
Hunton Bridge
Abbots Langley
Bricket Wood
Colney Street
South Mimms
POTTERS BAR
CHESHAM
Waterside
Hyde Heath
Chesham Bois
Sarratt
Langleybury
Micklefield Green
Chenies
Latimer
Little Kingshill
Great Kingshill
Little Missenden
Beamond End
Holmer Green
AMERSHAM
RADLETT
Shenley
Shenleybury
Ridge
Aldenham
Letchmore Heath
Patchetts Green
Green Street
BOREHAMWOOD
Bentley Heath
Monken Hadley
Hadley Wood
High Barnet
Chandler's Cross
WATFORD
Little Chalfont
CHORLEYWOOD
Croxley Green
BUSHEY
Elstree
BARNET
Arkley
Totteridge
Widmer End
Hazlemere
Penn Street
Coleshill
Winchmore Hill
Tylers Green
Penn
Knotty Green
Chalfont St. Giles
Heronsgate
RICKMANSWORTH
Batchworth
Maple Cross
South Oxhey
Oxhey
Bushey Heath
LONDON GATEWAY
Whetstone
Seer Green
Jordans
Forty Green
Chalfont Common
West Hyde
Eastbury
NORTHWOOD
Hatch End
STANMORE
Mill Hill
FINCHLEY
Wycombe Marsh
Loudwater
BEACONSFIELD
Flackwell Heath
Layter's Green
Chalfont St. Peter
Harefield
Harrow Weald
Wealdstone
EDGWARE
Burnt Oak
Wooburn Green
Wooburn
Gerrards Cross
Denham
Ruislip Common
PINNER
HARROW
KENTON
Kingsbury
HENDON
Golders Green
Little Marlow
Bourne End
Hedgerley
Denham Green
Newyears Green
Eastcote
RUISLIP
Rayners Lane
Harrow on the Hill
Brent Cross
Cookham Dean
Cookham
Cookham Rise
Egypt
Farnham Common
Fulmer
Tatling End
Ickenham
Stoke Poges
New Denham
UXBRIDGE
NORTHOLT
WEMBLEY
Neasden
Cricklewood
HAMPSTEAD
WILLESDEN
Kilburn
East Burnham
Burnham
Taplow
SLOUGH
Farnham Royal
Wexham Street
Iver Heath
Hillingdon
Cowley
GREENFORD
Yeading
EALING
ACTON
Shepherd's Bush
PADDINGTON
MARYLEBONE
MAIDENHEAD
Bray
Bray Wick
Cippenham
Shreding Green
George Green
Richings Park
West Drayton
Yiewsley
HAYES
SOUTHALL
Hanwell
KENSINGTON
Dorney
Eton Wick
Boveney
Eton
Upton
Langley
Sutton
Harmondsworth
Sipson
HESTON
Harlington
Brentford
CHISWICK
HAMMERSMITH
Holyport
Fifield
Oakley Green
Moneyrow Green
Touchen-end
WINDSOR
Datchet
Colnbrook
Poyle
Longford
LONDON-HEATHROW
Cranford
Osterley
Kew
North Sheen
BARNES
FULHAM
Paley Street
Horton
Wraysbury
Old Windsor
Stanwell Moor
Hatton
ISLEWORTH
HOUNSLOW
RICHMOND
PUTNEY
WANDSWORTH
Legoland
Hawthorn Hill
Maiden's Green
Cranbourne
WINDSOR GREAT PARK
Hythe End
Stanwell
East Bedfont
TWICKENHAM
Roehampton
Ham
Richmond Park
Warfield
Newell Green
Winkfield
Winkfield Row
Woodside
Englefield Green
Egham Hythe
ASHFORD
FELTHAM
Hanworth
TEDDINGTON
WIMBLEDON
Priestwood
Budleigh
North Ascot
Cheapside
Ascot
Savill
STAINES-UPON-THAMES
Queen Mary Resr.
Hampton
Hampton Wick
MERTON
EGHAM
Thorpe
SUNBURY
Upper Halliford
West Molesey
East Molesey
Hampton Court
KINGSTON UPON THAMES
MORDEN
BRACKNELL
South Ascot
Sunningdale
Virginia Water
Laleham
Littleton
Shepperton
Thames Ditton
SURBITON
NEW MALDEN
Sunninghill
Broomhall
Trumps Green
Lyne
CHERTSEY
WALTON-ON-THAMES
Tolworth
Long Ditton
Look Out Discovery Centre
Windlesham
Longcross
WEYBRIDGE
ESHER
Worcester Park
CARSHALTON
Crowthorne
Bagshot
Addlestone
New Haw
Hersham
Hook
Chessington
SUTTON
Valley End
Burrowhill
Ottershaw
Row Town
St. George's Hill
Whiteley Village
Claygate
Cheam
Lightwater
Chobham
Mimbridge
Woodham
Fairoaks
CAMBERLEY
Donkey Town
West End
Castle Green
Sheerwater
West Byfleet
Byfleet
Cobham
Fairmile
Oxshott
Malden Rushett
EWELL
EPSOM
Blackwater
Bisley
Horsell
Pyrford Village
Wisley
Stoke D'Abernon
Pachesham
Ashtead
BANSTEAD
Chipstead
Frimley
Frimley Green
Knaphill
Brookwood
Deepcut
WOKING
Old Woking
Ripley
Martyr's Green
Downside
COBHAM
Ockham
LEATHERHEAD
Burgh Heath
Tadworth
West Heath
Mytchett
Pirbright
Mayford
Send Marsh
Cartbridge
Effingham Common
Fetcham
Headley
Walton on the Hill
Kingswood
Mugswell
Cove
Fox Corner
Pyle Hill
Send
Burntcommon
West Horsley
East Horsley
Little Bookham
Great Bookham
Lower Kingswood
Worplesdon
Pitch Place
Sutton Green
Jacobswell
West Clandon
East Clandon
Effingham
Mickleham
Westhumble
Margery
Willey Green
Fairlands
Stoughton
Burpham
Merrow
Hatchlands Park
Polesden Lacey
Box Hill
Ranmore Common
Buckland
Wyke
Normandy
Wood Street Village
Ash
Flexford
Onslow Village
Newlands Corner
Silent Pool
Betchworth
Brockham
Westcott
Tongham
GUILDFORD
Artington
Littleton
Chilworth
Gomshall
Wotton
DORKING
REIGATE
Strood Green
Gadbrook
Doversgreen
Puttenham
Runfold
Seale
Compton
Shalford
Albury
Shere
Abinger Hammer
North Holmwood
Stonebridge
Dawesgreen
Leigh
FARNHAM
SURREY

39
40
ESSEX
KENT
LONDON
Hammond Street
Cuffley
Northaw
Goff's Oak
CHESHUNT
Wormley
Turnford
Waltham Cross
WALTHAM ABBEY
Holyfield
Bumble's Green
Epping Upland
EPPING
Upshire
Thornwood Common
Coopersale Common
Coopersale Street
North Weald Bassett
Greensted Green
Toot Hill
Stanford Rivers
High Ongar
Norton Heath
Mandeville
Chipping Ongar
Nine Ashes
Elkins Green
Blackmore
Loves Green
Beggar Hill
Margaretting
Margaretting Tye
Mill Green
Stondon Massey
Ingatestone
Stock
Crews Hill
Forty Hill
Botany Bay
Enfield Wash
Sewardstone
ENFIELD
Theydon Bois
Debden Green
High Beech
Hobbs Cross
Stapleford Tawney
Kelvedon Hatch
Wyatt's Green
Doddinghurst
Fox Hatch
Mountnessing
Heybridge
Navestock
Navestock Side
Crow Green
Pilgrims Hatch
LOUGHTON
Abridge
Passingford Bridge
Stapleford Abbotts
Havering's
Hutton
Shenfield
BRENTWOOD
Winchmore Hill
SOUTHGATE
EDMONTON
CHINGFORD
Ponders End
CHIGWELL
Lambourne End
Noak Hill
South Weald
Buckhurst Hill
Grange Hill
Chigwell Row
Havering-atte-Bower
Brook Street
Ingrave
Little Burstead
Woodford Green
WOODFORD
Hainault
Harold Hill
Great Warley
Little Warley
Herongate
WOOD GREEN
TOTTENHAM
WALTHAMSTOW
HORNSEY
Collier Row
Gidea Park
Harold Wood
Laindon
Gants Hill
Barkingside
Chadwell Heath
ROMFORD
Cranham
UPMINSTER
West Horndon
Langdon Hills
Dry Street
STOKE NEWINGTON
LEYTON
Leytonstone
WANSTEAD
Goodmayes
HORNCHURCH
Bulphan
Manor Park
ILFORD
Becontree
Elm Park
North Ockendon
ISLINGTON
HACKNEY
STRATFORD
BARKING
FINSBURY
BETHNAL GREEN
SHOREDITCH
WEST HAM
EAST HAM
South Hornchurch
Horndon on the Hill
STEPNEY
DAGENHAM
Rainham
South Ockendon
Baker Street
Orsett
WEST END
CITY
POPLAR
Beckton
Creekmouth
North Stifford
Stanford-le-Hope
LONDON CITY
Thamesmead
Wennington
Aveley
THURROCK
Little Thurrock
Mucking
Chadwell St. Mary
Linford
BERMONDSEY
Abbey Wood
Belvedere
East Tilbury
LAMBETH
DEPTFORD
GREENWICH
WOOLWICH
Charlton
Plumstead
ERITH
Purfleet
Chafford Hundred
Tilbury
CAMBERWELL
Dartford-Thurrock River Crossing
South Stifford
West Thurrock
GRAYS
Coalhouse Fort
BRIXTON
Blackheath
Kidbrooke
Welling
Slade Green
Bexleyheath
Crayford
TILBURY
CLAPHAM
LEWISHAM
Lee
ELTHAM
Blackfen
DARTFORD
Greenhithe
Stone
Swanscombe
Northfleet
Ebbsfleet
Chalk
Bexley
Old Bexley
GRAVESEND
CATFORD
New Eltham
Dulwich
Grove Park
SIDCUP
North Cray
Wilmington
Bean
Perry Street
Singlewell
West Norwood
Sydenham
Mottingham
Foots Cray
Hextable
Hawley
Darenth
Betsham
Southfleet
Shorne
STREATHAM
Crystal Palace
Penge
South Darenth
Green St. Green
Hook Green
Istead Rise
Thong
South Norwood
CHISLEHURST
Swanley
Sutton at Hone
Longfield
New Barn
MITCHAM
Thornton Heath
BECKENHAM
BROMLEY
St. Paul's Cray
Petts Wood
St. Mary Cray
Horton Kirby
Sole Street
Cobham
Crockenhill
Hartley
Longfield Hill
Meopham Station
Henley Street
Hayes
ORPINGTON
Farningham
Hook Green
Beddington
Addiscombe
West Wickham
Meopham
Luddesdown
Fawkham Green
New Ash Green
Meopham Green
CROYDON
Addington
Keston
Chelsfield
Well Hill
Eynsford
Maplescombe
Ash
Priestwood
Upper Halling
WALLINGTON
Farnborough
Green Street Green
Lullingstone Castle
West Kingsdown
Ridley
Harvel
Selsdon
New Addington
Pratt's Bottom
Badgers Mount
Knatts Valley
Stansted
Hodsoll Street
Culverstone Green
Leaves Green
Downe
Halstead
Shoreham
Fairseat
Vigo Village
Snodland
PURLEY
Sanderstead
Farleigh
Woodlands
Trottiscliffe
Birling
Ryarsh
Berry's Green
Cudham
Knockholt
Knockholt Pound
Otford
Kemsing
Heaverham
Wrotham
Leybourne
Hamsey Green
Kenley
Whyteleafe
Old Coulsdon
Chelsham
Biggin Hill
Tatsfield
Chevening
Dunton Green
Borough Green
Addington
West Malling
COULSDON
Wrotham Heath
Offham
Platt
WARLINGHAM
Chipstead
Riverhead
Seal
Ightham
Claygate Cross
Crouch
Kings Hill
Chaldon
Woldingham
CATERHAM
Titsey
CLACKET LANE
Brasted
Westerham
Sundridge
Brasted Chart
SEVENOAKS
Ivy Hatch
Stone Street
Plaxtol
Mereworth
Kent Street
Limpsfield
Oxted
Moorhouse
The Chart
French Street
Ide Hill
Goathurst Common
Underriver
Dunk's Green
Wateringbury
Merstham
Warwick Wold
Brewer Street
Godstone
Limpsfield Chart
Shipbourne
West Peckham
Nettlestead Green
REDHILL
Nutfield
Bletchingley
Tandridge
Hurst Green
Toy's Hill
Sevenoaks Weald
Crockham Hill
Coldharbour
Peckham Bush
Hadlow
South Godstone
Pootings
Cooper's Corner
Fletcher's Green
Hildenborough
Pittswood
Hale Street
South Nutfield
Four Elms
Marlpit Hill
Bough Beech Reservoir
Higham Wood
Barnes Street
East Peckham
Golden Green
Laddingford
Crowhurst Lane End
Crowhurst
Chiddingstone Causeway
Edenbridge
Bough Beech
TONBRIDGE
Beltring
M11
M25
M20
M26
M23
A10
A12
A13
A127
A414
A2
A20
A21
A22
A23
A25
A26
A228
A232

40
Great Baddow
Sandon
Danbury
Gay Bowers
Butt's Green
Galleyend
Galleywood
Howe Green
Woodham Mortimer
Hazeleigh
New Hall Vineyards
Cock Clarks
Bicknacre
Rudley Green
Purleigh
Howegreen
Cold Norton
Mundon
Steeple
St. Lawrence
Rural Discovery
Tillingham
Dengie
Maylandsea
Mayland
Asheldham
Latchingdon
Southminster
Althorne
Mangapps Railway
Stoneyhills
Ostend
Burnham-on-Crouch
River Crouch
Loves Green
Elkins Green
Beggar Hill
Margaretting
Margaretting Tye
Fryerning
Ingatestone
Ingatestone Hall
Stock
Heybridge
Mountnessing
East Hanningfield
West Hanningfield
Hanningfield Reservoir
South Hanningfield
Coalhill
RHS Hyde Hall
Rettendon
Tropical Wings
Woodham Ferrers
Stow Maries
South Woodham Ferrers
North Fambridge
South Fambridge
Ramsden Heath
Downham
Havering's Grove
Hutton
Shenfield
BRENTWOOD
BILLERICAY
Ramsden Bellhouse
South Green
Wickford
Runwell
Battlesbridge
Rawreth
Hullbridge
Hockley
Ashingdon
Canewdon
Paglesham Churchend
Paglesham Eastend
Wallasea Island
Churchend
FOULNESS ISLAND
Potton Island
Ballards Gore
Great Stambridge
Stroud Green
Rochford
LONDON SOUTHEND
Hawkwell
Rayleigh Mount
RAYLEIGH
Eastwood
Ingrave
Great Burstead
Crays Hill
Shotgate
Nevendon
Little Burstead
Herongate
Little Warley
Laindon
BASILDON
North Benfleet
Bowers Gifford
Pitsea
Thundersley
Daws Heath
Hadleigh
Tarpots
Prittlewell Priory
Prittlewell
Barling
Little Wakering
Great Wakering
Bournes Green
North Shoebury
West Horndon
Langdon Hills
Dry Street
Vange
Bulphan
Hope's Green
South Benfleet
Winter Gardens
Leigh-on-Sea
Beecroft Gallery
Westcliff-on-Sea
Southchurch
Thorpe Bay
Sea Life
Pier
Shoeburyness
SOUTHEND-ON-SEA
SHOEBURY NESS
Horndon on the Hill
Balstonia
Fobbing
Corringham
Coryton
Dutch Cottage
Newlands
Leigh Beck
Canvey Island Transport
CANVEY ISLAND
Heritage Centre
Baker Street
Orsett
Stanford-le-Hope
Thames Haven
Mucking
Walton Hall
Little Thurrock
Chadwell St. Mary
Linford
East Tilbury
River Thames
Blythe Sands
The Lower Hope
Cliffe Marshes
Halstow Marshes
St. Mary's Marshes
Allhallows-on-Sea
Allhallows
West Tilbury
Coalhouse Fort
TILBURY
Tilbury Fort
St. Mary Hoo
Lower Stoke
Grain
Cliffe
Cooling
High Halstow
Fenn Street
Stoke
Wallend
Isle of Grain
Thamesport
SHEERNESS
Heritage Cen.
Mile Town
Marine Town
Minster
East End
Halfway Houses
Queenborough
Chetney Marshes
Rushenden
Brambledown
Eastchurch
Warden
ISLE OF SHEPPE
Elmley Island
Isle of
Northfleet
GRAVESEND
Chantry
Chalk
Lower Higham
Church Street
Cooling Street
Cliffe Woods
Sharnal Street
North Street
Hoo St. Werburgh
Kingsnorth
Perry Street
Singlewell
Betsham
Southfleet
Hook Green
Istead Rise
Higham
Shorne
Shorne Ridgeway
Thong
Wainscott
Chattenden
Lower Upnor
Upper Upnor
RIVER MEDWAY
Longfield
New Barn
Owletts
Sole Street
Cobham
STROOD
Frindsbury
Brompton
Lower Rainham
Upchurch
Ham Green
Lower Halstow
Iwade
Longfield Hill
Meopham Station
Hook Green
Henley Street
Cuxton
Borstal
ROCHESTER
GILLINGHAM
Otterham Quay
Kemsley
The Swale
Meopham
Luddesdown
MEDWAY TOWNS
CHATHAM
Rainham
Howt Green
Bobbing
Milton Regis
Sittingbourne & Kemsley Light Railway
Conyer
Uplees
New Ash Green
Priestwood
Upper Halling
North Halling
Halling
Wouldham
Hempstead
Wigmore
Hartlip
Newington
SITTINGBOURNE
Teynham Street
Oare
Ridley
Harvel
Walderslade
Danaway
Oad Street
Key Street
Borden
Bapchild
Teynham
Luddenham
FAVERSHAM
Hodsoll Street
Culverstone Green
Burham
Blue Bell Hill
Yelsted
Tunstall
Rodmersham
Snodland
Kit's Coty House
Bredhurst
Stockbury
Highsted
Rodmersham Green
Lynsted
Lewson Street
Ospringe
Fairseat
Vigo Village
Trottiscliffe
Birling
Ham Hill
New Hythe
Eccles
Kent County Showground
South Green
Bredgar
Dungate
Erriottwood
Ryarsh
Lunsford
The Friars
Aylesford
Boxley
Hucking
Bicknor
Swanton Street
Milstead
Painter's Forstal
Brogdale
Addington
Leybourne
Larkfield
Bredgar & Wormshill Light Railway
Bluetown
Newnham
North Street
Platt
Wrotham Heath
West Malling
Offham
East Malling
Ditton
Allington
Sandling
Detling
Thurnham
Broad Street
Wormshill
Frinsted
Doddington
Doddington Place
Eastling
Sheldwich
Belmont
Great Comp
Crouch
Mereworth Woods
Kings Hill
MAIDSTONE
Hollingbourne
Eyhorne Street
Ringlestone
Wichling
Throwley
Throwley Forstal
Badlesm
Herne Pound
Old Soar Manor
Kent Street
Barming Heath
Bearsted
Stoneacre
West Street
Mereworth
Teston
Barming
East Farleigh
Shepway
Leeds
Otham
Leeds Castle
Harrietsham
Lenham
Warren Street
Stalisfield Green
Leaveland
Wateringbury
West Farleigh
Nettlestead
Loose
West Peckham
Boughton Green
Langley
Broomfield
Langley Heath
Kingswood
Leadingcross Green
Sandway
Platt's Heath
Nettlestead Green
Chart Corner
Stocker's Head
Challock
Charing Hill
Paddock
The Lees
Peckham Bush
Yalding
Coxheath
Linton
Boughton Monchelsea
Chart Sutton
Lenham Heath
Fairbourne Heath
Hadlow
Hale Street
Hunton
Sutton Valence
Ulcombe
Grafty Green
Boughton Malherbe
Charing Heath
Charing
Beech Court
Pittswood
Barnes Street
East Peckham
Laddingford
Benover
Westwell Leacon
Golden Green
Hop Farm Family Park
Chainhurst
Egerton
Boughton Lees
Westwell
TONBRIDGE
Whetsted
Beltring
Egerton Forstal
ESSEX
NORTH DOWNS
DANGER AREA
A414
A12
A130
A127
A13
A129
A132
A228
A229
A249
A2
M2
M20
A20
A26
B1018
B1010
B1012
53
54
39
28

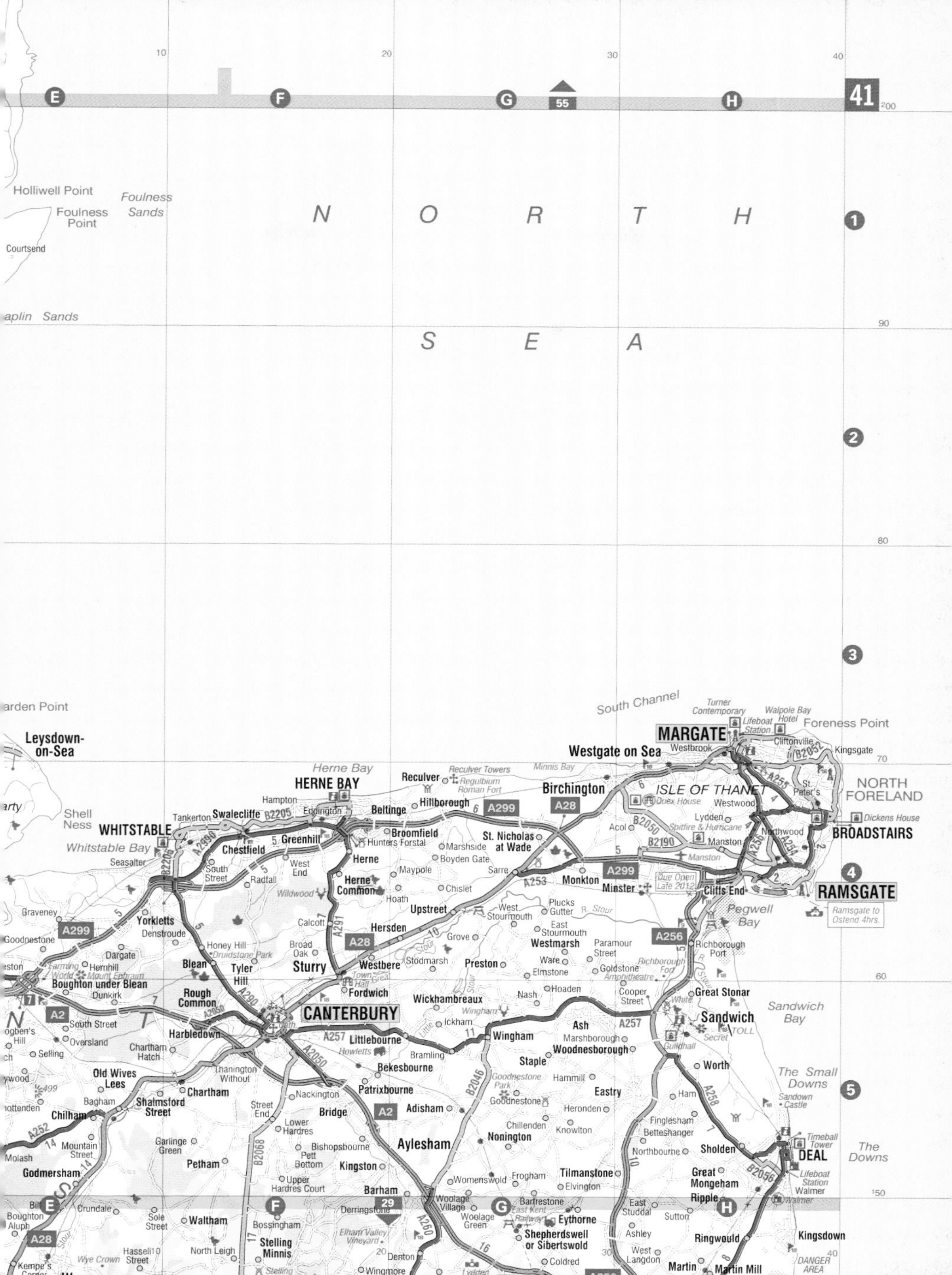

55
NORTH SEA
Holliwell Point
Foulness Point
Foulness Sands
Courtsend
Maplin Sands
South Channel
Leysdown-on-Sea
MARGATE
Westgate on Sea
Westbrook
Turner Contemporary
Lifeboat Station
Walpole Bay Hotel
Foreness Point
Cliftonville
Kingsgate
NORTH FORELAND
Herne Bay
HERNE BAY
Reculver
Reculver Towers Regulbium Roman Fort
Minnis Bay
Birchington
ISLE OF THANET
Quex House
St. Peter's
Westwood
Lydden
Spitfire & Hurricane
Dickens House
BROADSTAIRS
Acol
Manston
Northwood
Shell Ness
WHITSTABLE
Whitstable Bay
Seasalter
Tankerton
Swalecliffe
Hampton
Eddington
Beltinge
Hillborough
Chestfield
Greenhill
Broomfield
Hunters Forstal
Herne
Marshside
Boyden Gate
St. Nicholas at Wade
Sarre
Monkton
Minster
Due Open Late 2012
Cliffs End
RAMSGATE
Ramsgate to Ostend 4hrs.
South Street
Radfall
West End
Maypole
Herne Common
Wildwood
Chislet
Hoath
Upstreet
West Stourmouth
Plucks Gutter
Pegwell Bay
Graveney
Yorkletts
Denstroude
Calcott
Hersden
East Stourmouth
Westmarsh
Paramour Street
Richborough Port
Goodnestone
Dargate
Honey Hill
Druidstone Park
Broad Oak
Grove
Sturry
Westbere
Stodmarsh
Preston
Ware
Elmstone
Goldstone
Richborough Fort
Amphitheatre
Farming World
Hernhill
Mount Ephraim
Blean
Tyler Hill
Boughton under Blean
Dunkirk
Rough Common
Fordwich
Wickhambreaux
Nash
Hoaden
Cooper Street
Great Stonar
CANTERBURY
Wingham
Ickham
Ash
Sandwich
Sandwich Bay
South Street
Oversland
Harbledown
Chartham Hatch
Selling
Littlebourne
Howletts
Bramling
Marshborough
Woodnesborough
Staple
Guildhall
Secret
Worth
Old Wives Lees
Thanington Without
Chartham
Bekesbourne
Patrixbourne
Goodnestone Park
Hammill
Eastry
The Small Downs
Sandown Castle
Bagham
Shalmsford Street
Nackington
Street End
Bridge
Adisham
Goodnestone
Heronden
Ham
Chilham
Lower Hardres
Chillenden
Knowlton
Finglesham
Betteshanger
Timeball Tower
Mountain Street
Garlinge Green
Bishopsbourne
Pett Bottom
Aylesham
Nonington
Northbourne
Sholden
DEAL
The Downs
Molash
Godmersham
Petham
Kingston
Womenswold
Frogham
Tilmanstone
Elvington
Great Mongeham
Lifeboat Station
Walmer
Upper Hardres Court
Barham
Woolage Village
Barfrestone
East Studdal
Ripple
Crundale
Sole Street
Waltham
Bossingham
Derringstone
Woolage Green
East Kent Railway
Eythorne
Sutton
Boughton Aluph
Stelling Minnis
Elham Valley Vineyard
Shepherdswell or Sibertswold
Ashley
Ringwould
Kingsdown
Wye Crown
Hassell Street
North Leigh
Denton
West Langdon
Coldred
Lydden
Wingmore
Kempe's Corner
Martin
Martin Mill
DANGER AREA
A299
A28
A2
A257
A256
A253
B2205
A2990
B2050
B2190
A255
A254
B2052
A291
A290
A2050
A252
B2046
B2068
A258
B2056
A260
29

Fishguard to Rosslare 3hrs. 30mins.
STRUMBLE HEAD
Carregwastad Point
Pen Brush
Llanwnda
Goodwick (Wdig)
Ocean Lab
Trefasser
Penbwchdy
Dyffryn
Manorowen
Fishguard (Abergwaun)
St. Nicholas
Melin Tregwynt
Granston
Scleddau
Abercastle
Penclegyr
Porthgain
Trefin
Mathry
Jordanston
Llangloffan
Blue Lagoon
Abereiddy
Llanrian
Carreg-gwylan-fach
Castlemorris
Newbridge
Croes-Goch
Penclegyr
Penllechwen
ST. DAVID'S HEAD
Letterston
Treffynnon
Tretio
Treleddyd-fawr
Rhodiad-Y-Brenin
Carnhedryn
Welsh Hook
Wolf's Castle
Wolfscastle Pottery
Whitesand Bay or Porth-mawr
R. Alun
R. Solva
Caerfarchell
St. David's Solva Woollen Mill
Llandeloy
Rhosson
St. David's (Tyddewi)
Oriel y Parc
Whitchurch
Hayscastle
Hayscastle Cross
Cathedral & Bishop's Palace
Brimaston
Ramsey Island
Ramsey Sound
St. Non's Chapel
Solva
Gignog
Mountain Water
Treffgarne
Western Cleddau
Penycwm
Leweston
Green Scar
Newgale
Wood
Wolfsdale
Ynys Bery
Roch
Dudwells
Camrose
Simpson Cross
Keeston
Rickets Head
Cuttybridge
Pelcomb Cross
Pelcomb Bridge
Tangiers
ST. BRIDES BAY
Nolton Haven
Simpson
Nolton
Motor
Druidston
Lambston
Sutton
Portfield Gate
Haroldston West
Dreenhill
Albert Town
Merlin's Bridge
Uzmaston
Hangstone Davey
Broad Haven
Broadway
Stack Rocks
Little Haven
Walton West
Pope Hill
Talbenny
Freystrop
Tower Point
Walwyn's Castle
Skomer Island
Harold Stone
Wooltack Point
St. Brides
Hasguard
Robeston West
Tiers Cross
Johnston
Grassholm Island
PEMBROKESHIRE COAST NATIONAL PARK (PARC CENEDLAETHOL ARFORDIR PENFRO)
Midland Isle
Marloes
Herbrandston
Thornton
Steynton
Rosemarket
Priory
MILFORD HAVEN (Aberdaugleddau)
BROAD SOUND
Sandy Haven
St. Ishmael's
Hubberston
Gateholm Island
Dale
Dale Point
Hakin
Waterston
Llanstadwell
Neyland
Skokholm Island
Milford Haven
West Blockhouse
Thorn Island
Pembroke Dock (Doc Penfro)
Angle
DANGER AREA
Angle Bay
Pembroke to Rosslare 3hrs. 45mins.
St. Ann's Head
Sheep Island
Rhoscrowther
Pwllcrochan
Wallaston Green
Hundleton
Freshwater West
Castlemartin
Warren
St. Twynnells
Merrion
Linney Head
DANGER AREA
Crow Rock
Toes
The Wash
Bosherston
St. Govan's Head
A40
A487
A4076
A477
B4583
B4330
B4331
B4341
B4327
B4320
B4319
B4325

43
44
30
E
F
G
H
1
2
3
4
5
DINAS HEAD
Dinas Island
Trwyn-y-bwa
Moylgrove
(Trewyddel)
Monington
A487
Pen-y-bryn
A478
Cilgerran
Cwm Plysgog
Cnwcau
Llechryd
Llandygwydd
Brongest
Brongwyn
Coed-y-bryn
Maes Llyn
Cross-
Horeb
Aber-banc
Llandyfriog
Penrhiw-llan
Gethsemane
Glanrhyd
Bridell
Llantood
Cwm-cou
Adpar
Cenarth
Newport Bay
(Bae Trefdraeth)
Nevern
(Nanhyfer)
Berry Hill
Bryn-henllan
Dinas Cross
Parrog
Newport
(Trefdraeth)
Castle
Felindre Farchog
Castell Henllys Iron Age Fort
Eglwyswrw
Rhos-hill
Newchapel
(Capel Newydd)
Abercych
Penrhiw
Newcastle Emlyn
(Castell Newydd Emlyn)
Aberarad
Pentrecagal
Drefach
Llangeler
Waungilwen
Felindre
Glynteg
Saron
Boncath
Cilwendeg Shell House
Penrherber
Cawš Cenarth Cheese
PEMBROKESHIRE COAST
NATIONAL PARK
(PARC CENEDLAETHOL
ARFORDIR PENFRO)
Llanfair-Nant-Gwyn
Shire Horse Farm
Bro Meigan
Pentre Ifan Burial Chamber
Blaenffos
Cwmhiraeth
Mynydd Carningli
Mynydd Caregog
Cilgwyn
Brynberian
Crosswell
Pontyglazier
Whitechurch
Penygroes
Bwlch-y-groes
Cwmcych
Capel Iwan
Moelfre
Llanychaer
Star
Clydey
Cilrhedyn
Cwmorgan
Rhos
Pontfaen
Tafarn-y-bwlch
PRESELI
MYNYDD
Frenni Fawr
Crymych
Tegryn
Foeleryr
Glan-rhyd
Foel-cwmcerwyn
Pentre Galar
Hermon
Llanfyrnach
Henfeddau Fawr
Trelech
Dinas
Hermon
Cwmduad
Morvil
Puncheston
(Cas-Mael)
Greenway
Rosebush
Mynachlog-ddu
Gors Fawr Stone Circle
Foel-drych
Little Newcastle
Castlebythe
Glandwr
Esgair
Cynwyl Elfed
Tufton
Henry's Moat
(Castell Hendre)
Maenclochog
Glandy Cross
Hebron
Blaenwaun
Pen-y-bont
Blaen-y-coed
Llandilo
Llangolman
Llanglydwen
Llanwinio
Ambleston
Wallis
Woodstock Slop
Llys-y-fran Resr.
New Moat
Efailwen
Pant-y-Caws
Welsh Chocolate Farm
Cwmbach
Gwastad
Llys-y-fran
Cefn-y-pant
Cwmfelin Mynach
Talog
Bwlchnewydd
CARMARTHENSHIRE
Walton East
Llanycefn
Login
Crosshands
Llanboidy
Gellywen
Abernant
Scolton
Penffordd
Cwm-miles
Caerlleon
Dyffryn
Nant Cynnen
Tre-vaughan
Clarbeston
Bletherston
Llandissilio
Hiraeth
Meidrim
Drefach
Merthyr
CARMARTHEN
(Caerfyrddin)
Clarbeston Road
Llanfallteg
Henllan Amgoed
Esgair
B4298
Clunderwen
Llangynin
Llanfallteg West
Cwmfelin Boeth
Gelli
Plain Dealings
Wiston
Grove Land Adventure World
Glyn-Coch Craft Centre
A40
Llanllwch
Bethesda
Llanddewi Velfrey
Bancyfelin
Llawhaden
Robeston Wathen
Whitland
Pwlltrap
Canaston Bridge
St. Clears
Llangynog
Llangain
HAVERFORDWEST
Hywel Dda Centre
Backe
Narberth
(Arberth)
Robeston Back
Lampeter Velfrey
Lampeter Vale
Trevaughan
Llwyn-y-brain
The Rhos
Blackpool Mill
Crinow
Minwear
Bluestone
Narberth Bridge
Llan-mill
Cold Blow
Princes Gate
Tavernspite
Llanddowror
Morfa Bach
Picton
Oakwood
PEMBROKESHIRE COAST NATIONAL PARK
Templeton
Halfpenny Furze
Llanybri
Landshipping
Ludchurch
Red Roses
Dylan Thomas Boathouse
Llandawke
Martletwy
Cwm Deri Vineyard
Llanteg
Laugharne
Llansteffan
Black Tar
Yerbeston
Reynalton
Thomas Chapel
Marros
Llansadurnen
Brook
Broadway
Ferryside
(PARC CENEDLAETHOL ARFORDIR PENFRO)
Loveston
Kilgetty
(Cilgeti)
Stepaside
Colby Woodland
Summerhill
Pendine
(Pentywyn)
Museum of Speed
Llanmiloe
DANGER AREA
Ginst Point
St. Ishmael
Broadlay
Kidwelly
Houghton
Lawrenny
Cresswell
Begelly
Sardis
Amroth
West Williamston
Cresselly
Cresswell Quay
Jeffreyston
Gwendraeth
Burton
Upton Castle
Broadmoor
Pentlepoir
Carew Newton
Saundersfoot
Pembroke Ferry
Upton
East Williamston
Waterloo
Cosheston
Redberth
Milton
Carew
Broadfield
Monkstone Point
Sageston
Heatherton World of Activities
A478
Carew Cheriton
Control Tower
New Hedges
Silent World
CARMARTHEN BAY
(BAE CAERFYRDDIN)
Pembroke
(Penfro)
Upper Nash
The Dinosaur Park
Manor House
Tenby
(Dinbych-y-Pysgod)
Bishop's Palace
St. Florence
Gumfreston
Lamphey
Manorbier Newton
Jameston
Penally
(Penalun)
Tudor Merchant's House
National Park Centre
Hodgeston
Freshwater East
Lydstep
Giltar Point
Caldey Sound
Cheriton or Stackpole Elidor
Manorbier
Abbey
Trewent Point
St. Margaret's Island
Caldey Island
Old Priory
Chapel Point
Stackpole
Old Castle Head
Stackpole Head
Burry Holms
Rhossili Bay
WORMS HEAD
(Penrhyn-gwyr)
A477
A4139
A4075
A4115
B4313
B4314
B4315
B4316
B4318
B4328
B4329
B4332
B4333
B4335
B4299
B4312
B4582
B4585
B5484
A4066
A484
A486
A475
B4571
B4570
B4334
B4319
200
10
20
30
90

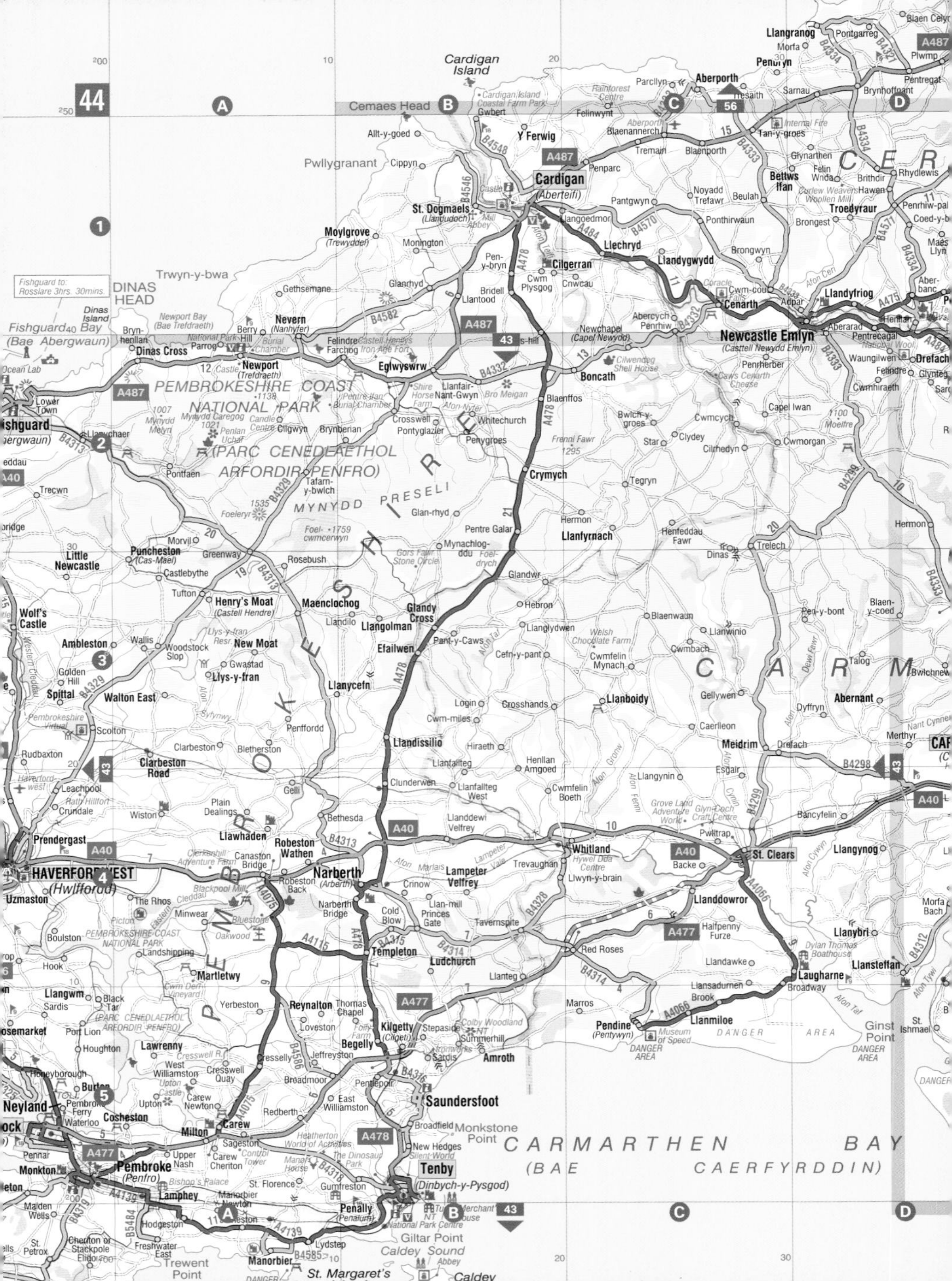
44
Cardigan Island
Cemaes Head
Cardigan Island Coastal Farm Park
Gwbert
Y Ferwig
Allt-y-goed
Pwllygranant
Cippyn
Cardigan
(Aberteifi)
St. Dogmaels
(Llandudoch)
Moylgrove
(Trewyddel)
Monington
Trwyn-y-bwa
DINAS HEAD
Dinas Island
Fishguard to: Rosslare 3hrs. 30mins.
Fishguard Bay
(Bae Abergwaun)
Ocean Lab
Lower Town
Fishguard
Gethsemane
Glanrhyd
Llantood
Bridell
Pen-y-bryn
Cilgerran
Cwm Plysgog
Cnwcau
Llechryd
Llandygwydd
Llangoedmor
Nevern
(Nanhyfer)
Newport Bay
(Bae Trefdraeth)
Bryn-henllan
Dinas Cross
Parrog
Berry Hill
Newport
(Trefdraeth)
Felindre Farchog
Castell Henllys Iron Age Fort
Eglwyswrw
PEMBROKESHIRE COAST NATIONAL PARK
(PARC CENEDLAETHOL ARFORDIR PENFRO)
Mynydd Carningli
Mynydd Caregog
Penlan Uchaf
Candle Centre
Cilgwyn
Brynberian
Crosswell
Pontyglazier
Whitechurch
Penygroes
Llanfair-Nant-Gwyn
Bro Meigan
Shire Horse Farm
Pentre Ifan Burial Chamber
Llanychaer
Pontfaen
Trecwn
Tafarn-y-bwlch
MYNYDD PRESELI
Foelcwmcerwyn
Foeleryr
Glan-rhyd
Pentre Galar
Crymych
Blaenffos
Boncath
Newchapel
(Capel Newydd)
Cilwendeg Shell House
Frenni Fawr
Hermon
Llanfyrnach
Tegryn
Bwlch-y-groes
Star
Clydey
Cwmcych
Cilrhedyn
Cwmorgan
Capel Iwan
Moelfre
Penrherber
Caws Cenarth Cheese
Abercych
Penrhiw
Cenarth
Cwm-cou
Adpar
Newcastle Emlyn
(Castell Newydd Emlyn)
Aberarad
Pentrecagal
National Wool
Waungilwen
Felindre
Cwmhiraeth
Drefach
Llandyfriog
Henllan
Aber-banc
Llangranog
Pontgarreg
Morfa
Penbryn
Aberporth
Parcllyn
Rainforest Centre
Sarnau
Tresaith
Brynhoffnant
Pentregat
Plwmp
Blaen Celyn
Felinwynt
Blaenannerch
Tan-y-groes
Internal Fire
Tremain
Blaenporth
Penparc
Glynarthen
Felin Wnda
Brithdir
Rhydlewis
Hawen
Betws Ifan
Curlew Weavers Woollen Mill
Troedyraur
Brongest
Penrhiw-pal
Coed-y-bryn
Maesllyn
Noyadd Trefawr
Beulah
Pantgwyn
Ponthirwaun
Brongwyn
CER
Little Newcastle
Puncheston
(Cas-Mael)
Castlebythe
Morvil
Greenway
Rosebush
Tufton
Henry's Moat
(Castell Hendre)
Maenclochog
Mynachlog-ddu
Gors Fawr Stone Circle
Foel-drych
Glandwr
Hebron
Glandy Cross
Llangolman
Llandilo
Efailwen
Pant-y-Caws
Llanglydwen
Welsh Chocolate Farm
Cefn-y-pant
Cwmfelin Mynach
Blaenwaun
Llanwinio
Cwmbach
Henfeddau Fawr
Dinas
Trelech
Pen-y-bont
Blaen-y-coed
Talog
Bwlchnewydd
Wolf's Castle
Ambleston
Wallis
Woodstock Slop
Llys-y-fran Resr.
New Moat
Gwastad
Llys-y-fran
Golden Hill
Spittal
Walton East
Llanycefn
Login
Crosshands
Llanboidy
Gellywen
Abernant
Dyffryn
CARM
Pembrokeshire Virtual
Scolton
Penffordd
Cwm-miles
Caerlleon
Meidrim
Drefach
Nant Cynnen
Merthyr
Rudbaxton
Clarbeston
Bletherston
Llandissilio
Hiraeth
Henllan Amgoed
Llanfallteg
Esgair
Llangynin
Clarbeston Road
Haverfordwest
Leachpool
Rath Hillfort
Crundale
Gelli
Clunderwen
Llanfallteg West
Cwmfelin Boeth
Grove Land Adventure World
Glyn-Coch Craft Centre
Bancyfelin
Plain Dealings
Wiston
Bethesda
Llawhaden
Llanddewi Velfrey
Prendergast
Robeston Wathen
Whitland
Pwlltrap
St. Clears
Llangynog
HAVERFORDWEST
(Hwlffordd)
Clerkenhill Adventure Farm
Canaston Bridge
Narberth
(Arberth)
Lampeter Vale
Hywel Dda Centre
Trevaughan
Llwyn-y-brain
Backe
Uzmaston
The Rhos
Blackpool Mill
Robeston Back
Crinow
Lampeter Velfrey
Llan-mill
Llanddowror
Morfa Bach
Picton
Minwear
Bluestone
Narberth Bridge
Cold Blow
Princes Gate
Tavernspite
Halfpenny Furze
Boulston
Oakwood
Templeton
Red Roses
Llanybri
Hook
Landshipping
Ludchurch
Llandawke
Dylan Thomas Boathouse
Llansteffan
Martletwy
Llanteg
Laugharne
Llansadurnen
Broadway
Brook
Llangwm
Black Tar
Sardis
Yerbeston
Reynalton
Thomas Chapel
Marros
Llanmiloe
Pendine
(Pentywyn)
Museum of Speed
DANGER AREA
Ginst Point
St. Ishmael
Rosemarket
Port Lion
Loveston
Folly Farm
Kilgetty
(Cilgeti)
Stepaside
Colby Woodland
Summerhill
Amroth
Houghton
Lawrenny
Cresswell R.
West Williamston
Cresswell Quay
Cresselly
Jeffreyston
Begelly
Ironworks
Sardis
Honeyborough
Burton
Pembroke Ferry
Neyland
Waterloo
Cosheston
Upton
Upton Castle
Carew Newton
Broadmoor
Redberth
Pentlepoir
East Williamston
Saundersfoot
Milton
Carew
Sageston
Heatherton World of Activities
Broadfield
Monkstone Point
New Hedges
Silent World
CARMARTHEN BAY
(BAE CAERFYRDDIN)
Pennar
Monkton
Pembroke
(Penfro)
Upper Nash
Carew Cheriton
Control Tower
Manor House
The Dinosaur Park
Tenby
(Dinbych-y-Pysgod)
Bishop's Palace
St. Florence
Gumfreston
Lamphey
Manorbier Newton
Penally
(Penalun)
Tudor Merchant's House
National Park Centre
Maiden Wells
Hodgeston
Jameston
Lydstep
Giltar Point
Caldey Sound
Freshwater East
Cheriton or Stackpole Elidor
St. Petrox
Trewent Point
Manorbier
St. Margaret's
Caldey
Abbey
DANGER

45
Synod Inn (Post-Mawr)
Mydroilyn
Temple Bar
Ffynnon-oer
Olmarch
Llanddewi Brefi
Esgair Llethr 1543
CAMBRIAN MOUNTAINS
Pen Rhiw-clochdy
Bryn 70 Brawd 1589
Llangybi
Bettws Bledrws
Silian
Cribyn
Llanfair Clydogau
Talgarreg
Gorsgoch
Capel Cynon
Bwlch-y-fadfa
Maestir
Lampeter (Llanbedr Pont Steffan)
Cellan
Pentrefelin
Craig Twrch
1497 Pen y Gurnos
Llyn Brianne
CEREDIGION
Aber
Cwrtnewydd
Llanwnnen
Pentre-bach
Cwmann
Pont-sian
Cwmsychpant
Drefach
Alltyblacca
Llanwenog
Rhydowen
Tre-groes
Croes-lan
Pren-gwyn
Pencarreg
Glan Duar
Llanybydder
Rhuddlan
Rock Mill Woollen Mill
Capel Dewi
Maesycrugiau
Horeb
Llandysul
Pontwelly
Norwood
Aber-Giâr
Llanfihangel-ar-Arth
Llanllwni
Mynydd Pencarreg 1360
Ffaldybrenin
Ffarmers
Afon Twrch
Cwrt-y-Cadno
1515 Mynydd Mallaen
Afon Cothi
Five Saints Stone
Pumsaint
Caio
Dolaucothi Gold Mines
Aberbowlan
Porthyrhyd
Crugybar
Cilycwm
Nant-y-bai
Rhandirmwyn
Afon Gwenlais
Afon Tywi
Cynghordy
Ystradffin
Pentre-cwrt
Banc-y-ffordd
New Inn
Pencader
Dol-gran
Gwyddgrug
Mynydd Llanllwni
1339 Mynydd Llanybyther
Rhydcymerau
Llidiad-Nenog
FOREST OF BRECHFA
Llansawel
Edwinsford
Abergorlech
Gwernogle
Abbey
Talley
Alltwalis
Llandovery (Llanymddyfri)
Mail Coach Pillar
Fron
Llansadwrn
Llanwrda
Mynydd Figyn
Cwmdu
Halfway
Felindre
Cilgwyn
Myddfai
Brechfa
Afon Cothi
Llanllawddog
Llanpumsaint
Pontarsais
Horeb
Llanfynydd
Capel Isaac
Soar
Maerdy
Hermon
Llangadog
Afon Bran
Afon Gwili
Gwili
Rhydargaeau
Salem
Tyle
Dyffryn Ceidrych
Cwmifor
Bethlehem
Caledfwlch
Talsam
CARMARTHENSHIRE
Sarnau
Pant-teg
Feling-wmuchaf
Pantgwyn
Pen-y-banc
Rhosmaen
Pontarllechau
Twynllanan
Llanddeusant
Afon Sawdde
Newchurch
Bronwydd Arms
Peniel
Llanfihangel-uwch-Gwili
Felingwmisaf
Court Henry
Broad Oak
Pentrefelin
Llangathen
Dinefwr Park
Cilsan
Dyffryn
Llandeilo
Y Garn Goch Hill Forts 1360
Trichrug
Capel Gwynfe
Ffynnon-ddrain
Henallt
Merlin's Hill Centre
White Mill
Aberglasney
Gelli Aur Arboretum
BRECON BEACONS NATIONAL PARK
Neuadd
Y Fan Fach
CARMARTHEN (Caerfyrddin)
Amphitheatre
Tanerdy
Abergwili
Carmarthenshire County Museum
Nantgaredig
Capel Dewi
Pont-ar-gothi
Llanegwad
Felindre
Dryslwyn
Ffairfach
Truman
Gareg Las 2076
Llangunnor
Llanarthne
Golden Grove
Trapp
Carreg Cennen
Pensarn
Johnstown
Pibwrlwyd
Paxton's Tower
National Botanic Garden of Wales
Temple Bar
Pant-y-llyn
BLACK MOUNTAIN
2022 Bylchau Rhos-faen
1982 Foel Fraith
Cefn Carn-Fadog 1657
Afon Twrch
Cwmffrwd
Llanddarog
Maesybont
Carmel
Llandyfan
Pentre Gwenlais
Croesyceiliog
Cwmisfael
Porthyrhyd
Idole
Bancycapel
Llangendeirne
Gwendraeth Fach
Mynydd Cerrig
Cefneithin
Gorslas
Cae'r-bryn
Llandybie
Black Mountain Centre
Upper Brynamman
Brynamman
Rhosaman
Crwbin
Capel Seion
Drefach
Cross Hands
Pen-y-groes
Ammanford (Rhydaman)
Glanaman
Tir-y-dail
Lower Brynamman
Cefn-bryn-brain
Cwmllynfell
Ystradowen
Cwmgiedd
Pontantwn
Cwm-mawr
Saron
Garnant
Gwaun-Cae-Gurwen
Pontamman
Betws
Tairgwaith
Llandyfaelog
Bancffosfelen
Tumble (Y Tymbl)
Capel Hendre
Penybanc
Banc Cwmhelen
Mynydd y Betws
Cwmgors
Cwm-twrch Uchaf
Pen Rhiwfawr
Pontyberem
Cwmgwili
Pantyffynnon
Tycroes
Meinciau
Pont-Henri
Tournos
Ystradgynlais
Four Roads
Pontyates (Pont-iets)
Broadway
Llansaint
Mynyddygarreg
Kidwelly (Cydweli)
Llangadog
Pont-newydd
Carway
Cynheidre
Mynydd Sylen 933
Sylen
Llannon
PONT ABRAHAM
Llwyn-Teg
Garnswllt
Mynydd y Gwair
Cwmcerdinen 974
Mynydd Garn-fach
Upper Lliw Resr
Cwm-twrch Isaf
Ystalyfera
Mynydd Allt-y-grug
Glan-rhyd
Godre'r-graig
Cilmaengwyn
Swansea Valley
Carn Llechart
Ring Cairn
Burial Chamber
Rhyd-y-fro
Llangiwg
Ynysmeudwy
Graig Fawr 907
R. Loughor (Afon Llwchwr)
Sardis
DANGER AREA
Ffos Las
Five Roads
Horeb
Trimsaran
Pinged
Waun-y-Clyn
Pen-y-Mynydd
Mynydd Pen-bre
Pembrey
Cwm Capel
Graig
Burry Port (Porth Tywyn)
Parc Howard
Pentrebach
Cefn Drum
Lower Lliw Resr
Pontarddulais
Pontardawe
Cilybebyll
Gellinudd
SWANSEA
Rhos
Tyn-y-cwm
Cynghordy
Craig-cefn-parc
Trebanos
Alltwen
1370 Cefn Coed Colliery Museum
Mynydd Marchywel
Hendy
Cwm Dulais
Felindre
Fagwyr
Craig-y-Duke
Pembrey Forest
Pembrey
Sandy
Furnace
Felinfoel
Allt
Llangennech
Llwyncelyn
Clydach
Fforest Goch
Cilfrew
Aberdulais
Falls
Pwll
Dafen
Bryn
Pontlliw
SWANSEA WEST
Ynystawe
Glais
Ynysforgan
Bryn-coch
Cadoxton-Juxta-Neath
Vale of Neath
Millennium Coastal Park
Discovery Centre
Cefncaeau
Pemberton
Llwynhendy
Grovesend
Penyrheol
Tircoed
Pant-lasau
Rhydding
Neath Abbey
Tonna (Tonnau)
LLANELLI
Bynea
GORSEINON
Yspitty
Penllergaer
Llangyfelach
Morriston
Birchgrove
NEATH (Castell-nedd)
Loughor
National Wetland Centre Wales
Garden Village
Llansamlet
Skewen
Cimla
Whiteford
Cadle
Port Mead
Lower Loughor
A40
A48
A483
A484
A485
A486
A475
A476
A482
A474
A4069
A4067
A4068
A4138
A4240
A4109
B4337
B4338
B4343
B4459
B4476
B4336
B4301
B4310
B4302
B4297
B4300
B4312
B4306
B4309
B4317
B4311
B4308
B4304
B4296
B4556
B4603
B4291
B4599
M4
30
46
57
E
F
G
H
1
2
3
4
5

46
CAMBRIAN MOUNTAINS
Esgair Llethr 1543
1641 Cefn-Coch
Bryn
Pentre-llwyn-llwyd
B4358
Abergwesyn
Cefn Fannog 1476
Tywi Forest
Llyn Brianne
57
Troedrhiwdalar
Builth Road
Cwmbach Llechrhyd
Llansantffraed-in-Elwel
A483
A481
Llanelwedd
Cregrina
Cilmery (Cilmeri)
Llywelyn the Last Monument
Royal Welsh Showground
Beulah
Llanafan-fechan
Builth Wells 58
(Llanfair-ym-Muallt)
Llanfaredd
Caerau Roman Fort
Garth
A470
B4567
A483
Cambrian Woollen Mill
Llanwrtyd
Mynydd Trawsnant 1695
Llanwrtyd Wells
(Llanwrtud)
Llangammarch Wells
DANGER AREA
Maesmynis
B4520
Llanddewi'r Cwm
Alltmawr
Aberedw
Church Aberedw Rocks
Llandeilo Graban
Llanbadarn-y-garreg
Ystradffin
1515 Mynydd Mallaen
Nant-y-bai
Rhandirmwyn
Cefngorwydd
Bryn Nicol
Cefn Llwydlo
Crychan Forest
Drum-ddu 1554
B4519
EPPYNT
MYNYDD
1559
Pentre Dolau Honddu
Erwood
Gwenddwr
Crickadarn
Bryn-du 1519
Twyn Rhyd-car
Tirabad
Afon Gwenlas
Afon Tywi
Cilycwm
Cynghordy
Upper Chapel
A470
Fforest
CARMARTHENSHIRE
Llandovery
(Llanymddyfri)
A483
Pentre-ty-gwyn
Babel
MYNYDD BWLCH-Y-GROES
Merthyr Cynog
Llaneglwys
Landefalle Hill
Ponde
Lower Chapel
Llandefalle
Llandeilo'r Fan
POWYS
Llanfihangel Nant Bran
Pont-faen
Pwllgloyw
Trawscoed
Garthbrengy
Felinfach
A40
A4069
Mail Coach Pillar
Fron
Pentrebach
Halfway
Pentre-bach
Afon Gwydderig
Sarnau
Talachddu
Llanwrda
Mynydd Aberscir 1204
Soar
Llandefaelog Fach
Battle
Llanddew
Trefeitha
Myddfai
1443 Mynydd Myddfai
Usk Resr.
A40
Llywel
Trecastle
Pentre'r-felin
Yr Allt 1156
Sennybridge
Trallong
Aberbran
Penpont
Brecon Gaer Roman Fort
Cradoc
Pen-y-Crug Hillfort
Aberyscir
Llanfaes
Brecon
(Aberhonddu)
Llechfaen
Llanywern
Groesffordd
Llangadog
Cwmwysg
R. Usk
Pont ar Hydfer
Defynnog
Llanspyddid
Ffrwdgrech
Mynydd Illtyd
Brecon Beacons National Park
Cantref Adventure Farm
Llanhamlach
Talsarn
A4067
Forest Fach
Libanus
Llanfrynach
Twynllanan
Pontarllechau
Llanddeusant
Source of R. Usk
Afon Sawdde
Glas Fynydd Forest
Crai
A4215
Afon Senni
1845 Allt Ddu
Pencelli
B4558
Capel Gwynfe
Moel Feity 1940
Llyn y Fan Fach
Llyn y Fan-Fawr
Heol Senni
Pen Milan
Glyn Tarell
Afon Tarell
Cross Oak
Talybont-on-Usk
Bryn 1842
Aber Village
Cray Resr.
A470
PEN Y FAN 2906
BRECON BEACONS
Gareg Las 2076
BLACK MOUNTAIN
Brest Twrch
2366 Fan Hir
FFOREST FAWR
BRECON BEACONS NATIONAL PARK
Fan Fawr 2409
Beacons Reservoir
Fan Llia 2071
Ystradfellte Reservoir
Fan Gihirych
Neuadd Reservoirs
Torpantau
Talybont Reservoir
1982 Foel Fraith
2022 Bylchau Rhos-faen
A4069
Carreg-lem 1832
Cefn Carn-Fadog 1657
Castell-y-geifr
National Showcaves Centre for Wales
Glyntawe
(PARC CENEDLAETHOL BANNAU BRYCHEINIOG)
Wern
Cefn Mawr
Afon Twrch
Craig-y-nos
Penwyllt
1763
Carreg-lwydd
R. Neath
Cantref Resr.
Waun Lysiog
Taf Fechan
Pentwyn Reservoir
Black Mountain Centre
Upper Amman
Rhosamman
Pen-y-cae
Nant-ddu
Pontsticill Reservoir
Brecon Mountain Railway
Lower Brynamman
Cefn-bryn-brain
A4068
Cwmllynfell
Ystradowen
Abercraf
Ynyswen
Henrhyd Waterfall
Ystradfellte
A4059
R. Hepste
Garwnant
MERTHYR
Tairgwaith
Cwm-twrch Uchaf
Cwmgiedd
Caehopkin
Cae'r-bont
Penrhos
A4221
Coelbren
Porth yr Ogof Cave
Cader Fawr
Llwyn-on Resr.
Llwyn-on Village
Pontsticill
Vaynor
Cwmgors
Pen-rhiwfawr
Gurnos
Ystradgynlais
Onllwyn
Nedd Fechan Waterfalls
Afon Mellte Waterfalls
Pant Sychbant
MERTHYR TYDFIL
Tafarnaubach
Morlais Castle
A474
Cwm-twrch Isaf
977 Mynydd y Drum
B4599
Dyffryn Cellwen
Afon Pyrddin Waterfalls
Sgwd yr Eira Waterfall
RHONDDA
Ystalyfera
Glan-rhyd
A4067
A4109
Seven Sisters
(Blaendulais)
Glyn-neath
Waterfalls Centre
Pontneddfechan
Penderyn
Mynydd-y-glog 1376
Cefn-coed-y-cymmer
Trefechan
(Merthyr Tudful)
Bute Town
RHYMNEY
(Rhymni)
Godre'r-graig
Swansea Valley
Dulais
Hirfynydd
Morfa Glas
Pontbren Llwyd
A465
Pen-y-Darren
Dowlais
A4060
Rhaslas Pond
Pontlottyn
Cilmaengwyn
Mynydd Marchywel
Pont-Walby
B4242
Rhigos
Hirwaun
CYNON
Clwydfagwyr
Pen-yr-Heolgerrig
Fochriw
Troedrhiw
Llangiwg
Rhyd-y-fro
B4603
Pontardawe
Cilybebyll
Gellinudd
Crynant
Pentreclwydau
Blaengwrach
Cwmgwrach
A465
A4059
Penywaun
Cwmdare
B4276
Llwydcoed
Robertstown
Gethin Woodland Park
Pentrebach
Pentwyn
Alltwen
Rhos
1370 Cefn Coed Colliery
A4109
B4242
Abergarwed
Resolven
(Resolfen)
1257 Mynydd Resolfen
Cefn Grug
Craig y Llyn
Llyn-Fawr
1969
Hirwaun Common
Trecynon
Abernant
Abercanaid
1611 Mynydd Merthyr
Cwmbach
Troedyrhiw
Bedlinog
Craig-y-Duke
A474
Fforest Goch
Melincourt
Melincourt Waterfall
NEATH
A4061
ABERDARE
(Aberdar)
Lluest-wen Resrvoir
TAFF
Aberaman
Cwmpennar
TYDFIL
Glais
A4067
Cilfrew
Aberdulais Falls
Vale of Neath
Clyne
(Y Clun)
Blaenrhondda
Cwmaman
Aberfan
Merthyr Vale
(Ynysowen)
Dryn-coch
Cadoxton-Juxta-Neath
AFAN FOREST PARK
Bryncorrwg
32
Tynewydd
Treherbert
A4233
Abercwmboi
MOUNTAIN ASH
(Aberpennar)
A470
B4275
Newtown
Treharris
Birchgrove
Rhyddings Neath Abbey
Tonna
(Tonnau)
B4434
Blaencwm
Maerdy
Ynys-wen
Blaenllechau
Penrhiwceiber
Skewen
NEATH
(Castell-nedd)
Cimla
PORT TALBOT
Abercregan
Cymmer
Blaengwynfi
Treorchy
(Treorci)
Ferndale
Pentre
RHONDDA
Tonmawr
St. Gwynno Forest
A4059
Edwardsville

47
HEREFORDSHIRE
MONMOUTHSHIRE
BLACK MOUNTAINS
BLAENAU GWENT
TORFAEN
ENGLAND
WALES
HEREFORD
ABERGAVENNY
(Y Fenni)
MONMOUTH
(Trefynwy)
Hay-on-Wye
(Y Gelli Gandryll)
Kingswood
Huntington
Glascwm
Newchurch
Michaelchurch-on-Arrow
Bryngwyn
Rhosgoch
Clyro
Clifford
Llowes
Glasbury
Talgarth
Three Cocks
Velindre
Tregoyd
Llanigon
Cusop
Dorstone
Peterchurch
Vowchurch
Turnastone
Michaelchurch Escley
St. Margarets
Newton
Bacton
Abbey Dore
Ewyas Harold
Pontrilas
Rowlstone
Longtown
Clodock
Llanthony
Capel-y-ffin
Oldcastle
Walterstone
Cwmyoy
Pandy
Llanvihangel Crucorney
Grosmont
Kentchurch
Skenfrith
Cross Ash
Llanvetherine
Crickhowell
(Crughywel)
Gilwern
Govilon
Brynmawr
Beaufort
Nantyglo
EBBW VALE
(Glyn Ebwy)
Blaina
Blaenavon
Abersychan
ABERTILLERY
(Abertyleri)
New Tredegar
Llanhilleth
Oakdale
Blackwood
Crumlin
Newbridge
(Cefn Bychan)
PONTYPOOL
(Pontypwl)
Griffithstown
Usk
(Brynbuga)
Raglan
Llangwm
Llantrisant
Devauden
Trellech
Llandogo
Tintern
Whitebrook
Redbrook
Wyesham
Dixton
Whitchurch
Welsh Newton
Llangarron
Llangrove
St. Weonards
St. Owen's Cross
Much Dewchurch
Kilpeck
Wormbridge
King's Thorn
Callow
Kingstone
Allensmore
Clehonger
Madley
Peterchurch
Moccas
Blakemere
Bredwardine
Staunton on Wye
Bishopstone
Credenhill
Bridge Sollers
Weobley
Dilwyn
Almeley
Eardisley
Kinnersley
Whitney
Winforton
Canon Pyon
Wellington
Moreton on Lugg
Burghill
Holmer
Bodenham
Hope under Dinmore
Lugwardine
Lower Bullingham
Dinedor
A438
A4112
A480
A4110
A49
A465
A479
A40
A4042
A449
A466
A4137
A4103
B4348
B4352
B4347
B4521
B4233
B4350
B4558
B4246
59
48
33
E
F
G
H
1
2
3
4
5

48
A
B
C
D
Birley
Upper Hill
Hope under Dinmore
Bush Bank
Westhope
Queenswood
Hampton Court
Bodenham
59
Newton
Risbury
Broadfield Court
Bowley
Stannett
Hegdon Hill
Pencombe
Bromyard Downs
Bromyard
A44
Bringsty Common
Linley Green
Yearsett
A44
Broadwas
Cotheridge
Ravenhills Green
Alfrick
Brockamin
Leigh Court Barn
Leigh
Rushwick
St. Johns
St. Peter the Great
Whittington
A4440
A417
Maund Bryan
Ullingswick
Little Cowarne
Shortwood Family Farm
A465
Munderfield Row
Munderfield Stocks
Stanford Bishop
Suckley Knowl
Suckley
Alfrick Pound
Smith End Green
Bransford
Coles Green
Dawshill
Bowling Green
Powick
Leigh Sinton
A4103
60
A449
Bastonford
Pole Elm
Brook End
Highway
Canon Pyon
Wellington
Auberrow
Moreton on Lugg
Tillington
Portway
Burghill
Stretton Sugwas
Monmarsh
The Vauld
Venn's Green
Urdimarsh
Marden
Walker's Green
Preston Wynne
Sutton Walls Hillfort
Sutton St. Michael
Sutton St. Nicholas
A49
Felton
Preston Marsh
Ocle Pychard
Moreton Jeffries
Upper Town
Stoke Cross
Stoke Lacy
Burley Gate
Much Cowarne
Lower Egleton
Bishop's Frome
Five Bridges
Acton Beauchamp
Acton Green
Longley Green
Evesbatch
Halmond's Frome
Stony Cross
Ridgeway Cross
Stifford's Bridge
Storridge
Cradley
Upper Howsell
Pins Green
Newland
Malvern Link
Madresfield
GREAT MALVERN
West Malvern
Callow End
Kempsey
Draycott
Clevelode
Kerswell Green
M5
Pipe and Lyde
Kenchester Water
Shelwick
White Stone
Shelwick Green
Withington Marsh
Withington
Shucknall
Westhide
Newtown
Monkhide
Yarkhill
Lower Town
Stretton Grandison
A4103
Castle Frome
Fromes Hill
Stanley Hill
Canon Frome
Bosbury
Norbridge
Mathon
Coddington
Ham Green
Upper Wyche
Lower Wyche
Worcestershire Beacon 1394
Picton
Colwall
Three Counties Showground
Guarlford
B4211
Hanley Swan
Severn Stoke
Clifton
Rhydd
A38
Holmer
King's Acre
Swainshill
A4103
HEREFORDSHIRE
Lugwardine
Hagley
Weston Beggard
Tarrington
Ashperton
Swinmore Common
Munsley
Staplow
Wellington Heath
Colwall Green
Evendine
Malvern Wells
Gilbert's End
Hook Bank
Brotheridge Green
Hanley Castle
Heritage Centre
Ryall
Upton upon Severn
Upper Breinton
Breinton
Tupsley
Bartestree
HEREFORD
Dormington
Prior's Frome
Larport
Stoke Edith
A438
Durlow Common
Trumpet
Plaistow
Bradlow
Herefordshire Beacon
Little Malvern
Little Malvern Court
A449
Welland
Newbridge Green
Lower Bullingham
Bullinghope
Hampton Bishop
Sufton Court
Mordiford
Checkley
Pixley
Aylton
Butchers Row House
Ledbury
Heritage Centre
MALVERN
Chandler's Cross
Druggers End
Uckinghall
Gorsty Common
Grafton
A465
Dinedor
Putley
Farm Park
Little Marcle
Preston Cross
Eastnor
Eastnor Castle
Hollybush
Birts Street
Castlemorton
Queenhill
Allensmore
Dinedor Cross
Holme Lacy
Shipley
Woolhope
Kynaston
Rushall
Parkway
A417
Camer's Green
Rye Street
Longdon
M50
Bushley Green
Callow
Twyford Common
Fownhope
Common Hill
Donnington
Bromsberrow
Birtsmorton
White End
A438
Dewsall Court
Kivernoll
Aconbury
Newtown
Bolstone
Little Dewchurch
R. Wye
Sollers Hope
Westons Cider
Bounds
Hallwood Green
Tillers Green
Bromsberrow Heath
King's Green
Long Green
Tewkesbury
Didley
King's Thorn
Little Birch
Much Birch
Ballingham
Falcon
Much Marcle
Hellens
B4024
Broom's Green
Ryton
Pendock
Playley Green
Eldersfield
Chaceley
Much Dewchurch
Kilpeck
Wormelow Tump
Violette Szabo
A49
Brockhampton
How Caple Court
How Caple
Carey
Stocking
Yatton
Lyne Down
Shakesfield
Dymock
Redmarley D'Abitot
Lowbands
Linkend
Lime Street
Corse Lawn
Odda's Chapel
Orcop Hill
Hoarwithy
Penalt
Kings Caple
Fawley Chapel
Old Gore
Fishpool
Church
Kempley
Kempley Green
M50
Hawcross
Hethelpit Cross
Staunton
Tirley
Apperley
Llandinabo
Harewood End
Foy
Strangford
Poolhill
Botloe's Green
Brand Green
Four Oaks
Corse
Llanwarne
Sellack
Brampton Abbotts
A449
Crow Hill
Upton Crews
Upton Bishop
Oxenhall
Upleadon
Oridge Street
Hasfield
Netherton
Upper Grove Common
Phocle Green
Gorsley
Picklenash
Newent
Ashleworth
The Leigh
Garway Hill
Orcop
Sandyway
Michaelchurch
ROSS SPUR
Rudhall
A417
Malswick
St. Owen's Cross
Poolmill
Bridstow
Ross-on-Wye
Linton
Linton Hill
Gorsley Common
Kilcot
Birds of Prey Centre
Hartpury
Tithe Barn
Bishop's Norton
Prior's Norton
St. Weonards
Treaddow
Peterstow
Wilson
Tretire
A40
Ashfield
Bromsash
Aston Crews
Aston Ingham
Kent's Green
Highleadon
Woolridge
Norton
Wallsworth
Garway Common
Three Ashes
A4137
Glewstone
Tudorville
Weston under Penyard
Ryeford
A40
Lea
Clifford's Mesne
Tibberton
Sandhurst
Twigworth
Nature in Art
Down Hatherley
Hom Green
Coughton
Pontshill
Luxley
Glasshouse
Taynton
Rudford
Maisemore
Longford
Innsworth
Llancloudy
Llangarron
Broad Oak
Pencraig
Walford
Howle Hill
East Dean
Boxbush
Dursley Cross
Huntley
Highnam
Wharf House
Over
Kingsholm
Ruxton Green
Goodrich
Kiln Green
Hope Mansell
Llanrothal
Llangrove
Marstow
Welsh Newton
Welsh Newton Common
Kerne Bridge
Drybrook
Forest of Dean Mechanical Organ
Puddlebrook
Longhope
Birdwood
A40
Churcham
GLOUCESTER
Wotton
Barnwood
Hucclecote
Old Forge
Whitchurch
Maze
Leisure Park
Symonds Yat
Ruardean
Ruardean Hill
Drybrook
Mitcheldean
Abenhall
Dick Whittington Farm Park
Blaisdon
Oakle Street
High Orchard
Hempsted
Linden
St. Maughan's Green
Maypole
Ganarew
Buckholt
Crocker's Ash
Gt. Doward
Lower Lydbrook
English Bicknor
Ruardean Woodside
Nailbridge
Northwood Green
Lower Ley
Minsterworth
Elmore Back
Elmore
A40
King Arthur's Cave
Upper Lydbrook
Brierley
Flaxley
Pope's Hill
A48
Rockfield
Dixton
Hillersland
Bilson Green
Cinderford
Westbury-on-Severn
Chaxhill
Farley's End
Quedgeley
MONMOUTH
(Trefynwy)
Christchurch
Staunton
Berry Hill
Edge End
B4227
Littledean
Elton
Westbury Court
Whaddon
Over Monnow
Kymin
The Buck Stone
Hopewell Colliery
Ruspidge
Cyril Hart Arboretum
Broadoak
Newnham
Longney
Hardwicke
Hardwicke Court
Brookthorpe
Wyesham
Jingle Street
Penallt
Coleford
Broadwell
Coalway
Upper Soudley
Dean Heritage Centre
Lower Soudley
St. Augustine's Farm
Arlingham
Rodley
Epney
Upper Framilode
Colethrop
Haresfield
Rococo
Mitchel Troy
Redbrook
Perrygrove Railway
Puzzlewood
FOREST OF DEAN
Moreton Valence
Little Haresfield
Harescombe
Edge
A40
Mitchel Troy Common
Newland
Milkwall
Roman Road
Two Bridges
A48
Fretherne
Saul
Whitminster
Standish
Haresfield Beacon
Pitchcombe
Cwmcarvan
New Mills
Clearwell Caves
Clearwell
Ellwood
Parkend
Yorkley
Viney Hill
Awre
Frampton on Severn
Church End
Nupend
OLDBURY
Whiteshill
Randwick
The North
Offa's Dyke
Stowe
Whitebrook
Bream's Meend
Pillowell
Whitecroft
Blakeney
Etloe
SEVERN
Claypits
Stonehouse
Ebley
Llangovan
Trelleck
Harold's Stones
Cotland
Bream
Allaston
Primrose Hill
Slimbridge Wetland Centre
Eastington
King's Stanley
Dudbridge
Rodborough
Lower Meend
Llandogo
St. Briavels
Dean Forest Railway
Lydney
Lydney Park
Purton
Purton
Sharpness
Canal
Slimbridge
Cambridge
Moorend
Middle Street
Leonard Stanley
Selsley
Thrupp
Brimscombe
Llanishen
Parkhouse
Coldharbour
Catbrook
Aylburton Common
Hewelsfield
Aylburton
Brookend
Halmore
Gossington
Frocester
Tithe Barn
Middleyard
Woodchester
Newtown
Coaley
Nympsfield Long Barrow
Woodchester Mansion
Dunkirk Mill
Trelleck Grange
Angiddy Furnace
Tintern
Brockweir
Old Station
Tintern Abbey
Netherend
Alvington
Wanswell
Breadstone
BERKELEY
Lower Cam
Far Green
Nympsfield
Ashmead Green
Amberley
Inchbrook
Burleigh
Dew Inn
Devauden
Chepstow Park Wood
Chapel Hill
Woolaston
Hook Street
34
Berkeley
Dr Jenner's House
A48
The Quarry
Cam
Dursley
Uley Bury
Hetty Pegler's Tump
Forest Green
Nailsworth
Newchurch
Stroat
Ham
Newport
Stinchcombe
Uley
Horsley
St. Arvans
Boughspring
Wibdon
RIVER
M5
A4135
Kingscote
Tiltups End
Bevington

49
A422
Upton Snodsbury
Churchill
Spetchley
Sneachill
White Ladies Aston
North Piddle
Flyford Flavell
Radford
Abberton
Rous Lench
Goom's Hill
Naunton Beauchamp
Bishampton
Church Lench
Ab Lench
Atch Lench
Iron Cross
Dunnington
A46
Salford Priors
Abbot's Salford
Ardens Grafton
Broom
Bidford-on-Avon
Marlcliff
Temple Grafton
Binton
Welford-on-Avon
Luddington
Weston-on-Avon
B439
Clifford Chambers
STRATFORD UPON-AVON
Bridge Town
Wellesbourne Mountford
Loxley
Walton
A4390
A422
Atherstone on Stour
Preston on Stour
A44
Egdon
Peopleton
Stoulton
E
F
G
H
Throckmorton
Harvington
Barton
Bickmarsh
61
Dorsington
Pinvin
Drakes Broughton
Hawbridge
Wadborough
Pirton
Hill
Hill Furze
A44
Norton
Lenchwick
Cleeve Prior
Long Marston
Pebworth
Wimpstone
Alderminster
A3400
Ettington
A429
Lower Quinton
Crimscote
Pillerton Priors
Wyre Piddle
Lower Moor
Fladbury
Pershore
Wick
Ramsden
Offenham
Evesham Vale
North Littleton
Middle Littleton
South Littleton
Broad Marston
Upper Quinton
Meon Hill
Admington
Newbold on Stour
Halford
Croome
Besford
Defford
Cropthorne
Charlton
Offenham Cross
EVESHAM
Bretforton
Honeybourne
Mickleton
Armscote
Idlicote
Tredington
Pensham
Little Comberton
Aldington
Bengeworth
Ilmington
Kiftsgate Court
Hidcote Bartrim
Hidcote Boyce
Blackwell
Birlingham
Bricklehampton
Hampton
Badsey
Honington
Darlingscott
Woodmancote
Great Comberton
Elmley Castle
Netherton
Wickhamford
Weston-sub-Edge
Aston Subedge
Shipston-on-Stour
STRENSHAM
Eckington
Lower Strensham
WORCESTERSHIRE
VALE OF EVESHAM
Murcot
Ebrington
Bredon Hill
Parson's Folly 961
Kersoe
Hinton on the Green
A46
Saintbury
Ernest Wilson Memorial
Naunton
Upper Strensham
Bredon's Norton
Ashton under Hill
Childswickham
Willersey
Littleworth
Market Hall
Chipping Campden
Charingworth
B4035
Barcheston
Willington
Tidmington
Burmington
Westmancote
Sedgeberrow
Aston Somerville
Broadway
Stretton-on-Fosse
Paxford
Twyning
Bredon
Overbury
Grafton
Broad Campden
Kemerton
Conderton
Dumbleton
Wormington
West End
Bury End
Buckland
Laverton
Broadway Tower
B4081
Draycott
Aston Magna
Todenham
Cherington
Twyning Green
Shuthonger
The Mythe
Kinsham
Northway
Aston on Carrant
Aston Cross
Beckford
Great Washbourne
Little Washbourne
Alderton
B4077
Snowshill Manor
Stanton
Snowshill
A44
Mill Dene
Blockley
Batsford Arboretum
Batsford
Lower Lemington
Great Wolford
A46
Ashchurch
Pamington
Teddington
Toddington
Stanway House & Fountain
Stanway
Moreton-in-Marsh
Cotswold Falconry Centre
Barton-on-the-Heath
Four Shire Stone
M5
Newtown
Walton Cardiff
Bengrove
Alstone
Alderton Fields
Gloucestershire Warwickshire Railway
Didbrook
Hailes
Wood Stanway
Taddington
Bourton-on-the-Hill
Wellington Aviation
Sezincote
A44
A429
Oxenton
Woolstone
Dixton
Fiddington
Tredington
Greet
Gretton
Hailes Abbey
Farmcote
Cutsdean
Ford
Hinchwick
Longborough
Chastleton
Compton
Little Rollright
Stoke Orchard
Gotherington
Winchcombe
Langley
Hyde
B4077
Ganborough
Condicote
Donnington
Evenlode
Chastleton House
Hardwicke
Bishop's Cleeve
Woodmancote
Postlip
Folk & Police
Sudeley Castle
Temple Guiting
Kineton
Broadwell
Adlestrop
Cornwell
Chipping Norton
Elmstone Hardwicke
Brockhampton
Cleeve Hill
Cotswold Farm Park
Upper Swell
Stow-on-the-Wold
Lower Oddington
Daylesford
Boddington
A4019
Swindon
Southam
Cleeve Cloud 1040
Belas Knap Long Barrow
Charlton Abbots
Guiting Power
Barton
Chalk Hill
Lower Swell
Maugersbury
Upper Oddington
Kingham
Uckington
Hall of Fame
Prestbury
B4068
Naunton
Wyck Hill
Golden Valley
Hester's Way
Pittville
Hawling
Brockhampton
Upper Slaughter
Lower Slaughter
Icomb
Bledington
Foscot
CHELTENHAM
Lansdown
A40
The Reddings
Battledown
Sevenhampton
Whittington Court
Whittington
Aylworth
Wyck Rissington
Model Railway Exhibition
Model Village
Church Westcote
Nether Westcote
Lyneham
Bruern Abbey
Idbury
Up Hatherley
Charlton Kings
Syreford
Hampen
Long Barrow
Salperton
Cotswold Motoring
Bourton-on-the-Water
Little Rissington
Birdland Park & Gardens
Leckhampton
Little Herbert's
Dowdeswell
Andoversford
Notgrove
Cold Aston
Nethercote
Badgeworth
Devil's Chimney
Shipton
A40
Hazleton
A429
Clapton-on-the-Hill
Fifield
Milton-under-Wychwood
Shurdington
Seven Springs
A436
Foxcote
Turkdean
Great Rissington
Shipton-under-Wychwood
Bentham
Seven Springs
Compton Abdale
Hampnett
Coberley
A417
Little Witcombe
Birdlip
Great Witcombe
Upper Coberley
Cowley
Withington
Farmington
Northleach
Mill End
Mechanical Music
Sherborne
Great Barrington
Taynton
Cranham
A435
Colesbourne
Yanworth
Chedworth Roman Villa
Eastington
Windrush
Little Barrington
A40
Lodge Park
Burford
Fulbrook
Brimpsfield
Elkstone
Chedworth
Pancakehill
Fossebridge
Coln St. Dennis
Swinbrook
Asthall
Caudle Green
Syde
Rendcomb
Calcot
Coln Rogers
Aldsworth
B4425
Westwell
Signet
A40
Sheepscombe
Whiteway
Winstone
Miserden Castle
Miserden
Woodmancote
Calmsden
Winson
Ablington
Trout Farm
Holwell
Cotswold Wildlife Park
Shilton
The Camp
Throughams
Duntisbourne Abbots
A417
North Cerney
Cerney House
A429
Arlington
Bibury
Arlington Row
Sudgrove
Duntisbourne Leer
Middle Duntisbourne
Bagendon
The Giant's Stone
Edgeworth
Duntisbourne Rouse
Perrott's Brook
Coln St. Aldwyns
Hatherop
Eastleach Turville
Eastleach Martin
Swinford
Kencot
Broadwell
Alvescot
Bisley
Waterlane
Daglingworth
Baunton
Barnsley
Abbey Home Farm
Cotswold Woollen Weavers
Fyfield
Filkins
Eastcombe
Bournes Green
Far Oakridge
Bussage
Chalford
Oakridge
Sapperton
Stratton
B4425
Quenington
Southrop
Broughton Poggs
Langford
Frampton Mansell
A419
Roman Wall
Ampney Crucis
Ampney St. Mary
Little Faringdon
Little Clanfield
Hyde
CIRENCESTER
Corinium Museum
Roman Amphitheatre
Preston
A417
Fairford
Milton End
Horcott
Clanfield
Minchinhampton
Aston Down
Coates
A429
Harnhill
Ampney St. Peter
Poulton
A417
Grafton
Long Stone
Hampton Fields
Cherington
Chesterton
Siddington
Meysey Hampton
Marston Hill
Whelford
Lechlade on Thames
Kelmscott
Kelmscott Manor
Source of R. Thames
A433
South Cerney
Butts Farm
35
Fairford
Father Thames Statue
Eaton Hastings
Avening
Rodmarton
Kemble
Ewen
South Cerney
Down Ampney
Marston Meysey
Kempsford
Upper Inglesham
Buscot
Buscot Park
Windmill Tump
Cotswold
Poole
Somerford
Shorncote
A419
A417
A4095
COTSWOLD
HILLS
GLOUCESTERSHIRE

UPON-AVON
WARWICKSHIRE
OXFORDSHIRE
NORTHAMP
Ettington
Kineton
Gaydon
Fenny Compton
Upper Boddington
Byfield
Hinton
Woodford Halse
Eydon
Chipping Warden
Claydon
Farnborough
Warmington
Ratley
Mollington
Cropredy
Upper Wardington
Culworth
Weston
Sulgrave
Alderminster
Pillerton Hersey
Halford
Tredington
Oxhill
Middle Tysoe
Upper Tysoe
Shenington
Hornton
Shotteswell
Hanwell
BANBURY
Wroxton
Drayton
Middleton Cheney
Marston St. Lawrence
Greatworth
Helmdon
Chacombe
Shipston-on-Stour
Upper Brailes
Lower Brailes
Shutford
North Newington
Broughton
Sibford Gower
Swalcliffe
Tadmarton
Bodicote
Adderbury
Bloxham
King's Sutton
Charlton
Brackley
Farthinghoe
Stretton-on-Fosse
Todenham
Cherington
Stourton
Whichford
Hook Norton
Great Wolford
Moreton-in-Marsh
Long Compton
South Newington
Barford St. Michael
Deddington
Aynho
Croughton
Evenley
Souldern
Great Rollright
Little Compton
Great Tew
Fritwell
Stoke Lyne
Fringford
Broadwell
Over Norton
Salford
Chipping Norton
Middle Barton
Steeple Aston
Upper Heyford
Ardley
Bucknell
Kingham
Churchill
Enstone
Bicester
Bledington
Icomb
Chadlington
Charlbury
Tackley
Kirtlington
Chesterton
Ambrosden
Milton-under-Wychwood
Ascott-under-Wychwood
Shipton-under-Wychwood
Woodstock
Stonesfield
Finstock
Leafield
Ramsden
Kidlington
Weston-on-the-Green
Bletchingdon
Charlton-on-Otmoor
Islip
OT MOOR
Burford
Taynton
North Leigh
Long Hanborough
Freeland
Hailey
WITNEY
Yarnton
Eynsham
Carterton
Brize Norton
Ducklington
OXFORD
Marston
Headington
Wheatley
Stanton Harcourt
Cumnor
Kennington
Littlemore
Bampton
Clanfield
Langford
Kelmscott
Buckland
Kingston Bagpuize
Marcham
ABINGDON
Stadhampton
A422
A423
A429
A3400
A361
A44
A34
A40
A41
A43
A420
A415
A4095
A4260
A4142
A421
M40
B4035
B4031
B4030
B4026
B4022
B4437
B4449
B4027
B4100
61
62
36
49

51
Grimscote
Dalscote
Eastcote
Astcote
Cold Higham
Foxley
Duncote
Caldecote
A5
A43
Blisworth
Roade
Courteenhall
Quinton
Horton
CHASE
The Menagerie
Warrington
B5388
Lavendon
Church Path Oak
Salcey Forest
Hartwell
Eakley Lanes
Ravenstone
Weston Underwood
Olney
Clifton Reynes
Cold Brayfield
Newton Blossomville
Turvey
West End
Stevington
Oakley
Clapham
Bromham
A428
A4280
Biddenham
Box End
B560
Greens Norton
Bradden
Shutlanger
Stoke Bruerne
Ashton
Towcester
Stoke Park Pavilions
Heathencote
TONSHIRE
Hulcote
Canal
63
Emberton
Petsoe End
Stagsden
Kempston
Stoke Goldington
A508
Grafton Regis
Long Street
Hanslope
Tathall End
Gayhurst
Filgrave
Tyringham
Sherington
A509
Hardmead
Astwood
A422
Abthorpe
Wood Burcote
Alderton
Wappenham
Pury End
Paulerspury
A5
Yardley Gobion
M1
Castlethorpe
Little Linford
NEWPORT PAGNELL
Lathbury
Chicheley
Little Crawley
North Crawley
Bourne End
Upper Shelton
Hall End
Keeley Green
Wootton
Kempston Hardwick
A421
Silverstone
Whittlebury
Potterspury
Whittlewood Forest
Cosgrove
Haversham
Great Linford
Wharley End
Broad Green
Lower Shelton
Moulsoe
Cranfield
Stewartby
Brackley Hatch
Lillingstone Lovell
Old Stratford
Wolverton
Bradwell
Willen
Willen Lake
Marston Moretaine
How End
Biddlesden
Lillingstone Dayrell
Deanshanger
Wicken
Passenham
Stony Stratford
Calverton
Gulliver's
Milton Keynes Village
Broughton
Salford
Lidlington
Millbrook
Katherine's Cross
Houghton House
Dadford
Stowe House
Akeley
Leckhampstead
Upper Weald
Loughton
Shenley Church End
MILTON KEYNES
Brogborough
A421
Ampthill
Stowe Landscape
Chackmore
Foxcote Res
Maids Moreton
Beachampton
Thornton
Wavendon
A4146
Walton
Woburn Sands
Aspley Heath
Aspley Guise
Husborne Crawley
Ridgmont
Segenhoe Church
Steppingley
Flitwick
Water Stratford
Buffler's Holt
Radclive
Buckingham
Mount Pleasant
Shenley Brook End
Whaddon
Nash
BLETCHLEY
Bletchley Park
Bow Brickhill
Birchmoor Green
Woburn
Woburn Safari Park
Froxfield
Eversholt
Tingewick
Thornborough
Thornborough Bridge
A421
B4034
Fenny Stratford
Little Brickhill
Heritage Centre
Woburn Abbey
Tingrith
Westoning
Gawcott
Barton Hartshorn
Singleborough
Great Horwood
Little Horwood
Newton Longville
Great Brickhill
Grand Union Canal
A5
A4012
Milton Bryan
M1
Padbury
Adstock
B4033
Stoke Hammond
Potsgrove
Battlesden
Toddington
Chetwode
Preston Bissett
Hillesden
A413
Addington
Drayton Parslow
A4146
Heath and Reach
Watergate Farm
Upper Sundon
Steeple Claydon
Winslow
Mursley
Soulbury
Hollingdon
Leighton Buzzard Railway
Hockliffe
Tebworth
Twyford
Middle Claydon
Shipton
Swanbourne
Stewkley Dean
B4032
Stewkley
Chalton
Wingfield
Poundon
Grebe Lake
Claydon
East Claydon
Granborough
Hoggeston
Eggington
Tilsworth
Houghton Regis
Charndon
Calvert
Botolph Claydon
Littlecote
Linslade
Leighton Buzzard
A505
Stanbridge
Marsh Gibbon
North Marston
Dunton
Burcott
Sewell
BUCKINGHAMSHIRE
Edgcott
Cublington
Wing
Ascott
Billington
Little Billington
DUNSTABLE
Totternhoe
Grendon Underwood
Oving
Whitchurch
Aston Abbotts
A418
Ledburn
Slapton
Honeywick
Eaton Bray
Church End
Quainton
Pitchcott
Mentmore
Northall
Edlesborough
Chilterns Gateway
Kensworth
Blackthorn
Kingswood
A41
Buckinghamshire Railway Centre
Hardwick
Crafton
Wingrave
Horton
Ivinghoe Aston
A5
Ludgershall
Weedon
Rowsham
Whipsnade
Kensworth Common
Piddington
Westcott
Waddesdon
Waddesdon Manor
The Lake
Wotton House
Wotton Underwood
Upper Winchendon
Watermead
Hulcott
Cheddington
Long Marston
Ford End Watermill
Ivinghoe
Ivinghoe Beacon
Pitstone
Gubblecote
Dagnall
Studham
Boarstall
Dorton
Ashendon
Pollicott
Quarrendon
A4157
Bierton
Puttenham
Marsworth
Wilstone
Ringshall
Bridgewater Monument
Ashridge Estate
Little Gaddesden
Jockey End
Brill
Little London
AYLESBURY
Stone
A41
Grand Union Canal
Buckland
Drayton Beauchamp
Tring
New Mill
Bulbourne
Aldbury
Great Gaddesden
St. Margaret's
Nether Winchendon
Nether Winchendon House
Cuddington
Upton
Southcourt
Stoke Mandeville
Weston Turville
Aston Clinton
Halton
A413
Upper Dunsley
B486
Oakley
Chilton
Chearsley
Gibraltar
Dinton
Westlington
Bishopstone
Easington
Bucks Goat Centre
West Leith
Natural History
Wigginton
Nettleden
Frithsden
Potten End
Worminghall
Long Crendon
Courthouse
Haddenham
Aylesbury (Thame)
Ford
Marsh
Nash Lee
Terrick
Wendover
Wendover Woods
Hastoe
Northchurch
Ickford
Tiggywinkles Wildlife Hospital
Aston Sandford
Kimble Wick
North Lee
A4010
A4009
Cholesbury Camp
Cholesbury
BERKHAMSTED
Warners End
Chaulden
Bourne End
Boxmoor
Shabbington
North Weston
Kingsey
Owlswick
Little Kimble
Ellesborough
St. Leonards
Buckland Common
A4251
A41
Waterstock
Draycot
A4129
Thame
Towersey
Ilmer
Meadle
Askett
Great Kimble
Coombe Hill Monument
Chequers
Kingsash
HUNDREDS
Bellingdon
Ashley Green
Whelpley Hill
Tiddington
A329
Longwick
Monks Risborough
THREE HILLS
Dunsmore
The Lee
Lee Clump
Bovingdon
Felden
B4505
Moreton
B4012
B4445
Pitch Green
Skittle Green
Horsenden
Princes Risborough
Little Hampden
Chartridge
Chesham
Milton Common
Great Haseley
Emmington
Henton
Chinnor & Princes Risborough Railway
Bledlow
Saunderton
Great Hampden
Hampden Monument
AYLESBURY
Ballinger Common
South Heath
B485
Lye Green
Ley Hill
Botley
CHESHAM
Waterside
Chipperfield
M40
Tetsworth
Latchford
Sydenham
Kingston Stert
Kingston Blount
B4009
Chinnor
Cross
Loosley Row
Lacey Green
Speen
Prestwood
Great Missenden
Roald Dahl
Hyde Heath
Flaunden
Belsize
Little Haseley
Stoke Talmage
Adwell
Postcombe
37
Saunderton Lee
Lacey Green
Horse Trust
Bryant's Bottom
Upper North Dean
Little Kingshill
Great Kingshill
A413
Chesham Bois
38
Sarratt
Chalgrove
Chalgrove 1643
South Weston
Aston Rowant
Radnage
Walter's Ash
A4128
Little Missenden
Beamond End
Latimer
Chenies Manor
Chenies
Mickle Green
Easington
Bledlow Ridge
Bradenham
Naphill
Cryers Hill
Hughenden Valley
Hazlemere
Holmer Green
AMERSHAM
A404
Little Chalfont
Pyrton
Shirburn
The City
Stokenchurch
A4010
Widmer End
Penn Street
CHORLEYWOOD
CHILTERN

52
BEDFORD
Kempston
Wootton
Bromham
Oakley
Clapham
Great Barford
Blunham
Sandy
Potton
Gamlingay
Biggleswade
Shefford
Ampthill
Flitwick
Toddington
DUNSTABLE
Houghton Regis
LUTON
HARPENDEN
Wheathampstead
Redbourn
HEMEL HEMPSTEAD
ST. ALBANS
HATFIELD
WELWYN GARDEN CITY
Welwyn
Knebworth
STEVENAGE
HITCHIN
LETCHWORTH GARDEN CITY
BALDOCK
Stotfold
Arlesey
Henlow
HERTFORD
HODDESDON
CHESHUNT
POTTERS BAR
BOREHAMWOOD
RADLETT
WATFORD
Kings Langley
Abbots Langley
Bovingdon
CHESHAM
CHORLEYWOOD
ENFIELD
Waltham Cross
London Colney
Brookmans Park
Cuffley
Barton-le-Clay
Woburn
Stewartby
Cranfield
Ashwell
Guilden Morden
Steeple Morden
Bassingbourn
Litlington
Kneesworth
Wrestlingworth
Old Warden
CENTRAL BEDFORDSHIRE
HERTFORDS
CAM
M1
A1
A1(M)
A5
A6
A10
A41
A414
A505
A507
A602
M25
A
B
C
D
1
2
3
4
5
63
64
38

CAMBRIDGESHIRE
ESSEX
HERTFORDSHIRE
M11
Great Shelford
Gog Magog Hills
Wandlebury
A11
Fleam Dyke
Harlton
Haslingfield
Hauxton
Stapleford
Little Shelford
Harston
Babraham
Balsham
West Wratting
Weston Colville
Weston Green
Willingham Green
Brinkley
Carlton
Great Bradley
Little Bradley
East Green
Cowlinge
Pound Green
Wickhambrook
Farley Green
Hobbles Green
Clopton Green
Denston
Hawkedon
Stradishall
Stansfield
Little Thurlow
Great Thurlow
Sowley Green
Thurston End
A10
Barrington
Shepreth
Foxton
Newton
FOURWENTWAYS
Sawston
Little Abington
Great Abington
Hildersham
Burton End
West Wickham
Streetly End
Horseheath
Withersfield
Great Wratting
Little Wratting
Barnardiston
Chimney Street
Hundon
Poslingford
Brockley Green
Kedington
Chilton Street
Cavendish
A505
Whittlesford
Pampisford
Thriplow
Heathfield
Duxford
Fowlmere
Linton
Cardinal's Green
Haverhill
Calford Green
Ancient House
Clare
A1092
Castle
Imperial War Museum
Hinxton
Ickleton
Hadstock
Bartlow
Bartlow Hills
Shudy Camps
Castle Camps
Wiggens Green
Sturmer
Boyton End
Wixoe
Stoke by Clare
Priory
Melbourn
Great Chesterford
Steventon End
Helions Bumpstead
Steeple Bumpstead
New England
Baythorn End
Ovington
Belchamp St. Paul
Little Chesterford
Church End
Ashdon
Camps End
Water End
Olmstead Green
Birdbrook
Ridgewell
Ashen
Tilbury Green
Little Walden
Heydon
Crawley End
Elmdon
Chrishall
Great Chishill
Strethall
Littlebury
Audley End
Turf Maze
Sewards End
Stocking Green
Hempstead
Tilbury Juxta Clare
Little Yeldham
Great Yeldham
North End
Ridgewell Airfield
Stambourne
Toppesfield
Barley
Littlebury Green
Pond Street
Little Chishill
Duddenhoe End
Bridge Green
Saffron Walden
Radwinter
Wimbish
Cornish Hall End
Robinhood End
Pool Street
Colne Valley Railway
Wendens Ambo
Langley
Upper Green
Nuthampstead
Lower Green
Arkesden
Newport
Tye Green
Howlett End
Wimbish Green
Great Sampford
Gainsford End
Delvin End
Howe Street
Highstreet Green
Castle Hedingham
Sible Hedingham
Elder Street
Debden
Anstey
Meesden
Stickling Green
Wicken Bonhunt
Priors Hall Barn
Widdington
Mole Hall
Debden Green
Boyton End
Little Sampford
Finchingfield
Wethersfield
Morris Green
Southey Green
School Green
Brent Pelham
Starling's Green
Hill Green
Clavering
Rickling
Quendon
Hamperden End
Cutlers Green
Thaxted
Little Bardfield
Bardfield End Green
Great Bardfield
Waltham's Cross
Blackmore End
Boydell's Dairy Farm
Gosfield
Great Hormead
Hare Street
Little Hormead
Berden
Stocking Pelham
Furneux Pelham
East End
Rickling Green
Woodend Green
Henham
Ugley
Ugley Green
Monk Street
Holder's Green
Oxen End
Shalford
Church End
Beazley End
Dassels
Hay Street
Mallows Green
Manuden
Pledgdon Green
Elsenham
Broxted
Duton Hill
Lindsell
Shalford Green
Bardfield Saling
Jasper's Green
Bocking Churchstreet
High Garrett
A131
Braughing
Patmore Heath
Farnham Green
Stansted Mountfitchet
Albury
Clapgate
Farnham
Mountfitchet Castle
Molehill Green
Great Easton
Little Easton
Bran End
Duck End
Great Saling
Panfield
Upwick Green
Tye Green
LONDON STANSTED
Andrewsfield
Stebbing
Stebbing Green
Blake End
Bocking
Braintree
Puckeridge
Standon
A120
Little Hadham
BISHOP'S STORTFORD
Birchanger
Burton End
Bamber's Green
Great Dunmow
Churchend
Rayne
Wellpond Green
Hadham Ford
Latchford
Bromley
Bury Green
Takeley
Start Hill
Takeley Street
BIRCHANGER GREEN
Smith's Green
Little Canfield
Little Dunmow
Bannister Green
Bartholomew Green
Great Notley
Black Notley
Cressing
Barwick
Much Hadham
Thorley Street
Thorley
Rhodes
Bedlar's Green
Great Hallingbury
Puttock's End
Bacon End
Barnston
Felsted
Cock Green
Willows Green
Young's End
Hadham Cross
Perry Green
Green Tye
Little Hallingbury
Spellbrook
Hatfield Broad Oak
Taverners Green
Great Canfield
High Roding
Bishop's Green
Onslow Green
North End
Hartford End
Littley Green
Great Leighs
Rank's Green
White Notley
Faulkbourne
Fairstead
Babb's Green
Allen's Green
Wright's Green
Hatfield Heath
THE RODINGS
Aythorpe Roding
Roundbush Green
High Easter
Stagden Cross
Pleshey
Ford End
Little Leighs
Chatham Green
Fuller Street
Terling
Widford
Wareside
Sawbridgeworth
Hunsdon
High Wych
Hunsdonbury
Sheering
White Roding
Leaden Roding
Howe Street
Great Waltham
Hack's Green
Witham
Stanstead Abbotts
Eastwick
Pye Corner
A414
Nether Street
Margaret Roding
Good Easter
Fanner's Green
Broad's Green
Little Waltham
A130
A12
Hatfield Peverel
HARLOW
Roydon
Matching
Matching Tye
Matching Green
Abbess Roding
Beauchamp Roding
Marshbury
Chalk End
Chignall Smealy
Broomfield
Parsonage Green
Boreham
Hare Street
Church Langley
Potter Street
Great Parndon
Foster Street
Magdalen Laver
High Laver
Little Laver
Birds Green
Shellow Bowells
Boyton Cross
Chignall St. James
Roxwell
Ulting
Roydon Hamlet
Broadley Common
Hastingwood
Fyfield
Willingale
Great Oxney Green
Little Baddow
Nazeing
Lower Nazeing
Moreton
Tyler's Green
Bovinger
Bobbingworth
Norton Mandeville
Cooksmill Green
Writtle
Widford
CHELMSFORD
Danbury
Epping Green
Bumble's Green
Holyfield Hall Farm
Thornwood Common
Epping Upland
North Weald Bassett
High Ongar
Norton Heath
Edney Common
Hylands House
Great Baddow
Sandon
Gay Bowers
Butt's Green
Greensted Green
Loves Green
Galleywood
Howe Green
Holyfield
Hayes Hill Farm
WALTHAM ABBEY
EPPING
Coopersale Common
Coopersale Street
Toot Hill
Saxon Wooden Church
Chipping Ongar
Nine Ashes
Elkins Green
Blackmore
Beggar Hill
Mill Green
Margaretting
Margaretting Tye
East Hanningfield
Bicknacre
Upshire
Fiddlers Hamlet
Stanford Rivers
Little End
Stondon Massey
Fryerning
Ingatestone
Ingatestone Hall
Stock
West Hanningfield
Copthall Green
Theydon Bois
Stapleford Tawney
Nuclear Bunker
Wyatt's Green
Doddinghurst
Kelvedon Hatch
Heybridge
Mountnessing
Hanningfield Reservoir
South Hanningfield
RHS Hyde Hall
Rettendon
Coalhill
Tropical Wings
High Beech
Epping Forest
Debden Green
Hobbs Cross
Passingford Bridge
Navestock
Navestock Side
Fox Hatch
Crow Green
Pilgrims Hatch
Ramsden Heath
Abridge
Stapleford
LOUGHTON
M25
A113
Queen's Lodge
54

54
Wickhambrook
Pound Green
Farley Green
Denston
Hawkedon
Somerton
Lawshall
Thorpe Green
Thorpe Morieux
Brettenham
Battisford
Market
Stradishall
Stansfield
Hartest
Shimpling Street
Smithwood Green
Rooksey Green
Cross Green
Charles Tye
Ringshall
Barking Tye
Barking
Darmsden
Assington Green
Thurston End
Boxted
Shimpling
Alpheton
Hitcham
Wattisham
Ringshall Stocks
Baylham
Willisham Tye
Great Blakenham
A
B
C
D
65
66
Hundon
Chimney Street
Brockley Green
Kedington
Poslingford
Glemsford
Stanstead
Bridge Street
Kentwell
Lavenham
Little Hall
Guildhall NT
Brent Eleigh
Kettlebaston
Monks Eleigh
Bildeston
Nedging Tye
Naughton
Nedging
Greenstreet Green
Offton
Somersham
Blakenham Woodland
Little Blakenham
Chilton Street
Cavendish
Long Melford
Melford Hall
Chelsworth
Semer
Ash Street
Whatfield
Elmsett
Flowton
Bramford
Milden
Swingleton Green
Lindsey
Lindsey Tye
Aldham
Sproughton
Ancient House
Clare
Castle
Priory
Liston
Pentlow
Foxearth
Acton
Little Waldingfield
Round Maple
Rose Green
Kersey
Chapel
Rowland Taylor Monument
Burstall
Hintlesham
Calford Green
Boyton End
Stoke by Clare
Wixoe
Baythorn End
Ovington
Ashen
Belchamp St. Paul
Belchamp Otten
Borley Green
Borley
Newman's Green
Great Waldingfield
Mill Green
Wicker Street Green
Hadleigh Heath
Guildhall
Hadleigh
Washbrook
Chattisham
Copdock
Ridgewell
Tilbury Green
Belchamp Walter
Puttock End
Sudbury
Gainsborough's House
Ballingdon
Bulmer
Great Cornard
Newton
Edwardstone
Groton
Boxford
Calais Street
Lower Layham
Upper Layham
Little Yeldham
Tilbury Juxta Clare
Ridgewell Airfield
Middleton
Little Cornard
Stone Street
Whitestreet Green
Polstead Heath
Little Wenham
Capel St. Mary
Stambourne
Toppesfield
Great Yeldham
North End
Gestingthorpe
Bulmer Tye
Great Henny
Henny Street
Workhouse Green
Assington
Leavenheath
Polstead
Shelley
Raydon
Lower Raydon
Great Wenham
Bentley
Pool Street
Colne Valley Railway
Hedingham
Wickham St. Paul
Twinstead Green
Twinstead
Dorking Tye
Withermarsh Green
Holton St. Mary
Gainsford End
Delvin End
Castle Hedingham
Great Maplestead
Long Gardens
Lamarsh
Alphamstone
Honey Tye
Stoke-by-Nayland
Higham
East Bergholt Place
East End
Highstreet Green
Sible Hedingham
Alderford Mill
Little Maplestead
Cross End
Bures
Nayland
Thorington Street
Stratford St. Mary
East Bergholt
Bridge Cottage NT
Morris Green
Wethersfield
Pebmarsh
Boxted
Boxted Cross
Dedham
Munnings
Cattawade
Manningtree
Southey Green
Mount Bures
Little Horkesley
School Green
Blackmore End
Whiteash Green
Countess Cross
Carter's Vineyards
Langham
Lamb Corner
Dedham Heath
Lawford
Mistley
Boydell's Dairy Farm
Buntings Green
Colne Engaine
Wormingford
Great Horkesley
Gnome Magic
Shalford
Church End
Beazley End
Gosfield
Halstead
White Colne
Wakes Colne
East Anglian Railway
Hemp's Green
Horkesley Heath
Ardleigh Resr
Ardleigh
Little Bromley
Earls Colne
Chappel
Rose Green
Fordham
West Bergholt
Mile End
Fox Street
Burnt Heath
Horsley Cross
Jasper's Green
Bocking Churchstreet
High Garrett
Greenstead Green
Burton's Green
Swan Street
Ford Street
Fordham Heath
Crockleford Heath
Great Bromley
Panfield
Tumbler's Green
Marks Hall
Aldham
Great Tey
Eight Ash Green
COLCHESTER
Elmstead
Stisted
Pattiswick
East Gores
Marks Tey
Stanway
Lexden Earthworks
Beacon End
Beth Chatto
Hare Green
Blake End
Rayne
Bocking
BRAINTREE
Coggeshall
Copford
Shrub End
Elmstead Market
Frating Green
Bradwell
Stockstreet
Grange Barn
Paycocke's NT
Surrex
Skye Green
Little Tey
Copford Green
Easthorpe
Bourne Mill NT
Rowhedge
Wivenhoe
Elmstead Heath
Alresford
Bartholomew Green
Great Notley
Tye Green
Cressing
Perry Green
Coggeshall Hamlet
Feering
Feeringbury Manor
Colchester Zoo
Heckfordbridge
Blackheath
Felsted Brewery
Willows Green
Row Green
Young's End
Black Notley
Cressing Temple
Hardy's Green
Birch
Layer-de-la-Haye
Fingringhoe
Thorrington
Tide Mill
Silver End
Kelvedon
Messing
Birch Green
Abberton
South Green
Langenhoe
Great Leighs
Rank's Green
White Notley
Local History
Inworth
Smyth's Green
Layer Marney
Layer Breton
Abberton Resr
Little Leighs
Faulkbourne
Fairstead
Rivenhall
Layer Marney Tower
Brightlingsea
Fuller Street
Terling
Chipping Hill
Rivenhall End
Tiptree
Peldon
Hurst Green
Flack's Green
Dorothy L Sayers Centre
Tiptree Heath
Great Braxted
Tolleshunt Knights
Great Wigborough
Blue Row
East Mersea
Aviation
Point Clear
WITHAM
Oxley Green
Salcott
MERSEA ISLAND
Little Waltham
Wickham Bishops
Great Totham North
Great Totham South
Little Totham
Tolleshunt D'Arcy
West Mersea
Colne Point
Hatfield Peverel
Tolleshunt Major
Virley Channel
Tollesbury
Nounsley
Boreham
Ulting
Langford
Broad Street Green
Agricultural & Domestic
Goldhanger
Sales Point
St. Peter's Chapel
Heybridge
Little Baddow
Woodham Walter
Maeldune Cen
Heybridge Basin
Bradwell Waterside
Osea Island
RIVER BLACKWATER
CHELMSFORD
MALDON
Northey Island
Bradwell-on-Sea
Great Baddow
Sandon
Danbury
Gay Bowers
Woodham Mortimer
Hazeleigh
Ramsey Island
St. Lawrence
Galleyend
Galleywood
Butt's Green
Howe Green
Cock Clarks
Bicknacre
New Hall Vineyards
Rudley Green
Purleigh
Mundon
Steeple
Rural Discovery
Tillingham
Dengie
East Hanningfield
Howegreen
Cold Norton
Maylandsea
Mayland
Asheldham
Latchingdon
West Hanningfield
Woodham Ferrers
Stow Maries
Southminster
Althorne
Mangapps Railway
RHS Hyde Hall
Hanningfield Reservoir
Coalhill
Rettendon
South Hanningfield
Tropical Wings
South Woodham Ferrers
North Fambridge
Stoneyhills
Ostend
Burnham-
Holliwell Point
Foulness
A143
A1092
A1017
B1063
B1064
B1065
B1066
A134
A1141
B1115
B1078
B1113
B1071
B7115
A1141
A1071
A131
B1508
A1124
B1068
B1087
B1070
A12
A137
B1029
B1035
B1352
A120
B1053
B1024
A1232
B1028
B1027
B1025
B1026
B1408
B1022
B1018
B1019
B1023
B1389
A130
B1137
B1008
A414
A1060
A1114
B1010
B1012
B1418
B1021
B1256
B1018
B1029
A133

IPSWICH
WOODBRIDGE
FELIXSTOWE
Harwich
CLACTON-ON-SEA
Walton-on-the-Naze
Frinton-on-Sea
Orford Ness
Hollesley Bay
Harwich to:
Esbjerg 18hrs.
Hook of Holland 6hrs. 15mins.
Horsey Island
Hamford Water
The Naze
NORTH SEA
Kesgrave
Rushmere St. Andrew
Martlesham
Melton
Bromeswell
Ufford
Rendlesham
Sudbourne
Chillesford
Butley
Orford
Sutton
Hollesley
Shottisham
Alderton
Bawdsey
Trimley St. Martin
Trimley St. Mary
Shotley Gate
Parkeston
Little Oakley
Great Oakley
Wix
Kirby-le-Soken
Thorpe-le-Soken
Weeley
Little Clacton
Great Holland
Holland-on-Sea
Jaywick

CARDIGAN BAY

(BAE CEREDIGION)

Aberaeron

New Quay
(Ceinewydd)
Marine Wildlife Centre
Ffos-y-ffin
Gilfachreda
Llwyncelyn
Maen-y-groes
Llanarth
Oakford
(Derwen Gam)
Cross Inn
New Quay Honey Farm
Geneva
Cwmtudu
Nanternis
Caerwedros
Pen-cae
Llwyndafydd
Mydroilyn
Ynys-Lochtyn
Blaen Celyn
Synod Inn
(Post-Mawr)
A487
Pontgarreg
Plwmp
Llangranog
Morfa
Penbryn
Pentregat
Brynhoffnant
Talgarreg
Sarnau
Cardigan Island
Parcllyn
Aberporth
Tresaith
Brithdir
Rhydlewis
C
Cardigan Island Coastal Farm Park
Rainforest Centre
Felinwynt
Internal Fire
Cemaes Head
Glanrhyd
Gwbert
Blaenannerch
A
Allt-y-goed
Y Ferwig
A4548
44
Blaenporth
15
B
Fan-y-groes
Cardigan Wool len Mill
C
Bwlch-y-fadfa
A459
Pwllygranant
Cippyn
A487
Penparc
Tremain
Capel Cynon
Ffostrasol
Cardigan
(Aberteifi)
Pantgwyn
Noyadd Trefawr
Beulah
Felin Wnda
Bettws Ifan
Hawen
Pont-sian

Tonfanau
Bryncrug
Dolgoch
Dolgoch Falls
Railway
2076
Torrenhendre
Pantperthog
Centre for Alternative Technology
Llanwrin
B4404
Road
A470
A487
Aber Dysynni
Broad Water
Pandy
Rhyd-yr-onen
70
Machynlleth
Penegoes
A489
Abercegir
Commins Coch
Darowen
Tafolwern
57
Trum Gelli
Pennal
A493
Tywyn
E
F
69
G
H
Tal-y-Wern
Llan
Bont Dolgad
Narrow Gauge Railway
Cwrt
Forge
Afon Dulas
Corlan-fraith
Derwenlas
Melinbyrhedyn
Moelfre 1537
B4518
River Dovey (Afon Dyfi)
Glandyfi
Glaspwll
Aberhosan
Pennant
Penhelig
Ynys-hir
Snowdonia National Park
Aberdovey (Aberdyfi)
A487
Eglwys Fach
Furnace
Dyfi Furnace
Pencarreggopa 1467
POWYS
1
Dylife
Ynyslas
Llyn Conach
Glaslyn
Ynyslas
B4353
Tre'r-ddol
Llancynfelyn
Tre Taliesin
Llyn Dwfn
Moel y-Llyn 1708
Llyn Plas-y-mynydd
Bugeilyn
Llwynygog
Stayl (Penff
Station
Borth
Animalarium
Tal-y-bont
Upper Borth
Dol-y-Bont
Afon Leri
Source of R. Severn
Pen Pumlumon Arwystli 2431
Hafren Forest
Llyn Clywedog (Reservoir)
Drosgol 1806
Nant-y-moch Reservoir 2467
Source of R. Wye (Afon Gwy)
PLYNLIMON (PUMLUMON FAWR)
Esgair y Maesnant
R. Severn
Llandre
Rhyd-meirionydd
Bontgoch
Llyn Craigypistyll
Drum Peithnant
B4572
Pen-y-garn
Bow Street
Llyn Syfydrin
2
Afon Rheidol
Y Foel
Afon Bidno
Garth
Salem
Penrhyn-coch
Cwmsymlog
Llangorwen
Camera Obscura Cliff Railway
A4159
Cefn Llwyd
Pen-bont Rhydybeddau
Cwmerfyn
Dinas Resr.
A44
12
Wye Valley
R. Wye (Afon Gwy)
ABERYSTWYTH
Comins Coch
Capel Dewi
Bwlch Nant yr Arian Forest
Llywernog Silver-Lead Mine
Waun Fawr
A44
Blaen-geuffordd
Dollwen
Goginan
Ponterwyd
Dyffryn Castell
The Bar
Llanbadarn Fawr
Penparcau
Southgate
Afon Rheidol
13
Cwmbrwyno
Llywernog
B4343
1849
80
Llang
Capel Bangor
Moriah
A4120
Esgair Ychion
Rhydyfelin
Capel Seion
Vale of Rheidol
Aberffrwd
Rheidol Power Station
Falls
Ystumtuen
Ysbyty Cynfyn
Banc Nant Rhys
Llanfarian
Gors
12
Falls
58
Llaniwared
Chancery
New Cross
Llanfihangel-y-Creuddyn
Devil's Bridge (Pontarfynach)
Three Bridges
Bryn Garw
A485
Blaenplwyf
Trisant
B4574
Jubilee Arch
Yr Allt
Llanilar
Cnwch Coch
B4343
3
Elan
B4340
9
A487
B4576
Rhos-y-garth
B4575
New Row
B4574
Cwmystwyth
Crosswood (Trawsgoed)
Llanafan
Afon Ystwyth
Pont-rhyd-y-groes
Afon Elan
Llanddeiniol
Wenallt
Geifas 1873
Ysbyty Ystwyth
Llyn Fyrddon-Fawr
Nant Hirin
Carreg Ti-pw
Llangwyryfon
Lledrod
Mynydd Bach 1092
Marchnant
Trawsallt
Llyn Fyrddon-Fach 1944
Llyn Cerrigllwydion Isaf
70
Clawdd-du-bach
Llanrhystud
Llyn Du
Llyn Cerrigllwydion Uchaf
18
Tynygraig
15
Trefenter
Rhyd-Rosser
1183
Ystradmeurig
Ffair Rhos
Llyn Teifi
Llyn Hir
Trumau
Llansantffraed
Bronnant
B4340
Llan-non
B4337
Rhydfudr
MYNYDD BACH
Pontrhydfendigaid
Llyn Egnant
Llyn y Gorlan
Swyddffynnon
1738
B4343
Dibyn Du
Bontnewydd
Strata Florida
Abbey
4
Rhos
Nebo
Haminiog
A487
Cors-goch Glan Teifi
Afon Teifi
Esgair Garthen
Claerwen Reservoir
Cross Inn
B4577
17
B4576
Bethania
Blaenpennal
Pen-y-bwlch
Llyn Gynon
Aberarth
Pennant
A485
Penuwch
B4577
Ty'n-yr-eithin
Monachty
Afon Claerwen
Esgair Llyn-du
11
Afon Aeron
Bryn Garw 1827
Llanaeron
Llanerchaeron NT
Cilcennin
Llangeitho
B4578
Tregaron
60
B4576
B4342
Y Drum 1668
Esgair Ambor
Drum yr Eira
Newbridge
Red Kite Centre & Museum
2104
Drygarn Fawr
Ciliau Aeron
Afon Aeron
Bwlch-Llan
Capel Betws Lleucu
Bryn Crwn 1732
B4339
Trefilan
Llundain-fach
Gartheli
Llwyn-y-groes
1592
Esgair Fraith
Llyn Berwyn
Esgair Cerrig
1588
Gamallt
Ystrad Aeron
Talsarn
B4342
Abermeurig
Dihewyd
Felinfach
B4337
Olmarch
B4343
Llanddewi Brefi
Camddwr
5
Temple Bar
Ffynnon-oer
Esgair Llethr 1543
Irfon
1641
Cefn-Coch
Llangybi
A485
Abergwesyn
Bettws Bledrws
Llanfair Clydogau
Bryn Brawd 1589
Pen Rhiw-clochdy
Cefn Fannog 1476
Cribyn
Silian
A482
1497
Pen y Gurnos
Llyn Brianne
Tywi Forest
250
Gorsgoch
Afon Teifi
45
F
G
46
H
Maesycrugiau
Lampeter (Llanbedr Pont Steffan)
Cellan
Pentrefelin
B4343
Craig Twrch
Mynydd Trawsnant 1695
Cambrian Woollen Mill
Llanwrtyd
Cwrtnewydd
B4337
8
60
70
80
Llanwnnen
A475
B4338
Pentre-bach
A485
Cwmann
CARMARTHENSHIRE
Ystradffin
Llanwrtyd Wells (Llanwrtud)
CEREDIGION
CAMBRIAN MOUNTAINS

58
A
B
C
D
1
2
3
4
5
CAMBRIAN MOUNTAINS
P O W Y S
RADNOR FORES
A470
A44
A483
A489
A488
A481
A4081
B4518
B4568
B4569
B4355
B4356
B4358
B4368
B4386
B4389
B4390
B4567
B4520
70
57
46
Llanbrynmair
Pandy
Commins Coch
Abercegir
Dar
Tafolwern
Dol-fâch
Llan
Bont Dolgadfan
Talerddig
Melinbyrhedyn
Moelfre 1537
Pennant
Aberhosan
Brynamiwg 1602
Trannon
Carno
Esgair Rhiciau
Ffridd
Cefn Coch
Llanllugan
Llanwyddelan
Glan-yr-afon
Adfa
Mynydd Clogau
Gwgla
Llyn Mawr
Llyn y Tarw
Bwlch y Garreg
Bwlch-y-ffridd
Tregynon
Manafon
New Mills
(Felin Newydd)
Pant-y-ffridd
Llwynderw
Berriew
(Aberriw)
Garthmyl
Brooks
Pentre Llifior
Fron
Hendomen
Bettws Cedewain
Highgate
Dolforwyn
Llandyssil
Abermule
(Aber-miwl)
Cefn-y-coed
Aberbechan
Llanmerwig
Hodley
Llanllwchaiarn
Aberhafesp
Milford
Newtown
(Y Drenewydd)
Maesyrhandir
Garth Owen
Kerry
(Ceri)
Glanmule
Sarn
Bryniiywarch
Pentre
Mochdre
Dolfor
Kerry Hill
Cross Dyke
1732
Cilfaesty Hill
Anchor
Black Mountain
1468
R. Clun
Crug-y-byddar
Felindre
Beguildy
Quabbs
Dutlas
Black Mountain 1584
Beacon Hill 1796
Pool Hill 1690
1736
Gors Lydan
Dylife
Glaslyn
Bugeilyn
Staylittle
(Penffordd-Lâs)
Llwynygog
Gors-goch
Clatter
Llanwnog
Pontdolgoch
Caersws
Waen
Llawryglyn
Gleiniant
Trefeglwys
Afon Trannon
Little London
Llandinam
Pentre
Source of R. Severn
Pen Pumlumon Arwystli 2431
Hafren Forest
Source of R. Wye (Afon Gwy)
Esgairy Maesnant
Biga
Llyn Clywedog (Reservoir)
Bryn y Fan 1583
Llyn Ebyr
Cerist
Van
Oakley Park
Bryntail Lead Mine
R. Severn
Glan-y-nant
Afon Clywedog
Y Foel
Afon Biga
Llanidloes
Newchapel
Glynbrochan
Cwmbelan
Afon Dulas
Oldchapel Hill
Tylwch
Llandinam Wind Farm
Dethenydd
Llyn-dwr Hill
1921
Rhydyhywel
A44
Wye Valley
R. Wye (Afon Gwy)
1849
Banc Nant Rhys
Esgair Ychion
Llangurig
Foel Gurig
Llaniwared
Llaithddu
David's Well
Red Lion Hill
Llanbadarn Fynydd
R. Ithon
Dolfach
Sychnant
Nantgwyn
1618
Ddyle
Yr Allt
Bryn Titli
Dwrysgol
Pant-y-dwr
Afon Marteg
Bwlch-y-sarnau
Llananno
Llanbister
Llancoch
Crug
Llangunllo
Elan
Valley
Dolhelfa
St. Harmon
Cefn-crin
Afon Elan
Geifas 1873
Nant Hirin
Llyn Cerrigllwydion Isaf
Llyn Cerrigllwydion Uchaf
Clawdd-du-bach
Craig Goch Reservoir
(Cwm Elan)
Gamallt
Moel Hywel
Abbey-cwm-hir
Abbey
Camlo Hill 1670
Clywedog Brook
Maelienydd
Heartsease
Llanddewi Ystradenni
Penygarreg Resr.
Trumau
Rhayader
(Rhaeadr Gwy)
Llansantffraed Cwmdeuddwr
Gaufron
Gigrin Farm
Welsh Royal Crystal
Garreg-ddu Resr.
Lower Llanfadog
Elan Village
Elan Valley
Gwastedyn Hill 1566
Nantmel
Coedglasson
Gwystre
Fron
Little Hill
Fishpools
Bleddfa
Dolau
Llanfihangel Rhydithon
Esgair Garthen
Claerwen Reservoir
Nant Glas
Llanwrthwl
Crossgates
Penybont
Argoed Mill
Castell Collen Roman Fort
Llanyre
Llandrindod Wells
(Llandrindod)
Cefnllys Castle
Ridgebourne
Llandegley
2166
AREA
DANGER
Esgairnantau
Bache Hill
New Radnor
DANGER AREA
Water Break-its-Neck Waterfall
Yardro
Afon Claerwen
Caban Coch Reservoir
Gamriw
Drum-ddu 1761
Bryn Garw 1827
Drum yr Eira
2104
Drygarn Fawr
Gorllwyn 2010
Newbridge on Wye
Disserth
Howey
Crossway
Gilwern Hill 1440
Llandegley Rhos
Llanfihangel-Nant-Melan
Bryn-y-maen
Bryn Crwn 1732
1572
Bryn
Llanafan-fawr
Irfon
1641
Cefn-Coch
Pentre-llwyn-llwyd
R. Wye (Afon Gwy)
Cwmbach Llechrhyd
Carneddau
Frank's Bridge
Gwaunceste Hill 1777
Llansantffraed-in-Elwel
Hundred House
Glascwm
Abergwesyn
Troedrhiwdalar
Chwefru
Builth Road
Royal Welsh Showground
Llewelyn the Last Monument
Cilmery
(Cilmeri)
Llanelwedd
Cregrina
R. Edw
1718
Glascwm Hill
Cefn Fannog 1476
Tywi Forest
Beulah
Dulas
Llanafan-fechan
Builth Wells
(Llanfair-ym-Muallt)
Oaklands
Llanfaredd
Red Hill 1671
Rhulen
Bryngwyn
Arrow
Newchurch
Caerau Roman Fort
Garth
Cambrian Woollen Mill
Llanwrtyd
DANGER AREA
Maesmynis
Llanddewi'r Cwm
Alltmawr
Aberedw
Church
Aberedw Rocks
Llandeilo Hill
Llanbadarn-y-garreg
Llanbedr Hill
Rhosgoch
Clyro Hill 1276
Llanbedr
Mynydd Trawsnant 1695
Llanwrtyd Wells
(Llanwrtud)
Llangammarch Wells
DANGER AREA

59
Binweston
Brockton
B4499
Longden Common
Wrentnall
Great Ryton
Pitchford
Cound
Harnage
Cressage
Sheinton
Buildwas
Abbey
Trelystan
Leigh
Ploxgreen
Habberley
Dorrington
Little Ryton
Acton Burnell
Golding
Acton Pigott
Harley
Homer
Farley
Wyke
Fron
Kingswood
Marton
B4386
Snailbeach
Pulverbatch
Church Pulverbatch
Castle
A49
Netley
Meadowtown
Bentlawnt
Hope
Stockton
Rorrington
Stiperstones
71
Longnor
Frodesley
Ruckley
Kenley
A458
Much Wenlock
The Bank
Wotherton
Langley Chapel
Priory
E
F
G
H
Offa's Dyke
Mitchell's Fold Stone Circle
Picklescott
Woolstaston
Leebotwood
Church Preen
Stretton Westwood
Chirbury
Shelve
Pennerley
Stiperstones
Broome
Hughley
The Bog
Chatwall
Presthope
Dudston
Priest Weston
The Marsh
Kinnerton
Ratlinghope
Comley
Plaish
Callaughton
Montgomery
(Trefaldwyn)
Corndon Hill
Enchmarsh
Bourton
Muckley
Alport
All Stretton
Caer Caradoc
Cardington
Gretton
Eastthope
Acton Round
Church Stoke
Hyssington
Medlicott
Long Mynd
Ashbrook
Longville in the Dale
Astonlane
Hurdley
Llanerch
Linley Hill
Norbury
Church Stretton
Worldsend
Stoneacton
East Wall
Brockton
Weston
Monkhopton
B4368
Linley
Wentnor
Hazler
Hope Bowdler
Wall under Heywood
Wilderhope Manor
Shipton
Upper Netchwood
Bachelore
Pentre
B4385
Owlbury
Snead
Little Stretton
Ragdon
Rushbury
Lower Netchwood
Cwm
More
Whitcot
Long Mynd
Minton
Chelmick
Soudley
Ticklerton
Roman Bank
Stanton Long
Derrington
Hopton
Lydham
Asterton
Hardwick
Hatton
Eaton
Broadstone
Holdgate Castle
Middleton Priors
Historic Working Farm
Bishop's Castle
Railway
B4383
Lea
Eaton
Marshbrook
Acton Scott
Upper Millichope
Holdgate
Ashfield
Choulton
Hamperley
Henley
Harton
Middlehope
Hungerford
Ditton Priors
Plowden
Whittingslow
B4370
Munslow
Mainstone
Colebatch
Eyton
Bushmoor
Felhampton
Alcaston
Tugford
Abdon
Hillside
Neenton
Churchtown
Reilth
Lydbury North
Horderley
Woolston
Wistanstow
Upper Affcot
Aston Munslow
Broncroft
Upper Heath
Cleobury North
Forest
Cefn Einion
A488
Edgton
Strefford
Westhope
Diddlebury
Heath Chapel
Nordy Bank
Cockshutford
Wrickton
Bryn
Brockton
Walcot Hall Arboretum
Cheney Longville
Corfton
Bouldon
Clee St. Margaret
Burwarton
Acton
Round Oak
Peaton
Mardu
Lower Down
S H R O P S H I R E
Upper Dinchope
Halford
Aston Botterell
Whitcott Keysett
Bury Ditches
Sibdon Carwood
Brown Clee Hill
Newcastle
Guilden Down
Hopesay
Long Meadowend
Craven Arms
Shropshire Hills Discovery Centre
Great Sutton
Seifton
Blackford
Loughton
Bicton
Kempton
Little Brampton
B4368
Stokesay
Norton Camp
Culmington
Stoke St. Milborough
Wheathill
Clunton
Aston on Clun
Broome
Norton
Upper Hayton
Hopton Cangeford
Weston Hill
Cleedownton
Clun
R. Clun
Purslow
Clunbury
Rowton
Aldon
Vernolds Common
Lower Hayton
Hayton's Bent
Bromdon
Farlow
Silvington
Brandhill
Wernlas Collection
Onibury
B4365
B4364
Cleestanton
Black Hill
Twitchen
Hopton Castle
Clungunford
Stanton Lacy
Titterstone Clee Hill
Cleeton St. Mary
Crumpsbrook
Hobarris
Abcott
Hoptonheath
Shelderton
Wootton
Ludlow
Middleton
Bitterley
Angelbank
Foxwood
60
Llanfair Waterdine
Pentre Hodre
Hopton Titterhill
Marlow
Bromfield
Henley
Doddington
Purlogue
New Invention
Chapel Lawn
Bedstone
Todding
A4113
Priors Halton
Rockgreen
Snitton
Knowbury
Cleehill
Hints
Lloyney
Heyop
Knucklas Castle
Skyborry Green
Caer Caradoc
Coxall
Kinton
Ludlow
Ludford
Lower Ledwyche
Hope Bagot
Knowle
Coreley
Knucklas
Knighton
(Tref-Y-Clawdd)
Stowe
Weston
Bucknell
B4367
Leintwardine
Buckton
Downton on the Rock
Bringewood Chase
Caynham
Whitton
Garth
Milebrook
A4113
Brampton Bryan
Walford
Burrington
Pipe Aston
Overton
Nash
Milson
Bailey Hill
A488
Spaceguard Centre
WALES
ENGLAND
Grange
Adforton
Elton
Ashford Carbonel
Greete
Whatmore
Knighton Common
Rhos-y-meirch
B4355
Llan-wen Hill
Letton
Birtley
Richard's Castle
Ashford Bowdler
Dean Park
Boraston
Monaughty
Pilleth
Wigmore
A4110
Leinthall Starkes
Middleton
Richards Castle
Little Hereford
Burford
Woofferton
Burford House
Tenbury Wells
Kyrewood
Ongar Street
Leinthall Earls
Orleton Common
B4362
Wyson
Brimfield
A456
Whitton
Offa's Dyke
Norton
Lingen
Croft Ambrey Hillfort
Comberton
Orleton
Stony Cross
Berrington
Berrington Green
Oldwood Common
Upper Rochford
Dolley Green
Lower Lye
Upper Lye
Yatton
Ashley Moor
Cock Gate
Bircher
A49
Sutton
Discoed
Stapleton
Priory
Aymestrey
Croft NT
Middleton on the Hill
St. Michaels
Hanley Child
Beggar's Bush
Judge's Lodging
Kinsham
Byton
Water Mill
Mortimer's Cross
Lucton
Yarpole
Moreton
Ashton
Miles Hope
Kyre Park
Presteigne
(Llanandras)
B4362
Combe
Uphampton
Mortimer's Cross 1461
Bicton
Eye
Berrington NT Hall
The Hundred
Laysters Pole
Romers Common
Thorn
Kinnerton
Evenjobb
Rodd
Easthampton
Luston
A4112
Combe Moor
Lugg Green
Aston
Kyre Green
Bank Street
Four Stones
Nash
Staunton Park
Shobdon
Ledicot
Kingsland
Eyton
Kimbolton
Woonton
Pie Corner
Womaston
Knill
Stansbatch
B4360
The Broad
Stockton
Stockton Cross
Whyle
Grafton
Burcher
Titley
Staunton on Arrow
Shobdon
Shirl Heath
Cobnash
R. Lugg
Hatfield
Old Radnor
Walton
Offa's Dyke
The Forge
Old Chapel
Lawton
Cholstrey
Pudleston
Thornbury
Burlingjobb
Flintsham
Bradnor Hill
Howe Ditch
Eardisland
B4529
Barons Cross
Leominster
Dolyhir
Pembridge
Marston
A44
Monkland
Stretford
Docklow
Grendon Green
Weythel
A44
Nextend
New Street
Upper Hardwick
Ivington Green
Ivington
Steen's Bridge
Buckland
Bredenbury
Hergest Croft
Kington
Westonbury Mill Water
Lower Hardwick
Stoke Prior
Humber
Hergest Ridge
Upper Hergest
Lower Hergest
Penrhos
Weston
Barewood
Brierley
Wharton
Marston Stannett
Gladestry
Lyonshall
Holme Marsh
Moorcot
Haven
Sollers Dilwyn
Aulden
Risbury
Huntington Castle
Kingswood
Small Breeds Farm Park & Owl Centre
Broxwood
Dilwyn
H E R E F O R D S H I R E
Newton
Hegdon Hill
Huntington
Chickward
Hopley's Green
Birley
Upper Hill
Broadfield Court
Pencombe
Almeley Wooton
A4112
Knapton Green
Hope under Dinmore
Bowley
Almeley
Woonton
Weobley
Weobley Marsh
Bush Bank
Hampton Court
Lugg
A417
Little Cowarne
Lower Welson
Logaston
Upcott
Queenswood Arboretum
Westhope
Bodenham
Shortwood Family Farm
Newchurch
Ledgemoor
Michaelchurch-on-Arrow
Sarnesfield
King's Pyon
Pool Head
Maund Bryan
Ullingswick
Stoke Cross
Woods Eaves
Hurstway Common
47
Ennersley
Eardisley
Highway
A49
Monmarsh
The Vauld
48
Moreton Jeffries
Stoke Lacy
Brilley
Ennersley Castle
Hurstley
Eccles Green
Canon Pyon
Venn's Green
Felton
Upper Town
A438
Millhalf
Ailey
Wormsley
Wellington
Urdimarsh
Whitney
Willersley
Waterloo
Norton Canon
Yarsop
Marden
Walker's Green
Preston Wynne
Preston Marsh
Burley Gate
Much Cowarne
Five Bridges
Spence
TOLL
Winforton
A438
Moorhampton
Tillington Common
Auberrow
Sutton Walls Hillfort
Ocle Pychard
Clifford
B4350
Letton
Staunton
Yazor
Mansell
Moreton
Lower

60
WOLVERHAMPTON
Bridgnorth
KIDDERMINSTER
WORCESTER
STOURBRIDGE
HALESOWEN
Bewdley
Stourport-on-Severn
DROITWICH SPA
BROMSGROVE
Tenbury Wells
Bromyard
Much Wenlock
Ironbridge
SHROPSHIRE
WORCESTERSHIRE
WYRE FOREST
GREAT MALVERN
Malvern Link
72
48
59
61

61
TAMWORTH
Polesworth
Warton
Orton-on-the-Hill
Newtown
Pelsall
Clayhanger
Stonnall
Shenstone
Weeford
Hints
Walsall Wood
BLOXWICH
Rushall
ALDRIDGE
WALSALL
Fazeley
Drayton Bassett
Two Gates
Glascote
Wilnecote
Dordon
St. Helena
Sheepy Magna
Sheepy Parva
Wellsborough
Upton
Atherstone
ATHERSTONE
Witherley
Fenny Drayton
Grendon
Baddesley Ensor
Grendon Common
Baxterley
Mancetter
Stoke Golding
Higham on the Hill
Caldecote
Hartshill
Oldbury
Weddington
NUNEATON
Stockingford
Galley Common
Ansley
Nether Whitacre
Over Whitacre
Old Arley
New Arley
Kingsbury
Hurley
Wood End
Piccadilly
Middleton
Streetly
Mere Green
Roughley
SUTTON COLDFIELD
Banners Gate
New Oscott
Great Barr
WEDNESBURY
WEST BROMWICH
Wishaw
Curdworth
Minworth
Water Orton
Erdington
Castle Bromwich
Kingshurst
Coleshill
Maxstoke
Fillongley
Corley
Corley Ash
Astley
BEDWORTH
Bulkington
Marston Jabbett
OLDBURY
SMETHWICK
BIRMINGHAM
BLACKHEATH
Harborne
Edgbaston
Ladywood
Small Heath
Yardley
Sheldon
Marston Green
Acocks Green
Olton
Elmdon
Bickenhill
Catherine-de-Barnes
Hampton in Arden
Meriden
Allesley
Keresley
COVENTRY
Longford
Foleshill
Hall Green
Moseley
Selly Oak
Bournville
Northfield
Longbridge
Rubery
King's Norton
Shirley
SOLIHULL
Knowle
Dorridge
Balsall Common
Berkswell
Canley
Earlsdon
Stivichall
Baginton
Stoneleigh
Kenilworth
KENILWORTH
Leek Wootton
Hollywood
Wythall
Drakes Cross
Hockley Heath
Lapworth
Kingswood
Rowington
Shrewley
Haseley
Hatton
Alvechurch
Barnt Green
Cofton Hackett
Redditch
REDDITCH
Headless Cross
Studley
Tanworth-in-Arden
Henley-in-Arden
Wootton Wawen
Claverdon
Norton Lindsey
Hampton Magna
WARWICK
Milverton
ROYAL LEAMINGTON SPA
Offchurch
Cubbington
Radford Semele
Whitnash
Bishop's Tachbrook
Barford
Sherbourne
Wasperton
Snitterfield
Bearley
Astwood Bank
Feckenham
Inkberrow
Alcester
Great Alne
Wilmcote
Stratford-upon-Avon
STRATFORD-UPON-AVON
Tiddington
Alveston
Charlecote
Hampton Lucy
Wellesbourne
Kineton
Gaydon
Lighthorne
Bishop's Itchington
Harbury
Ufton
Salford Priors
Bidford-on-Avon
Welford-on-Avon
Clifford Chambers
Atherstone on Stour
Ettington
Pillerton Hersey
Pillerton Priors
Long Marston
Lower Quinton
Pebworth
Cleeve Prior
Harvington
Offenham
Fladbury
Lower Moor
WARWICKSHIRE
M6
M6 TOLL
M42
M40
M5
A5
A38
A45
A46
A422
A429
A435
A441
A444
A446
A452
A453
A4177
A4189

62
A
B
C
D
LEICESTER
LEICESTER FOREST EAST
Braunstone Town
Newton Unthank
Kirby Fields
Leicester Forest East
Market Bosworth
Bosworth Water Trust
Wellsborough
Cadeby
Newbold Verdon
Desford
Sheepy Magna
Orton-on-the-Hill
Sibson
Upton
Sutton Cheney
Bosworth Battlefield
Peckleton
Kirkby Mallory
Thurlaston
Enderby
Glen Parva
Aylestone
Knighton
Oadby
WIGSTON
Stoneygate
North Evington
Evington
Thurnby
Bushby
Houghton on the Hill
Stoughton
Billesdon
King's Norton
Frisby
Gaulby
Little Stretton
Great Glen
Illston on the Hill
Carlton Curlieu
Burton Overy
Newton Harcourt
Ratcliffe Culey
Whittington
ATHERSTONE
Atterton
Witherley
Fenny Drayton
Stapleton
Dadlington
Earl Shilton
Barwell
Stoke Golding
Narborough
Huncote
Blaby
South Wigston
Whetstone
Littlethorpe
Countesthorpe
Kilby
Foston
Wistow Rural Centre
Shangton
Kibworth Harcourt
Tur Langton
Kibworth Beauchamp
Smeeton Westerby
Saddington
Mancetter
Higham on the Hill
Wykin
Elmesthorpe
Croft
Cosby
Sutton in the Elms
LEICESTERSH
Oldbury
Hartshill
Caldecote
Weddington
HINCKLEY
Burbage
Stoney Stanton
Sapcote
Broughton Astley
Primethorpe
Willoughby Waterleys
Peatling Magna
Arnesby
Fleckney
Whittleford
Stockingford
NUNEATON
Sketchley
Aston Flamville
Sharnford
Frolesworth
Dunton Bassett
Ashby Magna
Shearsby
Bruntingthorpe
Peatling Parva
Saddington Resr.
Gumley
Foxton
Foxton Locks
Laughton
Mowsley
Attleborough
Burton Hastings
Smockington
Claybrooke Magna
Claybrooke Parva
Leire
Ashby Parva
Gilmorton
Walton
Lubenham
Astley
Arbury Hall
Marston Jabbett
Bramcote
Shelford
Wolvey Heath
Copston Magna
Wibtoft
Ullesthorpe
Kimcote
Theddingworth
Marston Trussell
BEDWORTH
Howe Green
Griff
Marston Junction
Weston in Arden
Ryton
Wolvey
Market End
Bulkington
Bitteswell
Lutterworth
East Farndon
CORLEY
Ash Green
Keresley Newland
Neal's Green
Keresley
Longford
Little Heath
Radford
Barnacle
Hawkesbury
Shilton
Ansty
Withybrook
Willey
Magna Park
Misterton
Walcote
North Kilworth
Husbands Bosworth
Sibbertoft
Foleshill
Wyken
Monks Kirby
Pailton
Cotesbach
South Kilworth
Clipston
Great Heath
Walsgrave on Sowe
Stretton under Fosse
Churchover
Shawell
Stanford Resr.
Welford
Naseby
Spon End
Stoke
Brinklow
Easenhall
Harborough Magna
Newton
Swinford
Stanford Hall
Stanford on Avon
Catthorpe
Obelisk
Earlsdon
Binley
COVENTRY
Bretford
King's Newnham
Little Lawford
Newbold on Avon
Clifton upon Dunsmore
Lilbourne
Clay Coton
Cold Ashby
Naseby Resr.
Stivichall
Pinley
Willenhall
Church Lawford
Long Lawford
Elkington
Thornby
Brandon
Ryton-on-Dunsmore
Wolston
Knightlow Hill
RUGBY
Yelvertoft
NORTHA
Baginton
Coventry
Midland Air
Stoneleigh
Bubbenhall
Bilton
Cawston
Hillmorton
Winwick
Guilsborough
Hollowell Resr.
Cottesbrooke
Stareton
Stretton-on-Dunsmore
Dunchurch
Barby Nortoft
Kilsby
Crick
West Haddon
Coton
Hollowell
Princethorpe
Thurlaston
Bourton on Dunsmore
Draycote Water
Barby
Coton Manor
Ravensthorpe
Ravensthorpe Resr.
Ashow
Weston under Wetherley
Frankton
Draycote
Teeton
Eathorpe
Wappenbury
Marton
Kites Hardwick
Watford
Hunningham
Birdingbury
Woolscott
Ashby St. Ledgars
Long Buckby
East Haddon
Cubbington
Leamington Hastings
Hill
Willoughby
WATFORD GAP
Holdenby
ROYAL LEAMINGTON SPA
Grandborough
Braunston
Welton
Holdenby Ho. Gdns. & Falconry
WARWICKSHIRE
Sawbridge
Long Buckby Wharf
Church Brampton
Offchurch
Long Itchington
Broadwell
Whilton
Althorp
Little Brington
Great Brington
Harlestone
Radford Semele
Whitnash
Nethercote
Drayton Resr.
Norton
Muscott
Nobottle
Warwickshire Exhibition Centre
Bascote
Stockton
Lower Shuckburgh
Flecknoe
Brockhall
Tachbrook Mallory
Bishop's Tachbrook
Ufton
Southam
Napton on the Hill
Drayton
DAVENTRY
New Duston
Staverton
Chapel Green
Dodford
Flore
Harpole
Duston
Harbury
Lower Catesby
Upper Catesby
Badby
Newnham
Little Everdon
Weedon Bec
Road Weedon
Upper Heyford
Kislingbury
Upton
Chesterton Green
WARWICK
Bishop's Itchington
Ladbroke
Marston Doles
Hellidon
Arbury Hill
Upper Weedon
Church Stowe
Nether Heyford
NORTHAMPTON
Rothersthorpe
Lighthorne
Priors Hardwick
Priors Marston
Charwelton
Everdon
Upper Stowe
Bugbrooke
Oxford Canal
Preston Capes
Farthingstone
Litchborough
Pattishall
Gayton
Heritage Motor Centre
Knightcote
Wormleighton
Upper Boddington
Byfield
Little Preston
Grimscote
Dalscote
Eastcote
Astcote
Compton Verney
Chadshunt
Gaydon
Northend
Burton Dassett Beacon
Fenny Compton
Wormleighton Resr.
Lower Boddington
Westhorp
Boddington Resr.
Hinton
Woodford Halse
Maidford
Cold Higham
Tiffield
Kineton
West Farndon
Adstone
Foxley
Duncote
Avon Dassett
Aston le Walls
Canons Ashby House NT
Canons Ashby
Caldecote
Little Kineton
Claydon
Eydon
Blakesley
Shutlanger
Edgehill
Arlescote
Farnborough
Chipping Warden
Woodend
Moreton Pinkney
Greens Norton
Hulcote
Towcester
Radway
Warmington
Farnborough Hall NT
Plumpton
Bradden
Ratley
Mollington
Cropredy
Upper Wardington
Culworth
Weston
Milthorpe
Weedon Lois
Slapton
Abthorpe
Wood Burcote
Heathencote
Lower Tysoe
Shotteswell
National Herb Centre
Wardington
Sulgrave
Bosworth Field
Canal
Aircraft
Grand Union Canal

63
Lyndon
North Luffenham
Ketton
Geeston
Wothorpe
Barnack
Ufford
A6003
A1
A47
Ridlington
Preston
Wing
Pilton
South Luffenham
A6121
A43
Collyweston
White Water Resr.
Southorpe
Loddington
Belton-in-Rutland
Ayston
Morcott
Duddington
Wittering
Marholm
Skeffington
Tugby
East Norton
Glaston
Thornhaugh
Rollesto
Allexton
Wardley
Bisbrooke
Barrowden
Tixover
Wansford
Stibbington
Ailsworth
Castor
Wakerley
Sutton
Noseley
Goadby
Uppingham
Seaton
King's Cliffe
Yarwell
Water Newton
Orton Wistow
Horninghold
Stockerston
Stoke Dry
Lyddington
Harringworth
Sibson
Alwalton
Glooston
Hallaton
Lyddington Bede House
Thorpe by Water
Laxton
Nassington
Peterborough (Sibson)
Stonton Wyville
Eyebrook Reservoir
Blatherwycke Lake
Blatherwycke
Apethorpe
Prebendal Manor House
Chesterton
Cranoe
Blaston
Slawston
A6003
Gretton
Bulwick
Woodnewton
East of England Showground
Church Langton
Thorpe Langton
Medbourne
Great Easton
Caldecott
Kirby Hall
Deene
Fotheringhay
Elton
Elton Hall
Over End
Haddon
PETERBOROUGH
East Langton
Welham
Drayton
Bringhurst
Deene Park
Southwick
Southwick Hall
Deenethorpe
A605
Morborne
Weston by Welland
Rockingham
Rockingham Motor Speedway
Tansor
Eaglethorpe
Warmington
Sutton Bassett
Ashley
Cottingham
Middleton
Upper Benefield
Glapthorn
Cotterstock
Folksworth
Great Bowden
Stoke Albany
Wilbarston
East Carlton
A6116
Weldon
A427
Lower Benefield
Oundle
Ashton
Caldecote
Dingley
Little Bowden
B6481
CORBY
Stanion
ROCKINGHAM
Polebrook
Lutton
Brampton Ash
A427
A6014
Great Oakley
Fermynwoods Contemporary Art
Stoke Doyle
Armston
MARKET HARBOROUGH
A6
Pipewell
Little Oakley
Brigstock
NT Lyveden New Bield
Hemington
West Lodge Rural Centre
A43
A6116
Pilton
Barnwell
Luddington in the Brook
Braybrooke
Newton
Wadenhoe
Great Gidding
Desborough
Triangular Lodge
Geddington
Eleanor Cross
Achurch
Wigsthorpe
Thurning
A508
Rushton
A6003
Sudborough
Aldwincle
Little Gidding
Arthingworth
Rothwell
Boughton
USAAF Memorial
Lowick
Thorpe Waterville
Steeple Gidding
Harrington
Weekley
Warkton
Grafton Underwood
Clopton
Winwick
A605
Titchmarsh
Hamerton
Kelmarsh
Orton
Thorpe Malsor Resr.
A14
KETTERING
Slipton
Islip
Loddington
Harrington Aviation
Thorpe Malsor
Cransley Resr.
Barton Seagrave
Cranford St. Andrew
Cranford St. John
Twywell
A14
Thrapston
Old Weston
Maidwell
Great Cransley
Woodford
Denford
Buckworth
Draughton
Mawsley Village
Broughton
Wicksteed Park
Molesworth
Bythorn
Brington
A43
Burton Latimer
Great Addington
Ringstead
Keyston
Leighton Bromswold
NORTHAMPTONSHIRE
Lamport
Lamport Hall
A6
A45
A14
Hanging Houghton
Pytchley
Isham
Little Addington
Old
A509
A510
Catworth
Scaldwell
Walgrave
Orlingbury
Finedon
Stanwick
Raunds
Little Catworth
Spaldwick
Saxon Church
Little Harrowden
B574
Hargrave
Three Shire Stone
Covington
Easton
Brixworth
Great Harrowden
Irthlingborough
Stow Longa
Hannington
Pitsford Resr.
Holcot
Hardwick
A510
B571
Chichele College
B663
B645
Chelveston
Tilbrook
Higham Ferrers
Caldecott
Shelton
Lower Dean
Newtown
Sywell
A508
WELLINGBOROUGH
A5193
Pitsford
Northampton and Lamport Railway
Sywell
A509
Kimbolton
Yielden
Upper Dean
Stonely
Chapel Brampton
Boughton House
Moulton
Sywell Aviation
Overstone
Mears Ashby
Wilby
A45
Little Irchester
Knuston
Transport
Newton Bromswold
Swineshead
Wood End
Boughton
Sywell Res.
Earls Barton
A4500
Little Wymington
Melchbourne
RUSHDEN
A5028
B569
Pertenhall
A5076
A43
Irchester
B570
A6
Great Staughton
Staughton Highway
Kingsthorpe
Boothville
Great Billing
Ecton
Great Doddington
Wymington
Farndish
Knotting
Riseley
Green End
Keysoe
A5123
Cottarville
Little Billing
B573
A45
Wollaston
Podington
Souldrop
Knotting Green
Little Staughton
Weston Favell
Strixton
Hinwick
306th Bombardment Group
Keysoe Row
NORTHAMPTON
Cogenhoe
Whiston
Lower End
Grendon
A509
Santa Pod Raceway
Sharnbrook
Bourne End
Bedford
Staploe
St. James' End
Far Cotton
Brafield-on-the-Green
Castle Ashby
Chadstone
Bozeat
Thurleigh
Thurleigh Farm Centre
Bolnhurst
Bushmead
Great Houghton
Little Houghton
A428
Denton
Easton Maudit
Odell
Felmersham
Bletsoe
Colmworth
Honeydon
Hardingstone
Yardley Hastings
Harrold
Radwell
BEDFORD
Rootham's Green
Wootton
Collingtree
Carlton
Chellington
Pavenham
Milton Ernest
Channel's End
Milton Malsor
Hackleton
YARDLEY CHASE
Colesden
Piddington
Horton
Quinton
Wilden
Ravensden
Blisworth
Courteenhall
The Menagerie
Warrington
Lavendon
West End
Stevington
Oakley
A6
Glenn Miller
Renhold
A421
Church Path Oak
Salcey Forest
Turvey
Stevington
Clapham
Salph End
Roade
B5388
B565
Clifton Reynes
Cold Brayfield
Goldington
Great Barford
Ravenstone
Weston Underwood
Olney
Cowper & Newton
Newton Blossomville
A428
Bromham
BEDFORD
A4280
Blunham
Hartwell
Eakley Lanes
Bridge End
Danish Camp
Ashton
Stoke Bruerne
Emberton
Box End
Biddenham
Dovecote & Stables NT
Willington
Chalton
Stoke Goldington
Petsoe End
Stagsden
A422
A428
Moggerhanger
Long Street
B560
Cople
A508
Grafton Regis
Hanslope
Filgrave
Tyringham
Sherington
A509
Hardmead
Astwood
Green End
Kempston
Elstow
Cardington
Harrowden
Shortstown
Airship Hangars
Moggerhanger Park
Gayhurst
Tathall
A422
A600
B531
52
51
64
75

64
Ufford
Clare Cottage
BEDFORD (NORTH LEVEL)
Eye Green
14
Thorney
Thorney Toll
Pigeons Farm
Guyhirn Gull
Guyhirn
Friday Bridge
B1101
Werrington
A15
Southorpe
Gunthorpe
Walton
A47
Eye
A47
Ring's End
Coldham
Laddus
A1
10
Marholm
Bretton
30
R. Nene
New England
Dogsthorpe
Stone Bridge Corner
A141
Upton
A
Newark
B
76
C
Chainbridge
D
A47
Longthorpe Tower
Millfield
PETERBOROUGH
Euximoor
Stibbington
Ailsworth
Longthorpe
Westwood
B1040
Eldernell
A605
West Fen
Sutton
Castor
Coates
Westry
Norwoodside
Yarwell
Railway
Nene Valley Railway
Water Newton
Woodston
A1139
Flag Fen
West End
March
Sibson
Orton Wistow
Alwalton
Orton Longueville
Old Fletton
Stanground
Eastrea
Oldeamere
Binnimoor Fen
B671
Peterborough (Sibson)
Orton Waterville
Whittlesey
R. Nene
Chesterton
A605
King's Delph
B1093
Town End
B1099
East of England Showground
Farcet
Flag Fen
Twenty Foot R.
Knight's End
Elton
Over End
3
Hampton Hargate
A15
B1095
Flood's Ferry
Hook
Stonea Camp
Elton Hall
17
B1091
Chapelbridge
Eastwood End
Stone
Haddon
PETERBOROUGH
Norman Cross
White Fen
Wimblington
A605
Morborne
Yaxley
Farcet Fen
Pondersbridge
Copalder Corner
New World
B1093
Sixteen Foot Drain
Eaglethorpe
16
Gallery
B1093
Warmington
Whittlesey Mere
BEDFORD (MIDDLE LEVEL)
Benwick
Doddington
Folksworth
B1043
The Herne
Middle Moor
Ramsey Mereside
Wimblington Fen
Stilton
Mere Side
B1096
Swingbrow
Chatteris
Caldecote
Denton
Ramsey St. Mary's
A141
Polebrook
Lutton
Holme
B660
Ramsey Forty Foot
Forty Foot Drain
Vermudens Drain
Slade Field
A1(M)
Armston
Glatton
Peterborough Airport (Conington)
Chatteris
B1098
Horseway
Hemington
Conington
Ramsey
Ramsey Rural
Hollow
Langwood Fen
Welches Dam
B660
Abbey Gatehouse
A142
Luddington in the Brook
Ramsey Heights
Upwood
Bury
Tick Fen
Sawtry
Ferry Hill
Great Gidding
Thurning
Church End
Upwood
15
A141
Horseley Fen
New Bedford R.
Little Gidding
B1090
B1040
Somersham High North Fen
B1050
Wardy Hill
Steeple Gidding
Winwick
Hamerton
Woodwalton
Great Raveley
Wistow
Mepal
Clopton
Hamerton
Warboys
Pidley Fen
Sutton Gault
Witcham
Coppingford
Little Raveley
Fenton
Upton
Wennington
B1043
13
Somersham
Sutton
Old West
63
Alconbury Weston
14
Abbots Ripton
Broughton
B1040
B1089
Pidley
A1421
C A M B R I D G E S H
Molesworth
Buckworth
Alconbury
Kings Ripton
Oldhurst
B1086
B1050
B1381
A1123
Haddenham End
Brington
B660
Leighton Bromswold
Barham
Alconbury
Little Stukeley
13a
Woodhurst
Raptor Foundation
Colne
Hade
Great Stukeley
A14
18
17
Woolley
A141
Wyton
B1040
Bluntisham
Earith
10
Great Mill
Catworth
18
A1
A14
Sapley
East End
B1090
Aldreth
Little Catworth
19
Spaldwick
Huntingdon
Hartford
Wyton
R. Great Ouse
Easton
HUNTINGDON
Houghton
St. Ives
A1123
Needingworth
Covington
Stow Longa
Ellington
Ellington Thorpe
21
22
Cromwell
Mill NT
Bridge Chapel
Hemingford Abbots
Hemingford Grey
Norris
Church End
Willingham
Tilbrook
B1514
The Manor
A1096
Holywell
Over
Smithey Fen
Lower Dean
B645
Grafham
Brampton
Godmanchester
24
25
Fen Drayton
Fenstanton
Swavesey
Newtown
Grafham Water
26
27
Rampton
Kimbolton
West Perry
East Perry
Towers
Buckden
Offord Cluny
A1198
B1050
Boxworth End
Longstanton
Cottenham
Stonely
Wood End
B660
B661
Offord D'Arcy
B1040
Turf Maze
Conington
Northstowe
Dillington
Hilton
CAMBRIDGE
28
Westwick
B1049
Pertenhall
Great Staughton
Staughton Green
Diddington
Oakington
Landbeach
Staughton Highway
Southoe
Graveley
Papworth St. Agnes
Boxworth
28a
Lolworth
29
A14
Histon
Green End
B645
Great Paxton
Elsworth
Bar Hill
30
Keysoe
Little Staughton
Hail Weston
Little Paxton
Papworth Everard
Knapwell
Dry Drayton
Girton
Impington
Little Staughton
Toseland
Yelling
31
32
Keysoe Row
St. Neots
B1041
B1043
A428
Duloe
Staploe
B1428
Croxton
Caxton Gibbet
17
A428
Madingley
14
A1307
A1309
Bolnhurst
Upper Staploe
Eynesbury
Cambourne
Chesterton
A1134
Thurleigh Farm Centre
B660
Bushmead
Eltisley
Bourn
Highfields Caldecote
Coton
Eaton Socon
A1
Honeydon
Caxton
Hardwick
A1303
13
The Backs
Barnwell
Colmworth
Bourn
Crow End
M11
Rootham's Green
R. Gt. Ouse
B1046
B1040
Newnham
Botanic
Wyboston
Little Barford
Abbotsley
Caldecote
Channel's End
Chawston
Great Gransden
Bourn
Comberton
12
A603
A1134
A1307
Toft
Grantchester
Colesden
B1046
Barton
Wilden
Ravensden
A421
Roxton
Little Gransden
Longstowe
21
Kingston
Trumpington
Renhold
Waresley
Little Eversden
Great Eversden
Great Shelford
Salph End
Tempsford
Gamlingay Cinques
Great Barford
Gransden
11
Haslingfield
Hauxton
A1301
Blunham
Gamlingay Great Heath
Gamlingay
Wimpole Home Farm
Hatley St. George
Harlton
Little Shelford
Goldington
A4280
Dovecote & Stables
Danish Camp
Everton
Wimpole Hall
Harston
BEDFORD
Willington
Chalton
Sandy
Arrington
Orwell
A10
Caesar's Camp
Potton
52
East Hatley
A603
A
B
C
D
Moggerhanger
A603
B1042
Cockayne Hatley
Croydon
A603
Barrington
Newton
Cople
Moggerhanger Park
Hatch
Shepreth
Foxton
Cardington
Thorncote Green
Beeston
The Lodge
Wrestlingworth
B1042
R. Cam or Rhee
Crossing House
Harrowden
Shortstown
Airship Hangars
Tadlow
Wendy
A1198
Docwra's Manor
B1368
Whittle
Elstow
Northill
Upper Caldecote
Sutton
A1
DANGER AREA
Meldreth
Whaddon
Thriplow
Heathfield
Cotton

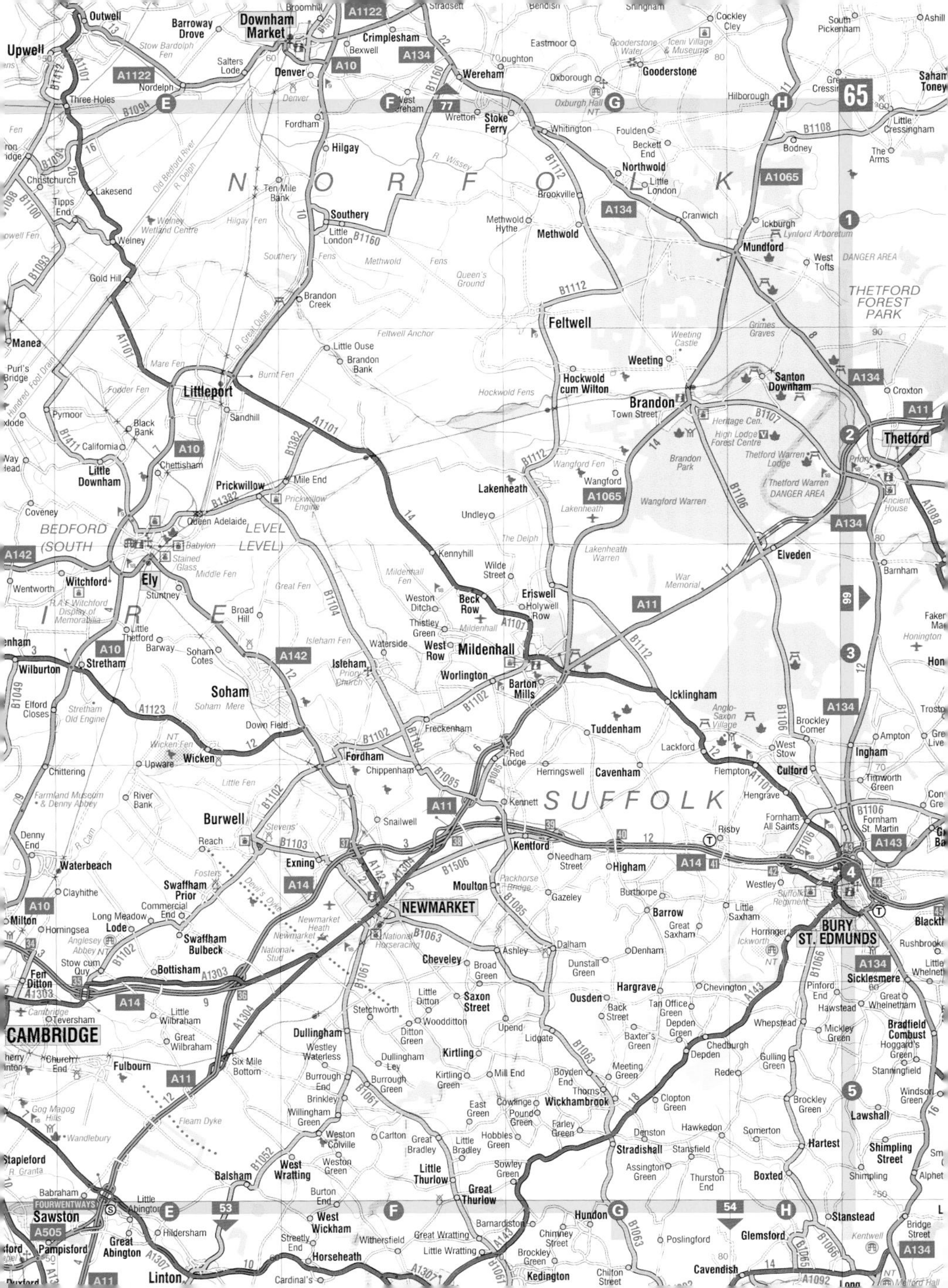
65
N O R F O L K
S U F F O L K
Outwell
Upwell
Barroway Drove
Downham Market
Crimplesham
Bexwell
Stow Bardolph Fen
Salters Lode
Nordelph
Denver
Three Holes
West Dereham
Wereham
Stoke Ferry
Wretton
Whitington
Oxborough
Oxburgh Hall NT
Gooderstone
Eastmoor
Cockley Cley
South Pickenham
Ashill
Hilborough
Great Cressingham
Little Cressingham
Foulden
Beckett End
Bodney
The Arms
Northwold
Little London
Brookville
Methwold
Methwold Hythe
Cranwich
Ickburgh
Mundford
Lynford Arboretum
West Tofts
DANGER AREA
THETFORD FOREST PARK
Fordham
Hilgay
Ten Mile Bank
Southery
Little London
Brandon Creek
Christchurch
Lakesend
Tipps End
Welney
Welney Wetland Centre
Hilgay Fen
Southery Fens
Methwold Fens
Queen's Ground
Gold Hill
Manea
Purl's Bridge
Little Ouse
Brandon Bank
Feltwell Anchor
Feltwell
Weeting
Weeting Castle
Grimes Graves
Santon Downham
Croxton
Hockwold cum Wilton
Hockwold Fens
Brandon
Town Street
Heritage Cen.
High Lodge Forest Centre
Brandon Park
Thetford Warren Lodge
Thetford Warren DANGER AREA
Thetford
Priory
Ancient House
Mare Fen
Burnt Fen
Littleport
Sandhill
Fodder Fen
Pymoor
Black Bank
California
Little Downham
Chettisham
Prickwillow
Prickwillow Engine
Mile End
Lakenheath
Wangford Fen
Wangford
Wangford Warren
Lakenheath Warren
Undley
The Delph
Elveden
Barnham
Coveney
BEDFORD (SOUTH LEVEL)
Queen Adelaide
Babylon
Stained Glass
Ely
Middle Fen
Kennyhill
Wilde Street
Eriswell
Holywell Row
War Memorial
Wentworth
Witchford
RAF Witchford Display of Memorabilia
Stuntney
Broad Hill
Great Fen
Mildenhall Fen
Weston Ditch
Beck Row
Thistley Green
West Row
Mildenhall
Little Thetford
Barway
Soham Cotes
Isleham Fen
Waterside
Isleham
Priory Church
Worlington
Barton Mills
Icklingham
Honington
Wilburton
Stretham
Soham
Soham Mere
Elford Closes
Stretham Old Engine
Down Field
Freckenham
Tuddenham
Anglo-Saxon Village
Lackford
West Stow
Brockley Corner
Ampton
Ingham
Wicken
Wicken Fen NT
Upware
Chittering
Fordham
Chippenham
Red Lodge
Herringswell
Cavenham
Flempton
Culford
Timworth Green
Little Fen
Farmland Museum & Denny Abbey
River Bank
Burwell
Snailwell
Kennett
Hengrave
Fornham All Saints
Fornham St. Martin
Denny End
Reach
Stevens'
Kentford
Risby
Waterbeach
Exning
Needham Street
Higham
Westley
Clayhithe
Swaffham Prior
Fosters
Devil's Dyke
Moulton
Packhorse Bridge
Gazeley
Burthorpe
Barrow
Little Saxham
Great Saxham
Suffolk Regiment
Milton
Horningsea
Long Meadow
Commercial End
Lode
NEWMARKET
Newmarket Heath
National Horseracing
National Stud
Anglesey Abbey NT
Swaffham Bulbeck
Stow cum Quy
Fen Ditton
Bottisham
Cheveley
Broad Green
Ashley
Dalham
Dunstall Green
Denham
Horringer
Ickworth NT
BURY ST. EDMUNDS
Rushbrooke
Sicklesmere
Little Whelnetham
Great Whelnetham
Pinford End
Hawstead
Cambridge
Teversham
CAMBRIDGE
Little Wilbraham
Great Wilbraham
Little Ditton
Saxon Street
Stetchworth
Woodditton
Ditton Green
Upend
Lidgate
Ousden
Hargrave
Chevington
Back Street
Tan Office Green
Depden Green
Baxter's Green
Whepstead
Mickley Green
Bradfield Combust
Hoggard's Green
Stanningfield
Cherry Hinton
Church End
Fulbourn
Six Mile Bottom
Dullingham
Westley Waterless
Dullingham Ley
Kirtling
Burrough End
Burrough Green
Kirtling Green
Mill End
Boyden End
Thorns
Meeting Green
Chedburgh
Depden
Rede
Gulling Green
Wickhambrook
Clopton Green
Brockley Green
Lawshall
Windsor Green
Gog Magog Hills
Wandlebury
Fleam Dyke
Brinkley
Willingham Green
East Green
Cowlinge
Pound Green
Farley Green
Weston Colville
Carlton
Great Bradley
Little Bradley
Hobbles Green
Denston
Hawkedon
Somerton
Hartest
Shimpling Street
Shimpling
Stapleford
Balsham
West Wratting
Weston Green
Little Thurlow
Sowley Green
Stradishall
Stansfield
Assington Green
Thurston End
Boxted
Great Thurlow
Burton End
Babraham
Little Abington
FOURWENTWAYS
Sawston
Hildersham
West Wickham
Barnardiston
Hundon
Stanstead
Bridge Street
Great Abington
Pampisford
Streetly End
Withersfield
Great Wratting
Little Wratting
Chimney Street
Poslingford
Glemsford
Kentwell
Horseheath
Brockley Green
Linton
Cardinal's
Kedington
Chilton Street
Cavendish
Melford Hall
A1122
A134
A10
A1101
A1065
A11
A1088
A142
A1123
B1102
B1104
B1085
A14
A1303
A1304
A505
A1307
A143
B1063
B1061
B1052
B1066
B1106
A1092
B1065

66
A
B
C
D
78
South Pickenham
Ashill
Saham Hills
Saham Toney
Ovington
Neaton
Carbrooke
Woodrising
Cranworth
Southburgh
Hardingham
Kimberley
Forehoe
Crownthorpe
Kidd's Moor
Hethersett
Intwood
Lower East Carleton
East Carleton
Ketteringham
Swardeston
Swainsthorpe
Mulbarton
Wicklewood
Hackford
Hingham
Wymondham
Deopham
Watton
Scoulton
Little Cressingham
Griston
Northacre
Little Ellingham
Morley St. Botolph
Suton
Silfield
Wreningham
Bracon Ash
Newton Flotman
Merton
The Arms
Bodney
Rockland St. Peter
Deopham Green
Bush Green
Caston
Spooner Row
Ashwellthorpe
Toprow
Flordon
Fundenhall
Thompson
Stow Bedon
Rockland All Saints
Great Ellingham
Besthorpe
Hapton
Tasburgh
Attleborough
Black Carr
Tacolneston
Tharston
Ickburgh
Lynford Arboretum
Mundford
West Tofts
DANGER AREA
Breckles
Lower Stow Bedon
Mount Pleasant
Shropham
Old Buckenham
Bunwell
Forncett St. Mary
Forncett St. Peter
Stratton St. Michael
Forncett End
Long Stratton
North End
Puddledock
Upgate Street
Carleton Rode
THETFORD FOREST PARK
Great Hockham
World Horse Welfare Rail Farm
Fen Street
Old Buckenham
Pottergate Street
Great Moulton
Aslacton
Wacton
East Wretham
Snetterton
Eccles Road
Wilby
Stacksford
New Buckenham
Hargate
Grimes Graves
Larling
Illington
Snetterton
Tibenham
Pristow Green
Santon Downham
Harling Road
English Whisky Company
Quidenham
Hunt's Corner
Banham
Short Green
Tivetshall St. Margaret
Colegate End
Bush Green
Croxton
East Harling
Kenninghall
Winfarthing
Tivetshall St. Mary
Pulham Market
Hall Green
Gissing
Bridgham
Middle Harling
Dam Green
Thetford Warren Lodge
Thetford Warren DANGER AREA
Brettenham
Shadwell
R. Thet
Shelfanger
Mill Green
Burston
Shimpling
Rushall
Thetford
Ancient House
Priory
North Lopham
Fersfield
Garboldisham
South Lopham
Wilney Green
Snow Street
Dickleburgh
Walcot Green
Thelveton
100th Bomb Group Memorial
Rushford
Smallworth
Bressingham
Frenze
Thorpe Abbotts
Elveden
Gasthorpe
Roydon
Diss
Palgrave
Billingford
Scole
Euston
Euston Hall
Barnham
Coney Weston
Hopton
Blo' Norton
Thelnetham
Magpie Green
Green Street
Oakley
Hoxne
Wingfield
Market Weston
Redgrave
Wortham
Stuston
Great Green
Brome
Brome Street
Chickering
Fakenham Magna
Barningham
Hinderclay
Botesdale
Burgate Great Green
Thrandeston
Heckfield Green
Cross Street
Honington
Rickinghall
Hepworth
Stanton Chare
Sapiston
Bardwell
Burgate Little Green
Yaxley
Denham
Reading Green
Candle Street
Wattisfield
Mellis
Eye
Thornham Parva
Little Green
Braiseworth
Cranley
Denham Street
Horham
Stanton
Upthorpe
Walsham le Willows
Cranmer Green
Ixworth Thorpe
Troston
Brockley Corner
West Stow
Ampton
Great Livermere
Wyken Hall
Gislingham
Thornham Magna
Athelington
Ingham
Ixworth
Pakenham Water Mill
Four Ashes
Wickham Street
Stoke Ash
Sandwell Green
Occold
Redlingfield
Culford
Crowland
Langham
Wickham Green
Thorndon
Southolt
Timworth Green
Conyer's Green
Westhorpe
Finningham
Hengrave
Hunston
Badwell Ash
Wyverstone Street
Wyverstone
Wickham Skeith
Thwaite
Rishangles
Bedingfield
Fornham All Saints
Fornham St. Martin
Grimstone End
Stowlangtoft
Long Thurlow
Mechanical Music
Great Barton
Pakenham
Stanton Street
Great Ashfield
Bacton
Cotton
Brockford Street
Wetheringsett
Monk Soham Green
Earl's Green
Mid-Suffolk Light Railway
Kenton
Norton
Norton Little Green
Mendlesham
Blacksmith's Green
Westley
BURY ST. EDMUNDS
Thurston
Canham's Green
Monk Soham
Suffolk Regiment
Tostock
Elmswell
Haughley Green
Ward Green
Gipping
Wetherup Street
Debenham
Little Saxham
Horringer
Ickworth NT
Blackthorpe
Beyton
Woolpit
Wetherden
Haughley
Old Newton
Mendlesham Green
Ashfield
Rushbrooke
Kingshall Street
Drinkstone
Saxham Street
Mickfield
Rougham
Hessett
Borley Green
Winston
Little Whelnetham
Sicklesmere
Bradfield St. George
Drinkstone Green
Harleston
Onehouse
Stowupland
Middlewood Green
Forward Green
Little Stonham
Stonham Aspal
Peats Corner
Pinford End
Hawstead
Great Whelnetham
Maypole Green
Rattlesden
Stowmarket
Creeting St. Peter
Earl Stonham
Pettaugh
Framsden
Whepstead
Mickley Green
Bradfield St. Clare
Bradfield Combust
Hoggard's Green
Gedding
Granary Crafts
East Anglian Life
Poystreet Green
Buxhall
Great Finborough
Creeting St. Mary
Suffolk Owl Sanctuary
Crowfield
Helmingham Hall
Helmingham
Gulling Green
Stanningfield
Bush Green
Felsham
Great Green
Hightown Green
Combs
Combs Ford
R. Gipping
Coddenham Green
Otley Hall
Cross Green
Rattlesden
High Street Green
Moats Tye
Needham Market
Gosbeck
Ashbocking
Otley
Brockley Green
Windsor Green
Cockfield
Thorpe Green
Battisford Tye
Battisford
Coddenham
Gibraltar
Lawshall
Thorpe Morieux
Brettenham
Cross Green
Ringshall
Barking Tye
Barking
Darmsden
Hemingstone
Swilland
Somerton
Hartest
Shimpling Street
Smithwood Green
Charles Tye
Wattisham
Ringshall Stocks
Baylham
Bell's Cross
Boxted
Shimpling
Alpheton
Rooksey Green
Hitcham
Wattisham
Willisham Tye
Great Blakenham
Barham
Henley
Witnesham
Grundisburgh
Preston
Kettlebaston
Great Bricett
Greenstreet Green
Claydon
Stanstead
Lavenham
Little Hall
Guildhall NT
Brent Eleigh
Bildeston
Nedging Tye
Naughton
Offton
Blakenham Woodland
Akenham
Tuddenham St. Martin
Bridge Street
Glemsford
Kentwell
Monks Eleigh
Nedging
Somersham
Little Blakenham
Westerfield
Playford
Chelsworth
Semer
Ash Street
Whatfield
Elmsett
Flowton
Bramford
Castle Hill
IPSWICH
Rushmere
Long Melford
Melford Hall
Milden
Swingleton Green
54
N O R F O L K
S U F F O L K
A11
A140
A1065
A134
A1075
A1066
A143
A1088
A14
A1120
A1141
A1092
A1101
B1108
B1077
B1111
B1113
B1134
B1527
B1172
B1135
B1107
B1106
B1118
B1117
B1066
B1065
B1071
B1115
B1078
B1079
B1135
1
2
3
4
5
65

67
St. Mary
Arminghall
Caistor St. Edmund
Upper Stoke
A146
Hellington
Claxton
Cantley
Limpenhoe
Burgh Castle
Bradwell
Lifeboat Station
Gorleston-on-Sea
Framingham Pigot
Ashby St. Mary
Langley Green
Abbey
Langley Street
Carleton St. Peter
Framingham Earl
Yelverton
Hardley Street
Reedham
Pettitts
R. Yare
Belton
A143
Browston Green
Stoke Holy Cross
Poringland
Bergh Apton
Alpington
Thurton
Nogdam End
79
Redwings Horse Sanctuary
Fritton Priory
Fritton
Fritton Lake
Bunker's Hill
Hopton on Sea
West Poringland
Howe
Chedgrave
Norton Subcourse
Lower Thurlton
St. Olaves
The Dell
Lound
Hawes Green
Shotesham
Brooke
The Ling
Sisland
Loddon
Thurlton
Herringfleet
Somerleyton
Blundeston
A12
Mundham
Hales
Thorpe
Haddiscoe
Somerleyton
Corton
Saxlingham Nethergate
Kirstead Green
Seething
Stubbs Green
B1136
Raveningham
Maypole Green
A1117
Pleasurewood Hills
B1385
Saxlingham Green
Seething
Station 146 Control Tower
A146
Brundish
Toft Monks
LOWESTOFT
Maritime
Royal Naval Patrol
Hempnall
Road Green
B1527
Thwaite St. Mary
Kirby Green
Wheatacre
Oulton
Hempnall Green
Silver Green
Woodton
Hedenham
A143
Stockton
Burgh St. Peter
Aldeby
Oulton Broad
A1144
B1531
Lifeboat Station
Topcroft
Bedingham Green
Ellingham
Kirby Cane
Geldeston
R. Waveney
Kirkley
B1532
Lundy Green
Topcroft Street
B1332
Gillingham
A146
Shelton Green
Ditchingham
Broome
Hardwick
Great Green
Bungay
Shipmeadow
Worlingham
Barnby
Pakefield
A1145
Carlton Colville
Earsham
Mettingham
B1062
Barsham
East Anglia Transport
Darrow Green
Beccles
North Cove
Mutford
A12
Castle
Ringsfield
Beccles
Gisleham
Denton
Ilketshall St. Andrew
Weston
Rushmere
Black Street
DANGER AREA
Alburgh
B1062
Flixton
St. Peter's Brewery
Ringsfield Corner
Ellough
B1127
Hulver Street
Henstead
Kessingland
Piccadilly Corner
Norfolk & Suffolk Aviation
Ilketshall St. Margaret
A144
B1437
Kessingland Beach
Africa Alive!
Homersfield
High Street
Cider Place
Redisham
A145
Sotterley
Benacre
Wortwell
St. Margaret South Elmham
Ilketshall St. Lawrence
Shadingfield
Redenhall
St. Cross South Elmham
St. Michael South Elmham
Stone Street
Cox Common
Church Corner
Wrentham
St. Andrew's
Mendham
Minster (ruins)
St. Nicholas South Elmham
All Saints South Elmham
Mill Common
Brampton
Stoven
Covehithe
B1123
Rumburgh
Clay Common
South Cove
Withersdale Street
Metfield
St. James South Elmham
Spexhall
Westhall
B1127
Uggeshall
B1116
Chediston Green
Wissett
Broadway Airfield
B1124
Wangford
Earsham Street
Little Whittingham Green
Linstead Parva
Chediston
B1123
B1126
Reydon
Fressingfield
North Green
Holton
Blyford
A1095
Southwold
Halesworth
Wenhaston
Blythburgh
R. Blyth
Sailor's Reading Room
Alfred Corry Lifeboat Station
Pixey Green
Silverley's Green
Cratfield
Cookley
Old Chapel
Walpole
Blackheath
Walberswick
Stradbroke
Ashfield Green
Huntingfield
B1117
B1387
B1117
Queen's Oak
Thorington
Bramfield
Russel's Green
Banyard's Green
A144
A12
Laxfield
Heveningham
Wilby
B1118
Ubbeston Green
High Street
B1125
Dunwich
Brundish Street
Darsham
Greyfriars
Crown Corner
B1116
Brundish
Sibton
Goddard's Corner
A1120
Peasenhall
Yoxford
Westleton
Worlingworth
B1122
Middleton
NORTH SEA
Badingham
Rotten End
Minsmere
Tannington
Dennington
Bruisyard Street
North Green
Minsmere Haven
Saxtead
B1120
Bruisyard
Theberton
East Bridge
Post Mill
Brabling Green
Cransford
Kelsale
B1121
Rendham
Leiston Abbey
B1119
Carlton
Saxtead Green
Framlingham
Swefling
B1119
Saxmundham
Long Shop
Earl Soham
North Green
Great Glemham
B1119
Knodishall
Sizewell
Leiston
Parham Airfield
Sternfield
Aldringham
Brandeston
Coldfair Green
B1116
Parham
Stratford St. Andrew
Benhall Green
B1121
B1069
B1353
Thorpeness
Kettleburgh
Friston
A12
Farnham
Thorpeness Windmill
Hoo
Easton
Hacheston
A1094
B1122
Easton Farm Park
Marlesford
Gromford
Monewden
Letheringham
Little Glemham
Snape
Moot Hall
Blaxhall
Maltings
R. Alde
Lifeboat Station
Charsfield
Iken
Aldeburgh
Campsea Ashe
B1069
Aldeburgh Bay
Wickham Market
B1078
High Street
B1078
Dallinghoo
Tunstall Forest
Debach
Tunstall
Martello Tower
Pettistree
B1069
Rendlesham
Sudbourne
Bredfield
A1152
Chillesford
Ufford
Burgh
Eyke
Dunwich Underwater Exploration
Hasketon
Melton
Bromeswell
B1084
Butley
B1084
Orford
B1079
55
Rendlesham Forest
Capel Green
Butley High Corner
R. Alde
Orford Ness
B1438
WOODBRIDGE
DANGER AREA
Capel St. Andrew
Little Bealings
Tide Mill
Sutton Hoo NT
Martlesham
Boyton
Sutton

CAERNARFON BAY
(BAE CAERNARFON)
CARDIGAN BAY
(BAE CEREDIGION)
LLEYN PENINSULA
(PENRHYN LLYN)
Pwllheli
Abersoch
Aberdaron
Nefyn
Morfa Nefyn
Tudweiliog
Botwnnog
Llanbedrog
Trefor
Y Ffor
Chwilog
Llanystumdwy
Llannor
Bardsey Island
(Ynys Enlli)
BARDSEY SOUND
(SWNT ENLLI)
St. Tudwal's Islands
Ynys Gwylan-fawr
Braich Anelog
Braich y Pwll
Pen y Cil
Penrhyn Mawr
Trwyn y Gorlech
Carreg Ddu
Trwyn Llanbedrog
Trwyn yr Wylfa
Trwyn Cilan
Carreg yr Imbill
Pen-ychain
Porth Neigwl or Hell's Mouth
A499
A497
A487
B4417
B4413
B4415
B4412
B4354
B4411
80
56

69
SNOWDON (YR WYDDFA)
3559
CONWY
GWYNEDD
SNOWDONIA NATIONAL PARK
(PARC CENEDLAETHOL ERYRI)
TREMADOG BAY
(BAE TREMADOG)
COED Y BRENIN FOREST PARK
CAMBRIAN MOUNTAINS
CADAIR IDRIS
POWYS
DYFI FOREST
Barmouth Bay (Bae Bermo)
Talysarn
Nantlle
Rhyd-Ddu
Beddgelert
Nantmor
Bethania
Dolwyddelan
Pont-y-pant
Pentre-bont
Blaenau Dolwyddelan
Penmachno
Rhydlanfair
Glan-Conwy
Pentrefoelas
Rhydlydan
Ysbyty Ifan
Carrog
Cwm Penmachno
Tal-y-waenydd
Rhiwbryfdir
Blaenau Ffestiniog
Tanygrisiau
Congl-y-wal
Llan Ffestiniog
Bont Newydd
Croesor
Tan-lan
Rhyd
Garreg
Llanfrothen
Tan-y-bwlch
Maentwrog
Gellilydan
Penmorfa
Tremadog
Prenteg
Wern
Pentrefelin
Porthmadog
Minffordd
Penrhyndeudraeth
Llandecwyn
Garth
Borth-y-Gest
Portmeirion
Morfa Bychan
Criccieth
Y Dref
Bryncir
Garndolbenmaen
Dolbenmaen
Glan-Dwyfach
Golan
Rhoslan
Llanfihangel-y-pennant
Talsarnau
Soar
Llanfihangel-y-traethau
Glan-y-wern
Eisingrug
Harlech
Llanfair
Pen-sarn
Llandanwg
Pentre Gwynfryn
Llanbedr
Coed Ystumgwern
Llanenddwyn
Dyffryn Ardudwy
Llanddwywe
Tal-y-bont
Llanaber
Barmouth (Abermaw)
Cutiau
Caerdeon
Bontddu
Penmaenpool
Llanelltyd
Dolgellau
Arthog
Fairbourne
Friog
Llwyngwril
Llangelynin
Rhoslefain
Llanfendigaid
Tonfanau
Llanegryn
Peniarth
Bryncrug
Pandy
Rhyd-yr-onen
Tywyn
Cwrt
Pennal
Machynlleth
Penegoes
Forge
Derwenlas
Glandyfi
Glaspwll
Penhelig
Trawsfynydd
Fronoleu
Bronaber
Bryn Eden
Ganllwyd
Llanfachreth
Rhydymain
Brithdir
Cross Foxes
Tal-y-llyn
Abergynolwyn
Dolgoch
Llanfihangel-y-pennant
Corris Uchaf
Corris
Aberllefenni
Esgairgeiliog
Pantperthog
Llanwrin
Cemmaes Road
Cemmaes
Cwm-Llinau
Aberangell
Mallwyd
Dinas Mawddwy
Minllyn
Cwm-Cewydd
Aber-Cywarch
Cywarch
Llanuwchllyn
Pandy
Rhosdylluan
Parc
Llidiardau
Abercegir
Commins Coch
Darowen
Tafolwern
Tal-y-Wern
Melinbyrhedyn
Aberhosan
Pennant
A487
A470
A496
A497
A498
A4085
A4212
A494
A493
A489
A5
B4391
B4410
B4405
B4404
B4416
B4407
B4406
B4513
B4418

70
82
69
58
A
B
C
D
1
2
3
4
5
Capel Garmon Burial Chamber
Rhydlanfair
Glan-Conwy
Pentrefoelas Castle
Pentrefoelas
Rhydlydan
Glasfryn
Cefn-brith
Ysbyty Ifan
Llyn Brenig
Pentre-llyn-cymmer
CLOCAENOG FOREST
Cefn Du
Clocaenog
Pwll-glas
Bird Gardens
Graig-fechan
Pentre-celyn
Llandegla
Pen-y-stryt
Clawdd-newydd
Derwen
Churchyard Cross
Bryn-Saith Marchog
Llanelidan
Rhyd-y-meudwy
Llanfihangel Glyn Myfyr
Cerrigydrudion
Melin-y-wig
Bettws Gwerfil Goch
Gwyddelwern
Bryneglwys
Horseshoe Pass
Llantysilio Mountain
Llandynan
Rhewl
Eliseg's Pillar
Valle Cr
Moel Morfydd
Llangollen
Berwyn
Falls
Garn Prys
Gylchedd
Carnedd y Filiast
Ewe-phoria Sheepdog Centre
Ty-nant
Llangwm
Dinmael
Maerdy
Rug Chapel
Druid
Carrog
Corwen
Cynwyd Forest
Llidiart y parc
Glyndyfrdwy
Llangar Church
Glasgoed
Llyn Arenig Fach
Arenig Fach
Foel Goch
Wenallt
Glan-yr-afon
Cynwyd
DENBIGHSHIRE
Llyn Celyn
Ciltalgarth
Frongoch
Craig yr Hyrddod
Llyn Arenig fawr
Llidiardau
Arenig Fawr
Sarnau
Bethel
Cefn-ddwysarn
Rhiwlas
Llanfor
Rhyd-uchaf
Llandderfel
Moel Fferna
Ceiriog Forest
Glyn Ceiriog
Tyn-y-celyn
Bala
(Y Bala)
Llanycil
Pale
Llandrillo
Cefn Coch
Cadwst
Pennant
Rhos-y-gwaliau
Afon Llafar
Parc
Bryn Du
Pandy
Pentre
Llechryda
Llyn Tegid or Bala Lake
Llangower
GWYNEDD
Penllyn Forest
B E R W Y N
Foel Wen
Mynydd Tarw
Llanarmon Dyffryn Ceiriog
Tregeiriog
Foel Rhiwlas
Rhiwlas
Mynydd Tyn-llech
Bala Lake Railway
Pentre-piod
Tyn-y-ffridd
Llangadwaladr
Cefn C
Castell Carndochan
Llanuwchllyn
Pandy
Ty Issa
Tan-y-pistyll
Pistyll Rhaeadr
Y Clogydd
Tyn-y-wern
Tai-bach
Moelfre
Llansilin
Dyrysgol
Rhosdylluan
Foel Figenau
Foel y Geifr
Talardd
Cwm Cynllwyd
Commins
Cefn-coch
Efail-rhyd
Pencraig
Llangynog
Pennant Melangell
Llanrhaeadr-ym-Mochnant
Mynydd-y-briw
Sycharth Castle
Sycharth
A494
CAMBRIAN MOUNTAINS
Aran Benllyn
Cwm Croes
Foel Rhudd
Afon Tanat
Tanat Valley
Penybontfawr
Pedair-ffordd
Penygarnedd
Llangedwyn
Golfa
Pen-y-
Afon Wnion
Bwlch y Groes
Hirnant
Rhos-y-brithdir
Aran Fawddwy
Llyn Efyrnwy (Lake Vyrnwy)
Bwlchyddar
Pennant
Llanfechain
Llansantffraid-ym-Mechain
Lake Vyrnwy
Llanwddyn
Abertridwr
Llanfyllin
Llanymawddwy
Cywarch
Afon Dyfi
Pen y Ffridd Cownwy
Ddol Cownwy
Tycrwyn
Bwlch-y-cibau
Waen F
Dyfnant Forest
Llanfihangel-yng-Ngwynfa
Nant-y-meichiaid
Tir Rhiwiog
Afon Cerist
Aber-Cywarch
Dinas Mawddwy
Cae Afon
Afon Twrch
Pont Llogel
Mynydd y Gadfa
Afon Efyrnwy (R. Vyrnwy)
Pentre'r beirdd
Minllyn
Pont Minllyn
Cwm-Cewydd
Nant-y-dugoed
Mallwyd
Wern
Dugoed
Dolanog
Pontrobert
Meifod
Foel-y-ffridd
Esgair Ddu
Llyn Coch-hwyad
Tyn-y-rhyd
Maesgwyn-Isaf
Clipiau
Foel
Llangadfan
Groes-lwyd
Aberangell
Llanerfyl
Pen Coed
Four Crosses
Heniarth
Cloddiau
Frochas
Cwm-Llinau
Cemmaes Windfarm (Fferm wynt Cemmaes)
P O W Y S
Neuadd
Welshpool
(Y Trallwng)
Mynydd Rhiw-Saeson
Sychtyn
Llyn Gwyddior
Melin-y-ddol
Llanfair Caereinion
Sylfaen
Powis Castle
Cemmaes
Nant yr Eira
Bryn y Castell
Mynydd Waun Fawr
Llyn Hir
Welshpool & Llanfair Light Railway
Castle Caereinion
Pwll
Cemmaes Road
Esgair Rriciau
Pandy
Llwynderw
Abercegir
Commins Coch
Tafolwern
Llanbrynmair
Ffridd
Cefn Coch
Manafon
Pant-y-ffridd
Darowen
Dol-fâch
Llanllugan
Tal-y-Wern
Llan
Llanwyddelan
New Mills
(Felin Newydd)
Berriew
(Aberriw)
Bont Dolgadfan
Talerddig
Esgair Cwmowen
Glan-yr-afon
Adfa
Sculpture
Melinbyrhedyn
Moelfre
Mynydd Clogau
Brooks
Garthmyl
Tregynon
Pentre Llifior
Abernosan
Pennant
Brynamlwg
Gwgia
Llyn Mawr
Llyn y Tarw
Fron
Hendomen
Trannon
Carno
Bwlch y Garreg
Bettws Cedewain
A5
A5104
A525
A542
B5105
B5113
B4501
B5437
B5436
B5429
A4212
B4402
B4401
B4391
B4403
B4393
B4396
B4580
B4395
B4382
B4389
B4390
B4385
B4388
B4518
B4386
A458
A470
A489
A490
A495
A483
A543
B4407
B4500
B4392
B4381

71
WREXHAM
(Wrecsam)
CHESHIRE EAST
W R E X H A M
S H R O P S H I R E
WALES
ENGLAND
NANTWICH
Whitchurch
OSWESTRY
(Croesoswallt)
SHREWSBURY
Ellesmere
Wem
Malpas
Ruabon (Rhiwabon)
Rhosllanerchrugog
Chirk
(Y Waun)
Overton (Owrtyn)
Bangor-is-y-coed
Marchwiel
Rhostyllen
Coedpoeth
Minera
Brymbo
Bwlchgwyn
Rhydtalog
Gresford
Holt
Farndon
Acton
Burland
Wrenbury
Aston
Newhall
Penley
Hanmer
Bronington
Welshampton
Bettisfield
Tetchill
Whittington
Gobowen
St. Martin's
Weston Rhyn
Selattyn
Froncysyllte
Cefn-mawr
Acrefair
Penycae
Trevor Uchaf
Pontfadog
Morda
Trefonen
Llanymynech
Pant
Llandysilio
Four Crosses
Llandrinio
Melverley
Knockin
Kinnerley
Ruyton-XI-Towns
Baschurch
Little Ness
Wilcott
Montford
Shrawardine
Alberbury
Ford
Middletown
Wollaston
Westbury
Yockleton
Hanwood
Bayston Hill
Condover
Pontesbury
Minsterley
Worthen
Chirbury
Shelve
Woolstaston
Leebotwood
Church Preen
Hughley
Acton Burnell
Dorrington
Longnor
Cressage
Buildwas
Much Wenlock
Atcham
Upton Magna
Withington
High Ercall
Shawbury
Hadnall
Harlescott
Bomere Heath
Myddle
Burlton
Petton
Cockshutt
Loppington
Clive
Grinshill
Lee Brockhurst
Stanton upon Hine Heath
Hodnet
Marchamley
Prees
Prees Higher Heath
Moreton Say
Bletchley
Grindley Brook
No Man's Heath
Threapwood
Tallarn Green
Shocklach
Tilston
Hopton
Hordley
West Felton
Uppington
Cross Houses
A5
A41
A49
A53
A458
A483
A495
A525
A528
A534
A539
83
59
E
F
G
H
1
2
3
4
5

72
84
71
60
A
B
C
D
1
2
3
4
5
CHESHIRE EAST
SHROPSHIRE
STOKE-ON-TRENT
NEWCASTLE-UNDER-LYME
STAFFORD
TELFORD
WOLVERHAMPTON
WEDNESFIELD
WILLENHALL
BILSTON
STONE
NANTWICH
MARKET DRAYTON
Whitchurch
Alsager
Kidsgrove
Wood
Brindley Ford
Packmoor
Goldenhill
Endon Bank
Brown Edge
Endon
Stanley
Horse Bridge
Cheddleton
Flint Mill
Ridgeway
Norton Green
Tunstall
Norton in the Moors
Stockton Brook
Bagnall
Burslem
Milton
Baddeley Green
Light Oaks
Abbey Hulton
Wetley Rocks
Northwood
Hanley
City Centre
Bucknall
Washerwall
Cellarhead
Werrington
Fenton
Hulme
Roughcote
Weston Coyney
Cookshill
Caverswall
Longton
Meir
Blythe Bridge
Lightwood
Stallington
Meir Heath
Rough Close
Cresswell
Fulford
Crossgate
Mossgate
Barlaston
Oulton
Moddershall
Cotwalton
Meaford
Hilderstone
Garshall Green
Dayhills
Little Stoke
Milwich
Smallrice
Walton
Aston-by-Stone
Norton Bridge
Shallowford
Chebsey
Yarlet
Whitgreave
Sandonbank
Burston
Sandon
Enson
Marston
Salt
Hopton Heath
Hopton
Holmcroft
Doxey
Littleworth
Weeping Cross
Milford
Forebridge
Wildwood
Walton-on-the-Hill
Rickerscote
Hyde Lea
Billington
Coppenhall
Bednall
Acton Trussell
Dunston
Dunston Heath
Levedale
Penkridge
Longridge
Mitton
Bickford
Longnor
Whiston
Congreve
Lapley
Wolgarston
Pillaton
Huntington
Otherton
Oldfallow
Stretton
Gailey
Hatherton
Four Crosses
Great Saredon
Four Ashes
Calf Heath
Slade Heath
Little Saredon
Shareshill
Cross Green
Featherstone
Coven
Coven Heath
Somerford
Standeford
Lower Green
Brewood
Chillington Hall
Park Lane
Gunstone
Bilbrook
Fordhouses
Moseley
Bushbury
Essington
Oxley
Old Fallings
Wood Hayes
Pendeford
Codsall
Oaken
Kingswood Common
Palmers Cross
Wergs
Tettenhall
Pattingham
Dunstall
Heath Town
Wightwick
Bradmore
Trescott
Lower
Blakenhall
Shipley
Dunkirk
Talke
Radway Green
Barthomley
Englesea-brook
Weston
Shavington
Hough
Chorlton
Balterley
Audley
Red Street
Crackley
Bignall End
Halmer End
Miles Green
Chesterton
Wolstanton
Scot Hay
Alsagers Bank
Leycett
Silverdale
Betley
Wrinehill
Madeley Heath
Keele
Madeley
Onneley
Woore
Pipe Gate
Aston
Willoughbridge
Baldwin's Gate
Whitmore
Acton
Hanchurch
Butterton
Shutlanehead
Seabridge
Clayton
Stoke Town
Hanford
Trentham
Blurton
Tittensor
Beech
Beech Caves
Maer
Chapel Chorlton
Cranberry
Swynnerton
Burybank
Cotes
Cotes Heath
Standon
Bowers
Podmore
Chatcull
Walford
Millmeece
Coldmeece
Slindon
Yarnfield
Croxtonbank
Croxton
Brockton
Little Sugnall
Sugnall
Sturbridge
Pershall
Offleyhay
Bishop's Offley
Offleymarsh
Eccleshall
Garmelow
Wootton
Walton
Little Bridgeford
Great Bridgeford
Ellenhall
Broad Heath
Whitley Heath
Knightley
Seighford
Ranton
Coton Clanford
Long Compton
Derrington
Ranton Green
Shut Heath
Audmore
Haughton
Gnosall
Gnosall Heath
Coton
Cowley
Allimore Green
Bradley
Apeton
Wood Eaton
Church Eaton
Little Onn
High Onn
Orslow
Marston
Brineton
Wheaton Aston
Blymhill
Blymhill Lawns
Ivetsey Bank
Weston under Lizard
Burlington
Kiddemore Green
Shutt Green
Horsebrook
Bishops Wood
Coldham
Boscobel House
White Ladies Priory
Shackerley
Tong
Tong Norton
Tong Forge
Crackleybank
Redhill
Priorslee
Haughton
Stafford Park
Shifnal
Hollinswood
Malinslee
Dawley
Stirchley
The Wyke
The Hem
Little Dawley
Horsehay
Tweedale
Madeley
Kemberton
Brockton
Grindle
Ryton
Donington
Cosford
Albrighton
Whiston Cross
Boningale
Beckbury
Burnhill Green
Ackleton
Stableford
Higford
Norton
Stockton
Sutton Maddock
Coalport
Jackfield
Blists Hill
Broseley
Benthall
Ironbridge
Coalbrookdale
Buildwas
Sheinton
Leighton
Cressage
Harley
Homer
Farley
Wyke
Much Wenlock
Barrow
Willey
Linley
Colemore Green
Ewdness
Newton
Nordley
Astley
Allscott
Worfield
Rudge
Chesterton
The Smithies
Atterley
Callaughton
Bourton
Mucklev
Stretton Westwood
Hughley
Kenley
The Bank
Presthope
Eyton on Severn
Dryton
Garmston
Eaton Constantine
Little Wenlock
Upper Longwood
Rushton
Huntington
Lawley
Cluddley
Aston
Uppington
Wroxeter Roman City
Donnington
Uckington
Norton
Charlton
Leaton
Wellington
Arleston
Walcot
Upton Magna
Wrockwardine
Admaston
Hadley
Oakengates
Trench
Leegomery
Hortonwood
Donnington
Muxton
Lilleshall
Honnington
Heath Hill
Lilyhurst
Sheriffhales
Weston Heath
Chadwell
Great Chatwell
Lynn
Stockton
Moreton
Bromstead Heath
Beffcote
Outwoods
Pave Lane
Chetwynd Aston
Cheswell
Brockton
Church Aston
Longford
Newport
Edgmond
Adeney
Kynnersley
Preston upon the Weald Moors
Eyton upon the Weald Moors
Long Lane
Bratton
Shawbirch
Marsh Green
Isombridge
Withington
Rodington
Rodington Heath
Longdon on Tern
Roden
Crudgington
Rodway
Moortown
Waters Upton
Rowton
Cherrington
Tibberton
Edgmond Marsh
Islington
Meretown
Aqualate Mere
Cotonwood
Sutton
Forton
Oulton
Norbury
Weston Jones
Puleston
Pickstock
Standford Bridge
Sambrook
Howle
Meeson
Great Bolas
Little Bolas
Cold Hatton
Cold Hatton Heath
Ellerdine
Ellerdine Heath
Eaton upon Tern
High Hatton
Ollerton
Peplow
Child's Ercall
The Marsh
Hinstock
Ellerton
Shebdon
High Offley
Woodseaves
Grub Street
Littleworth
Lawnhead
Knightley Dale
Adbaston
Tunstall
Knighton
Woodlane
Lockleywood
Little Soudley
Soudley
Goldstone
Doley
Outlands
Lipley
Cheswardine
Chipnall
The Four Alls
Woodseaves
Rosehill
Hungryhatton
Mill Green
Stoke on Tern
Wistanswick
Stoke Heath
Hodnet
Hodnet Hall
Wollerton
Tern Hill
Sutton
Little Drayton
Ternhill
Bletchley
Moreton Say
Longford
Longslow
Brownhills
Almington
Hales
Hookgate
Loggerheads
Ashley
Ashley Heath
Gerrard's Bromley
Broughton
Wetwood
Fairoak
Mucklestone
Winnington
Betton
Blackbrook
Ridgwardine
Norton in Hales
Knighton
Bearstone
Adderley
Calverhall
Newstreet Lane
Cloverley Pool
Coxbank
Kinsey Heath
Lightwood Green
Royal's Green
Wilkesley
Audlem
Buerton
Hankelow
Bridgemere
Bridgemere Garden World
Checkley
Doddington Castle
Blakenhall
Hatherton
Walgherton
Wybunbury
Stapeley
Butt Green
Willaston
Wistaston
Wells Green
Stoneley Green
Ravensmoor
Burland
Acton
Brindley
Faddiley
Larden Green
Chorley
Sound
Broomhall
Hack Green Secret Nuclear Bunker
Wrenbury
Aston
Norbury
Marley Green
Pinsley Green
Marbury
Newhall
Hollyhurst
Burleydam
Broughall
Edgeley
Ash Magna
Ash Parva
Ightfield
Tilstock
Prees Higher Heath
Sandford
Prees
Darliston
Fauls
Prees Green
Marchamley
Weston
Wixhill
Kenstone
Moston
Hopton
Booley
Stanton upon Hine Heath
Moreton Corbet
Morton Mill
Edgebolton
Muckleton
Great Wytheford
Poynton Green
Poynton
Walton
High Ercall
Green Lane
M6
M54
A534
A49
A530
A529
A51
A500
A5020
A531
A525
A53
A34
A52
A520
A5009
A50
A5035
A5005
B5029
A519
A5013
A513
A518
A449
A41
A442
A5
A464
A4169
A458
A460
A454
A5026
B5026
B5027
B5066
B5062
B5063
B5065
B4394
B4380
B4371
B4375
B4376
B4373
B4379
B4176
B5314
B5405
B5415
B5044
B5367
B5500
B5077
B5078
B5061
KEELE
STAFFORD NORTH
STAFFORD SOUTH
HILTON PARK
Stafford Castle
Izaak Walton's Cottage
Gentleshaw Wildlife Centre
Cop Mere
Devil's Ring & Finger
Dorothy Clive
Weston Park
Belvide Resr
The Wrekin
Wenlock Priory
Benthall Hall
Wonderland
Tar Tunnel
Jackfield Tile
Wedgwood
Trentham
Gladstone Pottery
Foxfield Steam Railway
Staffordshire County Showground
Shropshire Union Canal
Staffs. & Worc. Canal
Whitmore Hall
Betley Mere
Monument
Hoo Farm
Chetwynd
RAF Cosford
The Pool
The Great Pool
Royal Oak
Mosty Lea Watermill
Hawk Lake
Hawkstone Park & Follies
Combermere
Oss Mere
Dorfold Hall
Berry Ring
Mill Meece Pumping Station
Castle

73
Onecote
Grindon
Parwich
Brassington
Wirksworth
Crich
Ashbourne
Tissington
Waterhouses
Ipstones
Cauldon
Kniveton
Mapleton
Froghall
Kingsley
Cotton
Stanton
Mayfield
Hulland
BELPER
Cheadle
Oakamoor
Ramshorn
Church Mayfield
Clifton
Osmaston
Ellastone
Alton
Denstone
Rocester
Duffield
Brailsford
DERBYSHIRE
Allestree
Upper Tean
Great Gate
Stubwood
Hollington
Yeaveley
Rodsley
Kirk Langley
Chaddesden
Marston Montgomery
Longford
Mackworth
Mickleover
Church Leigh
Somersal Herbert
Church Broughton
Sutton on the Hill
DERBY
Uttoxeter
Doveridge
Sudbury
Etwall
Marchington
Hatton
Hilton
Findern
Chellaston
Tutbury
Rolleston on Dove
Willington
Stretton
Repton
Newborough
Abbots Bromley
Horninglow
BURTON UPON TRENT
NEEDWOOD
FOREST
Shobnall
Winshill
Stapenhill
Newhall
Great Haywood
Colwich
Little Haywood
Colton
Hamstall Ridware
Yoxall
Barton-under-Needwood
Branston
SWADLINCOTE
RUGELEY
CANNOCK CHASE
Walton-on-Trent
Ashby-de-la-Zouch
Brereton
Armitage
Handsacre
Kings Bromley
Alrewas
Fradley
Linton
Overseal
Hazelslade
Cannock Wood
Hednesford
Netherseal
Measham
CANNOCK
LICHFIELD
Elford
Clifton Campville
Heath Hayes
Chase Terrace
Burntwood
Boney Hay
Chorley
Leamonsley
Whittington
Thorpe Constantine
Appleby Magna
Newton Burgoland
Norton Canes
Chasetown
Great Wyrley
BROWNHILLS
Hopwas
Newton Regis
Austrey
Walsall Wood
Shenstone
Weeford
TAMWORTH
Polesworth
Twycross
BLOXWICH
Fazeley
Sheepy Magna
Rushall
ALDRIDGE
Drayton Bassett
Dordon
WALSALL
Streetly
Wood End
Grendon Common
Baddesley Ensor
ATHERSTONE
M6
M6 TOLL
M42
A38
A5
A50
A52
A515
A444
85
61
74

74
73
NOTTINGHAMSHIRE
DERBYSHIRE
LEICESTERSHIRE
CHARNWOOD FOREST
NOTTINGHAM
DERBY
LEICESTER
LOUGHBOROUGH
HUCKNALL
ARNOLD
CARLTON
BEESTON
WEST BRIDGFORD
STAPLEFORD
LONG EATON
ILKESTON
EASTWOOD
HEANOR
BELPER
COALVILLE
WIGSTON
ATHERSTONE
Ripley
Somercotes
Ravenshead
Southwell
Calverton
Bulwell
Kimberley
Nuthall
Bingham
Radcliffe on Trent
Cotgrave
Ruddington
Clifton
Keyworth
East Leake
Kegworth
Castle Donington
Melbourne
Spondon
Chellaston
Allestree
Duffield
Chaddesden
Sandiacre
Draycott
Breaston
Shepshed
Whitwick
Quorn
Mountsorrel
Barrow upon Soar
Sileby
Syston
Thurmaston
Birstall
Anstey
Glenfield
Ibstock
Market Bosworth
Oadby
Blaby
Earl Shilton
Barwell
Ashby-de-la-Zouch
Measham
Twycross
Braunstone Town
Hinckley
M1
A52
A6
A38
A42
A50
A46
A60
A453
A606
A607
A511
A512
A610
A6006
A6097
M69
EAST MIDLANDS
DONINGTON PARK
SHARDLOW
TROWELL
LEICESTER (MARKFIELD)
LEICESTER FOREST EAST

75
87
63
LINCOLNSHIRE
RUTLAND
NEWARK-ON-TRENT
GRANTHAM
MELTON MOWBRAY
STAMFORD
Sleaford
Bourne
Oakham
Uppingham
Upton
Staythorpe
Averham
Coddington
Beckingham
Brant Broughton
Welbourn
Digby
Billing
Bloxholm
Dorrington
Temple Bruer Tower
Rolleston
Farndon
New Balderton
Barnby in the Willows
Stragglethorpe
Leadenham
Fiskerton
Hawton
Balderton
Fenton
Fulbeck
Cranwell
Ruskington
Leasingham
Anwick
East Stoke
Thorpe
Stubton
Claypole
Elston
Syerston
Cotham
Brandon
Caythorpe
Frieston
Dry Doddington
North Rauceby
South Rauceby
Holdingham
Evedon
Ewerby
Kirkby la Thorpe
Howell
Asgarby
Flintham
Sibthorpe
Shelton
Hough-on-the-Hill
Gelston
Normanton
Carlton Scroop
Sudbrook
Ancaster
Cogglesford Watermill
Quarrington
Screveton
Hawksworth
Staunton in the Vale
Long Bennington
Westborough
Hougham
Marston
Honington
West Willoughby
Wilsford
Silk Willoughby
Heckington
Burton Pedwardine
Thoroton
Flawborough
Kilvington
Foston
Scarrington
Alverton
Barkston Heath
Barkston
Kelby
Orston
Normanton
Allington
Syston
Culverthorpe
Heydour
Swarby
Scredington
Aswarby
Northbeck
Thorpe Latimer
Whatton
Elton
Bottesford
Easthorpe
Grantham North
Great Gonerby
Manthorpe
Belton
Belton House NT
Londonthorpe
Welby
Oasby
Aisby
Aunsby
Osbournby
Spanby
Swaton
Sutton
Muston
Sedgebrook
Dembleby
Gonerby Hill Foot
Grantham House NT
Earlesfield
Barrowby
Stenwith
Redmile
Granby
Barnstone
Barkestone-le-Vale
Naturescape
Plungar
Woolsthorpe By Belvoir
Belvoir
Denton
Denton Resr.
Harlaxton
Old Somerby
Ropsley
Braceby
Haceby
Newton
Walcot
Threekingham
Sapperton
Pickworth
Folkingham
Stow
Horbling
Billingborough
Birthorpe
Sempringham
Woodnook
Little Ponton
Humby
Hanby
Laughton
Pointon
Little Wisbeach
Knipton
Harston
Stathern
Harby
Knipton Resr.
Stroxton
Boothby Pagnell
Norman Manor House
Lenton
Ingoldsby
Aslackby
Millthorpe
Great Ponton
Hungerton
Wyville
Hose
Eastwell
Eaton
Branston
Croxton Kerrial
Water Spout
Bassingthorpe
Westby
Bitchfield
Keisby
Dowsby
Graby
Rippingale
Stoke Rochford
Easton
Walled
Burton Coggles
Irnham
Hawthorpe
Bulby
Kirkby Underwood
Dunsby
Goadby Marwood
Bescaby
Saltby
Skillington
Waltham on the Wolds
Woolsthorpe-by-Colsterworth
Woolsthorpe Manor NT
Colsterworth
Willoughby Memorial Trust
Corby Glen
Stainfield
Hacconby
Morton
Scalford
Chadwell
Stonesby
Sproxton
Elsthorpe
Hanthorpe
Holwell
Potter Hill
Buckminster
Stainby
Birkholme
Swayfield
Swinstead
Grimsthorpe
Grimsthorpe Castle
Dyke
Cawthorpe
Twinlakes Theme Park
Coston
Sewstern
Gunby
North Witham
Edenham
Scottlethorpe
Thorpe Arnold
Garthorpe
Freeby
Saxby
Wyfordby
Brentingby
Stapleford
Wymondham
South Witham
Creeton
Thistleton
Castle Bytham
Little Bytham
Lound
Northorpe
Burton Lazars
Edmondthorpe
Market Overton
Clipsham
Stretton
Careby
Toft
Manthorpe
Witham on the Hill
Thurlby
Obthorpe
Great Dalby
Teigh
Cottesmore
Barrow
Rutland Railway
Whissendine
Ashwell
Aunby
Carlby
Thetford
Baston
Little Dalby
Greetham
Lime Kiln
Pickworth
Wilsthorpe
Braceborough
Burley Castle
Essendine
Greatford
Langtoft
Thorpe Satchville
Pickwell
Somerby
Burrough on the Hill
Langham
Burley
Exton
Ryhall
Belmesthorpe
Barnsdale
Little Casterton
Barholm
Towngate
Cold Overton
Barleythorpe
Vale of Catmose
Tickencote
Great Casterton
Deeping Gate
Marefield
Owston
Knossington
Drought Gdn. & Arboretum
Whitwell
Empingham
Ingthorpe
Uffington
West Deeping
Maxey
Braunston-in-Rutland
Rutland County
Egleton
Upper Hambleton
Tinwell
Tallington
Etton
Halstead
Rutland Water
Normanton Church
Bainton
Pilsgate
Ashton
Burghley
Tilton on the Hill
Brooke
Edith Weston
Easton on the Hill
Wothorpe
Barnack
Helpston
Manton
Lyndon
North Luffenham
Ketton
Aldgate
Geeston
Priest's House NT
White Water Resr.
Hills & Holes
Ufford
Clare Cottage
Wing
Pilton
Collyweston
Southorpe
Ridlington
Preston
Turf Maze
South Luffenham
Wittering
Keffington
Loddington
Belton-in-Rutland
Morcott
Duddington
Marholm
Tugby
East Norton
Ayston
Thornhaugh
Sacrewell Farm
Rolleston
Allexton
Wardley
Glaston
Barrowden
Tixover
Upton
Noseley
Goadby
Bisbrooke
Wakerley
Wansford
Ailsworth
Castor
Stibbington
Sutton
Nene Valley Railway
Water Newton
Orton
Wistow
Alwalton
Hallaton
Horninghold
Stockerston
Stoke Dry
Seaton
Lyddington
Lyddington Bede House
Viaduct
Harringworth
King's Cliffe
Laxton
Thorpe
Yarwell
Sibson
Peterborough
Glooston
Blatherwycke
Nassington
Fotheringhay
A1
A15
A17
A46
A52
A151
A153
A606
A607
A6003
A6006
A6121
A47
A43
A1175
B1429
B1209
B1188
B1191
B1394
B1517
B1518
B1397
B1177
B1176
B1174
B6403
B6326
B676
B668
B640
B1081
B1443
B672
B6047
B1193
B1524

76
88
64
Digby
Billinghay
Dogdyke
Chapel Hill
Hundle Houses
New York
Bunkers Hill
Lade Bank
Dorrington
North Kyme
Haven Bank
West Fen
Northlands
Leake Common Side
Sibsey Fen Side
Frithville
Sibsey
Old Leake
Wrangle
Wrangle Lowgate
Anwick
South Kyme
Leasingham
Holland Fen
Bubble Car
Gipsey Bridge
Langrick
Fishtoft Drove
Anton's Gowt
High Ferry
Leake Hurn's End
Leverton Outgate
Evedon
Ewerby
Amber Hill
Frith Bank
Hilldyke
Leverton
West End
Benington
Leverton Lucasgate
Benington Sea End
Howell
Kirkby la Thorpe
Asgarby
Brothertoft
Burton Corner
Haltoft End
Butterwick
Sleaford
Quarrington
East Heckington
Garwick
Swineshead Bridge
Hubbert's Bridge
BOSTON
Skirbeck
Brand End
Freiston
Heckington
Great Hale
Burton Pedwardine
Silk Willoughby
Little Hale
North End
Baythorpe
Kirton Holme
Frampton West End
Chain Bridge
Skirbeck Quarter
Fishtoft
Tamworth Green
Freiston Shore
Scrane End
Northbeck
Helpringham
Wyberton
Kirton End
Fenhouses
Scredington
Thorpe Latimer
Swineshead
Drayton
Blackjack
Frampton
Aswarby
Osbournby
Spanby
Bicker Gauntlet
Bicker Bar
Kirton
Swaton
Bicker
Asperton
Strugg's Hill
Sandholme
Skeldyke
Hoffleet Stow
Wigtoft
Sutterton
Northorpe
Donington Eaudike
Donington
Seadyke
Bucklegate
Threekingham
Stow
Bridge End
Horbling
Walcot
Burtoft
Algarkirk
Church End
Billingborough
Donington South Ing
Fosdyke
Birthorpe
Sempringham
Quadring Eaudike
Sutterton Dowdyke
Quadring
Holbeach St. Matthew
Laughton
Pointon
Little Wisbeach
LINCOLNSHIRE
Gosberton
Westhorpe
Aslackby
Millthorpe
Holbeach St. Marks
Risegate
Belnie
Wargate
Dowsby
Graby
Gosberton Cheal
Surfleet Seas End
Holbeach Marsh
Dawsmere
Gosberton Clough
Surfleet
Gedney Drove End
Rippingale
Moulton Seas End
Saracen's Head
Holbeach Bank
Holbeach Hurn
Black Barn
Kirkby Underwood
Dunsby
Pinchbeck
Wykeham
Halesgate
Penny Hill
Gedney Dyke
Sutton Corner
Northgate
Holbeach Clough
Loosegate
Fleet Hargate
Stainfield
Haconby
Pinchbeck Bars
Weston
Lutton
Lutton Gowts
Chapelgate
Hanthorpe
Morton
Pinchbeck West
Moulton
Whaplode
Holbeach
Long Sutton
SPALDING
Fulney
Springfields
Fleet
Gedney
Little London
Dyke
Grimsthorpe
Cawthorpe
Clay Lake
Low Fulney
Gedney Broadgate
Garnsgate
Little Sutton
Guthram Gowt
Pode Hole
Bourne
Twenty
Little London
Fen End
Clark's Hill
Sutton Crosses
Weston Hills
Whaplode St. Catherine
Tydd St. Mary
Tydd Gote
Tongue End
Lound
Northorpe
Cowbit
Moulton Chapel
Holbeach St. Johns
Sutton St. James
Four Anchor
Toft
Peak Hill
Fenland
Tydd St. Giles
Four Gotes
Manthorpe
Thurlby
Moulton Eaugate
Obthorpe
Deeping Fen
Deeping St. Nicholas
Thetford
Baston
Brotherhouse Bar
Newton
Wilsthorpe
Braceborough
Hop Pole
Crowland
Postland
Whaplode Drove
Sutton St. Edmund
Fitton End
Greatford
Langtoft
Holbeach Drove
Leverington
Gorefield
Market Deeping
Shepeau Stow
Gedney Hill
Barholm
Towngate
Frognall
Crowland
Dowsdale
Cranmore
Trinity Bridge
Throckenholt
Church End
WISBECH
Deeping Gate
Deeping St. James
West Deeping
Nene Terrace
North Fen
Sutton St. Edmund's Common
Parson Drove
Uffington
Tallington
Maxey
Northborough
Murrow
Bunker's Hill
Wisbech St. Mary
Elm
Etton
Morris Fen
Glinton
Peakirk
Newborough
Wryde Croft
Tholomas Drove
Pilsgate
Bainton
Ashton
Helpston
Rogue's Alley
Begdale
Barnack
Ufford
BEDFORD (NORTH LEVEL)
Eye Green
Thorney
Thorney Toll
Guyhirn Gull
Guyhirn
Southorpe
Werrington
Gunthorpe
Walton
Eye
Ring's End
Coldham
Marholm
Bretton
Thornhaugh
New England
Dogsthorpe
Newark
Stone Bridge Corner
Upton
Chainbridge
Wansford
Stibbington
Ailsworth
Longthorpe
Westwood
Millfield
PETERBOROUGH
Eldernell
West Fen
Norwoodside
Sutton
Castor
Coates
Westry
March
Yarwell
Water Newton
Orton Waterville
Woodston
Stanground
Eastrea
Oldeamere
West End
Sibson
Alwalton
Old Fletton
Whittlesey
A15
A17
A52
A16
A151
A1121
A152
A1175
A153
A1101
A141
A47
A1
A605
A1139
A6121
B1192
B1183
B1184
B1395
B1209
B1517
B1391
B1397
B1357
B1356
B1180
B1172
B1165
B1168
B1166
B1167
B1187
B1169
B1390
B1359
B1040
B1443
B1524
B1525
B1177
B1394
B1193

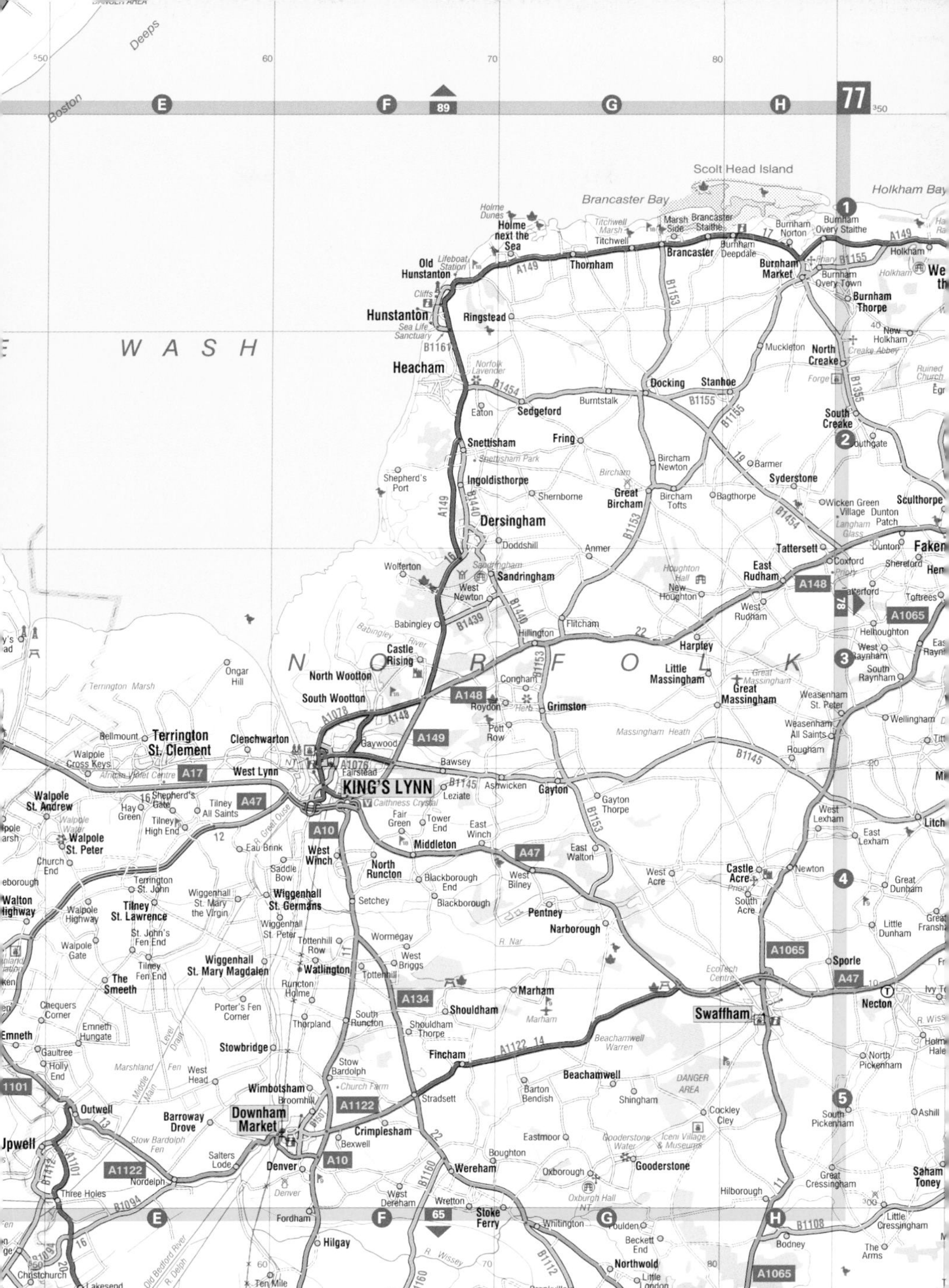
Boston Deeps
W A S H
N O R F O L K
Scolt Head Island
Brancaster Bay
Holkham Bay
Holme next the Sea
Old Hunstanton
Hunstanton
Heacham
Thornham
Brancaster
Burnham Market
Burnham Thorpe
North Creake
South Creake
Docking
Stanhoe
Ringstead
Sedgeford
Snettisham
Ingoldisthorpe
Dersingham
Sandringham
Fring
Great Bircham
Syderstone
Sculthorpe
Tattersett
East Rudham
Castle Rising
North Wootton
South Wootton
Hillington
Harpley
Little Massingham
Great Massingham
Grimston
Terrington St. Clement
Clenchwarton
West Lynn
KING'S LYNN
Gayton
Walpole St. Andrew
Walpole St. Peter
Middleton
West Winch
North Runcton
Wiggenhall St. Germans
Tilney St. Lawrence
Wiggenhall St. Mary Magdalen
The Smeeth
Watlington
Marham
Shouldham
Pentney
Narborough
Castle Acre
Swaffham
Sporle
Necton
Stowbridge
Fincham
Beachamwell
Outwell
Barroway Drove
Downham Market
Crimplesham
Denver
Wereham
Gooderstone
Stoke Ferry
Hilgay
Northwold
Saham Toney
A149
A148
A17
A47
A10
A134
A1122
A1065
B1153
B1155
B1454
B1145
B1440
B1439
B1161
B1355
B1108
B1160
B1112
B1094
89
65
78

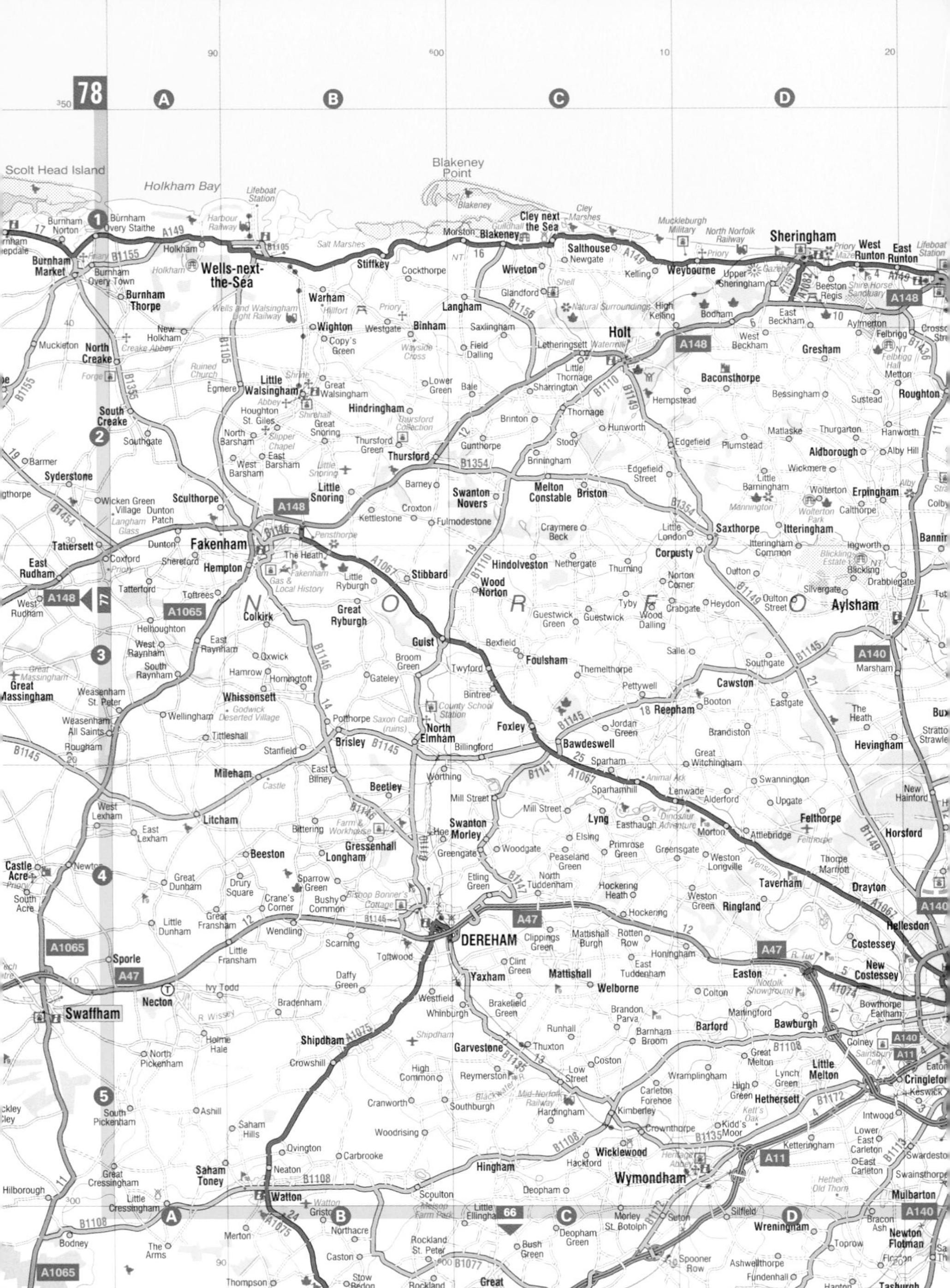
78
A
B
C
D
90
600
10
20
350
Scolt Head Island
Holkham Bay
Blakeney Point
Lifeboat Station
Harbour Railway
Blakeney
Cley Marshes
Muckleburgh Military
North Norfolk Railway
Burnham Overy Staithe
Burnham Norton
Burnham Market
Burnham Overy Town
Burnham Thorpe
Holkham
Wells-next-the-Sea
Salt Marshes
Stiffkey
Morston
Blakeney
Cley next the Sea
Salthouse
Newgate
Kelling
Weybourne
Sheringham
Upper Sheringham
West Runton
East Runton
Lifeboat Station
Beeston Regis
Shire Horse Sanctuary
Cockthorpe
Wiveton
Glandford
Shell
Natural Surroundings
High Kelling
Bodham
East Beckham
Aylmerton
Felbrigg
Cromer
Warham
Langham
Wighton
Westgate
Binham
Saxlingham
Letheringsett
Holt
West Beckham
Gresham
Wells and Walsingham Light Railway
Copy's Green
Wayside Cross
Field Dalling
New Holkham
Muckleton
North Creake
Creake Abbey
Forge
Ruined Church
Egmere
Little Walsingham
Great Walsingham
Lower Green
Bale
Little Thornage
Sharrington
Baconsthorpe
Hempstead
Bessingham
Sustead
Roughton
Houghton St. Giles
Shirehall
Hindringham
Thursford Collection
Brinton
Thornage
Hunworth
Matlaske
Thurgarton
Hanworth
South Creake
Southgate
North Barsham
Slipper Chapel
Great Snoring
Thursford Green
Thursford
Gunthorpe
Stody
Edgefield
Plumstead
Aldborough
Alby Hill
Barmer
Syderstone
West Barsham
East Barsham
Little Snoring
Briningham
Edgefield Street
Wickmere
Little Barningham
Wolterton
Erpingham
Barney
Swanton Novers
Melton Constable
Briston
Mannington
Wolterton Park
Calthorpe
Wicken Green Village
Dunton Patch
Sculthorpe
Croxton
Kettlestone
Fulmodestone
Craymere Beck
Little London
Saxthorpe
Itteringham
Langham Glass
Tattersett
Dunton
Fakenham
Pensthorpe
Corpusty
Itteringham Common
Ingworth
Blickling Estate
Blickling
East Rudham
Coxford Priory
Sherford
Hempton
The Heath
Gas & Local History
Fakenham
Little Ryburgh
Stibbard
Hindolveston
Nethergate
Thurning
Norton Corner
Oulton
Drabblegate
Silvergate
West Rudham
Tatterford
Toftrees
Colkirk
Great Ryburgh
Wood Norton
Tyby
Wood Dalling
Crabgate
Heydon
Oulton Street
Aylsham
NORFOLK
Helhoughton
East Raynham
West Raynham
South Raynham
Oxwick
Hamrow
Horningtoft
Guist
Bexfield
Guestwick Green
Guestwick
Salle
Broom Green
Gateley
Twyford
Foulsham
Themelthorpe
Southgate
Marsham
Great Massingham
Weasenham St. Peter
Whissonsett
Bintree
Pettywell
Cawston
Booton
Eastgate
Wellingham
Godwick Deserted Village
County School Station
Weasenham All Saints
Tittleshall
Potthorpe
Saxon Cath. (ruins)
North Elmham
Foxley
Jordan Green
Reepham
The Heath
Brandiston
Rougham
Stanfield
Brisley
Billingford
Bawdeswell
Hevingham
Great Witchingham
Mileham
Castle
East Bilney
Worthing
Sparham
Beetley
Mill Street
Sparhamhill
Animal Ark
Lenwade
Alderford
Swannington
Upgate
New Hainford
West Lexham
Litcham
Mill Street
Lyng
Dinosaur Adventure
Easthaugh
Morton
Attlebridge
Felthorpe
Horsford
East Lexham
Bittering
Farm & Workhouse
Hoe
Swanton Morley
Elsing
Primrose Green
Greengate
Weston Longville
Wensum
Thorpe Marriott
Beeston
Gressenhall
Longham
Greengate
Woodgate
Peaseland Green
Castle Acre
Priory
Newton
Great Dunham
Drury Square
Sparrow Green
Etling Green
North Tuddenham
Hockering Heath
Weston Green
Ringland
Taverham
Drayton
South Acre
Crane's Corner
Bushy Common
Bishop Bonner's Cottage
Hockering
Hellesdon
Little Dunham
Great Fransham
Wendling
Scarning
DEREHAM
Clippings Green
Mattishall Burgh
Rotten Row
Honingham
Costessey
Little Fransham
Toftwood
Clint Green
East Tuddenham
Easton
New Costessey
Sporle
Swaffham
Necton
Ivy Todd
Daffy Green
Yaxham
Mattishall
Welborne
Colton
Norfolk Showground
Marlingford
Bowthorpe
Earlham
Bradenham
Westfield
Whinburgh
Brakefield Green
Brandon Parva
Barford
Bawburgh
R. Wissey
Holme Hale
Shipdham
Garvestone
Thuxton
Runhall
Barnham Broom
Colney
North Pickenham
Crowshill
High Common
Reymerston
Low Street
Coston
Great Melton
Little Melton
Lynch Green
Cringleford
Keswick
Wramplingham
Blackwater R.
Mid-Norfolk Railway
Carleton Forehoe
High Green
Hethersett
South Pickenham
Ashill
Cranworth
Southburgh
Hardingham
Kimberley
Kett's Oak
Kidd's Moor
Intwood
Saham Hills
Woodrising
Crownthorpe
Lower East Carleton
Ovington
Carbrooke
Wicklewood
Heritage Abbey
Ketteringham
Swardeston
Great Cressingham
Saham Toney
Neaton
Hingham
Hackford
Wymondham
East Carleton
Swainsthorpe
Hilborough
Watton
Scoulton
Deopham
Hethel Old Thorn
Mulbarton
Little Cressingham
Griston
Wayland Farm Park
Little Ellingham
Morley St. Botolph
Silfield
Wreningham
Bracon Ash
Newton Flotman
Bodney
Merton
Northacre
Rockland St. Peter
Deopham Green
Bush Green
Spooner Row
Toprow
The Arms
Caston
Ashwellthorpe
Fundenhall
Flordon
Thompson
Stow Bedon
Rockland
Great Ellingham
Hapton
Tasburgh
A149
A148
A1065
A47
A1067
A1075
A140
A11
A1074
A1082
B1155
B1105
B1156
B1355
B1110
B1149
B1354
B1454
B1146
B1145
B1147
B1110
B1108
B1135
B1172
B1113
B1436
B1077
B1145
A148 77
66

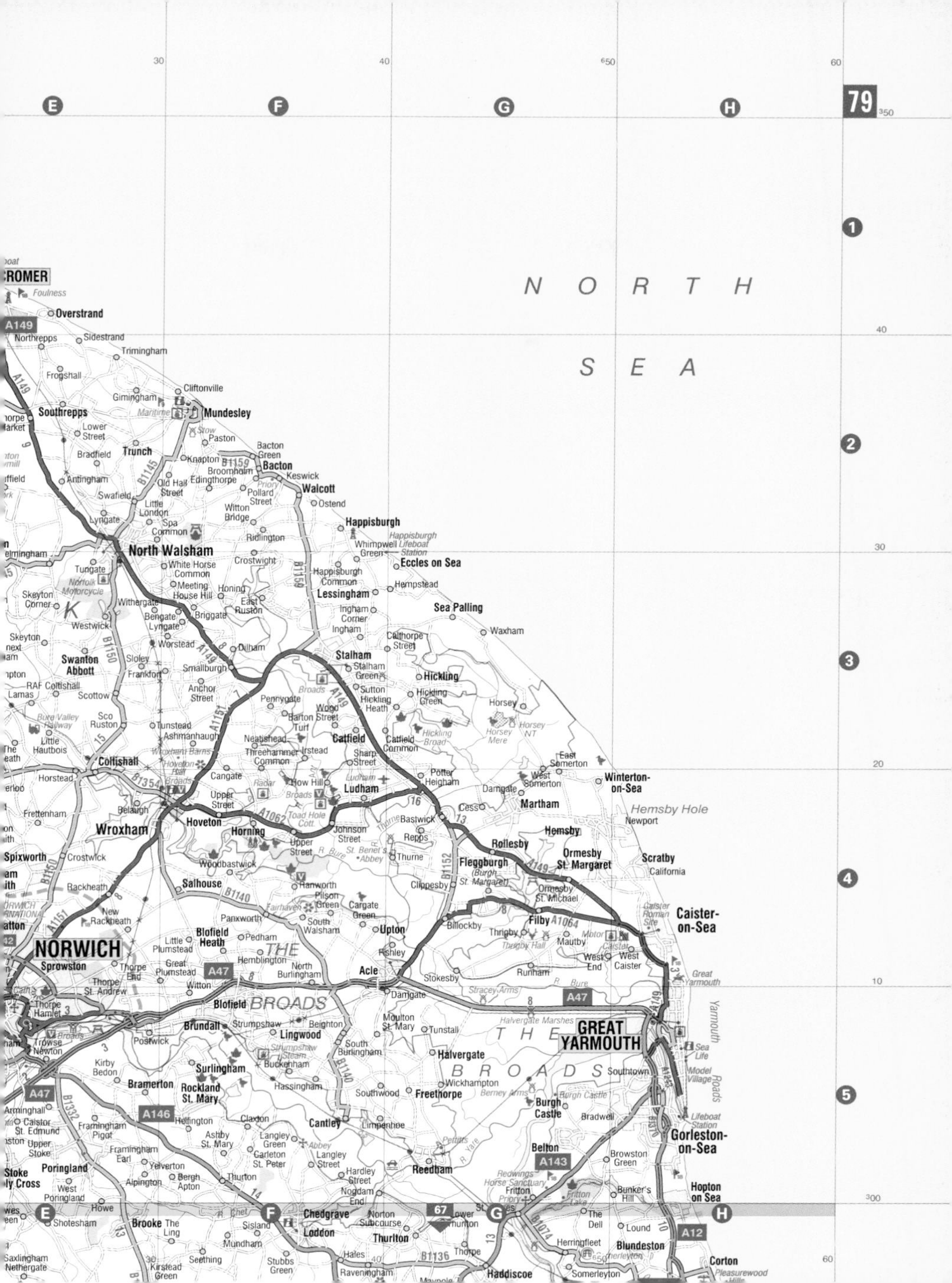

30
40
650
60
E
F
G
H
350
1
2
3
4
5
NORTH SEA
40
30
20
10
300
CROMER
Foulness
Overstrand
A149
Northrepps
Sidestrand
Trimingham
Frogshall
Cliftonville
Gimingham
Mundesley
Maritime
Southrepps
Lower Street
Stow
Paston
Bacton Green
Bradfield
Trunch
Knapton
B1159
Bacton
Broomholm
Keswick
Antingham
B1145
Old Hall Street
Edingthorpe
Priory
Walcott
Swafield
Pollard Street
Ostend
Little London
Witton Bridge
Lyngate
Spa Common
Happisburgh
Ridlington
Happisburgh Lifeboat Station
Whimpwell Green
North Walsham
Tungate
White Horse Common
Crostwight
Eccles on Sea
Norfolk Motorcycle
Happisburgh Common
Hempstead
Skeyton Corner
Meeting House Hill
Honing
Lessingham
Withergate
East Ruston
Sea Palling
Westwick
Bengate
Briggate
Ingham Corner
Lyngate
Ingham
Waxham
Skeyton
Worstead
Calthorpe Street
Swanton Abbott
Dilham
Stalham
Sloley
Smallburgh
Stalham Green
Frankfort
Hickling
RAF Coltishall
Scottow
Anchor Street
Sutton
Hickling Green
Lamas
Broads
Pennygate
Hickling Heath
Horsey
Bure Valley Railway
Sco Ruston
Wood Street
Barton Turf
Tunstead
Horsey NT
Little Hautbois
Ashmanhaugh
Neatishead
Catfield
Catfield Common
Hickling Broad
Horsey Mere
Coltishall
Wroxham Barns
Threehammer Common
Irstead
Sharp Street
East Somerton
Winterton-on-Sea
Horstead
Hoveton Hall
Cangate
Radar
How Hill
Ludham
Potter Heigham
West Somerton
Damgate
B1354
Broads
Belaugh
Upper Street
Toad Hole Cott.
Cess
Martham
Hemsby Hole
Newport
Frettenham
Wroxham
Hoveton
A1062
Horning
Johnson Street
Bastwick
Repps
Hemsby
Spixworth
Crostwick
Upper Street
R. Bure
St. Benet's Abbey
Thurne
Rollesby
Ormesby St. Margaret
Scratby
California
Woodbastwick
B1152
Fleggburgh (Burgh St. Margaret)
A149
Rackheath
Salhouse
Ranworth
Clippesby
Ormesby St. Michael
B1140
Pilson Green
Caister Roman Site
Caister-on-Sea
New Rackheath
Fairhaven
Cargate Green
South Walsham
Panxworth
Billockby
Filby
A1064
Thrigby
Thrigby Hall
Mautby
Motor
Caister
NORWICH
Little Plumstead
Blofield Heath
Pedham
Upton
THE
Fishley
West End
West Caister
Sprowston
Thorpe End
Great Plumstead
Hemblington
North Burlingham
Acle
Great Yarmouth
Thorpe St. Andrew
A47
Witton
Stokesby
Runham
R. Bure
Damgate
Stracey Arms
A47
Thorpe Hamlet
Blofield
BROADS
Brundall
Strumpshaw
Beighton
Moulton St. Mary
Tunstall
Halvergate Marshes
THE
GREAT YARMOUTH
Yarmouth
Trowse Newton
Postwick
Lingwood
Strumpshaw Steam
South Burlingham
Halvergate
Sea Life
Kirby Bedon
Surlingham
Buckenham
B1140
BROADS
Southtown
Model Village
Roads
Bramerton
Rockland St. Mary
Hassingham
Wickhampton
A47
Southwood
Freethorpe
Berney Arms
Burgh Castle
Arminghall
B1332
A146
Burgh Castle
Bradwell
Caistor St. Edmund
Framingham Pigot
Helllington
Claxton
Cantley
Limpenhoe
Lifeboat Station
Upper Stoke
Ashby St. Mary
Langley Green
Abbey
Gorleston-on-Sea
Framingham Earl
Carleton St. Peter
Langley Street
Pettitts
R. Yare
Belton
A143
Browston Green
Stoke Holy Cross
Poringland
Yelverton
Hardley Street
Reedham
Redwings Horse Sanctuary
West Poringland
Alpington
Bergh Apton
Thurton
Nogdam End
Fritton
Fritton Lake
Bunker's Hill
Hopton on Sea
Howe
Priory
Shotesham
Brooke
The Ling
R. Chet
Sisland
Chedgrave
Norton Subcourse
67
Lower Thurlton
St. Olaves
The Dell
Lound
A12
Mundham
Loddon
Thurlton
B1074
Herringfleet
Blundeston
Saxlingham Nethergate
Seething
Hales
B1136
Thorpe
Somerleyton
Kirstead Green
Stubbs Green
Ravenningham
Haddiscoe
Corton
Pleasurewood Hill

Holyhead to
Dublin 3hrs. 15mins.
Dublin 1hr. 50mins.
(Fast Ferry)
Dun Laoghaire 1hr. 50mins.
(Fast Ferry. Seasonal)

HOLYHEAD BAY
(BAE CAERGYBI)

Middle Mouse
(Ynys Badrig)

West Mouse
(Maen y Bugael)

The Skerries
(Ynysoedd y Moelrhoniaid)

Carmel Head
(Trwyn y Gader)

East Mou
(Ynys Amlwc

Bull Bay
(Porthllechog)

Amlwch
Port

Amlwch

Penyl

Cemaes

Llanbadrig

Cemlyn
Bay

Penrhos

Burwen

Tregele

Llanfechell

Mynydd
Mechell

Rhosgoch

Gadfa

Church Bay
(Porth Swtan)

Llanfairynghornwy

Llanrhyddlad

Llanfflewyn

Rhosybol

Penygraigwen

City Dulas

Rhyd wyn

Carreglefn

Rhosgoch

Rh

Llantaethlu

Llanbabo

Llynnon

Gwredog

Llandyfrydog

Llanddeusant

Melin Hywel

Llyn Alaw

Llanerchymedd

Maenaddwyn

Bachau

Llanfwrog

Carmel

Pen-llyn

Station

Cape
Coch

ANGLESEY

(YNYS

MÔN

Breakwater

Salt Island

HOLYHEAD
(Caergybi)

Llanfachraeth

Llyn Llywenan

Tryfil

Llangwyllog

Bodffordd

Llangefni

Rhos

Gogarth
Bay

Porth-y-felin

Caer y Twr

Holt

Llangoch

Penrhos

Tregwehelyth
Standing Stone

Llanynghenedl

Trefor

B5109

Llyntaes

Cefn
Pres

ISLE

Ellin's Tower

Penrhos Feilw
Standing Stones

Ty Mawr
Standing
Stone

Stryd

Kingsland

Newlands
Park

Y Fali

Presaddfed
Burial Chambers

Bryngwran

Bodedern

A5

Gwalchmai

Henblas

Rhostrehwfa

St. Gwenfaen's
Well

Trearddur

Four Mile
Bridge

Caergeiliog

Llanfairyn-
heubwll

Llyn Dinam

Llanfihangel
yn Nhowyn

Capel
Gwyn

Dothan

Cerrigceinwen

Llangristiolus

Rhoscolyn

Valley

Ty Newydd
Burial
Chamber

Pentre Berw

Cymyran
Bay

Rhosneigr

Llanfaelog

Bryn Du

Soar

Capel Mawr

Gwalchmai

A5

Llyn
Maelog

Pencarnisiog

Das Dryfol
Tomb

Trefdraeth

Barclodiad Y Gawres
Grave

Llangwyfan
-isaf

Bethel

Llangadwaladr

Malltraeth

Llangaffo

Bodow
Dolme
Castell
Bryn Gw

Aberffraw

St. Cwyfan's
'The Church in the Sea'

A4080

Hermon

Bodorgan

Dwyran

Aberffraw
Bay

Newborough
(Niwbwrch)

Newborough
Model Village

Anglesey
Model Village

Foe
Farm F

Malltraeth
Bay

Newborough
Forest

Abermenai
Point

Llanddwyn Island
(Ynys Llanddwyn)

Llanddwyn
Bay

Llanfagla

CAERNARFON   BAY

Foryd
Bay

Llandwrog

Saron

Caernarfon

(BAE   CAERNARFON)

Dinas
Dinlle

Llandwrog

A499

Iniqo Jones
Slate Works

A487

Pontllyfni

Aberdesach

Tai'n Lon

Clynnog-fawr

Capel

Trefor

St. Beuno's
Well

St. Beuno's

Bwlch Mawr
1671

Bwlchderwin

E
F
G
H
250
60
70
80
400
1
2
3
4
5
90
Point Lynas
(Trwyn Eilian)
Ynys Dulas
Dulas Bay
Lligwy Bay
Brynrefail
Moelfre
Seawatch Centre
Lligwy Burial Chamber
Llanallgo
A5108
Marian-glas
Tynygongl
Benllech
Red Wharf Bay
(Traeth-coch)
Red Wharf Bay
Pentrellwyn
Llanbedrgoch
Llanddyfnan
Pentraeth
Mariandyrys
Glan-yr-afon
Priory
Cairn
Penmon
Haulfre Stables
Llanddona
Llangoed
Castell Aberlleiniog
Puffin Island
(Ynys Seiriol)
Penmaen Swatch
Llyn Bodgylched
Bulkeley Mon.
Llanfaes
B5109
Pen-y-garnedd
Talwrn
Stone Science
Rhoscefnhir
A5025
Llansadwrn
Beaumaris
Courthouse
Gaol
Llandegfan
A545
Penmynydd
B5420
Menai Bridge
(Porthaethwy)
Pili Palas
Llanfair Pwllgwyngyll
Upper Bangor
BANGOR
Penrhyn Castle
NT
Lavan Sands
(Traeth Lafan)
Llandygai
Penrhos Garnedd
Vaynol
Nelson Statue
A5
A487
A4087
A4080
Llanddaniel Fab
Bryn Celli Ddu Burial Chamber
Newydd
Glasinfryn
A4244
Tal-y-bont
Llanllechid
Rachub
Bethesda
Gerlan
Tregarth
B4409
Bryn Eglwys
Mynydd Llandegai
Braichmelyn
Y Felinheli
(Port Dinorwig)
Greenwood Forest Pk
Saron
Llanddeiniolen
Pentir
Rhiwlas
Bethel
B4366
B4547
Pont-Rhythallt
Penisa'r Waun
Clwt-y-bont
Deiniolen
Pont-rug
Llanrug
Segontium Roman Fort
CAERNARFON
Caeathro
Cwm-y-glo
Brynrefail
Dinorwig
Ceunant
Llanberis Lake Railway
Llyn Padarn
A4086
Bontnewydd
A4085
Bryn Pistyll
Llanberis
Slate
Dinorwig Power Station
Electric Mountain
Llyn Peris
Croesywaun
Waunfawr
GWYNEDD
Rhostryfan
Rhosgadfan
Waterfall
Llyn Dwythwch
Nant Peris
(Old Llanberis)
Betws Garmon
Penyffridd
Snowdon Mountain Railway
Pass of Llanberis
Carmel
Welsh Highland Railway
Y Fron
Llyn Cwellyn
Talysarn
B4418
Nantlle
Rhyd-Ddu
Llyn y Gader
Craig Cwm Silyn
2408
2299
Garnedd-goch
Hafod Eryri
SNOWDON
(YR WYDDFA)
3559
Glaslyn
Llyn Llydaw
Yr Aran 2451
Waterfalls
Llyn Gwynant
Bethania
Castell Dinas Emrys
Llyn Dinas
Sygun Copper Mine
Welsh Highland Railway
Beddgelert
Snowdonia National Park
Gelert's Grave
2566
Moel Hebog
Pass of Aberglaslyn
Nantmor
Cnicht
2265
SNOWDONIA NATIONAL PARK
(PARC CENEDLAETHOL ERYRI)
Llanfairfechan
Nant-y-Pandy
Nant-y-felin
Abergwyngregyn
A55
Moel Wnion 1902
Aber Falls
Llyn Anafon
2526
Drum
2484
Drosgl
3091
FOEL-FRAS
CAMBRIAN MOUNTAINS
3485
CARNEDD LLEWELYN
3425
CARNEDD DAFYDD
Marchlyn Mawr Resr.
2665
Mynydd Perfedd
Nant Ffrancon
Llyn Ogwen
Pont Pen-y-benglog
Llyn Idwal
Tryfan 3002
3279
GLYDER FAWR
Cwmffynnon
A4086
Capel Curig
A5
Llugwy
Dulyn Resr.
Melynllyn
Llyn Eigiau Resr.
Pen Llithrig y wrach 2620
Llyn Cowlyd Resr.
Carnedd Moel-siabod
2861
Llyn y Foel
Llynnau Mymbyr
Pont Cyfyng
Llynnau Diwaunedd
Y Cribau
Dolwyddelan
Blaenau Dolwyddelan
Pentre-bont
Ty Mawr Wybrnant
NT
Pont-y-pant
A470
Yr Ardu
69
1978
Moel Penamnen
Llyn Conglog
Tal-y-waenydd
Llechwedd Slate Caverns
Llyn Newydd
Rhiwbryfdir
Blaenau
Cwm Penmachno
Carrog
Penmachno
Great Ormes Head
(Pen-y-Gogarth)
Cable Cars & Tramway
Gogarth Abbey
Haulfre
TOLL
Ormes Bay or Llandudno Bay
Little Ormes Head
LLANDUDNO
B5115
Penrhyn Bay
(Bae Penrhyn)
St. Trillo's
Penrhyn Side
Rhos-on-Sea
(Llandrillo-yn-Rhos)
A470
CONWY BAY
Conwy Sands
Deganwy
Castle
Llanrhos
A546
Colwyn Bay
COLWYN BAY
Llandudno Junction
Tywyn
Mochdre
A55
Old Colwyn
Penmaen Rhos
Llanddulas
82
Conwy
Gyffin
Dwygyfylchi
Penmaenmawr
Cefn Coch Stone Circle
Henryd
Llansanffraid Glan Conwy
A547
B5113
Bryn-y-maen
Llanelian-yn-Rhos
B5383
B5381
Dolwen
Pentrefelin
Felin Isaf Watermill
Tal y fan 2000
Maen y bardd Burial Chamber
Rowen
Tyn-y-groes
B5279
Bodnant
NT
Bodnant
Graig
Brymbo
Dawn
Moelfre Uchaf 1298
Canovium Roman Fort
Pontwgan
Ty-y-cafn
Eglwysbach
Pen-y-Gaer Hillfort
Llanbedr-y-cennin
Castell
Tal-y-Bont
Vale of Conwy
B5106
Gell
A548
1277
Mwdwl Eithin
Llangernyw
B5382
Dulyn
CONWY
Dolgarrog
Afon Porth-llwyd
Trefriw Wells Spa
Afon Ddu
A470
Llanddoged
Trefriw
Woollen Mills
Tan-lan
A548
Pandy Tudur
Pente-tafarn-y-fedw
Llyn Crafnant Resr.
Llyn Geirionydd
Chapel
Llanrwst
Gwydir Castle
Gwytherin
GWYDYR FOREST PARK
Ty Hyll
Swallow Falls
Llyn y Parc
Snowdonia National Park
Melin-y-coed
Railway
B5427
Betws-y-Coed
Waterloo Bridge
Capel Garmon
Capel Garmon Burial Chamber
Nebo
Moel Seisiog
1514
1528
Mynydd Cribau 1132
Llyn Elsi Resr.
Fairy Glen
Conwy & Machno Falls
Pont Rhyd-y-Gynnen
Ty-n-y-Coed Uchaf
B4406
Rhydlanfair
Glan-Conwy
A5
B5113
Pentrefoelas Castle
Pentrefoelas
Rhydlydan
Ysbyty Ifan
B4407
Afon Machno
1751
Garn Prys
Llyn Alwen

A
B
C
D
1
2
3
4
5
81
70
LIVERP
BAY
Little Ormes Head
Penrhyn Bay (Bae Penrhyn)
Rhos-on-Sea
Colwyn Bay
Abergele Roads
COLWYN BAY (Bae Colwyn)
Mochdre
Old Colwyn
Llanddulas
Llysfaen
Llansanffraid Glan Conwy
Llanelian -yn-Rhos
Betws -yn-Rhos
Dolwen
Pentrefelin
Bodnant
Graig
Brymbo
Dawn
Moelfre Uchaf 1298
Llanfair Talhaiarn
Gell
1277 Mwdwl Eithin
Llangernyw
Llansannan
Llanddoged
Pandy Tudur
Llanrwst
Gwydir Castle
Melin-y-coed
Gwytherin
CONWY
Nebo
Capel Garmon
Capel Garmon Burial Chamber
Waterloo Bridge
Rhydlanfair
Glan-Conwy
Pentrefoelas
Pentrefoelas Castle
Rhydlydan
Glasfryn
Cefn-brith
Ysbyty Ifan
1751 Garn Prys
Moel Seisiog 1514
1528 Moel Llyn
Aled Isaf Resr.
Llyn Aled
Llyn Aled
Llyn Alwen
Bryn Trillyn 1627
Llyn Bran
Mynydd Hiraethog
Llyn Brenig
Alwen Resr.
CLOCAENOG FOREST
Pentre-llyn-cymmer
Cerrigydrudion
Llanfihangel Glyn Myfyr
Melin-y-wig
Bettws Gwerfil Goch
Kinmel Bay (Bae Cinmel)
RHYL
SeaQuarium
Sky Tower
Belgrano
Towyn
Abergele
Plas Llwyd
Rhuddlan
St. George
Kimmel Park
Bodelwyddan
'Marble' Church
Pengwern
Moelfre
Glascoed
Mynydd Bodrochwyn
Llannefydd
Plas yn Cefn
Bont-newydd
Dolwen Resr.
Cefn Berain
Henllan
Gwaenynog Bach
Tan-y-fron
Groes
Bylchau
Nantglyn
Waen
Prestatyn
Gronant
Gwespyr
Meliden (Gallt Melyd)
Bryn-llwyn
Gwaenysgor
Tan-yr-allt
Dyserth
Trelawnyd
Bodrhyddan Hall
Marian Cwm
Cwm
Rhuallt
St. Asaph (Llanelwy)
Cathedral
Waen Goleugoed
Trefnant
Denbigh (Dinbych)
Friary
Town Walls
Point of Ayr
Talacre
Llawndy
Picton
Ffynnongroyw
Pen-y-ffordd
Mostyn Quay
Llanasa
Trelogan
Berthengam
Mostyn
Rhewl-Mostyn
Maen Achwyfan Cross
Glan-y-don
Whitford (Chwitffordd)
Lloc
Pant y Waco
Gorsedd
Carmel
Pantasaph
Greenfield (Maes-glas)
Basingwerk Abbey
Holywell (Treffynnon)
Pen-y-cefn
Tremeirchion
Caerwys
Bodfari
Afon-wen
Ddol
Ysceifiog
Brynford
Babell
Lixwm
Pentre Halkyn
Halkyn (Helygain)
Halkyn Mountains
Dolphin
Nannerch
FLINTSHIRE
Rhosesmor
Castell
Waen
Llangwyfan
Llandyrnog
Rhydymwyn
Cilcain
Pont-newydd
Moel Llys -y-Coed 1524
Clwyd Forest
Cefn-bychan
Gwernaffield
Gwernymynydd
Llanrhaeadr
Pentre-Llanrhaeadr
Llangynhafal
Llanynys
Gellifor
Moel Famau Jubilee Tower 1818
Tafarn-y-Gelyn
Cadole
Prion
Pant-pastynog
Bachymbyd Fawr
Rhewl
Hirwaen
Llanferres
Maeshafn
Ffridd Fawr
Ruthin (Rhuthun)
Llanbedr-Dyffryn -Clwyd
Cyffylliog
Llanfwrog
Bontuchel
Nantclwyd
Gaol
DENBIGHSHIRE
Eryrys
Graianrhyd
Efenechtyd
Llanarmon-yn-Ial
Llanfair Dyffryn Clwyd
Pen-Y-Ffrith Bird Gardens
Pwll-glas
Clocaenog
Cefn Du
Graig-fechan
Pentre-celyn
Llandegla
Clawdd-newydd
Derwen
Churchyard Cross
Bryn-Saith Marchog
Rhyd-y-meudwy
Llanelidan
Gwyddelwern
Bryneglwys
Horseshoe Pass
1848
CLWYDIAN RANGE
Vale of Clwyd
HOYLAKE
Hilbre Islands
West Kirby
Lifeboat Station
Lifeboat
RIVER
A55
A5
A470
A494
A548
A547
A543
A544
A525
A541
A5151
A5026
A5104
A5119
B5118
B5119
B5381
B5382
B5383
B5384
B5428
B5429
B5435
B5105
B4501
B5113
B5106
B5427
B5431
B5121
B5122
B4407
B5430
B5401

83
LIVERPOOL
CHESTER
WARRINGTON
BIRKENHEAD
WALLASEY
BOOTLE
CROSBY
LITHERLAND
MAGHULL
KIRKBY
ST. HELENS
HUYTON
PRESCOT
WIDNES
RUNCORN
ELLESMERE PORT
BEBINGTON
HESWALL
NESTON
CONNAH'S QUAY
BUCKLEY
Mold
WREXHAM
(Wrecsam)
FRODSHAM
Helsby
NORTHWICH
NANTWICH
HINDLEY
LEIGH
GOLBORNE
HAYDOCK
NEWTON-LE-WILLOWS
ASHTON IN-MAKERFIELD
Ince-in-Makerfield
Up Holland
Rainford
Billinge
Aintree
Fazakerley
Bootle
Seaforth
Waterloo
Hightown
Ince Blundell
Lydiate
Walton
Everton
Anfield
West Derby
Knowsley
Wavertree
Toxteth
Childwall
Allerton
Woolton
Garston
Speke
Halewood
Hale
Hale Bank
Cronton
Rainhill
Whiston
Eccleston
Moreton
Upton
Greasby
Hoylake
Irby
Thingwall
Barnston
Brimstage
Bromborough
Port Sunlight
Rock Ferry
New Ferry
Eastham
Hooton
Willaston
Little Neston
Ness
Parkgate
Gayton
Burton
Puddington
Capenhurst
Saughall
Sealand
Blacon
Hoole
Upton
Mollington
Backford
Mickle Trafford
Guilden Sutton
Stamford Bridge
Great Barrow
Tarvin
Kelsall
Delamere
Mouldsworth
Manley
Ashton Hayes
Christleton
Waverton
Saltney
Lache
Handbridge
Huntington
Eccleston
Saighton
Aldford
Pulford
Dodleston
Higher Kinnerton
Penyffordd
Hope
Caergwrle
Llay
Gresford
Rossett
Marford
Holt
Farndon
Churton
Coddington
Tattenhall
Handley
Beeston
Peckforton
Bunbury
Tarporley
Tiverton
Alpraham
Malpas
Tilston
Broxton
Clutton
Harthill
Bickerton
Hawarden
Ewloe
Queensferry
Shotton
Broughton
Bretton
Flint
Northop
Leeswood
Brymbo
Coedpoeth
Minera
Gwersyllt
Marchwiel
Rhosllanerchrugog
Bangor-is-y-coed
Sutton Weaver
Preston Brook
Daresbury
Stretton
Appleton Thorn
Grappenhall
Weaverham
Cuddington
Sandiway
Little Budworth
Cotebrook
Eaton
Acton
Burland
Wrenbury
LIVERPOOL JOHN LENNON
RIVER MERSEY
Manchester Ship Canal
ENGLAND
WALES
CHESHIRE WEST & CHESTER
DELAMERE FOREST PARK
BURTONWOOD
M53
M56
M57
M58
M62
M6
A41
A49
A51
A54
A55
A56
A57
A58
A59
A483
A494
A534
A550
A557
A561
A562
A565
A570
A580
A5300
E
F
G
H
90
71
84

84
HINDLEY
Ince-in-Makerfield
ATHERTON
WORSLEY
SWINTON
PRESTWICH
OLDHAM
Tyldesley
FAILSWORTH
LEIGH
ECCLES
MANCHESTER
ASHTON-IN-MAKERFIELD
ASHTON UNDER-LYNE
GOLBORNE
SALFORD
DROYLSDEN
DUKINFIELD
NEWTON-LE-WILLOWS
URMSTON
STRETFORD
DENTON
Culcheth
Irlam
SALE
WARRINGTON
STOCKPORT
ALTRINCHAM
Gatley
CHEADLE
Cheadle Hulme
Marple
Hazel Grove
Lymm
Hale
Bramhall
Poynton
WILMSLOW
KNUTSFORD
Alderley Edge
BOLLINGTON
NORTHWICH
Weaverham
MACCLESFIELD
Middlewich
WINSFORD
Holmes Chapel
CONGLETON
SANDBACH
BIDDULPH
CREWE
Alsager
KIDSGROVE
NANTWICH
Audley
Tunstall
Burslem
Hanley
STOKE-ON-TRENT
Silverdale
Tarporley
M6
M56
M62
M60

85
PEAK DISTRICT
HIGH PEAK
Kinder Scout
2088
PEAK DISTRICT
NATIONAL PARK
DERBYSHIRE
RDSHIRE
SHEFFIELD
CHESTERFIELD
DRONFIELD
BUXTON
GLOSSOP
LEEK
MATLOCK
Ashbourne
BELPER
ALFRETON
Mossley
Hadfield
Tintwistle
Hollingworth
Gamesley
Charlesworth
Chunal
Crowden
Rowarth
Little Hayfield
Hayfield
Birch Vale
Thornsett
New Mills
Low Leighton
Newtown
Furness Vale
Chinley
Bridgemont
Whaley Bridge
Buxworth
Whitehough
Lower Crossings
Chapel-en-le-Frith
Horwich End
Combs
Fernilee
Dove Holes
Peak Dale
Peak Forest
Sparrowpit
Malcoff
Wash
Slackhall
Chapel Milton
Edale
Upper Booth
Barber Booth
Castleton
Hope
Aston
Thornhill
Bamford
Brough
Shatton
Bradwell
Hathersage
Hathersage Booths
Upper Padley
Nether Padley
Grindleford
Great Hucklow
Little Hucklow
Windmill
Grindlow
Foolow
Eyam
Froggatt
Curbar
Calver
Stoney Middleton
Tideswell
Litton
Wardlow
Wormhill
Cressbrook
Miller's Dale
Blackwell
Priestcliffe
Taddington
Chelmorton
Little Longstone
Great Longstone
Rowland
Hassop
Baslow
Nether End
Pilsley
Edensor
Ashford in the Water
Bakewell
Sheldon
Flagg
Monyash
Over Haddon
Rowsley
Beeley
Youlgreave
Alport
Bradford
Middleton
Stanton in Peak
Birchover
Winster
Elton
Darley Dale
Darley Bridge
Two Dales
Churchtown
Northwood
Wensley
Upper Hackney
Tansley
Riber
Starkholmes
Matlock Bath
Bonsall
Upper Town
Cromford
Middleton
Wirksworth
Bolehill
Brassington
Carsington
Hopton
Gorseybank
Millers Green
Hognaston
Kirk Ireton
Idridgehay
Kniveton
Atlow
Biggin
Tissington
Fenny Bentley
Thorpe
Ilam
Mapleton
Parwich
Alsop en le Dale
Ballidon
Longcliffe
Aldwark
Grangemill
Ible
Newhaven
Pikehall
Friden
Hartington
Heathcote
Biggin
Sheen
Pilsbury
Crowdecote
Longnor
Earl Sterndale
Glutton Bridge
Hollinsclough
Flash
Morridge Top
Fawfieldhead
Newtown
Upper Hulme
Blackshaw Moor
Upper Elkstone
Warslow
Hulme End
Thorncliffe
Mixon
Butterton
Wetton
Alstonefield
Hope
Hopedale
Milldale
Stanshope
Onecote
Grindon
Morridge Side
Bradnop
Birchall
Leekbrook
Basford Green
Ford
Winkhill
Waterfall
Waterhouses
Calton
Ipstones
Cauldon
Cauldon Lowe
Blore
Swinscoe
Foxt
Froghall
Kingsley
Whiston
Cotton
Stanton
Burbage
Fairfield
Staden
King Sterndale
Harpur Hill
Sterndale Moor
Wheston
Hargatewall
Tunstead
Bibbington
Upper End
Smalldale
Old Dam
Coplow Dale
Abney
Leam
Owler Bar
Holmesfield
Dronfield Woodhouse
Unstone
Unstone Green
Common Side
Barlow
Cutthorpe
Overgreen
Old Brampton
Newbold
Wadshelf
Holymoorside
Walton
Wingerworth
Uppertown
Kelstedge
Ashover
Clay Cross
Milltown
Dethick
Lea
Holloway
Wessington
South Wingfield
Crich
Whatstandwell
Alderwasley
Ambergate
Toadmoor
Shottle
Belper Lane End
Blackbrook
Cowers Lane
Turnditch
Hulland Ward
Hulland
Penistone
Oxspring
Thurlstone
Carlecotes
Hazlehead
Dunford Bridge
Langsett
Midhopestones
Stocksbridge
Deepcar
Bolsterstone
Wharncliffe Side
Grenoside
Oughtibridge
Ecclesfield
Chapeltown
High Green
Thurgoland
Wortley
Silkstone Common
Worsbrough
Wombwell
Hoyland
Birdwell
Tankersley
High Bradfield
Low Bradfield
Dungworth
Stannington
Loxley
Hollow Meadows
Ringinglow
Fulwood
Greystones
Totley
Dore
Bradway
Norton
Hillsborough
Crookes
Walkley
Ladybower Reservoir
Howden Moors
Bleaklow Hill
2077
Snake Pass
Featherbed Top
Stanage Edge
A6
A57
A61
A515
A523
A52
A623
A619
A621
A625
A628
A616
A629
A6020
A5012
M1
E
F
G
H
92
73

86
WORSBROUGH
Darfield
WOMBWELL
Goldthorpe
Bolton upon Dearne
DONCASTER
A1(M)
A635
A18
M18
Bessacarr
Cantley
Branton
Birdwell
Hoyland
HOYLAND
Elsecar
WATH UPON DEARNE
MEXBOROUGH
Sprotbrough
Warmsworth
Conisbrough
CONISBROUGH
SWINTON
Denaby Main
New Edlington
Old Edlington
Loversall
Rossington
New Rossington
Finningley
ROBIN HOOD DONCASTER SHEFFIELD
Auckley
Blaxton
Wentworth
Chapeltown
High Green
Tankersley
Harley
Upper Haugh
RAWMARSH
Kilnhurst
Hooton Roberts
Thrybergh
Ravenfield
Wadworth
Greasbrough
Thorpe Hesley
Grenoside
Oughtibridge
Ecclesfield
ROTHERHAM
Dalton
Bramley
MALTBY
Braithwell
Stainton
Tickhill
Austerfield
Misson
Bawtry
Newington
Parson Cross
Shiregreen
Wadsley Bridge
Hillsborough
Moorgate
Wickersley
Whiston
Hooton Levitt
Harworth
Bircotes
Everton
Scrooby
Styrrup
Oldcotes
BLYTH
Blyth
Ranskill
Mattersey
Brinsworth
Catcliffe
Treeton
Thurcroft
Laughton en le Morthen
Firbeck
Roche Abbey
Langold
Torworth
SHEFFIELD
Handsworth
Aughton
Dinnington
Letwell
Laughton Common
Swallownest
Carlton in Lindrick
North Anston
South Anston
Gildingwells
Woodsetts
Barnby Moor
Sutton cum Lound
Lound
Ecclesall
Millhouses
Beighton
Aston
Wales
Todwick
Kiveton Park
Hackenthorpe
Gleadless
Norton
Abbeydale
Ridgeway
Holbrook
Halfway
Killamarsh
Harthill
Thorpe Salvin
Shireoaks
Rhodesia
WORKSOP
Scofton
Ranby
Babworth
Bilby
Dronfield
DRONFIELD
Eckington
Mosborough
Woodall
WOODALL
Renishaw
Spinkhill
Barlborough
Clowne
Whitwell
Manton
Ordsall
Eaton
Unstone
Common Side
Mastin Moor
Staveley
Barrow Hill
Creswell
Elmton
Hodthorpe
Belph
Clumber Park
Hardwick Village
Elkesley
West Drayton
Sheepbridge
Whittington
Newbold
Brimington
Tapton
Calow
DERBYSHIRE
Duckmanton
Holbeck
Whaley Thorns
Welbeck
Norton
Cuckney
Carburton
THE DUKERIES
Perlethorpe
Thoresby
Bothamsall
Haughton
MARKHAM MOOR
Walesby
Bevercotes
CHESTERFIELD
Hady
Bolsover
Langwith
Nether Langwith
Meden Vale
Church Warsop
Budby
New Ollerton
Boughton
Kirton
Holymoorside
Hasland
Sutton Scarsdale
Palterton
Hillstown
Scarcliffe
Upper Langwith
Shirebrook
Warsop
Warsop Vale
Edwinstowe
Ollerton
Wellow
Grassmoor
Temple Normanton
Wingerworth
Heath
Glapwell
Stony Houghton
Sookholme
Kings Clipstone
Clipstone
Old Tupton
North Wingfield
Holmewood
Pleasley
New Houghton
MANSFIELD WOODHOUSE
Rufford Abbey
Ompton
Kneesall
Ashover
Clay Cross
Danesmoor
Hardstoft
Pilsley
Teversal
Skegby
Forest Town
NOTTINGHAM
Eakring
Kersall
Stretton
Morton
Tibshelf
TIBSHELF
Newton
Stanton Hill
Huthwaite
SUTTON IN ASHFIELD
MANSFIELD
Bilsthorpe
Maplebeck
Tansley
Matlock Bath
Wessington
Stonebroom
Higham
Shirland
Blackwell
Rainworth
Kirklington
South Wingfield
ALFRETON
South Normanton
KIRKBY IN ASHFIELD
Blidworth
Farnsfield
Hockerton
Edingley
Crich
Pinxton
Somercotes
Annesley Woodhouse
Annesley
Newstead Abbey
Ravenshead
Halam
SWANWICK
Swanwick
Selston
Newstead
Linby
Papplewick
Oxton
Southwell
Halloughton
Ripley
Codnor
Underwood
Heage
Jacksdale
Hucknall
HUCKNALL
Calverton
Woodborough
Thurgarton
Epperstone
Belper
BELPER
Heanor
HEANOR
EASTWOOD
Loscoe
Moorgreen
Bulwell
Lowdham
Gonalston
Hoveringham
Bestwood

87
94
88
75
E
F
G
H
1
2
3
4
5
Epworth
Old Rectory
Epworth Turbary
A161
Low Burnham
Messingham
Manton
B1398
A159
B1400
Scotterthorpe
Susworth
Kelfield
Owston Ferry
Scotter
Sturton
A15
Hibaldstow
Cadney
Howsham
Owmby
Clixby
Pelham's Pillar
A1084
North Kelsey Moor
North Kelsey
North Kelsey Beck
Caistor
Cabourne
A46
B1434
Redbourne
Raventhorpe Medieval Village
B1206
Woodside
Epperthorpe
Haxey
B1396
East Lound
Graiselound
East Ferry
Wildsworth
Laughton
Gunthorpe
Scotton
Mount Pleasant
Kirton in Lindsey
B1400
Northorpe
Brandy Wharf
South Kelsey
Moortown
Nettleton
Rothwell
B1225
B1205
Holton le Moor
Heckdyke
West Stockwith
Misterton
B1403
East Stockwith
Walkerith
Blyton
Pilham
Aisby
Grayingham
Blyborough
Willoughton
B1398
Waddingham
Snitterby
Atterby
Bishop Norton
Thornton le Moor
North Owersby
South Owersby
Usselby
Kingerby
Kirkby
Osgodby
Horse World
Normanby le Wold
Claxby
Otby
Walesby
Walkeringham
Morton
GAINSBOROUGH
A159
Beckingham
Corringham
Hemswell
York Model Railway
Spital in the Street
Glentham
Bishopbridge
A1103
Middle Rasen
Market Rasen
Old Hall
B1433
A631
Springthorpe
Sturgate
Harpswell
Hemswell Cliff
Caenby
West Rasen
Clayworth
Saundby
Heapham
Glentworth
Normanby-by-Spital
Toft next Newton
Newton by Toft
Market Rasen
B1202
A156
A620
Bole
Lea
Upton
Owmby-by-Spital
North Wheatley
Knaith Park
B1241
Fillingham
Saxby
Linwood
South Wheatley
Hayton
Sturton le Steeple
Kexby
Spridlington
Buslingthorpe
Faldingworth
Bleasby
Knaith
Willingham by Stow
Clarborough
Gate Burton
Coates
Cold Hanworth
Lissington
Bleasby Moor
Fenton
Littleborough
Ingham
Hackthorn
Friesthorpe
West Torrington
North Leverton
Marton
Stow
Cammeringham
Snarford
Welham
Habblesthorpe
Sturton by Stow
Thorpe in the Fallows
Brattleby
Welton Hill
Wickenby
Holton cum Beckering
South Leverton
Cottam
Scampton
A1500
Aisthorpe
Welton
Snelland
Grove
Brampton
Scampton
A15
Dunholme
Reasby
Fulnetby
Sundown Adventureland
Torksey
Bransby
Home of Rest for Horses
Treswell
Rampton
Stainton by Langworth
Rand
Wragby
Woodbeck
North Carlton
Lincolnshire Agricultural Showground
A46
Scothern
Church Laneham
Fenton
Broxholme
Headon
Stokeham
Laneham
A1133
South Carlton
LINCOLNSHIRE
Langworth
Langton by Wragby
Upton
Fossdyke Navigation
Laughterton
Saxilby
B1398
Riseholme
Sudbrooke
Apley
A156
A57
Burton-by-Lincoln
A158
Kettlethorpe
Kingthorpe
East Drayton
Dunham-on-Trent
Newton on Trent
Barlings
Nettleham
Reepham
Low Barlings
Ermine
A57
Darlton
Ragnall
Broadholme
North Greetwell
Abbey
Toll
Stainfield
East Markham
North Clifton
Thorney
Cherry Willingham
LINCOLN
Skellingthorpe
A46
Fledborough
Fiskerton
Harby
New Boultham
Washingborough
High Marnham
B1378
B1308
Young Wood
Skegby
Wigsley
Doddington Hall
Swanpool
B1190
Branston Booths
Normanton on Trent
South Clifton
Doddington
Birchwood
Canwick
Bardney
Low Marnham
Spalford
Boultham
Heighington
Egmanton
Weston
A1133
Eagle Moor
Swallow Beck
B1190
B1190
B1164
Bracebridge
B1188
Moorhouse
Grassthorpe
North Scarle
Eagle
Whisby
Road Transport
B1131
Bracebridge Heath
Branston
Potterhanworth Booths
A1
Sutton on Trent
Girton
Weecar
Natural World Centre
North Hykeham
A607
Potterhanworth
South
Eagle Barnsdale
Thorpe on the Hill
A1434
B1178
B1202
Ossington
Carlton-on-Trent
Besthorpe
South Hykeham
Waddington
Nocton
Wasps Nest
Sots Hole
Tanvats
SHIRE
South Scarle
Morton
Haddington
Waddington
Norwell
Collingham
Swinderby
A46
Witham St. Hughs
Aubourn
Harmston
B1178
A15
Dunston
Dolls
Cromwell
Thurlby
B1189
Caunton
Bassingham
Coleby
Blankney
Metheringham
B1191
Martin
A616
Bathley
Holme
B1202
Metheringham Airfield
Little Carlton
North Muskham
Langford
Brough
Norton Disney
Boothby Graffoe
Scopwick
Timberland
Winthorpe
Stapleford
Carlton-le-Moorland
Navenby
Kirkby Green
B1189
A617
South Muskham
Newark Showground
Winthorpe
Newark Air
Wellingore
Rowston
Thorpe Tilney
Walcott
Kelham
A616
A17
Ashby de la Launde
Averham
Town Hall
Coddington
Heritage Room
Brant Broughton
Welbourn
Castle
Digby
Billinghay
Staythorpe
Millgate
Beckingham
A607
Temple Bruer Tower
B1191
Bloxholm
B1188
Dorrington
North Ings Farm
Rolleston
A46
Gilstrap Cen.
New Balderton
Farndon
NEWARK-ON-TRENT
A1
Barnby in the Willows
Stragglethorpe
Leadenham
Ruskington
Fiskerton
Hawton
Balderton
A17
A15
A153
East Stoke
Fenton
Manor
Fulbeck
Cranwell
Anwick
Thorpe
Stoke Field 1487
B6326
Claypole
Stubton
B1429
Cranwell
Leasingham
Slea
Elston
Brandon
Caythorpe
Frieston
B1209
Cotham
Syerston
Dry Doddington
Aviation Heritage
North Rauceby
Holdingham
Evedon
Ewerby
A17
Kirkby la Thorpe
Flintham
Hough-on-the-Hill
Normanton
B6403
Trent
Witham
Brant
Devon
Idle
Canal
Eau
Till
Sturgate
Kirton in Lindsey
Wickenby
Waddington

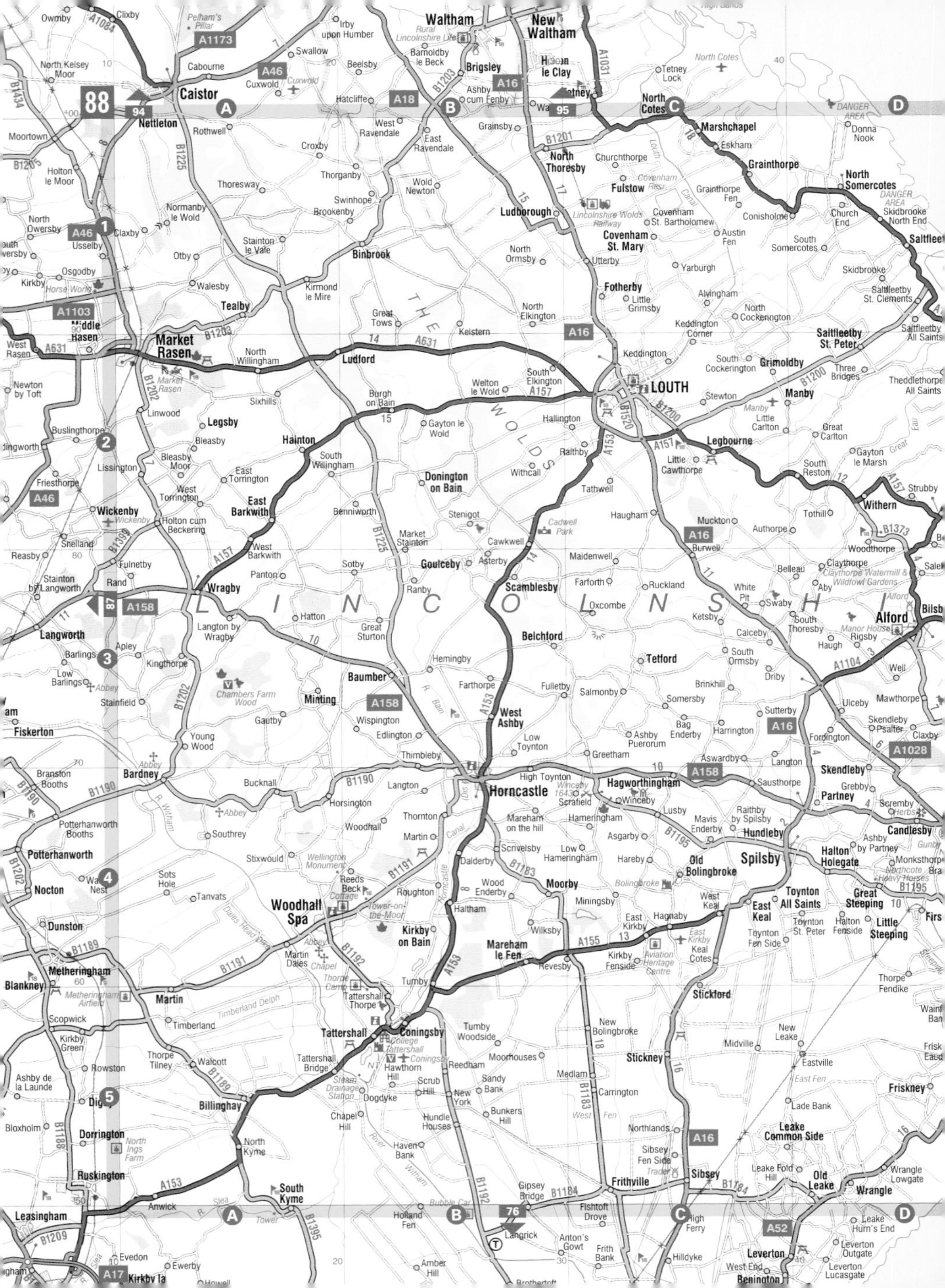

88
94
95
87
76
A
B
C
D
Ownby
Clixby
A1084
Pelham's Pillar
A1173
Irby upon Humber
Swallow
Waltham
New Waltham
Rural Lincolnshire Life
Barnoldby le Beck
Brigsley
Humberston le Clay
Tetney
Tetney Lock
North Cotes
North Kelsey Moor
Cabourne
A46
Cuxwold
Beelsby
Caistor
Nettleton
Hatcliffe
A18
Ashby cum Fenby
A16
A1031
B1434
Moortown
Rothwell
West Ravendale
East Ravendale
Croxby
Grainsby
B1201
North Thoresby
Churchthorpe
Marshchapel
Eskham
Grainthorpe
DANGER AREA
Donna Nook
B1205
Holton le Moor
B1225
Thorganby
Thoresway
Wold Newton
Fulstow
Covenham Resr
Grainthorpe Fen
North Somercotes
Normanby le Wold
Swinhope
Brookenby
Ludborough
Lincolnshire Wolds Railway
Covenham St. Bartholomew
Conisholme
Church End
Skidbrooke North End
North Owersby
Claxby
Usselby
Stainton le Vale
Binbrook
Covenham St. Mary
Austin Fen
South Somercotes
Saltfleet
Otby
North Ormsby
Utterby
Yarburgh
Osgodby
Kirkby
Horse World
Walesby
Kirmond le Mire
Fotherby
Little Grimsby
Alvingham
Skidbrooke
Saltfleetby St. Clements
A1103
Middle Rasen
Tealby
B1203
Great Tows
THE WOLDS
North Elkington
North Cockerington
Kelstern
Keddington Corner
Saltfleetby St. Peter
Saltfleetby All Saints
West Rasen
A631
Market Rasen
North Willingham
Ludford
Keddington
South Cockerington
Grimoldby
Three Bridges
Theddlethorpe All Saints
Newton by Toft
B1202
Sixhills
Burgh on Bain
Welton le Wold
South Elkington
A157
LOUTH
Stewton
Manby
B1200
Linwood
Legsby
Gayton le Wold
Hallington
B1520
Little Carlton
Great Carlton
Buslingthorpe
Bleasby
Hainton
Raithby
A153
Legbourne
Gayton le Marsh
Bleasby Moor
South Willingham
Little Cawthorpe
South Reston
Friesthorpe
Lissington
East Torrington
Withcall
Donington on Bain
Tathwell
Strubby
West Torrington
East Barkwith
Benniworth
Haugham
Withern
Tothill
Wickenby
Holton cum Beckering
Stenigot
Cadwell Park
Muckton
Authorpe
B1373
B1399
Snelland
Market Stainton
Cawkwell
Burwell
Woodthorpe
Reasby
West Barkwith
Asterby
Maidenwell
Claythorpe
Fulnetby
Sotby
Goulceby
Belleau
Claythorpe Watermill & Wildfowl Gardens
Stainton by Langworth
Panton
Scamblesby
Farforth
Ruckland
Aby
Rand
Wragby
Ranby
White Pit
Swaby
A158
LINCOLNSHIRE
Langworth
Langton by Wragby
Hatton
Oxcombe
Ketsby
South Thoresby
Alford
Great Sturton
Belchford
Calceby
Manor House
Rigsby
Haugh
Apley
Barlings
Kingthorpe
Hemingby
Tetford
South Ormsby
Low Barlings
Abbey
Baumber
Farthorpe
Driby
A1104
Well
Stainfield
Chambers Farm Wood
Minting
Fulletby
Salmonby
Brinkhill
Mawthorpe
Ulceby
Fiskerton
Gautby
Wispington
West Ashby
Somersby
Sutterby
Skendleby Psalter
Edlington
Bag Enderby
Ashby Puerorum
Harrington
Fordington
Young Wood
Low Toynton
Greetham
Aswardby
Langton
A1028
Thimbleby
Branston Booths
Bardney
Bucknall
B1190
Langton
High Toynton
Horncastle
Winceby 1643
Scrafield
Hagworthingham
Winceby
Sausthorpe
Skendleby
Grebby
Partney
Scremby
Horsington
Lusby
Raithby by Spilsby
Potterhanworth Booths
Thornton
Mareham on the hill
Hameringham
Mavis Enderby
Hundleby
Candlesby
Ashby by Partney
Southrey
Woodhall
Martin
Asgarby
Spilsby
Halton Holegate
Monksthorpe
Potterhanworth
Stixwould
Wellington Monument
Scrivelsby
Low Hameringham
Hareby
Old Bolingbroke
B1195
B1202
Reeds Beck
Cottage
B1191
Dalderby
Wood Enderby
Moorby
Toynton All Saints
Great Steeping
Sots Hole
Tanvats
Roughton
Tower-on-the-Moor
Horncastle Canal
Miningsby
West Keal
East Keal
Nocton
Wasps Nest
Woodhall Spa
Haltham
East Kirkby
Hagnaby
Toynton St. Peter
Halton Fenside
Little Steeping
Dunston
Kirkby on Bain
Mareham le Fen
Wilksby
A155
Toynton Fen Side
B1189
Martin Dales
Abbey
B1192
Revesby
Kirkby Fenside
Aviation Heritage Centre
Keal Cotes
Metheringham
Chapel
Thorpe Camp
Blankney
Metheringham Airfield
Tumby
Stickford
Thorpe Fendike
Martin
Tattershall Thorpe
Timberland Delph
Scopwick
Timberland
Tumby Woodside
New Bolingbroke
Tattershall
Coningsby
College
Kirkby Green
New Leake
Midville
Thorpe Tilney
Walcott
Tattershall Bridge
Moorhouses
Stickney
Eastville
Rowston
Reedham
Ashby de la Launde
Steam Drainage Station
Hawthorn Hill
Scrub Hill
Sandy Bank
Medlam
Carrington
East Fen
Digby
Billinghay
Dogdyke
New York
B1183
Friskney
Bunkers Hill
Lade Bank
Bloxholm
B1188
Dorrington
Chapel Hill
Hundle Houses
West Fen
Northlands
North Ings Farm
North Kyme
Haven Bank
Leake Common Side
A16
River Witham
Sibsey Fen Side
Trader
Ruskington
Gipsey Bridge
Leake Fold Hill
Old Leake
Wrangle Lowgate
A153
South Kyme
B1184
Frithville
Sibsey
Wrangle
Anwick
Slea
Bubble Car
Fishtoft Drove
Leasingham
Tower
Holland Fen
High Ferry
Leake Hurn's End
B1395
A52
B1209
Langrick
Anton's Gowt
Frith Bank
Leverton
Leverton Outgate
Evedon
Hilldyke
Ewerby
Amber Hill
West End
Leverton Lucasgate
A17
Kirkby la Thorpe
Benington

1

^{9}50 60 70 80

90

N O R T H

S E A

2

80

ddlethorpe
St. Helen
*Seal Sanctuary &
Wildlife Centre*
Mablethorpe
Lifeboat Station
Ye Olde
Curiosity
Thorpe
Trusthorpe
Sutton on Sea
y
sh
Sandilands
A1111
Hannah
Markby
A52
80

R E
Thurlby **Huttoft**
B1449 13 Drainage Anderby
Creek
horpe Cumberworth Anderby
15 **Mumby**
Authorpe
Row
Helsey
**Chapel
St. Leonards**
onthorpe **Hogsthorpe**
ughby
3

70

Sloothby
Hasthorpe Slackholme
End
*Hardys
Animal
Farm*
an Addlethorpe **Ingoldmells**
sh **Ingoldmells
Point**
Orby *Skegness
(Ingoldmells)* *Butlin's*
Orby Marsh *Water
Leisure Park*
Winthorpe **Seathorne**

**Burgh
le Marsh** A158 Church
Farm *Natureland
Seal Sanctuary*
Model Village *Bottons
Pleasure Beach*
Thorpe Croft **SKEGNESS**
St. Peter
5
Seacroft
Croft Marsh
4

60

Moptalen *Gibraltar Point*
fleet **Wainfleet
Mary All Saints** Gibraltar
Toft

A52

DANGER AREA

5

Deeps

^{3}50

Boston

^{9}50 60 70

Scolt Head
80 Island

Holkham Bay

Brancaster Bay

90
96
83
CLEVELEYS
Thornton
Hambleton
Out Rawcliffe
St. Michael's on Wyre
Nateby
Churchtown
Catterall
Claughton
Bowland
Great Eccleston
Bilsborrow
Inglewhite
Poulton-le-Fydle
Singleton
Elswick
Inskip
Barton
Longridge
THE FYLDE
Goosnargh
BLACKPOOL
Great Marton
Staining
Weeton
Kirkham
Woodplumpton
Broughton
Grimsargh
South Shore
Pleasure Beach
Wrea Green
FULWOOD
St. Anne's
Warton
Freckleton
PRESTON
LYTHAM ST. ANNE'S
Lytham
Higher Penwortham
River Ribble
Hutton
Longton
Bamber Bridge
Hesketh Bank
Much Hoole
LEYLAND
West Lancashire Light Railway
Hesketh
Tarleton
Banks
Bretherton
Southport Sands
SOUTHPORT
Churchtown
Mere Brow
Croston
Eccleston
Birkdale
Holmeswood
Rufford
Mawdesley
Charnock Richard
Coppull
Burscough
Burscough Bridge
Adlington
Ainsdale
Woodvale
Parbold
STANDISH
Halsall
ORMSKIRK
Newburgh
FORMBY
Haskayne
SKELMERSDALE
ORRELL
WIGAN
Hightown
Maghull
Up Holland
Ince-in-Makerfield
LIVERPOOL BAY
Rainford
Billinge
ASHTON-IN-MAKERFIELD
CROSBY
LITHERLAND
Aintree
KIRKBY
BOOTLE
ST. HELENS
HAYDOCK
GOLBORNE
Liverpool to: Dublin 8hrs.
Liverpool to: Douglas 2hrs. 30mins. (Fast Ferry, Seasonal)
Birkenhead to: Belfast 8hrs. Douglas 4hrs. 15mins. (Seasonal)
WALLASEY
New Brighton
West Derby
PRESCOT
NEWTON-LE-WILLOWS
HUYTON
Rainhill
Whiston
WARRINGTON
HOYLAKE
BIRKENHEAD
LIVERPOOL
Wavertree
Toxteth
Childwall
Woolton
Great Sankey
M6
M55
M58
M57
M62
A583
A585
A565
A59
A570
A5209
A580
A58
A57
A49
A577

91
97
98
92
84
85
Waddington
Horrocksford
Downham
Twiston
Bashall Eaves
Bashall Town
Clitheroe
Worston
Low Moor
Walker Fold
Longridge Fell
Pendleton
Woodfields
Great Mitton
Barrow
Wiswell
Sabden
Whalley
Billington
Hurst Green
Dinckley
Stydd
Ribchester
Copster Green
Langho
Read
Simonstone
Altham
Padiham
Hapton
Huncoat
Salesbury
Wilpshire
Great Harwood
Clayton -le-Moors
Rishton
Brownhill
Osbaldeston
Mellor
Balderstone
Beardwood
Church
BLACKBURN
Pleasington
Mill Hill
Shadsworth
Guide
Lower Darwen
Feniscowles
Oswaldtwistle
ACCRINGTON
Scaitcliffe
Haworth
Dunnockshaw
Goodshaw Fold
Baxenden
Goodshaw
Love Clough
Crawshawbooth
Acre
Haslingden
RAWTENSTALL
Newchurch
Waterfoot
Cowpe
Helmshore
Ewood Bridge
Edenfield
Stubbins
RAMSBOTTOM
Holcombe
Shuttleworth
Nuttall
Hawkshaw
Summerseat
Walmersley
Tottington
BURY
Chesham
Elton
Walshaw
Starling
Ainsworth
Redvales
Fishpool
Black Lane
Hollins
RADCLIFFE
WHITEFIELD
Little Lever
Kearsley
Prestwich
Park Lane
Clifton
Heaton Park
Crumpsall
Cheetham Hill
Harpurhey
Broughton Park
Pendlebury
SWINTON
WORSLEY
Walkden
Little Hulton
FARNWORTH
Daubhill
BOLTON
Breightmet
Harwood
Bradshaw
Astley Bridge
Bromley Cross
Eagley
Toppings
Dunscar
Egerton
Turton Bottoms
Chapeltown
Edgworth
Dimple
Belmont
Winter Hill
Rivington
Lever Park
HORWICH
Barrow Bridge
Horrocks Fold
Bottom o' th' Moor
Lostock Junction
Chew Moor
Hunger Hill
Wingates
Over Hulton
Daisy Hill
ATHERTON
Tyldesley
Astley
Westleigh
Bedford
Blackmoor
Boothstown
LEIGH
Pennington
Glazebury
Twiss Green
Fowley Common
Chat Moss
Culcheth
Croft
Glazebrook
Risley
Birchwood
Hollinfare
Cadishead
Irlam
Partington
Carrington
Warburton
Mossbrow
Heatley
Oughtrington
Lymm
Thelwall
Martinscroft
Woolston
Dunham Woodhouses
Dunham Town
Little Bollington
Bowdon
ALTRINCHAM
Hale
Timperley
Broadheath
Brooklands
SALE
Woodhouses
Ashton upon Mersey
Flixton
URMSTON
Davyhulme
Trafford Park
STRETFORD
Old Trafford
Hulme
Moss Side
Rusholme
Chorlton -cum- Hardy
Fallowfield
Withington
Burnage
Heaton Moor
Didsbury
Wythenshawe
Gatley
CHEADLE
Cheadle Hulme
Benchill
Heald Green
ECCLES
Pendleton
SALFORD
MANCHESTER
Newton Heath
Woodhouses
Clayton
DROYLSDEN
Gorton
Levenshulme
Reddish
DENTON
Audenshaw
Haughton Green
STOCKPORT
Bredbury
Romiley
Offerton
Marple
Hazel Grove
Hawk Green
Strines
New Mills
Compstall
Woodley
Gee Cross
HYDE
Broadbottom
Charlesworth
Chisworth
Mellor
Rowarth
Little Hayfield
Birch Vale
Hayfield
GLOSSOP
Chunal
Lee Head
Gamesley
Hadfield
Tintwistle
Hollingworth
Mottram in Longdendale
Hattersley
Newton
DUKINFIELD
STALYBRIDGE
ASHTON-UNDER-LYNE
Mossley
Buckton Vale
Buckton Castle
Chew Resr.
Greenfield
Uppermill
Grasscroft
Lees
Lydgate
OLDHAM
Hollinwood
Bardsley
Hurst
FAILSWORTH
Charlestown
Blackley
CHADDERTON
MIDDLETON
Rhodes
Birch
Langley
Slattocks
ROYTON
SHAW
Gravel Hole
Castleton
HEYWOOD
Hooley Bridge
Hooley Brow
Birtle
ROCHDALE
Norden
Nangreaves
Milnrow
Lower Place
Firgrove
Newhey
Ogden
Denshaw
Delph
Dobcross
Diggle
Harrop Dale
SADDLEWORTH
Scouthead
Moorside
Sholver
Acre
Castleshaw Moor
Standedge Tunnel
Smallbridge
Smithy Bridge
LITTLEBOROUGH
Rakewood
Wardle
Clough
Syke
Healey
Broadley
Whitworth
Calderbrook
Summit
Millgate
Shawforth
Britannia
Bacup
Stacksteads
Sharneyford
Weir
Water
Lumb
Whitewell Bottom
Edgeside
Portsmouth
Cornholme
Lydgate
Todmorden
Walsden
Mankinholes
Clough Foot
Walk Mill
Holme Chapel
Cliviger
Worsthorne
Hurstwood
Mereclough
BURNLEY
Rose Hill
Habergham
Briercliffe
Lane Bottom
Haggate
NELSON
Brierfield
Higham
Fence
Wheatley Lane
Newchurch
Barrowford
Barley
Roughlee
Blacko
Foulridge
Colne
Laneshaw Bridge
Trawden
Cowling
Sutton-in-Craven
Cross Hills
Steeton
Eastburn
Beechcliffe
Braithwaite
Laycock
Oakworth
Lees
Stanbury
Haworth
Oxenhope
Keighley Moor
THE FOREST OF TRAWDEN
THE FOREST OF PENDLE
FOREST OF ROSSENDALE
ROSSENDALE
Boulsworth Hill
Widdop Moor
Walshaw Dean Resrs.
Wadsworth Moor
Haworth Moor
Pecket Well
Slack
Colden
Heptonstall
Blackshaw Head
Charlestown
Hebden Bridge
Mytholmroyd
Midgley
Chiserley
Wainstalls
Booth
Luddenden
Luddenden Foot
Sowerby
Steep Lane
Triangle
Cragg Vale
Mill Bank
Lumb
Soyland Town
Ripponden
Rishworth
Booth Wood
Rishworth Moor
Moss Moor
Stoodley Pike Monument
Heptonstall Moor
Darwen
BLACKBURN WITH DARWEN
Hoddlesden
Blacksnape
Sunnyhurst
Earcroft
Grimshaw
Belthorn
Tockholes
Withnell
Whittlestone Head
Haslingden Grane
Turton Tower
Holcombe Brook
Greenmount
Bradshaw
M65
M66
M62
M61
M60
M6
M602
M67
A627(M)
A56
A59
A682
A6068
A671
A680
A666
A646
A6114
A6033
A58
A672
A640
A673
A6027
A676
A579
A6
A577
A580
A57
A572
A576
A663
A627
A635
A6010
A6018
A628
A5103
A34
A560
A6053
A62
A669
A6104
B6243
B6246
B6245
B6232
B6236
B6391
B6214
B6527
B6238
B6222
B6225
B6197
B6138
B6114
B6265
B6143
B6105
B5160
B5158
B5165
B5212
B5213

92
KEIGHLEY
BINGLEY
BAILDON
GUISELEY
YEADON
Menston
Bramhope
HORSFORTH
SHIPLEY
BRADFORD
PUDSEY
LEEDS
Queensbury
HALIFAX
Mytholmroyd
Hebden Bridge
SOWERBY BRIDGE
BRIGHOUSE
Elland
CLECKHEATON
LIVERSEDGE
Heckmondwike
DEWSBURY
BATLEY
MORLEY
ROTHWELL
Middleton
Gildersome
Drighlington
Birstall
Ossett
Horbury
MIRFIELD
Thornhill
HUDDERSFIELD
Ripponden
Slaithwaite
Marsden
Meltham
Holmfirth
Honley
Kirkburton
Skelmanthorpe
Clayton West
Denby Dale
Darton
ROYSTON
Penistone
Dodworth
STOCKSBRIDGE
Chapeltown
Grenoside
SHEFFIELD
Stannington
Mossley
STALYBRIDGE
HYDE
Hadfield
GLOSSOP
Uppermill
Delph
Denshaw
Greenfield
Marple
KEIGHLEY MOOR
PEAK DISTRICT NATIONAL PARK
DERBYSHIRE
PEAK DISTRICT
HIGH PEAK
Kinder Scout
M62
M606
M621
M1
M67
A629
A650
A660
A61
A58
A646
A640
A644
A642
A637
A638
A635
A628
A616
A6018
A6120
A6068
A6036
A6110
A653
A57
98
91
85

93
Kyme
Rigton
Clifford
Tadcaster
A659
A64
Oxton
Appleton Roebuck
Deighton
Escrick
Storwood
B1228
Melbourne
Bramham
Bramham Park
1408
Stutton
Kirkby Wharfe
Bolton Percy
Acaster Selby
River Ouse
B1222
Stillingfleet
Thorganby
East Cottingwith
Seaton Ross
Thorner
99
E
B1223
Ulleskelf
F
G
100
Ellerton
H
Laytham
Holme on Spalding
44
Towton
Towton 1461
Ryther
Kelfield
Aughton
A64
Barwick in Elmet
A1(M)
Church Fenton
Cawood
Riccall
A19
Skipwith
North Duffield
Harlthorpe
A163
Water End
Aberford
B1217
Foggathorpe
Bubwith
Highfield
Saxton
NORTH YORKSHIRE
Lotherton Hall
48
Barkston Ash
Wistow
A163
Breighton
Gunby
Gribthorpe
M1
47
43
Biggin
Little Fenton
Barlby
Menthorpe
Willitoft
1
Sherburn in Elmet
Osgodby
River
West Garforth
East Garforth
Old Micklefield
Micklefield
B1222
Abbey
South Duffield
Breighton
Spaldington
Garforth
New Micklefield
Sherburn in Elmet
Newthorpe
SELBY
Lund
Thorpe Willoughby
A1238
East Common
Cliffe
A63
Wressle
B1228
A614
Holmthorpe
B6137
Steeton Hall Gateway
South Milford
Monk Fryston
A63
Brayton
A63
Hemingbrough
Brind
Portington
Kippax
A656
42
Lumby
Hambleton
Newsholme
Great Preston
Ledsham
Barmby on the Marsh
Howden
Eastrington
Ledston
Fairburn
A1246
A162
Hillam
Burn
Burn
A1041
Barlow
Long Drax
Asselby
Allerton Bywater
Burton Salmon
Gateforth
A19
Knedlington
M62
Balkholme
Wood Row
Mickletown
New Fryston
Water Fryston
Birkin
B1228
37
Kilpin
Methley
Poole
Chapel Haddlesey
Camblesforth
R. Ouse
Kilpin Pike
Methley Junction
A6032
CASTLEFORD
Brotherton
West Haddlesey
Little Airmyn
A614
Skelton
Laxton
Airedale
Byram
Beal
Temple Hirst
Drax
2
Whitwood
Red Hill
B6136
Kellington
A645
Newland
Airmyn
31
32
32a
41
Ferrybridge
KNOTTINGLEY
A645
Hut Green
Hirst Courtney
Carlton
62
Kellingley
Hensall
Rawcliffe
A614
36
Saltmarshe
Altofts
A6539
B6421
New Town
FERRYBRIDGE
Eggborough
Little Heck
Gowdall
R. Aire
Snaith
East Cowick
GOOLE
North Featherstone
Pontefract
PONTEFRACT
Waterways
Old Goole
Swinefleet
Old Snydale
B6134
Ackton
Chequerfield
33
Cridling Stubbs
34
High Eggborough
A645
West Cowick
Rawcliffe Bridge
Dutch R
A161
Streethouse
FEATHERSTONE
Carleton
40
Whitley Thorpe
Whitley
Great Heck
M62
35
Marshland
Snydale
Darrington
Goole Fields
94
Sharlston Common
Purston Jaglin
West Hardwick
East Hardwick
Pollington
Southfield Resr.
Aire & Calder Navigation
Sharlston
Womersley
B6428
High Ackworth
Wentbridge
A1
A614
M18
NT Nostell Priory
Wragby
Low Ackworth
A639
Little Smeaton
Walden Stubbs
R. Went
Sykehouse
Ackworth Moor Top
Kirk Smeaton
Fenwick
Moorends
Wintersett
Fitzwilliam
Thorpe Audlin
New Junction Canal
R. Don
Badsworth
BARNSDALE BAR
Thorn Waste or Moors
Ryhill
A628
B6474
Norton
Moss
3
Kinsley
B6273
Wrangbrook
Campsall
Fishlake
Crowle
Havercroft
A638
Upton
North Elmsall
Askern
A161
South Hiendley
Hemsworth
A6021
Braithwaite
Stainforth
Thorne
Old R. Don
Burghwallis
Sutton
Kirk Bramwith
Stainforth & Keadby Canal
Skelbrooke
Thorpe in Balne
A161
Shafton
Brierley
B6422
South Elmsall
Owston
DONCASTER NORTH
Ealand
Skellow
A18
A628
South Kirkby
Carcroft
Hatfield
Hatfield Chase
Upper Cudworth
Hampole
A19
Barnby Dun
M180
2
Cudworth
Grimethorpe
B6422
38
ADWICK LE STREET
Toll Bar
Dunscroft
Clayton
Hooton Pagnell
Kirk Sandall
Hatfield Woodhouse
Sandtoft
Grey Green
Almholme
Dunsville
Trolleybus
Westgate
A6195
Great Houghton
A1(M)
Woodlands
New Village
Hatfield Moors
Belton
Brodsworth
Brodsworth Hall
A18
Edenthorpe
West Carr
Bracon
A635
Little Houghton
B6411
Thurnscoe
A638
Rostholme
Arksey
Carrhouse
Church Town
Middlecliffe
B6273
DEARNE
Marr
BENTLEY
A630
ISLE OF AXHOLME
Darfield
Billingley
Hickleton
A635
37
A630
Wheatley Park
Armthorpe
4
A614
Old Rectory
Goldthorpe
Scawsby
Cusworth
Cusworth Hall
Wheatley
Nutwell
Epworth
Wombwell
Bolton upon Dearne
Broomhill
Barnburgh
A18
M18
Wroot
Epworth Turbary
A6195
Adwick upon Dearne
Harlington
DONCASTER
Doncaster
Cantley
A161
DEARNE VALLEY
Bessacarr
Branton
Low Burnham
High Melton
Sprotbrough
Hyde Park
Hemingfield
Brampton
MEXBOROUGH
Balby
B1396
B6097
36
A6182
Auckley
Blaxton
Westwoodside
Upperthorpe
Cadeby
Warmsworth
Elsecar
WATH UPON DEARNE
A6023
86
3
Finningley
87
Haxey
East Lound
B6089
Denaby Main
New Edlington
2
A60
B1396
Wentworth
SWINTON
CONISBROUGH
Loversall
Rossington
ROBIN HOOD DONCASTER SHEFFIELD
Graiselound
A630
Old Edlington
B6376
Wentworth Woodhouse
Upper Haugh
B6090
Kilnhurst
35
New Rossington
A614
Mausoleum
Nether Haugh
RAWMARSH
Hooton Roberts
R. Idle
Heckdyke
Thorpe Common
Wadworth
West Stockwith
Clifton
B6094
Greasbrough
Thrybergh
Ravenfield
Austerfield
Misson
Misson
5
Ravenfield Common
Braithwell
Dalton
Sunnyside
A1(M)
B6463
A638
B1403
A629
Micklebring
East Stockwith
ROTHERHAM
Stainton
Newington
A6109
A6123
B6376
MALTBY
B6427
Tickhill
Bawtry
Walkerith
Dalton Magna
Bramley
1
Castle
Canal
Magna
A631
Bircotes
Walkeringham
Tinsley
Moorgate
Wickersley
Whiston
M18
Hooton Levitt
A631
Harworth
Scaftworth
Everton
Gringley on the Hill
A631
A631
Styrrup
A614
Chesterfield
Beckingham
Brinsworth
B6410
Slade Hooton
Scrooby
Old Hall
Morthen
A634
Mattersey Thorpe
Wiseton
Mattersey Priory
Treeton
Thurcroft
86
F
Roche Abbey (remains of)
Serlby
G
H
87
Catcliffe
Brookhouse
Mattersey
Upper Whiston
B6060
Laughton en le Morthen
Firbeck
B6463
Oldcotes
BLYTH
B6045
Clayworth
Brampton en le Morthen
A1
Ranskill
Saundby
A630
B6067
Ulley
Letwell
Langold
Blyth
Handsworth
Aughton
Laughton Common
Dinnington
A60
Torworth
Lound
North Wheatley
A620
Bole

94
A
B
C
D
100
87
93
1
2
3
4
5
Melbourne
Bielby
Thorpe le Street
Shiptonthorpe
Goodmanham
Market Weighton
Kiplingcotes
Dalton
Etton
Gardham
Cherry Burton
Leconfield
Arram
Routh
Tickton
BEVERLEY
Molescroft
Grovehill
Weel
Meaux
Woodmansey
Thearne
Wawne
Seaton Ross
Everingham
Harswell
Arras
Laytham
Holme-on-Spalding-Moor
Sancton
Bishop Burton
Walkington
Harlthorpe
Foggathorpe
Water End
Sand Hole
Moor End
Rascal Moor
North Newbald
South Newbald
North Cliffe
South Cliffe
EAST RIDING OF YORKSHIRE
Bubwith
Highfield
Breighton
Gunby
Willitoft
Gribthorpe
Spaldington
Bursea
Hotham
High Hunsley
Little Weighton
Risby
Skidby
COTTINGHAM
Bentley
Dunswell
Bransholme
Stoneferry
New Village
Inglemire
Newland
Sculcoates
North Cave
Rowley
Riplingham
Eppleworth
Willerby
Brind
Portington
Hive
Sandholme
Everthorpe
West End
South Cave
Brantingham
Wauldby
West Ella
Kirk Ella
East Ella
Newsholme
Howden
Asselby
Knedlington
Eastrington
Gilberdyke
Scalby
Staddlethorpe
Newport
Walling Fen
Ellerker
Swanland
Anlaby
Anlaby Park
Northfield
KINGSTON UPON HULL
Balkholme
Kilpin
Kilpin Pike
Ellougton
Welton
Melton
Brough
Broomfleet
North Ferriby
HESSLE
South Field
Humber Bridge
TOLL
Little Airmyn
Airmyn
Hook
Skelton
Laxton
GOOLE
Yokefleet
Blacktoft
Faxfleet
Whitton
Saltmarshe
Reedness
Whitgift
Ousefleet
Redcliff Channel
Read's Island
Barton Waterside
New Holland
Barrow Haven
Barton upon Humber
Far Ings
Swinefleet
Old Goole
Rawcliffe Bridge
Alkborough
Winteringham
Goxhill
West Halton
Adlingfleet
Walcot
Marshland
Goole Fields
Ferriby Sluice
South Ferriby
Baysgarth House
Barrow upon Humber
Kingsforth
The Hallands
Deepdale
Garthorpe
Fockerby
Coleby
Burton upon Stather
Burton Stather
Winterton
Horkstow
Thornton Curtis
Thealby
Normanby
Normanby Hall
Roxby
Saxby All Saints
Burnham
Eastoft
Luddington
Moorends
Thorn Waste or Moors
Flixborough
Risby
Wootton
NORTH LINCOLNSHIRE
Bonby
Ulceby
Amcotts
Appleby
Worlaby
Crowle
Neap House
Dragonby
Thorne
Stainforth & Keadby Canal
Keadby
Elsham
Elsham Hall
Croxton
Gunness
Crosby
Frodingham
Ealand
Melton Ross
Kirmington
Althorpe
SCUNTHORPE
HUMBERSIDE INTERNATIONAL
Hatfield Chase
Coskills
New Barnetby
Derrythorpe
Burringham
Brumby
Broughton
Wressle
Sandtoft
Trolleybus
Ashby
Wrawby
Wrawby Postmill
Barnetby le Wold
Grey Green
Westgate
Bracon
Belton
Beltoft
Yaddlethorpe
Holme
Bottesford
Pink Pig Farm
Brigg
Island Carr
Scawby Brook
Bigby
Somerby
Monument
Hatfield Moors
West Carr
Carrhouse
Church Town
East Butterwick
West Butterwick
Scawby
Sturton
Searby
Grasby
Clixby
ISLE OF AXHOLME
Epworth
Messingham
Old Rectory
Cadney
Howsham
Owmby
Wroot
Epworth Turbary
Manton
Hibaldstow
Low Burnham
Susworth
Scotterthorpe
North Kelsey Moor
North Kelsey
Kelfield
Owston Ferry
Scotter
Gainsthorpe Medieval Village
Redbourne
Caistor
Westwoodside
Upperthorpe
Haxey
East Lound
East Ferry
Scotton
Mount Pleasant
Kirton in Lindsey
Moortown
South Kelsey
Graiseland
Wildsworth
Laughton
Brandy Wharf
Holton le Moor
Gunthorpe
Northorpe
R. Idle
Heckdyke
West Stockwith
Grayingham
Waddingham
Thornton le Moor
Blyton
North Owersby
Misterton
East Stockwith
Blyborough
Snitterby
Claxby
Usselby
South Owersby
Pilham
Aisby
Willoughton
Atterby
Kingerby
Osgodby
Walkerith
Bishop Norton
Kirkby
Horse World
Walkeringham
Morton
Gringley on the Hill
Corringham
Hemswell
Bishopbridge
Glentham
GAINSBOROUGH
Beckingham
York Model Railway
Spital in the Street
Middle Rasen
Wiseton
Old Hall
Springthorpe
Sturgate
Hemswell Cliff
Caenby
West Rasen
Clayworth
Heapham
Glentworth
Normanby-by-Spital
Owmby-by-Spital
Toft next Newton
Newton by Toft
Saundby
Bole
Lea
Knaith Park
Upton
Fillingham
Saxby
North Wheatley
LINCOLNSHIRE
A614
A1035
A164
A1079
A1174
A163
A1034
B1230
A614
B1228
A63
M62
A1105
A1166
B1231
B1232
B1233
B1237
A161
A15
B1206
B1218
B1204
B1207
A1077
B1430
B1392
B1216
A18
M180
M181
B1450
A159
A180
A1084
B1398
B1400
B1205
B1396
B1403
A631
A156
A620
A1103
A46
B1433
B1434
B1248
B1208

NORTH SEA
RIVER HUMBER
Mouth of the Humber
NORTH EAST LINCOLNSHIRE
LINCOLNSHIRE
THE WOLDS
Withernwick
Aldbrough
Sproatley
Bilton
Preston
Elstronwick
Burton Pidsea
Roos
Marfleet
Hedon
Burstwick
Withernsea
Havenside
Thorngumbald
Keyingham
Hollym
Ottringham
Patrington
Holmpton
Welwick
Skeffling
Easington
Sunk Island Sands
Kilnsea
Spurn Heritage Coast
Trinity Sands
Grimsby Roads
SPURN HEAD
Immingham Dock
South Killingholme
Immingham
Brocklesby
Stallingborough
Keelby
Healing
GRIMSBY
CLEETHORPES
Discovery Centre
Jungle Zoo
Cleethorpes Coast Light Railway
Pleasure Island
Humberston
Scartho
Laceby
Bradley
Waltham
New Waltham
Holton le Clay
Tetney
North Cotes
Marshchapel
Grainthorpe
North Somercotes
Saltfleet
North Thoresby
Fulstow
Ludborough
Covenham St. Mary
Binbrook
Tealby
Fotherby
Ludford
LOUTH
Grimoldby
Manby
Saltfleetby St. Peter
Theddlethorpe St. Helen
Seal Sanctuary & Wildlife Centre
Hull to:
Rotterdam (Europoort) 10hrs.
Zeebrugge 12hrs. 30mins.
A165
A1033
A160
A1173
A180
A46
A16
A18
A1031
A631
A157
B1240
B1362
B1445
B1242
B1238
B1239
B1210
B1211
B1203
B1201
B1200
B1225
101
88
89

96
LAKE
DISTRICT
NATIONAL
PARK
FURNESS
ULVERSTON
BARROW-IN-FURNESS
Dalton-in-Furness
Millom
Grange-over-Sands
MORECAMBE
LANCASTER
Heysham
FLEETWOOD
CLEVELEYS
BLACKPOOL
Poulton-le-Fylde
Thornton
MORECAMBE
BAY
Lancaster Sound
Walney Island
Foulney Island
Piel Island
Chapel Island
Heysham to Douglas 3hrs. 30mins.
Wyre Light
Heysham Lake
Rossall Point
THE FYLDE

97
KENDAL
Kentrigg
Fisher Tarn Resr.
A684
A591
Fox's Pulpit
Winder 1552
Marthwaite
Sedbergh
Baugh Fell
East Baugh Fell 2217
Garsdale Head
Cotterdale
High Shaw
Hardraw
Sedbusk
Appersett
Hawes
Gayle
Burtersett
Wensleydale Creamery
Oxenholme
New Hutton
KILLINGTON LAKE
Millholme
Hallbank
Millthrop
Brigflatts
Fairfield Mill
Garsdale
Mossdale Moor
Lenacre
Killington
Rise Hill 1825
Natland
Middleshaw
Barrows Green
Halfpenny
Old Hutton
Sedgwick
Beckside
Gawthrop
Dent
Cowgill
Lea Yeat
Stone House
Widdale Fell
Wether
Stainton
Gatebeck
Middleton
Calf Top
Dodd Fell
Marsett
Hincaster
Endmoor
Goose Green
Warth Hill
Crooklands
Leasgill
Heversham
Milton
Nook
Scout Hill 935
Mansergh
Barbon
Crag Hill 2250
Deepdale
Wold Fell 1829
2192
Gayle Moor
Oughtershaw
Ackenthwaite
Whasset
Farleton
Lupton
Kearstwick
Casterton
Ruskin's View
Kirkby Lonsdale
WHERNSIDE 2414
Blea Moor
YORKSHIRE DALES
Deepdale
Beetham
Holme
Slack Head
Hale
Lakeland Wildlife Oasis
Hutton Roof
High Biggins
Cowan Bridge
Leck
Leck Fell 2057
Ribblehead Viaduct
Ribblehead Station
LANGSTROTHDALE CHASE
Sike Moor
Foxup
Halton Gill
BURTON-IN-KENDAL
Burton-in-Kendal
Yealand Storrs
Yealand Redmayne
Leighton Hall
Whittington
Overtown
Ireby
Masongill
Chapel le Dale
High Birkwith
Selside
NATIONAL PARK
Yealand Conyers
Priest Hutton
Newton
Nether Burrow
Westhouse
Thornton Force
Thornton in Lonsdale
White Scar Cave
Ingleborough 2376
Simon Fell
Horton Moor
Hull Pot
Pen-y-ghent Side
Pen-y-ghent 2277
Warton
Borwick
Tunstall
Arkholme
Cantsfield
A687
Skirwith
Ingleton
Ingleborough Common
Gaping Gill
NORTH
New Houses
New Inn
Horton in Ribblesdale
Darnbrook Fell
Millhead
Carnforth
Capernwray
Wrayton
Burton in Lonsdale
Melling
Cold Cotes
Newby Cote
Newby
Ingleborough Cave
YORKSHIRE
Fountains Fell 2191
Over Kellet
Gressingham
Wennington
Tatham
Low Bentham
High Bentham
A65
Clapham
Wharfe
Helwith Bridge
Nether Kellet
Hornby
Wray
Farleton
Butt Yeats
B6480
R. Wenning
Austwick
Feizor
Little Stainforth
Stainforth Force
Stainforth
86
Aughton
Bolton Town End
Claughton
R. Hindburn
Keasden
Lawkland
Eldroth
Stackhouse
Langcliffe
Halton
Caton
Brookhouse
Whit Moor
Caton Moor
Lowgill
Tatham Fells
1318
Burn Moor Fell
Giggleswick
Settle
1815
Malham Cove
Kirkby Fell
Malham
M6
A683
Goodber Common
Salter
Thrushgill
Botton Head
Wham
Scaleber Force
Crossgill
Mearbeck
Quernmore
Blanch Fell
Haylot Fell
1595
Catlow Fell
Black Hill
Rathmell
Long Preston
Kirkby Malham
Airton
Clougha Pike
1839 Ward's Stone
Mallowdale Fell
1786 White Hill
Croasdale Fell
Otterburn
Lee Fell
LANCASHIRE
Stocks Resr.
Tosside
Wigglesworth
Hellifield
Smith Green
Lee
Tambrook
FOREST
A682
Halton West
Conistone Cold
Four Lane Ends
Five Lane Ends
Dolphinholme
Abbeystead
R. Wyre
Marshaw
Trough of Bowland
1561 Whins Brow
Slaidburn
Nappa
LANCASTER
Hawthornthwaite Fell Top 1572
Street
Sykes
OF
Paythorne
Newsholme
West Marton
Hareden
Dunsop Bridge
Newton
Lane Ends
Horton
Scorton
Calder Fell
R. Calder
Sykes Fell
Easington Fell 1300
Holden
Bolton-by-Bowland
Gisburn
Bracewell
Thornton in Craven
BOWLAND
A59
Cabus
Oakenclough
Whitewell
Sawley
Rimington
Barnoldswick
Bancroft Mill Engine
Salterforth
Fair Snape Fell
Browsholme Hall
Grindleton
West Bradford
Chatburn
Howgill
Calder Vale
Bowland Wild Boar Park
Horrocksford
Downham
Twiston
Weets Hill
Whitemoor Resr.
Bonds
Bowgreave
Catterall
Chipping
Waddington
Bashall Eaves
Bashall Town
Clitheroe
Worston
Pendle Hill 1827
Claughton
Bowland
Beacon Fell
Blacko
Foulridge
White Chapel
Hesketh Lane
Walker Fold
Longridge Fell
Low Moor
Barley
Roughlee
Colne
PENDLE
Bilsborrow
Inglewhite
Woodfields
91
Pendleton
Newchurch
Barrowford
Knowle Green
New Row
B6243
Great Mitton
Barrow
FOREST OF PENDLE
Wheatley Lane
Longridge
Hurst Green
Wiswell
Sabden
Fence
Barton
Ward Green Cross
Dinckley
Whalley
Higham
NELSON
Brierfield
Newsham
Goosnargh
Stydd
M65
E
F
G
H
1
2
3
4
5
103
104

98
104
105
97
91
92
Cotterdale
Askrigg Common
East Bolton Moor
Redmire Moor
Barden
East Hauxwell
Appleton
Hornby
Arrathorne
Bellerby
Garriston
Constable Burton Hall
Hunton
High Shaw
Hardraw
Sedbusk
Askrigg
Newbiggin
Castle Bolton
Bolton
Bellerby Camp
Leyburn
Mossdale Moor
Hawes
Gayle
Yorkshire Dales National Park
Wensleydale Creamery
Bainbridge
Worton
Woodhall
Carperby
Redmire
Preston-under-Scar
Constable Burton
Finghall
Newton-le-Willows
Burtersett
Thornton Rust
Aysgarth
Aysgarth Falls
Swinithwaite
West Witton
Wensley
Harmby
Spennithorne
Middleham
Countersett
Wether
Semer Water
Stalling Busk
Marsett
Thoralby
West Burton
Newbiggin
Penhill
Agglethorpe
Harland Hill
Coverham
Corbidden Corner
Melmerby
Braithwaite Hall
Caldbergh
Carlton
Carlton Moor
St. Simon's Chapel
East Witton
Thornton Steward
Jervaulx Abbey
Dodd Fell
YORKSHIRE DALES
NATIONAL PARK
WENSLEYDALE
Bishopdale Beck
Gammersgill
West Scrafton
Walden
Ellingstring
High Ellington
Oughtershaw
Cam Beck
Kidstones
Horsehouse
Hindlethwaite Moor
Colsterdale Moor
Colsterdale
Gollinglith Foot
Fearby
Theakston Brewery
Healey
Walden Head
Bradley
Great Haw
Masham Moor
Leighton
Deepdale
Yockenthwaite
Cray
Woodale
LANGSTROTHDALE CHASE
Hubberholme
Buckden
Buckden Pike
Cover Head Bents
Little Whernside
Scar House Reservoir
Angram Reservoir
Druid's Temple
Ilton
Warthermarske
Foxup
Halton Gill
High Birkwith
Brown Ridge
NORTH YORKSHIRE
Grewelthorpe
Pen-y-ghent Side
Horton Moor
Hull Pot
Pen-y-ghent
New Houses
New Inn
Horton in Ribblesdale
Litton
Starbotton
River Wharfe
GREAT WHERNSIDE
Riggs Moor
Middlesmoor
How Stean Gorge
Stean
Lofthouse
Hambleton Hill
Carlesmoor
Swetton
Darnbrook Fell
Arncliffe
Kettlewell
Nidderdale
Greygarth
Dallowgill Moor
Dallow
Lumley Moor Reservoir
Fountains Fell
Hawkswick
Arncliffe Cote
Conistone Moor
Stean Moor
Bouthwaite
Ramsgill
Gouthwaite Reservoir
Helwith Bridge
WHARFEDALE
Heathfield Moor
Pateley Moor
Little Stainforth
Stainforth
Kilnsey
Kilnsey Crag
Conistone
Malham Tarn
Wath
Stackhouse
Hebden Moor
Nidderdale
Pateley Bridge
Langcliffe
Malham Cove
Gordale Scar
Bordley
Grimwith Resr.
Greenhow Hill
Brimham Rocks
Giggleswick
Settle
Kirkby Fell
Grassington
Bewerley
Wilsill
Glasshouses
Scaleber Force
Malham
Janet's Foss
Threshfield
Hebden
Stump Cross Caverns
Summerbridge
Boss Moor
Linton
Burnsall
Parcevall Hall
Pock Stones Moor
Dacre Banks
Mearbeck
Kirkby Malham
Hanlith
Winterburn Reservoir
Thorpe
Cracoe
Threapland
Appletreewick
Dacre
Long Preston
Airton
Calton
Winterburn
Hetton
Rylstone
Howgill
Barden Fell
Bramley Head
Padside
Thornthwaite
Darley Head
Darley
Otterburn
Drebley
Earl Seat
West End
Thruscross Resr.
Hellifield
Barden Resrs.
Barden Tower
Brown Bank Head
Wigglesworth
Bell Busk
Eshton
Flasby
Embsay Moor
Barden Scale
Blubberhouses
Kettlesing
Halton West
Coniston Cold
Embsay & Bolton Abbey Steam Railway
Halton East
Hesketh Farm Park
Bolton Priory
Hill End
Reservoir
Gargrave
Embsay
Eastby
Bolton Abbey
Round Hill
Fewston
Nappa
Bank Newton
Skipton
Draughton
Beamsley
Kex Beck
Timble
Swinsty Resr.
Paythorne
Newsholme
Thorlby
Broughton
Craven
SKIPTON
Chelker Res.
Langbar
March Ghyll Reservoir
Jack Hill
Horton
West Marton
East Marton
Elslack
Carleton
Nesfield
Middleton
Denton
Clifton
Bracewell
Thornton in Craven
Low Bradley
Addingham
Askwith
Gisburn
Yorkshire Dales Mining Museum
Earby
Cononley
Silsden
ILKLEY
Swartha
Newall
Otley
Barnoldswick
Bancroft Mill Engine
Lothersdale
Farnhill
Kildwick
White Wells Spa Cottage
Ilkley Moor
Burley in Wharfedale
Howgill
Salterforth
Glusburn
Brunthwaite
Weets Hill
Kelbrook
Eastburn
Cross Hills
Steeton
RUMBALDS MOOR
Burley Woodhead
Twiston
Whitemoor Resr.
Cowling
Sutton-in-Craven
Riddlesden
East Riddlesden Hall
Menston
Guiseley
LANCASHIRE
Beechcliffe
Stockbridge
East Morton
Yeadon
Pendle Hill
Blacko
Foulridge
Braithwaite
Micklethwaite
Hawksworth
Barley
Roughlee
Colne
Laneshaw Resr.
Laycock
Thwaites
KEIGHLEY
Newchurch
Barrowford
Laneshaw Bridge
Eldwick
BAILDON
Esholt
Wheatley Lane
Trawden
KEIGHLEY MOOR
Ingrow
Bingley
Harden
Baildon Green
THE FOREST OF TRAWDEN
Water Sheddles Reservoir
Brontë Parsonage
Oakworth
Hainworth
Lees
Saltaire
Salts Mill
Fence
NELSON
Stanbury
Ponden Resr.
Cottingley
Cullingworth
Nab Wood
Shipley
Calverley
Brierfield
Haworth
Keighley &
A684
A6108
B6255
B6160
B6479
B6480
A65
A682
A59
A56
B6251
B6252
B6383
A629
A6131
A6034
A6068
B6265
B6165
B6451
A650
A682
B6248
M65
A658
A657
B6429
B6143

99
NORTH YORK MOORS
NATIONAL PARK
HAMBLETON HILLS
Hackforth
Great Fencote
Little Fencote
Thrintoft
Yafforth
Romanby
NORTHALLERTON
Kirby Sigston
Fangdale Beck
East Moors
Langthorne
Scruton
Ainderby Steeple
Over Silton
Arden Great Moor
Little Crakehall
Kirkbridge
Morton-on-Swale
Warlaby
Crosby Court
Nether Silton
Kepwick
Arden Hall
Leake
Thornton-le-Beans
North Otterington
Borrowby
Hawnby
Rievaulx Moor
Leeming Bar
Leeming
Aiskew
Bedale
LEEMING
Londonderry
Gatenby
Newby Wiske
Thornton-le-Moor
South Otterington
Cowesby
Knayton
Upsall
Kirby Knowle
Boltby
Old Byland
Exelby
Firby
Thorp Perrow Arboretum
Theakston
Burneston
Snape
Maunby
Kirby Wiske
Newsham
Thornton-le-Street
North Kilvington
South Kilvington
Felixkirk
Carlton
Pockley
Wytherstone
Rievaulx
NT Terrace
Abbey
Carthorpe
Pickhill
Thirlby
North York Moors National Park
Cold Kirby
Scawton
Helmsley
Well
Holme
Sinderby
Ainderby Quernhow
Sandhutton
Norby
Thirsk
Sutton-under-Whitestonecliffe
Duncombe Park
Kilburn White Horse
Sutton Bank
Kirklington
Skipton-on-Swale
Carlton Miniott
Sowerby
Monk Park Farm
Balk
Sproxton
Binsoe
Nosterfield
Thornborough
Marmion Tower
West Tanfield
Sutton Howgrave
Howe
Bagby
Great Thirkleby
Little Thirkleby
Kilburn
Mouseman
High Kilburn
Oldstead
Wass
Byland Abbey
Ampleforth
Ampleforth College
Oswaldkirk
East Newton
Middleton Quernhow
Baldersby
Topcliffe
Catton
Baldersby St. James
Cod Beck
Shandy Hall
Coxwold
Newburgh Priory
Thorpe Hall
Gilling East
Stonegrave
Cawton
Mickley
North Stainley
Wath
Melmerby
Norton Conyers
Lightwater Valley
Topcliffe
Asenby
Dalton
Hutton Sessay
Carlton Husthwaite
Husthwaite
Kirkby Malzeard
Azerley
Nunwick
Rainton
Sessay
Thormanby
Oulston
Yearsley
Coulton
Sutton Grange
Hutton Conyers
Crakehill
Fawdington
Brandsby
North Lees
Ure Bank
Sharow
Dishforth
Cundall
Scackleton
Galphay
Winksley
Bishopton
RIPON
Copt Hewick
Marton-le-Moor
Norton-le-Clay
Raskelf
Crayke
Stearsby
Howard
Skewsby
Low Grantley
Brafferton
Easingwold
Marton Abbey
Whenby
Studley Roger
Studley Royal NT
Fountains Abbey
Aldfield
Bridge Hewick
Ripon
Kirby Hill
Helperby
Risplith
Littlethorpe
Skelton
Boroughbridge 1322
Milby
Myton 1319
Stillington
Farlington
Sawley
Markenfield Hall
Newby Hall
Devil's Arrows
Langthorpe
Boroughbridge
Tholthorpe
Aldborough
Roman Site
Myton-on-Swale
Bishop Monkton
Roecliffe
Markington
Lower Dunsforth
Flawith
Alne
Huby
Minskip
Tollerton
Cross Lanes
Sutton-on-the-Forest
Sutton Park
Burton Leonard
Bishop Thornton
Copgrove
Grafton
Upper Dunsforth
Aldwark
Youlton
South Stainley
Staveley
Shaw Mills
Marton
Branton Green
Great Ouseburn
Linton-on-Ouse
Bedlam
Burnt Yates
Brearton
Ferrensby
Little Ouseburn
Strensall
Strensall Camp
Farnham
Arkendale
Ripley
Clint
Nidd
Scotton
Thorpe Underwood
Newton-on-Ouse
Beningbrough Hall NT
Shipton
Wigginton
Towthorpe
Hampsthwaite
Killinghall
Coneythorpe
Scriven
Allerton Mauleverer
Nun Monkton
Swincliffe
HARROGATE
Henshaws
Flaxby
KNARESBOROUGH
Whixley
Green Hammerton
Beningbrough
Haxby
Earswick
Bilton
Starbeck
Goldsborough
Hopperton
Moor Monkton
Skelton
Huntington
New Park
Mother Shipton's Cave
Overton
Nether Poppleton
Rawcliffe
New Earswick
Dyke Res.
RHS Harlow Carr
Woodlands
Kirk Hammerton
Upper Poppleton
Nidd
Cattal
Marston Moor
Marston Moor 1644
Hessay
Clifton
Heworth
Tang Hall
Yorkshire Farm
Beckwithshaw
Pannal Ash
Oatlands
Follifoot
Walshford
Little Ribston
Hunsingore
Cowthorpe
Tockwith
Long Marston
Knapton
Rufforth
Acomb
Bunker
Osbaldwick
Daw Cross
Pannal
Spofforth Castle
North Deighton
YORK
Clifford's Tower
Grimston
Brackenthwaite
Spacey Houses
Spofforth
Kirk Deighton
Bickerton
WETHERBY
Hutton Wandesley
Rufforth
Heslington
North Rigton
Kirkby Overblow
Stockeld Park
Sicklinghall
Bilton in Ainsty
Askham Bryan
Woodthorpe
Nunthorpe
Fulford
Stainburn
Huby
Weeton
Wetherby
Linton
Walton
Angram
Askham Richard
Dunkeswick
Healaugh
Bishopthorpe
Leathley
Wighill
Castley
Collingham
Boston Spa
Thorp Arch
Bilbrough
Copmanthorpe
Crockey Hill
Pool
Harewood
Catterton
Acaster Malbis
Naburn
Weardley
Harewood House
East Keswick
Newton Kyme
Colton
Deighton
Arthington
East Rigton
Clifford
Tadcaster
Oxton
Escrick
Bramhope
Bardsey
Bramham
Appleton Roebuck
Eccup
Eccup Resr.
Wike
Bramham Park
Alwoodley
Stutton
Kirkby Wharfe
Bolton Percy
Acaster Selby
Slaid Hill
Scarcroft
1408
Stillingfleet
Tinshill
Thorner
Ulleskelf
Ryther
Moor Allerton
Shadwell
Towton
Moortown
Roundhay Park
Roundhay
Barwick in Elmet
Towton 1461
Cock Beck
Church Fenton
Kelfield
Chapel Allerton
Meanwood
Abbey House
Oakwood
Potternewton
Headingley
LEEDS
Scholes
Aberford
Saxton
Cawood
Riccall
RSFORTH
A1
A1(M)
A19
A61
A168
A167
A684
A6055
A6108
A170
A59
A658
A661
A660
A6120
A64
A659
A162
A1237
A1036
B1257
B1363
B6267
B6268
B6285
B1448
B6265
B6165
B6161
B6162
B6164
B1224
B1223
B1222
B1217
106
93
100

100
106
107
A
B
C
D
NORTH YORK MOORS NATIONAL PARK
Fangdale Beck
Bilsdale
River Seph
East Moors
Rudland Rigg
Hodge Beck
River Seven
Cross
TOLL
Blakey Topping
Spaunton Moor
Hartoft End
Stape
Hole of Horcum
Skelton Tower
Ryedale Folk
Lastingham
Gillamoor
Hutton-le-Hole
Spaunton
Levisham
Lockton
Newton-on-Rawcliffe
Newton Dale
Stain Dale
Bickley
Langdale End
Silpho
Broxa
Rievaulx Moor
Fadmoor
Kirk Dale
Cropton Brewery
Cropton
Cawthorne
Appleton-le-Moors
North Yorkshire Moors Railway
Low Dalby
Dalby Forest Drive
Dalby Forest
Troutsdale
Wykeham Forest
North Moor
Old Byland
Kirkbymoorside
Kirkdale Cave
Keldholme
Sinnington
Wrelton
Carlton
Pockley
Wytherstone
Rievaulx
NT Terrace
Abbey
Rye Dale
Beadlam
Nawton
Welburn
Kirkby Mills
Aislaby
Middleton
Beck Isle
Newbridge
Pickering
Ellerburn
Sawdon
Scawton
Helmsley
Duncombe Park
Wombleton
Great Edstone
Marton
Costa Beck
A170
A169
Ruston
Wilton
Allerston
Ebberston
Thornton-le-Dale
Snainton
Brompton
B1257
B1415
B1258
Harome
Normanby
Spraxton
Riccal
NORTH YORK
Muscoates
Salton
Little Barugh
Flamingo Land
Kirby Misperton
Yedingham
East Newton
Nunnington
Nunnington Hall
East Ness
West Ness
Great Barugh
High Marishes
R. Derwent
Ampleforth
Byland Abbey
Ampleforth College
Oswaldkirk
Stonegrave
South Holme
Brawby
Butterwick
Little Habton
Low Marishes
East Heslerton
Sherburn
Gilling East
Thorpe Hall
Newburgh Priory
Cawton
Hovingham Hall
Hovingham
Great Habton
River Rye
Ryton
Wykeham
Scampston
Scampston Hall
East Knapton
West Knapton
West Heslerton
A64
B1363
Oulston
Yearsley
Fryton
Slingsby
Rillington
Coulton
Barton-le-Street
Appleton-le-Street
Amotherby
Swinton
Eden Camp
Broughton
Wintringham
Brandsby
Scackleton
Malton
Old Malton
Scagglethorpe
Thorpe Bassett
Place Newton
Stearsby
Howardian Hills
Terrington
Coneysthorpe
Castle Howard
Norton-on-Derwent
Settrington
Crayke
Skewsby
Yorkshire Lavender
Ganthorpe
Whenby
Marton Abbey
Whitewall Corner
Helperthorpe
Stillington
Farlington
Sheriff Hutton
Castle
Bulmer
Welburn
High Hutton
Menethorpe
Crambeck
Huttons Ambo
Langton
North Grimston
High Mowthorpe
East Lutton
West Lutton
Duggleby
B1248
B1253
Kirby Grindalythe
Huby
Sutton-on-the-Forest
Sutton Park
Thornton-le-Clay
Whitwell-on-the-Hill
Firby
Kirkham
Priory
Kennythorpe
Birdsall
Wharram-le-Street
Sledmere
Sledmere House
West Lilling
Foston
Crambe
Westow
Burythorpe
Wharram Percy Deserted Medieval Village
Barton Hill
Barton-le-Willows
Flaxton
Harton
Howsham
Leavening
Towthorpe
Burdale
B1252
B1251
Strensall
Danger Area
Bossall
Acklam
Thixendale
Sir Tatton Sykes's Monument
Strensall Camp
Claxton
Scrayingham
Leppington
Fimber
Wetwang
Towthorpe
Sand Hutton
Painsthorpe
Kirby Underdale
Fridaythorpe
A166
Wigginton
Haxby
Buttercrambe
Bugthorpe
Earswick
A19
Skelton
A1237
Stockton-on-the-Forest
Upper Helmsley
Skirpenbeck
Huntington
Gate Helmsley
Youlthorpe
Bishop Wilton
Huggate
Tibthorpe
Nether Poppleton
Rawcliffe
New Earswick
Warthill
Stamford Bridge 1066
Full Sutton
Gowthorpe
EAST RIDING OF YORKSHIRE
Brockfield Hall
Holtby
Stamford Bridge
High Catton
Low Catton
Fangfoss
Great Givendale
North Dalton
B1246
Clifton
Heworth
Tang Hall
Yorkshire Farm
Murton
Meltonby
Knapton
B1224
Bunker
Osbaldwick
Dunnington
Bolton
Yapham
Millington
Acomb
YORK
Grimston
A1036
A1079
Kexby
Wilberfoss
Warter
Middleton-on-the-Wolds
Clifford's Tower
Woodthorpe
Heslington
Nunthorpe
Fulford
B1228
Newton upon Derwent
Barmby Moor
Pocklington
Burnby Hall
B1247
Elvington
Yorkshire Air
Allerthorpe
Nunburnholme
Bishopthorpe
Copmanthorpe
Crockey Hill
Sutton upon Derwent
Pocklington Canal
Burnby
Holme on the Wolds
Acaster Malbis
Naburn
Wheldrake
Hayton
Londesborough
A614
Kiplingcotes
South Dalton
Deighton
Thornton
Thorpe le Street
Storwood
Melbourne
Bielby
Shiptonthorpe
Goodmanham
Appleton Roebuck
Escrick
River Ouse
Market Weighton
Gardham
Everingham
Thorganby
East Cottingwith
Arras
B1222
Acaster Selby
Stillingfleet
Seaton Ross
Harswell
Ryther
Ellerton
93
Laytham
Holme-on-Spalding-Moor
Sancton
94
Kelfield
Aughton
Riccall
Skipwith
North Duffield
Harlthorpe
Moor End
Water End
Sand Hole
North Newbald
A1034
Cawood
B1223
Foggathorpe
Bubwith
A163
Highfield
Rascal Moor
North Cliffe

NORTH SEA
Cloughton
Burniston
Scalby
Scalby Mills
Throxenby
Newby
Barrowcliff
SCARBOROUGH
Falsgrave
East Ayton
West Ayton
Osgodby
Cayton Bay
Crossgates
Eastfield
Irton
Seamer
Cayton
The Wyke
Lebberston
Gristhorpe
Newbiggin
Lifeboat Station
Filey
Flixton
Folkton
Muston
Willerby
Staxton
Ganton
Primrose Valley
Royal Oak
Hunmanby
Hunmanby Sands
Fordon
Reighton
Speeton
Wold Newton
Foxholes
Burton Fleming
Buckton
Bempton
FLAMBOROUGH HEAD
Danes Dyke
Flamborough
Butterwick
Grindale
Thwing
Octon
Marton
Sewerby Hall
Sewerby
Lifeboat Station
Boynton
Rudston
Rudston Monolith
Gypsey Race
Bondville Miniature Village
BRIDLINGTON
Harbour
Langtoft
Carnaby
John Bull World of Rock
Bessingby
West Hill
Lifeboat Station
Hilderthorpe
Bridlington Bay
Cottam
Haisthorpe
Park Rose Birds of Prey
Wilsthorpe
West End
Kilham
Norman Manor House
Thornholme
Burton Agnes
Ruston Parva
Harpham
Fraisthorpe
Great Kendale
Garton-on-the-Wolds
Lowthorpe
Little Kelk
Gransmoor
Barmston
Nafferton
DRIFFIELD
Elmswell
Little Driffield
Great Kelk
Lissett
East End
Gembling
Wansford
Foston on the Wolds
West End
Ulrome
Skipsea
Skerne
Southburn
Dringhoe
Beeford
Upton
Skipsea Brough
Brigham
Church End
North Frodingham
Hutton
Hutton Cranswick
Dunnington
Atwick
Rotsea
Kilnwick
Watton
Hempholme
Bewholme
Beswick
Lockington
Burshill
Little Burton
Hornsea
Brandesburton
Hornsea Burton
Hornsea Mere
Thorpe
Aike
Seaton
Little Leven
Sigglesthorne
Goxhill
Scorborough
Leven
Catwick
Rolston
Arram
Leven Canal
Little Catwick
Mappleton
Leconfield
Routh
Long Riston
Little Hatfield
Great Hatfield
Great Cowden
Rise
Tickton
Arnold
Beverley
BEVERLEY
Withernwick
Molescroft
Grovehill
DANGER AREA
Meaux
New Ellerby
Marton
Weel
Skirlaugh
West Newton
Aldbrough
Minster
Woodmansey
Old Ellerby
East Newton
Walkington
Thearne
Burton Constable
Wawne
Flinton
Bentley
Wood
A171
A165
A170
A64
A165
B1261
B1267
A1039
B1249
B1229
A165
B1255
B1259
B1253
A614
B1242
B1249
A164
A165
B1244
A1035
B1243
B1242
B1248
A164
A1174
A1079
B1238
95
E
F
G
H
1
2
3
4
5
10
20
30
90
80
70
60
50
40

102
A
B
C
D
1
2
3
4
5
Westnewton
Yearngill
Heathfield
A596
Crookdake
Bolton New Houses
Bolton Wood Lane
Allonby
Allonby Bay
Hayton
Aspatria
Watchill
Fletchertown
B5299
Blennerhasset
Mealsgate
A595
Harriston
Kirkland Guards
Boltongate
Prospect
112
Allerby
Westmoor End
Parsonby
Threapland
Plumbland
Bothel
Torpenhow
Whitrigg
Ireby
Aughertree
Uldale
High Ireby
Ruthwaite
Longlands
Fell Side
Branthwaite
Whelpo
A596
Crosscanonby
Crosby Villa
Senhouse Roman
Alauna Roman Fort
Crosby
Bullgill
Gilcrux
Birkby
Greengill
R. Ellen
B5301
A591
Maryport
Maritime
Netherton
A594
Dearham
Townhead
Moota Hill
Sunderland
Binsey 1467
Bewaldeth
Ellenborough
Tallentire
A595
Blindcrake
Over Water
Orthwaite
Fothergill
Flimby
Broughton Moor
Dovenby
Bridekirk
Redmain
Isel Hall
River Derwent
Trotters World of Animals
Kilnhill
North Row
Bassenthwaite
St. Helens
Little Broughton
Belle Vue
Wordsworth House NT
Elva Plain Stone Circle
B5291
Chapel
Siddick
Camerton
Great Broughton
Papcastle
Cockermouth
Embleton
Whitewater Dash
Great Calva 2265
A596
North Side
Seaton
Great Clifton
Broughton Cross
Brigham
Wythop Mill
High Side
SKIDDAW FOREST
SKIDDAW
3054
Bridgefoot
Stainburn
Greysouthen
A66
WORKINGTON
A66
Little Clifton
Eaglesfield
B5292
Bassenthwaite Lake
Mirehouse
Little Crosthwaite
Moss Bay
Westfield
A596
WHINLATTER FOREST PARK
Lord's Seat 1811
Winscales
Deanscales
A5086
Low Lorton
Spout Force
Millbeck
Applethwaite
High Harrington
11
Thornthwaite
A591
Harrington
Branthwaite
Dean
High Lorton
Whinlatter Forest
Ormathwaite
Threlkeld
Grayson Green
A597
Pardshaw
Lorton Yew
Whinlatter Pass
A66
Distington
Ullock
R. Cocker
B5292
Braithwaite
Portinscale
Keswick
A595
Mockerkin
Grisedale Pike 2595
Hope Park
Castlerigg Stone Circle
Lowca
Common End
Pica
Gilgarran
Friar's Crag
Castlerigg
Dale Bottom
B5306
Kidburngill
Loweswater
Causey Pike
Centenary Stone
A591
B5289
Parton
Asby
Lamplugh
Loweswater
Grasmoor 2795
Stair
Derwent Water
Brandelhow Memorial
Barrow Falls
A5094
Bransty
Moresby Parks
Arlecdon
Loweswater Fell
1880
Little Town
Legburthwaite
The Beacon
A5086
Murton Fell
Crummock Water
WHITEHAVEN
Rowrah
Kirkland
Scale Force
Derwent Fells
Lodore Falls
High Seat 1996
Saltom Pit
Frizington
Moss Force
Grange
Saltom Bay
Kells
Hensingham
B5294
C
U
M
Great Borne 2021
Buttermere
Sour Milk Gill
Hassness
Buttermere Fell
Dale Head 2470
Bowder Stone
Watendlath
Sandwith
B5345
Keekle
R. Ehen
Ennerdale Bridge
Red Pike 2648
High Stile
Gatesgarth
B5289
Rosthwaite
Launchy Gill Force
St. Bees Head
Mirehouse
B5295
Moor Row
Lourdes Grotto
Wath Brow
Cleator Moor
Blakeley Raise (Kinniside) Stone Circle
Ennerdale Water
Ennerdale Fell
R. Liza
Scarth Gap Pass
Hay Stacks
Honister Pass
Seatoller
Stonethwaite
Blea Tarn
Honister Slate Mine
LAKE
Rottington
Bigrigg
A5086
Cleator
A595
Borrowdale Fells
Borrowdale Yews
Ullscarf 2382
Wythburn Fells
Priory
St. Bees
L
A
K
E
D
I
Kinniside Common
Pillar 2927
Seathwaite
Lifeboat Station
Lowes Court Gallery
Egremont
Wilton
2100
Black Sail Pass
Great Gable 2949
Taylorgill Force
Seathwaite Fell
Glaramara 2569
R. Derwent
Scoat Fell
Caw Fell
Haycock
Monks Bridge
NATIO
Carleton
High Raise 2500
Coulderton
B5345
Thornhill
Haile
Wasdale Head
St. Olaf's
Packhorse Bridge
Great End
Stake Pass
Easedale Tarn
Middletown
Nethertown
Seatallan 2270
Lingmell
Langdale Pikes 2415
COPELAND
FOREST
3209
SCAFELL PIKE
3162
SCA FELL
Bow Fell 2960
Dungeon Ghyll Force
B5343
Beckermet
R. Calder
Calder Abbey
Braystones
Calder Bridge
Great Langdale
Chapel Stile
Little Langdale
Nether Wasdale
Wellington
The Screes
Wast Water
1998
Burnmoor Tarn
Cross
Gosforth
R. Irt
Eskdale Moor Stone Circles
Lingcove Packhorse Bridge
Three Shire Stone
Wrynose Pass
Grey Croft Stone Circle
Santon
Santon Bridge
Whillan Beck
A595
C
U
M
B
R
I
A
N
Seascale
Hardknott Pass
Cockley Beck
Giggle Alley Japanese
Eskdale Mill
Boot
Hardknott Roman Fort
Tilberthwaite Gill
B5344
Irton Cross
Beckfoot
Eskdale
FURNESS FELLS
Holmrook
Birker Force
Harter Fell 2142
Levers Water
Levers Waterfall
Stubble Green
Eskdale Green
Stanley Ghyll Force
Birks Bridge Rapids
Seathwaite Tarn
THE OLD MAN OF CONISTON
2635
Drigg
R. Mite
Ravenglass & Eskdale Railway
R. Esk
24
DANGER AREA
Saltcoats
Devoke Water
Muncaster Castle
Railway
Ravenglass
Roman Bath House
Woodend
Seathwaite
Bowmanstead
Conis
Hall Waberthwaite
Broad Oak
Hall Dunnerdale
Caw 1735
Ulpha Fell
Stainton Fell
Torver
A593
Newbiggin
Waberthwaite
Whitfell 1880
Ulpha
R. Duddon
1231
Stickle Pike
A5084
Sunny Bank
Corney Fell
DANGER AREA
Corney
Ulpha Park
F
U
R
N
E
S
S
Broughton Mills
Bridge End
836 Beacon
A
B
C
D
96
High Nibthwaite
Hycemoor
Beckfoot
Lower Hawthwaite
A593
Selker Bay
Bootle
Duddon Bridge
Broughton in Furness
Bootle Fell
Swinside Stone Circle
Duddon Ironworks
Blawith
Hyton
A595
Annaside
Broadgate
A595
Lowick Bridge

103
GILDERDALE FOREST
INGLEWOOD FOREST
Grassgarth
Welton
Stockdalewath
Southwaite
Hesket
Old Town
Ruckcroft
Dale
Staffield
Houses
Renwick
Haresceugh
Leadgate
Garrigill
Thethwaite
Highbridge
Ivegill
Low Braithwaite
Middlesceugh
Churchtown
Sebergham
High Bankhill
Busk
Unthank
Kirkoswald
Kirkoswald Castle
Sour Nook
Thomas Close
Sowerby Row
Newlands
Morton
Fieldhead
Plumpton Foot
Townhead
Lazonby
Glassonby
Glassonby Cairn Circle
Lacy's Caves
Gamblesby
Melmerby Fell
2331
Black Burn
Alston Moor
Hutton End
Millhouse
Hattcliff Bridge
New Rent
Hutton-in-the-Forest
Plumpton
Brockleymoor
Great Salkeld
Little Salkeld
Long Meg & Her Daughters Stone Circle
Melmerby
Calebrack
Lamonby
Ellonby
Unthank
High Row
Skelton
Unthank End
Plumpton Head
Salkeld Dykes
Hunsonby
Shire
Row
Winskill
Ousby
Townhead
Cross Fell
2930
R. Tees
Hutton Roof
Greystoke Forest
Catterlen
Laithes
Johnby
Little Blencow
Great Blencow
Newton Reigny
Newton Rigg
Fair Hill
Langwathby
Skirwith
Kirkland
MILBURN FOREST
Mosedale
Bowscale
Mungrisdale
PENRITH
Edenhall
R. Eden
Blencarn
Castletown
St Ninian's Church
Greystoke
Greystoke Gill
Berrier
Motherby
Newbiggin
Penruddock
Carleton
Countess Pillar
Winderwath
Culgaith
Milburn
Eamont Bridge
Brougham
Brougham Hall
Mayburgh Henge
Stainton
Dalemain
Yanwath
Sockbridge
Watermill
Acorn Bank
Newbiggin
Scales
Troutbeck
Hutton
Dacre
Barton
Tirril
Clifton
Clifton Hall Pele Tower
Wetheriggs Pottery
Temple Sowerby
Kirkby Thore
Knock
High Cup Nick
Dufton
Thackthwaite
Sparket
Soulby
Dunmallard Hillfort
Lakeland Bird of Prey Centre
Melkinthorpe
Abbott Lodge Farm
Cliburn
Town End
Long Marton
Keisley
Brampton
Threlkeld Quarry & Mining
Matterdale End
Bennethead
Wreay
Pooley Bridge
Askham
Newtown
Lowther Castle
Hackthorpe
Great Strickland
Bolton
Crackenthorpe
Watermill
Ulcat Row
Longthwaite
Thornythwaite
Watermillock
The Cockpit Stone Circle
Helton
Morland
Newby Head
Newby
King's Meaburn
Colby
Murton
Knotts
Dockray
Aira Force
Whale
Low Knipe
High Knipe
Little Strickland
Littlebeck
Appleby-in-Westmorland
Hilton
Great Dodd
2812
Dowthwaitehead
Arboretum
Ullswater
Sandwick
Martindale
St. Martin's
Yew Tree
2205 Loadpot Hill
Bampton Grange
Sweetholme
Sleagill
Gunnerkeld Stone Circle
Brackenber
Coupland
Burrells
Great Ormside
Hoff
104
Raise
2897
Glenridding
Lake District National Park
Bampton
Bampton Common
Burnbanks
Beda Fell
Rooking
Dale Head
Rosgill
Reagill
Little Ormside
Eden Valley Railway
Sandford
Warcop
HELVELLYN
3117
Striking Edge
Patterdale
Shap Abbey
Shap
Keld
Keld Chapel
Haweswater Reservoir
Swindale Beck
Maulds Meaburn
Drybeck
Butter Force
Bridgend
DISTRICT
Crosby Ravensworth
Great Asby
Grisedale Tarn
Hartsop
Brothers Water
Hayeswater
LAKE DISTRICT NATIONAL PARK
Fairfield
2864
High Street
2717
Mardale Common
Wet Sleddale Reservoir
Oddendale Stone Circle
Black Dub
1315
Town Head
Soulby
Britannia Pillar
Crosby Ravensworth Fell
Little Asby
Crosby Garrett
Rydal Fell
2552 Harter Fell
Gatescarth Pass
Kentmere Reservoir
Shap Fells
Birk Beck
Gamelands Stone Circle
Orton
Raisbeck
Nettle Hill
1253
Smardale
Kirkstone Pass
Wordsworth Dove Cottage
Rydal
Rydal Mount
Rydal Hall
Scout Green
TEBAY (EAST)
TEBAY (WEST)
Old Tebay
Sadgill
Bretherdale Head
Gaisgill
Kelleth
Wath
Newbiggin-on-Lune
Ash Fell
1264
Ravenstonedale
Rydal Cave
Rydal Water
Elterwater
Skelwith Bridge
Armitt
Stockghyll Force
Bridge House
Ambleside
High Green
Kentmere
Tebay
Longdale
Bowderdale
Weasdale
Clappersgate
Waterhead
Troutbeck
Jesus Church
Roundthwaite
Tebay Fell
Borrowdale
Stagshaw
Townend
Town End
Low Borrowbridge
West Fell
Low Wray
Brockhole
Blelham Tarn
Troutbeck Bridge
Holehird
High Borrans
Forest Hall
Whinfell Beacon
High Carlingill
Langdale Fell
1925
Uldale Head
Ravenstonedale Common
Courthouse
Hawkshead Hill
Outgate
High Wray
Elfhowe
Garnett Bridge
Selside
Watchgate
HOWGILL FELLS
Fell End
Hawkshead
Colthouse
Bowness-on-Windermere
Windermere
Ings
Staveley
Cowan Head
Garth Row
Patton Bridge
Meal Bank
Grayrigg
Lowgill
2219
Narthwaite
The Calf
Cautley Spout
Roger Ground
Esthwaite Water
Claife Heights
Belle Isle
World of Beatrix Potter
Bowston
Burneside
Beck Foot
Near Sawrey
Far Sawrey
Grizedale
Hill Top
B5284
Crook
Plumgarths
Kentrigg
KENDAL
Lambrigg Fell
1109
Fisher Tarn Resr
Brant Fell
Cautley
West Baugh Fell
Storrs
Blackwell
Winster
Fox's Pulpit
GRIZEDALE FOREST
Cunsey Beck Forge
Underbarrow
Winder
1552
Baugh Fell
Marthwaite
Sedbergh
Fairfield Mill
Graythwaite Hall
Crosthwaite
New Hutton
KILLINGTON LAKE
Briggflatts
Hallbank
Millthrop
East Baugh Fell
2217
Garsdale
Thwaite Head
Ludderburn
Oxenholme
Millholme
Holme Open Farm
Brigsteer
Rise Hill
1825
Lenacre
R. Dee
Satterthwaite
Rusland
Stott Park Bobbin Mill
Bowland Bridge
Middleshaw
Natland
Barrows Green
Killington
Finsthwaite
Lakes Aquarium
Cartmel Fell
Howe
Sizergh Castle
Cotes
Halfpenny
Old Hutton
Beckside
Gawthrop
Dent
Cowgill
Town End
Lakeside & Haverthwaite Railway
Lakeside
Fell Foot Park
Staveley-in-Cartmel
Levens
Sedgwick
Force Falls
Stainton
Gatebeck
Middleton
Lune
M6
A6
A66
A686
A591
A592
A5091
A685
A683
A684
A5074
B5305
B6413
B6412
B5288
B5320
B6260
B6261
B5286
B5285
B6257
B6256
B6254
113
97
E
F
G
H
1
2
3
4
5

104
ILDERDALE FOREST
A686
Leadgate
Garrigill
B6277
Nenthead
Nenthead Mines Heritage Centre
A689
Killhope (North of England Lead Mining)
Lanehead
Cornriggs
Copthill
B6295
Middlehope Moor
Rookhope
Lintzgarth
Stanhope Common
B6278
Waskerley Reservoir
1694 Collier Law
Crawley Side
Durham Dales
Wolsingham Moor
Stanhope
Wolsingham
Cows
114
Burnhope Reservoir
Wearhead
West Blackdene
Weardale
Ireshopeburn
High House Chapel
St. John's Chapel
Daddry Shield
Westgate
Eastgate
Brotherlee
Burnhope Seat 2448
Ireshope Moor
Alston Moor
Round Hill 2249
Black Burn
R. Tees
Cross Fell 2930
Frosterley
Hill End
White Kirkley
Weardale Railway
St. John's Hall
Three Pikes
Viewing Hill 2099
Harwood
2284 Chapelfell Top
Snowhope Hill
Bollihope Common
Newbiggin Common
1599 Pawlaw Pike
Pikeston Fell
Hamsterley Forest Dr
MILBURN FOREST
Widdybank Fell
Langdon Beck
Ettersgill
Forest-in-Teesdale
Summerhill Force
Gibson's Cave
Bowlees
Newbiggin
High Force
Low Force
Wynch Suspension Bridge
Holwick
Skears Limekilns
HAMSTERLEY FOREST
Eggleston Common
Milburn
Dufton Fell 2518
Cow Green Reservoir
Cauldron Snout
Cronkley Fell
Knock
High Cup Nick
Mickle Fell 2591
Middleton-in-Teesdale
B6282
1511 Woodland Fell
Woodland
Dufton
Long Marton
Keisley
Murton Fell 2207
Lune Moor
Bowbank
Mickleton
Laithkirk
Hill Top
Eggleston
Eggleston Hall
Brampton
Watermill
Crackenthorpe
Thringarth
B6276
B6281
B6279
A66
Colby
Appleby-in-Westmorland
Murton
Hilton
LUNE FOREST
Warcop Fell
Grassholme
Grassholme Reservoir
Romaldkirk
Kinninvie
B6278
River Lune
Selset Reservoir
Hunderthwaite
Hury
Cotherstone
Brackenber
Coupland
Burrells
Great Ormside
Little Ormside
Eden Valley Railway
Hoff
B6260
103
CUMBRIA
Dow Crag 1843
Stainmore Common
Hunderthwaite Moor
Balderhead Reservoir
Blackton Reservoir
Hury Reservoir
East Briscoe
DANGER AREA
Lartington
BARNARD CASTLE
Startforth
River Balder
Cotherstone Moor
Sandford
Warcop
Hillbeck
Brough
North Stainmore
Deep Dale
A67
Boldron
Drybeck
Great Musgrave
Little Musgrave
B6259
Church Brough
Bowes Moor
Bowes
Gilmonby
Cross Lanes
Great Asby
Town Head
Brough Sowerby
A685
South Stainmore
A66
Old Spital
God's Bridge
Lavatrae Roman Fort
Stainmore Forest
Kaber
Moudy Mea
Thwaite
Brignall
Scargill
Soulby
Rookby
Winton
Sleightholme
Little Asby
Crosby Garrett
Kirkby Stephen
Hartley
Winton Fell
Sleightholme Moor
1674 Cleasby Hill
Nettle Hill 1253
Smardale
Waitby
Nateby
Tan Hill Inn
Tan Hill
Arkengarthdale Moor
Kelleth
Wath
Newbiggin-on-Lune
Bowderdale
Weasdale
Ravenstonedale
Ash Fell 1264
B6270
Whaw
Stonesdale Moor
2203 Rogan's Seat
Ravenseat
West Stonesdale
1914 Great Pinseat
Langthwaite
Arkle Town
Booze
Hurst
Washfold
West Fell
Pendragon
Outhgill
Shoregill
Ravenstonedale Common
YORKSHIRE DALES
Keld
Melbecks Moor
Yorkshire Dales National Park
Swaledale
Kearton
Healaugh
Reeth
Fremington
Grinton
A683
Fell End
2324
Mallerstang Common
Angram
Angram Common
Thwaite
Muker
Ivelet
Gunnerside
Feetham
Low Row
Satron
Crackpot
Maiden Castle
Harkerside Moor
Gibbon Hill
Northwaite
2219 The Calf
Cautley Spout
2349 Great Shunner Fell
The Buttertubs
NATIONAL PARK
Whitaside Moor
Cautley
West Baugh Fell
Abbotside Common
Askrigg Common
East Bolton Moor
Redmire Moor
Sedbergh
Baugh Fell
Cotterdale
NORTH
Fairfield Mill
Hallbank
Millthrop
East Baugh Fell 2217
Garsdale Head
A684
High Shaw
Hardraw
Dales Countryside
Sedbusk
Askrigg
Newbiggin
Castle Bolton
Bolton
Redmire
Preston-under-Scar
Mossdale Moor
Appersett
Hawes
Gayle
Wensleydale Creamery
Yorkshire Dales National Park
Burtersett
Bainbridge
Worton
Woodhall
Carperby
Aysgarth Falls
98
Swinithwaite
Thornton Rust
Aysgarth
West Witton
Rise Hill 1825
97
Garsdale
Lenacre
R. Dee
Gawthrop
Dent
Cowgill
Lea Yeat
Widdale Fell
B6255
Countersett
Semer Water
Wether Fell
Thoralby
West Burton
1792 Penhill
B6160
Stalling
Stone

105
Butsfield
Park
Hill Top
A691
Moor
Pittington
High Haswell
Colliery
Hall Hill Farm
Quebec
Esh
Ushaw Moor
Bearpark
Aykley Heads
Carrville
Littletown
Satley
Cornsay
Cornsay Colliery
DURHAM
Hallgarth
Haswell Plough
Haswell
Easington
Horden Point
Gilesgate Moor
Sherburn
Sherburn Hill
A68
Esh Winning
New Brancepeth
Broompark
Byers Garth
Shotton Colliery
Ludworth
High Stoop
Waterhouses
115
Langley Moor
Shincliffe
High Shincliffe
Botanic Garden
Shadforth
Thornley
Wheatley Hill
Shotton
PETERLEE
Blackhall Colliery
East Hedleyhope
A1(M)
Dan's Castle
Brandon
Meadowfield
A167
Bowburn
Old Cassop
Old Quarrington
Cassop
Castle Eden
Blackhall Rocks
Tow Law
Sunniside
Stanley Crook
Brancepeth
Sunderland Bridge
DURHAM
Croxdale
Wingate
High Hesleden
Crimdon Park
Hesleden
Quarrington Hill
Deaf Hill
Eden Vale
Station Town
Monk Hesleden
Thornley
Billy Row
Oakenshaw
Hett
A688
Town Kelloe
Hart Station
Roddymoor
Page Bank
Tudhoe
Tursdale
Kelloe
Trimdon Grange
Trimdon Colliery
Hutton Henry
A19
River Wear
Helmington Row
Tudhoe Grange
Coxhoe
Sheraton
Hart
A689
Crook
Willington
Byers Green
Spennymoor
Garmondsway
Fir Tree
Cornforth
West Cornforth
A179
Howden-le-Wear
North Bitchburn
Lane Ends
Newfield
A688
Dean Bank
Trimdon
High Throston
Weardale Railway
Middlestone Moor
Ferryhill
Elwick
A68
Witton-le-Wear
High Grange
Hunwick
Binchester
BISHOP AUCKLAND
North Close
Kirk Merrington
Mainsforth
Fishburn
West Park
Bedburn
Hamsterley
Low Barns
Westerton
Ferryhill Station
Bishop Middleham
Dalton Piercy
Rift House
Redford
Witton Park
Toronto
Escomb
Middlestone
Leasingthorne
Chilton Lane
Butterwick
Etherley Dene
Great Chilton
Brierton
Woodside
Coundon
Chilton
Sedgefield
Embleton
Owton Manor
Low Etherley
High Etherley
Tindale Crescent
Coundon Grange
A689
Rushyford
Morley
Toft Hill
South Church
Eldon
Old Eldon
Bradbury
Newton Bewley
Greatham
St. Helen Auckland
Thorpe Larches
Wynyard Village
Lynesack
Butterknowle
West Auckland
Shildon
Middridge
Locomotion
A167
Mordon
Shotton
Wolviston
High Lands
Evenwood
NEWTON AYCLIFFE
Fulthorpe
Cowpen Bewley
The Slack
A6072
A1(M)
Preston-le-Skerne
Foxton
Chimney Smeltmill
Cockfield
A688
Evenwood Gate
Bildershaw
Royal Oak
School Aycliffe
Stillington
Thorpe Thewles
BILLINGHAM
Burnt Houses
Redworth
Aycliffe Village
Elstob
Whitton
Haverton Hill
Raby
Wackerfield
Bolam
Houghton Bank
B6444
Great Stainton
Carlton
Morton Tinmouth
Heighington
Brafferton
Port Clarence
Staindrop
Hilton
Ingleton
Houghton-le-Side
Bishopton
Redmarshall
Hardwick
Norton
Killerby
Walworth Gate
A68
Coatham Mundeville
Newton Ketton
STOCKTON-ON-TEES
Langton
Denton
Little Stainton
Cleatlam
Headlam
Summerhouse
Walworth
A167
Whinny Hill
South Cleatlam
Beaumont Hill
Barmpton
Little Newsham
106
Hartburn
MIDD
Winston
Gainford
Archdeacon Newton
Harrowgate Hill
Great Burdon
Sadberge
Elton
A66
Acklam
A1150
Thornaby-on-Tees
East Shaws
Faverdale
Long Newton
Carlbury
High Coniscliffe
Haughton Le Skerne
Suspension Bridge
Piercebridge
Roman Bridge
Cliffe
Mowden
Butterfly World
Preston Hall
Whorlton
Wycliffe
Ovington
Low Coniscliffe
DARLINGTON
Urlay Nook
Eaglescliffe
Merrybent
Ingleby Barwick
Hemlington
Stainton
Thornton
Caldwell
Eppleby
Manfield
Cleasby
B6280
Eastbourne
A167
A67
Egglescliffe
Hutton Magna
Forcett
Stanwick Fortifications
Blackwell
Middleton St. George
Oak Tree
DURHAM TEES VALLEY
Aislaby
Yarm
High Leven
Maltby
Lane Head
Stapleton
A66(M)
A66
Middleton One Row
West Layton
East Layton
Aldbrough St. John
Hurworth Place
Neasham
Low Dinsdale
Low Worsall
Hilton
Barningham
A1(M)
A19
Newsham
Croft-on-Tees
Newton Morrell
Hurworth-on-Tees
Seamer
High Worsall
Kirklevington
Middleton-on-Leven
Dalton
Ravensworth
Melsonby
Barton
Dalton-on-Tees
Eryholme
Girsby
Sockburn
Gayles
Picton
Crathorne
Croft
Rudby
Kirby Hill
Whashton
SCOTCH CORNER
Middleton Tyas
Appleton Wiske
Hutton Rudby
DANGER AREA
Gilling West
A66
Scotch Corner
Hornby
Great Smeaton
North Cowton
Moulton
R. Wiske
West Rounton
Potto
East Rounton
Skeeby
Georgian Theatre Royal
A1
Uckerby
East Cowton
Birkby
Welbury
Whorlton
Richmond
Pepper Arden
Deighton
A19
Swainby
Ingleby Arncliffe
Skelton
Marske
Holly Hill
Scorton
Forest
Hutton Bonville
A172
Hudswell
Easby
East Harlsey
Abbey
Green Howards
Colburn
Brompton-on-Swale
Catterick Bridge
Bolton-on-Swale
Whitwell
Streetlam
Harlsey Castle
Marrick
Whorlton Moor
Mount Grace Priory
Cod Beck
Downholme
Hipswell
Walkerville
Ellerton
Danby Wiske
Battle of the Standard 1138
Osmotherley
Catterick Garrison
Catterick
Kiplin Hall
Great Langton
Brompton
A684
Ellerbeck
Stainton
DANGER AREA
Hipswell Moor
Tunstall
East Appleton
Foxton
Scotton
Kirkby Fleetham
Thimbleby
DANGER AREA
Bullamoor
Kirby Sigston
West Appleton
Yafforth
Y O R K S H I R E
Barden
East Hauxwell
Hornby
Hackforth
Great Fencote
Romanby
NORTHALLERTON
Over Silton
Arrathorne
Thrintoft
Ainderby Steeple
Bellerby
Garriston
Little Fencote
Scruton
Constable Burton Hall
Hunton
Langthorne
A19
Nether Silton
Bellerby Camp
Patrick Brompton
Morton-on-Swale
Warlaby
Crosby Court
Kepwick
Leyburn
Little Crakehall
Kirkbridge
A684
North Otterington
Thornton-le-Beans
Leake
Constable Burton
Great Crakehall
Wensley
Harmby
Finghall
Leeming Bar
Borrowby
Cowesby
Spennithorne
Newton-le-Willows
Wensleydale Railway
Aiskew
Leeming
99
Thornton-le-Moor
Middleham
Bedale
LEEMING
Londonderry
Newby Wiske
South Otterington
Knayton
Kirby Knowle
Cowling
Gatenby
Upsall
Coverham
Thornton Steward
Burrill
Firby
Exelby
A1(M)
Boltby
Maunby
Thornton-
North

106
115
105
99
DURHAM
Carrville
Littletown
Haswell
Haswell Plough
High Haswell
Easington
Colliery
Horden Point
Horden
Dene Mouth
Sherburn
Sherburn Hill
Hallgarth
Gilesgate Moor
Byers Garth
Ludworth
Shadforth
Shotton Colliery
Shotton
PETERLEE
Thornley
Wheatley Hill
Blackhall Colliery
Blackhall Rocks
Crimdon Park
Hart Station
Old Cassop
Old Quarrington
Cassop
Castle Eden
Wingate
Hesleden
High Hesleden
Monk Hesleden
Eden Vale
Bowburn
Croxdale
Hett
Tudhoe
Quarrington Hill
Town Kelloe
Kelloe
Deaf Hill
Station Town
Hutton Henry
Sheraton
Hart
Coxhoe
Trimdon Grange
Trimdon Colliery
Tursdale
Garmondsway
West View
Middleton
Maritime Experience
HARTLEPOOL
Hartlepool Bay
Cornforth
West Cornforth
Dean Bank
Ferryhill
Kirk Merrington
Mainsforth
Trimdon
DURHAM
High Throston
West Park
Elwick
Dalton Piercy
Rift House
Ferryhill Station
Chilton Lane
Bishop Middleham
Fishburn
Seaton Carew
Middlestone
Leasingthorne
Coundon
Great Chilton
Chilton
Sedgefield
Butterwick
Embleton
Brierton
Owton Manor
Tees Bay
Rushyford
Old Eldon
Bradbury
Mordon
Thorpe Larches
Wynyard Village
Newton Bewley
Greatham
Graythorp
Middridge
NEWTON AYCLIFFE
Preston-le-Skerne
Shotton
Foxton
Fulthorpe
Wolviston
Cowpen Bewley
TEESSIDE
Warrenby
Coatham
Zetland Lifeboat
REDCAR
Marske-by-the-Sea
Saltburn-by-the-Sea
Aycliffe Village
Elstob
Stillington
Thorpe Thewles
Whitton
BILLINGHAM
Haverton Hill
Teesport
Dormanstown
Kirkleatham Owl Centre
Kirkleatham
Great Stainton
Carlton
Port Clarence
Transporter Bridge
South Bank
New Marske
Brafferton
Bishopton
Redmarshall
Hardwick
Roseworth
Norton
Yearby
Coatham Mundeville
Newton Ketton
Little Stainton
STOCKTON-ON-TEES
Grangetown
Lazenby
Wilton
North Ormesby
Eston
Upleatham
Tocketts Water Mill
Skelton
Beaumont Hill
Whinny Hill
Barmpton
MIDDLESBROUGH
Normanby
Dunsdale
Skelton Green
Harrowgate Hill
Great Burdon
Sadberge
Hartburn
Elton
Thornaby-on-Tees
Acklam
Nature's World
Ormesby
REDCAR & CLEVELAND
Boosbeck
Lingdale
Faverdale
Haughton Le Skerne
Long Newton
Marton
Priory
Mowden
Low Coniscliffe
DARLINGTON
Urlay Nook
Butterfly World
Preston Hall
Eaglescliffe
Ingleby Barwick
Hemlington
Coulby Newham
Newham Grange Country Farm
Nunthorpe
Hutton Gate
GUISBOROUGH
Cleasby
Eastbourne
Middleton St. George
Oak Tree
DURHAM TEES VALLEY
Egglescliffe
High Leven
Stainton
Thornton
Maltby
Newton under Roseberry
Hutton Village
Guisborough Moor
Blackwell
Stapleton
Aislaby
Yarm
Newby
Roseberry Topping
Middleton One Row
Hilton
Tanton
Captain Cook Schoolroom
Great Ayton
Guisborough Forest
Captain Cook's Monument
Commondale
Hurworth Place
Neasham
Low Dinsdale
Low Worsall
Seamer
New Row
Croft-on-Tees
Hurworth-on-Tees
Kirklevington
Middleton-on-Leven
Stokesley
Little Ayton
Kildale
Kildale Moor
Dalton-on-Tees
Eryholme
Girsby
High Worsall
Easby
Croft
Sockburn
Picton
Crathorne
Battersby
Baysdale Beck
Rudby
River Leven
Great Busby
Kirkby
Great Broughton
Ingleby Greenhow
Westerdale
Hornby
Appleton Wiske
Hutton Rudby
North Cowton
Great Smeaton
R. Wiske
West Rounton
East Rounton
Potto
Carlton in Cleveland
Faceby
East Cowton
Birkby
Welbury
Whorlton
Urra
Westerdale Moor
Pepper Arden
Deighton
Ingleby Arncliffe
Swainby
NORTH
Forest
Hutton Bonville
Scugdale Beck
Seave Green
Chop Gate
1410 Cockayne Ridge
Farndale Moor
Bolton-on-Swale
Whitwell
Streetlam
East Harlsey
Harlsey Castle
Mount Grace Priory
Cod Beck
Whorlton Moor
NORTH
Cockayne
Danby Wiske
Battle of the Standard 1138
Osmotherley
CLEVELAND HILLS
Catterick
Kiplin Hall
Great Langton
Brompton
Ellerbeck
Snilesworth Moor
Cross Holme
The Grange
Bilsdale East Moor
NATIONAL
Low Mill
Kirkby Fleetham
NORTH YORK
Foxton
Thimbleby
Cow Ridge
Bransdale
Rudland Rigg
Great Fencote
Yafforth
Bullamoor
Kirby Sigston
Fangdale Beck
East Moors
Little Fencote
Thrintoft
Romanby
NORTHALLERTON
Over Silton
Arden Great Moor
Langthorne
Scruton
Ainderby Steeple
Morton-on-Swale
Warlaby
Crosby Court
Nether Silton
Helmsley Moor
Bilsdale
River Seph
Kirkbridge
Thornton-le-Beans
Kepwick
Arden Hall
Leeming Bar
North Otterington
Leake
Hawnby
Leeming
Londonderry
Borrowby
Cowesby
Rievaulx Moor
Aiskew
LEEMING
Gatenby
Newby Wiske
Thornton-le-Moor
South Otterington
Knayton
Kirby Knowle
Upsall
Boltby
Old Byland
Exelby
Firby
Maunby
Carlton
Pockley
Thornton-
Gilling
Fadmoor
A1(M)
A19
A167
A688
A689
A179
A66
A68
A1150
A67
A172
A174
A171
A173
A1043
A1053
A684
A168
A181
A178
A1086
A1185
B1264
B1263
B6271
B1257
B1365
B1292

NORTH SEA
Brotton
Skinningrove
Carlin How
Loftus
Boulby
Cowbar
Staithes
Easington
Liverton Mines
Kilton Thorpe
Liverton
Moorsholm
Port Mulgrave
Hinderwell
Runswick Bay
Runswick
Kettleness
Goldsborough
Roxby
Borrowby
Newton Mulgrave
Ellerby
Scaling Dam
Scaling
Mickleby
West Barnby
East Barnby
Lythe
Sandsend
East Row
WHITBY
Captain Cook Memorial
Saltwick Bay
Raithwaite
Castle Park
Dunsley
Newholm
Ugthorpe
Danby
Stonegate
Hutton Mulgrave
Briggswath
Ruswarp
Golden Grove
Long Lease
High Hawsker
Aislaby
Stainsacre
Sneaton
Low Hawsker
Sleights
Ugglebarnby
Sneatonthorpe
Ness Point or North Cheek
Robin Hood's Bay
Fylingthorpe
Castleton
Ainthorpe
Houlsyke
Lealholm
Egton
Glaisdale
Egton Bridge
Grosmont
Lease Rigg
Esk Valley
Key Green
Danby Botton
Botton
Street
Green End
Beck Hole
Goathland
Old Peak or South Cheek
Ravenscar
YORK MOORS
NORTH YORK MOORS
PARK
Staintondale
Crowdon
Harwood Dale
Cloughton Newlands
Cloughton
Burniston
Thorgill
Low Bell End
Rosedale Abbey
Langdale Forest
Stape
Hartoft End
Silpho
Broxa
Bickley
Suffield
Hackness
Langdale End
Scalby
Scalby Mills
SCARBOROUGH
Lastingham
Levisham
Hutton-le-Hole
Spaunton
Newton-on-Rawcliffe
Lockton
Cropton
Cawthorne
Appleton-le-Moors
Low Dalby
Everley
Barrowcliff
Falsgrave
Kirkbymoorside
Keldholme
Sinnington
Wrelton
North Moor
East
A174
A171
A169
A165
A170
B1266
B1416
B1447
B1410
100
101

ISLE OF MAN

POINT OF AYRE

Rue Point
The Ayres
The Lhen
Dhowin
Bride
Cranstal

Shellag Point

Jurby East
Andreas
Crosses
Jurby West
Jurby Head
Ballasalla
Sandygate
Regaby
Ramsey
Bay
The Cronk
St. Judes
Sulby
Churchtown
Ramsey
Orrisdale
Ballaugh
Lhergy Frissel
Port e Vullen
Orrisdale Head
Ravensdale
Glen
Auldyn
Maughold
Head
Bishopscourt
Glen
Glen Wyllin
Kirk Michael
Maughold
Lewaigue
Ballajora
Port Mooar
Ballaleigh
Cornaa
Ballacarnane
1854
North Barrule
Corrany
Cornaa
Manx
Electric
Railway
Barregarrow
Sulby
Glen Mona
Port Cornaa
Gob y Deigan
SNAEFELL
1601
Knocksharry
Cronk-y-Voddy
Clagh Ouyr
Dhoon
Bulgham Bay
St. Patrick's Isle
Lambfell
Moar
Rhenass
Waterfall
1599
Colden
Snaefell
Mountain
Railway
Dhoon Glen
Laxey
Glen
Peel
Ballagyr
Glen Helen
Injebreck
Resr.
Great Laxey Mine Railway
Laxey
Wheel
Minorca
Contrary Head
Ballaugh
Mill
Ballig
St. John's
Silverdale
1570
Baldwin
Ballaheannagh
Old
Laxey
Laxey Head
Patrick
Greeba
Castle
Ballacannell
Laxey Bay
ISLE   OF   MAN
Crosby
Hillberry
Baldrine
Glen Maye
Glen
Maye
Lower
Foxdale
Glen
Vine
Strang
Onchan
Clay Head
Dalby Point
Dalby
Foxdale
Garth
Union Mills
Whitebridge
Douglas Bay
Groudie
Railway
Port Groudle
Groudle Glen
Niarbyl Bay
Cooil
Braaid
Spring
Valley
DOUGLAS
Onchan Head
Stroin Vuigh
Close
Clark
Newtown
Kewaigue
Douglas Head
St.
Mark
Horse's
Hill
Ballamodha
Quine's
Hill
Fleshwick
Bay
Ronague
Grenaby
Kerrstal
Little Ness
Lingague
Ballabeg
Port
Soderick
Bradda Head
Bradda
Surby
Colby
Ballasalla
Isle of Man
Steam railway
Santon Head
Port Erin
Port
St. Mary
Four
Roads
Ballasalla
Ship Burial
ISLE OF MAN
The Howe
Castletown
Chambered Cairn
The Sound
Cregneash
Derby
Fort
St. Michael's Island
Kitterland
National
Folk
Derbyhaven
Nautical
SPANISH HEAD
Old House
of Keys
Calf of Man
Dreswick
Point

Douglas to:
Belfast 2hrs. 45mins.
(Fast Ferry, Seasonal)
Birkenhead 4hrs. 15mins.
(Seasonal)
Heysham 3hrs. 30mins.
Dublin 2hrs. 45mins.
(Fast Ferry, Seasonal)
Liverpool 2hrs. 30mins.
(Fast Ferry, Seasonal)

PAGE NOT CONTINUED

109
SOUTH AYRSHIRE
DUMFRIES & GALLOWAY
THE RHINNS
LUCE BAY
PAGE NOT CONTINUED
Cairnryan to:
Belfast 2hrs. 15mins.
(Fast Ferry, Seasonal)
Larne 1hr
(Fast Ferry, Seasonal)
Larne 2hrs.
Stranraer
Lendalfoot
Colmonell
Ballantrae
Pinwherry
Barrhill
Cairnryan
Kirkcolm
Leswalt
Portpatrick
Lochans
Stoneykirk
Sandhead
Dunragit
Glenluce
New Luce
Auchenmalg
Port William
Ardwell
Kirkmaiden
Drummore
CHANGUE FOREST
Bennane Head
Ballantrae Bay
Downan Point
Currarie Port
Milleur Point
Corsewall Point
Finnarts Bay
Dounan Bay
Portobello
Slouchnawen Bay
Broadsea Bay
Black Head
Port of Spittal Bay
Loch Ryan
Cairngarroch Bay
Money Head
Float Bay
Ardwell Point
Chapel Rossan Bay
Balgowan Point
Mull of Logan
Port Logan Bay
Terally Point
Cairnywellan Head
Clanyard Bay
Laggantalluch Head
Kilstay Bay
Auchenmalg Bay
Garheugh Port
Milton Point
Barsalloch Point
Monreith Bay
MULL OF GALLOWAY
Kilstay Bay
Cailiness Point
Maryport Bay
Crammag Head
Port Kemin
Mull of Galloway
Maryport
INSET

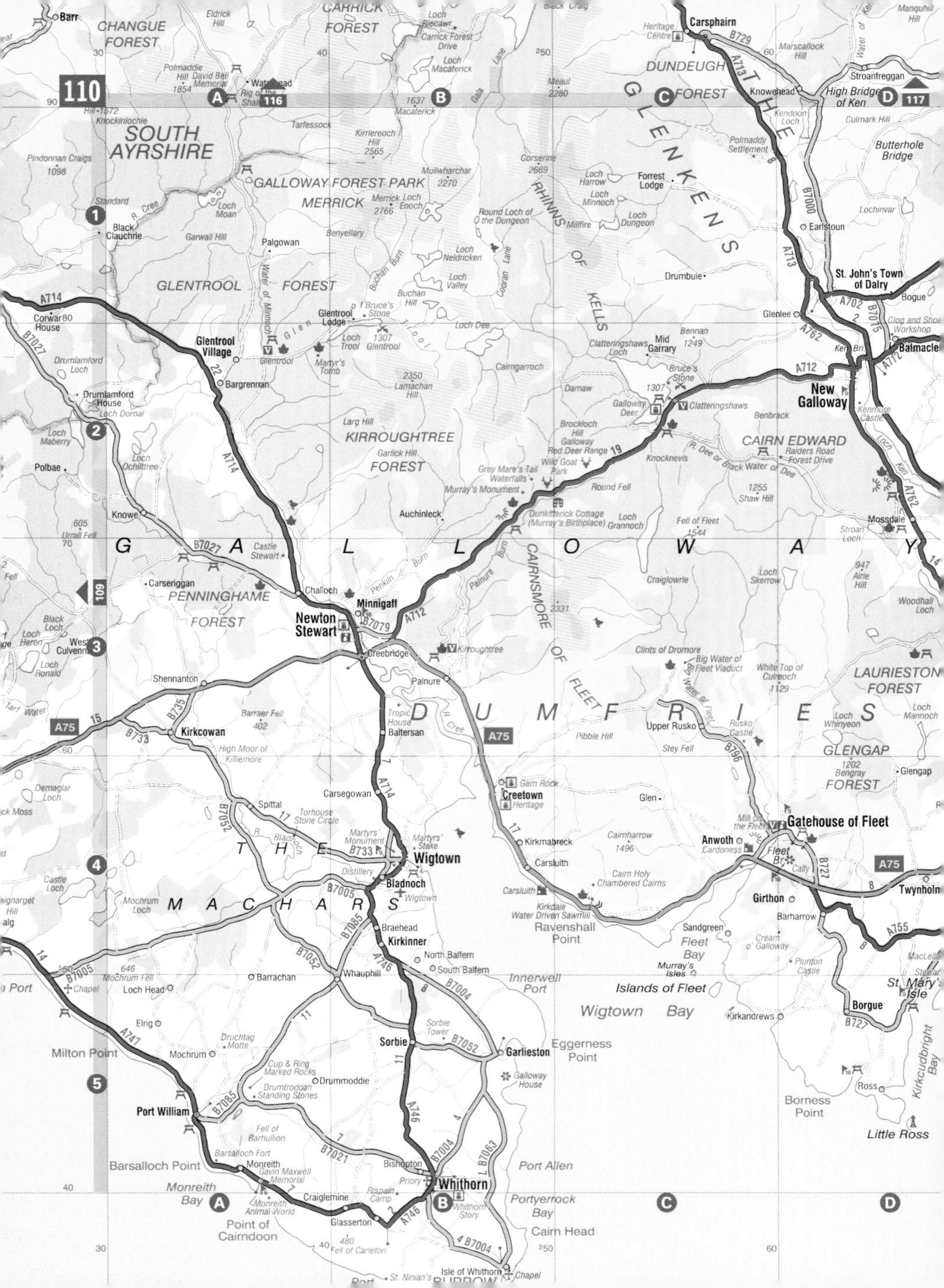
Barr
CHANGUE FOREST
Eldrick Hill
CARRICK FOREST
Loch Riecawr
Carrick Forest Drive
Loch Macaterick
Black Craig
Carsphairn
Heritage Centre
B729
Marscallock Hill
Manquhill Hill
Polmaddie Hill 1854
David Bell Memorial
Waterhead
Rig of the Shalloch
116
1637 Macaterick
Meaul 2280
DUNDEUGH FOREST
A713
Knowehead
Stroanfreggan
High Bridge of Ken
117
Hill 1572
Knockinlochie
SOUTH AYRSHIRE
Tarfessock
Kirriereoch Hill 2565
Kendoon Loch
Culmark Hill
THE GLENKENS
Pindonnan Craigs 1098
Corserine 2669
Polmaddy Settlement
Butterhole Bridge
GALLOWAY FOREST PARK
Mullwharchar 2270
Loch Harrow
Forrest Lodge
MERRICK
Merrick 2766
Loch Enoch
Loch Minnoch
RHINNS OF KELLS
B7000
Standard
R. Cree
Loch Moan
Round Loch of the Dungeon
Millfire
Loch Dungeon
Lochinvar
Black Clauchrie
Garwall Hill
Benyellary
Earlstoun
Palgowan
Loch Neldricken
Loch Valley
A713
GLENTROOL FOREST
Water of Minnoch
Buchan Burn
Buchan Hill
Cooran Lane
Drumbuie
St. John's Town of Dalry
A714
Glentrool Lodge
Bruce's Stone
Loch Dee
Glenlee
A702
B7075
Bogue
Corwar House
Glen Trool
Clog and Shoe Workshop
B7027
Glentrool Village
Glentrool
Loch Trool
1307 Glentrool
Martyr's Tomb
Clatteringshaws Loch
Mid Garrary
Bennan 1249
A762
Ken Bri.
Balmaclellan
Drumlamford Loch
Bargrennan
Cairngarroch
Bruce's Stone
A712
Drumlamford House
2350 Lamachan Hill
Darnaw
New Galloway
Loch Dornal
1307
Galloway Deer
Clatteringshaws
Kenmure Castle
Loch Maberry
Larg Hill
Brockloch Hill
Galloway Red Deer Range
Benbrack
KIRROUGHTREE FOREST
Garlick Hill
CAIRN EDWARD
Raiders Road Forest Drive
Loch Ochiltree
Wild Goat Park
Knocknevis
R. Dee or Black Water of Dee
Loch Ken
Polbae
A714
Grey Mare's Tail Waterfalls
Murray's Monument
Round Fell
1255 Shaw Hill
Knowe
Auchinleck
Dunkitterick Cottage (Murray's Birthplace)
Loch Grannoch
Fell of Fleet 1544
Mossdale
605 Urrall Fell
Stroan Loch
GALLOWAY
Castle Stewart
Penkiln Burn
Palnure Burn
CAIRNSMORE OF FLEET
947 Airie Hill
Carseriggan
PENNINGHAME FOREST
Challoch
Craiglowrie
Loch Skerrow
109
Minnigaff
Woodhall Loch
Newton Stewart
B7079
2331
Black Loch
Loch Heron
West Culvennan
Kirroughtree
Clints of Dromore
Big Water of Fleet Viaduct
White Top of Culreoch 1129
LAURIESTON FOREST
Loch Ronald
Creebridge
Shennanton
Palnure
Tarf Water
B735
Barraer Fell 402
Tropic House
DUMFRIES
R. Cree
Loch Whinyeon
Loch Mannoch
A75
B733
Kirkcowan
Baltersan
A75
Pibble Hill
Upper Rusko
Rusko Castle
High Moor of Killiemore
Stey Fell
B796
GLENGAP
Demaglar Loch
1202 Bengray
Glengap
FOREST
Carsegowan
Gem Rock
Creetown
Heritage
Glen
Spittal
Torhouse Stone Circle
B7052
R. Bladnoch
Martyrs' Monument
Martyrs' Stake
Mill on the Fleet
Gatehouse of Fleet
Anwoth
Cardoness
Kirkmabreck
Cairnharrow 1496
THE MACHARS
B733
Wigtown
Carsluith
Fleet Br.
Cally
B727
A75
Castle Loch
Distillery
Bladnoch
Cairn Holy Chambered Cairns
Carsluith
Twynholm
Mochrum Loch
B7005
Wigtown
Kirkdale Water Driven Sawmill
Girthon
Barharrow
Ravenshall Point
Sandgreen
Braehead
B7085
Kirkinner
Fleet Bay
Cream o' Galloway
A755
B7052
North Balfern
South Balfern
Murray's Isles
Plunton Castle
646 Mochrum Fell
B7005
Chapel
Barrachan
Whauphill
A746
Innerwell Port
Islands of Fleet
Loch Head
B7004
St. Mary's Isle
Wigtown Bay
Borgue
Kirkandrews
B727
Elrig
Sorbie Tower
Milton Point
Sorbie
B7052
Garlieston
Eggerness Point
Druchtag Motte
Mochrum
Cup & Ring Marked Rocks
Galloway House
Kirkcudbright Bay
Drummoddie
Drumtroddan Standing Stones
Ross
Borness Point
Port William
B7085
A746
Fell of Barhullion
Little Ross
B7021
B7063
Barsalloch Fort
Barsalloch Point
Monreith
Gavin Maxwell Memorial
Bishopton
B7004
Port Allen
Monreith Bay
Priory
Whithorn
Craiglemine
Rispain Camp
Portyerrock Bay
Monreith Animal World
Whithorn Story
Point of Cairndoon
Glasserton
A746
Cairn Head
480 Fell of Carleton
B7004
Isle of Whithorn
Chapel
St. Ninian's
A
B
C
D
1
2
3
4
5
30
40
250
60
90
80
70
60
50
40

111
Tynron
Dalwhat Water
Keir Mill
A76
Closeburn
Cample
FOREST OF AE
St. Ann's
A701
Hill
1157 Great Hill
James Renwick Monument
B729
Moniaive
A702
Kirkland
1172 Keir Hills
Park
Kirkpatrick
118
Brownmoor Hill
Johnstonebridge
Courance
E
F
G
H
Glenmaid Moor
Ae
Parkgate
Wallaceton
Blackwood
High Auldgirth
Glenmidge
Nethermill
Templand
Kinnel Water
Water of Ae
B7020
Craigmuie
1471 Bogrie Hill
Auldgirth
Dalswinton
Auchencairn
Shieldhill
1
Marjoriebanks
Dunscore
Throughgate
Glenesslin
Loch Urr
Ellisland Farm
Duncow
Amisfield
Craigenputtock
Cairn Water
Stepford
Morrington
787 Steilston Hill
Newtonairds
Tinwald
Barr Hill
Kirkton
Holywood
Locharbriggs
A701
Castle Loch
Lochmaben
Garcrogo Forest
Brockloch Hill
B729
A76
Heathhall
Dumfries & Galloway Aviation
Twelve Apostles Stone Circle
New Bridge
Dalscone Farm Fun
Lincluden
The Grove
Cruck Cottage
Torthorwald
Torthorwald Castle
Mossburn Animal Centre
Glenkiln Resr.
Glenkiln
Terregles
Corsock
Craig
Shawhead
Maxwelltown
A780
A709
Collin
Woodside
A75
Cargenbridge
DUMFRIES
Greenlea
Elizafield
Racks
2
B724
Troqueer
Crofts
A712
Lochfoot
Drumsleet
B726
Crichton Grounds
Kingholm Quay
Islesteps
Mouswald
A75
Falbae Loch
Crocketford or Ninemile Bar
Auchenreoch Loch
Milton Loch
Lochrutton Loch
B725
Lochar Water
Carrutherstown
Loch Lukie
Knockvennie
B794
Kirkpatrick Durham
Milton
Lochaber Loch
Mabie
Mabie Forest
Mabie Farm Park
A710
River Nith
Kelton
Parton
Springholm
Loch Roan
Beeswing
Loch Arthur
Drumcoltran Tower
112
Glencaple
Bankend
Clarencefield
Old Bridge of Urr
Erncrogo Loch
A711
Lotus Hill
National Costume
Kirkconnell
B725
Crossmichael
Hardgate
Kirkgunzeon
Brow-Well
Ruthwell
Clarebrand
Corn Mill
Shearington
Dornell Loch
Townhead of Greenlaw
Haugh of Urr
Corra
New Abbey
Sweetheart Abbey
Blackshaw
Laurieston
B795
Mote of Urr
Waterloo Monument
Caerlaverock
3
Glenlochar
A75
B794
Loch Kindar
Castle Douglas
Leaths
Long Fell 1256
Glentoo Loch
Threave
Meikle Hard Hill
Old Buittle Tower
Dalbeattie
G A L L O W A Y
Criffel 1868
Drumburn
Bargatton Loch
Sulwath Brewery
Carlingwark Loch
1032 Maidenpap
Boreland Hill
Bridge of Dee
Craignair
A745
Threave NTS
B727
A711
B793
Carsethorn
Rhonehouse or Kelton Hill
60
A762
B736
Kirkbean
Gelston
A710
DALBEATTIE FOREST
Caulkerbush
Prestonmill
B793
John Paul Jones Birthplace
A711
R. Dee
Palnackie
Barnbarroch
A710
Mainsriddle
Orchardton Tower
Loaningfoot
1283 Bengairn
Screel Hill
Colvend
Sandyhills
4
Tongland
Tongland Bridge
Kippford or Scaur
Mote of Mark
Rockcliffe
Portling
Southerness
Southerness Point
Rough Island
Castlehill Point
Barcloy Hill
A762
Galloway
B727
Auchencairn
Kirkcudbright
Auchencairn Bay
Hestan Island
Broughton House NTS
Balcary Point
550
Beckfoot
Rascarrel
Dundrennan
A711
Abbey
Rascarrel Bay
SOLWAY FIRTH
Townhead
Mawbray
Dubmill Point
Salta
Netherlaw
Port Mary
5
DANGER AREA
Abbey Head
Allonby
Allonby Bay
Milefortlet 21 Salt Pans
B5300
Allerby
A596
Crosscanonby
Senhouse Roman
Alauna Roman Fort
Crosby
Birkby
R. Ellen
Maryport
Maritime
A594
Dearham
70
80
90
300

112
Cample
FOREST OF AE
St. Ann's
1157 Great Hill
A701
Johnstonebridge
ANNANDALE WATER
16
Berryscaur
Boreland
CASTLE O'ER FOREST
Castle O'er
Bentpath
Park
Kirkpatrick
A
B
C
D
Brownmoor Hill
Courance
118
Broomhillbank
Glenmaid Moor
Ae
A74(M)
Telford Memorial
The Shin
1087 Hart Fell
A76
Parkgate
Sibbaldbie
High Auldgirth
Nethermill
Claydaubing Bridge
1478 Calkin Rig
Corrie Common
Auldgirth
Templand
D U M F R I E S & G A L L O
Dalswinton
NITHSDALE
Millhousebridge
Glentenmont Height
Auchencairn
Shieldhill
Applegarthtown
Paddockhole
Ellisland Farm
Marjoriebanks
B7068
Raes Knowes
Duncow
Amisfield
Lochmaben
Lockerbie
Tinwald
Dryfesdale Lodge
Bankshill
1047 Grange Fell
B729
Kirkton
Castle Loch
A709
Holywood
Locharbriggs
A701
Heck
18
B7068
Kirtleton
Greenhill
Heathhall
Dumfries & Galloway Aviation
Twelve Apostles Stone Circle
Dalscone Farm Fun
Howat's Hill
A76
Mossburn Animal Centre
Hightae
New Bridge
Lincluden
Cruck Cottage
Burnswark
Craigs
The Grove
Torthorwald
Torthorwald Castle
Waterbeck
B722
Terregles
Smallholm
B725
Maxwelltown
A780
A709
Collin
Kettleholm
Middlebie
Kirkconnel
A75
19
Cargenbridge
DUMFRIES
Greenlea
Ecclefechan
Eaglesfield
Troqueer
Elizafield
Woodside
Dalton Pottery
Dalton
Drumsleet
Crichton Grounds
Racks
Hoddom Castle
Carlyle's Birthplace NTS
Hoddomcross
Chapelknowe
B726
Kingholm Quay
B724
A75
Merkland Cross
A711
Islesteps
Mouswald
20
Kirtlebridge
Repentance Tower
B725
Lochar Water
Carrutherstown
Kelton
Mabie
Brydekirk
Moorend
Lochaber Loch
Mabie Forest
Mabie Farm Park
River Nith
Newton
Bruce's Cave
Kirkpatrick-Fleming
A74(M)
21
A710
Charlesfield
Creca
Loch Arthur
Warmanbie
Stapleton Tower
Bankend
B723
GRETNA
Glencaple
Clarencefield
Ruthwell Cross
B6357
Gretna Green
Kirkconnell
B725
Ruthwell
Savings Banks
A75
Rigg
National Costume
Brow Well
Howes
ANNAN
Shearington
Corn Mill
Sweetheart Abbey
Cummertrees
B724
Gretna
New Abbey
Blackshaw
Welldale
Dornock
Eastriggs
B721
Waterloo Monument
Caerlaverock
Powfoot
Newbie
Devil's Porridge
Loch Kindar
SCOTLAND
ENGLAND
Barnkirk Point
Redkirk Point
Torduff Point
1256
Meikle Hard Hill
Criffel 1868
Port Carlisle
Bowness-on-Solway
Drumburn
Boreland Hill
Glasson
Drumburgh
F I R T H
Carsethorn
Dykesfield
Kirkbean
Easton
Cardurnock
Anthorn
Longcroft
Boustead Hill
Longburgh
B793
Prestonmill
Whitrigg
Caulkerbush
John Paul Jones Birthplace
Angerton
B5307
A710
Mainsriddle
Fingland
Kirkbampton
Kirkbride
Skinburness
Loaningfoot
Thurstonfield
Little Bampton
Oughterby
Southerness
Lifeboat Station
Newton Arlosh
Wampool
Southerness Point
Calvo
Silloth
Seaville
Aikton
Greenrow
B5302
Wedholme Flow
Biglands
Wiggonby
Blackdyke
B5301
Moss Side
Thornby
Blitterlees
Gamelsby
Raby
Moorhouse
Knowsley Wildlife Rescue Trust
Low Whinnow
R. Waver
Parton
Oulton
Micklethwaite
Crofton
Kelsick
Abbeytown
B5302
Dundraw
Lessonhall
Standingstone
A596
Beckfoot
Wolsty
Highlaws
Pelutho
Moor Row
Aikhead
Thornby Moor Dairy
West Woodside
Southerfield
Aldoth
Blencogo
Waverbridge
Wigton
Kirkland
Newtown
Tarns
Waverton
Highmoor
A595
Bromfield
A596
Parkgate
Brackenlands
Carwath
Mawbray
Holme St. Cuthbert
Langrigg
High Scales
High Longthwaite
Brackenthwaite
Dubmill Point
Mealrigg
Waterside
Red Dial
Old Carlisle Roman Fort
B5305
Salta
Woodrow
Edderside
New Cowper
Low Row
Bolton Low Houses
Westward
Rosley
S O L W A Y
Heathfield
Bolton Wood Lane
Westnewton
Yearngill
Crookdake
Bolton New Houses
Allonby
C U M
Watchill
Fletchertown
Allonby Bay
Aspatria
B5299
Blennerhasset
Mealsgate
Hayton
Harriston
Prospect
Kirkland Guards
Boltongate
Sandale
Milefortlet 21 Salt Pans
Oughterside
Howk Bobbin Mill
Allerby
102
Westmoor
Plumbland
Whelpo
Crosscanonby
A596
Crosby Villa
Parsonby
Torpenhow
Ireby
B5299
Senhouse Roman Museum
Bothel
Whitrigg
The Howk
Crosby
Bullgill
Gilcrux
B5301
Aughertree
Fell Side
Alauna Roman Fort
A591
Birkby
Greengill
R. Ellen
High Ireby
Maryport
Maritime
Dearham
Ruthwaite
Uldale
Branthwaite
A594
Moota Hill
A595
Longlands

KIELDER FOREST
KIELDER WATER & FOREST PARK
NORTHUMBERLAND
Kielder
Kielder Castle
Butteryhaugh
Kielder Viaduct
Newcastleton or Copshaw Holm
Liddesdale Heritage Centre
Newcastleton Forest
Langholm
Skipper's Bridge
Kershope Bri.
Kershopefoot
KERSHOPE FOREST
Baileyhead
Bewcastle Fells
WARK FOREST
Canonbie
Bewcastle
DANGER AREA
Butterburn
Longtown
Gilsland
Greenhead
Haltwhistle
Brampton
CARLISLE
Hayton
Warwick Bridge
Wetheral
Castle Carrock
Dalston
Armathwaite
Kirkoswald
Alston
GILDERDALE FOREST
Melmerby
Gamblesby
Glassonby
Great Salkeld
Hunsonby
Plumpton
Southwaite
Raise
Ayle
Blagill
Leadgate
Garrigill
Knarsdale
Slaggyford
Lambley
Halton Lea Gate
Featherstone Castle
Whiteside
A7
A6071
A689
A69
A6
A686
A595
M6
B6318
B6357
B6413

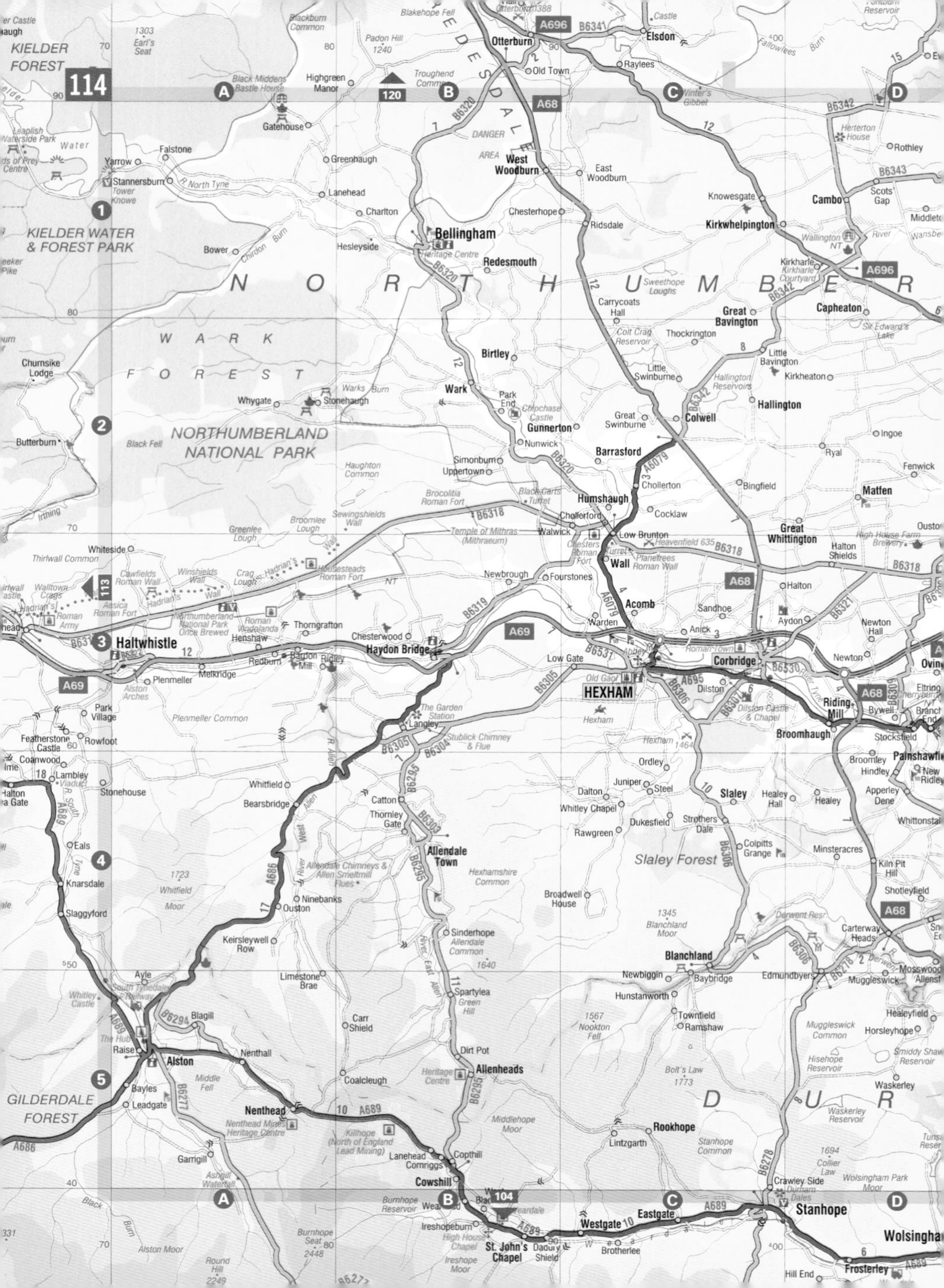

115
Longhorsley
Rayburn Lake
Fenrother
Tritlington
Widdrington Station
Cresswell
Ulgham
Ellington
Linton Colliery
Lynemouth
A697
A1
A1068
Bide-a-Wee Cottage
121
Stanton
The Sanctuary Wildlife Care Centre
A189
Hebron
Longhirst
Woodhorn
Beacon Point
Heritage
ASHINGTON
Pigdon
Pegswood
Newbiggin-by-the-Sea
Hartburn
Throphill
Mitford
MORPETH
Bothal
North Seaton
Sheepwash
West Sleekburn
North Seaton Colliery
High Angerton
B6343
Castle
High Church
Guide Post
Stakeford
Low Angerton
Meldon
Molesden
Loansdean
Hepscott
Choppington
Bomarsund
Earth Balance
Cambois
Clifton
Tranwell
B6524
East Sleekburn
North Blyth
Bolam
Nedderton
B1331
Bebside
Whalton
Shilvington
Whitehouse Farm Centre
BEDLINGTON
Cowpen
BLYTH
Isabella Pit
B1329
B1523
East Hartford
South Newsham
Newsham
NORTH SEA
Saltwick
Stannington
A192
A1061
Belsay
Belsay Hall
Ogle
Shankhouse
Nelson Village
Shotton
Kirkley Hall
R. Blyth
R. Pont
New Hartley
Seaton Sluice
Black Heddon
Horton Grange
Cramlington
East Cramlington
Seaton
A190
Higham Dykes
Seaton Delaval
NT Seaton Delaval Hall
Hartley
St. Mary's Lighthouse
St. Mary's or Bait Island
Milbourne
Berwick Hill
A19
Holywell
DANGER AREA
Seaton Burn
Seghill
B1325
Ponteland
Dudley
A696
Dinnington
Brunswick Village
Wide Open
Backworth
Earsdon
WHITLEY BAY
Heugh
Stamfordham
Darras Hall
Prestwick
NEWCASTLE INTERNATIONAL
Hazlerigg
Burradon
Monkseaton
Dalton
A1056
Killingworth
Shiremoor
Lifeboat Station
Cullercoats
Blue Reef Aquarium
Eachwick
Medburn
B6545
High Callerton
B6918
New York
Woolsington
Black Callerton
LONGBENTON
TYNEMOUTH
Kenton Bankfoot
GOSFORTH
Newcastle to Amsterdam (IJmuiden) 15hrs
NEWCASTLE UPON TYNE
A1058
North Walbottle
B6323
B6324
Willington
North Shields
Arbeia Roman Fort
SOUTH SHIELDS
B6318
B6528
A69
Jesmond
Tyne Tunnel
Marsden Bay
Houghton
Heddon-on-the-Wall
Throckley
Walbottle
Heaton
WALLSEND
Westoe
Marsden
Horsley
George Stephenson's Birthplace NT
NEWBURN
A191
A167(M)
Walker
A185
Harton
Souter NT
Lizard Point
Clara Vale
Ryton
Lemington
Fenham
Benwell
A186
Byker
West Harton
A1300
Whitburn Colliery
Wylam
Scotswood
HEBBURN
JARROW
A1018
Crawcrook
B6317
Elswick
FELLING
Dunston
A194
Boldon Colliery
Cleadon
Whitburn
West Wylam
Ryton Woodside
BLAYDON
Winlaton
A695
Prudhoe
Greenside
B5317
Teams
B1426
Heworth
B1298
B1299
South Bents
Coalburns
Barlow
Thornley Woodlands
GATESHEAD
A184
Boldon
Winlaton Mill
WHICKHAM
Bowes
B1288
A195
Seaburn
Leadgate
High Spen
A692
Fulwell
Roker
Rowlands Gill
Hooker Gate
Gibside NT
Marley Hill
Street Gate
Wrekenton
A194(M)
A1290
Southwick
Castletown
A1231
Chopwell
Highfield
Sunniside
Angel of the North
Springwell
Usworth
WASHINGTON
Monkwearmouth
National Glass Centre
Blackhall Mill
Derwentcote Steel Furnace
Lintzford
Leazes
Sheep Hill
Tanfield
Byermoor
Lamesley
South Hylton
SUNDERLAND
Hamsterley
Hamsterley Mill
Crookgate Bank
A6076
Kibblesworth
Old Hall
Washington Village
Pennywell
Low Westwood
High Westwood
Burnopfield
Hobson
Causey Arch
Birtley
WASHINGTON
Offerton
Hendon
B6310
Beamish
Fatfield
Cox Green
A183
A690
High Newport
A1018
Ebchester
Hill Top
Tantobie
Tanfield Lea
Ouston
Barley Mow
Penshaw
Herrington
Tunstall
Ryhope Colliery
Ryhope
Medomsley
Dipton
Beamish
Perkinsville
Rickleton
New Herrington
Benfieldside
Leadgate
Harelaw
Catchgate
Greencroft
STANLEY
West Pelton
Pelton
Newfield
A693
The Middles
Grange Villa
B6313
Shiney Row
Philadelphia
Silksworth
Ryhope Engines
CONSETT
South Moor
Quaking Houses
Craghead
CHESTER-LE-STREET
Bournmoor
Newbottle
Fence Houses
HOUGHTON-LE-SPRING
Crookhall
Annfield Plain
Iveston
Waldridge
A167
Templetown
Delves
Greencroft Park
Maiden Law
Holmside
B6532
Chester Moor
Great Lumley
Colliery Row
Rainton Meadows
Great Eppleton
Seaton
SEAHAM
Castleside
Knitsley
A691
Edmondsley
Dawdon
Rowley
Newbiggin
Burnhope
Nettlesworth
Plawsworth
West Rainton
East Rainton
Hetton-le-Hole
Murton
Dalton-le-Dale
Lanchester
Sacriston
Witton Gilbert
Kimblesworth
Finchale Priory
Middle Rainton
Low Moorsley
South Hetton
Cold Hesleden
EASINGTON
East Butsfield
B6312
Pity Me
Newton Hall
A1(M)
Leamside
Easington Lane
Hawthorn
Beacon Point
Diggerland
Langley Park
Wall Nook
Framwellgate Moor
Pittington
High Haswell
A19
Easington Colliery
West Butsfield
Hill Top
Quebec
A691
Carrville
Littletown
Haswell
Hall Hill Farm
Cornsay
Cornsay Colliery
Esh
Ushaw Moor
Bearpark
Aykley Heads
Hallgarth
Haswell Plough
Easington
Horden Point
Satley
DURHAM
Sherburn
B6302
Esh Winning
New Brancepeth
Gilesgate Moor
Sherburn Hill
Shotton Colliery
PETERLEE
Horden
A68
Broompark
Byers Garth
Ludworth
East Hedleyhope
Waterhouses
Langley Moor
Shincliffe
High Shincliffe
Botanic Garden
Shadforth
Dene Mouth
High Stoop
B6301
105
Thornley
Wheatley Hill
106
Shotton
Blackhall Colliery
Dan's Castle
Brandon
Meadowfield
Old Cassop
Castle Eden
Blackhall Rocks
Sunniside
Bowburn
Quarrington
Cassop
Crimdon Park
Tow Law
Stanley Crook
B6299
Brancepeth
B6300
A181
Wingate
High Hesleden
Billy Row
Quarrington Hill
Eden Vale
Monk Hesleden
Thornley
Roddymoor
Oakenshaw
Sunderland Bridge
Croxdale
Town Kelloe
Deaf Hill
Station Town
Hart Station
Page
Hett
A688
Kelloe
A19

Kilwinning
Horse Isle
Ardrossan
Stevenston
Saltcoats
North Ayrshire
Montgreenan
Torranyard
Doura
Cunninghamhead
Kilmaurs
Rowallan Castle
Ardrossan to Brodick 55mins.
Irvine Mains
Girdle Toll
Stanecastle
Dreghorn
Springside
Knockentiber
Altonhill
Onthank
Knockinlaw
KILMARNOC
Crookedholm
IRVINE
Scottish Maritime
Beach Park
Crosshouse
Grange
Laigh Milton Viaduct
Drybridge
Gatehead
Irvine Bay
Earlston
Riccarton
Hurlford
Crossroads
Dundonald
Clauchlands Point
Holy Island
Barassie
Troon to Larne 1hr. 50mins. (Fast Ferry, Seasonal)
Loans
Symington
Bogend
Craigie
Troon
Lady Isle
Kingscross Point
Kingscross
Whiting
Monktonhill
Fail
Monkton
GLASGOW PRESTWICK INTERNATIONAL
Tarbolton
Bachelors' Club NTS
Failford
Prestwick
New Prestwick
Mossblown
Newton upon Ayr
St. Quivox
Largybeg Point
Yett
Milton
Stair
Whitletts
Annbank
Dippin Head
Newton Steeple
AYR
Dalmilling
Wallacetown
Gadgirth
Trabboch
Wallace Tower
Seafield
Belston
Cunning Park
Greenan Castle
Doonfoot
Belmont
Joppa
Coalhall
Coylton
Hillhead
Drongan
Heads of Ayr
Heads of Ayr Farm Park
Alloway
Robert Burns Birthplace NTS
Brig o' Doon
Low Coylton
Fisherton
Doonholm
Barbieston
Martnaham Loch
Dunure
943 Brown Carrick Hill
Carclule
Hayhill
Culroy
Knockdon
Dalrymple
Minishant
Hollybush
Littlemill
Knockshinnoch
Rankinston
Electric Brae
Knoweside
Culzean Bay
Polnessan
1408 Kilmein Hill
Culzean Castle NTS
Maidenhead Bay
Whitefaulds
Maybole
Patna
Lethanhill
Burnfoot
Scottish Industrial Railway Centre
Kirkmichael
Maidens
Turnberry Castle
Crossraguel Abbey
Kirkoswald
Souter Johnnie's Cottage NTS
Turnberry Bay
Loch Spallander Resr.
Waterside
River Doon
Turnberry
Crosshill
Blairquhan Castle
Bogton Loch
Straiton
Matthew's Port
Ruglen
Kilkerran
Dersalloch Hill
Dipple
Wallacetown
Kilgrammie
Dalquharran Castle
Dailly
1395 Glenalla Fell
Big Hill of Glenmount 1252
Bargany
Old Dailly
Hadyard Hill 1060
Derclach Loch
Loch Finlas
Tairlaw Ring
1408 Garleffin Fell
Tairlaw Plantation
Girvan
Penkill
Linfern Loch
Tallaminnock
Loch Bradan Resr.
McKechnie Institute
Saugh Hill 971
Penwhapple Reservoir
Glendoune
Stinchar Falls
Woodland Bay
Dalquhairn
1165 Mull of Miljoan
Black Hill
Craiglee
Byne Hill
Tormitchell
CARRICK FOREST
Barr
Eldrick Hill
CHANGUE FOREST
Loch Riecawr
Carrick Forest Drive
Grey Hill 975
River Stinchar
Pinmore
Loch Macaterick
Polmaddie Hill 1854
David Bell Memorial
Waterhead
Rig of the Shalloch
Merkland
Straid
Lendalfoot
853 Knockdaw Hill
Cairn Hill 1572
Knockinlochie
1637 Macaterick
Tarfessock
Kirriereoch Hill 2565
Bennane Head
Poundland
Pinwherry
Pindonnan Craigs 1098
Mullwharchar 2270
Colmonell
Bellamore
Ballantrae Bay
GALLOWAY FOREST PARK
SOUTH AYRSHIRE
CARRICK
126
123
109

117
127
128
118
110
111
EAST AYRSHIRE
SOUTH LANARKSHIRE
SOUTHERN UPLANDS
NITHSDALE
DUMFRIES & GALLOWAY
Newmilns
Darvel
Greenholm
Priestland
Drumclog
Caldermill
Sandford
Blackwood
Kirkmuirhill
Auchenheath
Stonebyres
Kirkfieldbank
New Lanark
Boghead
Dillarburn
Lesmahagow
Brocketsbrae
Turfholm
Auchlochan
Douglas Water
Rigside
Coalburn
Bellfield
Braehead
HAPPENDON
Happendon
Uddington
Douglas
Glenbuck
Glespin
Muirkirk
Smallburn
Kames
Sorn
Catrine
Ballochmyle
Auchinleck
Lugar
Cronberry
Holmhead
Cumnock
Logan
Craigens
Netherthird
Garrallan
Skares
Ochiltree
Dalblair
Fingland
Crawfordjohn
Leadhills
Wanlockhead
Mansfield
Pathhead
New Cumnock
Bankglen
Connel Park
Burnside
Dalleagles
Waterhead
Kirkland
Kirkconnel
Crawick
Kelloholm
Sanquhar
Barr
Mennock
Pennyvenie
Dalmellington
Craigdarroch
Enterkinfoot
Polskeoch
Chanlockfoot
Enoch
Holm of Drumlanrig
Carronbridge
Corlae
Benbuie
Auchenbrack
Burnhead
Thornhill
Penpont
Tynron
Keir Mill
Closeburn
Carsphairn
Craigmalloch
Knowehead
Stroanfreggan
Moniaive
Kirkland
Wallaceton
Glenmidge
Forrest Lodge
Sornhill
Crossbands
Auchmillan
Montgarswood
Haugh
Shawwood
Roddenloft
Waterside
DUNDEUGH FOREST
GLENKENS
High Bridge of Ken
Butterhole Bridge
Kendoon Loch
Polmaddy Settlement
M74
A71
A70
A76
A713
A702
B7086
B743
B745
B7037
B705
B7036
B7046
B741
B740
B797
B729
B7078
B7055
B7018
B731
B732

LANARK
Kirkfieldbank
Stonebyres
New Lanark
Bankhead
Falls of Clyde
Hyndford Bridge
Pettinain
Libberton
Elsrickle
Kirkurd
Candy Mill
Kaimrig End
Broughton Heights 1874
Black Meldon 1334
Lyne
Hallyne
Shieldhill
Tower
Covington
Quothquan
Discover Carmichael
Thankerton
Carmichael
Greenhill Covenanters' House
Ewe Hill
Skirling
Puppet Theatre
Biggar
Cormiston
Coulter Motte
Causewayend
Broughton Gallery
Trahenna Hill 1792
Dreva Wood
Stobo
Stobo Castle
Dawyck Botanic Garden
Bellspool
1563 Whitelaw Hill
Broughton
Drumelzier
Rachan Mill
Goseland Hill 1427
Kilbucho Place
John Buchan Centre
Douglas Water
Rigside
Howgate Hill 1456
Tinto Hills
2334 Tinto
Symington
Coulter
Bellfield
Braehead
HAPPENDON
Happendon
Uddington
Wiston
Newton
Lamington
Snaip Hill
Common Law
Glenholm Wildlife Project
Glenholm
Finglen Rig
Heritage
Douglas Water
St. Bride's Church
Douglas
Scaur Hill
1673 Dungavel Hill
SOUTH
Blakehope Head 1783
Stanhope
2417 Pykestone Hill
Horse Hill
Pagie Hill
Roberton Law 1238
Backstane Hill
Roberton
Startup Hill
Broad Hill
Culter Fell 2455
Glenkirk
Glenlood Hill
Kingledores
2089 Taberon Law
2682 Dollar Law
LANARKSHIRE
Wandel
ABINGTON
Culter Waterhead Reservoir
Duncangill Head
2257 Gathersnow Hill
Crawfordjohn
Heritage Venture
Abington
1868 Tewsgill Hill
Tweedsmuir
Glenmuck Height
Common Hill
Camps Water
Culter Cleuch Shank
Camps Resr.
2756 Broad Law
Drake Law 1586
Kirkton
Castle
Crawford
Glenbreck
Megget Reservoir
White Hill
Talla Resr.
Talla Linnfoots
1392 Spango Hill
Spango Bridge
1814 Wellgrain Dod
Fruid Resr.
1813 Craigmaid
Lochcraig Head 2625
1621 Rake Law
Elvanfoot
Birk Craigs
Wedder Dod 1460
Leadhills
Miners' Library
1790 Clyde Law
Cape Law
Loch Skeen
Grey Mare's Tail Waterfall
Wanlockhead
Beam Engine
Dun Law
Leadhills & Wanlockhead Railway
Postie Stone (Mail Coach Memorial)
Nether Howcleugh
Devil's Beef Tub
John Hunter Memorial
2651 Hart Fell
2696 White Coomb
2413 Saddle Yoke
Bell Craig
1591 Conrig Hill
1926 Stood Hill
Lead Mining
2403 Green Lowther
Nunnerie
Ericstane
Swatte Fell
Wintercleuch Fell
Bodesbeck Law
1912 Thirstane Hill
Capplegill
Auldton Fell
2270 Ettrick Pen
Comb Law 2108
Daer Resr.
1473 Cairn Hill
1987 Well Hill
Ballencleuch Law 2268
Kirkhope
Auldton Mote
Moffat
Craigieburn
Capel Fell 2223
Selcoth Burn
Holmend
Woollen Mill
Croft Head
2256 Loch Fell
Craiglochan
Cornal Burn
ESKDALEMUIR
Enterkinfoot
Durisdeermill
Church
Durisdeer
Wedder Law
Craighoar Hill 1898
Kinnelhead
Beattock
Broomlands
Wamphray Water
Ewelairs Hill
Garwald
Enoch
Bellybought Hill 1453
2191 Gana Hill
Lochan Burn
Queensberry 2286
Wee Queensberry
Black Hill
Holm of Drumlanrig
Drumlanrig Castle
Morton
DUMFRIES & GALLOWAY
Laverhay
Milne Height
Black Esk Reservoir
Tibbers Castle
Carronbridge
Locherben
Minnygap Height 1308
Gatelawbridge
Scaur Water
Burnhead
Thornhill
Penpont
Holehouse Hill
Whitefauld Hill
Newton
Fingland Fell
Cample
Keir Mill
FOREST OF AE
St. Ann's
ANNANDALE WATER
Closeburn
1157 Great Hill
Johnstonebridge
1172 Keir Hills
Park
Kirkpatrick
Brownmoor Hill
Berryscaur
Boreland
Courance
Broomhillbank
Glenmaid Moor
Ae
Parkgate
Sibbaldbie
Claydaubing Bridge
Wallaceton
Blackwood
Glenmidge
High Auldgirth
Auldgirth
Nethermill
Water of Ae
Kinnel Water
Templand
Dryfe Water
Corrie Common
NITHSDALE
LOWTHER HILLS
ANNANDALE
SOUTHERN UPLANDS
SCOTTISH BORDERS
M74
A74(M)
A702
A701
A70
A73
A72
A76
A708
A721
B7016
B7055
B7078
B740
B797
B7040
B7076
B719
B7020
B712
B732
B731
B729
128
117
111
112

119
Peebles
Glentress Forest
Dunslair Heights
1975
Whitehope Law 2038
2163 Windlestraw Law
1764 Black Law
Stow
Old Kirk & Bishop's House
Nether Blainslie
Ledgerwood
Huntlywood
Greenknowe Tower
Gordon
Cross Kirk
Beltane
Glentress
Horsbrugh Ford
Tweeddale
Kings Muir
Kailzie
Cademuir Hill
Cardrona Forest
Lee Pen 1648
St. Ronan's Wells
Pirn Hill Fort
Priesthorpe Hill
1666 Great Law
William Law
1314
Buckholm
Langshaw
Earlston
Fans
Mellerstain House
LAUDERDALE
1222 Knowes Hill
Walkerburn
Robert Smail's Printing Works
Clovenfords
GALASHIELS
Preston Law
1507 Wallace's Hill
Traquair House
Innerleithen
Elibank and Traquair Forest
Meigle 1389 Hill
Old Gala House
Lowood
Gattonside
Redpath
Smailholm Tower
Hundleshope Heights
Traquair
Ashiestiel Hill
Peel
Caddonfoot
Yair Hill Forest
Darnick
Melrose
Newstead
Leaderfoot
Scott's View
Bemersyde
Glen House
Kirkhouse
1859 Minch Moor
Boleside
Abbotsford
Dingleton
Eildon Hills
Eildon
Clintmains
Newtown St. Boswells
Dryburgh
Mertoun Bridge
Mertoun
Dun Rig 2441
Blake Muir
Broomy Law
Lindean Mill Glass
Lindean
Cauldshiels Hill
Bowden
Abbey
St. Boswells
1779 Deuchar Law
Yarrow Ford
Linglie Hill
Selkirk Glass
Lochcarron Mill
Maxton
Sir Walter Scott's Courtroom
Newark Castle
Yarrow
Fastheugh Hill 1645
Bowhill House & Country Estate
Philiphaugh
Selkirk
Halliwells Ho.
Philiphaugh 1645
Midlem
Longnewton
Ancrum Moor 1545
Longnewton Forest
Sandystones
Waterloo Monument
Mountbenger
Yarrow Feus
Aikwood Tower
Brockhill
Lilliesleaf
Ancrum
Cappercleuch
ETTRICK FOREST
Ettrickbridge
Bloomfield
St. Mary's Loch
1933 The Wiss
Black Knowe Head 1805
Gilmanscleuch
Caver's Hill 1209
Essenside Loch
Ashkirk
Minto Hills 905
Fatlips Castle
Lanton
Mary, Queen of Scots' Ho.
Akermoor Loch
Minto
Spittal-on-Rule
Newton
Castle Jail
Loch of the Lowes
Shaws Under Loch
Hassendean
Horsleyhill
Leyden Monument
Dunion Hill
Tushielaw
Dun Knowe
Drinkstone Hill
Clarilaw
Appletreehall
Denholm
Bedrule
Ramsey Knowe
Hellmoor Loch
Smasha Hill
Scottish Borders Art Glass
Redfordgreen
Burnfoot
Cauldmill
1391 Rubers Law
James Hogg Monument
Ettrick
Alemoor Loch
Roberton
Wilton
HAWICK
Buccleuch
Borders Textile Towerhouse
Kirkton
Leyden Obelisk
Law Kneis 1634
Burnfoot
Motte
Bonchester Bridge
Hobkirk
Branxholme
987 White Hill
Deanburnhaugh
Glenkerry
Sauchie Law
1278 Redcleuch Edge
Hott Hill
Newmill
Chesters
Southdean
CRAIK FOREST
Stobs Castle
Cross Hill
Craik
Dryden Fell
Craik Cross Hill
Pike Hill 1369
Allan Water
Green Law
WAUCHOPE FOREST
TEVIOTDALE
Teviothead
River Teviot
Skelfhill
The Pike 1516
Langburnshiels
Wyndburgh Hill
1688 Fanna Hill
Carlin Tooth
FOREST
1746 Skelfhill Pen
Maiden Paps
Leap Hill
Needs Law
Davington
Blaeberry Hill
Eweslees Knowe
Comb Hill
Millstone Edge
1996 Cauldcleuch Head
1966 Greatmoor Hill
Sandy Edge
Lamblair Hill
Hartshorn Pike
Kagyu Samye Ling
Causeway Grain Head
Mosspaul
Tudhope Hill 1965
Saughtree Fell
1975 Peel Fell
Eskdalemuir
1953 Wisp Hill
White Hope Edge
Jamestown
1722 Faw Side
Geordie's Hill
1737 Din Fell
Hermitage Chapel
Hermitage
1464 Arnton Fell
Saughtree
Deadwater
Hog Hill
Broad Head 1614
Pike Fell
Foulmire Heights
CASTLE O'ER FOREST
Castle O'er
Crumpton Hill 1575
1862 Roan Fell
Steele Road
902 North Birny Fell
Kielder
Buttery
Kielder Viaduct
Larriston Fells 1678
SCOTLAND
ENGLAND
KIELDER FOREST
Black Knowe
Dinmont Lairs
Kirkstile or Ewes
Watch Hill
Bentpath
ESKDALE
LIDDESDALE
Telford Memorial
Hog Fell
Wilson's Pike
The Shin
Black Edge 1464
Newcastleton or Copshaw Holm
Liddesdale Heritage Centre
Newcastleton Forest
Black Knowe
1478 Calkin Rig
Clan Armstrong
McDiarmid Memorial
Lewis
Rough Pike
Millholm
Glendhu
129
130
120
113

120
130
119
113
114
A
B
C
D
1
2
3
4
5
LAUDERDALE
SCOTTISH BORDERS
THE CHEVIOT HILLS
NORTHUMBERLAND NATIONAL PARK
THE REDESDALE
SCOTLAND
ENGLAND
Ledgerwood
Huntlywood
Gordon
Greenknowe Tower
Hume
Hume Castle
Lambden
Leitholm
Eccles
Coldstream
Lennel
Hirsel
Twizel Bridge
Felkington
Duddo
Stone Circle
Castle Heaton
Melkington
Cornhill-on-Tweed
Etal
Lady Waterford Hall
Heatherslaw Light Railway
Crookham
Ford
Branxton
Flodden Field Monument
1513 Flodden Field
Flodden
Kimmerston
Maelmin Heritage Trail
Milfield
Fans
Earlston
Redpath
Mellerstain House
Nenthorn
Stichill
Sweethope Hill
Smailholm
Smailholm Tower
Ednam
James Thomson Obelisk
Kelso
Floors Castle
Abbey
Birgham
Carham
Wark
West Learmouth
East Learmouth
Hadden
Pressen
Sprouston
Downham
Thornington
Mindrum
Pawston
Kilham
Howtel
Housedon Hill
Lanton
Coupland
Yeavering
Yeavering Bell
Kirknewton
Westnewton
Akeld
Hethpool
Newstead
Leaderfoot
Bemersyde
Scott's View
Eildon
Newtown St. Boswells
Dryburgh
St. Boswells
Clintmains
Mertoun Bridge
Mertoun
Makerstoun
Maxwellheugh
Roxburgh
Heiton
Lempitlaw
Hoselaw Loch
Shotton
Maxton
Longnewton
Longnewton Forest
Ancrum Moor
1545
Teviot Game Fare Smokery & Water Gardens
Bowmount Forest
Linton Hill
Town Yetholm
Kirk Yetholm
Coldsmouth Hill
Sandystones
Waterloo Monument
Peniel Heugh
Nisbet
Eckford
Kale Water
Linton
Primsidemill
White Law
Newton Tors
Fredden Hill
Ancrum
Bloomfield
Monteviot House
Harestanes
Crailing
Morebattle
Steer Rig
Timpendean Tower
Bonjedward
Cessford
Castle
Crookedshaws Hill
The Curr
The Schil
Preston Hill
Cold Law
Lanton
Crailinghall
Whitton
Hownam Law
THE CHEVIOT
Langleeford
Minto Hills
Minto
Fatlips Castle
Mary, Queen of Scots' Ho
Jedburgh
Spittal-on-Rule
Newton
Castle Jail
Whitton Loch
Mowhaugh
Sourhope
Hedgehope Hill
Leyden Monument
Denholm
Dunion Hill
Bedrule
Hownam
Craik Moor
Comb Fell
Ferniehirst
Oxnam
Swinside Hall
Cock Law
R. Breamish
Rubers Law
Mossburnford
Mozie Law
Whitestone Hill
Windy Gyle
Bloodybush Edge
Shill Moor
Leyden Obelisk
Jedforest Deer & Farm Park
Camptown
Beefstand Hill
Loft Hill
Cushat Law
Bonchester Bridge
Hobkirk
Woden Law
Kidland Forest
Wether Cairn
Chesters
Jed Water
Blindburn
Barrowburn
Southdean
Upper Hindhope
Deerlee Knowe
Leithope Forest
Bell Hill
Biddlestone
Grindstone Law
Carter Bar
Redeswire Fray
Leap Hill
Hungry Law
Green Law
WAUCHOPE FOREST
DANGER AREA
Shillmoor
R. Coquet
Linshiels
Alwinton
Clennell
Harbottle
Carlin Tooth
Fanna Hill
Catcleugh
Byrness
Dour Hill
Catcleugh Resr.
Needs Law
Holystone
Hartshorn Pike
Girdle Fell
Ellis Crag
Lamblair Hill
Kielderhead Moor
REDESDALE FOREST
Sills
North Yardhope
Redesdale Camp
Brigantium
Rochester
Peel Fell
Rushy Knowe
Hindhope Law
Saughtree
Deadwater
Kielder Forest Drive
Horsley
Blakeman's Law
Otterburn Camp
Foulmire Heights
Emblehope Moor
Rooken Edge
Elishaw
Otterburn Hall
Blakehope Fell
Kielder
Kielder Castle
Butteryhaugh
Kielder Viaduct
Blackburn Common
Earl's Seat
Padon Hill
Otterburn
Elsdon
Larriston Fells
KIELDER FOREST
Black Knowe
Dinmont Lairs
Highgreen Manor
Troughend Common
Old Town
Raylees
Black Middens Bastle House
Gatehouse
Winter's Gibbet
Leaplish Waterside Park
Birds of Prey Centre
Rough Pike
Falstone
Yarrow
Stannersburn
R. North Tyne
Greenhaugh
West Woodburn
East Woodburn
TOLL
A68
A697
A698
A699
A6105
A6089
A6091
A6088
A696
A6112
B6461
B6364
B6397
B6356
B6360
B6404
B6398
B6350
B6352
B6396
B6436
B6401
B6400
B6358
B6405
B6357
B6354
B6351
B6437
B6341
B6320

121
HOLY ISLAND
Keel Head
Holy Island
Lindisfarne Centre
NT Lindisfarne Priory
Castle Point
Burrows Hole
Longstone
Staple Sound
FARNE ISLANDS
Chapel NT
Inner Sound
NORTH SEA
NORTHUMBERLAND
Haggerston
Berrington
Beal
Bowsden
Fenham
Barmoor
Lowick
West Kyloe
East Kyloe
Kyloe Hills
Buckton
Elwick
Ross
Budle Bay
Holburn
Detchant
St. Cuthbert's Cave
Hetton Steads
North Hazelrigg
Middleton
Waren Mill
Bamburgh
Budle
Grace Darling
Nesbit
Belford
Easington
Burton
New Shoreston
Lifeboat Station
Seahouses
Heritage
Carr End
Spindlestone
Bradford
Doddington
South Hazelrigg
West Horton
East Horton
Lyham
Warenton
Bellshill
ADDERSTONE
Adderstone
Lucker
Elford
North Sunderland
Beadnell
Lime Kilns
Beadnell Bay
Weetwood Hall
Chatton
Greendykes
Warenford
Newham
Swinhoe
West Fleetham
Wooler
Earle
Haugh Head
Chillingham
Wild Cattle
Ros Castle
Chathill
Tughall
Ellingham
Snook Point
High Newton-by-the-Sea
Low Newton-by-the-Sea
Preston
Brunton
Tower
Middleton Hall
North Middleton
Newtown
Lilburn Tower
Hepburn
876 Cateran Hill
Middle Moor
South Middleton
East Lilburn
North Charlton
Armstrong's Household & Farming
Doxford
Christon Bank
Embleton
Embleton Bay
Dunstanburgh NT
Ilderton
Old Bewick
Roseden
Roddam
South Charlton
Wooperton
B6346
New Bewick
Harehope
Eglingham
Rock
Dunstan
Craster
1464 Hedgeley Moor
Percy's Cross
Beanley
Heiferlaw Tower
Rennington
Stamford
Littlemill
Howick
Howick Hall
Brandon
Powburn
East Bolton
Shipley
Greensidehill
Ingram
Northumberland National Park
Branton
Titlington
Hulne Priory
Littlehoughton
Longhoughton
Glanton Pyke
Shawdon Hall
Hulne Park
Abbey
Boulmer
Glanton
Denwick
ALNWICK
1093
A1068
Great Ryle
Eslington Hall
Bolton
Broome Park
Abberwick
Prendwick
House of Hardy
Hipsburn
Lesbury
Little Ryle
Whittingham
Lemmington Hall
Bilton
Alnmouth
Alnham
Thrunton
Yetlington
High Buston
Alnmouth Bay
Scrainwood
Callaly
Edlingham
Shilbottle
Shilbottle Grange
Lorbottle Hall
Lorbottle
Burradon
Newton-on-the-Moor
Eastfield Hall
Birling
Hermitage
Warkworth
High Trewhitt
Cartington
Hazon
Guyzance
Gloster Hill
Lifeboat Station
Coquet Island
Amble
Snitter
Warton
Northumberland National Park
Swarland
Morwick Hall
Hauxley
Hauxley Haven
Flotterton
Rothbury
Thropton
Old Swarland
Acklington
Radcliffe
Cragside NT
Caistron
Newtown
Whitton
Longframlington
Felton
North Broomhill
Togston
South Broomhill
Great Tosson
Bickerton
Pauperhaugh
West Thirston
East Thirston
Hadston
Red Row
Weldon
Brinkburn Priory
1444 Tosson Hill
Low Hesleyhurst
Eshott
Druridge Bay
HARWOOD FOREST
ROTHBURY FOREST
Forestburn Gate
West Chevington
Fontburn Reservoir
Wingates
Causey Park
Widdrington
Longhorsley
Stobswood
Fallowlees Burn
Rayburn Lake
Nunnykirk
Widdrington Station
Tritlington
Cresswell
Ulgham
Ellington
Ewesley
Fenrother
Linton Colliery
Lynemouth
Espley Hall
The Sanctuary Wildlife Care Centre
Bide-a-Wee Cottage
Stanton
Netherwitton
Hebron
Longhirst
Woodhorn
Beacon Point
Heritage
Longwitton
ASHINGTON
Newbiggin-by-the-Sea
Herterton House
Rothley
Pigdon
Pegswood
North Seaton
Bothal
Hartburn
Throphill
Mitford
MORPETH
Sheepwash
West Sleekburn
North Seaton
Hirst
Scots Gap
Cambo
A1
A697
A189
A696
A1068
A196
A197
B1340
B1339
B1338
B1341
B1342
B6341
B6342
B6343
B6344
B6345
B6346
B6347
B6348
B6349
B6353
B6525
B1337
B1334
131
115

ISLE OF GIGHA
Gigha
Sound of Gigha
West Tarbert Bay
East Tarbert Bay
Druimyeon Bay
Ardminish
Achamore
Craro Island
Gigalum Island
Cara Island
Mull of Cara
A' Chleit
Tayinloan
Killean
Muasdale
Ballochroy
Rhunahaorine
Glenacardoch Point
Port a' Bhorrain
Glenbarr
Glenbarr Abbey
Bellochantuy Bay
Bellochantuy
Port Corbert
Machrihanish Bay
Machrihanish
CAMPBELTOWN
Campbeltown
Springbank Distillery
Kilchenzie
Skeroblingarry
Drumlemble
Stewarton
Earadale Point
Rubha Dùin Bhàin
Rubha' a' Mharaiche
Dalsmirren
Killellan
Southend
Carskiey
Lephenstrath
High Keil
Feorlan
Port Mean
MULL OF KINTYRE
Rubha Chlachan
Brunerican Bay
Cove Point
Sheep Island
Black Point
Sanda Island
Polliwilline Bay
Macharioch
Feochaig
Johnston's Point
Achinhoan Head
Island Davaar
Mill Knowe
Peninver
Ardnacross Bay
Black Bay
Ugadale
Ugadale Point
Saddell
Saddell Bay
Rubha nan Sgarbh
Torrisdale
Carradale
Carradale Point
Port Righ
Dippen
Grogport
Cour
Crossaig
Eascairt Point
KILBRANNAN SOUND
ARGYLL & BUTE
ISLE OF ARRAN
NORTH AYRSHIRE
Rubha Creagan Dubha
Lochranza
Catacol
Rubha Airigh Bheirg
Lenimore
Thundergay
Pirnmill
Alltgobhlach
Whitefarland Point
Whitefarland
Imachar
Dougarie Point
Dougarie
Machrie Bay
Machrie
Tormore
Ballymichael
Shedog
Shiskine
Torbeg
Drumadoon Point
Blackwaterfoot
Drumadoon Bay
Kilpatrick
Brown Head
Glenree
Corriecravie
Bennecarrigan
Sliddery
Lagg
Kilmory
A83
B842
B843
B879
B880
125

123
Arran
Dunagoil Bay
Dunagoil
St. Blane's
Garroch Head
Little Cumbrae Island
The Tan
Robertson Museum & Aquarium
Millstone Point
126
Gull Point
FIRTH OF CLYDE
Campbelton
Portencross
Farland Head
Ardneil Bay
Seamill
West Kilbride
Southannan
Kaim Hill
Knockendon Resr.
Baidland Hill
Glengarnock
Longbar
Gateside
Hessilhead
Highgate
The Den
Drakemyre
Highfield
Dalry
Crosbie
NORTH AYRSHIRE
CUNNINGHAME
Auchenmade
Auchentiber
North Sannox
Sannox Bay
Sannox
Corrie
GOATFELL
Mill Glen Reservoir
Dalgarven
Lylestone
Kilwinning
Torranyard
Montgreenan
Doura
Horse Isle
Ardrossan
Saltcoats
Stevenston
Perceton
Irvine Mains
Girdle Toll
Stanecastle
Knockentiber
Springside
Crosshouse
IRVINE
Dreghorn
Drybridge
Merkland Point
Brodick Castle
Isle of Arran Brewery
Glenrosa
Brodick Bay
Brodick
Strathwhillan
Corrygills
Ardrossan to Brodick 55mins.
Irvine Bay
Dundonald
Barassie
Troon to Larne 1hr. 50mins. (Fast Ferry, Seasonal)
Loans
Symington
Troon
Clauchlands Point
Margnaheglish
Lamlash
Holy Island
Monamore Br.
Cordon
Lady Isle
Monktonhill
Monkton
GLASGOW PRESTWICK INTERNATIONAL
Prestwick
New Prestwick
Newton upon Ayr
St. Quivox
Kingscross Point
Kingscross
Knockenkelly
Whiting Bay
Glenashdale Falls
Largymore
Largymeanoch
Largybeg
Largybeg Point
Dippin
Dippin Head
Levencorroch
East Bennan
Kildonan
West Bennan
Sound of Pladda
Bennan Head
Pladda
Newton Steeple
AYR
Whitletts
Dalmilling
Wallacetown
Wallace Tower
Seafield
Cunning Park
Greenan Castle
Doonfoot
Heads of Ayr
Heads of Ayr Farm Park
Belmont
Alloway
Doonholm
116
Fisherton
Dunure
Brown Carrick Hill
Carcluie
Dalrymple
Culroy
Knockdon
Minishant
Electric Brae
Knoweside
SOUTH
Culzean Bay
Culzean Castle
Maidenhead Bay
Whitefaulds
Maybole
Kirkmichael
Maidens
Turnberry Castle
Turnberry
Turnberry Bay
Crossraguel Abbey
Kirkoswald
Souter Johnnie's Cottage NTS
AYRSHIRE
Crosshill
Blairquhan Castle
Straiton
Matthew's Port
Rugles
Kilkerran
Dipple
Wallacetown
Kilgrammie
Dalquharran Castle
Dailly
Glenalla Field
Bargany
Old Dailly
Penkill
Hadyard Hill
Ailsa Craig
Girvan
McKechnie Institute
Glendoune
Saugh Hill
Penwhapple Reservoir
Woodland Bay
Dalquhairn
Garleffin Fell
Linfern Loch
Stinchar Falls
A78
A737
A736
A738
A71
A759
A77
A719
A70
A713
A841
B7023
B741
B734
B742
B7034
B7045

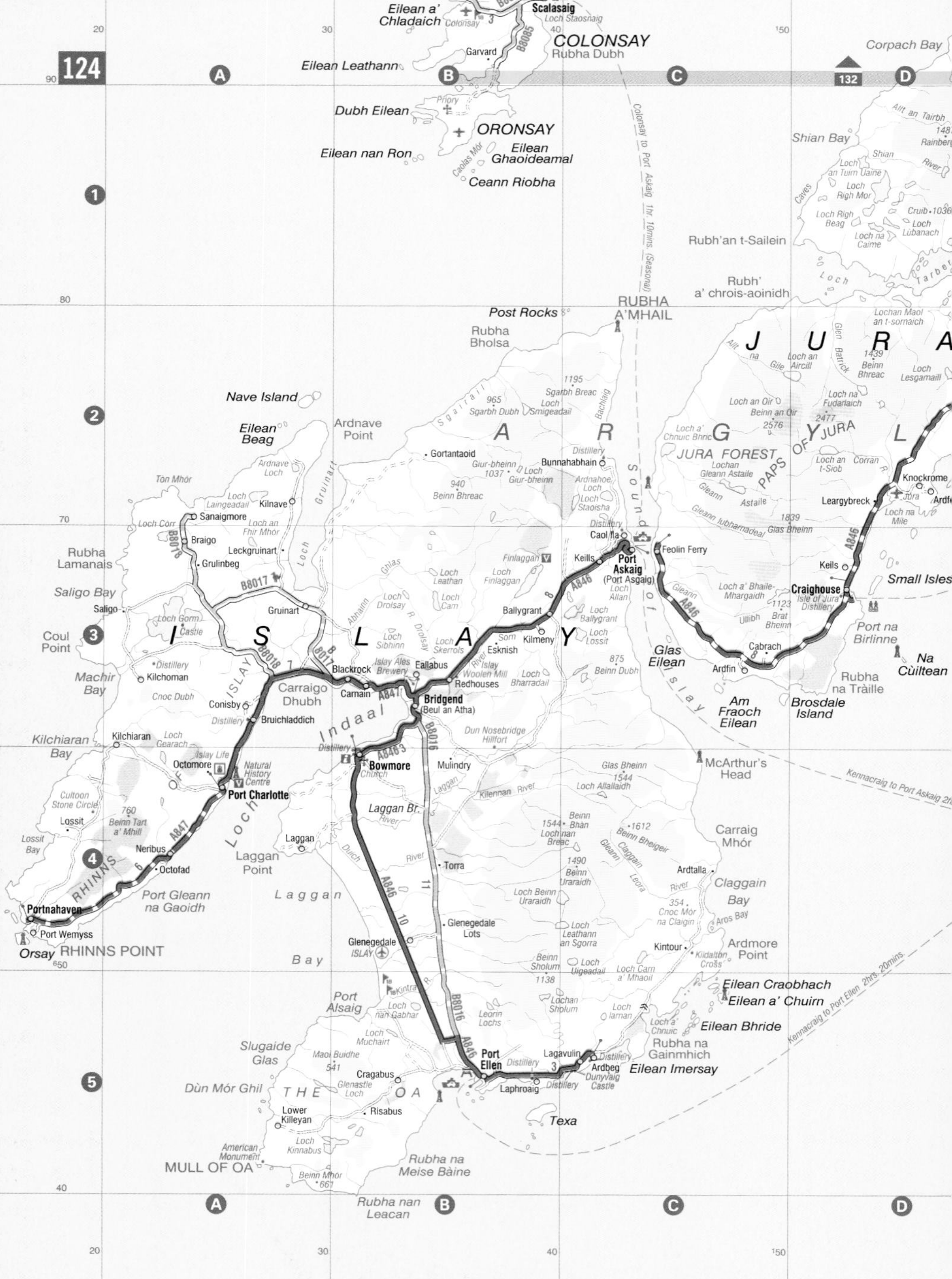

COLONSAY
Scalasaig
Eilean a' Chladaich
Eilean Leathann
Garvard
Rubha Dubh
Corpach Bay
Dubh Eilean
ORONSAY
Eilean Ghaoideamal
Eilean nan Ron
Ceann Riobha
Colonsay to Port Askaig 1hr. 10mins. (Seasonal)
Shian Bay
Rubh'an t-Sailein
Rubh' a' chrois-aoinidh
Post Rocks
RUBHA A'MHAIL
Rubha Bholsa
JURA
Nave Island
Eilean Beag
Ardnave Point
ARGYLL
ISLAY
JURA FOREST
PAPS OF JURA
Bunnahabhain
Gortantaoid
Sanaigmore
Braigo
Kilnave
Leckgruinart
Grulinbeg
Rubha Lamanais
Saligo Bay
Saligo
Gruinart
Caol Ila
Port Askaig (Port Asgaig)
Feolin Ferry
Keills
Finlaggan
Ballygrant
Kilmeny
Esknish
Craighouse
Small Isles
Knockrome
Leargybreck
Coul Point
Machir Bay
Kilchoman
Carraigo Dhubh
Blackrock
Carnain
Eallabus
Redhouses
Bridgend (Beul an Atha)
Conisby
Bruichladdich
Glas Eilean
Am Fraoch Eilean
Brosdale Island
Rubha na Tràille
Na Cùiltean
Ardfin
Cabrach
Kilchiaran Bay
Kilchiaran
Octomore
Port Charlotte
Loch Indaal
Bowmore
Mulindry
McArthur's Head
Kennacraig to Port Askaig 2hrs.
Lossit
Neribus
Octofad
RHINNS OF ISLAY
Laggan
Laggan Point
Laggan Bay
Torra
Carraig Mhór
Ardtalla
Claggain Bay
Portnahaven
Port Wemyss
Orsay
RHINNS POINT
Port Gleann na Gaoidh
Glenegedale
Glenegedale Lots
Kintour
Ardmore Point
Eilean Craobhach
Eilean a' Chuirn
Eilean Bhride
Port Alsaig
Slugaide Glas
Port Ellen
Lagavulin
Ardbeg
Laphroaig
Rubha na Gainmhich
Eilean Imersay
Kennacraig to Port Ellen 2hrs. 20mins.
Dùn Mór Ghil
THE OA
Cragabus
Risabus
Lower Killeyan
Texa
MULL OF OA
American Monument
Rubha na Meise Bàine
Rubha nan Leacan
A846
A847
B8016
B8017
B8018

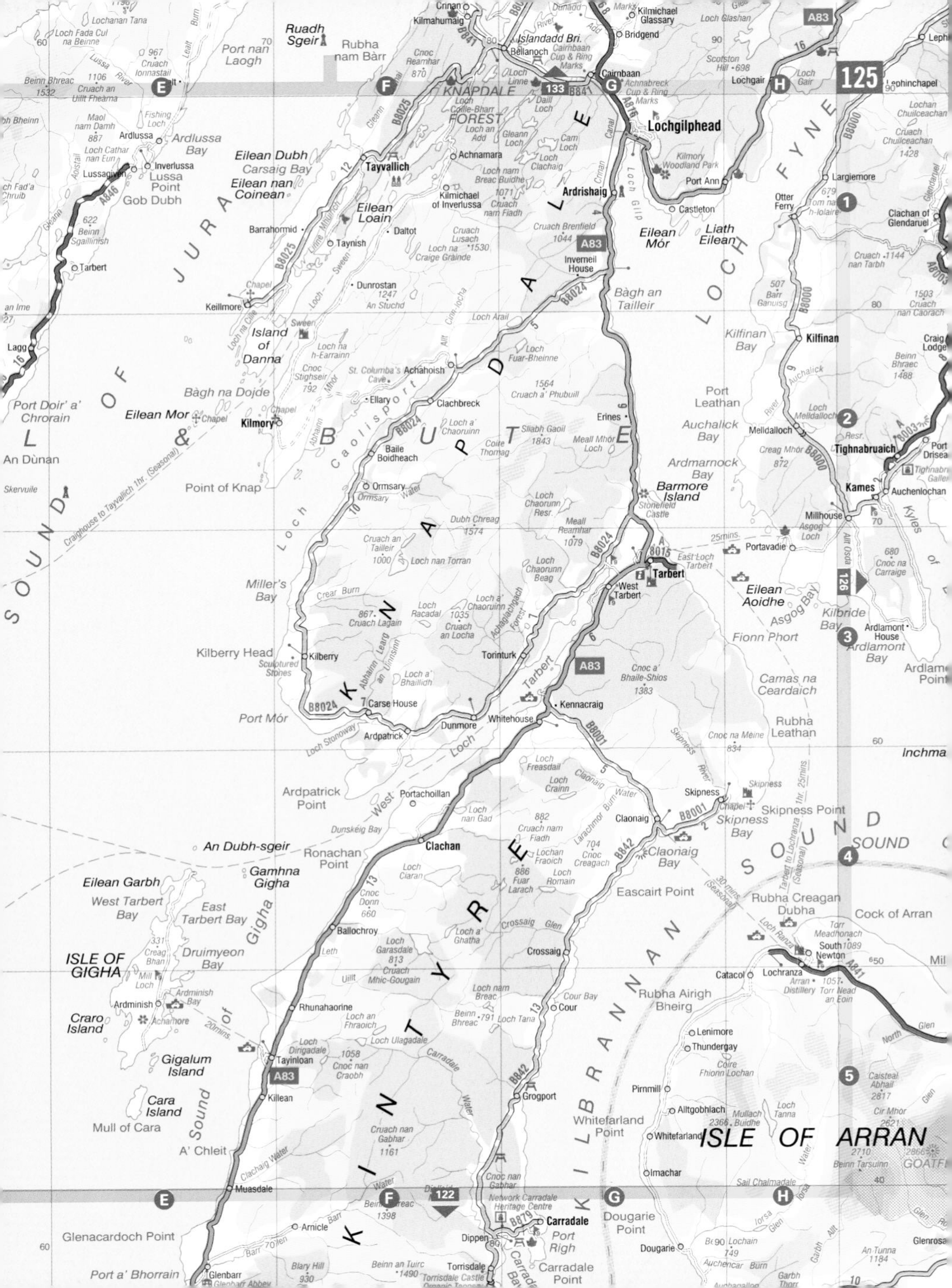
Crinan
Kilmahumaig
Kilmichael Glassary
Bridgend
Loch Glashan
A83
Ruadh Sgeir
Rubha nam Bàrr
Port nan Laogh
Lochanan Tana
Loch Fada Cul na Beinne
Cruach Ionnastail
Beinn Bhreac 1532
Cruach an Uillt Fheàrna
Islandadd Bri.
Bellanoch
Cairnbaan Cup & Ring Marks
Cairnbaan
Achnabreck Cup & Ring Marks
Scotston Hill 698
Lochgair
Loch Gair
Lephinchapel
KNAPDALE
FOREST
133
B841
A816
Loch Coille-Bharr
Daill Loch
Lochgilphead
Kilmory Woodland Park
Port Ann
Largiemore
Otter Ferry
Castleton
Maol nam Damh 887
Ardlussa
Ardlussa Bay
Loch Cathar nan Eun
Inverlussa
Lussagiven
Lussa Point
Gob Dubh
Eilean Dubh
Carsaig Bay
Eilean nan Coinean
Tayvallich
Achnamara
Kilmichael of Inverlussa
Ardrishaig
Loch Gilp
Eilean Loain
Barrahormid
Taynish
Daltot
Cruach Brenfield 1044
Eilean Mór
Liath Eilean
Clachan of Glendaruel
Cruach nan Tarbh 1144
Beinn Sgaillinish
Tarbert
Dunrostan
An Stuchd
Inverneil House
Bàgh an Tailleir
Keillmore
Chapel
Loch Arail
Kilfinan Bay
Kilfinan
Lagg
Island of Danna
Loch Fuar-Bheinne
Achahoish
St. Columba's Cave
Ellary
Clachbreck
Cruach a' Phubuill
Port Leathan
Beinn Bhreac 1488
Bàgh na Dojde
Port Doir' a' Chrorain
Eilean Mor
Kilmory
Sliabh Gaoil 1843
Erines
Meall Mhòr Loch
Auchalick Bay
Melldalloch
Tighnabruaich
An Dùnan
Baile Boidheach
Ardmarnock Bay
Creag Mhòr 872
Skervuile
Point of Knap
Ormsary
Barmore Island
Stonefield Castle
Kames
Auchenlochan
Millhouse
Craighouse to Tayvallich 1hr. (Seasonal)
Dubh Chreag 1574
Meall Reamhar 1079
Loch Chaorunn Resr.
Asgog Loch
Portavadie
Cruach an Tailleir 1000
Loch nan Torran
B8015
East Loch Tarbert
Tarbert
West Tarbert
Eilean Aoidhe
Asgog Bay
Kilbride Bay
Ardlamont House
Ardlamont Bay
Miller's Bay
Cruach Lagain
Loch Racadal
Cruach an Locha
Fionn Phort
Kilberry Head
Kilberry
Sculptured Stones
Torinturk
A83
Cnoc a' Bhaile-Shios 1383
Camas na Ceardaich
Port Mór
Carse House
B8024
Dunmore
Whitehouse
Kennacraig
B8001
Ardpatrick
Loch Stornoway
Rubha Leathan
Cnoc na Meine 834
Loch Freasdail
Loch Crainn
Claonaig Water
Skipness
Ardpatrick Point
Portachoillan
West Loch Tarbert
Claonaig
Skipness Point
Skipness Bay
Dunskeig Bay
An Dubh-sgeir
Clachan
Cruach nam Fiadh
Cnoc Creagach
SOUND OF JURA
Gamhna Gigha
Ronachan Point
Claonaig Bay
Eilean Garbh
West Tarbert Bay
East Tarbert Bay
Loch Ciaran
Fuar Larach
Eascairt Point
Rubha Creagan Dubha
Cock of Arran
Tarbert to Lochranza 1hr. 25mins. (Seasonal)
Ballochroy
Loch Garasdale
Cruach Mhic-Gougain
Crossaig
Crossaig Glen
Loch Ranza
South Newton
ISLE OF GIGHA
Druimyeon Bay
Mill Loch
Catacol
Lochranza
Arran Distillery
Torr Nead an Eoin
A841
Ardminish
Ardminish Bay
Achamore
Craro Island
Rhunahaorine
Loch nam Breac
Beinn Bhreac 791
Loch Tana
Cour Bay
Cour
Rubha Airigh Bheirg
Lenimore
Thundergay
Loch Dirigadale
Loch Ulagadale
Cnoc nan Craobh
Carradale Water
Tayinloan
Gigalum Island
Cara Island
Mull of Cara
Killean
Sound of Gigha
Grogport
B842
Coire Fhionn Lochan
Pirnmill
Alltgobhlach
Mullach Buidhe
Whitefarland Point
Whitefarland
ISLE OF ARRAN
Caisteal Abhail 2817
Cir Mhor
A' Chleit
Cruach nan Gabhar 1161
Imachar
Beinn Tarsuinn
GOATFELL
Clachaig Water
Muasdale
Beinn Bhreac 1398
122
Network Carradale Heritage Centre
Carradale
B879
Dougarie Point
Dougarie
Sail Chalmadale
Glenacardoch Point
Arnicle
Dippen
Port Righ
Beinn an Tuirc 1490
Blary Hill
Torrisdale
Torrisdale Castle
Carradale Point
Port a' Bhorrain
Glenbarr
Glenbarr Abbey
An Tunna 1184
Glenrosa
KINTYRE
KILBRANNAN SOUND
KNAPDALE
LOCH FYNE
126

126
133
134
125
123
116
ISLE OF BUTE
ARGYLL
FIRTH OF CLYDE
ISLE OF ARRAN
NORTH AYRSHIRE
INVERCL
SOUND OF BUTE
ROTHESAY
DUNOON
GREENOCK
HELENSBURGH
Tighnabruaich
Port Bannatyne
Largs
Millport
Gourock
Garelochhead
Kilcreggan
Ardrossan
Saltcoats
Stevenston
Kilwinning
IRVINE
West Kilbride
Kilbirnie
Dalry
Wemyss Bay
Skelmorlie
Fairlie
Kingarth
Colintraive
Kames
Innellan
Sandbank
Blairmore
Strone
Ardentinny
Cove
Rosneath
Clynder
Shandon
GREAT CUMBRAE ISLAND
Little Cumbrae Island
Inchmarnock
GOATFELL
Glendaruel Forest
Corlarach Forest
Loch Striven
Kyles of Bute
Ardrossan to Brodick 55mins.
Tarbert to Lochranza 1hr. 25mins. (Seasonal)
CLYDE MUIRSHIEL REGIONAL PARK

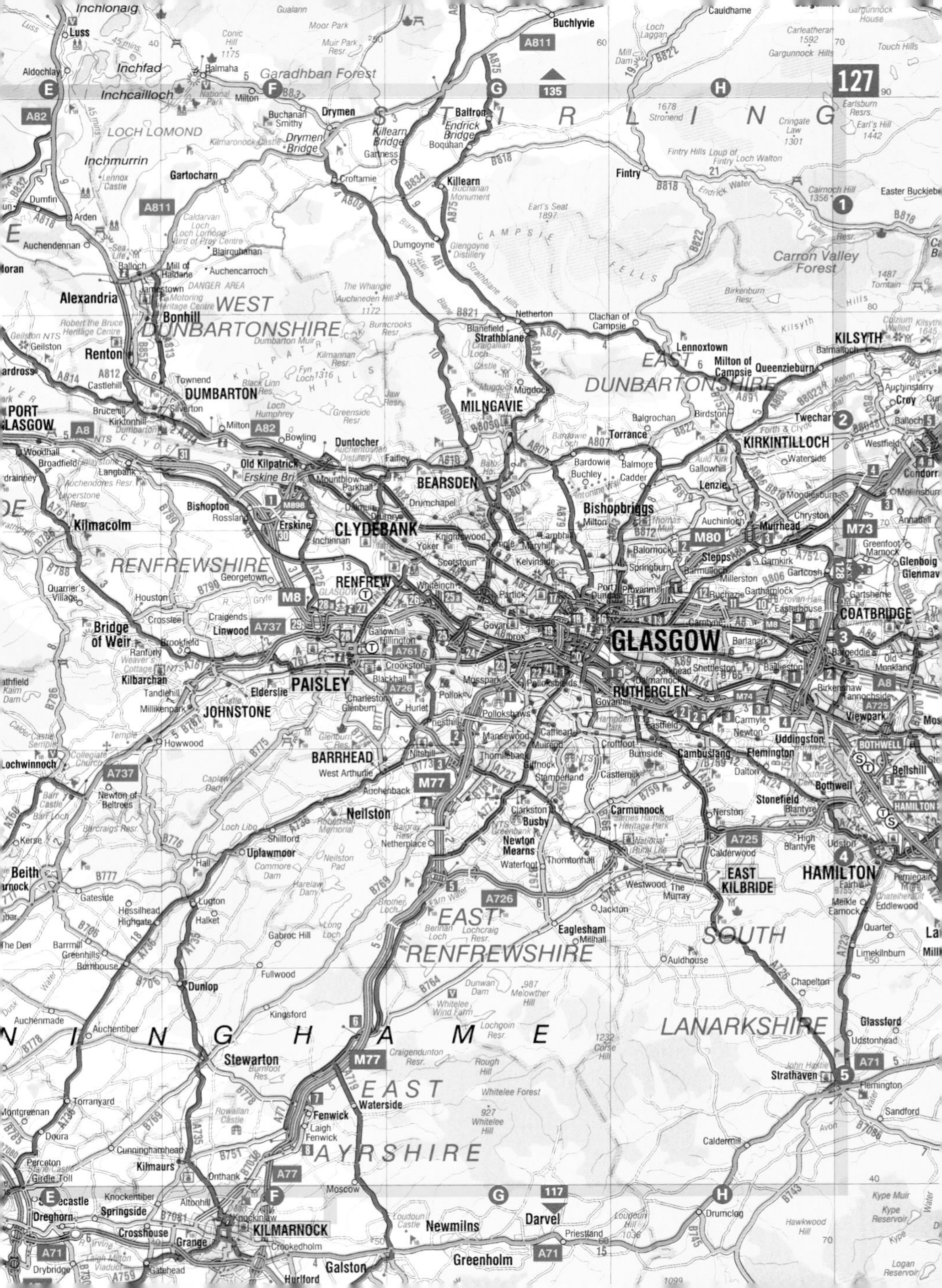
127
135
117
E
F
G
H
STIRLING
EAST DUNBARTONSHIRE
WEST DUNBARTONSHIRE
RENFREWSHIRE
EAST RENFREWSHIRE
SOUTH LANARKSHIRE
EAST AYRSHIRE
LOCH LOMOND
Garadhban Forest
Carron Valley Forest
Campsie Fells
Kilpatrick Hills
Inchlonaig
Luss
Inchfad
Inchcailloch
Balmaha
Milton
Aldochlay
Inchmurrin
Buchlyvie
Drymen
Drymen Bridge
Balfron
Endrick Bridge
Killearn Bridge
Killearn
Croftamie
Gartness
Boquhan
Buchanan Smithy
Gartocharn
Fintry
Dumfin
Arden
Auchendennan
Balloch
Mill of Haldane
Blairquhanan
Auchencarroch
Jamestown
Alexandria
Bonhill
Renton
Geilston
Castlehill
Townend
DUMBARTON
Silverton
Brucehill
Kirktonhill
PORT GLASGOW
Woodhall
Broadfield
Langbank
Bowling
Old Kilpatrick
Erskine Bri
Duntocher
Faifley
Mountblow
Parkhall
Dumgoyne
Netherton
Blanefield
Strathblane
Clachan of Campsie
Lennoxtown
Milton of Campsie
Queenzieburn
KILSYTH
Mugdock
MILNGAVIE
Torrance
Balgrochan
Birdston
Twechar
Croy
KIRKINTILLOCH
Bardowie
Balmore
Buchley
Cadder
Gallowhill
Lenzie
Waterside
BEARSDEN
Drumchapel
Bishopbriggs
Auchinloch
Muirhead
Chryston
Bishopton
Rossland
Erskine
Kilmacolm
CLYDEBANK
Inchinnan
Knightswood
Yoker
Scotstoun
Temple
Maryhill
Kelvinside
Lambhill
Milton
Balornock
Springburn
Stepps
Garnkirk
Gartcosh
Glenboig
Coatbridge
COATBRIDGE
Georgetown
RENFREW
Whiteinch
Partick
Port Dundas
Provanmill
Millerston
Barmulloch
Riddrie
Garthamlock
Easterhouse
Quarrier's Village
Houston
Crosslee
Craigends
Linwood
Bridge of Weir
Brookfield
Ranfurly
Kilbarchan
Govan
Ibrox
GLASGOW
Barlanark
Camtyne
Gallowhill
Hillington
Crookston
Blackhall
Mosspark
Pollokshields
PAISLEY
Elderslie
Tandlehill
Millikenpark
JOHNSTONE
Charleston
Glenburn
Hurlet
Pollok
Pollokshaws
Priesthill
Mansewood
Cathcart
Muirend
Thornliebank
Giffnock
Stamperland
Croftfoot
Castlemilk
Burnside
Cambuslang
Flemington
RUTHERGLEN
Govanhill
Dalmarnock
Parkhead
Shettleston
Baillieston
Eastfield
Carmyle
Newton
Uddingston
Viewpark
Birkenshaw
Tannochside
Old Monkland
Bargeddie
Howwood
BARRHEAD
West Arthurlie
Nitshill
Auchenback
Neilston
Newton of Beltrees
Clarkston
Busby
Newton Mearns
Waterfoot
Thorntonhall
Carmunnock
Nerston
Dalton
Stonefield
Blantyre
High Blantyre
Bothwell
BOTHWELL
Bellshill
HAMILTON
Udston
Calderwood
EAST KILBRIDE
Westwood
The Murray
Jackton
Eaglesham
Millhall
Auldhouse
Chapelton
Limekilnburn
Quarter
Meikle Earnock
Eddlewood
Fairhill
Glassford
Udstonhead
Strathaven
Flemington
Sandford
Caldermill
Drumclog
Kype Muir
Kype Reservoir
Logan Reservoir
Lochwinnoch
Beith
Kerse
Uplawmoor
Shillford
Hall
Lugton
Halket
Gateside
Hessilhead
Highgate
Barrmill
Greenhills
Burnhouse
Gabroc Hill
Fullwood
Dunlop
Kingsford
Auchentiber
Auchenmade
Stewarton
Torranyard
Montgreenan
Doura
Cunninghamhead
Kilmaurs
Perceton
Girdle Toll
Onthank
Fenwick
Laigh Fenwick
Waterside
Moscow
Knockentiber
Altonhill
Springside
Dreghorn
Crosshouse
Knockinlaw
KILMARNOCK
Grange
Crookedholm
Gatehead
Drybridge
Hurlford
Galston
Newmilns
Greenholm
Darvel
Priestland
Whitelee Forest
Whitelee Wind Farm
A82
A811
A8
M8
M80
M73
M74
M77
A737
A761
A726
A725
A71
A77
B818
B822
B821
A81
A891
A803
A809
A875
A807

128
135
136
117
118
127
STIRLING
FALKIRK
NORTH LANARKSHIRE
SOUTH LANARKSHIRE
WEST LOTH
CLYDESDALE
Stirling
Cambusbarron
St. Ninians
Bannockburn
Fallin
Alloa
Clackmannan
Clackmannanshire Bridge
Kincardine
Kincardine Bridge
Culross
Oakley
Dunfermlin
Saline
Carnock
Comrie
Blairhall
Devilla Forest
Cowie
Plean
Airth
Dunipace
Denny
Larbert
Stenhousemuir
Carron
Grangemouth
Bo'ness
Linlithgow
Falkirk
Laurieston
Polmont
Bonnybridge
Banknock
Kilsyth
Queenzieburn
Twechar
Kirkintilloch
Croy
Cumbernauld
Condorrat
Airdrie
Coatbridge
Slamannan
Avonbridge
Torphichen
Bathgate
Armadale
Livingston
Uphall
Caldercruix
Blackridge
Whitburn
Blackburn
Harthill
Shotts
Fauldhouse
Stoneyburn
Addiewell
West Calder
Polbeth
Chapelhall
Calderbank
Mossend
Holytown
Uddingston
Bellshill
Bothwell
Motherwell
Wishaw
Newmains
Cleland
Hamilton
East Kilbride
Larkhall
Carluke
Braidwood
Crossford
Stonehouse
Strathaven
Lanark
New Lanark
Kirkfieldbank
Carstairs
Carstairs Junction
Carnwath
Forth
Lesmahagow
Biggar
Thankerton
Douglas Water
Carron Valley Forest
Heart of Scotland
M9
M80
M876
M73
M8
M74
A985
A876
A71
A725
A8
A70
A73
A706

EDINBURGH
FIRTH OF FORTH
MIDLOTHIAN
SCOTTISH BORDERS
SOUTHERN UPLANDS
MOORFOOT HILLS
KIRKCALDY
Dysart
Cowdenbeath
Lumphinnans
Lochgelly
Auchtertool
Kinghorn
Pettycur
Burntisland
Aberdour
Dalgety Bay
Hillend
Rosyth
Inverkeithing
Jamestown
North Queensferry
Forth Bridge
Forth Road Bridge
South Queensferry
Dalmeny
Inchkeith
Inchcolm
Inchmickery
Cramond Island
Cramond
Newhaven
Granton
Trinity
Leith
Portobello
Joppa
MUSSELBURGH
Fisherrow
Inveresk
Prestonpans
Cockenzie and Port Seton
Longniddry
Aberlady
Aberlady Bay
Gullane Bay
Eyebroughy
Gosford Bay
Tranent
Macmerry
Gladsmuir
Penston
Elphinstone
New Winton
Ormiston
Pencaitland
East Saltoun
West Saltoun
Crossgatehall
Cousland
Whitecraig
Newcraighall
Niddrie
Craigmillar
Danderhall
Millerhill
DALKEITH
Eskbank
Gilmerton
Liberton
Kaimes
Fairmilehead
Straiton
Loanhead
Lasswade
Bonnyrigg
Newbattle
Easthouses
Mayfield
Edgehead
Pathhead
Newtongrange
Gorebridge
Arniston
Hunterfield
Newlandrig
Crichton
Borthwick
North Middleton
Middleton
Temple
Tynehead
Fala
Fala Dam
Humbie
Gilchriston
Peaston
Roslin
Rosewell
Bilston
Penicuik
Auchendinny
Carrington
Howgate
Mount Lothian
Leadburn
Milton Bridge
Silverburn
Eight Mile Burn
Nine Mile Burn
Carlops
West Linton
Cowdenburn
Lamancha
Macbiehill
Waterheads
Earlyvale
Eddleston
Romannobridge
Mountain Cross
Bordlands
Blyth Bridge
Kirkurd
Dolphinton
Skirling
Broughton
Stobo
Lyne
Hallyne
Peebles
Kings Muir
Horsbrugh Ford
Walkerburn
Innerleithen
Clovenfords
Stow
Killochyett
Fountainhall
Heriot
Oxton
Gilston
Corstorphine
Murrayfield
Dalry
Gorgie
Merchiston
Morningside
Newington
Colinton
Oxgangs
Juniper Green
Currie
Balerno
Hermiston
Sighthill
Ratho
Ratho Station
Gogar
Newbridge
Kirkliston
Broxburn
Newton
East Calder
Kirknewton
Wilkieston
Bonnington
Burnwynd
Linburn
Glentress Forest
Cardrona Forest
Pentland Hills

North Berwick
Dirleton
Gullane
Aberlady
Dunbar
East Linton
Haddington
Tranent
Longniddry
Gifford
Pencaitland
Lauder
Stow
Duns
Greenlaw
Gordon
Earlston
Galashiels
Fidra
Craigleith
Bass Rock
Eyebroughy
Lamb
Gullane Bay
Aberlady Bay
Gosford Bay
Barns Ness
Reed Point
EAST LOTHIAN
LAMMERMUIR HILLS
LAMMERMUIR UPLANDS
LAUDERDALE
SOUTHERN
SCOTTISH
BORDERS
MERSE
137
129
119
120

E   F   G   H

90   400   10   20   90

1

80

N O R T H   S E A

2

70

Fast Castle
Head
Point   Fast
              Castle
Telegraph
Hill   **ST. ABB'S HEAD**
Lumsdaine
Cross Law •744   St. Abb's
              Head   St. Abbs
Coldingham Moor   Lifeboat   *Coldingham*
                              Station   *Bay*
11   Coldingham   Priory   Lifeboat Station
              Priory

Houndwood   Eyemouth
                                        Gunsgreenhill   **3**
859   A1107
Horseley   Reston   18
Hill   Ayton   Burnmouth
Auchencrow   Ross   60

                        Lamberton   Marshall
Chirnside   Meadows
                Tithe   Conundrum
              Barn Clappers   Farm
Edrom   Chirnside-   15   Foulden   Halidon   A1
              bridge   Hill 1333   **4**
Allanton   A6105   Bell
                        Tower   BERWICK-
Hutton   B6460   Castle   UPON-TWEED   50
              B6461   Paxton   Tweedmouth
B6460   Paxton Ho.   Tweed   Lifeboat Station
              Fishwick   Chain Bridge   Spittal
Whitsome   Honey Farm   East
B6461   Horncliffe   Ord   Redshin
                                        Doom Do   Cove
Horndean   Scremerston
                Murton
Ladykirk   Norham   Thornton
              Norham   Cheswick
Swinton   B6470   Station   Shoreswood   West
              Upsettlington   Shoresdean   Allerdean   Goswick   **5**
E   Simprim   Wizel   Grindon   LINDISFARNE
              Bridge   Ancroft   HOLY ISLAND
                Felkington   Berrington Law   Berrington   Keel
                Stone Circle   Duddo   Haggerston   Head
Castle   Beal   Holy
Heaton   NORTHUMBERLAND   Island   Castle Point
Hirsel Lennel   Fenham   Lindisfarne   NT Lindisfarne   Burrows
dstream   Melkington   Centre   Priory   Hole   40
Cornhill-   Heatherslaw   B6353   West   Fenwick
on-Tweed   Light Railway   Etal   Lowick   Kyloe   121   FARNE
West   Bareless   Waterford   East   Buckton   ISLANDS
Learmouth   A697   Hall   Ford   Kyloe   Staple
East   Crookham   Kyloe   Elwick   Ross   Sound
Learmouth   Branxton   Hills   Budle   Inner
Flodden Field   Holburn   Detchant   Bay   Chapel NT
Monument 1513   St. Cuthbert's   20

E   F   G   H

BEN MORE
3171
ISLE OF MULL
Erisgeir
Corra-bheinn
2311
ARDMEANACH
Rubha na h Uamha
MacCulloch's Fossil Tree
Tavool House
Tiroran
Loch Scridain
Port na Croise
Pennyghael
Rubha nan Cearc
Garbh Phort
Kintra
Creich
Eorabus
Ardchrishnish
Torrans
Knockan
Aridhglas
Loch Poit na h-I
Bunessan
BROLASS
ROSS OF MULL
Ross of Mull Historical Centre
Loch Assopol
Knockvologan
Ardalanish
Uisken
Ardchiavaig
Ardalanish Bay
Rubh' Ardalanish
Cruachan Min 1232
Beinn Chreagach
Carsaig
Carsaig Bay
Carsaig Arches
Malcolm's Point
Rubha nam Bràithrean
Loch Fuaran
Beinn na Croise 1649
Lochbuie
Standing Stone Circle
Moy Castle
Loch Uisg
Loch Buie
Kinlochspelve
Loch Spelve
Croggan
Ben Buie 2354
Creach Beinn 2290
Loch Airdeglais
Loch Squabain
Strathcoil
Oakbank
Lussa River
Glen Coladoir
Frank Lockwood's Island
FIRTH OF LORN
Oban to Colonsay 2hrs 20mins
Dubh-fheith
Garbh Eileach
Garvellachs
Eileach an Naoimh
Belnahua
Fladda
Eilean Dubh Mór
Lunga
Guirasdeal
SLATE ISLANDS
Kilmory Lodge
Rubha nam Faoilean
SCARBA
Cruach Scarba 1474
Corryvreckan Whirlpool
Gulf of Corryvreckan
Glengarrisdale Bay
Glendebadel Bay
Corpach Bay
Beinn Bhreac 1532
Lealt
Rubh' a' Bhacain
Ruadh Sgeir
Port nan Laogh
Shian Bay
Rainberg Mór 1487
Ardlussa
Ardlussa Bay
Inverlussa
Lussagiven
Lussa Point
Gob Dubh
Eilean Dubh
Carsaig Bay
Eilean nan Coinean
Beinn Sgaillinish 622
Tarbert
Loch Tarbert
Rubh'an t-Sailein
Rubh' a' chrois-aoinidh
SOUND OF JURA
JURA
Lagg
Barrahormid
Keillmore
Island of Danna
Bàgh na Dojde
IONA
Réidh Eilean
Eilean Annraidh
Baile Mór
Fionnphort
Sound of Iona
Stac an Aoineidh
Eilean nah-Aon Chaorach
Greave
Soa Island
Erraid
Fidden
Eilean nam Muc
Eilean a' Chalmain
Port na Cuilce
Kiloran Bay
Balnahard
Uragaig
Port Ceann a' Gharraidh
Kiloran
Colonsay House
COLONSAY
Port a' Bhàta
Sgreadan
Kilchattan
Loch Fada
Glas Aird
Scalasaig
Loch Staosnaig
Eilean a' Chladaich
Eilean Leathann
Garvard
Rubha Dubh
Dubh Eilean
ORONSAY
Eilean nan Ron
Eilean Ghaoideamal
Ceann Riobha
Colonsay to Port Askaig 1hr 10mins (Seasonal)
Post Rocks
RUBHA A'MHAIL
Rubha Bholsa
124
139
A849
B8035
B8086
B8085
A846
B8025

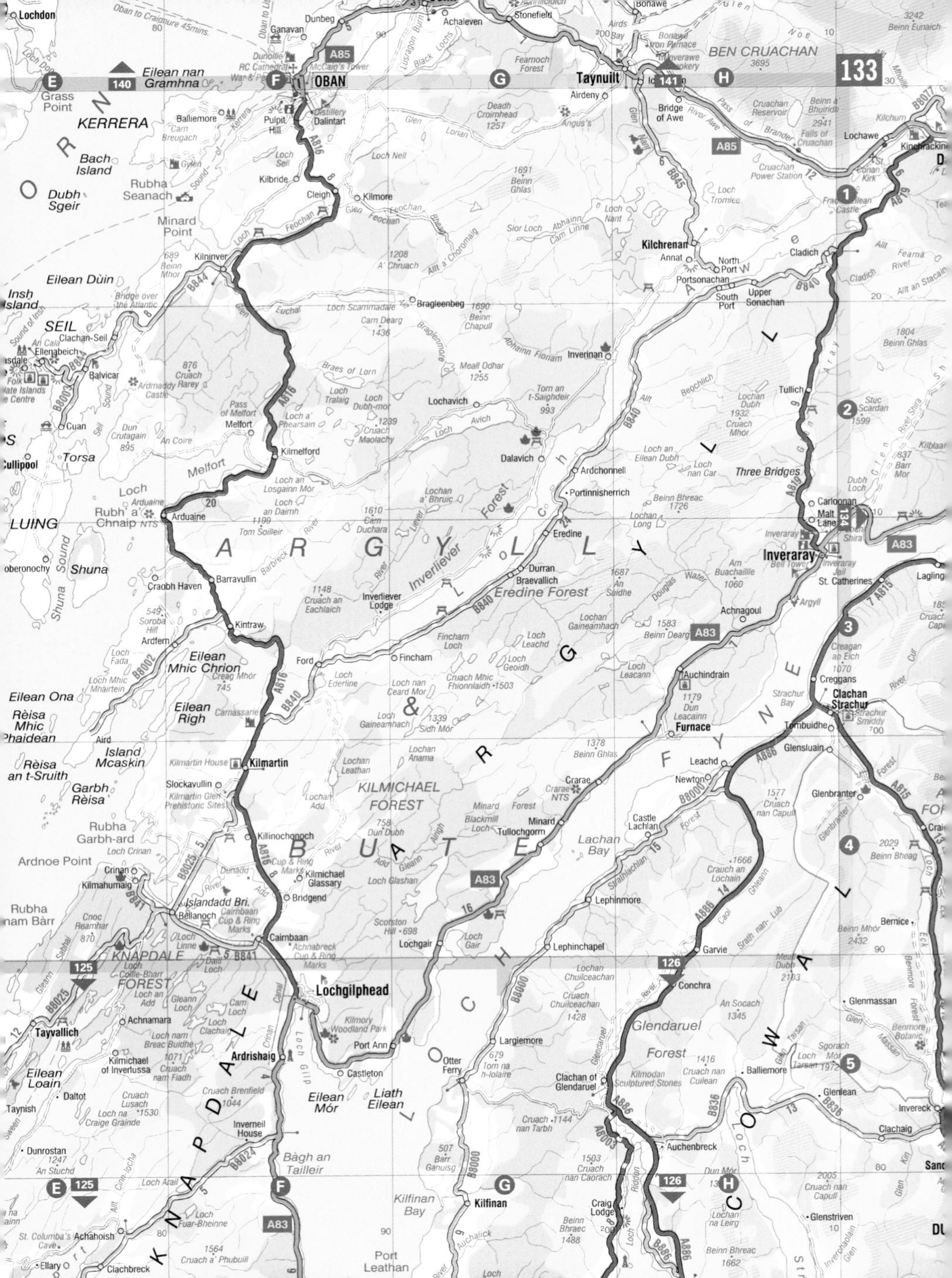

Lochdon
Oban to Craignure 45mins.
Ganavan
Dunbeg
Achaleven
Stonefield
Bonawe
Airds Bay
Bonawe Iron Furnace
Inverawe Smokery
BEN CRUACHAN
3695
3242
Beinn Eunaich
Eilean nan Gamhna
Dunollie
RC Cathedral
McCaig's Tower
A85
OBAN
Fearnoch Forest
Taynuilt
Grass Point
KERRERA
Balliemore
Pulpit Hill
Distillery
Dalintart
Deadh Choimhead
1257
Airdeny
Angus's
Bridge of Awe
River Awe
Pass of Brander
Cruachan Reservoir
Beinn a' Bhuiridh
2941
Falls of Cruachan
Lochawe
Kilchurn
Kinchrackine
Carn Breugach
Bach Island
Gylen
Loch Seil
Loch Nell
Glen Lonan
Cruachan Power Station
B845
Rubha Seanach
Dubh Sgeir
Kilbride
Cleigh
Kilmore
1691
Beinn Ghlas
Loch Tromlee
Fraoch Eilean Castle
Minard Point
Loch Feochan
Glen Feochan
Sior Loch
Abhainn Cam Linne
Loch Nant
Kilchrenan
Annat
North Port
Cladich
689
Beinn Mhor
Kilninver
1208
A' Chruach
Allt a' Choromaig
Portsonachan
South Port
Upper Sonachan
B840
Eilean Dùin
Insh Island
B844
Bridge over the Atlantic
Glen Euchar
Loch Scammadale
Bragleenbeg
1690
Beinn Chapull
SEIL
Sound of Insh
Clachan-Seil
An Cala
Ellenabeich
Easdale Folk
Slate Islands Centre
Carn Dearg
1436
Braglenmore
Abhainn Fionain
Inverinan
1804
Beinn Ghlas
876
Cruach Rarey
Ardmaddy Castle
Balvicar
B8003
Braes of Lorn
Meall Odhar
1255
Tullich
Loch Tralaig
Loch Dubh-mor
Lochavich
Tom an t-Saighdeir
993
Beochlich
Lochan Dubh
1932
Cruach Mhor
Stuc Scardan
1599
Pass of Melfort
Melfort
A816
Loch a' Phearsain
1239
Cruach Maolachy
Loch Avich
Cuan
Seil Sound
Dun Crutagain
895
An Coire
Kilmelford
Dalavich
Loch an Eilean Dubh
Loch nan Car
Three Bridges
837
Barr Mor
Cullipool
Torsa
Melfort
Loch an Losgainn Mòr
Ardchonnell
Portinnisherrich
Dubh Loch
Loch
Rubh' a' Chnaip
Arduaine
NTS
Lochan a' Bhruic
Inverliever Forest
Beinn Bhreac
1726
Carloonan
Malt Lane
LUING
20
Loch an Daimh
1199
Tom Soilleir
1610
Carn Duchara
Lochan Long
Eredine
Inveraray
Shira
A83
Cuan Sound
Shuna
ARGYLL
Barbreck River
River Liever
Durran
Braevallich
Eredine Forest
1687
An Suidhe
Douglas Water
Am Buachaille
1060
Inveraray Bell Tower
Inveraray Jail
St. Catherines
Lagling
Craobh Haven
Barravullin
1148
Cruach an Eachlaich
Inverliever Lodge
Argyll
Achnagoul
A815
Shuna Sound
549
Soroba Hill
Ardfern
Kintraw
Fincharn Loch
Loch Leachd
Lochan Gaineamhach
1583
Beinn Dearg
A83
Creagan an Eich
1070
Loch Fada
B8002
Eilean Mhic Chrion
Creag Mhòr
745
Ford
Fincharn
Loch Geoidh
Loch Leacann
Auchindrain
Creggans
Loch Mhic Mhàirtein
Eilean Ona
Rèisa Mhic Phaidean
Eilean Righ
Carnassarie
Loch Ederline
Loch nan Ceard Mor
Cruach Mhic Fhionnlaidh
1503
1179
Dun Leacainn
Strachur Bay
Clachan Strachur
Strachur Smiddy
Tombuidhe
Loch Gaineamhach
1339
Sidh Mòr
&
Furnace
Glensluain
Aird
Island Mcaskin
Kilmartin House
Kilmartin
Lochan Leathan
Lochan Anama
1378
Beinn Ghlas
Leachd
Newton
A886
Rèisa an t-Sruith
Garbh Rèisa
Slockavullin
Kilmartin Glen Prehistoric Sites
KILMICHAEL FOREST
Lochan Add
Crarae NTS
Crarae
B8000
1577
Cruach nan Capull
Glenbranter
Rubha Garbh-ard
758
Dun Dubh
Minard Forest
Blackmill Loch
Tullochgorm
Minard
Castle Lachlan
Ardnoe Point
Loch Crinan
Killinochonoch
BUTE
Lachan Bay
Strathlachlan
1666
Crauch an Lochain
2029
Beinn Bheag
Crinan
Kilmahumaig
B8025
Dunadd
Cup & Ring Marks
Kilmichael Glassary
Loch Glashan
A83
Lephinmore
Caol Ghleann
Rubha nam Bàrr
B841
Islandadd Bri.
Bellanoch
Cairnbaan Cup & Ring Marks
Bridgend
16
Cnoc Reamhar
870
Loch Linne
Daill Loch
Cairnbaan
Achnabreck Cup & Ring Marks
Scotston Hill
698
Lochgair
Loch Gair
Lephinchapel
Garvie
Srath nan Lub
Beinn Mhòr
2432
Bernice
KNAPDALE FOREST
B841
125
Loch Coille-Bharr
Lochgilphead
LOCH
126
Conchra
Meall Dubh
2103
Lochan Chuilceachan
Gleann Sabhal
B8025
Loch an Add
Gleann Loch
Carn Loch
Kilmory Woodland Park
B8000
Cruach Chuilceachan
1428
An Socach
1345
Glenmassan
Benmore Forest
Tayvallich
Achnamara
Loch Clachaig
Loch nam Breac Buidhe
Canal
Loch Gilp
Port Ann
Largiemore
Glendaruel Forest
Benmore Botanic
Sgorach Mor
1972
Kilmichael of Inverlussa
1071
Cruach nam Fiadh
Ardrishaig
Castleton
Otter Ferry
679
Tom na h-Iolaire
1416
Cruach nan Cuilean
Loch Tarsan
Balliemore
Glenlean
Eilean Loain
Daltot
Cruach Brenfield
1044
Eilean Mòr
Liath Eilean
Clachan of Glendaruel
Kilmodan Sculptured Stones
B836
Invereck
Taynish
Cruach Lusach
1530
Loch na Craige Grainde
Cruach nan Tarbh
1144
A886
Clachaig
KNAPDALE
Inverneil House
Auchenbreck
Dunrostan
1247
An Stuchd
B8024
Bàgh an Tailleir
507
Barr Ganuisg
1503
Cruach nan Caorach
Dun Mor
2005
Cruach nan Capull
Loch Arail
Kilfinan
Craig Lodge
Kilfinan Bay
Lochan na Leirg
Glenstriven
St. Columba's Cave
Achahoish
Loch Fuar-Bheinne
A83
758
Port Leathan
Auchalick
Beinn Bhraec
1488
B836
Ellary
Clachbreck
1564
Cruach a' Phubuill
Loch
Beinn Bhreac
1662
Inverchaolain Glen
COWAL
LOCH FYNE
LOCH AWE

Tyndrum
Clifton
Crianlarich
Dalmally
Lochawe
Inveraray
Cairndow
Arrochar
Tarbet
Lochgoilhead
Garelochhead
HELENSBURGH
DUNOON
Gourock
GREENOCK
DUMBARTON
Alexandria
Bonhill
Renton
Balloch
Luss
Cove
Kilcreggan
Strone
Blairmore
Ardentinny
Strachur
Shandon
Rhu
Cardross
Craigendoran
BEN MORE
BEN VORLICH
BEN LOMOND
BEINN IME
LOCH LOMOND AND THE TROSSACHS NATIONAL PARK
QUEEN ELIZABETH FOREST PARK
ARGYLL FOREST PARK
ARGYLL & BUTE
LOCH FYNE
LOCH LOMOND
A82
A83
A85
A815
A814
A817
A818
A811
A886
A880
A885
B828
B839
B833
B836
B8074
B8077
B840
141
133
126

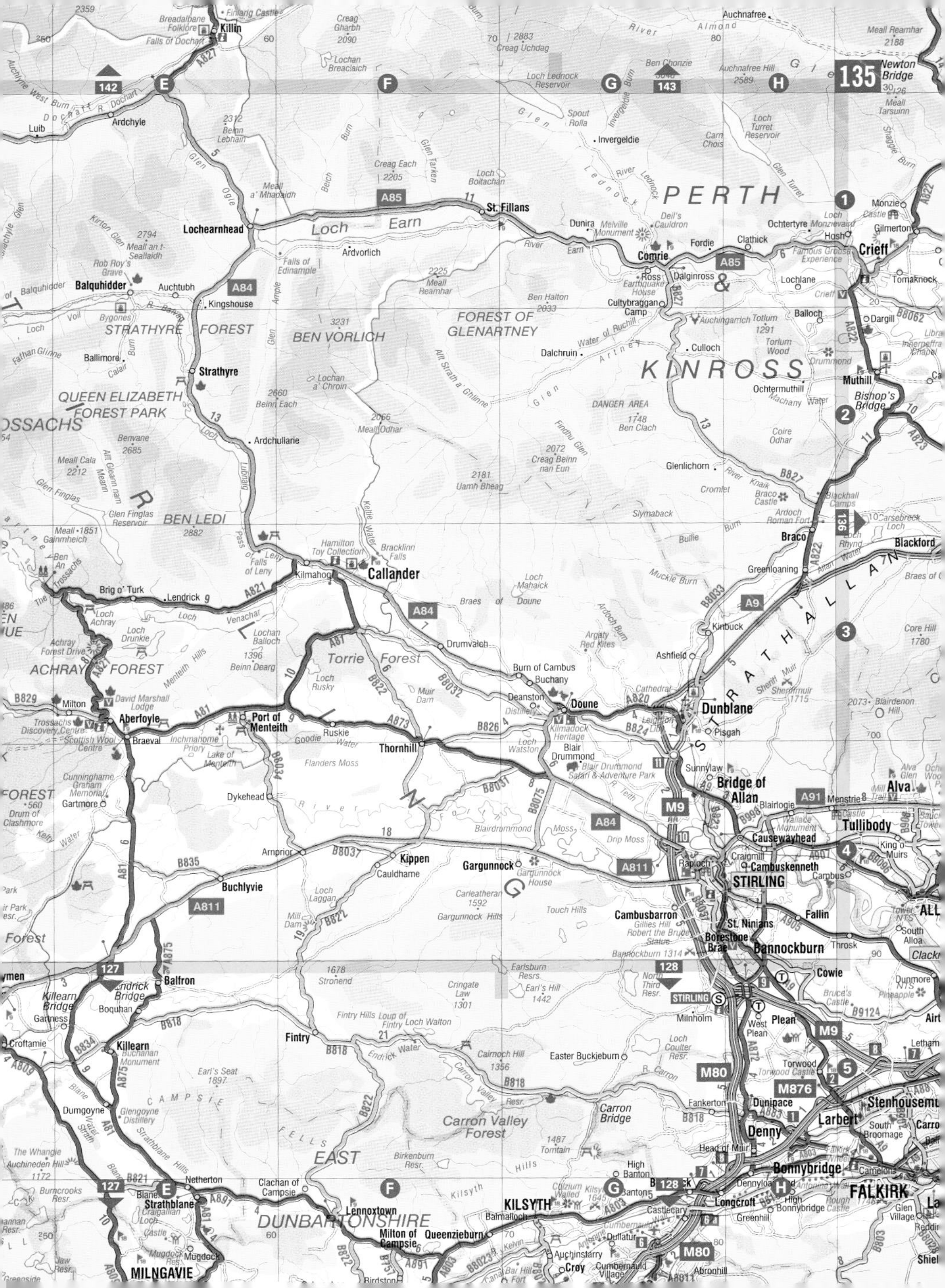

135
136
142
143
127
128
PERTH
&
KINROSS
STRATHALLAN
DUNBARTONSHIRE
EAST
Killin
Finlarig Castle
Breadalbane Folklore
Falls of Dochart
Creag Gharbh 2090
Lochan Breaclaich
Creag Uchdag 2883
River Almond
Auchnafree
Meall Reamhar 2188
Newton Bridge
Ben Chonzie
Auchnafree Hill 2589
Loch Lednock Reservoir
Luib
Ardchyle
Glen Dochart
Auchlyne West Burn
Beinn Lebhain 2312
Glen Ogle
Spout Rolla
Invergeldie
Loch Turret Reservoir
Carn Chois
Meall Tarsuinn
Creag Each 2205
Glen Tarken
Loch Boltachan
Meall a' Mhadaidh
A85
St. Fillans
Loch Earn
Lochearnhead
Ardvorlich
Falls of Edinample
Deil's Cauldron
Melville Monument
Dunira
Comrie
Fordie
Clathick
Ochtertyre
Loch Monzievaird
Monzie Castle
Gilmerton
Hosh
Crieff
Famous Grouse Experience
Kirkton Glen
Meall an t-Seallaidh 2794
Rob Roy's Grave
Balquhidder
Auchtubh
A84
Kingshouse
Meall Reamhar 2225
Ross
Earthquake House
Dalginross
Cultybraggan Camp
Ben Halton 2033
Lochlane
Tomaknock
B827
B8062
Dargill
Balloch
Bygones
STRATHYRE FOREST
BEN VORLICH 3231
FOREST OF GLENARTNEY
Auchingarrich
Totlum 1291
Torlum Wood
Drummond
Water of Ruchill
Glen Artney
Dalchruin
Culloch
Ballimore
Strathyre
Lochan a' Chroin
Allt Strath a' Ghlinne
Muthill
Ochtermuthill
Machany Water
Bishop's Bridge
A822
A823
QUEEN ELIZABETH FOREST PARK
TROSSACHS
Beinn Each 2660
Meall Odhar 2066
DANGER AREA
Ben Clach 1748
Coire Odhar
Benvane 2685
Ardchullarie
Creag Beinn nan Eun 2072
Findhu Glen
Meall Cala 2212
Allt Gleann nam Meann
Glen Finglas
Uamh Bheag 2181
Glenlichorn
River Knaik
Braco Castle
Cromlet
Blackhall Camps
Glen Finglas Reservoir
BEN LEDI 2882
Slymaback
Ardoch Roman Fort
Carsebreck Loch
Meall Gainmheich 1851
Ben An
The Trossachs
Pass of Leny
Falls of Leny
Hamilton Toy Collection
Bracklinn Falls
Keltie Water
Callander
Kilmahog
Braco
Loch Rhynd
Blackford
Greenloaning
Allan Water
Bullie Burn
Loch Mahaick
Braes of Doune
Muckle Burn
B8033
A9
Brig o' Turk
Lendrick
A821
Loch Achray
Loch Venachar
Loch Drunkie
Lochan Balloch
Beinn Dearg 1396
Achray Forest Drive
ACHRAY FOREST
Menteith Hills
Torrie Forest
A87
Drumvaich
Argaty Red Kites
Ardoch Burn
Kinbuck
Ashfield
Core Hill 1780
Burn of Cambus
Buchany
Deanston
Distillery
Doune
Loch Rusky
Muir Dam
B822
B8032
A820
Cathedral
Dunblane
Pisgah
Sheriff Muir
Sheriffmuir 1715
Blairdenon Hill 2073
B829
Milton
David Marshall Lodge
Aberfoyle
Trossachs Discovery Centre
Scottish Wool Centre
Braeval
A81
Port of Menteith
Inchmahome Priory
Lake of Menteith
Goodie Water
Ruskie
A873
Thornhill
B826
Kilmadock Heritage
Loch Watson
B824
Leighton Library
Blair Drummond
Blair Drummond Safari & Adventure Park
Sunnylaw
Bridge of Allan
Alva Glen
Alva
Flanders Moss
B8034
Cunninghame Graham Memorial
Gartmore
Dykehead
B8031
B8075
River Teith
M9
A91
Menstrie
Blairlogie
Wallace Monument
Tullibody
Drum of Clashmore
Kelty Water
River Forth
Blairdrummond Moss
Drip Moss
Causewayhead
Craigmill
Cambuskenneth
King o' Muirs
Arnprior
B8037
Kippen
Cauldhame
B835
Gargunnock
Gargunnock House
A811
Raploch
STIRLING
Campus
Buchlyvie
Loch Laggan
Carleatheran 1592
Gargunnock Hills
Touch Hills
Cambusbarron
Gillies Hill
Robert the Bruce Statue
St. Ninians
Fallin
A905
Tower NTS
South Alloa
Mill Dam
Forest
Borestone Brae
Bannockburn
Throsk
Bannockburn 1314
A875
Stronend 1678
Earlsburn Resrs.
North Third Resr.
Cowie
Dunmore
Endrick Bridge
Balfron
Killearn Bridge
Gartness
Boquhan
Cringate Law 1301
Earl's Hill 1442
Bruce's Castle
NTS Pineapple
B9124
Croftamie
Fintry Hills
Loup of Fintry
Loch Walton
Milnholm
West Plean
Plean
B818
Fintry
Endrick Water
Cairnoch Hill 1356
Easter Buckieburn
Loch Coulter Resr.
B834
Killearn
Buchanan Monument
Earl's Seat 1897
CAMPSIE FELLS
Carron Valley Resr.
R. Carron
M80
Torwood
Torwood Castle
M876
Blane Water
Dumgoyne
Glengoyne Distillery
Strathblane Hills
Carron Valley Forest
Carron Bridge
Fankerton
Dunipace
Denny
Larbert
Stenhousemuir
South Broomage
The Whangie
Auchineden Hill 1172
Birkenburn Resr.
Tomtain 1487
Head of Muir
Bonnybridge
Camelon
FALKIRK
Burncrooks Resr.
B821
Netherton
Clachan of Campsie
High Banton
Banton
Kilsyth Hills
Colzium Walled Garden
Kilsyth 1645
Dennyloanhead
Antonine Wall
High Bonnybridge
Rough Castle
Blanefield
Strathblane
Craigallian Loch
Lennoxtown
KILSYTH
Balmalloch
A803
Castlecary
Longcroft
Greenhill
Glen Village
Milton of Campsie
Queenzieburn
Dullatur
A891
Mugdock Castle
Mugdock
Jaw Resr.
MILNGAVIE
B822
B757
B8023
Bar Hill
Auchinstarry
Croy
Cumbernauld Village
Abronhill
Birdston
Canal

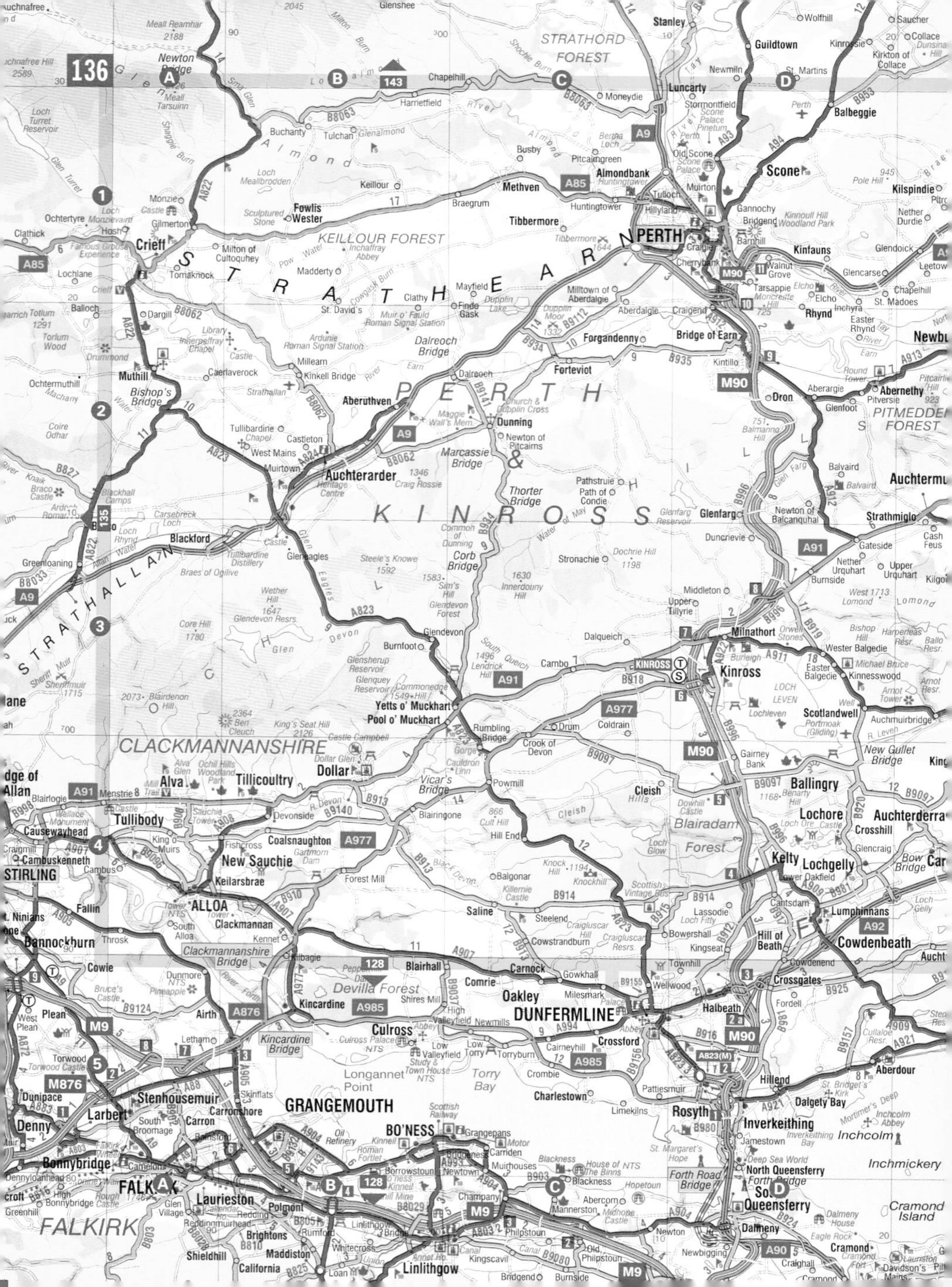
Glenshee
Meall Reamhar 2188
Newton Bridge
Glen Almond
Sma' Glen
Loch Turret Reservoir
Meall Tarsuinn
Shaggie Burn
Glen Turret
STRATHORD FOREST
Stanley
Guildtown
Wolfhill
Saucher
Collace
Kinrossie
Kirkton of Collace
Chapelhill
Moneydie
Harrietfield
Buchanty
Tulchan
Glenalmond
Luncarty
Newmiln
St. Martins
Stormontfield
Scone Palace Pinetum
Balbeggie
Perth
Bertha Loch
Busby
Pitcairngreen
Almondbank
Huntingtower
Old Scone
Scone Palace
Scone
Pole Hill
Kilspindie
Loch Meallbrodden
Keillour
Methven
Braegrum
Monzie Castle
Gilmerton
Sculptured Stone
Fowlis Wester
KEILLOUR FOREST
Tibbermore
Huntingtower
Hillyland
Tulloch
Muirton
Gannochy
Bridgend
Kinnoull Hill Woodland Park
Nether Durdie
Ochtertyre
Loch Monzievaird
Hosh
Clathick
Famous Grouse Experience
Crieff
Milton of Cultoquhey
Inchaffray Abbey
PERTH
Craigie
Barnhill
Kinfauns
Glendoick
A85
Lochlane
Tomaknock
STRATHEARN
Madderty
Cherrybank
Walnut Grove
Glencarse
Leetown
Mayfield
Dupplin Lake
Clathy
Finde Gask
St. David's
Muir o' Fauld Roman Signal Station
Milltown of Aberdalgie
Aberdalgie
Craigend
Tarsappie
Moncreiffe Hill
Elcho
Chapelhill
Inchyra
St. Madoes
Rhynd
Easter Rhynd
Balloch
Totlum 1291
Dargill
Torlum Wood
Drummond
Library
Innerpeffray Chapel
Castle
Ardunie Roman Signal Station
Dalreoch Bridge
Dupplin Moor
Forgandenny
Bridge of Earn
Newburgh
Millearn
Kinkell Bridge
Caerlaverock
Strathallan
Forteviot
Kintillo
Ochtermuthill
Machany
Muthill
Bishop's Bridge
Aberuthven
Dalreoch
PERTH
Church & Dupplin Cross
Dunning
Maggie Wall's Mem.
Round Tower
Aberargie
Abernethy
Pitcairlie
Pitversie
Glenfoot
Dron
PITMEDDEN FOREST
Coire Odhar
Tullibardine Chapel
Castleton
West Mains
Newton of Pitcairns
Balmanno Hill
Knaik
Braco Castle
Blackhall Camps
Ardoch Roman
Muirtown
Auchterarder
Heritage Centre
Marcassie Bridge
&
Craig Rossie
Thorter Bridge
Pathstruie
Path of Condie
Balvaird
Auchtermuchty
Carsebreck Loch
Loch Rhynd
Braco
Blackford
KINROSS
Glenfarg Reservoir
Glenfarg
Newton of Balcanquhal
Strathmiglo
Greenloaning
Allan Water
Tullibardine Distillery
Gleneagles
Castle
Steele's Knowe 1592
Common of Dunning
Corb Bridge
Water of May
Dochrie Hill 1198
Stronachie
Duncrievie
Gateside
Cash Feus
Braes of Ogilive
Glen Eagles
1583 Sim's Hill
Glendevon Forest
1630 Innerdouny Hill
Nether Urquhart
Upper Urquhart
Burnside
Kilgour
STRATHALLAN
Wether Hill 1647
Glendevon Resrs.
Middleton
Upper Tillyrie
West 1713 Lomond
Lomond
Core Hill 1780
Glendevon
Glen Devon
Burnfoot
Dalqueich
Milnathort
Orwell Stones
Bishop Hill
Harperleas Resr.
Ballo Resr.
Wester Balgedie
Sheriff Muir
Sheriffmuir 1715
Glensherup Reservoir
Glenquey Reservoir
1496 Lendrick Hill
South Queich
Cambo
KINROSS
Burleigh
Michael Bruce
Easter Balgedie
Kinnesswood
Kinross
Arnot Tower
LOCH LEVEN
Lochleven
2073 Blairdenon Hill
Commonedge 1549 Hill
Yetts o' Muckhart
Pool o' Muckhart
Well
Scotlandwell
Portmoak (Gliding)
Auchmuirbridge
2364 Ben Cleuch
King's Seat Hill 2126
Castle Campbell
Rumbling Bridge
Gorge
Drum
Coldrain
Crook of Devon
R. Leven
CLACKMANNANSHIRE
Dollar Glen
Dollar
Cauldron Linn
Gairney Bank
New Gullet Bridge
Kinglassie
Bridge of Allan
Alva Glen
Ochil Hills Woodland Park
Alva
Tillicoultry
Mill Trail
Vicar's Bridge
Powmill
Cleish Hills
Ballingry
Benarty Hill
Blairlogie
Menstrie
Wallace Monument
Castle
Sauchie Tower
Devonside
Coalsnaughton
Blairingone
866 Cult Hill
Cleish
Dowhill Castle
Blairadam Forest
Lochore
Loch Ore Castle
Auchterderran
Crosshill
Causewayhead
Tullibody
Craigmill
Cambuskenneth
King o' Muirs
Fishcross
New Sauchie
Gartmorn Dam
Hill End
Glencraig
Loch Glow
STIRLING
Cambus
Keilarsbrae
Forest Mill
Black Devon
Balgonar
Knock Hill 1194
Knockhill
Scottish Vintage Bus
Kelty
Lochgelly
Lower Oakfield
Bow Bridge
Cardenden
ALLOA
Tower NTS
Fallin
St. Ninians
Killernie Castle
Saline
Steelend
Craigluscar Hill
Lassodie
Loch Fitty
Cantsdam
Lumphinnans
Loch Gelly
South Alloa
Clackmannan
Bannockburn
Throsk
Kennet
Cowstrandburn
Craigluscar Resrs.
Bowershall
Kingseat
Hill of Beath
Cowdenbeath
Clackmannanshire Bridge
Kilbagie
Cowie
River Forth
Dunmore NTS Pineapple
Bruce's Castle
Blairhall
Devilla Forest
Comrie
Carnock
Gowkhall
Oakley
Milesmark
Townhill
Wellwood
Cowdenend
Crossgates
Fordell
Plean
West Plean
Airth
Kincardine
Shires Mill
High Valleyfield
Newmills
DUNFERMLINE
Palace
Abbey
Halbeath
Culross
Culross Palace NTS
Low Valleyfield
Low Torry
Torryburn
Cairneyhill
Crossford
Cullaloe Resr.
Letham
Kincardine Bridge
Torwood
Torwood Castle
Study & Town House NTS
Longannet Point
Torry Bay
Crombie
Pattiesmuir
Hillend
Aberdour
St. Bridget's Kirk
Dunipace
Larbert
Stenhousemuir
Skinflats
Carronshore
GRANGEMOUTH
Charlestown
Limekilns
Rosyth
Dalgety Bay
Mortimer's Deep
Inchcolm Abbey
Denny
South Broomage
Carron
Scottish Railway
BO'NESS
Grangepans
Inverkeithing
Jamestown
Inchcolm
Bainsford
Oil Refinery
Kinneil
Roman Fortlet
Motor
Carriden
Bridgeness
Newtown
Muirhouses
Blackness
House of The Binns NTS
St. Margaret's Hope
Deep Sea World
North Queensferry
Inchmickery
Bonnybridge
Camelon
Falkirk Wheel
Borrowstoun
Bo'ness Kinneil Mill
Blackness
Hopetoun
Forth Road Bridge
Forth Bridge
South Queensferry
Dennyloanhead
High Bonnybridge
Rough Castle
FALKIRK
Glen Village
Laurieston
Polmont
Callendar Ho.
Redding
Reddingmuirhead
Champany
Abercorn
Mannerston
Midhope Castle
Dalmeny House
Cramond Island
Greenhill
FALKIRK
Brightons
Rumford
Linlithgow Bridge
Philpstoun
Newton
Dalmeny
Eagle Rock
Shieldhill
Maddiston
Whitecross
Annet Ho.
Canal
Old Philpstoun
Newbigging
Cramond
California
Linlithgow
Loan
Kingscavil
Union Canal
Bridgend
Burnside
Craighall
Davidson's Mains
M9
M90
M876
A9
A91
A977
A985
A876
A92
A90
A823(M)

DUNDEE
Broughty Ferry
Carnoustie
Monifieth
BUDDON NESS
Newport-on-Tay
Tayport
TENTSMUIR FOREST
FIRTH OF TAY
Leuchars
Guardbridge
ST. ANDREWS BAY
St. Andrews
Cupar
Boarhills
Kingsbarns
FIFE NESS
Crail
Anstruther Easter
Anstruther Wester
Pittenweem
St. Monans
Elie
Largo Bay
Leven
Methil
Buckhaven
GLENROTHES
Markinch
Kennoway
Falkland
Ladybank
HOWE OF FIFE
Dysart
KIRKCALDY
Kinghorn
Burntisland
FIRTH OF FORTH
North Berwick
Dirleton
Gullane
EAST LOTHIAN
Aberlady
East Linton
Cockenzie and Port Seton
Longniddry
EDINBURGH
Leith
Newhaven
Bass Rock
Fidra
Inchkeith
A90
A92
A91
A915
A917
A921
A198
A1
144
145
129
130

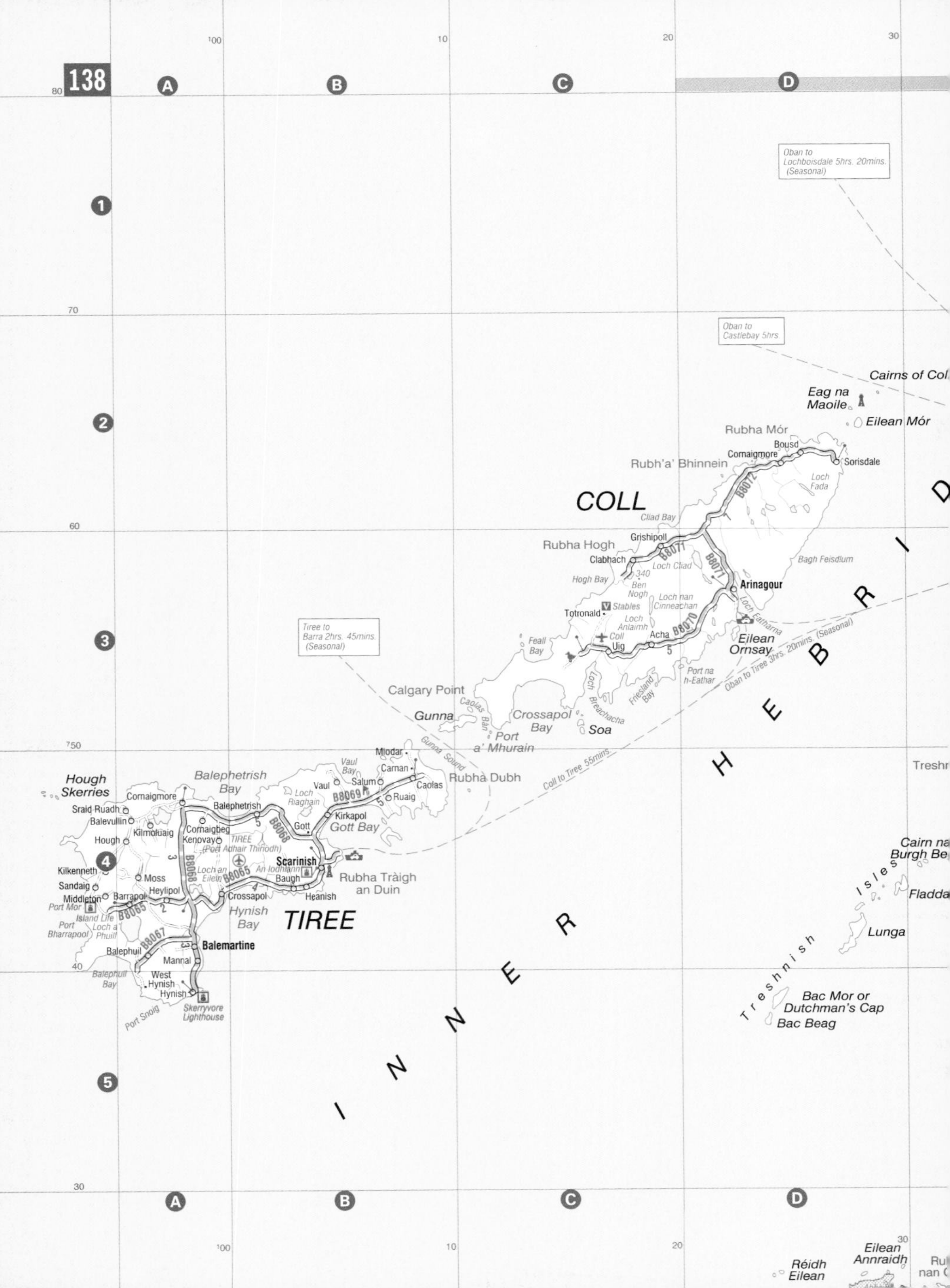

80

A B C D

100 10 20 30

1

Oban to
Lochboisdale 5hrs. 20mins.
(Seasonal)

70

Oban to
Castlebay 5hrs

Cairns of Col

2

Eag na
Maoile

Eilean Mór

Rubha Mór
Bousd
Cornaigmore

Sorisdale

Rubh'a' Bhinnein

Loch
Fada

COLL

Cliad Bay

B8072

60

Rubha Hogh

Grishipoll

Bagh Feisdlum

Clabhach

Loch Cliad

Hogh Bay

340

Arinagour

Ben
Nogh

Loch nan
Cinneachan

Totronald

Stables

Loch
Anlaimh

3

Tiree to
Barra 2hrs. 45mins.
(Seasonal)

Feall
Bay

Uig

Acha B8070

Coll

Eilean
Ornsay

Port na
h-Eathar

Calgary Point

Gunna

Cadhac Bay

Gunna Sound

Crossapol
Bay

Port
a' Mhurain

Soa

Loch Breachacha

Friesland Bay

Oban to Tiree 3hrs. 20mins. (Seasonal)

Treshr

H
E
B
R
I
D

50

Hough
Skerries

Cornaigmore

Balephetrish
Bay

Vaul
Bay

Mlodar

Caman

Rubhà Dubh

Coll to Tiree 55mins.

Sraid Ruadh

Balevullin

Balephetrish

Loch
Riaghain

Salum

Caolas

Cairn na
Burgh Be

Hough

Kilmoluaig

Cornaigbeg

TIREE
(Port Adhair Thiriodh)

Ruaig

Kenovay

Gott

Kirkapol

Fladda

4

Kilkenneth

Moss

Loch an
Eilein

An Iodhlann

Gott Bay

Heylipol

Scarinish

Sandaig

Baugh

Rubha Tràigh
an Duin

Lunga

Middleton
Port Mòr

Barrapol

Crossapol

Heanish

Port
Bharrapool

Balephuil

Island Life
Loch 4
Phuill

Hynish Bay

TIREE

Balemartine

Mannal

West
Hynish

Treshnish
Isles

Bac Mor or
Dutchman's Cap
Bac Beag

Balephuil
Bay

Hynish

Skerryvore
Lighthouse

Port Snoig

I
N
N
E
R

5

40

30

A B C D

100 10 20 30

Réidh
Eilean

Eilean
Annraidh

Ru
nan C

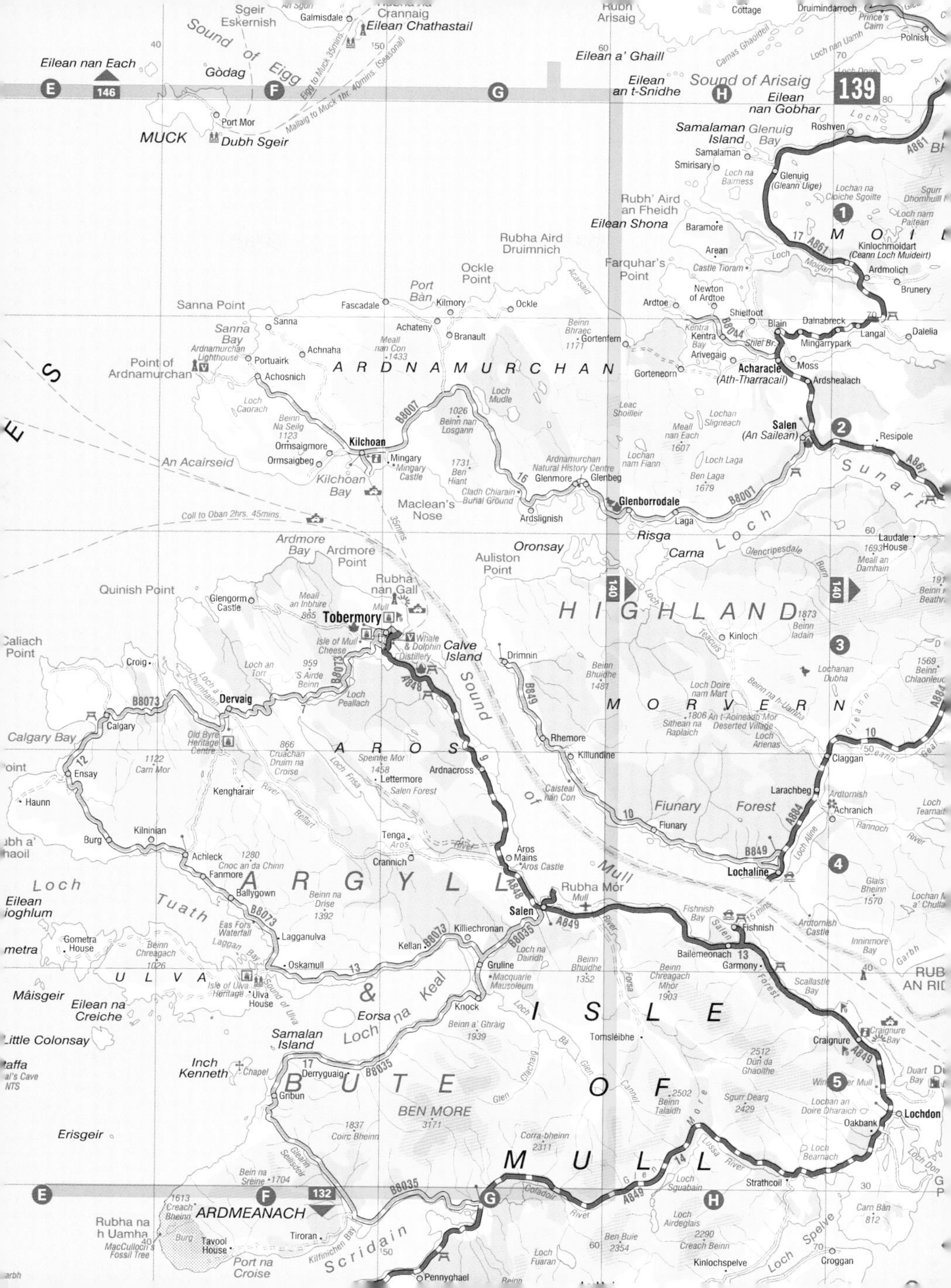

139
Sound of Eigg
Sgeir Eskernish
Galmisdale
Eilean Chathastail
Eilean nan Each
Gòdag
Eigg to Muck 35mins.
Mallaig to Muck 1hr. 40mins. (Seasonal)
146
Port Mor
MUCK
Dubh Sgeir
Rubh Arisaig
Eilean a' Ghaill
Eilean an t-Snidhe
Sound of Arisaig
Cottage
Druimindarroch
Prince's Cairn
Polnish
Loch nan Uamh
Eilean nan Gobhar
Samalaman Island
Glenuig Bay
Roshven
Samalaman
Smirisary
Glenuig (Gleann Uige)
Loch na Bairness
Lochan na Cloiche Sgoilte
A861
MOIDART
Rubh' Aird an Fheidh
Eilean Shona
Baramore
Arean
Castle Tioram
Loch Moidart
Kinlochmoidart (Ceann Loch Muideirt)
Ardmolich
Brunery
Rubha Aird Druimnich
Farquhar's Point
Ockle Point
Port Bàn
Sanna Point
Fascadale
Kilmory
Ockle
Newton of Ardtoe
Ardtoe
Shielfoot
Blain
Dalnabreck
Langal
Dalelia
Sanna
Sanna Bay
Achateny
Branault
Beinn Bhraec 1171
Gortenfern
Kentra
Kentra Bay
Arivegaig
B8044
Shiel Br.
Mingarrypark
Ardnamurchan Lighthouse
Point of Ardnamurchan
Achnaha
Portuairk
Meall nan Con 1433
ARDNAMURCHAN
Gorteneorn
Acharacle (Ath-Tharracail)
Moss
Ardshealach
Achosnich
Loch Caorach
Beinn Na Seilg 1123
B8007
1026 Beinn nan Losgann
Loch Mudle
Leac Shoilleir
Lochan Sligneach
Meall nan Each 1607
Salen (An Sailean)
Resipole
Ormsaigmore
Ormsaigbeg
Kilchoan
Mingary
Mingary Castle
An Acairseid
Kilchoan Bay
1731 Ben Hiant
Ardnamurchan Natural History Centre
Glenmore
Glenbeg
Lochan nam Fiann
Loch Laga
Ben Laga 1679
Loch Sunart
Maclean's Nose
Cladh Chiarain Burial Ground
Ardslignish
Glenborrodale
Laga
B8007
Coll to Oban 2hrs. 45mins.
Ardmore Bay
Ardmore Point
Auliston Point
Oronsay
Risga
Carna
Glencripesdale Burn
Laudale House
1693 Meall an Damhain
Quinish Point
Glengorm Castle
Rubha nan Gall
Meall an Inbhire 865
Tobermory
Mull
140
HIGHLAND
1873 Beinn Iadain
Kinloch
Teacuis
Caliach Point
Croig
Isle of Mull Cheese
Whale & Dolphin Distillery
Calve Island
Drimnin
Loch an Torr
959 'S Airde Beinn
Loch a' Chumhainn
Dervaig
B8073
Loch Peallach
A848
Sound of Mull
B849
Beinn Bhuidhe 1481
Loch Doire nam Mart
Lochanan Dubha
MORVERN
1569 Beinn Chlaonleud
Calgary
Calgary Bay
Old Byre Heritage Centre
866 Cruachan Druim na Croise
AROS
1806 Sithean na Raplaich
An t-Aoineadh Mòr Deserted Village
Loch Arienas
Rhemore
Killundine
Claggan
1122 Carn Mor
Ensay
Speinne Mor 1458
Lettermore
Salen Forest
Loch Frisa
Ardnacross
Kengharair
Bellart River
Caisteal nan Con
Larachbeg
Ardtornish
Achranich
Haunn
Fiunary Forest
Fiunary
Rannoch River
Kilninian
Burg
Tenga
Aros River
Crannich
Aros Mains
Aros Castle
Lochaline
Achleck
1280 Cnoc an da Chinn
Fanmore
ARGYLL
Loch Tuath
Eilean Ioghlum
Ballygown
Beinn na Drise 1392
Salen
Rubha Mòr
Mull
Fishnish Bay
Fishnish
Glais Bheinn 1570
Gometra House
Eas Fors Waterfall
Lagganulva
Killiechronan
B8035
A849
Ardtornish Castle
Beinn Chreagach 1026
Kellan
B8073
Loch na Dairidh
Beinn Bhuidhe 1352
Bailemeonach
Garmony
Inninmore Bay
ULVA
Oskamull
Gruline
Macquarie Mausoleum
Forsa River
Beinn Chreagach Mhor 1903
Scallastle Bay
Mâisgeir
Isle of Ulva Heritage
Ulva House
Sound of Ulva
Eilean na Creiche
Knock
Eorsa
Loch na Keal
ISLE
Craignure
Craignure Bay
Little Colonsay
Samalan Island
Beinn a' Ghràig 1939
Tomsléibhe
Inch Kenneth
Chapel
Derryguaig
B8035
BUTE
Glen Clachaig
Glen Cannel
2512 Dùn da Ghaoithe
OF
Duart Bay
Gribun
BEN MORE 3171
2502 Beinn Talaidh
Sgurr Dearg 2429
Lochan an Doire Dharaich
Lochdon
Oakbank
Erisgeir
1837 Coirc Bheinn
Corra-bheinn 2311
Glen Seilisdeir
MULL
Lussa River
Loch Bearnach
Glen More
Bein na Sreine 1704
132
B8035
Coladoir River
Loch Sguabain
Strathcoil
1613 Creach Bheinn
ARDMEANACH
Rubha na h Uamha
MacCulloch's Fossil Tree
Burg
Tiroran
Tavool House
Loch Scridain
Kilfinichen Bay
Port na Croise
Loch Airdeglais
2290 Creach Beinn
Ben Buie 2354
Loch Fuaran
Loch Spelve
Kinlochspelve
Croggan
Carn Bàn 812
Pennyghael

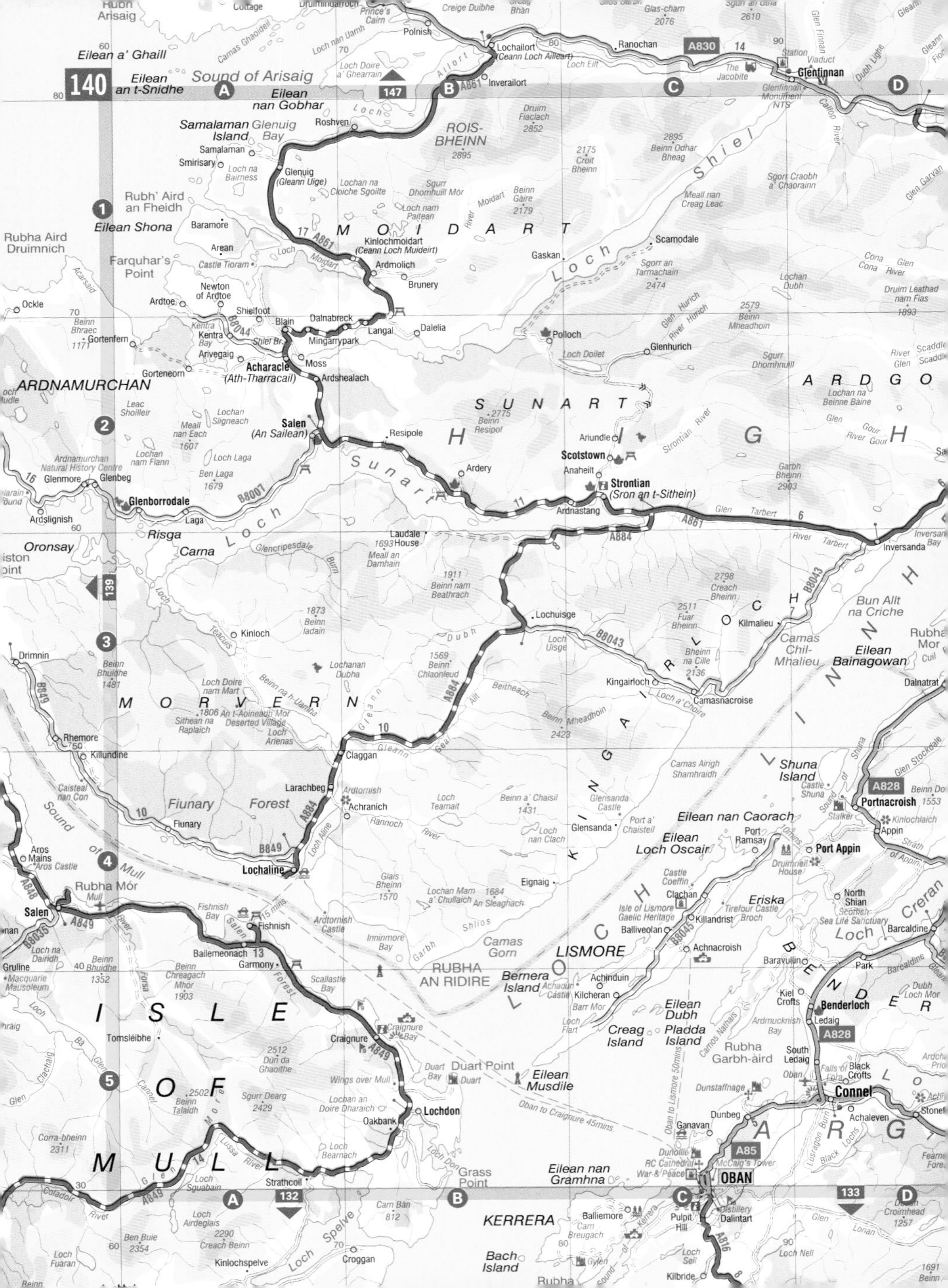

140
139
147
132
133
A
B
C
D
1
2
3
4
5
Rubh Arisaig
Eilean a' Ghaill
Eilean an t-Snidhe
Sound of Arisaig
Eilean nan Gobhar
Prince's Cairn
Creige Duibhe
Glas-charn
2076
2610
Loch nan Uamh
Polnish
Loch Doire a' Ghearrain
Lochailort (Ceann Loch Ailleart)
Inverailort
Ranochan
Loch Eilt
A830
The Jacobite
Station
Viaduct
Glenfinnan
Glenfinnan Monument NTS
Dubh Lighe
Callop River
Samalaman Island
Glenuig Bay
Roshven
Samalaman
Smirisary
Loch na Bairness
Glenuig (Gleann Uige)
Rubh' Aird an Fheidh
Eilean Shona
Rubha Aird Druimnich
ROIS-BHEINN
2895
Druim Fiaclach
2852
Beinn Odhar Bheag
2175 Croit Bheinn
Shiel
Sgorr Craobh a' Chaorainn
Glen Garvan
Lochan na Cloiche Sgoilte
Sgurr Dhomhuill Mór
Loch nam Paitean
Beinn Gaire
2179
River Moidart
Meall nan Creag Leac
MOIDART
Baramore
Arean
Castle Tioram
Farquhar's Point
A861
Kinlochmoidart (Ceann Loch Muideirt)
Ardmolich
Brunery
Gaskan
Scamodale
Loch
Sgorr an Tarmachain
2474
Cona Glen
Cona River
Lochan Dubh
Druim Leathad nam Fias
1893
Ockle
Ardtoe
Newton of Ardtoe
Shielfoot
Beinn Bhraec
1171
Gortenfern
Kentra
Kentra Bay
B8044
Blain
Dalnabreck
Langal
Dalelia
Mingarrypark
Shiel Br.
Arivegaig
Acharacle (Ath-Tharracail)
Moss
Gorteneorn
Ardshealach
Polloch
Loch Doilet
Glen Hurich
River Hurich
2579 Beinn Mheadhoin
Glenhurich
Sgurr Dhomhnuill
River Scaddle
Glen Scaddle
ARDNAMURCHAN
ARDGOUR
Lochan na Beinne Bàine
Leac Shoilleir
Lochan Sligneach
Meall nan Each
1607
Salen (An Sailean)
Resipole
SUNART
2775 Beinn Resipol
Ariundle
Strontian River
Glen Gour
River Gour
HIGHLAND
Lochan nam Fiann
Loch Laga
Ben Laga
1679
Ardnamurchan Natural History Centre
Glenmore
Glenbeg
Glenborrodale
Laga
B8007
Ardslignish
Sunart
Ardery
Scotstown
Anaheilt
Strontian (Sron an t-Sithein)
Ardnastang
Garbh Bheinn
2903
Glen Tarbert
River Tarbert
Inversanda
Inversanda Bay
Oronsay
Risga
Carna
Loch
Glencripesdale
Laudale House
1693
Meall an Damhain
A884
1911 Beinn nam Beathrach
2798 Creach Bheinn
B8043
Bun Allt na Criche
Rubha Mor
2511 Fuar Bheinn
Kilmalieu
Camas Chil-Mhalieu
Eilean Bainagowan
Kinloch
Loch Teacuis
1873 Beinn Iadain
Lochuisge
Loch Uisge
Bheinn na Cille
2136
Drimnin
Beinn Bhuidhe
1481
B849
Lochanan Dubha
1569 Beinn Chlaonleud
Dubh
Beitheach
Kingairloch
Camasnacroise
Loch a' Choire
Dalnatrat
MORVERN
Loch Doire nam Mart
Beinn na h-Uamha
1806 An t-Aoineadh Mór Deserted Village
Sithean na Raplaich
Loch Arienas
Gleann
Beinn Mheadhoin
2423
KINGAIRLOCH
Rhemore
Killundine
Claggan
Gleann Geal
Camas Airigh Shamhraidh
Shuna Island
Glen Stockdale
Castle Shuna
Sound of Shuna
A828
Portnacroish
Beinn Donn
1553
Caisteal nan Con
Larachbeg
Ardtornish
Achranich
Loch Teamait
Beinn a' Chaisil
1431
Glensanda Castle
Stalker
Kinlochlaich
Appin
Sound of Mull
Fiunary Forest
Fiunary
Rannoch River
Loch nan Clach
Glensanda
Port a' Chaisteil
Eilean nan Caorach
Eilean Loch Oscair
Port Ramsay
Port Appin
Strath of Appin
Aros Mains
Aros Castle
Lochaline
Loch Aline
Glais Bheinn
1570
Eignaig
Druimneil House
A848
Rubha Mór
Mull
Salen
Fishnish Bay
Lochan Mam a' Chullaich
1684 An Sleaghach
Castle Coeffin
Clachan
North Shian
Isle of Lismore Gaelic Heritage
Tirefour Castle Broch
Eriska
Scottish Sea Life Sanctuary
Loch Creran
B8035
A849
Fishnish
Ardtornish Castle
Inninmore Bay
Shlios
Balliveolan
Killandrist
Barcaldine
Bailemeonach
Garmony
Forest
Camas Gorn
LISMORE
Achnacroish
Baravullin
Park
Loch na Dairidh
Gruline
Beinn Bhuidhe
1352
Macquarie Mausoleum
Beinn Chreagach Mhór
1903
Scallastle Bay
Garbh
RUBHA AN RIDIRE
Bernera Island
Achadun Castle
Achinduin
Kilcheran
Barr Mor
Dubh Loch Mor
Kiel Crofts
Benderloch
Ledaig
BENDERLOCH
ISLE OF MULL
Tomsléibhe
Craignure
Craignure Bay
2512 Dùn da Ghaoithe
Loch Fiart
Creag Island
Eilean Dubh
Pladda Island
Camas Nathais
Ardmucknish Bay
Rubha Garbh-àird
South Ledaig
Black Crofts
Falls of Lora
Duart Bay
Duart
Duart Point
Eilean Musdile
Dunstaffnage
Connel
Glen Cannel
2502 Beinn Talaidh
Sgurr Dearg
2429
Wings over Mull
Lochan an Doire Dharaich
Lochdon
Oban to Craignure 45mins.
Oban to Lismore 50mins
Dunbeg
Achaleven
Ganavan
Corra-bheinn
2311
Oakbank
Loch Bearnach
Lussa River
Glen More
Loch Don
Grass Point
ARGYLL
A85
Dunollie
RC Cathedral
War & Peace
McCaig's Tower
OBAN
Lusragan Burn
Black Lochs
Eilean nan Gramhna
Strathcoil
Loch Sguabain
Glen Coladoir
Coladoir River
Carn Ban
812
KERRERA
Balliemore
Sound of Kerrera
Carn Breugach
Pulpit Hill
Distillery
Dalintart
Glen Lonan
Deadh Croimhead
1257
Loch Airdeglais
2290
Creach Beinn
Ben Buie
2354
Loch Spelve
Loch Fuaran
Kinlochspelve
Croggan
Bach Island
Gylen
Loch Seil
A816
Kilbride
Loch Nell
1691
Rubha

Stronenaba
Gleann Suileag
An t-Suileag
Stob a' Ghrianain
Druim Fada
River Loy
B8004
Caledonian Canal
Brackletter
Commando Memorial
Spean Bridge
A86
Bohenie
Inverroy
Roybridge
Creag Dhubh
Glen Spean
Achluachrach
Highbridge
A82
Alltour
Commando
Bunroy
Monessie Falls
Braes o' Lochaber
Inverlair Falls
Tulloch
Beinn an t-Sneachda
148
Muirshearlich
149
Achdalieu
Fassfern
Corribeg
Treasures of the Earth
Tor Castle
Leanachan Forest
Loch Eil
A830
The Jacobite
Corpach
Banavie
Neptune's Staircase
Crofting
Creig Aoil
Nevis Range Gondola
Beinn Chlianaig
2343
Fersit
South Garvan
Duisky
A861
Blaich
Caol
Carnaghael
Torlundy
Allt Coire an Eoin
The Cour
Allt Laire
Allt Loraich
Achaphubuil
Camusnagaul
B8006
Lochyside
Ben Nevis Distillery
Victoria Bridge
1645 Inverlochy
Trislaig
Inverlochy
Claggan
Bridge of Nevis
Glen Nevis
Stob Choire Claurigh
3858
Killiechonate Forest
Stob Coire a' Chearcaill
2528
Stronchreggan
West Highland Fired Art
FORT WILLIAM
Lochan Meall an t-Suidhe
Stob Coire Easain
3545
Stob Coire Easain
3658
Chno Dearg
3433
Ach' an Todhair
Rocking Stone
Nevis Forest
BEN NEVIS
4406
AONACH BEAG
4048
Lairig Leacach
Allt na Lairige
Loch Treig
Druimarbin
Loch Na Lap
Allt Feith Thuill
Beinn na Lap
Blarmachfoldach
Glen Nevis Waterslide
Uamh Shomhairle
Water of Nevis
Conaglen
River Kiachnish
Achriabhach
Glen Nevis Lower Falls
Steall Falls
Creaguaineach Lodge
Inverscaddle Bay
A82
Achriabhach Falls
Sgurr a' Mhàim
3601
Abhainn Rath
Loch Ossian
MAMORE
FOREST
Mullach nan Coirean
Binnein Mòr
3700
Loch Eilde Beag
Loch na Sgeallaig
Sgurr na h-Eanchainne
2395
Beinn na Gucaig
2022
Lochan Lùnn Dà-Bhrà
Narrows
Ardgour
Clovullin
Corran
Inchree
Inchrigh Falls
Glenrigh Forest
Allt na Lairige Moire
LAND
Loch Eilde Mòr
2971
Leum Uilleim
Allt Cam
Bunree
Mam na Gualainn
2611
Grey Mare's Tail
Ice Factor
Kinlochmore
Aluminium Story
Ciaran Water
Onich
B863
Sallachan Point
North Ballachulish
Loch Leven
Kinlochleven
Garbh Bheinn
2844
River Leven
Blackwater Reservoir
Black Water
Bridge of Coe
Folk
Glencoe
Pap of Glencoe
2430
3173
3118
Aonach Eagach
2120
Meall nan Ruadhag
A828
South Ballachulish
Ballachulish
Monument
Glencoe
A82
Clachaig
2811
Beinn a' Chrùlaiste
Altnafeadh
Stob na Cruaiche
2423
A' CHRUACH
Kentallen
Achindarroch
Beinn a' Bheithir
Meall Mòr
The Three Sisters
Ossian's Cave
Glencoe Gorge
Black Corries
Glenduror Forest
Gleann an Fhiodh
Glen Duror
3766
Bidean nam Bian
Buachaille Etive Beag
River Coupall
Buachaille Etive Mòr
Kingshouse
Royal Forest
White Corries
Lochan Gaineamhach
Lochan Coire na Mèinne
2883
Fraochaidh
Creran Forest
Sgor na h-Ulaidh
3258
Beinn Maol Chaluim
2774
Dalness
RANNOCH
A82
Glen Etive
Beinn Fhionnlaidh
3145
Loch Ba'
MOOR
Elleric
Stob Dubh
2897
Aonach Mòr
Allt Coire a' Chaolain
3602
Clach Leathad
Fasnacloich
Invercharnan
River Bà
Lochan na h-Achlaise
Loch Baile Mhic Chailein
Glen Ure
BLACK MOUNT
Invercreran
3059
Tulla
Gualachulain
3565
Stob Ghabhar
Water of Tulla
Beinn Sgulaird
2807
Allt Dochard
2752
Beinn Trilleachan
3425
Stob Coir an Albannaich
Achallader
3540
Beinn a' Chreachain
3404
Beinn Achaladair
Creach Bheinn
2656
3541
Ben Starav
Black Mount
Loch Tulla
Loch Dochard
Victoria Bri.
Beinn an Dothaidh
3267
3125
Beinn Mhanach
Abhainn Dalach
Allt Easach
3141
Beinn nan Aighenan
2215
Beinn Suidhe
Tolaghan
Bridge of Orchy
Dail
Allt Hallater
Glenkinglass Lodge
Glen Kinglass
2327
Beinn nan Lus
2087
Beinn Inverveigh
3524
Beinn Dorain
Allt Chonoghlais
River Esragan
Beinn Mheadhonach
2344
2283
Meall Garbh
B8074
3387
Creag Mhòr
Inveresragan
Inverliver
Glen Liver
Beinn Mhic-Mhonaidh
2602
Glen Orchy
Craig
Glennoe
Glen Noe
B845
Bonawe
Airds Bay
3242
Beinn Eunaich
Glen Strae
River Strae
Beinn Udlaidh
2759
Beinn Bhreac-liath
2633
2948
Beinn Odhar
Bonawe Iron Furnace
Inverawe Smokery
Beinn Donachain
2127
A82
Ben Challum
3354
Loch Lochy
ARGYLL & BUTE
3695
Allt Mhoille
River Lochy
Lochan na Bi
Clifton
Taynuilt
Ichrachan
BEN CRUACHAN
Tyndrum
Bridge of Awe
River Awe
Cruachan Reservoir
Beinn a' Bhuiridh
2941
B8077
134
Beinn na Sròine
Glen Nant
Pass of Brander
Falls of Cruachan
Kilchurn
Stronmilchan
Edendonich
River Orchy
Arinabalnich
Cononish
A85
Lochawe
Kinchrackine
A85
A82
Cruachan Power Station
St. Conan's Kirk
Dalmally
Duncan Ban MacIntyre Monument
3708
Ben Lui
2132
Strath Fillan
142
E
F
G
H
1
2
3
4
5

HIGHLAND
RANNOCH
RANNOCH MOOR
GRAMPIAN
BREADALBANE
STIRLING
TAY FOREST PARK
Loch Rannoch
Loch Ericht
Loch Ossian
Loch Tay
Loch Lyon
Glen Lyon
Glen Lochay
Kinloch Rannoch
Rannoch Station
Bridge of Gaur
Bridge of Ericht
Killichonan
Carie
Camghouran
Dall House
Finnart
Tempar
Dunalastair
Craiganour Lodge
Corrour Shooting Lodge
Ben Alder Lodge
Corrievarkie Lodge
Dalnaspidal Lodge
Sronphadruig Lodge
Moy Lodge
Fersit
Achluachrach
Bohenie
Innerwick
Bridge of Balgie
Camusvrachan
Invervar
Gallin
Cashlie
Kenknock
Killin
Lawers
Milton Morenish
Morenish
Ardeonaig
Ardtalnaig
Carie
Ardchyle
Luib
Lochdochart House
Tyndrum
Clifton
Bridge of Orchy
Achallader
BEN LAWERS
3984
Ben Alder
3765
Sgor Gaibhre
3124
Carn Dearg
3080
Chno Dearg
3433
Stob Coire Easain
3658
Meall Ghaordie
3410
Meall nan Tarmachon
3421
Stuchd an Lochain
3144
Beinn Dorain
3524
Carn Mairg
3419
Schiehallion
A86
A9
A82
A85
A827
B846
B847
142
149
141
134
135
A
B
C
D
1
2
3
4
5

143
150
151
144
136
E
F
G
H
1
2
3
4
5
Loch Errochty
Forest
Uchd a' Chlarsair
2587
3276
An Sgarsoch
3300
2992
Beinn Bhreac
Carn Bhac
3014
Baddoch
2908
Sgor Mòr
Loch Mhairc
Tarf Water
Allt Garbh Buidhe
3424
Beinn Iutharn Mhòr
Loch nan Eun
Loch Vrotachan
3059
The Cairnwell
BEINN DEARG
3307
2882
Braigh Sròn Ghorm
Dalnamein Forest
Sròn a' Chleirich
2678
OF ATHOLL
3377
Carn an Righ
3449
Glas Tulaichean
Gleann Mòr
Carn a' Gheoidh
3194
Bruar Lodge
CAIRNGORMS NATIONAL PARK
Forest Lodge
HOLL
MOUNTAINS
Beinn a' Ghlo
3673
Glen Loch
Glenlochsie Lodge
2641
Ben Gulabin
2470
Carn an Daimh
Allt a' Chireachain
Glen Tilt
River Tilt
1850
Meall Reamhar
Carn Liath
3197
Loch Valigan
Ben Vuirich
2962
2846
Meall a' Choire Bhuidhe
Spittal of Glenshee
2627
Ben Earb
Dalnamein Lodge
Falls of Bruar
Clan Donnachaidh
Tirinie
Fender Burn
Gleann Fearnach
2600
Meall Uaine
Old Blair
Blair
Old Bridge of Tilt
Loch Moraig
Glen Girnaig
Creag an-t Sithein
2075
Calvine
Struan
Pitagowan
B8079
Blair Atholl
Ballentoul
Atholl Country Life
1689
Glen Errochty
B847
Errochty Water
Aldclune
Claverhouse Stone
Ben Vrackie
2760
Straloch
Glen Brerachan
Dirnanean
Enochdhu
Lamh Dearg
1879
Glen Shee
1542
Tulach Hill
Killiecrankie
Tummel Forest
Loch Bhac
Lochan nan Nighean
Craig nan Caisean
1566
Tenandry
Pass of Killiecrankie
A924
Whitefield Castle
2092
Creag Dhubh
Loch Curran
Tressait
B8019
Linn of Tummel
Craigower Hill
Tummel Bridge
Loch Tummel
Queen's View Centre
Cammoch Hill
Moulin
Kirkmichael
B950
Tummel Aqueduct
B846
Foss
Loch Faskally
Explorers
Caisteal Dubh
Pitlochry
Edradour Distillery
Loch Broom
1751
Meall Reamhar
River Ardle
Pitlochry Hydro Electric
A9
STRATHARDLE
1458
Knock of Balmyle
Loch Kinardochy
TAY FOREST PARK
Lochan a' Chait
2559
Farragon Hill
Loch Derculich
Dunfallandy Stone
River Tummel
Lochan Oisinneach Mòr
Ballintuim
Black Water
ERTH
White Bridge
2583
Meall Tairneachan
Strathtay
Pitnacree
Haugh of Ballechin
1842
Creag nam Mial
Blackcraig Hill
1573
Allt Mòr
Grandtully
Derculich
A827
Ballinluig
Tulliemet
Loch Glassie
Loch Farleyer
Weem Hill
Cluny House
Little Ballinluig
Balnaguard
Logierait
B898
Forest of Clunie
Bridge of Cally
Keltney Burn
APPIN
Castle Menzies
Boltachan
Weem
Camserney
Dull
World of Whisky
Wade's Br
Pitcairn
Balnaguard Burn
Loch Ordie
Kindallachan
Blackcraig Forest
Loch Benachally
Keltneyburn
OF DULL
Aberfeldy
Kincraigie
Bishopric
Benachally
1594
Guay
Deuchary Hill
1676
Riemore Lodge
Cochrage Muir
Fortingall
Comrie Castle
Fortingall Yew Tree
Standing Stones
Drummond Hill
A827
Bolfracks
Black Watch Memorial
Falls of Moness
1747
Grandtully Hill
Loch Scoly
Loch Skiach
Dowally
Lornty Burn
1857
Craig Hill
Urlar Burn
Loch na Craigie
Dalguise
B898
Loch Kennard
Butterstone
Forneth
A923
Kinloch
Kenmore
Scottish Crannog Centre
ROSS
Craigvinean Forest
Loch of Butterstone
Loch of the Lowes
Loch of Clunie
Clunie
Clunie Castle
Loch of Drumellie
Craigie
Acham
Falls of Acham
Loch Hoil
Cochill Burn
A826
Glen Cochill
Ballinloan Burn
Scottish Horse Regimental
Loch of Craiglush
Dunkeld
Little Dunkeld
Snaigow House
Kirkton of Lethendy
B947
Loch Fender
2264
Meall Dearg
Tombane Burn
Ossian's Hall
Inver
Beatrix Potter Centre
1041
Newtyle hill
Ben Bhreac
Hermitage
Ossian's Cave
Birnam
Birnam Hill
1324
A984
Spittalfield
Wester Shian
Garrow
River Quaich
Glen Quaich
Trochry
River Braan
Obney Hills
Stare Dam
Caputh
Gellyburn
River Tay
Meikleour
Beech Hedge
A822
Strathbraan
Loch Freuchie
Croftmill
Kingswood Mill Dam
Murthly
Ardoch
B867
Tullybeagles Lodge
Waterloo
B9099
Cargill
2641
Meall nam Fuaran
Lochan a' Mhuilinn
Amulree
Glen Shee
Bankfoot
Airntully
Meall nan Caorach
2045
Little Glenshee
Ordie Burn
Stobhall
Auchnafree
River Almond
Meall Reamhar
2188
Milton Burn
Stanley
STRATHORD FOREST
Guildtown
Ben Chonzie
3048
Auchnafree Hill
2589
Glen Almond
Newton Bridge
Logiealmond
Chapelhill
Shochie Burn
B8063
Newmiln
2126
Meall Tarsuinn
Sma Glen
Harrietfield
River Almond
Moneydie
Luncarty
Stormontfield
Scone Palace
Pinetum
Invergeldie
Loch Turret Reservoir
Carn Chois
Shaggie Burn
Buchanty
Tulchan
Glenalmond
B8063
Busby
Bertha Loch
Pitcairngreen
A9
A93
A94
Old Scone
Perth
Scone Palace
Scone
Loch Meallbrodden
Keillour
Almondbank
Huntingtower
A85

144
151
143
136
137
A
B
C
D
1
2
3
4
5
CAIRNGORMS NATIONAL PARK
PERTH & KINROSS
ANGUS
STRATHARDLE
SIDLAW HILLS
GOWRIE
GLAS MAOL
Baddoch
2736 Creag nan Gabhar
Loch Callater
White Mounth
Dubh Loch
3314 Cairn Bannoch
Glas-allt Shiel
Loch Muick
2908 Sgor Mor
3268 Broad Cairn
3340 Carn an Tuirc
3143 Tolmount
Loch Esk
Loch Vrotachan
3059 The Cairnwell
Carn a' Gheoidh 3194
Devil's Elbow
3504 Caenlochan Forest
3238 Creag Leacach
2954 Finalty Hill
3043 Mayar
3108 Driesh
Glendoll Forest
Acharn
Glen Doll
Black Hill of Mark
2731 Easter Balloch
Glen Lee
Water of Mark
2276 Monawee
Kirkton
Carlochy
2726 Lair of Aldararie
Water of Unich
2699 Muckle Cairn
2424 Cruys
Loch Brandy
Loch Wharral
2941 Ben Tirran
Clova
River South Esk
2544 White Hill
Glen Clova
2483 Cairn Inks
2129 Cairn of Barns
Cairn Baddoch 1915
2641 Ben Gulabin
2470 Carn an Daimh
2643 Monamenach
Auchavan
Spittal of Glenshee
2627 Ben Earb
2600 Meall Uaine
2301 Mealna Letter or Duchray Hill
Loch Beanie
2428 Badandum Hill
Glen Isla
Glen Finlet
Glen Damff
Runtaleave
1992 Eskielawn
Glen Prosen
Balnaboth
Glenprosen Village
Hill of Couternach 1676
B955
Rottal
2478 Finbracks
2381 Hill of Glansie
Hunthill Lodge
Hill of Berran
1788 Auld Darkney
Glenmoy
1682 Pinderachy
Auchnacree
Glenogil
Easter Ogil
Mountains Animal Sanctuary
Deuchar
Glen Shee
Clach na Coileach
Lamh Dearg 1879
Cray
Folda
Auchintaple Loch
Dirnanean
Enochdhu
Whitefield Castle
2442 Mount Blair
B951
Brewlands Bridge
Kirkton of Glenisla
Loch Shandra
Glenhead Farm
Backwater Reservoir
Easter Lednathie
Cat Law 2202
Captain Scott & Dr. Wilson Cairn
Dykehead
Cortachy
Kirkmichael
B950
Blacklunans
1706 Cairn Gibbs
1630 Creigh Hill
Balintore
Pearsie
Prosen Bridge
Memus
Shielhill Bridge
Shielhill
Dykend
Braes of Coul
1341 Mile Hill
1458 Knock of Balmyle
Forest of Alyth
1383 Drumderg
Loch of Lintrathen
Bridgend of Lintrathen
B951
Kirkton of Kingoldrum
Kinnordy
Camera Obscura
Northmuir
J.M. Barrie's Birthplace NTS
Kirriemuir
B957
Bogindollo
Oathlaw
Ballintuim
A924
Blackcraig Hill 1573
Black Water
Milnacraig
Bridge of Craigisla
Reekie Linn
Craigyloch
1395 Baldruff Hill
Westmuir
Maryton
Ballinshoe Tower
Lunan
Netherton
Strone Bridge
Tullymurdoch
Kirkton of Airlie
A926
Padanaram
Drumgley
Forest of Clunie
Loch Benachally
Bridge of Cally
Blackcraig Forest
B954
Hill of Alyth 968
Craigton
Roundyhill
Gateside
St. Orland's Stone
FORFAR
Benachally 1594
Riemore Lodge
Cochrage Muir
Alyth
Ruthven
Eassie Sculptured Stone
Dean Water
Glasclune Castle
B952
New Alyth
Eassie
Bridgend
Glamis
Angus Folk
Douglastown
A90
Thornton
Kirkton
Carterhaugh
B9127
Fothringham Hill
Westfields of Rattray
Blairgowrie
Rattray
Bridge of Crathies
Charleston
Foffarty
Forneth
Loch of Butterstone
Loch of the Lowes
Loch of Clunie
Clunie
Loch of Drumellie
Kinloch
A923
Craigie
Leitfie
Balkeerie
Eassie and Nevay
Meigle
Sculptured Stone
Kirkinch
Milton
Gateside
Inverarity
Rosemount
Muirton of Ardblair
Snaigow House
Kirkton of Lethendy
B947
Monk Myre
Arthurstone
Ardler
Ark Hill 1116
Kinpurney Hill 1133
Over Finlarg
Gallowfauld
Beatrix Potter Centre
1041 Newtyle hill
Coupar Angus
Newbigging
Newtyle
Gallow Hill
Happas
Carrot Hill
A984
Spittalfield
Caputh
Gellyburn
Meikleour
Beech Hedge
Keillor
Hill of Keillor
Markethill
Kettins
Long Loch
Hillside of Prieston
Tealing
Kingswood
Murthly
Ardoch
Kinclaven Castle
Bridge of Isla
Woodside
Campmuir
Leys
Bonnyton
Kirkton of Auchterhouse
Kirkton
Dovecot & Earth House
Newbigging
Wellbank
A9
B9099
Cargill
Burrelton
Pitcur
Lundie
Auchterhouse
North Dronley
Westhall Terrace
Bankfoot
Airntully
Gallowhill
Laird's Loch
A923
Dronley
Bridgefoot
Kellas
Stobhall
Piperdam Osprey Centre
Woodland
Clatto Reservoir
Muirhead
Balmuir
Stanley
Wolfhill
Saucher
Fowlis
Liff
Birkhill
Downfield
Whitfield
Fintry
STRATHORD FOREST
Guildtown
Kinrossie
Collace
Dunsinane Hill
Kirkton of Collace
Knapp
Benvie
Lochee
Camperdown
Mills Observatory
Craigie
Claypotts
Newmiln
St. Martins
B953
Abernyte
Castlehill
Carse of Gowrie
DUNDEE
Broughty Ferry
Discovery
Unicorn
Moneydie
Luncarty
Stormontfield
Balbeggie
Kinnaird
Craigdallie
Inchture
Longforgan
Invergowrie
Kingoodie
Botanic
Tay Bridge
Tay Road Bridge
Newport-on-Tay
Perth
Scone Palace Pinetum
Bertha Loch
Pitcairngreen
Old Scone
Scone Palace
Almondbank
Huntingtower
A85
Scone
A94
Westown
Rait
Braes of the Carse
Winery
Grange
Inchmichael
Pole Hill
Kilspindie
B946
Woodhaven
Wormit
A92
A914
B945

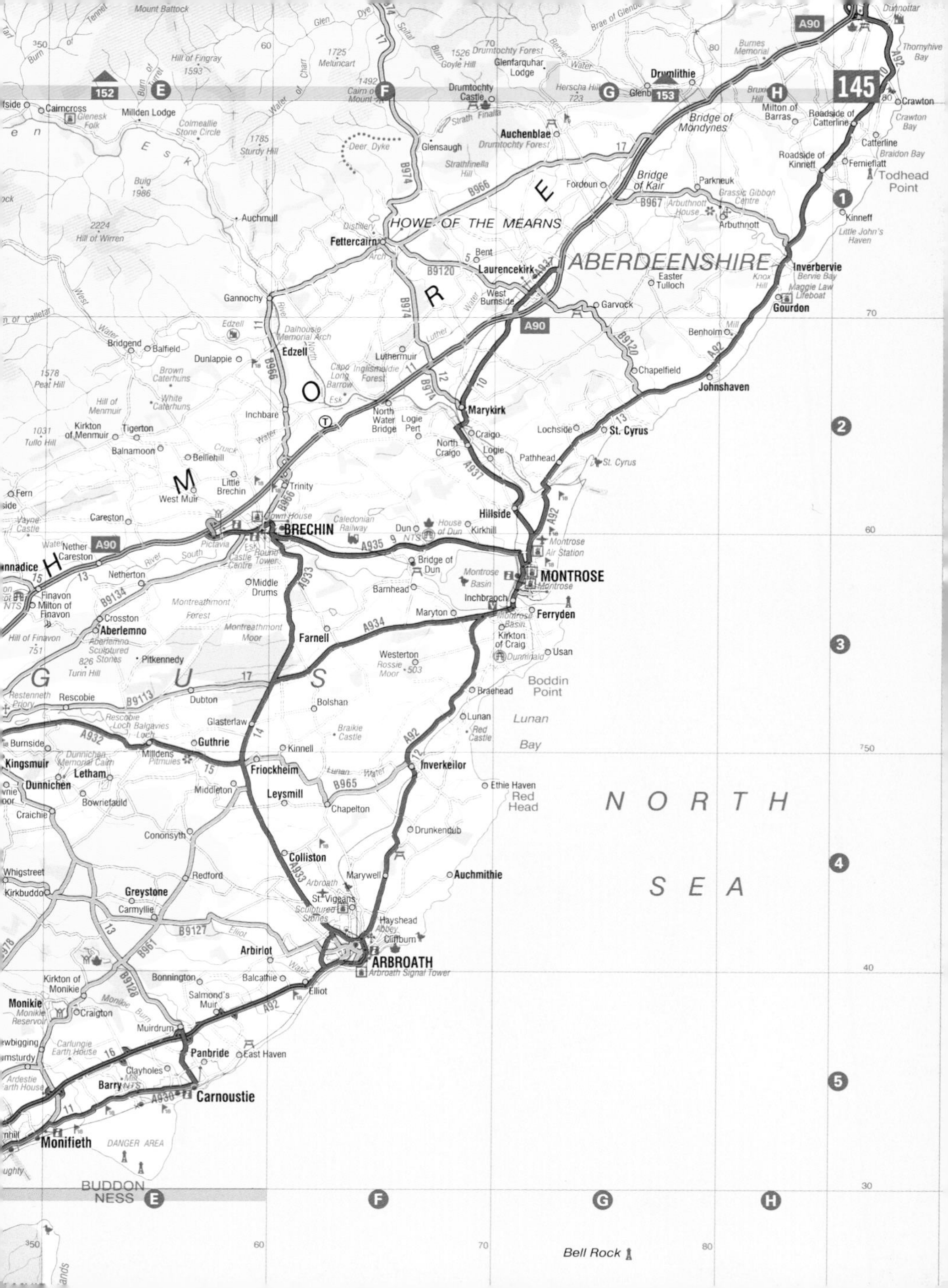

Mount Battock
Hill of Fingray
1593
Glen Dye
1725
Meluncart
1492
Cairn o' Mount
Drumtochty Forest
1526
Goyle Hill
Glenfarquhar Lodge
Bervie Water
Brae of Glenbervie
Dunnottar
A90
80
Burnes Memorial
Thornyhive Bay
A92
Drumlithie
Herscha Hill
723
Bruxie Hill
152
E
F
G
H
153
145
Crawton
Crawton Bay
Milton of Barras
Roadside of Catterline
Catterline
Braidon Bay
Cairncross
Glenesk Folk
Millden Lodge
Colmeallie Stone Circle
1785
Sturdy Hill
Esk
Drumtochty Castle
Strath Finalla
Auchenblae
Drumtochty Forest
Glensaugh
Deer Dyke
B974
Strathfinella Hill
Bridge of Mondynes
Roadside of Kinneff
Fernieflatt
Todhead Point
Bridge of Kair
Fordoun
Parkneuk
Grassic Gibbon Centre
B966
B967
Arbuthnott House
Arbuthnott
Kinneff
Little John's Haven
Buig
1986
Auchmull
HOWE OF THE MEARNS
Distillery
Fettercairn
2224
Hill of Wirren
Arch
Bent
Laurencekirk
A937
ABERDEENSHIRE
B9120
Inverbervie
Bervie Bay
Knox Hill
Maggie Law Lifeboat
Gourdon
Easter Tulloch
Gannochy
West Burnside
Garvock
70
A90
Edzell
Dalhousie Memorial Arch
Bridgend
Balfield
Dunlappie
Brown Caterthuns
White Caterthuns
1578
Peat Hill
Hill of Menmuir
Luthermuir
Capo Long Barrow
Inglismaldie Forest
Benholm
Chapelfield
Johnshaven
Inchbare
North Water Bridge
Logie Pert
Marykirk
Craigo
North Craigo
Logie
Lochside
St. Cyrus
Pathhead
1031
Tullo Hill
Kirkton of Menmuir
Tigerton
Balnamoon
Cruick Water
Belliehill
Little Brechin
West Muir
Trinity
Fern
Careston
Vayne Castle
Nether Careston
A90
Pictavia
Castle Centre
Round Tower
Town House
BRECHIN
Caledonian Railway
A935
Dun
House of Dun
NTS
Kirkhill
Hillside
Montrose Air Station
MONTROSE
Montrose Basin
Bridge of Dun
Barnhead
Inchbraoch
Ferryden
60
Finavon
Milton of Finavon
Netherton
River South Esk
B9134
Middle Drums
A933
Montreathmont Forest
Montreathmont Moor
Maryton
Crosston
Aberlemno
Aberlemno Sculptured Stones
Hill of Finavon
751
826
Turin Hill
Pitkennedy
Farnell
A934
Westerton
Rossie Moor
503
Kirkton of Craig
Dunninald
Usan
Boddin Point
Braehead
Restenneth Priory
Rescobie
B9113
Dubton
Bolshan
Lunan
Lunan Bay
Red Castle
Rescobie Loch
Balgavies Loch
A932
Glasterlaw
Braikie Castle
Burnside
Guthrie
Kinnell
Kingsmuir
Dunnichen Memorial Cairn
Milldens
Pitmuies
Friockheim
Lunan Water
Inverkeilor
Letham
Dunnichen
B965
Ethie Haven
Red Head
NORTH SEA
Bowriefauld
Middleton
Leysmill
Chapelton
Craichie
Cononsyth
Drunkendub
Colliston
Whigstreet
Redford
Marywell
Auchmithie
Kirkbuddo
Greystone
Carmyllie
Arbroath
St. Vigeans
Sculptured Stones
Hayshead
Abbey
Cliffburn
B9127
Elliot Water
Arbirlot
ARBROATH
Arbroath Signal Tower
B961
B9128
Kirkton of Monikie
Bonnington
Balcathie
Elliot
Monikie
Monikie Reservoir
Craigton
Salmond's Muir
A92
Muirdrum
Newbigging
Carlungie Earth House
Panbride
East Haven
Ardestie Earth House
Clayholes
Barry Mill NTS
Barry
A930
Carnoustie
Monifieth
DANGER AREA
BUDDON NESS
Bell Rock
350
60
70
80
40
50
30
1
2
3
4
5

ISLE OF SKYE
MINGINISH
CUILLIN HILLS
BLA BHEINN
SOAY
SEA OF THE HEBRIDES
INNER HEBRIDES
HIGH
CANNA
Sanday
Canna Harbour
Sound of Canna
RÙM
NATIONAL NATURE RESERVE
SOUND OF RÙM
EIGG
MUCK
Sound of Eigg
Talisker Bay
Talisker
Carbost
Drynoch
Merkadale
Sligachan
Sconser
GLAMAIG
Glenbrittle
Bualintur
Camasunary
Kilmarie
Elgol
Glasnakille
Eynort
Loch Eynort
An Dubh-sgeir
Stac an Tuill
Loch Brittle
Soay Sound
Loch Scavaig
Moi-chlach
Eilean na h-Airde
Rubha na h-Easgainne
Tarskavaig Point
Garrisdale Point
A' Chill
An Coroghon
Kilmory
Guirdil Bay
Kinloch
Kinloch Castle
Loch Scresort
Schooner Point
Rubha Shamhnan Insir
Camas Pliasgaig
Rubha nam Meirleach
Oigh-sgeir
Cleadale
Bay of Laig
Rubha nan Tri Chlach
Rubha an Fhasaidh
Kildonnan
Sandavore
Galmisdale
Eilean Chathastail
Rubha na Crannaig
Sgeir Eskernish
Eilean nan Each
Gòdag
Port Mor
Dubh Sgeir
Inver Dalav
Rubha Charn nan Cearc
Geur Rubha
Point of Sleat
Rùm to Canna 55mins.
Mallaig to Canna 2hrs. (Seasonal)
Mallaig to Rùm 1hr. 20mins.
Muck to Canna 1hr. 35mins. (Seasonal)
Eigg to Rùm 1hr. (Seasonal)
Rùm to Muck 1hr. 10mins. (Seasonal)
Eigg to Muck 35mins.
Mallaig to Muck
A863
A87
B8009
B8083
154
170
138
139

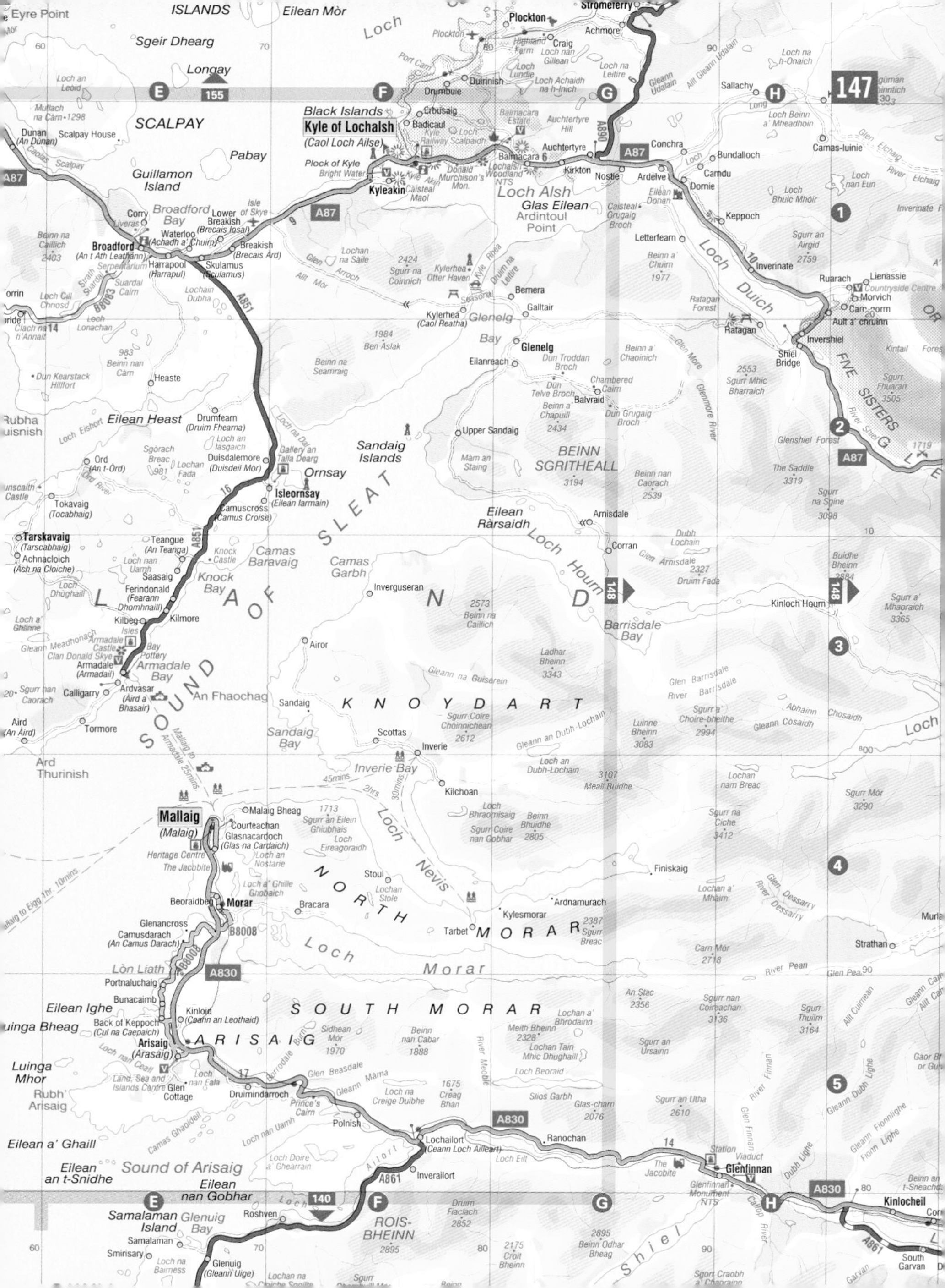
147
Eyre Point
ISLANDS
Eilean Mòr
Sgeir Dhearg
Longay
155
SCALPAY
Scalpay House
Dunan
(An Dùnan)
Mullach na Càrn 1298
Pabay
Guillamon Island
Broadford Bay
Corry
Lower Breakish
(Brecais Iosal)
Isle of Skye
Waterloo
(Achadh a' Chuim)
Breakish
(Brecais Àrd)
Broadford
(An t Ath Leathann)
Harrapool
(Harrapul)
Skulamus
(Sculamus)
Beinn na Caillich 2403
Suardal Cairn
Loch Cill Chriosd
Loch Lonachan
983 Beinn nan Càrn
Dun Kearstack Hillfort
Heaste
Rubha Suisnish
Eilean Heast
Loch Eishort
Drumfearn
(Druim Fhearna)
Sgòrach Breac 981
Lochan Fada
Duisdalemore
(Duisdeil Mòr)
Ord
(An t-Òrd)
Tokavaig
(Tocabhaig)
Camuscross
(Camus Croise)
Isleornsay
(Eilean Iarmain)
Ornsay
Gallery an Talla Dearg
Tarskavaig
(Tarscabhaig)
Achnacloich
(Ach na Cloiche)
Teangue
(An Teanga)
Saasaig
Ferindonald
(Fearann Dhomhnaill)
Knock Bay
Knock Castle
Camas Baravaig
Kilbeg
Kilmore
Armadale Castle
Clan Donald Skye
Armadale Bay
Armadale
(Armadail)
Ardvasar
(Àird a Bhasair)
Calligarry
Aird
(An Àird)
Tormore
An Fhaochag
SOUND OF SLEAT
Ard Thurinish
Mallaig to Armadale 25mins
Mallaig
(Malaig)
Heritage Centre
The Jacobite
Malaig Bheag
Courteachan
Glasnacardoch
(Glas na Cardaich)
Beoraidbeg
Morar
Bracara
Glenancross
Camusdarach
(An Camus Darach)
B8008
Lòn Liath
A830
Portnaluchaig
Bunacaimb
Eilean Ighe
Luinga Bheag
Back of Keppoch
(Cul na Caepaich)
Kinloid
(Ceann an Leothaid)
Arisaig
(Arasaig)
ARISAIG
Luinga Mhor
Rubh' Arisaig
Land, Sea and Islands Centre
Glen Cottage
Druimindarroch
Prince's Cairn
Polnish
Eilean a' Ghaill
Eilean an t-Snidhe
Sound of Arisaig
Eilean nan Gobhar
Samalaman Island
Glenuig Bay
Samalaman
Smirisary
Roshven
Glenuig
(Gleann Uige)
140
Plockton
Achmore
Stromeferry
Craig
Port Cam
Duirinish
Drumbuie
Erbusaig
Badicaul
Black Islands
Kyle of Lochalsh
(Caol Loch Ailse)
Plock of Kyle
Bright Water
Kyleakin
Caisteal Maol
Balmacara Estate
Auchtertyre Hill
Balmacara
Auchtertyre
Lochalsh Woodland NTS
Donald Murchison's Mon.
A87
A890
Conchra
Kirkton
Nostie
Ardelve
Bundalloch
Carndu
Dornie
Eilean Donan
Loch Alsh
Glas Eilean
Ardintoul Point
Caisteal Grugaig Broch
Keppoch
Letterfearn
Beinn a' Chuirn 1977
Loch Duich
Inverinate
Sgurr an Airgid 2759
Ruarach
Lienassie
Morvich
Countryside Centre
Camas-luinie
Sallachy
Loch Long
Aultachruinn
Invershiel
Shiel Bridge
Ratagan
Ratagan Forest
FIVE SISTERS
Sgurr Fhuaran 3505
Glenshiel Forest
The Saddle 3319
Sgurr na Sgine 3098
Lochan na Sàile
Sgurr na Coinnich 2424
Kylerhea Otter Haven
Kylerhea
(Caol Reatha)
Glenelg Bay
Bernera
Galltair
Glenelg
Eilanreach
Dun Troddan Broch
Dun Telve Broch
Chambered Cairn
Balvraid
Dun Grugaig Broch
Beinn a' Chapuill 2434
Beinn a' Chaoinich
Glen More
Glenmore River
Sgurr Mhic Bharraich 2553
Ben Aslak 1984
Beinn na Seamraig
Upper Sandaig
Sandaig Islands
Màm an Staing
BEINN SGRITHEALL 3194
Beinn nan Caorach 2539
Eilean Ràrsaidh
Loch Hourn
Arnisdale
Corran
Glen Arnisdale
Dubh Lochain
Druim Fada 2327
Buidhe Bheinn 2884
Kinloch Hourn
Sgurr a' Mhaoraich 3365
148
Camas Garbh
Inverguseran
LAND OF NOYDART
Beinn na Caillich 2573
Barrisdale Bay
Airor
Ladhar Bheinn 3343
Glen Barrisdale
Gleann na Guiserein
KNOYDART
Sandaig
Sandaig Bay
Sgurr Coire Choinnichean 2612
Luinne Bheinn 3083
Sgurr a' Choire-bheithe 2994
Gleann Cosaidh
Scottas
Inverie
Inverie Bay
Kilchoan
Meall Buidhe 3107
Loch an Dubh-Lochain
Lochan nam Breac
Sgurr Mòr 3290
Sgurr an Eilein Ghiubhais 1713
Loch Eireagoraidh
Loch Bhraomisaig
Sgurr Coire nan Gobhar
Beinn Bhuidhe 2805
Sgurr na Ciche 3412
Loch Nevis
Stoul
Lochan Stole
NORTH MORAR
Finiskaig
Glen Dessarry
River Dessarry
Kylesmorar
Ardnamurach
Tarbet
Sgurr Breac 2387
Loch Morar
Carn Mòr 2718
Strathan
River Pean
Glen Pean
SOUTH MORAR
An Stac 2356
Lochan a' Bhrodainn
Sgurr nan Coireachan 3136
Sgurr Thuilm 3164
Sidhean Mòr 1970
Beinn nan Cabar 1888
Meith Bheinn 2328
Lochan Tain Mhic Dhughaill
Sgurr an Ursainn
Loch Beoraid
Glen Beasdale
Gleann Màma
Loch na Creige Duibhe
Creag Bhan 1675
Slios Garbh
Glas-charn 2076
Sgurr an Utha 2610
River Meoble
Loch nan Uamh
Lochailort
(Ceann Loch Ailleart)
Ranochan
Loch Eilt
Inverailort
A861
Glenfinnan
Station
Viaduct
The Jacobite
Glenfinnan Monument NTS
Callop River
Kinlocheil
South Garvan
Druim Fiaclach 2852
ROIS-BHEINN 2895
Croit Bheinn 2175
Beinn Odhar Bheag 2895
Loch Shiel

148
Plockton
Stromeferry
Achmore
Craig
Highland Farm
Loch na Gillean
Loch Lundie
Loch na Beiste
Gleann Udalain
Allt Gleann Udalain
Balmacara Estate
Auchtertyre Hill
Auchtertyre
Balmacara
Kirkton
Nostie
Conchra
A87
A890
Bundalloch
Carndu
Ardelve
Dornie
Eilean Donan
Loch Alsh
Glas Eilean
Ardintoul Point
Caisteal Grugaig Broch
Keppoch
Letterfearn
Beinn a' Chuirn
1977
Loch Duich
Inverinate
Sallachy
Long
Killilan
Loch Beinn a' Mheadhoin
Camas-luinie
Glen Elchaig
River Elchaig
Loch na h-Oanaich
Loch nan Eun
Loch Bhuic Mhòir
Sgurr an Airgid
2759
Sgùman Coinntich
2883
Killilan Forest
156
Loch nan Ealachan
Allt na Doire Cairbhe
Carnach
Loch na Leitreach
Falls of Glomach
Inverinate Forest
3006
A' Ghlas-bheinn
Loch a' Bhealaich
2949
Aonach Buidhe
Loch Mhoicean
3508
3696
An Riabh
HIGHLANDS
Mullardoch
Glen Cannich
Glencannich Forest
Toll Creagach
3457
Tom a' Chòinich
3646
Coire Lochan
Carn Eighe
3880
Gleann nam Fiadh
West Benula Forest
Gleann Sithidh
Abhainn Sithidh
Glean a' Choilich
Abhainn a Choilich
Sgurr nan Ceathreamhnan
3771
Sgurr na Lapaich
3401
Affric Lodge
Loch Affric
Glen Affric
River Affric
Glenaffric Forest
NORTH WEST
Gleann Gniomhaidh
Ruarach
Lienassie
Countryside Centre
Morvich
Carn-gorm
Ault a' chruinn
Invershiel
Shiel Bridge
Ratagan
Ratagan Forest
Bernera
Galltair
Glenelg
Dun Troddan Broch
Dun Telve Broch
Chambered Cairn
Balvraid
Dun Grugaig Broch
Beinn a' Chaoinich
Glen More
Glenmore River
2553
Sgurr Mhic Bharraich
BEINN FHADA OR BEN ATTOW
3385
Kintail Forest
FIVE SISTERS
Sgurr Fhuaran
3505
River Shiel
Glenshiel Forest
GLEN SHIEL
1719
Allt Garbh
Aonach Shasuinn
2913
Mullach Fraoch-choire
3614
Ciste Dhubh
3218
A' Chràlaig
3673
Sgurr nan Conbhairean
3634
Ceannacroc Forest
River Doe
Beinn a' Chapuill
2434
Sandaig
BEINN SGRITHEALL
3194
Beinn nan Caorach
2539
The Saddle
3319
Sgurr na Sgine
3098
Sgurr an Lochain
3282
Cluanie Inn
Cluanie Lodge
Loch Cluanie
A87
Eilean Iarsaidh
Arnisdale
Corran
Loch Hourn
Dubh Lochain
Glen Arnisdale
2327
Druim Fada
147
Buidhe Bheinn
2884
Kinloch Hourn
Sgurr a' Mhaoraich
3365
Glen Quoich
Glenquoich Forest
Cluanie Forest
Aonach air Chrith
3342
Maol Chinn-dearg
Beinn Loinne
Bunloinn Forest
River Loyne
Loch Loyne
Glen Loyne
Barrisdale Bay
Ladhar Bheinn
3343
Glen Barrisdale
River Barrisdale
Gleouraich
3394
HIGH
East Glenquoich Forest
Ardochy House
Loch Fearna
Abhainn Chosaidh
Gleann Cosaidh
Sgurr a' Choire-bheithe
2994
Luinne Bheinn
3083
Gleann an Dubh-Lochain
Loch Quoich
Gearr Garry
Kingie
Tomdoun
Inchlaggan
River Garry
Glen Garry
Beinn Bheag
Gairich
3015
Loch an Dubh-Lochain
3107
Meall Buidhe
Lochan nam Breac
Sgurr Mòr
3290
Lochan nan Sgùd
Allt Choire a' Bhalachain
Glas Bheinn
1825
River Kingie
Glen Kingie
Beinn Bhuidhe
2805
Sgurr na Ciche
3412
Lochan Dubh
Loch Blàir
Meall Blàir
2154
Finiskaig
Sgurr Mhurlagain
2885
Geal Charn
Lochan a' Mhaim
Glen Dessarry
River Dessarry
Ardnamurach
Kylesmorar
2387
Sgurr Breac
MORAR
LOCH
Murlaggan
Strathan
Loch Arkaig
Ardechive
Gleann Cia-aig
Carn Mòr
2718
River Pean
Glen Pean
An Stac
2356
Sgurr nan Coireachan
3136
Sgurr Thuilm
3164
Allt Cuirnean
Gleann Camgharaidh
Allt Camgharaidh
Chia-aig Falls
Clunes
Locheil Forest
Inver Mallie
Glen Mallie
River Mallie
Achnacarry
Clan Cameron
Bunarkaig
B8005
Lochan a' Bhrodainn
Meith Bheinn
2328
Lochan Tain Mhic Dhughaill
Sgurr an Ursainn
Gaor Bheinn or Gulvain
Meall a' Phubuill
2533
Druim Gleann Laoigh
Achnanellan
Glen Loy
River Loy
Beinn Bhàn
2612
Gairlochy
Stronenaba
Loch Beoraid
Slios Garbh
Glas-charn
2076
Sgurr an Utha
2610
River Finnan
Glen Finnan
Gleann Dubh Lighe
Gleann Fionnlighe
Fionn Lighe
Gleann Suileag
An t-Suileag
Stob a' Ghrianain
Druim Fada
B8004
Caledonian Canal
Bracklettet
Commando Memorial
Ranochan
A830
Loch Eilt
The Jacobite
Station
Viaduct
Glenfinnan
Glenfinnan Monument NTS
Dubh Lighe
Beinn an t-Sneachda
Muirshearlich
Highbridge
A82
140
Kinlocheil
Corribeg
Fassfern
Achdalieu
A830
Treasures of the Earth
Corpach
Banavie
Neptune's Staircase
Caol
Camaghael
Torlundy
Tor Castle
River Lochy
141
Leanachan Forest
Crofting
Creag Aoil
Nevis Range Gondola
Loch Eil
The Jacobite
South Garvan
Duisky
Blaich
A861
B8006
Lochyside
Ben Nevis Distillery
Loch Shiel
2895
Beinn Odhar Bheag
2175
Croit Bheinn
Sgorr Craobh a' Chaorainn
Glen Garvan

149
150
Muchrachd
River Cannich
Balmore Forest
A831
Liatrie
Cannich
River Glass
Loch Sealbhanach
Corrimony
Buntait
Braefield
157
Balnaglaic
Balbeg
Rychraggan
Balnagrantach
Polmaily
Achmony
Drumnadrochit
Milton
Balnain
Loch Meiklie
River Enrick
Drum Farm Centre
Corrimony Chambered Cairn
Kerrow
Fasnakyle Forest
Caorach
1497
Lochan an Tairt
Loch Gorm
Nessieland Castle Monster Centre
Loch Ness Exhibition
A833
A82
Abriachan
Meall na h-Eilrig
1526
Dores
Ashie Moor
B852
B862
Stac na Cathaig
1463
Tom Baligeann
1522
Borlum
Urquhart Bay
Lewiston
Strone
Urquhart
Coiltie
Divach
Falls of Divach
Upper Lenie
Lower Lenie
John Cobb Memorial
Bunloit
Balbeg
Inverfarigaig
River Farigaig
Dun Deardull
Farigaig Forest
Errogie
Dunmaglass Lodge
Farraline
Loch Conagleann
Foyers
Falls of Foyers
Lyne of Gorthleck
Wester Aberchalder
Lochgarthside
Bunkegivie
Loch Ceo Glais
Torness
Loch Ruthven
River Nairn
Aberarder
B851
River Affric
Tomich
Suidhe Ghuirmain
1896
River Enrick
River Coiltie
Balmacaan Forest
Abhainn Deabhag
Mheadhoin
Loch nan Sean-each
Lochan Forest
Loch na Ruighe Duibhe
Loch a' Mhuilinn
Meall a' Chràthaich
2226
Loch Aslaich
Loch nam Meur
Loch nam Breac Dearga
Loch ma Stac
Loch nan Eun
Loch a' Chràthaich
Creag-nan-Eun Forest
Alltsigh
Loch na Beinne Bàine
Carn a' Chaochain
2314
Levishie Forest
Levishie
Allt Bhlàraidh
Achnaconeran
Moriston
Invermoriston
Invermoriston Falls
Portclair Forest
Dundreggan Forest
A887
Dundreggan
Glen Moriston
Dundreggan Reservoir
River Moriston
Burach
1986
Inverwick Forest
Dalchreichart
Torgyle
Allt na Muic
Ceannacroc Lodge
Ceannacroc Bridge
Allt Phocaichain
LOCH NESS
OR GLEN MOR
Strath Errick
River Foyers
Loch Mhor
Whitebridge
Upper Knockchoilum
Loch Knockie
Loch nan Lann
Knockie Lodge
B862
Glenbrein Lodge
River Fechlin
Garrogie Lodge
Loch Killin
Killin Lodge
River Killin
2618
Carn Odhar
Carn na Saobhaidhe
2658
Allt Uisg an t-Sidhein
Aberchalder Burn
Coignafearn
2658
Carn na Làraiche Maoile
MONADHLIA
Carn Coire na Creiche
2702
Burrach Mór
2686
Glen Markie
Abhainn Cro Chlach
Caledonian Canal
Bunoich
Fort Augustus
Jenkins Park
Inchnacardoch Forest
Auchteraw
Loch Tarff
Glendoebeg
Loch nan Eun
Allt Breineag
Allt Doe
Glen Brein
2554
Carn Easgann Bàna
Coire Odhar
Allt Càm Ban
Crom Allt
Allt Odhar
Lochan na Stairne
Glendoe Forest
Clansman Centre
River Oich
Caledonian Canal
Culachy Falls
Newtown
A82
Bridge of Oich
Loch a' Bhainne
Allt Lundie
Loch Lundie
Munerigie
Aberchalder
Garry
A87
Faichem
Invergarry
Allt na Cailliche Falls
Wester Mandally
Heritage Centre
Invergarry Castle
Loch Oich
Well of Seven Heads
Laggan Swing Bridge
Ben Tee
2957
Forest
Laggan
Kilfinnan
South Laggan Forest
Loch Lochy
A82
Altrua
GLEN ALBYN
GLEN
LAND
2677
Carn a' Chuilinn
Lochan Dearg Uillt
Loch Carn a' Chuilinn
River Glen Tarff
Culachy Forest
Calder Burn
Loch an Aonaich Odhair
Corrieyairack Pass
Gairbeinn
2929
Carn Leac
2889
Corrieyairack Forest
Carn Dearg
2677
2828
Meall na h-Aisre
Allt Coire Iain Òig
2498
Creag Mhòr
Feith Talagain
Loch na Lairige
Geal Charn
3036
Glen Markie
Melgarve
Drummin
River Spey
Garva Bridge
Garvamore
Loch Spey
Loch Crunachdain
Allt Crunachdain
Glenshero Lodge
Strathmashie House
Feagour
Cromra
Kinloch Laggan
Crathie
Laggan
A86
Balgowan
Drumgask
Catlodge
Strath Mashie
A889
Loch Caoldair
River Mashie
Carn Ban
3087
Carn Dearg
Loch Dubh
Allt Madagain
Marg na Craige
2731
River Turret
Brae Roy Lodge
Burn of Agie
Loch a' Bhànain
Carn Liath
3298
Coille Coire Chrannaig
River Gloy
Glen Gloy
Beinn Iaruinn
2636
Glen Roy
Carn Dearg
2736
Upper Glenfintaig
Lochan a' Choire
Creag Meagaidh
3700
Lochan Coire Choille-rais
Loch Laggan
Coire Ceirsle Hill
Caol Lairig
Parallel Roads
River Roy
Allt Glas Dhoire
2994
Beinn Teallach
Beinn a' Chaorainn
3437
A86
Moy Forest
Moy Lodge
Binnein Shuas
Lochan na h-Earba
Ardverikie Forest
River Pattack
2207
Beinn Eilde
Lochan na Doire-uaine
Distillery
Dalwhinnie
Cuaich
Bohenie
2160
Creag Dhubh
A86
Inverroy
Roybridge
Achluachrach
GLEN SPEAN
Bunroy
River Spean
Monessie Falls
Braes o' Lochaber
Tulloch
Inverlair Falls
Loch Laggan Resr.
Lochan an Turic
3443
Geal Charn
Meall Cruaidh
2941
Loch Ericht Forest
2520
Creagan Mòr
A9
Loch a' Bhealaich Leamhain
142
Pattack
Ben Alder Lodge
Beinn Chlianaig
2343
Meall Luidh Mòr
Allt Lòraich
Fersit
Allt Cam
3569
Beinn a' Chlachair
Allt Cam
An Lairig
3391
Càrn Dearg
Allt a' Chaoil-reidhe
3005
Geal Charn
R. Truim
Pass of Drumochter
2422
An Torc
BEER

150
158
149
142
143
A
B
C
D
1
2
3
4
5
Dores
Chlachain 1196
Dunlichity Lodge
Inverarnie
Castle
Ruthven
Ashie Moor
Farr
2022 Carn na h-Easgainn
Strathnairn Forest
2076 Carn an t-Sean-liathanaich
Loch Duntelchaig
Stac na Cathaig 1463
Loch Farr
Balvraid Lodge
Bailgeann 1522
Loch a' Choire
Brin Herb Nursery
Strathnairn
Distillery
Tomatin
Corrybrough
Raigbeg
2057 Carn a' Choire Mhòir
2182 Carn Glas-choire
B852
B862
B851
B9007
A938
A9
A95
A86
A889
B9152
B9153
B970
B9150
Loch Ceo Glais
Torness
Loch Ruthven
East Croachy
River Nairn
Beinn Bhreac 1969
Findhorn Bridge
Aberarder
Clune
Carn nam Bain-tighearna 2082
Duthil
River Dulnain
Glen Kyllachy
Carn na Saobhaidh 2321
Corrievorrie
Slochd
Errogie
Dunmaglass Lodge
Farraline
Glenmazeran Lodge
Carrbridge
Ellan
Landmark Forest Adventure Park
Glen Mazeran
Carn Phris Mhòir 2021
Sluggan
Loch Conagleann
Wester Aberchalder
2637 Carn Ghriogair
Beinn Bhreac Mhòr 2647
Carn Dubh 'Ic an Deòir 2461
Drumuillie
Boat of Garten
Dalmigavie
Chapelton
Kinveachy
Beinn Ghuilbin 1895
2618 Carn Odhar
River Findhorn
Strathdearn
Allt Lorgy
Carn Sleamhuinn 2217
Avielochan
Coignafearn Lodge
H I G H L A
Granish
West Croftmore
Strathspey Railway
Brewery
Aviemore
Loch Pityoulish
River Eskin
Carn Coire na h-Easgainn 2591
Cnoc Fraing 2444
Geal-charn Mòr 2703
Rothiemurchus Centre
Coignafearn Forest
Elrick Burn
Aberchalder Burn
2658 Carn na Làraiche Maoile
2668 Calpa Mòr
Lynwilg
Coylumbridge
Inverdruie
Loch Alvie
Alvie
Doune
Polchar
MONADHLIATH MOUNTAINS
2665 Carn Sgulain
Carn Coire na Creiche 2702
Burrach Mòr 2686
Glen Markie
Delfour
Loch an Eilein
Loch an Eilein Castle
Duke of Gordon's Monument
Inshriach Nursery
An Suidhe 1775
Leault Working Sheepdogs
Speybank
Loch Gamhna
Duchess of Gordon's Monument
Kincraig
2879 Carn an Fhreiceadain
Abhainn Cro Chlach
Allt Cam Ban
Carn Eilrig 2435
Castle Hill 2366
Raitts Burn
Highland
Allt Mòr
3045 A Chailleach
Carn Ban 3087
Loch Insh
Feshiebridge
Lagganlia
CAIRNGORMS
Farr
Loch Gynack
Carn Dearg
Loch Dubh
Loch na Lairige
Creag an Loin 1788
Kingussie
Lynchat
River Spey
Insh
Inshriach Forest
Loch Mhic Ghille-chaoil
Sgoran Dubh Mòr 3635
4248
BRAERIACH (Braigh Riabhach)
Waltzing Waters
Strone
Clan Macpherson
Newtonmore
Ruthven Barracks
Ruthven
Drumguish
3658 Sgòr Gaoith
Loch Einich
Geal Charn 3036
Allt Madagain
River Calder
Glen Banchor
Highland Folk
Ralia
Creag Dhubh
Marg na Craige 2731
Allt Chomhraig
Carn Ban Mòr 3443
CAIRN TOUL (Carn an t-Sabhail)
Creag nam Bodach 1610
Glentromie Lodge
Lynaberack Lodge
Meall Buidhe 2058
River Tromie
Monadh Mòr 3651
Crathie
Laggan
Balgowan
Glentruim House
Glenfeshie Lodge
Glen Feshie
River Feshie
Mullach Clach a' Bhlàir 3338
River Eidart
Beinn Bhrotain 3795
Glenshero Lodge
Drumgask
Strath Mashie
Catlodge
Cruban Beag 1935
Crubenbeg
Falls of Truim
Etteridge
1944 Garbh-mheall Mòr
Strathmashie House
Feagour
Meallach Mhòr 2521
B A D E N O C H
GLENFESHIE FOREST
Crubenmore Lodge
2813 Carn Dearg Mòr
Loch Caoldair
River Mashie
Allt Bhran
Loch Cuaich
Cuaich
Allt Cuaich
Loch an t-Seilich
Lochan na Doire-uaine
2207 Beinn Eilde
Dalwhinnie
Distillery
Glen Truim
Gaick Lodge
Carn an Fhidhleir or Carn Ealar 3276
An Sgarsoch 3300
Loch Bhrodainn
Gaick Forest
Allt Gharbh Ghaig
Loch Ericht Forest
Meall Cruaidh 2941
3087 Carn na Caim
Uchd a' Chlarsair 2587
2992 Beinn Bhreac
2522 Creagan Mòr
Loch Pattack
Loch an Duin
Loch Mhairc
Tarf Water
Ben Alder Lodge
3005 Geal Charn
A' Bhuidheanach Bheag 3072
Sronphadruig Lodge
Pass of Drumochter
PERTH & KINROSS
BEINN DEARG 3307
2882 Bràigh Sròn Ghorm
Dalnamein Forest
Sròn a' Chleirich 2678
Bruar Water
FOREST OF ATHOLL
3037 Glas Mheall Mòr
2422 An Torc or
Bruar Lodge

151
Grantown-on-Spey
Nethy Bridge
Dulnain Bridge
Tomintoul
Tomnavoulin
Braemar
Crathie
Ballater
Strathdon
Cock Bridge
Corgarff
Gairnshiel Lodge
HILLS OF CROMDALE
LADDER HILLS
CAIRNGORM NATIONAL PARK
GRAMPIAN MOUNTAINS
ABERDEENSHIRE
BRAEMAR
FOREST OF MAR
LOCHNAGAR
GLEN AVON
BEN AVON
BEINN A' BHUIRD
MORAY
AN SOCACH
GLAS MAOL
A95
A939
A93
A944
B976
B9008
B9136
152
159
144

MORAY
GARIOCH
ABERDEENSHIRE
ANGUS
CAIRNGORMS NATIONAL PARK
CORREEN HILLS
HOWE OF ALFORD
PITFICHIE FOREST
HILL OF FARE
Coynachie
Clashindarroch Forest
Clashindarroch
Kirkney
Gartly
Knockandy Hill 1425
Cults
Leith Hall NTS
Kennethmont
Bridgend
Inverharroch
Ardwell
Glenfiddich Forest
Cabrach
Mount of Haddoch 1708
Milton of Lesmore
Tap o' Noth 1848
Belhinnie
Rhynie
Craw Stane
Elrick
Clatt
Duncanston
Leslie
Insch
Kirkton of Culsalmond
Colpy
Lenchie
Largie
Upper Boddam
Picardy Symbol Stone
Knockenbaird
Dunnideer Castle
Kirkton of Rayne
Old Rayne
Pitmachie
Kirkton of Oyne
Oyne
Old Westhall
Kirkton
Auchleven
Chapel of Garioch
Maiden Stone
Bennachie
Bennachie Forest
Bennachie Centre
Millstone Hill
Glenton
Bograxie
Keig
Tullynessle
Syllavethy Gallery
Montgarrie
Alford Valley Railway
Bridge of Alford
Alford
Muir of Alford
Heritage Centre
Grampian Transport
Whitehouse
Monymusk
Arts Centre
Ramstone
Rorandle
Pitfichie
Cairn William
Grantlodge
Whitehill Stone Circle
Tillyfourie
Kirkton
Black Hill 608
Castle Fraser
Ordhead
Sauchen
Correnie Forest
Old Kinnernie
Bankhead
Comers
Tillybirloch
Midmar Kirk Stone Circle
Tornaveen
Drumlasie
Midmar Forest
Coldwells Croft
Whitehaugh Forest
Lord Arthur's Cairn 1699
Craig
St. Mary's Kirk
The Buck 2366
Clova
Lumsden
Mossatt
Kildrummy
Milltown
Rinmore
Belnacraig
Glenbuchat
Kirkton of Glenbuchat
Glenkindie
Sinnahard
Towie
Milltown of Towie
Frosty Hill
Milton of Cushnie
Leochel Cushnie
Muir of Fowlis
Mill of Craigievar
Noah's Ark Country Centre
Craigievar NTS
Correnie Moor
Benaquhame
Pressendye 2031
Corse Castle
Migvie
Coynach
Logie of Coldstone
Tarland
Culsh Earth-House
Craiglich 1562
Lumphanan
Peel Ring of Lumphanan
Milton of Auchinhove
Milton Auchlossan
Torphins
Milltown of Campfield
Mid Beltie
Craigton
Cluny Crichton Castle
Brathens
East Mains
Upper Lochton
Banchory
Arbeadie
Scolty Woodland Park
Deebank
Auchattie
Bridge of Feugh
Scolty Tower
Belts of Collonach
Strachan
Waulkmill
Whitestone
Finzean
Blackhall Forest
Tom's Cairn
Bridge of Canny
Potarch
Kincardine O'Neil
Belwade Farm
Birse
Birsemore
Marywell
Aboyne
Aboyne Castle
Loch of Aboyne
Mortlich 1248
Coull Castle
Tomnaverie Stone Circle
Ordie
Loch Davan
Scar Hill 984
New Kinord Settlement
Loch Kinord
Dinnet
Oakwood
Muir of Dinnet
Burn o' Vat
Cambus o' May
Milton of Tullich
Bridge of Gairn
McEwan Gallery
Ballater
Pannanich
Pannanich Wells
Littlemill
Knock Castle
Birkhall
Pannanich Hill
Millfield
Braeloine
Glen Tanar House
Black Craig 1742
Carnferg 1724
Glencat
Lamahip
Forest of Birse
Ballochan
Craigmahandle
Clachan Yell 2054
Cairn Leuchan
Aucholzie
The Coyles of Muick 1956
Culblean Hill 1983
Peter's Hill 1863
Morven 2861
Cairn Mona Gowan 2456
Lary
Glen Gairn
Glen Fenzie
Strathdon
Bellabeg
Forbestown
Doune of Invernochty
Heugh-head
Tornashean Forest
Craig of Bunzeach
Deskry Water
Breagach Hill 1825
Glenbuchat Lodge
Moss Hill 2159
Ladylea Hill 1998
Craig an Eunan 2073
Round Hill 1872
Cairnbrallan 2029
Hill of Three Stones 2073
Cock Cairn 2387
Hill of Cat
Mount Keen 3080
Fasheilach 2365
Spittal of Glenmuick
Hill of Saughs 2141
Mudlee Bracks 2259
Hill of Cammie 2028
Cock Hill 1960
White Hill
Peter Hill 2025
Mount Battock 2552
Hill of Edendocher 1944
Mount Shade 1662
Bridge of Dye
Tipperweir
Kerloch 1754
Craig of Dalfro
Hill of Fingray 1593
Mount Meluncart 1725
Cairn o' Mount 1492
Drumtochty Forest
Glenfarquhar Lodge
Goyle Hill
Drumtochty Castle
Strath Finella
Glensaugh
Deer Dyke
Strathfinella Hill
Auchenblae
Monawee 2276
Easter Balloch
Black Hill of Mark
Invermark Castle
Kirkton
Tarfside
Cairncross
Glenesk Folk
Millden
Colmeallie Stone Circle
Sturdy Hill
Glen Esk
Carlochy
Lair of Aldararie 2726
Muckle Cairn 2699
Bulg 1986
Water of Aven
Water of Feugh
Water of Tanar
Water of Mark
Water of Tarf
Water of Dye
River Dee
River Don
Water of Buchat
Water of Nochty
A941
A97
A944
A980
A93
A939
A96
A920
B9002
B992
B993
B9119
B9094
B976
B974
B972
B977
B966
151
160
144
145

153
F O R M A R T I N E
NORTH
SEA
Bay of Cruden
Whinnyfold
St. Katherines
Barthol Chapel
Earlsford
Ythanbank
Inverebrie
Folla Rule
Core Hill 804
Cross of Jackston
Wedderlairs
Thornroan
Medieval Tomb
Yonderton
Broomfield
Tulloch
Tarves
Prop of Ythsie
Ellon
Castle
Kinharrachie
Meikle Loch
Denhead
Craigdam
Heritage
South Ythsie Stone Circle
Pitmedden NTS
Esslemont Castle
Kirkton of Logie Buchan
Old Slains Castle
Kirktown of Slains
Collieston
Loanhead Stone Circle
Daviot
Glen Garioch Distillery
Tolquhon
Tolquhon Gallery
Pitmedden
Meikle Tarty
Oldmeldrum
Forvie
Tipperty
Hill of Barra 634
Udny Green
Knockhall Castle
Hackley Head or Forvie Ness
Harlaw 1411
Hattoncrook
Kirkton of Bourtie
Hill of Fiddes
Newburgh
Balhalgardy
Affleck
Whiterashes
Udny Station
Foveran Burn
Foveran
Newburgh Bar
Hillbrae
Carnegie
Tillery
Drums
Brandsbutt Symbol Stone
Bass of Inverurie
Inverurie
550 Beauty Hill
Reisque
Craigie
Port Elphinstone
Kinkell Church
Kinmuck
Newmachar
Burnhervie
Broomend
Clovenstone
Whitecairns
Belhelvie
Balmedie
Mill of Fintray
Cothall
Burgh Muir
Hallforest Castle
River Don
Hatton of Fintray
Dyce Symbol Stones
Corby Loch
Potterton
Kintore
DANGER AREA
Blackdog
Leylodge
Overton
Alky Brae Stone Circle
ABERDEEN (Dyce)
Fowlershill
Blackburn
821 Tyrebagger Hill
Dyce
Letter
Lyne of Skene
Stoneywood
Craibstone
Bankhead
Bridge of Don
Danestone
Woodside
Cruickshank
Hayton
Aberdeen to: Kirkwall (Hatston) 6hrs. Lerwick (Holmsgarth) 12hrs. 30mins
Dunecht
874 Brimmond Hill
Bucksburn
Old Aberdeen
Kirkton of Skene
Northfield
Loch of Skene
Gairloch
Westhill
Sheddocksley
Mastrick
Kittybrewster
ABERDEEN
Mill Power House
Masons Lodge
Kingswells
Summerhill
Footdee
Maritime
Elrick
Garlogie
Carnie
Mannofield
Ferryhill
Torry
Nigg Bay
Redhill
Leuchar Burn
Gordon Highlanders
Ruthrieston
Landerberry
Cullerlie Stone Circle
Easter Ord
Blacktop
Cults
Cullerlie Farm Park
Benthoul
Kincorth
Nigg
Doonies Farm
West Cullerlie
Bieldside
Hardgate
Craigton
Banchory-Devenick
Souter Head
Milltimber
Drum Castle
NTS
Cove Bay
Mains of Drum
Peterculter
Blairs
Crossroads
Charlestown
Coalford
Storybook Glen
River Dee
Kirkton of Maryculter
Myrebird
Drumoak
Park
Hillside
Findon
Crathes Castle
Portlethen
Crathes
Denside
558 Berry Top
Portlethen Village
Kirkton of Durris
Woodlands
Downies
Cammachmore Bay
Cammachmore
Durris Forest
Netherley
Cookney
Windyedge
Newtonhill
Damford
872 Meikle Carewe Hill
Muchalls
Lochton
1241 Cairn-mon-earn
Raedykes Roman Camp
Bridge of Muchalls
Doonie Point
1232 Mongour
Rickarton
New Mains of Ury
Garron Point
Cowie Water
1052 Hill of Trusta
Fetteresso Forest
Cowie
Kirktown of Fetteresso
Stonehaven
Tewel
Tolbooth
Castle Haven
Brae of Glenbervie
Dunnottar
Burnes Memorial
Thornyhive Bay
Drumlithie
Glenbervie
Bruxie Hill 711
Crawton
Milton of Barras
Bridge of Mondynes
Crawton Bay
Catterline
Braidon Bay
Roadside of Kinneff
Fernieflatt
Bridge of Kair
Parkneuk
Todhead Point
A90
A947
A948
A975
A920
A96
A944
A93
A956
A957
A92
B9170
B9005
B999
B9000
B9001
B9003
B993
B977
B979
B994
B987
B997
B9126
B9119
B9125
B9077
B9003
161

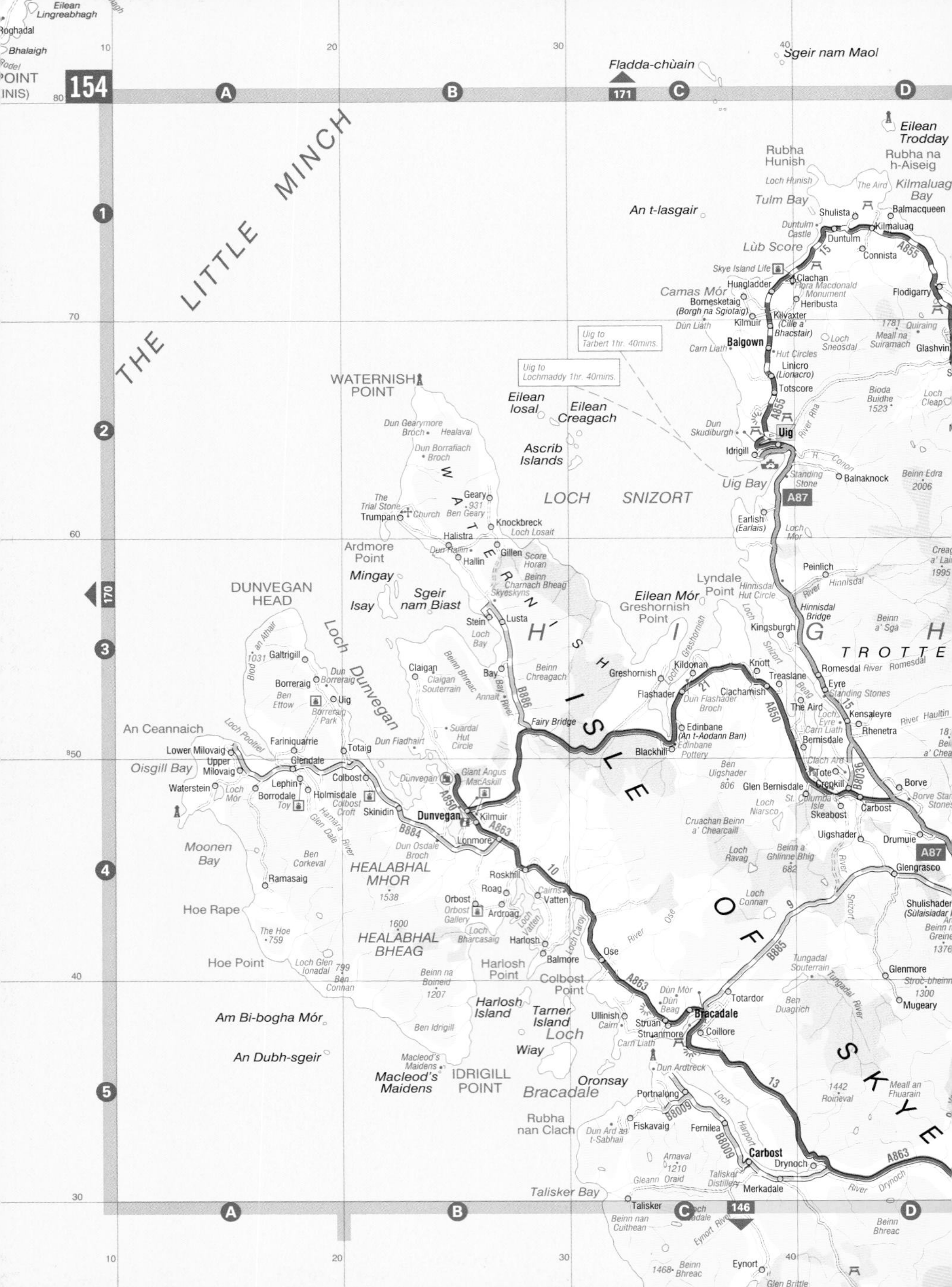
THE LITTLE MINCH
ISLE OF SKYE
WATERNISH
LOCH SNIZORT
Loch Dunvegan
DUNVEGAN HEAD
WATERNISH POINT
HEALABHAL MHOR
HEALABHAL BHEAG
IDRIGILL POINT
Macleod's Maidens
Dunvegan
Uig
Uig Bay
Balgown
Bracadale
Carbost
Kilmuir
Fladda-chùain
Sgeir nam Maol
Eilean Trodday
An t-Iasgair
Ascrib Islands
Eilean Iosal
Eilean Creagach
Isay
Mingay
Sgeir nam Biast
Eilean Mór
Oisgill Bay
Moonen Bay
Hoe Point
Harlosh Island
Tarner Island
Wiay
Oronsay
Loch Bracadale
Talisker Bay
Am Bi-bogha Mór
An Dubh-sgeir
Uig to Tarbert 1hr. 40mins.
Uig to Lochmaddy 1hr. 40mins.
A87
A850
A863
A855
B884
B885
B886
B8009
171
170
146

155
WESTER ROSS
Gairloch
Loch Gairloch
Port Henderson
Longa Island
Sgeir Eirin
Eilean Flodigarry
Staffin Island
Staffin (Stafainn)
Kilt Rock
Sgeir Ghlas
Sgeir na Trian
Rubha na Fearn
Loch Torridon
Lower Diabaig
Upper Diabaig
RONA
Rubha Chuaig
Eilean Garbh
Eilean Tigh
Garbh Eilean
Eilean Fladday
Holm Island
SOUND OF RAASAY
INNER SOUND
RAASAY
Applecross
Applecross Bay
Shieldaig
Shieldaig Island
Inveralligin
Kishorn Island
Plockton
Stromeferry
Loch Carron
CROWLIN ISLANDS
Eilean Mòr
Eilean Beag
Eilean na Bà
Sgeir Dhearg
Longay
SCALPAY
Pabay
Guillamon Island
Kyle of Lochalsh (Caol Loch Ailse)
Portree (Port Righ)
Sconser
Sligachan
GLAMAIG 2542
Eyre Point
Toscaig
Culduie
Camusterrach
Milton
Redpoint
South Erradale
Opinan
Badachro
Charlestown
Poolewe
A832
A896
A890
A87
A855
B8021
B8056
B883
162
156
147

156
A
B
C
D
162
163
155
148
1
2
3
4
5
WESTER ROSS
HIGH
WEST
NORTH
Poolewe
Londubh
Inverewe NTS
Naast
B8057
Loch Bad a' Chreamh
Mhic' ille Riabhaich
Loch na Mòine Buige
Meall na Mèine 820
Loch Ghiuragarstidh
Aird Dubh
Beinn a' Chàisgein Beag 2230
Toll a' Mhadaidh
Strathnasheallag Forest
Loch na Sealga
3484
Loch Toll an Lochain
Fisherfield Forest
Loch Ghiubsachain
Beinn Dearg Mòr 2974
Strath na Sealga
Loch Coire Chaorachain
Dundonnell Forest
Lochan Fada
Lochan Fraoich
Carn a' Bhiorain 1665
Loch Allt Eigin
Dundonnell River
Auchlunachan
Loch an Airceil
Lael Forest
River Broom
Loch an t-Sidheins
1270 Carn Breac Beag
Braemore
Corrieshalloch Gorge
Falls of Measach
Meall an t-Sithe 1971
Braemore Forest
A832
A835
Loch na Curra
River Ewe
Loch Kernsary
Tollie Farm
Loch Tollaidh
Gairloch
Strath
Charlestown
Marine Centre
Loch Shieldaig
B8056
River Kerry
Loch Bad an Sgalaig
Meall an Doirein 1381
Loch na Mòine
Fionn Loch
Lochan Beannach Mòr 2595
Beinn Airigh Charr
Dubh Loch
Lochan na Bearta
2802 Beinn a' Chàisgein Mòr
Loch Beinn Dearg
Beinn a' Chlaidheimh
Lochan Feith Mhic'illean
Fuar Loch Mòr
Loch a' Bhrisidh
Gorm Loch Mòr
Mullach Coire Mhic Fhearchair
2817 Beinn Làir
Letterewe Forest
Letterewe
Loch Garbhaig
Lochan Fada
Loch Maree
Eilean Sùbhainn
Victoria Falls
Talladale
River Sheil
Abhainn a' Gharbh Choire
2424 Groban
Loch an Sgeireach
Loch a' Bhraoin
Loch Toll an Lochain
3276 A' Chailleach
Meall a' Chrasgaidh 3062
Loch a' Mhadaidh
Sgurr Mòr 3637
Allt a' Mhadaidh
Allt a' Choire Mhòir
Fannich Forest
Fannich Lodge
SLIOCH 3215
Abhainn an Fhasaigh
Gleann Tanagaidh
Abhainn a' Chadh Bhuidhe
Loch Gaineamhach
Flowerdale Forest
Bridge of Grudie
River Grudie
Glen Grudie
Strath Lungard
Beinn a' Mhùinidh 2231
Kinlochewe Forest
Heights of Kinlochewe
Baosbheinn 2869
Loch na h-Oidhche
2805 Beinn an Eòin
Shieldaig
2333 Beinn nan Ramh
Lochan Sgeireach
Beinn Bhreac 2031
Loch a' Bhealaich
Beinn Eighe
Kinlochewe
Incheril
Abhainn Bruachaig
Loch na Mòine Mòr
Loch na Mòine Beag
Lochrosque
Fionn Bheinn 3062
Loch na h-Uamhaig
Beinn Alligin 3232
Ruadh-stac Mor 3313
Carn a' Ghlinne 1769
2313 Meall a' Chaorainn
Glen Docherty
Upper Diabaig
Loch Diabaigas Airde
BEINN EIGHE
A' Ghairbhe
Badavanich
Loch a' Chroisg
Achnasheen
River Bran
Alligin Shuas
Inverallig
Rechullin
Torridon Forest
3456
LIATHACH
A896
Loch Clair
Abhainn Dubh
Loch an Fhiarlaid
Upper Loch Torridon
Shieldaig Island
Fasag
Countryside Torridon Centre
Torridon
Deer
Glen Torridon
Loch Bharranch
2566 Sgurr Dubh
Coulin Lodge
Loch Coulin
River Torridon
Carn Beag 1804
Ledgowan
Loch Gowan
Ledgowan Forest
1765 Carn Mhartuin
Balgy
Falls of Balgy
Annat
Lochan Neimhe
Abhainn Thrail
Coulin Forest
River Coulin
A890
Ben-damph Forest
1692
Ben Shieldaig
Loch Damh
Lochan Uaine
Carn Breac 2223
Glen Carron
Loch Sgamhain
Loch Coire a' Bhuic
Loch Cnoc na Mointeich
Scardroy
Loch an Eoin
Beinn Damh 2957
Maol Chean-dearg 3060
Sgorr Ruadh 3142
River Lair
Loch Coire Lair
Glencarron Lodge
3026 Moruisg
Carn Gorm
Glencarron & Glenuig Forest
Creag na h-Iolaire
Glenshieldaig Forest
850
Craig
Achnashellach
Loch Coire an Ruadh-stic
Allt a' Chonais
Achnashellach Forest
Gleann Fhiodhaig
River Meig
Abhainn Dearg
An Gorm-loch
Loch Gaineamhach
Balnacra
Loch Dughaill
Loch Coire
2938
Loch Coultrie
Loch a' Mhuilinn
Coulags
Maoile Lunndaidh 3304
Sgurr a' Gharaidh 2396
Eagan
Sgurr na Feartaig
Sgurr a' Chaorachain 3455
River Carron
Glas Bheinn 2332
New Kelso
Creag a' Chaorainn
Beinn Tharsuinn
Tullich
Smithy Heritage Centre
Strathcarron
West Monar Forest
Loch Mhuilich
East Monar Forest
Loch Coire nan Arr
Kirkton
Achintee
Loch nan Creadha
Loch an Laoigh
Loch Monar
Monar Lodge
Kishorn
Carn Geuradainn 1950
Lurg Mhòr 3234
An Gead Loch
Ardarroch
Lochcarron
Attadale
Loch Kishorn
Achintraid
Bendronaig Lodge
Loch Calavie
Uisge Misgeach
Attadale Forest
Beinn Dronaig
Loch an Tachdaich
Meallan Buidhe
Bad a' Chreamha 1296
Lochcarron Weavers
Loch Cruoshie
Lochan Gobhlach
An Cruachan 2312
Stromemore
Strome NTS
Ardnarff
Carn nan Iomairean
Loch an Iasaich
Carn na Sean-luibe
Sgurr na Lapaich 3775
Ardaneaskan
Stromeferry
River Ling
Plockton
An Riabhachan 3696
Highland Farm
Craig
Loch nan Gillean
Achmore
3508
Glencannich Forest
Loch Lundie
Loch na Leitire
Loch na h-Onaich
Sgùman Coinntich 2883
Killilan Forest
2949 Aonach Buidhe
Loch Achaidh na h-Inich
Gleann Udalain
Allt Gleann Udalain
Loch Mhoicean
Loch Mullardoch
Sallachy
Killilan
Glen Cannich
Balmacara Estate
Auchtertyre Hill
Loch Beinn a' Mheadhoin
Loch Long
Loch nan Ealachan
Allt na Doire Gairbhe
Toll Creagach 3457
Auchtertyre
Conchra
Camas-luinie
Glen Elchaig
Carnach
West Benula Forest
Coire Lochan
Tom a' Choinich 3646
Balmacara
A87
Bundalloch
Carndu
Loch Long
Loch Leitreach
Lochalsh Woodland NTS
Kirkton
Nostie
Ardelve
Dornie
Loch nan Eun
River Elchaig
Falls of Glomach
Carn Eighe 3880
Loch Alsh

EASTER ROSS
HIGHLANDS
LAND
STRATHCONON
FOREST
CROMARTY
THE AIRD
INVERNESS
Beinn Dearg 3547
Loch Prille
Tollomuick Forest
Deanich Lodge
Beinn Tharsuinn 2330
Crom Loch
Diebidale Forest
Diebidale River
Glen Diebidale
Carn Chuinneag 2750
Meall Bhenneit 1744
Loch Muigh-bhlàraidh
Beinn a' Chaisteil 2404
Loch a' Choire Ghrènda
Loch Fèith nan Cleireach
Gorm Loch
Carn Cas nan Gabhar 1976
Black Water
Beinn Tharsuinn 2270
Loch Coire Làir
Allt Mhucarnaich
Meall Leacachain 2028
Meall a' Ghrianain 2531
Loch a' Chaorainn
Kildermorie Forest
Kildermorie Lodge
Loch Bad a' Bhathaich
Braeantra
Strath Rusdale
Loch Magharaidh
Loch nan Amhaichean
Inchbae Forest
Strathvaich Forest
Loch Vaich
Loch a' Gharbhrain
Loch Droma
Loch Sgeireach
Beinn nan Eun 2436
Carn nan Con Ruadha 2206
Strathrannoch
Loch Glascarnoch
Strathvaich Lodge
Strath Vaich
Strath Rannoch
Wyvis Lodge
Loch Glass
Meall Mòr 2421
Loch Morie
Boath
Ardross
Strathy
Loanreoch
Easter Ardross
River Averon
Beinn Liath Mhòr a' Ghiubhais Li 2464
Aultguish Inn
A835
Loch Bealach Cùlaidh
2095 Carn Mòr
Queen's Cairn 2109
Culzie Lodge
Bendeallt 1850
Cnoc Ceislein 1716
Fyrish Monument
Contullich
Crosshill
Carn Gorm
Loch Gorm
Kinlochluichart Forest
Beinn Dearg 2230
Inchbae Lodge
Carn na Dubh Choille 1571
Garbat Forest
BEN WYVIS 3433
Loch a' Choire Mhòir
Meall na Drochaide
Eileanach Lodge
Glen Glass
B9176
Meall Mhic Iomhair 1984
Corriemoillie Forest
3015 Coilleachan
Black Water
Allt nan Caorach
Black Rock Gorge
Alness Bay
Aultdearg
Loch Bad Leabhraidh
Achnaclerach
Meall na Speireig
River Glass
Swordale
Evanton
Drummond
B817
A9
An Cabar 1832
Loch na Curra
River Grudie
Corriemoillie
Strathgarve Forest
2497 Little Wyvis
Cloch Mhòr 1580
Strath Sgitheach
Clach Liath Forest
Storehouse of Foulis
Ardullie
Cullicudden
A832
Gorstan
Carn Gorm
Grudie
Lochluichart
Loch Luichart
Achanalt
Loch Achanalt
Loch a' Chuilinn
Garve
Heights of Brae
Heights of Fodderty
Mountgerald
A862
Findon Mains
Kinbeachie
Culbo
B9169
Loch Garve
Bottacks
Auchterneed
Fodderty
Upper Dochcarty
Castle Leod
Eagle Stone
Castle Doocot
DANGER AREA
Braefindon
Loch Culbokie
Culbokie
Loch Bhad Ghaineamhaich
1904 Sgurr Marcasaidh
Rogie Falls
A835
Tarvie
Strathpeffer
A834
Hill Fort
Dingwall
Knockfarrel
Highland Childhood
Glenmarksie
Craigdarroch
Lochussie
Alcaig
158
Little Scatwell
Loch Achilty
Contin
Torrachilty Wood
Jamestown
Loch Ussie
Tollie
Maryburgh
B9163
Duncanston
Knockbain
Sgurr a' Mhuilinn 2883
Milton
Porin
Achlorachan
Bridgend
Loch Meig
Scatwell
Conon Bridge
Corntown
Easter Kinkell
River Meig
Strathconon
River Conon
Loch Achonachie
Marybank
A832
Arcan
A835
Belmaduthy
Gleann Meinich
1936 Carn na Cloiche Mòire
Muir of Fairburn
Urray
A862
Newmore
Rootfield
Tore
Munlochy
Loch Aradaidh
Balvaird
Drynie Park
Kilcoy
B9161
Carn na Coinnich 2209
Chapelton
Arpafeelie
Bogallan
Inverchoran
Loch an Spàrdain
Cabaan Forest
Glen Ord Distillery
Urray Forest
Muir of Tarradale
Orrin Reservoir
River Orrin
Muir of Ord
Redcastle
Artafallie
Ardnagrask
Milton
Craigrory
Glen Orrin
Corriehallie Forest
Allt Goibhre
Loch nan Eun
Gleann Goibhre
Cnoc Eille Mòr
Corry of Ardnagrask
Rheindown
Windhill
Charlestown
Dolphin & Seal Centre
Beauly Firth
River Orrin
Loch nam Bonnach
Dunmore
Ruisaurie
Ruilick
Priory
South Kessock
Am Fiar-loch
An Gorm-loch
Drumindorsair
Beauly
Kirkhill
B9164
A862
Farley
Broallan
Balblair
Lentran
Clachnaharry
Bunchrew
Meallan Buidhe 2505
Erchless Forest
Breakachy
Drumchardine
Leachkin
Sgurr a' Choire Ghlais 3554
3254 Sgurr na Ruaidhe
Lochan Fada
2827 Beinn a' Bha'ach Ard
Kilmorack
Fanellan
Newtonhill
Balchraggan
Neaty Burn
A831
Crask of Aigas
Kiltarlity
Belladrum
AIRD
An Leacainn 1358
Carn Bàn
Erchless Castle
Leishmore
Craigdhu
Hughton
Culburnie
South Clunes
Dochgarroch
Struy
Craobhnaclag
Eskadale
Camault Muir
Glaichbea
Braulen Lodge
River Farrar
Culligran Falls
Caledonian Canal
River Ness
Scaniport
Glen Strathfarrar
Loch Beannacharan
Struy Forest
Boblainy Forest
Ardendrain
Lochend
B862
Loch a' Mhuillidh
2676 Sgorr na Diollaid
Loch Neaty
Cragganvallie
1642 Carn a' Bhodaich
Drumashie Moor
Carn Gorm 2218
Loch Garbh Iolachan
Loch Bruicheach
1401 Meall nan Caorach
Carn Mòr 1497
Lochan an Tairt
Glen Convinth
A82
Loch Ashie
Glassburn
Strathglass
Abriachan
Dores
Muchrachd
River Cannich
Balmore Forest
A831
A833
Liatrie
Loch Gorm
Balnagrantach
Meall na h-Eilrig 1526
Ashie Moor
Cannich
River Glass
Nessieland Castle Monster Centre
Loch Ness Exhibition
Loch Duntelchaig
Loch Bealbhanach
Buntait
Balbeg
Balnaglaic
Rychraggan
Polmaily
Achmony
B852
Corrimony
Braefield
Glen Urquhart
Drumnadrochit
Stac na Cathaig 1463
Kerrow
Corrimony Chambered Cairn
Balnain
149
Loch Meiklie
Milton
River Enrick
Drum Farm Centre
Borlum
Urquhart Bay
Tom Bailgeann 1522
Lewiston
Strone
Urquhart
River Affric
Tomich
Suidhe Ghuirmain 1896
River Enrick
Coiltie
Divach
Falls of Divach
Upper Lenie
John Cobb Mem.
Lower Lenie
Loch Ceo Glais
Loch Ruthven
Torness
River Nairn
A82
LOCH NESS
Aberarder
164

Edderton
Portmahomack
Bindal
Tarbat Discovery Centre
Seafield
Rockfield
Glenmorangie Distillery
Morangie
Tarlogie
DANGER AREA
Loch Muigh-bhlàraidh
Cnoc Muigh-bhlàraidh
Aultnamain Inn
Inver
Lower Arboll
Tarrel
Tain
Hilton
Toulvaddie
Tain Through Time
Morangie Forest
Loch Eye
Lower Pitkerrie
Geanies
Beinn Tharsuinn
2270
Cnoc an t-Sabhail
1243
Loch Sheilah
Glen Aldie
Hill of Fearn
Fearn
Tullich
Hilton of Cadboll Chapel
Hilton of Cadboll
Balintore
Shandwick
Braeantra
Strath Rusdale
Black Water
Strath Rory
Hartmount
Lamington
Marybank
Brenachie
Scotsburn
Pitmaduthy
Kildary
Arabella
Strathy
Loanreoch
Stittenham
Cnoc Corr Guinie
1301
Kinrive Hill
1056
Kinkhrive
Ardross Forest
Easter Ardross
Ardross
Boath
River Averon
Tullich Muir
Milton
Ankerville
Wester Rarichie
Port an Righ
Dalnavie
Badachonacher
Kilmuir
Nigg Bay
Pitcalnie
Bayfield Loch
Hill of Nigg
Nigg
Achandunie
Newmore
Coillemore
Delny
Barbaraville
Polio
Nonikiln
Rhicullen
Broomhill
Balintraid
Bendeallt
1850
Cnoc Ceislein
1716
Fyrish Monument
Contullich
Achnagarron
Tomich
Balnabruaich
Crosshills
Obsdale
Rosskeen
Saltburn
Balnapaling
Nigg Ferry
Castlecraig
Alness
Invergordon
Dalmore
Distillery
FIRTH
Cromarty
Hugh Miller NTS
Blue Head
Sutors of Cromarty
Courthouse
McFarquhar's Cave
Black Rock Gorge
Alness Bay
Ferryton
Balblair
Cromarty Bay
Udale Bay
Newton
Swordale
Evanton
Drummond
Alnessferry
Resolis
Jemimaville
Davidston
CROMARTY
Cullicudden
Newmills
Springfield
Mount High
Muirton
Clach Liath Forest
Ardullie
Easter Brae
Wester Brae
Millbuie Forest
Mountgerald
Findon Mains
Kinbeachie
Whitebog
Culbo
Braefindon
Mount Eagle
Whiteness Head
Castle Doocot
DANGER AREA
Loch Culbokie
Culbokie
BLACK
ISLE
Findon Forest
Killen
Groam House
Rosemarkie
Fortrose
Rosemarkie Bay
DANGER AREA
MORAY
FIRTH
Cran Loch
Loch Loy
Alcaig
Duncanston
Knockbain
Cathedral
Fort George
NAIRN
Kingsteps
Druim
Tradespark
Corntown
Easter Kinkell
Belmaduthy
Easter Suddie
Avoch
Chanonry Point
Ardersier
Househill
Auldearn
Blackhills
Connage Highland Dairy
Moss-side
Avoch Bay
Gollanfield
Muir of the Clans
Foynesfield
Rootfield
Tore
Munlochy
Munlochy Bay
Milton of Gollanfield
Lochside
Loch Flemington
Brackla
Geddes
Laiken Forest
Kilcoy
Drynie Park
Fisherton
INVERNESS
Regoul
Piperhill
Arpafeelie
Black Isle Wildlife Park
Bogallan
Kilmuir
Alturlie Point
Clephanton
Muir of Arradale
Redcastle
Artafallie
Drumsmittal
Tornagrain
Cawdor
Culcharry
Urchany
Littlemill
Milton
Craigrory
Craigton
Lifeboat Station
Dalcross
Croy
Kilravock
Newton
Beauly Firth
Charlestown
Dolphin & Seal Centre
North Kessock
Cantraywood
Cantray
Easter Galcantray
Wester Galcantray
Balloch
Redburn
Loch Belivat
Ardclach Bell Tower
South Kessock
Clunas
Kirkhill
Clachnaharry
Culloden
Feabuie
Assich Forest
Cantraybruich
Clunas Reservoir
Bunchrew
Craig Phadrig
Leachkin
Lentran
Well of the Dead
Smithton
Newlands
Memorial Cairn NTS
Ferness
Glenferness Mains
Drumchardine
Newtonhill
INVERNESS
Westhill
Culcabock
Culloden 1746 NTS
Clava Cairns
Saddle Hill
1227
Floral Hall
Lochardil
HIGHLAND
Carn a' Chrasgie
James Pringle Weavers
AIRD
An Leacainn
1358
Loch Kirkaldy
Caledonian Canal
South Clunes
Dochgarroch
Beinn Bhuidhe Mhòr
1799
Carn Sgumain
1370
River Ness
Scaniport
Essich
Drummossie Muir
Daviot
Craggiemore
Carn nan Tri-tighearnan
2016
Drynachan Lodge
Lochend
1675
Beinn Bhreac
Strath Dores
Drumashie Moor
Gask Ring Cairn
Moy Burn
Meall a' Bhreacraibh
1809
River Findhorn
Rhilean Burn
Tomlachan Burn
Lochindorb
Lochindorb Lodge
Leonach Burn
1642
Carn a' Bhodaich
Meall Mòr
1611
Loch Ashie
Creag a' Chlachain
1196
Inverarnie
Moy
Loch Moy
Castle
Funtack Burn
Abriachan
Dores
Dunlichity Lodge
Ashie Moor
Farr
Ruthven
Loch Duntelchaig
2022
Carn na h-Easgainn
2076
Carn an t-Sean-liathanaich
Strathnairn Forest
Stac na Cathaig
1463
Loch Farr
Balvraid Lodge
Loch a' Choire
Tom Baigeann
1522
Brin Herb Nursery
Strathnairn
Distillery
Tomatin
Corrybrough
Raigbeg
2057
Carn a' Choire Mhòir
2162
Carn Glas-choire
Loch Ceo Glais
Beinn Bhreac
1969
Findhorn Bridge
Torness
Loch Ruthven
River Nairn
East Croachy
Aberarder
Lochindorb Lodge
Loch Sidh
Newlands of Fleenas Wood
Muckle
164
165
150
157
A9
A96
A82
A835
A862
A832
A836
A939
B9176
B817
B9174
B9165
B9166
B9175
B9163
B9169
B9160
B9161
B9006
B9092
B9091
B9090
B9101
B9039
B8082
B862
B861
B851
B852
B9177
B9154
B9007
A
B
C
D
1
2
3
4
5

Branderburgh
Lossiemouth
Burghead
Hopeman
Cummingstown
Burghead Bay
Spey Bay
Findhorn
Kinloss
Findhorn Bay
Culbin Forest
Elgin
Bishopmill
New Elgin
Ashgrove
Lhanbryde
Urquhart
Kingston
Garmouth
Mosstodloch
Fochabers
FORRES
Rafford
Dallas
Rothes
Craigellachie
Archiestown
Charlestown of Aberlour
Dufftown
MORAY
Grantown-on-Spey
Tomnavoulin
Glenlivet
Bridge of Avon
BEN RINNES
2759
Cromdale
Dava
Knockando
Mulben
Orton
Coleburn
Longmorn
Alves
Duffus
Lochhill
A96
A95
A941
A940
A939
A920
B9102
B9009
B9008
B9010
B9015
B9103
B9040
B9012
B9013
B9089
B9011
B9135
B9136
B9137
B9138
B9154
B9104
B9014

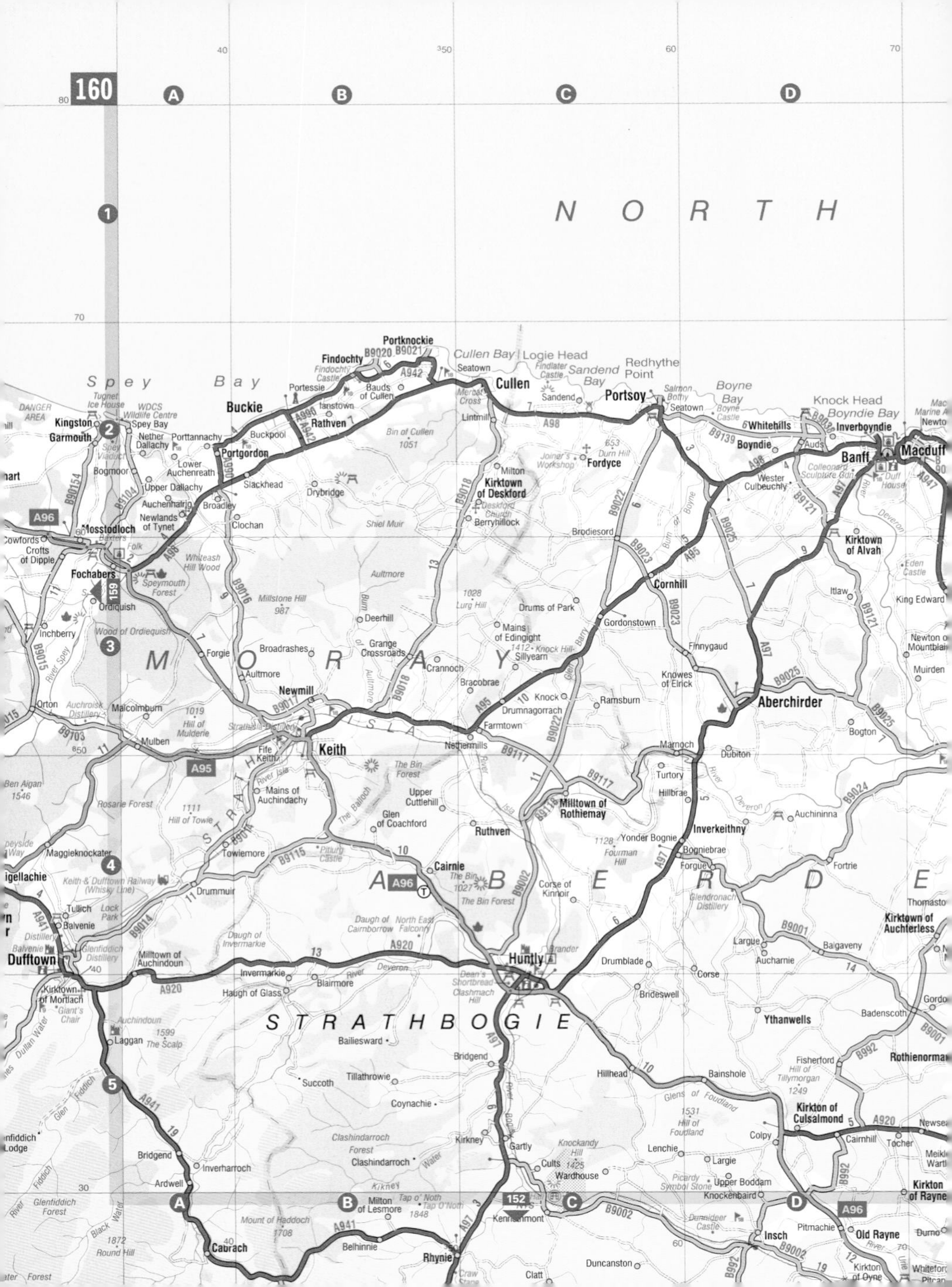

SEA
Troup Head
Pennan Head
Quarry Head
Head of Garness
Gamrie Bay
Rosehearty
Sandhaven
Pittulie
Kinnaird Head
Scottish Lighthouses
Broadsea
Fraserburgh
Fraserburgh Bay
Cairnbulg Point
Cairnbulg
Inverallochy
Charlestown
St. Combs
Inzie Head
Gardenstown
New Aberdour
Pennan
Crovie
Dubford
Longmanhill
New Pitsligo
Strichen
New Leeds
Crimond
Rattray Head
Loch of Strathbeg
New Byth
Garmond
Fintry
Cuminestown
Turriff
BUCHAN
Maud
New Deer
Old Deer
Mintlaw
Longside
St. Fergus
Buchanhaven
Peterhead
Keith Inch
Burnhaven
Boddam
Fetterangus
Stuartfield
Auchnagatt
ENSHIRE
Fyvie
Woodhead
Methlick
Tarves
Ellon
Hatton
Cruden Bay
Port Erroll
Bay of Cruden
Collieston
Oldmeldrum
Pitmedden
Daviot
FORMARTINE
Udny Green
Hackley Head or Forvie Ness
A90
A98
A950
A952
A981
A947
A948
A920
A975
Rora
Crimonmogate
Dunshillock
Milton Coldwells
Kinknockie
Clola
Whinnyfold
153

Seisiadar
Camas Eilean Ghlais
Reiff
Eilean Mullagrach
Isle Rist
Glas-leac Mór
Tanera Beg
Ullapool to Stornoway 2hrs. 40mins.
Glas-leac Beag
Eilean Dubh
Priest Island
Bottle Island
Greenstone Point
Rubha Beag
Loch na Doire Duinne
Opinan
Mellon Udrigle
Loch nan Clachan Geala
Loch a' Choire
Slaggan Bay
Loch an t-Slagain
Achgarve
Gruinard Island
Gruinard Bay
Mungasdale
Gruinard House
Eilean Furadh Mór
Rubha nan Sasan
513
Beinn Dearg Mhor
Mellon Charles
Laide
First Coast
Sand
Second Coast
Ormiscaig
Rubha Reidh
Camas Mór
Loch an Draing
Cove
Aultbea
Drumchork
An Cuaidh 972
Loch Airigh an Eilein
Mellangaun
Isle of Ewe
Beinn Dearg Bad Chailleach 897
Loch Sguod
Loch a' Bhaid-luachraich
Loch Fada
Melvaig
Aultgrishan
Midtown
Brae
Loch Ewe
Seana Chamas
Cnoc Breac 962
Peterburn
Naast
Loch Mhic' ille Riabhaich
Loch na Moine Buige
Aird Dubh
Inverewe NTS
Meall na Méine 820
Loch Ghiuragarstidh
Bad Bog
Port Erradale
North Erradale
River Sand
Loch nan Liagh
Loch Bad a' Chreamh
Londubh
Poolewe
River Ewe
Big Sand
Caolas Beag
Longa Island
Loch na Curra
Loch Kernsary
Loch na Moine
Lonemore
Mial
Strath
Tollie Farm
Loch Tollaidh
Smithstown
Heritage
Gairloch
Loch Gairloch
Meall an Doirein
Lochan Beannach Mór 2595
Little Gruinard River
Fionn Loch
A832
B8057
B8021
171
155

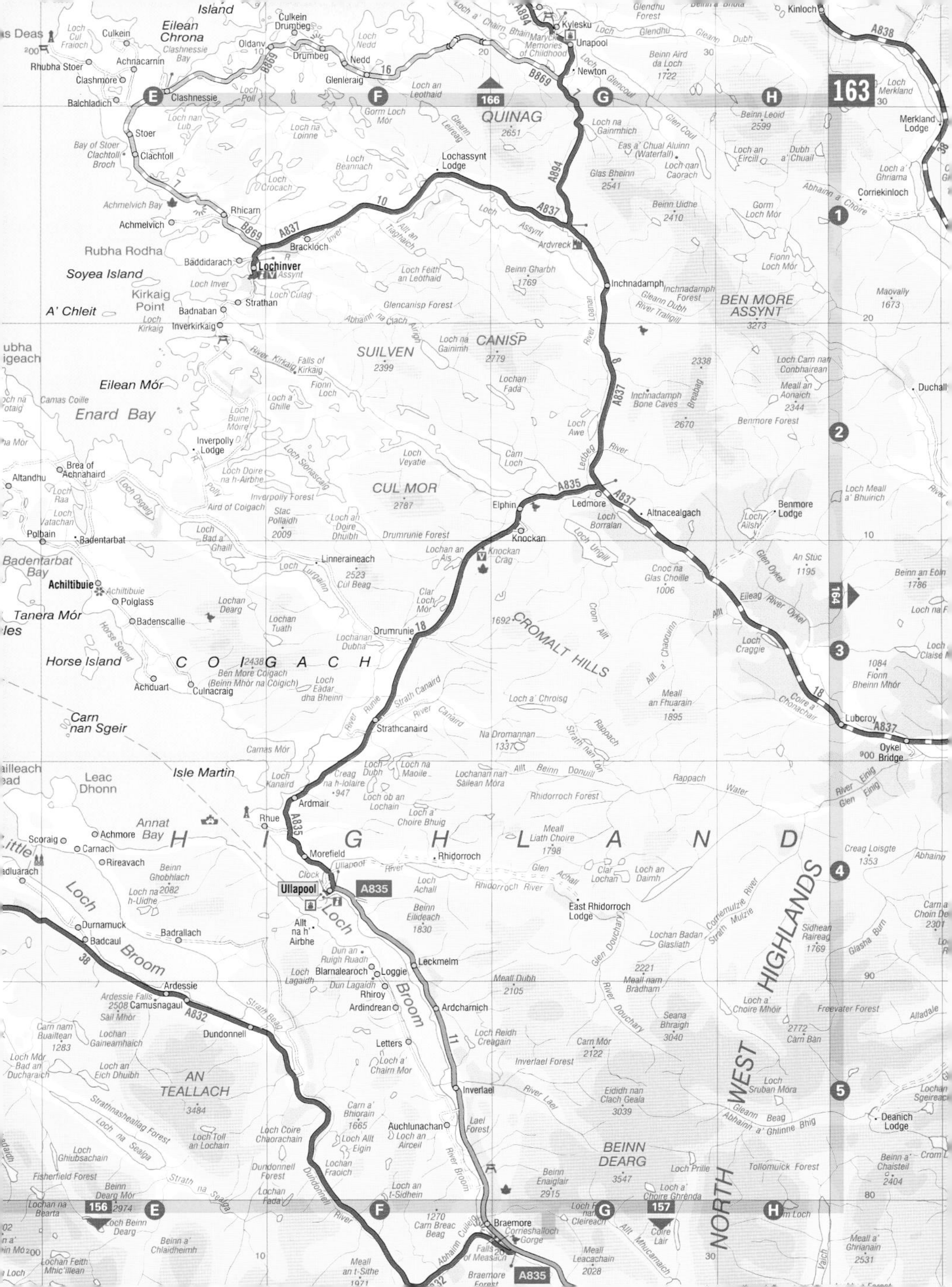
163
164
166
156
157
Lochinver
Ullapool
Achiltibuie
Kylesku
Unapool
Newton
Inchnadamph
Elphin
Ledmore
Altnacealgach
Knockan
Drumrunie
Strathcanaird
Ardmair
Rhue
Morefield
Leckmelm
Ardcharnich
Inverlael
Braemore
Dundonnell
Ardessie
Badcaul
Dundonnell
Oykel Bridge
Lubcroy
Stoer
Clachtoll
Clashnessie
Drumbeg
Nedd
Glenleraig
Culkein
Oldany
Achmelvich
Rhicarn
Brackloch
Strathan
Badnaban
Inverkirkaig
Polbain
Badentarbat
Polglass
Badenscallie
Achduart
Culnacraig
Scoraig
Achmore
Carnach
Rireavach
Durnamuck
Badrallach
Camusnagaul
Letters
Auchlunachan
Loggie
Rhiroy
Ardindrean
Blarnalearoch
Rhidorroch
East Rhidorroch Lodge
Deanich Lodge
Benmore Lodge
Merkland Lodge
Corriekinloch
Kinloch
Lochassynt Lodge
Inverpolly Lodge
Linneraineach
Altandhu
QUINAG
CANISP
SUILVEN
CUL MOR
BEN MORE ASSYNT
CROMALT HILLS
COIGACH
HIGHLAND
NORTH WEST HIGHLANDS
AN TEALLACH
BEINN DEARG
Loch Broom
Enard Bay
Isle Martin
Horse Island
Tanera Mór
Eilean Mór
Soyea Island
Eilean Chrona
A837
A835
A894
A832
A838
B869

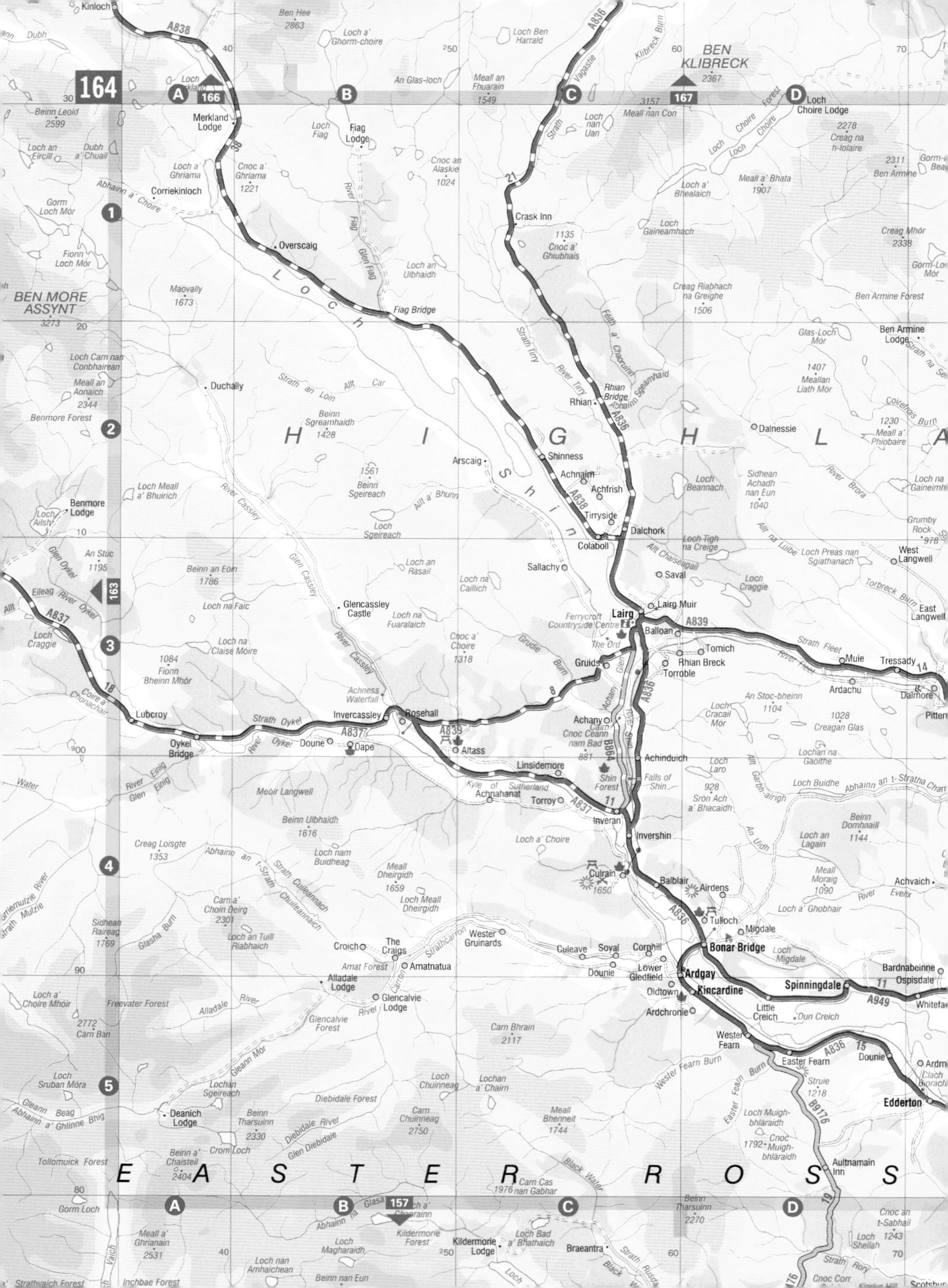
Kinloch
A838
Ben Hee
2863
Loch a' Ghorm-choire
Loch Ben Harrald
A836
Klibreck Burn
BEN KLIBRECK
2367
Loch
A
166
B
An Glas-loch
Meall an Fhuarain
1549
C
Vagastie
167
3157 Meall nan Con
D
Loch Choire Lodge
Beinn Leoid
2599
Merkland Lodge
Loch Fiag
Fiag Lodge
Strath
Loch nan Uan
Loch Choire Forest
2278
Creag na h-Iolaire
Loch an Eircill
Dubh Loch Chuail
Loch a' Ghriama
Cnoc a' Ghriama
1221
Cnoc an Alaskie
1024
2311
Ben Armine
Corriekinloch
Abhainn a' Choire
Loch a' Bhealaich
Meall a' Bhata
1907
Gorm Loch Mòr
Crask Inn
Loch Gaineamhach
Overscaig
1135
Cnoc a' Ghiubhais
Creag Mhòr
2338
Fionn Loch Mòr
Glen Fiag
Loch an Ulbhaidh
Gorm-Loch Mòr
Maovally
1673
Creag Riabhach na Greighe
1506
BEN MORE ASSYNT
3273
Loch Shin
Fiag Bridge
Ben Armine Forest
Strath Tirry
Feith a' Chaoruinn
Glas-Loch Mòr
Ben Armine Lodge
Loch Carn nan Conbhairean
Meall an Aonaich
2344
Duchally
Strath an Loin
Allt Car
River Tirry
Abhainn Sgeamhaid
1407
Meallan Liath Mòr
Rhian Bridge
Rhian
Coirefrois Burn
Benmore Forest
Beinn Sgreamhaidh
1428
1230
Meall a' Phiobaire
Dalnessie
H I G H L A
Arscaig
Shinness
Achnairn
Achfrish
Loch Beannach
Sidhean Achadh nan Eun
1040
River Brora
Loch na Gaineimh
1561
Beinn Sgeireach
Allt a' Bhunn
Loch Meall a' Bhuirich
River Cassley
Benmore Lodge
Loch Ailsh
Tirryside
Dalchork
Colaboll
Grumby Rock
976
Loch Sgeireach
Loch Tigh na Creige
Allt na Luibe
Loch Preas nan Sgiathanach
West Langwell
An Stùc
1195
Glen Oykel
Loch an Rasail
Loch na Caillich
Sallachy
Allt Chaiseagail
Saval
Beinn an Eoin
1786
163
Glen Cassley
Loch Craggie
Torbreck Burn
Eileag
River Oykel
Loch na Faic
Glencassley Castle
Loch na Fuaralaich
Lairg
Lairg Muir
East Langwell
A837
Ferrycroft Countryside Centre
Balloan
A839
Loch Craggie
Cnoc a' Choire
1318
The Ord
Tomich
Strath Fleet
Loch na Claise Mòire
River Cassley
Grudie Burn
Gruids
Rhian Breck
Torroble
River Fleet
Muie
Tressady
1084
Fionn Bheinn Mhòr
Achany Glen
A836
Ardachu
Dalmore
Coire a' Chonachair
Achness Waterfall
Loch Cracail Mòr
An Stoc-bheinn
1104
1028
Creagan Glas
Pitten
Lubcroy
Strath Oykel
Invercassley
Rosehall
Achany
Cnoc Ceann nam Bad
881
River Shin
Oykel Bridge
Doune
Oape
Altass
B864
Achinduich
Lochan na Gaoithe
Loch Laro
Allt Garbh-airigh
River Einig
Glen Einig
Linsidemore
Shin Forest
Falls of Shin
Loch Buidhe
Abhainn an t-Stratha Charnaig
Water
Meoir Langwell
Kyle of Sutherland
Achnahanat
Torroy
928
Sròn Ach a' Bhacaidh
Beinn Ulbhaidh
1616
Inveran
Invershin
Beinn Domhnaill
1144
Loch an Lagain
Creag Loisgte
1353
Abhainn an t-Strath
Loch nam Buidheag
Loch a' Choire
An Liath
Strath Cuileannach
Meall Dheirgidh
1659
Culrain
1650
Balblair
Airdens
Meall Moraig
1090
Achvaich
River Evelix
Loch Meall Dheirgidh
Carn a' Choin Deirg
2301
Loch a' Ghobhair
Sidhean Raireag
1769
Glasha Burn
Loch an Tuill Riabhaich
Tulloch
Migdale
Croich
The Craigs
Strathcarron
Wester Gruinards
Culeave
Soyal
Cornhill
Bonar Bridge
Loch Migdale
Amat Forest
Amatnatua
River Carron
Dounie
Lower Gledfield
Ardgay
Spinningdale
Bardnabeinne
Ospisdale
Alladale Lodge
Alladale River
Kincardine
Oldtown
A949
Whitefa
Loch a' Choire Mhòir
Freevater Forest
Glencalvie Lodge
Ardchronie
Little Creich
Dun Creich
2772
Càrn Bàn
Glencalvie Forest
Carn Bhrain
2117
Wester Fearn
Easter Fearn
Dounie
Loch Sruban Mòra
Gleann Mòr
Loch Chuinneag
Lochan a' Chairn
Wester Fearn Burn
Easter Fearn Burn
Struie
1218
Ardm
Clach Biorach
Gleann Beag
Lochan Sgeireach
Diebidale Forest
Edderton
Abhainn a' Ghlinne Bhig
Deanich Lodge
Beinn Tharsuinn
2330
Carn Chuinneag
2750
Meall Bhenneit
1744
Loch Muigh-bhlàraidh
Cnoc Muigh-bhlàraidh
1792
B9176
Diebidale River
Glen Diebidale
Crom Loch
Tollomuick Forest
Beinn a' Chaisteil
2404
Black Water
Aultnamain Inn
E A S T E R R O S S
Carn Cas nan Gabhar
1976
Gorm Loch
157
Loch a' Chaorainn
Beinn Tharsuinn
2270
Cnoc an t-Sabhail
1243
Abhainn na Glasa
Meall a' Ghrianain
2531
Loch Magharaidh
Kildermorie Forest
Kildermorie Lodge
Loch Bad a' Bhathaich
Braeantra
Loch Sheilah
Loch nan Amhaichean
Strath Rusdale
Strath Rory
Strathvaich Forest
Inchbae Forest
Beinn nan Eun
Cnoc Corr
Scotsbur

Badanloch
Badanloch Lodge
Loch an Alltan Fhearna
Achentoul
Loch Achnamoine
River Helmsdale
B871
Kinbrace
Loch na Gaineimh
A897
Cnoc Loch Mhadadh 1040
Feith Gaineimh Mhor
Gobernuisgeach
Dunbeath Water
Badnag
Berriedale Water
Braemore
Cnoc Coire na Fearna 1434
168
E
F
G
H
Balnabruich
Knockally
1423 Cnoc an Liath-bhaid Mhòir
Allt nan Achaidhean
Abhainn na Frithe
Kinbrace Burn
Cnoc an Eireannaich 1699
Morven 2313
Maiden Pap 1587
Meall na Caorach 1301
Scaraben 2055
Ramscraigs
Borgue
Borrobol Forest
Altanduin
Borrobol Lodge
Suisgill Burn
Wag
Loch Ascaig
1194 Cnoc na Breun-choille
Allt an Duin
1271 Creag nam Fiadh
Kildonan Burn
Creag Scalabsdale 1819
Langwell Forest
Aultibea
Newport
Langwell Water
Berriedale
Berriedale Castle
Kildonan
Beinn Dubhain 1365
Cnoc na Maoile 1315
A9
Boch-ailean
River Skinsdale
Strath Skinsdale
Tuarie Burn
Craggie
River Helmsdale
Ousdale
Badbea Clearance Village
Ousdale Broch
Torrish
Craggie Water
Strath of Kildonan or Strath Ullie
Cnoc Meadhonach 1134
1338 Eldrable Hill
Marrel
Navidale
Ord Point
Meallan Liath Beag 1512
Beinn Dhorain 2060
West Helmsdale
East Helmsdale
Helmsdale
Timespan
Gartymore
Portgower
N
D
Black Water
Allt Ach a' Bhathaich
Allt a' Mhuilinn
Allt Smeorail
Glen Sletdale
Glen Loth
Cnoc Leamhnachd 961
Balnacoil
Col-bheinn 1765
Lothmore
Kilmote
Crackaig
Lothbeg
River Brora
Gordonbush
Lothbeg Point
Dalreavoch
1063 Kilbraur Hill
Loch an Tubairnaich
Loch Brora
Rhilochan
Scottarie Burn
Achrimsdale
Knockarthur
Ben Horn 1706
Loch Horn
East Clyne
West Clyne
Dalchalm
Achvoan
Distillery
Clynelish
Cagar Feosaig 1239
Badnellan
Heritage Centre
Brora
Rogart
Doll
Beinn Lunndaidh 1463
Golspie Burn
Backies
Uppat
NORTH
Beinn a' Bhragaidh 1293
Duke of Sutherland Monument
Orcadian Stone Co.
Carn Liath
Morvich
Dunrobin
A839
River Fleet
Mound Rock
Kirkton
Little Torboll
Golspie
SEA
A9
Loch Laoigh
Loch Fleet
Littleferry
Skelbo
Skelbo Street
Badninish
Lednabirichen
Embo
Poles
Birichen
Fleuchary
Embo Street
Evelix
B9168
A949
Pitgrudy
Cathedral
Camore
Dornoch
Historylinks
Littletown
Lonemore
Loch Evelix
Dornoch
TARBAT NESS
DORNOCH FIRTH
Wilkhaven
Glenmorangie Distillery
DANGER AREA
Portmahomack
Bindal
Tarbat Discovery Centre
Tarlogie
Morangie
B9174
Seafield
Rockfield
Inver
Lower Arboll
B9165
Tarrel
Tain
Toulvaddie
Tain Through Time
Lochslin
Hilton
Loch Eye
Lower Pitkerrie
Geanies
158
159
B9165
Hill of Fearn
Hartmount
A9
Hilton of Cadboll Chapel
Fearn
B9166
Brenachie
Tullich
Hilton of Cadboll
1
2
3
4
5

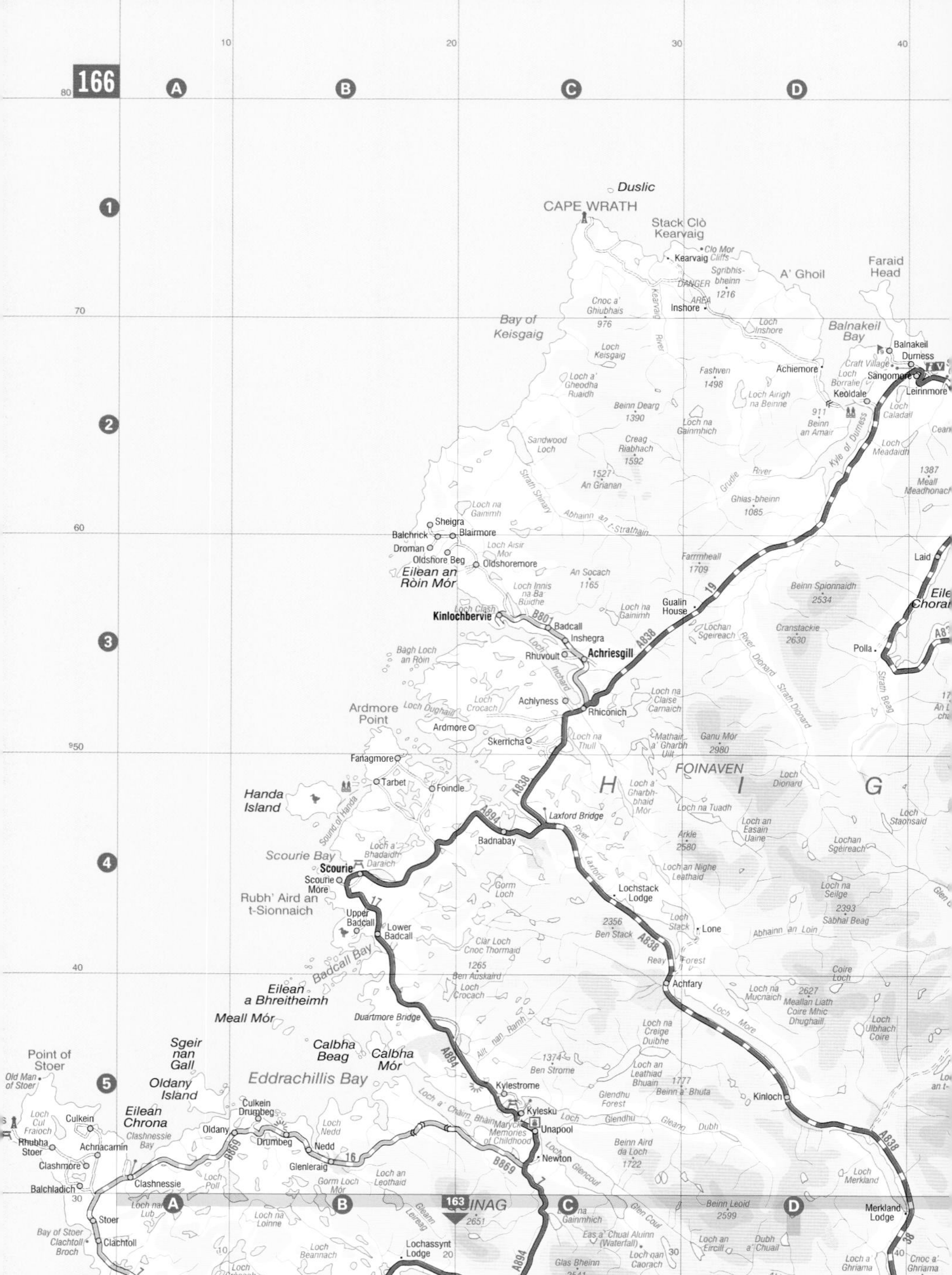

CAPE WRATH
Duslic
Stack Clò Kearvaig
Kearvaig
Clo Mor Cliffs
Sgribhis-bheinn 1216
DANGER AREA
A' Ghoil
Faraid Head
Inshore
Bay of Keisgaig
Balnakeil Bay
Balnakeil
Durness
Sangomore
Leirinmore
Keoldale
Achiemore
Kyle of Durness
Sandwood Loch
Sheigra
Balchrick
Blairmore
Droman
Oldshore Beg
Oldshoremore
Eilean an Ròin Mór
Kinlochbervie
Badcall
Inshegra
Rhuvoult
Achriesgill
Gualin House
Polla
Laid
Ardmore Point
Achlyness
Rhiconich
Ardmore
Skerricha
Fanagmore
Tarbet
Foindle
Handa Island
FOINAVEN
Laxford Bridge
Badnabay
Scourie Bay
Scourie
Scourie More
Rubh' Aird an t-Sionnaich
Upper Badcall
Lower Badcall
Lochstack Lodge
Lone
Badcall Bay
Achfary
Eilean a Bhreitheimh
Meall Mór
Duartmore Bridge
Sgeir nan Gall
Calbha Beag
Calbha Mór
Point of Stoer
Eddrachillis Bay
Oldany Island
Kylestrome
Kylesku
Kinloch
Eilean Chrona
Culkein
Culkein Drumbeg
Oldany
Drumbeg
Nedd
Unapool
Newton
Rhubha Stoer
Achnacarnin
Clashmore
Glenleraig
Balchladich
Clashnessie
Stoer
Clachtoll
Merkland Lodge
Lochassynt Lodge
A838
A894
B801
B869

Whiten Head or An Ceann Geal
Eilean Clùimhrig
Rispond
Ben Hutig 1338
Achininver
Midfield
Lubinvullin
Strathan
West Strathan
Achinahuagh
Talmine
Skinnet
Midtown
Rabbit Islands
Eilean nan Ron
Neave or Coombe Island
Clasheddy
Skerray
Achtoty
Modsarie
Torrisdale
Skullomie
Coldbackie
Blandy
Rhitongue
Dalcharn
Tongue
Braetongue
Hope
Achuvoldrach
Eriboll
Bettyhill
Farr Point
Kirtomy Point
Ardmore Point
STRATHY POINT
Totegan
Aultivullin
Brawl
Strathy
Armadale
Lednagullin
Clerkhill
Farr
Swordly
Kirtomy
Clachan
Crask
Achina
Invernaver
Leckfurin
Borgie
Skelpick
Archargary
Carnachy
Rhifail
Rough Haugh
Skail
Syre
Rimsdale
Garvault
Badanloch Lodge
Bowside Lodge
Strathy Forest
BEN HOPE 3040
Ben Loyal 2509
Loch Loyal Lodge
Kinloch Lodge
Ribigill
Alltnacaillich
Gobernuisgach Lodge
Mudale
Altnaharra
Grummore
BEN KLIBRECK 2367
Loch Choire Lodge
Fiag Lodge
Navar Forest
Rosal Clearance Village
Grumbeg Settlement
A838
A836
B871
B873
H L A N D
164
165
168

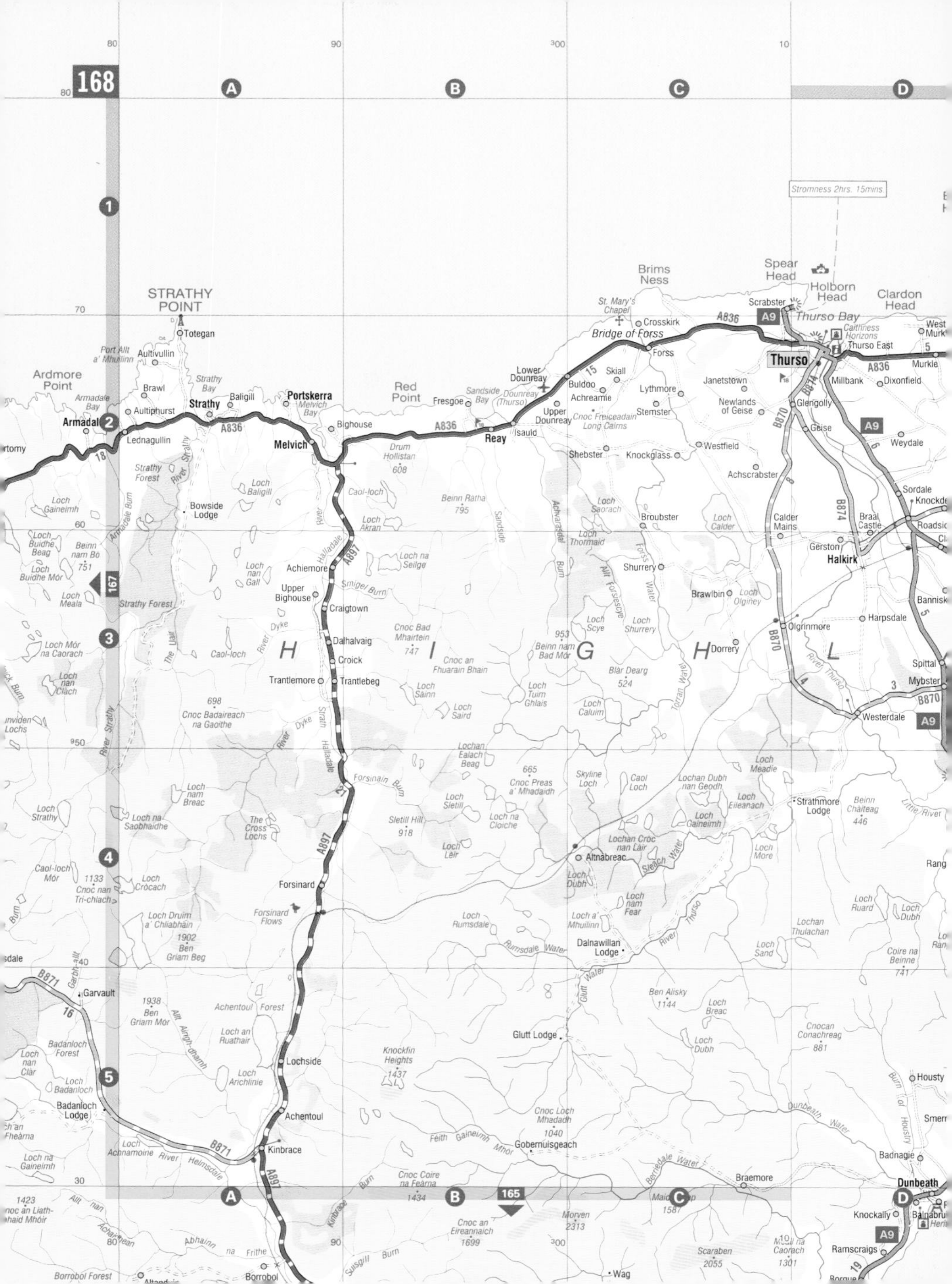

STRATHY POINT
Totegan
Port Allt a' Mhuilinn
Aultivullin
Ardmore Point
Armadale Bay
Brawl
Strathy Bay
Strathy
Baligill
Portskerra
Melvich Bay
Aultiphurst
Armadale
Lednagullin
A836
Melvich
Bighouse
Red Point
Fresgoe
Sandside Bay
Dounreay (Thurso)
Lower Dounreay
Reay
Isauld
Upper Dounreay
Buldoo
Skiall
Achreamie
Brims Ness
St. Mary's Chapel
Crosskirk
Bridge of Forss
Forss
Spear Head
Holborn Head
Scrabster
Thurso Bay
Clardon Head
Caithness Horizons
Thurso East
Thurso
Murkle
Millbank
Dixonfield
Janetstown
Lythmore
Stemster
Newlands of Geise
Glengolly
Geise
Weydale
Cnoc Freiceadain Long Cairns
Shebster
Knockglass
Westfield
Achscrabster
Sordale
Stromness 2hrs. 15mins
Drum Hollistan 608
Strathy Forest
River Strathy
Bowside Lodge
Loch Baligill
Caol-loch
Loch Akran
Beinn Ratha 795
Loch Saorach
Broubster
Loch Calder
Calder Mains
Braal Castle
Loch Gaineimh
Loch Buidhe Beag
Beinn nam Bò 751
Loch Buidhe Mór
Loch Meala
Armadale Burn
Halladale
A897
Achiemore
Loch nan Gall
Loch na Seilge
Loch Thormaid
Achvarasdal Burn
Allt Forsiescye
Forss Water
Shurrery
Gerston
Halkirk
Upper Bighouse
Smigel Burn
Craigtown
Brawlbin
Loch Olginey
Olgrinmore
Harpsdale
Loch Mór na Caorach
Loch nan Clach
Strathy Forest
The Uair
River Dyke
Caol-loch
Dalhalvaig
Croick
Cnoc Bad Mhairtein 747
Cnoc an Fhuarain Bhain
Beinn nam Bad Mór 953
Loch Scye
Loch Shurrery
Dorrery
Trantlemore
Trantlebeg
Loch Sàinn
Loch Saird
Loch Tuim Ghlais
Blàr Dearg 524
Torran Water
Loch Caluim
River Thurso
Spittal
Mybster
Westerdale
B870
B874
A9
H I G H L
698 Cnoc Badaireach na Gaoithe
Strath Halladale
Lochan Ealach Beag
Loch Meadie
Loch Strathy
Loch nam Breac
The Cross Lochs
Forsinain Burn
665 Cnoc Preas a' Mhadaidh
Skyline Loch
Caol Loch
Lochan Dubh nan Geodh
Loch Eileanach
Strathmore Lodge
Beinn Châiteag 446
Little River
Loch na Saobhaidhe
Loch Sletill
Sletill Hill 918
Loch na Cloiche
Loch Gaineimh
Lochan Cróc nan Lair
Loch Leir
Altnabreac
Sleach Water
Loch More
Caol-loch Mór
1133 Cnoc nan Tri-chlach
Loch Cròcach
Forsinard
Loch Dubh
Loch nam Fear
Loch Druim a' Chliabhain
Forsinard Flows
Loch Rumsdale
Loch a' Mhuilinn
Loch Ruard
Loch Dubh
Lochan Thulachan
1902 Ben Griam Beg
Rumsdale Water
Dalnawillan Lodge
Loch Sand
Coire na Beinne 741
B871
Garvault
Garbh-allt
1938 Ben Griam Mór
Achentoul Forest
Allt Airigh-dhamh
Loch an Ruathair
Glutt Water
Ben Alisky 1144
Loch Breac
Cnocan Conachreag 881
Glutt Lodge
Badanloch Forest
Loch nan Clàr
Loch Badanloch
Badanloch Lodge
Lochside
Knockfin Heights 1437
Loch Arichlinie
Loch Dubh
Housty
Burn of Housty
Achentoul
Cnoc Loch Mhadadh 1040
Dunbeath Water
Loch Achnamoine
River Helmsdale
Kinbrace
Feith Gaineimh Mhór
Gobernuisgeach
Badnagie
Loch na Gaineimh
Cnoc Coire na Fearna 1434
Berriedale Water
Braemore
Dunbeath
1423 Cnoc an Liath-bhaid Mhóir
Allt nan Achaidhean
Kinbrace Burn
Cnoc an Eireannaich 1699
Morven 2313
Maiden Pap 1587
Knockally
Balnabruich
Abhainn na Frithe
Suisgill Burn
Scaraben 2055
Meall na Caorach 1301
Ramscraigs
Borrobol Forest
Borrobol
Wag

167

165

PENTLAND FIRTH
172
Island of Stroma
Nethertown
Uppertown
Pentland Skerries
DUNNET HEAD
St. John's Point
Tang Head
DUNCANSBY HEAD
John o' Groats
Stacks of Duncansby
Dunnet
Dunnet Bay
Gills Bay
Mey
Castle of Mey
Brough
Ham
Scarfskerry
Rattar
East Mey
Gills
Kirkstyle
Huna
Seater
Canisbay
Warse
Upper Gills
Corsback
Barrock
Inkstack
Brabster
Warth Hill 406
Skirza
Skirza Head
Tofts
Freswick
Freswick Bay
Ness Head
Greenland
Greenland Mains
Lochend
Slickly
Olrig
Tain
Reaster
Alterwall
Durran
Bowermadden
Sortat
Lyth
Lyth Arts Centre
Caithness Broch Centre
Auckengill
Nybster
Brough Head
Bowertower
Howe
Keiss
Keiss Castle
Tang Head
Halcro
Hastigrow
Mireland
Corsback
Gillock
Kirk
North Watten
Myrelandhorn
Loch of Wester
Westerloch
Sinclair's Bay
Larel
Killimster
Knapperfield
Oldhall
Loch Watten
Watten
Winless
Reiss
Sinclair Girnigoe
Noss Head
Ackergillshore
Sealky Head
Ackergill
Bilbster
Sibster
WICK
Staxigoe
Papigoe
Broadhaven
Strath
Acharole
Haster
Milton
Janetstown
Wick
Wick Bay
Pulteney Distillery
South Head
Newton
Badlipster
Whiterow
Old Wick
Gote o' Tram
Loch Hempriggs
Tannach
Hempriggs
Helman Head
Hill of Oliclett 462
Gansclet
Thrumster
Loch of Yarrows
Raggra
Borrowston
Grey Cairns of Camster
Sarclet
Sarclet Head
South Yarrows Cairns
Cnoc an Earrannaiche 692
Camster
Cairn o' Get
Ulbster
Achavanich
Loch Stemster Standing Stones
815 Stemster Hill
Sheppardstown
Roster
East Clyth
Bruan
Crofts of Benachielt
Rumster Forest
Oscaly
Hill o' Many Stanes
Mid Clyth
Halberry Head
Upper Lybster
Achow
Overton
Clyth
Swiney
Lybster
Upper Latheron
Invershore
Waterlines
Burrigill
Forse
Forse Castle
Latheron
Clan Gunn Heritage Centre
Latheronwheel
Knockinnon
A836
A99
A882
A9
B855
B876
B874
B870
B9041
E
F
G
H
1
2
3
4
5

NA H-EILEANAN AN IAR
(WESTERN ISLES)
OUTER HEBRIDES
THE LITTLE MINCH
SEA OF THE HEBRIDES
NORTH UIST
(UIBHIST A TUATH)
BENBECULA
(BEINN NA FAOGHLA)
SOUTH UIST
(UIBHIST A DEAS)
BARRA
(BARRAIGH)
Vatersay
(Bhatarsaigh)
Sandray
(Sanndraigh)
Mingulay
(Miùghlaigh)
Eriskay
(Eiriosgaigh)
Heisker or Monach Islands
(Theisgeir no na H-Eileanan Monach)
Sound of Monach
(Caolas Mhonach)
Sound of Barra
(An Caolas Barrach)
Caolas Mhiùghlaigh
Baleshare
(Baile Sear)
Grimsay
(Griomasaigh)
Ronay
(Ronaigh)
Wiay
(Fuidhaigh)
Pabbay
(Pabaigh)
Boreray
(Boraraigh)
Berneray
(Bhearnaraigh)
Leverburgh
(An t-Ob)
Renish Point
(Rubha Reinis)
Lochmaddy
(Loch nam Madadh)
Lochboisdale (Loch Baghasdail)
Castlebay (Bàgh a' Chaisteil)
Dalabrog
Tochdar
Rubha Ghriminis
Rubha Shealllacro
Rubha na Creige Moire
Gob Sgùrabhal
Loch Eubhal
Loch Fada
Loch nan Eun
Loch Scadabhagh
Loch Bee
(Loch Bi)
Loch Aineort
Loch Baghasdail
Waternish Point
Dunvegan Head
Loch Pooltiel
Loch Dunvegan
ISLE OF SKYE
Lochmaddy to:
Uig 1hr. 40mins.
Lochboisdale to:
Castlebay 1hr. 45mins.
Oban 5hrs. 20mins.
(Seasonal)
Castlebay to:
Lochboisdale 1hr. 45mins.
Oban 5hrs.
Tiree 2hrs. 45mins.
(Seasonal)
40 mins.
A865
A867
B893
B894
B892
B891
B890
B888
A888
171
154
146
Scale: 9.72 miles to 1 inch 1:615,730
0 1 2 3 4 5 10 15 Miles
0 1 2 3 4 5 10 15 20 Kilometres

NA H-EILEANAN AN IAR
(WESTERN ISLES)
OUTER HEBRIDES
ISLE OF LEWIS (EILEAN LEODHAIS)
BUTT OF LEWIS
(RUBHA ROBHANAIS)
Eoropaidh
Coig Peighinnean
B8013
B8014
Tabost
Port Nis
Lional
Suainebost
Dail bho Dheas
Cros
Sgiogarstaigh
B8015
Gabhsann bho Thuath
Gabhsann bho Dheas
Mealabost
Coig Peighinnean Bhuirgh
Borgh
A857
Cuidhsiadar
Siadar
Baile an Truiseil
Steinacleit Cairn and Stone Circle
Cellar Head
Barabhas Iarach
Barbhas Uarach
Labost
Blackhouse
Bru
Barabhas
Siabost bho Thuath
Bragar
Arnol
Siabost bho Deas
Norse Mill & Kiln
Siabost
A858
Pairc Shiaboist
Blackhouse Village
Na Gearrannan
Dail Mor
Mullach Charlabhaigh
Borghastan
Carlabhagh
Loch Breabhat
Bail' Ur Tholastaidh
Tolstadh bho Thuath
Gleann Tholastaidh
B895
Tolsta Head
(Ceann Tholastaidh)
Griais
Bac
Broad Bay
Col
Col Uarach
Breibhig
Great Bernera
(Bearnaraigh)
An Caolas
Bostadh
Crothair
Dun Charlabhaigh
Tolastadh a Chaolais
Aird Uig
Bhaltos
Cnip
Tobson
Breacleit
Tunga
Aird Thunga
Port Nan Giuran
Port Mholair
Fleisirin
Aird
Newmarket
Grianan
Lacasdail
Sulaisiadar
Cliobh
Riof
Tacleit
Circebost
Breascleit
Calanais
Standing Stones
Timsgearraidh
Cradhlastadh
Miabhaig
Carnais
Cairisiadar
Iarsiadar
B8059
Bruach Mairi
STORNOWAY
(STEORNABHAGH)
Mealabost
Garrabost
Seisiadar
EYE PENINSULA
(AN RUBHA)
Coire an Fhuarain
Loch an Ois
Sanndabhaig
Pabail Uarach
Pabail Iarach
Mangurstadh
Eadar Dha Fhadhail
B8011
Geisiadar
Cruabhig
Linsiadar
Loch Suaineabhal
Loch Rog Beag
Acha Mor
A859
B897
Liurbost
Griomsiadar
Islibhig
Einacleit
B8011
Loch Fada Gobha
Stornoway to Ullapool 2hrs. 40mins.
Breanais
Giosla
Crosbost
Ranais
Lacasaidh
Ceos
Glib Cheois
Gromor
Loch Tamnabhaigh
Baile Ailein
Kinloch
Ceann Tarabhaigh
Gearraidh Bhaird
Marbhig
Tabost
Airidh a Bhruaich
B8060
Calbost
Loch Langabhat
Ceann Shiphoirt
Taobh a Ghlinne
Grabhair
Scarp
Loch Reasort
PARK
(PAIRC)
A' Chabag
Grasaigh
Leumrabhagh
Huisinis
Eisgein
Aird a Mhulaidh
B887
Scaladal
NORTH HARRIS
(CEANNA TUATH NA HEARADH)
Loch Claidh
Loch Shell
(Loch Sealg)
Gobhaig
Abhainn Suidhe
Cliasmol
Miabhaig
Loch Bhrolluim
Maraig
Loch Seaforth
(Loch Shiphoirt)
Bun Abhainn Eadarra
Loch a Siar
Taransay
(Tarasaigh)
Reinigeadal
SOUND OF SHIANT
(CAOLAS NAN EILEAN)
Tarbert
(Tairbeart)
Oban
Urgha
Paibeil
Losgaintir
Carragraich
Sound of Taransay
(Caolas Tharasaigh)
Camach
Miabhag
Scalpaigh
Horgabost
Seilebost
Drinisiadar
Toe Head
(Gob an Tobha)
Scarasta
Na Buirgh
Ceann a Bhaigh
Shiant Islands
(Na H-Eileanan Mora)
Greosabhagh
Plocropol
Tweed
Loch An Tairbeairt
Scalpay
(Scalpaigh)
Sgarasta Mhor
A859
Loch Langabhat
Ceann a Bhaigh
Geocrab
Scadabhagh
Cliuthar
Caolas Stocinis
Taobh Tuath
SOUTH HARRIS
(CEANNA DEAS NA HEARADH)
Tarbert to Uig 1hr. 40mins.
Seallam!
Beacrabhaic
Aird Shleibhe
Fleoideabhagh
Scale 9.72 miles to 1 inch 1:615,730
Leverburgh
(An t-Ob)
Aird Mhighe
Fionnsabhagh
Coidhtinis
Phabaigh
Berneray
(Bhearnaraigh)
SOUND OF HARRIS
(CAOLAS NA HEARADH)
Lingreabhagh
Cairminis
Srannda
Roghadal
Brusta
Ruisigearraidh
Borgh
Rennish Point
(Rubha Reinis)
170
154
155
Rubha na h-Aiseig
THE MINCH
LITTLE MINCH
B893
Tobha Beag
Bagh a Chaise
Kilmaluag
Lochmaddy to Uig 1hr. 40mins.
Uig to Lochmaddy 1hr. 40mins. Tarbert 1hr. 40mins.
Blathaisbhal
Lochportain
Struth Mor
A865
Lochmaddy
(Loch nam Madadh)
Kilvaxter
Staffin
Waternish Point
ISLE OF SKYE
Loch Scadabhagh
Loch Euphort
Idrigill
Uig
Culnaknock
Garros
Saighdinis
162

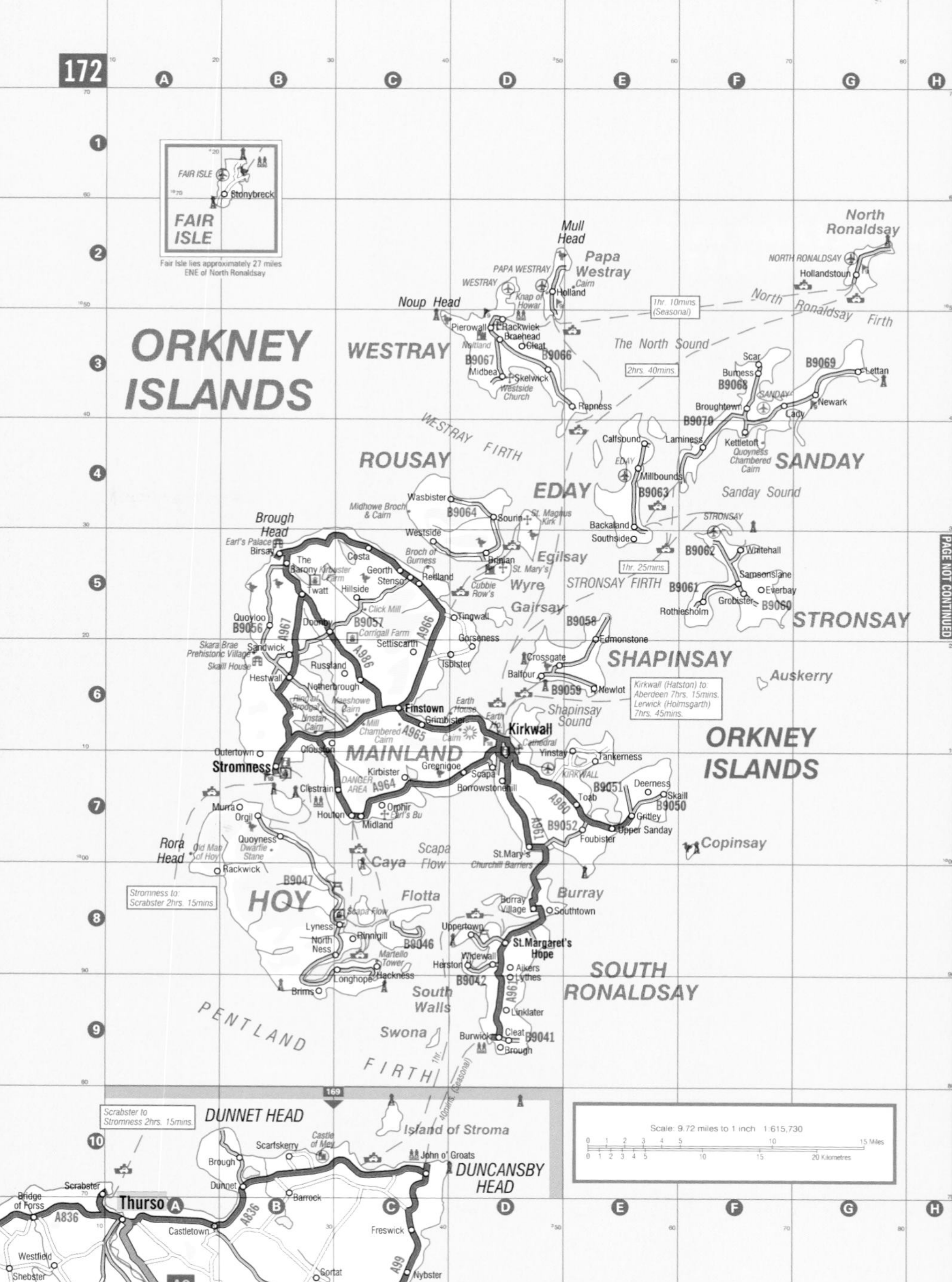

ORKNEY ISLANDS
FAIR ISLE
Stonybreck
Fair Isle lies approximately 27 miles ENE of North Ronaldsay
Mull Head
Papa Westray
PAPA WESTRAY
WESTRAY
Holland
Knap of Howar
Noup Head
Pierowall
Rackwick
Braehead
Cleat
Noltland
B9067
B9066
Midbea
Skelwick
Westside Church
Rapness
WESTRAY
North Ronaldsay
NORTH RONALDSAY
Hollandstoun
North Ronaldsay Firth
1hr. 10mins. (Seasonal)
The North Sound
2hrs. 40mins.
Scar
Burness
B9068
B9069
Lettan
SANDAY
Newark
Broughtown
Lady
B9070
Laminess
Kettletoft
Quoyness Chambered Cairn
SANDAY
Sanday Sound
WESTRAY FIRTH
ROUSAY
Calfsound
EDAY
Millbounds
B9063
Backaland
Southside
EDAY
Wasbister
B9064
Midhowe Broch & Cairn
Sourin
St. Magnus Kirk
Westside
Broch of Gurness
Brinian
Egilsay
St. Mary's
1hr. 25mins.
STRONSAY
B9062
Whitehall
Samsonslane
B9061
Everbay
Grobister
Rothiesholm
B9060
STRONSAY
Brough Head
Earl's Palace
Birsay
The Barony
Kirbuster Farm
Twatt
Costa
Georth
Stenso
Hillside
Redland
Cubbie Row's
Wyre
STRONSAY FIRTH
Gairsay
Click Mill
Quoyloo
B9056
A967
Dounby
B9057
A966
Tingwall
Corrigall Farm
Settiscarth
Gorseness
B9058
Edmonstone
Skara Brae Prehistoric Village
Sandwick
Skaill House
A986
Russland
Isbister
Crossgate
SHAPINSAY
Hestwall
Balfour
B9059
Newlot
Netherbrough
Ring of Brodgar
Maeshowe Cairn
Stenness
Stones of Stenness
Unstan Cairn
Finstown
Earth House
Grimbister
Mill Chambered Cairn
A965
Cairn
Kirkwall
Cathedral
Shapinsay Sound
Kirkwall (Hatston) to: Aberdeen 7hrs. 15mins. Lerwick (Holmsgarth) 7hrs. 45mins.
Auskerry
ORKNEY ISLANDS
Outertown
Stromness
Clouston
MAINLAND
Yinstay
Tankerness
Kirbister
Greenigoe
Scapa
KIRKWALL
Clestrain
DANGER AREA
A964
Borrowstonehill
B9051
Deerness
Skaill
B9050
Orphir
Earl's Bu
Toab
A960
Murra
Houton
Midland
Gritley
Orgil
A961
B9052
Upper Sanday
Foubister
Copinsay
Quoyness
Dwarfie Stane
Rora Head
Old Man of Hoy
Rackwick
St.Mary's
Churchill Barriers
Caya
Scapa Flow
B9047
Burray
Stromness to: Scrabster 2hrs. 15mins.
HOY
Flotta
Burray Village
Southtown
Scapa Flow
Lyness
Uppertown
North Ness
Rinnigill
St.Margaret's Hope
B9046
Martello Tower
Herston
Widewall
Aikers
Longhope
Hackness
B9042
Lythes
SOUTH RONALDSAY
Brims
South Walls
A961
Linklater
PENTLAND FIRTH
Swona
Burwick
Cleat
B9041
Brough
1hr.
40mins. (Seasonal)
169
Scrabster to Stromness 2hrs. 15mins.
DUNNET HEAD
Island of Stroma
Castle of Mey
Scarfskerry
John o' Groats
Brough
DUNCANSBY HEAD
Dunnet
Scrabster
Barrock
Bridge of Forss
Thurso
A836
A836
Castletown
Freswick
Westfield
Shebster
A99
Sortat
A9
Nybster
Scale: 9.72 miles to 1 inch 1:615,730
0 1 2 3 4 5 10 15 Miles
0 1 2 3 4 5 10 15 20 Kilometres
PAGE NOT CONTINUED

SHETLAND ISLANDS
UNST
YELL
FETLAR
MAINLAND
WHALSAY
Out Skerries
BRESSAY
Isle of Noss
Mousa
FOULA
Papa Stour
Vementry
MUCKLE ROE
ST. MAGNUS BAY
Vaila
West Burra
South Havra
Sumburgh Head
Lerwick
Scalloway
Voe
Brae
Aith
Tresta
Lerwick to Fair Isle 5hrs. (Seasonal)
Lerwick (Holmsgarth) to: Aberdeen 12hrs. Kirkwall (Hatston) 5hrs. 30mins.
Sumburgh to Fair Isle 2hrs. 30mins.
3hrs. 30mins. (Seasonal)
Scale: 9.72 miles to 1 inch 1:615,730
PAGE NOT CONTINUED

Aylesbury
St. Albans
Chelmsford
Watford
Maidenhead
Slough
LONDON
Dartford
Basildon
Southend-on-Sea
Reading
Windsor
Staines
Sheerness
Margate
Ramsgate
Woking
Croydon
Maidstone
Canterbury
Aldershot
Guildford
Royal Tunbridge Wells
Ashford
Dover
Folkestone
Channel Tunnel
Calais
Chichester
Brighton
Lewes
Hastings
Portsmouth
Newhaven
Eastbourne
Boulogne
Breda
Tilburg
HOLLAND
Roosendaal
Bergen op Zoom
Eindhoven
Vlissingen
Zeebrugge
Antwerpen
Mortsel
Oostende
Brugge
Mechelen
Gent
BELGIUM
Hasselt
Maastricht
Dunkerque
Bruxelles
Ieper
Kortrijk
Tourcoing
Liège
St. Omer
Lille
Roubaix
Tournai
Namur
Béthune
Mons
Charleroi
Montreuil
Lens
Douai
Denain
Valenciennes
St. Pol
Arras
Maubeuge
FRANCE
Cambrai
Abbeville
Charleville Mezières
Dieppe
Amiens
To Paris
St. Quentin
MOTORWAY AND AUTOROUTES
SELECTED MAIN ROUTES
SCALE
0 10 20 30 40 Miles
0 10 20 30 40 50 60 Kilometres

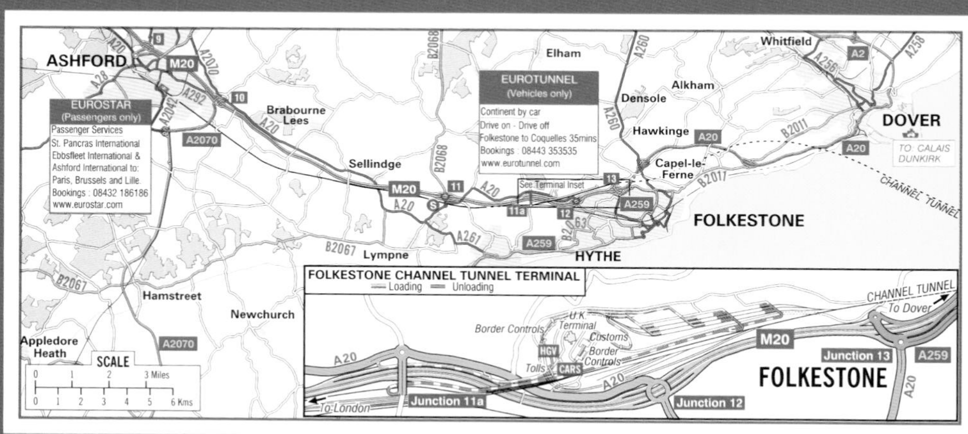

ASHFORD
M20
Elham
Whitfield
A2
EUROTUNNEL
(Vehicles only)
Continent by car
Drive on - Drive off
Folkestone to Coquelles 35mins
Bookings : 08443 353535
www.eurotunnel.com
Alkham
Densole
EUROSTAR
(Passengers only)
Passenger Services
St. Pancras International
Ebbsfleet International &
Ashford International to:
Paris, Brussels and Lille.
Bookings : 08432 186186
www.eurostar.com
Brabourne Lees
Hawkinge
DOVER
TO: CALAIS
DUNKIRK
Sellindge
Capel-le-Ferne
CHANNEL TUNNEL
See Terminal Inset
FOLKESTONE
Lympne
HYTHE
FOLKESTONE CHANNEL TUNNEL TERMINAL
Loading
Unloading
Hamstreet
Newchurch
Appledore Heath
SCALE
0 1 2 3 Miles
0 1 2 3 4 5 6 Kms
Border Controls
U.K. Terminal
Customs
Border Controls
Tolls
CARS
HGV
Junction 13
Junction 11a
Junction 12
To London
To Dover

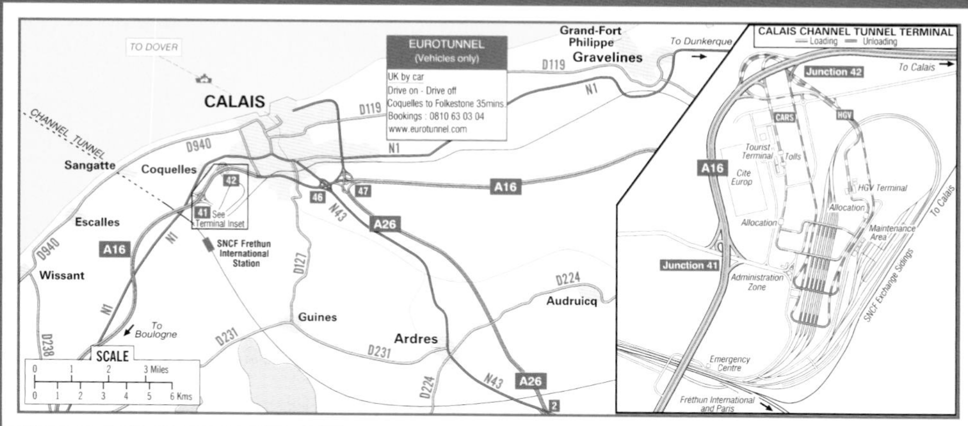

TO DOVER
Grand-Fort Philippe
Gravelines
To Dunkerque
EUROTUNNEL
(Vehicles only)
UK by car
Drive on - Drive off
Coquelles to Folkestone 35mins.
Bookings : 0810 63 03 04
www.eurotunnel.com
CALAIS
CHANNEL TUNNEL
Sangatte
Coquelles
See Terminal Inset
Escalles
SNCF Frethun International Station
Wissant
To Boulogne
Guines
Audruicq
Ardres
SCALE
0 1 2 3 Miles
0 1 2 3 4 5 6 Kms
CALAIS CHANNEL TUNNEL TERMINAL
Loading
Unloading
Junction 42
To Calais
CARS
HGV
Tourist Terminal
Tolls
Cite Europ
HGV Terminal
Allocation
Maintenance Area
Junction 41
Administration Zone
SNCF Exchange Sidings
Emergency Centre
Frethun International and Paris

Mileage Chart

The distances for the mileage chart have been compiled by using a combination of Primary Routes and Motorways between any two towns shown.

To find the distance between any two towns shown, follow the horizontal line of one town and the vertical line of the other; at the intersection read off the mileage.

ie : Horizontal - LONDON

                    Intersection 216 miles

Vertical - LIVERPOOL

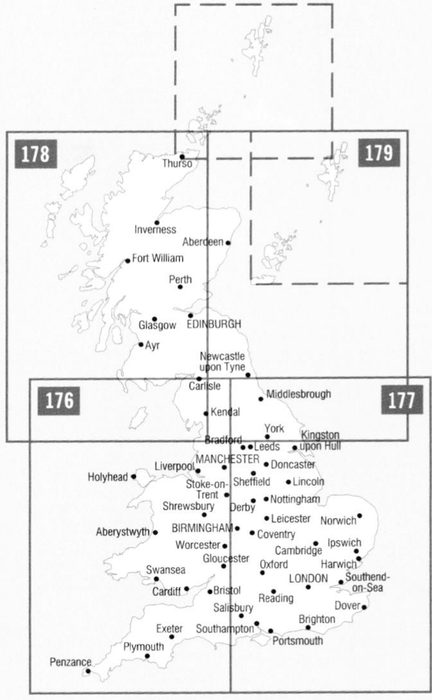

Key to Route Planning Map Pages

PRIMARY ROUTES, shown in green throughout this Atlas, are a national network of recommended through routes which complement the motorway system. Selected places of major traffic importance are known as Primary Route Destinations and, on road signs, have a green background.

ABERDEEN
449 ABERYSTWYTH
181 324 AYR
400 114 272 BIRMINGHAM
330 159 196 124 BRADFORD
562 258 441 169 263 BRIGHTON
503 122 375 88 215 129 BRISTOL
447 198 366 102 156 117 167 CAMBRIDGE
505 106 377 106 233 168 42 201 CARDIFF
217 232 89 183 107 345 286 256 288 CARLISLE
437 134 297 18 124 157 102 84 129 200 COVENTRY
397 137 269 41 88 188 134 99 159 180 43 DERBY
340 192 239 95 40 232 184 117 210 150 94 57 DONCASTER
558 315 477 195 284 81 194 118 233 393 180 208 244 DOVER
125 340 75 284 198 466 377 326 379 91 303 266 212 444 EDINBURGH
553 199 425 161 282 170 75 232 107 336 166 213 257 244 439 EXETER
148 430 136 391 305 568 478 456 486 198 415 387 345 591 131 549 FORT WILLIAM
148 322 36 291 203 468 378 355 384 96 313 282 245 491 46 449 100 GLASGOW
445 109 317 53 171 152 35 132 53 228 59 93 149 189 331 107 435 324 GLOUCESTER
520 258 411 170 224 130 203 64 234 323 152 167 185 129 397 262 524 419 171 HARWICH
443 96 315 151 158 330 204 252 209 226 167 156 169 358 316 279 423 323 189 331 HOLYHEAD
107 492 198 449 353 620 536 490 558 260 458 421 369 601 157 607 63 162 496 554 481 INVERNESS
505 268 420 156 210 125 206 54 240 311 138 155 171 127 381 264 510 409 177 21 307 538 IPSWICH
269 182 139 151 62 324 235 215 232 50 170 136 99 344 141 307 248 146 200 279 180 310 268 KENDAL
357 235 255 139 68 243 228 134 239 165 123 94 37 254 230 290 367 255 195 204 218 387 189 127 KINGSTON UPON HULL
316 171 198 119 9 256 209 144 226 111 117 74 32 275 190 279 309 208 167 217 162 345 197 72 60 LEEDS
407 155 294 43 99 163 118 70 140 214 24 30 73 183 282 189 412 312 83 146 182 431 125 166 98 97 LEICESTER
376 208 249 87 80 207 170 88 192 178 76 53 41 206 247 241 376 274 135 152 204 402 124 140 46 72 52 LINCOLN
327 120 199 99 67 267 180 179 110 113 90 89 294 201 240 308 213 142 265 95 370 236 75 126 73 110 118 LIVERPOOL
321 128 204 87 37 252 167 159 188 117 99 58 51 273 208 239 315 215 132 230 120 363 211 72 96 42 95 87 34 MANCHESTER
273 233 181 174 69 316 265 196 287 92 175 130 84 316 147 337 279 192 230 266 226 306 253 77 88 64 154 127 134 106 MIDDLESBROUGH
230 266 146 209 98 345 300 232 312 58 209 165 115 350 104 369 237 153 263 297 257 263 287 88 130 96 188 153 167 136 40 NEWCASTLE UPON TYNE
476 270 348 163 185 174 234 62 256 280 142 146 142 169 351 284 478 378 193 72 289 505 44 249 145 178 112 103 222 177 221 252 NORWICH
381 155 267 54 78 191 140 84 165 188 52 15 48 210 256 218 386 286 108 165 177 410 40 141 62 72 27 37 107 68 128 159 118 NOTTINGHAM
485 151 335 68 167 106 73 92 106 267 57 101 138 142 358 151 465 365 47 134 208 515 128 223 175 162 76 123 168 157 218 253 159 104 OXFORD
680 301 552 269 394 279 184 343 218 463 278 316 369 355 551 109 663 561 217 374 388 715 375 419 412 391 310 359 353 344 449 481 393 323 261 PENZANCE
87 366 85 336 245 509 412 370 422 134 346 309 254 485 43 487 103 59 362 439 360 113 424 184 273 233 326 290 244 254 191 148 394 290 404 598 PERTH
589 232 461 203 325 206 111 274 159 372 209 254 300 286 485 43 592 490 150 305 322 648 305 348 326 323 231 284 299 281 379 412 327 255 193 75 529 PLYMOUTH
575 231 440 147 274 50 95 132 138 357 132 184 231 137 448 127 554 451 100 137 223 617 119 264 216 209 254 237 315 360 200 191 33 235 486 170 PORTSMOUTH
526 180 399 103 213 79 77 90 112 309 90 138 184 115 402 141 506 406 75 129 264 554 126 263 209 207 113 168 193 197 264 295 152 129 25 251 445 184 60 READING
529 178 383 121 245 82 53 140 101 312 113 159 207 158 400 91 510 408 73 177 262 569 177 265 251 230 132 187 213 208 287 318 200 162 65 201 443 132 43 57 SALISBURY
355 173 235 79 40 225 163 121 193 154 75 35 21 268 230 245 352 250 139 185 164 387 176 102 66 33 46 74 40 102 133 144 37 137 361 273 293 228 160 203 SHEFFIELD
388 73 260 47 100 216 116 140 107 171 64 67 114 249 262 175 369 267 77 215 104 424 195 125 163 102 79 123 59 67 166 203 196 86 105 286 309 218 195 147 150 85 SHREWSBURY
547 213 401 128 235 64 75 129 122 330 114 167 201 150 433 106 528 426 98 127 287 590 162 276 249 230 136 189 235 215 288 320 190 162 76 217 476 149 20 47 23 206 175 SOUTHAMPTON
520 258 431 152 220 85 177 64 211 342 129 168 185 89 395 226 548 438 152 57 303 549 57 283 200 213 139 156 255 225 262 299 99 160 105 337 439 269 117 98 132 197 173 126 SOUTHEND-ON-SEA
374 108 243 47 75 217 127 137 140 150 64 36 74 236 241 202 348 248 95 201 122 410 179 121 117 78 55 87 56 36 142 173 171 55 118 311 287 241 201 147 168 50 35 183 199 STOKE-ON-TRENT
496 76 368 124 220 209 178 214 186 258 184 244 264 310 758 144 266 446 176 174 246 586 178 293 323 286 178 144 266 216 195 196 216 160 124 159 245 159 SWANSEA
213 584 304 557 461 728 644 589 640 352 552 529 475 706 262 715 169 268 604 657 589 108 654 402 492 453 544 510 463 471 410 367 613 519 621 823 220 758 709 662 664 506 523 682 659 502 631 THURSO
437 96 309 29 135 162 62 119 73 220 46 68 124 197 306 136 418 311 28 168 151 480 174 169 166 146 72 118 108 101 203 229 180 85 57 244 350 177 146 95 101 103 49 124 150 65 97 572 WORCESTER
312 193 201 129 34 269 227 151 237 116 129 84 33 269 187 289 314 214 181 232 185 344 200 81 38 24 108 76 96 65 48 83 176 114 140 400 230 331 257 217 244 54 132 244 214 116 268 450 164 YORK
501 206 390 118 203 53 118 58 150 305 97 128 165 76 373 171 503 403 101 79 264 527 76 264 188 196 102 143 216 200 246 278 114 130 55 282 416 214 74 39 84 161 160 87 84 161 187 636 110 203 LONDON

Newry
Newcastle
Warrenpoint
ISLE OF MAN
Peel
Douglas
Castletown
Kirkby Lonsdale
Ulverston
Barrow-in-Furness
Morecambe
Heysham
Lancaster
Dundalk
Carrickmacross
Drogheda
Kells
Navan
Mullingar
Fleetwood
Blackpool
Clitheroe
Blackburn
Preston
Lytham St.Anne's
Southport
Chorley
Darwen
Bolton
Bury
Burnley
Ormskirk
Wigan
Formby
St. Helens
IRISH SEA
LIVERPOOL
Wallasey
Birkenhead
Warrington
Sale
Runcorn
Northwich
Macclesfield
DUBLIN
Dun Laoghaire
Bray
Kildare
Naas
Portlaoise
REPUBLIC OF IRELAND
Wicklow
Carlow
Arklow
Gorey
Kilkenny
Enniscorthy
New Ross
Wexford
Waterford
Rosslare Harbour
Amlwch
Holyhead
(Caergybi)
Llangefni
Beaumaris
Llandudno
Rhyl
Conwy
Colwyn Bay
(Bae Colwyn)
Flint
(Y Fflint)
Ellesmere Port
Bangor
Llanrwst
Denbigh
(Dinbych)
Ruthin
(Rhuthun)
Mold
(Yr Wyddgrug)
Chester
Crewe
Caernarfon
Betws-y-Coed
Llan Ffestiniog
Wrexham
(Wrecsam)
Nantwich
Llangollen
Porthmadog
Pwllheli
Bala
(Y Bala)
Whitchurch
STOKE-ON-TRENT
Oswestry
(Croesoswallt)
Ellesmere
Wem
Market Drayton
Dolgellau
Barmouth
(Abermaw)
Llanfyllin
Shrewsbury
Newport
Oakengates
Welshpool
(Y Trallwng)
Telford
Montgomery
(Trefaldwyn)
Wolverhampton
Tywyn
Machynlleth
CARDIGAN BAY
Llanidloes
Newtown
(Y Drenewydd)
Church Stretton
Bridgnorth
Aberystwyth
Llangurig
Bishop's Castle
Ludlow
Kidderminster
Rhayader
(Rhaeadr Gwy)
Knighton
(Tref-Y-Clawdd)
Presteigne
(Llanandras)
Bromsgrove
Aberaeron
New Quay
(Ceinewydd)
Llandrindod Wells
Leominster
Worcester
Lampeter
(Llanbedr Pont Steffan)
Kington
Cardigan
(Aberteifi)
Builth Wells
(Llanfair-ym-Muallt)
Great Malvern
Fishguard
(Abergwaun)
Llandovery
(Llanymddyfri)
Brecon
(Aberhonddu)
Hereford
St. David's
(Tyddewi)
WALES
(CYMRU)
Carmarthen
(Caerfyrddin)
Ross-on-Wye
Tewkesbury
Llandeilo
Abergavenny
(Y Fenni)
Monmouth
(Trefynwy)
Gloucester
Haverfordwest
(Hwlffordd)
St. Clears
Ammanford
(Rhydaman)
Merthyr Tydfil
(Merthyr Tudful)
Ebbw Vale
Milford Haven
(Aberdaugleddau)
Tredegar
Aberdare
(Aberdar)
Abertillery
Chepstow
(Cas-gwent)
Pembroke
(Penfro)
Tenby
(Dinbych-y-Pysgod)
Llanelli
Neath
(Castell-nedd)
Pontypool
(Pontypwl)
Cwmbran
Nailsworth
SWANSEA
(Abertawe)
Pontypridd
Caerphilly
(Caerffili)
Newport
(Casnewydd)
Malmesbury
Port Talbot
Porthcawl
Bridgend
(Pen-y-Bont-Ar Ogwr)
Penarth
CARDIFF
(Caerdydd)
BRISTOL
Chippenham
BRISTOL CHANNEL
Barry
(Barri)
Weston-Super-Mare
Bath
Trowbridge
Radstock
Frome
Wells
Ilfracombe
Lynton
LUNDY
Watchet
Minehead
Burnham-on-Sea
Williton
Glastonbury
Shepton Mallet
Warminster
Barnstaple
Bridgwater
Bideford
Taunton
Wincanton
Great Torrington
South Molton
Wellington
Sherborne
Shaftesbury
Bude
Tiverton
Yeovil
Holsworthy
Chard
Crewkerne
Blandford Forum
Okehampton
Exeter
Honiton
Bridport
Sidmouth
Lyme Regis
Launceston
Exmouth
Dorchester
Wareham
Padstow
Wadebridge
Tavistock
Ashburton
Dawlish
Teignmouth
Weymouth
Bodmin
Liskeard
Newton Abbot
Fortuneswell
Newquay
Saltash
Buckfastleigh
Torquay
Lostwithiel
Devonport
Totnes
Paignton
Guernsey
Jersey
St. Malo
St. Austell
Looe
PLYMOUTH
Brixham
Redruth
Truro
Dartmouth
St. Ives
Kingsbridge
Camborne
Salcombe
Roscoff
Santander
St. Just
Falmouth
Penzance
Helston
LAND'S END
ENGLISH
ISLES OF SCILLY

REFERENCE

MOTORWAY WITH NUMBER	M4 —S— Service Area
MOTORWAY (Under Construction/Proposed)	
MOTORWAY JUNCTIONS	S 2a
PRIMARY ROUTE	A5
A ROAD	A272
NATIONAL BOUNDARY	
TOWNS SHOWN IN THE MILEAGE CHART	NORWICH

SCALE

0   10   20   30   40 Miles
0   10   20   30   40   50 Kilometres

OUTER HEBRIDES
INNER HEBRIDES
SCOTLAND
NORTHERN IRELAND
ISLE OF MAN
Scrabster
Thurso
Tongue
Wick
Scourie
Lochinver
Helmsdale
Lairg
Brora
Golspie
Ullapool
Bonar Bridge
Dornoch
Tain
Stornoway
(Steòrnabhagh)
ISLE OF LEWIS
(EILEAN LEODHAIS)
Tarbert
(Tairbeart)
Leverburgh
(An t-Ob)
HARRIS
(NA HEARADH)
Lochmaddy
(Loch nam Madadh)
NORTH UIST
(UIBHIST A TUATH)
BENBECULA
(BEINN NA FAOGHLA)
SOUTH UIST
(UIBHIST A DEAS)
Lochboisdale
(Loch Baghasdail)
BARRA
(BARRAIGH)
Castlebay
(Bàgh a' Chaisteil)
Poolewe
Gairloch
Alness
Invergordon
Moray Firth
Cromarty
Lossiemouth
Kinlochewe
Torridon
Achnasheen
Dingwall
Fortrose
Nairn
Forres
Elgin
Keith
Uig
Dunvegan
Portree
RAASAY
Shieldaig
Strathcarron
Inverness
Rothes
Dufftown
ISLE OF SKYE
Kyle of Lochalsh
Loch Ness
Grantown-on-Spey
Invermoriston
Aviemore
Fort Augustus
Kingussie
CANNA
RÙM
Mallaig
Invergarry
Newtonmore
Braemar
Ballater
Arisaig
EIGG
MUCK
Spean Bridge
Fort William
Kilchoan
Acharacle
COLL
Glencoe
Tobermory
Pitlochry
Kirriemuir
Lochaline
Aberfeldy
Blairgowrie
Forfar
TIREE
ISLE OF MULL
Dunkeld
Dundee
IONA
Oban
Crianlarich
Crieff
Perth
Auchterarder
Inveraray
Callander
Loch Lomond
Doune
Dunblane
Kinross
Cupar
Glenrothes
Methil
COLONSAY
JURA
Lochgilphead
Stirling
Alloa
Dunfermline
Kirkcaldy
Cowdenbeath
Firth of Forth
Helensburgh
Kilsyth
Dumbarton
GLASGOW
Falkirk
EDINBURGH
Dunoon
Greenock
Clydebank
Bathgate
Musselburgh
Wemyss Bay
Airdrie
Livingston
Dalkeith
Rothesay
Paisley
Kennacraig
Largs
Hamilton
Motherwell
ISLE OF BUTE
East Kilbride
Penicuik
ISLAY
Port Ellen
Tayinloan
Ardrossan
Lanark
Lauder
GIGHA
Irvine
Kilmarnock
Biggar
Peebles
Galashiels
Troon
Brodick
Prestwick
ISLE OF ARRAN
Ayr
Cumnock
Selkirk
Campbeltown
Hawick
Maybole
Sanquhar
Girvan
Moffat
Langholm
New Galloway
Lockerbie
Dumfries
Cairnryan
Newton Stewart
Castle Douglas
Annan
Gatehouse of Fleet
Dalbeattie
Stranraer
Wigtown
Kirkcudbright
Solway Firth
Carlisle
Whithorn
Maryport
Cockermouth
Workington
Keswick
Whitehaven
Egremont
Ambleside
Ravenglass
Coniston
Windermere
Kendal
Ramsey
Peel
Portrush
Portstewart
Ballycastle
Coleraine
Letterkenny
Londonderry
Strabane
Ballymena
Larne
Antrim
Lough Neagh
Omagh
Crumlin
Dungannon
BELFAST
Strangford Lough
Enniskillen
Armagh
Monaghan
Downpatrick
Newry
Newcastle

UNST
YELL
FETLAR
SHETLAND ISLANDS
WHALSAY
FOULA
Lerwick
Scalloway
BRESSAY
Sumburgh
FAIR ISLE
WESTRAY
EDAY
SANDAY
ROUSAY
STRONSAY
SHAPINSAY
Stromness
Kirkwall
ORKNEY ISLANDS
HOY
SOUTH RONALDSAY
John o'Groats
Scrabster
Thurso
NORTH SEA
Banff
Fraserburgh
Turriff
Peterhead
Ellon
Oldmeldrum
Inverurie
ABERDEEN
Peterculter
Stonehaven
Inverbervie
Montrose
Arbroath
Dunbar
Eyemouth
Duns
Berwick-upon-Tweed
Coldstream
Kelso
Wooler
Jedburgh
Alnwick
Amble
Ashington
Morpeth
Bedlington
Blyth
Whitley Bay
Amsterdam
NEWCASTLE UPON TYNE
Tynemouth
South Shields
Hexham
Gateshead
Washington
Stanley
Sunderland
Consett
Seaham
Alston
Tow Law
Durham
Peterlee
Hartlepool
Bishop Auckland
Appleby-in-Westmorland
Newton Aycliffe
Stockton-on-Tees
Redcar
Brough
MIDDLESBROUGH
Barnard Castle
Darlington
Whitby
Richmond
Catterick
Northallerton
Leyburn
Scarborough

INDEX TO CITIES, TOWNS, VILLAGES, HAMLETS & LOCATIONS

(1) A strict alphabetical order is used e.g. An Dùnan follows Andreas but precedes Andwell.

(2) The map reference given refers to the actual map square in which the town spot or built-up area is located and not to the place name.

(3) Where two or more places of the same name occur in the same County or Unitary Authority, the nearest large town is also given;
e.g. Achiemore. *High* . . . .2D **166** (nr. Durness) indicates that Achiemore is located in square 2D on page **166** and is situated near Durness in the Unitary Authority of Highland.

(4) Only one reference is given although due to page overlaps the place may appear on more than one page.

(5) Major towns are shown in bold, i.e. **Aberdeen.** *Aber* 3G **153**

COUNTIES and UNITARY AUTHORITIES with the abbreviations used in this index

Aberdeen : *Aber*
Aberdeenshire : *Abers*
Angus : *Ang*
Argyll & Bute : *Arg*
Bath & N E Somerset : *Bath*
Bedford : *Bed*
Blackburn with Darwen : *Bkbn*
Blackpool : *Bkpl*
Blaenau Gwent : *Blae*
Bournemouth : *Bour*
Bracknell Forest : *Brac*
Bridgend : *B'end*
Brighton & Hove : *Brig*
Bristol : *Bris*
Buckinghamshire : *Buck*
Caerphilly : *Cphy*
Cambridgeshire : *Cambs*
Cardiff : *Card*
Carmarthenshire : *Carm*
Central Bedfordshire : *C Beds*
Ceredigion : *Cdgn*
Cheshire East : *Ches E*
Cheshire West & Chester : *Ches W*
Clackmannanshire : *Clac*
Conwy : *Cnwy*
Cornwall : *Corn*
Cumbria : *Cumb*
Darlington : *Darl*
Denbighshire : *Den*
Derby : *Derb*
Derbyshire : *Derbs*
Devon : *Devn*
Dorset : *Dors*
Dumfries & Galloway : *Dum*
Dundee : *D'dee*
Durham : *Dur*
East Ayrshire : *E Ayr*
East Dunbartonshire : *E Dun*
East Lothian : *E Lot*
East Renfrewshire : *E Ren*
East Riding of Yorkshire : *E Yor*
East Sussex : *E Sus*
Edinburgh : *Edin*
Essex : *Essx*
Falkirk : *Falk*
Fife : *Fife*
Flintshire : *Flin*
Glasgow : *Glas*
Gloucestershire : *Glos*
Greater London : *G Lon*
Greater Manchester : *G Man*
Gwynedd : *Gwyn*
Halton : *Hal*
Hampshire : *Hants*
Hartlepool : *Hart*
Herefordshire : *Here*
Hertfordshire : *Herts*
Highland : *High*
Inverclyde : *Inv*
Isle of Anglesey : *IOA*
Isle of Man : *IOM*
Isle of Wight : *IOW*
Isles of Scilly : *IOS*
Kent : *Kent*
Kingston upon Hull : *Hull*
Lancashire : *Lanc*
Leicester : *Leic*
Leicestershire : *Leics*
Lincolnshire : *Linc*
Luton : *Lutn*
Medway : *Medw*
Merseyside : *Mers*
Merthyr Tydfil : *Mer T*
Middlesbrough : *Midd*
Midlothian : *Midl*
Milton Keynes : *Mil*
Monmouthshire : *Mon*
Moray : *Mor*
Neath Port Talbot : *Neat*
Newport : *Newp*
Norfolk : *Norf*
Northamptonshire : *Nptn*
North Ayrshire : *N Ayr*
North East Lincolnshire : *NE Lin*
North Lanarkshire : *N Lan*
North Lincolnshire : *N Lin*
North Somerset : *N Som*
Northumberland : *Nmbd*
North Yorkshire : *N Yor*
Nottingham : *Nott*
Nottinghamshire : *Notts*
Orkney : *Orkn*
Oxfordshire : *Oxon*
Pembrokeshire : *Pemb*
Perth & Kinross : *Per*
Peterborough : *Pet*
Plymouth : *Plym*
Poole : *Pool*
Portsmouth : *Port*
Powys : *Powy*
Reading : *Read*
Redcar & Cleveland : *Red C*
Renfrewshire : *Ren*
Rhondda Cynon Taff : *Rhon*
Rutland : *Rut*
Scottish Borders : *Bord*
Shetland : *Shet*
Shropshire : *Shrp*
Slough : *Slo*
Somerset : *Som*
Southampton : *Sotn*
South Ayrshire : *S Ayr*
Southend-on-Sea : *S'end*
South Gloucestershire : *S Glo*
South Lanarkshire : *S Lan*
South Yorkshire : *S Yor*
Staffordshire : *Staf*
Stirling : *Stir*
Stockton-on-Tees : *Stoc T*
Stoke-on-Trent : *Stoke*
Suffolk : *Suff*
Surrey : *Surr*
Swansea : *Swan*
Swindon : *Swin*
Telford & Wrekin : *Telf*
Thurrock : *Thur*
Torbay : *Torb*
Torfaen : *Torf*
Tyne & Wear : *Tyne*
Vale of Glamorgan, The : *V Glam*
Warrington : *Warr*
Warwickshire : *Warw*
West Berkshire : *W Ber*
West Dunbartonshire : *W Dun*
Western Isles : *W Isl*
West Lothian : *W Lot*
West Midlands : *W Mid*
West Sussex : *W Sus*
West Yorkshire : *W Yor*
Wiltshire : *Wilts*
Windsor & Maidenhead : *Wind*
Wokingham : *Wok*
Worcestershire : *Worc*
Wrexham : *Wrex*
York : *York*

INDEX

A

Abbas Combe. *Som* . . . 4C **22**
Abberley. *Worc* . . . 4B **60**
Abberley Common. *Worc* . . . 4B **60**
Abberton. *Essx* . . . 4D **54**
Abberton. *Worc* . . . 5D **61**
Abberwick. *Nmbd* . . . 3F **121**
Abbess Roding. *Essx* . . . 4F **53**
Abbey. *Devn* . . . 1E **13**
Abbey-cwm-hir. *Powy* . . . 3C **58**
Abbeydale. *S Yor* . . . 2H **85**
Abbeydale Park. *S Yor* . . . 2H **85**
Abbey Dore. *Here* . . . 2G **47**
Abbey Gate. *Devn* . . . 3F **13**
Abbey Hulton. *Stoke* . . . 1D **72**
Abbey St Bathans. *Bord* . . . 3D **130**
Abbeystead. *Lanc* . . . 4E **97**
Abbeytown. *Cumb* . . . 4C **112**
Abbey Village. *Lanc* . . . 2E **91**
Abbey Wood. *G Lon* . . . 3F **39**
Abbots Ann. *Hants* . . . 2B **24**
Abbots Bickington. *Devn* . . . 1D **11**
Abbots Bromley. *Staf* . . . 3E **73**
Abbotsbury. *Dors* . . . 4A **14**
Abbotsham. *Devn* . . . 4E **19**
Abbotskerswell. *Devn* . . . 2E **9**
Abbots Langley. *Herts* . . . 5A **52**
Abbots Leigh. *N Som* . . . 4A **34**
Abbotsley. *Cambs* . . . 5B **64**
Abbots Morton. *Worc* . . . 5E **61**
Abbots Ripton. *Cambs* . . . 3B **64**
Abbot's Salford. *Warw* . . . 5E **61**
Abbotstone. *Hants* . . . 3D **24**
Abbots Worthy. *Hants* . . . 3C **24**
Abcott. *Shrp* . . . 3F **59**
Abdon. *Shrp* . . . 2H **59**
Abenhall. *Glos* . . . 4B **48**
Aber. *Cdgn* . . . 1E **45**
Aberaeron. *Cdgn* . . . 4D **56**
Aberafan. *Neat* . . . 3G **31**
Aberaman. *Rhon* . . . 5D **46**
Aberangell. *Powy* . . . 4H **69**
Aberarad. *Carm* . . . 1H **43**
Aberarder. *High* . . . 1A **150**
Aberargie. *Per* . . . 2D **136**
Aberarth. *Cdgn* . . . 4D **57**
Aberavon. *Neat* . . . 3G **31**
Aber-banc. *Cdgn* . . . 1D **44**
Aberbargoed. *Cphy* . . . 2E **33**
Aberbechan. *Powy* . . . 1D **58**
Aberbeeg. *Blae* . . . 5F **47**
Aberbowlan. *Carm* . . . 2G **45**
Aberbran. *Powy* . . . 3C **46**
Abercanaid. *Mer T* . . . 5D **46**
Abercarn. *Cphy* . . . 2F **33**
Abercastle. *Pemb* . . . 1C **42**
Abercegir. *Powy* . . . 5H **69**
Aberchalder. *High* . . . 3F **149**
Aberchirder. *Abers* . . . 3D **160**
Abercorn. *W Lot* . . . 2D **129**
Abercraf. *Powy* . . . 4B **46**
Abercregan. *Neat* . . . 2B **32**
Abercrombie. *Fife* . . . 3H **137**
Abercwmboi. *Rhon* . . . 2D **32**
Abercych. *Pemb* . . . 1C **44**
Abercynon. *Rhon* . . . 2D **32**
Aber-Cywarch. *Gwyn* . . . 4A **70**
Aberdalgie. *Per* . . . 1C **136**
Aberdar. *Rhon* . . . 5C **46**
Aberdare. *Rhon* . . . 5C **46**
Aberdaron. *Gwyn* . . . 3A **68**
Aberdaugleddau. *Pemb* . . . 4D **42**
Aberdeen. *Aber* . . . 3G **153**
Aberdeen (Dyce) Airport. *Aber* . . . 2F **153**
Aberdesach. *Gwyn* . . . 5D **80**
Aberdour. *Fife* . . . 1E **129**
Aberdovey. *Gwyn* . . . 1F **57**
Aberdulais. *Neat* . . . 5A **46**
Aberdyfi. *Gwyn* . . . 1F **57**
Aberedw. *Powy* . . . 1D **46**
Abereiddy. *Pemb* . . . 1B **42**
Abererch. *Gwyn* . . . 2C **68**
Aberfan. *Mer T* . . . 5D **46**
Aberfeldy. *Per* . . . 4F **143**
Aberffraw. *IOA* . . . 4C **80**
Aberffrwd. *Cdgn* . . . 3F **57**
Aberford. *W Yor* . . . 1E **93**
Aberfoyle. *Stir* . . . 3E **135**
Abergarw. *B'end* . . . 3C **32**
Abergarwed. *Neat* . . . 5B **46**
Abergavenny. *Mon* . . . 4G **47**
Abergele. *Cnwy* . . . 3B **82**
Aber-Giar. *Carm* . . . 1F **45**
Abergorlech. *Carm* . . . 2F **45**
Abergwaun. *Pemb* . . . 1D **42**
Abergwesyn. *Powy* . . . 5A **58**
Abergwili. *Carm* . . . 3E **45**
Abergwynfi. *Neat* . . . 2B **32**
Abergwyngregyn. *Gwyn* . . . 3F **81**
Abergynolwyn. *Gwyn* . . . 5F **69**
Aberhafesp. *Powy* . . . 1C **58**
Aberhonddu. *Powy* . . . 3D **46**
Aberhosan. *Powy* . . . 1H **57**
Aberkenfig. *B'end* . . . 3B **32**
Aberlady. *E Lot* . . . 2A **130**
Aberlemno. *Ang* . . . 3E **145**
Aberllefenni. *Gwyn* . . . 5G **69**
Abermaw. *Gwyn* . . . 4F **69**
Abermeurig. *Cdgn* . . . 5E **57**
Aber-miwl. *Powy* . . . 1D **58**
Abermule. *Powy* . . . 1D **58**
Abernant. *Carm* . . . 2H **43**
Abernant. *Rhon* . . . 5D **46**
Abernethy. *Per* . . . 2D **136**
Abernyte. *Per* . . . 5B **144**
Aber-oer. *Wrex* . . . 1E **71**
Aberpennar. *Rhon* . . . 2D **32**
Aberporth. *Cdgn* . . . 5B **56**
Aberriw. *Powy* . . . 5D **70**
Abersoch. *Gwyn* . . . 3C **68**
Abersychan. *Torf* . . . 5F **47**
Abertawe. *Swan* . . . 3F **31**
Aberteifi. *Cdgn* . . . 1B **44**
Aberthin. *V Glam* . . . 4D **32**
Abertillery. *Blae* . . . 5F **47**
Abertridwr. *Cphy* . . . 3E **32**
Abertridwr. *Powy* . . . 4C **70**
Abertyleri. *Blae* . . . 5F **47**
Abertysswg. *Cphy* . . . 5E **47**
Aberuthven. *Per* . . . 2B **136**
Aber Village. *Powy* . . . 3E **46**
Aberyscir. *Powy* . . . 3D **46**
Aberystwyth. *Cdgn* . . . 2E **57**
Abhainn Suidhe. *W Isl* . . . 7C **171**
Abingdon. *Oxon* . . . 2C **36**
Abinger Common. *Surr* . . . 1C **26**
Abinger Hammer. *Surr* . . . 1B **26**
Abington. *S Lan* . . . 2B **118**
Abington Pigotts. *Cambs* . . . 1D **52**
Ab Kettleby. *Leics* . . . 3E **74**
Ab Lench. *Worc* . . . 5E **61**
Ablington. *Glos* . . . 5G **49**
Ablington. *Wilts* . . . 2G **23**
Abney. *Derbs* . . . 3F **85**
Aboyne. *Abers* . . . 4C **152**
Abram. *G Man* . . . 4E **90**
Abriachan. *High* . . . 5H **157**
Abridge. *Essx* . . . 1F **39**
Abronhill. *N Lan* . . . 2A **128**
Abson. *S Glo* . . . 4C **34**
Abthorpe. *Nptn* . . . 1E **51**
Aby. *Linc* . . . 3D **88**
Acaster Malbis. *York* . . . 5H **99**
Acaster Selby. *N Yor* . . . 5H **99**
Accott. *Devn* . . . 3G **19**
Accrington. *Lanc* . . . 2F **91**
Acha. *Arg* . . . 3C **138**
Achachork. *High* . . . 4D **155**
Achadh a' Chuirn. *High* . . . 1E **147**
Achahoish. *Arg* . . . 2F **125**
Achaleven. *Arg* . . . 5D **140**
Achallader. *Arg* . . . 4H **141**
Acha Mor. *W Isl* . . . 5F **171**
Achanalt. *High* . . . 2E **157**
Achandunie. *High* . . . 1A **158**
Ach'an Todhair. *High* . . . 1E **141**
Achany. *High* . . . 3C **164**
Achaphubuil. *High* . . . 1E **141**
Acharacle. *High* . . . 2A **140**
Acharn. *Ang* . . . 1B **144**
Acharn. *Per* . . . 4E **143**
Acharole. *High* . . . 3E **169**
Achateny. *High* . . . 2G **139**
Achavanich. *High* . . . 4D **169**
Achdalieu. *High* . . . 1E **141**
Achduart. *High* . . . 3E **163**
Achentoul. *High* . . . 5A **168**
Achfary. *High* . . . 5C **166**
Achfrish. *High* . . . 2C **164**
Achgarve. *High* . . . 4C **162**
Achiemore. *High* . . . 2D **166** (nr. Durness)
Achiemore. *High* . . . 3A **168** (nr. Thurso)
A'Chill. *High* . . . 3A **146**
Achiltibuie. *High* . . . 3E **163**
Achina. *High* . . . 2H **167**
Achinahuagh. *High* . . . 2F **167**
Achindarroch. *High* . . . 3E **141**
Achinduich. *High* . . . 3C **164**
Achinduin. *Arg* . . . 5C **140**
Achininver. *High* . . . 2F **167**
Achintee. *High* . . . 4B **156**

Achintraid. *High* 5H 155
Achleck. *Arg* 4F 139
Achlorachan. *High* 3F 157
Achluachrach. *High* 5E 149
Achlyness. *High* 3C 166
Achmelvich. *High* 1E 163
Achmony. *High* 5H 157
Achmore. *High* 5A 156
(nr. Stromeferry)
Achmore. *High* 4E 163
(nr. Ullapool)
Achnacarnin. *High* 1E 163
Achnacarry. *High* 5D 148
Achnaclerach. *High* 2G 157
Achnacloich. *High* 3D 147
Ach na Cloiche. *High* 3D 147
Achnaconeran. *High* 2G 149
Achnacroish. *Arg* 4C 140
Achnafalnich. *Arg* 1B 134
Achnagarron. *High* 1A 158
Achnaha. *High* 2F 139
Achnahanat. *High* 4C 164
Achnahannet. *High* 1D 151
Achnairn. *High* 2C 164
Achnamara. *Arg* 1F 125
Achnanellan. *High* 5C 148
Achnangoul. *Arg* 3H 133
Achnasheen. *High* 3D 156
Achnashellach. *High* 4C 156
Achosnich. *High* 2F 139
Achow. *High* 5E 169
Achranich. *High* 4B 140
Achreamie. *High* 2C 168
Achriabhach. *High* 2F 141
Achriesgill. *High* 3C 166
Achrimsdale. *High* 3G 165
Achscrabster. *High* 2C 168
Achtoty. *High* 2G 167
Achurch. *Nptn* 2H 63
Achuvoldrach. *High* 3F 167
Achvaich. *High* 4E 164
Achvoan. *High* 3E 165
Ackenthwaite. *Cumb* 1E 97
Ackergill. *High* 3F 169
Ackergillshore. *High* 3F 169
Acklam. *Midd* 3B 106
Acklam. *N Yor* 3B 100
Ackleton. *Shrp* 1B 60
Acklington. *Nmbd* 4G 121
Ackton. *W Yor* 2E 93
Ackworth Moor Top. *W Yor* 3E 93
Acle. *Norf* 4G 79
Acocks Green. *W Mid* 2F 61
Acol. *Kent* 4H 41
Acomb. *Nmbd* 3C 114
Acomb. *York* 4H 99
Aconbury. *Here* 2A 48
Acre. *G Man* 4H 91
Acre. *Lanc* 2F 91
Acrefair. *Wrex* 1E 71
Acrise. *Kent* 1F 29
Acton. *Ches E* 5A 84
Acton. *Dors* 5E 15
Acton. *G Lon* 2C 38
Acton. *Shrp* 2F 59
Acton. *Staf* 1C 72
Acton. *Suff* 1B 54
Acton. *Worc* 4C 60
Acton. *Wrex* 5F 83
Acton Beauchamp. *Here* 5A 60
Acton Bridge. *Ches W* 3H 83
Acton Burnell. *Shrp* 5H 71
Acton Green. *Here* 5A 60
Acton Pigott. *Shrp* 5H 71
Acton Round. *Shrp* 1A 60
Acton Scott. *Shrp* 2G 59
Acton Trussell. *Staf* 4D 72
Acton Turville. *S Glo* 3D 34
Adam's Hill. *Worc* 3D 60
Adbaston. *Staf* 3B 72
Adber. *Dors* 4B 22
Adderbury. *Oxon* 2C 50
Adderley. *Shrp* 2A 72
Adderstone. *Nmbd* 1F 121
Addiewell. *W Lot* 3C 128
Addingham. *W Yor* 5C 98
Addington. *Buck* 3F 51
Addington. *G Lon* 4E 39
Addington. *Kent* 5A 40
Addinston. *Bord* 4B 130
Addiscombe. *G Lon* 4E 39
Addlestone. *Surr* 4B 38
Addlethorpe. *Linc* 4E 89
Adeney. *Telf* 4B 72
Adfa. *Powy* 5C 70
Adforton. *Here* 3G 59
Adgestone. *IOW* 4D 16
Adisham. *Kent* 5G 41
Adlestrop. *Glos* 3H 49
Adlingfleet. *E Yor* 2B 94
Adlington. *Ches E* 2D 84
Adlington. *Lanc* 3E 90
Admaston. *Staf* 3E 73
Admaston. *Telf* 4A 72
Admington. *Warw* 1G 49
Adpar. *Cdgn* 1D 44
Adsborough. *Som* 4F 21
Adstock. *Buck* 2F 51
Adstone. *Nptn* 5C 62
Adversane. *W Sus* 3B 26
Advie. *High* 5F 159
Adwalton. *W Yor* 2C 92
Adwell. *Oxon* 2E 37
Adwick le Street. *S Yor* 4F 93
Adwick upon Dearne. *S Yor* 4E 93
Adziel. *Abers* 3G 161
Ae. *Dum* 1A 112
Affleck. *Abers* 1F 153
Affpuddle. *Dors* 3D 14
Affric Lodge. *High* 1D 148
Afon-wen. *Flin* 3D 82
Agglethorpe. *N Yor* 1C 98
Aglionby. *Cumb* 4F 113
Aigburth. *Mers* 2F 83
Aike. *E Yor* 5E 101
Aikers. *Orkn* 8D 172
Aiketgate. *Cumb* 5F 113
Aikhead. *Cumb* 5D 112
Aikton. *Cumb* 4D 112
Ailey. *Here* 1G 47
Ailsworth. *Pet* 1A 64
Ainderby Quernhow. *N Yor* 1F 99
Ainderby Steeple. *N Yor* 5A 106
Aingers Green. *Essx* 3E 54
Ainsdale. *Mers* 3B 90
Ainsdale-on-Sea. *Mers* 3B 90
Ainstable. *Cumb* 5G 113
Ainsworth. *G Man* 3F 91
Ainthorpe. *N Yor* 4E 107
Aintree. *Mers* 1F 83
Aird. *Arg* 3E 133
Aird. *Dum* 3F 109
Aird. *High* 1G 155
(nr. Port Henderson)
Aird. *High* 3D 147
(nr. Tarskavaig)
Aird. *W Isl* 3C 170
(on Benbecula)
Aird. *W Isl* 4H 171
(on Isle of Lewis)
Àird a Bhasair. *High* 3E 147
Aird a Mhachair. *W Isl* 4C 170
Aird a Mhulaidh. *W Isl* 6D 171
Airdens. *High* 4D 164
Airdeny. *Arg* 1G 133
Aird Mhidhinis. *W Isl* 8C 170
Aird Mhighe. *W Isl* 9C 171
Aird Mhor. *W Isl* 8C 170
(on Barra)
Aird Mhor. *W Isl* 4C 170
(on South Uist)
Airdrie. *N Lan* 3A 128
Aird Shleibhe. *W Isl* 9D 171
Aird, The. *High* 3D 154
Aird Thunga. *W Isl* 4G 171
Aird Uig. *W Isl* 4C 171
Airedale. *W Yor* 2E 93
Airidh a Bhruaich. *W Isl* 6E 171
Airies. *Dum* 3E 109
Airmyn. *E Yor* 2H 93
Airntully. *Per* 5H 143
Airor. *High* 3F 147
Airth. *Falk* 1C 128
Airton. *N Yor* 4B 98
Aisby. *Linc* 1F 87
(nr. Gainsborough)
Aisby. *Linc* 2H 75
(nr. Grantham)
Aisgernis. *W Isl* 6C 170
Aish. *Devn* 2C 8
(nr. Buckfastleigh)
Aish. *Devn* 3E 9
(nr. Totnes)
Aisholt. *Som* 3E 21
Aiskew. *N Yor* 1E 99
Aislaby. *N Yor* 1B 100
(nr. Pickering)
Aislaby. *N Yor* 4F 107
(nr. Whitby)
Aislaby. *Stoc T* 3B 106
Aisthorpe. *Linc* 2G 87
Aith. *Shet* 2H 173
(on Fetlar)
Aith. *Shet* 6E 173
(on Mainland)
Akeld. *Nmbd* 2D 120
Akeley. *Buck* 2F 51
Akenham. *Suff* 1E 55
Albaston. *Corn* 5E 11
Alberbury. *Shrp* 4F 71
Albert Town. *Pemb* 3D 42
Albert Village. *Leics* 4H 73
Albourne. *W Sus* 4D 26
Albrighton. *Shrp* 4G 71
(nr. Shrewsbury)
Albrighton. *Shrp* 5C 72
(nr. Telford)
Alburgh. *Norf* 2E 67
Albury. *Herts* 3E 53
Albury. *Surr* 1B 26
Albyfield. *Cumb* 4G 113
Alby Hill. *Norf* 2D 78
Alcaig. *High* 3H 157
Alcaston. *Shrp* 2G 59
Alcester. *Warw* 5E 61
Alciston. *E Sus* 5G 27
Alcombe. *Som* 2C 20
Alconbury. *Cambs* 3A 64
Alconbury Weston. *Cambs* 3A 64
Aldborough. *Norf* 2D 78
Aldborough. *N Yor* 3G 99
Aldbourne. *Wilts* 4A 36
Aldbrough. *E Yor* 1F 95
Aldbrough St John. *N Yor* 3F 105
Aldbury. *Herts* 4H 51
Aldcliffe. *Lanc* 3D 96
Aldclune. *Per* 2G 143
Aldeburgh. *Suff* 5G 67
Aldeby. *Norf* 1G 67
Aldenham. *Herts* 1C 38
Alderbury. *Wilts* 4G 23
Aldercar. *Derbs* 1B 74
Alderford. *Norf* 4D 78
Alderholt. *Dors* 1G 15
Alderley. *Glos* 2C 34
Alderley Edge. *Ches E* 3C 84
Aldermaston. *W Ber* 5D 36
Aldermaston Stoke. *W Ber* 5E 36
Aldermaston Wharf. *W Ber* 5E 36
Alderminster. *Warw* 1H 49
Alder Moor. *Staf* 3G 73
Aldersey Green. *Ches W* 5G 83
Aldershot. *Hants* 1G 25
Alderton. *Glos* 2E 49
Alderton. *Nptn* 1F 51
Alderton. *Shrp* 3G 71
Alderton. *Suff* 1G 55
Alderton. *Wilts* 3D 34
Alderton Fields. *Glos* 2F 49
Alderwasley. *Derbs* 5H 85
Aldfield. *N Yor* 3E 99
Aldford. *Ches W* 5G 83
Aldgate. *Rut* 5G 75
Aldham. *Essx* 3C 54
Aldham. *Suff* 1D 54
Aldingbourne. *W Sus* 5A 26
Aldingham. *Cumb* 2B 96
Aldington. *Kent* 2E 29
Aldington. *Worc* 1F 49
Aldington Frith. *Kent* 2E 29
Aldochlay. *Arg* 4C 134
Aldon. *Shrp* 3G 59
Aldoth. *Cumb* 5C 112
Aldreth. *Cambs* 3D 64
Aldridge. *W Mid* 5E 73
Aldringham. *Suff* 4G 67
Aldsworth. *Glos* 4G 49
Aldsworth. *W Sus* 2F 17
Aldwark. *Derbs* 5G 85
Aldwark. *N Yor* 3G 99
Aldwick. *W Sus* 3H 17
Aldwincle. *Nptn* 2H 63
Aldworth. *W Ber* 4D 36
Alexandria. *W Dun* 1E 127
Aley. *Som* 3E 21
Aley Green. *C Beds* 4A 52
Alfardisworthy. *Devn* 1C 10
Alfington. *Devn* 3E 12
Alfold. *Surr* 2B 26
Alfold Bars. *W Sus* 2B 26
Alfold Crossways. *Surr* 2B 26
Alford. *Abers* 2C 152
Alford. *Linc* 3D 88
Alford. *Som* 3B 22
Alfreton. *Derbs* 5B 86
Alfrick. *Worc* 5B 60
Alfrick Pound. *Worc* 5B 60
Alfriston. *E Sus* 5G 27
Algarkirk. *Linc* 2B 76
Alhampton. *Som* 3B 22
Alkborough. *N Lin* 2B 94
Alkerton. *Oxon* 1B 50
Alkham. *Kent* 1G 29
Alkington. *Shrp* 2H 71
Alkmonton. *Derbs* 2F 73
Alladale Lodge. *High* 5B 164
Allaleigh. *Devn* 3E 9
Allanbank. *N Lan* 4B 128
Allanton. *N Lan* 4B 128
Allanton. *Bord* 4E 131
Allaston. *Glos* 5B 48
Allbrook. *Hants* 4C 24
All Cannings. *Wilts* 5F 35
Allendale Town. *Nmbd* 4B 114
Allen End. *Warw* 1F 61
Allenheads. *Nmbd* 5B 114
Allensford. *Dur* 5D 115
Allen's Green. *Herts* 4E 53
Allensmore. *Here* 2H 47
Allenton. *Derb* 2A 74
Aller. *Som* 4H 21
Allerby. *Cumb* 1B 102
Allercombe. *Devn* 3D 12
Allerford. *Som* 2C 20
Allerston. *N Yor* 1C 100
Allerthorpe. *E Yor* 5B 100
Allerton. *Mers* 2G 83
Allerton. *W Yor* 1B 92
Allerton Bywater. *W Yor* 2E 93
Allerton Mauleverer. *N Yor* 4G 99
Allesley. *W Mid* 2G 61
Allestree. *Derb* 2H 73
Allet. *Corn* 4B 6
Allexton. *Leics* 5F 75
Allgreave. *Ches E* 4D 84
Allhallows. *Medw* 3C 40
Allhallows-on-Sea. *Medw* 3C 40
Alligin Shuas. *High* 3H 155
Allimore Green. *Staf* 4C 72
Allington. *Kent* 5B 40
Allington. *Linc* 1F 75
Allington. *Wilts* 3H 23
(nr. Amesbury)
Allington. *Wilts* 5F 35
(nr. Devizes)
Allithwaite. *Cumb* 2C 96
Alloa. *Clac* 4A 136
Allonby. *Cumb* 5B 112
Allostock. *Ches W* 3B 84
Alloway. *S Ayr* 3C 116
Allowenshay. *Som* 1G 13
All Saints South Elmham. *Suff* 2F 67
Allscott. *Shrp* 1B 60
Allscott. *Telf* 4A 72
All Stretton. *Shrp* 1G 59
Allt. *Carm* 5F 45
Alltami. *Flin* 4E 83
Alltgobhlach. *N Ayr* 5G 125
Alltmawr. *Powy* 1D 46
Alltnacaillich. *High* 4E 167
Allt na h-Airbhe. *High* 4F 163
Alltour. *High* 5E 148
Alltsigh. *High* 2G 149
Alltwalis. *Carm* 2E 45
Alltwen. *Neat* 5H 45
Alltyblacca. *Cdgn* 1F 45
Allt-y-goed. *Pemb* 1B 44
Almeley. *Here* 5F 59
Almeley Wooton. *Here* 5F 59
Almer. *Dors* 3E 15
Almholme. *S Yor* 4F 93
Almington. *Staf* 2B 72
Alminstone Cross. *Devn* 4D 18
Almodington. *W Sus* 3G 17
Almondbank. *Per* 1C 136
Almondbury. *W Yor* 3B 92
Almondsbury. *S Glo* 3B 34
Alne. *N Yor* 3G 99
Alness. *High* 2A 158
Alnessferry. *High* 2A 158
Alnham. *Nmbd* 3D 121
Alnmouth. *Nmbd* 3G 121
Alnwick. *Nmbd* 3F 121
Alphamstone. *Essx* 2B 54
Alpheton. *Suff* 5A 66
Alphington. *Devn* 3C 12
Alpington. *Norf* 5E 79
Alport. *Derbs* 4G 85
Alport. *Powy* 1E 59
Alpraham. *Ches E* 5H 83
Alresford. *Essx* 3D 54
Alrewas. *Staf* 4F 73
Alsager. *Ches E* 5B 84
Alsagers Bank. *Staf* 1C 72
Alsop en le Dale. *Derbs* 5F 85
Alston. *Cumb* 5A 114
Alston. *Devn* 2G 13
Alstone. *Glos* 2E 49
Alstone. *Som* 2G 21
Alstonefield. *Staf* 5F 85
Alston Sutton. *Som* 1H 21
Alswear. *Devn* 4H 19
Altandhu. *High* 2D 163
Altanduin. *High* 1F 165
Altarnun. *Corn* 4C 10
Altass. *High* 3B 164
Alterwall. *High* 2E 169
Altgaltraig. *Arg* 2B 126
Altham. *Lanc* 1F 91
Althorne. *Essx* 1D 40
Althorpe. *N Lin* 4B 94
Altnabreac. *High* 4C 168
Altnacealgach. *High* 2G 163
Altnafeadh. *High* 3G 141
Altnaharra. *High* 5F 167
Altofts. *W Yor* 2D 92
Alton. *Derbs* 4A 86
Alton. *Hants* 3F 25
Alton. *Staf* 1E 73
Alton Barnes. *Wilts* 5G 35
Altonhill. *E Ayr* 1D 116
Alton Pancras. *Dors* 2C 14
Alton Priors. *Wilts* 5G 35
Altrincham. *G Man* 2B 84
Altrua. *High* 4E 149
Alva. *Clac* 4A 136
Alvanley. *Ches W* 3G 83
Alvaston. *Derb* 2A 74
Alvechurch. *Worc* 3E 61
Alvecote. *Warw* 5G 73

Alvediston. Wilts 4E 23
Alveley. Shrp 2B 60
Alverdiscott. Devn 4F 19
Alverstoke. Hants 3D 16
Alverstone. IOW 4D 16
Alverthorpe. W Yor 2D 92
Alverton. Notts 1E 75
Alves. Mor 2F 159
Alvescot. Oxon 5A 50
Alveston. S Glo 3B 34
Alveston. Warw 5G 61
Alvie. High 3C 150
Alvingham. Linc 1C 88
Alvington. Glos 5B 48
Alwalton. Cambs 1A 64
Alweston. Dors 1B 14
Alwington. Devn 4E 19
Alwinton. Nmbd 4D 120
Alwoodley. W Yor 5E 99
Alyth. Per 4B 144
Amatnatua. High 4B 164
Am Baile. W Isl 7C 170
Ambaston. Derbs 2B 74
Ambergate. Derbs 5H 85
Amber Hill. Linc 1B 76
Amberley. Glos 5D 48
Amberley. W Sus 4B 26
Amble. Nmbd 4G 121
Amblecote. W Mid 2C 60
Ambler Thorn. W Yor 2A 92
Ambleside. Cumb 4E 103
Ambleston. Pemb 2E 43
Ambrosden. Oxon 4E 50
Amcotts. N Lin 3B 94
Amersham. Buck 1A 38
Amerton. Staf 3D 73
Amesbury. Wilts 2G 23
Amisfield. Dum 1B 112
Amlwch. IOA 1D 80
Amlwch Port. IOA 1D 80
Ammanford. Carm 4G 45
Amotherby. N Yor 2B 100
Ampfield. Hants 4B 24
Ampleforth. N Yor 2H 99
Ampleforth College. N Yor 2H 99
Ampney Crucis. Glos 5F 49
Ampney St Mary. Glos 5F 49
Ampney St Peter. Glos 5F 49
Amport. Hants 2A 24
Ampthill. C Beds 2A 52
Ampton. Suff 3A 66
Amroth. Pemb 4F 43
Amulree. Per 5G 143
Amwell. Herts 4B 52
Anaheilt. High 2C 140
An Aird. High 3D 147
An Camus Darach. High 4E 147
Ancaster. Linc 1G 75
Anchor. Shrp 2D 58
Anchorsholme. Bkpl 5C 96
Anchor Street. Norf 3F 79
An Cnoc. W Isl 4G 171
An Coroghon. High 3A 146
Ancroft. Nmbd 5G 131
Ancrum. Bord 2A 120
Ancton. W Sus 5A 26
Anderby. Linc 3E 89
Anderby Creek. Linc 3E 89
Anderson. Dors 3D 15
Anderton. Ches W 3A 84
Andertons Mill. Lanc 3D 90
Andover. Hants 2B 24
Andover Down. Hants 2B 24
Andoversford. Glos 4F 49
Andreas. IOM 2D 108
An Dùnan. High 1D 147
Andwell. Hants 1E 25
Anelog. Gwyn 3A 68
Anfield. Mers 1F 83
Angarrack. Corn 3C 4
Angelbank. Shrp 3H 59
Angersleigh. Som 1F 13
Angerton. Cumb 4D 112
Angle. Pemb 4C 42
Angmering. W Sus 5B 26
Angmering-on-Sea. W Sus 5B 26
Angram. N Yor 5B 104 (nr. Keld)
Angram. N Yor 5H 99 (nr. York)
Anick. Nmbd 3C 114
Ankerbold. Derbs 4A 86
Ankerville. High 1C 158
Anlaby. E Yor 2D 94
Anlaby Park. Hull 2D 94
An Leth Meadhanach. W Isl 7C 170
Anmer. Norf 3G 77
Anmore. Hants 1E 17
Annan. Dum 3D 112
Annaside. Cumb 1A 96
Annat. Arg 1H 133
Annat. High 3A 156
Annathill. N Lan 2A 128
Anna Valley. Hants 2B 24
Annbank. S Ayr 2D 116
Annesley. Notts 5C 86
Annesley Woodhouse. Notts 5C 86
Annfield Plain. Dur 4E 115
Annscroft. Shrp 5G 71
An Sailean. High 2A 140
Ansdell. Lanc 2B 90
Ansford. Som 3B 22
Ansley. Warw 1G 61
Anslow. Staf 3G 73
Anslow Gate. Staf 3F 73
Ansteadbrook. Surr 2A 26
Anstey. Herts 2E 53
Anstey. Leics 5C 74
Anston. S Lan 5D 128
Anstruther Easter. Fife 3H 137
Anstruther Wester. Fife 3H 137
Ansty. Warw 2A 62
Ansty. W Sus 3D 27
Ansty. Wilts 4E 23
An Taobh Tuath. W Isl 9B 171
An t-Aodann Ban. High 3C 154
An t Ath Leathann. High 1E 147
An Teanga. High 3E 147
Anthill Common. Hants 1E 17
Anthorn. Cumb 4C 112
Antingham. Norf 2E 79
An t-Ob. W Isl 9C 171
Anton's Gowt. Linc 1B 76
Antony. Corn 3A 8
An t-Òrd. High 2E 147
Antrobus. Ches W 3A 84
Anvil Corner. Devn 2D 10
Anwick. Linc 5A 88
Anwoth. Dum 4C 110
Apethorpe. Nptn 1H 63
Apeton. Staf 4C 72
Apley. Linc 3A 88
Apperknowle. Derbs 3A 86
Apperley. Glos 3D 48
Apperley Dene. Nmbd 4D 114
Appersett. N Yor 5B 104
Appin. Arg 4D 140
Appleby. N Lin 3C 94
Appleby-in-Westmorland. Cumb 2H 103
Appleby Magna. Leics 5H 73
Appleby Parva. Leics 5H 73
Applecross. High 4G 155
Appledore. Devn 3E 19 (nr. Bideford)
Appledore. Devn 1D 12 (nr. Tiverton)
Appledore. Kent 3D 28
Appledore Heath. Kent 2D 28
Appleford. Oxon 2D 36
Applegarthtown. Dum 1C 112
Applemore. Hants 2B 16
Appleshaw. Hants 2B 24
Applethwaite. Cumb 2D 102
Appleton. Hal 2H 83
Appleton. Oxon 5C 50
Appleton-le-Moors. N Yor 1B 100
Appleton-le-Street. N Yor 2B 100
Appleton Roebuck. N Yor 5H 99
Appleton Thorn. Warr 2A 84
Appleton Wiske. N Yor 4A 106
Appletree. Nptn 1C 50
Appletreehall. Bord 3H 119
Appletreewick. N Yor 3C 98
Appley. Som 4D 20
Appley Bridge. Lanc 4D 90
Apse Heath. IOW 4D 16
Apsley End. C Beds 2B 52
Apuldram. W Sus 2G 17
Arabella. High 1C 158
Arasaig. High 5E 147
Arbeadie. Abers 4D 152
Arberth. Pemb 3F 43
Arbirlot. Ang 4F 145
Arborfield. Wok 5F 37
Arborfield Cross. Wok 5F 37
Arborfield Garrison. Wok 5F 37
Arbourthorne. S Yor 2A 86
Arbroath. Ang 4F 145
Arbuthnott. Abers 1H 145
Arcan. High 3H 157
Archargary. High 3H 167
Archdeacon Newton. Darl 3F 105
Archiestown. Mor 4G 159
Arclid. Ches E 4B 84
Arclid Green. Ches E 4B 84
Ardachu. High 3D 164
Ardalanish. Arg 2A 132
Ardaneaskan. High 5H 155
Ardarroch. High 5H 155
Ardbeg. Arg 1C 126 (nr. Dunoon)
Ardbeg. Arg 5C 124 (on Islay)
Ardbeg. Arg 3B 126 (on Isle of Bute)
Ardcharnich. High 5F 163
Ardchiavaig. Arg 2A 132
Ardchonnell. Arg 2G 133
Ardchrishnish. Arg 1B 132
Ardchronie. High 5D 164
Ardchullarie. Stir 2E 135
Ardchyle. Stir 1E 135
Ard-dhubh. High 4G 155
Arddleen. Powy 4E 71
Arddlin. Powy 4E 71
Ardechive. High 4D 148
Ardeley. Herts 3D 52
Ardelve. High 1A 148
Arden. Arg 1E 127
Ardendrain. High 5H 157
Arden Hall. N Yor 5C 106
Ardens Grafton. Warw 5F 61
Ardentinny. Arg 1C 126
Ardeonaig. Stir 5D 142
Ardersier. High 3B 158
Ardery. High 2B 140
Ardessie. High 5E 163
Ardfern. Arg 3F 133
Ardfernal. Arg 2D 124
Ardfin. Arg 3C 124
Ardgartan. Arg 3B 134
Ardgay. High 4C 164
Ardgour. High 2E 141
Ardheslaig. High 3G 155
Ardindrean. High 5F 163
Ardingly. W Sus 3E 27
Ardington. Oxon 3C 36
Ardlamont House. Arg 3A 126
Ardleigh. Essx 3D 54
Ardler. Per 4B 144
Ardley. Oxon 3D 50
Ardlui. Arg 2C 134
Ardlussa. Arg 1E 125
Ardmair. High 4F 163
Ardmay. Arg 3B 134
Ardminish. Arg 5E 125
Ardmolich. High 1B 140
Ardmore. High 3C 166 (nr. Kinlochbervie)
Ardmore. High 5E 164 (nr. Tain)
Ardnacross. Arg 4G 139
Ardnadam. Arg 1C 126
Ardnagrask. High 4H 157
Ardnamurach. High 4G 147
Ardnarff. High 5A 156
Ardnastang. High 2C 140
Ardoch. Per 5H 143
Ardochy House. High 3E 148
Ardpatrick. Arg 3F 125
Ardrishaig. Arg 1G 125
Ardroag. High 4B 154
Ardross. High 1A 158
Ardrossan. N Ayr 5D 126
Ardshealach. High 2A 140
Ardsley. S Yor 4D 93
Ardslignish. High 2G 139
Ardtalla. Arg 4C 124
Ardtalnaig. Per 5E 142
Ardtoe. High 1A 140
Arduaine. Arg 2E 133
Ardullie. High 2H 157
Ardvasar. High 3E 147
Ardvorlich. Per 1F 135
Ardwell. Dum 5G 109
Ardwell. Mor 5A 160
Arean. High 1A 140
Areley Common. Worc 3C 60
Areley Kings. Worc 3B 60
Arford. Hants 3G 25
Argoed. Cphy 2E 33
Argoed Mill. Powy 4B 58
Aridhglas. Arg 2B 132
Arinacrinachd. High 3G 155
Arinagour. Arg 3D 138
Arisaig. High 5E 147
Ariundle. High 2C 140
Arivegaig. High 2A 140
Arkendale. N Yor 3F 99
Arkesden. Essx 2E 53
Arkholme. Lanc 2E 97
Arkle Town. N Yor 4D 104
Arkley. G Lon 1D 38
Arksey. S Yor 4F 93
Arkwright Town. Derbs 3B 86
Arlecdon. Cumb 3B 102
Arlescote. Warw 1B 50
Arlesey. C Beds 2B 52
Arleston. Telf 4A 72
Arley. Ches E 2A 84
Arlingham. Glos 4C 48
Arlington. Devn 2G 19
Arlington. E Sus 5G 27
Arlington. Glos 5G 49
Arlington Beccott. Devn 2G 19
Armadail. High 3E 147
Armadale. High 3E 147 (nr. Isleornsay)
Armadale. High 2H 167 (nr. Strathy)
Armadale. W Lot 3C 128
Armathwaite. Cumb 5G 113
Arminghall. Norf 5E 79
Armitage. Staf 4E 73
Armitage Bridge. W Yor 3B 92
Armley. W Yor 1C 92
Armscote. Warw 1H 49
Arms, The. Norf 1A 66
Armston. Nptn 2H 63
Armthorpe. S Yor 4G 93
Arncliffe. N Yor 2B 98
Arncliffe Cote. N Yor 2B 98
Arncroach. Fife 3H 137
Arne. Dors 4E 15
Arnesby. Leics 1D 62
Arnicle. Arg 2B 122
Arnisdale. High 2G 147
Arnish. High 4E 155
Arniston. Midl 3G 129
Arnol. W Isl 3F 171
Arnold. E Yor 5F 101
Arnold. Notts 1C 74
Arnprior. Stir 4F 135
Arnside. Cumb 2D 96
Aros Mains. Arg 4G 139
Arpafeelie. High 3A 158
Arrad Foot. Cumb 1C 96
Arram. E Yor 5E 101
Arras. E Yor 5D 100
Arrathorne. N Yor 5E 105
Arreton. IOW 4D 16
Arrington. Cambs 5C 64
Arrochar. Arg 3B 134
Arrow. Warw 5E 61
Arscaig. High 2C 164
Artafallie. High 4A 158
Arthington. W Yor 5E 99
Arthingworth. Nptn 2E 63
Arthog. Gwyn 4F 69
Arthrath. Abers 5G 161
Arthurstone. Per 4B 144
Artington. Surr 1A 26
Arundel. W Sus 5B 26
Asby. Cumb 2B 102
Ascog. Arg 3C 126
Ascot. Wind 4A 38
Ascott-under-Wychwood. Oxon 4B 50
Asenby. N Yor 2F 99
Asfordby. Leics 4E 74
Asfordby Hill. Leics 4E 74
Asgarby. Linc 4C 88 (nr. Horncastle)
Asgarby. Linc 1A 76 (nr. Sleaford)
Ash. Devn 4E 9
Ash. Dors 1D 14
Ash. Kent 5G 41 (nr. Sandwich)
Ash. Kent 4H 39 (nr. Swanley)
Ash. Som 4H 21
Ash. Surr 1G 25
Ashampstead. W Ber 4D 36
Ashbocking. Suff 5D 66
Ashbourne. Derbs 1F 73
Ashbrittle. Som 4D 20
Ashbrook. Shrp 1G 59
Ashburton. Devn 2D 8
Ashbury. Devn 3F 11
Ashbury. Oxon 3A 36
Ashby. N Lin 4B 94
Ashby by Partney. Linc 4D 88
Ashby cum Fenby. NE Lin 4F 95
Ashby de la Launde. Linc 5H 87
Ashby-de-la-Zouch. Leics 4A 74
Ashby Folville. Leics 4E 74
Ashby Magna. Leics 1C 62
Ashby Parva. Leics 2C 62
Ashby Puerorum. Linc 3C 88
Ashby St Ledgars. Nptn 4C 62
Ashby St Mary. Norf 5F 79
Ashchurch. Glos 2E 49
Ashcombe. Devn 5C 12
Ashcott. Som 3H 21
Ashdon. Essx 1F 53
Ashe. Hants 1D 24
Asheldham. Essx 5C 54
Ashen. Essx 1H 53
Ashendon. Buck 4F 51
Ashey. IOW 4D 16
Ashfield. Hants 1B 16
Ashfield. Here 3A 48
Ashfield. Shrp 2H 59
Ashfield. Stir 3G 135
Ashfield. Suff 4E 66
Ashfield Green. Suff 3E 67
Ashfold Crossways. W Sus 3D 26
Ashford. Devn 3F 19 (nr. Barnstaple)
Ashford. Devn 4C 8 (nr. Kingsbridge)
Ashford. Hants 1G 15
Ashford. Kent 1E 28
Ashford. Surr 3B 38
Ashford Bowdler. Shrp 3H 59
Ashford Carbonel. Shrp 3H 59
Ashford Hill. Hants 5D 36
Ashford in the Water. Derbs 4F 85

Ashgill—Bagby

Ashgill. S Lan 5A 128
Ash Green. Warw 2H 61
Ashgrove. Mor 2G 159
Ashill. Devn 1D 12
Ashill. Norf 5A 78
Ashill. Som 1G 13
Ashingdon. Essx 1C 40
Ashington. Nmbd 1F 115
Ashington. W Sus 4C 26
Ashkirk. Bord 2G 119
Ashlett. Hants 2C 16
Ashleworth. Glos 3D 48
Ashley. Cambs 4F 65
Ashley. Ches E 2B 84
Ashley. Dors 2G 15
Ashley. Glos 2E 35
Ashley. Hants 3A 16
(nr. New Milton)
Ashley. Hants 3B 24
(nr. Winchester)
Ashley. Kent 1H 29
Ashley. Nptn 1E 63
Ashley. Staf 2B 72
Ashley. Wilts 5D 34
Ashley Green. Buck 5H 51
Ashley Heath. Dors 2G 15
Ashley Heath. Staf 2B 72
Ashley Moor. Here 4G 59
Ash Magna. Shrp 2H 71
Ashmanhaugh. Norf 3F 79
Ashmansworth. Hants 1C 24
Ashmansworthy. Devn 1D 10
Ashmead Green. Glos 2C 34
Ashmill. Devn 3D 11
(nr. Holsworthy)
Ash Mill. Devn 4A 20
(nr. South Molton)
Ashmore. Dors 1E 15
Ashmore Green. W Ber 5D 36
Ashover. Derbs 4A 86
Ashow. Warw 3H 61
Ash Parva. Shrp 2H 71
Ashperton. Here 1B 48
Ashprington. Devn 3E 9
Ash Priors. Som 4E 21
Ashreigney. Devn 1G 11
Ash Street. Suff 1D 54
Ashtead. Surr 5C 38
Ash Thomas. Devn 1D 12
Ashton. Corn 4D 4
Ashton. Here 4H 59
Ashton. Inv 2D 126
Ashton. Nptn 2H 63
(nr. Oundle)
Ashton. Nptn 1F 51
(nr. Roade)
Ashton. Pet 5A 76
Ashton Common. Wilts 1E 23
Ashton Hayes. Ches W 4H 83
Ashton-in-Makerfield. G Man 4D 90
Ashton Keynes. Wilts 2F 35
Ashton under Hill. Worc 2E 49
Ashton-under-Lyne. G Man 1D 84
Ashton upon Mersey. G Man 1B 84
Ashurst. Hants 1B 16
Ashurst. Kent 2G 27
Ashurst. Lanc 4C 90
Ashurst. W Sus 4C 26
Ashurst Wood. W Sus 2F 27
Ash Vale. Surr 1G 25
Ashwater. Devn 3D 11
Ashwell. Herts 2C 52
Ashwell. Rut 4F 75
Ashwellthorpe. Norf 1D 66
Ashwick. Som 2B 22
Ashwicken. Norf 4G 77
Ashwood. Staf 2C 60
Askam in Furness. Cumb 2B 96
Askern. S Yor 3F 93
Askerswell. Dors 3A 14
Askett. Buck 5G 51
Askham. Cumb 2G 103
Askham. Notts 3E 87
Askham Bryan. York 5H 99
Askham Richard. York 5H 99
Askrigg. N Yor 5C 104
Askwith. N Yor 5D 98
Aslackby. Linc 2H 75
Aslacton. Norf 1D 66
Aslockton. Notts 1E 75
Aspatria. Cumb 5C 112
Aspenden. Herts 3D 52
Asperton. Linc 2B 76
Aspley Guise. C Beds 2H 51
Aspley Heath. C Beds 2H 51
Aspull. G Man 4E 90
Asselby. E Yor 2H 93
Assington. Suff 2C 54
Assington Green. Suff 5G 65
Astbury. Ches E 4C 84
Astcote. Nptn 5D 62
Asterby. Linc 3B 88
Asterley. Shrp 5F 71
Asterton. Shrp 1F 59
Asthall. Oxon 4A 50
Asthall Leigh. Oxon 4B 50
Astle. High 4E 165
Astley. G Man 4F 91
Astley. Shrp 4H 71
Astley. Warw 2H 61
Astley. Worc 4B 60
Astley Abbotts. Shrp 1B 60
Astley Bridge. G Man 3F 91
Astley Cross. Worc 4C 60
Aston. Ches E 1A 72
Aston. Ches W 3H 83
Aston. Derbs 2F 85
(nr. Hope)
Aston. Derbs 2F 73
(nr. Sudbury)
Aston. Flin 4F 83
Aston. Here 4G 59
Aston. Herts 3C 52
Aston. Oxon 5B 50
Aston. Shrp 1C 60
(nr. Bridgnorth)
Aston. Shrp 3H 71
(nr. Wem)
Aston. S Yor 2B 86
Aston. Staf 1B 72
Aston. Telf 5A 72
Aston. W Mid 1E 61
Aston. Wok 3F 37
Aston Abbotts. Buck 3G 51
Aston Botterell. Shrp 2A 60
Aston-by-Stone. Staf 2D 72
Aston Cantlow. Warw 5F 61
Aston Clinton. Buck 4G 51
Aston Crews. Here 3B 48
Aston Cross. Glos 2E 49
Aston End. Herts 3C 52
Aston Eyre. Shrp 1A 60
Aston Fields. Worc 4D 60
Aston Flamville. Leics 1B 62
Aston Ingham. Here 3B 48
Aston juxta Mondrum. Ches E 5A 84
Astonlane. Shrp 1A 60
Aston le Walls. Nptn 5B 62
Aston Magna. Glos 2G 49
Aston Munslow. Shrp 2H 59
Aston on Carrant. Glos 2E 49
Aston on Clun. Shrp 2F 59
Aston-on-Trent. Derbs 3B 74
Aston Pigott. Shrp 5F 71
Aston Rogers. Shrp 5F 71
Aston Rowant. Oxon 2F 37
Aston Sandford. Buck 5F 51
Aston Somerville. Worc 2F 49
Aston Subedge. Glos 1G 49
Aston Tirrold. Oxon 3D 36
Aston Upthorpe. Oxon 3D 36
Astrop. Nptn 2D 50
Astwick. C Beds 2C 52
Astwood. Mil 1H 51
Astwood Bank. Worc 4E 61
Aswarby. Linc 2H 75
Aswardby. Linc 3C 88
Atcham. Shrp 5H 71
Atch Lench. Worc 5E 61
Athelhampton. Dors 3C 14
Athelington. Suff 3E 66
Athelney. Som 4G 21
Athelstaneford. E Lot 2B 130
Atherfield Green. IOW 5C 16
Atherington. Devn 4F 19
Atherington. W Sus 5B 26
Athersley. S Yor 4D 92
Atherstone. Warw 1H 61
Atherstone on Stour. Warw 5G 61
Atherton. G Man 4E 91
Ath-Tharracail. High 2A 140
Atlow. Derbs 1G 73
Attadale. High 5B 156
Attenborough. Notts 2C 74
Atterby. Linc 1G 87
Atterley. Shrp 1A 60
Atterton. Leics 1A 62
Attleborough. Norf 1C 66
Attleborough. Warw 1A 62
Attlebridge. Norf 4D 78
Atwick. E Yor 4F 101
Atworth. Wilts 5D 34
Auberrow. Here 1H 47
Aubourn. Linc 4G 87
Aucharnie. Abers 4D 160
Auchattie. Abers 4D 152
Auchavan. Ang 2A 144
Auchbreck. Mor 1G 151
Auchenback. E Ren 4G 127
Auchenblae. Abers 1G 145
Auchenbrack. Dum 5G 117
Auchenbreck. Arg 1B 126
Auchencairn. Dum 4E 111
(nr. Dalbeattie)
Auchencairn. Dum 1A 112
(nr. Dumfries)
Auchencarroch. W Dun 1F 127
Auchencrow. Bord 3E 131
Auchendennan. W Dun 1E 127
Auchendinny. Midl 3F 129
Auchengray. S Lan 4C 128
Auchenhalrig. Mor 2A 160
Auchenheath. S Lan 5B 128
Auchenlochan. Arg 2A 126
Auchenmade. N Ayr 5E 127
Auchenmalg. Dum 4H 109
Auchentiber. N Ayr 5E 127
Auchenvennel. Arg 1D 126
Auchindrain. Arg 3H 133
Auchininna. Abers 4D 160
Auchinleck. Dum 2B 110
Auchinleck. E Ayr 2E 117
Auchinloch. N Lan 2H 127
Auchinstarry. N Lan 2A 128
Auchleven. Abers 1D 152
Auchlochan. S Lan 1H 117
Auchlunachan. High 5F 163
Auchmillan. E Ayr 2E 117
Auchmithie. Ang 4F 145
Auchmuirbridge. Per 3E 136
Auchmull. Ang 1E 145
Auchnacree. Ang 4G 161
Auchnafree. Per 5F 143
Auchnagallin. High 5E 159
Auchnagatt. Abers 4G 161
Aucholzie. Abers 4H 151
Auchreddie. Abers 4F 161
Auchterarder. Per 2B 136
Auchteraw. High 3F 149
Auchterderran. Fife 4E 136
Auchterhouse. Ang 5C 144
Auchtermuchty. Fife 2E 137
Auchterneed. High 3G 157
Auchtertool. Fife 4E 136
Auchtertyre. High 1G 147
Auchtubh. Stir 1E 135
Auckengill. High 2F 169
Auckley. S Yor 4G 93
Audenshaw. G Man 1D 84
Audlem. Ches E 1A 72
Audley. Staf 5B 84
Audley End. Essx 2F 53
Audmore. Staf 3C 72
Auds. Abers 2D 160
Aughertree. Cumb 1D 102
Aughton. E Yor 1H 93
Aughton. Lanc 3E 97
(nr. Lancaster)
Aughton. Lanc 4B 90
(nr. Ormskirk)
Aughton. S Yor 2B 86
Aughton. Wilts 1H 23
Aughton Park. Lanc 4C 90
Auldearn. High 3D 158
Aulden. Here 5G 59
Auldgirth. Dum 1G 111
Auldhouse. S Lan 4H 127
Ault a' chruinn. High 1B 148
Aultbea. High 5C 162
Aultdearg. High 2E 157
Aultgrishan. High 5B 162
Aultguish Inn. High 1F 157
Ault Hucknall. Derbs 4B 86
Aultibea. High 1H 165
Aultiphurst. High 2A 168
Aultivullin. High 2A 168
Aultmore. Mor 3B 160
Aultnamain Inn. High 5D 164
Aunby. Linc 4H 75
Aunsby. Linc 2H 75
Aust. S Glo 3A 34
Austerfield. S Yor 1D 86
Austin Fen. Linc 1C 88
Austrey. Warw 5G 73
Austwick. N Yor 3G 97
Authorpe. Linc 2D 88
Authorpe Row. Linc 3E 89
Avebury. Wilts 5G 35
Avebury Trusloe. Wilts 5F 35
Aveley. Thur 2G 39
Avening. Glos 2D 35
Averham. Notts 5E 87
Aveton Gifford. Devn 4C 8
Avielochan. High 2D 150
Aviemore. High 2C 150
Avington. Hants 3D 24
Avoch. High 3B 158
Avon. Hants 3G 15
Avonbridge. Falk 2C 128
Avon Dassett. Warw 5B 62
Avonmouth. Bris 4A 34
Avonwick. Devn 3D 8
Awbridge. Hants 4B 24
Awliscombe. Devn 2E 13
Awre. Glos 5C 48
Awsworth. Notts 1B 74
Axbridge. Som 1H 21
Axford. Hants 2E 24
Axford. Wilts 5H 35
Axminster. Devn 3F 13
Axmouth. Devn 3F 13
Aycliffe Village. Dur 2F 105
Aydon. Nmbd 3D 114
Aykley Heads. Dur 5F 115
Aylburton. Glos 5B 48
Aylburton Common. Glos 5B 48
Ayle. Nmbd 5A 114
Aylesbeare. Devn 3D 12
Aylesbury. Buck 4G 51
Aylesby. NE Lin 4F 95
Aylescott. Devn 1G 11
Aylesford. Kent 5B 40
Aylesham. Kent 5G 41
Aylestone. Leic 5C 74
Aylmerton. Norf 2D 78
Aylsham. Norf 3D 78
Aylton. Here 2B 48
Aylworth. Glos 3G 49
Aymestrey. Here 4G 59
Aynho. Nptn 2D 50
Ayot Green. Herts 4C 52
Ayot St Lawrence. Herts 4B 52
Ayot St Peter. Herts 4C 52
Ayr. S Ayr 2C 116
Ayreville. Torb 2E 9
Aysgarth. N Yor 1C 98
Ayshford. Devn 1D 12
Ayside. Cumb 1C 96
Ayston. Rut 5F 75
Ayton. Bord 3F 131
Aywick. Shet 3G 173
Azerley. N Yor 2E 99

B

Babbacombe. Torb 2F 9
Babbinswood. Shrp 3F 71
Babb's Green. Herts 4D 53
Babcary. Som 4A 22
Babel. Carm 2B 46
Babell. Flin 3D 82
Babingley. Norf 3F 77
Bablock Hythe. Oxon 5C 50
Babraham. Cambs 5E 65
Babworth. Notts 2D 86
Bac. W Isl 3G 171
Bachau. IOA 2D 80
Bacheldre. Powy 1E 59
Bachymbyd Fawr. Den 4C 82
Backaland. Orkn 4E 172
Backbarrow. Cumb 1C 96
Backe. Carm 3G 43
Backfolds. Abers 3H 161
Backford. Ches W 3G 83
Backhill. Abers 5E 161
Backhill of Clackriach. Abers 4G 161
Backies. High 3F 165
Backmuir of New Gilston. Fife 3G 137
Back of Keppoch. High 5E 147
Back Street. Suff 5G 65
Backwell. N Som 5H 33
Backworth. Tyne 2G 115
Bacon End. Essx 4G 53
Baconsthorpe. Norf 2D 78
Bacton. Here 2G 47
Bacton. Norf 2F 79
Bacton. Suff 4C 66
Bacton Green. Norf 2F 79
Bacup. Lanc 2G 91
Badachonacher. High 1A 158
Badachro. High 1G 155
Badanloch Lodge. High 5H 167
Badavanich. High 3D 156
Badbury. Swin 3G 35
Badby. Nptn 5C 62
Badcall. High 3C 166
Badcaul. High 4E 163
Baddeley Green. Stoke 5D 84
Baddesley Clinton. W Mid 3G 61
Baddesley Ensor. Warw 1G 61
Baddidarach. High 1E 163
Baddoch. Abers 5F 151
Badenscallie. High 3E 163
Badenscoth. Abers 5E 160
Badentarbat. High 2E 163
Badgall. Corn 4C 10
Badgers Mount. Kent 4F 39
Badgeworth. Glos 4E 49
Badgworth. Som 1G 21
Badicaul. High 1F 147
Badingham. Suff 4F 67
Badlesmere. Kent 5E 40
Badlipster. High 4E 169
Badluarach. High 4D 163
Badminton. S Glo 3D 34
Badnaban. High 1E 163
Badnabay. High 4C 166
Badnagie. High 5D 168
Badnellan. High 3F 165
Badninish. High 4E 165
Badrallach. High 4E 163
Badsey. Worc 1F 49
Badshot Lea. Surr 2G 25
Badsworth. W Yor 3E 93
Badwell Ash. Suff 4B 66
Bae Cinmel. Cnwy 2B 82
Bae Colwyn. Cnwy 3A 82
Bae Penrhyn. Cnwy 2H 81
Bagby. N Yor 1G 99

Bag Enderby. *Linc* 3C 88
Bagendon. *Glos* 5F 49
Bagginswood. *Shrp* 2A 60
Bàgh a Chàise. *W Isl* 1E 170
Bàgh a' Chaisteil. *W Isl* 9B 170
Bagham. *Kent* 5E 41
Baghasdal. *W Isl* 7C 170
Bagh Mor. *W Isl* 3D 170
Bagh Shiarabhagh. *W Isl* 8C 170
Bagillt. *Flin* 3E 83
Baginton. *Warw* 3H 61
Baglan. *Neat* 2A 32
Bagley. *Shrp* 3G 71
Bagley. *Som* 2H 21
Bagnall. *Staf* 5D 84
Bagnor. *W Ber* 5C 36
Bagshot. *Surr* 4A 38
Bagshot. *Wilts* 5B 36
Bagstone. *S Glo* 3B 34
Bagthorpe. *Norf* 2G 77
Bagthorpe. *Notts* 5B 86
Bagworth. *Leics* 5B 74
Bagwy Llydiart. *Here* 3H 47
Baildon. *W Yor* 1B 92
Baildon Green. *W Yor* 1B 92
Baile Ailein. *W Isl* 5E 171
Baile an Truiseil. *W Isl* 2F 171
Baile Boidheach. *Arg* 2F 125
Baile Glas. *W Isl* 3D 170
Bailemeonach. *Arg* 4A 140
Baile Mhanaich. *W Isl* 3C 170
Baile Mhartainn. *W Isl* 1C 170
Baile Mor. *Arg* 2A 132
Baile Mor. *W Isl* 2C 170
Baile nan Cailleach. *W Isl* 3C 170
Baile Raghaill. *W Isl* 2C 170
Bailey Green. *Hants* 4E 25
Baileyhead. *Cumb* 1G 113
Bailiesward. *Abers* 5B 160
Bail' Iochdrach. *W Isl* 3D 170
Baillieston. *Glas* 3H 127
Bailrigg. *Lanc* 4D 97
Bail' Uachdraich. *W Isl* 2D 170
Bail Ur Tholastaidh. *W Isl* 3H 171
Bainbridge. *N Yor* 5C 104
Bainsford. *Falk* 1B 128
Bainshole. *Abers* 5D 160
Bainton. *E Yor* 4D 100
Bainton. *Oxon* 3D 50
Bainton. *Pet* 5H 75
Baintown. *Fife* 3F 137
Baker Street. *Thur* 2H 39
Bakewell. *Derbs* 4G 85
Bala. *Gwyn* 2B 70
Balachuirn. *High* 4E 155
Balbeg. *High* 5G 157
(nr. Cannich)
Balbeg. *High* 1G 149
(nr. Loch Ness)
Balbeggie. *Per* 1D 136
Balblair. *High* 4C 164
(nr. Bonar Bridge)
Balblair. *High* 2B 158
(nr. Invergordon)
Balblair. *High* 4H 157
(nr. Inverness)
Balby. *S Yor* 4F 93
Balcathie. *Ang* 5F 145
Balchladich. *High* 1E 163
Balchraggan. *High* 4H 157
Balchrick. *High* 3B 166
Balcombe. *W Sus* 2E 27
Balcombe Lane. *W Sus* 2E 27
Balcurvie. *Fife* 3F 137
Baldersby. *N Yor* 2F 99
Baldersby St James. *N Yor* 2F 99
Balderstone. *Lanc* 1E 91
Balderton. *Ches W* 4F 83
Balderton. *Notts* 5F 87
Baldinnie. *Fife* 2G 137
Baldock. *Herts* 2C 52
Baldrine. *IOM* 3D 108
Baldslow. *E Sus* 4C 28
Baldwin. *IOM* 3C 108
Baldwinholme. *Cumb* 4E 113
Baldwin's Gate. *Staf* 2B 72
Bale. *Norf* 2C 78
Balearn. *Abers* 3H 161
Balemartine. *Arg* 4A 138
Balephretrish. *Arg* 4B 138
Balephuil. *Arg* 4A 138
Balerno. *Edin* 3E 129
Balevullin. *Arg* 4A 138
Balfield. *Ang* 2E 145
Balfour. *Orkn* 6D 172
Balfron. *Stir* 1G 127
Balgaveny. *Abers* 4D 160
Balgonar. *Fife* 4C 136
Balgowan. *High* 4A 150
Balgown. *High* 2C 154
Balgrochan. *E Dun* 2H 127
Balgy. *High* 3H 155
Balhalgardy. *Abers* 1E 153
Baliasta. *Shet* 1H 173
Baligill. *High* 2A 168
Balintore. *Ang* 3B 144
Balintore. *High* 1C 158
Balintraid. *High* 1B 158
Balk. *N Yor* 1G 99
Balkeerie. *Ang* 4C 144
Balkholme. *E Yor* 2A 94
Ball. *Shrp* 3F 71
Ballabeg. *IOM* 4B 108
Ballacannell. *IOM* 3D 108
Ballacarnane Beg. *IOM* 3C 108
Ballachulish. *High* 3E 141
Ballagyr. *IOM* 3B 108
Ballajora. *IOM* 2D 108
Ballaleigh. *IOM* 3C 108
Ballamodha. *IOM* 4B 108
Ballantrae. *S Ayr* 1F 109
Ballards Gore. *Essx* 1D 40
Ballasalla. *IOM* 4B 108
(nr. Castletown)
Ballasalla. *IOM* 2C 108
(nr. Kirk Michael)
Ballater. *Abers* 4A 152
Ballaugh. *IOM* 2C 108
Ballencrieff. *E Lot* 2A 130
Ballencrieff Toll. *W Lot* 2C 128
Ballentoul. *Per* 2F 143
Ball Hill. *Hants* 5C 36
Ballidon. *Derbs* 5G 85
Balliemore. *Arg* 1B 126
(nr. Dunoon)
Balliemore. *Arg* 1F 133
(nr. Oban)
Ballieward. *High* 5E 159
Ballig. *IOM* 3B 108
Ballimore. *Stir* 2E 135
Ballingdon. *Suff* 1B 54
Ballinger Common. *Buck* 5H 51
Ballingham. *Here* 2A 48
Ballingry. *Fife* 4D 136
Ballinluig. *Per* 3G 143
Ballintuim. *Per* 3A 144
Balliveolan. *Arg* 4C 140
Balloan. *High* 3C 164
Balloch. *High* 4B 158
Balloch. *N Lan* 2A 128
Balloch. *Per* 2H 135
Balloch. *W Dun* 1E 127
Ballochan. *Abers* 4C 152
Ballochgoy. *Arg* 3B 126
Ballochmyle. *E Ayr* 2E 117
Ballochroy. *Arg* 4F 125
Balls Cross. *W Sus* 3A 26
Ball's Green. *E Sus* 2F 27
Ballygown. *Arg* 4F 139
Ballygrant. *Arg* 3B 124
Ballymichael. *N Ayr* 2D 122
Balmacara. *High* 1G 147
Balmaclellan. *Dum* 2D 110
Balmacqueen. *High* 1D 154
Balmaha. *Stir* 4D 134
Balmalcolm. *Fife* 3F 137
Balmalloch. *N Lan* 2A 128
Balmeanach. *High* 5E 155
Balmedie. *Abers* 2G 153
Balmerino. *Fife* 1F 137
Balmerlawn. *Hants* 2B 16
Balmore. *E Dun* 2H 127
Balmore. *High* 4B 154
Balmuir. *Ang* 5D 144
Balmullo. *Fife* 1G 137
Balmurrie. *Dum* 3H 109
Balnaboth. *Ang* 2C 144
Balnabruaich. *High* 1B 158
Balnabruich. *High* 5D 168
Balnacoil. *High* 2F 165
Balnacra. *High* 4B 156
Balnacroft. *Abers* 4G 151
Balnageith. *Mor* 3E 159
Balnaglaic. *High* 5G 157
Balnagrantach. *High* 5G 157
Balnaguard. *Per* 3G 143
Balnahard. *Arg* 4B 132
Balnain. *High* 5G 157
Balnakeil. *High* 2D 166
Balnaknock. *High* 2D 154
Balnamoon. *Abers* 3G 161
Balnamoon. *Ang* 2E 145
Balnapaling. *High* 2B 158
Balornock. *Glas* 3H 127
Balquhidder. *Stir* 1E 135
Balsall. *W Mid* 3G 61
Balsall Common. *W Mid* 3G 61
Balscote. *Oxon* 1B 50
Balsham. *Cambs* 5E 65
Balstonia. *Thur* 2A 40
Baltasound. *Shet* 1H 173
Balterley. *Staf* 5B 84
Baltersan. *Dum* 3B 110
Balthangie. *Abers* 3F 161
Baltonsborough. *Som* 3A 22
Balvaird. *High* 3H 157
Balvaird. *Per* 2D 136
Balvenie. *Mor* 4H 159
Balvicar. *Arg* 2E 133
Balvraid. *High* 2G 147
Balvraid Lodge. *High* 5C 158
Bamber Bridge. *Lanc* 2D 90
Bamber's Green. *Essx* 3F 53
Bamburgh. *Nmbd* 1F 121
Bamford. *Derbs* 2G 85
Bamfurlong. *G Man* 4D 90
Bampton. *Cumb* 3G 103
Bampton. *Devn* 4C 20
Bampton. *Oxon* 5B 50
Bampton Grange. *Cumb* 3G 103
Banavie. *High* 1F 141
Banbury. *Oxon* 1C 50
Bancffosfelen. *Carm* 4E 45
Banchory. *Abers* 4D 152
Banchory-Devenick. *Abers* 3G 153
Bancycapel. *Carm* 4E 45
Bancyfelin. *Carm* 3H 43
Banc-y-ffordd. *Carm* 2E 45
Banff. *Abers* 2D 160
Bangor. *Gwyn* 3E 81
Bangor-is-y-coed. *Wrex* 1F 71
Bangors. *Corn* 3C 10
Bangor's Green. *Lanc* 4B 90
Banham. *Norf* 2C 66
Bank. *Hants* 2A 16
Bankend. *Dum* 3B 112
Bankfoot. *Per* 5H 143
Bankglen. *E Ayr* 3E 117
Bankhead. *Aber* 2F 153
Bankhead. *Abers* 3D 152
Bankhead. *S Lan* 5B 128
Bankland. *Som* 4G 21
Bank Newton. *N Yor* 4B 98
Banknock. *Falk* 2A 128
Banks. *Cumb* 3G 113
Banks. *Lanc* 2B 90
Bankshill. *Dum* 1C 112
Bank Street. *Worc* 4A 60
Bank, The. *Ches E* 5C 84
Bank, The. *Shrp* 1A 60
Bank Top. *Lanc* 4D 90
Banners Gate. *W Mid* 1E 61
Banningham. *Norf* 3E 78
Banniskirk. *High* 3D 168
Bannister Green. *Essx* 3G 53
Bannockburn. *Stir* 4H 135
Banstead. *Surr* 5D 38
Bantham. *Devn* 4C 8
Banton. *N Lan* 2A 128
Banwell. *N Som* 1G 21
Banyard's Green. *Suff* 3F 67
Bapchild. *Kent* 4D 40
Bapton. *Wilts* 3E 23
Barabhas. *W Isl* 3F 171
Barabhas Iarach. *W Isl* 2F 171
Baramore. *High* 1A 140
Barassie. *S Ayr* 1C 116
Baravullin. *Arg* 4D 140
Barbaraville. *High* 1B 158
Barber Booth. *Derbs* 2F 85
Barber Green. *Cumb* 1C 96
Barbhas Uarach. *W Isl* 2F 171
Barbieston. *S Ayr* 3D 116
Barbon. *Cumb* 1F 97
Barbourne. *Worc* 5C 60
Barbridge. *Ches E* 5A 84
Barbrook. *Devn* 2H 19
Barby. *Nptn* 3C 62
Barby Nortoft. *Nptn* 3C 62
Barcaldine. *Arg* 4D 140
Barcheston. *Warw* 1A 50
Barclose. *Cumb* 3F 113
Barcombe. *E Sus* 4F 27
Barcombe Cross. *E Sus* 4F 27
Barden. *N Yor* 5E 105
Barden Scale. *N Yor* 4C 98
Bardfield End Green. *Essx* 2G 53
Bardfield Saling. *Essx* 3G 53
Bardnabeinne. *High* 4E 164
Bardney. *Linc* 4A 88
Bardon. *Leics* 4B 74
Bardon Mill. *Nmbd* 3A 114
Bardowie. *E Dun* 2G 127
Bardrainney. *Inv* 2E 127
Bardsea. *Cumb* 2C 96
Bardsey. *W Yor* 5F 99
Bardsley. *G Man* 4H 91
Bardwell. *Suff* 3B 66
Bare. *Lanc* 3D 96
Barelees. *Nmbd* 1C 120
Barewood. *Here* 5F 59
Barford. *Hants* 3G 25
Barford. *Norf* 5D 78
Barford. *Warw* 4G 61
Barford St John. *Oxon* 2C 50
Barford St Martin. *Wilts* 3F 23
Barford St Michael. *Oxon* 2C 50
Barfrestone. *Kent* 5G 41
Bargeddie. *N Lan* 3A 128
Bargod. *Cphy* 2E 33
Bargoed. *Cphy* 2E 33
Bargrennan. *Dum* 2A 110
Barham. *Cambs* 3A 64
Barham. *Kent* 5G 41
Barham. *Suff* 5D 66
Barharrow. *Dum* 4D 110
Bar Hill. *Cambs* 4C 64
Barholm. *Linc* 4H 75
Barkby. *Leics* 4D 74
Barkestone-le-Vale. *Leics* 2E 75
Barkham. *Wok* 5F 37
Barking. *G Lon* 2F 39
Barking. *Suff* 5C 66
Barkingside. *G Lon* 2F 39
Barking Tye. *Suff* 5C 66
Barkisland. *W Yor* 3A 92
Barkston. *Linc* 1G 75
Barkston Ash. *N Yor* 1E 93
Barkway. *Herts* 2D 53
Barlanark. *Glas* 3H 127
Barlaston. *Staf* 2C 72
Barlavington. *W Sus* 4A 26
Barlborough. *Derbs* 3B 86
Barlby. *N Yor* 1G 93
Barlestone. *Leics* 5B 74
Barley. *Herts* 2D 53
Barley. *Lanc* 5H 97
Barley Mow. *Tyne* 4F 115
Barleythorpe. *Rut* 5F 75
Barling. *Essx* 2D 40
Barlings. *Linc* 3H 87
Barlow. *Derbs* 3H 85
Barlow. *N Yor* 2G 93
Barlow. *Tyne* 3E 115
Barmby Moor. *E Yor* 5B 100
Barmby on the Marsh. *E Yor* 2G 93
Barmer. *Norf* 2H 77
Barming. *Kent* 5B 40
Barming Heath. *Kent* 5B 40
Barmoor. *Nmbd* 1E 121
Barmouth. *Gwyn* 4F 69
Barmpton. *Darl* 3A 106
Barmston. *E Yor* 4F 101
Barmulloch. *Glas* 3H 127
Barnack. *Pet* 5H 75
Barnacle. *Warw* 2A 62
Barnard Castle. *Dur* 3D 104
Barnard Gate. *Oxon* 4C 50
Barnardiston. *Suff* 1H 53
Barnbarroch. *Dum* 4F 111
Barnburgh. *S Yor* 4E 93
Barnby. *Suff* 2G 67
Barnby Dun. *S Yor* 4G 93
Barnby in the Willows. *Notts* 5F 87
Barnby Moor. *Notts* 2D 86
Barnes. *G Lon* 3D 38
Barnes Street. *Kent* 1H 27
Barnet. *G Lon* 1D 38
Barnetby le Wold. *N Lin* 4D 94
Barney. *Norf* 2B 78
Barnham. *Suff* 3A 66
Barnham. *W Sus* 5A 26
Barnham Broom. *Norf* 5C 78
Barnhead. *Ang* 3F 145
Barnhill. *D'dee* 5D 145
Barnhill. *Mor* 3F 159
Barnhill. *Per* 1D 136
Barnhills. *Dum* 2E 109
Barningham. *Dur* 3D 105
Barningham. *Suff* 3B 66
Barnoldby le Beck. *NE Lin* 4F 95
Barnoldswick. *Lanc* 5A 98
Barns Green. *W Sus* 3C 26
Barnsley. *Glos* 5F 49
Barnsley. *Shrp* 1B 60
Barnsley. *S Yor* 4D 92
Barnstaple. *Devn* 3F 19
Barnston. *Essx* 4G 53
Barnston. *Mers* 2E 83
Barnstone. *Notts* 2E 75
Barnt Green. *Worc* 3E 61
Barnton. *Ches W* 3A 84
Barnwell. *Cambs* 5D 64
Barnwell. *Nptn* 2H 63
Barnwood. *Glos* 4D 48
Barons Cross. *Here* 5G 59
Barony, The. *Orkn* 5B 172
Barr. *Dum* 4G 117
Barr. *S Ayr* 5B 116
Barra Airport. *W Isl* 8C 170
Barrachan. *Dum* 5A 110
Barrahormid. *Arg* 1F 125
Barrapol. *Arg* 4A 138
Barrasford. *Nmbd* 2C 114
Barravullin. *Arg* 3F 133
Barregarrow. *IOM* 3C 108
Barrhead. *E Ren* 4G 127
Barrhill. *S Ayr* 1H 109
Barri. *V Glam* 5E 32
Barrington. *Cambs* 1D 53
Barrington. *Som* 1G 13
Barripper. *Corn* 3D 4
Barrmill. *N Ayr* 4E 127
Barrock. *High* 1E 169
Barrow. *Lanc* 1F 91
Barrow. *Rut* 4F 75
Barrow. *Shrp* 5A 72
Barrow. *Som* 3C 22
Barrow. *Suff* 4G 65
Barroway Drove. *Norf* 5E 77

Barrow Bridge. *G Man* 3E 91
Barrowburn. *Nmbd* 3C 120
Barrowby. *Linc* 2F 75
Barrowcliff. *N Yor* 1E 101
Barrow Common. *N Som* 5A 34
Barrowden. *Rut* 5G 75
Barrowford. *Lanc* 1G 91
Barrow Gurney. *N Som* 5A 34
Barrow Haven. *N Lin* 2D 94
Barrow Hill. *Derbs* 3B 86
Barrow-in-Furness. *Cumb* 3B 96
Barrow Nook. *Lanc* 4C 90
Barrows Green. *Cumb* 1E 97
Barrow's Green. *Hal* 2H 83
Barrow Street. *Wilts* 3D 22
Barrow upon Humber. *N Lin* 2D 94
Barrow upon Soar. *Leics* 4C 74
Barrow upon Trent. *Derbs* 3A 74
Barry. *Ang* 5E 145
Barry. *V Glam* 5E 32
Barry Island. *V Glam* 5E 32
Barsby. *Leics* 4D 74
Barsham. *Suff* 2F 67
Barston. *W Mid* 3G 61
Bartestree. *Here* 1A 48
Barthol Chapel. *Abers* 5F 161
Bartholomew Green. *Essx* 3H 53
Barthomley. *Ches E* 5B 84
Bartley. *Hants* 1B 16
Bartley Green. *W Mid* 2E 61
Bartlow. *Cambs* 1F 53
Barton. *Cambs* 5D 64
Barton. *Ches W* 5G 83
Barton. *Cumb* 2F 103
Barton. *Glos* 3F 49
Barton. *IOW* 4D 16
Barton. *Lanc* 4B 90
(nr. Ormskirk)
Barton. *Lanc* 1D 90
(nr. Preston)
Barton. *N Som* 1G 21
Barton. *N Yor* 4F 105
Barton. *Oxon* 5D 50
Barton. *Torb* 2F 9
Barton. *Warw* 5F 61
Barton Bendish. *Norf* 5G 77
Barton Gate. *Staf* 4F 73
Barton Green. *Staf* 4F 73
Barton Hartsthorn. *Buck* 2E 51
Barton Hill. *N Yor* 3B 100
Barton in Fabis. *Notts* 2C 74
Barton in the Beans. *Leics* 5A 74
Barton-le-Clay. *C Beds* 2A 52
Barton-le-Street. *N Yor* 2B 100
Barton-le-Willows. *N Yor* 3B 100
Barton Mills. *Suff* 3G 65
Barton on Sea. *Hants* 3H 15
Barton-on-the-Heath. *Warw* 2A 50
Barton St David. *Som* 3A 22
Barton Seagrave. *Nptn* 3F 63
Barton Stacey. *Hants* 2C 24
Barton Town. *Devn* 2G 19
Barton Turf. *Norf* 3F 79
Barton-under-Needwood. *Staf* 4F 73
Barton-upon-Humber. *N Lin* 2D 94
Barton Waterside. *N Lin* 2D 94
Barugh Green. *S Yor* 4D 92
Barway. *Cambs* 3E 65
Barwell. *Leics* 1B 62
Barwick. *Herts* 4D 53
Barwick. *Som* 1A 14
Barwick in Elmet. *W Yor* 1D 93
Baschurch. *Shrp* 3G 71
Bascote. *Warw* 4B 62
Basford Green. *Staf* 5D 85
Bashall Eaves. *Lanc* 5F 97
Bashall Town. *Lanc* 5G 97
Bashley. *Hants* 3H 15
Basildon. *Essx* 2B 40
Basingstoke. *Hants* 1E 25
Baslow. *Derbs* 3G 85
Bason Bridge. *Som* 2G 21
Bassaleg. *Newp* 3F 33
Bassendean. *Bord* 5C 130
Bassenthwaite. *Cumb* 1D 102
Bassett. *Sotn* 1C 16
Bassingbourn. *Cambs* 1D 52
Bassingfield. *Notts* 2D 74
Bassingham. *Linc* 4G 87
Bassingthorpe. *Linc* 3G 75
Bassus Green. *Herts* 3D 52
Basta. *Shet* 2G 173
Baston. *Linc* 4A 76
Bastonford. *Worc* 5C 60
Bastwick. *Norf* 4G 79
Batchley. *Worc* 4E 61
Batchworth. *Herts* 1B 38
Batcombe. *Dors* 2B 14
Batcombe. *Som* 3B 22
Bate Heath. *Ches E* 3A 84
Bath. *Bath* 5C 34
Bathampton. *Bath* 5C 34
Bathealton. *Som* 4D 20
Batheaston. *Bath* 5C 34
Bathford. *Bath* 5C 34
Bathgate. *W Lot* 3C 128
Bathley. *Notts* 5E 87
Bathpool. *Corn* 5C 10
Bathpool. *Som* 4F 21
Bathville. *W Lot* 3C 128
Bathway. *Som* 1A 22
Batley. *W Yor* 2C 92
Batsford. *Glos* 2G 49
Batson. *Devn* 5D 8
Battersby. *N Yor* 4C 106
Battersea. *G Lon* 3D 39
Battisborough Cross. *Devn* 4C 8
Battisford. *Suff* 5C 66
Battisford Tye. *Suff* 5C 66
Battle. *E Sus* 4B 28
Battle. *Powy* 2D 46
Battleborough. *Som* 1G 21
Battledown. *Glos* 3E 49
Battlefield. *Shrp* 4H 71
Battlesbridge. *Essx* 1B 40
Battlesden. *C Beds* 3H 51
Battlesea Green. *Suff* 3E 66
Battleton. *Som* 4C 20
Battram. *Leic* 5B 74
Battramsley. *Hants* 3B 16
Batt's Corner. *Surr* 2G 25
Bauds of Cullen. *Mor* 2B 160
Baugh. *Arg* 4B 138
Baughton. *Worc* 1D 49
Baughurst. *Hants* 5D 36
Baulking. *Oxon* 2B 36
Baumber. *Linc* 3B 88
Baunton. *Glos* 5F 49
Baverstock. *Wilts* 3F 23
Bawburgh. *Norf* 5D 78
Bawdeswell. *Norf* 3C 78
Bawdrip. *Som* 3G 21
Bawdsey. *Suff* 1G 55
Bawdsey Manor. *Suff* 2G 55
Bawsey. *Norf* 4F 77
Bawtry. *S Yor* 1D 86
Baxenden. *Lanc* 2F 91
Baxterley. *Warw* 1G 61
Baxter's Green. *Suff* 5G 65
Baybridge. *Hants* 4D 24
Baybridge. *Nmbd* 4C 114
Baycliff. *Cumb* 2B 96
Baydon. *Wilts* 4A 36
Bayford. *Herts* 5D 52
Bayford. *Som* 4C 22
Bayles. *Cumb* 5A 114
Baylham. *Suff* 5D 66
Baynard's Green. *Oxon* 3D 50
Bayston Hill. *Shrp* 5G 71
Baythorn End. *Essx* 1H 53
Baythorpe. *Linc* 1B 76
Bayton. *Worc* 3A 60
Bayton Common. *Worc* 3B 60
Bayworth. *Oxon* 5D 50
Beach. *S Glo* 4C 34
Beachampton. *Buck* 2F 51
Beachamwell. *Norf* 5G 77
Beachley. *Glos* 2A 34
Beacon. *Devn* 2E 13
Beacon End. *Essx* 3C 54
Beacon Hill. *Surr* 3G 25
Beacon's Bottom. *Buck* 2F 37
Beaconsfield. *Buck* 1A 38
Beacontree. *G Lon* 2F 39
Beacrabhaicg. *W Isl* 8D 171
Beadlam. *N Yor* 1A 100
Beadnell. *Nmbd* 2G 121
Beaford. *Devn* 1F 11
Beal. *Nmbd* 5G 131
Beal. *N Yor* 2F 93
Bealsmill. *Corn* 5D 10
Beam Hill. *Staf* 3G 73
Beamhurst. *Staf* 2E 73
Beaminster. *Dors* 2H 13
Beamish. *Dur* 4F 115
Beamond End. *Buck* 1A 38
Beamsley. *N Yor* 4C 98
Bean. *Kent* 3G 39
Beanacre. *Wilts* 5E 35
Beanley. *Nmbd* 3E 121
Beanshanger. *Nptn* 2F 51
Beardwood. *Bkbn* 2E 91
Beare Green. *Surr* 1C 26
Bearley. *Warw* 4F 61
Bearpark. *Dur* 5F 115
Bearsbridge. *Nmbd* 4A 114
Bearsden. *E Dun* 2G 127
Bearsted. *Kent* 5B 40
Bearstone. *Shrp* 2B 72
Bearwood. *Pool* 3F 15
Bearwood. *W Mid* 2E 61
Beattock. *Dum* 4C 118
Beauchamp Roding. *Essx* 5F 53
Beauchief. *S Yor* 2H 85
Beaufort. *Blae* 4E 47
Beaulieu. *Hants* 2B 16
Beauly. *High* 4H 157
Beaumaris. *IOA* 3F 81
Beaumont. *Cumb* 4E 113
Beaumont. *Essx* 3E 55
Beaumont Hill. *Darl* 3F 105
Beaumont Leys. *Leic* 5C 74
Beausale. *Warw* 3G 61
Beauvale. *Notts* 1B 74
Beauworth. *Hants* 4D 24
Beaworthy. *Devn* 3E 11
Beazley End. *Essx* 3H 53
Bebington. *Mers* 2F 83
Bebside. *Nmbd* 1F 115
Beccles. *Suff* 2G 67
Becconsall. *Lanc* 2C 90
Beckbury. *Shrp* 5B 72
Beckenham. *G Lon* 4E 39
Beckermet. *Cumb* 4B 102
Beckett End. *Norf* 1G 65
Beckfoot. *Cumb* 1A 96
(nr. Broughton in Furness)
Beck Foot. *Cumb* 5H 103
(nr. Kendal)
Beckfoot. *Cumb* 4C 102
(nr. Seascale)
Beckfoot. *Cumb* 5B 112
(nr. Silloth)
Beckford. *Worc* 2E 49
Beckhampton. *Wilts* 5F 35
Beck Hole. *N Yor* 4F 107
Beckingham. *Linc* 5F 87
Beckingham. *Notts* 1E 87
Beckington. *Som* 1D 22
Beckley. *E Sus* 3C 28
Beckley. *Hants* 3H 15
Beckley. *Oxon* 4D 50
Beck Row. *Suff* 3F 65
Beck Side. *Cumb* 1C 96
(nr. Cartmel)
Beckside. *Cumb* 1F 97
(nr. Sedbergh)
Beck Side. *Cumb* 1B 96
(nr. Ulverston)
Beckton. *G Lon* 2F 39
Beckwithshaw. *N Yor* 4E 99
Becontree. *G Lon* 2F 39
Bedale. *N Yor* 1E 99
Bedburn. *Dur* 1E 105
Bedchester. *Dors* 1D 14
Beddau. *Rhon* 3D 32
Beddgelert. *Gwyn* 1E 69
Beddingham. *E Sus* 5F 27
Beddington. *G Lon* 4D 39
Bedfield. *Suff* 4E 66
Bedford. *Bed* 1A 52
Bedford. *G Man* 4E 91
Bedham. *W Sus* 3B 26
Bedhampton. *Hants* 2F 17
Bedingfield. *Suff* 4D 66
Bedingham Green. *Norf* 1E 67
Bedlam. *N Yor* 3E 99
Bedlar's Green. *Essx* 4F 53
Bedlington. *Nmbd* 1F 115
Bedlinog. *Mer T* 5D 46
Bedminster. *Bris* 4A 34
Bedmond. *Herts* 5A 52
Bednall. *Staf* 4D 72
Bedrule. *Bord* 3A 120
Bedstone. *Shrp* 3F 59
Bedwas. *Cphy* 3E 33
Bedwellty. *Cphy* 5E 47
Bedworth. *Warw* 2A 62
Beeby. *Leics* 5D 74
Beech. *Hants* 3E 25
Beech. *Staf* 2C 72
Beechcliffe. *W Yor* 5C 98
Beech Hill. *W Ber* 5E 37
Beechingstoke. *Wilts* 1F 23
Beedon. *W Ber* 4C 36
Beeford. *E Yor* 4F 101
Beeley. *Derbs* 4G 85
Beelsby. *NE Lin* 4F 95
Beenham. *W Ber* 5D 36
Beeny. *Corn* 3B 10
Beer. *Devn* 4F 13
Beer. *Som* 3H 21
Beercrocombe. *Som* 4G 21
Beer Hackett. *Dors* 1B 14
Beesands. *Devn* 4E 9
Beesby. *Linc* 2D 88
Beeson. *Devn* 4E 9
Beeston. *C Beds* 1B 52
Beeston. *Ches W* 5H 83
Beeston. *Norf* 4B 78
Beeston. *Notts* 2C 74
Beeston. *W Yor* 1C 92
Beeston Regis. *Norf* 1D 78
Beeswing. *Dum* 3F 111
Beetham. *Cumb* 2D 97
Beetham. *Som* 1F 13
Beetley. *Norf* 4B 78
Beffcote. *Staf* 4C 72
Began. *Card* 3F 33
Begbroke. *Oxon* 4C 50
Begdale. *Cambs* 5D 76
Begelly. *Pemb* 4F 43
Beggar Hill. *Essx* 5G 53
Beggar's Bush. *Powy* 4E 59
Beggearn Huish. *Som* 3D 20
Beguildy. *Powy* 3D 58
Beighton. *Norf* 5F 79
Beighton. *S Yor* 2B 86
Beighton Hill. *Derbs* 5G 85
Beith. *N Ayr* 4E 127
Bekesbourne. *Kent* 5F 41
Belaugh. *Norf* 4E 79
Belbroughton. *Worc* 3D 60
Belchalwell. *Dors* 2C 14
Belchalwell Street. *Dors* 2C 14
Belchamp Otten. *Essx* 1B 54
Belchamp St Paul. *Essx* 1A 54
Belchamp Walter. *Essx* 1B 54
Belchford. *Linc* 3B 88
Belfatton. *Abers* 3H 161
Belford. *Nmbd* 1F 121
Belgrano. *Cnwy* 3B 82
Belhaven. *E Lot* 2C 130
Belhelvie. *Abers* 2G 153
Belhinnie. *Abers* 1B 152
Bellabeg. *Abers* 2A 152
Belladrum. *High* 4H 157
Bellamore. *S Ayr* 1H 109
Bellanoch. *Arg* 4F 133
Bell Busk. *N Yor* 4B 98
Belleau. *Linc* 3D 88
Belleheiglash. *Mor* 5F 159
Bell End. *Worc* 3D 60
Bellerby. *N Yor* 5E 105
Bellerby Camp. *N Yor* 5D 105
Bellever. *Devn* 5G 11
Belle Vue. *Cumb* 1C 102
Belle Vue. *Shrp* 4G 71
Bellfield. *S Lan* 1H 117
Belliehill. *Ang* 2E 145
Bellingdon. *Buck* 5H 51
Bellingham. *Nmbd* 1B 114
Bellmount. *Norf* 3E 77
Bellochantuy. *Arg* 2A 122
Bellsbank. *E Ayr* 4D 117
Bell's Cross. *Suff* 5D 66
Bellshill. *N Lan* 4A 128
Bellshill. *Nmbd* 1F 121
Bellside. *N Lan* 4B 128
Bellspool. *Bord* 1D 118
Bellsquarry. *W Lot* 3D 128
Bells Yew Green. *E Sus* 2H 27
Belmaduthy. *High* 3A 158
Belmesthorpe. *Rut* 4H 75
Belmont. *Bkbn* 3E 91
Belmont. *Shet* 1G 173
Belmont. *S Ayr* 3C 116
Belnacraig. *Abers* 2A 152
Belnie. *Linc* 2B 76
Belowda. *Corn* 2D 6
Belper. *Derbs* 1A 74
Belper Lane End. *Derbs* 1H 73
Belph. *Derbs* 3C 86
Belsay. *Nmbd* 2E 115
Belsford. *Devn* 3D 8
Belsize. *Herts* 5A 52
Belstead. *Suff* 1E 55
Belston. *S Ayr* 2C 116
Belstone. *Devn* 3G 11
Belstone Corner. *Devn* 3G 11
Belthorn. *Lanc* 2F 91
Beltinge. *Kent* 4F 41
Beltoft. *N Lin* 4B 94
Belton. *Leics* 3B 74
Belton. *Linc* 2G 75
Belton. *Norf* 5G 79
Belton. *N Lin* 4A 94
Belton-in-Rutland. *Rut* 5F 75
Beltring. *Kent* 1A 28
Belts of Collonach. *Abers* 4D 152
Belvedere. *G Lon* 3F 39
Belvoir. *Leics* 2F 75
Bembridge. *IOW* 4E 17
Bemersyde. *Bord* 1H 119
Bemerton. *Wilts* 3G 23
Bempton. *E Yor* 2F 101
Benacre. *Suff* 2H 67
Ben Alder Lodge. *High* 1C 142
Ben Armine Lodge. *High* 2E 164
Benbuie. *Dum* 5G 117
Benchill. *G Man* 2C 84
Benderloch. *Arg* 5D 140
Bendish. *Herts* 3B 52
Bendronaig Lodge. *High* 5C 156
Benenden. *Kent* 2C 28
Benera. *High* 1G 147
Benfieldside. *Dur* 4D 115
Bengate. *Norf* 3F 79
Bengeworth. *Worc* 1F 49
Bengrove. *Glos* 2E 49
Benhall Green. *Suff* 4F 67
Benholm. *Abers* 2H 145
Benington. *Herts* 3C 52
Benington. *Linc* 1C 76
Benington Sea End. *Linc* 1D 76
Benllech. *IOA* 2E 81
Benmore Lodge. *High* 2H 163
Bennacott. *Corn* 3D 10
Bennah. *Devn* 4B 12
Bennecarngan. *N Ayr* 3D 122

Bennethead. Cumb 2F 103
Benningbrough. N Yor 4H 99
Benniworth. Linc 2B 88
Benover. Kent 1B 28
Benson. Oxon 2E 36
Bent. Abers 1F 145
Benthall. Shrp 5A 72
Bentham. Glos 4E 49
Benthoul. Aber 3F 153
Bentlawnt. Shrp 5F 71
Bentley. E Yor 1D 94
Bentley. Hants 2F 25
Bentley. S Yor 4F 93
Bentley. Suff 2E 54
Bentley. Warw 1G 61
Bentley. W Mid 1D 61
Bentley Heath. Herts 1D 38
Bentley Heath. W Mid 3F 61
Bentpath. Dum 5F 119
Bents. W Lot 3C 128
Bentworth. Hants 2E 25
Benvie. D'dee 5C 144
Benville. Dors 2A 14
Benwell. Tyne 3F 115
Benwick. Cambs 1C 64
Beoley. Worc 4E 61
Beoraidbeg. High 4E 147
Bepton. W Sus 1G 17
Berden. Essx 3E 53
Bere Alston. Devn 2A 8
Bere Ferrers. Devn 2A 8
Berepper. Corn 4D 4
Bere Regis. Dors 3D 14
Bergh Apton. Norf 5F 79
Berinsfield. Oxon 2D 36
Berkeley. Glos 2B 34
Berkhamsted. Herts 5H 51
Berkley. Som 2D 22
Berkswell. W Mid 3G 61
Bermondsey. G Lon 3E 39
Bernice. Arg 4A 134
Bernisdale. High 3D 154
Berrick Salome. Oxon 2E 36
Berriedale. High 1H 165
Berrier. Cumb 2F 103
Berriew. Powy 5D 70
Berrington. Nmbd 5G 131
Berrington. Shrp 5H 71
Berrington. Worc 4H 59
Berrington Green. Worc 4H 59
Berrington Law. Nmbd 5F 131
Berrow. Som 1G 21
Berrow Green. Worc 5B 60
Berry Cross. Devn 1E 11
Berry Down Cross. Devn 2F 19
Berry Hill. Glos 4A 48
Berry Hill. Pemb 1A 44
Berryhillock. Mor 2C 160
Berrynarbor. Devn 2F 19
Berry Pomeroy. Devn 2E 9
Berryscaur. Dum 5D 118
Berry's Green. G Lon 5F 39
Bersham. Wrex 1F 71
Berthengam. Flin 3D 82
Berwick. E Sus 5G 27
Berwick Bassett. Wilts 4G 35
Berwick Hill. Nmbd 2E 115
Berwick St James. Wilts 3F 23
Berwick St John. Wilts 4E 23
Berwick St Leonard. Wilts 3E 23
Berwick-upon-Tweed. Nmbd 4G 131
Berwyn. Den 1D 70
Bescaby. Leics 3F 75
Bescar. Lanc 3B 90
Besford. Worc 1E 49
Bessacarr. S Yor 4G 93
Bessels Leigh. Oxon 5C 50
Bessingby. E Yor 3F 101
Bessingham. Norf 2D 78
Best Beech Hill. E Sus 2H 27
Besthorpe. Norf 1C 66
Besthorpe. Notts 4F 87
Bestwood Village. Notts 1C 74
Beswick. E Yor 5E 101
Betchworth. Surr 5D 38
Bethania. Cdgn 4E 57
Bethania. Gwyn 1G 69
(nr. Blaenau Ffestiniog)
Bethania. Gwyn 5F 81
(nr. Caernarfon)
Bethel. Gwyn 2B 70
(nr. Bala)
Bethel. Gwyn 4E 81
(nr. Caernarfon)
Bethel. IOA 3C 80
Bethersden. Kent 1D 28
Bethesda. Gwyn 4F 81
Bethesda. Pemb 3E 43
Bethlehem. Carm 3G 45
Bethnal Green. G Lon 2E 39
Betishill. N Lan 3A 128
Betley. Staf 1B 72
Betsham. Kent 3H 39
Betteshanger. Kent 5H 41
Bettiscombe. Dors 3H 13
Bettisfield. Wrex 2G 71
Betton. Shrp 2A 72
Betton Strange. Shrp 5H 71
Bettws. B'end 3C 32
Bettws. Newp 2F 33
Bettws Bledrws. Cdgn 5E 57
Bettws Cedewain. Powy 1D 58
Bettws Gwerfil Goch. Den 1C 70
Bettws Ifan. Cdgn 1D 44
Bettws Newydd. Mon 5G 47
Bettyhill. High 2H 167
Betws. Carm 4G 45
Betws Garmon. Gwyn 5E 81
Betws-y-Coed. Cnwy 5G 81
Betws-yn-Rhos. Cnwy 3B 82
Beulah. Cdgn 1C 44
Beulah. Powy 5B 58
Beul an Atha. Arg 3B 124
Bevendean. Brig 5E 27
Bevercotes. Notts 3E 86
Beverley. E Yor 1D 94
Beverston. Glos 2D 34
Bevington. Glos 2B 34
Bewaldeth. Cumb 1D 102
Bewcastle. Cumb 2G 113
Bewdley. Worc 3B 60
Bewerley. N Yor 3D 98
Bewholme. E Yor 4F 101
Bexfield. Norf 3C 78
Bexhill. E Sus 5B 28
Bexley. G Lon 3F 39
Bexleyheath. G Lon 3F 39
Bexleyhill. W Sus 3A 26
Bexwell. Norf 5F 77
Beyton. Suff 4B 66
Bhalton. W Isl 4C 171
Bhatarsaigh. W Isl 9B 170
Bibbington. Derbs 3E 85
Bibury. Glos 5G 49
Bicester. Oxon 3D 50
Bickenhall. Som 1F 13
Bickenhill. W Mid 2F 61
Bicker. Linc 2B 76
Bicker Bar. Linc 2B 76
Bicker Gauntlet. Linc 2B 76
Bickershaw. G Man 4E 91
Bickerstaffe. Lanc 4C 90
Bickerton. Ches E 5H 83
Bickerton. Nmbd 4D 121
Bickerton. N Yor 4G 99
Bickford. Staf 4C 72
Bickington. Devn 3F 19
(nr. Barnstaple)
Bickington. Devn 5B 12
(nr. Newton Abbot)
Bickleigh. Devn 2B 8
(nr. Plymouth)
Bickleigh. Devn 2C 12
(nr. Tiverton)
Bickleton. Devn 3F 19
Bickley. N Yor 5G 107
Bickley Moss. Ches W 1H 71
Bickmarsh. Warw 5F 61
Bicknacre. Essx 5A 54
Bicknoller. Som 3E 20
Bicknor. Kent 5C 40
Bickton. Hants 1G 15
Bicton. Here 4G 59
Bicton. Shrp 2E 59
(nr. Bishop's Castle)
Bicton. Shrp 4G 71
(nr. Shrewsbury)
Bicton Heath. Shrp 4G 71
Bidborough. Kent 1G 27
Biddenden. Kent 2C 28
Biddenden Green. Kent 1C 28
Biddenham. Bed 1A 52
Biddestone. Wilts 4D 34
Biddisham. Som 1G 21
Biddlesden. Buck 1E 51
Biddlestone. Nmbd 4D 120
Biddulph. Staf 5C 84
Biddulph Moor. Staf 5D 84
Bideford. Devn 4E 19
Bidford-on-Avon. Warw 5E 61
Bidlake. Devn 4F 11
Bidston. Mers 2E 83
Bielby. E Yor 5B 100
Bieldside. Aber 3F 153
Bierley. IOW 5D 16
Bierley. W Yor 1B 92
Bierton. Buck 4G 51
Bigbury. Devn 4C 8
Bigbury-on-Sea. Devn 4C 8
Bigby. Linc 4D 94
Biggar. Cumb 3A 96
Biggar. S Lan 1C 118
Biggin. Derbs 5F 85
(nr. Hartington)
Biggin. Derbs 1G 73
(nr. Hulland)
Biggin. N Yor 1F 93
Biggings. Shet 5C 173
Biggin Hill. G Lon 5F 39
Biggleswade. C Beds 1B 52
Bighouse. High 2A 168
Bighton. Hants 3E 24
Biglands. Cumb 4D 112
Bignall End. Staf 5C 84
Bignor. W Sus 4A 26
Bigrigg. Cumb 3B 102
Big Sand. High 1G 155
Bigton. Shet 9E 173
Bilberry. Corn 2E 6
Bilborough. Nott 1C 74
Bilbrook. Som 2D 20
Bilbrook. Staf 5C 72
Bilbrough. N Yor 5H 99
Bilbster. High 3E 169
Bilby. Notts 2D 86
Bildershaw. Dur 2F 105
Bildeston. Suff 1C 54
Billericay. Essx 1A 40
Billesdon. Leics 5E 74
Billesley. Warw 5F 61
Billingborough. Linc 2A 76
Billinge. Mers 4D 90
Billingford. Norf 3C 78
(nr. Dereham)
Billingford. Norf 3D 66
(nr. Diss)
Billingham. Stoc T 2B 106
Billinghay. Linc 5A 88
Billingley. S Yor 4E 93
Billingshurst. W Sus 3B 26
Billingsley. Shrp 2B 60
Billington. C Beds 3H 51
Billington. Lanc 1F 91
Billington. Staf 3C 72
Billockby. Norf 4G 79
Billy Row. Dur 1E 105
Bilsborrow. Lanc 5E 97
Bilsby. Linc 3D 88
Bilsham. W Sus 5A 26
Bilsington. Kent 2E 29
Bilson Green. Glos 4B 48
Bilsthorpe. Notts 4D 86
Bilston. Midl 3F 129
Bilston. W Mid 1D 60
Bilstone. Leics 5A 74
Bilting. Kent 1E 29
Bilton. E Yor 1E 95
Bilton. Nmbd 3G 121
Bilton. N Yor 4E 99
Bilton. Warw 3B 62
Bilton in Ainsty. N Yor 5G 99
Binbrook. Linc 1B 88
Binchester. Dur 1F 105
Bincombe. Dors 4B 14
Bindal. High 5G 165
Binegar. Som 2B 22
Bines Green. W Sus 4C 26
Binfield. Brac 4G 37
Binfield Heath. Oxon 4F 37
Bingfield. Nmbd 2C 114
Bingham. Notts 1E 74
Bingham's Melcombe. Dors 2C 14
Bingley. W Yor 1B 92
Bings Heath. Shrp 4H 71
Binham. Norf 2B 78
Binley. Hants 1C 24
Binley. W Mid 3A 62
Binnegar. Dors 4D 15
Binniehill. Falk 2B 128
Binsoe. N Yor 2E 99
Binstead. IOW 3D 16
Binstead. W Sus 5A 26
Binsted. Hants 2F 25
Binton. Warw 5F 61
Bintree. Norf 3C 78
Binweston. Shrp 5F 71
Birch. Essx 4C 54
Birchall. Staf 5D 85
Bircham Newton. Norf 2G 77
Bircham Tofts. Norf 2G 77
Birchanger. Essx 3F 53
Birchburn. N Ayr 3D 122
Birch Cross. Staf 2F 73
Bircher. Here 4G 59
Birch Green. Essx 4C 54
Birchgrove. Card 4E 33
Birchgrove. Swan 3G 31
Birch Heath. Ches W 4H 83
Birch Hill. Ches W 3H 83
Birchill. Devn 2G 13
Birchington. Kent 4G 41
Birch Langley. G Man 4G 91
Birchley Heath. Warw 1G 61
Birchmoor. Warw 5G 73
Birchmoor Green. C Beds 2H 51
Birchover. Derbs 4G 85
Birch Vale. Derbs 2E 85
Birchview. Mor 5F 159
Birchwood. Linc 4G 87
Birchwood. Som 1F 13
Birchwood. Warr 1A 84
Bircotes. Notts 1D 86
Birdbrook. Essx 1H 53
Birdham. W Sus 2G 17
Birdholme. Derbs 4A 86
Birdingbury. Warw 4B 62
Birdlip. Glos 4E 49
Birdsall. N Yor 3C 100
Birds Edge. W Yor 4C 92
Birds Green. Essx 5F 53
Birdsgreen. Shrp 2B 60
Birdsmoorgate. Dors 2G 13
Birdston. E Dun 2H 127
Birdwell. S Yor 4D 92
Birdwood. Glos 4C 48
Birgham. Bord 1B 120
Birichen. High 4E 165
Birkby. Cumb 1B 102
Birkby. N Yor 4A 106
Birkdale. Mers 3B 90
Birkenhead. Mers 2F 83
Birkenhills. Abers 4E 161
Birkenshaw. N Lan 3H 127
Birkenshaw. W Yor 2C 92
Birkhall. Abers 4H 151
Birkhill. Ang 5C 144
Birkholme. Linc 3G 75
Birkin. N Yor 2F 93
Birley. Here 5G 59
Birling. Kent 4A 40
Birling. Nmbd 4G 121
Birling Gap. E Sus 5G 27
Birlingham. Worc 1E 49
Birmingham. W Mid 2E 61
Birmingham Airport. W Mid 2F 61
Birnam. Per 4H 143
Birsay. Orkn 5B 172
Birse. Abers 4C 152
Birsemore. Abers 4C 152
Birstall. Leics 5C 74
Birstall. W Yor 2C 92
Birstall Smithies. W Yor 2C 92
Birstwith. N Yor 4E 99
Birthorpe. Linc 2A 76
Birtle. Lanc 3G 91
Birtley. Here 4F 59
Birtley. Nmbd 2B 114
Birtley. Tyne 4F 115
Birtsmorton. Worc 2D 48
Birts Street. Worc 2C 48
Bisbrooke. Rut 1F 63
Bisham. Wind 3G 37
Bishampton. Worc 5D 61
Bish Mill. Devn 4H 19
Bishop Auckland. Dur 2F 105
Bishopbridge. Linc 1H 87
Bishopbriggs. E Dun 2H 127
Bishop Burton. E Yor 1C 94
Bishopdown. Wilts 3G 23
Bishop Middleham. Dur 1A 106
Bishopmill. Mor 2G 159
Bishop Monkton. N Yor 3F 99
Bishop Norton. Linc 1G 87
Bishopsbourne. Kent 5F 41
Bishops Cannings. Wilts 5F 35
Bishop's Castle. Shrp 2F 59
Bishop's Caundle. Dors 1B 14
Bishop's Cleeve. Glos 3E 49
Bishop's Down. Dors 1B 14
Bishop's Frome. Here 1B 48
Bishop's Green. Essx 4G 53
Bishop's Green. Hants 5D 36
Bishop's Hull. Som 4F 21
Bishop's Itchington. Warw 5A 62
Bishops Lydeard. Som 4E 21
Bishop's Norton. Glos 3D 48
Bishop's Nympton. Devn 4A 20
Bishop's Offley. Staf 3B 72
Bishop's Stortford. Herts 3E 53
Bishops Sutton. Hants 3E 24
Bishop's Tachbrook. Warw 4H 61
Bishop's Tawton. Devn 3F 19
Bishopsteignton. Devn 5C 12
Bishopstoke. Hants 1C 16
Bishopston. Swan 4E 31
Bishopstone. Buck 4G 51
Bishopstone. E Sus 5F 27
Bishopstone. Here 1H 47
Bishopstone. Swin 3H 35
Bishopstone. Wilts 4F 23
Bishopstrow. Wilts 2D 23
Bishop Sutton. Bath 1A 22
Bishop's Waltham. Hants 1D 16
Bishopswood. Som 1F 13
Bishops Wood. Staf 5C 72
Bishopsworth. Bris 5A 34
Bishop Thornton. N Yor 3E 99
Bishopthorpe. York 5H 99
Bishopton. Darl 2A 106
Bishopton. Dum 5B 110
Bishopton. N Yor 2F 99
Bishopton. Ren 2F 127
Bishopton. Warw 5F 61
Bishop Wilton. E Yor 4B 100
Bishton. Newp 3G 33
Bishton. Staf 3E 73
Bisley. Glos 5E 49
Bisley. Surr 5A 38
Bispham. Bkpl 5C 96
Bispham Green. Lanc 3C 90

Bissoe. *Corn* 4B **6**
Bisterne. *Hants* 2G **15**
Bisterne Close. *Hants* 2H **15**
Bitchfield. *Linc* 3G **75**
Bittadon. *Devn* 2F **19**
Bittaford. *Devn* 3C **8**
Bittering. *Norf* 4B **78**
Bitterley. *Shrp* 3H **59**
Bitterne. *Sotn* 1C **16**
Bitteswell. *Leics* 2C **62**
Bitton. *S Glo* 5B **34**
Bix. *Oxon* 3F **37**
Bixter. *Shet* 6E **173**
Blaby. *Leics* 1C **62**
Blackawton. *Devn* 3E **9**
Black Bank. *Cambs* 2E **65**
Black Barn. *Linc* 3D **76**
Blackborough. *Devn* 2D **12**
Blackborough. *Norf* 4F **77**
Blackborough End. *Norf* 4F **77**
Black Bourton. *Oxon* 5A **50**
Blackboys. *E Sus* 3G **27**
Blackbrook. *Derbs* 1H **73**
Blackbrook. *Mers* 1H **83**
Blackbrook. *Staf* 2B **72**
Blackbrook. *Surr* 1C **26**
Blackburn. *Abers* 2F **153**
Blackburn. *Bkbn* 2E **91**
Blackburn. *W Lot* 3C **128**
Black Callerton. *Tyne* 3E **115**
Black Carr. *Norf* 1C **66**
Black Clauchrie. *S Ayr* 1H **109**
Black Corries. *High* 3G **141**
Black Crofts. *Arg* 5D **140**
Black Cross. *Corn* 2D **6**
Blackden Heath. *Ches E* 3B **84**
Blackditch. *Oxon* 5C **50**
Blackdog. *Abers* 2G **153**
Black Dog. *Devn* 2B **12**
Blackdown. *Dors* 2G **13**
Blackdyke. *Cumb* 4C **112**
Blacker Hill. *S Yor* 4D **92**
Blackfen. *G Lon* 3F **39**
Blackfield. *Hants* 2C **16**
Blackford. *Cumb* 3E **113**
Blackford. *Per* 3A **136**
Blackford. *Shrp* 2H **59**
Blackford. *Som* 2H **21**
(nr. Burnham-on-Sea)
Blackford. *Som* 4B **22**
(nr. Wincanton)
Blackfordby. *Leics* 4H **73**
Blackgang. *IOW* 5C **16**
Blackhall. *Edin* 2F **129**
Blackhall. *Ren* 3F **127**
Blackhall Colliery. *Dur* 1B **106**
Blackhall Mill. *Tyne* 4E **115**
Blackhall Rocks. *Dur* 1B **106**
Blackham. *E Sus* 2F **27**
Blackheath. *Essx* 3D **54**
Blackheath. *G Lon* 3E **39**
Blackheath. *Suff* 3G **67**
Blackheath. *Surr* 1B **26**
Blackheath. *W Mid* 2D **61**
Black Heddon. *Nmbd* 2D **115**
Blackhill. *Abers* 4H **161**
Blackhill. *High* 3C **154**
Black Hill. *Warw* 5G **61**
Blackhills. *Abers* 2G **161**
Blackhills. *High* 3D **158**
Blackjack. *Linc* 2B **76**
Blackland. *Wilts* 5F **35**
Black Lane. *G Man* 4F **91**
Blackleach. *Lanc* 1C **90**
Blackley. *G Man* 4G **91**
Blackley. *W Yor* 3B **92**
Blacklunans. *Per* 2A **144**
Blackmill. *B'end* 3C **32**
Blackmoor. *G Man* 4E **91**
Blackmoor. *Hants* 3F **25**
Blackmoor Gate. *Devn* 2G **19**
Blackmore. *Essx* 5G **53**
Blackmore End. *Essx* 2H **53**
Blackmore End. *Herts* 4B **52**
Black Mount. *Arg* 4G **141**
Blackness. *Falk* 2D **128**
Blacknest. *Hants* 2F **25**
Blackney. *Dors* 3H **13**
Blacknoll. *Dors* 4D **14**
Black Notley. *Essx* 3A **54**
Blacko. *Lanc* 5A **98**
Black Pill. *Swan* 3F **31**
Blackpool. *Bkpl* 1B **90**
Blackpool. *Devn* 4E **9**
Blackpool Airport. *Lanc* 1B **90**
Blackpool Corner. *Devn* 3G **13**
Blackpool Gate. *Cumb* 2G **113**
Blackridge. *W Lot* 3C **128**
Blackrock. *Arg* 3B **124**
Blackrock. *Mon* 4F **47**
Blackrod. *G Man* 3E **90**
Blackshaw. *Dum* 3B **112**
Blackshaw Head. *W Yor* 2H **91**
Blackshaw Moor. *Staf* 5E **85**
Blacksmith's Green. *Suff* 4D **66**
Blacksnape. *Bkbn* 2F **91**
Blackstone. *W Sus* 4D **26**
Black Street. *Suff* 2H **67**
Black Tar. *Pemb* 4D **43**
Blackthorn. *Oxon* 4E **50**
Blackthorpe. *Suff* 4B **66**
Blacktoft. *E Yor* 2B **94**
Blacktop. *Aber* 3F **153**
Black Torrington. *Devn* 2E **11**
Blacktown. *Newp* 3F **33**
Blackwall Tunnel. *G Lon* 2E **39**
Blackwater. *Corn* 4B **6**
Blackwater. *Hants* 1G **25**
Blackwater. *IOW* 4D **16**
Blackwater. *Som* 1F **13**
Blackwaterfoot. *N Ayr* 3C **122**
Blackwell. *Darl* 3F **105**
Blackwell. *Derbs* 5B **86**
(nr. Alfreton)
Blackwell. *Derbs* 3F **85**
(nr. Buxton)
Blackwell. *Som* 4D **20**
Blackwell. *Warw* 1H **49**
Blackwell. *Worc* 3D **61**
Blackwood. *Cphy* 2E **33**
Blackwood. *Dum* 1G **111**
Blackwood. *S Lan* 5A **128**
Blackwood Hill. *Staf* 5D **84**
Blacon. *Ches W* 4F **83**
Bladnoch. *Dum* 4B **110**
Bladon. *Oxon* 4C **50**
Blaenannerch. *Cdgn* 1C **44**
Blaenau Dolwyddelan. *Cnwy* 5F **81**
Blaenau Ffestiniog. *Gwyn* 1G **69**
Blaenavon. *Torf* 5F **47**
Blaenawey. *Mon* 4F **47**
Blaen Celyn. *Cdgn* 5C **56**
Blaen Clydach. *Rhon* 2C **32**
Blaendulais. *Neat* 5B **46**
Blaenffos. *Pemb* 1F **43**
Blaengarw. *B'end* 2C **32**
Blaen-geuffordd. *Cdgn* 2F **57**
Blaengwrach. *Neat* 5B **46**
Blaengwynfi. *Neat* 2B **32**
Blaenllechau. *Rhon* 2D **32**
Blaenpennal. *Cdgn* 4F **57**
Blaenplwyf. *Cdgn* 3E **57**
Blaenporth. *Cdgn* 1C **44**
Blaenrhondda. *Rhon* 2C **32**
Blaenwaun. *Carm* 2G **43**
Blaen-y-coed. *Carm* 2H **43**
Blaenycwm. *Rhon* 2C **32**
Blagdon. *N Som* 1A **22**
Blagdon. *Torb* 2E **9**
Blagdon Hill. *Som* 1F **13**
Blagill. *Cumb* 5A **114**
Blaguegate. *Lanc* 4C **90**
Blaich. *High* 1E **141**
Blain. *High* 2A **140**
Blaina. *Blae* 5F **47**
Blair Atholl. *Per* 2F **143**
Blair Drummond. *Stir* 4G **135**
Blairgowrie. *Per* 4A **144**
Blairhall. *Fife* 1D **128**
Blairingone. *Per* 4B **136**
Blairlogie. *Stir* 4H **135**
Blairmore. *Abers* 5B **160**
Blairmore. *Arg* 1C **126**
Blairmore. *High* 3B **166**
Blairquhanan. *W Dun* 1F **127**
Blaisdon. *Glos* 4C **48**
Blakebrook. *Worc* 3C **60**
Blakedown. *Worc* 3C **60**
Blake End. *Essx* 3H **53**
Blakemere. *Here* 1G **47**
Blakeney. *Glos* 5B **48**
Blakeney. *Norf* 1C **78**
Blakenhall. *Ches E* 1B **72**
Blakenhall. *W Mid* 1C **60**
Blakeshall. *Worc* 2C **60**
Blakesley. *Nptn* 5D **62**
Blanchland. *Nmbd* 4C **114**
Blandford Camp. *Dors* 2E **15**
Blandford Forum. *Dors* 2D **15**
Blandford St Mary. *Dors* 2D **15**
Bland Hill. *N Yor* 4E **98**
Blandy. *High* 3G **167**
Blanefield. *Stir* 2G **127**
Blankney. *Linc* 4H **87**
Blantyre. *S Lan* 4H **127**
Blarmachfoldach. *High* 2E **141**
Blarnalearoch. *High* 4F **163**
Blashford. *Hants* 2G **15**
Blaston. *Leics* 1F **63**
Blatchbridge. *Som* 2C **22**
Blathaisbhal. *W Isl* 1D **170**
Blatherwycke. *Nptn* 1G **63**
Blawith. *Cumb* 1B **96**
Blaxhall. *Suff* 5F **67**
Blaxton. *S Yor* 4G **93**
Blaydon. *Tyne* 3E **115**
Bleadney. *Som* 2H **21**
Bleadon. *N Som* 1G **21**
Blean. *Kent* 4F **41**
Bleasby. *Linc* 2A **88**
Bleasby. *Notts* 1E **74**
Bleasby Moor. *Linc* 2A **88**
Blebocraigs. *Fife* 2G **137**
Bleddfa. *Powy* 4E **58**
Bledington. *Glos* 3H **49**
Bledlow. *Buck* 5F **51**
Bledlow Ridge. *Buck* 2F **37**
Blencarn. *Cumb* 1H **103**
Blencogo. *Cumb* 5C **112**
Blendworth. *Hants* 1F **17**
Blenheim. *Oxon* 5D **50**
Blennerhasset. *Cumb* 5C **112**
Bletchingdon. *Oxon* 4D **50**
Bletchingley. *Surr* 5E **39**
Bletchley. *Mil* 2G **51**
Bletchley. *Shrp* 2A **72**
Bletherston. *Pemb* 2E **43**
Bletsoe. *Bed* 5H **63**
Blewbury. *Oxon* 3D **36**
Blickling. *Norf* 3D **78**
Blidworth. *Notts* 5C **86**
Blindburn. *Nmbd* 3C **120**
Blindcrake. *Cumb* 1C **102**
Blindley Heath. *Surr* 1E **27**
Blindmoor. *Som* 1F **13**
Blisland. *Corn* 5A **10**
Blissford. *Hants* 1G **15**
Bliss Gate. *Worc* 3B **60**
Blists Hill. *Telf* 5A **72**
Blisworth. *Nptn* 5E **63**
Blithbury. *Staf* 3E **73**
Blitterlees. *Cumb* 4C **112**
Blockley. *Glos* 2G **49**
Blofield. *Norf* 5F **79**
Blofield Heath. *Norf* 4F **79**
Blo' Norton. *Norf* 3C **66**
Bloomfield. *Bord* 2H **119**
Blore. *Staf* 1F **73**
Blount's Green. *Staf* 2E **73**
Bloxham. *Oxon* 2C **50**
Bloxholm. *Linc* 5H **87**
Bloxwich. *W Mid* 5E **73**
Bloxworth. *Dors* 3D **15**
Blubberhouses. *N Yor* 4D **98**
Blue Anchor. *Som* 2D **20**
Blue Anchor. *Swan* 3E **31**
Blue Bell Hill. *Kent* 4B **40**
Blue Row. *Essx* 4D **54**
Bluetown. *Kent* 5D **40**
Blundeston. *Suff* 1H **67**
Blunham. *C Beds* 5A **64**
Blunsdon St Andrew. *Swin* 3G **35**
Bluntington. *Worc* 3C **60**
Bluntisham. *Cambs* 3C **64**
Blunts. *Corn* 2H **7**
Blurton. *Stoke* 1C **72**
Blyborough. *Linc* 1G **87**
Blyford. *Suff* 3G **67**
Blymhill. *Staf* 4C **72**
Blymhill Lawns. *Staf* 4C **72**
Blyth. *Nmbd* 1G **115**
Blyth. *Notts* 2D **86**
Blyth. *Bord* 5E **129**
Blyth Bank. *Bord* 5E **129**
Blyth Bridge. *Bord* 5E **129**
Blythburgh. *Suff* 3G **67**
Blythe Bridge. *Staf* 1D **72**
Blythe Marsh. *Staf* 1D **72**
Blythe, The. *Staf* 3E **73**
Blyton. *Linc* 1F **87**
Boarhills. *Fife* 2H **137**
Boarhunt. *Hants* 2E **16**
Boarshead. *E Sus* 2G **27**
Boar's Head. *G Man* 4D **90**
Boars Hill. *Oxon* 5C **50**
Boarstall. *Buck* 4E **51**
Boasley Cross. *Devn* 3F **11**
Boath. *High* 1H **157**
Boat of Garten. *High* 2D **150**
Bobbing. *Kent* 4C **40**
Bobbington. *Staf* 1C **60**
Bobbingworth. *Essx* 5F **53**
Bocaddon. *Corn* 3F **7**
Bocking. *Essx* 3A **54**
Bocking Churchstreet. *Essx* 3A **54**
Boddam. *Abers* 4H **161**
Boddam. *Shet* 10E **173**
Boddington. *Glos* 3D **49**
Bodedern. *IOA* 2C **80**
Bodelwyddan. *Den* 3C **82**
Bodenham. *Here* 5H **59**
Bodenham. *Wilts* 4G **23**
Bodewryd. *IOA* 1C **80**
Bodfari. *Den* 3C **82**
Bodffordd. *IOA* 3D **80**
Bodham. *Norf* 1D **78**
Bodiam. *E Sus* 3B **28**
Bodicote. *Oxon* 2C **50**
Bodieve. *Corn* 1D **6**
Bodinnick. *Corn* 3F **7**
Bodle Street Green. *E Sus* 4A **28**
Bodmin. *Corn* 2E **7**
Bodnant. *Cnwy* 3H **81**
Bodney. *Norf* 1H **65**
Bodorgan. *IOA* 4C **80**
Bodrane. *Corn* 2G **7**
Bodsham. *Kent* 1F **29**
Boduan. *Gwyn* 2C **68**
Bodymoor Heath. *Warw* 1F **61**
Bogallan. *High* 3A **158**
Bogbrae Croft. *Abers* 5H **161**
Bogend. *S Ayr* 1C **116**
Boghall. *Midl* 3F **129**
Boghall. *W Lot* 3C **128**
Boghead. *S Lan* 5A **128**
Bogindollo. *Ang* 3D **144**
Bogmoor. *Mor* 2A **160**
Bogniebrae. *Abers* 4C **160**
Bognor Regis. *W Sus* 3H **17**
Bograxie. *Abers* 2E **152**
Bogside. *N Lan* 4B **128**
Bog, The. *Shrp* 1F **59**
Bogton. *Abers* 3D **160**
Bogue. *Dum* 1D **110**
Bohenie. *High* 5E **149**
Bohortha. *Corn* 5C **6**
Bokiddick. *Corn* 2E **7**
Bolam. *Dur* 2E **105**
Bolam. *Nmbd* 1D **115**
Bolberry. *Devn* 5C **8**
Bold Heath. *Mers* 2H **83**
Boldon. *Tyne* 3G **115**
Boldon Colliery. *Tyne* 3G **115**
Boldre. *Hants* 3B **16**
Boldron. *Dur* 3D **104**
Bole. *Notts* 2E **87**
Bolehall. *Staf* 5G **73**
Bolehill. *Derbs* 5G **85**
Bolenowe. *Corn* 5A **6**
Boleside. *Bord* 1G **119**
Bolham. *Devn* 1C **12**
Bolham Water. *Devn* 1E **13**
Bolingey. *Corn* 3B **6**
Bollington. *Ches E* 3D **84**
Bolney. *W Sus* 3D **26**
Bolnhurst. *Bed* 5H **63**
Bolshan. *Ang* 3F **145**
Bolsover. *Derbs* 3B **86**
Bolsterstone. *S Yor* 1G **85**
Bolstone. *Here* 2A **48**
Boltachan. *Per* 3F **143**
Boltby. *N Yor* 1G **99**
Bolton. *Cumb* 2H **103**
Bolton. *E Lot* 2B **130**
Bolton. *E Yor* 4B **100**
Bolton. *G Man* 4F **91**
Bolton. *Nmbd* 3F **121**
Bolton Abbey. *N Yor* 4C **98**
Bolton-by-Bowland. *Lanc* 5G **97**
Boltonfellend. *Cumb* 3F **113**
Boltongate. *Cumb* 5D **112**
Bolton Green. *Lanc* 3D **90**
Bolton-le-Sands. *Lanc* 3D **97**
Bolton Low Houses. *Cumb* 5D **112**
Bolton New Houses. *Cumb* 5D **112**
Bolton-on-Swale. *N Yor* 5F **105**
Bolton Percy. *N Yor* 5H **99**
Bolton Town End. *Lanc* 3D **97**
Bolton upon Dearne. *S Yor* 4E **93**
Bolton Wood Lane. *Cumb* 5D **112**
Bolventor. *Corn* 5B **10**
Bomarsund. *Nmbd* 1F **115**
Bomere Heath. *Shrp* 4G **71**
Bonar Bridge. *High* 4D **164**
Bonawe. *Arg* 5E **141**
Bonby. *N Lin* 3D **94**
Boncath. *Pemb* 1G **43**
Bonchester Bridge. *Bord* 3H **119**
Bonchurch. *IOW* 5D **16**
Bond End. *Staf* 4F **73**
Bondleigh. *Devn* 2G **11**
Bonds. *Lanc* 5D **97**
Bonehill. *Devn* 5H **11**
Bonehill. *Staf* 5F **73**
Bo'ness. *Falk* 1C **128**
Boney Hay. *Staf* 4E **73**
Bonham. *Wilts* 3C **22**
Bonhill. *W Dun* 2E **127**
Boningale. *Shrp* 5C **72**
Bonjedward. *Bord* 2A **120**
Bonkle. *N Lan* 4B **128**
Bonnington. *Ang* 5E **145**
Bonnington. *Edin* 3E **129**
Bonnington. *Kent* 2E **29**
Bonnybank. *Fife* 3F **137**
Bonnybridge. *Falk* 1B **128**
Bonnykelly. *Abers* 3F **161**
Bonnyrigg. *Midl* 3G **129**
Bonnyton. *Ang* 5C **144**
Bonnytown. *Fife* 2H **137**
Bonsall. *Derbs* 5G **85**
Bont. *Mon* 4G **47**
Bontddu. *Gwyn* 4F **69**
Bont Dolgadfan. *Powy* 5A **70**
Bontgoch. *Cdgn* 2F **57**
Bonthorpe. *Linc* 3D **89**
Bontnewydd. *Cdgn* 4F **57**
Bont-newydd. *Cnwy* 3C **82**

Bontnewydd. *Gwyn* 4D 81
(nr. Caernarfon)
Bont Newydd. *Gwyn* 1G 69
(nr. Llan Ffestiniog)
Bontuchel. *Den* 5C 82
Bonvilston. *V Glam* 4D 32
Bon-y-maen. *Swan* 3F 31
Booker. *Buck* 2G 37
Booley. *Shrp* 3H 71
Boorley Green. *Hants* 1D 16
Boosbeck. *Red C* 3D 106
Boot. *Cumb* 4C 102
Booth. *W Yor* 2A 92
Boothby Graffoe. *Linc* 5G 87
Boothby Pagnell. *Linc* 2G 75
Booth Green. *Ches E* 2D 84
Booth of Toft. *Shet* 4F 173
Boothstown. *G Man* 4F 91
Boothville. *Nptn* 4E 63
Booth Wood. *W Yor* 3A 92
Bootle. *Cumb* 1A 96
Bootle. *Mers* 1F 83
Booton. *Norf* 3D 78
Booze. *N Yor* 4D 104
Boquhan. *Stir* 1G 127
Boraston. *Shrp* 3A 60
Borden. *Kent* 4C 40
Borden. *W Sus* 4G 25
Bordlands. *Bord* 5E 129
Bordley. *N Yor* 3B 98
Bordon. *Hants* 3G 25
Boreham. *Essx* 5A 54
Boreham. *Wilts* 2D 23
Boreham Street. *E Sus* 4A 28
Borehamwood. *Herts* 1C 38
Boreland. *Dum* 5D 118
Boreston. *Devn* 3D 8
Borestone Brae. *Stir* 4H 135
Boreton. *Shrp* 5H 71
Borgh. *W Isl* 8B 170
(on Barra)
Borgh. *W Isl* 3C 170
(on Benbecula)
Borgh. *W Isl* 1E 170
(on Berneray)
Borgh. *W Isl* 2G 171
(on Isle of Lewis)
Borghastan. *W Isl* 3D 171
Borgh na Sgiotaig. *High* 1C 154
Borgie. *High* 3G 167
Borgue. *Dum* 5D 110
Borgue. *High* 1H 165
Borley. *Essx* 1B 54
Borley Green. *Essx* 1B 54
Borley Green. *Suff* 4B 66
Borlum. *High* 1H 149
Bornais. *W Isl* 6C 170
Bornesketaig. *High* 1C 154
Boroughbridge. *N Yor* 3F 99
Borough Green. *Kent* 5H 39
Borras Head. *Wrex* 5F 83
Borreraig. *High* 3A 154
Borrobol Lodge. *High* 1F 165
Borrodale. *High* 4A 154
Borrowash. *Derb* 2B 74
Borrowby. *N Yor* 1G 99
(nr. Northallerton)
Borrowby. *N Yor* 3E 107
(nr. Whitby)
Borrowston. *High* 4F 169
Borrowstonehill. *Orkn* 7D 172
Borrowstoun. *Falk* 1C 128
Borstal. *Medw* 4B 40
Borth. *Cdgn* 2F 57
Borthwick. *Midl* 4G 129
Borth-y-Gest. *Gwyn* 2E 69
Borve. *High* 4D 154
Borwick. *Lanc* 2E 97
Bosbury. *Here* 1B 48
Boscastle. *Corn* 3A 10
Boscombe. *Bour* 3G 15
Boscombe. *Wilts* 3H 23
Boscoppa. *Corn* 3E 7
Bosham. *W Sus* 2G 17
Bosherston. *Pemb* 5D 42
Bosley. *Ches E* 4D 84
Bossall. *N Yor* 3B 100
Bossiney. *Corn* 4A 10
Bossingham. *Kent* 1F 29
Bossington. *Som* 2B 20
Bostadh. *W Isl* 4D 171
Bostock Green. *Ches W* 4A 84
Boston. *Linc* 1C 76
Boston Spa. *W Yor* 5G 99
Boswarthen. *Corn* 3B 4
Boswinger. *Corn* 4D 6
Botallack. *Corn* 3A 4
Botany Bay. *G Lon* 1D 39
Botcheston. *Leics* 5B 74
Botesdale. *Suff* 3C 66
Bothal. *Nmbd* 1F 115
Bothampstead. *W Ber* 4D 36
Bothamsall. *Notts* 3D 86
Bothel. *Cumb* 1C 102
Bothenhampton. *Dors* 3H 13
Bothwell. *S Lan* 4H 127
Botley. *Buck* 5H 51
Botley. *Hants* 1D 16
Botley. *Oxon* 5C 50
Botloe's Green. *Glos* 3C 48
Botolph Claydon. *Buck* 3F 51
Botolphs. *W Sus* 5C 26
Bottacks. *High* 2G 157
Bottesford. *Leics* 2F 75
Bottesford. *N Lin* 4B 94
Bottisham. *Cambs* 4E 65
Bottlesford. *Wilts* 1G 23
Bottomcraig. *Fife* 1F 137
Bottom o' th' Moor. *G Man* 3E 91
Botton. *N Yor* 4D 107
Botton Head. *Lanc* 3F 97
Bottreaux Mill. *Devn* 4B 20
Botus Fleming. *Corn* 2A 8
Botwnnog. *Gwyn* 2B 68
Bough Beech. *Kent* 1F 27
Boughrood. *Powy* 2E 47
Boughspring. *Glos* 2A 34
Boughton. *Norf* 5F 77
Boughton. *Nptn* 4E 63
Boughton. *Notts* 4D 86
Boughton Aluph. *Kent* 1E 29
Boughton Green. *Kent* 5B 40
Boughton Lees. *Kent* 1E 28
Boughton Malherbe. *Kent* 1C 28
Boughton Monchelsea. *Kent* 5B 40
Boughton under Blean. *Kent* 5E 41
Boulby. *Red C* 3E 107
Bouldnor. *IOW* 4B 16
Bouldon. *Shrp* 2H 59
Boulmer. *Nmbd* 3G 121
Boulston. *Pemb* 3D 42
Boultham. *Linc* 4G 87
Boulton. *Derb* 2A 74
Boundary. *Staf* 1D 73
Bounds. *Here* 2B 48
Bourn. *Cambs* 5C 64
Bournbrook. *W Mid* 2E 61
Bourne. *Linc* 3H 75
Bourne End. *Bed* 4H 63
Bourne End. *Buck* 3G 37
Bourne End. *C Beds* 1H 51
Bourne End. *Herts* 5A 52
Bournemouth. *Bour* 3F 15
Bournemouth Airport. *Dors* 3G 15
Bournes Green. *Glos* 5E 49
Bournes Green. *S'end* 2D 40
Bourne, The. *Surr* 2G 25
Bournheath. *Worc* 3D 60
Bournmoor. *Dur* 4G 115
Bournville. *W Mid* 2E 61
Bourton. *Dors* 3C 22
Bourton. *N Som* 5G 33
Bourton. *Oxon* 3H 35
Bourton. *Shrp* 1H 59
Bourton. *Wilts* 5F 35
Bourton on Dunsmore. *Warw* 3B 62
Bourton-on-the-Hill. *Glos* 2G 49
Bourton-on-the-Water. *Glos* 3G 49
Bousd. *Arg* 2D 138
Boustead Hill. *Cumb* 4D 112
Bouth. *Cumb* 1C 96
Bouthwaite. *N Yor* 2D 98
Boveney. *Buck* 3A 38
Boveridge. *Dors* 1F 15
Boverton. *V Glam* 5C 32
Bovey Tracey. *Devn* 5B 12
Bovingdon. *Herts* 5A 52
Bovingdon Green. *Buck* 3G 37
Bovinger. *Essx* 5F 53
Bovington Camp. *Dors* 4D 14
Bow. *Devn* 2H 11
Bowbank. *Dur* 2C 104
Bow Brickhill. *Mil* 2H 51
Bowbridge. *Glos* 5D 48
Bowburn. *Dur* 1A 106
Bowcombe. *IOW* 4C 16
Bowd. *Devn* 4E 12
Bowden. *Devn* 4E 9
Bowden. *Bord* 1H 119
Bowden Hill. *Wilts* 5E 35
Bowdens. *Som* 4H 21
Bowderdale. *Cumb* 4H 103
Bowdon. *G Man* 2B 84
Bower. *Nmbd* 1A 114
Bowerchalke. *Wilts* 4F 23
Bowerhill. *Wilts* 5E 35
Bower Hinton. *Som* 1H 13
Bowermadden. *High* 2E 169
Bowers. *Staf* 2C 72
Bowers Gifford. *Essx* 2B 40
Bowershall. *Fife* 4C 136
Bowertower. *High* 2E 169
Bowes. *Dur* 3C 104
Bowgreave. *Lanc* 5D 97
Bowhousebog. *N Lan* 4B 128
Bowithick. *Corn* 4B 10
Bowland Bridge. *Cumb* 1D 96
Bowlees. *Dur* 2C 104
Bowley. *Here* 5H 59
Bowlhead Green. *Surr* 2A 26
Bowling. *W Dun* 2F 127
Bowling. *W Yor* 1B 92
Bowling Bank. *Wrex* 1F 71
Bowling Green. *Worc* 5C 60
Bowlish. *Som* 2B 22
Bowmanstead. *Cumb* 5E 102
Bowmore. *Arg* 4B 124
Bowness-on-Solway. *Cumb* 3D 112
Bowness-on-Windermere.
Cumb 5F 103
Bow of Fife. *Fife* 2F 137
Bowriefauld. *Ang* 4E 145
Bowscale. *Cumb* 1E 103
Bowsden. *Nmbd* 5F 131
Bowside Lodge. *High* 2A 168
Bowston. *Cumb* 5F 103
Bow Street. *Cdgn* 2F 57
Bowthorpe. *Norf* 5D 78
Box. *Glos* 5D 48
Box. *Wilts* 5D 34
Boxbush. *Glos* 3B 48
Box End. *Bed* 1A 52
Boxford. *Suff* 1C 54
Boxford. *W Ber* 4C 36
Boxgrove. *W Sus* 5A 26
Boxley. *Kent* 5B 40
Boxmoor. *Herts* 5A 52
Box's Shop. *Corn* 2C 10
Boxted. *Essx* 2C 54
Boxted. *Suff* 5H 65
Boxted Cross. *Essx* 2D 54
Boxworth. *Cambs* 4C 64
Boxworth End. *Cambs* 4C 64
Boyden End. *Suff* 5G 65
Boyden Gate. *Kent* 4G 41
Boylestone. *Derbs* 2F 73
Boylestonfield. *Derbs* 2F 73
Boyndie. *Abers* 2D 160
Boynton. *E Yor* 3F 101
Boys Hill. *Dors* 1B 14
Boythorpe. *Derbs* 4A 86
Boyton. *Corn* 3D 10
Boyton. *Suff* 1G 55
Boyton. *Wilts* 3E 23
Boyton Cross. *Essx* 5G 53
Boyton End. *Essx* 2G 53
Boyton End. *Suff* 1H 53
Bozeat. *Nptn* 5G 63
Braaid. *IOM* 4C 108
Braal Castle. *High* 2D 168
Brabling Green. *Suff* 4E 67
Brabourne. *Kent* 1F 29
Brabourne Lees. *Kent* 1E 29
Brabster. *High* 2F 169
Bracadale. *High* 5C 154
Bracara. *High* 4F 147
Braceborough. *Linc* 4H 75
Bracebridge. *Linc* 4G 87
Bracebridge Heath. *Linc* 4G 87
Braceby. *Linc* 2H 75
Bracewell. *Lanc* 5A 98
Brackenber. *Cumb* 3A 104
Brackenfield. *Derbs* 5A 86
Brackenlands. *Cumb* 5D 112
Brackenthwaite. *Cumb* 5D 112
Brackenthwaite. *N Yor* 4E 99
Brackla. *B'end* 4C 32
Brackla. *High* 3C 158
Bracklesham. *W Sus* 3G 17
Brackletter. *High* 5D 148
Brackley. *Nptn* 2D 50
Brackley Hatch. *Nptn* 1E 51
Brackloch. *High* 1F 163
Bracknell. *Brac* 5G 37
Braco. *Per* 3H 135
Bracobrae. *Mor* 3C 160
Bracon. *N Lin* 4A 94
Bracon Ash. *Norf* 1D 66
Bradbourne. *Derbs* 5G 85
Bradbury. *Dur* 2A 106
Bradda. *IOM* 4A 108
Bradden. *Nptn* 1E 51
Bradenham. *Buck* 2G 37
Bradenham. *Norf* 5B 78
Bradenstoke. *Wilts* 4F 35
Bradfield. *Essx* 2E 55
Bradfield. *Norf* 2E 79
Bradfield. *W Ber* 4E 36
Bradfield Combust. *Suff* 5A 66
Bradfield Green. *Ches E* 5A 84
Bradfield Heath. *Essx* 3E 55
Bradfield St Clare. *Suff* 5B 66
Bradfield St George. *Suff* 4B 66
Bradford. *Derbs* 4G 85
Bradford. *Devn* 2E 11
Bradford. *Nmbd* 1F 121
Bradford. *W Yor* 1B 92
Bradford Abbas. *Dors* 1A 14
Bradford Barton. *Devn* 1B 12
Bradford Leigh. *Wilts* 5D 34
Bradford-on-Avon. *Wilts* 5D 34
Bradford-on-Tone. *Som* 4E 21
Bradford Peverell. *Dors* 3B 14
Bradiford. *Devn* 3F 19
Brading. *IOW* 4E 16
Bradley. *Ches W* 3H 83
Bradley. *Derbs* 1G 73
Bradley. *Glos* 2C 34
Bradley. *Hants* 2E 25
Bradley. *NE Lin* 4F 95
Bradley. *N Yor* 1C 98
Bradley. *Staf* 4C 72
Bradley. *W Mid* 1D 60
Bradley. *W Yor* 2B 92
Bradley. *Wrex* 5F 83
Bradley Cross. *Som* 1H 21
Bradley Green. *Ches W* 1H 71
Bradley Green. *Som* 3F 21
Bradley Green. *Warw* 5G 73
Bradley Green. *Worc* 4D 61
Bradley in the Moors. *Staf* 1E 73
Bradley Mount. *Ches E* 3D 84
Bradley Stoke. *S Glo* 3B 34
Bradlow. *Here* 2C 48
Bradmore. *Notts* 2C 74
Bradmore. *W Mid* 1C 60
Bradninch. *Devn* 2D 12
Bradnop. *Staf* 5E 85
Bradpole. *Dors* 3H 13
Bradshaw. *G Man* 3F 91
Bradstone. *Devn* 4D 11
Bradwall Green. *Ches E* 4B 84
Bradway. *S Yor* 2H 85
Bradwell. *Derbs* 2F 85
Bradwell. *Essx* 3B 54
Bradwell. *Mil* 2G 51
Bradwell. *Norf* 5H 79
Bradwell-on-Sea. *Essx* 5D 54
Bradwell Waterside. *Essx* 5C 54
Bradworthy. *Devn* 1D 10
Brae. *High* 5C 162
Brae. *Shet* 5E 173
Braeantra. *High* 1H 157
Braefield. *High* 5G 157
Braefindon. *High* 3A 158
Braegrum. *Per* 1C 136
Braehead. *Ang* 3F 145
Braehead. *Dum* 4B 110
Braehead. *Mor* 4G 159
Braehead. *Orkn* 3D 172
Braehead. *S Lan* 1H 117
(nr. Coalburn)
Braehead. *S Lan* 4C 128
(nr. Forth)
Braehoulland. *Shet* 4D 173
Braemar. *Abers* 4F 151
Braemore. *High* 5C 168
(nr. Dunbeath)
Braemore. *High* 1D 156
(nr. Ullapool)
Brae of Achnahaird. *High* 2E 163
Brae Roy Lodge. *High* 4F 149
Braeside. *Abers* 5G 161
Braeside. *Inv* 2D 126
Braes of Coul. *Ang* 3B 144
Braetongue. *High* 3F 167
Braeval. *Stir* 3E 135
Braevallich. *Arg* 3G 133
Brafferton. *Darl* 2F 105
Brafferton. *N Yor* 2G 99
Brafield-on-the-Green. *Nptn* 5F 63
Bragar. *W Isl* 3E 171
Bragbury End. *Herts* 3C 52
Bragleenbeg. *Arg* 1G 133
Braichmelyn. *Gwyn* 4F 81
Braides. *Lanc* 4D 96
Braidwood. *S Lan* 5B 128
Braigo. *Arg* 3A 124
Brailsford. *Derbs* 1G 73
Braintree. *Essx* 3A 54
Braiseworth. *Suff* 3D 66
Braishfield. *Hants* 4B 24
Braithwaite. *Cumb* 2D 102
Braithwaite. *S Yor* 3G 93
Braithwaite. *W Yor* 5C 98
Braithwell. *S Yor* 1C 86
Brakefield Green. *Norf* 5C 78
Bramber. *W Sus* 4C 26
Brambledown. *Kent* 3D 40
Brambridge. *Hants* 4C 24
Bramcote. *Notts* 2C 74
Bramcote. *Warw* 2B 62
Bramdean. *Hants* 4E 24
Bramerton. *Norf* 5E 79
Bramfield. *Herts* 4C 52
Bramfield. *Suff* 3F 67
Bramford. *Suff* 1E 54
Bramhall. *G Man* 2C 84
Bramham. *W Yor* 5G 99
Bramhope. *W Yor* 5E 99
Bramley. *Hants* 1E 25
Bramley. *S Yor* 1B 86
Bramley. *Surr* 1B 26
Bramley. *W Yor* 1C 92
Bramley Green. *Hants* 1E 25
Bramley Head. *N Yor* 4D 98
Bramley Vale. *Derbs* 4B 86
Bramling. *Kent* 5G 41
Brampford Speke. *Devn* 3C 12
Brampton. *Cambs* 3B 64

Brampton—Broad Street

Brampton. Cumb 2H 103
(nr. Appleby-in-Westmorland)
Brampton. Cumb 3G 113
(nr. Carlisle)
Brampton. Linc 3F 87
Brampton. Norf 3E 78
Brampton. S Yor 4E 93
Brampton. Suff 2G 67
Brampton Abbotts. Here 3B 48
Brampton Ash. Nptn 2E 63
Brampton Bryan. Here 3F 59
Brampton en le Morthen. S Yor 2B 86
Bramshall. Staf 2E 73
Bramshaw. Hants 1A 16
Bramshill. Hants 5F 37
Bramshott. Hants 3G 25
Branault. High 2G 139
Brancaster. Norf 1G 77
Brancaster Staithe. Norf 1G 77
Brancepeth. Dur 1F 105
Branch End. Nmbd 3D 114
Branchill. Mor 3E 159
Brand End. Linc 1C 76
Branderburgh. Mor 1G 159
Brandesburton. E Yor 5F 101
Brandeston. Suff 4E 67
Brand Green. Glos 3C 48
Brandhill. Shrp 3G 59
Brandis Corner. Devn 2E 11
Brandish Street. Som 2C 20
Brandiston. Norf 3D 78
Brandon. Dur 1F 105
Brandon. Linc 1G 75
Brandon. Nmbd 3E 121
Brandon. Suff 2G 65
Brandon. Warw 3B 62
Brandon Bank. Cambs 2F 65
Brandon Creek. Norf 1F 65
Brandon Parva. Norf 5C 78
Brandsby. N Yor 2H 99
Brandy Wharf. Linc 1H 87
Brane. Corn 4B 4
Bran End. Essx 3G 53
Branksome. Pool 3F 15
Bransbury. Hants 2C 24
Bransby. Linc 3G 87
Branscombe. Devn 4E 13
Bransford. Worc 5B 60
Bransgore. Hants 3G 15
Bransholme. Hull 1D 94
Bransley. Shrp 3A 60
Branston. Leics 3F 75
Branston. Linc 4H 87
Branston. Staf 3G 73
Branston Booths. Linc 4H 87
Branstone. IOW 4D 16
Bransty. Cumb 3A 102
Brant Broughton. Linc 5G 87
Brantham. Suff 2E 54
Branthwaite. Cumb 1D 102
(nr. Caldbeck)
Branthwaite. Cumb 2B 102
(nr. Workington)
Brantingham. E Yor 2C 94
Branton. Nmbd 3E 121
Branton. S Yor 4G 93
Branton Green. N Yor 3G 99
Branxholme. Bord 3G 119
Branxton. Nmbd 1C 120
Brassington. Derbs 5G 85
Brasted. Kent 5F 39
Brasted Chart. Kent 5F 39
Bratch, The. Staf 1C 60
Brathens. Abers 4D 152
Bratoft. Linc 4D 88
Brattleby. Linc 2G 87
Bratton. Som 2C 20
Bratton. Telf 4A 72
Bratton. Wilts 1E 23
Bratton Clovelly. Devn 3E 11
Bratton Fleming. Devn 3G 19
Bratton Seymour. Som 4B 22
Braughing. Herts 3D 53
Braulen Lodge. High 5E 157
Braunston. Nptn 4C 62
Braunstone Town. Leic 5C 74
Braunston-in-Rutland. Rut 5F 75
Braunton. Devn 3E 19
Brawby. N Yor 2B 100
Brawl. High 2A 168
Brawlbin. High 3C 168
Bray. Wind 3A 38
Braybrooke. Nptn 2E 63
Brayford. Devn 3G 19
Bray Shop. Corn 5D 10
Braystones. Cumb 4B 102
Brayton. N Yor 1G 93
Bray Wick. Wind 4G 37
Brazacott. Corn 3C 10
Brea. Corn 4A 6
Breach. W Sus 2F 17
Breachwood Green. Herts 3B 52
Breacleit. W Isl 4D 171
Breaden Heath. Shrp 2G 71
Breadsall. Derbs 1A 74
Breadstone. Glos 5C 48
Breage. Corn 4D 4
Breakachy. High 4G 157
Breakish. High 1E 147
Bream. Glos 5B 48
Breamore. Hants 1G 15
Bream's Meend. Glos 5B 48
Brean. Som 1F 21
Breanais. W Isl 5B 171
Brearton. N Yor 3F 99
Breascleit. W Isl 4E 171
Breaston. Derbs 2B 74
Brecais Àrd. High 1E 147
Brecais Iosal. High 1E 147
Brechfa. Carm 2F 45
Brechin. Ang 3F 145
Breckles. Norf 1B 66
Brecon. Powy 3D 46
Brecon Beacons. Powy 3C 46
Bredbury. G Man 1D 84
Brede. E Sus 4C 28
Bredenbury. Here 5A 60
Breden's Norton. Worc 2E 49
Bredfield. Suff 5E 67
Bredgar. Kent 4C 40
Bredhurst. Kent 4B 40
Bredicot. Worc 5D 60
Bredon. Worc 2E 49
Bredwardine. Here 1G 47
Breedon on the Hill. Leics 3B 74
Breibhig. W Isl 9B 170
(on Barra)
Breibhig. W Isl 4G 171
(on Isle of Lewis)
Breich. W Lot 3C 128
Breightmet. G Man 3F 91
Breighton. E Yor 1H 93
Breinton. Here 2H 47
Breinton Common. Here 2H 47
Breiwick. Shet 7F 173
Brelston Green. Here 3A 48
Bremhill. Wilts 4E 35
Brenachie. High 1B 158
Brenchley. Kent 1A 28
Brendon. Devn 2A 20
Brent Cross. G Lon 2D 38
Brent Eleigh. Suff 1C 54
Brentford. G Lon 3C 38
Brentingby. Leics 4E 75
Brent Knoll. Som 1G 21
Brent Pelham. Herts 2E 53
Brentwood. Essx 1H 39
Brenzett. Kent 3E 28
Brereton. Staf 4E 73
Brereton Cross. Staf 4E 73
Brereton Green. Ches E 4B 84
Brereton Heath. Ches E 4C 84
Bressingham. Norf 2C 66
Bretby. Derbs 3G 73
Bretford. Warw 3B 62
Bretforton. Worc 1F 49
Bretherdale Head. Cumb 4G 103
Bretherton. Lanc 2C 90
Brettenham. Norf 2B 66
Brettenham. Suff 5B 66
Bretton. Flin 4F 83
Bretton. Pet 5A 76
Brewer Street. Surr 5E 39
Brewlands Bridge. Ang 2A 144
Brewood. Staf 5C 72
Briantspuddle. Dors 3D 14
Bricket Wood. Herts 5B 52
Bricklehampton. Worc 1E 49
Bride. IOM 1D 108
Bridekirk. Cumb 1C 102
Bridell. Pemb 1B 44
Bridestowe. Devn 4F 11
Brideswell. Abers 5C 160
Bridford. Devn 4B 12
Bridge. Corn 4A 6
Bridge. Kent 5F 41
Bridge. Som 2G 13
Bridge End. Bed 5H 63
Bridge End. Cumb 5D 102
(nr. Broughton in Furness)
Bridge End. Cumb 5E 113
(nr. Dalston)
Bridge End. Linc 2A 76
Bridge End. Shet 8E 173
Bridgefoot. Ang 5C 144
Bridgefoot. Cumb 2B 102
Bridge Green. Essx 2E 53
Bridgehampton. Som 4A 22
Bridge Hewick. N Yor 2F 99
Bridgehill. Dur 4D 115
Bridgemary. Hants 2D 16
Bridgemere. Ches E 1B 72
Bridgemont. Derbs 2E 85
Bridgend. Abers 5C 160
(nr. Huntly)
Bridgend. Abers 5H 161
(nr. Peterhead)
Bridgend. Ang 2E 145
(nr. Brechin)
Bridgend. Ang 4C 144
(nr. Kirriemuir)
Bridgend. Arg 4F 133
(nr. Lochgilphead)
Bridgend. Arg 3B 124
(on Islay)
Bridgend. B'end 3C 32
Bridgend. Cumb 3F 103
Bridgend. Devn 4B 8
Bridgend. Fife 2F 137
Bridgend. High 3F 157
Bridgend. Mor 5A 160
Bridgend. Per 1D 136
Bridgend. W Lot 2D 128
Bridgend of Lintrathen. Ang 3B 144
Bridgeness. Falk 1D 128
Bridge of Alford. Abers 2C 152
Bridge of Allan. Stir 4G 135
Bridge of Avon. Mor 5F 159
Bridge of Awe. Arg 1H 133
Bridge of Balgie. Per 4C 142
Bridge of Brown. High 1F 151
Bridge of Cally. Per 3A 144
Bridge of Canny. Abers 4D 152
Bridge of Dee. Dum 3E 111
Bridge of Don. Aber 2G 153
Bridge of Dun. Ang 3F 145
Bridge of Dye. Abers 5D 152
Bridge of Earn. Per 2D 136
Bridge of Ericht. Per 3C 142
Bridge of Feugh. Abers 4E 152
Bridge of Forss. High 2C 168
Bridge of Gairn. Abers 4A 152
Bridge of Gaur. Per 3C 142
Bridge of Muchalls. Abers 4F 153
Bridge of Oich. High 3F 149
Bridge of Orchy. Arg 5H 141
Bridge of Walls. Shet 6D 173
Bridge of Weir. Ren 3E 127
Bridge Reeve. Devn 1G 11
Bridgerule. Devn 2C 10
Bridge Sollers. Here 1H 47
Bridge Street. Suff 1B 54
Bridgetown. Devn 2E 9
Bridgetown. Som 3C 20
Bridge Town. Warw 5G 61
Bridge Trafford. Ches W 3G 83
Bridgeyate. S Glo 4B 34
Bridgham. Norf 2B 66
Bridgnorth. Shrp 1B 60
Bridgtown. Staf 5D 73
Bridgwater. Som 3G 21
Bridlington. E Yor 3F 101
Bridport. Dors 3H 13
Bridstow. Here 3A 48
Brierfield. Lanc 1G 91
Brierley. Glos 4B 48
Brierley. Here 5G 59
Brierley. S Yor 3E 93
Brierley Hill. W Mid 2D 60
Brierton. Hart 1B 106
Briestfield. W Yor 3C 92
Brigg. N Lin 4D 94
Briggate. Norf 3F 79
Briggswath. N Yor 4F 107
Brigham. Cumb 1B 102
Brigham. E Yor 4E 101
Brighouse. W Yor 2B 92
Brighstone. IOW 4C 16
Brightgate. Derbs 5G 85
Brighthampton. Oxon 5B 50
Brightholmlee. S Yor 1G 85
Brightley. Devn 3G 11
Brightling. E Sus 3A 28
Brightlingsea. Essx 4D 54
Brighton. Brig 5E 27
Brighton. Corn 3D 6
Brighton Hill. Hants 2E 24
Brightons. Falk 2C 128
Brightwalton. W Ber 4C 36
Brightwalton Green. W Ber 4C 36
Brightwell. Suff 1F 55
Brightwell Baldwin. Oxon 2E 37
Brightwell-cum-Sotwell. Oxon 2D 36
Brigmerston. Wilts 2G 23
Brignall. Dur 3D 104
Brig o'Turk. Stir 3E 135
Brigsley. NE Lin 4F 95
Brigsteer. Cumb 1D 97
Brigstock. Nptn 2G 63
Brill. Buck 4E 51
Brill. Corn 4E 5
Brilley. Here 1F 47
Brimaston. Pemb 2D 42
Brimfield. Here 4H 59
Brimington. Derbs 3B 86
Brimley. Devn 5B 12
Brimpsfield. Glos 4E 49
Brimpton. W Ber 5D 36
Brims. Orkn 9B 172
Brimscombe. Glos 5D 48
Brimstage. Mers 2F 83
Brincliffe. S Yor 2H 85
Brind. E Yor 1H 93
Brindle. Lanc 2E 90
Brindley. Ches E 5H 83
Brindley Ford. Stoke 5C 84
Brineton. Staf 4C 72
Bringhurst. Leics 1F 63
Brington. Cambs 3H 63
Brinian. Orkn 5D 172
Briningham. Norf 2C 78
Brinkhill. Linc 3C 88
Brinkley. Cambs 5F 65
Brinklow. Warw 3B 62
Brinkworth. Wilts 3F 35
Brinscall. Lanc 2E 91
Brinscombe. Som 1H 21
Brinsley. Notts 1B 74
Brinsty Common. Here 5A 60
Brinsworth. S Yor 2B 86
Brinton. Norf 2C 78
Brisco. Cumb 4F 113
Brisley. Norf 3B 78
Brislington. Bris 4B 34
Brissenden Green. Kent 2D 28
Bristol. Bris 4A 34
Bristol International Airport. N Som 5A 34
Briston. Norf 2C 78
Britannia. Lanc 2G 91
Britford. Wilts 4G 23
Brithdir. Cphy 5E 47
Brithdir. Cdgn 1D 44
Brithdir. Gwyn 4G 69
Briton Ferry. Neat 3G 31
Britwell Salome. Oxon 2E 37
Brixham. Torb 3F 9
Brixton. Devn 3B 8
Brixton. G Lon 3E 39
Brixton Deverill. Wilts 3D 22
Brixworth. Nptn 3E 63
Brize Norton. Oxon 5B 50
Broad Alley. Worc 4C 60
Broad Blunsdon. Swin 2G 35
Broadbottom. G Man 1D 85
Broadbridge. W Sus 2G 17
Broadbridge Heath. W Sus 2C 26
Broad Campden. Glos 2G 49
Broad Chalke. Wilts 4F 23
Broadclyst. Devn 3C 12
Broadfield. Inv 2E 127
Broadfield. Pemb 4F 43
Broadfield. W Sus 2D 26
Broadford. High 1E 147
Broadford Bridge. W Sus 3B 26
Broadgate. Cumb 1A 96
Broad Green. Cambs 5F 65
Broad Green. C Beds 1H 51
Broad Green. Worc 3D 61
(nr. Bromsgrove)
Broad Green. Worc 5B 60
(nr. Worcester)
Broadhaven. High 3F 169
Broad Haven. Pemb 3C 42
Broadheath. G Man 2B 84
Broad Heath. Staf 3C 72
Broadheath. Worc 4A 60
Broadhembury. Devn 2E 12
Broadhempston. Devn 2E 9
Broad Hill. Cambs 3E 65
Broad Hinton. Wilts 4G 35
Broadholm. Derbs 1A 74
Broadholme. Linc 3F 87
Broadlay. Carm 5D 44
Broad Laying. Hants 5C 36
Broadley. Lanc 3G 91
Broadley. Mor 2A 160
Broadley Common. Essx 5E 53
Broad Marston. Worc 1G 49
Broadmayne. Dors 4C 14
Broadmere. Hants 2E 24
Broadmoor. Pemb 4E 43
Broad Oak. Carm 3F 45
Broad Oak. Cumb 5C 102
Broad Oak. Devn 3D 12
Broadoak. Dors 3H 13
(nr. Bridport)
Broad Oak. Dors 1C 14
(nr. Sturminster Newton)
Broad Oak. E Sus 4C 28
(nr. Hastings)
Broad Oak. E Sus 3H 27
(nr. Heathfield)
Broadoak. Glos 4B 48
Broadoak. Hants 1C 16
Broad Oak. Here 3H 47
Broad Oak. Kent 4F 41
Broadrashes. Mor 3B 160
Broads. Norf 5G 79
Broadsea. Abers 2G 161
Broad's Green. Essx 4G 53
Broadshard. Som 1H 13
Broadstairs. Kent 4H 41
Broadstone. Pool 3F 15
Broadstone. Shrp 2H 59
Broad Street. E Sus 4C 28
Broad Street. Kent 1F 29
(nr. Ashford)
Broad Street. Kent 5C 40
(nr. Maidstone)

Broad Street Green. *Essx* 5B **54**
Broad, The. *Here* 4G **59**
Broad Town. *Wilts* 4F **35**
Broadwas. *Worc* 5B **60**
Broadwath. *Cumb* 4F **113**
Broadway. *Carm* 5D **45**
(nr. Kidwelly)
Broadway. *Carm* 3G **43**
(nr. Laugharne)
Broadway. *Pemb* 3C **42**
Broadway. *Som* 1G **13**
Broadway. *Suff* 3F **67**
Broadway. *Worc* 2G **49**
Broadwell. *Glos* 4A **48**
(nr. Cinderford)
Broadwell. *Glos* 3H **49**
(nr. Stow-on-the-Wold)
Broadwell. *Oxon* 5A **50**
Broadwell. *Warw* 4B **62**
Broadwell House. *Nmbd* 4C **114**
Broadwey. *Dors* 4B **14**
Broadwindsor. *Dors* 2H **13**
Broadwoodkelly. *Devn* 2G **11**
Broadwoodwidger. *Devn* 4E **11**
Broallan. *High* 4G **157**
Brobury. *Here* 1G **47**
Brochel. *High* 4E **155**
Brockamin. *Worc* 5B **60**
Brockbridge. *Hants* 1E **16**
Brockdish. *Norf* 3E **66**
Brockencote. *Worc* 3C **60**
Brockenhurst. *Hants* 2A **16**
Brocketsbrae. *S Lan* 1H **117**
Brockford Street. *Suff* 4D **66**
Brockhall. *Nptn* 4D **62**
Brockham. *Surr* 1C **26**
Brockhampton. *Glos* 3E **49**
(nr. Bishop's Cleeve)
Brockhampton. *Glos* 3F **49**
(nr. Sevenhampton)
Brockhampton. *Here* 2A **48**
Brockhill. *Bord* 2F **119**
Brockholes. *W Yor* 3B **92**
Brockhouse. *S Yor* 2C **86**
Brockhurst. *Hants* 2D **16**
Brocklesby. *Linc* 3E **95**
Brockley. *N Som* 5H **33**
Brockley Corner. *Suff* 3H **65**
Brockley Green. *Suff* 1H **53**
(nr. Bury St Edmunds)
Brockley Green. *Suff* 5H **65**
(nr. Haverhill)
Brockleymoor. *Cumb* 1F **103**
Brockmoor. *W Mid* 2C **60**
Brockton. *Shrp* 2F **59**
(nr. Bishop's Castle)
Brockton. *Shrp* 5B **72**
(nr. Madeley)
Brockton. *Shrp* 1H **59**
(nr. Much Wenlock)
Brockton. *Shrp* 5F **71**
(nr. Pontesbury)
Brockton. *Staf* 2C **72**
Brockton. *Telf* 4B **72**
Brockweir. *Glos* 5A **48**
Brockworth. *Glos* 4D **49**
Brocton. *Staf* 4D **72**
Brodick. *N Ayr* 2E **123**
Brodie. *Mor* 3D **159**
Brodiesord. *Abers* 3C **160**
Brodsworth. *S Yor* 4F **93**
Brogaig. *High* 2D **154**
Brogborough. *C Beds* 2H **51**
Brokenborough. *Wilts* 3E **35**
Broken Cross. *Ches E* 3C **84**
Bromborough. *Mers* 2F **83**
Bromdon. *Shrp* 2A **60**
Brome. *Suff* 3D **66**
Brome Street. *Suff* 3D **66**
Bromeswell. *Suff* 5F **67**
Bromfield. *Cumb* 5C **112**
Bromfield. *Shrp* 3G **59**
Bromford. *W Mid* 1F **61**
Bromham. *Bed* 5H **63**
Bromham. *Wilts* 5E **35**
Bromley. *G Lon* 4F **39**
Bromley. *Herts* 3E **53**
Bromley. *Shrp* 1B **60**
Bromley Cross. *G Man* 3F **91**
Bromley Green. *Kent* 2D **28**
Bromley Wood. *Staf* 3F **73**
Brompton. *Medw* 4B **40**
Brompton. *N Yor* 5A **106**
(nr. Northallerton)
Brompton. *N Yor* 1D **100**
(nr. Scarborough)
Brompton. *Shrp* 5H **71**
Brompton-on-Swale. *N Yor* 5F **105**
Brompton Ralph. *Som* 3D **20**
Brompton Regis. *Som* 3C **20**
Bromsash. *Here* 3B **48**
Bromsberrow. *Glos* 2C **48**
Bromsberrow Heath. *Glos* 2C **48**
Bromsgrove. *Worc* 3D **60**
Bromstead Heath. *Staf* 4B **72**
Bromyard. *Here* 5A **60**
Bromyard Downs. *Here* 5A **60**
Bronaber. *Gwyn* 2G **69**
Broncroft. *Shrp* 2H **59**
Brongest. *Cdgn* 1D **44**
Brongwyn. *Cdgn* 1C **44**
Bronington. *Wrex* 2G **71**
Bronllys. *Powy* 2E **47**
Bronnant. *Cdgn* 4F **57**
Bronwydd Arms. *Carm* 3E **45**
Bronydd. *Powy* 1F **47**
Bronygarth. *Shrp* 2E **71**
Brook. *Carm* 4G **43**
Brook. *Hants* 1A **16**
(nr. Cadnam)
Brook. *Hants* 4B **24**
(nr. Romsey)
Brook. *IOW* 4B **16**
Brook. *Kent* 1E **29**
Brook. *Surr* 1B **26**
(nr. Guildford)
Brook. *Surr* 2A **26**
(nr. Haslemere)
Brooke. *Norf* 1E **67**
Brooke. *Rut* 5F **75**
Brookenby. *Linc* 1B **88**
Brookend. *Glos* 5B **48**
Brook End. *Worc* 1D **48**
Brookfield. *Lanc* 1D **90**
Brookfield. *Ren* 3F **127**
Brookhouse. *Lanc* 3E **97**
Brookhouse Green. *Ches E* 4C **84**
Brookhouses. *Staf* 1D **73**
Brookhurst. *Mers* 2F **83**
Brookland. *Kent* 3D **28**
Brooklands. *G Man* 1B **84**
Brooklands. *Shrp* 1H **71**
Brookmans Park. *Herts* 5C **52**
Brooks. *Powy* 1D **58**
Brooksby. *Leics* 4D **74**
Brooks Green. *W Sus* 3C **26**
Brook Street. *Essx* 1G **39**
Brook Street. *Kent* 2D **28**
Brook Street. *W Sus* 3E **27**
Brookthorpe. *Glos* 4D **48**
Brookville. *Norf* 1G **65**
Brookwood. *Surr* 5A **38**
Broom. *C Beds* 1B **52**
Broom. *Fife* 3F **137**
Broom. *Warw* 5E **61**
Broome. *Norf* 1F **67**
Broome. *Shrp* 1H **59**
(nr. Cardington)
Broome. *Shrp* 2G **59**
(nr. Craven Arms)
Broome. *Worc* 3D **60**
Broomedge. *Warr* 2B **84**
Broomend. *Abers* 2E **153**
Broome Park. *Nmbd* 3F **121**
Broomer's Corner. *W Sus* 3C **26**
Broomfield. *Abers* 5G **161**
Broomfield. *Essx* 4H **53**
Broomfield. *Kent* 4F **41**
(nr. Herne Bay)
Broomfield. *Kent* 5C **40**
(nr. Maidstone)
Broomfield. *Som* 3F **21**
Broomfleet. *E Yor* 2B **94**
Broom Green. *Norf* 3B **78**
Broomhall. *Ches E* 1A **72**
Broomhall. *Wind* 4A **38**
Broomhaugh. *Nmbd* 3D **114**
Broomhill. *Bris* 4B **34**
Broom Hill. *Dors* 2F **15**
Broomhill. *High* 1D **151**
(nr. Grantown-on-Spey)
Broomhill. *High* 1B **158**
(nr. Invergordon)
Broomhill. *Norf* 5F **77**
Broomhill. *S Yor* 4E **93**
Broom Hill. *Worc* 3D **60**
Broomhillbank. *Dum* 5D **118**
Broomholm. *Norf* 2F **79**
Broomlands. *Dum* 4C **118**
Broomley. *Nmbd* 3D **114**
Broom of Moy. *Mor* 3E **159**
Broompark. *Dur* 5F **115**
Broom's Green. *Glos* 2C **48**
Brora. *High* 3G **165**
Broseley. *Shrp* 5A **72**
Brotherhouse Bar. *Linc* 4B **76**
Brotheridge Green. *Worc* 1D **48**
Brotherlee. *Dur* 1C **104**
Brothertoft. *Linc* 1B **76**
Brotherton. *N Yor* 2E **93**
Brotton. *Red C* 2D **107**
Broubster. *High* 2C **168**
Brough. *Cumb* 3A **104**
Brough. *Derbs* 2F **85**
Brough. *E Yor* 2C **94**
Brough. *High* 1E **169**
Brough. *Notts* 5F **87**
Brough. *Orkn* 9D **172**
Brough. *Shet* 4F **173**
(nr. Booth of Toft)
Brough. *Shet* 5G **173**
(on Whalsay)
Broughall. *Shrp* 1H **71**
Brougham. *Cumb* 2G **103**
Brough Sowerby. *Cumb* 3A **104**
Broughton. *Cambs* 3B **64**
Broughton. *Flin* 4F **83**
Broughton. *Hants* 3B **24**
Broughton. *Lanc* 1D **90**
Broughton. *Mil* 2G **51**
Broughton. *Nptn* 3F **63**
Broughton. *N Lin* 4C **94**
Broughton. *N Yor* 2B **100**
(nr. Malton)
Broughton. *N Yor* 4B **98**
(nr. Skipton)
Broughton. *Oxon* 2C **50**
Broughton. *Bord* 1D **118**
Broughton. *Staf* 2B **72**
Broughton. *V Glam* 4C **32**
Broughton Astley. *Leics* 1C **62**
Broughton Beck. *Cumb* 1B **96**
Broughton Cross. *Cumb* 1B **102**
Broughton Gifford. *Wilts* 5D **35**
Broughton Green. *Worc* 4D **60**
Broughton Hackett. *Worc* 5D **60**
Broughton in Furness. *Cumb* 1B **96**
Broughton Mills. *Cumb* 5D **102**
Broughton Moor. *Cumb* 1B **102**
Broughton Park. *G Man* 4G **91**
Broughton Poggs. *Oxon* 5H **49**
Broughtown. *Orkn* 3F **172**
Broughty Ferry. *D'dee* 5D **144**
Brownbread Street. *E Sus* 4A **28**
Brown Candover. *Hants* 3D **24**
Brown Edge. *Lanc* 3B **90**
Brown Edge. *Staf* 5D **84**
Brownhill. *Bkbn* 1E **91**
Brownhill. *Shrp* 3G **71**
Brownhills. *Shrp* 2A **72**
Brownhills. *W Mid* 5E **73**
Brown Knowl. *Ches W* 5G **83**
Brownlow. *Ches E* 4C **84**
Brownlow Heath. *Ches E* 4C **84**
Brown's Green. *W Mid* 1E **61**
Brownshill. *Glos* 5D **49**
Brownston. *Devn* 3C **8**
Brownstone. *Devn* 2A **12**
Browston Green. *Norf* 5G **79**
Broxa. *N Yor* 5G **107**
Broxbourne. *Herts* 5D **52**
Broxburn. *E Lot* 2C **130**
Broxburn. *W Lot* 2D **129**
Broxholme. *Linc* 3G **87**
Broxted. *Essx* 3F **53**
Broxton. *Ches W* 5G **83**
Broxwood. *Here* 5F **59**
Broyle Side. *E Sus* 4F **27**
Brù. *W Isl* 3F **171**
Bruach Mairi. *W Isl* 4F **171**
Bruairnis. *W Isl* 8C **170**
Bruan. *High* 5F **169**
Bruar Lodge. *Per* 1F **143**
Brucehill. *W Dun* 2E **127**
Brucklay. *Abers* 3G **161**
Bruera. *Ches W* 4G **83**
Bruern Abbey. *Oxon* 3A **50**
Bruichladdich. *Arg* 3A **124**
Bruisyard. *Suff* 4F **67**
Bruisyard Street. *Suff* 4F **67**
Brumby. *N Lin* 4B **94**
Brund. *Staf* 4F **85**
Brundall. *Norf* 5F **79**
Brundish. *Norf* 1F **67**
Brundish. *Suff* 4E **67**
Brundish Street. *Suff* 3E **67**
Brunery. *High* 1B **140**
Brunswick Village. *Tyne* 2F **115**
Brunthwaite. *W Yor* 5C **98**
Bruntingthorpe. *Leics* 1D **62**
Brunton. *Fife* 1F **137**
Brunton. *Nmbd* 2G **121**
Brunton. *Wilts* 1H **23**
Brushford. *Devn* 2G **11**
Brushford. *Som* 4C **20**
Brusta. *W Isl* 1E **170**
Bruton. *Som* 3B **22**
Bryanston. *Dors* 2D **15**
Bryant's Bottom. *Buck* 2G **37**
Brydekirk. *Dum* 2C **112**
Brymbo. *Cnwy* 3H **81**
Brymbo. *Wrex* 5E **83**
Brympton D'Evercy. *Som* 1A **14**
Bryn. *Carm* 5F **45**
Bryn. *G Man* 4D **90**
Bryn. *Neat* 2B **32**
Bryn. *Shrp* 2E **59**
Brynamman. *Carm* 4H **45**
Brynberian. *Pemb* 1F **43**
Brynbryddan. *Neat* 2A **32**
Bryncae. *Rhon* 3C **32**
Bryncethin. *B'end* 3C **32**
Bryncir. *Gwyn* 1D **69**
Bryn-coch. *Neat* 3G **31**
Bryncroes. *Gwyn* 2B **68**
Bryncrug. *Gwyn* 5F **69**
Bryn Du. *IOA* 3C **80**
Bryn Eden. *Gwyn* 3G **69**
Bryneglwys. *Den* 1D **70**
Bryn Eglwys. *Gwyn* 4F **81**
Brynford. *Flin* 3D **82**
Bryn Gates. *G Man* 4D **90**
Bryn Golau. *Rhon* 3D **32**
Bryngwran. *IOA* 3C **80**
Bryngwyn. *Mon* 5G **47**
Bryngwyn. *Powy* 1E **47**
Bryn-henllan. *Pemb* 1E **43**
Brynhoffnant. *Cdgn* 5C **56**
Bryn-llwyn. *Flin* 2C **82**
Brynllywarch. *Powy* 2D **58**
Brynmawr. *Blae* 4E **47**
Bryn-mawr. *Gwyn* 2B **68**
Brynmenyn. *B'end* 3C **32**
Brynmill. *Swan* 3F **31**
Brynna. *Rhon* 3C **32**
Brynrefail. *Gwyn* 4E **81**
Brynrefail. *IOA* 2D **81**
Brynsadler. *Rhon* 3D **32**
Bryn-Saith Marchog. *Den* 5C **82**
Brynsiencyn. *IOA* 4D **81**
Brynteg. *IOA* 2D **81**
Brynteg. *Wrex* 5F **83**
Brynygwenyn. *Mon* 4G **47**
Bryn-y-maen. *Cnwy* 3H **81**
Buaile nam Bodach. *W Isl* 8C **170**
Bualintur. *High* 1C **146**
Bubbenhall. *Warw* 3A **62**
Bubwith. *E Yor* 1H **93**
Buccleuch. *Bord* 3F **119**
Buchanan Smithy. *Stir* 1F **127**
Buchanhaven. *Abers* 4H **161**
Buchanty. *Per* 1B **136**
Buchany. *Stir* 3G **135**
Buchley. *E Dun* 2G **127**
Buchlyvie. *Stir* 4E **135**
Buckabank. *Cumb* 5E **113**
Buckden. *Cambs* 4A **64**
Buckden. *N Yor* 2B **98**
Buckenham. *Norf* 5F **79**
Buckerell. *Devn* 2E **13**
Buckfast. *Devn* 2D **8**
Buckfastleigh. *Devn* 2D **8**
Buckhaven. *Fife* 4F **137**
Buckholm. *Bord* 1G **119**
Buckholt. *Here* 4A **48**
Buckhorn Weston. *Dors* 4C **22**
Buckhurst Hill. *Essx* 1F **39**
Buckie. *Mor* 2B **160**
Buckingham. *Buck* 2E **51**
Buckland. *Buck* 4G **51**
Buckland. *Glos* 2F **49**
Buckland. *Here* 5H **59**
Buckland. *Herts* 2D **52**
Buckland. *Kent* 1H **29**
Buckland. *Oxon* 2B **36**
Buckland. *Surr* 5D **38**
Buckland Brewer. *Devn* 4E **19**
Buckland Common. *Buck* 5H **51**
Buckland Dinham. *Som* 1C **22**
Buckland Filleigh. *Devn* 2E **11**
Buckland in the Moor. *Devn* 5H **11**
Buckland Monachorum. *Devn* 2A **8**
Buckland Newton. *Dors* 2B **14**
Buckland Ripers. *Dors* 4B **14**
Buckland St Mary. *Som* 1F **13**
Buckland-tout-Saints. *Devn* 4D **8**
Bucklebury. *W Ber* 4D **36**
Bucklegate. *Linc* 2C **76**
Buckleigh. *Devn* 4E **19**
Buckler's Hard. *Hants* 3C **16**
Bucklesham. *Suff* 1F **55**
Buckley. *Flin* 4E **83**
Buckley Green. *Warw* 4F **61**
Buckley Hill. *Mers* 1F **83**
Bucklow Hill. *Ches E* 2B **84**
Buckminster. *Leics* 3F **75**
Bucknall. *Linc* 4A **88**
Bucknall. *Stoke* 1D **72**
Bucknell. *Oxon* 3D **50**
Bucknell. *Shrp* 3F **59**
Buckpool. *Mor* 2B **160**
Bucksburn. *Aber* 3F **153**
Buck's Cross. *Devn* 4D **18**
Bucks Green. *W Sus* 2B **26**
Buckshaw Village. *Lanc* 2D **90**
Bucks Hill. *Herts* 5A **52**
Bucks Horn Oak. *Hants* 2G **25**
Buck's Mills. *Devn* 4D **18**
Buckton. *E Yor* 2F **101**
Buckton. *Here* 3F **59**
Buckton. *Nmbd* 1E **121**
Buckton Vale. *G Man* 4H **91**
Buckworth. *Cambs* 3A **64**
Budby. *Notts* 4D **86**
Bude. *Corn* 2C **10**
Budge's Shop. *Corn* 3H **7**
Budlake. *Devn* 2C **12**
Budle. *Nmbd* 1F **121**
Budleigh Salterton. *Devn* 4D **12**

Budock Water. *Corn* 5B 6
Buerton. *Ches E* 1A 72
Buffler's Holt. *Buck* 2E 51
Bugbrooke. *Nptn* 5D 62
Buglawton. *Ches E* 4C 84
Bugle. *Corn* 3E 6
Bugthorpe. *E Yor* 4B 100
Buildwas. *Shrp* 5A 72
Builth Road. *Powy* 5C 58
Builth Wells. *Powy* 5C 58
Bulbourne. *Herts* 4H 51
Bulby. *Linc* 3H 75
Bulcote. *Notts* 1D 74
Buldoo. *High* 2B 168
Bulford. *Wilts* 2G 23
Bulford Camp. *Wilts* 2G 23
Bulkeley. *Ches E* 5H 83
Bulkington. *Warw* 2A 62
Bulkington. *Wilts* 1E 23
Bulkworthy. *Devn* 1D 11
Bullamoor. *N Yor* 5A 106
Bull Bay. *IOA* 1D 80
Bullbridge. *Derbs* 5A 86
Bullgill. *Cumb* 1B 102
Bull Hill. *Hants* 3B 16
Bullinghope. *Here* 2A 48
Bull's Green. *Herts* 4C 52
Bullwood. *Arg* 2C 126
Bulmer. *Essx* 1B 54
Bulmer. *N Yor* 3A 100
Bulmer Tye. *Essx* 2B 54
Bulphan. *Thur* 2H 39
Bulverhythe. *E Sus* 5B 28
Bulwark. *Abers* 4G 161
Bulwell. *Nott* 1C 74
Bulwick. *Nptn* 1G 63
Bumble's Green. *Essx* 5E 53
Bun Abhainn Eadarra. *W Isl* 7D 171
Bunacaimb. *High* 5E 147
Bun a' Mhuillinn. *W Isl* 7D 170
Bunarkaig. *High* 5D 148
Bunbury. *Ches E* 5H 83
Bunchrew. *High* 4A 158
Bundalloch. *High* 1A 148
Bunessan. *Arg* 1A 132
Bungay. *Suff* 2F 67
Bunkegivie. *High* 2H 149
Bunker's Hill. *Cambs* 5D 76
Bunkers Hill. *Linc* 5B 88
Bunker's Hill. *Norf* 5H 79
Bunloit. *High* 1H 149
Bunnahabhain. *Arg* 2C 124
Bunny. *Notts* 3C 74
Bunoich. *High* 3F 149
Bunree. *High* 2E 141
Bunroy. *High* 5E 149
Buntait. *High* 5F 157
Buntingford. *Herts* 3D 52
Buntings Green. *Essx* 2B 54
Bunwell. *Norf* 1D 66
Burbage. *Derbs* 3E 85
Burbage. *Leics* 1B 62
Burbage. *Wilts* 5H 35
Burcher. *Here* 4F 59
Burchett's Green. *Wind* 3G 37
Burcombe. *Wilts* 3F 23
Burcot. *Oxon* 2D 36
Burcot. *Worc* 3D 61
Burcote. *Shrp* 1B 60
Burcott. *Buck* 3G 51
Burcott. *Som* 2A 22
Burdale. *N Yor* 3C 100
Burdrop. *Oxon* 2B 50
Bures. *Suff* 2C 54
Burford. *Oxon* 4A 50
Burford. *Shrp* 4H 59
Burf, The. *Worc* 4C 60
Burg. *Arg* 4E 139
Burgate Great Green. *Suff* 3C 66
Burgate Little Green. *Suff* 3C 66
Burgess Hill. *W Sus* 4E 27
Burgh. *Suff* 5E 67
Burgh by Sands. *Cumb* 4E 113
Burgh Castle. *Norf* 5G 79

Burghclere. *Hants* 5C 36
Burghead. *Mor* 2F 159
Burghfield. *W Ber* 5E 37
Burghfield Common.
  W Ber 5E 37
Burghfield Hill. *W Ber* 5E 37
Burgh Heath. *Surr* 5D 38
Burghill. *Here* 1H 47
Burgh le Marsh. *Linc* 4E 89
Burgh Muir. *Abers* 2E 153
Burgh next Aylsham. *Norf* 3E 78
Burgh on Bain. *Linc* 2B 88
Burgh St Margaret. *Norf* 4G 79
Burgh St Peter. *Norf* 1G 67
Burghwallis. *S Yor* 3F 93
Burgie. *Mor* 3E 159
Burham. *Kent* 4B 40
Buriton. *Hants* 4F 25
Burland. *Ches E* 5A 84
Burland. *Shet* 8E 173
Burlawn. *Corn* 2D 6
Burleigh. *Brac* 3A 38
Burleigh. *Glos* 5D 48
Burlescombe. *Devn* 1D 12
Burleston. *Dors* 3C 14
Burlestone. *Devn* 4E 9
Burley. *Hants* 2H 15
Burley. *Rut* 4F 75
Burley. *W Yor* 1C 92
Burley Gate. *Here* 1A 48
Burley in Wharfedale.
  W Yor 5D 98
Burley Street. *Hants* 2H 15
Burley Woodhead. *W Yor* 5D 98
Burlingjobb. *Powy* 5E 59
Burlton. *Shrp* 3G 71
Burmantofts. *W Yor* 1D 92
Burmarsh. *Kent* 2F 29
Burmington. *Warw* 2A 50
Burn. *N Yor* 2F 93
Burnage. *G Man* 1C 84
Burnaston. *Derbs* 2G 73
Burnbanks. *Cumb* 3G 103
Burnby. *E Yor* 5C 100
Burncross. *S Yor* 1H 85
Burneside. *Cumb* 5G 103
Burness. *Orkn* 3F 172
Burneston. *N Yor* 1F 99
Burnett. *Bath* 5B 34
Burnfoot. *E Ayr* 4D 116
Burnfoot. *Per* 3B 136
Burnfoot. *Bord* 3H 119
  (nr. Hawick)
Burnfoot. *Bord* 3G 119
  (nr. Roberton)
Burngreave. *S Yor* 2A 86
Burnham. *Buck* 2A 38
Burnham. *N Lin* 3D 94
Burnham Deepdale. *Norf* 1H 77
Burnham Green. *Herts* 4C 52
Burnham Market. *Norf* 1H 77
Burnham Norton. *Norf* 1H 77
Burnham-on-Crouch. *Essx* 1D 40
Burnham-on-Sea. *Som* 2G 21
Burnham Overy Staithe. *Norf* 1H 77
Burnham Overy Town. *Norf* 1H 77
Burnham Thorpe. *Norf* 1A 78
Burnhaven. *Abers* 4H 161
Burnhead. *Dum* 5A 118
Burnhervie. *Abers* 2E 153
Burnhill Green. *Staf* 5B 72
Burnhope. *Dur* 5E 115
Burnhouse. *N Ayr* 4E 127
Burniston. *N Yor* 5H 107
Burnlee. *W Yor* 4B 92
Burnley. *Lanc* 1G 91
Burnleydam. *Ches E* 1A 72
Burnmouth. *Bord* 3F 131
Burn Naze. *Lanc* 5C 96
Burn of Cambus. *Stir* 3G 135
Burnopfield. *Dur* 4E 115
Burnsall. *N Yor* 3C 98
Burnside. *Ang* 3E 145

Burnside. *E Ayr* 3E 117
Burnside. *Per* 3D 136
Burnside. *Shet* 4D 173
Burnside. *S Lan* 4H 127
Burnside. *W Lot* 2D 129
  (nr. Broxburn)
Burnside. *W Lot* 2D 128
  (nr. Winchburgh)
Burntcommon. *Surr* 5B 38
Burntheath. *Derbs* 2G 73
Burnt Heath. *Essx* 3D 54
Burnt Hill. *W Ber* 4D 36
Burnt Houses. *Dur* 2E 105
Burntisland. *Fife* 1F 129
Burnt Oak. *G Lon* 1D 38
Burnton. *E Ayr* 4D 117
Burntstalk. *Norf* 2G 77
Burntwood. *Staf* 5E 73
Burntwood Green. *Staf* 5E 73
Burnt Yates. *N Yor* 3E 99
Burnwynd. *Edin* 3E 129
Burpham. *Surr* 5B 38
Burpham. *W Sus* 5B 26
Burradon. *Nmbd* 4D 121
Burradon. *Tyne* 2F 115
Burrafirth. *Shet* 1H 173
Burras. *Corn* 5A 6
Burraton. *Corn* 3A 8
Burravoe. *Shet* 3E 173
  (nr. North Roe)
Burravoe. *Shet* 4G 173
  (on Yell)
Burray Village. *Orkn* 8D 172
Burrells. *Cumb* 3H 103
Burrelton. *Per* 5A 144
Burridge. *Devn* 2G 13
Burridge. *Hants* 1D 16
Burrigill. *High* 5E 169
Burrill. *N Yor* 1E 99
Burringham. *N Lin* 4B 94
Burrington. *Devn* 1G 11
Burrington. *Here* 3G 59
Burrington. *N Som* 1H 21
Burrough End. *Cambs* 5F 65
Burrough Green. *Cambs* 5F 65
Burrough on the Hill.
  Leics 4E 75
Burrow. *Devn* 4D 12
Burrow. *Som* 2C 20
Burrowbridge. *Som* 4G 21
Burrowhill. *Surr* 4A 38
Burry. *Swan* 3D 30
Burry Green. *Swan* 3D 30
Burry Port. *Carm* 5E 45
Burscough. *Lanc* 3C 90
Burscough Bridge. *Lanc* 3C 90
Bursea. *E Yor* 1B 94
Burshill. *E Yor* 5E 101
Bursledon. *Hants* 2C 16
Burslem. *Stoke* 1C 72
Burstall. *Suff* 1D 54
Burstock. *Dors* 2H 13
Burston. *Devn* 2H 11
Burston. *Norf* 2D 66
Burston. *Staf* 2D 72
Burstow. *Surr* 1E 27
Burstwick. *E Yor* 2F 95
Burtersett. *N Yor* 1A 98
Burtholme. *Cumb* 3G 113
Burthorpe. *Suff* 4G 65
Burthwaite. *Cumb* 5F 113
Burtle. *Som* 2H 21
Burtoft. *Linc* 2B 76
Burton. *Ches W* 4H 83
  (nr. Kelsall)
Burton. *Ches W* 3F 83
  (nr. Neston)
Burton. *Dors* 3G 15
  (nr. Christchurch)
Burton. *Dors* 3B 14
  (nr. Dorchester)
Burton. *Nmbd* 1F 121
Burton. *Pemb* 4D 43
Burton. *Som* 2E 21

Burton. *Wilts* 4D 34
  (nr. Chippenham)
Burton. *Wilts* 3D 22
  (nr. Warminster)
Burton. *Wrex* 5F 83
Burton Agnes. *E Yor* 3F 101
Burton Bradstock. *Dors* 4H 13
Burton-by-Lincoln. *Linc* 3G 87
Burton Coggles. *Linc* 3G 75
Burton Constable. *E Yor* 1E 95
Burton Corner. *Linc* 1C 76
Burton End. *Cambs* 1G 53
Burton End. *Essx* 3F 53
Burton Fleming. *E Yor* 2E 101
Burton Green. *W Mid* 3G 61
Burton Green. *Wrex* 5F 83
Burton Hastings. *Warw* 2B 62
Burton-in-Kendal. *Cumb* 2E 97
Burton in Lonsdale. *N Yor* 2F 97
Burton Joyce. *Notts* 1D 74
Burton Latimer. *Nptn* 3G 63
Burton Lazars. *Leics* 4E 75
Burton Leonard. *N Yor* 3F 99
Burton on the Wolds. *Leics* 3C 74
Burton Overy. *Leics* 1D 62
Burton Pedwardine. *Linc* 1A 76
Burton Pidsea. *E Yor* 1F 95
Burton Salmon. *N Yor* 2E 93
Burton's Green. *Essx* 3B 54
Burton Stather. *N Lin* 3B 94
Burton upon Stather. *N Lin* 3B 94
Burton upon Trent. *Staf* 3G 73
Burton Wolds. *Leics* 3D 74
Burtonwood. *Warr* 1H 83
Burwardsley. *Ches W* 5H 83
Burwarton. *Shrp* 2A 60
Burwash. *E Sus* 3A 28
Burwash Common. *E Sus* 3H 27
Burwash Weald. *E Sus* 3A 28
Burwell. *Cambs* 4E 65
Burwell. *Linc* 3C 88
Burwen. *IOA* 1D 80
Burwick. *Orkn* 9D 172
Bury. *Cambs* 2B 64
Bury. *G Man* 3G 91
Bury. *Som* 4C 20
Bury. *W Sus* 4B 26
Burybank. *Staf* 2C 72
Bury End. *Worc* 2F 49
Bury Green. *Herts* 3E 53
Bury Hill. *S Glo* 3C 34
Bury St Edmunds. *Suff* 4A 66
Burythorpe. *N Yor* 3B 100
Busbridge. *Surr* 1A 26
Busby. *E Ren* 4G 127
Busby. *Per* 1C 136
Buscot. *Oxon* 2H 35
Bush. *Corn* 2C 10
Bush Bank. *Here* 5G 59
Bushbury. *W Mid* 5D 72
Bushby. *Leics* 5D 74
Bushey. *Dors* 4E 15
Bushey. *Herts* 1C 38
Bushey Heath. *Herts* 1C 38
Bush Green. *Norf* 1C 66
  (nr. Attleborough)
Bush Green. *Norf* 2E 66
  (nr. Harleston)
Bush Green. *Suff* 5B 66
Bushley. *Worc* 2D 48
Bushley Green. *Worc* 2D 48
Bushmead. *Bed* 4A 64
Bushmoor. *Shrp* 2G 59
Bushton. *Wilts* 4F 35
Bushy Common. *Norf* 4B 78
Busk. *Cumb* 5H 113
Buslingthorpe. *Linc* 2H 87
Bussage. *Glos* 5D 49
Bussex. *Som* 3G 21
Busta. *Shet* 5E 173
Bustard Green. *Essx* 3G 53
Butcher's Cross. *E Sus* 3G 27
Butcombe. *N Som* 5A 34
Bute Town. *Cphy* 5E 46

Butleigh. *Som* 3A 22
Butleigh Wootton. *Som* 3A 22
Butlers Marston. *Warw* 5H 61
Butley. *Suff* 5F 67
Butley High Corner. *Suff* 1G 55
Butlocks Heath. *Hants* 2C 16
Butterburn. *Cumb* 2H 113
Buttercrambe. *N Yor* 4B 100
Buttergask. *Suff* 2E 105
Butterknowle. *Dur* 2E 105
Butterleigh. *Devn* 2C 12
Buttermere. *Cumb* 3C 102
Buttermere. *Wilts* 5B 36
Buttershaw. *W Yor* 2B 92
Butterstone. *Per* 4H 143
Butterton. *Staf* 5E 85
  (nr. Leek)
Butterton. *Staf* 1C 72
  (nr. Stoke-on-Trent)
Butterwick. *Dur* 2A 106
Butterwick. *Linc* 1C 76
Butterwick. *N Yor* 2B 100
  (nr. Malton)
Butterwick. *N Yor* 2D 101
  (nr. Weaverthorpe)
Butteryhaugh. *Nmbd* 5A 120
Butt Green. *Ches E* 5A 84
Buttington. *Powy* 5E 71
Buttonbridge. *Shrp* 3B 60
Buttonoak. *Shrp* 3B 60
Buttsash. *Hants* 2C 16
Butt's Green. *Essx* 5A 54
Butt Yeats. *Lanc* 3E 97
Buxhall. *Suff* 5C 66
Buxted. *E Sus* 3F 27
Buxton. *Derbs* 3E 85
Buxton. *Norf* 3E 79
Buxworth. *Derbs* 2E 85
Bwcle. *Flin* 4E 83
Bwlch. *Powy* 3E 47
Bwlchderwin. *Gwyn* 1D 68
Bwlchgwyn. *Wrex* 5E 83
Bwlch-Llan. *Cdgn* 5E 57
Bwlchnewydd. *Carm* 3D 44
Bwlchtocyn. *Gwyn* 3C 68
Bwlch-y-cibau. *Powy* 4D 70
Bwlchyddar. *Powy* 3D 70
Bwlch-y-fadfa. *Cdgn* 1E 45
Bwlch-y-ffridd. *Powy* 1C 58
Bwlch y Garreg. *Powy* 1C 58
Bwlch-y-groes. *Pemb* 1G 43
Bwlch-y-sarnau. *Powy* 3C 58
Bybrook. *Kent* 1E 28
Byermoor. *Tyne* 4E 115
Byers Garth. *Dur* 5G 115
Byers Green. *Dur* 1F 105
Byfield. *Nptn* 5C 62
Byfleet. *Surr* 4B 38
Byford. *Here* 1G 47
Bygrave. *Herts* 2C 52
Byker. *Tyne* 3F 115
Byland Abbey. *N Yor* 2H 99
Bylchau. *Cnwy* 4B 82
Byley. *Ches W* 4B 84
Bynea. *Carm* 3E 31
Byram. *N Yor* 2E 93
Byrness. *Nmbd* 4B 120
Bystock. *Devn* 4D 12
Bythorn. *Cambs* 3H 63
Byton. *Here* 4F 59
Bywell. *Nmbd* 3D 114
Byworth. *W Sus* 3A 26

C

Cabourne. *Linc* 4E 95
Cabrach. *Arg* 3C 124
Cabrach. *Mor* 1A 152
Cabus. *Lanc* 5D 97
Cadbury. *Devn* 2C 12
Cadder. *E Dun* 2H 127
Caddington. *C Beds* 4A 52
Caddonfoot. *Bord* 1G 119
Cadeby. *Leics* 5B 74

Cadeby. *S Yor* 4F 93
Cadeleigh. *Devn* 2C 12
Cade Street. *E Sus* 3H 27
Cadgwith. *Corn* 5E 5
Cadham. *Fife* 3E 137
Cadishead. *G Man* 1B 84
Cadle. *Swan* 3F 31
Cadley. *Lanc* 1D 90
Cadley. *Wilts* 1H 23
(nr. Ludgershall)
Cadley. *Wilts* 5H 35
(nr. Marlborough)
Cadmore End. *Buck* 2F 37
Cadnam. *Hants* 1A 16
Cadney. *N Lin* 4D 94
Cadole. *Flin* 4E 82
Cadoxton-Juxta-Neath. *Neat* 2A 32
Cadwell. *Herts* 2B 52
Cadwst. *Den* 2C 70
Caeathro. *Gwyn* 4E 81
Caehopkin. *Powy* 4B 46
Caenby. *Linc* 2H 87
Caerau. *B'end* 2B 32
Caerau. *Card* 4E 33
Cae'r-bont. *Powy* 4B 46
Cae'r-bryn. *Carm* 4F 45
Caerdeon. *Gwyn* 4F 69
Caerdydd. *Card* 4E 33
Caerfarchell. *Pemb* 2B 42
Caerffili. *Cphy* 3E 33
Caerfyrddin. *Carm* 4E 45
Caergeiliog. *IOA* 3C 80
Caergwrle. *Flin* 5F 83
Caergybi. *IOA* 2B 80
Caerlaverock. *Per* 2A 136
Caerleon. *Newp* 2G 33
Caerlleon. *Carm* 2G 43
Caerllion. *Newp* 2G 33
Caernarfon. *Gwyn* 4D 81
Caerphilly. *Cphy* 3E 33
Caersws. *Powy* 1C 58
Caerwedros. *Cdgn* 5C 56
Caerwent. *Mon* 2H 33
Caerwys. *Flin* 3D 82
Caim. *IOA* 2F 81
Caio. *Carm* 2G 45
Cairinis. *W Isl* 2D 170
Cairisiadar. *W Isl* 4C 171
Cairminis. *W Isl* 9C 171
Cairnbaan. *Arg* 4F 133
Cairnbulg. *Abers* 2H 161
Cairncross. *Ang* 1D 145
Cairndow. *Arg* 2A 134
Cairness. *Abers* 2H 161
Cairneyhill. *Fife* 1D 128
Cairngarroch. *Dum* 5F 109
Cairngorms. *High* 3D 151
Cairnhill. *Abers* 5D 160
Cairnie. *Abers* 4B 160
Cairnorrie. *Abers* 4F 161
Cairnryan. *Dum* 3F 109
Caister-on-Sea. *Norf* 4H 79
Caistor. *Linc* 4E 95
Caistor St Edmund. *Norf* 5E 79
Caistron. *Nmbd* 4D 121
Cakebole. *Worc* 3C 60
Calais Street. *Suff* 1C 54
Calanais. *W Isl* 4E 171
Calbost. *W Isl* 6G 171
Calbourne. *IOW* 4C 16
Calceby. *Linc* 3C 88
Calcot. *Glos* 4F 49
Calcot Row. *W Ber* 4E 37
Calcott. *Kent* 4F 41
Calcott. *Shrp* 4G 71
Caldback. *Shet* 1H 173
Caldbeck. *Cumb* 1E 102
Caldbergh. *N Yor* 1C 98
Caldecote. *Cambs* 5C 64
(nr. Cambridge)
Caldecote. *Cambs* 2A 64
(nr. Peterborough)
Caldecote. *Herts* 2C 52
Caldecote. *Warw* 1A 62
Caldecott. *Nptn* 4G 63
Caldecott. *Oxon* 2C 36
Caldecott. *Rut* 1F 63
Calderbank. *N Lan* 3A 128
Calder Bridge. *Cumb* 4B 102
Calderbrook. *G Man* 3H 91
Caldercruix. *N Lan* 3B 128
Calder Grove. *W Yor* 3D 92
Calder Mains. *High* 3C 168
Caldermill. *S Lan* 5H 127
Calder Vale. *Lanc* 5E 97
Calderwood. *S Lan* 4H 127
Caldescote. *Nptn* 5D 62
Caldicot. *Mon* 3H 33
Caldwell. *Derbs* 4G 73
Caldwell. *N Yor* 3E 105
Caldy. *Mers* 2E 83
Calebrack. *Cumb* 1E 103
Caledfwlch. *Carm* 3G 45
Calf Heath. *Staf* 5D 72
Calford Green. *Suff* 1G 53
Calfsound. *Orkn* 4E 172
Calgary. *Arg* 3E 139
Califer. *Mor* 3E 159
California. *Cambs* 2E 65
California. *Falk* 2C 128
California. *Norf* 4H 79
California. *Suff* 1E 55
Calke. *Derbs* 3A 74
Callakille. *High* 3F 155
Callaly. *Nmbd* 4E 121
Callander. *Stir* 3F 135
Callaughton. *Shrp* 1A 60
Callendoun. *Arg* 1E 127
Callestick. *Corn* 3B 6
Calligarry. *High* 3E 147
Callington. *Corn* 2H 7
Callingwood. *Staf* 3F 73
Callow. *Here* 2H 47
Callowell. *Glos* 5D 48
Callow End. *Worc* 1D 48
Callow Hill. *Wilts* 3F 35
Callow Hill. *Worc* 3B 60
(nr. Bewdley)
Callow Hill. *Worc* 4E 61
(nr. Redditch)
Calmore. *Hants* 1B 16
Calmsden. *Glos* 5F 49
Calne. *Wilts* 4E 35
Calow. *Derbs* 3B 86
Calshot. *Hants* 2C 16
Calstock. *Corn* 2A 8
Calstone Wellington. *Wilts* 5F 35
Calthorpe. *Norf* 2D 78
Calthorpe Street. *Norf* 3G 79
Calthwaite. *Cumb* 5F 113
Calton. *N Yor* 4B 98
Calton. *Staf* 5F 85
Calveley. *Ches E* 5H 83
Calver. *Derbs* 3G 85
Calverhall. *Shrp* 2A 72
Calverleigh. *Devn* 1C 12
Calverley. *W Yor* 1C 92
Calvert. *Buck* 3E 51
Calverton. *Mil* 2F 51
Calverton. *Notts* 1D 74
Calvine. *Per* 2F 143
Calvo. *Cumb* 4C 112
Cam. *Glos* 2C 34
Camaghael. *High* 1F 141
Camas-luinie. *High* 1B 148
Camasnacroise. *High* 3C 140
Camastianavaig. *High* 5E 155
Camasunary. *High* 2D 146
Camault Muir. *High* 4H 157
Camb. *Shet* 2G 173
Camber. *E Sus* 4D 28
Camberley. *Surr* 5G 37
Camberwell. *G Lon* 3E 39
Camblesforth. *N Yor* 2G 93
Cambo. *Nmbd* 1D 114
Cambois. *Nmbd* 1G 115
Camborne. *Corn* 3D 4
Cambourne. *Cambs* 5C 64
Cambridge. *Cambs* 5D 64
Cambridge. *Glos* 5C 48
Cambrose. *Corn* 4A 6
Cambus. *Clac* 4A 136
Cambusbarron. *Stir* 4G 135
Cambuskenneth. *Stir* 4H 135
Cambuslang. *S Lan* 3H 127
Cambusnethan. *N Lan* 4B 128
Cambus o'May. *Abers* 4B 152
Camden Town. *G Lon* 2D 39
Cameley. *Bath* 1B 22
Camelford. *Corn* 4B 10
Camelon. *Falk* 1B 128
Camelsdale. *Surr* 2A 26
Camer's Green. *Worc* 2C 48
Camerton. *Bath* 1B 22
Camerton. *Cumb* 1B 102
Camerton. *E Yor* 2F 95
Camghouran. *Per* 3C 142
Cammachmore. *Abers* 4G 153
Cammeringham. *Linc* 2G 87
Camore. *High* 4E 165
Campbelton. *N Ayr* 4C 126
Campbeltown. *Arg* 3B 122
Campbeltown Airport. *Arg* 3A 122
Cample. *Dum* 5B 118
Campmuir. *Per* 5B 144
Campsall. *S Yor* 3F 93
Campsea Ashe. *Suff* 5F 67
Camps End. *Cambs* 1G 53
Camp, The. *Glos* 5E 49
Campton. *C Beds* 2B 52
Camptoun. *E Lot* 2B 130
Camptown. *Bord* 3A 120
Camrose. *Pemb* 2D 42
Camserney. *Per* 4F 143
Camster. *High* 4E 169
Camus Croise. *High* 2E 147
Camuscross. *High* 2E 147
Camusdarach. *High* 4E 147
Camusnagaul. *High* 1E 141
(nr. Fort William)
Camusnagaul. *High* 5E 163
(nr. Little Loch Broom)
Camusteel. *High* 4G 155
Camusterrach. *High* 4G 155
Camusvrachan. *Per* 4D 142
Canada. *Hants* 1A 16
Canadia. *E Sus* 4B 28
Canaston Bridge. *Pemb* 3E 43
Candlesby. *Linc* 4D 88
Candle Street. *Suff* 3C 66
Candy Mill. *S Lan* 5D 128
Cane End. *Oxon* 4E 37
Canewdon. *Essx* 1C 40
Canford Cliffs. *Pool* 4F 15
Canford Heath. *Pool* 3F 15
Canford Magna. *Pool* 3F 15
Cangate. *Norf* 3F 79
Canham's Green. *Suff* 4C 66
Canholes. *Derbs* 3E 85
Canisbay. *High* 1F 169
Canley. *W Mid* 3H 61
Cann. *Dors* 4D 22
Cann Common. *Dors* 4D 23
Cannich. *High* 5F 157
Cannington. *Som* 3F 21
Cannock. *Staf* 4D 73
Cannock Wood. *Staf* 4E 73
Canonbie. *Dum* 2E 113
Canon Bridge. *Here* 1H 47
Canon Frome. *Here* 1B 48
Canon Pyon. *Here* 1H 47
Canons Ashby. *Nptn* 5C 62
Canonstown. *Corn* 3C 4
Canterbury. *Kent* 5F 41
Cantley. *Norf* 5F 79
Cantley. *S Yor* 4G 93
Cantlop. *Shrp* 5H 71
Canton. *Card* 4E 33
Cantray. *High* 4B 158
Cantraybruich. *High* 4B 158
Cantraywood. *High* 4B 158
Cantsdam. *Fife* 4D 136
Cantsfield. *Lanc* 2F 97
Canvey Island. *Essx* 2B 40
Canwick. *Linc* 4G 87
Canworthy Water. *Corn* 3C 10
Caol. *High* 1F 141
Caolas. *W Isl* 9B 170
Caolas Liubharsaigh. *W Isl* 4D 170
Caolas Stocinis. *W Isl* 8D 171
Caoles. *Arg* 4B 138
Caol Ila. *Arg* 3C 124
Caol Loch Ailse. *High* 1F 147
Caol Reatha. *High* 1F 147
Capel. *Kent* 1H 27
Capel. *Surr* 1C 26
Capel Bangor. *Cdgn* 2F 57
Capel Betws Lleucu. *Cdgn* 5F 57
Capel Coch. *IOA* 2D 80
Capel Curig. *Cnwy* 5G 81
Capel Cynon. *Cdgn* 1D 45
Capel Dewi. *Carm* 3E 45
Capel Dewi. *Cdgn* 2F 57
(nr. Aberystwyth)
Capel Dewi. *Cdgn* 1E 45
(nr. Llandysul)
Capel Garmon. *Cnwy* 5H 81
Capel Green. *Suff* 1G 55
Capel Gwyn. *IOA* 3C 80
Capel Gwynfe. *Carm* 3H 45
Capel Hendre. *Carm* 4F 45
Capel Isaac. *Carm* 3F 45
Capel Iwan. *Carm* 1G 43
Capel-le-Ferne. *Kent* 2G 29
Capel Llanilterne. *Card* 4D 32
Capel Mawr. *IOA* 3D 80
Capel Newydd. *Pemb* 1G 43
Capel St Andrew. *Suff* 1G 55
Capel St Mary. *Suff* 2D 54
Capel Seion. *Carm* 4F 45
Capel Seion. *Cdgn* 3F 57
Capel Uchaf. *Gwyn* 1D 68
Capel-y-ffin. *Powy* 2F 47
Capenhurst. *Ches W* 3F 83
Capernwray. *Lanc* 2E 97
Capheaton. *Nmbd* 1D 114
Cappercleuch. *Bord* 2E 119
Capplegill. *Dum* 4D 118
Capton. *Devn* 3E 9
Capton. *Som* 3D 20
Caputh. *Per* 5H 143
Caradon Town. *Corn* 5C 10
Carbis Bay. *Corn* 3C 4
Carbost. *High* 5C 154
(nr. Loch Harport)
Carbost. *High* 4D 154
(nr. Portree)
Carbrook. *S Yor* 2A 86
Carbrooke. *Norf* 5B 78
Carburton. *Notts* 3D 86
Carcluie. *S Ayr* 3C 116
Car Colston. *Notts* 1E 74
Carcroft. *S Yor* 3F 93
Cardenden. *Fife* 4E 136
Cardeston. *Shrp* 4F 71
Cardewlees. *Cumb* 4E 113
Cardiff. *Card* 4E 33
Cardiff International Airport. *V Glam* 5D 32
Cardigan. *Cdgn* 1B 44
Cardinal's Green. *Cambs* 1G 53
Cardington. *Bed* 1A 52
Cardington. *Shrp* 1H 59
Cardinham. *Corn* 2F 7
Cardno. *Abers* 2G 161
Cardow. *Mor* 4F 159
Cardross. *Arg* 2E 127
Cardurnock. *Cumb* 4C 112
Careby. *Linc* 4H 75
Careston. *Ang* 2E 145
Carew. *Pemb* 4E 43
Carew Cheriton. *Pemb* 4E 43
Carew Newton. *Pemb* 4E 43
Carey. *Here* 2A 48
Carfin. *N Lan* 4A 128
Carfrae. *Bord* 4B 130
Cargate Green. *Norf* 4F 79
Cargenbridge. *Dum* 2G 111
Cargill. *Per* 5A 144
Cargo. *Cumb* 4E 113
Cargreen. *Corn* 2A 8
Carham. *Nmbd* 1B 120
Carhampton. *Som* 2D 20
Carharrack. *Corn* 4B 6
Carie. *Per* 3D 142
(nr. Loch Rannah)
Carie. *Per* 5D 142
(nr. Loch Tay)
Carisbrooke. *IOW* 4C 16
Cark. *Cumb* 2C 96
Carkeel. *Corn* 2A 8
Carlabhagh. *W Isl* 3E 171
Carland Cross. *Corn* 3C 6
Carlbury. *Darl* 3F 105
Carlby. *Linc* 4H 75
Carlecotes. *S Yor* 4B 92
Carleen. *Corn* 4D 4
Carlesmoor. *N Yor* 2D 98
Carleton. *Cumb* 4F 113
(nr. Carlisle)
Carleton. *Cumb* 4B 102
(nr. Egremont)
Carleton. *Cumb* 2G 103
(nr. Penrith)
Carleton. *Lanc* 1B 90
Carleton. *N Yor* 5B 98
Carleton. *W Yor* 2E 93
Carleton Forehoe. *Norf* 5C 78
Carleton Rode. *Norf* 1D 66
Carleton St Peter. *Norf* 5F 79
Carlidnack. *Corn* 4E 5
Carlingcott. *Bath* 1B 22
Carlin How. *Red C* 3E 107
Carlisle. *Cumb* 4F 113
Carloonan. *Arg* 2H 133
Carlops. *Bord* 4E 129
Carlton. *Bed* 5G 63
Carlton. *Cambs* 5F 65
Carlton. *Leics* 5A 74
Carlton. *N Yor* 1A 100
(nr. Helmsley)
Carlton. *N Yor* 1C 98
(nr. Middleham)
Carlton. *N Yor* 2G 93
(nr. Selby)
Carlton. *Notts* 1D 74
Carlton. *S Yor* 3D 92
Carlton. *Stoc T* 2A 106
Carlton. *Suff* 4F 67
Carlton. *W Yor* 2D 92
Carlton Colville. *Suff* 1H 67
Carlton Curlieu. *Leics* 1D 62
Carlton Husthwaite. *N Yor* 2G 99
Carlton in Cleveland. *N Yor* 4C 106
Carlton in Lindrick. *Notts* 2C 86
Carlton-le-Moorland. *Linc* 5G 87
Carlton Miniott. *N Yor* 1F 99
Carlton-on-Trent. *Notts* 4F 87
Carlton Scroop. *Linc* 1G 75
Carluke. *S Lan* 4B 128
Carlyon Bay. *Corn* 3E 7
Carmarthen. *Carm* 4E 45
Carmel. *Carm* 4F 45
Carmel. *Flin* 3D 82
Carmel. *Gwyn* 5D 81
Carmel. *IOA* 2C 80
Carmichael. *S Lan* 1B 118
Carmunnock. *Glas* 4H 127
Carmyle. *S Lan* 3H 127
Carmyllie. *Ang* 4E 145
Carnaby. *E Yor* 3F 101
Carnach. *High* 1C 148
(nr. Lochcarron)
Carnach. *High* 4E 163
(nr. Ullapool)
Carnach. *Mor* 4E 159
Carnach. *W Isl* 8E 171
Carnachy. *High* 3H 167
Carnain. *Arg* 3B 124
Carnais. *W Isl* 4C 171

Carnan—Charing Hill

Carnan. *Arg* 4B 138
Carnbee. *Fife* 3H 137
Carnbo. *Per* 3C 136
Carn Brea Village. *Corn* 4A 6
Carndu. *High* 1A 148
Carne. *Corn* 5D 6
Carnell. *S Ayr* 1D 116
Carnforth. *Lanc* 2E 97
Carn-gorm. *High* 1B 148
Carnhedryn. *Pemb* 2B 42
Carnhell Green. *Corn* 3D 4
Carnie. *Abers* 3F 153
Carnkie. *Corn* 5B 6 (nr. Falmouth)
Carnkie. *Corn* 5A 6 (nr. Redruth)
Carnkief. *Corn* 3B 6
Carno. *Powy* 1B 58
Carnock. *Fife* 1D 128
Carnon Downs. *Corn* 4B 6
Carnoustie. *Ang* 5E 145
Carntyne. *Glas* 3H 127
Carnwath. *S Lan* 5C 128
Carnyorth. *Corn* 3A 4
Carol Green. *W Mid* 3G 61
Carpalla. *Corn* 3D 6
Carperby. *N Yor* 1C 98
Carradale. *Arg* 2C 122
Carragraich. *W Isl* 8D 171
Carrbridge. *High* 1D 150
Carr Cross. *Lanc* 3B 90
Carreglefn. *IOA* 2C 80
Carrhouse. *N Lin* 4A 94
Carrick Castle. *Arg* 4A 134
Carriden. *Falk* 1D 128
Carrington. *G Man* 1B 84
Carrington. *Linc* 5C 88
Carrington. *Midl* 3G 129
Carrog. *Cnwy* 1G 69
Carrog. *Den* 1D 70
Carron. *Falk* 1B 128
Carron. *Mor* 4G 159
Carronbridge. *Dum* 5A 118
Carronshore. *Falk* 1B 128
Carrow Hill. *Mon* 2H 33
Carr Shield. *Nmbd* 5B 114
Carrutherstown. *Dum* 2C 112
Carr Vale. *Derbs* 4B 86
Carrville. *Dur* 5G 115
Carrycoats Hall. *Nmbd* 2C 114
Carsaig. *Arg* 1C 132
Carscreugh. *Dum* 3H 109
Carsegowan. *Dum* 4B 110
Carse House. *Arg* 3F 125
Carseriggan. *Dum* 3A 110
Carsethorn. *Dum* 4A 112
Carshalton. *G Lon* 4D 38
Carsington. *Derbs* 5G 85
Carskiey. *Arg* 5A 122
Carsluith. *Dum* 4B 110
Carsphairn. *Dum* 5E 117
Carstairs. *S Lan* 5C 128
Carstairs Junction. *S Lan* 5C 128
Cartbridge. *Surr* 5B 38
Carterhaugh. *Ang* 4D 144
Carter's Clay. *Hants* 4B 24
Carterton. *Oxon* 5A 50
Carterway Heads. *Nmbd* 4D 114
Carthew. *Corn* 3E 6
Carthorpe. *N Yor* 1F 99
Cartington. *Nmbd* 4E 121
Cartland. *S Lan* 5B 128
Cartmel. *Cumb* 2C 96
Cartmel Fell. *Cumb* 1D 96
Cartworth. *W Yor* 4B 92
Carwath. *Cumb* 5E 112
Carway. *Carm* 5E 45
Carwinley. *Cumb* 2F 113
Cascob. *Powy* 4E 59
Cas-gwent. *Mon* 2A 34
Cash Feus. *Fife* 3E 136
Cashlie. *Per* 4B 142
Cashmoor. *Dors* 1E 15
Cas-Mael. *Pemb* 2E 43
Casnewydd. *Newp* 3G 33
Cassington. *Oxon* 4C 50
Cassop. *Dur* 1A 106
Castell. *Cnwy* 4G 81
Castell. *Den* 4D 82
Castell Hendre. *Pemb* 2E 43
Castell-nedd. *Neat* 2A 32
Castell Newydd Emlyn. *Carm* 1D 44
Castell-y-bwch. *Torf* 2F 33
Casterton. *Cumb* 2F 97
Castle. *Som* 2A 22
Castle Acre. *Norf* 4H 77
Castle Ashby. *Nptn* 5F 63
Castlebay. *W Isl* 9B 170
Castle Bolton. *N Yor* 5D 104
Castle Bromwich. *W Mid* 2F 61
Castle Bytham. *Linc* 4G 75
Castlebythe. *Pemb* 2E 43
Castle Caereinion. *Powy* 5D 70
Castle Camps. *Cambs* 1G 53
Castle Carrock. *Cumb* 4G 113
Castlecary. *N Lan* 2A 128
Castle Cary. *Som* 3B 22
Castle Combe. *Wilts* 4D 34
Castlecraig. *High* 2C 158
Castle Donington. *Leics* 3B 74
Castle Douglas. *Dum* 3E 111
Castle Eaton. *Swin* 2G 35
Castle Eden. *Dur* 1B 106
Castleford. *W Yor* 2E 93
Castle Frome. *Here* 1B 48
Castle Green. *Surr* 4A 38
Castle Green. *Warw* 3G 61
Castle Gresley. *Derbs* 4G 73
Castle Heaton. *Nmbd* 5F 131
Castle Hedingham. *Essx* 2A 54
Castle Hill. *Kent* 1A 28
Castlehill. *Per* 5B 144
Castlehill. *S Lan* 4B 128
Castle Hill. *Suff* 1E 55
Castlehill. *W Dun* 2E 127
Castle Kennedy. *Dum* 4G 109
Castle Lachlan. *Arg* 4H 133
Castlemartin. *Pemb* 5D 42
Castlemilk. *Glas* 4H 127
Castlemorris. *Pemb* 1D 42
Castlemorton. *Worc* 2C 48
Castle O'er. *Dum* 5E 119
Castle Park. *N Yor* 3F 107
Castlerigg. *Cumb* 2D 102
Castle Rising. *Norf* 3F 77
Castleside. *Dur* 5D 115
Castlethorpe. *Mil* 1F 51
Castleton. *Abers* 4F 151
Castleton. *Arg* 1G 125
Castleton. *Derbs* 2F 85
Castleton. *G Man* 3G 91
Castleton. *Mor* 1F 151
Castleton. *Newp* 3F 33
Castleton. *N Yor* 4D 107
Castleton. *Per* 2B 136
Castletown. *Cumb* 1G 103
Castletown. *Dors* 5B 14
Castletown. *High* 2D 169
Castletown. *IOM* 5B 108
Castletown. *Tyne* 4G 115
Castley. *N Yor* 5E 99
Caston. *Norf* 1B 66
Castor. *Pet* 1A 64
Caswell. *Swan* 4E 31
Catacol. *N Ayr* 5H 125
Catbrook. *Mon* 5A 48
Catchems End. *Worc* 3B 60
Catchgate. *Dur* 4E 115
Catcleugh. *Nmbd* 4B 120
Catcliffe. *S Yor* 2B 86
Catcott. *Som* 3G 21
Caterham. *Surr* 5E 39
Catfield. *Norf* 3F 79
Catfield Common. *Norf* 3F 79
Catford. *G Lon* 3E 39
Catforth. *Lanc* 1C 90
Cathcart. *Glas* 3G 127
Cathedine. *Powy* 3E 47
Catherine-de-Barnes. *W Mid* 2F 61
Catherington. *Hants* 1E 17
Catherston Leweston. *Dors* 3G 13
Catherton. *Shrp* 3A 60
Catisfield. *Hants* 2D 16
Catlodge. *High* 4A 150
Catlowdy. *Cumb* 2F 113
Catmore. *W Ber* 3C 36
Caton. *Devn* 5A 12
Caton. *Lanc* 3E 97
Catrine. *E Ayr* 2E 117
Cat's Ash. *Newp* 2G 33
Catsfield. *E Sus* 4B 28
Catsgore. *Som* 4A 22
Catshill. *Worc* 3D 60
Cattal. *N Yor* 4G 99
Cattawade. *Suff* 2E 54
Catterall. *Lanc* 5D 97
Catterick. *N Yor* 5F 105
Catterick Bridge. *N Yor* 5F 105
Catterick Garrison. *N Yor* 5E 105
Catterlen. *Cumb* 1F 103
Catterline. *Abers* 1H 145
Catterton. *N Yor* 5H 99
Catteshall. *Surr* 1A 26
Catthorpe. *Leics* 3C 62
Cattistock. *Dors* 3A 14
Catton. *Nmbd* 4B 114
Catton. *N Yor* 2F 99
Catwick. *E Yor* 5F 101
Catworth. *Cambs* 3H 63
Caudle Green. *Glos* 4E 49
Caulcott. *Oxon* 3D 50
Cauldhame. *Stir* 4F 135
Cauldmill. *Bord* 3H 119
Cauldon. *Staf* 1E 73
Cauldon Lowe. *Staf* 1E 73
Cauldwells. *Abers* 3E 161
Caulkerbush. *Dum* 4G 111
Caulside. *Dum* 1F 113
Caunsall. *Worc* 2C 60
Caunton. *Notts* 4E 87
Causewayend. *S Lan* 1C 118
Causewayhead. *Stir* 4H 135
Causey Park. *Nmbd* 5F 121
Caute. *Devn* 1E 11
Cautley. *Cumb* 5H 103
Cavendish. *Suff* 1B 54
Cavendish Bridge. *Derbs* 2B 74
Cavenham. *Suff* 4G 65
Caversfield. *Oxon* 3D 50
Caversham. *Read* 4F 37
Caversham Heights. *Read* 4E 37
Caverswall. *Staf* 1D 72
Cawdor. *High* 4C 158
Cawkwell. *Linc* 2B 88
Cawood. *N Yor* 1F 93
Cawsand. *Corn* 3A 8
Cawston. *Norf* 3D 78
Cawston. *Warw* 3B 62
Cawthorne. *N Yor* 1B 100
Cawthorne. *S Yor* 4C 92
Cawthorpe. *Linc* 3H 75
Cawton. *N Yor* 2A 100
Caxton. *Cambs* 5C 64
Caynham. *Shrp* 3H 59
Caythorpe. *Linc* 1G 75
Caythorpe. *Notts* 1D 74
Cayton. *N Yor* 1E 101
Ceallan. *W Isl* 3D 170
Ceann a Bhàigh. *W Isl* 9C 171 (on Harris)
Ceann a Bhaigh. *W Isl* 2C 170 (on North Uist)
Ceann a Bhaigh. *W Isl* 8E 171 (on Scalpay)
Ceann a Bhaigh. *W Isl* 8D 171 (on South Harris)
Ceannacroc Lodge. *High* 2E 149
Ceann an Leothaid. *High* 5E 147
Ceann a Tuath Loch Baghasdail. *W Isl* 6C 170
Ceann Loch Ailleart. *High* 5F 147
Ceann Loch Muideirt. *High* 1B 140
Ceann Shiphoirt. *W Isl* 6E 171
Ceann Tarabhaigh. *W Isl* 6E 171
Ceathramh Meadhanach. *W Isl* 1D 170
Cefn Berain. *Cnwy* 4B 82
Cefn-brith. *Cnwy* 5B 82
Cefn-bryn-brain. *Carm* 4H 45
Cefn Bychan. *Cphy* 2F 33
Cefn-bychan. *Flin* 4D 82
Cefncaeau. *Carm* 3E 31
Cefn Canol. *Powy* 2E 71
Cefn Coch. *Powy* 5C 70 (nr. Llanfair Caereinion)
Cefn-coch. *Powy* 3D 70 (nr. Llanrhaeadr-ym-Mochnant)
Cefn-coed-y-cymmer. *Mer T* 5D 46
Cefn Cribwr. *B'end* 3B 32
Cefn-ddwysarn. *Gwyn* 2B 70
Cefn Einion. *Shrp* 2E 59
Cefneithin. *Carm* 4F 45
Cefn Glas. *B'end* 3B 32
Cefngorwydd. *Powy* 1C 46
Cefn Llwyd. *Cdgn* 2F 57
Cefn-mawr. *Wrex* 1E 71
Cefn-y-bedd. *Flin* 5F 83
Cefn-y-coed. *Powy* 1D 58
Cefn-y-pant. *Carm* 2F 43
Cegidfa. *Powy* 4E 70
Ceinewydd. *Cdgn* 5C 56
Cellan. *Cdgn* 1G 45
Cellardyke. *Fife* 3H 137
Cellarhead. *Staf* 1D 72
Cemaes. *IOA* 1C 80
Cemmaes. *Powy* 5H 69
Cemmaes Road. *Powy* 5H 69
Cenarth. *Carm* 1C 44
Cenin. *Gwyn* 1D 68
Ceos. *W Isl* 5F 171
Ceres. *Fife* 2G 137
Ceri. *Powy* 2D 58
Cerist. *Powy* 2B 58
Cerne Abbas. *Dors* 2B 14
Cerney Wick. *Glos* 2F 35
Cerrigceinwen. *IOA* 3D 80
Cerrigydrudion. *Cnwy* 1B 70
Cess. *Norf* 4G 79
Cessford. *Bord* 2B 120
Ceunant. *Gwyn* 4E 81
Chaceley. *Glos* 2D 48
Chacewater. *Corn* 4B 6
Chackmore. *Buck* 2E 51
Chacombe. *Nptn* 1C 50
Chadderton. *G Man* 4H 91
Chaddesden. *Derb* 2A 74
Chaddesden Common. *Derb* 2A 74
Chaddesley Corbett. *Worc* 3C 60
Chaddlehanger. *Devn* 5E 11
Chaddleworth. *W Ber* 4C 36
Chadlington. *Oxon* 3B 50
Chadshunt. *Warw* 5H 61
Chadstone. *Nptn* 5F 63
Chad Valley. *W Mid* 2E 61
Chadwell. *Leics* 3E 75
Chadwell. *Shrp* 4B 72
Chadwell Heath. *G Lon* 2F 39
Chadwell St Mary. *Thur* 3H 39
Chadwick End. *W Mid* 3G 61
Chadwick Green. *Mers* 1H 83
Chaffcombe. *Som* 1G 13
Chafford Hundred. *Thur* 3H 39
Chagford. *Devn* 4H 11
Chailey. *E Sus* 4E 27
Chainbridge. *Cambs* 5D 76
Chain Bridge. *Linc* 1C 76
Chainhurst. *Kent* 1B 28
Chalbury. *Dors* 2F 15
Chalbury Common. *Dors* 2F 15
Chaldon. *Surr* 5E 39
Chaldon Herring. *Dors* 4C 14
Chale. *IOW* 5C 16
Chale Green. *IOW* 5C 16
Chalfont Common. *Buck* 1B 38
Chalfont St Giles. *Buck* 1A 38
Chalfont St Peter. *Buck* 2B 38
Chalford. *Glos* 5D 49
Chalgrove. *Oxon* 2E 37
Chalk. *Kent* 3A 40
Chalk End. *Essx* 4G 53
Chalk Hill. *Glos* 3G 49
Challaborough. *Devn* 4C 8
Challacombe. *Devn* 2G 19
Challoch. *Dum* 3A 110
Challock. *Kent* 5E 40
Chalton. *C Beds* 5A 64 (nr. Bedford)
Chalton. *C Beds* 3A 52 (nr. Luton)
Chalton. *Hants* 1F 17
Chalvington. *E Sus* 5G 27
Champany. *Falk* 2D 128
Chance Inn. *Fife* 2F 137
Chancery. *Cdgn* 3E 57
Chandler's Cross. *Herts* 1B 38
Chandler's Cross. *Worc* 2C 48
Chandler's Ford. *Hants* 4C 24
Chanlockfoot. *Dum* 4G 117
Channel's End. *Bed* 5A 64
Channel Tunnel. *Kent* 2F 29
Chantry. *Som* 2C 22
Chantry. *Suff* 1E 55
Chapel. *Cumb* 1D 102
Chapel. *Fife* 4E 137
Chapel Allerton. *Som* 1H 21
Chapel Allerton. *W Yor* 1D 92
Chapel Amble. *Corn* 1D 6
Chapel Brampton. *Nptn* 4E 63
Chapelbridge. *Cambs* 1B 64
Chapel Chorlton. *Staf* 2C 72
Chapel Cleeve. *Som* 2D 20
Chapel End. *C Beds* 1A 52
Chapel-en-le-Frith. *Derbs* 2E 85
Chapelfield. *Abers* 2G 145
Chapelgate. *Linc* 3D 76
Chapel Green. *Warw* 2G 61 (nr. Coventry)
Chapel Green. *Warw* 4B 62 (nr. Southam)
Chapel Haddlesey. *N Yor* 2F 93
Chapelhall. *N Lan* 3A 128
Chapel Hill. *Abers* 5H 161
Chapel Hill. *Linc* 5B 88
Chapel Hill. *Mon* 5A 48
Chapelhill. *Per* 1E 136 (nr. Glencarse)
Chapelhill. *Per* 5H 143 (nr. Harrietfield)
Chapelknowe. *Dum* 2E 112
Chapel Lawn. *Shrp* 3F 59
Chapel le Dale. *N Yor* 2G 97
Chapel Milton. *Derbs* 2E 85
Chapel of Garioch. *Abers* 1E 152
Chapel Row. *W Ber* 5D 36
Chapels. *Cumb* 1B 96
Chapel St Leonards. *Linc* 3E 89
Chapel Stile. *Cumb* 4E 102
Chapelthorne. *W Yor* 3D 92
Chapelton. *Ang* 4F 145
Chapelton. *Devn* 4F 19
Chapelton. *High* 2D 150 (nr. Grantown-on-Spey)
Chapelton. *High* 3H 157 (nr. Inverness)
Chapelton. *S Lan* 5H 127
Chapeltown. *Bkbn* 3F 91
Chapel Town. *Corn* 3C 6
Chapeltown. *Mor* 1G 151
Chapeltown. *S Yor* 1H 85
Chapmanslade. *Wilts* 2D 22
Chapmans Well. *Devn* 3D 10
Chapmore End. *Herts* 4D 52
Chappel. *Essx* 3B 54
Chard. *Som* 2G 13
Chard Junction. *Dors* 2G 13
Chardstock. *Devn* 2G 13
Charfield. *S Glo* 2C 34
Charing. *Kent* 1D 28
Charing Heath. *Kent* 1D 28
Charing Hill. *Kent* 5D 40

Charingworth. Glos 2G 49
Charlbury. Oxon 4B 50
Charlcombe. Bath 5C 34
Charlcutt. Wilts 4E 35
Charlecote. Warw 5G 61
Charles. Devn 3G 19
Charlesfield. Dum 3C 112
Charleshill. Surr 2G 25
Charleston. Ang 4C 144
Charleston. Ren 3F 127
Charlestown. Aber 3G 153
Charlestown. Abers 2H 161
Charlestown. Corn 3E 7
Charlestown. Dors 5B 14
Charlestown. Fife 1D 128
Charlestown. G Man 4G 91
Charlestown. High 1H 155
(nr. Gairloch)
Charlestown. High 4A 158
(nr. Inverness)
Charlestown. W Yor 2H 91
Charlestown of Aberlour. Mor 4G 159
Charles Tye. Suff 5C 66
Charlesworth. Derbs 1E 85
Charlton. G Lon 3F 39
Charlton. Hants 2B 24
Charlton. Herts 3B 52
Charlton. Nptn 2D 50
Charlton. Nmbd 1B 114
Charlton. Oxon 3C 36
Charlton. Som 1B 22
(nr. Radstock)
Charlton. Som 2B 22
(nr. Shepton Mallet)
Charlton. Som 4F 21
(nr. Taunton)
Charlton. Telf 4H 71
Charlton. W Sus 1G 17
Charlton. Wilts 3E 35
(nr. Malmesbury)
Charlton. Wilts 1G 23
(nr. Pewsey)
Charlton. Wilts 4G 23
(nr. Salisbury)
Charlton. Wilts 4E 23
(nr. Shaftesbury)
Charlton. Worc 1F 49
(nr. Evesham)
Charlton. Worc 3C 60
(nr. Stourport-on-Severn)
Charlton Abbots. Glos 3F 49
Charlton Adam. Som 4A 22
Charlton Down. Dors 3B 14
Charlton Horethorne. Som 4B 22
Charlton Kings. Glos 3E 49
Charlton Mackrell. Som 4A 22
Charlton Marshall. Dors 2E 15
Charlton Musgrove. Som 4C 22
Charlton-on-Otmoor. Oxon 4D 50
Charlton on the Hill. Dors 2D 15
Charlwood. Hants 3E 25
Charlwood. Surr 1D 26
Charlynch. Som 3F 21
Charminster. Dors 3B 14
Charmouth. Dors 3G 13
Charndon. Buck 3E 51
Charney Bassett. Oxon 2B 36
Charnock Green. Lanc 3D 90
Charnock Richard. Lanc 3D 90
Charsfield. Suff 5E 67
Chart Corner. Kent 5B 40
Charter Alley. Hants 1D 24
Charterhouse. Som 1H 21
Charterville Allotments. Oxon 4B 50
Chartham. Kent 5F 41
Chartham Hatch. Kent 5F 41
Chartridge. Buck 5H 51
Chart Sutton. Kent 5B 40
Chart, The. Kent 5F 39
Charvil. Wok 4F 37
Charwelton. Nptn 5C 62
Chase Terrace. Staf 5E 73
Chasetown. Staf 5E 73
Chastleton. Oxon 3H 49

Chasty. Devn 2D 10
Chatburn. Lanc 5G 97
Chatcull. Staf 2B 72
Chatham. Medw 4B 40
Chatham Green. Essx 4H 53
Chathill. Nmbd 2F 121
Chatley. Worc 4C 60
Chattenden. Medw 3B 40
Chatteris. Cambs 2C 64
Chattisham. Suff 1D 54
Chatton. Nmbd 2E 121
Chatwall. Shrp 1H 59
Chaulden. Herts 5A 52
Chaul End. C Beds 3A 52
Chawleigh. Devn 1H 11
Chawley. Oxon 5C 50
Chawston. Bed 5A 64
Chawton. Hants 3F 25
Chaxhill. Glos 4C 48
Cheadle. G Man 2C 84
Cheadle. Staf 1E 73
Cheadle Hulme. G Man 2C 84
Cheam. Surr 4D 38
Cheapside. Wind 4A 38
Chearsley. Buck 4F 51
Chebsey. Staf 3C 72
Checkendon. Oxon 3E 37
Checkley. Ches E 1B 72
Checkley. Here 2A 48
Checkley. Staf 2E 73
Chedburgh. Suff 5G 65
Cheddar. Som 1H 21
Cheddington. Buck 4H 51
Cheddleton. Staf 5D 84
Cheddon Fitzpaine. Som 4F 21
Chedglow. Wilts 2E 35
Chedgrave. Norf 1F 67
Chedington. Dors 2H 13
Chediston. Suff 3F 67
Chediston Green. Suff 3F 67
Chedworth. Glos 4F 49
Chedzoy. Som 3G 21
Cheeseman's Green. Kent 2E 29
Cheetham Hill. G Man 4G 91
Cheglinch. Devn 2F 19
Cheldon. Devn 1H 11
Chelford. Ches E 3C 84
Chellaston. Derb 2A 74
Chellington. Bed 5G 63
Chelmarsh. Shrp 2B 60
Chelmick. Shrp 1G 59
Chelmondiston. Suff 2F 55
Chelmorton. Derbs 4F 85
Chelmsford. Essx 5H 53
Chelsea. G Lon 3D 39
Chelsfield. G Lon 4F 39
Chelsham. Surr 5E 39
Chelston. Som 4E 21
Chelsworth. Suff 1C 54
Cheltenham. Glos 3E 49
Chelveston. Nptn 4G 63
Chelvey. N Som 5H 33
Chelwood. Bath 5B 34
Chelwood Common. E Sus 3F 27
Chelwood Gate. E Sus 3F 27
Chelworth. Wilts 2E 35
Chelworth Lower Green. Wilts 2F 35
Chelworth Upper Green. Wilts 2F 35
Chelynch. Som 2B 22
Cheney Longville. Shrp 2G 59
Chenies. Buck 1B 38
Chepstow. Mon 2A 34
Chequerfield. W Yor 2E 93
Chequers Corner. Norf 5D 77
Cherhill. Wilts 4F 35
Cherington. Glos 2E 35
Cherington. Warw 2A 50
Cheriton. Devn 2H 19
Cheriton. Hants 4D 24
Cheriton. Kent 2G 29
Cheriton. Pemb 5D 43
Cheriton. Swan 3D 30
Cheriton Bishop. Devn 3A 12
Cheriton Cross. Devn 3A 12

Cheriton Fitzpaine. Devn 2B 12
Cherrington. Telf 3A 72
Cherrybank. Per 1D 136
Cherry Burton. E Yor 5D 101
Cherry Green. Herts 3D 52
Cherry Hinton. Cambs 5D 65
Cherry Willingham. Linc 3H 87
Chertsey. Surr 4B 38
Cheselbourne. Dors 3C 14
Chesham. Buck 5H 51
Chesham. G Man 3G 91
Chesham Bois. Buck 1A 38
Cheshunt. Herts 5D 52
Cheslyn Hay. Staf 5D 73
Chessetts Wood. Warw 3F 61
Chessington. G Lon 4C 38
Chester. Ches W 4G 83
Chesterblade. Som 2B 22
Chesterfield. Derbs 3A 86
Chesterfield. Staf 5F 73
Chesterhope. Nmbd 1C 114
Chester-le-Street. Dur 4F 115
Chester Moor. Dur 5F 115
Chesters. Bord 3A 120
Chesterton. Cambs 4D 64
(nr. Cambridge)
Chesterton. Cambs 1A 64
(nr. Peterborough)
Chesterton. Glos 5F 49
Chesterton. Oxon 3D 50
Chesterton. Shrp 1B 60
Chesterton. Staf 1C 72
Chesterton Green. Warw 5H 61
Chesterwood. Nmbd 3B 114
Chestfield. Kent 4F 41
Cheston. Devn 3C 8
Cheswardine. Shrp 2B 72
Cheswell. Telf 4B 72
Cheswick. Nmbd 5G 131
Cheswick Green. W Mid 3F 61
Chetnole. Dors 2B 14
Chettiscombe. Devn 1C 12
Chettisham. Cambs 2E 65
Chettle. Dors 1E 15
Chetton. Shrp 1A 60
Chetwode. Buck 3E 51
Chetwynd Aston. Telf 4B 72
Cheveley. Cambs 4F 65
Chevening. Kent 5F 39
Chevington. Suff 5G 65
Chevithorne. Devn 1C 12
Chew Magna. Bath 5A 34
Chew Moor. G Man 4E 91
Chew Stoke. Bath 5A 34
Chewton Keynsham. Bath 5B 34
Chewton Mendip. Som 1A 22
Chichacott. Devn 3G 11
Chicheley. Mil 1H 51
Chichester. W Sus 2G 17
Chickerell. Dors 4B 14
Chickering. Suff 3E 66
Chicklade. Wilts 3E 23
Chicksands. C Beds 2B 52
Chickward. Here 5E 59
Chidden. Hants 1E 17
Chiddingfold. Surr 2A 26
Chiddingly. E Sus 4G 27
Chiddingstone. Kent 1G 27
Chiddingstone Causeway. Kent 1G 27
Chiddingstone Hoath. Kent 1F 27
Chideock. Dors 3H 13
Chidgley. Som 3D 20
Chidham. W Sus 2F 17
Chieveley. W Ber 4C 36
Chignall St James. Essx 5G 53
Chignall Smealy. Essx 4G 53
Chigwell. Essx 1F 39
Chigwell Row. Essx 1F 39
Chilbolton. Hants 2B 24
Chilcomb. Hants 4D 24
Chilcombe. Dors 3A 14
Chilcompton. Som 1B 22
Chilcote. Leics 4G 73
Childer Thornton. Ches W 3F 83

Child Okeford. Dors 1D 14
Childrey. Oxon 3B 36
Child's Ercall. Shrp 3A 72
Childswickham. Worc 2F 49
Childwall. Mers 2G 83
Childwick Green. Herts 4B 52
Chilfrome. Dors 3A 14
Chilgrove. W Sus 1G 17
Chilham. Kent 5E 41
Chilhampton. Wilts 3F 23
Chilla. Devn 2E 11
Chilland. Hants 3D 24
Chillaton. Devn 4E 11
Chillenden. Kent 5G 41
Chillerton. IOW 4C 16
Chillesford. Suff 5F 67
Chillingham. Nmbd 2E 121
Chillington. Devn 4D 9
Chillington. Som 1G 13
Chilmark. Wilts 3E 23
Chilmington Green. Kent 1D 28
Chilson. Oxon 4B 50
Chilsworthy. Corn 5E 11
Chilsworthy. Devn 2D 10
Chiltern Green. C Beds 4B 52
Chilthorne Domer. Som 1A 14
Chilton. Buck 4E 51
Chilton. Devn 2B 12
Chilton. Dur 2F 105
Chilton. Oxon 3C 36
Chilton Candover. Hants 2D 24
Chilton Cantelo. Som 4A 22
Chilton Foliat. Wilts 4B 36
Chilton Lane. Dur 1A 106
Chilton Polden. Som 3G 21
Chilton Street. Suff 1A 54
Chilton Trinity. Som 3F 21
Chilwell. Notts 2C 74
Chilworth. Hants 1C 16
Chilworth. Surr 1B 26
Chimney. Oxon 5B 50
Chimney Street. Suff 1H 53
Chineham. Hants 1E 25
Chingford. G Lon 1E 39
Chinley. Derbs 2E 85
Chinnor. Oxon 5F 51
Chipley. Som 4E 20
Chipnall. Shrp 2B 72
Chippenham. Cambs 4F 65
Chippenham. Wilts 4E 35
Chipperfield. Herts 5A 52
Chipping. Herts 2D 52
Chipping. Lanc 5F 97
Chipping Campden. Glos 2G 49
Chipping Hill. Essx 4B 54
Chipping Norton. Oxon 3B 50
Chipping Ongar. Essx 5F 53
Chipping Sodbury. S Glo 3C 34
Chipping Warden. Nptn 1C 50
Chipstable. Som 4D 20
Chipstead. Kent 5G 39
Chipstead. Surr 5D 38
Chirbury. Shrp 1E 59
Chirk. Wrex 2E 71
Chirmorie. S Ayr 2H 109
Chirnside. Bord 4E 131
Chirnsidebridge. Bord 4E 131
Chirton. Wilts 1F 23
Chisbridge Cross. Buck 3G 37
Chisbury. Wilts 5A 36
Chiselborough. Som 1H 13
Chiseldon. Swin 4G 35
Chiselhampton. Oxon 2D 36
Chiserley. W Yor 2A 92
Chislehurst. G Lon 4F 39
Chislet. Kent 4G 41
Chiswell. Dors 5B 14
Chiswell Green. Herts 5B 52
Chiswick. G Lon 3D 38
Chisworth. Derbs 1D 85
Chitcombe. E Sus 3C 28
Chithurst. W Sus 4G 25
Chittering. Cambs 4D 65
Chitterley. Devn 2C 12

Chitterne. Wilts 2E 23
Chittlehamholt. Devn 4G 19
Chittlehampton. Devn 4G 19
Chittoe. Wilts 5E 35
Chivelstone. Devn 5D 9
Chivenor. Devn 3F 19
Chobham. Surr 4A 38
Cholderton. Wilts 2H 23
Cholesbury. Buck 5H 51
Chollerford. Nmbd 2C 114
Chollerton. Nmbd 2C 114
Cholsey. Oxon 3D 36
Cholstrey. Here 5G 59
Chop Gate. N Yor 5C 106
Choppington. Nmbd 1F 115
Chopwell. Tyne 4E 115
Chorley. Ches E 5H 83
Chorley. Lanc 3D 90
Chorley. Shrp 2A 60
Chorley. Staf 4E 73
Chorleywood. Herts 1B 38
Chorlton. Ches E 5B 84
Chorlton-cum-Hardy. G Man 1C 84
Chorlton Lane. Ches W 1G 71
Choulton. Shrp 2F 59
Chrishall. Essx 2E 53
Christchurch. Cambs 1D 65
Christchurch. Dors 3G 15
Christchurch. Glos 4A 48
Christian Malford. Wilts 4E 35
Christleton. Ches W 4G 83
Christmas Common. Oxon 2F 37
Christon. N Som 1G 21
Christon Bank. Nmbd 2G 121
Christow. Devn 4B 12
Chryston. N Lan 2H 127
Chuck Hatch. E Sus 2F 27
Chudleigh. Devn 5B 12
Chudleigh Knighton. Devn 5B 12
Chulmleigh. Devn 1G 11
Chunal. Derbs 1E 85
Church. Lanc 2F 91
Churcham. Glos 4C 48
Church Aston. Telf 4B 72
Church Brampton. Nptn 4E 62
Church Brough. Cumb 3A 104
Church Broughton. Derbs 2G 73
Church Corner. Suff 2G 67
Church Crookham. Hants 1G 25
Churchdown. Glos 4D 48
Church Eaton. Staf 4C 72
Church End. Cambs 5D 65
(nr. Cambridge)
Church End. Cambs 2B 64
(nr. Sawtry)
Church End. Cambs 3C 64
(nr. Willingham)
Church End. Cambs 5C 76
(nr. Wisbech)
Church End. C Beds 3H 51
(nr. Dunstable)
Church End. C Beds 2B 52
(nr. Stotfold)
Church End. E Yor 4E 101
Church End. Essx 3H 53
(nr. Braintree)
Church End. Essx 3G 53
(nr. Great Dunmow)
Church End. Essx 1F 53
(nr. Saffron Walden)
Churchend. Essx 1E 40
(nr. Southend-on-Sea)
Church End. Glos 5C 48
Church End. Hants 1E 25
Church End. Linc 2B 76
(nr. Donington)
Church End. Linc 1D 88
(nr. North Somercotes)
Church End. Norf 4E 77
Church End. Warw 1G 61
(nr. Coleshill)
Church End. Warw 1G 61
(nr. Nuneaton)
Church End. Wilts 4F 35

Church Enstone—Clyst St George

Church Enstone. *Oxon* 3B 50
Church Fenton. *N Yor* 1F 93
Church Green. *Devn* 3E 13
Church Gresley. *Derbs* 4G 73
Church Hanborough. *Oxon* 4C 50
Church Hill. *Ches W* 4A 84
Church Hill. *Worc* 4E 61
Church Hougham. *Kent* 1G 29
Church Houses. *N Yor* 5D 106
Churchill. *Devn* 2G 13 (nr. Axminster)
Churchill. *Devn* 2F 19 (nr. Barnstaple)
Churchill. *N Som* 1H 21
Churchill. *Oxon* 3A 50
Churchill. *Worc* 3C 60 (nr. Kidderminster)
Churchill. *Worc* 5D 60 (nr. Worcester)
Churchinford. *Som* 1F 13
Church Knowle. *Dors* 4E 15
Church Laneham. *Notts* 3F 87
Church Langley. *Essx* 5E 53
Church Langton. *Leics* 1E 62
Church Lawford. *Warw* 3B 62
Church Lawton. *Ches E* 5C 84
Church Leigh. *Staf* 2E 73
Church Lench. *Worc* 5E 61
Church Mayfield. *Staf* 1F 73
Church Minshull. *Ches E* 4A 84
Church Norton. *W Sus* 3G 17
Churchover. *Warw* 2C 62
Church Preen. *Shrp* 1H 59
Church Pulverbatch. *Shrp* 5G 71
Churchstanton. *Som* 1E 13
Church Stoke. *Powy* 1E 59
Churchstow. *Devn* 4D 8
Church Stowe. *Nptn* 5D 62
Church Street. *Kent* 3B 40
Church Stretton. *Shrp* 1G 59
Churchthorpe. *Linc* 1C 88
Churchtown. *Cumb* 5E 113
Churchtown. *Derbs* 4G 85
Churchtown. *Devn* 2G 19
Churchtown. *IOM* 2D 108
Churchtown. *Lanc* 5D 97
Church Town. *Leics* 4A 74
Churchtown. *Mers* 3B 90
Church Town. *N Lin* 4A 94
Churchtown. *Shrp* 2E 59
Church Village. *Rhon* 3D 32
Church Warsop. *Notts* 4C 86
Church Westcote. *Glos* 3H 49
Church Wilne. *Derbs* 2B 74
Churnsike Lodge. *Nmbd* 2H 113
Churston Ferrers. *Torb* 3F 9
Churt. *Surr* 3G 25
Churton. *Ches W* 5G 83
Churwell. *W Yor* 2C 92
Chute Standen. *Wilts* 1B 24
Chwilog. *Gwyn* 2D 68
Chwittfordd. *Flin* 3D 82
Chyandour. *Corn* 3B 4
Cilan Uchaf. *Gwyn* 3B 68
Cilcain. *Flin* 4D 82
Cilcennin. *Cdgn* 4E 57
Cilfrew. *Neat* 5A 46
Cilfynydd. *Rhon* 2D 32
Cilgerran. *Pemb* 1B 44
Cilgeti. *Pemb* 4F 43
Cilgwyn. *Carm* 3H 45
Cilgwyn. *Pemb* 1E 43
Ciliau Aeron. *Cdgn* 5D 57
Cill Amhlaidh. *W Isl* 4C 170
Cill Donnain. *High* 1G 165
Cill Donnain. *W Isl* 6C 170
Cille a' Bhacstair. *High* 2C 154
Cille Bhrighde. *W Isl* 7C 170
Cille Pheadair. *W Isl* 6C 170
Cilmaengwyn. *Neat* 5H 45
Cilmeri. *Powy* 5C 58
Cilmery. *Powy* 5C 58
Cilrhedyn. *Pemb* 1G 43
Cilsan. *Carm* 3F 45
Ciltalgarth. *Gwyn* 1A 70
Ciltwrch. *Powy* 1E 47
Cilybebyll. *Neat* 5H 45
Cilycwm. *Carm* 2A 46
Cimla. *Neat* 2A 32
Cinderford. *Glos* 4B 48
Cinderhill. *Derbs* 1A 74
Cippenham. *Slo* 2A 38
Cippyn. *Pemb* 1B 44
Cirbhig. *W Isl* 3E 171
Circebost. *W Isl* 4D 171
Cirencester. *Glos* 5F 49
City. *Powy* 1E 58
City. *V Glam* 4C 32
City Centre. *Stoke* 1C 72
City Dulas. *IOA* 2D 80
City (London) Airport. *G Lon* 2F 39
City of London. *G Lon* 2E 39
City, The. *Buck* 2F 37
Clabhach. *Arg* 3C 138
Clachaig. *Arg* 1C 126
Clachaig. *High* 3F 141 (nr. Kinlochleven)
Clachaig. *High* 2E 151 (nr. Nethy Bridge)
Clachamish. *High* 3C 154
Clachan. *Arg* 4F 125 (on Kintyre)
Clachan. *Arg* 4C 140 (on Lismore)
Clachan. *High* 2H 167 (nr. Bettyhill)
Clachan. *High* 2D 155 (nr. Staffin)
Clachan. *High* 1C 154 (nr. Uig)
Clachan. *High* 5E 155 (on Raasay)
Clachan Farm. *Arg* 2A 134
Clachan na Luib. *W Isl* 2D 170
Clachan of Campsie. *E Dun* 2H 127
Clachan of Glendaruel. *Arg* 1A 126
Clachan-Seil. *Arg* 2E 133
Clachan Shannda. *W Isl* 1D 170
Clachan Strachur. *Arg* 3H 133
Clachbreck. *Arg* 2F 125
Clachnaharry. *High* 4A 158
Clachtoll. *High* 1E 163
Clackmannan. *Clac* 4B 136
Clackmarras. *Mor* 3G 159
Clacton-on-Sea. *Essx* 4E 55
Cladach a Chaolais. *W Isl* 2C 170
Cladach Chairinis. *W Isl* 3D 170
Cladach Chirceboist. *W Isl* 2C 170
Cladich. *Arg* 1H 133
Cladswell. *Worc* 5E 61
Claggan. *High* 1F 141 (nr. Fort William)
Claggan. *High* 4A 140 (nr. Lochaline)
Claigan. *High* 3B 154
Clandown. *Bath* 1B 22
Clanfield. *Hants* 1E 17
Clanfield. *Oxon* 5A 50
Clanville. *Hants* 2B 24
Clanville. *Som* 3B 22
Claonaig. *Arg* 4G 125
Clapgate. *Dors* 2F 15
Clapgate. *Herts* 3E 53
Clapham. *Bed* 5H 63
Clapham. *Devn* 4B 12
Clapham. *G Lon* 3D 39
Clapham. *N Yor* 3G 97
Clapham. *W Sus* 5B 26
Clap Hill. *Kent* 2E 29
Clappers. *Bord* 4F 131
Clappersgate. *Cumb* 4E 103
Clapton. *Som* 2H 13 (nr. Crewkerne)
Clapton. *Som* 1B 22 (nr. Radstock)
Clapton-in-Gordano. *N Som* 4H 33
Clapton-on-the-Hill. *Glos* 4G 49
Clapworthy. *Devn* 4G 19
Clara Vale. *Tyne* 3E 115
Clarbeston. *Pemb* 2E 43
Clarbeston Road. *Pemb* 2E 43
Clarborough. *Notts* 2E 87
Clare. *Suff* 1A 54
Clarebrand. *Dum* 3E 111
Clarencefield. *Dum* 3B 112
Clarilaw. *Bord* 3H 119
Clark's Green. *Surr* 2C 26
Clark's Hill. *Linc* 3C 76
Clarkston. *E Ren* 4G 127
Clasheddy. *High* 2G 167
Clashindarroch. *Abers* 5B 160
Clashmore. *High* 5E 165 (nr. Dornoch)
Clashmore. *High* 1E 163 (nr. Stoer)
Clashnessie. *High* 5A 166
Clashnoir. *Mor* 1G 151
Clathick. *Per* 1H 135
Clathy. *Per* 2B 136
Clatt. *Abers* 1C 152
Clatter. *Powy* 1B 58
Clatterford. *IOW* 4C 16
Clatworthy. *Som* 3D 20
Claughton. *Lanc* 3E 97 (nr. Caton)
Claughton. *Lanc* 5E 97 (nr. Garstang)
Claughton. *Mers* 2F 83
Claverdon. *Warw* 4F 61
Claverham. *N Som* 5H 33
Clavering. *Essx* 2E 53
Claverley. *Shrp* 1B 60
Claverton. *Bath* 5C 34
Clawdd-coch. *V Glam* 4D 32
Clawdd-newydd. *Den* 5C 82
Clawson Hill. *Leics* 3E 75
Clawton. *Devn* 3D 10
Claxby. *Linc* 3D 88 (nr. Alford)
Claxby. *Linc* 1A 88 (nr. Market Rasen)
Claxton. *Norf* 5F 79
Claxton. *N Yor* 4A 100
Claybrooke Magna. *Leics* 2B 62
Claybrooke Parva. *Leics* 2B 62
Clay Common. *Suff* 2G 67
Clay Coton. *Nptn* 3C 62
Clay Cross. *Derbs* 4A 86
Claydon. *Oxon* 5B 62
Claydon. *Suff* 5D 66
Clay End. *Herts* 3D 52
Claygate. *Dum* 2E 113
Claygate. *Kent* 1B 28
Claygate. *Surr* 4C 38
Claygate Cross. *Kent* 5H 39
Clayhall. *Hants* 3E 16
Clayhanger. *Devn* 4D 20
Clayhanger. *W Mid* 5E 73
Clayhidon. *Devn* 1E 13
Clay Hill. *Bris* 4B 34
Clayhill. *E Sus* 3C 28
Clayhill. *Hants* 2B 16
Clayhithe. *Cambs* 4E 65
Clayholes. *Ang* 5E 145
Clay Lake. *Linc* 3B 76
Clayock. *High* 3D 168
Claypits. *Glos* 5C 48
Claypole. *Linc* 1F 75
Claythorpe. *Linc* 3D 88
Clayton. *G Man* 1C 84
Clayton. *S Yor* 4E 93
Clayton. *Staf* 1C 72
Clayton. *W Sus* 4E 27
Clayton. *W Yor* 1B 92
Clayton Green. *Lanc* 2D 90
Clayton-le-Moors. *Lanc* 1F 91
Clayton-le-Woods. *Lanc* 2D 90
Clayton West. *W Yor* 3C 92
Clayworth. *Notts* 2E 87
Cleadale. *High* 5C 146
Cleadon. *Tyne* 3G 115
Clearbrook. *Devn* 2B 8
Clearwell. *Glos* 5A 48
Cleasby. *N Yor* 3F 105
Cleat. *Orkn* 3D 172 (nr. Braehead)
Cleat. *Orkn* 9D 172 (nr. St Margaret's Hope)
Cleatlam. *Dur* 3E 105
Cleator. *Cumb* 3B 102
Cleator Moor. *Cumb* 3B 102
Cleckheaton. *W Yor* 2B 92
Cleedownton. *Shrp* 2H 59
Cleehill. *Shrp* 3H 59
Cleekhimin. *N Lan* 4A 128
Clee St Margaret. *Shrp* 2H 59
Cleestanton. *Shrp* 3H 59
Cleethorpes. *NE Lin* 4G 95
Cleeton St Mary. *Shrp* 3A 60
Cleeve. *N Som* 5H 33
Cleeve. *Oxon* 3E 36
Cleeve Hill. *Glos* 3E 49
Cleeve Prior. *Worc* 1F 49
Clehonger. *Here* 2H 47
Cleigh. *Arg* 1F 133
Cleish. *Per* 4C 136
Cleland. *N Lan* 4B 128
Clench Common. *Wilts* 5G 35
Clenchwarton. *Norf* 3E 77
Clennell. *Nmbd* 4D 120
Clent. *Worc* 3D 60
Cleobury Mortimer. *Shrp* 3A 60
Cleobury North. *Shrp* 2A 60
Clephanton. *High* 3C 158
Clerkhill. *High* 2H 167
Clestrain. *Orkn* 7C 172
Clevancy. *Wilts* 4F 35
Clevedon. *N Som* 4H 33
Cleveley. *Oxon* 3B 50
Cleveleys. *Lanc* 5C 96
Clevelode. *Worc* 1D 48
Cleverton. *Wilts* 3E 35
Clewer. *Som* 1H 21
Cley next the Sea. *Norf* 1C 78
Cliaid. *W Isl* 8B 170
Cliasmol. *W Isl* 7C 171
Clibberswick. *Shet* 1H 173
Cliburn. *Cumb* 2G 103
Cliddesden. *Hants* 2E 25
Clieves Hills. *Lanc* 4B 90
Cliff. *Warw* 1G 61
Cliffburn. *Ang* 4F 145
Cliffe. *Medw* 3B 40
Cliffe. *N Yor* 3F 105 (nr. Darlington)
Cliffe. *N Yor* 1G 93 (nr. Selby)
Cliff End. *E Sus* 4C 28
Cliffe Woods. *Medw* 3B 40
Clifford. *Here* 1F 47
Clifford. *W Yor* 5G 99
Clifford Chambers. *Warw* 5F 61
Clifford's Mesne. *Glos* 3B 48
Cliffs End. *Kent* 4H 41
Clifton. *Bris* 4A 34
Clifton. *C Beds* 2B 52
Clifton. *Cumb* 2G 103
Clifton. *Derbs* 1F 73
Clifton. *Devn* 2G 19
Clifton. *G Man* 4F 91
Clifton. *Lanc* 1C 90
Clifton. *Nmbd* 1F 115
Clifton. *N Yor* 5D 98
Clifton. *Nott* 2C 74
Clifton. *Oxon* 2C 50
Clifton. *S Yor* 1C 86
Clifton. *Stir* 5H 141
Clifton. *W Yor* 2B 92
Clifton. *Worc* 1D 48
Clifton. *York* 4H 99
Clifton Campville. *Staf* 4G 73
Clifton Hampden. *Oxon* 2D 36
Clifton Hill. *Worc* 4B 60
Clifton Reynes. *Mil* 5G 63
Clifton upon Dunsmore. *Warw* 3C 62
Clifton upon Teme. *Worc* 4B 60
Cliftonville. *Kent* 3H 41
Cliftonville. *Norf* 2F 79
Climping. *W Sus* 5A 26
Climpy. *S Lan* 4C 128
Clint. *N Yor* 4E 99
Clint Green. *Norf* 4C 78
Clintmains. *Bord* 1A 120
Cliobh. *W Isl* 4C 171
Clipiau. *Gwyn* 4H 69
Clippesby. *Norf* 4G 79
Clippings Green. *Norf* 4C 78
Clipsham. *Rut* 4G 75
Clipston. *Nptn* 2E 62
Clipston. *Notts* 2D 74
Clipstone. *Notts* 4C 86
Clitheroe. *Lanc* 5G 97
Cliuthar. *W Isl* 8D 171
Clive. *Shrp* 3H 71
Clivocast. *Shet* 1H 173
Clixby. *Linc* 4D 94
Clocaenog. *Den* 5C 82
Clochan. *Mor* 2B 160
Clochforbie. *Abers* 3F 161
Clock Face. *Mers* 1H 83
Cloddiau. *Powy* 5E 70
Cloddymoss. *Mor* 2D 159
Clodock. *Here* 3G 47
Cloford. *Som* 2C 22
Clola. *Abers* 4H 161
Clophill. *C Beds* 2A 52
Clopton. *Nptn* 2H 63
Clopton Corner. *Suff* 5E 66
Clopton Green. *Suff* 5G 65
Closeburn. *Dum* 5A 118
Close Clark. *IOM* 4B 108
Closworth. *Som* 1A 14
Clothall. *Herts* 2C 52
Clotton. *Ches W* 4H 83
Clough. *G Man* 3H 91
Clough. *W Yor* 3A 92
Clough Foot. *W Yor* 2H 91
Cloughton. *N Yor* 5H 107
Cloughton Newlands. *N Yor* 5H 107
Clouston. *Orkn* 6B 172
Clova. *Abers* 1B 152
Clova. *Ang* 1C 144
Clovelly. *Devn* 4D 18
Clovenfords. *Bord* 1G 119
Clovenstone. *Abers* 2E 153
Clovullin. *High* 2E 141
Clowne. *Derbs* 3B 86
Clows Top. *Worc* 3B 60
Cloy. *Wrex* 1F 71
Cluanie Inn. *High* 2C 148
Cluanie Lodge. *High* 2C 148
Cluddley. *Telf* 5A 72
Clun. *Shrp* 2F 59
Clunas. *High* 4C 158
Clunbury. *Shrp* 2F 59
Clunderwen. *Pemb* 3F 43
Clune. *High* 1B 150
Clunes. *High* 5E 148
Clungunford. *Shrp* 3F 59
Clunie. *Per* 4A 144
Clunton. *Shrp* 2F 59
Cluny. *Fife* 4E 137
Clutton. *Bath* 1B 22
Clutton. *Ches W* 5G 83
Clwt-y-bont. *Gwyn* 4E 81
Clwydfagwyr. *Mer T* 5D 46
Clydach. *Mon* 4F 47
Clydach. *Swan* 5G 45
Clydach Vale. *Rhon* 2C 32
Clydebank. *W Dun* 2G 127
Clydey. *Pemb* 1G 43
Clyffe Pypard. *Wilts* 4F 35
Clynder. *Arg* 1D 126
Clyne. *Neat* 5B 46
Clynelish. *High* 3F 165
Clynnog-fawr. *Gwyn* 1D 68
Clyro. *Powy* 1F 47
Clyst Honiton. *Devn* 3C 12
Clyst Hydon. *Devn* 2D 12
Clyst St George. *Devn* 4C 12

Clyst St Lawrence—Coombe

Clyst St Lawrence. *Devn* 2D 12
Clyst St Mary. *Devn* 3C 12
Clyth. *High* 5E 169
Cnip. *W Isl* 4C 171
Cnwcau. *Pemb* 1C 44
Cnwch Coch. *Cdgn* 3F 57
Coad's Green. *Corn* 5C 10
Coal Aston. *Derbs* 3A 86
Coalbrookdale. *Telf* 5A 72
Coalbrookvale. *Blae* 5F 47
Coalburn. *S Lan* 1H 117
Coalburns. *Tyne* 3E 115
Coalcleugh. *Nmbd* 5B 114
Coaley. *Glos* 5C 48
Coalford. *Abers* 4F 153
Coalhall. *E Ayr* 3D 116
Coalhill. *Essx* 1B 40
Coalpit Heath. *S Glo* 3B 34
Coal Pool. *W Mid* 5E 73
Coalport. *Telf* 5B 72
Coalsnaughton. *Clac* 4B 136
Coaltown of Balgonie. *Fife* 4F 137
Coaltown of Wemyss. *Fife* 4F 137
Coalville. *Leics* 4B 74
Coalville. *Mil* 5F 63
Coalway. *Glos* 4A 48
Coanwood. *Nmbd* 4H 113
Coat. *Som* 4H 21
Coatbridge. *N Lan* 3A 128
Coatdyke. *N Lan* 3A 128
Coate. *Swin* 3G 35
Coate. *Wilts* 5F 35
Coates. *Cambs* 1C 64
Coates. *Glos* 5E 49
Coates. *Linc* 2G 87
Coates. *W Sus* 4A 26
Coatham. *Red C* 2C 106
Coatham Mundeville. *Darl* 2F 105
Cobbaton. *Devn* 4G 19
Coberley. *Glos* 4E 49
Cobhall Common. *Here* 2H 47
Cobham. *Kent* 4A 40
Cobham. *Surr* 4C 38
Cobnash. *Here* 4G 59
Coburg. *Devn* 5B 12
Cockayne. *N Yor* 5D 106
Cockayne Hatley. *C Beds* 1C 52
Cock Bank. *Wrex* 1F 71
Cock Bridge. *Abers* 3G 151
Cockburnspath. *Bord* 2D 130
Cock Clarks. *Essx* 5B 54
Cockenzie and Port Seton. *E Lot* 2H 129
Cockerham. *Lanc* 4D 96
Cockermouth. *Cumb* 1C 102
Cockernhoe. *Herts* 3B 52
Cockfield. *Dur* 2E 105
Cockfield. *Suff* 5B 66
Cockfosters. *G Lon* 1D 39
Cock Gate. *Here* 4G 59
Cock Green. *Essx* 4G 53
Cocking. *W Sus* 1G 17
Cocking Causeway. *W Sus* 1G 17
Cockington. *Torb* 2F 9
Cocklake. *Som* 2H 21
Cocklaw. *Abers* 4H 161
Cocklaw. *Nmbd* 2C 114
Cockley Beck. *Cumb* 4D 102
Cockley Cley. *Norf* 5G 77
Cockmuir. *Abers* 3G 161
Cockpole Green. *Wind* 3G 37
Cockshutford. *Shrp* 2H 59
Cockshutt. *Shrp* 3G 71
Cockthorpe. *Norf* 1B 78
Cockwood. *Devn* 4C 12
Cockyard. *Derbs* 3E 85
Cockyard. *Here* 2H 47
Codda. *Corn* 5B 10
Coddenham. *Suff* 5D 66
Coddenham Green. *Suff* 5D 66
Coddington. *Ches W* 5G 83
Coddington. *Here* 1C 48
Coddington. *Notts* 5F 87
Codford St Mary. *Wilts* 3E 23
Codford St Peter. *Wilts* 3E 23
Codicote. *Herts* 4C 52
Codmore Hill. *W Sus* 3B 26
Codnor. *Derbs* 1B 74
Codrington. *S Glo* 4C 34
Codsall. *Staf* 5C 72
Codsall Wood. *Staf* 5C 72
Coed Duon. *Cphy* 2E 33
Coedely. *Rhon* 3D 32
Coedglasson. *Powy* 4C 58
Coedkernew. *Newp* 3F 33
Coed Morgan. *Mon* 4G 47
Coedpoeth. *Wrex* 5E 83
Coedway. *Powy* 4F 71
Coed-y-bryn. *Cdgn* 1D 44
Coed-y-paen. *Mon* 2G 33
Coed-yr-ynys. *Powy* 3E 47
Coed Ystumgwern. *Gwyn* 3E 69
Coelbren. *Powy* 4B 46
Coffinswell. *Devn* 2E 9
Cofton Hackett. *Worc* 3E 61
Cogan. *V Glam* 4E 33
Cogenhoe. *Nptn* 4F 63
Cogges. *Oxon* 5B 50
Coggeshall. *Essx* 3B 54
Coggeshall Hamlet. *Essx* 3B 54
Coggins Mill. *E Sus* 3G 27
Coignafearn Lodge. *High* 2A 150
Coig Peighinnean. *W Isl* 1H 171
Coig Peighinnean Bhuirgh. *W Isl* 2G 171
Coilleag. *W Isl* 7C 170
Coilliemore. *High* 1A 158
Coillore. *High* 5C 154
Coire an Fhuarain. *W Isl* 4E 171
Coity. *B'end* 3C 32
Cokhay Green. *Derbs* 3G 73
Col. *W Isl* 4G 171
Colaboll. *High* 2C 164
Colan. *Corn* 2C 6
Colaton Raleigh. *Devn* 4D 12
Colbost. *High* 4B 154
Colburn. *N Yor* 5E 105
Colby. *Cumb* 2H 103
Colby. *IOM* 4B 108
Colby. *Norf* 2E 78
Colchester. *Essx* 3D 54
Cold Ash. *W Ber* 5D 36
Cold Ashby. *Nptn* 3D 62
Cold Ashton. *S Glo* 4C 34
Cold Aston. *Glos* 4G 49
Coldbackie. *High* 3G 167
Cold Blow. *Pemb* 3F 43
Cold Brayfield. *Mil* 5G 63
Cold Cotes. *N Yor* 2G 97
Coldean. *Brig* 5E 27
Coldeast. *Devn* 5B 12
Colden. *W Yor* 2H 91
Colden Common. *Hants* 4C 24
Coldfair Green. *Suff* 4G 67
Coldham. *Cambs* 5D 76
Coldham. *Staf* 5C 72
Cold Hanworth. *Linc* 2H 87
Coldharbour. *Corn* 4B 6
Cold Harbour. *Dors* 3E 15
Coldharbour. *Glos* 5A 48
Coldharbour. *Kent* 5G 39
Coldharbour. *Surr* 1C 26
Cold Hatton. *Telf* 3A 72
Cold Hatton Heath. *Telf* 3A 72
Cold Hesledon. *Dur* 5H 115
Cold Hiendley. *W Yor* 3D 92
Cold Higham. *Nptn* 5D 62
Coldingham. *Bord* 3F 131
Cold Kirby. *N Yor* 1H 99
Coldmeece. *Staf* 2C 72
Cold Northcott. *Corn* 4C 10
Cold Norton. *Essx* 5B 54
Cold Overton. *Leics* 4F 75
Coldrain. *Per* 3C 136
Coldred. *Kent* 1G 29
Coldridge. *Devn* 2G 11
Cold Row. *Lanc* 5C 96
Coldstream. *Bord* 5E 131
Coldwaltham. *W Sus* 4B 26
Coldwell. *Here* 2H 47
Coldwells. *Abers* 5H 161
Coldwells Croft. *Abers* 1C 152
Cole. *Som* 3B 22
Colebatch. *Shrp* 2F 59
Colebrook. *Devn* 2D 12
Colebrooke. *Devn* 2A 12
Coleburn. *Mor* 3G 159
Coleby. *Linc* 4G 87
Coleby. *N Lin* 3B 94
Cole End. *Warw* 2G 61
Coleford. *Devn* 2A 12
Coleford. *Glos* 4A 48
Coleford. *Som* 2B 22
Colegate End. *Norf* 2D 66
Cole Green. *Herts* 4C 52
Cole Henley. *Hants* 1C 24
Colehill. *Dors* 2F 15
Coleman Green. *Herts* 4B 52
Coleman's Hatch. *E Sus* 2F 27
Colemere. *Shrp* 2G 71
Colemore. *Hants* 3F 25
Colemore Green. *Shrp* 1B 60
Coleorton. *Leics* 4B 74
Colerne. *Wilts* 4D 34
Colesbourne. *Glos* 4E 49
Colesden. *Bed* 5A 64
Coles Green. *Worc* 5B 60
Coleshill. *Buck* 1A 38
Coleshill. *Oxon* 2H 35
Coleshill. *Warw* 2G 61
Colestocks. *Devn* 2D 12
Colethrop. *Glos* 4D 48
Coley. *Bath* 1A 22
Colgate. *W Sus* 2D 26
Colinsburgh. *Fife* 3G 137
Colinton. *Edin* 3F 129
Colintraive. *Arg* 2B 126
Colkirk. *Norf* 3B 78
Collace. *Per* 5B 144
Collaton. *Devn* 5D 8
Collaton St Mary. *Torb* 2E 9
College of Roseisle. *Mor* 2F 159
Collessie. *Fife* 2E 137
Collier Row. *G Lon* 1F 39
Colliers End. *Herts* 3D 52
Collier Street. *Kent* 1B 28
Colliery Row. *Tyne* 5G 115
Collieston. *Abers* 1H 153
Collin. *Dum* 2B 112
Collingbourne Ducis. *Wilts* 1H 23
Collingbourne Kingston. *Wilts* 1H 23
Collingham. *Notts* 4F 87
Collingham. *W Yor* 5F 99
Collingtree. *Nptn* 5E 63
Collins Green. *Warr* 1H 83
Collins Green. *Worc* 5B 60
Colliston. *Ang* 4F 145
Colliton. *Devn* 2D 12
Collydean. *Fife* 3E 137
Collyweston. *Nptn* 5G 75
Colmonell. *S Ayr* 1G 109
Colmworth. *Bed* 5A 64
Colnbrook. *Slo* 3B 38
Colne. *Cambs* 3C 64
Colne. *Lanc* 5A 98
Colne Engaine. *Essx* 2B 54
Colney. *Norf* 5D 78
Colney Heath. *Herts* 5C 52
Colney Street. *Herts* 5B 52
Coln Rogers. *Glos* 5F 49
Coln St Aldwyns. *Glos* 5G 49
Coln St Dennis. *Glos* 4F 49
Colpitts Grange. *Nmbd* 4C 114
Colpy. *Abers* 5D 160
Colscott. *Devn* 1D 10
Colsterdale. *N Yor* 1D 98
Colsterworth. *Linc* 3G 75
Colston Bassett. *Notts* 2D 74
Colstoun House. *E Lot* 2B 130
Coltfield. *Mor* 2F 159
Colthouse. *Cumb* 5E 103
Coltishall. *Norf* 4E 79
Coltness. *N Lan* 4A 128
Colton. *Cumb* 1C 96
Colton. *Norf* 5D 78
Colton. *N Yor* 5H 99
Colton. *Staf* 3E 73
Colton. *W Yor* 1D 92
Colt's Hill. *Kent* 1H 27
Col Uarach. *W Isl* 4G 171
Colvend. *Dum* 4F 111
Colwall. *Here* 1C 48
Colwall Green. *Here* 1C 48
Colwell. *Nmbd* 2C 114
Colwich. *Staf* 3E 73
Colwick. *Notts* 1D 74
Colwinston. *V Glam* 4C 32
Colworth. *W Sus* 5A 26
Colwyn Bay. *Cnwy* 3A 82
Colyford. *Devn* 3F 13
Colyton. *Devn* 3F 13
Combe. *Devn* 2D 8
Combe. *Here* 4F 59
Combe. *Oxon* 4C 50
Combe. *W Ber* 5B 36
Combe Almer. *Dors* 3E 15
Combebow. *Devn* 4E 11
Combe Down. *Bath* 5C 34
Combe Fishacre. *Devn* 2E 9
Combe Florey. *Som* 3E 21
Combe Hay. *Bath* 1C 22
Combeinteignhead. *Devn* 5C 12
Combe Martin. *Devn* 2F 19
Combe Moor. *Here* 4F 59
Combe Raleigh. *Devn* 2E 13
Comberbach. *Ches W* 3A 84
Comberford. *Staf* 5F 73
Comberton. *Cambs* 5C 64
Comberton. *Here* 4G 59
Combe St Nicholas. *Som* 1G 13
Combpyne. *Devn* 3F 13
Combridge. *Staf* 2E 73
Combrook. *Warw* 5H 61
Combs. *Derbs* 3E 85
Combs. *Suff* 5C 66
Combs Ford. *Suff* 5C 66
Combwich. *Som* 2F 21
Comers. *Abers* 3D 152
Comhampton. *Worc* 4C 60
Comins Coch. *Cdgn* 2F 57
Comley. *Shrp* 1G 59
Commercial End. *Cambs* 4E 65
Commins. *Powy* 3D 70
Commins Coch. *Powy* 5H 69
Commondale. *N Yor* 3D 106
Common End. *Cumb* 2B 102
Common Hill. *Here* 2A 48
Common Moor. *Corn* 2G 7
Commonside. *Ches W* 3H 83
Common Side. *Derbs* 3H 85
(nr. Chesterfield)
Commonside. *Derbs* 1G 73
(nr. Derby)
Common, The. *Wilts* 3H 23
(nr. Salisbury)
Common, The. *Wilts* 3F 35
(nr. Swindon)
Compstall. *G Man* 1D 84
Compton. *Devn* 2E 9
Compton. *Hants* 4C 24
Compton. *Staf* 2C 60
Compton. *Surr* 1A 26
Compton. *W Ber* 3D 36
Compton. *W Sus* 1F 17
Compton. *Wilts* 1G 23
Compton Abbas. *Dors* 1D 14
Compton Abdale. *Glos* 4F 49
Compton Bassett. *Wilts* 4F 35
Compton Beauchamp. *Oxon* 3A 36
Compton Bishop. *Som* 1G 21
Compton Chamberlayne. *Wilts* 4F 23
Compton Dando. *Bath* 5B 34
Compton Dundon. *Som* 3H 21
Compton Greenfield. *S Glo* 3A 34
Compton Martin. *Bath* 1A 22
Compton Pauncefoot. *Som* 4B 22
Compton Valence. *Dors* 3A 14
Comrie. *Fife* 1D 128
Comrie. *Per* 1G 135
Conaglen. *High* 2E 141
Conchra. *Arg* 1B 126
Conchra. *High* 1A 148
Conder Green. *Lanc* 4D 96
Conderton. *Worc* 2E 49
Condicote. *Glos* 3G 49
Condorrat. *N Lan* 2A 128
Condover. *Shrp* 5G 71
Coneyhurst Common. *W Sus* 3C 26
Coneysthorpe. *N Yor* 2B 100
Coneythorpe. *N Yor* 4F 99
Coney Weston. *Suff* 3B 66
Conford. *Hants* 3G 25
Congdon's Shop. *Corn* 5C 10
Congerstone. *Leics* 5A 74
Congham. *Norf* 3G 77
Congleton. *Ches E* 4C 84
Congl-y-wal. *Gwyn* 1G 69
Congresbury. *N Som* 5H 33
Congreve. *Staf* 4D 72
Conham. *S Glo* 4B 34
Conicavel. *Mor* 3D 159
Coningsby. *Linc* 5B 88
Conington. *Cambs* 4C 64
(nr. Fenstanton)
Conington. *Cambs* 2A 64
(nr. Sawtry)
Conisbrough. *S Yor* 1C 86
Conisby. *Arg* 3A 124
Conisholme. *Linc* 1D 88
Coniston. *Cumb* 5E 102
Coniston. *E Yor* 1E 95
Coniston Cold. *N Yor* 4B 98
Conistone. *N Yor* 3B 98
Connah's Quay. *Flin* 4E 83
Connel. *Arg* 5D 140
Connel Park. *E Ayr* 3F 117
Connista. *High* 1D 154
Connor Downs. *Corn* 3C 4
Conock. *Wilts* 1F 23
Conon Bridge. *High* 3H 157
Cononley. *N Yor* 5B 98
Cononsyth. *Ang* 4E 145
Conordan. *High* 5E 155
Consall. *Staf* 1D 73
Consett. *Dur* 4E 115
Constable Burton. *N Yor* 5E 105
Constantine. *Corn* 4E 5
Constantine Bay. *Corn* 1C 6
Contin. *High* 3G 157
Contullich. *High* 1A 158
Conwy. *Cnwy* 3G 81
Conyer. *Kent* 4D 40
Conyer's Green. *Suff* 4A 66
Cooden. *E Sus* 5B 28
Cooil. *IOM* 4C 108
Cookbury. *Devn* 2E 11
Cookbury Wick. *Devn* 2D 11
Cookham. *Wind* 3G 37
Cookham Dean. *Wind* 3G 37
Cookham Rise. *Wind* 3G 37
Cookhill. *Worc* 5E 61
Cookley. *Suff* 3F 67
Cookley. *Worc* 2C 60
Cookley Green. *Oxon* 2E 37
Cookney. *Abers* 4F 153
Cooksbridge. *E Sus* 4F 27
Cooksey Green. *Worc* 4D 60
Cookshill. *Staf* 1D 72
Cooksmill Green. *Essx* 5G 53
Coolham. *W Sus* 3C 26
Cooling. *Medw* 3B 40
Cooling Street. *Medw* 3B 40
Coombe. *Corn* 1C 10
(nr. Bude)
Coombe. *Corn* 3D 6
(nr. St Austell)
Coombe. *Corn* 4C 6
(nr. Truro)

Coombe. *Devn* 3E **12** (nr. Sidmouth)
Coombe. *Devn* 5C **12** (nr. Teignmouth)
Coombe. *Glos* 2C **34**
Coombe. *Hants* 4E **25**
Coombe. *Wilts* 1G **23**
Coombe Bissett. *Wilts* 4G **23**
Coombe Hill. *Glos* 3D **49**
Coombe Keynes. *Dors* 4D **14**
Coombes. *W Sus* 5C **26**
Coopersale Common. *Essx* 5E **53**
Coopersale Street. *Essx* 5E **53**
Cooper's Corner. *Kent* 1F **27**
Cooper Street. *Kent* 5H **41**
Cootham. *W Sus* 4B **26**
Copalder Corner. *Cambs* 1C **64**
Copdock. *Suff* 1E **54**
Copford. *Essx* 3C **54**
Copford Green. *Essx* 3C **54**
Copgrove. *N Yor* 3F **99**
Copister. *Shet* 4F **173**
Cople. *Bed* 1B **52**
Copley. *Dur* 2D **105**
Coplow Dale. *Derbs* 3F **85**
Copmanthorpe. *York* 5H **99**
Copp. *Lanc* 1C **90**
Coppathorne. *Corn* 2C **10**
Coppenhall. *Ches E* 5B **84**
Coppenhall. *Staf* 4D **72**
Coppenhall Moss. *Ches E* 5B **84**
Copperhouse. *Corn* 3C **4**
Coppicegate. *Shrp* 2B **60**
Coppingford. *Cambs* 2A **64**
Copplestone. *Devn* 2A **12**
Coppull. *Lanc* 3D **90**
Coppull Moor. *Lanc* 3D **90**
Copsale. *W Sus* 3C **26**
Copster Green. *Lanc* 1E **91**
Copston Magna. *Warw* 2B **62**
Copt Green. *Warw* 4F **61**
Copthall Green. *Essx* 5E **53**
Copt Heath. *W Mid* 3F **61**
Copt Hewick. *N Yor* 2F **99**
Copthill. *Dur* 5B **114**
Copthorne. *W Sus* 2E **27**
Coptiviney. *Shrp* 2G **71**
Copy's Green. *Norf* 2B **78**
Copythorne. *Hants* 1B **16**
Corbridge. *Nmbd* 3C **114**
Corby. *Nptn* 2F **63**
Corby Glen. *Linc* 3H **75**
Cordon. *N Ayr* 2E **123**
Coreley. *Shrp* 3A **60**
Corfe. *Som* 1F **13**
Corfe Castle. *Dors* 4E **15**
Corfe Mullen. *Dors* 3E **15**
Corfton. *Shrp* 2G **59**
Corgarff. *Abers* 3G **151**
Corhampton. *Hants* 4E **24**
Corlae. *Dum* 5F **117**
Corlannau. *Neat* 2A **32**
Corley. *Warw* 2H **61**
Corley Ash. *Warw* 2G **61**
Corley Moor. *Warw* 2G **61**
Cormiston. *S Lan* 1C **118**
Cornaa. *IOM* 3D **108**
Cornaigbeg. *Arg* 4A **138**
Cornaigmore. *Arg* 2D **138** (on Coll)
Cornaigmore. *Arg* 4A **138** (on Tiree)
Corner Row. *Lanc* 1C **90**
Corney. *Cumb* 5C **102**
Cornforth. *Dur* 1A **106**
Cornhill. *Abers* 3C **160**
Cornhill. *High* 4C **164**
Cornhill-on-Tweed. *Nmbd* 1C **120**
Cornholme. *W Yor* 2H **91**
Cornish Hall End. *Essx* 2G **53**
Cornriggs. *Dur* 5B **114**
Cornsay. *Dur* 5E **115**
Cornsay Colliery. *Dur* 5E **115**
Corntown. *High* 3H **157**
Corntown. *V Glam* 4C **32**
Cornwell. *Oxon* 3A **50**
Cornwood. *Devn* 3C **8**
Cornworthy. *Devn* 3E **9**
Corpach. *High* 1E **141**
Corpusty. *Norf* 3D **78**
Corra. *Dum* 3F **111**
Corran. *High* 2E **141** (nr. Arnisdale)
Corran. *High* 3A **148** (nr. Fort William)
Corrany. *IOM* 3D **108**
Corribeg. *High* 1D **141**
Corrie. *N Ayr* 5B **126**
Corrie Common. *Dum* 1D **112**
Corriecravie. *N Ayr* 3D **122**
Corriekinloch. *High* 1A **164**
Corriemoillie. *High* 2F **157**
Corrievarkie Lodge. *Per* 1C **142**
Corrievorrie. *High* 1B **150**
Corrimony. *High* 5F **157**
Corringham. *Linc* 1F **87**
Corringham. *Thur* 2B **40**
Corris. *Gwyn* 5G **69**
Corris Uchaf. *Gwyn* 5G **69**
Corrour Shooting Lodge. *High* 2B **142**
Corry. *High* 1E **147**
Corrybrough. *High* 1C **150**
Corrygills. *N Ayr* 2E **123**
Corry of Ardnagrask. *High* 4H **157**
Corsback. *High* 1E **169** (nr. Dunnet)
Corsback. *High* 3E **169** (nr. Halkirk)
Corscombe. *Dors* 2A **14**
Corse. *Abers* 4D **160**
Corse. *Glos* 3C **48**
Corsehill. *Abers* 3G **161**
Corse Lawn. *Worc* 2D **48**
Corse of Kinnoir. *Abers* 4C **160**
Corsham. *Wilts* 4D **34**
Corsley. *Wilts* 2D **22**
Corsley Heath. *Wilts* 2D **22**
Corsock. *Dum* 2E **111**
Corston. *Bath* 5B **34**
Corston. *Wilts* 3E **35**
Corstorphine. *Edin* 2F **129**
Cortachy. *Ang* 3C **144**
Corton. *Suff* 1H **67**
Corton. *Wilts* 2E **23**
Corton Denham. *Som* 4B **22**
Corwar House. *S Ayr* 1H **109**
Corwen. *Den* 1C **70**
Coryates. *Dors* 4B **14**
Coryton. *Devn* 4E **11**
Coryton. *Thur* 2B **40**
Cosby. *Leics* 1C **62**
Coscote. *Oxon* 3D **36**
Coseley. *W Mid* 1D **60**
Cosgrove. *Nptn* 1F **51**
Cosham. *Port* 2E **17**
Cosheston. *Pemb* 4E **43**
Coskills. *N Lin* 3D **94**
Cosmeston. *V Glam* 5E **33**
Cossall. *Notts* 1B **74**
Cossington. *Leics* 4D **74**
Cossington. *Som* 2G **21**
Costa. *Orkn* 5C **172**
Costessey. *Norf* 4D **78**
Costock. *Notts* 3C **74**
Coston. *Leics* 3F **75**
Coston. *Norf* 5C **78**
Cote. *Oxon* 5B **50**
Cotebrook. *Ches W* 4H **83**
Cotehill. *Cumb* 4F **113**
Cotes. *Cumb* 1D **97**
Cotes. *Leics* 3C **74**
Cotes. *Staf* 2C **72**
Cotesbach. *Leics* 2C **62**
Cotes Heath. *Staf* 2C **72**
Cotford St Luke. *Som* 4E **21**
Cotgrave. *Notts* 2D **74**
Cothall. *Abers* 2F **153**
Cotham. *Notts* 1E **75**
Cothelstone. *Som* 3E **21**
Cotheridge. *Worc* 5B **60**
Cotherstone. *Dur* 3D **104**
Cothill. *Oxon* 2C **36**
Cotland. *Mon* 5A **48**
Cotleigh. *Devn* 2F **13**
Cotmanhay. *Derbs* 1B **74**
Coton. *Cambs* 5D **64**
Coton. *Nptn* 3D **62**
Coton. *Staf* 3C **72** (nr. Gnosall)
Coton. *Staf* 2D **73** (nr. Stone)
Coton. *Staf* 5F **73** (nr. Tamworth)
Coton Clanford. *Staf* 3C **72**
Coton Hayes. *Staf* 2D **73**
Coton Hill. *Shrp* 4G **71**
Coton in the Clay. *Staf* 3F **73**
Coton in the Elms. *Derbs* 4G **73**
Cotonwood. *Shrp* 2H **71**
Cotonwood. *Staf* 3C **72**
Cott. *Devn* 2D **9**
Cottam. *E Yor* 3D **101**
Cottam. *Lanc* 1D **90**
Cottam. *Notts* 3F **87**
Cottartown. *High* 5E **159**
Cottarville. *Nptn* 4E **63**
Cottenham. *Cambs* 4D **64**
Cotterdale. *N Yor* 5B **104**
Cottered. *Herts* 3D **52**
Cotterstock. *Nptn* 1H **63**
Cottesbrooke. *Nptn* 3E **62**
Cottesmore. *Rut* 4G **75**
Cotteylands. *Devn* 1C **12**
Cottingham. *E Yor* 1D **94**
Cottingham. *Nptn* 1F **63**
Cottingley. *W Yor* 1B **92**
Cottisford. *Oxon* 2D **50**
Cotton. *Staf* 1E **73**
Cotton. *Suff* 4C **66**
Cotton End. *Bed* 1A **52**
Cottown. *Abers* 4F **161**
Cotts. *Devn* 2A **8**
Cotwalton. *Staf* 2D **72**
Couch's Mill. *Corn* 3F **7**
Coughton. *Here* 3A **48**
Coughton. *Warw* 4E **61**
Coulags. *High* 4B **156**
Coulby Newham. *Midd* 3C **106**
Coulderton. *Cumb* 4A **102**
Coulin Lodge. *High* 3C **156**
Coull. *Abers* 3C **152**
Coulport. *Arg* 1D **126**
Coulsdon. *Surr* 5D **39**
Coulter. *S Lan* 1C **118**
Coultershaw Bridge. *W Sus* 4A **26**
Coultings. *Som* 2F **21**
Coulton. *N Yor* 2A **100**
Cound. *Shrp* 5H **71**
Coundon. *Dur* 2F **105**
Coundon Grange. *Dur* 2F **105**
Countersett. *N Yor* 1B **98**
Countess. *Wilts* 2G **23**
Countess Cross. *Essx* 2B **54**
Countesthorpe. *Leics* 1C **62**
Countisbury. *Devn* 2H **19**
Coupar Angus. *Per* 4B **144**
Coupe Green. *Lanc* 2D **90**
Coupland. *Cumb* 3A **104**
Coupland. *Nmbd* 1D **120**
Cour. *Arg* 5G **125**
Courance. *Dum* 5C **118**
Court-at-Street. *Kent* 2E **29**
Courteachan. *High* 4E **147**
Courteenhall. *Nptn* 5E **63**
Court Henry. *Carm* 3F **45**
Courtsend. *Essx* 1E **41**
Courtway. *Som* 3F **21**
Cousland. *Midl* 3G **129**
Cousley Wood. *E Sus* 2A **28**
Coustonn. *Arg* 2B **126**
Cove. *Arg* 1D **126**
Cove. *Devn* 1C **12**
Cove. *Hants* 1G **25**
Cove. *High* 4C **162**
Cove. *Bord* 2D **130**
Cove Bay. *Aber* 3G **153**
Covehithe. *Suff* 2H **67**
Coven. *Staf* 5D **72**
Coveney. *Cambs* 2D **65**
Covenham St Bartholomew. *Linc* 1C **88**
Covenham St Mary. *Linc* 1C **88**
Coven Heath. *Staf* 5D **72**
Coventry. *W Mid* 3H **61**
Coverack. *Corn* 5E **5**
Coverham. *N Yor* 1D **98**
Covesea. *Mor* 1F **159**
Covingham. *Swin* 3G **35**
Covington. *Cambs* 3H **63**
Covington. *S Lan* 1B **118**
Cowan Bridge. *Lanc* 2F **97**
Cowan Head. *Cumb* 5F **103**
Cowbar. *Red C* 3E **107**
Cowbeech. *E Sus* 4H **27**
Cowbit. *Linc* 4B **76**
Cowbridge. *V Glam* 4C **32**
Cowden. *Kent* 1F **27**
Cowdenbeath. *Fife* 4D **136**
Cowdenburn. *Bord* 4F **129**
Cowdenend. *Fife* 4D **136**
Cowers Lane. *Derbs* 1H **73**
Cowes. *IOW* 3C **16**
Cowesby. *N Yor* 1G **99**
Cowfold. *W Sus* 3D **26**
Cowfords. *Mor* 3H **159**
Cowgill. *Cumb* 1G **97**
Cowie. *Abers* 5F **153**
Cowie. *Stir* 1B **128**
Cowlam. *E Yor* 3D **100**
Cowley. *Devn* 3C **12**
Cowley. *Glos* 4E **49**
Cowley. *G Lon* 2B **38**
Cowley. *Oxon* 5D **50**
Cowley. *Staf* 4C **72**
Cowleymoor. *Devn* 1C **12**
Cowling. *Lanc* 3D **90**
Cowling. *N Yor* 1E **99** (nr. Bedale)
Cowling. *N Yor* 5B **98** (nr. Glusburn)
Cowlinge. *Suff* 5G **65**
Cowmes. *W Yor* 3B **92**
Cowpe. *Lanc* 2G **91**
Cowpen. *Nmbd* 1F **115**
Cowpen Bewley. *Stoc T* 2B **106**
Cowplain. *Hants* 1E **17**
Cowshill. *Dur* 5B **114**
Cowslip Green. *N Som* 5H **33**
Cowstrandburn. *Fife* 4C **136**
Cowthorpe. *N Yor* 4G **99**
Coxall. *Here* 3F **59**
Coxbank. *Ches E* 1A **72**
Coxbench. *Derbs* 1A **74**
Cox Common. *Suff* 2G **67**
Coxford. *Norf* 3H **77**
Coxgreen. *Staf* 2C **60**
Cox Green. *Surr* 2B **26**
Cox Green. *Tyne* 4G **115**
Coxheath. *Kent* 5B **40**
Coxhoe. *Dur* 1A **106**
Coxley. *Som* 2A **22**
Coxwold. *N Yor* 2H **99**
Coychurch. *V Glam* 3C **32**
Coylton. *S Ayr* 3D **116**
Coylumbridge. *High* 2D **150**
Coynach. *Abers* 3B **152**
Coynachie. *Abers* 5B **160**
Coytrahen. *B'end* 3B **32**
Crabbs Cross. *Worc* 4E **61**
Crabgate. *Norf* 3C **78**
Crab Orchard. *Dors* 2F **15**
Crabtree. *W Sus* 3D **26**
Crabtree Green. *Wrex* 1F **71**
Crackaig. *High* 2G **165**
Crackenthorpe. *Cumb* 2H **103**
Crackington Haven. *Corn* 3B **10**
Crackley. *Staf* 5C **84**
Crackley. *Warw* 3G **61**
Crackleybank. *Shrp* 4B **72**
Crackpot. *N Yor* 5C **104**
Cracoe. *N Yor* 3B **98**
Craddock. *Devn* 1D **12**
Cradhlastadh. *W Isl* 4C **171**
Cradley. *Here* 1C **48**
Cradley. *W Mid* 2D **60**
Cradoc. *Powy* 2D **46**
Crafthole. *Corn* 3H **7**
Crafton. *Buck* 4G **51**
Cragabus. *Arg* 5B **124**
Crag Foot. *Lanc* 2D **97**
Craggan. *High* 1E **151**
Cragganmore. *Mor* 5F **159**
Cragganvallie. *High* 5H **157**
Craggie. *High* 1F **165**
Craggiemore. *High* 5B **158**
Cragg Vale. *W Yor* 2A **92**
Craghead. *Dur* 4F **115**
Crai. *Powy* 3B **46**
Craibstone. *Aber* 2F **153**
Craichie. *Ang* 4E **145**
Craig. *Arg* 5E **141**
Craig. *Dum* 2D **111**
Craig. *High* 4C **156** (nr. Achnashellach)
Craig. *High* 2G **155** (nr. Lower Diabaig)
Craig. *High* 5H **155** (nr. Stromeferry)
Craiganour Lodge. *Per* 3D **142**
Craigbrack. *Arg* 4A **134**
Craig-cefn-parc. *Swan* 5G **45**
Craigdallie. *Per* 1E **137**
Craigdam. *Abers* 5F **161**
Craigdarroch. *E Ayr* 4F **117**
Craigdarroch. *High* 3G **157**
Craigdhu. *High* 4G **157**
Craigearn. *Abers* 2E **152**
Craigellachie. *Mor* 4G **159**
Craigend. *Per* 1D **136**
Craigendoran. *Arg* 1E **126**
Craigends. *Ren* 3F **127**
Craigenputtock. *Dum* 1E **111**
Craigens. *E Ayr* 3E **117**
Craighall. *Edin* 2E **129**
Craighead. *Fife* 2H **137**
Craighouse. *Arg* 3D **124**
Craigie. *Abers* 2G **153**
Craigie. *D'dee* 5D **144**
Craigie. *Per* 4A **144** (nr. Blairgowrie)
Craigie. *Per* 1D **136** (nr. Perth)
Craigie. *S Ayr* 1D **116**
Craigielaw. *E Lot* 2A **130**
Craiglemine. *Dum* 5B **110**
Craig-llwyn. *Shrp* 3E **71**
Craiglockhart. *Edin* 2F **129**
Craig Lodge. *Arg* 2B **126**
Craigmalloch. *E Ayr* 5D **117**
Craigmaud. *Abers* 3F **161**
Craigmill. *Stir* 4H **135**
Craigmillar. *Edin* 2F **129**
Craigmore. *Arg* 3C **126**
Craigmuie. *Dum* 1E **111**
Craignair. *Dum* 3F **111**
Craignant. *Shrp* 2E **71**
Craigneuk. *N Lan* 3A **128** (nr. Airdrie)
Craigneuk. *N Lan* 4A **128** (nr. Motherwell)
Craignure. *Arg* 5B **140**
Craigo. *Abers* 2F **145**
Craigrory. *High* 4A **158**
Craigrothie. *Fife* 2F **137**
Craigs. *Dum* 2D **112**
Craigshill. *W Lot* 3D **128**
Craigs, The. *High* 4B **164**
Craigton. *Aber* 3F **153**

Craigton. *Abers* 3E 152
Craigton. *Ang* 5E 145
(nr. Carnoustie)
Craigton. *Ang* 3C 144
(nr. Kirriemuir)
Craigton. *High* 4A 158
Craigtown. *High* 3A 168
Craig-y-Duke. *Neat* 5H 45
Craigyloch. *Ang* 3B 144
Craig-y-nos. *Powy* 4B 46
Craik. *Bord* 4F 119
Crail. *Fife* 3H 137
Crailing. *Bord* 2A 120
Crailinghall. *Bord* 2A 120
Crakehill. *N Yor* 2G 99
Crakemarsh. *Staf* 2E 73
Crambe. *N Yor* 3B 100
Crambeck. *N Yor* 3B 100
Cramlington. *Nmbd* 2F 115
Cramond. *Edin* 2E 129
Cramond Bridge. *Edin* 2E 129
Cranage. *Ches E* 4B 84
Cranberry. *Staf* 2C 72
Cranborne. *Dors* 1F 15
Cranbourne. *Brac* 3A 38
Cranbrook. *Devn* 3D 12
Cranbrook. *Kent* 2B 28
Cranbrook Common. *Kent* 2B 28
Crane Moor. *S Yor* 4D 92
Crane's Corner. *Norf* 4B 78
Cranfield. *C Beds* 1H 51
Cranford. *G Lon* 3B 38
Cranford St Andrew. *Nptn* 3G 63
Cranford St John. *Nptn* 3G 63
Cranham. *Glos* 4D 49
Cranham. *G Lon* 2G 39
Crank. *Mers* 1H 83
Cranleigh. *Surr* 2B 26
Cranley. *Suff* 3D 66
Cranloch. *Mor* 3G 159
Cranmer Green. *Suff* 3C 66
Cranmore. *IOW* 3B 16
Cranmore. *Linc* 5A 76
Crannich. *Arg* 4G 139
Crannoch. *Mor* 3B 160
Cranoe. *Leics* 1E 63
Cransford. *Suff* 4F 67
Cranshaws. *Bord* 3C 130
Cranstal. *IOM* 1D 108
Crantock. *Corn* 2B 6
Cranwell. *Linc* 5H 87
Cranwich. *Norf* 1G 65
Cranworth. *Norf* 5B 78
Craobh Haven. *Arg* 3E 133
Craobhnaclag. *High* 4G 157
Crapstone. *Devn* 2B 8
Crarae. *Arg* 4G 133
Crask. *High* 2H 167
Crask Inn. *High* 1C 164
Crask of Aigas. *High* 4G 157
Craster. *Nmbd* 3G 121
Cratfield. *Suff* 3F 67
Crathes. *Abers* 4E 153
Crathie. *Abers* 4G 151
Crathie. *High* 4H 149
Crathorne. *N Yor* 4B 106
Craven Arms. *Shrp* 2G 59
Crawcrook. *Tyne* 3E 115
Crawford. *Lanc* 4D 90
Crawford. *S Lan* 2B 118
Crawforddyke. *S Lan* 4B 128
Crawfordjohn. *S Lan* 2A 118
Crawick. *Dum* 3G 117
Crawley. *Devn* 2F 13
Crawley. *Hants* 3C 24
Crawley. *Oxon* 4B 50
Crawley. *W Sus* 2D 26
Crawley Down. *W Sus* 2E 27
Crawley Side. *Dur* 5C 114
Crawshawbooth. *Lanc* 2G 91
Crawton. *Abers* 5F 153
Cray. *N Yor* 2B 98
Cray. *Per* 2A 144
Crayford. *G Lon* 3G 39
Crayke. *N Yor* 2H 99
Craymere Beck. *Norf* 2C 78
Crays Hill. *Essx* 1B 40
Cray's Pond. *Oxon* 3E 37
Crazies Hill. *Wok* 3F 37
Creacombe. *Devn* 1B 12
Creagan. *Arg* 4D 141
Creag Aoil. *High* 1F 141
Creag Ghoraidh. *W Isl* 4D 170
Creaguaineach Lodge. *High* 2H 141
Creamore Bank. *Shrp* 2H 71
Creaton. *Nptn* 3E 62
Creca. *Dum* 2D 112
Credenhill. *Here* 1H 47
Crediton. *Devn* 2B 12
Creebridge. *Dum* 3B 110
Creech. *Dors* 4E 15
Creech Heathfield. *Som* 4F 21
Creech St Michael. *Som* 4F 21
Creed. *Corn* 4D 6
Creekmoor. *Pool* 3E 15
Creekmouth. *G Lon* 2F 39
Creeting St Mary. *Suff* 5C 66
Creeting St Peter. *Suff* 5C 66
Creeton. *Linc* 3H 75
Creetown. *Dum* 4B 110
Creggans. *Arg* 3H 133
Cregneash. *IOM* 5A 108
Cregrina. *Powy* 5D 58
Creich. *Arg* 2B 132
Creich. *Fife* 1F 137
Creighton. *Staf* 2E 73
Creigiau. *Card* 3D 32
Cremyll. *Corn* 3A 8
Crendell. *Dors* 1F 15
Crepkill. *High* 4D 154
Cressage. *Shrp* 5H 71
Cressbrook. *Derbs* 3F 85
Cresselly. *Pemb* 4E 43
Cressing. *Essx* 3A 54
Cresswell. *Nmbd* 5G 121
Cresswell. *Staf* 2D 73
Cresswell Quay. *Pemb* 4E 43
Creswell. *Derbs* 3C 86
Creswell Green. *Staf* 4E 73
Cretingham. *Suff* 4E 67
Crewe. *Ches E* 5B 84
Crewe-by-Farndon. *Ches W* 5G 83
Crewgreen. *Powy* 4F 71
Crewkerne. *Som* 2H 13
Crews Hill. *G Lon* 5D 52
Crewton. *Derb* 2A 74
Crianlarich. *Stir* 1C 134
Cribbs Causeway. *S Glo* 3A 34
Cribyn. *Cdgn* 5E 57
Criccieth. *Gwyn* 2D 69
Crich. *Derbs* 5A 86
Crichton. *Midl* 3G 129
Crick. *Mon* 2H 33
Crick. *Nptn* 3C 62
Crickadarn. *Powy* 1D 46
Cricket Hill. *Hants* 5G 37
Cricket Malherbie. *Som* 1G 13
Cricket St Thomas. *Som* 2G 13
Crickham. *Som* 2H 21
Crickheath. *Shrp* 3E 71
Crickhowell. *Powy* 4F 47
Cricklade. *Wilts* 2F 35
Cricklewood. *G Lon* 2D 38
Cridling Stubbs. *N Yor* 2F 93
Crieff. *Per* 1A 136
Criftins. *Shrp* 2F 71
Criggion. *Powy* 4E 71
Crigglestone. *W Yor* 3D 92
Crimchard. *Som* 2G 13
Crimdon Park. *Dur* 1B 106
Crimond. *Abers* 3H 161
Crimonmogate. *Abers* 3H 161
Crimplesham. *Norf* 5F 77
Crimscote. *Warw* 1H 49
Crinan. *Arg* 4E 133
Cringleford. *Norf* 5D 78
Crinow. *Pemb* 3F 43
Cripplesease. *Corn* 3C 4
Cripplestyle. *Dors* 1F 15
Cripp's Corner. *E Sus* 3B 28
Croanford. *Corn* 5A 10
Crockenhill. *Kent* 4G 39
Crocker End. *Oxon* 3F 37
Crockerhill. *Hants* 2D 16
Crockernwell. *Devn* 3A 12
Crocker's Ash. *Here* 4A 48
Crockerton. *Wilts* 2D 22
Crocketford. *Dum* 2F 111
Crockey Hill. *York* 5A 100
Crockham Hill. *Kent* 5F 39
Crockhurst Street. *Kent* 1H 27
Crockleford Heath. *Essx* 3D 54
Croeserw. *Neat* 2B 32
Croes-Goch. *Pemb* 1C 42
Croes Hywel. *Mon* 4G 47
Croes-lan. *Cdgn* 1D 45
Croesor. *Gwyn* 1F 69
Croesoswallt. *Shrp* 3E 71
Croesyceiliog. *Carm* 4E 45
Croesyceiliog. *Torf* 2F 33
Croes-y-mwyalch. *Torf* 2G 33
Croesywaun. *Gwyn* 5E 81
Croford. *Som* 4E 20
Croft. *Leics* 1C 62
Croft. *Linc* 4E 89
Croft. *Warr* 1A 84
Croftamie. *Stir* 1F 127
Croftfoot. *Glas* 3G 127
Croftmill. *Per* 5F 143
Crofton. *Cumb* 4E 112
Crofton. *W Yor* 3D 93
Crofton. *Wilts* 5A 36
Croft-on-Tees. *N Yor* 4F 105
Crofts. *Dum* 2E 111
Crofts of Benachielt. *High* 5D 169
Crofts of Dipple. *Mor* 3H 159
Crofty. *Swan* 3E 31
Croggan. *Arg* 1E 132
Croglin. *Cumb* 5G 113
Croich. *High* 4B 164
Croick. *High* 3A 168
Croig. *Arg* 3E 139
Cromarty. *High* 2B 158
Crombie. *Fife* 1D 128
Cromdale. *High* 1E 151
Cromer. *Herts* 3C 52
Cromer. *Norf* 1E 79
Cromford. *Derbs* 5G 85
Cromhall. *S Glo* 2B 34
Cromhall Common. *S Glo* 3B 34
Cromor. *W Isl* 5G 171
Cromra. *High* 5H 149
Cromwell. *Notts* 4E 87
Cronberry. *E Ayr* 2F 117
Crondall. *Hants* 2F 25
Cronk, The. *IOM* 2C 108
Cronk-y-Voddy. *IOM* 3C 108
Cronton. *Mers* 2G 83
Crook. *Cumb* 5F 103
Crook. *Dur* 1E 105
Crookdake. *Cumb* 5C 112
Crooke. *G Man* 4D 90
Crookedholm. *E Ayr* 1D 116
Crooked Soley. *Wilts* 4B 36
Crookes. *S Yor* 2H 85
Crookgate Bank. *Dur* 4E 115
Crookhall. *Dur* 4E 115
Crookham. *Nmbd* 1D 120
Crookham. *W Ber* 5D 36
Crookham Village. *Hants* 1F 25
Crooklands. *Cumb* 1E 97
Crook of Devon. *Per* 3C 136
Crookston. *Ren* 3G 127
Cropredy. *Oxon* 1C 50
Cropston. *Leics* 4C 74
Cropthorne. *Worc* 1E 49
Cropton. *N Yor* 1B 100
Cropwell Bishop. *Notts* 2D 74
Cropwell Butler. *Notts* 2D 74
Cros. *W Isl* 1H 171
Crosbie. *N Ayr* 5D 126
Crosbost. *W Isl* 5F 171
Crosby. *Cumb* 1B 102
Crosby. *IOM* 4C 108
Crosby. *Mers* 1F 83
Crosby. *N Lin* 3B 94
Crosby Court. *N Yor* 5A 106
Crosby Garrett. *Cumb* 4A 104
Crosby Ravensworth. *Cumb* 3H 103
Crosby Villa. *Cumb* 1B 102
Croscombe. *Som* 2A 22
Crosland Moor. *W Yor* 3B 92
Cross. *Som* 1H 21
Crossaig. *Arg* 4G 125
Crossapol. *Arg* 4A 138
Cross Ash. *Mon* 4H 47
Cross-at-Hand. *Kent* 1B 28
Crossbush. *W Sus* 5B 26
Crosscanonby. *Cumb* 1B 102
Crossdale Street. *Norf* 2E 79
Cross End. *Essx* 2B 54
Crossens. *Mers* 3B 90
Crossford. *Fife* 1D 128
Crossford. *S Lan* 5B 128
Cross Foxes. *Gwyn* 4G 69
Crossgate. *Orkn* 6D 172
Crossgate. *Staf* 2D 72
Crossgatehall. *E Lot* 3G 129
Crossgates. *Fife* 1E 129
Crossgates. *N Yor* 1E 101
Crossgates. *Powy* 4C 58
Cross Gates. *W Yor* 1D 92
Crossgill. *Lanc* 3E 97
Cross Green. *Devn* 4D 11
Cross Green. *Staf* 5D 72
Cross Green. *Suff* 5A 66
(nr. Cockfield)
Cross Green. *Suff* 5B 66
(nr. Hitcham)
Cross Hands. *Carm* 4F 45
(nr. Ammanford)
Crosshands. *Carm* 2F 43
(nr. Whitland)
Crosshands. *E Ayr* 1D 117
Cross Hill. *Derbs* 1B 74
Crosshill. *E Ayr* 2D 117
Crosshill. *Fife* 4D 136
Cross Hill. *Glos* 2A 34
Crosshill. *S Ayr* 4C 116
Crosshills. *High* 1A 158
Cross Hills. *N Yor* 5C 98
Cross Holme. *N Yor* 5C 106
Crosshouse. *E Ayr* 1C 116
Cross Houses. *Shrp* 5H 71
Crossings. *Cumb* 2G 113
Cross in Hand. *E Sus* 3G 27
Cross Inn. *Cdgn* 4E 57
(nr. Aberaeron)
Cross Inn. *Cdgn* 5C 56
(nr. New Quay)
Cross Inn. *Rhon* 3D 32
Crosskeys. *Cphy* 2F 33
Crosskirk. *High* 2C 168
Crosslands. *Cumb* 1C 96
Cross Lane Head. *Shrp* 1B 60
Cross Lanes. *Corn* 4D 5
Cross Lanes. *Dur* 3D 104
Cross Lanes. *N Yor* 3H 99
Crosslanes. *Shrp* 4F 71
Cross Lanes. *Wrex* 1F 71
Crosslee. *Ren* 3F 127
Crossmichael. *Dum* 3E 111
Crossmoor. *Lanc* 1C 90
Cross Oak. *Powy* 3E 46
Cross of Jackston. *Abers* 5E 161
Cross o' th' Hands. *Derbs* 1G 73
Crossroads. *Abers* 3G 153
(nr. Aberdeen)
Crossroads. *Abers* 4E 153
(nr. Banchory)
Crossroads. *E Ayr* 1D 116
Cross Side. *Devn* 4B 20
Cross Street. *Suff* 3D 66
Crosston. *Ang* 3E 145
Cross Town. *Ches E* 3B 84
Crossway. *Mon* 4H 47
Crossway. *Powy* 5C 58
Crossway Green. *Mon* 2A 34
Crossway Green. *Worc* 4C 60
Crossways. *Dors* 4C 14
Crosswell. *Pemb* 1F 43
Crosswood. *Cdgn* 3F 57
Crosthwaite. *Cumb* 5F 103
Croston. *Lanc* 3C 90
Crostwick. *Norf* 4E 79
Crostwight. *Norf* 3F 79
Crothair. *W Isl* 4D 171
Crouch. *Kent* 5H 39
Croucheston. *Wilts* 4F 23
Crouch Hill. *Dors* 1C 14
Croughton. *Nptn* 2D 50
Crovie. *Abers* 2F 161
Crow. *Hants* 2G 15
Crowan. *Corn* 3D 4
Crowborough. *E Sus* 2G 27
Crowcombe. *Som* 3E 21
Crowcroft. *Worc* 5B 60
Crowdecote. *Derbs* 4F 85
Crowden. *Derbs* 1E 85
Crowden. *Devn* 3E 11
Crowdhill. *Hants* 1C 16
Crowdon. *N Yor* 5G 107
Crow Edge. *S Yor* 4B 92
Crow End. *Cambs* 5C 64
Crowfield. *Nptn* 1E 50
Crowfield. *Suff* 5D 66
Crow Green. *Essx* 1G 39
Crow Hill. *Here* 3B 48
Crowhurst. *E Sus* 4B 28
Crowhurst. *Surr* 1E 27
Crowhurst Lane End. *Surr* 1E 27
Crowland. *Linc* 4B 76
Crowland. *Suff* 3C 66
Crowlas. *Corn* 3C 4
Crowle. *N Lin* 3A 94
Crowle. *Worc* 5D 60
Crowle Green. *Worc* 5D 60
Crowmarsh Gifford. *Oxon* 3E 36
Crown Corner. *Suff* 3E 67
Crownthorpe. *Norf* 5C 78
Crowntown. *Corn* 3D 4
Crows-an-wra. *Corn* 4A 4
Crowshill. *Norf* 5B 78
Crowthorne. *Brac* 5G 37
Crowton. *Ches W* 3H 83
Croxall. *Staf* 4F 73
Croxby. *Linc* 1A 88
Croxdale. *Dur* 1F 105
Croxden. *Staf* 2E 73
Croxley Green. *Herts* 1B 38
Croxton. *Cambs* 4B 64
Croxton. *Norf* 2B 78
(nr. Fakenham)
Croxton. *Norf* 2A 66
(nr. Thetford)
Croxton. *N Lin* 3D 94
Croxton. *Staf* 2B 72
Croxtonbank. *Staf* 2B 72
Croxton Green. *Ches E* 5H 83
Croxton Kerrial. *Leics* 3F 75
Croy. *High* 4B 158
Croy. *N Lan* 2A 128
Croyde. *Devn* 3E 19
Croydon. *Cambs* 1D 52
Croydon. *G Lon* 4E 39
Crubenbeg. *High* 4A 150
Crubenmore Lodge. *High* 4A 150
Cruckmeore. *Shrp* 5G 71
Cruckton. *Shrp* 4G 71
Cruden Bay. *Abers* 5H 161
Crudgington. *Telf* 4A 72
Crudie. *Abers* 3E 161
Crudwell. *Wilts* 2E 35
Cruft. *Devn* 3F 11
Crug. *Powy* 3D 58
Crughywel. *Powy* 4F 47
Crugmeer. *Corn* 1D 6
Crugybar. *Carm* 2G 45
Crug-y-byddar. *Powy* 2D 58
Crulabhig. *W Isl* 4D 171

Crumlin. *Cphy* 2F **33**
Crumpsall. *G Man* 4G **91**
Crumpsbrook. *Shrp* 3A **60**
Crundale. *Kent* 1E **29**
Crundale. *Pemb* 3D **42**
Cruwys Morchard. *Devn* 1B **12**
Crux Easton. *Hants* 1C **24**
Cruxton. *Dors* 3B **14**
Crwbin. *Carm* 4E **45**
Cryers Hill. *Buck* 2G **37**
Crymych. *Pemb* 1F **43**
Crynant. *Neat* 5A **46**
Crystal Palace. *G Lon* 3E **39**
Cuaich. *High* 5A **150**
Cuaig. *High* 3G **155**
Cuan. *Arg* 2E **133**
Cubbington. *Warw* 4H **61**
Cubert. *Corn* 3B **6**
Cubley. *S Yor* 4C **92**
Cubley Common. *Derbs* 2F **73**
Cublington. *Buck* 3G **51**
Cublington. *Here* 2H **47**
Cuckfield. *W Sus* 3E **27**
Cucklington. *Som* 4C **22**
Cuckney. *Notts* 3C **86**
Cuddesdon. *Oxon* 5E **50**
Cuddington. *Buck* 4F **51**
Cuddington. *Ches W* 3A **84**
Cuddington Heath. *Ches W* 1G **71**
Cuddy Hill. *Lanc* 1C **90**
Cudham. *G Lon* 5F **39**
Cudlipptown. *Devn* 5F **11**
Cudworth. *Som* 1G **13**
Cudworth. *S Yor* 4D **93**
Cudworth. *Surr* 1D **26**
Cuerdley Cross. *Warr* 2H **83**
Cuffley. *Herts* 5D **52**
Cuidhsiadar. *W Isl* 2H **171**
Cuidhtinis. *W Isl* 9C **171**
Culbo. *High* 2A **158**
Culbokie. *High* 3A **158**
Culburnie. *High* 4G **157**
Culcabock. *High* 4A **158**
Culcharry. *High* 3C **158**
Culcheth. *Warr* 1A **84**
Culduie. *High* 4G **155**
Culeave. *High* 4C **164**
Culford. *Suff* 4H **65**
Culgaith. *Cumb* 2H **103**
Culham. *Oxon* 2D **36**
Culkein. *High* 1E **163**
Culkein Drumbeg. *High* 5B **166**
Culkerton. *Glos* 2E **35**
Cullen. *Mor* 2C **160**
Cullercoats. *Tyne* 2G **115**
Cullicudden. *High* 2A **158**
Cullingworth. *W Yor* 1A **92**
Cullipool. *Arg* 2E **133**
Cullivoe. *Shet* 1G **173**
Culloch. *Per* 2G **135**
Culloden. *High* 4B **158**
Cullompton. *Devn* 2D **12**
Culm Davy. *Devn* 1E **13**
Culmington. *Shrp* 2G **59**
Culmstock. *Devn* 1E **12**
Cul na Caepaich. *High* 5E **147**
Culnacnoc. *High* 2E **155**
Culnacraig. *High* 3E **163**
Culrain. *High* 4C **164**
Culross. *Fife* 1C **128**
Culroy. *S Ayr* 3C **116**
Culswick. *Shet* 7D **173**
Cults. *Aber* 3F **153**
Cults. *Abers* 5C **160**
Cults. *Fife* 3F **137**
Cultybraggan Camp. *Per* 1G **135**
Culver. *Devn* 3B **12**
Culverlane. *Devn* 2D **8**
Culverstone Green. *Kent* 4H **39**
Culverthorpe. *Linc* 1H **75**
Culworth. *Nptn* 1D **50**
Culzie Lodge. *High* 1H **157**
Cumberlow Green. *Herts* 2D **52**
Cumbernauld. *N Lan* 2A **128**
Cumbernauld Village. *N Lan* 2A **128**
Cumberworth. *Linc* 3E **89**
Cumdivock. *Cumb* 5E **113**
Cuminestown. *Abers* 3F **161**
Cumledge Mill. *Bord* 4D **130**
Cummersdale. *Cumb* 4E **113**
Cummertrees. *Dum* 3C **112**
Cummingstown. *Mor* 2F **159**
Cumnock. *E Ayr* 3E **117**
Cumnor. *Oxon* 5C **50**
Cumrew. *Cumb* 4G **113**
Cumwhinton. *Cumb* 4F **113**
Cumwhitton. *Cumb* 4G **113**
Cundall. *N Yor* 2G **99**
Cunninghamhead. *N Ayr* 5E **127**
Cunning Park. *S Ayr* 3C **116**
Cunningsburgh. *Shet* 9F **173**
Cunnister. *Shet* 2G **173**
Cupar. *Fife* 2F **137**
Cupar Muir. *Fife* 2F **137**
Cupernham. *Hants* 4B **24**
Curbar. *Derbs* 3G **85**
Curborough. *Staf* 4F **73**
Curbridge. *Hants* 1D **16**
Curbridge. *Oxon* 5B **50**
Curdridge. *Hants* 1D **16**
Curdworth. *Warw* 1F **61**
Curland. *Som* 1F **13**
Curland Common. *Som* 1F **13**
Curridge. *W Ber* 4C **36**
Currie. *Edin* 3E **129**
Curry Mallet. *Som* 4G **21**
Curry Rivel. *Som* 4G **21**
Curtisden Green. *Kent* 1B **28**
Curtisknowle. *Devn* 3D **8**
Cury. *Corn* 4D **5**
Cusgarne. *Corn* 4B **6**
Cusop. *Here* 1F **47**
Cusworth. *S Yor* 4F **93**
Cutcombe. *Som* 3C **20**
Cuthill. *E Lot* 2G **129**
Cutiau. *Gwyn* 4F **69**
Cutlers Green. *Essx* 2F **53**
Cutmadoc. *Corn* 2E **7**
Cutnall Green. *Worc* 4C **60**
Cutsdean. *Glos* 2F **49**
Cutthorpe. *Derbs* 3H **85**
Cuttiford's Door. *Som* 1G **13**
Cuttivett. *Corn* 2H **7**
Cuttybridge. *Pemb* 3D **42**
Cuttyhill. *Abers* 3H **161**
Cuxham. *Oxon* 2E **37**
Cuxton. *Medw* 4B **40**
Cuxwold. *Linc* 4E **95**
Cwm. *Blae* 5E **47**
Cwm. *Den* 3C **82**
Cwm. *Powy* 1E **59**
Cwmafan. *Neat* 2A **32**
Cwmaman. *Rhon* 2C **32**
Cwmann. *Carm* 1F **45**
Cwmbach. *Carm* 2G **43**
Cwmbach. *Powy* 2E **47**
Cwmbach. *Rhon* 5D **46**
Cwmbach Llechryd. *Powy* 5C **58**
Cwmbelan. *Powy* 2B **58**
Cwmbran. *Torf* 2F **33**
Cwmbrwyno. *Cdgn* 2G **57**
Cwm Capel. *Carm* 5E **45**
Cwmcarn. *Cphy* 2F **33**
Cwmcarvan. *Mon* 5H **47**
Cwm-celyn. *Blae* 5F **47**
Cwmcerdinen. *Swan* 5G **45**
Cwm-Cewydd. *Gwyn* 4A **70**
Cwmcoy. *Cdgn* 1C **44**
Cwmcrawnon. *Powy* 4E **47**
Cwmcych. *Pemb* 1G **43**
Cwmdare. *Rhon* 5C **46**
Cwmdu. *Carm* 2G **45**
Cwmdu. *Powy* 3E **47**
Cwmduad. *Carm* 2D **45**
Cwm Dulais. *Swan* 5G **45**
Cwmerfyn. *Cdgn* 2F **57**
Cwmfelin. *B'end* 3B **32**
Cwmfelin Boeth. *Carm* 3F **43**
Cwmfelinfach. *Cphy* 2E **33**
Cwmfelin Mynach. *Carm* 2G **43**
Cwmffrwd. *Carm* 4E **45**
Cwmgiedd. *Powy* 4A **46**
Cwmgors. *Neat* 4H **45**
Cwmgwili. *Carm* 4F **45**
Cwmgwrach. *Neat* 5B **46**
Cwmhiraeth. *Carm* 1H **43**
Cwmifor. *Carm* 3G **45**
Cwmisfael. *Carm* 4E **45**
Cwm-Llinau. *Powy* 5H **69**
Cwmllynfell. *Neat* 4H **45**
Cwm-mawr. *Carm* 4F **45**
Cwm-miles. *Carm* 2F **43**
Cwmorgan. *Carm* 1G **43**
Cwmparc. *Rhon* 2C **32**
Cwm Penmachno. *Cnwy* 1G **69**
Cwmpennar. *Rhon* 5D **46**
Cwm Plysgog. *Pemb* 1B **44**
Cwmrhos. *Powy* 3E **47**
Cwmsychpant. *Cdgn* 1E **45**
Cwmsyfiog. *Cphy* 5E **47**
Cwmsymlog. *Cdgn* 2F **57**
Cwmtillery. *Blae* 5F **47**
Cwm-twrch Isaf. *Powy* 5A **46**
Cwm-twrch Uchaf. *Powy* 4A **46**
Cwmwysg. *Powy* 3B **46**
Cwm-y-glo. *Gwyn* 4E **81**
Cwmyoy. *Mon* 3G **47**
Cwmystwyth. *Cdgn* 3G **57**
Cwrt. *Gwyn* 1F **57**
Cwrtnewydd. *Cdgn* 1E **45**
Cwrt-y-Cadno. *Carm* 1G **45**
Cydweli. *Carm* 5E **45**
Cyffylliog. *Den* 5C **82**
Cymau. *Flin* 5E **83**
Cymer. *Neat* 2B **32**
Cymmer. *Neat* 2B **32**
Cymmer. *Rhon* 2D **32**
Cyncoed. *Card* 3E **33**
Cynghordy. *Carm* 2B **46**
Cynghordy. *Swan* 5G **45**
Cynheidre. *Carm* 5E **45**
Cynonville. *Neat* 2B **32**
Cynwyd. *Den* 1C **70**
Cynwyl Elfed. *Carm* 3D **44**
Cywarch. *Gwyn* 4A **70**

D

Dacre. *Cumb* 2F **103**
Dacre. *N Yor* 3D **98**
Dacre Banks. *N Yor* 3D **98**
Daddry Shield. *Dur* 1B **104**
Dadford. *Buck* 2E **51**
Dadlington. *Leics* 1B **62**
Dafen. *Carm* 5F **45**
Daffy Green. *Norf* 5B **78**
Dagdale. *Staf* 2E **73**
Dagenham. *G Lon* 2F **39**
Daggons. *Dors* 1G **15**
Daglingworth. *Glos* 5E **49**
Dagnall. *Buck* 4H **51**
Dagtail End. *Worc* 4E **61**
Dail. *Arg* 5E **141**
Dail bho Dheas. *W Isl* 1G **171**
Dailly. *S Ayr* 4B **116**
Dail Mor. *W Isl* 3E **171**
Dairsie. *Fife* 2G **137**
Daisy Bank. *W Mid* 1E **61**
Daisy Hill. *G Man* 4E **91**
Daisy Hill. *W Yor* 1B **92**
Dalabrog. *W Isl* 6C **170**
Dalavich. *Arg* 2G **133**
Dalbeattie. *Dum* 3F **111**
Dalblair. *E Ayr* 3F **117**
Dalbury. *Derbs* 2G **73**
Dalby. *IOM* 4B **108**
Dalby Wolds. *Leics* 3D **74**
Dalchalm. *High* 3G **165**
Dalcharn. *High* 3G **167**
Dalchork. *High* 2C **164**
Dalchreichart. *High* 2E **149**
Dalchruin. *Per* 2G **135**
Dalcross. *High* 4B **158**
Dalderby. *Linc* 4B **88**
Dale. *Cumb* 5G **113**
Dale. *Pemb* 4C **42**
Dale Abbey. *Derbs* 2B **74**
Dalebank. *Derbs* 4A **86**
Dale Bottom. *Cumb* 2D **102**
Dale Head. *Cumb* 3F **103**
Dalehouse. *N Yor* 3E **107**
Dalelia. *High* 2B **140**
Dale of Walls. *Shet* 6C **173**
Dalgarven. *N Ayr* 5D **126**
Dalgety Bay. *Fife* 1E **129**
Dalginross. *Per* 1G **135**
Dalguise. *Per* 4G **143**
Dalhalvaig. *High* 3A **168**
Dalham. *Suff* 4G **65**
Dalintart. *Arg* 1F **133**
Dalkeith. *Midl* 3G **129**
Dallas. *Mor* 3F **159**
Dalleagles. *E Ayr* 3E **117**
Dall House. *Per* 3C **142**
Dallinghoo. *Suff* 5E **67**
Dallington. *E Sus* 4A **28**
Dallow. *N Yor* 2D **98**
Dalmally. *Arg* 1A **134**
Dalmarnock. *Glas* 3H **127**
Dalmellington. *E Ayr* 4D **117**
Dalmeny. *Edin* 2E **129**
Dalmigavie. *High* 2B **150**
Dalmilling. *S Ayr* 2C **116**
Dalmore. *High* 2A **158** (nr. Alness)
Dalmore. *High* 3E **164** (nr. Rogart)
Dalmuir. *W Dun* 2F **127**
Dalmunach. *Mor* 4G **159**
Dalnabreck. *High* 2B **140**
Dalnacardoch Lodge. *Per* 1E **142**
Dalnamein Lodge. *Per* 2E **143**
Dalnaspidal Lodge. *Per* 1D **142**
Dalnatrat. *High* 3D **140**
Dalnavie. *High* 1A **158**
Dalnawillan Lodge. *High* 4C **168**
Dalness. *High* 3F **141**
Dalnessie. *High* 2D **164**
Dalqueich. *Per* 3C **136**
Dalquhairn. *S Ayr* 5C **116**
Dalreavoch. *High* 3E **165**
Dalreoch. *Per* 2C **136**
Dalry. *Edin* 2F **129**
Dalry. *N Ayr* 5D **126**
Dalrymple. *E Ayr* 3C **116**
Dalscote. *Nptn* 5D **62**
Dalserf. *S Lan* 4A **128**
Dalsmirren. *Arg* 4A **122**
Dalston. *Cumb* 4E **113**
Dalswinton. *Dum* 1G **111**
Dalton. *Dum* 2C **112**
Dalton. *Lanc* 4C **90**
Dalton. *Nmbd* 4C **114** (nr. Hexham)
Dalton. *Nmbd* 2E **115** (nr. Ponteland)
Dalton. *N Yor* 4E **105** (nr. Richmond)
Dalton. *N Yor* 2G **99** (nr. Thirsk)
Dalton. *S Lan* 4H **127**
Dalton. *S Yor* 1B **86**
Dalton-in-Furness. *Cumb* 2B **96**
Dalton-le-Dale. *Dur* 5H **115**
Dalton Magna. *S Yor* 1B **86**
Dalton-on-Tees. *N Yor* 4F **105**
Dalton Piercy. *Hart* 1B **106**
Daltot. *Arg* 1F **125**
Dalvey. *High* 5F **159**
Dalwhinnie. *High* 5A **150**
Dalwood. *Devn* 2F **13**
Damerham. *Hants* 1G **15**
Damgate. *Norf* 5G **79** (nr. Acle)
Damgate. *Norf* 4G **79** (nr. Martham)
Dam Green. *Norf* 2C **66**
Damhead. *Mor* 3E **159**
Danaway. *Kent* 4C **40**
Danbury. *Essx* 5A **54**
Danby. *N Yor* 4E **107**
Danby Botton. *N Yor* 4D **107**
Danby Wiske. *N Yor* 5A **106**
Danderhall. *Midl* 3G **129**
Danebank. *Ches E* 2D **85**
Danebridge. *Ches E* 4D **84**
Dane End. *Herts* 3D **52**
Danehill. *E Sus* 3F **27**
Danesford. *Shrp* 1B **60**
Daneshill. *Hants* 1E **25**
Danesmoor. *Derbs* 4A **86**
Danestone. *Aber* 2G **153**
Dangerous Corner. *Lanc* 3D **90**
Daniel's Water. *Kent* 1D **28**
Dan's Castle. *Dur* 1E **105**
Danzey Green. *Warw* 4F **61**
Dapple Heath. *Staf* 3E **73**
Daren. *Powy* 4F **47**
Darenth. *Kent* 3G **39**
Daresbury. *Hal* 2H **83**
Darfield. *S Yor* 4E **93**
Dargate. *Kent* 4E **41**
Dargill. *Per* 2A **136**
Darite. *Corn* 2G **7**
Darlaston. *W Mid* 1D **60**
Darley. *N Yor* 4E **98**
Darley Abbey. *Derb* 2A **74**
Darley Bridge. *Derbs* 4G **85**
Darley Dale. *Derbs* 4G **85**
Darley Head. *N Yor* 4D **98**
Darlingscott. *Warw* 1H **49**
Darlington. *Darl* 3F **105**
Darliston. *Shrp* 2H **71**
Darlton. *Notts* 3E **87**
Darmsden. *Suff* 5C **66**
Darnall. *S Yor* 2A **86**
Darnford. *Abers* 4E **153**
Darnford. *Staf* 5F **73**
Darnhall. *Ches W* 4A **84**
Darnick. *Bord* 1H **119**
Darowen. *Powy* 5H **69**
Darra. *Abers* 4E **161**
Darracott. *Devn* 3E **19**
Darras Hall. *Nmbd* 2E **115**
Darrington. *W Yor* 3E **93**
Darrow Green. *Norf* 2E **67**
Darsham. *Suff* 4G **67**
Dartfield. *Abers* 3H **161**
Dartford. *Kent* 3G **39**
Dartford-Thurrock River Crossing. *Kent* 3G **39**
Dartington. *Devn* 2D **9**
Dartmeet. *Devn* 5G **11**
Dartmoor. *Devn* 4F **11**
Dartmouth. *Devn* 3E **9**
Darton. *S Yor* 3D **92**
Darvel. *E Ayr* 1E **117**
Darwen. *Bkbn* 2E **91**
Dassels. *Herts* 3D **53**
Datchet. *Wind* 3A **38**
Datchworth. *Herts* 4C **52**
Datchworth Green. *Herts* 4C **52**
Daubhill. *G Man* 4F **91**
Dauntsey. *Wilts* 3E **35**
Dauntsey Green. *Wilts* 3E **35**
Dauntsey Lock. *Wilts* 3E **35**
Dava. *Mor* 5E **159**
Davenham. *Ches W* 3A **84**
Daventry. *Nptn* 4C **62**
Davidson's Mains. *Edin* 2F **129**
Davidston. *High* 2B **158**
Davidstow. *Corn* 4B **10**
David's Well. *Powy* 3C **58**
Davington. *Dum* 4E **119**
Daviot. *Abers* 1E **153**
Daviot. *High* 5B **158**

Davyhulme—Dounie

Davyhulme. *G Man* 1B **84**
Daw Cross. *N Yor* 4E **99**
Dawdon. *Dur* 5H **115**
Dawesgreen. *Surr* 1D **26**
Dawley. *Telf* 5A **72**
Dawlish. *Devn* 5C **12**
Dawlish Warren. *Devn* 5C **12**
Dawn. *Cnwy* 3A **82**
Daws Heath. *Essx* 2C **40**
Dawshill. *Worc* 5C **60**
Daw's House. *Corn* 4D **10**
Dawsmere. *Linc* 2D **76**
Dayhills. *Staf* 2D **72**
Dayhouse Bank. *Worc* 3D **60**
Daylesford. *Glos* 3H **49**
Daywall. *Shrp* 2E **71**
Ddol. *Flin* 3D **82**
Ddol Cownwy. *Powy* 4C **70**
Deadman's Cross. *C Beds* 1B **52**
Deadwater. *Nmbd* 5A **120**
Deaf Hill. *Dur* 1A **106**
Deal. *Kent* 5H **41**
Dean. *Cumb* 2B **102**
Dean. *Devn* 2G **19**
(nr. Combe Martin)
Dean. *Devn* 2H **19**
(nr. Lynton)
Dean. *Dors* 1E **15**
Dean. *Hants* 1D **16**
(nr. Bishop's Waltham)
Dean. *Hants* 3C **24**
(nr. Winchester)
Dean. *Oxon* 3B **50**
Dean. *Som* 2B **22**
Dean Bank. *Dur* 1F **105**
Deanburnhaugh. *Bord* 3F **119**
Dean Cross. *Devn* 2F **19**
Deane. *Hants* 1D **24**
Deanich Lodge. *High* 5A **164**
Deanland. *Dors* 1E **15**
Deanlane End. *W Sus* 1F **17**
Dean Park. *Shrp* 4H **59**
Dean Prior. *Devn* 2D **8**
Dean Row. *Ches E* 2C **84**
Deans. *W Lot* 3D **128**
Deanscales. *Cumb* 2B **102**
Deanshanger. *Nptn* 2F **51**
Deanston. *Stir* 3G **135**
Dearham. *Cumb* 1B **102**
Dearne. *S Yor* 4E **93**
Dearne Valley. *S Yor* 4D **93**
Debach. *Suff* 5E **67**
Debden. *Essx* 2F **53**
Debden Green. *Essx* 1F **39**
(nr. Loughton)
Debden Green. *Essx* 2F **53**
(nr. Saffron Walden)
Debenham. *Suff* 4D **66**
Dechmont. *W Lot* 2D **128**
Deddington. *Oxon* 2C **50**
Dedham. *Essx* 2D **54**
Dedham Heath. *Essx* 2D **54**
Deebank. *Abers* 4D **152**
Deene. *Nptn* 1G **63**
Deenethorpe. *Nptn* 1G **63**
Deepcar. *S Yor* 1G **85**
Deepcut. *Surr* 5A **38**
Deepdale. *Cumb* 1G **97**
Deepdale. *N Lin* 3D **94**
Deepdale. *N Yor* 2A **98**
Deeping Gate. *Pet* 5A **76**
Deeping St James. *Linc* 5A **76**
Deeping St Nicholas. *Linc* 4B **76**
Deerhill. *Mor* 3B **160**
Deerhurst. *Glos* 3D **48**
Deerhurst Walton. *Glos* 3D **49**
Deerness. *Orkn* 7E **172**
Defford. *Worc* 1E **49**
Defynnog. *Powy* 3C **46**
Deganwy. *Cnwy* 3G **81**
Deighton. *N Yor* 4A **106**
Deighton. *W Yor* 3B **92**
Deighton. *York* 5A **100**
Deiniolen. *Gwyn* 4E **81**
Delabole. *Corn* 4A **10**
Delamere. *Ches W* 4H **83**
Delfour. *High* 3C **150**
Dellieture. *High* 5E **159**
Dell, The. *Suff* 1G **67**
Delly End. *Oxon* 4B **50**
Delny. *High* 1B **158**
Delph. *G Man* 4H **91**
Delves. *Dur* 5E **115**
Delves, The. *W Mid* 1E **61**
Delvin End. *Essx* 2A **54**
Dembleby. *Linc* 2H **75**
Demelza. *Corn* 2D **6**
Denaby Main. *S Yor* 1B **86**
Denbeath. *Fife* 4F **137**
Denbigh. *Den* 4C **82**
Denbury. *Devn* 2E **9**
Denby. *Derbs* 1A **74**
Denby Common. *Derbs* 1B **74**
Denby Dale. *W Yor* 4C **92**
Denchworth. *Oxon* 2B **36**
Dendron. *Cumb* 2B **96**
Deneside. *Dur* 5H **115**
Denford. *Nptn* 3G **63**
Dengie. *Essx* 5C **54**
Denham. *Buck* 2B **38**
Denham. *Suff* 4G **65**
(nr. Bury St Edmunds)
Denham. *Suff* 3D **66**
(nr. Eye)
Denham Green. *Buck* 2B **38**
Denham Street. *Suff* 3D **66**
Denhead. *Abers* 5G **161**
(nr. Ellon)
Denhead. *Abers* 3G **161**
(nr. Strichen)
Denhead. *Fife* 2G **137**
Denholm. *Bord* 3H **119**
Denholme. *W Yor* 1A **92**
Denholme Clough. *W Yor* 1A **92**
Denholme Gate. *W Yor* 1A **92**
Denio. *Gwyn* 2C **68**
Denmead. *Hants* 1E **17**
Dennington. *Suff* 4E **67**
Denny. *Falk* 1B **128**
Denny End. *Cambs* 4D **65**
Dennyloanhead. *Falk* 1B **128**
Den of Lindores. *Fife* 2E **137**
Denshaw. *G Man* 3H **91**
Denside. *Abers* 4F **153**
Densole. *Kent* 1G **29**
Denston. *Suff* 5G **65**
Denstone. *Staf* 1F **73**
Denstroude. *Kent* 4F **41**
Dent. *Cumb* 1G **97**
Den, The. *N Ayr* 4E **127**
Denton. *Cambs* 2A **64**
Denton. *Darl* 3F **105**
Denton. *E Sus* 5F **27**
Denton. *G Man* 1D **84**
Denton. *Kent* 1G **29**
Denton. *Linc* 2F **75**
Denton. *Norf* 2E **67**
Denton. *Nptn* 5F **63**
Denton. *N Yor* 5D **98**
Denton. *Oxon* 5D **50**
Denver. *Norf* 5F **77**
Denwick. *Nmbd* 3G **121**
Deopham. *Norf* 5C **78**
Deopham Green. *Norf* 1C **66**
Depden. *Suff* 5G **65**
Depden Green. *Suff* 5G **65**
Deptford. *G Lon* 3E **39**
Deptford. *Wilts* 3F **23**
Derby. *Derb* 2A **74**
Derbyhaven. *IOM* 5B **108**
Derculich. *Per* 3F **143**
Dereham. *Norf* 4B **78**
Deri. *Cphy* 5E **47**
Derril. *Devn* 2D **10**
Derringstone. *Kent* 1G **29**
Derrington. *Shrp* 1A **60**
Derrington. *Staf* 3C **72**
Derriton. *Devn* 2D **10**
Derryguaig. *Arg* 5F **139**
Derry Hill. *Wilts* 4E **35**
Derrythorpe. *N Lin* 4B **94**
Dersingham. *Norf* 2F **77**
Dervaig. *Arg* 3F **139**
Derwen. *Den* 5C **82**
Derwen Gam. *Cdgn* 5D **56**
Derwenlas. *Powy* 1G **57**
Desborough. *Nptn* 2F **63**
Desford. *Leics* 5B **74**
Detchant. *Nmbd* 1E **121**
Dethick. *Derbs* 5H **85**
Detling. *Kent* 5B **40**
Deuchar. *Ang* 2D **144**
Deuddwr. *Powy* 4E **71**
Devauden. *Mon* 2H **33**
Devil's Bridge. *Cdgn* 3G **57**
Devitts Green. *Warw* 1G **61**
Devizes. *Wilts* 5F **35**
Devonport. *Plym* 3A **8**
Devonside. *Clac* 4B **136**
Devoran. *Corn* 5B **6**
Dewartown. *Midl* 3G **129**
Dewlish. *Dors* 3C **14**
Dewsbury. *W Yor* 2C **92**
Dewshall Court. *Here* 2H **47**
Dexbeer. *Devn* 2C **10**
Dhoon. *IOM* 3D **108**
Dhoor. *IOM* 2D **108**
Dhowin. *IOM* 1D **108**
Dial Green. *W Sus* 3A **26**
Dial Post. *W Sus* 4C **26**
Dibberford. *Dors* 2H **13**
Dibden. *Hants* 2C **16**
Dibden Purlieu. *Hants* 2C **16**
Dickleburgh. *Norf* 2D **66**
Didbrook. *Glos* 2F **49**
Didcot. *Oxon* 2D **36**
Diddington. *Cambs* 4A **64**
Diddlebury. *Shrp* 2H **59**
Didley. *Here* 2H **47**
Didling. *W Sus* 1G **17**
Didmarton. *Glos* 3D **34**
Didsbury. *G Man* 1C **84**
Didworthy. *Devn* 2C **8**
Digby. *Linc* 5H **87**
Digg. *High* 2D **154**
Diggle. *G Man* 4A **92**
Digmoor. *Lanc* 4C **90**
Digswell. *Herts* 4C **52**
Dihewyd. *Cdgn* 5D **57**
Dilham. *Norf* 3F **79**
Dilhorne. *Staf* 1D **72**
Dillarburn. *S Lan* 5B **128**
Dillington. *Cambs* 4A **64**
Dilston. *Nmbd* 3C **114**
Dilton Marsh. *Wilts* 2D **22**
Dilwyn. *Here* 5G **59**
Dimmer. *Som* 3B **22**
Dimple. *G Man* 3F **91**
Dinas. *Carm* 1G **43**
Dinas. *Gwyn* 5D **81**
(nr. Caernarfon)
Dinas. *Gwyn* 2B **68**
(nr. Tudweiliog)
Dinas Cross. *Pemb* 1E **43**
Dinas Dinlle. *Gwyn* 5D **80**
Dinas Mawddwy. *Gwyn* 4A **70**
Dinas Powys. *V Glam* 4E **33**
Dinbych. *Den* 4C **82**
Dinbych-y-Pysgod. *Pemb* 4F **43**
Dinckley. *Lanc* 1E **91**
Dinder. *Som* 2A **22**
Dinedor. *Here* 2A **48**
Dinedor Cross. *Here* 2A **48**
Dingestow. *Mon* 4H **47**
Dingle. *Mers* 2F **83**
Dingleden. *Kent* 2C **28**
Dingleton. *Bord* 1H **119**
Dingley. *Nptn* 2E **63**
Dingwall. *High* 3H **157**
Dinmael. *Cnwy* 1C **70**
Dinnet. *Abers* 4B **152**
Dinnington. *Som* 1H **13**
Dinnington. *S Yor* 2C **86**
Dinnington. *Tyne* 2F **115**
Dinorwig. *Gwyn* 4E **81**
Dinton. *Buck* 4F **51**
Dinton. *Wilts* 3F **23**
Dinworthy. *Devn* 1D **10**
Dipley. *Hants* 1F **25**
Dippen. *Arg* 2B **122**
Dippenhall. *Surr* 2G **25**
Dippertown. *Devn* 4E **11**
Dippin. *N Ayr* 3E **123**
Dipple. *S Ayr* 4B **116**
Diptford. *Devn* 3D **8**
Dipton. *Dur* 4E **115**
Dirleton. *E Lot* 1B **130**
Dirt Pot. *Nmbd* 5B **114**
Discoed. *Powy* 4E **59**
Diseworth. *Leics* 3B **74**
Dishforth. *N Yor* 2F **99**
Disley. *Ches E* 2D **85**
Diss. *Norf* 3D **66**
Disserth. *Powy* 5C **58**
Distington. *Cumb* 2B **102**
Ditchampton. *Wilts* 3F **23**
Ditcheat. *Som* 3B **22**
Ditchingham. *Norf* 1F **67**
Ditchling. *E Sus* 4E **27**
Ditteridge. *Wilts* 5D **34**
Dittisham. *Devn* 3E **9**
Ditton. *Hal* 2G **83**
Ditton. *Kent* 5B **40**
Ditton Green. *Cambs* 5F **65**
Ditton Priors. *Shrp* 2A **60**
Divach. *High* 1G **149**
Dixonfield. *High* 2D **168**
Dixton. *Glos* 2E **49**
Dixton. *Mon* 4A **48**
Dizzard. *Corn* 3B **10**
Dobcross. *G Man* 4H **91**
Dobs Hill. *Flin* 4F **83**
Dobson's Bridge. *Shrp* 2G **71**
Dobwalls. *Corn* 2G **7**
Doccombe. *Devn* 4A **12**
Dochgarroch. *High* 4A **158**
Docking. *Norf* 2G **77**
Docklow. *Here* 5H **59**
Dockray. *Cumb* 2E **103**
Doc Penfro. *Pemb* 4D **42**
Dodbrooke. *Devn* 4D **8**
Doddenham. *Worc* 5B **60**
Doddinghurst. *Essx* 1G **39**
Doddington. *Cambs* 1C **64**
Doddington. *Kent* 5D **40**
Doddington. *Linc* 4G **87**
Doddington. *Nmbd* 1D **121**
Doddington. *Shrp* 3A **60**
Doddiscombsleigh. *Devn* 4B **12**
Doddshill. *Norf* 2G **77**
Dodford. *Nptn* 4D **62**
Dodford. *Worc* 3D **60**
Dodington. *Som* 2E **21**
Dodington. *S Glo* 4C **34**
Dodleston. *Ches W* 4F **83**
Dods Leigh. *Staf* 2E **73**
Dodworth. *S Yor* 4D **92**
Doe Lea. *Derbs* 4B **86**
Dogdyke. *Linc* 5B **88**
Dogmersfield. *Hants* 1F **25**
Dogsthorpe. *Pet* 5B **76**
Dog Village. *Devn* 3C **12**
Dolanog. *Powy* 4C **70**
Dolau. *Powy* 4D **58**
Dolau. *Rhon* 3D **32**
Dolbenmaen. *Gwyn* 1E **69**
Doley. *Staf* 3B **72**
Dol-fach. *Powy* 5B **70**
(nr. Llanbrynmair)
Dolfach. *Powy* 3B **58**
(nr. Llanidloes)
Dolfor. *Powy* 2D **58**
Dolgarrog. *Cnwy* 4G **81**
Dolgellau. *Gwyn* 4G **69**
Dolgoch. *Gwyn* 5F **69**
Dol-gran. *Carm* 2E **45**
Dolhelfa. *Powy* 3B **58**
Doll. *High* 3F **165**
Dollar. *Clac* 4B **136**
Dolley Green. *Powy* 4E **59**
Dollwen. *Cdgn* 2F **57**
Dolphin. *Flin* 3D **82**
Dolphingstone. *E Lot* 2G **129**
Dolphinholme. *Lanc* 4E **97**
Dolphinton. *S Lan* 5E **129**
Dolton. *Devn* 1F **11**
Dolwen. *Cnwy* 3A **82**
Dolwyddelan. *Cnwy* 5G **81**
Dol-y-Bont. *Cdgn* 2F **57**
Dolyhir. *Powy* 5E **59**
Domgay. *Powy* 4E **71**
Doncaster. *S Yor* 4F **93**
Donhead St Andrew. *Wilts* 4E **23**
Donhead St Mary. *Wilts* 4E **23**
Doniford. *Som* 2D **20**
Donington. *Linc* 2B **76**
Donington. *Shrp* 5C **72**
Donington Eaudike. *Linc* 2B **76**
Donington le Heath. *Leics* 4B **74**
Donington on Bain. *Linc* 2B **88**
Donington South Ing. *Linc* 2B **76**
Donisthorpe. *Leics* 4H **73**
Donkey Street. *Kent* 2F **29**
Donkey Town. *Surr* 4A **38**
Donna Nook. *Linc* 1D **88**
Donnington. *Glos* 3G **49**
Donnington. *Here* 2C **48**
Donnington. *Shrp* 5H **71**
Donnington. *Telf* 4B **72**
Donnington. *W Ber* 5C **36**
Donnington. *W Sus* 2G **17**
Donyatt. *Som* 1G **13**
Doomsday Green. *W Sus* 2C **26**
Doonfoot. *S Ayr* 3C **116**
Doonholm. *S Ayr* 3C **116**
Dorback Lodge. *High* 2E **151**
Dorchester. *Dors* 3B **14**
Dorchester on Thames. *Oxon* 2D **36**
Dordon. *Warw* 5G **73**
Dore. *S Yor* 2H **85**
Dores. *High* 5H **157**
Dorking. *Surr* 1C **26**
Dorking Tye. *Suff* 2C **54**
Dormansland. *Surr* 1F **27**
Dormans Park. *Surr* 1E **27**
Dormanstown. *Red C* 2C **106**
Dormington. *Here* 1A **48**
Dormston. *Worc* 5D **61**
Dorn. *Glos* 2H **49**
Dorney. *Buck* 3A **38**
Dornie. *High* 1A **148**
Dornoch. *High* 5E **165**
Dornock. *Dum* 3D **112**
Dorrery. *High* 3C **168**
Dorridge. *W Mid* 3F **61**
Dorrington. *Linc* 5H **87**
Dorrington. *Shrp* 5G **71**
Dorsington. *Warw* 1G **49**
Dorstone. *Here* 1G **47**
Dorton. *Buck* 4E **51**
Dotham. *IOA* 3C **80**
Dottery. *Dors* 3H **13**
Doublebois. *Corn* 2F **7**
Dougarie. *N Ayr* 2C **122**
Doughton. *Glos* 2D **35**
Douglas. *IOM* 4C **108**
Douglas. *S Lan* 1H **117**
Douglastown. *Ang* 4D **144**
Douglas Water. *S Lan* 1A **118**
Doulting. *Som* 2B **22**
Dounby. *Orkn* 5B **172**
Doune. *High* 3C **150**
(nr. Kingussie)
Doune. *High* 3B **164**
(nr. Lairg)
Doune. *Stir* 3G **135**
Dounie. *High* 4C **164**
(nr. Bonar Bridge)
Dounie. *High* 5D **164**
(nr. Tain)

Dounreay—Durran

Dounreay. *High* 2B **168**
Doura. *N Ayr* 5E **127**
Dousland. *Devn* 2B **8**
Dovaston. *Shrp* 3F **71**
Dove Holes. *Derbs* 3E **85**
Dovenby. *Cumb* 1B **102**
Dover. *Kent* 1H **29**
Dovercourt. *Essx* 2F **55**
Doverdale. *Worc* 4C **60**
Doveridge. *Derbs* 2F **73**
Doversgreen. *Surr* 1D **26**
Dowally. *Per* 4H **143**
Dowbridge. *Lanc* 1C **90**
Dowdeswell. *Glos* 4F **49**
Dowlais. *Mer T* 5D **46**
Dowland. *Devn* 1F **11**
Dowlands. *Devn* 3F **13**
Dowles. *Worc* 3B **60**
Dowlesgreen. *Wok* 5G **37**
Dowlish Wake. *Som* 1G **13**
Downall Green. *Mers* 4D **90**
Down Ampney. *Glos* 2F **35**
Downderry. *Corn* 3H **7** (nr. Looe)
Downderry. *Corn* 3D **6** (nr. St Austell)
Downe. *G Lon* 4F **39**
Downend. *IOW* 4D **16**
Downend. *S Glo* 4B **34**
Downend. *W Ber* 4C **36**
Down Field. *Cambs* 3F **65**
Downfield. *D'dee* 5C **144**
Downgate. *Corn* 5D **10** (nr. Kelly Bray)
Downgate. *Corn* 5C **10** (nr. Upton Cross)
Downham. *Essx* 1B **40**
Downham. *Lanc* 5G **97**
Downham. *Nmbd* 1C **120**
Downham Market. *Norf* 5F **77**
Down Hatherley. *Glos* 3D **48**
Downhead. *Som* 2B **22** (nr. Frome)
Downhead. *Som* 4A **22** (nr. Yeovil)
Downholland Cross. *Lanc* 4B **90**
Downholme. *N Yor* 5E **105**
Downies. *Abers* 4G **153**
Downley. *Buck* 2G **37**
Down St Mary. *Devn* 2H **11**
Downside. *Som* 1B **22** (nr. Chilcompton)
Downside. *Som* 2B **22** (nr. Shepton Mallet)
Downside. *Surr* 5C **38**
Down, The. *Shrp* 1A **60**
Down Thomas. *Devn* 3B **8**
Downton. *Hants* 3A **16**
Downton. *Wilts* 4G **23**
Downton on the Rock. *Here* 3G **59**
Dowsby. *Linc* 3A **76**
Dowsdale. *Linc* 4B **76**
Dowthwaitehead. *Cumb* 2E **103**
Doxey. *Staf* 3D **72**
Doxford. *Nmbd* 2F **121**
Doynton. *S Glo* 4C **34**
Drabblegate. *Norf* 3E **78**
Draethen. *Cphy* 3F **33**
Draffan. *S Lan* 5A **128**
Dragonby. *N Lin* 3C **94**
Dragons Green. *W Sus* 3C **26**
Drakelow. *Worc* 2C **60**
Drakemyre. *N Ayr* 4D **126**
Drakes Broughton. *Worc* 1E **49**
Drakes Cross. *Worc* 3E **61**
Drakewalls. *Corn* 5E **11**
Draughton. *Nptn* 3E **63**
Draughton. *N Yor* 4C **98**
Drax. *N Yor* 2G **93**
Draycot. *Oxon* 5E **51**
Draycote. *Warw* 4B **62**
Draycot Foliat. *Swin* 4G **35**
Draycott. *Derbs* 2B **74**
Draycott. *Glos* 2G **49**
Draycott. *Shrp* 1C **60**
Draycott. *Som* 1H **21** (nr. Cheddar)
Draycott. *Som* 4A **22** (nr. Yeovil)
Draycott. *Worc* 1D **48**
Draycott in the Clay. *Staf* 3F **73**
Draycott in the Moors. *Staf* 1D **73**
Drayford. *Devn* 1A **12**
Drayton. *Leics* 1F **63**
Drayton. *Linc* 2B **76**
Drayton. *Norf* 4D **78**
Drayton. *Nptn* 4C **62**
Drayton. *Oxon* 2C **36** (nr. Abingdon)
Drayton. *Oxon* 1C **50** (nr. Banbury)
Drayton. *Port* 2E **17**
Drayton. *Som* 4H **21**
Drayton. *Warw* 5F **61**
Drayton. *Worc* 3D **60**
Drayton Bassett. *Staf* 5F **73**
Drayton Beauchamp. *Buck* 4H **51**
Drayton Parslow. *Buck* 3G **51**
Drayton St Leonard. *Oxon* 2D **36**
Drebley. *N Yor* 4C **98**
Dreenhill. *Pemb* 3D **42**
Drefach. *Carm* 4F **45** (nr. Meidrim)
Drefach. *Carm* 2D **44** (nr. Newcastle Emlyn)
Drefach. *Carm* 2G **43** (nr. Tumble)
Drefach. *Cdgn* 1E **45**
Dreghorn. *N Ayr* 1C **116**
Drellingore. *Kent* 1G **29**
Drem. *E Lot* 2B **130**
Dreumasdal. *W Isl* 5C **170**
Drewsteignton. *Devn* 3H **11**
Driby. *Linc* 3C **88**
Driffield. *E Yor* 4E **101**
Driffield. *Glos* 2F **35**
Drift. *Corn* 4B **4**
Drigg. *Cumb* 5B **102**
Drighlington. *W Yor* 2C **92**
Drimnin. *High* 3G **139**
Drimpton. *Dors* 2H **13**
Dringhoe. *E Yor* 4F **101**
Drinisiadar. *W Isl* 8D **171**
Drinkstone. *Suff* 4B **66**
Drinkstone Green. *Suff* 4B **66**
Drointon. *Staf* 3E **73**
Droitwich Spa. *Worc* 4C **60**
Droman. *High* 3B **166**
Dron. *Per* 2D **136**
Dronfield. *Derbs* 3A **86**
Dronfield Woodhouse. *Derbs* 3H **85**
Drongan. *E Ayr* 3D **116**
Dronley. *Ang* 5C **144**
Droop. *Dors* 2C **14**
Drope. *V Glam* 4E **32**
Droxford. *Hants* 1E **16**
Droylsden. *G Man* 1C **84**
Druggers End. *Worc* 2C **48**
Druid. *Den* 1C **70**
Druid's Heath. *W Mid* 5E **73**
Druidston. *Pemb* 3C **42**
Druim. *High* 3D **158**
Druimarbin. *High* 1E **141**
Druim Fhearna. *High* 2E **147**
Druimindarroch. *High* 5E **147**
Drum. *Per* 3C **136**
Drumbeg. *High* 5B **166**
Drumblade. *Abers* 4C **160**
Drumbuie. *Dum* 1C **110**
Drumbuie. *High* 5G **155**
Drumburgh. *Cumb* 4D **112**
Drumburn. *Dum* 3A **112**
Drumchapel. *Glas* 2G **127**
Drumchardine. *High* 4H **157**
Drumchork. *High* 5C **162**
Drumclog. *S Lan* 1F **117**
Drumeldrie. *Fife* 3G **137**
Drumelzier. *Bord* 1D **118**
Drumfearn. *High* 2E **147**
Drumgask. *High* 4A **150**
Drumgelloch. *N Lan* 3A **128**
Drumgley. *Ang* 3D **144**
Drumguish. *High* 4B **150**
Drumin. *Mor* 5F **159**
Drumindorsair. *High* 4G **157**
Drumlamford House. *S Ayr* 2H **109**
Drumlasie. *Abers* 3D **152**
Drumlemble. *Arg* 4A **122**
Drumlithie. *Abers* 5E **153**
Drummoddie. *Dum* 5A **110**
Drummond. *High* 2A **158**
Drummore. *Dum* 5E **109**
Drummuir. *Mor* 4A **160**
Drumnadrochit. *High* 5H **157**
Drumnagorrach. *Mor* 3C **160**
Drumoak. *Abers* 4E **153**
Drumrunie. *High* 3F **163**
Drumry. *W Dun* 2G **127**
Drums. *Abers* 1G **153**
Drumsleet. *Dum* 2G **111**
Drumsmittal. *High* 4A **158**
Drums of Park. *Abers* 3C **160**
Drumsturdy. *Ang* 5D **145**
Drumtochty Castle. *Abers* 5D **152**
Drumuie. *High* 4D **154**
Drumuillie. *High* 1D **150**
Drumvaich. *Stir* 3F **135**
Drumwhindle. *Abers* 5G **161**
Drunkendub. *Ang* 4F **145**
Drury. *Flin* 4E **83**
Drury Square. *Norf* 4B **78**
Drybeck. *Cumb* 3H **103**
Drybridge. *Mor* 2B **160**
Drybridge. *N Ayr* 1C **116**
Drybrook. *Glos* 4B **48**
Drybrook. *Here* 4A **48**
Dryburgh. *Bord* 1H **119**
Dry Doddington. *Linc* 1F **75**
Dry Drayton. *Cambs* 4C **64**
Drym. *Corn* 3D **4**
Drymen. *Stir* 1F **127**
Drymuir. *Abers* 4G **161**
Drynachan Lodge. *High* 5C **158**
Drynie Park. *High* 3H **157**
Drynoch. *High* 5D **154**
Dry Sandford. *Oxon* 5C **50**
Dryslwyn. *Carm* 3F **45**
Dry Street. *Essx* 2A **40**
Dryton. *Shrp* 5H **71**
Dubford. *Abers* 2E **161**
Dubiton. *Abers* 3D **160**
Dubton. *Ang* 3E **145**
Duchally. *High* 2A **164**
Duck End. *Essx* 3G **53**
Duckington. *Ches W* 5G **83**
Ducklington. *Oxon* 5B **50**
Duckmanton. *Derbs* 3B **86**
Duck Street. *Hants* 2B **24**
Dudbridge. *Glos* 5D **48**
Duddenhoe End. *Essx* 2E **53**
Duddingston. *Edin* 2F **129**
Duddington. *Nptn* 5G **75**
Duddleswell. *E Sus* 3F **27**
Duddo. *Nmbd* 5F **131**
Duddon. *Ches W* 4H **83**
Duddon Bridge. *Cumb* 1A **96**
Dudleston. *Shrp* 2F **71**
Dudleston Heath. *Shrp* 2F **71**
Dudley. *Tyne* 2F **115**
Dudley. *W Mid* 2D **60**
Dudston. *Shrp* 1E **59**
Dudwells. *Pemb* 2D **42**
Duffield. *Derbs* 1H **73**
Duffryn. *Neat* 2B **32**
Dufftown. *Mor* 4H **159**
Duffus. *Mor* 2F **159**
Dufton. *Cumb* 2H **103**
Duggleby. *N Yor* 3C **100**
Duirinish. *High* 5G **155**
Duisdalemore. *High* 2E **147**
Duisdeil Mòr. *High* 2E **147**
Duisky. *High* 1E **141**
Dukesfield. *Nmbd* 4C **114**
Dukestown. *Blae* 5E **47**
Dukinfield. *G Man* 1D **84**
Dulas. *IOA* 2D **81**
Dulcote. *Som* 2A **22**
Dulford. *Devn* 2D **12**
Dull. *Per* 4F **143**
Dullatur. *N Lan* 2A **128**
Dullingham. *Cambs* 5F **65**
Dullingham Ley. *Cambs* 5F **65**
Dulnain Bridge. *High* 1D **151**
Duloe. *Bed* 4A **64**
Duloe. *Corn* 3G **7**
Dulverton. *Som* 4C **20**
Dulwich. *G Lon* 3E **39**
Dumbarton. *W Dun* 2F **127**
Dumbleton. *Glos* 2F **49**
Dumfin. *Arg* 1E **127**
Dumfries. *Dum* 2A **112**
Dumgoyne. *Stir* 1G **127**
Dummer. *Hants* 2D **24**
Dumpford. *W Sus* 4G **25**
Dun. *Ang* 2F **145**
Dunagoil. *Arg* 4B **126**
Dunalastair. *Per* 3E **142**
Dunan. *High* 1D **147**
Dunball. *Som* 2G **21**
Dunbar. *E Lot* 2C **130**
Dunbeath. *High* 5D **168**
Dunbeg. *Arg* 5C **140**
Dunblane. *Stir* 3G **135**
Dunbog. *Fife* 2E **137**
Dunbridge. *Hants* 4B **24**
Duncanston. *Abers* 1C **152**
Duncanston. *High* 3H **157**
Dun Charlabhaigh. *W Isl* 3D **171**
Dunchideock. *Devn* 4B **12**
Dunchurch. *Warw* 3B **62**
Duncote. *Nptn* 5D **62**
Duncow. *Dum* 1A **112**
Duncrievie. *Per* 3D **136**
Duncton. *W Sus* 4A **26**
Dundee. *D'dee* 5D **144**
Dundee Airport. *D'dee* 1F **137**
Dundon. *Som* 3H **21**
Dundonald. *S Ayr* 1C **116**
Dundonnell. *High* 5E **163**
Dundraw. *Cumb* 5D **112**
Dundreggan. *High* 2F **149**
Dundrennan. *Dum* 5E **111**
Dundridge. *Hants* 1D **16**
Dundry. *N Som* 5A **34**
Dunecht. *Abers* 3E **153**
Dunfermline. *Fife* 1D **129**
Dunford Bridge. *S Yor* 4B **92**
Dungate. *Kent* 5D **40**
Dunge. *Wilts* 1D **23**
Dungeness. *Kent* 4E **29**
Dungworth. *S Yor* 2G **85**
Dunham-on-the-Hill. *Ches W* 3G **83**
Dunham-on-Trent. *Notts* 3F **87**
Dunhampton. *Worc* 4C **60**
Dunham Town. *G Man* 2B **84**
Dunham Woodhouses. *G Man* 2B **84**
Dunholme. *Linc* 3H **87**
Dunino. *Fife* 2H **137**
Dunipace. *Falk* 1B **128**
Dunira. *Per* 1G **135**
Dunkeld. *Per* 4H **143**
Dunkerton. *Bath* 1C **22**
Dunkeswell. *Devn* 2E **13**
Dunkeswick. *N Yor* 5F **99**
Dunkirk. *Kent* 5E **41**
Dunkirk. *S Glo* 3C **34**
Dunkirk. *Staf* 5C **84**
Dunkirk. *Wilts* 5E **35**
Dunk's Green. *Kent* 5H **39**
Dunlappie. *Ang* 2E **145**
Dunley. *Hants* 1C **24**
Dunley. *Worc* 4B **60**
Dunlichity Lodge. *High* 5A **158**
Dunlop. *E Ayr* 5F **127**
Dunmaglass Lodge. *High* 1H **149**
Dunmore. *Arg* 3F **125**
Dunmore. *Falk* 1B **128**
Dunmore. *High* 4H **157**
Dunnet. *High* 1E **169**
Dunnichen. *Ang* 4E **145**
Dunning. *Per* 2C **136**
Dunnington. *E Yor* 4F **101**
Dunnington. *Warw* 5E **61**
Dunnington. *York* 4A **100**
Dunningwell. *Cumb* 1A **96**
Dunnockshaw. *Lanc* 2G **91**
Dunoon. *Arg* 2C **126**
Dunphail. *Mor* 4E **159**
Dunragit. *Dum* 4G **109**
Dunrostan. *Arg* 1F **125**
Duns. *Bord* 4D **130**
Dunsby. *Linc* 3A **76**
Dunscar. *G Man* 3F **91**
Dunscore. *Dum* 1F **111**
Dunscroft. *S Yor* 4G **93**
Dunsdale. *Red C* 3D **106**
Dunsden Green. *Oxon* 4F **37**
Dunsfold. *Surr* 2B **26**
Dunsford. *Devn* 4B **12**
Dunshalt. *Fife* 2E **137**
Dunshillock. *Abers* 4G **161**
Dunsley. *N Yor* 3F **107**
Dunsley. *Staf* 2C **60**
Dunsmore. *Buck* 5G **51**
Dunsop Bridge. *Lanc* 4F **97**
Dunstable. *C Beds* 3A **52**
Dunstal. *Staf* 3E **73**
Dunstall. *Staf* 3F **73**
Dunstall Green. *Suff* 4G **65**
Dunstall Hill. *W Mid* 1D **60**
Dunstan. *Nmbd* 3G **121**
Dunster. *Som* 2C **20**
Duns Tew. *Oxon* 3C **50**
Dunston. *Linc* 4H **87**
Dunston. *Norf* 5E **79**
Dunston. *Staf* 4D **72**
Dunston. *Tyne* 3F **115**
Dunstone. *Devn* 3B **8**
Dunston Heath. *Staf* 4D **72**
Dunsville. *S Yor* 4G **93**
Dunswell. *E Yor* 1D **94**
Dunsyre. *S Lan* 5D **128**
Dunterton. *Devn* 5D **11**
Duntisbourne Abbots. *Glos* 5E **49**
Duntisbourne Leer. *Glos* 5E **49**
Duntisbourne Rouse. *Glos* 5E **49**
Duntish. *Dors* 2B **14**
Duntocher. *W Dun* 2F **127**
Dunton. *Buck* 3G **51**
Dunton. *C Beds* 1C **52**
Dunton. *Norf* 2A **78**
Dunton Bassett. *Leics* 1C **62**
Dunton Green. *Kent* 5G **39**
Dunton Patch. *Norf* 2A **78**
Duntulm. *High* 1D **154**
Dunure. *S Ayr* 3B **116**
Dunvant. *Swan* 3E **31**
Dunvegan. *High* 4B **154**
Dunwich. *Suff* 3G **67**
Dunwood. *Staf* 5D **84**
Durdar. *Cumb* 4F **113**
Durgates. *E Sus* 2H **27**
Durham. *Dur* 5F **115**
Durham Tees Valley Airport. *Darl* 3A **106**
Durisdeer. *Dum* 4A **118**
Durisdeermill. *Dum* 4A **118**
Durkar. *W Yor* 3D **92**
Durleigh. *Som* 3F **21**
Durley. *Hants* 1D **16**
Durley. *Wilts* 5H **35**
Durley Street. *Hants* 1D **16**
Durlow Common. *Here* 2B **48**
Durnamuck. *High* 4E **163**
Durness. *High* 2E **166**
Durno. *Abers* 1E **152**
Durns Town. *Hants* 3A **16**
Duror. *High* 3D **141**
Durran. *Arg* 3G **133**
Durran. *High* 2D **169**

Durrant Green. *Kent* 2C **28**
Durrants. *Hants* 1F **17**
Durrington. *W Sus* 5C **26**
Durrington. *Wilts* 2G **23**
Dursley. *Glos* 2C **34**
Dursley Cross. *Glos* 4B **48**
Durston. *Som* 4F **21**
Durweston. *Dors* 2D **14**
Duston. *Nptn* 4E **62**
Duthil. *High* 1D **150**
Dutlas. *Powy* 3E **58**
Duton Hill. *Essx* 3G **53**
Dutson. *Corn* 4D **10**
Dutton. *Ches W* 3H **83**
Duxford. *Cambs* 1E **53**
Duxford. *Oxon* 2B **36**
Dwygyfylchi. *Cnwy* 3G **81**
Dwyran. *IOA* 4D **80**
Dyce. *Aber* 2F **153**
Dyffryn. *B'end* 2B **32**
Dyffryn. *Carm* 2H **43**
Dyffryn. *Pemb* 1D **42**
Dyffryn. *V Glam* 4D **32**
Dyffryn Ardudwy. *Gwyn* 3E **69**
Dyffryn Castell. *Cdgn* 2G **57**
Dyffryn Ceidrych. *Carm* 3H **45**
Dyffryn Cellwen. *Neat* 5B **46**
Dyke. *Linc* 3A **76**
Dyke. *Mor* 3D **159**
Dykehead. *Ang* 2C **144**
Dykehead. *N Lan* 3B **128**
Dykehead. *Stir* 4E **135**
Dykend. *Ang* 3B **144**
Dykesfield. *Cumb* 4E **112**
Dylife. *Powy* 1A **58**
Dymchurch. *Kent* 3F **29**
Dymock. *Glos* 2C **48**
Dyrham. *S Glo* 4C **34**
Dysart. *Fife* 4F **137**
Dyserth. *Den* 3C **82**

E

Eachwick. *Nmbd* 2E **115**
Eadar Dha Fhadhail. *W Isl* 4C **171**
Eagland Hill. *Lanc* 5D **96**
Eagle. *Linc* 4F **87**
Eagle Barnsdale. *Linc* 4F **87**
Eagle Moor. *Linc* 4F **87**
Eaglescliffe. *Stoc T* 3B **106**
Eaglesfield. *Cumb* 2B **102**
Eaglesfield. *Dum* 2D **112**
Eaglesham. *E Ren* 4G **127**
Eaglethorpe. *Nptn* 1H **63**
Eagley. *G Man* 3F **91**
Eairy. *IOM* 4B **108**
Eakley Lanes. *Mil* 5F **63**
Eakring. *Notts* 4D **86**
Ealand. *N Lin* 3A **94**
Ealing. *G Lon* 2C **38**
Eallabus. *Arg* 3B **124**
Eals. *Nmbd* 4H **113**
Eamont Bridge. *Cumb* 2G **103**
Earby. *Lanc* 5B **98**
Earcroft. *Bkbn* 2E **91**
Eardington. *Shrp* 1B **60**
Eardisland. *Here* 5G **59**
Eardisley. *Here* 1G **47**
Eardiston. *Shrp* 3F **71**
Eardiston. *Worc* 4A **60**
Earith. *Cambs* 3C **64**
Earlais. *High* 2C **154**
Earle. *Nmbd* 2D **121**
Earlesfield. *Linc* 2G **75**
Earlestown. *Mers* 1H **83**
Earley. *Wok* 4F **37**
Earlham. *Norf* 5D **78**
Earlish. *High* 2C **154**
Earls Barton. *Nptn* 4F **63**
Earls Colne. *Essx* 3B **54**
Earls Common. *Worc* 5D **60**
Earl's Croome. *Worc* 1D **48**
Earlsdon. *W Mid* 3H **61**
Earlsferry. *Fife* 3G **137**
Earlsford. *Abers* 5F **161**
Earl's Green. *Suff* 4C **66**
Earlsheaton. *W Yor* 2C **92**
Earl Shilton. *Leics* 1B **62**
Earl Soham. *Suff* 4E **67**
Earl Sterndale. *Derbs* 4E **85**
Earlston. *E Ayr* 1D **116**
Earlston. *Bord* 1H **119**
Earl Stonham. *Suff* 5D **66**
Earlstoun. *Dum* 1D **110**
Earlswood. *Mon* 2H **33**
Earlswood. *Warw* 3F **61**
Earlyvale. *Bord* 4F **129**
Earnley. *W Sus* 3G **17**
Earsairidh. *W Isl* 9C **170**
Earsdon. *Tyne* 2G **115**
Earsham. *Norf* 2F **67**
Earsham Street. *Suff* 3E **67**
Earswick. *York* 4A **100**
Eartham. *W Sus* 5A **26**
Earthcott Green. *S Glo* 3B **34**
Easby. *N Yor* 4C **106**
(nr. Great Ayton)
Easby. *N Yor* 4E **105**
(nr. Richmond)
Easdale. *Arg* 2E **133**
Easebourne. *W Sus* 4G **25**
Easenhall. *Warw* 3B **62**
Eashing. *Surr* 1A **26**
Easington. *Buck* 4E **51**
Easington. *Dur* 5H **115**
Easington. *E Yor* 3G **95**
Easington. *Nmbd* 1F **121**
Easington. *Oxon* 2C **50**
(nr. Banbury)
Easington. *Oxon* 2E **37**
(nr. Watlington)
Easington. *Red C* 3E **107**
Easington Colliery. *Dur* 5H **115**
Easington Lane. *Tyne* 5G **115**
Easingwold. *N Yor* 3H **99**
Easole Street. *Kent* 5G **41**
Eassie. *Ang* 4C **144**
Eassie and Nevay. *Ang* 4C **144**
East Aberthaw. *V Glam* 5D **32**
Eastacombe. *Devn* 4F **19**
Eastacott. *Devn* 4G **19**
East Allington. *Devn* 4D **8**
East Anstey. *Devn* 4B **20**
East Anton. *Hants* 2B **24**
East Appleton. *N Yor* 5F **105**
East Ardsley. *W Yor* 2D **92**
East Ashley. *Devn* 1G **11**
East Ashling. *W Sus* 2G **17**
East Aston. *Hants* 2C **24**
East Ayton. *N Yor* 1D **101**
East Barkwith. *Linc* 2A **88**
East Barnby. *N Yor* 3F **107**
East Barnet. *G Lon* 1D **39**
East Barns. *E Lot* 2D **130**
East Barsham. *Norf* 2B **78**
East Beach. *W Sus* 3G **17**
East Beckham. *Norf* 1D **78**
East Bedfont. *G Lon* 3B **38**
East Bennan. *N Ayr* 3D **123**
East Bergholt. *Suff* 2D **54**
East Bierley. *W Yor* 2B **92**
East Blatchington. *E Sus* 5F **27**
East Bliney. *Norf* 4B **78**
East Bloxworth. *Dors* 3D **15**
East Boldre. *Hants* 2B **16**
East Bolton. *Nmbd* 3F **121**
Eastbourne. *Darl* 3F **105**
Eastbourne. *E Sus* 5H **27**
East Brent. *Som* 1G **21**
East Bridge. *Suff* 4G **67**
East Bridgford. *Notts* 1D **74**
East Briscoe. *Dur* 3C **104**
East Buckland. *Devn* 3G **19**
(nr. Barnstaple)
East Buckland. *Devn* 4C **8**
(nr. Thurlestone)
East Budleigh. *Devn* 4D **12**
Eastburn. *W Yor* 5C **98**
East Burnham. *Buck* 2A **38**
East Burrafirth. *Shet* 6E **173**
East Burton. *Dors* 4D **14**
Eastbury. *Herts* 1B **38**
Eastbury. *W Ber* 4B **36**
East Butsfield. *Dur* 5E **115**
East Butterleigh. *Devn* 2C **12**
East Butterwick. *N Lin* 4B **94**
Eastby. *N Yor* 4C **98**
East Calder. *W Lot* 3D **129**
East Carleton. *Norf* 5D **78**
East Carlton. *Nptn* 2F **63**
East Carlton. *W Yor* 5E **98**
East Chaldon. *Dors* 4C **14**
East Challow. *Oxon* 3B **36**
East Charleton. *Devn* 4D **8**
East Chelborough. *Dors* 2A **14**
East Chiltington. *E Sus* 4E **27**
East Chinnock. *Som* 1H **13**
East Chisenbury. *Wilts* 1G **23**
Eastchurch. *Kent* 3D **40**
East Clandon. *Surr* 5B **38**
East Claydon. *Buck* 3F **51**
East Clevedon. *N Som* 4H **33**
East Clyne. *High* 3F **165**
East Clyth. *High* 5E **169**
East Coker. *Som* 1A **14**
Eastcombe. *Glos* 5D **49**
East Combe. *Som* 3E **21**
East Common. *N Yor* 1G **93**
East Compton. *Som* 2B **22**
East Cornworthy. *Devn* 3E **9**
Eastcote. *G Lon* 2C **38**
Eastcote. *Nptn* 5D **62**
Eastcote. *W Mid* 3F **61**
Eastcott. *Corn* 1C **10**
Eastcott. *Wilts* 1F **23**
East Cottingwith. *E Yor* 5B **100**
East Coulston. *Wilts* 1E **23**
Eastcourt. *Wilts* 5H **35**
(nr. Pewsey)
Eastcourt. *Wilts* 2E **35**
(nr. Tetbury)
East Cowes. *IOW* 3D **16**
East Cowick. *E Yor* 2G **93**
East Cowton. *N Yor* 4A **106**
East Cramlington. *Nmbd* 2F **115**
East Cranmore. *Som* 2B **22**
East Creech. *Dors* 4E **15**
East Croachy. *High* 1A **150**
East Dean. *E Sus* 5G **27**
East Dean. *Glos* 3B **48**
East Dean. *Hants* 4A **24**
East Dean. *W Sus* 4A **26**
East Down. *Devn* 2G **19**
East Drayton. *Notts* 3E **87**
East Dundry. *N Som* 5A **34**
East Ella. *Hull* 2D **94**
East End. *Cambs* 3C **64**
East End. *Dors* 3E **15**
East End. *E Yor* 4F **101**
(nr. Ulrome)
East End. *E Yor* 2F **95**
(nr. Withernsea)
East End. *Hants* 3B **16**
(nr. Lymington)
East End. *Hants* 5C **36**
(nr. Newbury)
East End. *Herts* 3E **53**
East End. *Kent* 3D **40**
(nr. Minster)
East End. *Kent* 2C **28**
(nr. Tenterden)
East End. *N Som* 4H **33**
East End. *Oxon* 4B **50**
East End. *Som* 1A **22**
East End. *Suff* 2E **54**
Easter Ardross. *High* 1A **158**
Easter Balgedie. *Per* 3D **136**
Easter Balmoral. *Abers* 4G **151**
Easter Brae. *High* 2A **158**
Easter Buckieburn. *Stir* 1A **128**
Easter Bush. *Midl* 3F **129**
Easter Compton. *S Glo* 3A **34**
Easter Fearn. *High* 5D **164**
Easter Galcantray. *High* 4C **158**
Eastergate. *W Sus* 5A **26**
Easterhouse. *Glas* 3H **127**
Easter Howgate. *Midl* 3F **129**
Easter Kinkell. *High* 3H **157**
Easter Lednathie. *Ang* 2C **144**
Easter Ogil. *Ang* 2D **144**
Easter Ord. *Abers* 3F **153**
Easter Quarff. *Shet* 8F **173**
Easter Rhynd. *Per* 2D **136**
Easter Skeld. *Shet* 7E **173**
Easter Suddie. *High* 3A **158**
Easterton. *Wilts* 1F **23**
Eastertown. *Som* 1G **21**
Easter Tulloch. *Abers* 1G **145**
East Everleigh. *Wilts* 1H **23**
East Farleigh. *Kent* 5B **40**
East Farndon. *Nptn* 2E **62**
East Ferry. *Linc* 1F **87**
Eastfield. *N Lan* 3B **128**
(nr. Caldercruix)
Eastfield. *N Lan* 3B **128**
(nr. Harthill)
Eastfield. *N Yor* 1E **101**
Eastfield. *S Lan* 3H **127**
Eastfield Hall. *Nmbd* 4G **121**
East Fortune. *E Lot* 2B **130**
East Garforth. *W Yor* 1E **93**
East Garston. *W Ber* 4B **36**
Eastgate. *Dur* 1C **104**
Eastgate. *Norf* 3D **78**
East Ginge. *Oxon* 3C **36**
East Gores. *Essx* 3B **54**
East Goscote. *Leics* 4D **74**
East Grafton. *Wilts* 5A **36**
East Green. *Suff* 5F **65**
East Grimstead. *Wilts* 4H **23**
East Grinstead. *W Sus* 2E **27**
East Guldeford. *E Sus* 3D **28**
East Haddon. *Nptn* 4D **62**
East Hagbourne. *Oxon* 3D **36**
East Halton. *N Lin* 2E **95**
East Ham. *G Lon* 2F **39**
Eastham. *Mers* 2F **83**
Eastham. *Worc* 4A **60**
Eastham Ferry. *Mers* 2F **83**
Easthampstead. *Brac* 5G **37**
Easthampton. *Here* 4G **59**
East Hanney. *Oxon* 2C **36**
East Hanningfield. *Essx* 5A **54**
East Hardwick. *W Yor* 3E **93**
East Harling. *Norf* 2B **66**
East Harlsey. *N Yor* 5B **106**
East Harnham. *Wilts* 4G **23**
East Harptree. *Bath* 1A **22**
East Hartford. *Nmbd* 2F **115**
East Harting. *W Sus* 1G **17**
East Hatch. *Wilts* 4E **23**
East Hatley. *Cambs* 5B **64**
Easthaugh. *Norf* 4C **78**
East Hauxwell. *N Yor* 5E **105**
East Haven. *Ang* 5E **145**
Eastheath. *Wok* 5G **37**
East Heckington. *Linc* 1A **76**
East Hedleyhope. *Dur* 5E **115**
East Helmsdale. *High* 2H **165**
East Hendred. *Oxon* 3C **36**
East Heslerton. *N Yor* 2D **100**
East Hoathly. *E Sus* 4G **27**
East Holme. *Dors* 4D **15**
Easthope. *Shrp* 1H **59**
Easthorpe. *Essx* 3C **54**
Easthorpe. *Leics* 2F **75**
East Horrington. *Som* 2A **22**
East Horsley. *Surr* 5B **38**
East Horton. *Nmbd* 1E **121**
Easthouses. *Midl* 3G **129**
East Howe. *Bour* 3F **15**
East Huntspill. *Som* 2G **21**
East Hyde. *C Beds* 4B **52**
East Ilsley. *W Ber* 3C **36**
Eastington. *Devn* 2H **11**
Eastington. *Glos* 4G **49**
(nr. Northleach)
Eastington. *Glos* 5C **48**
(nr. Stonehouse)
East Keal. *Linc* 4C **88**
East Kennett. *Wilts* 5G **35**
East Keswick. *W Yor* 5F **99**
East Kilbride. *S Lan* 4H **127**
East Kirkby. *Linc* 4C **88**
East Knapton. *N Yor* 2C **100**
East Knighton. *Dors* 4D **14**
East Knowstone. *Devn* 4B **20**
East Knoyle. *Wilts* 3D **23**
East Kyloe. *Nmbd* 1E **121**
East Lambrook. *Som* 1H **13**
East Langdon. *Kent* 1H **29**
East Langton. *Leics* 1E **63**
East Langwell. *High* 3E **164**
East Lavant. *W Sus* 2G **17**
East Lavington. *W Sus* 4A **26**
East Layton. *N Yor* 4E **105**
Eastleach Martin. *Glos* 5H **49**
Eastleach Turville. *Glos* 5G **49**
East Leake. *Notts* 3C **74**
East Learmouth. *Nmbd* 1C **120**
Eastleigh. *Devn* 4E **19**
(nr. Bideford)
East Leigh. *Devn* 2H **11**
(nr. Crediton)
East Leigh. *Devn* 3C **8**
(nr. Modbury)
Eastleigh. *Hants* 1C **16**
East Lexham. *Norf* 4A **78**
East Lilburn. *Nmbd* 2E **121**
Eastling. *Kent* 5D **40**
East Linton. *E Lot* 2B **130**
East Liss. *Hants* 4F **25**
East Lockinge. *Oxon* 3C **36**
East Looe. *Corn* 3G **7**
East Lound. *N Lin* 1E **87**
East Lulworth. *Dors* 4D **14**
East Lutton. *N Yor* 3D **100**
East Lydford. *Som* 3A **22**
East Lyng. *Som* 4G **21**
East Mains. *Abers* 4D **152**
East Malling. *Kent* 5B **40**
East Marden. *W Sus* 1G **17**
East Markham. *Notts* 3E **87**
East Marton. *N Yor* 4B **98**
East Meon. *Hants* 4E **25**
East Mersea. *Essx* 4D **54**
East Mey. *High* 1F **169**
East Midlands Airport. *Leics* 3B **74**
East Molesey. *Surr* 4C **38**
Eastmoor. *Norf* 5G **77**
East Morden. *Dors* 3E **15**
East Morton. *W Yor* 5D **98**
East Ness. *N Yor* 2A **100**
East Newton. *E Yor* 1F **95**
East Newton. *N Yor* 2A **100**
Eastney. *Port* 3E **17**
Eastnor. *Here* 2C **48**
East Norton. *Leics* 5E **75**
East Nynehead. *Som* 4E **21**
East Oakley. *Hants* 1D **24**
Eastoft. *N Lin* 3B **94**
East Ogwell. *Devn* 5B **12**
Easton. *Cambs* 3A **64**
Easton. *Cumb* 4D **112**
(nr. Burgh by Sands)
Easton. *Cumb* 2F **113**
(nr. Longtown)
Easton. *Devn* 4H **11**
Easton. *Dors* 5B **14**
Easton. *Hants* 3D **24**
Easton. *Linc* 3G **75**
Easton. *Norf* 4D **78**
Easton. *Som* 2A **22**
Easton. *Suff* 5E **67**
Easton. *Wilts* 4D **35**
Easton Grey. *Wilts* 3D **35**
Easton-in-Gordano. *N Som* 4A **34**
Easton Maudit. *Nptn* 5F **63**

Easton on the Hill. *Nptn* 5H 75
Easton Royal. *Wilts* 5H 35
East Orchard. *Dors* 1D 14
East Ord. *Nmbd* 4F 131
East Panson. *Devn* 3D 10
East Peckham. *Kent* 1A 28
East Pennard. *Som* 3A 22
East Perry. *Cambs* 4A 64
East Pitcorthie. *Fife* 3H 137
East Portlemouth. *Devn* 5D 8
East Prawle. *Devn* 5D 9
East Preston. *W Sus* 5B 26
East Putford. *Devn* 1D 10
East Quantoxhead. *Som* 2E 21
East Rainton. *Tyne* 5G 115
East Ravendale. *NE Lin* 1B 88
East Raynham. *Norf* 3A 78
Eastrea. *Cambs* 1B 64
East Rhidorroch Lodge.
            High 4G 163
Eastriggs. *Dum* 3D 112
East Rigton. *W Yor* 5F 99
Eastrington. *E Yor* 1A 94
East Rounton. *N Yor* 4B 106
East Row. *N Yor* 3F 107
East Rudham. *Norf* 3H 77
East Runton. *Norf* 1D 78
East Ruston. *Norf* 3F 79
Eastry. *Kent* 5H 41
East Saltoun. *E Lot* 3A 130
East Shaws. *Dur* 3D 105
East Shefford. *W Ber* 4B 36
Eastshore. *Shet* 10E 173
East Sleekburn. *Nmbd* 1F 115
East Somerton. *Norf* 4G 79
East Stockwith. *Linc* 1E 87
East Stoke. *Dors* 4D 14
East Stoke. *Notts* 1E 75
East Stoke. *Som* 1H 13
East Stour. *Dors* 4D 22
East Stourmouth. *Kent* 4G 41
East Stowford. *Devn* 4G 19
East Stratton. *Hants* 2D 24
East Studdal. *Kent* 1H 29
East Taphouse. *Corn* 2F 7
East-the-Water. *Devn* 4E 19
East Thirston. *Nmbd* 5F 121
East Tilbury. *Thur* 3A 40
East Tisted. *Hants* 3F 25
East Torrington. *Linc* 2A 88
East Tuddenham.
            Norf 4C 78
East Tytherley. *Hants* 4A 24
East Tytherton. *Wilts* 4E 35
East Village. *Devn* 2B 12
Eastville. *Linc* 5D 88
East Wall. *Shrp* 1H 59
East Walton. *Norf* 4G 77
East Week. *Devn* 3G 11
Eastwell. *Leics* 3E 75
East Wellow. *Hants* 4B 24
East Wemyss. *Fife* 4F 137
East Whitburn. *W Lot* 3C 128
Eastwick. *Herts* 4E 53
Eastwick. *Shet* 4E 173
East Williamston. *Pemb* 4E 43
East Winch. *Norf* 4F 77
East Winterslow. *Wilts* 3H 23
East Wittering. *W Sus* 3F 17
East Witton. *N Yor* 1D 98
Eastwood. *Notts* 1B 74
Eastwood. *S'end* 2C 40
East Woodburn. *Nmbd* 1C 114
Eastwood End. *Cambs* 1D 64
East Woodhay. *Hants* 5C 36
East Woodlands. *Som* 2C 22
East Worldham. *Hants* 3F 25
East Wretham. *Norf* 1B 66
East Worlington. *Devn* 1A 12
East Youlstone. *Devn* 1C 10
Eathorpe. *Warw* 4A 62
Eaton. *Ches E* 4C 84
Eaton. *Ches W* 4H 83
Eaton. *Leics* 3E 75

Eaton. *Norf* 2F 77
            (nr. Heacham)
Eaton. *Norf* 5E 78
            (nr. Norwich)
Eaton. *Notts* 3E 86
Eaton. *Oxon* 5C 50
Eaton. *Shrp* 2F 59
            (nr. Bishop's Castle)
Eaton. *Shrp* 1H 59
            (nr. Church Stretton)
Eaton Bishop. *Here* 2H 47
Eaton Bray. *C Beds* 3H 51
Eaton Constantine. *Shrp* 5H 71
Eaton Hastings. *Oxon* 2A 36
Eaton Socon. *Cambs* 5A 64
Eaton upon Tern. *Shrp* 3A 72
Eau Brink. *Norf* 4E 77
Eaves Green. *W Mid* 2G 61
Ebberley Hill. *Devn* 1F 11
Ebberston. *N Yor* 1C 100
Ebbesbourne Wake. *Wilts* 4E 23
Ebblake. *Dors* 2G 15
Ebbsfleet. *Kent* 3H 39
Ebbw Vale. *Blae* 5E 47
Ebchester. *Dur* 4E 115
Ebernoe. *W Sus* 3A 26
Ebford. *Devn* 4C 12
Ebley. *Glos* 5D 48
Ebnal. *Ches W* 1G 71
Ebrington. *Glos* 1G 49
Ecchinswell. *Hants* 1D 24
Ecclefechan. *Dum* 2C 112
Eccles. *G Man* 1B 84
Eccles. *Kent* 4B 40
Eccles. *Bord* 5D 130
Ecclesall. *S Yor* 2H 85
Ecclesfield. *S Yor* 1A 86
Eccles Green. *Here* 1G 47
Eccleshall. *Staf* 3C 72
Eccleshill. *W Yor* 1B 92
Ecclesmachan. *W Lot* 2D 128
Eccles on Sea. *Norf* 3G 79
Eccles Road. *Norf* 1C 66
Eccleston. *Ches W* 4G 83
Eccleston. *Lanc* 3D 90
Eccleston. *Mers* 1G 83
Eccup. *W Yor* 5E 99
Echt. *Abers* 3E 153
Eckford. *Bord* 2B 120
Eckington. *Derbs* 3B 86
Eckington. *Worc* 1E 49
Ecton. *Nptn* 4F 63
Edale. *Derbs* 2F 85
Eday Airport. *Orkn* 4E 172
Edburton. *W Sus* 4D 26
Edderside. *Cumb* 5C 112
Edderton. *High* 5E 164
Eddington. *Kent* 4F 41
Eddington. *W Ber* 5B 36
Eddleston. *Bord* 5F 129
Eddlewood. *S Lan* 4A 128
Edenbridge. *Kent* 1F 27
Edendonich. *Arg* 1A 134
Edenfield. *Lanc* 3G 91
Edenhall. *Cumb* 1G 103
Edenham. *Linc* 3H 75
Edensor. *Derbs* 4G 85
Edentaggart. *Arg* 4C 134
Edenthorpe. *S Yor* 4G 93
Eden Vale. *Dur* 1B 106
Edern. *Gwyn* 2B 68
Edgarley. *Som* 3A 22
Edgbaston. *W Mid* 2E 61
Edgcott. *Buck* 3E 51
Edgcott. *Som* 3B 20
Edge. *Glos* 5D 48
Edge. *Shrp* 5F 71
Edgebolton. *Shrp* 3H 71
Edge End. *Glos* 4A 48
Edgefield. *Norf* 2C 78
Edgefield Street. *Norf* 2C 78
Edge Green. *Ches W* 5G 83
Edgehead. *Midl* 3G 129
Edgeley. *Shrp* 1H 71

Edgeside. *Lanc* 2G 91
Edgeworth. *Glos* 5E 49
Edgiock. *Worc* 4E 61
Edgmond. *Telf* 4B 72
Edgmond Marsh. *Telf* 3B 72
Edgton. *Shrp* 2F 59
Edgware. *G Lon* 1C 38
Edgworth. *Bkbn* 3F 91
Edinbane. *High* 3C 154
Edinburgh. *Edin* 2F 129
Edinburgh Airport. *Edin* 2E 129
Edingale. *Staf* 4G 73
Edingley. *Notts* 5D 86
Edingthorpe. *Norf* 2F 79
Edington. *Som* 3G 21
Edington. *Wilts* 1E 23
Edingworth. *Som* 1G 21
Edistone. *Devn* 4C 18
Edithmead. *Som* 2G 21
Edith Weston. *Rut* 5G 75
Edlaston. *Derbs* 1F 73
Edlesborough. *Buck* 4H 51
Edlingham. *Nmbd* 4F 121
Edlington. *Linc* 3B 88
Edmondsham. *Dors* 1F 15
Edmondsley. *Dur* 5F 115
Edmondthorpe. *Leics* 4F 75
Edmonstone. *Orkn* 5E 172
Edmonton. *Corn* 1D 6
Edmonton. *G Lon* 1E 39
Edmundbyers. *Dur* 4D 114
Ednam. *Bord* 1B 120
Ednaston. *Derbs* 1G 73
Edney Common. *Essx* 5G 53
Edrom. *Bord* 4E 131
Edstaston. *Shrp* 2H 71
Edstone. *Warw* 4F 61
Edvin Loach. *Here* 5A 60
Edwalton. *Notts* 2D 74
Edwardstone. *Suff* 1C 54
Edwardsville. *Mer T* 2D 32
Edwinsford. *Carm* 2G 45
Edwinstowe. *Notts* 4D 86
Edworth. *C Beds* 1C 52
Edwyn Ralph. *Here* 5A 60
Edzell. *Ang* 2F 145
Efail-fach. *Neat* 2A 32
Efail Isaf. *Rhon* 3D 32
Efailnewydd. *Gwyn* 2C 68
Efail-rhyd. *Powy* 3D 70
Efailwen. *Carm* 2F 43
Efenechtyd. *Den* 5D 82
Effingham. *Surr* 5C 38
Effingham Common. *Surr* 5C 38
Effirth. *Shet* 6E 173
Efflinch. *Staf* 4F 73
Efford. *Devn* 2B 12
Egbury. *Hants* 1C 24
Egdon. *Worc* 5D 60
Egerton. *G Man* 3F 91
Egerton. *Kent* 1D 28
Egerton Forstal. *Kent* 1C 28
Eggborough. *N Yor* 2F 93
Eggbuckland. *Plym* 3A 8
Eggesford. *Devn* 1G 11
Eggington. *C Beds* 3H 51
Egginton. *Derbs* 3G 73
Egglescliffe. *Stoc T* 3B 106
Eggleston. *Dur* 2C 104
Egham. *Surr* 3B 38
Egham Hythe. *Surr* 3B 38
Egleton. *Rut* 5F 75
Eglingham. *Nmbd* 3F 121
Egloshayle. *Corn* 5A 10
Egloskerry. *Corn* 4C 10
Eglwysbach. *Cnwy* 3H 81
Eglwys Brewis. *V Glam* 5D 32
Eglwys Fach. *Cdgn* 1F 57
Eglwyswrw. *Pemb* 1F 43
Egmanton. *Notts* 4E 87
Egmere. *Norf* 2B 78
Egremont. *Cumb* 3B 102
Egremont. *Mers* 1F 83
Egton. *N Yor* 4F 107
Egton Bridge. *N Yor* 4F 107

Egypt. *Buck* 2A 38
Egypt. *Hants* 2C 24
Eight Ash Green. *Essx* 3C 54
Eight Mile Burn. *Midl* 4E 129
Eignaig. *High* 4B 140
Eilanreach. *High* 2G 147
Eildon. *Bord* 1H 119
Eileanach Lodge. *High* 2H 157
Eilean Iarmain. *High* 2F 147
Einacleit. *W Isl* 5D 171
Eisgein. *W Isl* 6F 171
Eisingrug. *Gwyn* 2F 69
Elan Village. *Powy* 4B 58
Elberton. *S Glo* 3B 34
Elbridge. *W Sus* 5A 26
Elburton. *Plym* 3B 8
Elcho. *Per* 1D 136
Elcombe. *Swin* 3G 35
Elcot. *W Ber* 5B 36
Eldernell. *Cambs* 1C 64
Eldersfield. *Worc* 2D 48
Elderslie. *Ren* 3F 127
Elder Street. *Essx* 2F 53
Eldon. *Dur* 2F 105
Eldroth. *N Yor* 3G 97
Eldwick. *W Yor* 5D 98
Elford. *Nmbd* 1F 121
Elford. *Staf* 4F 73
Elford Closes. *Cambs* 3D 65
Elgin. *Mor* 2G 159
Elgol. *High* 2D 146
Elham. *Kent* 1F 29
Elie. *Fife* 3G 137
Eling. *Hants* 1B 16
Eling. *W Ber* 4D 36
Elishaw. *Nmbd* 5C 120
Elizafield. *Dum* 2B 112
Elkesley. *Notts* 3D 86
Elkington. *Nptn* 3D 62
Elkins Green. *Essx* 5G 53
Elkstone. *Glos* 4E 49
Ellan. *High* 1C 150
Elland. *W Yor* 2B 92
Ellary. *Arg* 2F 125
Ellastone. *Staf* 1F 73
Ellbridge. *Corn* 2A 8
Ellel. *Lanc* 4D 97
Ellemford. *Bord* 3D 130
Ellenabeich. *Arg* 2E 133
Ellenborough. *Cumb* 1B 102
Ellenbrook. *Herts* 5C 52
Ellenhall. *Staf* 3C 72
Ellen's Green. *Surr* 2B 26
Ellerbec. *N Yor* 5B 106
Ellerburn. *N Yor* 1C 100
Ellerby. *N Yor* 3E 107
Ellerdine. *Telf* 3A 72
Ellerdine Heath. *Telf* 3A 72
Ellerhayes. *Devn* 2C 12
Elleric. *Arg* 4E 141
Ellerker. *E Yor* 2C 94
Ellerton. *E Yor* 1H 93
Ellerton. *N Yor* 5F 105
Ellerton. *Shrp* 3B 72
Ellesborough. *Buck* 5G 51
Ellesmere. *Shrp* 2F 71
Ellesmere Port. *Ches W* 3G 83
Ellingham. *Hants* 2G 15
Ellingham. *Norf* 1F 67
Ellingham. *Nmbd* 2F 121
Ellingstring. *N Yor* 1D 98
Ellington. *Cambs* 3A 64
Ellington. *Nmbd* 5G 121
Ellington Thorpe. *Cambs* 3A 64
Elliot. *Ang* 5F 145
Ellisfield. *Hants* 2E 25
Ellishadder. *High* 2E 155
Ellistown. *Leics* 4B 74
Ellon. *Abers* 5G 161
Ellonby. *Cumb* 1F 103
Ellough. *Suff* 2G 67
Elloughton. *E Yor* 2C 94
Ellwood. *Glos* 5A 48

Elm. *Cambs* 5D 76
Elmbridge. *Glos* 4D 48
Elmbridge. *Worc* 4D 60
Elmdon. *Essx* 2E 53
Elmdon. *W Mid* 2F 61
Elmdon Heath. *W Mid* 2F 61
Elmesthorpe. *Leics* 1B 62
Elmfield. *IOW* 3D 16
Elm Hill. *Dors* 4D 22
Elmhurst. *Staf* 4F 73
Elmley Castle. *Worc* 1E 49
Elmley Lovett. *Worc* 4C 60
Elmore. *Glos* 4C 48
Elmore Back. *Glos* 4C 48
Elm Park. *G Lon* 2G 39
Elmscott. *Devn* 4C 18
Elmsett. *Suff* 1D 54
Elmstead. *Essx* 3D 54
Elmstead Heath. *Essx* 3D 54
Elmstead Market. *Essx* 3D 54
Elmsted. *Kent* 1F 29
Elmstone. *Kent* 4G 41
Elmstone Hardwicke. *Glos* 3E 49
Elmswell. *E Yor* 4D 101
Elmswell. *Suff* 4B 66
Elmton. *Derbs* 3C 86
Elphin. *High* 2G 163
Elphinstone. *E Lot* 2G 129
Elrick. *Abers* 3F 153
Elrick. *Mor* 1B 152
Elrig. *Dum* 5A 110
Elsecar. *S Yor* 1A 86
Elsenham. *Essx* 3F 53
Elsfield. *Oxon* 4D 50
Elsham. *N Lin* 3D 94
Elsing. *Norf* 4C 78
Elslack. *N Yor* 5B 98
Elsrickle. *S Lan* 5D 128
Elstead. *Surr* 1A 26
Elsted. *W Sus* 1G 17
Elsted Marsh. *W Sus* 4G 25
Elsthorpe. *Linc* 3H 75
Elstob. *Dur* 2A 106
Elston. *Devn* 2A 12
Elston. *Lanc* 1E 90
Elston. *Notts* 1E 75
Elston. *Wilts* 2F 23
Elstone. *Devn* 1G 11
Elstow. *Bed* 1A 52
Elstree. *Herts* 1C 38
Elstronwick. *E Yor* 1F 95
Elswick. *Lanc* 1C 90
Elswick. *Tyne* 3F 115
Elsworth. *Cambs* 4C 64
Elterwater. *Cumb* 4E 103
Eltham. *G Lon* 3F 39
Eltisley. *Cambs* 5B 64
Elton. *Cambs* 1H 63
Elton. *Ches W* 3G 83
Elton. *Derbs* 4G 85
Elton. *Glos* 4C 48
Elton. *G Man* 3F 91
Elton. *Here* 3G 59
Elton. *Notts* 2E 75
Elton. *Stoc T* 3B 106
Elton Green. *Ches W* 3G 83
Eltringham. *Nmbd* 3D 115
Elvanfoot. *S Lan* 3B 118
Elvaston. *Derbs* 2B 74
Elveden. *Suff* 3H 65
Elvetham Heath. *Hants* 1F 25
Elvingston. *E Lot* 2A 130
Elvington. *Kent* 5G 41
Elvington. *York* 5B 100
Elwick. *Hart* 1B 106
Elwick. *Nmbd* 1F 121
Elworth. *Ches E* 4B 84
Elworthy. *Som* 4A 14
Elworthy. *Som* 3D 20
Ely. *Cambs* 2E 65
Ely. *Card* 4E 33
Emberton. *Mil* 1G 51
Embleton. *Cumb* 1C 102

Embleton. *Dur* 2B 106
Embleton. *Nmbd* 2G 121
Embo. *High* 4F 165
Emborough. *Som* 1B 22
Embo Street. *High* 4F 165
Embsay. *N Yor* 4C 98
Emery Down. *Hants* 2A 16
Emley. *W Yor* 3C 92
Emmbrook. *Wok* 5F 37
Emmer Green. *Read* 4F 37
Emmington. *Oxon* 5F 51
Emneth. *Norf* 5D 77
Emneth Hungate. *Norf* 5E 77
Empingham. *Rut* 5G 75
Empshott. *Hants* 3F 25
Emsworth. *Hants* 2F 17
Enborne. *W Ber* 5C 36
Enborne Row. *W Ber* 5C 36
Enchmarsh. *Shrp* 1H 59
Enderby. *Leics* 1C 62
Endmoor. *Cumb* 1E 97
Endon. *Staf* 5D 84
Endon Bank. *Staf* 5D 84
Enfield. *G Lon* 1E 39
Enfield Wash. *G Lon* 1E 39
Enford. *Wilts* 1G 23
Engine Common. *S Glo* 3B 34
Englefield. *W Ber* 4E 36
Englefield Green. *Surr* 3A 38
Engleseabrook. *Ches E* 5B 84
English Bicknor. *Glos* 4A 48
Englishcombe. *Bath* 5C 34
English Frankton. *Shrp* 3G 71
Enham Alamein. *Hants* 2B 24
Enmore. *Som* 3F 21
Ennerdale Bridge. *Cumb* 3B 102
Enniscaven. *Corn* 3D 6
Enoch. *Dum* 4A 118
Enochdhu. *Per* 2H 143
Ensay. *Arg* 4E 139
Ensbury. *Bour* 3F 15
Ensdon. *Shrp* 4G 71
Ensis. *Devn* 4F 19
Enson. *Staf* 3D 72
Enstone. *Oxon* 3B 50
Enterkinfoot. *Dum* 4A 118
Enville. *Staf* 2C 60
Eolaigearraidh. *W Isl* 8C 170
Eorabus. *Arg* 1A 132
Eoropaidh. *W Isl* 1H 171
Epney. *Glos* 4C 48
Epperstone. *Notts* 1D 74
Epping. *Essx* 5E 53
Epping Green. *Essx* 5E 53
Epping Green. *Herts* 5C 52
Epping Upland. *Essx* 5E 53
Eppleby. *N Yor* 3E 105
Eppleworth. *E Yor* 1D 94
Epsom. *Surr* 4D 38
Epwell. *Oxon* 1B 50
Epworth. *N Lin* 4A 94
Epworth Turbary. *N Lin* 4A 94
Erbistock. *Wrex* 1F 71
Erbusaig. *High* 1F 147
Erchless Castle. *High* 4G 157
Erdington. *W Mid* 1F 61
Eredine. *Arg* 3G 133
Eriboll. *High* 3E 167
Ericstane. *Dum* 3C 118
Eridge Green. *E Sus* 2G 27
Erines. *Arg* 2G 125
Eriswell. *Suff* 3G 65
Erith. *G Lon* 3G 39
Erlestoke. *Wilts* 1E 23
Ermine. *Linc* 3G 87
Ermington. *Devn* 3C 8
Ernesettle. *Plym* 3A 8
Erpingham. *Norf* 2D 78
Erriottwood. *Kent* 5D 40
Errogie. *High* 1H 149
Errol. *Per* 1E 137
Errol Station. *Per* 1E 137
Erskine. *Ren* 2F 127
Erskine Bridge. *Ren* 2F 127
Ervie. *Dum* 3F 109
Erwarton. *Suff* 2F 55
Erwood. *Powy* 1D 46
Eryholme. *N Yor* 4A 106
Eryrys. *Den* 5E 82
Escalls. *Corn* 4A 4
Escomb. *Dur* 1E 105
Escrick. *N Yor* 5A 100
Esgair. *Carm* 3D 45
(nr. Carmarthen)
Esgair. *Carm* 3G 43
(nr. St Clears)
Esgairgeiliog. *Powy* 5G 69
Esh. *Dur* 5E 115
Esher. *Surr* 4C 38
Esholt. *W Yor* 5D 98
Eshott. *Nmbd* 5G 121
Eshton. *N Yor* 4B 98
Esh Winning. *Dur* 5E 115
Eskadale. *High* 5G 157
Eskbank. *Midl* 3G 129
Eskdale Green. *Cumb* 4C 102
Eskdalemuir. *Dum* 5E 119
Eskham. *Linc* 1C 88
Esknish. *Arg* 3B 124
Esk Valley. *N Yor* 4F 107
Eslington Hall. *Nmbd* 3E 121
Espley Hall. *Nmbd* 5F 121
Esprick. *Lanc* 1C 90
Essendine. *Rut* 4H 75
Essendon. *Herts* 5C 52
Essich. *High* 5A 158
Essington. *Staf* 5D 72
Eston. *Red C* 3C 106
Estover. *Plym* 3B 8
Eswick. *Shet* 6F 173
Etal. *Nmbd* 1D 120
Etchilhampton. *Wilts* 5F 35
Etchingham. *E Sus* 3B 28
Etchinghill. *Kent* 2F 29
Etchinghill. *Staf* 4E 73
Etherley Dene. *Dur* 2E 105
Ethie Haven. *Ang* 4F 145
Etling Green. *Norf* 4C 78
Etloe. *Glos* 5B 48
Eton. *Wind* 3A 38
Eton Wick. *Wind* 3A 38
Etteridge. *High* 4A 150
Ettersgill. *Dur* 2B 104
Ettiley Heath. *Ches E* 4B 84
Ettington. *Warw* 1A 50
Etton. *E Yor* 5D 101
Etton. *Pet* 5A 76
Ettrick. *Bord* 3E 119
Ettrickbridge. *Bord* 2F 119
Etwall. *Derbs* 2G 73
Eudon Burnell. *Shrp* 2B 60
Eudon George. *Shrp* 2A 60
Euston. *Suff* 3A 66
Euxton. *Lanc* 3D 90
Evanstown. *B'end* 3C 32
Evanton. *High* 2A 158
Evedon. *Linc* 1H 75
Evelix. *High* 4E 165
Evendine. *Here* 1C 48
Evenjobb. *Powy* 4E 59
Evenley. *Nptn* 2D 50
Evenlode. *Glos* 3H 49
Even Swindon. *Swin* 3G 35
Evenwood. *Dur* 2E 105
Evenwood Gate. *Dur* 2E 105
Everbay. *Orkn* 5F 172
Evercreech. *Som* 3B 22
Everdon. *Nptn* 5C 62
Everingham. *E Yor* 5C 100
Everleigh. *Wilts* 1H 23
Everley. *N Yor* 1D 100
Eversholt. *C Beds* 2H 51
Evershot. *Dors* 2A 14
Eversley. *Hants* 5F 37
Eversley Centre. *Hants* 5F 37
Eversley Cross. *Hants* 5F 37
Everthorpe. *E Yor* 1C 94
Everton. *C Beds* 5B 64
Everton. *Hants* 3A 16
Everton. *Mers* 1F 83
Everton. *Notts* 1D 86
Evertown. *Dum* 2E 113
Evesbatch. *Here* 1B 48
Evesham. *Worc* 1F 49
Evington. *Leic* 5D 74
Ewden Village. *S Yor* 1G 85
Ewdness. *Shrp* 1B 60
Ewell. *Surr* 4D 38
Ewell Minnis. *Kent* 1G 29
Ewelme. *Oxon* 2E 37
Ewen. *Glos* 2F 35
Ewenny. *V Glam* 4C 32
Ewerby. *Linc* 1A 76
Ewes. *Dum* 5F 119
Ewesley. *Nmbd* 5E 121
Ewhurst. *Surr* 1B 26
Ewhurst Green. *E Sus* 3B 28
Ewhurst Green. *Surr* 2B 26
Ewlo. *Flin* 4F 83
Ewloe. *Flin* 4F 83
Ewood Bridge. *Lanc* 2F 91
Eworthy. *Devn* 3E 11
Ewshot. *Hants* 1G 25
Ewyas Harold. *Here* 3G 47
Exbourne. *Devn* 2G 11
Exbury. *Hants* 2C 16
Exceat. *E Sus* 5G 27
Exebridge. *Som* 4C 20
Exelby. *N Yor* 1E 99
Exeter. *Devn* 3C 12
Exeter International Airport. *Devn* 3D 12
Exford. *Som* 3B 20
Exfords Green. *Shrp* 5G 71
Exhall. *Warw* 5F 61
Exlade Street. *Oxon* 3E 37
Exminster. *Devn* 4C 12
Exmoor. *Som* 3B 20
Exmouth. *Devn* 4D 12
Exning. *Suff* 4F 65
Exton. *Devn* 4C 12
Exton. *Hants* 4E 24
Exton. *Rut* 4G 75
Exton. *Som* 3C 20
Exwick. *Devn* 3C 12
Eyam. *Derbs* 3G 85
Eydon. *Nptn* 5C 62
Eye. *Here* 4G 59
Eye. *Pet* 5B 76
Eye. *Suff* 3D 66
Eye Green. *Pet* 5B 76
Eyemouth. *Bord* 3F 131
Eyeworth. *C Beds* 1C 52
Eyhorne Street. *Kent* 5C 40
Eyke. *Suff* 5F 67
Eynesbury. *Cambs* 5A 64
Eynort. *High* 1B 146
Eynsford. *Kent* 4G 39
Eynsham. *Oxon* 5C 50
Eyre. *High* 3D 154
(on Isle of Skye)
Eyre. *High* 5E 155
(on Raasay)
Eythorne. *Kent* 1G 29
Eyton. *Here* 4G 59
Eyton. *Shrp* 2F 59
(nr. Bishop's Castle)
Eyton. *Shrp* 4F 71
(nr. Shrewsbury)
Eyton. *Wrex* 1F 71
Eyton on Severn. *Shrp* 5H 71
Eyton upon the Weald Moors. *Telf* 4A 72

F

Faccombe. *Hants* 1B 24
Faceby. *N Yor* 4B 106
Faddiley. *Ches E* 5H 83
Fadmoor. *N Yor* 1A 100
Fagwyr. *Swan* 5G 45
Faichem. *High* 3E 149
Faifley. *W Dun* 2G 127
Fail. *S Ayr* 2D 116
Failand. *N Som* 4A 34
Failford. *S Ayr* 2D 116
Failsworth. *G Man* 4H 91
Fairbourne. *Gwyn* 4F 69
Fairbourne Heath. *Kent* 5C 40
Fairburn. *N Yor* 2E 93
Fairfield. *Derbs* 3E 85
Fairfield. *Kent* 3D 28
Fairfield. *Worc* 3D 60
(nr. Bromsgrove)
Fairfield. *Worc* 1F 49
(nr. Evesham)
Fairford. *Glos* 5G 49
Fair Green. *Norf* 4F 77
Fair Hill. *Cumb* 1G 103
Fairhill. *S Lan* 4A 128
Fair Isle Airport. *Shet* 1B 172
Fairlands. *Surr* 5A 38
Fairlie. *N Ayr* 4D 126
Fairlight. *E Sus* 4C 28
Fairlight Cove. *E Sus* 4C 28
Fairmile. *Devn* 3D 12
Fairmile. *Surr* 4C 38
Fairmilehead. *Edin* 3F 129
Fair Oak. *Devn* 1D 12
Fair Oak. *Hants* 1C 16
(nr. Eastleigh)
Fair Oak. *Hants* 5D 36
(nr. Kingsclere)
Fairoak. *Staf* 2B 72
Fair Oak Green. *Hants* 5E 37
Fairseat. *Kent* 4H 39
Fairstead. *Essx* 4A 54
Fairstead. *Norf* 4F 77
Fairwarp. *E Sus* 3F 27
Fairwater. *Card* 4E 33
Fairy Cross. *Devn* 4E 19
Fakenham. *Norf* 3B 78
Fakenham Magna. *Suff* 3B 66
Fala. *Midl* 3H 129
Fala Dam. *Midl* 3H 129
Falcon. *Here* 2B 48
Faldingworth. *Linc* 2H 87
Falfield. *S Glo* 2B 34
Falkenham. *Suff* 2F 55
Falkirk. *Falk* 2B 128
Falkland. *Fife* 3E 137
Fallin. *Stir* 4H 135
Fallowfield. *G Man* 1C 84
Falmer. *E Sus* 5E 27
Falmouth. *Corn* 5C 6
Falsgrave. *N Yor* 1E 101
Falstone. *Nmbd* 1A 114
Fanagmore. *High* 4B 166
Fancott. *C Beds* 3A 52
Fanellan. *High* 4G 157
Fangdale Beck. *N Yor* 5C 106
Fangfoss. *E Yor* 4B 100
Fankerton. *Falk* 1A 128
Fanmore. *Arg* 4F 139
Fanner's Green. *Essx* 4G 53
Fannich Lodge. *High* 2E 156
Fans. *Bord* 5C 130
Farcet. *Cambs* 1B 64
Far Cotton. *Nptn* 5E 63
Fareham. *Hants* 2D 16
Farewell. *Staf* 4E 73
Far Forest. *Worc* 3B 60
Farforth. *Linc* 3C 88
Far Green. *Glos* 5C 48
Far Hoarcross. *Staf* 3F 73
Faringdon. *Oxon* 2A 36
Farington. *Lanc* 2D 90
Farlam. *Cumb* 4G 113
Farleigh. *N Som* 5H 33
Farleigh. *Surr* 4E 39
Farleigh Hungerford. *Som* 1D 22
Farleigh Wallop. *Hants* 2E 24
Farleigh Wick. *Wilts* 5D 34
Farlesthorpe. *Linc* 3D 88
Farleton. *Cumb* 1E 97
Farleton. *Lanc* 3E 97
Farley. *High* 4G 157
Farley. *N Som* 4H 33
Farley. *Shrp* 5F 71
(nr. Shrewsbury)
Farley. *Shrp* 5A 72
(nr. Telford)
Farley. *Staf* 1E 73
Farley. *Wilts* 4H 23
Farley Green. *Suff* 5G 65
Farley Green. *Surr* 1B 26
Farley Hill. *Wok* 5F 37
Farley's End. *Glos* 4C 48
Farlington. *N Yor* 3A 100
Farlington. *Port* 2E 17
Farlow. *Shrp* 2A 60
Farmborough. *Bath* 5B 34
Farmcote. *Glos* 3F 49
Farmcote. *Shrp* 1B 60
Farmington. *Glos* 4G 49
Far Moor. *G Man* 4D 90
Farmoor. *Oxon* 5C 50
Farmtown. *Mor* 3C 160
Farnah Green. *Derbs* 1H 73
Farnborough. *G Lon* 4F 39
Farnborough. *Hants* 1G 25
Farnborough. *Warw* 1C 50
Farnborough. *W Ber* 3C 36
Farncombe. *Surr* 1A 26
Farndish. *Bed* 4G 63
Farndon. *Ches W* 5G 83
Farndon. *Notts* 5E 87
Farnell. *Ang* 3F 145
Farnham. *Dors* 1E 15
Farnham. *Essx* 3E 53
Farnham. *N Yor* 3F 99
Farnham. *Suff* 4F 67
Farnham. *Surr* 2G 25
Farnham Common. *Buck* 2A 38
Farnham Green. *Essx* 3E 53
Farnham Royal. *Buck* 2A 38
Farnhill. *N Yor* 5C 98
Farningham. *Kent* 4G 39
Farnley. *N Yor* 5E 98
Farnley Tyas. *W Yor* 3B 92
Farnsfield. *Notts* 5D 86
Farnworth. *G Man* 4F 91
Farnworth. *Hal* 2H 83
Far Oakridge. *Glos* 5E 49
Farr. *High* 2H 167
(nr. Bettyhill)
Farr. *High* 5A 158
(nr. Inverness)
Farr. *High* 3C 150
(nr. Kingussie)
Farraline. *High* 1H 149
Farringdon. *Devn* 3D 12
Farrington. *Dors* 1D 14
Farrington Gurney. *Bath* 1B 22
Far Sawrey. *Cumb* 5E 103
Farsley. *W Yor* 1C 92
Farthinghoe. *Nptn* 2D 50
Farthingstone. *Nptn* 5D 62
Farthorpe. *Linc* 3B 88
Fartown. *W Yor* 3B 92
Farway. *Devn* 3E 13
Fasag. *High* 3A 156
Fascadale. *High* 1G 139
Fasnacloich. *Arg* 4E 141
Fassfern. *High* 1E 141
Fatfield. *Tyne* 4G 115
Faugh. *Cumb* 4G 113
Fauld. *Staf* 3F 73
Fauldhouse. *W Lot* 3C 128
Faulkbourne. *Essx* 4A 54
Faulkland. *Som* 1C 22
Fauls. *Shrp* 2H 71
Faverdale. *Darl* 3F 105
Faversham. *Kent* 4E 40
Fawdington. *N Yor* 2G 99
Fawfieldhead. *Staf* 4E 85
Fawkham Green. *Kent* 4G 39
Fawler. *Oxon* 4B 50
Fawley. *Buck* 3F 37

Fawley—Ford

Fawley. *Hants* 2C 16
Fawley. *W Ber* 3B 36
Fawley Chapel. *Here* 3A 48
Fawton. *Corn* 2F 7
Faxfleet. *E Yor* 2B 94
Faygate. *W Sus* 2D 26
Fazakerley. *Mers* 1F 83
Fazeley. *Staf* 5F 73
Feabuie. *High* 4B 158
Feagour. *High* 4H 149
Fearann Dhomhnaill. *High* 3E 147
Fearby. *N Yor* 1D 98
Fearn. *High* 1C 158
Fearnan. *Per* 4E 142
Fearnbeg. *High* 3G 155
Fearnhead. *Warr* 1A 84
Fearnmore. *High* 2G 155
Featherstone. *Staf* 5D 72
Featherstone. *W Yor* 2E 93
Featherstone Castle. *Nmbd* 3H 113
Feckenham. *Worc* 4E 61
Feering. *Essx* 3B 54
Feetham. *N Yor* 5C 104
Feizor. *N Yor* 3G 97
Felbridge. *Surr* 2E 27
Felbrigg. *Norf* 2E 78
Felcourt. *Surr* 1E 27
Felden. *Herts* 5A 52
Felhampton. *Shrp* 2G 59
Felindre. *Carm* 3F 45
(nr. Llandeilo)
Felindre. *Carm* 2G 45
(nr. Llandovery)
Felindre. *Carm* 2D 44
(nr. Newcastle Emlyn)
Felindre. *Powy* 2D 58
Felindre. *Swan* 5G 45
Felindre Farchog. *Pemb* 1F 43
Felinfach. *Cdgn* 5E 57
Felinfach. *Powy* 2D 46
Felinfoel. *Carm* 5F 45
Felingwmisaf. *Carm* 3F 45
Felingwmuchaf. *Carm* 3F 45
Felin Newydd. *Powy* 5C 70
(nr. Newtown)
Felin Newydd. *Powy* 3E 70
(nr. Oswestry)
Felin Wnda. *Cdgn* 1D 44
Felinwynt. *Cdgn* 5B 56
Felixkirk. *N Yor* 1G 99
Felixstowe. *Suff* 2F 55
Felixstowe Ferry. *Suff* 2G 55
Felkington. *Nmbd* 5F 131
Fell End. *Cumb* 5A 104
Felling. *Tyne* 3F 115
Fell Side. *Cumb* 1E 102
Felmersham. *Bed* 5G 63
Felmingham. *Norf* 3E 79
Felpham. *W Sus* 3H 17
Felsham. *Suff* 5B 66
Felsted. *Essx* 3G 53
Feltham. *G Lon* 3C 38
Felthamhill. *Surr* 3B 38
Felthorpe. *Norf* 4D 78
Felton. *Here* 1A 48
Felton. *N Som* 5A 34
Felton. *Nmbd* 4F 121
Felton Butler. *Shrp* 4F 71
Feltwell. *Norf* 1G 65
Fenay Bridge. *W Yor* 3B 92
Fence. *Lanc* 1G 91
Fence Houses. *Tyne* 4G 115
Fencott. *Oxon* 4D 50
Fen Ditton. *Cambs* 4D 65
Fen Drayton. *Cambs* 4C 64
Fen End. *Linc* 3B 76
Fen End. *W Mid* 3G 61
Fenham. *Nmbd* 5G 131
Fenham. *Tyne* 3F 115
Fenhouses. *Linc* 1B 76
Feniscowles. *Bkbn* 2E 91
Feniton. *Devn* 3D 12
Fenn Green. *Shrp* 2B 60
Fenn's Bank. *Wrex* 2H 71
Fenn Street. *Medw* 3B 40
Fenny Bentley. *Derbs* 5F 85
Fenny Bridges. *Devn* 3E 12
Fenny Compton. *Warw* 5B 62
Fenny Drayton. *Leics* 1A 62
Fenny Stratford. *Mil* 2G 51
Fenrother. *Nmbd* 5F 121
Fenstanton. *Cambs* 4C 64
Fen Street. *Norf* 1C 66
Fenton. *Cambs* 3C 64
Fenton. *Cumb* 4G 113
Fenton. *Linc* 5F 87
(nr. Caythorpe)
Fenton. *Linc* 3F 87
(nr. Saxilby)
Fenton. *Nmbd* 1D 120
Fenton. *Notts* 2E 87
Fenton. *Stoke* 1C 72
Fentonadle. *Corn* 5A 10
Fenton Barns. *E Lot* 1B 130
Fenwick. *E Ayr* 5F 127
Fenwick. *Nmbd* 5G 131
(nr. Berwick-upon-Tweed)
Fenwick. *Nmbd* 2D 114
(nr. Hexham)
Fenwick. *S Yor* 3F 93
Feochaig. *Arg* 4B 122
Feock. *Corn* 5C 6
Feolin Ferry. *Arg* 3C 124
Feorlan. *Arg* 5A 122
Ferindonald. *High* 3E 147
Feriniquarrie. *High* 3A 154
Fern. *Ang* 2D 145
Ferndale. *Rhon* 2C 32
Ferndown. *Dors* 2F 15
Ferness. *High* 4D 158
Fernham. *Oxon* 2A 36
Fernhill. *W Sus* 1D 27
Fernhill Heath. *Worc* 5C 60
Fernhurst. *W Sus* 4G 25
Fernieflatt. *Abers* 1H 145
Ferniegair. *S Lan* 4A 128
Fernilea. *High* 5C 154
Fernilee. *Derbs* 3E 85
Ferrensby. *N Yor* 3F 99
Ferriby Sluice. *N Lin* 2C 94
Ferring. *W Sus* 5C 26
Ferrybridge. *W Yor* 2E 93
Ferryden. *Ang* 3G 145
Ferryhill. *Aber* 3G 153
Ferry Hill. *Cambs* 2C 64
Ferryhill. *Dur* 1F 105
Ferryhill Station. *Dur* 1F 105
Ferryside. *Carm* 4D 44
Ferryton. *High* 2A 158
Fersfield. *Norf* 2C 66
Fersit. *High* 1A 142
Feshiebridge. *High* 3C 150
Fetcham. *Surr* 5C 38
Fetterangus. *Abers* 3G 161
Fettercairn. *Abers* 1F 145
Fewcott. *Oxon* 3D 50
Fewston. *N Yor* 4D 98
Ffairfach. *Carm* 3G 45
Ffair Rhos. *Cdgn* 4G 57
Ffaldybrenin. *Carm* 1G 45
Ffarmers. *Carm* 1G 45
Ffawyddog. *Powy* 4F 47
Ffodun. *Powy* 5E 71
Ffont-y-gari. *V Glam* 5D 32
Fforest. *Carm* 5F 45
Fforest-fach. *Swan* 3F 31
Fforest Goch. *Neat* 5H 45
Ffostrasol. *Cdgn* 1D 44
Ffos-y-ffin. *Cdgn* 4D 56
Ffrith. *Flin* 5E 83
Ffrwdgrech. *Powy* 3D 46
Ffwl-y-mwn. *V Glam* 5D 32
Ffynnon-ddrain. *Carm* 3E 45
Ffynnongroyw. *Flin* 2D 82
Ffynnon Gynydd. *Powy* 1E 47
Ffynnonoer. *Cdgn* 5E 57
Fiag Lodge. *High* 1B 164
Fidden. *Arg* 2B 132
Fiddington. *Glos* 2E 49
Fiddington. *Som* 2F 21
Fiddleford. *Dors* 1D 14
Fiddlers Hamlet. *Essx* 5E 53
Field. *Staf* 2E 73
Field Assarts. *Oxon* 4B 50
Field Broughton. *Cumb* 1C 96
Field Dalling. *Norf* 2C 78
Fieldhead. *Cumb* 1F 103
Field Head. *Leics* 5B 74
Fifehead Magdalen. *Dors* 4C 22
Fifehead Neville. *Dors* 1C 14
Fifehead St Quintin. *Dors* 1C 14
Fife Keith. *Mor* 3B 160
Fifield. *Oxon* 4H 49
Fifield. *Wilts* 1G 23
Fifield. *Wind* 3A 38
Fifield Bavant. *Wilts* 4F 23
Figheldean. *Wilts* 2G 23
Filby. *Norf* 4G 79
Filey. *N Yor* 1F 101
Filford. *Dors* 3H 13
Filgrave. *Mil* 1G 51
Filkins. *Oxon* 5H 49
Filleigh. *Devn* 1H 11
(nr. Crediton)
Filleigh. *Devn* 4G 19
(nr. South Molton)
Fillingham. *Linc* 2G 87
Fillongley. *Warw* 2G 61
Filton. *S Glo* 4B 34
Fimber. *E Yor* 3C 100
Finavon. *Ang* 3D 145
Fincham. *Norf* 5F 77
Finchampstead. *Wok* 5F 37
Fincharn. *Arg* 3G 133
Finchdean. *Hants* 1F 17
Finchingfield. *Essx* 2G 53
Finchley. *G Lon* 1D 38
Findern. *Derbs* 2H 73
Findhorn. *Mor* 2E 159
Findhorn Bridge. *High* 1C 150
Findochty. *Mor* 2B 160
Findo Gask. *Per* 1C 136
Findon. *Abers* 4G 153
Findon. *W Sus* 5C 26
Findon Mains. *High* 2A 158
Findon Valley. *W Sus* 5C 26
Finedon. *Nptn* 3G 63
Fingal Street. *Suff* 3E 66
Fingest. *Buck* 2F 37
Finghall. *N Yor* 1D 98
Fingland. *Cumb* 4D 112
Fingland. *Dum* 3G 117
Finglesham. *Kent* 5H 41
Fingringhoe. *Essx* 3D 54
Finiskaig. *High* 4A 148
Finmere. *Oxon* 2E 51
Finnart. *Per* 3C 142
Finningham. *Suff* 4C 66
Finningley. *S Yor* 1D 86
Finnyguad. *Abers* 3D 160
Finsbury. *G Lon* 2E 39
Finstall. *Worc* 3D 61
Finsthwaite. *Cumb* 1C 96
Finstock. *Oxon* 4B 50
Finstown. *Orkn* 6C 172
Fintry. *Abers* 3E 161
Fintry. *D'dee* 5D 144
Fintry. *Stir* 1H 127
Finwood. *Warw* 4F 61
Finzean. *Abers* 4D 152
Fionnphort. *Arg* 2B 132
Fionnsabhagh. *W Isl* 9C 171
Firbeck. *S Yor* 2C 86
Firby. *N Yor* 1E 99
(nr. Bedale)
Firby. *N Yor* 3B 100
(nr. Malton)
Firgrove. *G Man* 3H 91
Firle. *E Sus* 5F 27
Firsdown. *Wilts* 3H 23
First Coast. *High* 4D 162
Firth. *Shet* 4F 173
Fir Tree. *Dur* 1E 105
Fishbourne. *IOW* 3D 16
Fishbourne. *W Sus* 2G 17
Fishburn. *Dur* 1A 106
Fishcross. *Clac* 4B 136
Fisherford. *Abers* 5D 160
Fisherrow. *E Lot* 2G 129
Fisher's Pond. *Hants* 4C 24
Fisher's Row. *Lanc* 5D 96
Fisherstreet. *W Sus* 2A 26
Fisherton. *High* 3B 158
Fisherton. *S Ayr* 3B 116
Fisherton de la Mere. *Wilts* 3E 23
Fishguard. *Pemb* 1D 42
Fishlake. *S Yor* 3G 93
Fishley. *Norf* 4G 79
Fishnish. *Arg* 4A 140
Fishpond Bottom. *Dors* 3G 13
Fishponds. *Bris* 4B 34
Fishpool. *Glos* 3B 48
Fishpool. *G Man* 4G 91
Fishpools. *Powy* 4D 58
Fishtoft. *Linc* 1C 76
Fishtoft Drove. *Linc* 1C 76
Fishwick. *Bord* 4F 131
Fiskavaig. *High* 5C 154
Fiskerton. *Linc* 3H 87
Fiskerton. *Notts* 5E 87
Fitling. *E Yor* 1F 95
Fittleton. *Wilts* 2G 23
Fittleworth. *W Sus* 4B 26
Fitton End. *Cambs* 4D 76
Fitz. *Shrp* 4G 71
Fitzhead. *Som* 4E 20
Fitzwilliam. *W Yor* 3E 93
Fiunary. *High* 4A 140
Five Ash Down. *E Sus* 3F 27
Five Ashes. *E Sus* 3G 27
Five Bells. *Som* 2D 20
Five Bridges. *Here* 1B 48
Fivehead. *Som* 4G 21
Five Lane Ends. *Lanc* 4E 97
Fivelanes. *Corn* 4C 10
Five Oak Green. *Kent* 1H 27
Five Oaks. *W Sus* 3B 26
Five Roads. *Carm* 5E 45
Five Ways. *Warw* 3G 61
Flack's Green. *Essx* 4A 54
Flackwell Heath. *Buck* 3G 37
Fladbury. *Worc* 1E 49
Fladdabister. *Shet* 8F 173
Flagg. *Derbs* 4F 85
Flamborough. *E Yor* 2G 101
Flamstead. *Herts* 4A 52
Flansham. *W Sus* 5A 26
Flasby. *N Yor* 4B 98
Flash. *Staf* 4E 85
Flashader. *High* 3C 154
Flatt, The. *Cumb* 2G 113
Flaunden. *Herts* 5A 52
Flawborough. *Notts* 1E 75
Flawith. *N Yor* 3G 99
Flax Bourton. *N Som* 5A 34
Flaxby. *N Yor* 4F 99
Flaxholme. *Derbs* 1H 73
Flaxley. *Glos* 4B 48
Flaxley Green. *Staf* 4E 73
Flaxpool. *Som* 3E 21
Flaxton. *N Yor* 3A 100
Fleckney. *Leics* 1D 62
Flecknoe. *Warw* 4C 62
Fledborough. *Notts* 3F 87
Fleet. *Dors* 4B 14
Fleet. *Hants* 1G 25
(nr. Farnborough)
Fleet. *Hants* 2F 17
(nr. South Hayling)
Fleet. *Linc* 3C 76
Fleet Hargate. *Linc* 3C 76
Fleetville. *Herts* 5B 52
Fleetwood. *Lanc* 5C 96
Fleggburgh. *Norf* 4G 79
Fleisirin. *W Isl* 4H 171
Flemingston. *V Glam* 4D 32
Flemington. *S Lan* 3H 127
(nr. Glasgow)
Flemington. *S Lan* 5A 128
(nr. Strathaven)
Flempton. *Suff* 4H 65
Fleoideabhagh. *W Isl* 9C 171
Fletcher's Green. *Kent* 1G 27
Fletchertown. *Cumb* 5D 112
Fletching. *E Sus* 3F 27
Fleuchary. *High* 4E 165
Flexbury. *Corn* 2C 10
Flexford. *Surr* 5A 38
Flimby. *Cumb* 1B 102
Flimwell. *E Sus* 2B 28
Flint. *Flin* 3E 83
Flintham. *Notts* 1E 75
Flint Mountain. *Flin* 3E 83
Flinton. *E Yor* 1F 95
Flintsham. *Here* 5F 59
Flishinghurst. *Kent* 2B 28
Flitcham. *Norf* 3G 77
Flitton. *C Beds* 2A 52
Flitwick. *C Beds* 2A 52
Flixborough. *N Lin* 3B 94
Flixton. *G Man* 1B 84
Flixton. *N Yor* 2E 101
Flixton. *Suff* 2F 67
Flockton. *W Yor* 3C 92
Flodden. *Nmbd* 1D 120
Flodigarry. *High* 1D 154
Flood's Ferry. *Cambs* 1C 64
Flookburgh. *Cumb* 2C 96
Flordon. *Norf* 1D 66
Flore. *Nptn* 4D 62
Flotterton. *Nmbd* 4E 121
Flowton. *Suff* 1D 54
Flushing. *Abers* 4H 161
Flushing. *Corn* 5C 6
Fluxton. *Devn* 3D 12
Flyford Flavell. *Worc* 5D 61
Fobbing. *Thur* 2B 40
Fochabers. *Mor* 3H 159
Fochriw. *Cphy* 5E 46
Fockerby. *N Lin* 3B 94
Fodderty. *High* 3H 157
Foddington. *Som* 4A 22
Foel. *Powy* 4B 70
Foffarty. *Ang* 4D 144
Foggathorpe. *E Yor* 1A 94
Fogo. *Bord* 5D 130
Fogorig. *Bord* 5D 130
Foindle. *High* 4B 166
Folda. *Ang* 2A 144
Fole. *Staf* 2E 73
Foleshill. *W Mid* 2A 62
Foley Park. *Worc* 3C 60
Folke. *Dors* 1B 14
Folkestone. *Kent* 2G 29
Folkingham. *Linc* 2H 75
Folkington. *E Sus* 5G 27
Folksworth. *Cambs* 1A 64
Folkton. *N Yor* 2E 101
Folla Rule. *Abers* 5E 161
Follifoot. *N Yor* 4F 99
Folly Cross. *Devn* 2E 11
Folly Gate. *Devn* 3F 11
Folly, The. *Herts* 4B 52
Folly, The. *W Ber* 5C 36
Fonmon. *V Glam* 5D 32
Fonthill Bishop. *Wilts* 3E 23
Fonthill Gifford. *Wilts* 3E 23
Fontmell Magna. *Dors* 1D 14
Fontwell. *W Sus* 5A 26
Font-y-gary. *V Glam* 5D 32
Foodieash. *Fife* 2F 137
Foolow. *Derbs* 3F 85
Footdee. *Aber* 3G 153
Footherley. *Staf* 5F 73
Foots Cray. *G Lon* 3F 39
Forbestown. *Abers* 2A 152
Force Forge. *Cumb* 5E 103
Force Mills. *Cumb* 5E 103
Forcett. *N Yor* 3E 105
Ford. *Arg* 3F 133

Gairloch. *High* 1H **155**
Gairlochy. *High* 5D **148**
Gairney Bank. *Per* 4D **136**
Gairnshiel Lodge. *Abers* 3G **151**
Gaisgill. *Cumb* 4H **103**
Gaitsgill. *Cumb* 5E **113**
Galashiels. *Bord* 1G **119**
Galgate. *Lanc* 4D **97**
Galhampton. *Som* 4B **22**
Gallatown. *Fife* 4E **137**
Galley Common. *Warw* 1H **61**
Galleyend. *Essx* 5H **53**
Galleywood. *Essx* 5H **53**
Gallin. *Per* 4C **142**
Gallowfauld. *Ang* 4D **144**
Gallowhill. *E Dun* 2H **127**
Gallowhill. *Per* 5A **144**
Gallowhill. *Ren* 3F **127**
Gallowhills. *Abers* 3H **161**
Gallows Green. *Staf* 1E **73**
Gallows Green. *Worc* 4D **60**
Gallowstree Common. *Oxon* 3E **37**
Galltair. *High* 1G **147**
Gallt Melyd. *Den* 2C **82**
Galmington. *Som* 4F **21**
Galmisdale. *High* 5C **146**
Galmpton. *Devn* 4C **8**
Galmpton. *Torb* 3E **9**
Galmpton Warborough. *Torb* 3E **9**
Galphay. *N Yor* 2E **99**
Galston. *E Ayr* 1D **117**
Galton. *Dors* 4C **14**
Galtrigill. *High* 3A **154**
Gamblesby. *Cumb* 1H **103**
Gamelsby. *Cumb* 4D **112**
Gamesley. *Derbs* 1E **85**
Gamlingay. *Cambs* 5B **64**
Gamlingay Cinques. *Cambs* 5B **64**
Gamlingay Great Heath. *C Beds* 5B **64**
Gammaton. *Devn* 4E **19**
Gammersgill. *N Yor* 1C **98**
Gamston. *Notts* 2D **74** (nr. Nottingham)
Gamston. *Notts* 3E **86** (nr. Retford)
Ganarew. *Here* 4A **48**
Ganavan. *Arg* 5C **140**
Ganborough. *Glos* 3G **49**
Gang. *Corn* 2H **7**
Ganllwyd. *Gwyn* 3G **69**
Gannochy. *Ang* 1E **145**
Gannochy. *Per* 1D **136**
Gansclet. *High* 4F **169**
Ganstead. *E Yor* 1E **95**
Ganthorpe. *N Yor* 2A **100**
Ganton. *N Yor* 2D **101**
Gants Hill. *G Lon* 2F **39**
Gappah. *Devn* 5B **12**
Garafad. *High* 2D **155**
Garboldisham. *Norf* 2C **66**
Garden City. *Flin* 4F **83**
Gardeners Green. *Wok* 5G **37**
Gardenstown. *Abers* 2F **161**
Garden Village. *S Yor* 1G **85**
Garden Village. *Swan* 3E **31**
Garderhouse. *Shet* 7E **173**
Gardham. *E Yor* 5D **100**
Gare Hill. *Som* 2C **22**
Garelochhead. *Arg* 4B **134**
Garford. *Oxon* 2C **36**
Garforth. *W Yor* 1E **93**
Gargrave. *N Yor* 4B **98**
Gargunnock. *Stir* 4G **135**
Garleffin. *S Ayr* 1F **109**
Garlieston. *Dum* 5B **110**
Garlinge Green. *Kent* 5F **41**
Garlogie. *Abers* 3E **153**
Garmelow. *Staf* 3B **72**
Garmond. *Abers* 3F **161**
Garmondsway. *Dur* 1A **106**
Garmony. *Arg* 4A **140**
Garmouth. *Mor* 2H **159**
Garmston. *Shrp* 5A **72**
Garnant. *Carm* 4G **45**
Garndiffaith. *Torf* 5F **47**
Garndolbenmaen. *Gwyn* 1D **69**
Garnett Bridge. *Cumb* 5G **103**
Garnfadryn. *Gwyn* 2B **68**
Garnkirk. *N Lan* 3H **127**
Garnlydan. *Blae* 4E **47**
Garnsgate. *Linc* 3D **76**
Garnswllt. *Swan* 5G **45**
Garn-yr-erw. *Torf* 4F **47**
Garrabost. *W Isl* 4H **171**
Garrallan. *E Ayr* 3E **117**
Garras. *Corn* 4E **5**
Garreg. *Gwyn* 1F **69**
Garrigill. *Cumb* 5A **114**
Garriston. *N Yor* 5E **105**
Garrogie Lodge. *High* 2H **149**
Garros. *High* 2D **155**
Garrow. *Per* 4F **143**
Garsdale. *Cumb* 1G **97**
Garsdale Head. *Cumb* 5A **104**
Garsdon. *Wilts* 3E **35**
Garshall Green. *Staf* 2D **72**
Garsington. *Oxon* 5D **50**
Garstang. *Lanc* 5D **97**
Garston. *Mers* 2G **83**
Garswood. *Mers* 1H **83**
Gartcosh. *N Lan* 3H **127**
Garth. *B'end* 2B **32**
Garth. *Cdgn* 2F **57**
Garth. *Gwyn* 2E **69**
Garth. *IOM* 4C **108**
Garth. *Powy* 1C **46** (nr. Builth Wells)
Garth. *Powy* 3E **59** (nr. Knighton)
Garth. *Wrex* 1E **71**
Garthamlock. *Glas* 3H **127**
Garthbrengy. *Powy* 2D **46**
Gartheli. *Cdgn* 5E **57**
Garthmyl. *Powy* 1D **58**
Garthorpe. *Leics* 3F **75**
Garthorpe. *N Lin* 3B **94**
Garth Owen. *Powy* 1D **58**
Garth Row. *Cumb* 5G **103**
Gartly. *Abers* 5C **160**
Gartmore. *Stir* 4E **135**
Gartness. *N Lan* 3A **128**
Gartness. *Stir* 1G **127**
Gartocharn. *W Dun* 1F **127**
Garton. *E Yor* 1F **95**
Garton-on-the-Wolds. *E Yor* 4D **101**
Gartsherrie. *N Lan* 3A **128**
Gartymore. *High* 2H **165**
Garvald. *E Lot* 2B **130**
Garvamore. *High* 4H **149**
Garvard. *Arg* 4A **132**
Garvault. *High* 5H **167**
Garve. *High* 2F **157**
Garvestone. *Norf* 5C **78**
Garvie. *Arg* 4H **133**
Garvock. *Abers* 1G **145**
Garvock. *Inv* 2D **126**
Garway. *Here* 3H **47**
Garway Common. *Here* 3H **47**
Garway Hill. *Here* 3H **47**
Garwick. *Linc* 1A **76**
Gaskan. *High* 1C **140**
Gasper. *Wilts* 3C **22**
Gastard. *Wilts* 5D **35**
Gasthorpe. *Norf* 2B **66**
Gatcombe. *IOW* 4C **16**
Gateacre. *Mers* 2G **83**
Gatebeck. *Cumb* 1E **97**
Gate Burton. *Linc* 2F **87**
Gateforth. *N Yor* 2F **93**
Gatehead. *E Ayr* 1C **116**
Gate Helmsley. *N Yor* 4A **100**
Gatehouse. *Nmbd* 1A **114**
Gatehouse of Fleet. *Dum* 4D **110**
Gatelawbridge. *Dum* 5B **118**
Gateley. *Norf* 3B **78**
Gatenby. *N Yor* 1F **99**
Gatesgarth. *Cumb* 3C **102**
Gateshead. *Tyne* 3F **115**
Gatesheath. *Ches W* 4G **83**
Gateside. *Ang* 4D **144** (nr. Forfar)
Gateside. *Ang* 4C **144** (nr. Kirriemuir)
Gateside. *Fife* 3D **136**
Gateside. *N Ayr* 4E **127**
Gathurst. *G Man* 4D **90**
Gatley. *G Man* 2C **84**
Gatton. *Surr* 5D **39**
Gattonside. *Bord* 1H **119**
Gatwick (London) Airport. *W Sus* 1D **27**
Gaufron. *Powy* 4B **58**
Gaulby. *Leics* 5D **74**
Gauldry. *Fife* 1F **137**
Gaultree. *Norf* 5D **77**
Gaunt's Common. *Dors* 2F **15**
Gaunt's Earthcott. *S Glo* 3B **34**
Gautby. *Linc* 3A **88**
Gavinton. *Bord* 4D **130**
Gawber. *S Yor* 4D **92**
Gawcott. *Buck* 2E **51**
Gawsworth. *Ches E* 4C **84**
Gawthorpe. *W Yor* 2C **92**
Gawthrop. *Cumb* 1F **97**
Gawthwaite. *Cumb* 1B **96**
Gay Bowers. *Essx* 5A **54**
Gaydon. *Warw* 5A **62**
Gayhurst. *Mil* 1G **51**
Gayle. *N Yor* 1A **98**
Gayles. *N Yor* 4E **105**
Gay Street. *W Sus* 3B **26**
Gayton. *Mers* 2E **83**
Gayton. *Norf* 4G **77**
Gayton. *Nptn* 5E **62**
Gayton. *Staf* 3D **73**
Gayton le Marsh. *Linc* 2D **88**
Gayton le Wold. *Linc* 2B **88**
Gayton Thorpe. *Norf* 4G **77**
Gaywood. *Norf* 3F **77**
Gazeley. *Suff* 4G **65**
Geanies. *High* 1C **158**
Gearraidh Bhailteas. *W Isl* 6C **170**
Gearraidh Bhaird. *W Isl* 6F **171**
Gearraidh ma Monadh. *W Isl* 7C **170**
Geary. *High* 2B **154**
Geddes. *High* 3C **158**
Gedding. *Suff* 5B **66**
Geddington. *Nptn* 2F **63**
Gedintailor. *High* 5E **155**
Gedling. *Notts* 1D **74**
Gedney. *Linc* 3D **76**
Gedney Broadgate. *Linc* 3D **76**
Gedney Drove End. *Linc* 3D **76**
Gedney Dyke. *Linc* 3D **76**
Gedney Hill. *Linc* 4C **76**
Gee Cross. *G Man* 1D **84**
Geeston. *Rut* 5G **75**
Geilston. *Arg* 2E **127**
Geirinis. *W Isl* 4C **170**
Geise. *High* 2D **168**
Geisiadar. *W Isl* 4D **171**
Gelder Shiel. *Abers* 5G **151**
Geldeston. *Norf* 1F **67**
Gell. *Cnwy* 4A **82**
Gelli. *Pemb* 3E **43**
Gelli. *Rhon* 2C **32**
Gellifor. *Den* 4D **82**
Gelligaer. *Cphy* 2E **33**
Gellilydan. *Gwyn* 2F **69**
Gellinudd. *Neat* 5H **45**
Gellyburn. *Per* 5H **143**
Gellywen. *Carm* 2G **43**
Gelston. *Dum* 4E **111**
Gelston. *Linc* 1G **75**
Gembling. *E Yor* 4F **101**
Geneva. *Cdgn* 5D **56**
Gentleshaw. *Staf* 4E **73**
Geocrab. *W Isl* 8D **171**
George Green. *Buck* 2A **38**
Georgeham. *Devn* 3E **19**
George Nympton. *Devn* 4H **19**
Georgetown. *Blae* 5E **47**
Georgetown. *Ren* 3F **127**
Georth. *Orkn* 5C **172**
Gerlan. *Gwyn* 4F **81**
Germansweek. *Devn* 3E **11**
Germoe. *Corn* 4C **4**
Gerrans. *Corn* 5C **6**
Gerrard's Bromley. *Staf* 2B **72**
Gerrards Cross. *Buck* 2A **38**
Gerston. *High* 3D **168**
Gestingthorpe. *Essx* 2B **54**
Gethsemane. *Pemb* 1A **44**
Geuffordd. *Powy* 4E **70**
Gibraltar. *Buck* 4F **51**
Gibraltar. *Linc* 5E **89**
Gibraltar. *Suff* 5D **66**
Gibsmere. *Notts* 1E **74**
Giddeahall. *Wilts* 4D **34**
Gidea Park. *G Lon* 2G **39**
Gidleigh. *Devn* 4G **11**
Giffnock. *E Ren* 4G **127**
Gifford. *E Lot* 3B **130**
Giffordtown. *Fife* 2E **137**
Giggetty. *Staf* 1C **60**
Giggleswick. *N Yor* 3H **97**
Gignog. *Pemb* 2C **42**
Gilberdyke. *E Yor* 2B **94**
Gilbert's End. *Worc* 1D **48**
Gilbert's Green. *Warw* 3F **61**
Gilchriston. *E Lot* 3A **130**
Gilcrux. *Cumb* 1C **102**
Gildersome. *W Yor* 2C **92**
Gildingwells. *S Yor* 2C **86**
Gilesgate Moor. *Dur* 5F **115**
Gileston. *V Glam* 5D **32**
Gilfach. *Cphy* 2E **33**
Gilfach Goch. *Rhon* 2C **32**
Gilfachreda. *Cdgn* 5D **56**
Gilgarran. *Cumb* 2B **102**
Gillamoor. *N Yor* 5D **107**
Gillan. *Corn* 4E **5**
Gillar's Green. *Mers* 1G **83**
Gillen. *High* 3B **154**
Gilling East. *N Yor* 2A **100**
Gillingham. *Dors* 4D **22**
Gillingham. *Medw* 4B **40**
Gillingham. *Norf* 1G **67**
Gilling West. *N Yor* 4E **105**
Gillock. *High* 3E **169**
Gillow Heath. *Staf* 5C **84**
Gills. *High* 1F **169**
Gill's Green. *Kent* 2B **28**
Gilmanscleuch. *Bord* 2F **119**
Gilmerton. *Edin* 3F **129**
Gilmerton. *Per* 1A **136**
Gilmonby. *Dur* 3C **104**
Gilmorton. *Leics* 2C **62**
Gilsland. *Nmbd* 3H **113**
Gilsland Spa. *Cumb* 3H **113**
Gilston. *Midl* 4H **129**
Giltbrook. *Notts* 1B **74**
Gilwern. *Mon* 4F **47**
Gimingham. *Norf* 2E **79**
Giosla. *W Isl* 5D **171**
Gipping. *Suff* 4C **66**
Gipsey Bridge. *Linc* 1B **76**
Gipton. *W Yor* 1D **92**
Girdle Toll. *N Ayr* 5E **127**
Girlsta. *Shet* 6F **173**
Girsby. *N Yor* 4A **106**
Girthon. *Dum* 4D **110**
Girton. *Cambs* 4D **64**
Girton. *Notts* 4F **87**
Girvan. *S Ayr* 5A **116**
Gisburn. *Lanc* 5H **97**
Gisleham. *Suff* 2H **67**
Gislingham. *Suff* 3C **66**
Gissing. *Norf* 2D **66**
Gittisham. *Devn* 3E **13**
Gladestry. *Powy* 5E **59**
Gladsmuir. *E Lot* 2A **130**
Glaichbea. *High* 5H **157**
Glais. *Swan* 5H **45**
Glaisdale. *N Yor* 4E **107**
Glame. *High* 4E **155**
Glamis. *Ang* 4C **144**
Glamisdale. *High* 5C **146**
Glanaman. *Carm* 4G **45**
Glan-Conwy. *Cnwy* 5H **81**
Glandford. *Norf* 1C **78**
Glan Duar. *Carm* 1F **45**
Glandwr. *Blae* 5F **47**
Glandwr. *Pemb* 2F **43**
Glan-Dwyfach. *Gwyn* 1D **69**
Glandy Cross. *Carm* 2F **43**
Glandyfi. *Cdgn* 1F **57**
Glangrwyney. *Powy* 4F **47**
Glanmule. *Powy* 1D **58**
Glanrhyd. *Gwyn* 2B **68**
Glanrhyd. *Pemb* 1B **44** (nr. Cardigan)
Glan-rhyd. *Pemb* 1F **43** (nr. Crymych)
Glan-rhyd. *Powy* 5A **46**
Glanton. *Nmbd* 3E **121**
Glanton Pyke. *Nmbd* 3E **121**
Glanvilles Wootton. *Dors* 2B **14**
Glan-y-don. *Flin* 3D **82**
Glan-y-nant. *Powy* 2B **58**
Glan-yr-afon. *Gwyn* 1C **70**
Glan-yr-afon. *IOA* 2F **81**
Glan-yr-afon. *Powy* 5C **70**
Glan-y-wern. *Gwyn* 2F **69**
Glapthorn. *Nptn* 1H **63**
Glapwell. *Derbs* 4B **86**
Glas Aird. *Arg* 4A **132**
Glas-allt Shiel. *Abers* 5G **151**
Glasbury. *Powy* 2E **47**
Glaschoil. *Mor* 5E **159**
Glascoed. *Den* 3B **82**
Glascoed. *Mon* 5G **47**
Glascote. *Staf* 5G **73**
Glascwm. *Powy* 5D **58**
Glasfryn. *Cnwy* 5B **82**
Glasgow. *Glas* 3G **127**
Glasgow Airport. *Ren* 3F **127**
Glasgow Prestwick International Airport. *S Ayr* 2C **116**
Glashvin. *High* 2D **154**
Glasinfryn. *Gwyn* 4E **81**
Glas na Cardaich. *High* 4E **147**
Glasnacardoch. *High* 4E **147**
Glasnakille. *High* 2D **146**
Glaspwll. *Cdgn* 1G **57**
Glassburn. *High* 5F **157**
Glassenbury. *Kent* 2B **28**
Glasserton. *Dum* 5B **110**
Glassford. *S Lan* 5A **128**
Glassgreen. *Mor* 2G **159**
Glasshouse. *Glos* 3C **48**
Glasshouses. *N Yor* 3D **98**
Glasson. *Cumb* 3D **112**
Glasson. *Lanc* 4D **96**
Glassonby. *Cumb* 1G **103**
Glasterlaw. *Ang* 3E **145**
Glaston. *Rut* 5F **75**
Glastonbury. *Som* 3H **21**
Glatton. *Cambs* 2A **64**
Glazebrook. *Warr* 1A **84**
Glazebury. *Warr* 1A **84**
Glazeley. *Shrp* 2B **60**
Gleadless. *S Yor* 2A **86**
Gleadsmoss. *Ches E* 4C **84**
Gleann Dail bho Dheas. *W Isl* 7C **170**
Gleann Tholastaidh. *W Isl* 3H **171**
Gleann Uige. *High* 1A **140**
Gleaston. *Cumb* 2B **96**
Glecknabae. *Arg* 3B **126**
Gledrid. *Shrp* 2E **71**
Gleiniant. *Powy* 1B **58**
Glemsford. *Suff* 1B **54**
Glen. *Dum* 4C **110**
Glenancross. *High* 4E **147**
Glen Audlyn. *IOM* 2D **108**
Glenbarr. *Arg* 2A **122**
Glenbeg. *High* 2G **139**
Glen Bernisdale. *High* 4D **154**
Glenbervie. *Abers* 5E **153**

Glenboig. *N Lan* 3A 128
Glenborrodale. *High* 2A 140
Glenbranter. *Arg* 4A 134
Glenbreck. *Bord* 2C 118
Glenbrein Lodge. *High* 2G 149
Glenbrittle. *High* 1C 146
Glenbuchat Lodge. *Abers* 2H 151
Glenbuck. *E Ayr* 2G 117
Glenburn. *Ren* 3F 127
Glencalvie Lodge. *High* 5B 164
Glencaple. *Dum* 3A 112
Glencarron Lodge. *High* 3C 156
Glencarse. *Per* 1D 136
Glencassley Castle. *High* 3B 164
Glencat. *Abers* 4C 152
Glencoe. *High* 3F 141
Glen Cottage. *High* 5E 147
Glencraig. *Fife* 4D 136
Glendale. *High* 4A 154
Glendevon. *Per* 3B 136
Glendoebeg. *High* 3G 149
Glendoick. *Per* 1E 136
Glendoune. *S Ayr* 5A 116
Glenduckie. *Fife* 2E 137
Gleneagles. *Per* 3B 136
Glenegedale. *Arg* 4B 124
Glenegedale Lots. *Arg* 4B 124
Glenelg. *High* 2G 147
Glenernie. *Mor* 4E 159
Glenesslin. *Dum* 1F 111
Glenfarg. *Per* 2D 136
Glenfarquhar Lodge. *Abers* 5E 152
Glenferness Mains. *High* 4D 158
Glenfeshie Lodge. *High* 4C 150
Glenfiddich Lodge. *Mor* 5H 159
Glenfield. *Leics* 5C 74
Glenfinnan. *High* 5B 148
Glenfintaig Lodge. *High* 5E 149
Glenfoot. *Per* 2D 136
Glenfyne Lodge. *Arg* 2B 134
Glengap. *Dum* 4D 110
Glengarnock. *N Ayr* 4E 126
Glengolly. *High* 2D 168
Glengorm Castle. *Arg* 3F 139
Glengrasco. *High* 4D 154
Glenhead Farm. *Ang* 2B 144
Glenholm. *Bord* 1D 118
Glen House. *Bord* 1E 119
Glenhurich. *High* 2C 140
Glenkerry. *Bord* 3E 119
Glenkiln. *Dum* 2F 111
Glenkindie. *Abers* 2B 152
Glenkinglass Lodge. *Arg* 5F 141
Glenkirk. *Bord* 2C 118
Glenlean. *Arg* 1B 126
Glenlee. *Dum* 1D 110
Glenleraig. *High* 5B 166
Glenlichorn. *Per* 2G 135
Glenlivet. *Mor* 1F 151
Glenlochar. *Dum* 3E 111
Glenlochsie Lodge. *Per* 1H 143
Glenluce. *Dum* 4G 109
Glenmarskie. *High* 3F 157
Glenmassan. *Arg* 1C 126
Glenmavis. *N Lan* 3A 128
Glen Maye. *IOM* 4B 108
Glenmazeran Lodge. *High* 1B 150
Glenmidge. *Dum* 1F 111
Glen Mona. *IOM* 3D 108
Glenmore. *High* 2G 139
(nr. Glenborrodale)
Glenmore. *High* 3D 151
(nr. Kingussie)
Glenmore. *High* 4D 154
(on Isle of Skye)
Glenmoy. *Ang* 2D 144
Glennoe. *Arg* 5E 141
Glen of Coachford. *Abers* 4B 160
Glenogil. *Ang* 2D 144
Glen Parva. *Leics* 1C 62
Glenprosen Village. *Ang* 2C 144
Glenree. *N Ayr* 3D 122
Glenridding. *Cumb* 3E 103
Glenrosa. *N Ayr* 2E 123
Glenrothes. *Fife* 3E 137
Glensanda. *High* 4C 140
Glensaugh. *Abers* 1F 145
Glenshero Lodge. *High* 4H 149
Glensluain. *Arg* 4H 133
Glenstockadale. *Dum* 3F 109
Glenstriven. *Arg* 2B 126
Glen Tanar House. *Abers* 4B 152
Glentham. *Linc* 1H 87
Glenton. *Abers* 1D 152
Glentress. *Bord* 1E 119
Glentromie Lodge. *High* 4B 150
Glentrool Lodge. *Dum* 1B 110
Glentrool Village. *Dum* 2A 110
Glentruim House. *High* 4A 150
Glentworth. *Linc* 2G 87
Glenuig. *High* 1A 140
Glen Village. *Falk* 2B 128
Glen Vine. *IOM* 4C 108
Glenwhilly. *Dum* 2G 109
Glenzierfoot. *Dum* 2E 113
Glespin. *S Lan* 2H 117
Gletness. *Shet* 6F 173
Glewstone. *Here* 3A 48
Glib Cheois. *W Isl* 5F 171
Glinton. *Pet* 5A 76
Glooston. *Leics* 1E 63
Glossop. *Derbs* 1E 85
Gloster Hill. *Nmbd* 4G 121
Gloucester. *Glos* 4D 48
Gloucestershire Airport. *Glos* 3D 49
Gloup. *Shet* 1G 173
Glusburn. *N Yor* 5C 98
Glutt Lodge. *High* 5B 168
Glutton Bridge. *Staf* 4E 85
Gluvian. *Corn* 2D 6
Glympton. *Oxon* 3C 50
Glyn. *Cnwy* 3A 82
Glynarthen. *Cdgn* 1D 44
Glynbrochan. *Powy* 2B 58
Glyn Ceiriog. *Wrex* 2E 70
Glyncoch. *Rhon* 2D 32
Glyncorrwg. *Neat* 2B 32
Glynde. *E Sus* 5F 27
Glyndebourne. *E Sus* 4F 27
Glyndyfrdwy. *Den* 1D 70
Glyn Ebwy. *Blae* 5E 47
Glynllan. *B'end* 3C 32
Glyn-neath. *Neat* 5B 46
Glynogwr. *B'end* 3C 32
Glyntaff. *Rhon* 3D 32
Glyntawe. *Powy* 4B 46
Glynteg. *Carm* 2D 44
Gnosall. *Staf* 3C 72
Gnosall Heath. *Staf* 3C 72
Goadby. *Leics* 1E 63
Goadby Marwood. *Leics* 3E 75
Goatacre. *Wilts* 4F 35
Goathill. *Dors* 1B 14
Goathland. *N Yor* 4F 107
Goathurst. *Som* 3F 21
Goathurst Common. *Kent* 5F 39
Goat Lees. *Kent* 1E 28
Gobernuisgach Lodge. *High* 4E 167
Gobernuisgeach. *High* 5B 168
Gobhaig. *W Isl* 7C 171
Gobowen. *Shrp* 2F 71
Godalming. *Surr* 1A 26
Goddard's Corner. *Suff* 4E 67
Goddard's Green. *Kent* 2C 28
(nr. Benenden)
Goddard's Green. *Kent* 2B 28
(nr. Cranbrook)
Goddards Green. *W Sus* 3D 27
Godford Cross. *Devn* 2E 13
Godleybrook. *Staf* 1D 73
Godmanchester. *Cambs* 3B 64
Godmanstone. *Dors* 3B 14
Godmersham. *Kent* 5E 41
Godolphin Cross. *Corn* 3D 4
Godre'r-graig. *Neat* 5A 46
Godshill. *Hants* 1G 15
Godshill. *IOW* 4D 16
Godstone. *Staf* 2E 73
Godstone. *Surr* 5E 39
Goetre. *Mon* 5G 47
Goff's Oak. *Herts* 5D 52
Gogar. *Edin* 2E 129
Goginan. *Cdgn* 2F 57
Golan. *Gwyn* 1E 69
Golant. *Corn* 3F 7
Golberdon. *Corn* 5D 10
Golborne. *G Man* 1A 84
Golcar. *W Yor* 3A 92
Goldcliff. *Newp* 3G 33
Golden Cross. *E Sus* 4G 27
Golden Green. *Kent* 1H 27
Golden Grove. *Carm* 4F 45
Golden Grove. *N Yor* 4F 107
Golden Hill. *Pemb* 2D 43
Goldenhill. *Stoke* 5C 84
Golden Pot. *Hants* 2F 25
Golden Valley. *Glos* 3E 49
Golders Green. *G Lon* 2D 38
Goldhanger. *Essx* 5C 54
Gold Hill. *Norf* 1E 65
Golding. *Shrp* 5H 71
Goldington. *Bed* 5H 63
Goldsborough. *N Yor* 4F 99
(nr. Harrogate)
Goldsborough. *N Yor* 3F 107
(nr. Whitby)
Goldsithney. *Corn* 3C 4
Goldstone. *Kent* 4G 41
Goldstone. *Shrp* 3B 72
Goldthorpe. *S Yor* 4E 93
Goldworthy. *Devn* 4D 19
Golfa. *Powy* 3D 70
Gollanfield. *High* 3C 158
Gollinglith Foot. *N Yor* 1D 98
Golsoncott. *Som* 3D 20
Golspie. *High* 4F 165
Gomeldon. *Wilts* 3G 23
Gomersal. *W Yor* 2C 92
Gometra House. *Arg* 4E 139
Gomshall. *Surr* 1B 26
Gonalston. *Notts* 1D 74
Gonerby Hill Foot. *Linc* 2G 75
Good Easter. *Essx* 4G 53
Gooderstone. *Norf* 5G 77
Goodleigh. *Devn* 3G 19
Goodmanham. *E Yor* 5C 100
Goodmayes. *G Lon* 2F 39
Goodnestone. *Kent* 5G 41
(nr. Aylesham)
Goodnestone. *Kent* 4E 41
(nr. Faversham)
Goodrich. *Here* 4A 48
Goodrington. *Torb* 3E 9
Goodshaw. *Lanc* 2G 91
Goodshaw Fold. *Lanc* 2G 91
Goodstone. *Devn* 5A 12
Goodwick. *Pemb* 1D 42
Goodworth Clatford. *Hants* 2B 24
Goole. *E Yor* 2H 93
Goom's Hill. *Worc* 5E 61
Goonabarn. *Corn* 3D 6
Goonbell. *Corn* 4B 6
Goonhavern. *Corn* 3B 6
Goonvrea. *Corn* 4B 6
Goose Green. *Cumb* 1E 97
Goose Green. *S Glo* 3C 34
Gooseham. *Corn* 1C 10
Goosewell. *Plym* 3B 8
Goosey. *Oxon* 2B 36
Goosnargh. *Lanc* 1D 90
Goostrey. *Ches E* 3B 84
Gorcott Hill. *Warw* 4E 61
Gordon. *Bord* 5C 130
Gordonbush. *High* 3F 165
Gordonstown. *Abers* 3C 160
(nr. Cornhill)
Gordonstown. *Abers* 5E 160
(nr. Fyvie)
Gorebridge. *Midl* 3G 129
Gorefield. *Cambs* 4D 76
Gores. *Wilts* 1G 23
Gorgie. *Edin* 2F 129
Goring. *Oxon* 3E 36
Goring-by-Sea. *W Sus* 5C 26
Goring Heath. *Oxon* 4E 37
Gorleston-on-Sea. *Norf* 5H 79
Gornalwood. *W Mid* 1D 60
Gorran Churchtown. *Corn* 4D 6
Gorran Haven. *Corn* 4E 6
Gorran High Lanes. *Corn* 4D 6
Gors. *Cdgn* 3F 57
Gorsedd. *Flin* 3D 82
Gorseinon. *Swan* 3E 31
Gorseness. *Orkn* 6D 172
Gorseybank. *Derbs* 5G 85
Gorsgoch. *Cdgn* 5D 57
Gorslas. *Carm* 4F 45
Gorsley. *Glos* 3B 48
Gorsley Common. *Here* 3B 48
Gorstan. *High* 2F 157
Gorstella. *Ches W* 4F 83
Gorsty Common. *Here* 2H 47
Gorsty Hill. *Staf* 3E 73
Gortantaoid. *Arg* 2B 124
Gorteneorn. *High* 2A 140
Gortenfern. *High* 2A 140
Gorton. *G Man* 1C 84
Gosbeck. *Suff* 5D 66
Gosberton. *Linc* 2B 76
Gosberton Cheal. *Linc* 3B 76
Gosberton Clough. *Linc* 3A 76
Goseley Dale. *Derbs* 3H 73
Gosfield. *Essx* 3A 54
Gosford. *Oxon* 4D 50
Gosforth. *Cumb* 4B 102
Gosforth. *Tyne* 3F 115
Gosmore. *Herts* 3B 52
Gospel End Village. *Staf* 1C 60
Gosport. *Hants* 2E 16
Gossabrough. *Shet* 3G 173
Gossington. *Glos* 5C 48
Gossops Green. *W Sus* 2D 26
Goswick. *Nmbd* 5G 131
Gotham. *Notts* 2C 74
Gotherington. *Glos* 3E 49
Gott. *Arg* 4B 138
Goudhurst. *Kent* 2B 28
Goulceby. *Linc* 3B 88
Gourdon. *Abers* 1H 145
Gourock. *Inv* 2D 126
Govan. *Glas* 3G 127
Govanhill. *Glas* 3G 127
Goverton. *Notts* 1E 74
Goveton. *Devn* 4D 8
Govilon. *Mon* 4F 47
Gowanhill. *Abers* 2H 161
Gowdall. *E Yor* 2G 93
Gowerton. *Swan* 3E 31
Gowkhall. *Fife* 1D 128
Gowthorpe. *E Yor* 4B 100
Goxhill. *E Yor* 5F 101
Goxhill. *N Lin* 2E 94
Goxhill Haven. *N Lin* 2E 94
Goytre. *Neat* 3A 32
Grabhair. *W Isl* 6F 171
Graby. *Linc* 3H 75
Graffham. *W Sus* 4A 26
Grafham. *Cambs* 4A 64
Grafham. *Surr* 1B 26
Grafton. *Here* 2H 47
Grafton. *N Yor* 3G 99
Grafton. *Oxon* 5A 50
Grafton. *Shrp* 4G 71
Grafton. *Worc* 2E 49
(nr. Evesham)
Grafton. *Worc* 4H 59
(nr. Leominster)
Grafton Flyford. *Worc* 5D 60
Grafton Regis. *Nptn* 1F 51
Grafton Underwood. *Nptn* 2G 63
Grafty Green. *Kent* 1C 28
Graianrhyd. *Den* 5E 82
Graig. *Carm* 5E 45
Graig. *Cnwy* 3H 81
Graig. *Den* 3C 82
Graig-fechan. *Den* 5D 82
Graig Penllyn. *V Glam* 4C 32
Grain. *Medw* 3C 40
Grainsby. *Linc* 1B 88
Grainthorpe. *Linc* 1C 88
Grainthorpe Fen. *Linc* 1C 88
Graiselound. *N Lin* 1E 87
Gramasdail. *W Isl* 3D 170
Grampound. *Corn* 4D 6
Grampound Road. *Corn* 3D 6
Granborough. *Buck* 3F 51
Granby. *Notts* 2E 75
Grandborough. *Warw* 4B 62
Grandpont. *Oxon* 5D 50
Grandtully. *Per* 3G 143
Grange. *Cumb* 3D 102
Grange. *E Ayr* 1D 116
Grange. *Here* 3G 59
Grange. *Mers* 2E 83
Grange. *Per* 1E 137
Grange Crossroads. *Mor* 3B 160
Grange Hill. *G Lon* 1F 39
Grangemill. *Derbs* 5G 85
Grange Moor. *W Yor* 3C 92
Grangemouth. *Falk* 1C 128
Grange of Lindores. *Fife* 2E 137
Grange-over-Sands. *Cumb* 2D 96
Grangepans. *Falk* 1D 128
Grange, The. *N Yor* 5C 106
Grangetown. *Card* 4E 33
Grangetown. *Red C* 2C 106
Grange Villa. *Dur* 4F 115
Granish. *High* 2C 150
Gransmoor. *E Yor* 4F 101
Granston. *Pemb* 1C 42
Grantchester. *Cambs* 5D 64
Grantham. *Linc* 2G 75
Grantley. *N Yor* 3E 99
Grantlodge. *Abers* 2E 152
Granton. *Edin* 2F 129
Grantown-on-Spey. *High* 1E 151
Grantshouse. *Bord* 3E 130
Grappenhall. *Warr* 2A 84
Grasby. *Linc* 4D 94
Grasmere. *Cumb* 4E 103
Grasscroft. *G Man* 4H 91
Grassendale. *Mers* 2F 83
Grassgarth. *Cumb* 5E 113
Grassholme. *Dur* 2C 104
Grassington. *N Yor* 3C 98
Grassmoor. *Derbs* 4B 86
Grassthorpe. *Notts* 4E 87
Grateley. *Hants* 2A 24
Gratton. *Devn* 1D 11
Gratton. *Staf* 5D 84
Gratwich. *Staf* 2E 73
Graveley. *Cambs* 4B 64
Graveley. *Herts* 3C 52
Gravelhill. *Shrp* 4G 71
Gravel Hole. *G Man* 4H 91
Gravelly Hill. *W Mid* 1F 61
Graven. *Shet* 4F 173
Graveney. *Kent* 4E 41
Gravesend. *Kent* 3H 39
Grayingham. *Linc* 1G 87
Grayrigg. *Cumb* 5G 103
Grays. *Thur* 3H 39
Grayshott. *Hants* 3G 25
Grayson Green. *Cumb* 2A 102
Grayswood. *Surr* 2A 26
Graythorp. *Hart* 2C 106
Grazeley. *Wok* 5E 37
Grealin. *High* 2E 155
Greasbrough. *S Yor* 1B 86
Greasby. *Mers* 2E 83
Great Abington. *Cambs* 1F 53
Great Addington. *Nptn* 3G 63
Great Alne. *Warw* 5F 61
Great Altcar. *Lanc* 4B 90
Great Amwell. *Herts* 4D 52
Great Asby. *Cumb* 3H 103
Great Ashfield. *Suff* 4B 66
Great Ayton. *N Yor* 3C 106
Great Baddow. *Essx* 5H 53
Great Bardfield. *Essx* 2G 53

Great Barford. Bed 5A 64
Great Barr. W Mid 1E 61
Great Barrington. Glos 4H 49
Great Barrow. Ches W 4G 83
Great Barton. Suff 4A 66
Great Barugh. N Yor 2B 100
Great Bavington. Nmbd 1C 114
Great Bealings. Suff 1F 55
Great Bedwyn. Wilts 5A 36
Great Bentley. Essx 3E 54
Great Billing. Nptn 4F 63
Great Bircham. Norf 2G 77
Great Blakenham. Suff 5D 66
Great Blencow. Cumb 1F 103
Great Bolas. Telf 3A 72
Great Bookham. Surr 5C 38
Great Bosullow. Corn 3B 4
Great Bourton. Oxon 1C 50
Great Bowden. Leics 2E 63
Great Bradley. Suff 5F 65
Great Braxted. Essx 4B 54
Great Bricett. Suff 5C 66
Great Brickhill. Buck 2H 51
Great Bridgeford. Staf 3C 72
Great Brington. Nptn 4D 62
Great Bromley. Essx 3D 54
Great Broughton. Cumb 1B 102
Great Broughton. N Yor 4C 106
Great Budworth. Ches W 3A 84
Great Burdon. Darl 3A 106
Great Burstead. Essx 1A 40
Great Busby. N Yor 4C 106
Great Canfield. Essx 4F 53
Great Carlton. Linc 2D 88
Great Casterton. Rut 5H 75
Great Chalfield. Wilts 5D 34
Great Chart. Kent 1D 28
Great Chatwell. Staf 4B 72
Great Chesterford. Essx 1F 53
Great Cheverell. Wilts 1E 23
Great Chilton. Dur 1F 105
Great Chishill. Cambs 2E 53
Great Clacton. Essx 4E 55
Great Cliff. W Yor 3D 92
Great Clifton. Cumb 2B 102
Great Coates. NE Lin 3F 95
Great Comberton. Worc 1E 49
Great Corby. Cumb 4F 113
Great Cornard. Suff 1B 54
Great Cowden. E Yor 5G 101
Great Coxwell. Oxon 2A 36
Great Crakehall. N Yor 1E 99
Great Cransley. Nptn 3F 63
Great Cressingham. Norf 5H 77
Great Crosby. Mers 1F 83
Great Cubley. Derbs 2F 73
Great Dalby. Leics 4E 75
Great Doddington. Nptn 4F 63
Great Doward. Here 4A 48
Great Dunham. Norf 4A 78
Great Dunmow. Essx 3G 53
Great Durnford. Wilts 3G 23
Great Easton. Essx 3G 53
Great Easton. Leics 1F 63
Great Eccleston. Lanc 5D 96
Great Edstone. N Yor 1B 100
Great Ellingham. Norf 1C 66
Great Elm. Som 2C 22
Great Eppleton. Tyne 5G 115
Great Eversden. Cambs 5C 64
Great Fencote. N Yor 5F 105
Great Finborough. Suff 5C 66
Greatford. Linc 4H 75
Great Fransham. Norf 4A 78
Great Gaddesden. Herts 4A 52
Great Gate. Staf 1E 73
Great Gidding. Cambs 2A 64
Great Givendale. E Yor 4C 100
Great Glemham. Suff 4F 67
Great Glen. Leics 1D 62
Great Gonerby. Linc 2G 75
Great Gransden. Cambs 5B 64
Great Green. Norf 2E 67
Great Green. Suff 5B 66
(nr. Lavenham)
Great Green. Suff 3D 66
(nr. Palgrave)
Great Habton. N Yor 2B 100
Great Hale. Linc 1A 76
Great Hallingbury. Essx 4F 53
Greatham. Hants 3F 25
Greatham. Hart 2B 106
Greatham. W Sus 4B 26
Great Hampden. Buck 5G 51
Great Harrowden. Nptn 3F 63
Great Harwood. Lanc 1F 91
Great Haseley. Oxon 5E 51
Great Hatfield. E Yor 5F 101
Great Haywood. Staf 3D 73
Great Heath. W Mid 2H 61
Great Heck. N Yor 2F 93
Great Henny. Essx 2B 54
Great Hinton. Wilts 1E 23
Great Hockham. Norf 1B 66
Great Holland. Essx 4F 55
Great Horkesley. Essx 2C 54
Great Hormead. Herts 2E 53
Great Horton. W Yor 1B 92
Great Horwood. Buck 2F 51
Great Houghton. Nptn 5E 63
Great Houghton. S Yor 4E 93
Great Hucklow. Derbs 3F 85
Great Kelk. E Yor 4F 101
Great Kendale. E Yor 3E 101
Great Kimble. Buck 5G 51
Great Kingshill. Buck 2G 37
Great Langdale. Cumb 4D 102
Great Langton. N Yor 5F 105
Great Leighs. Essx 4H 53
Great Limber. Linc 4E 95
Great Linford. Mil 1G 51
Great Livermere. Suff 3A 66
Great Longstone. Derbs 3G 85
Great Lumley. Dur 5F 115
Great Lyth. Shrp 5G 71
Great Malvern. Worc 1C 48
Great Maplestead. Essx 2B 54
Great Marton. Bkpl 1B 90
Great Massingham. Norf 3G 77
Great Melton. Norf 5D 78
Great Milton. Oxon 5E 51
Great Missenden. Buck 5G 51
Great Mitton. Lanc 1F 91
Great Mongeham. Kent 5H 41
Great Moulton. Norf 1D 66
Great Munden. Herts 3D 52
Great Musgrave. Cumb 3A 104
Great Ness. Shrp 4F 71
Great Notley. Essx 3H 53
Great Oak. Mon 5G 47
Great Oakley. Essx 3E 55
Great Oakley. Nptn 2F 63
Great Offley. Herts 3B 52
Great Ormside. Cumb 3A 104
Great Orton. Cumb 4E 113
Great Ouseburn. N Yor 3G 99
Great Oxendon. Nptn 2E 63
Great Oxney Green. Essx 5G 53
Great Parndon. Essx 5E 53
Great Paxton. Cambs 4B 64
Great Plumpton. Lanc 1B 90
Great Plumstead. Norf 4F 79
Great Ponton. Linc 2G 75
Great Potheridge. Devn 1F 11
Great Preston. W Yor 2E 93
Great Raveley. Cambs 2B 64
Great Rissington. Glos 4G 49
Great Rollright. Oxon 2B 50
Great Ryburgh. Norf 3B 78
Great Ryle. Nmbd 3E 121
Great Ryton. Shrp 5G 71
Great Saling. Essx 3G 53
Great Salkeld. Cumb 1G 103
Great Sampford. Essx 2G 53
Great Sankey. Warr 2H 83
Great Saredon. Staf 5D 72
Great Saxham. Suff 4G 65
Great Shefford. W Ber 4B 36
Great Shelford. Cambs 5D 64
Great Shoddesden. Hants 2A 24
Great Smeaton. N Yor 4A 106
Great Snoring. Norf 2B 78
Great Somerford. Wilts 3E 35
Great Stainton. Darl 2A 106
Great Stambridge. Essx 1C 40
Great Staughton. Cambs 4A 64
Great Steeping. Linc 4D 88
Great Stonar. Kent 5H 41
Greatstone-on-Sea. Kent 3E 29
Great Strickland. Cumb 2G 103
Great Stukeley. Cambs 3B 64
Great Sturton. Linc 3B 88
Great Sutton. Ches W 3F 83
Great Sutton. Shrp 2H 59
Great Swinburne. Nmbd 2C 114
Great Tew. Oxon 3B 50
Great Tey. Essx 3B 54
Great Thirkleby. N Yor 2G 99
Great Thorness. IOW 3C 16
Great Thurlow. Suff 5F 65
Great Torr. Devn 4C 8
Great Torrington. Devn 1E 11
Great Tosson. Nmbd 4E 121
Great Totham North. Essx 4B 54
Great Totham South. Essx 4B 54
Great Tows. Linc 1B 88
Great Urswick. Cumb 2B 96
Great Wakering. Essx 2D 40
Great Waldingfield. Suff 1C 54
Great Walsingham. Norf 2B 78
Great Waltham. Essx 4G 53
Great Warley. Essx 1G 39
Great Washbourne. Glos 2E 49
Great Wenham. Suff 2D 54
Great Whelnetham. Suff 5A 66
Great Whittington. Nmbd 2D 114
Great Wigborough. Essx 4C 54
Great Wilbraham. Cambs 5E 65
Great Wilne. Derbs 2B 74
Great Wishford. Wilts 3F 23
Great Witchingham. Norf 3D 78
Great Witcombe. Glos 4E 49
Great Witley. Worc 4B 60
Great Wolford. Warw 2H 49
Greatworth. Nptn 1D 50
Great Wratting. Suff 1G 53
Great Wymondley. Herts 3C 52
Great Wyrley. Staf 5D 73
Great Wytheford. Shrp 4H 71
Great Yarmouth. Norf 5H 79
Great Yeldham. Essx 2A 54
Grebby. Linc 4D 88
Greeba Castle. IOM 3C 108
Greenbank. Shet 1G 173
Greenbottom. Corn 4B 6
Greenburn. W Lot 3C 128
Greencroft. Dur 4E 115
Greencroft Park. Dur 5E 115
Greendown. Som 1A 22
Greendykes. Nmbd 2E 121
Green End. Bed 1A 52
(nr. Bedford)
Green End. Bed 4A 64
(nr. St Neots)
Green End. Herts 2D 52
(nr. Buntingford)
Green End. Herts 3D 52
(nr. Stevenage)
Green End. N Yor 4F 107
Green End. Warw 2G 61
Greenfield. Arg 4B 134
Greenfield. C Beds 2A 52
Greenfield. Flin 3D 82
Greenfield. G Man 4H 91
Greenfield. Oxon 2F 37
Greenfoot. N Lan 3A 128
Greenford. G Lon 2C 38
Greengairs. N Lan 2A 128
Greengate. Norf 4C 78
Greengill. Cumb 1C 102
Greenhalgh. Lanc 1C 90
Greenham. Dors 2H 13
Greenham. Som 4D 20
Greenham. W Ber 5C 36
Green Hammerton. N Yor 4G 99
Greenhaugh. Nmbd 1A 114
Greenhead. Nmbd 3H 113
Green Heath. Staf 4D 73
Greenhill. Dum 2C 112
Greenhill. Falk 2B 128
Greenhill. Kent 4F 41
Greenhill. S Yor 2H 85
Greenhill. Worc 3C 60
Greenhills. N Ayr 4E 127
Greenhithe. Kent 3G 39
Greenholm. E Ayr 1E 117
Greenhow Hill. N Yor 3D 98
Greenigoe. Orkn 7D 172
Greenland. High 2E 169
Greenland Mains. High 2E 169
Greenlands. Worc 4E 61
Green Lane. Shrp 3A 72
Green Lane. Warw 4E 61
Greenlaw. Bord 5D 130
Greenlea. Dum 2B 112
Greenloaning. Per 3H 135
Greenmount. G Man 3F 91
Greenock. Inv 2D 126
Greenock Mains. E Ayr 2F 117
Greenodd. Cumb 1C 96
Green Ore. Som 1A 22
Greenrow. Cumb 4C 112
Greens. Abers 4F 161
Greensgate. Norf 4D 78
Greenside. Tyne 3E 115
Greensidehill. Nmbd 3D 121
Greens Norton. Nptn 1E 51
Greenstead Green. Essx 3B 54
Greensted Green. Essx 5F 53
Green Street. Herts 1C 38
Green Street. Suff 3D 66
Green Street Green. G Lon 4F 39
Green Street Green. Kent 3G 39
Greenstreet Green. Suff 1D 54
Green, The. Cumb 1A 96
Green, The. Wilts 3D 22
Green Tye. Herts 4E 53
Greenway. Pemb 2E 43
Greenway. V Glam 4D 32
Greenwell. Cumb 4G 113
Greenwich. G Lon 3E 39
Greet. Glos 2F 49
Greete. Shrp 3H 59
Greetham. Linc 3C 88
Greetham. Rut 4G 75
Greetland. W Yor 2A 92
Gregson Lane. Lanc 2D 90
Grein. W Isl 8B 170
Greinetobht. W Isl 1D 170
Greinton. Som 3H 21
Grenaby. IOM 4B 108
Grendon. Nptn 4F 63
Grendon. Warw 1G 61
Grendon Common. Warw 1G 61
Grendon Green. Here 5H 59
Grendon Underwood. Buck 3E 51
Grenofen. Devn 5E 11
Grenoside. S Yor 1H 85
Greosabhagh. W Isl 8D 171
Gresford. Wrex 5F 83
Gresham. Norf 2D 78
Greshornish. High 3C 154
Gressenhall. Norf 4B 78
Gressingham. Lanc 2E 97
Greta Bridge. Dur 3D 105
Gretna. Dum 3E 112
Gretna Green. Dum 3E 112
Gretton. Glos 2F 49
Gretton. Nptn 1G 63
Gretton. Shrp 1H 59
Grewelthorpe. N Yor 2E 99
Greygarth. N Yor 2D 98
Grey Green. N Lin 4A 94
Greylake. Som 3G 21
Greysouthen. Cumb 2B 102
Greystoke. Cumb 1F 103
Greystoke Gill. Cumb 2F 103
Greystone. Ang 4E 145
Greystones. S Yor 2H 85
Greywell. Hants 1F 25
Griais. W Isl 3G 171
Grianan. W Isl 4G 171
Gribthorpe. E Yor 1A 94
Gribun. Arg 5F 139
Griff. Warw 2A 62
Griffithstown. Torf 2F 33
Griffydam. Leics 4B 74
Griggs Green. Hants 3G 25
Grimbister. Orkn 6C 172
Grimeford Village. Lanc 3E 90
Grimethorpe. S Yor 4E 93
Griminis. W Isl 3C 170
(on Benbecula)
Griminis. W Isl 1C 170
(on North Uist)
Grimister. Shet 2F 173
Grimley. Worc 4C 60
Grimoldby. Linc 2C 88
Grimpo. Shrp 3F 71
Grimsargh. Lanc 1D 90
Grimsbury. Oxon 1C 50
Grimsby. NE Lin 3F 95
Grimscote. Nptn 5D 62
Grimscott. Corn 2C 10
Grimshaw. Bkbn 2F 91
Grimshaw Green. Lanc 3C 90
Grimsthorpe. Linc 3H 75
Grimston. E Yor 1F 95
Grimston. Leics 3D 74
Grimston. Norf 3G 77
Grimston. York 4A 100
Grimstone. Dors 3B 14
Grimstone End. Suff 4B 66
Grinacombe Moor. Devn 3E 11
Grindale. E Yor 2F 101
Grindhill. Devn 3E 11
Grindiscol. Shet 8F 173
Grindle. Shrp 5B 72
Grindleford. Derbs 3G 85
Grindleton. Lanc 5G 97
Grindley. Staf 3E 73
Grindley Brook. Shrp 1H 71
Grindlow. Derbs 3F 85
Grindon. Nmbd 5F 131
Grindon. Staf 5E 85
Gringley on the Hill. Notts 1E 87
Grinsdale. Cumb 4E 113
Grinshill. Shrp 3H 71
Grinton. N Yor 5D 104
Griomsidar. W Isl 5G 171
Grishipoll. Arg 3C 138
Grisling Common. E Sus 3F 27
Gristhorpe. N Yor 1E 101
Griston. Norf 1B 66
Gritley. Orkn 7E 172
Grittenham. Wilts 3F 35
Grittleton. Wilts 4D 34
Grizebeck. Cumb 1B 96
Grizedale. Cumb 5E 103
Grobister. Orkn 5F 172
Groby. Leics 5C 74
Groes. Cnwy 4C 82
Groes. Neat 3A 32
Groes-faen. Rhon 3D 32
Groesffordd. Gwyn 2B 68
Groesffordd. Powy 3D 46
Groeslon. Gwyn 5D 81
Groes-lwyd. Powy 4E 70
Groes-wen. Cphy 3E 33
Grogport. Arg 5G 125
Groigearraidh. W Isl 4C 170
Gromford. Suff 5F 67
Gronant. Flin 2C 82
Groombridge. E Sus 2G 27
Grosmont. Mon 3H 47
Grosmont. N Yor 4F 107
Groton. Suff 1C 54
Grove. Dors 5C 14
Grove. Kent 4G 41

Grove—Hannington

Grove. *Notts* 3E **87**
Grove. *Oxon* 2B **36**
Grovehill. *E Yor* 1D **94**
Grove Park. *G Lon* 3F **39**
Grovesend. *Swan* 5F **45**
Grove, The. *Dum* 2A **112**
Grove, The. *Worc* 1D **48**
Grub Street. *Staf* 3B **72**
Grudie. *High* 2F **157**
Gruids. *High* 3C **164**
Gruinard House. *High* 4D **162**
Gruinart. *Arg* 3A **124**
Grulinbeg. *Arg* 3A **124**
Gruline. *Arg* 4G **139**
Grummore. *High* 5G **167**
Grundisburgh. *Suff* 5E **66**
Gruting. *Shet* 7D **173**
Grutness. *Shet* 10F **173**
Gualachulain. *High* 4F **141**
Gualin House. *High* 3D **166**
Guardbridge. *Fife* 2G **137**
Guarlford. *Worc* 1D **48**
Guay. *Per* 4H **143**
Gubblecote. *Herts* 4H **51**
Guestling Green. *E Sus* 4C **28**
Guestling Thorn. *E Sus* 4C **28**
Guestwick. *Norf* 3C **78**
Guestwick Green. *Norf* 3C **78**
Guide. *Bkbn* 2F **91**
Guide Post. *Nmbd* 1F **115**
Guilden Down. *Shrp* 2F **59**
Guilden Morden. *Cambs* 1C **52**
Guilden Sutton. *Ches W* 4G **83**
Guildford. *Surr* 1A **26**
Guildtown. *Per* 5A **144**
Guilsborough. *Nptn* 3D **62**
Guilsfield. *Powy* 4E **70**
Guineaford. *Devn* 3F **19**
Guisborough. *Red C* 3D **106**
Guiseley. *W Yor* 5D **98**
Guist. *Norf* 3B **78**
Guiting Power. *Glos* 3F **49**
Gulberwick. *Shet* 8F **173**
Gullane. *E Lot* 1A **130**
Gulling Green. *Suff* 5H **65**
Gulval. *Corn* 3B **4**
Gumfreston. *Pemb* 4F **43**
Gumley. *Leics* 1D **62**
Gunby. *E Yor* 1H **93**
Gunby. *Linc* 3G **75**
Gundleton. *Hants* 3E **24**
Gun Green. *Kent* 2B **28**
Gun Hill. *E Sus* 4G **27**
Gunn. *Devn* 3G **19**
Gunnerside. *N Yor* 5C **104**
Gunnerton. *Nmbd* 2C **114**
Gunness. *N Lin* 3B **94**
Gunnislake. *Corn* 5E **11**
Gunsgreenhill. *Bord* 3F **131**
Gunstone. *Staf* 5C **72**
Gunthorpe. *Norf* 2C **78**
Gunthorpe. *N Lin* 1F **87**
Gunthorpe. *Notts* 1D **74**
Gunthorpe. *Pet* 5A **76**
Gunville. *IOW* 4C **16**
Gupworthy. *Som* 3C **20**
Gurnard. *IOW* 3C **16**
Gurney Slade. *Som* 2B **22**
Gurnos. *Powy* 5A **46**
Gussage All Saints. *Dors* 1F **15**
Gussage St Andrew. *Dors* 1E **15**
Gussage St Michael. *Dors* 1E **15**
Guston. *Kent* 1H **29**
Gutcher. *Shet* 2G **173**
Guthram Gowt. *Linc* 3A **76**
Guthrie. *Ang* 3E **145**
Guyhirn. *Cambs* 5D **76**
Guyhirn Gull. *Cambs* 5C **76**
Guy's Head. *Linc* 3D **77**
Guy's Marsh. *Dors* 4D **22**
Guyzance. *Nmbd* 4G **121**
Gwaelod-y-garth. *Card* 3E **32**
Gwaenynog Bach. *Den* 4C **82**
Gwaenysgor. *Flin* 2C **82**
Gwalchmai. *IOA* 3C **80**
Gwastad. *Pemb* 2E **43**
Gwaun-Cae-Gurwen. *Neat* 4H **45**
Gwaun-y-bara. *Cphy* 3E **33**
Gwbert. *Cdgn* 1B **44**
Gweek. *Corn* 4E **5**
Gwehelog. *Mon* 5G **47**
Gwenddwr. *Powy* 1D **46**
Gwennap. *Corn* 4B **6**
Gwenter. *Corn* 5E **5**
Gwernaffield. *Flin* 4E **82**
Gwernesney. *Mon* 5H **47**
Gwernogle. *Carm* 2F **45**
Gwern-y-go. *Powy* 1E **58**
Gwernymynydd. *Flin* 4E **82**
Gwersyllt. *Wrex* 5F **83**
Gwespyr. *Flin* 2D **82**
Gwinear. *Corn* 3C **4**
Gwithian. *Corn* 2C **4**
Gwredog. *IOA* 2D **80**
Gwyddelwern. *Den* 1C **70**
Gwyddgrug. *Carm* 2E **45**
Gwynfryn. *Wrex* 5E **83**
Gwystre. *Powy* 4C **58**
Gwytherin. *Cnwy* 4A **82**
Gyfelia. *Wrex* 1F **71**
Gyffin. *Cnwy* 3G **81**

H

Habberley. *Shrp* 5F **71**
Habblesthorpe. *Notts* 2E **87**
Habergham. *Lanc* 1G **91**
Habin. *W Sus* 4G **25**
Habrough. *NE Lin* 3E **95**
Haceby. *Linc* 2H **75**
Hacheston. *Suff* 5F **67**
Hackenthorpe. *S Yor* 2B **86**
Hackford. *Norf* 5C **78**
Hackforth. *N Yor* 5F **105**
Hackleton. *Nptn* 5F **63**
Hackman's Gate. *Worc* 3C **60**
Hackness. *N Yor* 5G **107**
Hackness. *Orkn* 8C **172**
Hackney. *G Lon* 2E **39**
Hackthorn. *Linc* 2G **87**
Hackthorpe. *Cumb* 2G **103**
Haclait. *W Isl* 4D **170**
Haconby. *Linc* 3A **76**
Hadden. *Bord* 1B **120**
Haddenham. *Buck* 5F **51**
Haddenham. *Cambs* 3D **64**
Haddenham End. *Cambs* 3D **64**
Haddington. *E Lot* 2B **130**
Haddington. *Linc* 4G **87**
Haddiscoe. *Norf* 1G **67**
Haddo. *Abers* 5F **161**
Haddon. *Cambs* 1A **64**
Hademore. *Staf* 5F **73**
Hadfield. *Derbs* 1E **85**
Hadham Cross. *Herts* 4E **53**
Hadham Ford. *Herts* 3E **53**
Hadleigh. *Essx* 2C **40**
Hadleigh. *Suff* 1D **54**
Hadleigh Heath. *Suff* 1C **54**
Hadley. *Telf* 4A **72**
Hadley. *Worc* 4C **60**
Hadley End. *Staf* 3F **73**
Hadley Wood. *G Lon* 1D **38**
Hadlow. *Kent* 1H **27**
Hadlow Down. *E Sus* 3G **27**
Hadnall. *Shrp* 3H **71**
Hadstock. *Essx* 1F **53**
Hadston. *Nmbd* 5G **121**
Hady. *Derbs* 3A **86**
Hadzor. *Worc* 4D **60**
Haffenden Quarter. *Kent* 1C **28**
Haggate. *Lanc* 1G **91**
Haggbeck. *Cumb* 2F **113**
Haggerston. *Nmbd* 5G **131**
Haggrister. *Shet* 4E **173**
Hagley. *Here* 1A **48**
Hagley. *Worc* 2D **60**
Hagnaby. *Linc* 4C **88**
Hagworthingham. *Linc* 4C **88**
Haigh. *G Man* 4E **90**
Haigh Moor. *W Yor* 2C **92**
Haighton Green. *Lanc* 1D **90**
Haile. *Cumb* 4B **102**
Hailes. *Glos* 2F **49**
Hailey. *Herts* 4D **52**
Hailey. *Oxon* 4B **50**
Hailsham. *E Sus* 5G **27**
Hail Weston. *Cambs* 4A **64**
Hainault. *G Lon* 1F **39**
Hainford. *Norf* 4E **78**
Hainton. *Linc* 2A **88**
Hainworth. *W Yor* 1A **92**
Haisthorpe. *E Yor* 3F **101**
Hakin. *Pemb* 4C **42**
Halam. *Notts* 5D **86**
Halbeath. *Fife* 1E **129**
Halberton. *Devn* 1D **12**
Halcro. *High* 2E **169**
Hale. *Cumb* 2E **97**
Hale. *G Man* 2B **84**
Hale. *Hal* 2G **83**
Hale. *Hants* 1G **15**
Hale. *Surr* 2G **25**
Hale Bank. *Hal* 2G **83**
Halebarns. *G Man* 2B **84**
Hales. *Norf* 1F **67**
Hales. *Staf* 2B **72**
Halesgate. *Linc* 3C **76**
Hales Green. *Derbs* 1F **73**
Halesowen. *W Mid* 2D **60**
Hale Street. *Kent* 1A **28**
Halesworth. *Suff* 3F **67**
Halewood. *Mers* 2G **83**
Halford. *Shrp* 2G **59**
Halford. *Warw* 1A **50**
Halfpenny. *Cumb* 1E **97**
Halfpenny Furze. *Carm* 3G **43**
Halfpenny Green. *Shrp* 1C **60**
Halfway. *Carm* 2G **45**
Halfway. *Powy* 2B **46**
Halfway. *S Yor* 2B **86**
Halfway. *W Ber* 5C **36**
Halfway House. *Shrp* 4F **71**
Halfway Houses. *Kent* 3D **40**
Halgabron. *Corn* 4A **10**
Halifax. *W Yor* 2A **92**
Halistra. *High* 3B **154**
Halket. *E Ayr* 4F **127**
Halkirk. *High* 3D **168**
Halkyn. *Flin* 3E **82**
Hall. *E Ren* 4F **127**
Hallam Fields. *Derbs* 1B **74**
Halland. *E Sus* 4G **27**
Hallands, The. *N Lin* 2D **94**
Hallaton. *Leics* 1E **63**
Hallatrow. *Bath* 1B **22**
Hallbank. *Cumb* 5H **103**
Hallbankgate. *Cumb* 4G **113**
Hall Dunnerdale. *Cumb* 5D **102**
Hallen. *S Glo* 3A **34**
Hall End. *Bed* 1A **52**
Hallgarth. *Dur* 5G **115**
Hall Green. *Ches E* 5C **84**
Hall Green. *Norf* 2D **66**
Hall Green. *W Mid* 2F **61**
Hall Green. *W Yor* 3D **92**
Hall Green. *Wrex* 1G **71**
Halliburton. *Bord* 5C **130**
Hallin. *High* 3B **154**
Halling. *Medw* 4B **40**
Hallington. *Linc* 2C **88**
Hallington. *Nmbd* 2C **114**
Halloughton. *Notts* 5D **86**
Hallow. *Worc* 5C **60**
Hallow Heath. *Worc* 5C **60**
Hallowsgate. *Ches W* 4H **83**
Hallsands. *Devn* 5E **9**
Hall's Green. *Herts* 3C **52**
Hallspill. *Devn* 4E **19**
Hallthwaites. *Cumb* 1A **96**
Hall Waberthwaite. *Cumb* 5C **102**
Hallwood Green. *Glos* 2B **48**
Hallworthy. *Corn* 4B **10**
Hallyne. *Bord* 5E **129**
Halmer End. *Staf* 1C **72**
Halmond's Frome. *Here* 1B **48**
Halmore. *Glos* 5B **48**
Halnaker. *W Sus* 5A **26**
Halsall. *Lanc* 3B **90**
Halse. *Nptn* 1D **50**
Halse. *Som* 4E **21**
Halsetown. *Corn* 3C **4**
Halsham. *E Yor* 2F **95**
Halsinger. *Devn* 3F **19**
Halstead. *Essx* 2B **54**
Halstead. *Kent* 4F **39**
Halstead. *Leics* 5E **75**
Halstock. *Dors* 2A **14**
Halsway. *Som* 3E **21**
Haltcliff Bridge. *Cumb* 1E **103**
Haltham. *Linc* 4B **88**
Haltoft End. *Linc* 1C **76**
Halton. *Buck* 5G **51**
Halton. *Hal* 2H **83**
Halton. *Lanc* 3E **97**
Halton. *Nmbd* 3C **114**
Halton. *W Yor* 1D **92**
Halton. *Wrex* 2F **71**
Halton East. *N Yor* 4C **98**
Halton Fenside. *Linc* 4D **88**
Halton Gill. *N Yor* 2A **98**
Halton Holegate. *Linc* 4D **88**
Halton Lea Gate. *Nmbd* 4H **113**
Halton Moor. *W Yor* 1D **92**
Halton Shields. *Nmbd* 3D **114**
Halton West. *N Yor* 4H **97**
Haltwhistle. *Nmbd* 3A **114**
Halvergate. *Norf* 5G **79**
Halwell. *Devn* 3D **9**
Halwill. *Devn* 3E **11**
Halwill Junction. *Devn* 3E **11**
Ham. *Devn* 2F **13**
Ham. *Glos* 2B **34**
Ham. *G Lon* 3C **38**
Ham. *High* 1E **169**
Ham. *Kent* 5H **41**
Ham. *Plym* 3A **8**
Ham. *Shet* 8A **173**
Ham. *Som* 1F **13** (nr. Ilminster)
Ham. *Som* 4F **21** (nr. Taunton)
Ham. *Som* 4E **21** (nr. Wellington)
Ham. *Wilts* 5B **36**
Hambleden. *Buck* 3F **37**
Hambledon. *Hants* 1E **17**
Hambledon. *Surr* 2A **26**
Hamble-le-Rice. *Hants* 2C **16**
Hambleton. *Lanc* 5C **96**
Hambleton. *N Yor* 1F **93**
Hambridge. *Som* 4G **21**
Hambrook. *S Glo* 4B **34**
Hambrook. *W Sus* 2F **17**
Ham Common. *Dors* 4D **22**
Hameringham. *Linc* 4C **88**
Hamerton. *Cambs* 3A **64**
Ham Green. *Here* 1C **48**
Ham Green. *Kent* 4C **40**
Ham Green. *N Som* 4A **34**
Ham Green. *Worc* 4E **61**
Ham Hill. *Kent* 4A **40**
Hamilton. *Leics* 5D **74**
Hamilton. *S Lan* 4A **128**
Hammer. *W Sus* 3G **25**
Hammersmith. *G Lon* 3D **38**
Hammerwich. *Staf* 5E **73**
Hammerwood. *E Sus* 2F **27**
Hammill. *Kent* 5G **41**
Hammond Street. *Herts* 5D **52**
Hammoon. *Dors* 1D **14**
Hamnavoe. *Shet* 8E **173** (nr. Burland)
Hamnavoe. *Shet* 3F **173** (on Yell)
Hamp. *Som* 3G **21**
Hampden Park. *E Sus* 5H **27**
Hampen. *Glos* 3F **49**
Hamperden End. *Essx* 2F **53**
Hamperley. *Shrp* 2G **59**
Hampnett. *Glos* 4F **49**
Hampole. *S Yor* 3F **93**
Hampreston. *Dors* 3F **15**
Hampstead. *G Lon* 2D **38**
Hampstead Norreys. *W Ber* 4D **36**
Hampsthwaite. *N Yor* 4E **99**
Hampton. *Devn* 3F **13**
Hampton. *G Lon* 3C **38**
Hampton. *Kent* 4F **41**
Hampton. *Shrp* 2B **60**
Hampton. *Swin* 2G **35**
Hampton. *Worc* 1F **49**
Hampton Bishop. *Here* 2A **48**
Hampton Fields. *Glos* 2D **35**
Hampton Hargate. *Pet* 1A **64**
Hampton Heath. *Ches W* 1H **71**
Hampton in Arden. *W Mid* 2G **61**
Hampton Loade. *Shrp* 2B **60**
Hampton Lovett. *Worc* 4C **60**
Hampton Lucy. *Warw* 5G **61**
Hampton Magna. *Warw* 4G **61**
Hampton on the Hill. *Warw* 4G **61**
Hampton Poyle. *Oxon* 4D **50**
Hampton Wick. *G Lon* 4C **38**
Hamptworth. *Wilts* 1H **15**
Hamrow. *Norf* 3B **78**
Hamsey. *E Sus* 4F **27**
Hamsey Green. *Surr* 5E **39**
Hamstall Ridware. *Staf* 4F **73**
Hamstead. *IOW* 3C **16**
Hamstead. *W Mid* 1E **61**
Hamstead Marshall. *W Ber* 5C **36**
Hamsterley. *Dur* 4E **115** (nr. Consett)
Hamsterley. *Dur* 1E **105** (nr. Wolsingham)
Hamsterley Mill. *Dur* 4E **115**
Hamstreet. *Kent* 2E **28**
Ham Street. *Som* 3A **22**
Hamworthy. *Pool* 3E **15**
Hanbury. *Staf* 3F **73**
Hanbury. *Worc* 4D **60**
Hanbury Woodend. *Staf* 3F **73**
Hanby. *Linc* 2H **75**
Hanchurch. *Staf* 1C **72**
Hand and Pen. *Devn* 3D **12**
Handbridge. *Ches W* 4G **83**
Handcross. *W Sus* 3D **26**
Handforth. *Ches E* 2C **84**
Handley. *Ches W* 5G **83**
Handley. *Derbs* 4A **86**
Handsacre. *Staf* 4E **73**
Handsworth. *S Yor* 2B **86**
Handsworth. *W Mid* 1E **61**
Handy Cross. *Buck* 2G **37**
Hanford. *Dors* 1D **14**
Hanford. *Stoke* 1C **72**
Hangersley. *Hants* 2G **15**
Hanging Houghton. *Nptn* 3E **63**
Hanging Langford. *Wilts* 3F **23**
Hangleton. *Brig* 5D **26**
Hangleton. *W Sus* 5B **26**
Hanham. *S Glo* 4B **34**
Hanham Green. *S Glo* 4B **34**
Hankelow. *Ches E* 1A **72**
Hankerton. *Wilts* 2E **35**
Hankham. *E Sus* 5H **27**
Hanley. *Stoke* 1C **72**
Hanley Castle. *Worc* 1D **48**
Hanley Childe. *Worc* 4A **60**
Hanley Swan. *Worc* 1D **48**
Hanley William. *Worc* 4A **60**
Hanlith. *N Yor* 3B **98**
Hanmer. *Wrex* 2G **71**
Hannaborough. *Devn* 2F **11**
Hannaford. *Devn* 4G **19**
Hannah. *Linc* 3E **89**
Hannington. *Hants* 1D **24**
Hannington. *Nptn* 3F **63**

Hannington. *Swin* 2G **35**
Hannington Wick. *Swin* 2G **35**
Hanscombe End. *C Beds* 2B **52**
Hanslope. *Mil* 1G **51**
Hanthorpe. *Linc* 3H **75**
Hanwell. *G Lon* 2C **38**
Hanwell. *Oxon* 1C **50**
Hanwood. *Shrp* 5G **71**
Hanworth. *G Lon* 3C **38**
Hanworth. *Norf* 2D **78**
Happas. *Ang* 4D **144**
Happendon. *S Lan* 1A **118**
Happisburgh. *Norf* 2F **79**
Happisburgh Common. *Norf* 3F **79**
Hapsford. *Ches W* 3G **83**
Hapton. *Lanc* 1F **91**
Hapton. *Norf* 1D **66**
Harberton. *Devn* 3D **9**
Harbertonford. *Devn* 3D **9**
Harbledown. *Kent* 5F **41**
Harborne. *W Mid* 2E **61**
Harborough Magna. *Warw* 3B **62**
Harbottle. *Nmbd* 4D **120**
Harbourneford. *Devn* 2D **8**
Harbours Hill. *Worc* 4D **60**
Harbridge. *Hants* 1G **15**
Harbury. *Warw* 4A **62**
Harby. *Leics* 2E **75**
Harby. *Notts* 3F **87**
Harcombe. *Devn* 3E **13**
Harcombe Bottom. *Devn* 3G **13**
Harcourt. *Corn* 5C **6**
Harden. *W Yor* 1A **92**
Hardenhuish. *Wilts* 4E **35**
Hardgate. *Abers* 3E **153**
Hardgate. *Dum* 3F **111**
Hardham. *W Sus* 4B **26**
Hardingham. *Norf* 5C **78**
Hardingstone. *Nptn* 5E **63**
Hardings Wood. *Ches E* 5C **84**
Hardington. *Som* 1C **22**
Hardington Mandeville. *Som* 1A **14**
Hardington Marsh. *Som* 2A **14**
Hardington Moor. *Som* 1A **14**
Hardley. *Hants* 2C **16**
Hardley Street. *Norf* 5F **79**
Hardmead. *Mil* 1H **51**
Hardraw. *N Yor* 5B **104**
Hardstoft. *Derbs* 4B **86**
Hardway. *Hants* 2E **16**
Hardway. *Som* 3C **22**
Hardwick. *Buck* 4G **51**
Hardwick. *Cambs* 5C **64**
Hardwick. *Norf* 2E **66**
Hardwick. *Nptn* 4F **63**
Hardwick. *Oxon* 3D **50**
(nr. Bicester)
Hardwick. *Oxon* 5B **50**
(nr. Witney)
Hardwick. *Shrp* 1F **59**
Hardwick. *S Yor* 2B **86**
Hardwick. *Stoc T* 2B **106**
Hardwick. *W Mid* 1E **61**
Hardwicke. *Glos* 3E **49**
(nr. Cheltenham)
Hardwicke. *Glos* 4C **48**
(nr. Gloucester)
Hardwicke. *Here* 1F **47**
Hardwick Village. *Notts* 3D **86**
Hardy's Green. *Essx* 3C **54**
Hare. *Som* 1F **13**
Hareby. *Linc* 4C **88**
Hareden. *Lanc* 4F **97**
Harefield. *G Lon* 1B **38**
Hare Green. *Essx* 3D **54**
Hare Hatch. *Wok* 4G **37**
Harehill. *Derbs* 2F **73**
Harehills. *W Yor* 1D **92**
Harehope. *Nmbd* 2E **121**
Harelaw. *Dum* 2F **113**
Harelaw. *Dur* 4E **115**
Hareplain. *Kent* 2C **28**
Haresceugh. *Cumb* 5H **113**
Harescombe. *Glos* 4D **48**
Haresfield. *Glos* 4D **48**
Haresfinch. *Mers* 1H **83**
Hareshaw. *N Lan* 3B **128**
Hare Street. *Essx* 5E **53**
Hare Street. *Herts* 3D **53**
Harewood. *W Yor* 5F **99**
Harewood End. *Here* 3A **48**
Harford. *Devn* 3C **8**
Hargate. *Norf* 1D **66**
Hargatewall. *Derbs* 3F **85**
Hargrave. *Ches W* 4G **83**
Hargrave. *Nptn* 3H **63**
Hargrave. *Suff* 5G **65**
Harker. *Cumb* 3E **113**
Harkstead. *Suff* 2E **55**
Harlaston. *Staf* 4G **73**
Harlaxton. *Linc* 2F **75**
Harlech. *Gwyn* 2E **69**
Harlequin. *Notts* 2D **74**
Harlescott. *Shrp* 4H **71**
Harleston. *Devn* 4D **9**
Harleston. *Norf* 2E **67**
Harleston. *Suff* 4C **66**
Harlestone. *Nptn* 4E **62**
Harley. *Shrp* 5H **71**
Harley. *S Yor* 1A **86**
Harling Road. *Norf* 2B **66**
Harlington. *C Beds* 2A **52**
Harlington. *G Lon* 3B **38**
Harlington. *S Yor* 4E **93**
Harlosh. *High* 4B **154**
Harlow. *Essx* 4E **53**
Harlow Hill. *Nmbd* 3D **115**
Harlsey Castle. *N Yor* 5B **106**
Harlthorpe. *E Yor* 1H **93**
Harlton. *Cambs* 5C **64**
Harlyn Bay. *Corn* 1C **6**
Harman's Cross. *Dors* 4E **15**
Harmby. *N Yor* 1D **98**
Harmer Green. *Herts* 4C **52**
Harmer Hill. *Shrp* 3G **71**
Harmondsworth. *G Lon* 3B **38**
Harmston. *Linc* 4G **87**
Harnage. *Shrp* 5H **71**
Harnham. *Nmbd* 1D **115**
Harnhill. *Glos* 5F **49**
Harold Hill. *G Lon* 1G **39**
Haroldston West. *Pemb* 3C **42**
Haroldswick. *Shet* 1H **173**
Harold Wood. *G Lon* 1G **39**
Harome. *N Yor* 1A **100**
Harpenden. *Herts* 4B **52**
Harpford. *Devn* 3D **12**
Harpham. *E Yor* 3E **101**
Harpley. *Norf* 3G **77**
Harpley. *Worc* 4A **60**
Harpole. *Nptn* 4D **62**
Harpsdale. *High* 3D **168**
Harpsden. *Oxon* 3F **37**
Harpswell. *Linc* 2G **87**
Harpurhey. *G Man* 4G **91**
Harpur Hill. *Derbs* 3E **85**
Harraby. *Cumb* 4F **113**
Harracott. *Devn* 4F **19**
Harrapool. *High* 1E **147**
Harrapul. *High* 1E **147**
Harrietfield. *Per* 1B **136**
Harrietsham. *Kent* 5C **40**
Harrington. *Cumb* 2A **102**
Harrington. *Linc* 3C **88**
Harrington. *Nptn* 2E **63**
Harringworth. *Nptn* 1G **63**
Harriseahead. *Staf* 5C **84**
Harriston. *Cumb* 5C **112**
Harrogate. *N Yor* 4F **99**
Harrold. *Bed* 5G **63**
Harrop Dale. *G Man* 4A **92**
Harrow. *G Lon* 2C **38**
Harrowbarrow. *Corn* 2H **7**
Harrowden. *Bed* 1A **52**
Harrowgate Hill. *Darl* 3F **105**
Harrow on the Hill. *G Lon* 2C **38**
Harrow Weald. *G Lon* 1C **38**
Harry Stoke. *S Glo* 4B **34**
Harston. *Cambs* 5D **64**
Harston. *Leics* 2F **75**
Harswell. *E Yor* 5C **100**
Hart. *Hart* 1B **106**
Hartburn. *Nmbd* 1D **115**
Hartburn. *Stoc T* 3B **106**
Hartest. *Suff* 5H **65**
Hartfield. *E Sus* 2F **27**
Hartford. *Cambs* 3B **64**
Hartford. *Ches W* 3A **84**
Hartford. *Som* 4C **20**
Hartfordbridge. *Hants* 1F **25**
Hartford End. *Essx* 4G **53**
Harthill. *Ches W* 5H **83**
Harthill. *N Lan* 3C **128**
Harthill. *S Yor* 2B **86**
Hartington. *Derbs* 4F **85**
Hartland. *Devn* 4C **18**
Hartland Quay. *Devn* 4C **18**
Hartle. *Worc* 3D **60**
Hartlebury. *Worc* 3C **60**
Hartlepool. *Hart* 1C **106**
Hartley. *Cumb* 4A **104**
Hartley. *Kent* 2B **28**
(nr. Cranbrook)
Hartley. *Kent* 4H **39**
(nr. Dartford)
Hartley. *Nmbd* 2G **115**
Hartley Green. *Staf* 2D **73**
Hartley Mauditt. *Hants* 3F **25**
Hartley Wespall. *Hants* 1E **25**
Hartley Wintney. *Hants* 1F **25**
Hartlip. *Kent* 4C **40**
Hartmount. *High* 1B **158**
Hartoft End. *N Yor* 5E **107**
Harton. *N Yor* 3B **100**
Harton. *Shrp* 2G **59**
Harton. *Tyne* 3G **115**
Hartpury. *Glos* 3C **48**
Hartshead. *W Yor* 2B **92**
Hartshill. *Warw* 1H **61**
Hartshorne. *Derbs* 3H **73**
Hartsop. *Cumb* 3F **103**
Hart Station. *Hart* 1B **106**
Hartswell. *Som* 4D **20**
Hartwell. *Nptn* 5E **63**
Hartwood. *Lanc* 3D **90**
Hartwood. *N Lan* 4B **128**
Harvel. *Kent* 4A **40**
Harvington. *Worc* 1F **49**
(nr. Evesham)
Harvington. *Worc* 3C **60**
(nr. Kidderminster)
Harwell. *Oxon* 3C **36**
Harwich. *Essx* 2F **55**
Harwood. *Dur* 1B **104**
Harwood. *G Man* 3F **91**
Harwood Dale. *N Yor* 5G **107**
Harworth. *Notts* 1D **86**
Hascombe. *Surr* 2A **26**
Haselbech. *Nptn* 3E **62**
Haselbury Plucknett. *Som* 1H **13**
Haseley. *Warw* 4G **61**
Haselor. *Warw* 5F **61**
Hasfield. *Glos* 3D **48**
Hasguard. *Pemb* 4C **42**
Haskayne. *Lanc* 4B **90**
Hasketon. *Suff* 5E **67**
Hasland. *Derbs* 4A **86**
Haslemere. *Surr* 2A **26**
Haslingden. *Lanc* 2F **91**
Haslingden Grane. *Lanc* 2F **91**
Haslingfield. *Cambs* 5D **64**
Haslington. *Ches E* 5B **84**
Hassall. *Ches E* 5B **84**
Hassall Green. *Ches E* 5B **84**
Hassell Street. *Kent* 1E **29**
Hassendean. *Bord* 2H **119**
Hassingham. *Norf* 5F **79**
Hassness. *Cumb* 3C **102**
Hassocks. *W Sus* 4E **27**
Hassop. *Derbs* 3G **85**
Haster. *High* 3F **169**
Hasthorpe. *Linc* 4D **89**
Hastigrow. *High* 2E **169**
Hastingleigh. *Kent* 1E **29**
Hastings. *E Sus* 5C **28**
Hastingwood. *Essx* 5E **53**
Hastoe. *Herts* 5H **51**
Haston. *Shrp* 3H **71**
Haswell. *Dur* 5G **115**
Haswell Plough. *Dur* 5G **115**
Hatch. *C Beds* 1B **52**
Hatch Beauchamp. *Som* 4G **21**
Hatch End. *G Lon* 1C **38**
Hatch Green. *Som* 1G **13**
Hatching Green. *Herts* 4B **52**
Hatchmere. *Ches W* 3H **83**
Hatch Warren. *Hants* 2E **24**
Hatcliffe. *NE Lin* 4F **95**
Hatfield. *Here* 5H **59**
Hatfield. *Herts* 5C **52**
Hatfield. *S Yor* 4G **93**
Hatfield. *Worc* 5C **60**
Hatfield Broad Oak. *Essx* 4F **53**
Hatfield Garden Village. *Herts* 5C **52**
Hatfield Heath. *Essx* 4F **53**
Hatfield Hyde. *Herts* 4C **52**
Hatfield Peverel. *Essx* 4A **54**
Hatfield Woodhouse. *S Yor* 4G **93**
Hatford. *Oxon* 2B **36**
Hatherden. *Hants* 1B **24**
Hatherleigh. *Devn* 2F **11**
Hathern. *Leics* 3C **74**
Hatherop. *Glos* 5G **49**
Hathersage. *Derbs* 2G **85**
Hathersage Booths. *Derbs* 2G **85**
Hatherton. *Ches E* 1A **72**
Hatherton. *Staf* 4D **72**
Hatley St George. *Cambs* 5B **64**
Hatt. *Corn* 2H **7**
Hattersley. *G Man* 1D **85**
Hattingley. *Hants* 3E **25**
Hatton. *Abers* 5H **161**
Hatton. *Derbs* 2G **73**
Hatton. *G Lon* 3B **38**
Hatton. *Linc* 3A **88**
Hatton. *Shrp* 1G **59**
Hatton. *Warr* 2H **83**
Hatton. *Warw* 4G **61**
Hattoncrook. *Abers* 1F **153**
Hatton Heath. *Ches W* 4G **83**
Hatton of Fintray. *Abers* 2F **153**
Haugh. *E Ayr* 2D **117**
Haugh. *Linc* 3D **88**
Haugham. *Linc* 2C **88**
Haugh Head. *Nmbd* 2E **121**
Haughley. *Suff* 4C **66**
Haughley Green. *Suff* 4C **66**
Haugh of Ballechin. *Per* 3G **143**
Haugh of Glass. *Mor* 5B **160**
Haugh of Urr. *Dum* 3F **111**
Haughton. *Ches E* 5H **83**
Haughton. *Notts* 3D **86**
Haughton. *Shrp* 1A **60**
(nr. Bridgnorth)
Haughton. *Shrp* 3F **71**
(nr. Oswestry)
Haughton. *Shrp* 5B **72**
(nr. Shifnal)
Haughton. *Shrp* 4H **71**
(nr. Shrewsbury)
Haughton. *Staf* 3C **72**
Haughton Green. *G Man* 1D **84**
Haughton le Skerne. *Darl* 3A **106**
Haultwick. *Herts* 3D **52**
Haunn. *Arg* 4E **139**
Haunn. *W Isl* 7C **170**
Haunton. *Staf* 4G **73**
Hauxton. *Cambs* 5D **64**
Havannah. *Ches E* 4C **84**
Havant. *Hants* 2F **17**
Haven. *Here* 5G **59**
Haven Bank. *Linc* 5B **88**
Havenside. *E Yor* 2E **95**
Havenstreet. *IOW* 3D **16**
Haven, The. *W Sus* 2B **26**
Havercroft. *W Yor* 3D **93**
Haverfordwest. *Pemb* 3D **42**
Haverhill. *Suff* 1G **53**
Haverigg. *Cumb* 2A **96**
Havering-atte-Bower. *G Lon* 1G **39**
Havering's Grove. *Essx* 1A **40**
Haversham. *Mil* 1G **51**
Haverthwaite. *Cumb* 1C **96**
Haverton Hill. *Stoc T* 2B **106**
Havyatt. *Som* 3A **22**
Hawarden. *Flin* 4F **83**
Hawbridge. *Worc* 1E **49**
Hawcoat. *Cumb* 2B **96**
Hawcross. *Glos* 2C **48**
Hawen. *Cdgn* 1D **44**
Hawes. *N Yor* 1A **98**
Hawes Green. *Norf* 1E **67**
Hawick. *Bord* 3H **119**
Hawkchurch. *Devn* 2G **13**
Hawkedon. *Suff* 5G **65**
Hawkenbury. *Kent* 1C **28**
Hawkeridge. *Wilts* 1D **22**
Hawkerland. *Devn* 4D **12**
Hawkesbury. *S Glo* 3C **34**
Hawkesbury. *W Mid* 2A **62**
Hawkesbury Upton. *S Glo* 3C **34**
Hawkes End. *W Mid* 2G **61**
Hawk Green. *G Man* 2D **84**
Hawkhurst. *Kent* 2B **28**
Hawkhurst Common.
E Sus 4G **27**
Hawkinge. *Kent* 1G **29**
Hawkley. *Hants* 4F **25**
Hawkridge. *Som* 3B **20**
Hawksdale. *Cumb* 5E **113**
Hawkshaw. *G Man* 3F **91**
Hawkshead. *Cumb* 5E **103**
Hawkshead Hill. *Cumb* 5E **103**
Hawkswick. *N Yor* 2B **98**
Hawksworth. *Notts* 1E **75**
Hawksworth. *W Yor* 5D **98**
Hawkwell. *Essx* 1C **40**
Hawley. *Hants* 1G **25**
Hawley. *Kent* 3G **39**
Hawling. *Glos* 3F **49**
Hawnby. *N Yor* 1H **99**
Haworth. *W Yor* 1A **92**
Hawstead. *Suff* 5A **66**
Hawthorn. *Dur* 5H **115**
Hawthorn Hill. *Brac* 4G **37**
Hawthorn Hill. *Linc* 5B **88**
Hawthorpe. *Linc* 3H **75**
Hawton. *Notts* 5E **87**
Haxby. *York* 4A **100**
Haxey. *N Lin* 1E **87**
Haybridge. *Shrp* 3A **60**
Haybridge. *Som* 2A **22**
Haydock. *Mers* 1H **83**
Haydon. *Bath* 1B **22**
Haydon. *Dors* 1B **14**
Haydon. *Som* 4F **21**
Haydon Bridge. *Nmbd* 3B **114**
Haydon Wick. *Swin* 3G **35**
Haye. *Corn* 2H **7**
Hayes. *G Lon* 4F **39**
(nr. Bromley)
Hayes. *G Lon* 2B **38**
(nr. Uxbridge)
Hayfield. *Derbs* 2E **85**
Hay Green. *Norf* 4E **77**
Hayhill. *E Ayr* 3D **116**
Haylands. *IOW* 3D **16**
Hayle. *Corn* 3C **4**
Hayley Green. *W Mid* 2D **60**
Hayling Island. *Hants* 3F **17**
Hayne. *Devn* 2B **12**
Haynes. *C Beds* 1A **52**
Haynes West End. *C Beds* 1A **52**
Hay-on-Wye. *Powy* 1F **47**
Hayscastle. *Pemb* 2C **42**
Hayscastle Cross. *Pemb* 2D **42**
Haysden. *Kent* 1G **27**
Hayshead. *Ang* 4F **145**
Hay Street. *Herts* 3D **53**
Hayton. *Aber* 3G **153**

Hayton. *Cumb* 5C 112
  (nr. Aspatria)
Hayton. *Cumb* 4G 113
  (nr. Brampton)
Hayton. *E Yor* 5C 100
Hayton. *Notts* 2E 87
Hayton's Bent. *Shrp* 2H 59
Haytor Vale. *Devn* 5A 12
Haytown. *Devn* 1D 11
Haywards Heath. *W Sus* 3E 27
Haywood. *S Lan* 4C 128
Hazelbank. *S Lan* 5B 128
Hazelbury Bryan. *Dors* 2C 14
Hazeleigh. *Essx* 5B 54
Hazeley. *Hants* 1F 25
Hazel Grove. *G Man* 2D 84
Hazelhead. *S Yor* 4B 92
Hazelslade. *Staf* 4E 73
Hazel Street. *Kent* 2A 28
Hazelton Walls. *Fife* 1F 137
Hazelwood. *Derbs* 1H 73
Hazlemere. *Buck* 2G 37
Hazler. *Shrp* 1G 59
Hazlerigg. *Tyne* 2F 115
Hazles. *Staf* 1E 73
Hazleton. *Glos* 4F 49
Hazon. *Nmbd* 4F 121
Heacham. *Norf* 2F 77
Headbourne Worthy.
  Hants 3C 24
Headcorn. *Kent* 1C 28
Headingley. *W Yor* 1C 92
Headington. *Oxon* 5D 50
Headlam. *Dur* 3E 105
Headless Cross. *Worc* 4E 61
Headley. *Hants* 5G 25
  (nr. Haslemere)
Headley. *Hants* 5D 36
  (nr. Kingsclere)
Headley. *Surr* 5D 38
Headley Down. *Hants* 3G 25
Headley Heath. *Worc* 3E 61
Headley Park. *Bris* 5A 34
Head of Muir. *Falk* 1B 128
Headon. *Notts* 3E 87
Heads Nook. *Cumb* 4F 113
Heage. *Derbs* 5A 86
Healaugh. *N Yor* 5D 104
  (nr. Grinton)
Healaugh. *N Yor* 5H 99
  (nr. York)
Heald Green. *G Man* 2C 84
Heale. *Devn* 2G 19
Healey. *G Man* 3G 91
Healey. *Nmbd* 4D 114
Healey. *N Yor* 1D 98
Healeyfield. *Dur* 5D 114
Healey Hall. *Nmbd* 4D 114
Healing. *NE Lin* 3F 95
Heamoor. *Corn* 3B 4
Heanish. *Arg* 4B 138
Heanor. *Derbs* 1B 74
Heanton Punchardon. *Devn* 3F 19
Heapham. *Linc* 2F 87
Heartsease. *Powy* 4D 58
Heasley Mill. *Devn* 3H 19
Heaste. *High* 2E 147
Heath. *Derbs* 4B 86
Heath and Reach. *C Beds* 3H 51
Heath Common. *W Sus* 4C 26
Heathcote. *Derbs* 4F 85
Heath Cross. *Devn* 3H 11
Heathencote. *Nptn* 1F 51
Heath End. *Derbs* 3A 74
Heath End. *Hants* 5D 36
Heath End. *W Mid* 5E 73
Heather. *Leics* 4A 74
Heatherfield. *High* 4D 155
Heatherton. *Derb* 2H 73
Heathfield. *Cambs* 1E 53
Heathfield. *Cumb* 5C 112
Heathfield. *Devn* 5B 12
Heathfield. *E Sus* 3G 27
Heathfield. *Ren* 3E 126

Heathfield. *Som* 3E 21
  (nr. Lydeard St Lawrence)
Heathfield. *Som* 4E 21
  (nr. Norton Fitzwarren)
Heath Green. *Worc* 3E 61
Heathhall. *Dum* 2A 112
Heath Hayes. *Staf* 4E 73
Heath Hill. *Shrp* 4B 72
Heath House. *Som* 2H 21
Heathrow (London) Airport.
  G Lon 3B 38
Heathstock. *Devn* 2F 13
Heath, The. *Norf* 3E 79
  (nr. Buxton)
Heath, The. *Norf* 2D 78
  (nr. Fakenham)
Heath, The. *Norf* 3D 78
  (nr. Hevingham)
Heath, The. *Staf* 2E 73
Heath, The. *Suff* 2E 55
Heathton. *Shrp* 1C 60
Heathtop. *Derbs* 2F 73
Heath Town. *W Mid* 1D 60
Heatley. *G Man* 2B 84
Heatley. *Staf* 3E 73
Heaton. *Lanc* 3D 96
Heaton. *Staf* 4D 84
Heaton. *Tyne* 3F 115
Heaton. *W Yor* 1B 92
Heaton Moor. *G Man* 1C 84
Heaton's Bridge. *Lanc* 3C 90
Heaverham. *Kent* 5G 39
Heavitree. *Devn* 3C 12
Hebburn. *Tyne* 3G 115
Hebden. *N Yor* 3C 98
Hebden Bridge. *W Yor* 2H 91
Hebden Green. *Ches W* 4A 84
Hebing End. *Herts* 3D 52
Hebron. *Carm* 2F 43
Hebron. *Nmbd* 1E 115
Heck. *Dum* 1B 112
Heckdyke. *Notts* 1E 87
Heckfield. *Hants* 5F 37
Heckfield Green. *Suff* 3D 66
Heckfordbridge. *Essx* 3C 54
Heckington. *Linc* 1A 76
Heckmondwike. *W Yor* 2C 92
Heddington. *Wilts* 5E 35
Heddon. *Devn* 4G 19
Heddon-on-the-Wall. *Nmbd* 3E 115
Hedenham. *Norf* 1F 67
Hedge End. *Hants* 1C 16
Hedgerley. *Buck* 2A 38
Hedging. *Som* 4G 21
Hedley on the Hill. *Nmbd* 4D 115
Hednesford. *Staf* 4E 73
Hedon. *E Yor* 2E 95
Hegdon Hill. *Here* 5H 59
Heighington. *Darl* 2F 105
Heighington. *Linc* 4H 87
Heightington. *Worc* 3B 60
Heights of Brae. *High* 2H 157
Heights of Fodderty. *High* 2H 157
Heights of Kinlochewe. *High* . . .2C 156
Heiton. *Bord* 1B 120
Hele. *Devn* 2C 12
  (nr. Exeter)
Hele. *Devn* 3D 10
  (nr. Holsworthy)
Hele. *Devn* 2F 19
  (nr. Ilfracombe)
Hele. *Torb* 2F 9
Helensburgh. *Arg* 1D 126
Helford. *Corn* 4E 5
Helhoughton. *Norf* 3A 78
Helions Bumpstead. *Essx* 1G 53
Helland. *Corn* 5A 10
Helland. *Som* 4G 21
Hellandbridge. *Corn* 5A 10
Hellesdon. *Norf* 4E 78
Hellesveor. *Corn* 2C 4
Hellidon. *Nptn* 5C 62
Hellifield. *N Yor* 4A 98
Hellingly. *E Sus* 4G 27

Hellington. *Norf* 5F 79
Helmdon. *Nptn* 1D 50
Helmingham. *Suff* 5D 66
Helmington Row. *Dur* 1E 105
Helmsdale. *High* 2H 165
Helmshore. *Lanc* 2F 91
Helmsley. *N Yor* 1A 100
Helperby. *N Yor* 3G 99
Helperthorpe. *N Yor* 2D 100
Helpringham. *Linc* 1A 76
Helpston. *Pet* 5A 76
Helsby. *Ches W* 3G 83
Helsey. *Linc* 3E 89
Helston. *Corn* 4D 4
Helstone. *Corn* 4A 10
Helton. *Cumb* 2G 103
Helwith. *N Yor* 4D 105
Helwith Bridge. *N Yor* 3H 97
Helygain. *Flin* 3E 82
Hemblington. *Norf* 4F 79
Hemel Hempstead. *Herts* 5A 52
Hemerdon. *Devn* 3B 8
Hemingbrough. *N Yor* 1G 93
Hemingby. *Linc* 3B 88
Hemingfield. *S Yor* 4D 93
Hemingford Abbots. *Cambs* 3B 64
Hemingford Grey. *Cambs* 3B 64
Hemingstone. *Suff* 5D 66
Hemington. *Leics* 3B 74
Hemington. *Nptn* 2H 63
Hemington. *Som* 1C 22
Hemley. *Suff* 1F 55
Hemlington. *Midd* 3B 106
Hempholme. *E Yor* 4E 101
Hempnall. *Norf* 1E 67
Hempnall Green. *Norf* 1E 67
Hempriggs. *High* 4F 169
Hemp's Green. *Essx* 3C 54
Hempstead. *Essx* 2G 53
Hempstead. *Medw* 4B 40
Hempstead. *Norf* 2D 78
  (nr. Holt)
Hempstead. *Norf* 3G 79
  (nr. Stalham)
Hempsted. *Glos* 4D 48
Hempton. *Norf* 3B 78
Hempton. *Oxon* 2C 50
Hemsby. *Norf* 4G 79
Hemswell. *Linc* 1G 87
Hemswell Cliff. *Linc* 2G 87
Hemsworth. *Dors* 2E 15
Hemsworth. *W Yor* 3E 93
Hem, The. *Shrp* 5B 72
Hemyock. *Devn* 1E 13
Henallt. *Carm* 3E 45
Henbury. *Bris* 4A 34
Henbury. *Ches E* 3C 84
Hendomen. *Powy* 1E 58
Hendon. *G Lon* 2D 38
Hendon. *Tyne* 4H 115
Hendra. *Corn* 3D 6
Hendre. *B'end* 3C 32
Hendreforgan. *Rhon* 3C 32
Hendy. *Carm* 5F 45
Heneglwys. *IOA* 3D 80
Henfeddau Fawr. *Pemb* 1G 43
Henfield. *S Glo* 4B 34
Henfield. *W Sus* 4D 26
Henford. *Devn* 3D 10
Hengoed. *Cphy* 2E 33
Hengoed. *Shrp* 2F 71
Hengrave. *Suff* 4H 65
Henham. *Essx* 3F 53
Heniarth. *Powy* 5D 70
Henlade. *Som* 4F 21
Henley. *Dors* 2B 14
Henley. *Shrp* 2G 59
  (nr. Church Stretton)
Henley. *Shrp* 3H 59
  (nr. Ludlow)
Henley. *Som* 3H 21
Henley. *Suff* 5D 66
Henley. *W Sus* 4G 25
Henley-in-Arden. *Warw* 4F 61

Henley-on-Thames. *Oxon* 3F 37
Henley's Down. *E Sus* 4B 28
Henley Street. *Kent* 4A 40
Henllan. *Cdgn* 1D 44
Henllan. *Den* 4C 82
Henllan. *Mon* 3F 47
Henllan Amgoed. *Carm* 3F 43
Henllys. *Torf* 2F 33
Henlow. *C Beds* 2B 52
Hennock. *Devn* 4B 12
Henny Street. *Essx* 2B 54
Henryd. *Cnwy* 3G 81
Henry's Moat. *Pemb* 2E 43
Hensall. *N Yor* 2F 93
Henshaw. *Nmbd* 3A 114
Hensingham. *Cumb* 3A 102
Henstead. *Suff* 2G 67
Hensting. *Hants* 4C 24
Henstridge. *Som* 1C 14
Henstridge Ash. *Som* 4C 22
Henstridge Bowden. *Som* 4B 22
Henstridge Marsh. *Som* 4C 22
Henton. *Oxon* 5F 51
Henton. *Som* 2H 21
Henwood. *Corn* 5C 10
Heogan. *Shet* 7F 173
Heol Senni. *Powy* 3C 46
Heol-y-Cyw. *B'end* 3C 32
Hepburn. *Nmbd* 2E 121
Hepple. *Nmbd* 4D 121
Hepscott. *Nmbd* 1F 115
Heptonstall. *W Yor* 2H 91
Hepworth. *Suff* 3B 66
Hepworth. *W Yor* 4B 92
Herbrandston. *Pemb* 4C 42
Hereford. *Here* 2A 48
Heribusta. *High* 1D 154
Heriot. *Bord* 4H 129
Hermiston. *Edin* 2E 129
Hermitage. *Dors* 2B 14
Hermitage. *Bord* 5H 119
Hermitage. *W Ber* 4D 36
Hermitage. *W Sus* 2F 17
Hermon. *Carm* 3G 45
  (nr. Llandeilo)
Hermon. *Carm* 2D 44
  (nr. Newcastle Emlyn)
Hermon. *IOA* 4C 80
Hermon. *Pemb* 1G 43
Herne. *Kent* 4F 41
Herne Bay. *Kent* 4F 41
Herne Common. *Kent* 4F 41
Herne Pound. *Kent* 5A 40
Herner. *Devn* 4F 19
Hernhill. *Kent* 4E 41
Herodsfoot. *Corn* 2G 7
Heronden. *Kent* 5G 41
Herongate. *Essx* 1H 39
Heronsford. *S Ayr* 1G 109
Heronsgate. *Herts* 1B 38
Heron's Ghyll. *E Sus* 3F 27
Herra. *Shet* 2H 173
Herriard. *Hants* 2E 25
Herringfleet. *Suff* 1G 67
Herringswell. *Suff* 4G 65
Herrington. *Tyne* 4G 115
Hersden. *Kent* 4G 41
Hersham. *Corn* 2C 10
Hersham. *Surr* 4C 38
Herstmonceux. *E Sus* 4H 27
Herston. *Dors* 5F 15
Herston. *Orkn* 8D 172
Hertford. *Herts* 4D 52
Hertford Heath. *Herts* 4D 52
Hertingfordbury. *Herts* 4D 52
Hesket. *Lanc* 2C 90
Hesketh Bank. *Lanc* 2C 90
Hesketh Lane. *Lanc* 5F 97
Hesket Newmarket. *Cumb* 1E 103
Heskin Green. *Lanc* 3D 90
Hesleden. *Dur* 1B 106
Hesleyside. *Nmbd* 1B 114
Heslington. *York* 4A 100
Hessay. *York* 4H 99

Hessenford. *Corn* 3H 7
Hessett. *Suff* 4B 66
Hessilhead. *N Ayr* 4E 127
Hessle. *Hull* 2D 94
Hestaford. *Shet* 6D 173
Hest Bank. *Lanc* 3D 96
Hester's Way. *Glos* 3E 49
Heston. *G Lon* 3C 38
Hestwall. *Orkn* 6B 172
Heswall. *Mers* 2E 83
Hethe. *Oxon* 3D 50
Hethelpit Cross. *Glos* 3C 48
Hethersett. *Norf* 5D 78
Hethersgill. *Cumb* 3F 113
Hetherside. *Cumb* 3F 113
Hethpool. *Nmbd* 2C 120
Hett. *Dur* 1F 105
Hetton. *N Yor* 4B 98
Hetton-le-Hole. *Tyne* 5G 115
Hetton Steads. *Nmbd* 1E 121
Heugh. *Nmbd* 2D 115
Heugh-head. *Abers* 2A 152
Heveningham. *Suff* 3F 67
Hever. *Kent* 1F 27
Heversham. *Cumb* 1D 97
Hevingham. *Norf* 3D 78
Hewas Water. *Corn* 4D 6
Hewelsfield. *Glos* 5A 48
Hewish. *N Som* 5G 33
Hewish. *Som* 2H 13
Hewood. *Dors* 2G 13
Heworth. *York* 4A 100
Hexham. *Nmbd* 3C 114
Hextable. *Kent* 3G 39
Hexton. *Herts* 2B 52
Hexworthy. *Devn* 5G 11
Heybridge. *Essx* 1H 39
  (nr. Brentwood)
Heybridge. *Essx* 5B 54
  (nr. Maldon)
Heybridge Basin. *Essx* 5B 54
Heybrook Bay. *Devn* 4A 8
Heydon. *Cambs* 1E 53
Heydon. *Norf* 3D 78
Heydour. *Linc* 2H 75
Heylipol. *Arg* 4A 138
Heyop. *Powy* 3E 59
Heysham. *Lanc* 3D 96
Heyshott. *W Sus* 1G 17
Heytesbury. *Wilts* 2E 23
Heythrop. *Oxon* 3B 50
Heywood. *G Man* 3G 91
Heywood. *Wilts* 1D 22
Hibaldstow. *N Lin* 4C 94
Hickleton. *S Yor* 4E 93
Hickling. *Norf* 3G 79
Hickling. *Notts* 3D 74
Hickling Green. *Norf* 3G 79
Hickling Heath. *Norf* 3G 79
Hickstead. *W Sus* 3D 26
Hidcote Bartrim. *Glos* 1G 49
Hidcote Boyce. *Glos* 1G 49
Higford. *Shrp* 5B 72
High Ackworth. *W Yor* 3E 93
Higham. *Derbs* 5A 86
Higham. *Kent* 3B 40
Higham. *Lanc* 1G 91
Higham. *S Yor* 4D 92
Higham. *Suff* 2D 54
  (nr. Ipswich)
Higham. *Suff* 4G 65
  (nr. Newmarket)
Higham Dykes. *Nmbd* 2E 115
Higham Ferrers. *Nptn* 4G 63
Higham Gobion. *C Beds* 2B 52
Higham on the Hill. *Leics* 1A 62
Highampton. *Devn* 2E 11
Higham Wood. *Kent* 1G 27
High Angerton. *Nmbd* 1D 115
High Auldgirth. *Dum* 1G 111
High Bankhill. *Cumb* 5G 113
High Banton. *N Lan* 1A 128
High Barnet. *G Lon* 1D 38
High Beech. *Essx* 1F 39

High Bentham. N Yor 3F 97
High Bickington. Devn 4G 19
High Biggins. Cumb 2F 97
High Birkwith. N Yor 2H 97
High Blantyre. S Lan 4H 127
High Bonnybridge. Falk 2B 128
High Borrans. Cumb 4F 103
High Bradfield. S Yor 1G 85
High Bray. Devn 3G 19
Highbridge. Cumb 5E 113
Highbridge. High 5D 148
Highbridge. Som 2G 21
Highbrook. W Sus 2E 27
High Brooms. Kent 1G 27
High Bullen. Devn 4F 19
Highburton. W Yor 3B 92
Highbury. Som 2B 22
High Buston. Nmbd 4G 121
High Callerton. Nmbd 2E 115
High Carlingill. Cumb 4H 103
High Catton. E Yor 4B 100
High Church. Nmbd 1E 115
Highclere. Hants 5C 36
Highcliffe. Dors 3H 15
High Cogges. Oxon 5B 50
High Common. Norf 5B 78
High Coniscliffe. Darl 3F 105
High Crosby. Cumb 4F 113
High Cross. Hants 4F 25
High Cross. Herts 4D 52
High Dougarie. N Ayr 2C 122
High Easter. Essx 4G 53
High Eggborough. N Yor 2F 93
High Ellington. N Yor 1D 98
Higher Alham. Som 2B 22
Higher Ansty. Dors 2C 14
Higher Ashton. Devn 4B 12
Higher Ballam. Lanc 1B 90
Higher Bartle. Lanc 1D 90
Higher Bockhampton. Dors 3C 14
Higher Bojewyan. Corn 3A 4
High Ercall. Telf 4H 71
Higher Cheriton. Devn 2E 12
Higher Clovelly. Devn 4D 18
Higher Compton. Plym 3A 8
Higher Dinting. Derbs 1E 85
Higher Dunstone. Devn 5H 11
Higher End. G Man 4D 90
Higher Gabwell. Devn 2F 9
Higher Halstock Leigh. Dors 2A 14
Higher Heysham. Lanc 3D 96
Higher Hurdsfield. Ches E 3D 84
Higher Kingcombe. Dors 3A 14
Higher Kinnerton. Flin 4F 83
Higher Melcombe. Dors 2C 14
Higher Penwortham. Lanc 2D 90
Higher Porthpean. Corn 3E 7
Higher Poynton. Ches E 2D 84
Higher Shotton. Flin 4F 83
Higher Shurlach. Ches W 3A 84
Higher Slade. Devn 2F 19
Higher Tale. Devn 2D 12
Highertown. Corn 4C 6
Higher Town. IOS 1B 4
Higher Town. Som 2C 20
Higher Vexford. Som 3E 20
Higher Walton. Lanc 2D 90
Higher Walton. Warr 2H 83
Higher Whatcombe. Dors 2D 14
Higher Wheelton. Lanc 2E 90
Higher Whiteleigh. Corn 3C 10
Higher Whitley. Ches W 3A 84
Higher Wincham. Ches W 3A 84
Higher Wraxall. Dors 2A 14
Higher Wych. Wrex 1G 71
Higher Yalberton. Torb 3E 9
High Etherley. Dur 2E 105
High Ferry. Linc 1C 76
Highfield. E Yor 1H 93
Highfield. N Ayr 4E 126
Highfield. Tyne 4E 115
Highfields Caldecote. Cambs 5C 64
High Garrett. Essx 3A 54
Highgate. G Lon 2D 39
Highgate. N Ayr 4E 127
Highgate. Powy 1D 58
High Grange. Dur 1E 105
High Green. Cumb 4F 103
High Green. Norf 5D 78
High Green. Shrp 2B 60
High Green. S Yor 1H 85
High Green. W Yor 3B 92
High Green. Worc 1D 49
Highgreen Manor. Nmbd 5C 120
High Halden. Kent 2C 28
High Halstow. Medw 3B 40
High Ham. Som 3H 21
High Harrington. Cumb 2B 102
High Haswell. Dur 5G 115
High Hatton. Shrp 3A 72
High Hawkser. N Yor 4G 107
High Hesket. Cumb 5F 113
High Hesleden. Dur 1B 106
High Hoyland. S Yor 3C 92
High Hunsley. E Yor 1C 94
High Hurstwood. E Sus 3F 27
High Hutton. N Yor 3B 100
High Ireby. Cumb 1D 102
High Keil. Arg 5A 122
High Kelling. Norf 1D 78
High Kilburn. N Yor 2H 99
High Knipe. Cumb 3G 103
High Lands. Dur 2E 105
Highlands, The. Shrp 2A 60
Highlane. Ches E 4C 84
Highlane. Derbs 2B 86
High Lane. G Man 2D 84
High Lane. Here 4A 60
High Laver. Essx 5F 53
Highlaws. Cumb 5C 112
Highleadon. Glos 3C 48
High Legh. Ches E 2A 84
Highleigh. W Sus 3G 17
High Leven. Stoc T 3B 106
Highley. Shrp 2B 60
High Littleton. Bath 1B 22
High Longthwaite. Cumb 5D 112
High Lorton. Cumb 2C 102
High Marishes. N Yor 2C 100
High Marnham. Notts 3F 87
High Melton. S Yor 4F 93
High Mickley. Nmbd 3D 115
Highmoor. Cumb 5D 112
High Moor. Lanc 3D 90
Highmoor. Oxon 3F 37
Highmoor Cross. Oxon 3F 37
Highmoor Hill. Mon 3H 33
High Mowthorpe. N Yor 3C 100
Highnam. Glos 4C 48
High Newport. Tyne 4G 115
High Newton. Cumb 1D 96
High Newton-by-the-Sea. Nmbd 2G 121
High Nibthwaite. Cumb 1B 96
High Offley. Staf 3B 72
High Ongar. Essx 5F 53
High Onn. Staf 4C 72
High Orchard. Glos 4D 48
High Park. Mers 3B 90
High Roding. Essx 4G 53
High Row. Cumb 1E 103
High Salvington. W Sus 5C 26
High Scales. Cumb 5C 112
High Shaw. N Yor 5B 104
High Shincliffe. Dur 5F 115
High Side. Cumb 1D 102
High Spen. Tyne 3E 115
Highsted. Kent 4D 40
High Stoop. Dur 5E 115
High Street. Corn 3D 6
High Street. Suff 5G 67 (nr. Aldeburgh)
High Street. Suff 2F 67 (nr. Bungay)
High Street. Suff 3G 67 (nr. Yoxford)
Highstreet Green. Essx 2A 54
High Street Green. Suff 5C 66
Highstreet Green. Surr 2A 26
Hightae. Dum 2B 112
High Throston. Hart 1B 106
Hightown. Ches E 4C 84
Hightown. Mers 4A 90
High Town. Staf 4D 73
Hightown Green. Suff 5B 66
High Toynton. Linc 4B 88
High Trewhitt. Nmbd 4E 121
High Valleyfield. Fife 1D 128
Highway. Here 1H 47
Highweek. Devn 5B 12
High Westwood. Dur 4E 115
Highwood. Staf 2E 73
Highwood. Worc 4A 60
High Worsall. N Yor 4A 106
Highworth. Swin 2H 35
High Wray. Cumb 5E 103
High Wych. Herts 4E 53
High Wycombe. Buck 2G 37
Hilborough. Norf 5H 77
Hilcott. Wilts 1G 23
Hildenborough. Kent 1G 27
Hildersham. Cambs 1F 53
Hilderstone. Staf 2D 72
Hilderthorpe. E Yor 3F 101
Hilfield. Dors 2B 14
Hilgay. Norf 1F 65
Hill. S Glo 2B 34
Hill. Warw 4B 62
Hill. Worc 1E 49
Hillam. N Yor 2F 93
Hillbeck. Cumb 3A 104
Hillberry. IOM 4C 108
Hillborough. Kent 4G 41
Hillbourne. Pool 3F 15
Hillbrae. Abers 4D 160 (nr. Aberchirder)
Hillbrae. Abers 1E 153 (nr. Inverurie)
Hillbrae. Abers 5F 161 (nr. Methlick)
Hill Brow. Hants 4F 25
Hillbutts. Dors 2E 15
Hillcliffane. Derbs 1G 73
Hillcommon. Som 4E 21
Hill Deverill. Wilts 2D 22
Hilldyke. Linc 1C 76
Hill End. Dur 1D 104
Hillend. Fife 1E 129 (nr. Inverkeithing)
Hill End. Fife 4C 136 (nr. Saline)
Hillend. N Lan 3B 128
Hill End. N Yor 4C 98
Hillend. Shrp 1C 60
Hillend. Swan 3D 30
Hillersland. Glos 4A 48
Hillerton. Devn 3H 11
Hillesden. Buck 3E 51
Hillesley. Glos 3C 34
Hillfarrance. Som 4E 21
Hill Furze. Worc 1E 49
Hill Gate. Here 3H 47
Hill Green. Essx 2E 53
Hillgreen. W Ber 4C 36
Hillhead. Abers 5C 160
Hill Head. Hants 2D 16
Hillhead. S Ayr 3D 116
Hillhead. Torb 3F 9
Hillhead of Auchentumb. Abers 3G 161
Hilliard's Cross. Staf 4F 73
Hilliclay. High 2D 168
Hillingdon. G Lon 2B 38
Hillington. Norf 3G 77
Hillington. Ren 3G 127
Hillmorton. Warw 3C 62
Hill of Beath. Fife 4D 136
Hill of Fearn. High 1C 158
Hill of Fiddes. Abers 1G 153
Hill of Keillor. Ang 4B 144
Hill of Overbrae. Abers 2F 161
Hill Ridware. Staf 4E 73
Hillsborough. S Yor 1H 85
Hillside. Abers 4G 153
Hillside. Ang 2G 145
Hillside. Devn 2D 8
Hillside. Mers 3B 90
Hillside. Orkn 5C 172
Hillside. Shet 5F 173
Hillside. Shrp 2A 60
Hill Side. W Yor 3B 92
Hillside. Worc 4B 60
Hillside of Prieston. Ang 5C 144
Hill Somersal. Derbs 2F 73
Hillstown. Derbs 4B 86
Hillstreet. Hants 1B 16
Hillswick. Shet 4D 173
Hill, The. Cumb 1A 96
Hill Top. Dur 2C 104 (nr. Barnard Castle)
Hill Top. Dur 5F 115 (nr. Durham)
Hill Top. Dur 4E 115 (nr. Stanley)
Hill Top. Hants 2C 16
Hill View. Dors 3E 15
Hill Wootton. Warw 4H 61
Hillyland. Per 1C 136
Hilmarton. Wilts 4F 35
Hilperton. Wilts 1D 22
Hilperton Marsh. Wilts 1D 22
Hilsea. Port 2E 17
Hilston. E Yor 1F 95
Hiltingbury. Hants 4C 24
Hilton. Cambs 4B 64
Hilton. Cumb 2A 104
Hilton. Derbs 2G 73
Hilton. Dors 2C 14
Hilton. Dur 2E 105
Hilton. High 5E 165
Hilton. Shrp 1B 60
Hilton. Staf 5E 73
Hilton. Stoc T 3B 106
Hilton of Cadboll. High 1C 158
Himbleton. Worc 5D 60
Himley. Staf 1C 60
Hincaster. Cumb 1E 97
Hinchcliffe Mill. W Yor 4B 92
Hinchwick. Glos 2G 49
Hinckley. Leics 1B 62
Hinderclay. Suff 3C 66
Hinderwell. N Yor 3E 107
Hindford. Shrp 2F 71
Hindhead. Surr 3G 25
Hindley. G Man 4E 90
Hindley. Nmbd 4D 114
Hindley Green. G Man 4E 91
Hindlip. Worc 5C 60
Hindolveston. Norf 3C 78
Hindon. Wilts 3E 23
Hindringham. Norf 2B 78
Hingham. Norf 5C 78
Hinksford. Staf 2C 60
Hinstock. Shrp 3A 72
Hintlesham. Suff 1D 54
Hinton. Hants 3H 15
Hinton. Here 2G 47
Hinton. Nptn 5C 62
Hinton. Shrp 5G 71
Hinton. S Glo 4C 34
Hinton Ampner. Hants 4D 24
Hinton Blewett. Bath 1A 22
Hinton Charterhouse. Bath 1C 22
Hinton-in-the-Hedges. Nptn 2D 50
Hinton Martell. Dors 2F 15
Hinton on the Green. Worc 1F 49
Hinton Parva. Swin 3H 35
Hinton St George. Som 1H 13
Hinton St Mary. Dors 1C 14
Hinton Waldrist. Oxon 2B 36
Hints. Shrp 3A 60
Hints. Staf 5F 73
Hinwick. Bed 4G 63
Hinxhill. Kent 1E 29
Hinxton. Cambs 1E 53
Hinxworth. Herts 1C 52
Hipley. Hants 1E 16
Hipperholme. W Yor 2B 92
Hipsburn. Nmbd 3G 121
Hipswell. N Yor 5E 105
Hiraeth. Carm 2F 43
Hirn. Abers 3E 153
Hirnant. Powy 3C 70
Hirst. N Lan 3B 128
Hirst. Nmbd 1F 115
Hirst Courtney. N Yor 2G 93
Hirwaen. Den 4D 82
Hirwaun. Rhon 5C 46
Hiscott. Devn 4F 19
Histon. Cambs 4D 64
Hitcham. Suff 5B 66
Hitchin. Herts 3B 52
Hittisleigh. Devn 3H 11
Hittisleigh Barton. Devn 3H 11
Hive. E Yor 1B 94
Hixon. Staf 3E 73
Hoaden. Kent 5G 41
Hoar Cross. Staf 3F 73
Hoarwithy. Here 3A 48
Hoath. Kent 4G 41
Hobarris. Shrp 3F 59
Hobbles Green. Suff 5G 65
Hobbs Cross. Essx 1F 39
Hobkirk. Bord 3H 119
Hobson. Dur 4E 115
Hoby. Leics 4D 74
Hockering. Norf 4C 78
Hockering Heath. Norf 4C 78
Hockerton. Notts 5E 86
Hockley. Essx 1C 40
Hockley. Staf 5G 73
Hockley. W Mid 3G 61
Hockley Heath. W Mid 3F 61
Hockliffe. C Beds 3H 51
Hockwold cum Wilton. Norf 2G 65
Hockworthy. Devn 1D 12
Hoddesdon. Herts 5D 52
Hoddlesden. Bkbn 2F 91
Hoddomcross. Dum 2C 112
Hodgeston. Pemb 5E 43
Hodley. Powy 1D 58
Hodnet. Shrp 3A 72
Hodsoll Street. Kent 4H 39
Hodson. Swin 3G 35
Hodthorpe. Derbs 3C 86
Hoe. Norf 4B 78
Hoe Gate. Hants 1E 17
Hoe, The. Plym 3A 8
Hoff. Cumb 3H 103
Hoffleet Stow. Linc 2B 76
Hogaland. Shet 4E 173
Hogben's Hill. Kent 5E 41
Hoggard's Green. Suff 5A 66
Hoggeston. Buck 3G 51
Hoggrill's End. Warw 1G 61
Hogha Gearraidh. W Isl 1C 170
Hoghton. Lanc 2E 90
Hoghton Bottoms. Lanc 2E 91
Hognaston. Derbs 5G 85
Hogsthorpe. Linc 3E 89
Hogstock. Dors 2E 15
Holbeach. Linc 3C 76
Holbeach Bank. Linc 3C 76
Holbeach Clough. Linc 3C 76
Holbeach Drove. Linc 4C 76
Holbeach Hurn. Linc 3C 76
Holbeach St Johns. Linc 4C 76
Holbeach St Marks. Linc 2C 76
Holbeach St Matthew. Linc 2D 76
Holbeck. Notts 3C 86
Holbeck. W Yor 1C 92
Holbeck Woodhouse. Notts 3C 86
Holberrow Green. Worc 5E 61
Holbeton. Devn 3C 8
Holborn. G Lon 2E 39
Holbrook. Derbs 1A 74
Holbrook. S Yor 2B 86
Holbrook. Suff 2E 55
Holburn. Nmbd 1E 121
Holbury. Hants 2C 16

Holcombe—Howden

Holcombe. *Devn* 5C 12
Holcombe. *G Man* 3F 91
Holcombe. *Som* 2B 22
Holcombe Brook. *G Man* 3F 91
Holcombe Rogus. *Devn* 1D 12
Holcot. *Nptn* 4E 63
Holden. *Lanc* 5G 97
Holdenby. *Nptn* 4D 62
Holder's Green. *Essx* 3G 53
Holdgate. *Shrp* 2H 59
Holdingham. *Linc* 1H 75
Holditch. *Dors* 2G 13
Holemoor. *Devn* 2E 11
Hole Street. *W Sus* 4C 26
Holford. *Som* 2E 21
Holker. *Cumb* 2C 96
Holkham. *Norf* 1A 78
Hollacombe. *Devn* 2D 11
Holland. *Orkn* 2D 172
Holland Fen. *Linc* 1B 76
Holland Lees. *Lanc* 4D 90
Holland-on-Sea. *Essx* 4F 55
Holland Park. *W Mid* 5E 73
Hollandstoun. *Orkn* 2G 172
Hollesley. *Suff* 1G 55
Hollinfare. *Warr* 1A 84
Hollingbourne. *Kent* 5C 40
Hollingbury. *Brig* 5E 27
Hollingdon. *Buck* 3G 51
Hollingrove. *E Sus* 3A 28
Hollington. *Derbs* 1G 73
Hollington. *E Sus* 4B 28
Hollington. *Staf* 2E 73
Hollington Grove. *Derbs* 2G 73
Hollingworth. *G Man* 1E 85
Hollins. *Derbs* 3H 85
Hollins. *G Man* 4G 91
(nr. Bury)
Hollins. *G Man* 4G 91
(nr. Middleton)
Hollinsclough. *Staf* 4E 85
Hollinswood. *Telf* 5A 72
Hollinthorpe. *W Yor* 1D 93
Hollinwood. *G Man* 4H 91
Hollinwood. *Shrp* 2H 71
Hollocombe. *Devn* 1G 11
Holloway. *Derbs* 5H 85
Hollow Court. *Worc* 5D 61
Hollowell. *Nptn* 3D 62
Hollow Meadows. *S Yor* 2G 85
Hollows. *Dum* 2E 113
Hollybush. *Cphy* 5E 47
Hollybush. *E Ayr* 3C 116
Hollybush. *Worc* 2C 48
Holly End. *Norf* 5D 77
Holly Hill. *N Yor* 4E 105
Hollyhurst. *Ches E* 1H 71
Hollym. *E Yor* 2G 95
Hollywood. *Worc* 3E 61
Holmacott. *Devn* 4F 19
Holmbridge. *W Yor* 4B 92
Holmbury St Mary. *Surr* 1C 26
Holmbush. *Corn* 3E 7
Holmcroft. *Staf* 3D 72
Holme. *Cambs* 2A 64
Holme. *Cumb* 2E 97
Holme. *N Lin* 4C 94
Holme. *N Yor* 1F 99
Holme. *Notts* 5F 87
Holme. *W Yor* 4B 92
Holmebridge. *Dors* 4D 15
Holme Chapel. *Lanc* 2G 91
Holme Hale. *Norf* 5A 78
Holme Lacy. *Here* 2A 48
Holme Marsh. *Here* 5F 59
Holmend. *Dum* 4C 118
Holme next the Sea. *Norf* 1G 77
Holme-on-Spalding-Moor.
E Yor 1B 94
Holme on the Wolds. *E Yor* 5D 100
Holme Pierrepont. *Notts* 2D 74
Holmer. *Here* 1A 48
Holmer Green. *Buck* 1A 38
Holmes. *Lanc* 3C 90
Holme St Cuthbert. *Cumb* 5C 112
Holmes Chapel. *Ches E* 4B 84
Holmesfield. *Derbs* 3H 85
Holmeswood. *Lanc* 3C 90
Holmewood. *Derbs* 4B 86
Holmfirth. *W Yor* 4B 92
Holmhead. *E Ayr* 2E 117
Holmisdale. *High* 4A 154
Holm of Drumlanrig. *Dum* 5H 117
Holmpton. *E Yor* 2G 95
Holmrook. *Cumb* 5B 102
Holmside. *Dur* 5F 115
Holmwrangle. *Cumb* 5G 113
Holne. *Devn* 2D 8
Holsworthy. *Devn* 2D 10
Holsworthy Beacon. *Devn* 2D 10
Holt. *Dors* 2F 15
Holt. *Norf* 2C 78
Holt. *Wilts* 5D 34
Holt. *Worc* 4C 60
Holt. *Wrex* 5G 83
Holtby. *York* 4A 100
Holt End. *Hants* 3E 25
Holt End. *Worc* 4E 61
Holt Fleet. *Worc* 4C 60
Holt Green. *Lanc* 4B 90
Holt Heath. *Dors* 2F 15
Holt Heath. *Worc* 4C 60
Holton. *Oxon* 5E 50
Holton. *Som* 4B 22
Holton. *Suff* 3F 67
Holton cum Beckering. *Linc* 2A 88
Holton Heath. *Dors* 3E 15
Holton le Clay. *Linc* 4F 95
Holton le Moor. *Linc* 1H 87
Holton St Mary. *Suff* 2D 54
Holt Pound. *Hants* 2G 25
Holtsmere End. *Herts* 4A 52
Holtye. *E Sus* 2F 27
Holwell. *Dors* 1C 14
Holwell. *Herts* 2B 52
Holwell. *Leics* 3E 75
Holwell. *Oxon* 5H 49
Holwell. *Som* 2C 22
Holwick. *Dur* 2C 104
Holworth. *Dors* 4C 14
Holybourne. *Hants* 2F 25
Holy City. *Devn* 2G 13
Holy Cross. *Worc* 3D 60
Holyfield. *Essx* 5D 53
Holyhead. *IOA* 2B 80
Holy Island. *Nmbd* 5H 131
Holymoorside. *Derbs* 4H 85
Holyport. *Wind* 4G 37
Holystone. *Nmbd* 4D 120
Holytown. *N Lan* 3A 128
Holywell. *Cambs* 3C 64
Holywell. *Dors* 2A 14
Holywell. *Flin* 3D 82
Holywell. *Glos* 2C 34
Holywell. *Nmbd* 2G 115
Holywell. *Warw* 4F 61
Holywell Bay. *Corn* 3B 6
Holywell Green. *W Yor* 3A 92
Holywell Lake. *Som* 4E 20
Holywell Row. *Suff* 3G 65
Holywood. *Dum* 1G 111
Homer. *Shrp* 5A 72
Homer Green. *Mers* 4B 90
Homersfield. *Suff* 2E 67
Hom Green. *Here* 3A 48
Homington. *Wilts* 4G 23
Honeyborough. *Pemb* 4D 42
Honeybourne. *Worc* 1G 49
Honeychurch. *Devn* 2G 11
Honeydon. *Bed* 5A 64
Honey Hill. *Kent* 4F 41
Honey Street. *Wilts* 5G 35
Honey Tye. *Suff* 2C 54
Honeywick. *C Beds* 3H 51
Honiley. *Warw* 3G 61
Honing. *Norf* 3F 79
Honingham. *Norf* 4D 78
Honington. *Linc* 1G 75
Honington. *Suff* 3B 66
Honington. *Warw* 1A 50
Honiton. *Devn* 2E 13
Honley. *W Yor* 3B 92
Honnington. *Telf* 4B 72
Hoo. *Suff* 5E 67
Hoobrook. *Worc* 3C 60
Hood Green. *S Yor* 4D 92
Hooe. *E Sus* 5A 28
Hooe. *Plym* 3B 8
Hooe Common. *E Sus* 4A 28
Hoohill. *Bkpl* 1B 90
Hook. *Cambs* 1D 64
Hook. *E Yor* 2A 94
Hook. *G Lon* 4C 38
Hook. *Hants* 1F 25
(nr. Basingstoke)
Hook. *Hants* 2D 16
(nr. Fareham)
Hook. *Pemb* 3D 43
Hook. *Wilts* 3F 35
Hook-a-Gate. *Shrp* 5G 71
Hook Bank. *Worc* 1D 48
Hooke. *Dors* 2A 14
Hooker Gate. *Tyne* 4E 115
Hookgate. *Staf* 2B 72
Hook Green. *Kent* 2A 28
(nr. Lamberhurst)
Hook Green. *Kent* 3H 39
(nr. Longfield)
Hook Green. *Kent* 4H 39
(nr. Meopham)
Hook Norton. *Oxon* 2B 50
Hook's Cross. *Herts* 3C 52
Hook Street. *Glos* 2B 34
Hookway. *Devn* 3B 12
Hookwood. *Surr* 1D 26
Hoole. *Ches W* 4G 83
Hooley. *Surr* 5D 39
Hooley Bridge. *G Man* 3G 91
Hooley Brow. *G Man* 3G 91
Hoo St Werburgh. *Medw* 3B 40
Hooton. *Ches W* 3F 83
Hooton Levitt. *S Yor* 1C 86
Hooton Pagnell. *S Yor* 4E 93
Hooton Roberts. *S Yor* 1B 86
Hope. *Derbs* 2F 85
Hope. *Flin* 5F 83
Hope. *High* 2E 167
Hope. *Powy* 5E 71
Hope. *Shrp* 5F 71
Hope. *Staf* 5F 85
Hope Bagot. *Shrp* 3H 59
Hope Bowdler. *Shrp* 1G 59
Hopedale. *Staf* 5F 85
Hope Green. *Ches E* 2D 84
Hopeman. *Mor* 2F 159
Hope Mansell. *Here* 4B 48
Hopesay. *Shrp* 2F 59
Hope's Green. *Essx* 2B 40
Hopetown. *W Yor* 2D 93
Hope under Dinmore. *Here* 5H 59
Hopley's Green. *Here* 5F 59
Hopperton. *N Yor* 4G 99
Hop Pole. *Linc* 4A 76
Hopstone. *Shrp* 1B 60
Hopton. *Derbs* 5G 85
Hopton. *Powy* 1E 59
Hopton. *Shrp* 3F 71
(nr. Oswestry)
Hopton. *Shrp* 3H 71
(nr. Wem)
Hopton. *Staf* 3D 72
Hopton. *Suff* 3B 66
Hopton Cangeford. *Shrp* 2H 59
Hopton Castle. *Shrp* 3F 59
Hoptonheath. *Shrp* 3F 59
Hopton Heath. *Staf* 3D 72
Hopton on Sea. *Norf* 5H 79
Hopton Wafers. *Shrp* 3A 60
Hopwas. *Staf* 5F 73
Hopwood. *Worc* 3E 61
Horam. *E Sus* 4G 27
Horbling. *Linc* 2A 76
Horbury. *W Yor* 3C 92
Horcott. *Glos* 5G 49
Horden. *Dur* 5H 115
Horderley. *Shrp* 2G 59
Hordle. *Hants* 3A 16
Hordley. *Shrp* 2F 71
Horeb. *Carm* 3F 45
(nr. Brechfa)
Horeb. *Carm* 5E 45
(nr. Llanelli)
Horeb. *Cdgn* 1D 45
Horfield. *Bris* 4B 34
Horgabost. *W Isl* 8C 171
Horham. *Suff* 3E 66
Horkesley Heath. *Essx* 3C 54
Horkstow. *N Lin* 3C 94
Horley. *Oxon* 1C 50
Horley. *Surr* 1D 27
Horn Ash. *Dors* 2G 13
Hornblotton Green. *Som* 3A 22
Hornby. *Lanc* 3E 97
Hornby. *N Yor* 4A 106
(nr. Appleton Wiske)
Hornby. *N Yor* 5F 105
(nr. Catterick Garrison)
Horncastle. *Linc* 4B 88
Hornchurch. *G Lon* 2G 39
Horncliffe. *Nmbd* 5F 131
Horndean. *Hants* 1E 17
Horndean. *Bord* 5E 131
Horndon. *Devn* 4F 11
Horndon on the Hill. *Thur* 2A 40
Horne. *Surr* 1E 27
Horner. *Som* 2C 20
Horning. *Norf* 4F 79
Horninghold. *Leics* 1F 63
Horninglow. *Staf* 3G 73
Horningsea. *Cambs* 4D 65
Horningsham. *Wilts* 2D 22
Horningtoft. *Norf* 3B 78
Hornsbury. *Som* 1G 13
Hornsby. *Cumb* 4G 113
Hornsbygate. *Cumb* 4G 113
Horns Corner. *Kent* 3B 28
Horns Cross. *Devn* 4D 19
Hornsea. *E Yor* 5G 101
Hornsea Burton. *E Yor* 5G 101
Hornsey. *G Lon* 2E 39
Hornton. *Oxon* 1B 50
Horpit. *Swin* 3H 35
Horrabridge. *Devn* 2B 8
Horringer. *Suff* 4H 65
Horringford. *IOW* 4D 16
Horrocks Fold. *G Man* 3F 91
Horrocksford. *Lanc* 5G 97
Horsbrugh Ford. *Bord* 1E 119
Horsebridge. *Devn* 5E 11
Horsebridge. *E Sus* 4G 27
Horsebridge. *Hants* 3B 24
Horse Bridge. *Staf* 5D 84
Horsebrook. *Staf* 4C 72
Horsecastle. *N Som* 5H 33
Horsehay. *Telf* 5A 72
Horseheath. *Cambs* 1G 53
Horsehouse. *N Yor* 1C 98
Horsell. *Surr* 5A 38
Horseman's Green. *Wrex* 1G 71
Horsenden. *Buck* 5F 51
Horseway. *Cambs* 2D 64
Horsey. *Norf* 3G 79
Horsey. *Som* 3G 21
Horsford. *Norf* 4D 78
Horsforth. *W Yor* 1C 92
Horsham. *W Sus* 2C 26
Horsham. *Worc* 5B 60
Horsham St Faith. *Norf* 4E 78
Horsington. *Linc* 4A 88
Horsington. *Som* 4C 22
Horsley. *Derbs* 1A 74
Horsley. *Glos* 2D 34
Horsley. *Nmbd* 3D 115
(nr. Prudhoe)
Horsley. *Nmbd* 5C 120
(nr. Rochester)
Horsley Cross. *Essx* 3E 54
Horsleycross Street. *Essx* 3E 54
Horsleyhill. *Bord* 3H 119
Horsleyhope. *Dur* 5D 114
Horsley Woodhouse. *Derbs* 1A 74
Horsmonden. *Kent* 1A 28
Horspath. *Oxon* 5D 50
Horstead. *Norf* 4E 79
Horsted Keynes. *W Sus* 3E 27
Horton. *Buck* 4H 51
Horton. *Dors* 2F 15
Horton. *Lanc* 4A 98
Horton. *Nptn* 5F 63
Horton. *Shrp* 2G 71
Horton. *Som* 1G 13
Horton. *S Glo* 3C 34
Horton. *Staf* 5D 84
Horton. *Swan* 4D 30
Horton. *Wilts* 5F 35
Horton. *Wind* 3B 38
Horton Cross. *Som* 1G 13
Horton-cum-Studley. *Oxon* 4D 50
Horton Grange. *Nmbd* 2F 115
Horton Green. *Ches W* 1G 71
Horton Heath. *Hants* 1C 16
Horton in Ribblesdale. *N Yor* 2H 97
Horton Kirby. *Kent* 4G 39
Hortonwood. *Telf* 4A 72
Horwich. *G Man* 3E 91
Horwich End. *Derbs* 2E 85
Horwood. *Devn* 4F 19
Hoscar. *Lanc* 3C 90
Hose. *Leics* 3E 75
Hosh. *Per* 1A 136
Hosta. *W Isl* 1C 170
Hoswick. *Shet* 9F 173
Hotham. *E Yor* 1B 94
Hothfield. *Kent* 1D 28
Hoton. *Leics* 3C 74
Houbie. *Shet* 2H 173
Hough. *Arg* 4A 138
Hough. *Ches E* 5B 84
(nr. Crewe)
Hough. *Ches E* 3C 84
(nr. Wilmslow)
Hougham. *Linc* 1F 75
Hough Green. *Hal* 2G 83
Hough-on-the-Hill. *Linc* 1G 75
Houghton. *Cambs* 3B 64
Houghton. *Cumb* 4F 113
Houghton. *Hants* 3B 24
Houghton. *Nmbd* 3E 115
Houghton. *Pemb* 4D 43
Houghton. *W Sus* 4B 26
Houghton Bank. *Darl* 2F 105
Houghton Conquest. *C Beds* 1A 52
Houghton Green. *E Sus* 3D 28
Houghton-le-Side. *Darl* 2F 105
Houghton-le-Spring. *Tyne* 5G 115
Houghton on the Hill. *Leics* 5D 74
Houghton Regis. *C Beds* 3A 52
Houghton St Giles. *Norf* 2B 78
Houlsyke. *N Yor* 4E 107
Hound. *Hants* 2C 16
Hound Green. *Hants* 1F 25
Houndslow. *Bord* 5C 130
Houndsmoor. *Som* 4E 21
Houndwood. *Bord* 3E 131
Hounsdown. *Hants* 1B 16
Hounslow. *G Lon* 3C 38
Housay. *Shet* 4H 173
Househill. *High* 3C 158
Housetter. *Shet* 3E 173
Houss. *Shet* 8E 173
Houston. *Ren* 3F 127
Housty. *High* 5D 168
Houton. *Orkn* 7C 172
Hove. *Brig* 5D 27
Hoveringham. *Notts* 1E 74
Hoveton. *Norf* 4F 79
Hovingham. *N Yor* 2A 100
How. *Cumb* 4G 113
How Caple. *Here* 2B 48
Howden. *E Yor* 2H 93

Howden-le-Wear. *Dur* 1E **105**
Howe. *High* 2F **169**
Howe. *Norf* 5E **79**
Howe. *N Yor* 1F **99**
Howe Green. *Essx* 5H **53**
(nr. Chelmsford)
Howegreen. *Essx* 5B **54**
(nr. Maldon)
Howe Green. *Warw* 2H **61**
Howell. *Linc* 1A **76**
How End. *C Beds* 1A **52**
Howe of Teuchar. *Abers* 4E **161**
Howes. *Dum* 3C **112**
Howe Street. *Essx* 4G **53**
(nr. Chelmsford)
Howe Street. *Essx* 2G **53**
(nr. Finchingfield)
Howe, The. *Cumb* 1D **96**
Howe, The. *IOM* 5A **108**
Howey. *Powy* 5C **58**
Howgate. *Midl* 4F **129**
Howgill. *Lanc* 5H **97**
Howgill. *N Yor* 4C **98**
How Green. *Kent* 1F **27**
How Hill. *Norf* 4F **79**
Howick. *Nmbd* 3G **121**
Howle. *Telf* 3A **72**
Howle Hill. *Here* 3B **48**
Howleigh. *Som* 1F **13**
Howlett End. *Essx* 2F **53**
Howley. *Som* 2F **13**
Howley. *Warr* 2A **84**
Hownam. *Bord* 3B **120**
Howsham. *N Lin* 4D **94**
Howsham. *N Yor* 3B **100**
Howtel. *Nmbd* 1C **120**
Howt Green. *Kent* 4C **40**
Howton. *Here* 3H **47**
Howwood. *Ren* 3E **127**
Hoxne. *Suff* 3D **66**
Hoylake. *Mers* 2E **82**
Hoyland. *S Yor* 4D **92**
Hoylandswaine. *S Yor* 4C **92**
Hoyle. *W Sus* 4A **26**
Hubberholme. *N Yor* 2B **98**
Hubberston. *Pemb* 4C **42**
Hubbert's Bridge. *Linc* 1B **76**
Huby. *N Yor* 5E **99**
(nr. Harrogate)
Huby. *N Yor* 3H **99**
(nr. York)
Hucclecote. *Glos* 4D **48**
Hucking. *Kent* 5C **40**
Hucknall. *Notts* 1C **74**
Huddersfield. *W Yor* 3B **92**
Huddington. *Worc* 5D **60**
Huddlesford. *Staf* 5F **73**
Hudswell. *N Yor* 4E **105**
Huggate. *E Yor* 4C **100**
Hugglescote. *Leics* 4B **74**
Hughenden Valley. *Buck* 2G **37**
Hughley. *Shrp* 1H **59**
Hughton. *High* 4G **157**
Hugh Town. *IOS* 1B **4**
Hugus. *Corn* 4B **6**
Huish. *Devn* 1F **11**
Huish. *Wilts* 5G **35**
Huish Champflower. *Som* 4D **20**
Huish Episcopi. *Som* 4H **21**
Huisinis. *W Isl* 6B **171**
Hulcote. *Nptn* 5E **62**
Hulcott. *Buck* 4G **51**
Hulham. *Devn* 4D **12**
Hull. *Hull* 2D **94**
Hulland. *Derbs* 1G **73**
Hulland Moss. *Derbs* 1G **73**
Hulland Ward. *Derbs* 1G **73**
Hullavington. *Wilts* 3D **35**
Hullbridge. *Essx* 1C **40**
Hulme. *G Man* 1C **84**
Hulme. *Staf* 1D **72**
Hulme End. *Staf* 5F **85**
Hulme Walfield. *Ches E* 4C **84**
Hulverstone. *IOW* 4B **16**
Hulver Street. *Suff* 2G **67**
Humber. *Devn* 5C **12**
Humber. *Here* 5H **59**
Humber Bridge. *N Lin* 2D **94**
Humberside International Airport. *N Lin* 3D **94**
Humberston. *NE Lin* 4G **95**
Humberstone. *Leic* 5D **74**
Humbie. *E Lot* 3A **130**
Humbleton. *E Yor* 1F **95**
Humbleton. *Nmbd* 2D **121**
Humby. *Linc* 2H **75**
Hume. *Bord* 5D **130**
Humshaugh. *Nmbd* 2C **114**
Huna. *High* 1F **169**
Huncoat. *Lanc* 1F **91**
Huncote. *Leics* 1C **62**
Hundall. *Derbs* 3A **86**
Hunderthwaite. *Dur* 2C **104**
Hundleby. *Linc* 4C **88**
Hundle Houses. *Linc* 5B **88**
Hundleton. *Pemb* 4D **42**
Hundon. *Suff* 1H **53**
Hundred Acres. *Hants* 1D **16**
Hundred House. *Powy* 5D **58**
Hundred, The. *Here* 4H **59**
Hungarton. *Leics* 5D **74**
Hungerford. *Hants* 1G **15**
Hungerford. *Shrp* 2H **59**
Hungerford. *Som* 2D **20**
Hungerford. *W Ber* 5B **36**
Hungerford Newtown. *W Ber* 4B **36**
Hunger Hill. *G Man* 4E **91**
Hungerton. *Linc* 2F **75**
Hungladder. *High* 1C **154**
Hungryhatton. *Shrp* 3A **72**
Hunmanby. *N Yor* 2E **101**
Hunmanby Sands. *N Yor* 2F **101**
Hunningham. *Warw* 4A **62**
Hunnington. *Worc* 2D **60**
Hunny Hill. *IOW* 4C **16**
Hunsdon. *Herts* 4E **53**
Hunsdonbury. *Herts* 4E **53**
Hunsingore. *N Yor* 4G **99**
Hunslet. *W Yor* 1D **92**
Hunslet Carr. *W Yor* 2D **92**
Hunsonby. *Cumb* 1G **103**
Hunspow. *High* 1E **169**
Hunstanton. *Norf* 1F **77**
Hunstanworth. *Dur* 5C **114**
Hunston. *Suff* 4B **66**
Hunston. *W Sus* 2G **17**
Hunstrete. *Bath* 5B **34**
Hunt End. *Worc* 4E **61**
Hunterfield. *Midl* 3G **129**
Hunters Forstal. *Kent* 4F **41**
Hunter's Quay. *Arg* 2C **126**
Huntham. *Som* 4G **21**
Hunthill Lodge. *Ang* 1D **144**
Huntingdon. *Cambs* 3B **64**
Huntingfield. *Suff* 3F **67**
Huntingford. *Wilts* 3D **22**
Huntington. *Ches W* 4G **83**
Huntington. *E Lot* 2A **130**
Huntington. *Here* 5E **59**
Huntington. *Staf* 4D **72**
Huntington. *Telf* 5A **72**
Huntington. *York* 4A **100**
Huntingtower. *Per* 1C **136**
Huntley. *Glos* 4C **48**
Huntley. *Staf* 1E **73**
Huntly. *Abers* 4C **160**
Huntlywood. *Bord* 5C **130**
Hunton. *Hants* 3C **24**
Hunton. *Kent* 1B **28**
Hunton. *N Yor* 5E **105**
Hunton Bridge. *Herts* 5A **52**
Hunt's Corner. *Norf* 2C **66**
Huntscott. *Som* 2C **20**
Hunt's Cross. *Mers* 2G **83**
Hunts Green. *Warw* 1F **61**
Huntsham. *Devn* 4D **20**
Huntshaw. *Devn* 4F **19**
Huntspill. *Som* 2G **21**
Huntstile. *Som* 3F **21**
Huntstrete. *Bath* 5B **34**
Huntworth. *Som* 3G **21**
Hunwick. *Dur* 1E **105**
Hunworth. *Norf* 2C **78**
Hurcott. *Som* 1G **13**
(nr. Ilminster)
Hurcott. *Som* 4A **22**
(nr. Somerton)
Hurdcott. *Wilts* 3G **23**
Hurdley. *Powy* 1E **59**
Hurdsfield. *Ches E* 3D **84**
Hurlet. *Glas* 3G **127**
Hurley. *Warw* 1G **61**
Hurley. *Wind* 3G **37**
Hurlford. *E Ayr* 1D **116**
Hurlston Green. *Lanc* 3B **90**
Hurn. *Dors* 3G **15**
Hursey. *Dors* 2H **13**
Hursley. *Hants* 4C **24**
Hurst. *G Man* 4H **91**
Hurst. *N Yor* 4D **104**
Hurst. *Som* 1H **13**
Hurst. *Wok* 4F **37**
Hurstbourne Priors. *Hants* 2C **24**
Hurstbourne Tarrant. *Hants* 1B **24**
Hurst Green. *Ches E* 1H **71**
Hurst Green. *E Sus* 3B **28**
Hurst Green. *Essx* 4D **54**
Hurst Green. *Lanc* 1E **91**
Hurst Green. *Surr* 5E **39**
Hurstley. *Here* 1G **47**
Hurstpierpoint. *W Sus* 4D **27**
Hurstway Common. *Here* 1F **47**
Hurst Wickham. *W Sus* 4D **27**
Hurstwood. *Lanc* 1G **91**
Hurtmore. *Surr* 1A **26**
Hurworth-on-Tees. *Darl* 3A **106**
Hurworth Place. *Darl* 3F **105**
Hury. *Dur* 3C **104**
Husbands Bosworth. *Leics* 2D **62**
Husborne Crawley. *C Beds* 2H **51**
Husthwaite. *N Yor* 2H **99**
Hutcherleigh. *Devn* 3D **9**
Hut Green. *N Yor* 2F **93**
Huthwaite. *Notts* 5B **86**
Huttoft. *Linc* 3E **89**
Hutton. *Cumb* 2F **103**
Hutton. *E Yor* 4E **101**
Hutton. *Essx* 1H **39**
Hutton. *Lanc* 2C **90**
Hutton. *N Som* 1G **21**
Hutton. *Bord* 4F **131**
Hutton Bonville. *N Yor* 4A **106**
Hutton Buscel. *N Yor* 1D **100**
Hutton Conyers. *N Yor* 2F **99**
Hutton Cranswick. *E Yor* 4E **101**
Hutton End. *Cumb* 1F **103**
Hutton Gate. *Red C* 3C **106**
Hutton Henry. *Dur* 1B **106**
Hutton-le-Hole. *N Yor* 1B **100**
Hutton Magna. *Dur* 3E **105**
Hutton Mulgrave. *N Yor* 4F **107**
Hutton Roof. *Cumb* 2E **97**
(nr. Kirkby Lonsdale)
Hutton Roof. *Cumb* 1E **103**
(nr. Penrith)
Hutton Rudby. *N Yor* 4B **106**
Huttons Ambo. *N Yor* 3B **100**
Hutton Sessay. *N Yor* 2G **99**
Hutton Village. *Red C* 3D **106**
Hutton Wandesley. *N Yor* 4H **99**
Huxham. *Devn* 3C **12**
Huxham Green. *Som* 3A **22**
Huxley. *Ches W* 4H **83**
Huyton. *Mers* 1G **83**
Hwlffordd. *Pemb* 3D **42**
Hycemoor. *Cumb* 1A **96**
Hyde. *Glos* 5D **49**
(nr. Stroud)
Hyde. *Glos* 3F **49**
(nr. Winchcombe)
Hyde. *G Man* 1D **84**
Hyde Heath. *Buck* 5H **51**
Hyde Lea. *Staf* 3D **72**
Hyde Park. *S Yor* 4F **93**
Hydestile. *Surr* 1A **26**
Hyndford Bridge. *S Lan* 5C **128**
Hynish. *Arg* 5A **138**
Hyssington. *Powy* 1F **59**
Hythe. *Hants* 2C **16**
Hythe. *Kent* 2F **29**
Hythe End. *Wind* 3B **38**
Hythie. *Abers* 3H **161**
Hyton. *Cumb* 1A **96**

I

Ianstown. *Mor* 2B **160**
Iarsiadar. *W Isl* 4D **171**
Ibberton. *Dors* 2C **14**
Ible. *Derbs* 5G **85**
Ibrox. *Glas* 3G **127**
Ibsley. *Hants* 2G **15**
Ibstock. *Leics* 4B **74**
Ibstone. *Buck* 2F **37**
Ibthorpe. *Hants* 1B **24**
Iburndale. *N Yor* 4F **107**
Ibworth. *Hants* 1D **24**
Icelton. *N Som* 5G **33**
Ichrachan. *Arg* 5E **141**
Ickburgh. *Norf* 1H **65**
Ickenham. *G Lon* 2B **38**
Ickenthwaite. *Cumb* 1C **96**
Ickford. *Buck* 5E **51**
Ickham. *Kent* 5G **41**
Ickleford. *Herts* 2B **52**
Icklesham. *E Sus* 4C **28**
Ickleton. *Cambs* 1E **53**
Icklingham. *Suff* 3G **65**
Ickwell. *C Beds* 1B **52**
Icomb. *Glos* 3H **49**
Idbury. *Oxon* 3H **49**
Iddesleigh. *Devn* 2F **11**
Ide. *Devn* 3B **12**
Ideford. *Devn* 5B **12**
Ide Hill. *Kent* 5F **39**
Iden. *E Sus* 3D **28**
Iden Green. *Kent* 2C **28**
(nr. Benenden)
Iden Green. *Kent* 2B **28**
(nr. Goudhurst)
Idle. *W Yor* 1B **92**
Idless. *Corn* 4C **6**
Idlicote. *Warw* 1A **50**
Idmiston. *Wilts* 3G **23**
Idole. *Carm* 4E **45**
Idridgehay. *Derbs* 1G **73**
Idrigill. *High* 2C **154**
Idstone. *Oxon* 3A **36**
Iffley. *Oxon* 5D **50**
Ifield. *W Sus* 2D **26**
Ifieldwood. *W Sus* 2D **26**
Ifold. *W Sus* 2B **26**
Iford. *E Sus* 5F **27**
Ifton Heath. *Shrp* 2F **71**
Ightfield. *Shrp* 2H **71**
Ightham. *Kent* 5G **39**
Iken. *Suff* 5G **67**
Ilam. *Staf* 5F **85**
Ilchester. *Som* 4A **22**
Ilderton. *Nmbd* 2E **121**
Ilford. *G Lon* 2F **39**
Ilford. *Som* 1G **13**
Ilfracombe. *Devn* 2F **19**
Ilkeston. *Derbs* 1B **74**
Ilketshall St Andrew. *Suff* 2F **67**
Ilketshall St Lawrence. *Suff* 2F **67**
Ilketshall St Margaret. *Suff* 2F **67**
Ilkley. *W Yor* 5D **98**
Illand. *Corn* 5C **10**
Illey. *W Mid* 2D **61**
Illidge Green. *Ches E* 4B **84**
Illington. *Norf* 2B **66**
Illingworth. *W Yor* 2A **92**
Illogan. *Corn* 4A **6**
Illogan Highway. *Corn* 4A **6**
Illston on the Hill. *Leics* 1E **62**
Ilmer. *Buck* 5F **51**
Ilmington. *Warw* 1H **49**
Ilminster. *Som* 1G **13**
Ilsington. *Devn* 5A **12**
Ilsington. *Dors* 3C **14**
Ilston. *Swan* 3E **31**
Ilton. *N Yor* 2D **98**
Ilton. *Som* 1G **13**
Imachar. *N Ayr* 5G **125**
Imber. *Wilts* 2E **23**
Immingham. *NE Lin* 3E **95**
Immingham Dock. *NE Lin* 3E **95**
Impington. *Cambs* 4D **64**
Ince. *Ches W* 3G **83**
Ince Blundell. *Mers* 4B **90**
Ince-in-Makerfield. *G Man* 4D **90**
Inchbae Lodge. *High* 2G **157**
Inchbare. *Ang* 2F **145**
Inchberry. *Mor* 3H **159**
Inchbraoch. *Ang* 3G **145**
Inchbrook. *Glos* 5D **48**
Incheril. *High* 2C **156**
Inchinnan. *Ren* 3F **127**
Inchlaggan. *High* 3D **148**
Inchmichael. *Per* 1E **137**
Inchnadamph. *High* 1G **163**
Inchree. *High* 2E **141**
Inchture. *Per* 1E **137**
Inchyra. *Per* 1D **136**
Indian Queens. *Corn* 3D **6**
Ingatestone. *Essx* 1H **39**
Ingbirchworth. *S Yor* 4C **92**
Ingestre. *Staf* 3D **73**
Ingham. *Linc* 2G **87**
Ingham. *Norf* 3F **79**
Ingham. *Suff* 3A **66**
Ingham Corner. *Norf* 3F **79**
Ingleborough. *Norf* 4D **76**
Ingleby. *Derbs* 3H **73**
Ingleby Arncliffe. *N Yor* 4B **106**
Ingleby Barwick. *Stoc T* 3B **106**
Ingleby Greenhow. *N Yor* 4C **106**
Ingleigh Green. *Devn* 2G **11**
Inglemire. *Hull* 1D **94**
Inglesbatch. *Bath* 5C **34**
Ingleton. *Dur* 2E **105**
Ingleton. *N Yor* 2F **97**
Inglewhite. *Lanc* 5E **97**
Ingoe. *Nmbd* 2D **114**
Ingol. *Lanc* 1D **90**
Ingoldisthorpe. *Norf* 2F **77**
Ingoldmells. *Linc* 4E **89**
Ingoldsby. *Linc* 2H **75**
Ingon. *Warw* 5G **61**
Ingram. *Nmbd* 3E **121**
Ingrave. *Essx* 1H **39**
Ingrow. *W Yor* 1A **92**
Ings. *Cumb* 5F **103**
Ingst. *S Glo* 3A **34**
Ingthorpe. *Rut* 5G **75**
Ingworth. *Norf* 3D **78**
Inkberrow. *Worc* 5E **61**
Inkford. *Worc* 3E **61**
Inkpen. *W Ber* 5B **36**
Inkstack. *High* 1E **169**
Innellan. *Arg* 3C **126**
Inner Hope. *Devn* 5C **8**
Innerleith. *Fife* 2E **137**
Innerleithen. *Bord* 1F **119**
Innerleven. *Fife* 3F **137**
Innermessan. *Dum* 3F **109**
Innerwick. *E Lot* 2D **130**
Innerwick. *Per* 4C **142**
Innsworth. *Glos* 3D **48**
Insch. *Abers* 1D **152**
Insh. *High* 3C **150**
Inshegra. *High* 3C **166**
Inshore. *High* 1D **166**
Inskip. *Lanc* 1C **90**
Instow. *Devn* 3E **19**
Intwood. *Norf* 5D **78**
Inver. *Abers* 4G **151**
Inver. *High* 5F **165**

Inver. Per 4H 143
Inverailort. High 5F 147
Inveralligin. High 3H 155
Inverallochy. Abers 2H 161
Inveramsay. Abers 1E 153
Inveran. High 4C 164
Inveraray. Arg 3H 133
Inverarish. High 5E 155
Inverarity. Ang 4D 144
Inverarnan. Arg 2C 134
Inverarnie. High 5A 158
Inverbeg. Arg 4C 134
Inverbervie. Abers 1H 145
Inverboyndie. Abers 2D 160
Invercassley. High 3B 164
Invercharnan. High 4F 141
Inverchoran. High 3E 157
Invercreran. Arg 4E 141
Inverdruie. High 2D 150
Inverebrie. Abers 5G 161
Invereck. Arg 1C 126
Inveresk. E Lot 2G 129
Inveresragan. Arg 5D 141
Inverey. Abers 5E 151
Inverfarigaig. High 1H 149
Invergarry. High 3F 149
Invergeldie. Per 1G 135
Invergordon. High 2B 158
Invergowrie. Per 5C 144
Inverguseran. High 3F 147
Inverharroch. Mor 5A 160
Inverie. High 3F 147
Inverinan. Arg 2G 133
Inverinate. High 1B 148
Inverkeilor. Ang 4F 145
Inverkeithing. Fife 1E 129
Inverkeithny. Abers 4D 160
Inverkip. Inv 2D 126
Inverkirkaig. High 2E 163
Inverlael. High 5F 163
Inverliever Lodge. Arg 3F 133
Inverliver. Arg 5E 141
Inverloch. High 1F 141
Inverlochlarig. Stir 2D 134
Inverlussa. Arg 1E 125
Inver Mallie. High 5D 148
Invermarkie. Abers 5B 160
Invermoriston. High 2G 149
Invernaver. High 2H 167
Inverneil House. Arg 1G 125
Inverness. High 4A 158
Inverness Airport. High 3B 158
Invernettie. Abers 4H 161
Inverpolly Lodge. High 2E 163
Inverquhomery. Abers 4H 161
Inverroy. High 5E 149
Inversanda. High 3D 140
Invershiel. High 2B 148
Invershin. High 4C 164
Invershore. High 5E 169
Inversnaid. Stir 3C 134
Inverugie. Abers 4H 161
Inveruglas. Arg 3C 134
Inverurie. Abers 1E 153
Invervar. Per 4D 142
Inverythan. Abers 4E 161
Inwardleigh. Devn 3F 11
Inworth. Essx 4B 54
Iochdar. W Isl 4C 170
Iping. W Sus 4G 25
Ipplepen. Devn 2E 9
Ipsden. Oxon 3E 37
Ipstones. Staf 1E 73
Ipswich. Suff 1E 55
Irby. Mers 2E 83
Irby in the Marsh. Linc 4D 88
Irby upon Humber. NE Lin 4E 95
Irchester. Nptn 4G 63
Ireby. Cumb 1D 102
Ireby. Lanc 2F 97
Ireland. Shet 9E 173
Ireleth. Cumb 2B 96
Ireshopeburn. Dur 1B 104
Ireton Wood. Derbs 1G 73
Irlam. G Man 1B 84
Irnham. Linc 3H 75
Iron Acton. S Glo 3B 34
Iron Bridge. Cambs 1D 65
Ironbridge. Telf 5A 72
Iron Cross. Warw 5E 61
Ironville. Derbs 5B 86
Irstead. Norf 3F 79
Irthington. Cumb 3F 113
Irthlingborough. Nptn 3G 63
Irton. N Yor 1E 101
Irvine. N Ayr 1C 116
Irvine Mains. N Ayr 1C 116
Isabella Pit. Nmbd 1G 115
Isauld. High 2B 168
Isbister. Orkn 6D 172
Isbister. Shet 5G 173
Isfield. E Sus 4F 27
Isham. Nptn 3F 63
Island Carr. N Lin 4C 94
Islay Airport. Arg 4B 124
Isle Abbotts. Som 4G 21
Isle Brewers. Som 4G 21
Isleham. Cambs 3F 65
Isle of Man Airport. IOM 5B 108
Isle of Thanet. Kent 4H 41
Isle of Whithorn. Dum 5B 110
Isleornsay. High 2F 147
Isles of Scilly (St Mary's) Airport. IOS 1B 4
Islesteps. Dum 2A 112
Isleworth. G Lon 3C 38
Isley Walton. Leics 3B 74
Islibhig. W Isl 5B 171
Islington. G Lon 2E 39
Islington. Telf 3B 72
Islip. Nptn 3G 63
Islip. Oxon 4D 50
Islwyn. Cphy 2F 33
Isombridge. Telf 4A 72
Istead Rise. Kent 4H 39
Itchen. Sotn 1C 16
Itchen Abbas. Hants 3D 24
Itchen Stoke. Hants 3D 24
Itchingfield. W Sus 3C 26
Itchington. S Glo 3B 34
Itlaw. Abers 3D 160
Itteringham. Norf 2D 78
Itteringham Common. Norf 3D 78
Itton. Devn 3G 11
Itton Common. Mon 2H 33
Ivegill. Cumb 5F 113
Ivelet. N Yor 5C 104
Iverchaolain. Arg 2B 126
Iver Heath. Buck 2B 38
Iveston. Dur 4E 115
Ivetsey Bank. Staf 4C 72
Ivinghoe. Buck 4H 51
Ivinghoe Aston. Buck 4H 51
Ivington. Here 5G 59
Ivington Green. Here 5G 59
Ivybridge. Devn 3C 8
Ivychurch. Kent 3E 29
Ivy Hatch. Kent 5G 39
Ivy Todd. Norf 5A 78
Iwade. Kent 4D 40
Iwerne Courtney. Dors 1D 14
Iwerne Minster. Dors 1D 14
Ixworth. Suff 3B 66
Ixworth Thorpe. Suff 3B 66

J

Jackfield. Shrp 5A 72
Jack Hill. N Yor 4E 98
Jacksdale. Notts 5B 86
Jackton. S Lan 4G 127
Jacobstow. Corn 3B 10
Jacobstowe. Devn 2F 11
Jacobswell. Surr 5A 38
Jameston. Pemb 5E 43
Jamestown. Dum 5F 119
Jamestown. Fife 1E 129
Jamestown. High 3G 157
Jamestown. W Dun 1E 127
Janetstown. High 2C 168 (nr. Thurso)
Janetstown. High 3F 169 (nr. Wick)
Jarrow. Tyne 3G 115
Jarvis Brook. E Sus 3G 27
Jasper's Green. Essx 3H 53
Jaywick. Essx 4E 55
Jedburgh. Bord 2A 120
Jeffreyston. Pemb 4E 43
Jemimaville. High 2B 158
Jenkins Park. High 3F 149
Jersey Marine. Neat 3G 31
Jesmond. Tyne 3F 115
Jevington. E Sus 5G 27
Jingle Street. Mon 4H 47
Jockey End. Herts 4A 52
Jodrell Bank. Ches E 3B 84
Johnby. Cumb 1F 103
John o' Gaunts. W Yor 2D 92
John o' Groats. High 1F 169
John's Cross. E Sus 3B 28
Johnshaven. Abers 2G 145
Johnson Street. Norf 4F 79
Johnston. Pemb 3D 42
Johnstone. Ren 3F 127
Johnstonebridge. Dum 5C 118
Johnstown. Carm 4D 45
Johnstown. Wrex 1F 71
Joppa. Edin 2G 129
Joppa. S Ayr 3D 116
Jordan Green. Norf 3C 78
Jordans. Buck 1A 38
Jordanston. Pemb 1D 42
Jump. S Yor 4D 93
Jumpers Common. Dors 3G 15
Juniper. Nmbd 4C 114
Juniper Green. Edin 3E 129
Jurby East. IOM 2C 108
Jurby West. IOM 2C 108
Jury's Gap. E Sus 4D 28

K

Kaber. Cumb 3A 104
Kaimend. S Lan 5C 128
Kaimes. Edin 3F 129
Kaimrig End. Bord 5D 129
Kames. Arg 2A 126
Kames. E Ayr 2F 117
Kea. Corn 4C 6
Keadby. N Lin 3B 94
Keal Cotes. Linc 4C 88
Kearsley. G Man 4F 91
Kearsney. Kent 1G 29
Kearstwick. Cumb 1F 97
Kearton. N Yor 5C 104
Kearvaig. High 1C 166
Keasden. N Yor 3G 97
Keason. Corn 2H 7
Keckwick. Hal 2H 83
Keddington. Linc 2C 88
Keddington Corner. Linc 2C 88
Kedington. Suff 1H 53
Kedleston. Derbs 1H 73
Kedlock Feus. Fife 2F 137
Keekle. Cumb 3B 102
Keelby. Linc 3E 95
Keele. Staf 1C 72
Keeley Green. Bed 1A 52
Keeston. Pemb 3D 42
Keevil. Wilts 1E 23
Kegworth. Leics 3B 74
Kehelland. Corn 2D 4
Keig. Abers 2D 152
Keighley. W Yor 5C 98
Keilarsbrae. Clac 4A 136
Keillmore. Arg 1E 125
Keillor. Per 4B 144
Keillour. Per 1B 136
Keills. Arg 3C 124
Keiloch. Abers 4F 151
Keils. Arg 3D 124
Keinton Mandeville. Som 3A 22
Keir Mill. Dum 5A 118
Keirsleywell Row. Nmbd 4A 114
Keisby. Linc 3H 75
Keisley. Cumb 2A 104
Keiss. High 2F 169
Keith. Mor 3B 160
Keith Inch. Abers 4H 161
Kelbrook. Lanc 5B 98
Kelby. Linc 1H 75
Keld. Cumb 3G 103
Keld. N Yor 4B 104
Keldholme. N Yor 1B 100
Kelfield. N Lin 4B 94
Kelfield. N Yor 1F 93
Kelham. Notts 5E 87
Kellacott. Devn 4E 11
Kellan. Arg 4G 139
Kellas. Ang 5D 144
Kellas. Mor 3F 159
Kellaton. Devn 5E 9
Kelleth. Cumb 4H 103
Kelling. Norf 1C 78
Kellingley. N Yor 2F 93
Kellington. N Yor 2F 93
Kelloe. Dur 1A 106
Kelloholm. Dum 3G 117
Kells. Cumb 3A 102
Kelly. Devn 4D 11
Kelly Bray. Corn 5D 10
Kelmarsh. Nptn 3E 63
Kelmscott. Oxon 2A 36
Kelsale. Suff 4F 67
Kelsall. Ches W 4H 83
Kelshall. Herts 2D 52
Kelsick. Cumb 4C 112
Kelso. Bord 1B 120
Kelstedge. Derbs 4H 85
Kelstern. Linc 1B 88
Kelsterton. Flin 3E 83
Kelston. Bath 5C 34
Keltneyburn. Per 4E 143
Kelton. Dum 2A 112
Kelton Hill. Dum 4E 111
Kelty. Fife 4D 136
Kelvedon. Essx 4B 54
Kelvedon Hatch. Essx 1G 39
Kelvinside. Glas 3G 127
Kelynack. Corn 3A 4
Kemback. Fife 2G 137
Kemberton. Shrp 5B 72
Kemble. Glos 2E 35
Kemerton. Worc 2E 49
Kemeys Commander. Mon 5G 47
Kemnay. Abers 2E 153
Kempe's Corner. Kent 1E 29
Kempley. Glos 3B 48
Kempley Green. Glos 3B 48
Kempsey. Worc 1D 48
Kempsford. Glos 2G 35
Kemps Green. Warw 3F 61
Kempshott. Hants 1E 24
Kempston. Bed 1A 52
Kempston Hardwick. Bed 1A 52
Kempton. Shrp 2F 59
Kemp Town. Brig 5E 27
Kemsing. Kent 5G 39
Kemsley. Kent 4D 40
Kenardington. Kent 2D 28
Kenchester. Here 1H 47
Kencot. Oxon 5A 50
Kendal. Cumb 5G 103
Kendleshire. S Glo 4B 34
Kendray. S Yor 4D 92
Kenfig. B'end 3B 32
Kenfig Hill. B'end 3B 32
Kengharair. Arg 4F 139
Kenilworth. Warw 3G 61
Kenknock. Stir 5B 142
Kenley. G Lon 5E 39
Kenley. Shrp 5H 71
Kenmore. High 3G 155
Kenmore. Per 4E 143
Kenn. Devn 4C 12
Kenn. N Som 5H 33
Kennacraig. Arg 3G 125
Kenneggy Downs. Corn 4C 4
Kennerleigh. Devn 2B 12
Kennet. Clac 4B 136
Kennethmont. Abers 1C 152
Kennett. Cambs 4G 65
Kennford. Devn 4C 12
Kenninghall. Norf 2C 66
Kennington. Kent 1E 29
Kennington. Oxon 5D 50
Kennoway. Fife 3F 137
Kennyhill. Suff 3F 65
Kennythorpe. N Yor 3B 100
Kenovay. Arg 4A 138
Kensaleyre. High 3D 154
Kensington. G Lon 3D 38
Kenstone. Shrp 3H 71
Kensworth. C Beds 4A 52
Kensworth Common. C Beds 4A 52
Kentallen. High 3E 141
Kentchurch. Here 3H 47
Kentford. Suff 4G 65
Kentisbeare. Devn 2D 12
Kentisbury. Devn 2G 19
Kentisbury Ford. Devn 2G 19
Kentmere. Cumb 4F 103
Kenton. Devn 4C 12
Kenton. G Lon 2C 38
Kenton. Suff 4D 66
Kenton Bankfoot. Tyne 3F 115
Kentra. High 2A 140
Kentrigg. Cumb 5G 103
Kents Bank. Cumb 2C 96
Kent's Green. Glos 3C 48
Kent's Oak. Hants 4B 24
Kent Street. E Sus 4B 28
Kent Street. Kent 5A 40
Kent Street. W Sus 3D 26
Kenwick. Shrp 2G 71
Kenwyn. Corn 4C 6
Kenyon. Warr 1A 84
Keoldale. High 2D 166
Keppoch. High 1B 148
Kepwick. N Yor 5B 106
Keresley. W Mid 2H 61
Keresley Newland. Warw 2H 61
Keristal. IOM 4C 108
Kerne Bridge. Here 4A 48
Kerridge. Ches E 3D 84
Kerris. Corn 4B 4
Kerrow. High 5F 157
Kerry. Powy 2D 58
Kerrycroy. Arg 3C 126
Kerry's Gate. Here 2G 47
Kersall. Notts 4E 86
Kersbrook. Devn 4D 12
Kerse. Ren 4E 127
Kersey. Suff 1D 54
Kershopefoot. Cumb 1F 113
Kersoe. Worc 2E 49
Kerswell. Devn 2D 12
Kerswell Green. Worc 1D 48
Kesgrave. Suff 1F 55
Kessingland. Suff 2H 67
Kessingland Beach. Suff 2H 67
Kestle. Corn 4D 6
Kestle Mill. Corn 3C 6
Keston. G Lon 4F 39
Keswick. Cumb 2D 102
Keswick. Norf 2F 79 (nr. North Walsham)
Keswick. Norf 5E 78 (nr. Norwich)
Ketsby. Linc 3C 88
Kettering. Nptn 3F 63
Ketteringham. Norf 5D 78
Kettins. Per 5B 144
Kettlebaston. Suff 5B 66
Kettlebridge. Fife 3F 137
Kettlebrook. Staf 5G 73
Kettleburgh. Suff 4E 67

Kettleholm. *Dum* 2C **112**
Kettleness. *N Yor* 3F **107**
Kettleshulme. *Ches E* 3D **85**
Kettlesing. *N Yor* 4E **99**
Kettlesing Bottom. *N Yor* 4E **99**
Kettlestone. *Norf* 2B **78**
Kettlethorpe. *Linc* 3F **87**
Kettletoft. *Orkn* 4F **172**
Kettlewell. *N Yor* 2B **98**
Ketton. *Rut* 5G **75**
Kew. *G Lon* 3C **38**
Kewaigue. *IOM* 4C **108**
Kewstoke. *N Som* 5G **33**
Kexbrough. *S Yor* 4D **92**
Kexby. *Linc* 2F **87**
Kexby. *York* 4B **100**
Keyford. *Som* 2C **22**
Key Green. *Ches E* 4C **84**
Key Green. *N Yor* 4F **107**
Keyham. *Leics* 5D **74**
Keyhaven. *Hants* 3B **16**
Keyhead. *Abers* 3H **161**
Keyingham. *E Yor* 2F **95**
Keymer. *W Sus* 4E **27**
Keynsham. *Bath* 5B **34**
Keysoe. *Bed* 4H **63**
Keysoe Row. *Bed* 4H **63**
Key's Toft. *Linc* 5D **89**
Keyston. *Cambs* 3H **63**
Key Street. *Kent* 4C **40**
Keyworth. *Notts* 2D **74**
Kibblesworth. *Tyne* 4F **115**
Kibworth Beauchamp. *Leics* 1D **62**
Kibworth Harcourt. *Leics* 1D **62**
Kidbrooke. *G Lon* 3F **39**
Kidburngill. *Cumb* 2B **102**
Kiddemore Green. *Staf* 5C **72**
Kidderminster. *Worc* 3C **60**
Kiddington. *Oxon* 3C **50**
Kidd's Moor. *Norf* 5D **78**
Kidlington. *Oxon* 4C **50**
Kidmore End. *Oxon* 4E **37**
Kidnal. *Ches W* 1G **71**
Kidsgrove. *Staf* 5C **84**
Kidstones. *N Yor* 1B **98**
Kidwelly. *Carm* 5E **45**
Kiel Crofts. *Arg* 5D **140**
Kielder. *Nmbd* 5A **120**
Kilbagie. *Fife* 4B **136**
Kilbarchan. *Ren* 3F **127**
Kilbeg. *High* 3E **147**
Kilberry. *Arg* 3F **125**
Kilbirnie. *N Ayr* 4E **126**
Kilbride. *Arg* 1F **133**
Kilbride. *High* 1D **147**
Kilbucho Place. *Bord* 1C **118**
Kilburn. *Derbs* 1A **74**
Kilburn. *G Lon* 2D **38**
Kilburn. *N Yor* 2H **99**
Kilby. *Leics* 1D **62**
Kilchattan. *Arg* 4A **132** (on Colonsay)
Kilchattan. *Arg* 4C **126** (on Isle of Bute)
Kilchattan Bay. *Arg* 4B **126**
Kilchenzie. *Arg* 3A **122**
Kilcheran. *Arg* 5C **140**
Kilchiaran. *Arg* 3A **124**
Kilchoan. *High* 4F **147** (nr. Inverie)
Kilchoan. *High* 2F **139** (nr. Tobermory)
Kilchoman. *Arg* 3A **124**
Kilchrenan. *Arg* 1H **133**
Kilconquhar. *Fife* 3G **137**
Kilcot. *Glos* 3B **48**
Kilcoy. *High* 3H **157**
Kilcreggan. *Arg* 1D **126**
Kildale. *N Yor* 4D **106**
Kildary. *High* 1B **158**
Kildermorie Lodge. *High* 1H **157**
Kildonan. *Dum* 4F **109**
Kildonan. *High* 1G **165** (nr. Helmsdale)
Kildonan. *High* 3C **154** (on Isle of Skye)
Kildonan. *N Ayr* 3E **123**
Kildonnan. *High* 5C **146**
Kildrummy. *Abers* 2B **152**
Kildwick. *N Yor* 5C **98**
Kilfillan. *Dum* 4H **109**
Kilfinan. *Arg* 2H **125**
Kilfinnan. *High* 4E **149**
Kilgetty. *Pemb* 4F **43**
Kilgour. *Fife* 3E **136**
Kilgrammie. *S Ayr* 4B **116**
Kilham. *E Yor* 3E **101**
Kilham. *Nmbd* 1C **120**
Kilkenneth. *Arg* 4A **138**
Kilkhampton. *Corn* 1C **10**
Killamarsh. *Derbs* 2B **86**
Killandrist. *Arg* 4C **140**
Killay. *Swan* 3F **31**
Killean. *Arg* 5E **125**
Killearn. *Stir* 1G **127**
Killellan. *Arg* 4A **122**
Killen. *High* 3A **158**
Killerby. *Darl* 3E **105**
Killichonan. *Per* 3C **142**
Killiechronan. *Arg* 4G **139**
Killiecrankie. *Per* 2G **143**
Killilan. *High* 5B **156**
Killimster. *High* 3F **169**
Killin. *Stir* 5C **142**
Killinghall. *N Yor* 4E **99**
Killington. *Cumb* 1F **97**
Killingworth. *Tyne* 2F **115**
Killin Lodge. *High* 3H **149**
Killinochonoch. *Arg* 4F **133**
Killochyett. *Bord* 5A **130**
Killundine. *High* 4G **139**
Kilmacolm. *Inv* 3E **127**
Kilmahog. *Stir* 3F **135**
Kilmahumaig. *Arg* 4E **133**
Kilmalieu. *High* 3C **140**
Kilmaluag. *High* 1D **154**
Kilmany. *Fife* 1F **137**
Kilmarie. *High* 2D **146**
Kilmarnock. *E Ayr* 1D **116**
Kilmaron. *Fife* 2F **137**
Kilmartin. *Arg* 4F **133**
Kilmaurs. *E Ayr* 5F **127**
Kilmelford. *Arg* 2F **133**
Kilmeny. *Arg* 3B **124**
Kilmersdon. *Som* 1B **22**
Kilmeston. *Hants* 4D **24**
Kilmichael Glassary. *Arg* 4F **133**
Kilmichael of Inverlussa. *Arg* 1F **125**
Kilmington. *Devn* 3F **13**
Kilmington. *Wilts* 3C **22**
Kilmoluag. *Arg* 4A **138**
Kilmorack. *High* 4G **157**
Kilmore. *Arg* 1F **133**
Kilmore. *High* 3E **147**
Kilmory. *Arg* 2F **125**
Kilmory. *High* 1G **139** (nr. Kilchoan)
Kilmory. *High* 3B **146** (on Rùm)
Kilmory. *N Ayr* 3D **122**
Kilmory Lodge. *Arg* 3E **132**
Kilmote. *High* 2G **165**
Kilmuir. *High* 4B **154** (nr. Dunvegan)
Kilmuir. *High* 1B **158** (nr. Invergordon)
Kilmuir. *High* 4A **158** (nr. Inverness)
Kilmuir. *High* 1C **154** (nr. Uig)
Kilmun. *Arg* 1C **126**
Kilnave. *Arg* 2A **124**
Kilncadzow. *S Lan* 5B **128**
Kilndown. *Kent* 2B **28**
Kiln Green. *Here* 4B **48**
Kiln Green. *Wind* 4G **37**
Kilnhill. *Cumb* 1D **102**
Kilnhurst. *S Yor* 1B **86**
Kilninian. *Arg* 4E **139**
Kilninver. *Arg* 1F **133**
Kiln Pit Hill. *Nmbd* 4D **114**
Kilnsea. *E Yor* 3H **95**
Kilnsey. *N Yor* 3B **98**
Kilnwick. *E Yor* 5D **101**
Kiloran. *Arg* 4A **132**
Kilpatrick. *N Ayr* 3D **122**
Kilpeck. *Here* 2H **47**
Kilpin. *E Yor* 2A **94**
Kilpin Pike. *E Yor* 2A **94**
Kilrenny. *Fife* 3H **137**
Kilsby. *Nptn* 3C **62**
Kilspindie. *Per* 1E **136**
Kilsyth. *N Lan* 2A **128**
Kiltarlity. *High* 4H **157**
Kilton. *Som* 2E **21**
Kilton Thorpe. *Red C* 3D **107**
Kilvaxter. *High* 2C **154**
Kilve. *Som* 2E **21**
Kilvington. *Notts* 1F **75**
Kilwinning. *N Ayr* 5D **126**
Kimberley. *Norf* 5C **78**
Kimberley. *Notts* 1B **74**
Kimblesworth. *Dur* 5F **115**
Kimble Wick. *Buck* 5G **51**
Kimbolton. *Cambs* 4H **63**
Kimbolton. *Here* 4H **59**
Kimcote. *Leics* 2C **62**
Kimmeridge. *Dors* 5E **15**
Kimmerston. *Nmbd* 1D **120**
Kimpton. *Hants* 2A **24**
Kimpton. *Herts* 4B **52**
Kinbeachie. *High* 2A **158**
Kinbrace. *High* 5A **168**
Kinbuck. *Stir* 3G **135**
Kincaple. *Fife* 2G **137**
Kincardine. *Fife* 1C **128**
Kincardine. *High* 5D **164**
Kincardine Bridge. *Fife* 1C **128**
Kincardine O'Neil. *Abers* 4C **152**
Kinchrackine. *Arg* 1A **134**
Kincorth. *Aber* 3G **153**
Kincraig. *High* 3C **150**
Kincraigie. *Per* 4G **143**
Kindallachan. *Per* 3G **143**
Kineton. *Glos* 3F **49**
Kineton. *Warw* 5H **61**
Kinfauns. *Per* 1D **136**
Kingairloch. *High* 3C **140**
Kingarth. *Arg* 4B **126**
Kingcoed. *Mon* 5H **47**
King Edward. *Abers* 3E **160**
Kingerby. *Linc* 1H **87**
Kingham. *Oxon* 3A **50**
Kingholm Quay. *Dum* 2A **112**
Kinghorn. *Fife* 1F **129**
Kingie. *High* 3D **148**
Kinglassie. *Fife* 4E **137**
Kingledores. *Bord* 2D **118**
Kingodie. *Per* 1F **137**
King o' Muirs. *Clac* 4A **136**
King's Acre. *Here* 1H **47**
Kingsand. *Corn* 3A **8**
Kingsash. *Buck* 5G **51**
Kingsbarns. *Fife* 2H **137**
Kingsbridge. *Devn* 4D **8**
Kingsbridge. *Som* 3C **20**
King's Bromley. *Staf* 4F **73**
Kingsburgh. *High* 3C **154**
Kingsbury. *G Lon* 2C **38**
Kingsbury. *Warw* 1G **61**
Kingsbury Episcopi. *Som* 4H **21**
Kings Caple. *Here* 3A **48**
Kingscavil. *W Lot* 2D **128**
Kingsclere. *Hants* 1D **24**
King's Cliffe. *Nptn* 1H **63**
Kings Clipstone. *Notts* 4D **86**
Kingscote. *Glos* 2D **34**
Kingscott. *Devn* 1F **11**
Kings Coughton. *Warw* 5E **61**
Kingscross. *N Ayr* 3E **123**
Kingsdon. *Som* 4A **22**
Kingsdown. *Kent* 1H **29**
Kingsdown. *Swin* 3G **35**
Kingsdown. *Wilts* 5D **34**
Kingseat. *Fife* 4D **136**
Kingsey. *Buck* 5F **51**
Kingsfold. *Lanc* 2D **90**
Kingsfold. *W Sus* 2C **26**
Kingsford. *E Ayr* 5F **127**
Kingsford. *Worc* 2C **60**
Kingsforth. *N Lin* 3D **94**
Kingsgate. *Kent* 3H **41**
King's Green. *Glos* 2C **48**
Kingshall Street. *Suff* 4B **66**
Kingsheanton. *Devn* 3F **19**
King's Heath. *W Mid* 2E **61**
Kings Hill. *Kent* 5A **40**
Kingsholm. *Glos* 4D **48**
Kingshouse. *High* 3G **141**
Kingshouse. *Stir* 1E **135**
Kingshurst. *W Mid* 2F **61**
Kingskerswell. *Devn* 2E **9**
Kingskettle. *Fife* 3F **137**
Kingsland. *Here* 4G **59**
Kingsland. *IOA* 2B **80**
Kings Langley. *Herts* 5A **52**
Kingsley. *Ches W* 3H **83**
Kingsley. *Hants* 3F **25**
Kingsley. *Staf* 1E **73**
Kingsley Green. *W Sus* 3G **25**
Kingsley Holt. *Staf* 1E **73**
King's Lynn. *Norf* 3F **77**
King's Meaburn. *Cumb* 2H **103**
Kings Moss. *Mers* 4D **90**
Kingsmuir. *Ang* 4D **145**
Kingsmuir. *Fife* 3H **137**
Kings Muir. *Bord* 1E **119**
King's Newnham. *Warw* 3B **62**
Kings Newton. *Derbs* 3A **74**
Kingsnorth. *Kent* 2E **28**
Kingsnorth. *Medw* 3C **40**
King's Norton. *Leics* 5D **74**
King's Norton. *W Mid* 3E **61**
King's Nympton. *Devn* 1G **11**
King's Pyon. *Here* 5G **59**
Kings Ripton. *Cambs* 3B **64**
King's Somborne. *Hants* 3B **24**
King's Stag. *Dors* 1C **14**
King's Stanley. *Glos* 5D **48**
King's Sutton. *Nptn* 2C **50**
Kingstanding. *W Mid* 1E **61**
Kingsteignton. *Devn* 5B **12**
Kingsteps. *High* 3D **158**
King Sterndale. *Derbs* 3E **85**
King's Thorn. *Here* 2A **48**
Kingsthorpe. *Nptn* 4E **63**
Kingston. *Cambs* 5C **64**
Kingston. *Devn* 4C **8**
Kingston. *Dors* 2C **14** (nr. Sturminster Newton)
Kingston. *Dors* 5E **15** (nr. Swanage)
Kingston. *E Lot* 1B **130**
Kingston. *Hants* 2G **15**
Kingston. *IOW* 4C **16**
Kingston. *Kent* 5F **41**
Kingston. *Mor* 2H **159**
Kingston. *W Sus* 5B **26**
Kingston Bagpuize. *Oxon* 2C **36**
Kingston Blount. *Oxon* 2F **37**
Kingston by Sea. *W Sus* 5D **26**
Kingston Deverill. *Wilts* 3D **22**
Kingstone. *Here* 2H **47**
Kingstone. *Som* 1G **13**
Kingstone. *Staf* 3E **73**
Kingston Lisle. *Oxon* 3B **36**
Kingston Maurward. *Dors* 3C **14**
Kingston near Lewes. *E Sus* 5E **27**
Kingston on Soar. *Notts* 3C **74**
Kingston Russell. *Dors* 3A **14**
Kingston St Mary. *Som* 4F **21**
Kingston Seymour. *N Som* 5H **33**
Kingston Stert. *Oxon* 5F **51**
Kingston upon Hull. *Hull* 2D **94**
Kingston upon Thames. *G Lon* 4C **38**
King's Walden. *Herts* 3B **52**
Kingswear. *Devn* 3E **9**
Kingswells. *Aber* 3F **153**
Kingswinford. *W Mid* 2C **60**
Kingswood. *Buck* 4E **51**
Kingswood. *Glos* 2C **34**
Kingswood. *Here* 5E **59**
Kingswood. *Kent* 5C **40**
Kingswood. *Per* 5H **143**
Kingswood. *Powy* 5E **71**
Kingswood. *Som* 3E **20**
Kingswood. *S Glo* 4B **34**
Kingswood. *Surr* 5D **38**
Kingswood. *Warw* 3F **61**
Kingswood Common. *Staf* 5C **72**
Kings Worthy. *Hants* 3C **24**
Kingthorpe. *Linc* 3A **88**
Kington. *Here* 5F **59**
Kington. *S Glo* 2B **34**
Kington. *Worc* 5D **61**
Kington Langley. *Wilts* 4E **35**
Kington Magna. *Dors* 4C **22**
Kington St Michael. *Wilts* 4E **35**
Kingussie. *High* 3B **150**
Kingweston. *Som* 3A **22**
Kinharrachie. *Abers* 5G **161**
Kinhrive. *High* 1B **158**
Kinkell Bridge. *Per* 2B **136**
Kinknockie. *Abers* 4H **161**
Kinkry Hill. *Cumb* 2G **113**
Kinlet. *Shrp* 2B **60**
Kinloch. *High* 5D **166** (nr. Loch More)
Kinloch. *High* 3A **140** (nr. Lochaline)
Kinloch. *High* 4C **146** (on Rùm)
Kinloch. *Per* 4A **144**
Kinlochard. *Stir* 3D **134**
Kinlochbervie. *High* 3C **166**
Kinlocheil. *High* 1D **141**
Kinlochewe. *High* 2C **156**
Kinloch Hourn. *High* 3B **148**
Kinloch Laggan. *High* 5H **149**
Kinlochleven. *High* 2F **141**
Kinloch Lodge. *High* 3F **167**
Kinlochmoidart. *High* 1B **140**
Kinlochmore. *High* 2F **141**
Kinloch Rannoch. *Per* 3D **142**
Kinlochspelve. *Arg* 1D **132**
Kinloid. *High* 5E **147**
Kinloss. *Mor* 2E **159**
Kinmel Bay. *Cnwy* 2B **82**
Kinmuck. *Abers* 2F **153**
Kinnadie. *Abers* 4G **161**
Kinnaird. *Per* 1E **137**
Kinneff. *Abers* 1H **145**
Kinnelhead. *Dum* 4C **118**
Kinnell. *Ang* 3F **145**
Kinnerley. *Shrp* 3F **71**
Kinnernie. *Abers* 2E **152**
Kinnersley. *Here* 1G **47**
Kinnersley. *Worc* 1D **48**
Kinnerton. *Powy* 4E **59**
Kinnerton. *Shrp* 1F **59**
Kinnesswood. *Per* 3D **136**
Kinninvie. *Dur* 2D **104**
Kinnordy. *Ang* 3C **144**
Kinoulton. *Notts* 2D **74**
Kinross. *Per* 3D **136**
Kinrossie. *Per* 5A **144**
Kinsbourne Green. *Herts* 4B **52**
Kinsey Heath. *Ches E* 1A **72**
Kinsham. *Here* 4F **59**
Kinsham. *Worc* 2E **49**
Kinsley. *W Yor* 3E **93**
Kinson. *Bour* 3F **15**
Kintbury. *W Ber* 5B **36**
Kintessack. *Mor* 2E **159**
Kintillo. *Per* 2D **136**
Kinton. *Here* 3G **59**
Kinton. *Shrp* 4F **71**
Kintore. *Abers* 2E **153**

Kintour. *Arg* 4C 124
Kintra. *Arg* 2B 132
Kintraw. *Arg* 3F 133
Kinveachy. *High* 2D 150
Kinver. *Staf* 2C 60
Kinwarton. *Warw* 5F 61
Kiplingcotes. *E Yor* 5D 100
Kippax. *W Yor* 1E 93
Kippen. *Stir* 4F 135
Kippford. *Dum* 4F 111
Kipping's Cross. *Kent* 1H 27
Kirbister. *Orkn* 7C 172
Kirby Bedon. *Norf* 5E 79
Kirby Bellars. *Leics* 4E 74
Kirby Cane. *Norf* 1F 67
Kirby Cross. *Essx* 3F 55
Kirby Fields. *Leics* 5C 74
Kirby Green. *Norf* 1F 67
Kirby Grindalythe. *N Yor* 3D 100
Kirby Hill. *N Yor* 4E 105
(nr. Richmond)
Kirby Hill. *N Yor* 3F 99
(nr. Ripon)
Kirby Knowle. *N Yor* 1G 99
Kirby-le-Soken. *Essx* 3F 55
Kirby Misperton. *N Yor* 2B 100
Kirby Muxloe. *Leics* 5C 74
Kirby Sigston. *N Yor* 5B 106
Kirby Underdale. *E Yor* 4C 100
Kirby Wiske. *N Yor* 1F 99
Kirdford. *W Sus* 3B 26
Kirk. *High* 3E 169
Kirkabister. *Shet* 6F 173
Kirkandrews. *Dum* 5D 110
Kirkandrews-on-Eden. *Cumb* 4E 113
Kirkapol. *Arg* 4B 138
Kirkbampton. *Cumb* 4E 112
Kirkbean. *Dum* 4A 112
Kirk Bramwith. *S Yor* 3G 93
Kirkbride. *Cumb* 4D 112
Kirkbridge. *N Yor* 5F 105
Kirkbuddo. *Ang* 4E 145
Kirkburn. *E Yor* 4D 101
Kirkburton. *W Yor* 3B 92
Kirkby. *Linc* 1H 87
Kirkby. *Mers* 1G 83
Kirkby. *N Yor* 4C 106
Kirkby Fenside. *Linc* 4C 88
Kirkby Fleetham. *N Yor* 5F 105
Kirkby Green. *Linc* 5H 87
Kirkby-in-Ashfield. *Notts* 5C 86
Kirkby Industrial Estate. *Mers* 1G 83
Kirkby-in-Furness. *Cumb* 1B 96
Kirkby la Thorpe. *Linc* 1A 76
Kirkby Lonsdale. *Cumb* 2F 97
Kirkby Malham. *N Yor* 3A 98
Kirkby Mallory. *Leics* 5B 74
Kirkby Malzeard. *N Yor* 2E 99
Kirkby Mills. *N Yor* 1B 100
Kirkbymoorside. *N Yor* 1A 100
Kirkby on Bain. *Linc* 4B 88
Kirkby Overblow. *N Yor* 5F 99
Kirkby Stephen. *Cumb* 4A 104
Kirkby Thore. *Cumb* 2H 103
Kirkby Underwood. *Linc* 3H 75
Kirkby Wharfe. *N Yor* 5H 99
Kirkcaldy. *Fife* 4E 137
Kirkcambeck. *Cumb* 3G 113
Kirkcolm. *Dum* 3F 109
Kirkconnel. *Dum* 3G 117
Kirkconnell. *Dum* 3A 112
Kirkcowan. *Dum* 3A 110
Kirkcudbright. *Dum* 4D 111
Kirkdale. *Mers* 1F 83
Kirk Deighton. *N Yor* 4F 99
Kirk Ella. *E Yor* 2D 94
Kirkfieldbank. *S Lan* 5B 128
Kirkforthar Feus. *Fife* 3E 137
Kirkgunzeon. *Dum* 3F 111
Kirk Hallam. *Derbs* 1B 74
Kirkham. *Lanc* 1C 90
Kirkham. *N Yor* 3B 100
Kirkhamgate. *W Yor* 2C 92
Kirk Hammerton. *N Yor* 4G 99

Kirkharle. *Nmbd* 1D 114
Kirkheaton. *Nmbd* 2D 114
Kirkheaton. *W Yor* 3B 92
Kirkhill. *Ang* 2F 145
Kirkhill. *High* 4H 157
Kirkhope. *S Lan* 4B 118
Kirkhouse. *Bord* 1F 119
Kirkibost. *High* 2D 146
Kirkinch. *Ang* 4C 144
Kirkinner. *Dum* 4B 110
Kirkintilloch. *E Dun* 2H 127
Kirk Ireton. *Derbs* 5G 85
Kirkland. *Cumb* 3B 102
(nr. Cleator Moor)
Kirkland. *Cumb* 1H 103
(nr. Penrith)
Kirkland. *Cumb* 5D 112
(nr. Wigton)
Kirkland. *Dum* 3G 117
(nr. Kirkconnel)
Kirkland. *Dum* 5H 117
(nr. Moniaive)
Kirkland Guards. *Cumb* 5C 112
Kirk Langley. *Derbs* 2G 73
Kirklauchline. *Dum* 4F 109
Kirkleatham. *Red C* 2C 106
Kirklevington. *Stoc T* 4B 106
Kirkley. *Suff* 1H 67
Kirklington. *N Yor* 1F 99
Kirklington. *Notts* 5D 86
Kirklinton. *Cumb* 3F 113
Kirkliston. *Edin* 2E 129
Kirkmabreck. *Dum* 4B 110
Kirkmaiden. *Dum* 5E 109
Kirk Merrington. *Dur* 1F 105
Kirk Michael. *IOM* 2C 108
Kirkmichael. *Per* 2H 143
Kirkmichael. *S Ayr* 4C 116
Kirkmuirhill. *S Lan* 5A 128
Kirknewton. *Nmbd* 1D 120
Kirknewton. *W Lot* 3E 129
Kirkney. *Abers* 5C 160
Kirk of Shotts. *N Lan* 3B 128
Kirkoswald. *Cumb* 5G 113
Kirkoswald. *S Ayr* 4B 116
Kirkpatrick. *Dum* 5B 118
Kirkpatrick Durham. *Dum* 2E 111
Kirkpatrick-Fleming. *Dum* 2D 112
Kirk Sandall. *S Yor* 4G 93
Kirksanton. *Cumb* 1A 96
Kirk Smeaton. *N Yor* 3F 93
Kirkstall. *W Yor* 1C 92
Kirkstile. *Dum* 5F 119
Kirkstyle. *High* 1F 169
Kirkthorpe. *W Yor* 2D 92
Kirkton. *Abers* 2D 152
(nr. Alford)
Kirkton. *Abers* 1D 152
(nr. Insch)
Kirkton. *Abers* 4F 161
(nr. Turriff)
Kirkton. *Ang* 5D 144
(nr. Dundee)
Kirkton. *Ang* 4D 144
(nr. Forfar)
Kirkton. *Ang* 5B 152
(nr. Tarfside)
Kirkton. *Dum* 1A 112
Kirkton. *Fife* 1F 137
Kirkton. *High* 4E 165
(nr. Golspie)
Kirkton. *High* 5H 147
(nr. Kyle of Lochalsh)
Kirkton. *High* 4B 156
(nr. Lochcarron)
Kirkton. *Bord* 3H 119
Kirkton. *S Lan* 2B 118
Kirktonhill. *W Dun* 2E 127
Kirkton Manor. *Bord* 1E 118
Kirkton of Airlie. *Ang* 3C 144
Kirkton of Auchterhouse. *Ang* 5C 144
Kirkton of Bourtie. *Abers* 1F 153
Kirkton of Collace. *Per* 5A 144
Kirkton of Craig. *Ang* 3G 145

Kirkton of Culsalmond. *Abers* 5D 160
Kirkton of Durris. *Abers* 4E 153
Kirkton of Glenbuchat. *Abers* 2A 152
Kirkton of Glenisla. *Ang* 2B 144
Kirkton of Kingoldrum. *Ang* 3C 144
Kirkton of Largo. *Fife* 3G 137
Kirkton of Lethendy. *Per* 4A 144
Kirkton of Logie Buchan.
Abers 1G 153
Kirkton of Maryculter. *Abers* 4F 153
Kirkton of Menmuir. *Ang* 2E 145
Kirkton of Monikie. *Ang* 5E 145
Kirkton of Oyne. *Abers* 1D 152
Kirkton of Rayne. *Abers* 5D 160
Kirkton of Skene. *Abers* 3F 153
Kirktown. *Abers* 2G 161
(nr. Fraserburgh)
Kirktown. *Abers* 3H 161
(nr. Peterhead)
Kirktown of Alvah. *Abers* 2D 160
Kirktown of Auchterless.
Abers 4E 160
Kirktown of Deskford. *Mor* 2C 160
Kirktown of Fetteresso. *Abers* 5F 153
Kirktown of Mortlach. *Mor* 5H 159
Kirktown of Slains. *Abers* 1H 153
Kirkurd. *Bord* 5E 129
Kirkwall. *Orkn* 6D 172
Kirkwall Airport. *Orkn* 7D 172
Kirkwhelpington. *Nmbd* 1C 114
Kirk Yetholm. *Bord* 2C 120
Kirmington. *N Lin* 3E 94
Kirmond le Mire. *Linc* 1A 88
Kirn. *Arg* 2C 126
Kirriemuir. *Ang* 3C 144
Kirstead Green. *Norf* 1E 67
Kirtlebridge. *Dum* 2D 112
Kirtleton. *Dum* 2D 112
Kirtling. *Cambs* 5F 65
Kirtling Green. *Cambs* 5F 65
Kirtlington. *Oxon* 4D 50
Kirtomy. *High* 2H 167
Kirton. *Linc* 2C 76
Kirton. *Notts* 4D 86
Kirton. *Suff* 2F 55
Kirton End. *Linc* 1B 76
Kirton Holme. *Linc* 1B 76
Kirton in Lindsey. *N Lin* 1G 87
Kishorn. *High* 4H 155
Kislingbury. *Nptn* 5D 62
Kite Hill. *IOW* 3D 16
Kites Hardwick. *Warw* 4B 62
Kittisford. *Som* 4D 20
Kittle. *Swan* 4E 31
Kittybrewster. *Aber* 3G 153
Kitwood. *Hants* 3E 25
Kivernoll. *Here* 2H 47
Kiveton Park. *S Yor* 2B 86
Knaith. *Linc* 2F 87
Knaith Park. *Linc* 2F 87
Knaphill. *Surr* 5A 38
Knapp. *Hants* 4C 24
Knapp. *Per* 5B 144
Knapp. *Som* 4G 21
Knapperfield. *High* 3E 169
Knapton. *Norf* 2F 79
Knapton. *York* 4H 99
Knapton Green. *Here* 5G 59
Knapwell. *Cambs* 4C 64
Knaresborough. *N Yor* 4F 99
Knarsdale. *Nmbd* 4H 113
Knatts Valley. *Kent* 4G 39
Knaven. *Abers* 4F 161
Knayton. *N Yor* 1G 99
Knebworth. *Herts* 3C 52
Knedlington. *E Yor* 2H 93
Kneesall. *Notts* 4E 86
Kneesworth. *Cambs* 1D 52
Kneeton. *Notts* 1E 74
Knelston. *Swan* 4D 30
Knenhall. *Staf* 2D 72
Knightacott. *Devn* 3G 19
Knightcote. *Warw* 5B 62
Knightcott. *N Som* 1G 21

Knightley. *Staf* 3C 72
Knightley Dale. *Staf* 3C 72
Knightlow Hill. *Warw* 3B 62
Knighton. *Devn* 4B 8
Knighton. *Dors* 1B 14
Knighton. *Leic* 5D 74
Knighton. *Powy* 3E 59
Knighton. *Som* 2E 21
Knighton. *Staf* 3B 72
(nr. Eccleshall)
Knighton. *Staf* 1B 72
(nr. Woore)
Knighton. *Warw* 5H 61
Knighton. *Wilts* 4A 36
Knighton. *Worc* 5E 61
Knighton Common. *Worc* 3A 60
Knight's End. *Cambs* 1D 64
Knightswood. *Glas* 3G 127
Knightwick. *Worc* 5B 60
Knill. *Here* 4E 59
Knipton. *Leics* 2F 75
Knitsley. *Dur* 5E 115
Kniveton. *Derbs* 5G 85
Knock. *Arg* 5G 139
Knock. *Cumb* 2H 103
Knock. *Mor* 3C 160
Knockally. *High* 5D 168
Knockan. *Arg* 1B 132
Knockan. *High* 2G 163
Knockandhu. *Mor* 1G 151
Knockando. *Mor* 4F 159
Knockarthur. *High* 3E 165
Knockbain. *High* 3A 158
Knockbreck. *High* 2B 154
Knockdee. *High* 2D 168
Knockdolian. *S Ayr* 1G 109
Knockdon. *S Ayr* 3C 116
Knockdown. *Glos* 3D 34
Knockenbaird. *Abers* 1D 152
Knockenkelly. *N Ayr* 3E 123
Knockentiber. *E Ayr* 1C 116
Knockfarrel. *High* 3H 157
Knockglass. *High* 2C 168
Knockholt. *Kent* 5F 39
Knockholt Pound. *Kent* 5F 39
Knockie Lodge. *High* 2G 149
Knockin. *Shrp* 3F 71
Knockinlaw. *E Ayr* 1D 116
Knockinnon. *High* 5D 169
Knockrome. *Arg* 2D 124
Knocksharry. *IOM* 3B 108
Knockshinnoch. *E Ayr* 3D 116
Knockvennie. *Dum* 2E 111
Knockvologan. *Arg* 3B 132
Knodishall. *Suff* 4G 67
Knole. *Som* 4H 21
Knollbury. *Mon* 3H 33
Knolls Green. *Ches E* 3C 84
Knolton. *Wrex* 2F 71
Knook. *Wilts* 2E 23
Knossington. *Leics* 5F 75
Knott. *High* 3C 154
Knott End-on-Sea. *Lanc* 5C 96
Knotting. *Bed* 4H 63
Knotting Green. *Bed* 4H 63
Knottingley. *W Yor* 2E 93
Knotts. *Cumb* 2F 103
Knotty Ash. *Mers* 1G 83
Knotty Green. *Buck* 1A 38
Knowbury. *Shrp* 3H 59
Knowe. *Dum* 2A 110
Knowefield. *Cumb* 4F 113
Knowehead. *Dum* 5F 117
Knowes. *E Lot* 2C 130
Knowesgate. *Nmbd* 1C 114
Knoweside. *S Ayr* 3B 116
Knowle. *Bris* 4A 34
Knowle. *Devn* 3E 19
(nr. Braunton)
Knowle. *Devn* 4D 12
(nr. Budleigh Salterton)
Knowle. *Devn* 2A 12
(nr. Crediton)
Knowle. *Shrp* 3H 59

Knowle. *W Mid* 3F 61
Knowle Green. *Lanc* 1E 91
Knowle St Giles. *Som* 1G 13
Knowlesands. *Shrp* 1B 60
Knowles of Elrick. *Abers* 3D 160
Knowle Village. *Hants* 2D 16
Knowl Hill. *Wind* 4G 37
Knowlton. *Kent* 5G 41
Knowsley. *Mers* 1G 83
Knowstone. *Devn* 4B 20
Knucklas. *Powy* 3E 59
Knuston. *Nptn* 4G 63
Knutsford. *Ches E* 3B 84
Knypersley. *Staf* 5C 84
Krumlin. *W Yor* 3A 92
Kuggar. *Corn* 5E 5
Kyleakin. *High* 1F 147
Kyle of Lochalsh. *High* 1F 147
Kylerhea. *High* 1F 147
Kylesku. *High* 5C 166
Kyles Lodge. *W Isl* 9B 171
Kylesmorar. *High* 4G 147
Kylestrome. *High* 5C 166
Kymin. *Mon* 4A 48
Kynaston. *Here* 2B 48
Kynaston. *Shrp* 3F 71
Kynnersley. *Telf* 4A 72
Kyre Green. *Worc* 4A 60
Kyre Park. *Worc* 4A 60
Kyrewood. *Worc* 4A 60

L

Labost. *W Isl* 3E 171
Lacasaidh. *W Isl* 5F 171
Lacasdail. *W Isl* 4G 171
Laceby. *NE Lin* 4F 95
Lacey Green. *Buck* 5G 51
Lach Dennis. *Ches W* 3B 84
Lache. *Ches W* 4F 83
Lackford. *Suff* 3G 65
Lacock. *Wilts* 5E 35
Ladbroke. *Warw* 5B 62
Laddingford. *Kent* 1A 28
Lade Bank. *Linc* 5C 88
Ladock. *Corn* 3C 6
Lady. *Orkn* 3F 172
Ladycross. *Corn* 4D 10
Lady Green. *Mers* 4B 90
Lady Hall. *Cumb* 1A 96
Ladykirk. *Bord* 5E 131
Ladysford. *Abers* 2G 161
Ladywood. *W Mid* 2E 61
Ladywood. *Worc* 4C 60
Laga. *High* 2A 140
Lagavulin. *Arg* 5C 124
Lagg. *Arg* 2D 125
Lagg. *N Ayr* 3D 122
Laggan. *Arg* 4A 124
Laggan. *High* 4E 149
(nr. Fort Augustus)
Laggan. *High* 4A 150
(nr. Newtonmore)
Laggan. *Mor* 5H 159
Lagganlia. *High* 3C 150
Lagganulva. *Arg* 4F 139
Laglingarten. *Arg* 3A 134
Lagness. *W Sus* 2G 17
Laid. *High* 3E 166
Laide. *High* 4D 162
Laigh Fenwick. *E Ayr* 5F 127
Laindon. *Essx* 2A 40
Lair. *High* 3C 156
Lairg. *High* 3C 164
Lairg Muir. *High* 3C 164
Laithes. *Cumb* 1F 103
Laithkirk. *Dur* 2C 104
Lake. *Devn* 3F 19
Lake. *IOW* 4D 16
Lake. *Wilts* 3G 23
Lake District. *Cumb* 3E 103
Lakenham. *Norf* 5E 79
Lakenheath. *Suff* 2G 65

Lakesend. *Norf* 1E **65**
Lakeside. *Cumb* 1C **96**
Laleham. *Surr* 4B **38**
Laleston. *B'end* 3B **32**
Lamancha. *Bord* 4F **129**
Lamarsh. *Essx* 2B **54**
Lamas. *Norf* 3E **79**
Lamb Corner. *Essx* 2D **54**
Lambden. *Bord* 5D **130**
Lamberhead Green. *G Man* 4D **90**
Lamberhurst. *Kent* 2A **28**
Lamberhurst Quarter. *Kent* 2A **28**
Lamberton. *Bord* 4F **131**
Lambeth. *G Lon* 3E **39**
Lambfell Moar. *IOM* 3B **108**
Lambhill. *Glas* 3G **127**
Lambley. *Nmbd* 4H **113**
Lambley. *Notts* 1D **74**
Lambourn. *W Ber* 4B **36**
Lambourne End. *Essx* 1F **39**
Lambourn Woodlands. *W Ber* 4B **36**
Lambrook. *Som* 4F **21**
Lambs Green. *Dors* 3E **15**
Lambs Green. *W Sus* 2D **26**
Lambston. *Pemb* 3D **42**
Lamellion. *Corn* 2G **7**
Lamerton. *Devn* 5E **11**
Lamesley. *Tyne* 4F **115**
Laminess. *Orkn* 4F **172**
Lamington. *High* 1B **158**
Lamington. *S Lan* 1B **118**
Lamlash. *N Ayr* 2E **123**
Lamonby. *Cumb* 1F **103**
Lamorick. *Corn* 2E **7**
Lamorna. *Corn* 4B **4**
Lamorran. *Corn* 4C **6**
Lampeter. *Cdgn* 1F **45**
Lampeter Velfrey. *Pemb* 3F **43**
Lamphey. *Pemb* 4E **43**
Lamplugh. *Cumb* 2B **102**
Lamport. *Nptn* 3E **63**
Lamyatt. *Som* 3B **22**
Lana. *Devn* . . . . . 3D **10** (nr. Ashwater)
Lana. *Devn* . . . . . 2D **10** (nr. Holsworthy)
Lanark. *S Lan* 5B **128**
Lanarth. *Corn* 4E **5**
Lancaster. *Lanc* 3D **97**
Lanchester. *Dur* 5E **115**
Lancing. *W Sus* 5C **26**
Landbeach. *Cambs* 4D **64**
Landcross. *Devn* 4E **19**
Landerberry. *Abers* 3E **153**
Landford. *Wilts* 1A **16**
Land Gate. *G Man* 4D **90**
Landhallow. *High* 5D **169**
Landimore. *Swan* 3D **30**
Landkey. *Devn* 3F **19**
Landkey Newland. *Devn* 3F **19**
Landore. *Swan* 3F **31**
Landport. *Port* 2E **17**
Landrake. *Corn* 2H **7**
Landscove. *Devn* 2D **9**
Land's End (St Just) Airport. *Corn* 4A **4**
Landshipping. *Pemb* 3E **43**
Landulph. *Corn* 2A **8**
Landywood. *Staf* 5D **73**
Lane. *Corn* 2C **6**
Laneast. *Corn* 4C **10**
Lane Bottom. *Lanc* 1G **91**
Lane End. *Buck* 2G **37**
Lane End. *Hants* 4D **24**
Lane End. *IOW* 4E **17**
Lane End. *Wilts* 2D **22**
Lane Ends. *Derbs* 2G **73**
Lane Ends. *Dur* 1E **105**
Lane Ends. *Lanc* 4G **97**
Laneham. *Notts* 3F **87**
Lanehead. *Dur* . . . . . 5B **114** (nr. Cowshill)
Lane Head. *Dur* . . . . . 3E **105** (nr. Hutton Magna)
Lane Head. *Dur* . . . . . 2D **105** (nr. Woodland)
Lane Head. *G Man* 1A **84**
Lanehead. *Nmbd* 1A **114**
Lane Head. *W Yor* 4B **92**
Lane Heads. *Lanc* 1C **90**
Lanercost. *Cumb* 3G **113**
Laneshaw Bridge. *Lanc* 5B **98**
Laney Green. *Staf* 5D **72**
Langais. *W Isl* 2D **170**
Langal. *High* 2B **140**
Langar. *Notts* 2E **74**
Langbank. *Ren* 2E **127**
Langbar. *N Yor* 4C **98**
Langburnshiels. *Bord* 4H **119**
Langcliffe. *N Yor* 3H **97**
Langdale End. *N Yor* 5G **107**
Langdon. *Corn* 3C **10**
Langdon Beck. *Dur* 1B **104**
Langdon Cross. *Corn* 4D **10**
Langdon Hills. *Essx* 2A **40**
Langdown. *Hants* 2C **16**
Langdyke. *Fife* 3F **137**
Langenhoe. *Essx* 4D **54**
Langford. *C Beds* 1B **52**
Langford. *Devn* 2D **12**
Langford. *Essx* 5B **54**
Langford. *Notts* 5F **87**
Langford. *Oxon* 5H **49**
Langford. *Som* 4F **21**
Langford Budville. *Som* 4E **20**
Langham. *Dors* 4C **22**
Langham. *Essx* 2D **54**
Langham. *Norf* 1C **78**
Langham. *Rut* 4F **75**
Langham. *Suff* 4B **66**
Langho. *Lanc* 1F **91**
Langholm. *Dum* 1E **113**
Langland. *Swan* 4F **31**
Langleeford. *Nmbd* 2D **120**
Langley. *Ches E* 3D **84**
Langley. *Derbs* 1B **74**
Langley. *Essx* 2E **53**
Langley. *Glos* 3F **49**
Langley. *Hants* 2C **16**
Langley. *Herts* 3C **52**
Langley. *Kent* 5C **40**
Langley. *Nmbd* 3B **114**
Langley. *Slo* 3B **38**
Langley. *Som* 4D **20**
Langley. *Warw* 4F **61**
Langley. *W Sus* 4G **25**
Langley Burrell. *Wilts* 4E **35**
Langleybury. *Herts* 5A **52**
Langley Common. *Derbs* 2G **73**
Langley Green. *Derbs* 2G **73**
Langley Green. *Norf* 5F **79**
Langley Green. *Warw* 4F **61**
Langley Green. *W Sus* 2D **26**
Langley Heath. *Kent* 5C **40**
Langley Marsh. *Som* 4D **20**
Langley Moor. *Dur* 5F **115**
Langley Park. *Dur* 5F **115**
Langley Street. *Norf* 5F **79**
Langney. *E Sus* 5H **27**
Langold. *Notts* 2C **86**
Langore. *Corn* 4D **10**
Langport. *Som* 4H **21**
Langrick. *Linc* 1B **76**
Langridge. *Bath* 5C **34**
Langridgeford. *Devn* 4F **19**
Langrigg. *Cumb* 5C **112**
Langrish. *Hants* 4F **25**
Langsett. *S Yor* 4C **92**
Langshaw. *Bord* 1H **119**
Langstone. *Hants* 2F **17**
Langthorne. *N Yor* 5F **105**
Langthorpe. *N Yor* 3F **99**
Langthwaite. *N Yor* 4D **104**
Langtoft. *E Yor* 3E **101**
Langtoft. *Linc* 4A **76**
Langton. *Dur* 3E **105**
Langton. *Linc* . . . . . 4B **88** (nr. Horncastle)
Langton. *Linc* . . . . . 3C **88** (nr. Spilsby)
Langton. *N Yor* 3B **100**
Langton by Wragby. *Linc* 3A **88**
Langton Green. *Kent* 2G **27**
Langton Herring. *Dors* 4B **14**
Langton Long Blandford. *Dors* 2E **15**
Langton Matravers. *Dors* 5F **15**
Langtree. *Devn* 1E **11**
Langwathby. *Cumb* 1G **103**
Langwith. *Derbs* 4C **86**
Langworth. *Linc* 3H **87**
Lanivet. *Corn* 2E **7**
Lanjeth. *Corn* 3D **6**
Lank. *Corn* 5A **10**
Lanlivery. *Corn* 3E **7**
Lanner. *Corn* 5B **6**
Lanreath. *Corn* 3F **7**
Lansallos. *Corn* 3F **7**
Lansdown. *Bath* 5C **34**
Lansdown. *Glos* 3E **49**
Lanteglos Highway. *Corn* 3F **7**
Lanton. *Nmbd* 1D **120**
Lanton. *Bord* 2A **120**
Lapford. *Devn* 2H **11**
Lapford Cross. *Devn* 2H **11**
Laphroaig. *Arg* 5B **124**
Lapley. *Staf* 4C **72**
Lapworth. *Warw* 3F **61**
Larachbeg. *High* 4A **140**
Larbert. *Falk* 1B **128**
Larden Green. *Ches E* 5H **83**
Larel. *High* 3D **169**
Largie. *Abers* 5D **160**
Largiemore. *Arg* 1H **125**
Largoward. *Fife* 3G **137**
Largs. *N Ayr* 4D **126**
Largue. *Abers* 4D **160**
Largybeg. *N Ayr* 3E **123**
Largymeanoch. *N Ayr* 3E **123**
Largymore. *N Ayr* 3E **123**
Larkfield. *Inv* 2D **126**
Larkfield. *Kent* 5A **40**
Larkhall. *Bath* 5C **34**
Larkhall. *S Lan* 4A **128**
Larkhill. *Wilts* 2G **23**
Larling. *Norf* 2B **66**
Larport. *Here* 2A **48**
Lartington. *Dur* 3D **104**
Lary. *Abers* 3H **151**
Lasham. *Hants* 2E **25**
Lashenden. *Kent* 1C **28**
Lassodie. *Fife* 4D **136**
Lasswade. *Midl* 3G **129**
Lastingham. *N Yor* 5E **107**
Latchford. *Herts* 3D **53**
Latchford. *Oxon* 5E **51**
Latchingdon. *Essx* 5B **54**
Latchley. *Corn* 5E **11**
Latchmere Green. *Hants* 5E **37**
Lathbury. *Mil* 1G **51**
Latheron. *High* 5D **169**
Latheronwheel. *High* 5D **169**
Lathom. *Lanc* 4C **90**
Lathones. *Fife* 3G **137**
Latimer. *Buck* 1B **38**
Latteridge. *S Glo* 3B **34**
Lattiford. *Som* 4B **22**
Latton. *Wilts* 2F **35**
Laudale House. *High* 3B **140**
Lauder. *Bord* 5B **130**
Laugharne. *Carm* 3H **43**
Laughterton. *Linc* 3F **87**
Laughton. *E Sus* 4G **27**
Laughton. *Leics* 2D **62**
Laughton. *Linc* . . . . . 1F **87** (nr. Gainsborough)
Laughton. *Linc* . . . . . 2H **75** (nr. Grantham)
Laughton Common. *S Yor* 2C **86**
Laughton en le Morthen. *S Yor* 2C **86**
Launcells. *Corn* 2C **10**
Launceston. *Corn* 4D **10**
Launcherley. *Som* 2A **22**
Launton. *Oxon* 3E **50**
Laurencekirk. *Abers* 1G **145**
Laurieston. *Dum* 3D **111**
Laurieston. *Falk* 2C **128**
Lavendon. *Mil* 5G **63**
Lavenham. *Suff* 1C **54**
Laverhay. *Dum* 5D **118**
Laversdale. *Cumb* 3F **113**
Laverstock. *Wilts* 3G **23**
Laverstoke. *Hants* 2C **24**
Laverton. *Glos* 2F **49**
Laverton. *N Yor* 2E **99**
Laverton. *Som* 1C **22**
Lavister. *Wrex* 5F **83**
Law. *S Lan* 4B **128**
Lawers. *Per* 5D **142**
Lawford. *Essx* 2D **54**
Lawhitton. *Corn* 4D **10**
Lawkland. *N Yor* 3G **97**
Lawley. *Shrp* 5A **72**
Lawnhead. *Staf* 3C **72**
Lawrenny. *Pemb* 4E **43**
Lawshall. *Suff* 5A **66**
Lawton. *Here* 5G **59**
Laxey. *IOM* 3D **108**
Laxfield. *Suff* 3E **67**
Laxfirth. *Shet* 6F **173**
Laxo. *Shet* 5F **173**
Laxton. *E Yor* 2A **94**
Laxton. *Nptn* 1G **63**
Laxton. *Notts* 4E **86**
Laycock. *W Yor* 5C **98**
Layer Breton. *Essx* 4C **54**
Layer-de-la-Haye. *Essx* 3C **54**
Layer Marney. *Essx* 4C **54**
Layland's Green. *W Ber* 5B **36**
Laymore. *Dors* 2G **13**
Laysters Pole. *Here* 4H **59**
Layter's Green. *Buck* 1A **38**
Laytham. *E Yor* 1H **93**
Lazenby. *Red C* 3C **106**
Lazonby. *Cumb* 1G **103**
Lea. *Derbs* 5H **85**
Lea. *Here* 3B **48**
Lea. *Linc* 2F **87**
Lea. *Shrp* . . . . . 2F **59** (nr. Bishop's Castle)
Lea. *Shrp* . . . . . 5G **71** (nr. Shrewsbury)
Lea. *Wilts* 3E **35**
Leabrooks. *Derbs* 5B **86**
Leachd. *Arg* 4H **133**
Leachkin. *High* 4A **158**
Leachpool. *Pemb* 3D **42**
Leadburn. *Midl* 4F **129**
Leadenham. *Linc* 5G **87**
Leaden Roding. *Essx* 4F **53**
Leaderfoot. *Bord* 1H **119**
Leadgate. *Cumb* 5A **114**
Leadgate. *Dur* 4E **115**
Leadgate. *Nmbd* 4E **115**
Leadhills. *S Lan* 3A **118**
Leadingcross Green. *Kent* 5C **40**
Lea End. *Worc* 3E **61**
Leafield. *Oxon* 4B **50**
Leagrave. *Lutn* 3A **52**
Lea Hall. *W Mid* 2F **61**
Lea Heath. *Staf* 3E **73**
Leake. *N Yor* 5B **106**
Leake Common Side. *Linc* 5C **88**
Leake Fold Hill. *Linc* 5D **88**
Leake Hurn's End. *Linc* 1D **76**
Lealholm. *N Yor* 4E **107**
Lealt. *Arg* 4D **132**
Lealt. *High* 2E **155**
Leam. *Derbs* 3G **85**
Lea Marston. *Warw* 1G **61**
Leamington Hastings. *Warw* 4B **62**
Leamington Spa, Royal. *Warw* 4H **61**
Leamonsley. *Staf* 5F **73**
Leamside. *Dur* 5G **115**
Leargybreck. *Arg* 2D **124**
Lease Rigg. *N Yor* 4F **107**
Leasgill. *Cumb* 1D **97**
Leasingham. *Linc* 1H **75**
Leasingthorne. *Dur* 1F **105**
Leasowe. *Mers* 1E **83**
Leatherhead. *Surr* 5C **38**
Leathley. *N Yor* 5E **99**
Leaths. *Dum* 3E **111**
Leaton. *Shrp* 4G **71**
Leaton. *Telf* 4A **72**
Lea Town. *Lanc* 1C **90**
Leaveland. *Kent* 5E **40**
Leavenheath. *Suff* 2C **54**
Leavening. *N Yor* 3B **100**
Leaves Green. *G Lon* 4F **39**
Lea Yeat. *Cumb* 1G **97**
Leazes. *Dur* 4E **115**
Lebberston. *N Yor* 1E **101**
Lechlade on Thames. *Glos* 2H **35**
Leck. *Lanc* 2F **97**
Leckford. *Hants* 3B **24**
Leckfurin. *High* 3H **167**
Leckgruinart. *Arg* 3A **124**
Leckhampstead. *Buck* 2F **51**
Leckhampstead. *W Ber* 4C **36**
Leckhampstead Street. *W Ber* 4C **36**
Leckhampton. *Glos* 4E **49**
Leckmelm. *High* 4F **163**
Leckwith. *V Glam* 4E **33**
Leconfield. *E Yor* 5E **101**
Ledaig. *Arg* 5D **140**
Ledburn. *Buck* 3H **51**
Ledbury. *Here* 2C **48**
Ledgemoor. *Here* 5G **59**
Ledgowan. *High* 3D **156**
Ledicot. *Here* 4G **59**
Ledmore. *High* 2G **163**
Lednabirichen. *High* 4E **165**
Lednagullin. *High* 2A **168**
Ledsham. *Ches W* 3F **83**
Ledsham. *W Yor* 2E **93**
Ledston. *W Yor* 2E **93**
Ledstone. *Devn* 4D **8**
Ledwell. *Oxon* 3C **50**
Lee. *Devn* . . . . . 2E **19** (nr. Ilfracombe)
Lee. *Devn* . . . . . 4B **20** (nr. South Molton)
Lee. *G Lon* 3F **39**
Lee. *Hants* 1B **16**
Lee. *Lanc* 4E **97**
Lee. *Shrp* 2G **71**
Leeans. *Shet* 7E **173**
Leebotten. *Shet* 9F **173**
Leebotwood. *Shrp* 1G **59**
Lee Brockhurst. *Shrp* 3H **71**
Leece. *Cumb* 3B **96**
Leechpool. *Mon* 3A **34**
Lee Clump. *Buck* 5H **51**
Leeds. *Kent* 5C **40**
Leeds. *W Yor* 1C **92**
Leeds Bradford International Airport. *W Yor* 5E **98**
Leedstown. *Corn* 3D **4**
Leegomery. *Telf* 4A **72**
Lee Head. *Derbs* 1E **85**
Leek. *Staf* 5D **85**
Leekbrook. *Staf* 5D **85**
Leek Wootton. *Warw* 4G **61**
Lee Mill. *Devn* 3B **8**
Leeming. *N Yor* 1E **99**
Leeming Bar. *N Yor* 5F **105**
Lee Moor. *Devn* 2B **8**
Lee Moor. *W Yor* 2D **92**
Lee-on-the-Solent. *Hants* 2D **16**
Lees. *Derbs* 2G **73**
Lees. *G Man* 4H **91**
Lees. *W Yor* 1A **92**
Lees, The. *Kent* 5E **40**
Leeswood. *Flin* 4E **83**
Lee, The. *Buck* 5H **51**

Leetown. *Per* 1E 136
Leftwich. *Ches W* 3A 84
Legbourne. *Linc* 2C 88
Legburthwaite. *Cumb* 3E 102
Legerwood. *Bord* 5B 130
Legsby. *Linc* 2A 88
Leicester. *Leic* 5C 74
Leicester Forest East. *Leics* 5C 74
Leigh. *Dors* 2B 14
Leigh. *G Man* 4E 91
Leigh. *Kent* 1G 27
Leigh. *Shrp* 5F 71
Leigh. *Surr* 1D 26
Leigh. *Wilts* 2F 35
Leigh. *Worc* 5B 60
Leigham. *Plym* 3B 8
Leigh Beck. *Essx* 2C 40
Leigh Common. *Som* 4C 22
Leigh Delamere. *Wilts* 4D 35
Leigh Green. *Kent* 2D 28
Leighland Chapel. *Som* 3D 20
Leigh-on-Sea. *S'end* 2C 40
Leigh Park. *Hants* 2F 17
Leigh Sinton. *Worc* 5B 60
Leighterton. *Glos* 2D 34
Leigh, The. *Glos* 3D 48
Leighton. *N Yor* 2D 98
Leighton. *Powy* 5E 71
Leighton. *Shrp* 5A 72
Leighton. *Som* 2C 22
Leighton Bromswold. *Cambs* 3A 64
Leighton Buzzard. *C Beds* 3H 51
Leigh-upon-Mendip. *Som* 2B 22
Leinthall Earls. *Here* 4G 59
Leinthall Starkes. *Here* 4G 59
Leintwardine. *Here* 3G 59
Leire. *Leics* 1C 62
Leirinmore. *High* 2E 166
Leishmore. *High* 4G 157
Leiston. *Suff* 4G 67
Leitfie. *Per* 4B 144
Leith. *Edin* 2F 129
Leitholm. *Bord* 5D 130
Lelant. *Corn* 3C 4
Lelant Downs. *Corn* 3C 4
Lelley. *E Yor* 1F 95
Lem Hill. *Worc* 3B 60
Lemington. *Tyne* 3E 115
Lemmington Hall. *Nmbd* 3F 121
Lempitlaw. *Bord* 1B 120
Lemsford. *Herts* 4C 52
Lenacre. *Cumb* 1F 97
Lenchie. *Abers* 5C 160
Lenchwick. *Worc* 1F 49
Lendalfoot. *S Ayr* 5A 116
Lendrick. *Stir* 3E 135
Lenham. *Kent* 5C 40
Lenham Heath. *Kent* 1D 28
Lenimore. *N Ayr* 5G 125
Lennel. *Bord* 5E 131
Lennoxtown. *E Dun* 2H 127
Lenton. *Linc* 2H 75
Lentran. *High* 4H 157
Lenwade. *Norf* 4C 78
Lenzie. *E Dun* 2H 127
Leochel Cushnie. *Abers* 2C 152
Leominster. *Here* 5G 59
Leonard Stanley. *Glos* 5D 48
Lepe. *Hants* 3C 16
Lephenstrath. *Arg* 5A 122
Lephin. *High* 4A 154
Lephinchapel. *Arg* 4G 133
Lephinmore. *Arg* 4G 133
Leppington. *N Yor* 3B 100
Lepton. *W Yor* 3C 92
Lerryn. *Corn* 3F 7
Lerwick. *Shet* 7F 173
Lerwick (Tingwall) Airport. *Shet* 7F 173
Lesbury. *Nmbd* 3G 121
Leslie. *Abers* 1C 152
Leslie. *Fife* 3E 137
Lesmahagow. *S Lan* 1H 117
Lesnewth. *Corn* 3B 10
Lessingham. *Norf* 3F 79
Lessonhall. *Cumb* 4D 112
Leswalt. *Dum* 3F 109
Letchmore Heath. *Herts* 1C 38
Letchworth Garden City. *Herts* 2C 52
Letcombe Bassett. *Oxon* 3B 36
Letcombe Regis. *Oxon* 3B 36
Letham. *Ang* 4E 145
Letham. *Falk* 1B 128
Letham. *Fife* 2F 137
Lethanhill. *E Ayr* 3D 116
Lethenty. *Abers* 4F 161
Letheringham. *Suff* 5E 67
Letheringsett. *Norf* 2C 78
Lettaford. *Devn* 4H 11
Lettan. *Orkn* 3G 172
Letter. *Abers* 2E 153
Letterewe. *High* 1B 156
Letterfearn. *High* 1A 148
Lettermore. *Arg* 4F 139
Letters. *High* 5F 163
Letterston. *Pemb* 2D 42
Letton. *Here* 1G 47 (nr. Kington)
Letton. *Here* 3F 59 (nr. Leintwardine)
Letty Green. *Herts* 4C 52
Letwell. *S Yor* 2C 86
Leuchars. *Fife* 1G 137
Leumrabhagh. *W Isl* 6F 171
Leusdon. *Devn* 5H 11
Levedale. *Staf* 4C 72
Leven. *E Yor* 5F 101
Leven. *Fife* 3F 137
Levencorroch. *N Ayr* 3E 123
Levenhall. *E Lot* 2G 129
Levens. *Cumb* 1D 97
Levens Green. *Herts* 3D 52
Levenshulme. *G Man* 1C 84
Levenwick. *Shet* 9F 173
Leverburgh. *W Isl* 9C 171
Leverington. *Cambs* 4D 76
Leverton. *Linc* 1C 76
Leverton. *W Ber* 4B 36
Leverton Lucasgate. *Linc* 1D 76
Leverton Outgate. *Linc* 1D 76
Levington. *Suff* 2F 55
Levisham. *N Yor* 5F 107
Levishie. *High* 2G 149
Lew. *Oxon* 5B 50
Lewaigue. *IOM* 2D 108
Lewannick. *Corn* 4C 10
Lewdown. *Devn* 4E 11
Lewes. *E Sus* 4F 27
Leweston. *Pemb* 2D 42
Lewisham. *G Lon* 3E 39
Lewiston. *High* 1H 149
Lewistown. *B'end* 3C 32
Lewknor. *Oxon* 2F 37
Leworthy. *Devn* 3G 19 (nr. Barnstaple)
Leworthy. *Devn* 2D 10 (nr. Holsworthy)
Lewson Street. *Kent* 4D 40
Lewthorn Cross. *Devn* 5A 12
Lewtrenchard. *Devn* 4E 11
Ley. *Corn* 2F 7
Leybourne. *Kent* 5A 40
Leyburn. *N Yor* 5E 105
Leycett. *Staf* 1B 72
Leyfields. *Staf* 5G 73
Ley Green. *Herts* 3B 52
Ley Hill. *Buck* 5H 51
Leyland. *Lanc* 2D 90
Leylodge. *Abers* 2E 153
Leymoor. *W Yor* 3B 92
Leys. *Per* 5B 144
Leysdown-on-Sea. *Kent* 3E 41
Leysmill. *Ang* 4F 145
Leyton. *G Lon* 2E 39
Leytonstone. *G Lon* 2F 39
Lezant. *Corn* 5D 10
Leziate. *Norf* 4F 77
Lhanbryde. *Mor* 2G 159
Lhen, The. *IOM* 1C 108
Liatrie. *High* 5E 157
Libanus. *Powy* 3C 46
Libberton. *S Lan* 5C 128
Libbery. *Worc* 5D 60
Liberton. *Edin* 3F 129
Lichfield. *Staf* 5F 73
Lickey. *Worc* 3D 61
Lickey End. *Worc* 3D 61
Lickfold. *W Sus* 3A 26
Liddaton. *Devn* 4E 11
Liddington. *Swin* 3H 35
Lidgate. *Suff* 5G 65
Lidgett. *Notts* 4D 86
Lidham Hill. *E Sus* 4C 28
Lidlington. *C Beds* 2H 51
Lidsey. *W Sus* 5A 26
Lidstone. *Oxon* 3B 50
Lienassie. *High* 1B 148
Liff. *Ang* 5C 144
Lifford. *W Mid* 2E 61
Lifton. *Devn* 4D 11
Liftondown. *Devn* 4D 10
Lighthorne. *Warw* 5H 61
Light Oaks. *Staf* 5D 84
Lightwater. *Surr* 4A 38
Lightwood. *Staf* 1E 73
Lightwood. *Stoke* 1D 72
Lightwood Green. *Ches E* 1A 72
Lightwood Green. *Wrex* 1F 71
Lilbourne. *Nptn* 3C 62
Lilburn Tower. *Nmbd* 2E 121
Lillesdon. *Som* 4G 21
Lilleshall. *Telf* 4B 72
Lilley. *Herts* 3B 52
Lilliesleaf. *Bord* 2H 119
Lillingstone Dayrell. *Buck* 2F 51
Lillingstone Lovell. *Buck* 1F 51
Lillington. *Dors* 1B 14
Lilstock. *Som* 2E 21
Lilybank. *Inv* 2E 126
Lilyhurst. *Shrp* 4B 72
Limbrick. *Lanc* 3E 90
Limbury. *Lutn* 3A 52
Limekilnburn. *S Lan* 4A 128
Limekilns. *Fife* 1D 129
Limerigg. *Falk* 2B 128
Limestone Brae. *Nmbd* 5A 114
Lime Street. *Worc* 2D 48
Limington. *Som* 4A 22
Limpenhoe. *Norf* 5F 79
Limpley Stoke. *Wilts* 5C 34
Limpsfield. *Surr* 5E 39
Limpsfield Chart. *Surr* 5F 39
Linburn. *W Lot* 3E 129
Linby. *Notts* 5C 86
Linchmere. *W Sus* 3G 25
Lincluden. *Dum* 2A 112
Lincoln. *Linc* 3G 87
Lincomb. *Worc* 4C 60
Lindale. *Cumb* 1D 96
Lindal in Furness. *Cumb* 2B 96
Lindean. *Bord* 1G 119
Linden. *Glos* 4D 48
Lindfield. *W Sus* 3E 27
Lindford. *Hants* 3G 25
Lindores. *Fife* 2E 137
Lindridge. *Worc* 4A 60
Lindsell. *Essx* 3G 53
Lindsey. *Suff* 1C 54
Lindsey Tye. *Suff* 1C 54
Linford. *Hants* 2G 15
Linford. *Thur* 3A 40
Lingague. *IOM* 4B 108
Lingdale. *Red C* 3D 106
Lingen. *Here* 4F 59
Lingfield. *Surr* 1E 27
Lingoed. *Mon* 3G 47
Lingreabhagh. *W Isl* 9C 171
Ling, The. *Norf* 1F 67
Lingwood. *Norf* 5F 79
Lingy Close. *Cumb* 4E 113
Linicro. *High* 2C 154
Linkend. *Worc* 2D 48
Linkenholt. *Hants* 1B 24
Linkinhorne. *Corn* 5D 10
Linklater. *Orkn* 9D 172
Linktown. *Fife* 4E 137
Linkwood. *Mor* 2G 159
Linley. *Shrp* 1F 59 (nr. Bishop's Castle)
Linley. *Shrp* 1A 60 (nr. Bridgnorth)
Linley Green. *Here* 5A 60
Linlithgow. *W Lot* 2C 128
Linlithgow Bridge. *Falk* 2C 128
Linneraineach. *High* 3F 163
Linshiels. *Nmbd* 4C 120
Linsiadar. *W Isl* 4E 171
Linsidemore. *High* 4C 164
Linslade. *C Beds* 3H 51
Linstead Parva. *Suff* 3F 67
Linstock. *Cumb* 4F 113
Linthwaite. *W Yor* 3B 92
Lintlaw. *Bord* 4E 131
Lintmill. *Mor* 2C 160
Linton. *Cambs* 1F 53
Linton. *Derbs* 4G 73
Linton. *Here* 3B 48
Linton. *Kent* 5B 40
Linton. *N Yor* 3B 98
Linton. *Bord* 2B 120
Linton. *W Yor* 5F 99
Linton Colliery. *Nmbd* 5G 121
Linton Hill. *Here* 3B 48
Linton-on-Ouse. *N Yor* 3G 99
Lintzford. *Tyne* 4E 115
Lintzgarth. *Dur* 5C 114
Linwood. *Hants* 2G 15
Linwood. *Linc* 2A 88
Linwood. *Ren* 3F 127
Lionacleit. *W Isl* 4C 170
Lionacro. *High* 2C 154
Lionacuidhe. *W Isl* 4C 170
Lional. *W Isl* 1H 171
Liphook. *Hants* 3G 25
Lipley. *Shrp* 2B 72
Lipyeate. *Som* 1B 22
Liquo. *N Lan* 4B 128
Liscard. *Mers* 1F 83
Liscombe. *Som* 3B 20
Liskeard. *Corn* 2G 7
Lisle Court. *Hants* 3B 16
Liss. *Hants* 4F 25
Lissett. *E Yor* 4F 101
Liss Forest. *Hants* 4F 25
Lissington. *Linc* 2A 88
Liston. *Essx* 1B 54
Lisvane. *Card* 3E 33
Liswerry. *Newp* 3G 33
Litcham. *Norf* 4A 78
Litchard. *B'end* 3C 32
Litchborough. *Nptn* 5D 62
Litchfield. *Hants* 1C 24
Litherland. *Mers* 1F 83
Litlington. *Cambs* 1D 52
Litlington. *E Sus* 5G 27
Littemill. *Nmbd* 3G 121
Litterty. *Abers* 3E 161
Little Abington. *Cambs* 1F 53
Little Addington. *Nptn* 3G 63
Little Airmyn. *N Yor* 2H 93
Little Alne. *Warw* 4F 61
Little Ardo. *Abers* 5F 161
Little Asby. *Cumb* 4H 103
Little Aston. *Staf* 5E 73
Little Atherfield. *IOW* 4C 16
Little Ayton. *N Yor* 3C 106
Little Baddow. *Essx* 5A 54
Little Badminton. *S Glo* 3D 34
Little Ballinluig. *Per* 3G 143
Little Bampton. *Cumb* 4D 112
Little Bardfield. *Essx* 2G 53
Little Barford. *Bed* 5A 64
Little Barningham. *Norf* 2D 78
Little Barrington. *Glos* 4H 49
Little Barrow. *Ches W* 4G 83
Little Barugh. *N Yor* 2B 100
Little Bavington. *Nmbd* 2C 114
Little Bealings. *Suff* 1F 55
Littlebeck. *Cumb* 3H 103
Little Bedwyn. *Wilts* 5A 36
Little Bentley. *Essx* 3E 54
Little Berkhamsted. *Herts* 5C 52
Little Billing. *Nptn* 4F 63
Little Billington. *C Beds* 3H 51
Little Birch. *Here* 2A 48
Little Bispham. *Bkpl* 5C 96
Little Blakenham. *Suff* 1E 54
Little Blencow. *Cumb* 1F 103
Little Bognor. *W Sus* 3B 26
Little Bolas. *Shrp* 3A 72
Little Bollington. *Ches E* 2B 84
Little Bookham. *Surr* 5C 38
Littleborough. *Devn* 1B 12
Littleborough. *G Man* 3H 91
Littleborough. *Notts* 2F 87
Littlebourne. *Kent* 5G 41
Little Bourton. *Oxon* 1C 50
Little Bowden. *Leics* 2E 63
Little Bradley. *Suff* 5F 65
Little Brampton. *Shrp* 2F 59
Little Brechin. *Ang* 2E 145
Littlebredy. *Dors* 4A 14
Little Brickhill. *Mil* 2H 51
Little Bridgeford. *Staf* 3C 72
Little Brington. *Nptn* 4D 62
Little Bromley. *Essx* 3D 54
Little Broughton. *Cumb* 1B 102
Little Budworth. *Ches W* 4H 83
Little Burstead. *Essx* 1A 40
Little Burton. *E Yor* 5F 101
Littlebury. *Essx* 2F 53
Littlebury Green. *Essx* 2E 53
Little Bytham. *Linc* 4H 75
Little Canfield. *Essx* 3F 53
Little Canford. *Dors* 3F 15
Little Carlton. *Linc* 2C 88
Little Carlton. *Notts* 5E 87
Little Casterton. *Rut* 5H 75
Little Catwick. *E Yor* 5F 101
Little Catworth. *Cambs* 3A 64
Little Cawthorpe. *Linc* 2C 88
Little Chalfont. *Buck* 1A 38
Little Chart. *Kent* 1D 28
Little Chesterford. *Essx* 1F 53
Little Cheverell. *Wilts* 1E 23
Little Chishill. *Cambs* 2E 53
Little Clacton. *Essx* 4E 55
Little Clanfield. *Oxon* 5A 50
Little Clifton. *Cumb* 2B 102
Little Coates. *NE Lin* 4F 95
Little Comberton. *Worc* 1E 49
Little Common. *E Sus* 5B 28
Little Compton. *Warw* 2A 50
Little Cornard. *Suff* 2B 54
Littlecote. *Buck* 3G 51
Littlecott. *Wilts* 1G 23
Little Cowarne. *Here* 5A 60
Little Coxwell. *Oxon* 2A 36
Little Crakehall. *N Yor* 5F 105
Little Crawley. *Mil* 1H 51
Little Creich. *High* 5D 164
Little Cressingham. *Norf* 5A 78
Little Crosby. *Mers* 4B 90
Little Crosthwaite. *Cumb* 2D 102
Little Cubley. *Derbs* 2F 73
Little Dalby. *Leics* 4E 75
Little Dawley. *Telf* 5A 72
Littledean. *Glos* 4B 48
Little Dens. *Abers* 4H 161
Little Dewchurch. *Here* 2A 48
Little Ditton. *Cambs* 5F 65
Little Down. *Hants* 1B 24
Little Downham. *Cambs* 2E 65
Little Drayton. *Shrp* 2A 72
Little Driffield. *E Yor* 4E 101
Little Dunham. *Norf* 4A 78
Little Dunkeld. *Per* 4H 143
Little Dunmow. *Essx* 3G 53
Little Easton. *Essx* 3G 53
Little Eaton. *Derbs* 1A 74

Little Eccleston. *Lanc* 5D **96**
Little Ellingham. *Norf* 1C **66**
Little Elm. *Som* 2C **22**
Little End. *Essx* 5F **53**
Little Everdon. *Nptn* 5C **62**
Little Eversden. *Cambs* 5C **64**
Little Faringdon. *Oxon* 5H **49**
Little Fencote. *N Yor* 5F **105**
Little Fenton. *N Yor* 1F **93**
Littleferry. *High* 4F **165**
Little Fransham. *Norf* 4B **78**
Little Gaddesden. *Herts* 4H **51**
Little Garway. *Here* 3H **47**
Little Gidding. *Cambs* 2A **64**
Little Glemham. *Suff* 5F **67**
Little Glenshee. *Per* 5G **143**
Little Gransden. *Cambs* 5B **64**
Little Green. *Suff* 3C **66**
Little Green. *Wrex* 1G **71**
Little Grimsby. *Linc* 1C **88**
Little Habton. *N Yor* 2B **100**
Little Hadham. *Herts* 3E **53**
Little Hale. *Linc* 1A **76**
Little Hallingbury. *Essx* 4E **53**
Littleham. *Devn* 4E **19** (nr. Bideford)
Littleham. *Devn* 4D **12** (nr. Exmouth)
Little Hampden. *Buck* 5G **51**
Littlehampton. *W Sus* 5B **26**
Little Haresfield. *Glos* 5D **48**
Little Harrowden. *Nptn* 3F **63**
Little Haseley. *Oxon* 5E **51**
Little Hatfield. *E Yor* 5F **101**
Little Hautbois. *Norf* 3E **79**
Little Haven. *Pemb* 3C **42**
Little Hay. *Staf* 5F **73**
Little Hayfield. *Derbs* 2E **85**
Little Haywood. *Staf* 3E **73**
Little Heath. *W Mid* 2H **61**
Little Heck. *N Yor* 2F **93**
Littlehempston. *Devn* 2E **9**
Little Herbert's. *Glos* 3E **49**
Little Hereford. *Here* 4H **59**
Little Horkesley. *Essx* 2C **54**
Little Hormead. *Herts* 3E **53**
Little Horsted. *E Sus* 4F **27**
Little Horton. *W Yor* 1B **92**
Little Horwood. *Buck* 2F **51**
Little Houghton. *Nptn* 5F **63**
Littlehoughton. *Nmbd* 3G **121**
Little Houghton. *S Yor* 4E **93**
Little Hucklow. *Derbs* 3F **85**
Little Hulton. *G Man* 4F **91**
Little Irchester. *Nptn* 4G **63**
Little Kelk. *E Yor* 3E **101**
Little Kimble. *Buck* 5G **51**
Little Kineton. *Warw* 5H **61**
Little Kingshill. *Buck* 2G **37**
Little Langdale. *Cumb* 4E **102**
Little Langford. *Wilts* 3F **23**
Little Laver. *Essx* 5F **53**
Little Lawford. *Warw* 3B **62**
Little Leigh. *Ches W* 3A **84**
Little Leighs. *Essx* 4H **53**
Little Leven. *E Yor* 5E **101**
Little Lever. *G Man* 4F **91**
Little Linford. *Mil* 1G **51**
Little London. *Buck* 4E **51**
Little London. *E Sus* 4G **27**
Little London. *Hants* 2B **24** (nr. Andover)
Little London. *Hants* 1E **24** (nr. Basingstoke)
Little London. *Linc* 3D **76** (nr. Long Sutton)
Little London. *Linc* 3B **76** (nr. Spalding)
Little London. *Norf* 2E **79** (nr. North Walsham)
Little London. *Norf* 1G **65** (nr. Northwold)
Little London. *Norf* 2D **78** (nr. Saxthorpe)
Little London. *Norf* 1F **65** (nr. Southery)
Little London. *Powy* 2C **58**
Little Longstone. *Derbs* 3F **85**
Little Malvern. *Worc* 1C **48**
Little Maplestead. *Essx* 2B **54**
Little Marcle. *Here* 2B **48**
Little Marlow. *Buck* 3G **37**
Little Massingham. *Norf* 3G **77**
Little Melton. *Norf* 5D **78**
Littlemill. *Abers* 4H **151**
Littlemill. *E Ayr* 3D **116**
Littlemill. *High* 4D **158**
Little Mill. *Mon* 5G **47**
Little Milton. *Oxon* 5E **50**
Little Missenden. *Buck* 1A **38**
Littlemoor. *Derbs* 4A **86**
Littlemoor. *Dors* 4B **14**
Littlemore. *Oxon* 5D **50**
Little Mountain. *Flin* 4E **83**
Little Musgrave. *Cumb* 3A **104**
Little Ness. *Shrp* 4G **71**
Little Neston. *Ches W* 3F **83**
Little Newcastle. *Pemb* 2D **43**
Little Newsham. *Dur* 3E **105**
Little Oakley. *Essx* 3F **55**
Little Oakley. *Nptn* 2F **63**
Little Onn. *Staf* 4C **72**
Little Ormside. *Cumb* 3A **104**
Little Orton. *Cumb* 4E **113**
Little Orton. *Leics* 5H **73**
Little Ouse. *Norf* 2F **65**
Little Ouseburn. *N Yor* 3G **99**
Littleover. *Derb* 2H **73**
Little Packington. *Warw* 2G **61**
Little Paxton. *Cambs* 4A **64**
Little Petherick. *Corn* 1D **6**
Little Plumpton. *Lanc* 1B **90**
Little Plumstead. *Norf* 4F **79**
Little Ponton. *Linc* 2G **75**
Littleport. *Cambs* 2E **65**
Little Posbrook. *Hants* 2D **16**
Little Potheridge. *Devn* 1F **11**
Little Preston. *Nptn* 5C **62**
Little Raveley. *Cambs* 3B **64**
Little Reynoldston. *Swan* 4D **31**
Little Ribston. *N Yor* 4F **99**
Little Rissington. *Glos* 4G **49**
Little Rogart. *High* 3E **165**
Little Rollright. *Oxon* 2A **50**
Little Ryburgh. *Norf* 3B **78**
Little Ryle. *Nmbd* 3E **121**
Little Ryton. *Shrp* 5G **71**
Little Salkeld. *Cumb* 1G **103**
Little Sampford. *Essx* 2G **53**
Little Sandhurst. *Brac* 5G **37**
Little Saredon. *Staf* 5D **72**
Little Saxham. *Suff* 4G **65**
Little Scatwell. *High* 3F **157**
Little Shelford. *Cambs* 5D **64**
Little Shoddesden. *Hants* 2A **24**
Little Singleton. *Lanc* 1B **90**
Little Smeaton. *N Yor* 3F **93**
Little Snoring. *Norf* 2B **78**
Little Sodbury. *S Glo* 3C **34**
Little Somborne. *Hants* 3B **24**
Little Somerford. *Wilts* 3E **35**
Little Soudley. *Shrp* 3B **72**
Little Stainforth. *N Yor* 3H **97**
Little Stainton. *Darl* 2A **106**
Little Stanney. *Ches W* 3G **83**
Little Staughton. *Bed* 4A **64**
Little Steeping. *Linc* 4D **88**
Littlester. *Shet* 4G **173**
Little Stoke. *Staf* 2D **72**
Littlestone-on-Sea. *Kent* 3E **29**
Little Stonham. *Suff* 4D **66**
Little Stretton. *Leics* 5D **74**
Little Stretton. *Shrp* 1G **59**
Little Strickland. *Cumb* 3G **103**
Little Stukeley. *Cambs* 3B **64**
Little Sugnall. *Staf* 2C **72**
Little Sutton. *Ches W* 3F **83**
Little Sutton. *Linc* 3D **76**
Little Swinburne. *Nmbd* 2C **114**
Little Tew. *Oxon* 3B **50**
Little Tey. *Essx* 3B **54**
Little Thetford. *Cambs* 3E **65**
Little Thirkleby. *N Yor* 2G **99**
Little Thornage. *Norf* 2C **78**
Little Thornton. *Lanc* 5C **96**
Littlethorpe. *Leics* 1C **62**
Littlethorpe. *N Yor* 3F **99**
Little Thorpe. *W Yor* 2B **92**
Little Thurlow. *Suff* 5F **65**
Little Thurrock. *Thur* 3H **39**
Littleton. *Ches W* 4G **83**
Littleton. *Hants* 3C **24**
Littleton. *Som* 3H **21**
Littleton. *Surr* 1A **26** (nr. Guildford)
Littleton. *Surr* 4B **38** (nr. Staines)
Littleton Drew. *Wilts* 3D **34**
Littleton Pannell. *Wilts* 1E **23**
Littleton-upon-Severn. *S Glo* 3A **34**
Little Torboll. *High* 4E **165**
Little Torrington. *Devn* 1E **11**
Little Totham. *Essx* 4B **54**
Little Town. *Cumb* 3D **102**
Littletown. *Dur* 5G **115**
Littletown. *High* 5E **165**
Little Town. *Lanc* 1E **91**
Little Twycross. *Leics* 5H **73**
Little Urswick. *Cumb* 2B **96**
Little Wakering. *Essx* 2D **40**
Little Walden. *Essx* 1F **53**
Little Waldingfield. *Suff* 1C **54**
Little Walsingham. *Norf* 2B **78**
Little Waltham. *Essx* 4H **53**
Little Warley. *Essx* 1H **39**
Little Washbourne. *Glos* 2E **49**
Little Weighton. *E Yor* 1C **94**
Little Wenham. *Suff* 2D **54**
Little Wenlock. *Telf* 5A **72**
Little Whelnetham. *Suff* 5A **66**
Little Whittingham Green. *Suff* 3E **67**
Littlewick Green. *Wind* 4G **37**
Little Wilbraham. *Cambs* 5E **65**
Littlewindsor. *Dors* 2H **13**
Little Wisbeach. *Linc* 2A **76**
Little Witcombe. *Glos* 4E **49**
Little Witley. *Worc* 4B **60**
Little Wittenham. *Oxon* 2D **36**
Little Wolford. *Warw* 2A **50**
Littleworth. *Bed* 1A **52**
Littleworth. *Glos* 2G **49**
Littleworth. *Oxon* 2B **36**
Littleworth. *Staf* 4E **73** (nr. Cannock)
Littleworth. *Staf* 3B **72** (nr. Eccleshall)
Littleworth. *Staf* 3D **72** (nr. Stafford)
Littleworth. *W Sus* 3C **26**
Littleworth. *Worc* 4D **61** (nr. Redditch)
Littleworth. *Worc* 1D **49** (nr. Worcester)
Little Wratting. *Suff* 1G **53**
Little Wymington. *Nptn* 4G **63**
Little Wymondley. *Herts* 3C **52**
Little Wyrley. *Staf* 5E **73**
Little Yeldham. *Essx* 2A **54**
Littley Green. *Essx* 4G **53**
Litton. *Derbs* 3F **85**
Litton. *N Yor* 2B **98**
Litton. *Som* 1A **22**
Litton Cheney. *Dors* 3A **14**
Liurbost. *W Isl* 5F **171**
Liverpool. *Mers* 1F **83**
Liverpool John Lennon Airport. *Mers* 2G **83**
Liversedge. *W Yor* 2B **92**
Liverton. *Devn* 5B **12**
Liverton. *Red C* 3E **107**
Liverton Mines. *Red C* 3E **107**
Livingston. *W Lot* 3D **128**
Livingston Village. *W Lot* 3D **128**
Lixwm. *Flin* 3D **82**
Lizard. *Corn* 5E **5**
Llaingoch. *IOA* 2B **80**
Llaithddu. *Powy* 2C **58**
Llampha. *V Glam* 4C **32**
Llan. *Powy* 5A **70**
Llanaber. *Gwyn* 4F **69**
Llanaelhaearn. *Gwyn* 1C **68**
Llanaeron. *Cdgn* 4D **57**
Llanafan. *Cdgn* 3F **57**
Llanafan-fawr. *Powy* 5B **58**
Llanafan-fechan. *Powy* 5B **58**
Llanallgo. *IOA* 2D **81**
Llanandras. *Powy* 4F **59**
Llananno. *Powy* 3C **58**
Llanarmon. *Gwyn* 2D **68**
Llanarmon Dyffryn Ceiriog. *Wrex* 2D **70**
Llanarmon-yn-Ial. *Den* 5D **82**
Llanarth. *Cdgn* 5D **56**
Llanarth. *Mon* 4G **47**
Llanarthne. *Carm* 3F **45**
Llanasa. *Flin* 2D **82**
Llanbabo. *IOA* 2C **80**
Llanbadarn Fawr. *Cdgn* 2F **57**
Llanbadarn Fynydd. *Powy* 3C **58**
Llanbadarn-y-garreg. *Powy* 1E **46**
Llanbadoc. *Mon* 5G **47**
Llanbadrig. *IOA* 1C **80**
Llanbeder. *Newp* 2G **33**
Llanbedr. *Gwyn* 3E **69**
Llanbedr. *Powy* 3F **47** (nr. Crickhowell)
Llanbedr. *Powy* 1E **47** (nr. Hay-on-Wye)
Llanbedr-Dyffryn-Clwyd. *Den* 5D **82**
Llanbedrgoch. *IOA* 2E **81**
Llanbedrog. *Gwyn* 2C **68**
Llanbedr Pont Steffan. *Cdgn* 1F **45**
Llanbedr-y-cennin. *Cnwy* 4G **81**
Llanberis. *Gwyn* 4E **81**
Llanbethery. *V Glam* 5D **32**
Llanbister. *Powy* 3D **58**
Llanblethian. *V Glam* 4C **32**
Llanboidy. *Carm* 2G **43**
Llanbradach. *Cphy* 2E **33**
Llanbrynmair. *Powy* 5A **70**
Llanbydderi. *V Glam* 5D **32**
Llancadle. *V Glam* 5D **32**
Llancarfan. *V Glam* 4D **32**
Llancatal. *V Glam* 5D **32**
Llancayo. *Mon* 5G **47**
Llancloudy. *Here* 3H **47**
Llancoch. *Powy* 3E **58**
Llancynfelyn. *Cdgn* 1F **57**
Llandaff. *Card* 4E **33**
Llandanwg. *Gwyn* 3E **69**
Llandarcy. *Neat* 3G **31**
Llandawke. *Carm* 3G **43**
Llanddaniel-Fab. *IOA* 3D **81**
Llanddarog. *Carm* 4F **45**
Llanddeiniol. *Cdgn* 3E **57**
Llanddeiniolen. *Gwyn* 4E **81**
Llandderfel. *Gwyn* 2B **70**
Llanddeusant. *Carm* 3A **46**
Llanddeusant. *IOA* 2C **80**
Llanddew. *Powy* 2D **46**
Llanddewi. *Swan* 4D **30**
Llanddewi Brefi. *Cdgn* 5F **57**
Llanddewi'r Cwm. *Powy* 1D **46**
Llanddewi Rhydderch. *Mon* 4G **47**
Llanddewi Velfrey. *Pemb* 3F **43**
Llanddewi Ystradenni. *Powy* 4D **58**
Llanddoged. *Cnwy* 4H **81**
Llanddona. *IOA* 3E **81**
Llanddowror. *Carm* 3G **43**
Llanddulas. *Cnwy* 3B **82**
Llanddwywe. *Gwyn* 3E **69**
Llanddyfnan. *IOA* 3E **81**
Llandecwyn. *Gwyn* 2F **69**
Llandefaelog Fach. *Powy* 2D **46**
Llandefaelog-tre'r-graig. *Powy* 2E **47**
Llandefalle. *Powy* 2E **46**
Llandegfan. *IOA* 3E **81**
Llandegla. *Den* 5D **82**
Llandegley. *Powy* 4D **58**
Llandegveth. *Mon* 2G **33**
Llandeilo. *Carm* 3G **45**
Llandeilo Graban. *Powy* 1D **46**
Llandeilo'r Fan. *Powy* 2B **46**
Llandeloy. *Pemb* 2C **42**
Llandenny. *Mon* 5H **47**
Llandevaud. *Newp* 2H **33**
Llandevenny. *Mon* 3G **33**
Llandilo. *Pemb* 2F **43**
Llandinabo. *Here* 3A **48**
Llandinam. *Powy* 2C **58**
Llandissilio. *Pemb* 2F **43**
Llandogo. *Mon* 5A **48**
Llandough. *V Glam* 4C **32** (nr. Cowbridge)
Llandough. *V Glam* 4E **33** (nr. Penarth)
Llandovery. *Carm* 2A **46**
Llandow. *V Glam* 4C **32**
Llandre. *Cdgn* 2F **57**
Llandrillo. *Den* 2C **70**
Llandrillo-yn-Rhos. *Cnwy* 2H **81**
Llandrindod. *Powy* 4C **58**
Llandrindod Wells. *Powy* 4C **58**
Llandrinio. *Powy* 4E **71**
Llandsadwrn. *Carm* 2G **45**
Llandudno. *Cnwy* 2G **81**
Llandudno Junction. *Cnwy* 3G **81**
Llandudoch. *Pemb* 1B **44**
Llandw. *V Glam* 4C **32**
Llandwrog. *Gwyn* 5D **80**
Llandybie. *Carm* 4G **45**
Llandyfaelog. *Carm* 4E **45**
Llandyfan. *Carm* 4G **45**
Llandyfriog. *Cdgn* 1D **44**
Llandyfrydog. *IOA* 2D **80**
Llandygai. *Gwyn* 3E **81**
Llandygwydd. *Cdgn* 1C **44**
Llandynan. *Den* 1D **70**
Llandyrnog. *Den* 4D **82**
Llandysilio. *Powy* 4E **71**
Llandyssil. *Powy* 1D **58**
Llandysul. *Cdgn* 1E **45**
Llanedeyrn. *Card* 3F **33**
Llaneglwys. *Powy* 2D **46**
Llanegryn. *Gwyn* 5F **69**
Llanegwad. *Carm* 3F **45**
Llaneilian. *IOA* 1D **80**
Llanelian-yn-Rhos. *Cnwy* 3A **82**
Llanelidan. *Den* 5D **82**
Llanelieu. *Powy* 2E **47**
Llanellen. *Mon* 4G **47**
Llanelli. *Carm* 3E **31**
Llanelltyd. *Gwyn* 4G **69**
Llanelly. *Mon* 4F **47**
Llanelly Hill. *Mon* 4F **47**
Llanelwedd. *Powy* 5C **58**
Llanelwy. *Den* 3C **82**
Llanenddwyn. *Gwyn* 3E **69**
Llanengan. *Gwyn* 3B **68**
Llanerch. *Powy* 1F **59**
Llanerchymedd. *IOA* 2D **80**
Llanerfyl. *Powy* 5C **70**
Llaneuddog. *IOA* 2D **80**
Llanfachraeth. *IOA* 2C **80**
Llanfaelog. *IOA* 3C **80**
Llanfaelrhys. *Gwyn* 3B **68**
Llanfaenor. *Mon* 4H **47**
Llanfaes. *IOA* 3F **81**
Llanfaes. *Powy* 3D **46**
Llanfaethlu. *IOA* 2C **80**
Llanfaglan. *Gwyn* 4D **80**
Llanfair. *Gwyn* 3E **69**
Llanfair. *Here* 1F **47**
Llanfair Caereinion. *Powy* 5D **70**
Llanfair Clydogau. *Cdgn* 5F **57**
Llanfair Dyffryn Clwyd. *Den* 5D **82**
Llanfairfechan. *Cnwy* 3F **81**
Llanfair-Nant-Gwyn. *Pemb* 1F **43**

Llanfair Pwllgwyngyll. *IOA* 3E **81**
Llanfair Talhaiarn. *Cnwy* 3B **82**
Llanfair Waterdine. *Shrp* 3E **59**
Llanfair-ym-Muallt. *Powy* 5C **58**
Llanfairyneubwll. *IOA* 3C **80**
Llanfairynghornwy. *IOA* 1C **80**
Llanfallteg. *Carm* 3F **43**
Llanfallteg West. *Carm* 3F **43**
Llanfaredd. *Powy* 5C **58**
Llanfarian. *Cdgn* 3E **57**
Llanfechain. *Powy* 3D **70**
Llanfechell. *IOA* 1C **80**
Llanfechreth. *Gwyn* 3G **69**
Llanfendigaid. *Gwyn* 5E **69**
Llanferres. *Den* 4D **82**
Llan Ffestiniog. *Gwyn* 1G **69**
Llanfflewyn. *IOA* 2C **80**
Llanfihangel Glyn Myfyr. *Cnwy* 1B **70**
Llanfihangel Nant Bran. *Powy* 2C **46**
Llanfihangel-Nant-Melan. *Powy* 5D **58**
Llanfihangel Rhydithon. *Powy* 4D **58**
Llanfihangel Rogiet. *Mon* 3H **33**
Llanfihangel Tal-y-llyn. *Powy* 3E **46**
Llanfihangel-uwch-Gwili. *Carm* 3E **45**
Llanfihangel-yng-Ngwynfa. *Powy* 4C **70**
Llanfihangel yn Nhowyn. *IOA* 3C **80**
Llanfihangel-y-pennant. *Gwyn* 1E **69** (nr. Golan)
Llanfihangel-y-pennant. *Gwyn* 5F **69** (nr. Tywyn)
Llanfilo. *Powy* 2E **46**
Llanfinhangel-ar-Arth. *Carm* 2E **45**
Llanfinhangel-y-Creuddyn. *Cdgn* 3F **57**
Llanfinhangel-y-traethau. *Gwyn* 2E **69**
Llanfleiddan. *V Glam* 4C **32**
Llanfoist. *Mon* 4F **47**
Llanfor. *Gwyn* 2B **70**
Llanfrechfa. *Torf* 2G **33**
Llanfrothen. *Gwyn* 1F **69**
Llanfrynach. *Powy* 3D **46**
Llanfwrog. *Den* 5D **82**
Llanfwrog. *IOA* 2C **80**
Llanfyllin. *Powy* 4D **70**
Llanfynydd. *Carm* 3F **45**
Llanfynydd. *Flin* 5E **83**
Llanfyrnach. *Pemb* 1G **43**
Llangadfan. *Powy* 4C **70**
Llangadog. *Carm* 3H **45** (nr. Llandovery)
Llangadog. *Carm* 5E **45** (nr. Llanelli)
Llangadwaladr. *IOA* 4C **80**
Llangadwaladr. *Powy* 2D **70**
Llangaffo. *IOA* 4D **80**
Llangain. *Carm* 4D **45**
Llangammarch Wells. *Powy* 1C **46**
Llangan. *V Glam* 4C **32**
Llangarron. *Here* 3A **48**
Llangasty-Talyllyn. *Powy* 3E **47**
Llangathen. *Carm* 3F **45**
Llangattock. *Powy* 4F **47**
Llangattock Lingoed. *Mon* 3G **47**
Llangattock-Vibon-Avel. *Mon* 4H **47**
Llangedwyn. *Powy* 3D **70**
Llangefni. *IOA* 3D **80**
Llangeinor. *B'end* 3C **32**
Llangeitho. *Cdgn* 5F **57**
Llangeler. *Carm* 2D **44**
Llangelynin. *Gwyn* 5E **69**
Llangendeirne. *Carm* 4E **45**
Llangennech. *Carm* 5F **45**
Llangennith. *Swan* 3D **30**
Llangenny. *Powy* 4F **47**
Llangernyw. *Cnwy* 4A **82**
Llangian. *Gwyn* 3B **68**
Llangiwg. *Neat* 5H **45**
Llangloffan. *Pemb* 1D **42**
Llanglydwen. *Carm* 2F **43**
Llangoed. *IOA* 3F **81**
Llangoedmor. *Cdgn* 1B **44**
Llangollen. *Den* 1E **70**
Llangolman. *Pemb* 2F **43**
Llangorse. *Powy* 3E **47**
Llangorwen. *Cdgn* 2F **57**
Llangovan. *Mon* 5H **47**
Llangower. *Gwyn* 2B **70**
Llangranog. *Cdgn* 5C **56**
Llangristiolus. *IOA* 3D **80**
Llangrove. *Here* 4A **48**
Llangua. *Mon* 3G **47**
Llangunllo. *Powy* 3E **58**
Llangunnor. *Carm* 3E **45**
Llangurig. *Powy* 3B **58**
Llangwm. *Cnwy* 1B **70**
Llangwm. *Mon* 5H **47**
Llangwm. *Pemb* 4D **43**
Llangwm-isaf. *Mon* 5H **47**
Llangwnnadl. *Gwyn* 2B **68**
Llangwyfan. *Den* 4D **82**
Llangwyfan-isaf. *IOA* 4C **80**
Llangwyllog. *IOA* 3D **80**
Llangwyryfon. *Cdgn* 3E **57**
Llangybi. *Cdgn* 5F **57**
Llangybi. *Gwyn* 1D **68**
Llangybi. *Mon* 2G **33**
Llangyfelach. *Swan* 3F **31**
Llangynhafal. *Den* 4D **82**
Llangynidr. *Powy* 4E **47**
Llangynin. *Carm* 3G **43**
Llangynog. *Carm* 3H **43**
Llangynog. *Powy* 3C **70**
Llangynwyd. *B'end* 3B **32**
Llanhamlach. *Powy* 3D **46**
Llanharan. *Rhon* 3D **32**
Llanharry. *Rhon* 3D **32**
Llanhennock. *Mon* 2G **33**
Llanhilleth. *Blae* 5F **47**
Llanidloes. *Powy* 2B **58**
Llaniestyn. *Gwyn* 2B **68**
Llanigon. *Powy* 1F **47**
Llanilar. *Cdgn* 3F **57**
Llanilid. *Rhon* 3C **32**
Llanilltud Fawr. *V Glam* 5C **32**
Llanishen. *Card* 3E **33**
Llanishen. *Mon* 5H **47**
Llanllawddog. *Carm* 3E **45**
Llanllechid. *Gwyn* 4F **81**
Llanllowell. *Mon* 2G **33**
Llanllugan. *Powy* 5C **70**
Llanllwch. *Carm* 4D **45**
Llanllwchaiarn. *Powy* 1D **58**
Llanllwni. *Carm* 2E **45**
Llanllyfni. *Gwyn* 5D **80**
Llanmadoc. *Swan* 3D **30**
Llanmaes. *V Glam* 5C **32**
Llanmartin. *Newp* 3G **33**
Llanmerwig. *Powy* 1D **58**
Llanmihangel. *V Glam* 4C **32**
Llan-mill. *Pemb* 3F **43**
Llanmiloe. *Carm* 4G **43**
Llanmorlais. *Swan* 3E **31**
Llannefydd. *Cnwy* 3B **82**
Llannon. *Carm* 5F **45**
Llan-non. *Cdgn* 4E **57**
Llannor. *Gwyn* 2C **68**
Llanpumsaint. *Carm* 3E **45**
Llanrhaeadr. *Den* 4C **82**
Llanrhaeadr-ym-Mochnant. *Powy* 3D **70**
Llanrhidian. *Swan* 3D **31**
Llanrhos. *Cnwy* 2G **81**
Llanrhyddlad. *IOA* 2C **80**
Llanrhystud. *Cdgn* 4E **57**
Llanrian. *Pemb* 1C **42**
Llanrothal. *Here* 4H **47**
Llanrug. *Gwyn* 4E **81**
Llanrumney. *Card* 3F **33**
Llanrwst. *Cnwy* 4G **81**
Llansadurnen. *Carm* 3G **43**
Llansadwrn. *IOA* 3E **81**
Llansaint. *Carm* 5D **45**
Llansamlet. *Swan* 3F **31**
Llansanffraid Glan Conwy. *Cnwy* 3H **81**
Llansannan. *Cnwy* 4B **82**
Llansannor. *V Glam* 4C **32**
Llansantffraed. *Cdgn* 4E **57**
Llansantffraed. *Powy* 3E **46**
Llansantffraed Cwmdeuddwr. *Powy* 4B **58**
Llansantffraed in Elwel. *Powy* 5C **58**
Llansantffraid-ym-Mechain. *Powy* 3E **70**
Llansawel. *Carm* 2G **45**
Llansawel. *Neat* 3G **31**
Llansilin. *Powy* 3E **70**
Llansoy. *Mon* 5H **47**
Llanspyddid. *Powy* 3D **46**
Llanstadwell. *Pemb* 4D **42**
Llansteffan. *Carm* 3H **43**
Llanstephan. *Powy* 1E **46**
Llantarnam. *Torf* 2F **33**
Llanteg. *Pemb* 3F **43**
Llanthony. *Mon* 3F **47**
Llantilio Crossenny. *Mon* 4G **47**
Llantilio Pertholey. *Mon* 4G **47**
Llantood. *Pemb* 1B **44**
Llantrisant. *Mon* 2G **33**
Llantrisant. *Rhon* 3D **32**
Llantrithyd. *V Glam* 4D **32**
Llantwit Fardre. *Rhon* 3D **32**
Llantwit Major. *V Glam* 5C **32**
Llanuwchllyn. *Gwyn* 2A **70**
Llanvaches. *Newp* 2H **33**
Llanvair Discoed. *Mon* 2H **33**
Llanvapley. *Mon* 4G **47**
Llanvetherine. *Mon* 4G **47**
Llanveynoe. *Here* 2G **47**
Llanvihangel Crucorney. *Mon* 3G **47**
Llanvihangel Gobion. *Mon* 5G **47**
Llanvihangel Ystern-Llewern. *Mon* 4H **47**
Llanwarne. *Here* 3A **48**
Llanwddyn. *Powy* 4C **70**
Llanwenarth. *Mon* 4F **47**
Llanwenog. *Cdgn* 1E **45**
Llanwern. *Newp* 3G **33**
Llanwinio. *Carm* 2G **43**
Llanwnda. *Gwyn* 5D **81**
Llanwnda. *Pemb* 1D **42**
Llanwnnen. *Cdgn* 1F **45**
Llanwnog. *Powy* 1C **58**
Llanwrda. *Carm* 2H **45**
Llanwrin. *Powy* 5G **69**
Llanwrthwl. *Powy* 4B **58**
Llanwrtud. *Powy* 1B **46**
Llanwrtyd. *Powy* 1B **46**
Llanwrtyd Wells. *Powy* 1B **46**
Llanwyddelan. *Powy* 5C **70**
Llanyblodwel. *Shrp* 3E **71**
Llanybri. *Carm* 3H **43**
Llanybydder. *Carm* 1F **45**
Llanycefn. *Pemb* 2E **43**
Llanychaer. *Pemb* 1D **43**
Llanycil. *Gwyn* 2B **70**
Llanymawddwy. *Gwyn* 4B **70**
Llanymddyfri. *Carm* 2A **46**
Llanymynech. *Shrp* 3E **71**
Llanynghenedl. *IOA* 2C **80**
Llanynys. *Den* 4D **82**
Llan-y-pwll. *Wrex* 5F **83**
Llanyrafon. *Torf* 2G **33**
Llanyre. *Powy* 4C **58**
Llanystumdwy. *Gwyn* 2D **68**
Llanywern. *Powy* 3E **46**
Llawhaden. *Pemb* 3E **43**
Llawndy. *Flin* 2D **82**
Llawnt. *Shrp* 2E **71**
Llawr Dref. *Gwyn* 3B **68**
Llawryglyn. *Powy* 1B **58**
Llay. *Wrex* 5F **83**
Llechfaen. *Powy* 3D **46**
Llechryd. *Cphy* 5E **46**
Llechryd. *Cdgn* 1C **44**
Llechrydau. *Wrex* 2E **71**
Lledrod. *Cdgn* 3F **57**
Llethrid. *Swan* 3E **31**
Llidiad-Nenog. *Carm* 2F **45**
Llidiardau. *Gwyn* 2A **70**
Llidiart y Parc. *Den* 1D **70**
Llithfaen. *Gwyn* 1C **68**
Lloc. *Flin* 3D **82**
Llong. *Flin* 4E **83**
Llowes. *Powy* 1E **47**
Lloyney. *Powy* 3E **59**
Llundain-fach. *Cdgn* 5E **57**
Llwydcoed. *Rhon* 5C **46**
Llwyncelyn. *Cdgn* 5D **56**
Llwyncelyn. *Swan* 5G **45**
Llwyndaffydd. *Cdgn* 5C **56**
Llwynderw. *Powy* 5E **70**
Llwyn-du. *Mon* 4F **47**
Llwyngwril. *Gwyn* 5E **69**
Llwynhendy. *Carm* 3E **31**
Llwynmawr. *Wrex* 2E **71**
Llwyn-on Village. *Mer T* 4D **46**
Llwyn-teg. *Carm* 5F **45**
Llwyn-y-brain. *Carm* 3F **43**
Llwynygog. *Powy* 1A **58**
Llwyn-y-groes. *Cdgn* 5E **57**
Llwynypia. *Rhon* 2C **32**
Llynclys. *Shrp* 3E **71**
Llynfaes. *IOA* 3D **80**
Llysfaen. *Cnwy* 3A **82**
Llyswen. *Powy* 2E **47**
Llysworney. *V Glam* 4C **32**
Llys-y-fran. *Pemb* 2E **43**
Llywel. *Powy* 2B **46**
Llywernog. *Cdgn* 2G **57**
Loan. *Falk* 2C **128**
Loanend. *Nmbd* 4F **131**
Loanhead. *Midl* 3F **129**
Loaningfoot. *Dum* 4A **112**
Loanreoch. *High* 1A **158**
Loans. *S Ayr* 1C **116**
Loansdean. *Nmbd* 1F **115**
Lobb. *Devn* 3E **19**
Lobhillcross. *Devn* 4E **11**
Lochaber. *Mor* 3E **159**
Loch a Charnain. *W Isl* 4D **170**
Lochailort. *High* 5F **147**
Lochaline. *High* 4A **140**
Lochans. *Dum* 4F **109**
Locharbriggs. *Dum* 1A **112**
Lochardil. *High* 4A **158**
Lochassynt Lodge. *High* 1F **163**
Lochavich. *Arg* 2G **133**
Lochawe. *Arg* 1A **134**
Loch Baghasdail. *W Isl* 7C **170**
Lochboisdale. *W Isl* 7C **170**
Lochbuie. *Arg* 1D **132**
Lochcarron. *High* 5A **156**
Loch Choire Lodge. *High* 5G **167**
Lochdochart House. *Stir* 1D **134**
Lochdon. *Arg* 5B **140**
Lochearnhead. *Stir* 1E **135**
Lochee. *D'dee* 5C **144**
Lochend. *High* 5H **157** (nr. Inverness)
Lochend. *High* 2E **169** (nr. Thurso)
Locherben. *Dum* 5B **118**
Loch Euphort. *W Isl* 2D **170**
Lochfoot. *Dum* 2F **111**
Lochgair. *Arg* 4G **133**
Lochgarthside. *High* 2H **149**
Lochgelly. *Fife* 4D **136**
Lochgilphead. *Arg* 1G **125**
Lochgoilhead. *Arg* 3A **134**
Loch Head. *Dum* 5A **110**
Lochhill. *Mor* 2G **159**
Lochindorb Lodge. *High* 5D **158**
Lochinver. *High* 1E **163**
Lochlane. *Per* 1H **135**
Loch Lomond. *Arg* 3C **134**
Loch Loyal Lodge. *High* 4G **167**
Lochluichart. *High* 2F **157**
Lochmaben. *Dum* 1B **112**
Lochmaddy. *W Isl* 2E **170**
Loch nam Madadh. *W Isl* 2E **170**
Lochore. *Fife* 4D **136**
Lochportain. *W Isl* 1E **170**
Lochranza. *N Ayr* 4H **125**
Loch Sgioport. *W Isl* 5D **170**
Lochside. *Abers* 2G **145**
Lochside. *High* 5A **168** (nr. Achentoul)
Lochside. *High* 3C **158** (nr. Nairn)
Lochslin. *High* 5F **165**
Lochstack Lodge. *High* 4C **166**
Lochton. *Abers* 4E **153**
Lochty. *Fife* 3H **137**
Lochuisge. *High* 3B **140**
Lochussie. *High* 3G **157**
Lochwinnoch. *Ren* 4E **127**
Lochyside. *High* 1F **141**
Lockengate. *Corn* 2E **7**
Lockerbie. *Dum* 1C **112**
Lockeridge. *Wilts* 5G **35**
Lockerley. *Hants* 4A **24**
Lockhills. *Cumb* 5G **113**
Locking. *N Som* 1G **21**
Lockington. *E Yor* 5D **101**
Lockington. *Leics* 3B **74**
Lockleywood. *Shrp* 3A **72**
Locksgreen. *IOW* 3C **16**
Locks Heath. *Hants* 2D **16**
Lockton. *N Yor* 5F **107**
Loddington. *Leics* 5E **75**
Loddington. *Nptn* 3F **63**
Loddiswell. *Devn* 4D **8**
Loddon. *Norf* 1F **67**
Lode. *Cambs* 4E **65**
Loders. *Dors* 3H **13**
Lodsworth. *W Sus* 3A **26**
Lofthouse. *N Yor* 2D **98**
Lofthouse. *W Yor* 2D **92**
Lofthouse Gate. *W Yor* 2D **92**
Loftus. *Red C* 3E **107**
Logan. *E Ayr* 2E **117**
Loganlea. *W Lot* 3C **128**
Logaston. *Here* 5F **59**
Loggerheads. *Staf* 2B **72**
Loggie. *High* 4F **163**
Logie. *Ang* 2F **145**
Logie. *Fife* 1G **137**
Logie. *Mor* 3E **159**
Logie Coldstone. *Abers* 3B **152**
Logie Pert. *Ang* 2F **145**
Logierait. *Per* 3G **143**
Login. *Carm* 2F **43**
Lolworth. *Cambs* 4C **64**
Lonbain. *High* 3F **155**
Londesborough. *E Yor* 5C **100**
London. *G Lon* 2E **39**
London Apprentice. *Corn* 3E **6**
London Ashford (Lydd) Airport. *Kent* 3E **29**
London City Airport. *G Lon* 2F **39**
London Colney. *Herts* 5B **52**
Londonderry. *N Yor* 1F **99**
London Gatwick Airport. *W Sus* 1D **27**
London Heathrow Airport. *G Lon* 3B **38**
London Luton Airport. *Lutn* 3B **52**
London Southend Airport. *Essx* 2C **40**
London Stansted Airport. *Essx* 3F **53**
Londonthorpe. *Linc* 2G **75**
Londubh. *High* 5C **162**
Lone. *High* 4D **166**
Lonemore. *High* 5E **165** (nr. Dornoch)
Lonemore. *High* 1G **155** (nr. Gairloch)
Long Ashton. *N Som* 4A **34**
Long Bank. *Worc* 3B **60**
Longbar. *N Ayr* 4E **127**
Long Bennington. *Linc* 1F **75**
Longbenton. *Tyne* 3F **115**
Longborough. *Glos* 3G **49**
Long Bredy. *Dors* 3A **14**
Longbridge. *Warw* 4G **61**
Longbridge. *W Mid* 3E **61**
Longbridge Deverill. *Wilts* 2D **22**

Long Buckby. *Nptn* 4D **62**
Long Buckby Wharf. *Nptn* 4D **62**
Longburgh. *Cumb* 4E **112**
Longburton. *Dors* 1B **14**
Long Clawson. *Leics* 3E **74**
Longcliffe. *Derbs* 5G **85**
Long Common. *Hants* 1D **16**
Long Compton. *Staf* 3C **72**
Long Compton. *Warw* 2A **50**
Longcot. *Oxon* 2A **36**
Long Crendon. *Buck* 5E **51**
Long Crichel. *Dors* 1E **15**
Longcroft. *Cumb* 4D **112**
Longcroft. *Falk* 2A **128**
Longcross. *Surr* 4A **38**
Longdale. *Cumb* 4H **103**
Longdales. *Cumb* 5G **113**
Longden. *Shrp* 5G **71**
Longden Common. *Shrp* 5G **71**
Long Ditton. *Surr* 4C **38**
Longdon. *Staf* 4E **73**
Longdon. *Worc* 2D **48**
Longdon Green. *Staf* 4E **73**
Longdon on Tern. *Telf* 4A **72**
Longdown. *Devn* 3B **12**
Longdowns. *Corn* 5B **6**
Long Drax. *N Yor* 2G **93**
Long Duckmanton. *Derbs* 3B **86**
Long Eaton. *Derbs* 2B **74**
Longfield. *Kent* 4H **39**
Longfield Hill. *Kent* 4H **39**
Longford. *Derbs* 2G **73**
Longford. *Glos* 3D **48**
Longford. *G Lon* 3B **38**
Longford. *Shrp* 2A **72**
Longford. *Telf* 4B **72**
Longford. *W Mid* 2H **61**
Longforgan. *Per* 1F **137**
Longformacus. *Bord* 4C **130**
Longframlington. *Nmbd* 4F **121**
Long Gardens. *Essx* 2B **54**
Long Green. *Ches W* 3G **83**
Long Green. *Worc* 2D **48**
Longham. *Dors* 3F **15**
Longham. *Norf* 4B **78**
Long Hanborough. *Oxon* 4C **50**
Longhedge. *Wilts* 2D **22**
Longhill. *Abers* 3H **161**
Longhirst. *Nmbd* 1F **115**
Longhope. *Glos* 4B **48**
Longhope. *Orkn* 8C **172**
Longhorsley. *Nmbd* 5F **121**
Longhoughton. *Nmbd* 3G **121**
Long Itchington. *Warw* 4B **62**
Longlands. *Cumb* 1D **102**
Longlane. *Derbs* 2G **73**
Long Lane. *Telf* 4A **72**
Longlane. *W Ber* 4C **36**
Long Lawford. *Warw* 3B **62**
Long Lease. *N Yor* 4G **107**
Longley Green. *Worc* 5B **60**
Long Load. *Som* 4H **21**
Longmanhill. *Abers* 2E **161**
Long Marston. *Herts* 4G **51**
Long Marston. *N Yor* 4H **99**
Long Marston. *Warw* 1G **49**
Long Marton. *Cumb* 2H **103**
Long Meadow. *Cambs* 4E **65**
Long Meadowend. *Shrp* 2G **59**
Long Melford. *Suff* 1B **54**
Longmoor Camp. *Hants* 3F **25**
Longmorn. *Mor* 3G **159**
Longmoss. *Ches E* 3C **84**
Long Newnton. *Glos* 2E **35**
Longnewton. *Bord* 2H **119**
Long Newton. *Stoc T* 3A **106**
Longney. *Glos* 4C **48**
Longniddry. *E Lot* 2H **129**
Longnor. *Shrp* 5G **71**
Longnor. *Staf* 4E **85**
(nr. Leek)
Longnor. *Staf* 4C **72**
(nr. Stafford)
Longparish. *Hants* 2C **24**
Longpark. *Cumb* 3F **113**
Long Preston. *N Yor* 4H **97**
Longridge. *Lanc* 1E **90**
Longridge. *Staf* 4D **72**
Longridge. *W Lot* 3C **128**
Longriggend. *N Lan* 2B **128**
Long Riston. *E Yor* 5F **101**
Longrock. *Corn* 3C **4**
Longsdon. *Staf* 5D **84**
Longshaw. *G Man* 4D **90**
Longshaw. *Staf* 1E **73**
Longside. *Abers* 4H **161**
Longslow. *Shrp* 2A **72**
Longstanton. *Cambs* 4C **64**
Longstock. *Hants* 3B **24**
Longstowe. *Cambs* 5C **64**
Long Stratton. *Norf* 1D **66**
Long Street. *Mil* 1F **51**
Longstreet. *Wilts* 1G **23**
Long Sutton. *Hants* 2F **25**
Long Sutton. *Linc* 3D **76**
Long Sutton. *Som* 4H **21**
Longthorpe. *Pet* 1A **64**
Long Thurlow. *Suff* 4C **66**
Longthwaite. *Cumb* 2F **103**
Longton. *Lanc* 2C **90**
Longton. *Stoke* 1D **72**
Longtown. *Cumb* 3E **113**
Longtown. *Here* 3G **47**
Longville in the Dale. *Shrp* 1H **59**
Long Whatton. *Leics* 3B **74**
Longwick. *Buck* 5F **51**
Long Wittenham. *Oxon* 2D **36**
Longwitton. *Nmbd* 1D **115**
Longworth. *Oxon* 2B **36**
Longyester. *E Lot* 3B **130**
Lonmore. *High* 4B **154**
Looe. *Corn* 3G **7**
Loose. *Kent* 5B **40**
Loosegate. *Linc* 3C **76**
Loosley Row. *Buck* 5G **51**
Lopcombe Corner. *Wilts* 3A **24**
Lopen. *Som* 1H **13**
Loppington. *Shrp* 3G **71**
Lorbottle. *Nmbd* 4E **121**
Lorbottle Hall. *Nmbd* 4E **121**
Lordington. *W Sus* 2F **17**
Loscoe. *Derbs* 1B **74**
Loscombe. *Dors* 3A **14**
Losgaintir. *W Isl* 8C **171**
Lossiemouth. *Mor* 2G **159**
Lossit. *Arg* 4A **124**
Lostock Gralam. *Ches W* 3A **84**
Lostock Green. *Ches W* 3A **84**
Lostock Hall. *Lanc* 2D **90**
Lostock Junction. *G Man* 4E **91**
Lostwithiel. *Corn* 3F **7**
Lothbeg. *High* 2G **165**
Lothersdale. *N Yor* 5B **98**
Lothianbridge. *Midl* 3G **129**
Lothianburn. *Edin* 3F **129**
Lothmore. *High* 2G **165**
Lottisham. *Som* 3A **22**
Loudwater. *Buck* 1A **38**
Loughborough. *Leics* 4C **74**
Loughor. *Swan* 3E **31**
Loughton. *Essx* 1F **39**
Loughton. *Mil* 2G **51**
Loughton. *Shrp* 2A **60**
Lound. *Linc* 4H **75**
Lound. *Notts* 2D **86**
Lound. *Suff* 1H **67**
Lount. *Leics* 4A **74**
Louth. *Linc* 2C **88**
Love Clough. *Lanc* 2G **91**
Lovedean. *Hants* 1E **17**
Lover. *Wilts* 4H **23**
Loversall. *S Yor* 1C **86**
Loves Green. *Essx* 5G **53**
Loveston. *Pemb* 4E **43**
Lovington. *Som* 3A **22**
Low Ackworth. *W Yor* 3E **93**
Low Angerton. *Nmbd* 1D **115**
Low Ardwell. *Dum* 5F **109**
Low Ballochdoan. *S Ayr* 2F **109**
Lowbands. *Glos* 2C **48**
Low Barlings. *Linc* 3H **87**
Low Bell End. *N Yor* 5E **107**
Low Bentham. *N Yor* 3F **97**
Low Borrowbridge. *Cumb* 4H **103**
Low Bradfield. *S Yor* 1G **85**
Low Bradley. *N Yor* 5C **98**
Low Braithwaite. *Cumb* 5F **113**
Low Brunton. *Nmbd* 2C **114**
Low Burnham. *N Lin* 4A **94**
Lowca. *Cumb* 2A **102**
Low Catton. *E Yor* 4B **100**
Low Coniscliffe. *Darl* 3F **105**
Low Coylton. *S Ayr* 3D **116**
Low Crosby. *Cumb* 4F **113**
Low Dalby. *N Yor* 1C **100**
Lowdham. *Notts* 1D **74**
Low Dinsdale. *Darl* 3A **106**
Lowe. *Shrp* 2G **71**
Low Ellington. *N Yor* 1E **98**
Lower Amble. *Corn* 1D **6**
Lower Ansty. *Dors* 2C **14**
Lower Arboll. *High* 5F **165**
Lower Arncott. *Oxon* 4E **50**
Lower Ashton. *Devn* 4B **12**
Lower Assendon. *Oxon* 3F **37**
Lower Auchenreath. *Mor* 2A **160**
Lower Badcall. *High* 4B **166**
Lower Ballam. *Lanc* 1B **90**
Lower Basildon. *W Ber* 4E **36**
Lower Beeding. *W Sus* 3D **26**
Lower Benefield. *Nptn* 2G **63**
Lower Bentley. *Worc* 4D **61**
Lower Beobridge. *Shrp* 1B **60**
Lower Bockhampton. *Dors* 3C **14**
Lower Boddington. *Nptn* 5B **62**
Lower Bordean. *Hants* 4E **25**
Lower Brailes. *Warw* 2B **50**
Lower Breakish. *High* 1E **147**
Lower Broadheath. *Worc* 5C **60**
Lower Brynamman. *Neat* 4H **45**
Lower Bullingham. *Here* 2A **48**
Lower Bullington. *Hants* 2C **24**
Lower Burgate. *Hants* 1G **15**
Lower Cam. *Glos* 5C **48**
Lower Catesby. *Nptn* 5C **62**
Lower Chapel. *Powy* 2D **46**
Lower Cheriton. *Devn* 2E **12**
Lower Chicksgrove. *Wilts* 3E **23**
Lower Chute. *Wilts* 1B **24**
Lower Clopton. *Warw* 5F **61**
Lower Common. *Hants* 2E **25**
Lower Cumberworth. *W Yor* 4C **92**
Lower Darwen. *Bkbn* 2E **91**
Lower Dean. *Bed* 4H **63**
Lower Dean. *Devn* 2D **8**
Lower Diabaig. *High* 2G **155**
Lower Dicker. *E Sus* 4G **27**
Lower Dounreay. *High* 2B **168**
Lower Down. *Shrp* 2F **59**
Lower Dunsforth. *N Yor* 3G **99**
Lower East Carleton. *Norf* 5D **78**
Lower Egleton. *Here* 1B **48**
Lower Ellastone. *Derbs* 1F **73**
Lower End. *Nptn* 4F **63**
Lower Everleigh. *Wilts* 1G **23**
Lower Eype. *Dors* 3H **13**
Lower Failand. *N Som* 4A **34**
Lower Faintree. *Shrp* 2A **60**
Lower Farringdon. *Hants* 3F **25**
Lower Foxdale. *IOM* 4B **108**
Lower Frankton. *Shrp* 2F **71**
Lower Froyle. *Hants* 2F **25**
Lower Gabwell. *Devn* 2F **9**
Lower Gledfield. *High* 4C **164**
Lower Godney. *Som* 2H **21**
Lower Gravenhurst. *C Beds* 2B **52**
Lower Green. *Essx* 2E **53**
Lower Green. *Norf* 2B **78**
Lower Green. *Staf* 5D **72**
Lower Green. *W Ber* 5B **36**
Lower Halstow. *Kent* 4C **40**
Lower Hardres. *Kent* 5F **41**
Lower Hardwick. *Here* 5G **59**
Lower Hartshay. *Derbs* 5A **86**
Lower Hawthwaite. *Cumb* 1B **96**
Lower Hayton. *Shrp* 2H **59**
Lower Hergest. *Here* 5E **59**
Lower Heyford. *Oxon* 3C **50**
Lower Heysham. *Lanc* 3D **96**
Lower Higham. *Kent* 3B **40**
Lower Holbrook. *Suff* 2E **55**
Lower Holditch. *Dors* 2G **13**
Lower Hordley. *Shrp* 3F **71**
Lower Horncroft. *W Sus* 4B **26**
Lower Kilcott. *Glos* 3C **34**
Lower Killeyan. *Arg* 5A **124**
Lower Kingcombe. *Dors* 3A **14**
Lower Kingswood. *Surr* 5D **38**
Lower Kinnerton. *Ches W* 4F **83**
Lower Langford. *N Som* 5H **33**
Lower Largo. *Fife* 3G **137**
Lower Layham. *Suff* 1D **54**
Lower Ledwyche. *Shrp* 3H **59**
Lower Leigh. *Staf* 2E **73**
Lower Lemington. *Glos* 2H **49**
Lower Lenie. *High* 1H **149**
Lower Ley. *Glos* 4C **48**
Lower Llanfadog. *Powy* 4B **58**
Lower Lode. *Glos* 2D **49**
Lower Lovacott. *Devn* 4F **19**
Lower Loxhore. *Devn* 3G **19**
Lower Loxley. *Staf* 2E **73**
Lower Lydbrook. *Glos* 4A **48**
Lower Lye. *Here* 4G **59**
Lower Machen. *Newp* 3F **33**
Lower Maes-coed. *Here* 2G **47**
Lower Meend. *Glos* 5A **48**
Lower Milovaig. *High* 3A **154**
Lower Moor. *Worc* 1E **49**
Lower Morton. *S Glo* 2B **34**
Lower Mountain. *Flin* 5F **83**
Lower Nazeing. *Essx* 5D **53**
Lower Netchwood. *Shrp* 1A **60**
Lower Nyland. *Dors* 4C **22**
Lower Oakfield. *Fife* 4D **136**
Lower Oddington. *Glos* 3H **49**
Lower Ollach. *High* 5E **155**
Lower Penarth. *V Glam* 5E **33**
Lower Penn. *Staf* 1C **60**
Lower Pennington. *Hants* 3B **16**
Lower Peover. *Ches W* 3B **84**
Lower Pilsley. *Derbs* 4B **86**
Lower Pitkerrie. *High* 1C **158**
Lower Place. *G Man* 3H **91**
Lower Quinton. *Warw* 1G **49**
Lower Rainham. *Medw* 4C **40**
Lower Raydon. *Suff* 2D **54**
Lower Seagry. *Wilts* 3E **35**
Lower Shelton. *C Beds* 1H **51**
Lower Shiplake. *Oxon* 4F **37**
Lower Shuckburgh. *Warw* 4B **62**
Lower Sketty. *Swan* 3F **31**
Lower Slade. *Devn* 2F **19**
Lower Slaughter. *Glos* 3G **49**
Lower Soudley. *Glos* 4B **48**
Lower Stanton St Quintin. *Wilts* 3E **35**
Lower Stoke. *Medw* 3C **40**
Lower Stondon. *C Beds* 2B **52**
Lower Stonnall. *Staf* 5E **73**
Lower Stow Bedon. *Norf* 1B **66**
Lower Street. *Norf* 2E **79**
Lower Strensham. *Worc* 1E **49**
Lower Sundon. *C Beds* 3A **52**
Lower Swanwick. *Hants* 2C **16**
Lower Swell. *Glos* 3G **49**
Lower Tale. *Devn* 2D **12**
Lower Tean. *Staf* 2E **73**
Lower Thurlton. *Norf* 1G **67**
Lower Thurnham. *Lanc* 4D **96**
Lower Thurvaston. *Derbs* 2G **73**
Lowertown. *Corn* 4D **4**
Lower Town. *Here* 1B **48**
Lower Town. *IOS* 1B **4**
Lower Town. *Pemb* 1D **42**
Lower Tysoe. *Warw* 1B **50**
Lower Upham. *Hants* 1D **16**
Lower Upnor. *Medw* 3B **40**
Lower Vexford. *Som* 3E **20**
Lower Walton. *Warr* 2A **84**
Lower Wear. *Devn* 4C **12**
Lower Weare. *Som* 1H **21**
Lower Welson. *Here* 5E **59**
Lower Whatcombe. *Dors* 2D **14**
Lower Whitley. *Ches W* 3A **84**
Lower Wield. *Hants* 2E **25**
Lower Withington. *Ches E* 4C **84**
Lower Woodend. *Buck* 3G **37**
Lower Woodford. *Wilts* 3G **23**
Lower Wraxall. *Dors* 2A **14**
Lower Wych. *Ches W* 1G **71**
Lower Wyche. *Worc* 1C **48**
Lowesby. *Leics* 5E **74**
Lowestoft. *Suff* 1H **67**
Loweswater. *Cumb* 2C **102**
Low Etherley. *Dur* 2E **105**
Lowfield Heath. *W Sus* 1D **26**
Lowford. *Hants* 1C **16**
Low Fulney. *Linc* 3B **76**
Low Gate. *Nmbd* 3C **114**
Lowgill. *Cumb* 5H **103**
Lowgill. *Lanc* 3F **97**
Low Grantley. *N Yor* 2E **99**
Low Green. *N Yor* 4E **98**
Low Habberley. *Worc* 3C **60**
Low Ham. *Som* 4H **21**
Low Hameringham. *Linc* 4C **88**
Low Hawkser. *N Yor* 4G **107**
Low Hesket. *Cumb* 5F **113**
Low Hesleyhurst. *Nmbd* 5E **121**
Lowick. *Cumb* 1B **96**
Lowick. *Nptn* 2G **63**
Lowick. *Nmbd* 1E **121**
Lowick Bridge. *Cumb* 1B **96**
Lowick Green. *Cumb* 1B **96**
Low Knipe. *Cumb* 3G **103**
Low Leighton. *Derbs* 2E **85**
Low Lorton. *Cumb* 2C **102**
Low Marishes. *N Yor* 2C **100**
Low Marnham. *Notts* 4F **87**
Low Mill. *N Yor* 5D **106**
Low Moor. *Lanc* 5G **97**
Low Moor. *W Yor* 2B **92**
Low Moorsley. *Tyne* 5G **115**
Low Newton-by-the-Sea. *Nmbd* 2G **121**
Lownie Moor. *Ang* 4D **145**
Lowood. *Bord* 1H **119**
Low Row. *Cumb* 3G **113**
(nr. Brampton)
Low Row. *Cumb* 5C **112**
(nr. Wigton)
Low Row. *N Yor* 5C **104**
Lowsonford. *Warw* 4F **61**
Low Street. *Norf* 5C **78**
Lowther. *Cumb* 2G **103**
Lowthorpe. *E Yor* 3E **101**
Lowton. *Devn* 2G **11**
Lowton. *G Man* 1A **84**
Lowton. *Som* 1E **13**
Lowton Common. *G Man* 1A **84**
Low Torry. *Fife* 1D **128**
Low Toynton. *Linc* 3B **88**
Low Valleyfield. *Fife* 1C **128**
Low Westwood. *Dur* 4E **115**
Low Whinnow. *Cumb* 4E **112**
Low Wood. *Cumb* 1C **96**
Low Worsall. *N Yor* 4A **106**
Low Wray. *Cumb* 4E **103**
Loxbeare. *Devn* 1C **12**
Loxhill. *Surr* 2B **26**
Loxhore. *Devn* 3G **19**
Loxley. *S Yor* 2H **85**
Loxley. *Warw* 5G **61**
Loxley Green. *Staf* 2E **73**
Loxton. *N Som* 1G **21**
Loxwood. *W Sus* 2B **26**
Lubcroy. *High* 3A **164**
Lubenham. *Leics* 2E **62**
Lubinvullin. *High* 2F **167**

Luccombe. Som	2C 20
Luccombe Village. IOW	4D 16
Lucker. Nmbd	1F 121
Luckett. Corn	5D 11
Luckington. Wilts	3D 34
Lucklawhill. Fife	1G 137
Luckwell Bridge. Som	3C 20
Lucton. Here	4G 59
Ludag. W Isl	7C 170
Ludborough. Linc	1B 88
Ludchurch. Pemb	3F 43
Luddenden. W Yor	2A 92
Luddenden Foot. W Yor	2A 92
Luddenham. Kent	4D 40
Ludderburn. Cumb	5F 103
Luddesdown. Kent	4A 40
Luddington. N Lin	3B 94
Luddington. Warw	5F 61
Luddington in the Brook. Nptn	2A 64
Ludford. Linc	2A 88
Ludford. Shrp	3H 59
Ludgershall. Buck	4E 51
Ludgershall. Wilts	1A 24
Ludgvan. Corn	3C 4
Ludham. Norf	4F 79
Ludlow. Shrp	3H 59
Ludstone. Shrp	1C 60
Ludwell. Wilts	4E 23
Ludworth. Dur	5G 115
Luffenhall. Herts	3C 52
Luffincott. Devn	3D 10
Lugar. E Ayr	2E 117
Luggate Burn. E Lot	2C 130
Lugg Green. Here	4G 59
Luggiebank. N Lan	2A 128
Lugton. E Ayr	4F 127
Lugwardine. Here	1A 48
Luib. High	1D 146
Luib. Stir	1D 135
Lulham. Here	1H 47
Lullington. Derbs	4G 73
Lullington. E Sus	5G 27
Lullington. Som	1C 22
Lulsgate Bottom. N Som	5A 34
Lulsley. Worc	5B 60
Lulworth Camp. Dors	4D 14
Lumb. Lanc	2G 91
Lumb. W Yor	2A 92
Lumby. N Yor	1E 93
Lumphanan. Abers	3C 152
Lumphinnans. Fife	4D 136
Lumsdaine. Bord	3E 131
Lumsden. Abers	1B 152
Lunan. Ang	3F 145
Lunanhead. Ang	3D 145
Luncarty. Per	1C 136
Lund. E Yor	5D 100
Lund. N Yor	1G 93
Lundie. Ang	5B 144
Lundin Links. Fife	3G 137
Lundy Green. Norf	1E 67
Lunna. Shet	5F 173
Lunning. Shet	5G 173
Lunnon. Swan	4E 31
Lunsford. Kent	5B 40
Lunsford's Cross. E Sus	4B 28
Lunt. Mers	4B 90
Luppitt. Devn	2E 13
Lupridge. Devn	3D 8
Lupset. W Yor	3D 92
Lupton. Cumb	1E 97
Lurgashall. W Sus	3A 26
Lurley. Devn	1C 12
Lusby. Linc	4C 88
Luscombe. Devn	3D 9
Luson. Devn	4C 8
Luss. Arg	4C 134
Lussagiven. Arg	1E 125
Lusta. High	3B 154
Lustleigh. Devn	4A 12
Luston. Here	4G 59
Luthermuir. Abers	2F 145
Luthrie. Fife	2F 137
Lutley. Staf	2C 60

Luton. Devn	2D 12
(nr. Honiton)	
Luton. Devn	5C 12
(nr. Teignmouth)	
Luton. Devn	3A 52
Luton (London) Airport.	
Lutn	3B 52
Lutterworth. Leics	2C 62
Lutton. Devn	3B 8
Lutton. Devn	2C 8
(nr. Ivybridge)	
Lutton. Devn	2C 8
(nr. South Brent)	
Lutton. Linc	3D 76
Lutton. Nptn	2A 64
Lutton Gowts. Linc	3D 76
Lutworthy. Devn	1A 12
Luxborough. Som	3C 20
Luxley. Glos	3B 48
Luxulyan. Corn	3E 7
Lybster. High	5E 169
Lydbury North. Shrp	2F 59
Lydcott. Devn	3G 19
Lydd. Kent	3E 29
Lydden. Kent	1G 29
(nr. Dover)	
Lydden. Kent	4H 41
(nr. Margate)	
Lyddington. Rut	1F 63
Lydd (London Ashford) Airport.	
Kent	3E 29
Lydd-on-Sea. Kent	3E 29
Lydeard St Lawrence. Som	3E 21
Lyde Green. Hants	1F 25
Lydford. Devn	4F 11
Lydford Fair Place. Som	3A 22
Lydgate. G Man	4H 91
Lydgate. W Yor	2H 91
Lydham. Shrp	1F 59
Lydiard Millicent. Wilts	3F 35
Lydiate. Mers	4B 90
Lydiate Ash. Worc	3D 61
Lydlinch. Dors	1C 14
Lydmarsh. Som	2G 13
Lydney. Glos	5B 48
Lydstep. Pemb	5E 43
Lye. W Mid	2D 60
Lye Green. Buck	5H 51
Lye Green. E Sus	2G 27
Lye Head. Worc	3B 60
Lye, The. Shrp	1A 60
Lyford. Oxon	2B 36
Lyham. Nmbd	1E 121
Lylestone. N Ayr	5E 127
Lymbridge Green. Kent	1F 29
Lyme Regis. Dors	3G 13
Lyminge. Kent	1F 29
Lymington. Hants	3B 16
Lyminster. W Sus	5B 26
Lymm. Warr	2A 84
Lymore. Hants	3A 16
Lympne. Kent	2F 29
Lympsham. Som	1G 21
Lympstone. Devn	4C 12
Lynaberack Lodge. High	4B 150
Lynbridge. Devn	2H 19
Lynch. Som	2C 20
Lynchat. High	3B 150
Lynch Green. Norf	5D 78
Lyndhurst. Hants	2B 16
Lyndon. Rut	5G 75
Lyne. Bord	5F 129
Lyne. Surr	4B 38
Lyneal. Shrp	2G 71
Lyne Down. Here	2B 48
Lyneham. Oxon	3A 50
Lyneham. Wilts	4F 35
Lyneholmeford. Cumb	2G 113
Lynemouth. Nmbd	5G 121
Lyne of Gorthleck.	
High	1H 149
Lyne of Skene. Abers	2E 153
Lynesack. Dur	2D 105
Lyness. Orkn	8C 172
Lyng. Norf	4C 78

Lyngate. Norf	2E 79
(nr. North Walsham)	
Lyngate. Norf	3F 79
(nr. Worstead)	
Lynmouth. Devn	2H 19
Lynn. Staf	5E 73
Lynn. Telf	4B 72
Lynsted. Kent	4D 40
Lynstone. Corn	2C 10
Lynton. Devn	2H 19
Lynwilg. High	2C 150
Lyon's Gate. Dors	2B 14
Lyonshall. Here	5F 59
Lytchett Matravers. Dors	3E 15
Lytchett Minster. Dors	3E 15
Lyth. High	2E 169
Lytham. Lanc	2B 90
Lytham St Anne's. Lanc	2B 90
Lythe. N Yor	3F 107
Lythes. Orkn	9D 172
Lythmore. High	2C 168

M

Mabe Burnthouse. Corn	5B 6
Mabie. Dum	2A 112
Mablethorpe. Linc	2E 89
Macbiehill. Bord	4E 129
Macclesfield. Ches E	3D 84
Macclesfield Forest. Ches E	3D 85
Macduff. Abers	2E 160
Machan. S Lan	4A 128
Macharioch. Arg	5B 122
Machen. Cphy	3F 33
Machrie. N Ayr	2C 122
Machrihanish. Arg	3A 122
Machroes. Gwyn	3C 68
Machynlleth. Powy	5G 69
Mackerye End. Herts	4B 52
Mackworth. Derb	2H 73
Macmerry. E Lot	2H 129
Madderty. Per	1B 136
Maddington. Wilts	2F 23
Maddiston. Falk	2C 128
Madehurst. W Sus	4A 26
Madeley. Staf	1B 72
Madeley. Telf	5A 72
Madeley Heath. Staf	1B 72
Madeley Heath. Worc	3D 60
Madford. Devn	1E 13
Madingley. Cambs	4C 64
Madley. Here	2H 47
Madresfield. Worc	1D 48
Madron. Corn	3B 4
Maenaddwyn. IOA	2D 80
Maenclochog. Pemb	2E 43
Maendy. V Glam	4D 32
Maenporth. Corn	4E 5
Maentwrog. Gwyn	1F 69
Maen-y-groes. Cdgn	5C 56
Maer. Staf	2B 72
Maerdy. Carm	3G 45
Maerdy. Cnwy	1C 70
Maerdy. Rhon	2C 32
Maesbrook. Shrp	3F 71
Maesbury. Shrp	3F 71
Maesbury Marsh. Shrp	3F 71
Maes-glas. Flin	3D 82
Maesgwyn-Isaf. Powy	4D 70
Maeshafn. Den	4E 82
Maes Llyn. Cdgn	1D 44
Maesmynis. Powy	1D 46
Maesteg. B'end	2B 32
Maestir. Cdgn	1F 45
Maesybont. Carm	4F 45
Maesycrugiau. Carm	1E 45
Maesycwmmer. Cphy	2E 33
Maesyrhandir. Powy	1C 58
Magdalen Laver. Essx	5F 53
Maggieknockater. Mor	4H 159
Magham Down. E Sus	4H 27
Maghull. Mers	4B 90
Magna Park. Leics	2C 62

Magor. Mon	3H 33
Magpie Green. Suff	3C 66
Magwyr. Mon	3H 33
Maidenbower. W Sus	2D 27
Maiden Bradley. Wilts	3D 22
Maidencombe. Torb	2F 9
Maidenhayne. Devn	3F 13
Maidenhead. Wind	3G 37
Maiden Law. Dur	5E 115
Maiden Newton. Dors	3A 14
Maidens. S Ayr	4B 116
Maiden's Green. Brac	4G 37
Maidensgrove. Oxon	3F 37
Maidenwell. Corn	5B 10
Maidenwell. Linc	3C 88
Maiden Wells. Pemb	5D 42
Maidford. Nptn	5D 62
Maids Moreton. Buck	2F 51
Maidstone. Kent	5B 40
Maidwell. Nptn	3E 63
Mail. Shet	9F 173
Maindee. Newp	3G 33
Mainsforth. Dur	1A 106
Mains of Auchindachy. Mor	4B 160
Mains of Auchnagatt. Abers	4G 161
Mains of Drum. Abers	4F 153
Mains of Edingight. Mor	3C 160
Mainsriddle. Dum	4G 111
Mainstone. Shrp	2E 59
Maisemore. Glos	3D 48
Major's Green. Worc	3F 61
Makeney. Derbs	1A 74
Makerstoun. Bord	1A 120
Malacleit. W Isl	1C 170
Malaig. High	4E 147
Malaig Bheag. High	4E 147
Malborough. Devn	5D 8
Malcoff. Derbs	2E 85
Malcolmburn. Mor	3A 160
Malden Rushett. G Lon	4C 38
Maldon. Essx	5B 54
Malham. N Yor	3B 98
Maligar. High	2D 155
Malinslee. Telf	5A 72
Mallaig. High	4E 147
Malleny Mills. Edin	3E 129
Mallows Green. Essx	3E 53
Malltraeth. IOA	4D 80
Mallwyd. Gwyn	4A 70
Malmesbury. Wilts	3E 35
Malmsmead. Devn	2A 20
Malpas. Ches W	1G 71
Malpas. Corn	4C 6
Malpas. Newp	2F 33
Malswick. Glos	3C 48
Maltby. S Yor	1C 86
Maltby. Stoc T	3B 106
Maltby le Marsh. Linc	2D 88
Malt Lane. Arg	3H 133
Maltman's Hill. Kent	1D 28
Malton. N Yor	2B 100
Malvern Link. Worc	1C 48
Malvern Wells. Worc	1C 48
Mamble. Worc	3A 60
Mamhilad. Mon	5G 47
Manaccan. Corn	4E 5
Manafon. Powy	5D 70
Manaton. Devn	4A 12
Manby. Linc	2C 88
Mancetter. Warw	1H 61
Manchester. G Man	1C 84
Manchester International Airport.	
G Man	2C 84
Mancot. Flin	4F 83
Manea. Cambs	2D 65
Maney. W Mid	1F 61
Manfield. N Yor	3F 105
Mangotsfield. S Glo	4B 34
Mangurstadh. W Isl	4C 171
Mankinholes. W Yor	2H 91
Manley. Ches W	3H 83
Manmoel. Cphy	5E 47
Mannal. Arg	4A 138
Mannerston. Falk	2D 128

Manningford Bohune. Wilts	1G 23
Manningford Bruce. Wilts	1G 23
Manningham. W Yor	1B 92
Mannings Heath. W Sus	3D 26
Mannington. Dors	2F 15
Manningtree. Essx	2E 54
Mannofield. Aber	3G 153
Manor. Pemb	5E 43
Manorbier. Pemb	5E 43
Manorbier Newton. Pemb	5E 43
Manorowen. Pemb	1D 42
Manor Park. G Lon	2F 39
Mansell Gamage. Here	1G 47
Mansell Lacy. Here	1H 47
Mansergh. Cumb	1F 97
Mansewood. Glas	3G 127
Mansfield. E Ayr	3F 117
Mansfield. Notts	4C 86
Mansfield Woodhouse. Notts	4C 86
Mansriggs. Cumb	1B 96
Manston. Dors	1D 14
Manston. Kent	4H 41
Manston. W Yor	1D 92
Manswood. Dors	2E 15
Manthorpe. Linc	4H 75
(nr. Bourne)	
Manthorpe. Linc	2G 75
(nr. Grantham)	
Manton. N Lin	4C 94
Manton. Notts	3C 86
Manton. Rut	5F 75
Manton. Wilts	5G 35
Manuden. Essx	3E 53
Maperton. Som	4B 22
Maplebeck. Notts	4E 86
Maple Cross. Herts	1B 38
Mapledurham. Oxon	4E 37
Mapledurwell. Hants	1E 25
Maplehurst. W Sus	3C 26
Maplescombe. Kent	4G 39
Mapperley. Derbs	1B 74
Mapperley. Notts	1C 74
Mapperley Park. Notts	1C 74
Mapperton. Dors	3A 14
(nr. Beaminster)	
Mapperton. Dors	3E 15
(nr. Poole)	
Mappleborough Green. Warw	4E 61
Mappleton. Derbs	1F 73
Mappleton. E Yor	5G 101
Mapplewell. S Yor	4D 92
Mappowder. Dors	2C 14
Maraig. W Isl	7E 171
Marazion. Corn	3C 4
Marbhig. W Isl	6G 171
Marbury. Ches E	1H 71
March. Cambs	1D 64
Marcham. Oxon	2C 36
Marchamley. Shrp	3H 71
Marchington. Staf	2F 73
Marchington Woodlands. Staf	3F 73
Marchwiel. Wrex	1F 71
Marchwood. Hants	1B 16
Marcross. V Glam	5C 32
Marden. Here	1A 48
Marden. Kent	1B 28
Marden. Wilts	1F 23
Marden Beech. Kent	1B 28
Marden Thorn. Kent	1B 28
Mardu. Shrp	2E 59
Mardy. Mon	4G 47
Marefield. Leics	5E 75
Mareham le Fen. Linc	4B 88
Mareham on the Hill. Linc	4B 88
Marehay. Derbs	1A 74
Marehill. W Sus	4B 26
Maresfield. E Sus	3F 27
Marfleet. Hull	2E 95
Marford. Wrex	5F 83
Margam. Neat	3A 32
Margaret Marsh. Dors	1D 14
Margaret Roding. Essx	4F 53
Margaretting. Essx	5G 53
Margaretting Tye. Essx	5G 53
Margate. Kent	3H 41

Margery—Mere Green

Margery. *Surr* 5D 38
Margnaheglish. *N Ayr* 2E 123
Marham. *Norf* 5G 77
Marhamchurch. *Corn* 2C 10
Marholm. *Pet* 5A 76
Marian Cwm. *Den* 3C 82
Mariandyrys. *IOA* 2F 81
Marian-glas. *IOA* 2E 81
Mariansleigh. *Devn* 4H 19
Marian-y-de. *Gwyn* 2C 68
Marine Town. *Kent* 3D 40
Marion-y-mor. *Gwyn* 2C 68
Marishader. *High* 2D 155
Marjoriebanks. *Dum* 1B 112
Mark. *Dum* 4G 109
Mark. *Som* 2G 21
Markbeech. *Kent* 1F 27
Markby. *Linc* 3D 89
Mark Causeway. *Som* 2G 21
Mark Cross. *E Sus* 2G 27
Markeaton. *Derb* 2H 73
Market Bosworth. *Leics* 5B 74
Market Deeping. *Linc* 4A 76
Market Drayton. *Shrp* 2A 72
Market End. *Warw* 2H 61
Market Harborough. *Leics* 2E 63
Markethill. *Per* 5B 144
Market Lavington. *Wilts* 1F 23
Market Overton. *Rut* 4F 75
Market Rasen. *Linc* 2A 88
Market Stainton. *Linc* 2B 88
Market Weighton. *E Yor* 5C 100
Market Weston. *Suff* 3B 66
Markfield. *Leics* 4B 74
Markham. *Cphy* 5E 47
Markinch. *Fife* 3E 137
Markington. *N Yor* 3E 99
Marksbury. *Bath* 5B 34
Mark's Corner. *IOW* 3C 16
Marks Tey. *Essx* 3C 54
Markwell. *Corn* 3H 7
Markyate. *Herts* 4A 52
Marlborough. *Wilts* 5G 35
Marlcliff. *Warw* 5E 61
Marldon. *Devn* 2E 9
Marle Green. *E Sus* 4G 27
Marlesford. *Suff* 5F 67
Marley Green. *Ches E* 1H 71
Marley Hill. *Tyne* 4F 115
Marlingford. *Norf* 5D 78
Mar Lodge. *Abers* 5E 151
Marloes. *Pemb* 4B 42
Marlow. *Buck* 3G 37
Marlow. *Here* 3G 59
Marlow Bottom. *Buck* 3G 37
Marlow Common. *Buck* 3G 37
Marlpit Hill. *Kent* 1F 27
Marlpits. *E Sus* 3F 27
Marlpool. *Derbs* 1B 74
Marnhull. *Dors* 1C 14
Marnoch. *Abers* 3C 160
Marnock. *N Lan* 3A 128
Marple. *G Man* 2D 84
Marr. *S Yor* 4F 93
Marrel. *High* 2H 165
Marrick. *N Yor* 5D 105
Marros. *Carm* 4G 43
Marsden. *Tyne* 3G 115
Marsden. *W Yor* 3A 92
Marsett. *N Yor* 1B 98
Marsh. *Buck* 5G 51
Marsh. *Devn* 1F 13
Marshall Meadows. *Nmbd* 4F 131
Marshalsea. *Dors* 2G 13
Marshalswick. *Herts* 5B 52
Marsham. *Norf* 3D 78
Marshaw. *Lanc* 4E 97
Marsh Baldon. *Oxon* 2D 36
Marsh Benham. *W Ber* 5C 36
Marshborough. *Kent* 5H 41
Marshbrook. *Shrp* 2G 59
Marshbury. *Essx* 4G 53
Marshchapel. *Linc* 1C 88
Marshfield. *Newp* 3F 33
Marshfield. *S Glo* 4C 34
Marshgate. *Corn* 3B 10
Marsh Gibbon. *Buck* 3E 51
Marsh Green. *Devn* 3D 12
Marsh Green. *Kent* 1F 27
Marsh Green. *Staf* 5C 84
Marsh Green. *Telf* 4A 72
Marsh Lane. *Derbs* 3B 86
Marshside. *Kent* 4G 41
Marshside. *Mers* 3B 90
Marsh Side. *Norf* 1G 77
Marsh Street. *Som* 2C 20
Marsh, The. *Powy* 1F 59
Marsh, The. *Shrp* 3A 72
Marshwood. *Dors* 3G 13
Marske. *N Yor* 4E 105
Marske-by-the-Sea. *Red C* 2D 106
Marston. *Ches W* 3A 84
Marston. *Here* 5F 59
Marston. *Linc* 1F 75
Marston. *Oxon* 5D 50
Marston. *Staf* 3D 72
(nr. Stafford)
Marston. *Staf* 4C 72
(nr. Wheaton Aston)
Marston. *Warw* 1G 61
Marston. *Wilts* 1E 23
Marston Doles. *Warw* 5B 62
Marston Green. *W Mid* 2F 61
Marston Hill. *Glos* 2G 35
Marston Jabbett. *Warw* 2A 62
Marston Magna. *Som* 4A 22
Marston Meysey. *Wilts* 2G 35
Marston Montgomery. *Derbs* 2F 73
Marston Moretaine. *C Beds* 1H 51
Marston on Dove. *Derbs* 3G 73
Marston St Lawrence. *Nptn* 1D 50
Marston Stannett. *Here* 5H 59
Marston Trussell. *Nptn* 2D 62
Marstow. *Here* 4A 48
Marsworth. *Buck* 4H 51
Marten. *Wilts* 5A 36
Marthall. *Ches E* 3C 84
Martham. *Norf* 4G 79
Marthwaite. *Cumb* 5H 103
Martin. *Hants* 1F 15
Martin. *Kent* 1H 29
Martin. *Linc* 4B 88
(nr. Horncastle)
Martin. *Linc* 5A 88
(nr. Metheringham)
Martindale. *Cumb* 3F 103
Martin Dales. *Linc* 4A 88
Martin Drove End. *Hants* 4F 23
Martinhoe. *Devn* 2G 19
Martinhoe Cross. *Devn* 2G 19
Martin Hussingtree. *Worc* 4C 60
Martin Mill. *Kent* 1H 29
Martinscroft. *Warr* 2A 84
Martin's Moss. *Ches E* 4C 84
Martinstown. *Dors* 4B 14
Martlesham. *Suff* 1F 55
Martlesham Heath. *Suff* 1F 55
Martletwy. *Pemb* 3E 43
Martley. *Worc* 5B 60
Martock. *Som* 1H 13
Marton. *Ches E* 4C 84
Marton. *Cumb* 2B 96
Marton. *E Yor* 3G 101
(nr. Bridlington)
Marton. *E Yor* 1E 95
(nr. Hull)
Marton. *Linc* 2F 87
Marton. *Midd* 3C 106
Marton. *N Yor* 3G 99
(nr. Boroughbridge)
Marton. *N Yor* 1B 100
(nr. Pickering)
Marton. *Shrp* 3G 71
(nr. Myddle)
Marton. *Shrp* 5E 71
(nr. Worthen)
Marton. *Warw* 4B 62
Marton Abbey. *N Yor* 3H 99
Marton-le-Moor. *N Yor* 2F 99
Martyr's Green. *Surr* 5B 38
Martyr Worthy. *Hants* 3D 24
Marwood. *Devn* 3F 19
Marybank. *High* 3G 157
(nr. Dingwall)
Marybank. *High* 1B 158
(nr. Invergordon)
Maryburgh. *High* 3H 157
Maryfield. *Corn* 3A 8
Maryhill. *Glas* 3G 127
Marykirk. *Abers* 2F 145
Marylebone. *G Lon* 2D 39
Marylebone. *G Man* 4D 90
Marypark. *Mor* 5F 159
Maryport. *Cumb* 1B 102
Maryport. *Dum* 5E 109
Marystow. *Devn* 4E 11
Mary Tavy. *Devn* 5F 11
Maryton. *Ang* 3C 144
(nr. Kirriemuir)
Maryton. *Ang* 3F 145
(nr. Montrose)
Marywell. *Abers* 4C 152
Marywell. *Ang* 4F 145
Masham. *N Yor* 1E 98
Mashbury. *Essx* 4G 53
Masongill. *N Yor* 2F 97
Masons Lodge. *Abers* 3F 153
Mastin Moor. *Derbs* 3B 86
Mastrick. *Aber* 3G 153
Matching. *Essx* 4F 53
Matching Green. *Essx* 4F 53
Matching Tye. *Essx* 4F 53
Matfen. *Nmbd* 2D 114
Matfield. *Kent* 1A 28
Mathern. *Mon* 2A 34
Mathon. *Here* 1C 48
Mathry. *Pemb* 1C 42
Matlaske. *Norf* 2D 78
Matlock. *Derbs* 4G 85
Matlock Bath. *Derbs* 5G 85
Matterdale End. *Cumb* 2E 103
Mattersey. *Notts* 2D 86
Mattersey Thorpe. *Notts* 2D 86
Mattingley. *Hants* 1F 25
Mattishall. *Norf* 4C 78
Mattishall Burgh. *Norf* 4C 78
Mauchline. *E Ayr* 2D 117
Maud. *Abers* 4G 161
Maudlin. *Corn* 2E 7
Maugersbury. *Glos* 3G 49
Maughold. *IOM* 2D 108
Maulden. *C Beds* 2A 52
Maulds Meaburn. *Cumb* 3H 103
Maunby. *N Yor* 1F 99
Maund Bryan. *Here* 5H 59
Mautby. *Norf* 4G 79
Mavesyn Ridware. *Staf* 4E 73
Mavis Enderby. *Linc* 4C 88
Mawbray. *Cumb* 5B 112
Mawdesley. *Lanc* 3C 90
Mawdlam. *B'end* 3B 32
Mawgan. *Corn* 4E 5
Mawgan Porth. *Corn* 2C 6
Maw Green. *Ches E* 5B 84
Mawla. *Corn* 4B 6
Mawnan. *Corn* 4E 5
Mawnan Smith. *Corn* 4E 5
Mawsley Village. *Nptn* 3F 63
Mawthorpe. *Linc* 3D 88
Maxey. *Pet* 5A 76
Maxstoke. *Warw* 2G 61
Maxted Street. *Kent* 1F 29
Maxton. *Kent* 1G 29
Maxton. *Bord* 1A 120
Maxwellheugh. *Bord* 1B 120
Maxwelltown. *Dum* 2A 112
Maxworthy. *Corn* 3C 10
Mayals. *Swan* 4F 31
Maybole. *S Ayr* 4C 116
Maybush. *Sotn* 1B 16
Mayes Green. *Surr* 2C 26
Mayfield. *E Sus* 3G 27
Mayfield. *Midl* 3G 129
Mayfield. *Per* 1C 136
Mayfield. *Staf* 1F 73
Mayford. *Surr* 5A 38
Mayhill. *Swan* 3F 31
Mayland. *Essx* 5C 54
Maylandsea. *Essx* 5C 54
Maynard's Green. *E Sus* 4G 27
Maypole. *IOS* 1B 4
Maypole. *Kent* 4G 41
Maypole. *Mon* 4H 47
Maypole Green. *Norf* 1G 67
Maypole Green. *Suff* 5B 66
Mayshill. *S Glo* 3B 34
Maywick. *Shet* 9E 173
Mead. *Devn* 1C 10
Meadgate. *Bath* 1B 22
Meadle. *Buck* 5G 51
Meadowbank. *Ches W* 4A 84
Meadowfield. *Dur* 1F 105
Meadow Green. *Here* 5B 60
Meadowmill. *E Lot* 2H 129
Meadows. *Nott* 2C 74
Meadowtown. *Shrp* 5F 71
Meadwell. *Devn* 4E 11
Meaford. *Staf* 2C 72
Mealabost. *W Isl* 2G 171
(nr. Borgh)
Mealabost. *W Isl* 4G 171
(nr. Stornoway)
Meal Bank. *Cumb* 5G 103
Mealrigg. *Cumb* 5C 112
Mealsgate. *Cumb* 5D 112
Meanwood. *W Yor* 1C 92
Mearbeck. *N Yor* 3H 97
Meare. *Som* 2H 21
Meare Green. *Som* 4F 21
(nr. Curry Mallet)
Meare Green. *Som* 4G 21
(nr. Stoke St Gregory)
Mears Ashby. *Nptn* 4F 63
Measham. *Leics* 4H 73
Meath Green. *Surr* 1D 27
Meathop. *Cumb* 1D 96
Meaux. *E Yor* 1D 94
Meavy. *Devn* 2B 8
Medbourne. *Leics* 1E 63
Medburn. *Nmbd* 2E 115
Meddon. *Devn* 1C 10
Meden Vale. *Notts* 4C 86
Medlam. *Linc* 5C 88
Medlicott. *Shrp* 1G 59
Medmenham. *Buck* 3G 37
Medomsley. *Dur* 4E 115
Medstead. *Hants* 3E 25
Medway Towns. *Medw* 4B 40
Meerbrook. *Staf* 4D 85
Meer End. *W Mid* 3G 61
Meers Bridge. *Linc* 2D 89
Meesden. *Herts* 2E 53
Meeson. *Telf* 3A 72
Meeth. *Devn* 2F 11
Meeting Green. *Suff* 5G 65
Meeting House Hill. *Norf* 3F 79
Meidrim. *Carm* 2G 43
Meifod. *Powy* 4D 70
Meigle. *Per* 4B 144
Meikle Earnock. *S Lan* 4A 128
Meikle Kilchattan Butts. *Arg* 4B 126
Meikleour. *Per* 5A 144
Meikle Tarty. *Abers* 1G 153
Meikle Wartle. *Abers* 5E 160
Meinciau. *Carm* 4E 45
Meir. *Stoke* 1D 72
Meir Heath. *Staf* 1D 72
Melbourn. *Cambs* 1D 53
Melbourne. *Derbs* 3A 74
Melbourne. *E Yor* 5B 100
Melbury Abbas. *Dors* 4D 23
Melbury Bubb. *Dors* 2A 14
Melbury Osmond. *Dors* 2A 14
Melbury Sampford. *Dors* 2A 14
Melby. *Shet* 6C 173
Melchbourne. *Bed* 4H 63
Melcombe Bingham. *Dors* 2C 14
Melcombe Regis. *Dors* 4B 14
Meldon. *Devn* 3F 11
Meldon. *Nmbd* 1E 115
Meldreth. *Cambs* 1D 53
Melfort. *Arg* 2F 133
Melgarve. *High* 4G 149
Meliden. *Den* 2C 82
Melinbyrhedyn. *Powy* 1H 57
Melincourt. *Neat* 5B 46
Melin-y-coed. *Cnwy* 4H 81
Melin-y-ddol. *Powy* 5C 70
Melin-y-wig. *Den* 1C 70
Melkington. *Nmbd* 5E 131
Melkinthorpe. *Cumb* 2G 103
Melkridge. *Nmbd* 3A 114
Melksham. *Wilts* 5E 35
Mellangaun. *High* 5C 162
Melldalloch. *Arg* 2H 125
Mellguards. *Cumb* 5F 113
Melling. *Lanc* 2E 97
Melling. *Mers* 4B 90
Melling Mount. *Mers* 4C 90
Mellis. *Suff* 3C 66
Mellon Charles. *High* 4C 162
Mellon Udrigle. *High* 4C 162
Mellor. *G Man* 2D 85
Mellor. *Lanc* 1E 91
Mellor Brook. *Lanc* 1E 91
Mells. *Som* 2C 22
Melmerby. *Cumb* 1H 103
Melmerby. *N Yor* 1C 98
(nr. Middleham)
Melmerby. *N Yor* 2F 99
(nr. Ripon)
Melplash. *Dors* 3H 13
Melrose. *Bord* 1H 119
Melsonby. *N Yor* 4E 105
Meltham. *W Yor* 3A 92
Meltham Mills. *W Yor* 3B 92
Melton. *E Yor* 2C 94
Melton. *Suff* 5E 67
Meltonby. *E Yor* 4B 100
Melton Constable. *Norf* 2C 78
Melton Mowbray. *Leics* 4E 75
Melton Ross. *N Lin* 3D 94
Melvaig. *High* 5B 162
Melverley. *Shrp* 4F 71
Melverley Green. *Shrp* 4F 71
Melvich. *High* 2A 168
Membury. *Devn* 2F 13
Memsie. *Abers* 2G 161
Memus. *Ang* 3D 144
Menabilly. *Corn* 3E 7
Menai Bridge. *IOA* 3E 81
Mendham. *Suff* 2E 67
Mendlesham. *Suff* 4D 66
Mendlesham Green. *Suff* 4C 66
Menethorpe. *N Yor* 3B 100
Menheniot. *Corn* 2G 7
Menithwood. *Worc* 4B 60
Menna. *Corn* 3D 6
Mennock. *Dum* 4H 117
Menston. *W Yor* 5D 98
Menstrie. *Clac* 4H 135
Menthorpe. *N Yor* 1H 93
Mentmore. *Buck* 4H 51
Meole Brace. *Shrp* 4G 71
Meols. *Mers* 2E 83
Meon. *Hants* 2D 16
Meonstoke. *Hants* 4E 24
Meopham. *Kent* 4H 39
Meopham Green. *Kent* 4H 39
Meopham Station. *Kent* 4H 39
Mepal. *Cambs* 2D 64
Meppershall. *C Beds* 2B 52
Merbach. *Here* 1G 47
Mercaston. *Derbs* 1G 73
Merchiston. *Edin* 2F 129
Mere. *Ches E* 2B 84
Mere. *Wilts* 3D 22
Mere Brow. *Lanc* 3C 90
Mereclough. *Lanc* 1G 91
Mere Green. *W Mid* 1F 61

A-Z Great Britain Handy Road Atlas 225

Mere Green—Milton Hill

Mere Green. Worc 4D 60
Mere Heath. Ches W 3A 84
Mereside. Bkpl 1B 90
Meretown. Staf 3B 72
Mereworth. Kent 5A 40
Meriden. W Mid 2G 61
Merkadale. High 5C 154
Merkland. S Ayr 5B 116
Merkland Lodge. High 1A 164
Merley. Pool 3F 15
Merlin's Bridge. Pemb 3D 42
Merridge. Som 3F 21
Merrington. Shrp 3G 71
Merrion. Pemb 5D 42
Merriott. Som 1H 13
Merrivale. Devn 5F 11
Merrow. Surr 5B 38
Merrybent. Darl 3F 105
Merry Lees. Leics 5B 74
Merrymeet. Corn 2G 7
Mersham. Kent 2E 29
Merstham. Surr 5D 39
Merston. W Sus 2G 17
Merstone. IOW 4D 16
Merther. Corn 4C 6
Merthyr. Carm 3D 44
Merthyr Cynog. Powy 2C 46
Merthyr Dyfan. V Glam 4E 32
Merthyr Mawr. B'end 4B 32
Merthyr Tudful. Mer T 5D 46
Merthyr Tydfil. Mer T 5D 46
Merthyr Vale. Mer T 5D 46
Merton. Devn 1F 11
Merton. G Lon 4D 38
Merton. Norf 1B 66
Merton. Oxon 4D 50
Meshaw. Devn 1A 12
Messing. Essx 4B 54
Messingham. N Lin 4B 94
Metcombe. Devn 3D 12
Metfield. Suff 2E 67
Metherell. Corn 2A 8
Metheringham. Linc 4H 87
Methil. Fife 4F 137
Methilhill. Fife 4F 137
Methley. W Yor 2D 93
Methley Junction. W Yor 2D 93
Methlick. Abers 5F 161
Methven. Per 1C 136
Methwold. Norf 1G 65
Methwold Hythe. Norf 1G 65
Mettingham. Suff 1F 67
Metton. Norf 2D 78
Mevagissey. Corn 4E 6
Mexborough. S Yor 4E 93
Mey. High 1E 169
Meysey Hampton. Glos 2G 35
Miabhag. W Isl 8D 171
Miabhaig. W Isl 7C 171
(nr. Cliasmol)
Miabhaig. W Isl 4C 171
(nr. Timsgearraidh)
Mial. High 1G 155
Michaelchurch. Here 3A 48
Michaelchurch Escley. Here 2G 47
Michaelchurch-on-Arrow. Powy 5E 59
Michaelston-le-Pit. V Glam 4E 33
Michaelston-y-Fedw. Newp 3F 33
Michaelstow. Corn 5A 10
Michelcombe. Devn 2C 8
Micheldever. Hants 3D 24
Micheldever Station. Hants 2D 24
Michelmersh. Hants 4B 24
Mickfield. Suff 4D 66
Micklebring. S Yor 1C 86
Mickleby. N Yor 3F 107
Micklefield. W Yor 1E 93
Micklefield Green. Herts 1B 38
Mickleham. Surr 5C 38
Mickleover. Derb 2H 73
Micklethwaite. Cumb 4D 112
Micklethwaite. W Yor 5D 98
Mickleton. Dur 2C 104
Mickleton. Glos 1G 49
Mickletown. W Yor 2D 93
Mickle Trafford. Ches W 4G 83
Mickley. N Yor 2E 99
Mickley Green. Suff 5H 65
Mickley Square. Nmbd 3D 115
Mid Ardlaw. Abers 2G 161
Midbea. Orkn 3D 172
Mid Beltie. Abers 3D 152
Mid Calder. W Lot 3D 129
Mid Clyth. High 5E 169
Middle Assendon. Oxon 3F 37
Middle Aston. Oxon 3C 50
Middle Barton. Oxon 3C 50
Middlebie. Dum 2D 112
Middle Chinnock. Som 1H 13
Middle Claydon. Buck 3F 51
Middlecliffe. S Yor 4E 93
Middlecott. Devn 4H 11
Middle Drums. Ang 3E 145
Middle Duntisbourne. Glos 5E 49
Middle Essie. Abers 3H 161
Middleforth Green. Lanc 2D 90
Middleham. N Yor 1D 98
Middle Handley. Derbs 3B 86
Middle Harling. Norf 2B 66
Middlehope. Shrp 2G 59
Middle Littleton. Worc 1F 49
Middle Maes-coed. Here 2G 47
Middlemarsh. Dors 2B 14
Middle Marwood. Devn 3F 19
Middle Mayfield. Staf 1F 73
Middlemoor. Devn 5E 11
Middlemuir. Abers 4F 161
(nr. New Deer)
Middlemuir. Abers 3G 161
(nr. Strichen)
Middle Rainton. Tyne 5G 115
Middle Rasen. Linc 2H 87
Middlesbrough. Midd 3B 106
Middlesceugh. Cumb 5E 113
Middleshaw. Cumb 1E 97
Middlesmoor. N Yor 2C 98
Middles, The. Dur 4F 115
Middlestone. Dur 1F 105
Middlestone Moor. Dur 1F 105
Middle Stoughton. Som 2H 21
Middlestown. W Yor 3C 92
Middle Street. Glos 5C 48
Middle Taphouse. Corn 2F 7
Middleton. Ang 4E 145
Middleton. Arg 4A 138
Middleton. Cumb 1F 97
Middleton. Derbs 4F 85
(nr. Bakewell)
Middleton. Derbs 5G 85
(nr. Wirksworth)
Middleton. Essx 2B 54
Middleton. G Man 4G 91
Middleton. Hants 2C 24
Middleton. Hart 1C 106
Middleton. Here 4H 59
Middleton. IOW 4B 16
Middleton. Lanc 4D 96
Middleton. Midl 4G 129
Middleton. Norf 4F 77
Middleton. Nptn 1F 63
Middleton. Nmbd 1F 121
(nr. Belford)
Middleton. Nmbd 1D 114
(nr. Morpeth)
Middleton. N Yor 5D 98
(nr. Ilkley)
Middleton. N Yor 1B 100
(nr. Pickering)
Middleton. Per 3D 136
Middleton. Shrp 3H 59
(nr. Ludlow)
Middleton. Shrp 3F 71
(nr. Oswestry)
Middleton. Suff 4G 67
Middleton. Swan 4D 30
Middleton. Warw 1F 61
Middleton. W Yor 2D 92
Middleton Cheney. Nptn 1D 50
Middleton Green. Staf 2D 73
Middleton Hall. Nmbd 2D 121
Middleton-in-Teesdale. Dur 2C 104
Middleton One Row. Darl 3A 106
Middleton-on-Leven. N Yor 4B 106
Middleton-on-Sea. W Sus 5A 26
Middleton on the Hill. Here 4H 59
Middleton-on-the-Wolds. E Yor 5D 100
Middleton Priors. Shrp 1A 60
Middleton Quernhow. N Yor 2F 99
Middleton St George. Darl 3A 106
Middleton Scriven. Shrp 2A 60
Middleton Stoney. Oxon 3D 50
Middleton Tyas. N Yor 4F 105
Middletown. Cumb 4A 102
Middle Town. IOS 1B 4
Middletown. Powy 4F 71
Middle Tysoe. Warw 1B 50
Middle Wallop. Hants 3A 24
Middlewich. Ches E 4B 84
Middle Winterslow. Wilts 3H 23
Middlewood. Corn 5C 10
Middlewood. S Yor 1H 85
Middle Woodford. Wilts 3G 23
Middlewood Green. Suff 4C 66
Middleyard. Glos 5D 48
Middlezoy. Som 3G 21
Middridge. Dur 2F 105
Midelney. Som 4H 21
Midfield. High 2F 167
Midford. Bath 5C 34
Mid Garrary. Dum 2C 110
Midge Hall. Lanc 2D 90
Midgeholme. Cumb 4H 113
Midgham. W Ber 5D 36
Midgley. W Yor 2A 92
(nr. Halifax)
Midgley. W Yor 3C 92
(nr. Horbury)
Midhopestones. S Yor 1G 85
Midhurst. W Sus 4G 25
Mid Kirkton. N Ayr 4C 126
Mid Lambrook. Som 1H 13
Midland. Orkn 7C 172
Mid Lavant. W Sus 2G 17
Midlem. Bord 2H 119
Midney. Som 4A 22
Midsomer Norton. Bath 1B 22
Midton. Inv 2D 126
Midtown. High 5C 162
(nr. Poolewe)
Midtown. High 2F 167
(nr. Tongue)
Midville. Linc 5C 88
Midway. Derbs 3H 73
Mid Yell. Shet 2G 173
Migdale. High 4D 164
Migvie. Abers 3B 152
Milborne Port. Som 1B 14
Milborne St Andrew. Dors 3D 14
Milborne Wick. Som 4B 22
Milbourne. Nmbd 2E 115
Milbourne. Wilts 3E 35
Milburn. Cumb 2H 103
Milbury Heath. S Glo 2B 34
Milby. N Yor 3G 99
Milcombe. Oxon 2C 50
Milden. Suff 1C 54
Mildenhall. Suff 3G 65
Mildenhall. Wilts 5H 35
Milebrook. Powy 3F 59
Milebush. Kent 1B 28
Mile End. Cambs 2F 65
Mile End. Essx 3C 54
Mileham. Norf 4B 78
Mile Oak. Brig 5D 26
Miles Green. Staf 5C 84
Miles Hope. Here 4H 59
Milesmark. Fife 1D 128
Mile Town. Kent 3D 40
Milfield. Nmbd 1D 120
Milford. Derbs 1A 74
Milford. Devn 4C 18
Milford. Powy 1C 58
Milford. Staf 3D 72
Milford. Surr 1A 26
Milford Haven. Pemb 4D 42
Milford on Sea. Hants 3A 16
Milkwall. Glos 5A 48
Milkwell. Wilts 4E 23
Milland. W Sus 4G 25
Millbank. High 2D 168
Mill Bank. W Yor 2A 92
Millbeck. Cumb 2D 102
Millbounds. Orkn 4E 172
Millbreck. Abers 4H 161
Millbridge. Surr 2G 25
Millbrook. C Beds 2A 52
Millbrook. Corn 3A 8
Millbrook. G Man 1D 85
Millbrook. Sotn 1B 16
Mill Common. Suff 2G 67
Mill Corner. E Sus 3C 28
Milldale. Staf 5F 85
Millden Lodge. Ang 1E 145
Milldens. Ang 3E 145
Millearn. Per 2B 136
Mill End. Buck 3F 37
Mill End. Cambs 5F 65
Millend. Glos 2C 34
(nr. Dursley)
Mill End. Glos 4G 49
(nr. Northleach)
Mill End. Herts 2D 52
Millerhill. Midl 3G 129
Miller's Dale. Derbs 3F 85
Millers Green. Derbs 5G 85
Millerston. N Lan 3H 127
Millfield. Abers 4B 152
Millfield. Pet 1A 64
Millgate. Lanc 3G 91
Mill Green. Essx 5G 53
Mill Green. Norf 2D 66
Mill Green. Shrp 3A 72
Mill Green. Staf 3E 73
Mill Green. Suff 1C 54
Millhalf. Here 1F 47
Millhall. E Ren 4G 127
Millhayes. Devn 2F 13
(nr. Honiton)
Millhayes. Devn 1E 13
(nr. Wellington)
Millhead. Lanc 2D 97
Millheugh. S Lan 4A 128
Mill Hill. Bkbn 2E 91
Mill Hill. G Lon 1D 38
Millholme. Cumb 5G 103
Millhouse. Arg 2A 126
Millhouse. Cumb 1E 103
Millhousebridge. Dum 1C 112
Millhouses. S Yor 2H 85
Millikenpark. Ren 3F 127
Millington. E Yor 4C 100
Millington Green. Derbs 1G 73
Mill Knowe. Arg 3B 122
Mill Lane. Hants 1F 25
Millmeece. Staf 2C 72
Mill of Craigievar. Abers 2C 152
Mill of Fintray. Abers 2F 153
Mill of Haldane. W Dun 1F 127
Millom. Cumb 1A 96
Millow. C Beds 1C 52
Millpool. Corn 5B 10
Millport. N Ayr 4C 126
Mill Side. Cumb 1D 96
Mill Street. Norf 4C 78
(nr. Lyng)
Mill Street. Norf 4C 78
(nr. Swanton Morley)
Millthorpe. Derbs 3H 85
Millthorpe. Linc 2A 76
Millthrop. Cumb 5H 103
Milltimber. Aber 3F 153
Milltown. Abers 3G 151
(nr. Corgarff)
Milltown. Abers 2B 152
(nr. Lumsden)
Milltown. Corn 3F 7
Milltown. Derbs 4A 86
Milltown. Devn 3F 19
Milltown. Dum 2E 113
Milltown. Mor 4C 160
Milltown of Aberdalgie. Per 1C 136
Milltown of Auchindoun. Mor 4A 160
Milltown of Campfield. Abers 3D 152
Milltown of Edinville. Mor 4G 159
Milltown of Towie. Abers 2B 152
Milnacraig. Ang 3B 144
Milnathort. Per 3D 136
Milngavie. E Dun 2G 127
Milnholm. Stir 1A 128
Milnrow. G Man 3H 91
Milnthorpe. Cumb 1D 97
Milnthorpe. W Yor 3D 92
Milson. Shrp 3A 60
Milstead. Kent 5D 40
Milston. Wilts 2G 23
Milthorpe. Nptn 1D 50
Milton. Ang 4C 144
Milton. Cambs 4D 65
Milton. Cumb 2C 50
(nr. Banbury)
Milton. Cumb 3G 113
(nr. Brampton)
Milton. Cumb 1E 97
(nr. Crooklands)
Milton. Derbs 3H 73
Milton. Dum 2F 111
(nr. Crocketford)
Milton. Dum 4H 109
(nr. Glenluce)
Milton. E Ayr 2D 116
Milton. Glas 2G 127
Milton. High 3F 157
(nr. Achnasheen)
Milton. High 4G 155
(nr. Applecross)
Milton. High 5G 157
(nr. Drumnadrochit)
Milton. High 1B 158
(nr. Invergordon)
Milton. High 4H 157
(nr. Inverness)
Milton. High 3F 169
(nr. Wick)
Milton. Mor 2C 160
(nr. Cullen)
Milton. Mor 2F 151
(nr. Tomintoul)
Milton. N Som 5G 33
Milton. Notts 3E 86
Milton. Oxon 2C 36
Milton. Pemb 4E 43
Milton. Port 3E 17
Milton. Som 4H 21
Milton. Stir 3E 135
(nr. Aberfoyle)
Milton. Stir 4D 134
(nr. Drymen)
Milton. Stoke 5D 84
Milton. W Dun 2F 127
Milton Abbas. Dors 2D 14
Milton Abbot. Devn 5E 11
Milton Auchlossan. Abers 3C 152
Milton Bridge. Midl 3F 129
Milton Bryan. C Beds 2H 51
Milton Clevedon. Som 3B 22
Milton Coldwells. Abers 5G 161
Milton Combe. Devn 2A 8
Milton Common. Oxon 5E 51
Milton Damerel. Devn 1D 11
Miltonduff. Mor 2F 159
Milton End. Glos 5G 49
Milton Ernest. Bed 5H 63
Milton Green. Ches W 5G 83
Milton Hill. Devn 5C 12
Milton Hill. Oxon 2C 36

Milton Keynes—Mountgerald

Milton Keynes. *Mil* 2G 51
Milton Keynes Village. *Mil* 2G 51
Milton Lilbourne. *Wilts* 5G 35
Milton Malsor. *Nptn* 5E 63
Milton Morenish. *Per* 5D 142
Milton of Auchinhove. *Abers* 3C 152
Milton of Balgonie. *Fife* 3F 137
Milton of Barras. *Abers* 1H 145
Milton of Campsie. *E Dun* 2H 127
Milton of Cultoquhey. *Per* 1A 136
Milton of Cushnie. *Abers* 2C 152
Milton of Finavon. *Ang* 3D 145
Milton of Gollanfield. *High* 3B 158
Milton of Lesmore. *Abers* 1B 152
Milton of Tullich. *Abers* 4A 152
Milton on Stour. *Dors* 4C 22
Milton Regis. *Kent* 4C 40
Milton Street. *E Sus* 5G 27
Milton-under-Wychwood. *Oxon* 4A 50
Milverton. *Som* 4E 20
Milverton. *Warw* 4H 61
Milwich. *Staf* 2D 72
Mimbridge. *Surr* 4A 38
Minard. *Arg* 4G 133
Minchington. *Dors* 1E 15
Minchinhampton. *Glos* 5D 49
Mindrum. *Nmbd* 1C 120
Minehead. *Som* 2C 20
Minera. *Wrex* 5E 83
Minety. *Wilts* 2F 35
Minffordd. *Gwyn* 2E 69
Mingarrypark. *High* 2A 140
Mingary. *High* 2G 139
Mingearraidh. *W Isl* 6C 170
Miningsby. *Linc* 4C 88
Minions. *Corn* 5C 10
Minishant. *S Ayr* 3C 116
Minllyn. *Gwyn* 4A 70
Minnigaff. *Dum* 3B 110
Minorca. *IOM* 3D 108
Minskip. *N Yor* 3F 99
Minstead. *Hants* 1A 16
Minsted. *W Sus* 4G 25
Minster. *Kent* 4H 41 (nr. Ramsgate)
Minster. *Kent* 3D 40 (nr. Sheerness)
Minsteracres. *Nmbd* 4D 114
Minsterley. *Shrp* 5F 71
Minster Lovell. *Oxon* 4B 50
Minsterworth. *Glos* 4C 48
Minterne Magna. *Dors* 2B 14
Minterne Parva. *Dors* 2B 14
Minting. *Linc* 3A 88
Mintlaw. *Abers* 4H 161
Minto. *Bord* 2H 119
Minton. *Shrp* 1G 59
Minwear. *Pemb* 3E 43
Minworth. *W Mid* 1F 61
Miodar. *Arg* 4B 138
Mirehouse. *Cumb* 3A 102
Mireland. *High* 2F 169
Mirfield. *W Yor* 3C 92
Miserden. *Glos* 5E 49
Miskin. *Rhon* 3D 32
Misson. *Notts* 1D 86
Misterton. *Leics* 2C 62
Misterton. *Notts* 1E 87
Misterton. *Som* 2H 13
Mistley. *Essx* 2E 54
Mistley Heath. *Essx* 2E 55
Mitcham. *G Lon* 4D 39
Mitcheldean. *Glos* 4B 48
Mitchell. *Corn* 3C 6
Mitchel Troy. *Mon* 4H 47
Mitcheltroy Common. *Mon* 5H 47
Mitford. *Nmbd* 1E 115
Mithian. *Corn* 3B 6
Mitton. *Staf* 4C 72
Mixbury. *Oxon* 2E 50
Mixenden. *W Yor* 2A 92
Mixon. *Staf* 5E 85
Moat. *Cumb* 2F 113
Moats Tye. *Suff* 5C 66
Mobberley. *Ches E* 3B 84
Mobberley. *Staf* 1E 73
Moccas. *Here* 1G 47
Mochdre. *Cnwy* 3H 81
Mochdre. *Powy* 2C 58
Mochrum. *Dum* 5A 110
Mockbeggar. *Hants* 2G 15
Mockerkin. *Cumb* 2B 102
Modbury. *Devn* 3C 8
Moddershall. *Staf* 2D 72
Modsarie. *High* 2G 167
Moelfre. *Cnwy* 3B 82
Moelfre. *IOA* 2E 81
Moelfre. *Powy* 3D 70
Moffat. *Dum* 4C 118
Moggerhanger. *C Beds* 1B 52
Mogworthy. *Devn* 1B 12
Moira. *Leics* 4H 73
Molash. *Kent* 5E 41
Mol-chlach. *High* 2C 146
Mold. *Flin* 4E 83
Molehill Green. *Essx* 3F 53
Molescroft. *E Yor* 5E 101
Molesden. *Nmbd* 1E 115
Molesworth. *Cambs* 3H 63
Moll. *High* 5E 155
Molland. *Devn* 4B 20
Mollington. *Ches W* 3F 83
Mollington. *Oxon* 1C 50
Mollinsburn. *N Lan* 2A 128
Monachty. *Cdgn* 4E 57
Monachyle. *Stir* 2D 134
Monar Lodge. *High* 4E 156
Monaughty. *Powy* 4E 59
Monewden. *Suff* 5E 67
Moneydie. *Per* 1C 136
Moneyrow Green. *Wind* 4G 37
Moniaive. *Dum* 5G 117
Monifieth. *Ang* 5E 145
Monikie. *Ang* 5E 145
Monimail. *Fife* 2E 137
Monington. *Pemb* 1B 44
Monk Bretton. *S Yor* 4D 92
Monken Hadley. *G Lon* 1D 38
Monk Fryston. *N Yor* 2F 93
Monk Hesleden. *Dur* 1B 106
Monkhide. *Here* 1B 48
Monkhill. *Cumb* 4E 113
Monkhopton. *Shrp* 1A 60
Monkland. *Here* 5G 59
Monkleigh. *Devn* 4E 19
Monknash. *V Glam* 4C 32
Monkokehampton. *Devn* 2F 11
Monkseaton. *Tyne* 2G 115
Monks Eleigh. *Suff* 1C 54
Monk's Gate. *W Sus* 3D 26
Monk's Heath. *Ches E* 3C 84
Monk Sherborne. *Hants* 1E 24
Monkshill. *Abers* 4E 161
Monksilver. *Som* 3D 20
Monks Kirby. *Warw* 2B 62
Monk Soham. *Suff* 4E 66
Monk Soham Green. *Suff* 4E 66
Monkspath. *W Mid* 3F 61
Monks Risborough. *Buck* 5G 51
Monksthorpe. *Linc* 4D 88
Monk Street. *Essx* 3G 53
Monkswood. *Mon* 5G 47
Monkton. *Devn* 2E 13
Monkton. *Kent* 4G 41
Monkton. *Pemb* 4D 42
Monkton. *S Ayr* 2C 116
Monkton Combe. *Bath* 5C 34
Monkton Deverill. *Wilts* 3D 22
Monkton Farleigh. *Wilts* 5D 34
Monkton Heathfield. *Som* 4F 21
Monktonhill. *S Ayr* 2C 116
Monkton Up Wimborne. *Dors* 1F 15
Monkton Wyld. *Dors* 3G 13
Monkwearmouth. *Tyne* 4H 115
Monkwood. *Dors* 3H 13
Monkwood. *Hants* 3E 25
Monmarsh. *Here* 1A 48
Monmouth. *Mon* 4A 48
Monnington on Wye. *Here* 1G 47
Monreith. *Dum* 5A 110
Montacute. *Som* 1H 13
Montford. *Arg* 3C 126
Montford. *Shrp* 4G 71
Montford Bridge. *Shrp* 4G 71
Montgarrie. *Abers* 2C 152
Montgarswood. *E Ayr* 2E 117
Montgomery. *Powy* 1E 58
Montgreenan. *N Ayr* 5E 127
Montrave. *Fife* 3F 137
Montrose. *Ang* 3G 145
Monxton. *Hants* 2B 24
Monyash. *Derbs* 4F 85
Monymusk. *Abers* 2D 152
Monzie. *Per* 1A 136
Moodiesburn. *N Lan* 2H 127
Moon's Green. *Kent* 3C 28
Moonzie. *Fife* 2F 137
Moor. *Som* 1H 13
Moor Allerton. *W Yor* 1C 92
Moorbath. *Dors* 3H 13
Moorby. *Linc* 4B 88
Moorcot. *Here* 5F 59
Moor Crichel. *Dors* 2E 15
Moor Cross. *Devn* 3C 8
Moordown. *Bour* 3F 15
Moore. *Hal* 2H 83
Moorend. *Dum* 2D 112
Moor End. *E Yor* 1B 94
Moorend. *Glos* 5C 48 (nr. Dursley)
Moorend. *Glos* 4D 48 (nr. Gloucester)
Moorends. *S Yor* 3G 93
Moorgate. *S Yor* 1B 86
Moorgreen. *Hants* 1C 16
Moorgreen. *Notts* 1B 74
Moor Green. *Wilts* 5D 34
Moorhaigh. *Notts* 4C 86
Moorhall. *Derbs* 3H 85
Moorhampton. *Here* 1G 47
Moorhouse. *Cumb* 4E 113 (nr. Carlisle)
Moorhouse. *Cumb* 4D 112 (nr. Wigton)
Moorhouse. *Notts* 4E 87
Moorhouse. *Surr* 5F 39
Moorhouses. *Linc* 5B 88
Moorland. *Som* 3G 21
Moorlinch. *Som* 3H 21
Moor Monkton. *N Yor* 4H 99
Moor of Granary. *Mor* 3E 159
Moor Row. *Cumb* 3B 102 (nr. Whitehaven)
Moor Row. *Cumb* 5D 112 (nr. Wigton)
Moorsholm. *Red C* 3D 107
Moorside. *Dors* 1C 14
Moorside. *G Man* 4H 91
Moor, The. *Kent* 3B 28
Moortown. *Devn* 3D 10
Moortown. *Hants* 2G 15
Moortown. *IOW* 4C 16
Moortown. *Linc* 1H 87
Moortown. *Telf* 4A 72
Moortown. *W Yor* 1D 92
Morangie. *High* 5E 165
Morar. *High* 4E 147
Morborne. *Cambs* 1A 64
Morchard Bishop. *Devn* 2A 12
Morcombelake. *Dors* 3H 13
Morcott. *Rut* 5G 75
Morda. *Shrp* 3E 71
Morden. *G Lon* 4D 38
Mordiford. *Here* 2A 48
Mordon. *Dur* 2A 106
More. *Shrp* 1F 59
Morebath. *Devn* 4C 20
Morebattle. *Bord* 2B 120
Morecambe. *Lanc* 3D 96
Morefield. *High* 4F 163
Moreleigh. *Devn* 3D 8
Morenish. *Per* 5C 142
Moresby Parks. *Cumb* 3A 102
Morestead. *Hants* 4D 24
Moreton. *Dors* 4D 14
Moreton. *Essx* 5F 53
Moreton. *Here* 4H 59
Moreton. *Mers* 1E 83
Moreton. *Oxon* 5E 51
Moreton. *Staf* 4B 72
Moreton Corbet. *Shrp* 3H 71
Moretonhampstead. *Devn* 4A 12
Moreton-in-Marsh. *Glos* 2H 49
Moreton Jeffries. *Here* 1B 48
Moreton Morrell. *Warw* 5H 61
Moreton on Lugg. *Here* 1A 48
Moreton Pinkney. *Nptn* 1D 50
Moreton Say. *Shrp* 2A 72
Moreton Valence. *Glos* 5C 48
Morfa. *Cdgn* 5C 56
Morfa Bach. *Carm* 4D 44
Morfa Bychan. *Gwyn* 2E 69
Morfa Glas. *Neat* 5B 46
Morfa Nefyn. *Gwyn* 1B 68
Morganstown. *Card* 3E 33
Morgan's Vale. *Wilts* 4G 23
Morham. *E Lot* 2B 130
Moriah. *Cdgn* 3F 57
Morland. *Cumb* 2G 103
Morley. *Ches E* 2C 84
Morley. *Derbs* 1A 74
Morley. *Dur* 2E 105
Morley. *W Yor* 2C 92
Morley St Botolph. *Norf* 1C 66
Morningside. *Edin* 2F 129
Morningside. *N Lan* 4B 128
Morningthorpe. *Norf* 1E 66
Morpeth. *Nmbd* 1F 115
Morrey. *Staf* 4F 73
Morridge Side. *Staf* 5E 85
Morridge Top. *Staf* 4E 85
Morrington. *Dum* 1F 111
Morris Green. *Essx* 2H 53
Morriston. *Swan* 3F 31
Morston. *Norf* 1C 78
Mortehoe. *Devn* 2E 19
Morthen. *S Yor* 2B 86
Mortimer. *W Ber* 5E 37
Mortimer's Cross. *Here* 4G 59
Mortimer West End. *Hants* 5E 37
Mortomley. *S Yor* 1H 85
Morton. *Cumb* 1F 103 (nr. Calthwaite)
Morton. *Cumb* 4E 113 (nr. Carlisle)
Morton. *Derbs* 4B 86
Morton. *Linc* 3H 75 (nr. Bourne)
Morton. *Linc* 1F 87 (nr. Gainsborough)
Morton. *Linc* 4F 87 (nr. Lincoln)
Morton. *Norf* 4D 78
Morton. *Notts* 5E 87
Morton. *Shrp* 3E 71
Morton. *S Glo* 2B 34
Morton Bagot. *Warw* 4F 61
Morton Mill. *Shrp* 3H 71
Morton-on-Swale. *N Yor* 5A 106
Morton Tinmouth. *Dur* 2E 105
Morvah. *Corn* 3B 4
Morval. *Corn* 3G 7
Morvich. *High* 3E 165 (nr. Golspie)
Morvich. *High* 1B 148 (nr. Shiel Bridge)
Morvil. *Pemb* 1E 43
Morville. *Shrp* 1A 60
Morwenstow. *Corn* 1C 10
Morwick Hall. *Nmbd* 4G 121
Mosborough. *S Yor* 2B 86
Moscow. *E Ayr* 5F 127
Mose. *Shrp* 1B 60
Mosedale. *Cumb* 1E 103
Moseley. *W Mid* 2E 61 (nr. Birmingham)
Moseley. *W Mid* 5D 72 (nr. Wolverhampton)
Moseley. *Worc* 5C 60
Moss. *Arg* 4A 138
Moss. *High* 2A 140
Moss. *S Yor* 3F 93
Moss. *Wrex* 5F 83
Mossatt. *Abers* 2B 152
Moss Bank. *Mers* 1H 83
Mossbank. *Shet* 4F 173
Mossblown. *S Ayr* 2D 116
Mossbrow. *G Man* 2B 84
Mossburnford. *Bord* 3A 120
Mossdale. *Dum* 2D 110
Mossedge. *Cumb* 3F 113
Mossend. *N Lan* 3A 128
Mossgate. *Staf* 2D 72
Moss Lane. *Ches E* 3D 84
Mossley. *Ches E* 4C 84
Mossley. *G Man* 4H 91
Mossley Hill. *Mers* 2F 83
Moss of Barmuckity. *Mor* 2G 159
Mosspark. *Glas* 3G 127
Mosspaul. *Bord* 5G 119
Moss Side. *Cumb* 4C 112
Moss Side. *G Man* 1C 84
Moss-side. *High* 3C 158
Moss Side. *Lanc* 1B 90 (nr. Blackpool)
Moss Side. *Lanc* 2D 90 (nr. Preston)
Moss Side. *Mers* 4B 90
Moss-side of Cairness. *Abers* 2H 161
Mosstodloch. *Mor* 2H 159
Mosswood. *Nmbd* 4D 114
Mossy Lea. *Lanc* 3D 90
Mosterton. *Dors* 2H 13
Moston. *Shrp* 3H 71
Moston Green. *Ches E* 4B 84
Mostyn. *Flin* 2D 82
Mostyn Quay. *Flin* 2D 82
Motcombe. *Dors* 4D 22
Mothecombe. *Devn* 4C 8
Motherby. *Cumb* 2F 103
Motherwell. *N Lan* 4A 128
Mottingham. *G Lon* 3F 39
Mottisfont. *Hants* 4B 24
Mottistone. *IOW* 4C 16
Mottram in Longdendale. *G Man* 1D 85
Mottram St Andrew. *Ches E* 3C 84
Mott's Mill. *E Sus* 2G 27
Mouldsworth. *Ches W* 3H 83
Moulin. *Per* 3G 143
Moulsecoomb. *Brig* 5E 27
Moulsford. *Oxon* 3D 36
Moulsoe. *Mil* 1H 51
Moulton. *Ches W* 4A 84
Moulton. *Linc* 3C 76
Moulton. *Nptn* 4E 63
Moulton. *N Yor* 4F 105
Moulton. *Suff* 4F 65
Moulton. *V Glam* 4D 32
Moulton Chapel. *Linc* 4B 76
Moulton Eugate. *Linc* 4B 76
Moulton St Mary. *Norf* 5F 79
Moulton Seas End. *Linc* 3C 76
Mount. *Corn* 2F 7 (nr. Bodmin)
Mount. *Corn* 3B 6 (nr. Newquay)
Mountain Ash. *Rhon* 2D 32
Mountain Cross. *Bord* 5E 129
Mountain Street. *Kent* 5E 41
Mountain Water. *Pemb* 2D 42
Mount Ambrose. *Corn* 4B 6
Mountbenger. *Bord* 2F 119
Mountblow. *W Dun* 2F 127
Mount Bures. *Essx* 2C 54
Mountfield. *E Sus* 3B 28
Mountgerald. *High* 2H 157

Mount Hawke. *Corn* 4B **6**
Mount High. *High* 2A **158**
Mountjoy. *Corn* 2C **6**
Mount Lothian. *Midl* 4F **129**
Mountnessing. *Essx* 1H **39**
Mounton. *Mon* 2A **34**
Mount Pleasant. *Buck* 2E **51**
Mount Pleasant. *Ches E* 5C **84**
Mount Pleasant. *Derbs* 1H **73** (nr. Derby)
Mount Pleasant. *Derbs* 4G **73** (nr. Swadlincote)
Mount Pleasant. *E Sus* 4F **27**
Mount Pleasant. *Fife* 2E **137**
Mount Pleasant. *Hants* 3A **16**
Mount Pleasant. *Norf* 1B **66**
Mount Skippett. *Oxon* 4B **50**
Mountsorrel. *Leics* 4C **74**
Mount Stuart. *Arg* 4C **126**
Mousehole. *Corn* 4B **4**
Mouswald. *Dum* 2B **112**
Mow Cop. *Ches E* 5C **84**
Mowden. *Darl* 3F **105**
Mowhaugh. *Bord* 2C **120**
Mowmacre Hill. *Leic* 5C **74**
Mowsley. *Leics* 2D **62**
Moy. *High* 5B **158**
Moylgrove. *Pemb* 1B **44**
Moy Lodge. *High* 5G **149**
Muasdale. *Arg* 5E **125**
Muchalls. *Abers* 4G **153**
Much Birch. *Here* 2A **48**
Much Cowarne. *Here* 1B **48**
Much Dewchurch. *Here* 2H **47**
Muchelney. *Som* 4H **21**
Muchelney Ham. *Som* 4H **21**
Much Hadham. *Herts* 4E **53**
Much Hoole. *Lanc* 2C **90**
Muchlarnick. *Corn* 3G **7**
Much Marcle. *Here* 2B **48**
Muchrachd. *High* 5E **157**
Much Wenlock. *Shrp* 1A **60**
Mucking. *Thur* 2A **40**
Muckleford. *Dors* 3B **14**
Mucklestone. *Staf* 2B **72**
Muckleton. *Norf* 2H **77**
Muckleton. *Shrp* 3H **71**
Muckley. *Shrp* 1A **60**
Muckley Corner. *Staf* 5E **73**
Muckton. *Linc* 2C **88**
Mudale. *High* 5F **167**
Muddiford. *Devn* 3F **19**
Mudeford. *Dors* 3G **15**
Mudford. *Som* 1A **14**
Mudgley. *Som* 2H **21**
Mugdock. *Stir* 2G **127**
Mugeary. *High* 5D **154**
Muggington. *Derbs* 1G **73**
Muggintonlane End. *Derbs* 1G **73**
Muggleswick. *Dur* 4D **114**
Mugswell. *Surr* 5D **38**
Muie. *High* 3D **164**
Muirden. *Abers* 3E **160**
Muirdrum. *Ang* 5E **145**
Muiredge. *Per* 1E **137**
Muirend. *Glas* 3G **127**
Muirhead. *Ang* 5C **144**
Muirhead. *Fife* 3E **137**
Muirhead. *N Lan* 3H **127**
Muirhouses. *Falk* 1D **128**
Muirkirk. *E Ayr* 2F **117**
Muir of Alford. *Abers* 2C **152**
Muir of Fairburn. *High* 3G **157**
Muir of Fowlis. *Abers* 2C **152**
Muir of Miltonduff. *Mor* 3F **159**
Muir of Ord. *High* 3H **157**
Muir of Tarradale. *High* 3H **157**
Muirshearlich. *High* 5D **148**
Muirtack. *Abers* 5G **161**
Muirton. *High* 2B **158**
Muirton. *Per* 1D **136**
Muirton of Ardblair. *Per* 4A **144**
Muirtown. *Per* 2B **136**
Muiryfold. *Abers* 3E **161**
Muker. *N Yor* 5C **104**
Mulbarton. *Norf* 5D **78**
Mulben. *Mor* 3A **160**
Mulindry. *Arg* 4B **124**
Mullach Charlabhaigh. *W Isl* 3E **171**
Mullacott. *Devn* 2F **19**
Mullion. *Corn* 5D **5**
Mullion Cove. *Corn* 5D **4**
Mumbles. *Swan* 4F **31**
Mumby. *Linc* 3E **89**
Munderfield Row. *Here* 5A **60**
Munderfield Stocks. *Here* 5A **60**
Mundesley. *Norf* 2F **79**
Mundford. *Norf* 1H **65**
Mundham. *Norf* 1F **67**
Mundon. *Essx* 5B **54**
Munerigie. *High* 3E **149**
Muness. *Shet* 1H **173**
Mungasdale. *High* 4D **162**
Mungrisdale. *Cumb* 1E **103**
Munlochy. *High* 3A **158**
Munsley. *Here* 1B **48**
Munslow. *Shrp* 2H **59**
Murchington. *Devn* 4G **11**
Murcot. *Worc* 1F **49**
Murcott. *Oxon* 4D **50**
Murdishaw. *Hal* 2H **83**
Murieston. *W Lot* 3D **128**
Murkle. *High* 2D **168**
Murlaggan. *High* 4C **148**
Murra. *Orkn* 7B **172**
Murrayfield. *Edin* 2F **129**
Murray, The. *S Lan* 4H **127**
Murrell Green. *Hants* 1F **25**
Murroes. *Ang* 5D **144**
Murrow. *Cambs* 5C **76**
Mursley. *Buck* 3G **51**
Murthly. *Per* 5H **143**
Murton. *Cumb* 2A **104**
Murton. *Dur* 5G **115**
Murton. *Nmbd* 5F **131**
Murton. *Swan* 4E **31**
Murton. *York* 4A **100**
Musbury. *Devn* 3F **13**
Muscoates. *N Yor* 1A **100**
Muscott. *Nptn* 4D **62**
Musselburgh. *E Lot* 2G **129**
Muston. *Leics* 2F **75**
Muston. *N Yor* 2E **101**
Mustow Green. *Worc* 3C **60**
Muswell Hill. *G Lon* 2D **39**
Mutehill. *Dum* 5D **111**
Mutford. *Suff* 2G **67**
Muthill. *Per* 2A **136**
Mutterton. *Devn* 2D **12**
Muxton. *Telf* 4B **72**
Mwmbwls. *Swan* 4F **31**
Mybster. *High* 3D **168**
Myddfai. *Carm* 2A **46**
Myddle. *Shrp* 3G **71**
Mydroilyn. *Cdgn* 5D **56**
Myerscough. *Lanc* 1C **90**
Mylor Bridge. *Corn* 5C **6**
Mylor Churchtown. *Corn* 5C **6**
Mynachlog-ddu. *Pemb* 1F **43**
Mynydd-bach. *Mon* 2H **33**
Mynydd Isa. *Flin* 4E **83**
Mynyddislwyn. *Cphy* 2E **33**
Mynydd Llandegai. *Gwyn* 4F **81**
Mynydd Mechell. *IOA* 1C **80**
Mynydd-y-briw. *Powy* 3D **70**
Mynyddygarreg. *Carm* 5E **45**
Mynytho. *Gwyn* 2C **68**
Myrebird. *Abers* 4E **153**
Myrelandhorn. *High* 3E **169**
Mytchett. *Surr* 1G **25**
Mythe, The. *Glos* 2D **49**
Mytholmroyd. *W Yor* 2A **92**
Myton-on-Swale. *N Yor* 3G **99**
Mytton. *Shrp* 4G **71**

N

Naast. *High* 5C **162**
Na Buirgh. *W Isl* 8C **171**
Naburn. *York* 5H **99**
Nab Wood. *W Yor* 1B **92**
Nackington. *Kent* 5F **41**
Nacton. *Suff* 1F **55**
Nafferton. *E Yor* 4E **101**
Na Gearrannan. *W Isl* 3D **171**
Nailbridge. *Glos* 4B **48**
Nailsbourne. *Som* 4F **21**
Nailsea. *N Som* 4H **33**
Nailstone. *Leics* 5B **74**
Nailsworth. *Glos* 2D **34**
Nairn. *High* 3C **158**
Nalderswood. *Surr* 1D **26**
Nancegollan. *Corn* 3D **4**
Nancledra. *Corn* 3B **4**
Nangreaves. *G Man* 3G **91**
Nanhyfer. *Pemb* 1E **43**
Nannerch. *Flin* 4D **82**
Nanpantan. *Leics* 4C **74**
Nanpean. *Corn* 3D **6**
Nanstallon. *Corn* 2E **7**
Nant-ddu. *Powy* 4D **46**
Nanternis. *Cdgn* 5C **56**
Nantgaredig. *Carm* 3E **45**
Nantgarw. *Rhon* 3E **33**
Nant Glas. *Powy* 4B **58**
Nantglyn. *Den* 4C **82**
Nantgwyn. *Powy* 3B **58**
Nantlle. *Gwyn* 5E **81**
Nantmawr. *Shrp* 3E **71**
Nantmel. *Powy* 4C **58**
Nantmor. *Gwyn* 1F **69**
Nant Peris. *Gwyn* 5F **81**
Nantwich. *Ches E* 5A **84**
Nant-y-bai. *Carm* 1A **46**
Nant-y-bwch. *Blae* 4E **47**
Nant-y-Derry. *Mon* 5G **47**
Nant-y-dugoed. *Powy* 4B **70**
Nant-y-felin. *Cnwy* 3F **81**
Nantyffyllon. *B'end* 2B **32**
Nantyglo. *Blae* 4E **47**
Nant-y-meichiaid. *Powy* 4D **70**
Nant-y-moel. *B'end* 2C **32**
Nant-y-Pandy. *Cnwy* 3F **81**
Naphill. *Buck* 2G **37**
Nappa. *Lanc* 4A **98**
Napton on the Hill. *Warw* 4B **62**
Narberth. *Pemb* 3F **43**
Narberth Bridge. *Pemb* 3F **43**
Narborough. *Leics* 1C **62**
Narborough. *Norf* 4G **77**
Narkurs. *Corn* 3H **7**
Narth, The. *Mon* 5A **48**
Narthwaite. *Cumb* 5A **104**
Nasareth. *Gwyn* 1D **68**
Naseby. *Nptn* 3D **62**
Nash. *Buck* 2F **51**
Nash. *Here* 4F **59**
Nash. *Kent* 5G **41**
Nash. *Newp* 3G **33**
Nash. *Shrp* 3A **60**
Nash Lee. *Buck* 5G **51**
Nassington. *Nptn* 1H **63**
Nasty. *Herts* 3D **52**
Natcott. *Devn* 4C **18**
Nateby. *Cumb* 4A **104**
Nateby. *Lanc* 5D **96**
Nately Scures. *Hants* 1F **25**
Natland. *Cumb* 1E **97**
Naughton. *Suff* 1D **54**
Naunton. *Glos* 3G **49**
Naunton. *Worc* 2D **49**
Naunton Beauchamp. *Worc* 5D **60**
Navenby. *Linc* 5G **87**
Navestock Heath. *Essx* 1G **39**
Navestock Side. *Essx* 1G **39**
Navidale. *High* 2H **165**
Nawton. *N Yor* 1A **100**
Nayland. *Suff* 2C **54**
Nazeing. *Essx* 5E **53**
Neacroft. *Hants* 3G **15**
Nealhouse. *Cumb* 4E **113**
Neal's Green. *W Mid* 2H **61**
Neap House. *N Lin* 3B **94**
Near Sawrey. *Cumb* 5E **103**
Neasden. *G Lon* 2D **38**
Neasham. *Darl* 3A **106**
Neath. *Neat* 2A **32**
Neath Abbey. *Neat* 3G **31**
Neatishead. *Norf* 3F **79**
Neaton. *Norf* 5B **78**
Nebo. *Cdgn* 4E **57**
Nebo. *Cnwy* 5H **81**
Nebo. *Gwyn* 5D **81**
Nebo. *IOA* 1D **80**
Necton. *Norf* 5A **78**
Nedd. *High* 5B **166**
Nedderton. *Nmbd* 1F **115**
Nedging. *Suff* 1D **54**
Nedging Tye. *Suff* 1D **54**
Needham. *Norf* 2E **67**
Needham Market. *Suff* 5C **66**
Needham Street. *Suff* 4G **65**
Needingworth. *Cambs* 3C **64**
Needwood. *Staf* 3F **73**
Neen Savage. *Shrp* 3A **60**
Neen Sollars. *Shrp* 3A **60**
Neenton. *Shrp* 2A **60**
Nefyn. *Gwyn* 1C **68**
Neilston. *E Ren* 4F **127**
Neithrop. *Oxon* 1C **50**
Nelly Andrews Green. *Powy* 5E **71**
Nelson. *Cphy* 2E **32**
Nelson. *Lanc* 1G **91**
Nelson Village. *Nmbd* 2F **115**
Nemphlar. *S Lan* 5B **128**
Nempnett Thrubwell. *Bath* 5A **34**
Nene Terrace. *Linc* 5B **76**
Nenthall. *Cumb* 5A **114**
Nenthead. *Cumb* 5A **114**
Nenthorn. *Bord* 1A **120**
Nercwys. *Flin* 4E **83**
Neribus. *Arg* 4A **124**
Nerston. *S Lan* 4H **127**
Nesbit. *Nmbd* 1D **121**
Nesfield. *N Yor* 5C **98**
Ness. *Ches W* 3F **83**
Nesscliffe. *Shrp* 4F **71**
Neston. *Ches W* 3E **83**
Neston. *Wilts* 5D **34**
Nethanfoot. *S Lan* 5B **128**
Nether Alderley. *Ches E* 3C **84**
Netheravon. *Wilts* 2G **23**
Nether Blainslie. *Bord* 5B **130**
Netherbrae. *Abers* 3E **161**
Netherbrough. *Orkn* 6C **172**
Nether Broughton. *Leics* 3D **74**
Netherburn. *S Lan* 5B **128**
Nether Burrow. *Lanc* 2F **97**
Netherbury. *Dors* 3H **13**
Netherby. *Cumb* 2E **113**
Nether Careston. *Ang* 3E **145**
Nether Cerne. *Dors* 3B **14**
Nether Compton. *Dors* 1A **14**
Nethercote. *Glos* 3G **49**
Nethercote. *Warw* 4C **62**
Nethercott. *Devn* 3E **19**
Nethercott. *Oxon* 3C **50**
Nether Dallachy. *Mor* 2A **160**
Nether Durdie. *Per* 1E **136**
Nether End. *Derbs* 3G **85**
Netherend. *Glos* 5A **48**
Nether Exe. *Devn* 2C **12**
Netherfield. *E Sus* 4B **28**
Netherfield. *Notts* 1D **74**
Nethergate. *Norf* 3C **78**
Netherhampton. *Wilts* 4G **23**
Nether Handley. *Derbs* 3B **86**
Nether Haugh. *S Yor* 1B **86**
Nether Heage. *Derbs* 5A **86**
Nether Heyford. *Nptn* 5D **62**
Netherhouses. *Cumb* 1B **96**
Nether Howcleugh. *Dum* 3C **118**
Nether Kellet. *Lanc* 3E **97**
Nether Kinmundy. *Abers* 4H **161**
Netherland Green. *Staf* 2F **73**
Nether Langwith. *Notts* 3C **86**
Netherlaw. *Dum* 5E **111**
Netherley. *Abers* 4F **153**
Nethermill. *Dum* 1B **112**
Nethermills. *Mor* 3C **160**
Nether Moor. *Derbs* 4A **86**
Nether Padley. *Derbs* 3G **85**
Netherplace. *E Ren* 4G **127**
Nether Poppleton. *York* 4H **99**
Netherseal. *Derbs* 4G **73**
Nether Silton. *N Yor* 5B **106**
Nether Stowey. *Som* 3E **21**
Nether Street. *Essx* 4F **53**
Netherstreet. *Wilts* 5E **35**
Netherthird. *E Ayr* 3E **117**
Netherthong. *W Yor* 4B **92**
Netherton. *Ang* 3E **145**
Netherton. *Cumb* 1B **102**
Netherton. *Devn* 5B **12**
Netherton. *Hants* 1B **24**
Netherton. *Here* 3A **48**
Netherton. *Mers* 1F **83**
Netherton. *N Lan* 4A **128**
Netherton. *Nmbd* 4D **121**
Netherton. *Per* 3A **144**
Netherton. *Shrp* 2B **60**
Netherton. *Stir* 2G **127**
Netherton. *W Mid* 2D **60**
Netherton. *W Yor* 3C **92** (nr. Horbury)
Netherton. *W Yor* 3B **92** (nr. Huddersfield)
Netherton. *Worc* 1E **49**
Nethertown. *Cumb* 4A **102**
Nethertown. *High* 1F **169**
Nethertown. *Staf* 4F **73**
Nether Urquhart. *Fife* 3D **136**
Nether Wallop. *Hants* 3B **24**
Nether Wasdale. *Cumb* 4C **102**
Nether Welton. *Cumb* 5E **113**
Nether Westcote. *Glos* 3H **49**
Nether Whitacre. *Warw* 1G **61**
Netherwhitton. *Nmbd* 5F **121**
Nether Winchendon. *Buck* 4F **51**
Nether Worton. *Oxon* 2C **50**
Nethy Bridge. *High* 1E **151**
Netley. *Hants* 2C **16**
Netley. *Shrp* 5G **71**
Netley Marsh. *Hants* 1B **16**
Nettlebed. *Oxon* 3F **37**
Nettlebridge. *Som* 2B **22**
Nettlecombe. *Dors* 3A **14**
Nettlecombe. *IOW* 5D **16**
Nettleden. *Herts* 4A **52**
Nettleham. *Linc* 3H **87**
Nettlestead. *Kent* 5A **40**
Nettlestead Green. *Kent* 5A **40**
Nettlestone. *IOW* 3E **16**
Nettlesworth. *Dur* 5F **115**
Nettleton. *Linc* 4E **94**
Nettleton. *Wilts* 4D **34**
Netton. *Devn* 4B **8**
Netton. *Wilts* 3G **23**
Neuadd. *Carm* 3H **45**
Neuadd. *Powy* 5C **70**
Neuk, The. *Abers* 4E **153**
Nevendon. *Essx* 1B **40**
Nevern. *Pemb* 1A **44**
New Abbey. *Dum* 3A **112**
New Aberdour. *Abers* 2F **161**
New Addington. *G Lon* 4E **39**
Newall. *W Yor* 5D **98**
New Alresford. *Hants* 3D **24**
New Alyth. *Per* 4B **144**
Newark. *Orkn* 3G **172**
Newark. *Pet* 5B **76**
Newark-on-Trent. *Notts* 5E **87**
New Arley. *Warw* 2G **61**

Newarthill. *N Lan* 4A **128**
New Ash Green. *Kent* 4H **39**
New Balderton. *Notts* 5F **87**
New Barn. *Kent* 4H **39**
New Barnetby. *N Lin* 3D **94**
Newbattle. *Midl* 3G **129**
New Bewick. *Nmbd* 2E **121**
Newbie. *Dum* 3C **112**
Newbiggin. *Cumb* 2H **103** (nr. Appleby)
Newbiggin. *Cumb* 3B **96** (nr. Barrow-in-Furness)
Newbiggin. *Cumb* 5G **113** (nr. Cumrew)
Newbiggin. *Cumb* 2F **103** (nr. Penrith)
Newbiggin. *Cumb* 5B **102** (nr. Seascale)
Newbiggin. *Dur* 5E **115** (nr. Consett)
Newbiggin. *Dur* 2C **104** (nr. Holwick)
Newbiggin. *Nmbd* 5C **114**
Newbiggin. *N Yor* 5C **104** (nr. Askrigg)
Newbiggin. *N Yor* 1F **101** (nr. Filey)
Newbiggin. *N Yor* 1B **98** (nr. Thoralby)
Newbiggin-by-the-Sea. *Nmbd* 1G **115**
Newbigging. *Ang* 5D **145** (nr. Monikie)
Newbigging. *Ang* 4B **144** (nr. Newtyle)
Newbigging. *Ang* 5D **144** (nr. Tealing)
Newbigging. *Edin* 2E **129**
Newbigging. *S Lan* 5D **128**
Newbiggin-on-Lune. *Cumb* 4A **104**
Newbold. *Derbs* 3A **86**
Newbold. *Leics* 4B **74**
Newbold on Avon. *Warw* 3B **62**
Newbold on Stour. *Warw* 1H **49**
Newbold Pacey. *Warw* 5G **61**
Newbold Verdon. *Leics* 5B **74**
New Bolingbroke. *Linc* 5C **88**
Newborough. *IOA* 4D **80**
Newborough. *Pet* 5B **76**
Newborough. *Staf* 3F **73**
Newbottle. *Nptn* 2D **50**
Newbottle. *Tyne* 4G **115**
New Boultham. *Linc* 3G **87**
Newbourne. *Suff* 1F **55**
New Brancepeth. *Dur* 5F **115**
Newbridge. *Cphy* 2F **33**
Newbridge. *Cdgn* 5E **57**
Newbridge. *Corn* 3B **4**
New Bridge. *Dum* 2G **111**
Newbridge. *Edin* 2E **129**
Newbridge. *Hants* 1A **16**
Newbridge. *IOW* 4C **16**
Newbridge. *N Yor* 1C **100**
Newbridge. *Pemb* 1D **42**
Newbridge. *Wrex* 1E **71**
Newbridge Green. *Worc* 2D **48**
Newbridge-on-Usk. *Mon* 2G **33**
Newbridge on Wye. *Powy* 5C **58**
New Brighton. *Flin* 4E **83**
New Brighton. *Hants* 2F **17**
New Brighton. *Mers* 1F **83**
New Brinsley. *Notts* 5B **86**
Newbrough. *Nmbd* 3B **114**
New Broughton. *Wrex* 5F **83**
New Buckenham. *Norf* 1C **66**
Newbuildings. *Devn* 2A **12**
Newburgh. *Abers* 1G **153**
Newburgh. *Fife* 2E **137**
Newburgh. *Lanc* 3C **90**
Newburn. *Tyne* 3E **115**
Newbury. *W Ber* 5C **36**
Newbury. *Wilts* 2D **22**
Newby. *Cumb* 2G **103**
Newby. *N Yor* 2G **97** (nr. Ingleton)
Newby. *N Yor* 1E **101** (nr. Scarborough)
Newby. *N Yor* 3C **106** (nr. Stokesley)
Newby Bridge. *Cumb* 1C **96**
Newby Cote. *N Yor* 2G **97**
Newby East. *Cumb* 4F **113**
Newby Head. *Cumb* 2G **103**
New Byth. *Abers* 3F **161**
Newby West. *Cumb* 4E **113**
Newby Wiske. *N Yor* 1F **99**
Newcastle. *B'end* 3B **32**
Newcastle. *Mon* 4H **47**
Newcastle. *Shrp* 2E **59**
Newcastle Emlyn. *Carm* 1D **44**
Newcastle International Airport. *Tyne* 2E **115**
Newcastleton. *Bord* 1F **113**
Newcastle-under-Lyme. *Staf* 1C **72**
Newcastle Upon Tyne. *Tyne* 3F **115**
Newchapel. *Pemb* 1G **43**
Newchapel. *Powy* 2B **58**
Newchapel. *Staf* 5C **84**
Newchapel. *Surr* 1E **27**
New Cheriton. *Hants* 4D **24**
Newchurch. *Carm* 3D **45**
Newchurch. *Here* 5F **59**
Newchurch. *IOW* 4D **16**
Newchurch. *Kent* 2E **29**
Newchurch. *Lanc* 1G **91** (nr. Nelson)
Newchurch. *Lanc* 2G **91** (nr. Rawtenstall)
Newchurch. *Mon* 2H **33**
Newchurch. *Powy* 5E **58**
Newchurch. *Staf* 3F **73**
New Costessey. *Norf* 4D **78**
Newcott. *Devn* 2F **13**
New Cowper. *Cumb* 5C **112**
Newcraighall. *Edin* 2G **129**
New Crofton. *W Yor* 3D **93**
New Cross. *Cdgn* 3F **57**
New Cross. *Som* 1H **13**
New Cumnock. *E Ayr* 3F **117**
New Deer. *Abers* 4F **161**
New Denham. *Buck* 2B **38**
Newdigate. *Surr* 1C **26**
New Duston. *Nptn* 4E **62**
New Earswick. *York* 4A **100**
New Edlington. *S Yor* 1C **86**
New Elgin. *Mor* 2G **159**
New Ellerby. *E Yor* 1E **95**
Newell Green. *Brac* 4G **37**
New Eltham. *G Lon* 3F **39**
New End. *Warw* 4F **61**
New End. *Worc* 5E **61**
Newenden. *Kent* 3C **28**
New England. *Essx* 1H **53**
New England. *Pet* 5A **76**
Newent. *Glos* 3C **48**
New Ferry. *Mers* 2F **83**
Newfield. *Dur* 4F **115** (nr. Chester-le-Street)
Newfield. *Dur* 1F **105** (nr. Willington)
New Forest. *Hants* 1H **15**
Newfound. *Hants* 1D **24**
New Fryston. *W Yor* 2E **93**
New Galloway. *Dum* 2D **110**
Newgate. *Norf* 1C **78**
Newgate. *Pemb* 2C **42**
Newgate Street. *Herts* 5D **52**
New Greens. *Herts* 5B **52**
New Grimsby. *IOS* 1A **4**
New Hainford. *Norf* 4E **78**
Newhall. *Ches E* 1A **72**
Newhall. *Staf* 3G **73**
Newham. *Nmbd* 2F **121**
New Hartley. *Nmbd* 2G **115**
Newhaven. *Derbs* 4F **85**
Newhaven. *E Sus* 5F **27**
Newhaven. *Edin* 2F **129**
New Haw. *Surr* 4B **38**
New Hedges. *Pemb* 4F **43**
New Herrington. *Tyne* 4G **115**
Newhey. *G Man* 3H **91**
New Holkham. *Norf* 2A **78**
New Holland. *N Lin* 2D **94**
Newholm. *N Yor* 3F **107**
New Houghton. *Derbs* 4C **86**
New Houghton. *Norf* 3G **77**
Newhouse. *N Lan* 3A **128**
New Houses. *N Yor* 2H **97**
New Hutton. *Cumb* 5G **103**
New Hythe. *Kent* 5B **40**
Newick. *E Sus* 3F **27**
Newingreen. *Kent* 2F **29**
Newington. *Edin* 2F **129**
Newington. *Kent* 2F **29** (nr. Folkestone)
Newington. *Kent* 4C **40** (nr. Sittingbourne)
Newington. *Notts* 1D **86**
Newington. *Oxon* 2E **36**
Newington Bagpath. *Glos* 2D **34**
New Inn. *Carm* 2E **45**
New Inn. *Mon* 5H **47**
New Inn. *N Yor* 2H **97**
New Inn. *Torf* 5G **47**
New Invention. *Shrp* 3E **59**
New Kelso. *High* 4B **156**
New Lanark. *S Lan* 5B **128**
Newland. *Glos* 5A **48**
Newland. *Hull* 1D **94**
Newland. *N Yor* 2G **93**
Newland. *Som* 3B **20**
Newland. *Worc* 1C **48**
Newlandrig. *Midl* 3G **129**
Newlands. *Cumb* 1E **103**
Newlands. *Essx* 2C **40**
Newlands. *High* 4B **158**
Newlands. *Nmbd* 4D **115**
Newlands. *Staf* 3E **73**
Newlands of Geise. *High* 2C **168**
Newlands of Tynet. *Mor* 2A **160**
Newlands Park. *IOA* 2B **80**
New Lane. *Lanc* 3C **90**
New Lane End. *Warr* 1A **84**
New Langholm. *Dum* 1E **113**
New Leake. *Linc* 5D **88**
New Leeds. *Abers* 3G **161**
New Lenton. *Nott* 2C **74**
New Longton. *Lanc* 2D **90**
Newlot. *Orkn* 6E **172**
New Luce. *Dum* 3G **109**
Newlyn. *Corn* 4B **4**
Newmachar. *Abers* 2F **153**
Newmains. *N Lan* 4B **128**
New Mains of Ury. *Abers* 5F **153**
New Malden. *G Lon* 4D **38**
Newman's Green. *Suff* 1B **54**
Newmarket. *Suff* 4F **65**
Newmarket. *W Isl* 4G **171**
New Marske. *Red C* 2D **106**
New Marton. *Shrp* 2F **71**
New Micklefield. *W Yor* 1E **93**
New Mill. *Abers* 4E **160**
New Mill. *Corn* 3B **4**
New Mill. *Herts* 4H **51**
Newmill. *Mor* 3B **160**
Newmill. *Bord* 3G **119**
New Mill. *W Yor* 4B **92**
New Mill. *Wilts* 5G **35**
Newmillerdam. *W Yor* 3D **92**
New Mills. *Corn* 3C **6**
New Mills. *Derbs* 2E **85**
Newmills. *Fife* 1D **128**
Newmills. *High* 2A **158**
New Mills. *Mon* 5A **48**
New Mills. *Powy* 5C **70**
Newmiln. *Per* 5A **144**
Newmilns. *E Ayr* 1E **117**
New Milton. *Hants* 3H **15**
New Mistley. *Essx* 2E **54**
New Moat. *Pemb* 2E **43**
Newmore. *High* 3H **157** (nr. Dingwall)
Newmore. *High* 1A **158** (nr. Invergordon)
Newnham. *Cambs* 5D **64**
Newnham. *Glos* 4B **48**
Newnham. *Hants* 1F **25**
Newnham. *Herts* 2C **52**
Newnham. *Kent* 5D **40**
Newnham. *Nptn* 5C **62**
Newnham. *Warw* 4F **61**
Newnham Bridge. *Worc* 4A **60**
New Ollerton. *Notts* 4D **86**
New Oscott. *W Mid* 1F **61**
Newpark. *Fife* 2G **137**
New Park. *N Yor* 4E **99**
New Pitsligo. *Abers* 3F **161**
New Polzeath. *Corn* 1D **6**
Newport. *Corn* 4D **10**
Newport. *Devn* 3F **19**
Newport. *E Yor* 1B **94**
Newport. *Essx* 2F **53**
Newport. *Glos* 2B **34**
Newport. *High* 1H **165**
Newport. *IOW* 4D **16**
Newport. *Newp* 3G **33**
Newport. *Norf* 4H **79**
Newport. *Pemb* 1E **43**
Newport. *Som* 4G **21**
Newport. *Telf* 4B **72**
Newport-on-Tay. *Fife* 1G **137**
Newport Pagnell. *Mil* 1G **51**
Newpound Common. *W Sus* 3B **26**
New Prestwick. *S Ayr* 2C **116**
New Quay. *Cdgn* 5C **56**
Newquay. *Corn* 2C **6**
Newquay Cornwall Airport. *Corn* 2C **6**
New Rackheath. *Norf* 4E **79**
New Radnor. *Powy* 4E **58**
New Rent. *Cumb* 1F **103**
New Ridley. *Nmbd* 4D **114**
New Romney. *Kent* 3E **29**
New Rossington. *S Yor* 1D **86**
New Row. *Cdgn* 3G **57**
New Row. *Lanc* 1E **91**
New Row. *N Yor* 3D **106**
New Sauchie. *Clac* 4A **136**
Newsbank. *Ches E* 4C **84**
Newseat. *Abers* 5E **160**
Newsham. *Lanc* 1D **90**
Newsham. *Nmbd* 2G **115**
Newsham. *N Yor* 3E **105** (nr. Richmond)
Newsham. *N Yor* 1F **99** (nr. Thirsk)
New Sharlston. *W Yor* 3D **93**
Newsholme. *E Yor* 2H **93**
Newsholme. *Lanc* 4H **97**
New Shoreston. *Nmbd* 1F **121**
New Springs. *G Man* 4D **90**
Newstead. *Notts* 5C **86**
Newstead. *Bord* 1H **119**
New Stevenston. *N Lan* 4A **128**
New Street. *Here* 5F **59**
Newstreet Lane. *Shrp* 2A **72**
New Swanage. *Dors* 4F **15**
New Swannington. *Leics* 4B **74**
Newthorpe. *N Yor* 1E **93**
Newthorpe. *Notts* 1B **74**
Newton. *Arg* 4H **133**
Newton. *B'end* 4B **32**
Newton. *Cambs* 1E **53** (nr. Cambridge)
Newton. *Cambs* 4D **76** (nr. Wisbech)
Newton. *Ches W* 4G **83** (nr. Chester)
Newton. *Ches W* 5H **83** (nr. Tattenhall)
Newton. *Cumb* 2B **96**
Newton. *Derbs* 5B **86**
Newton. *Dors* 1C **14**
Newton. *Dum* 2D **112** (nr. Annan)
Newton. *Dum* 5D **118** (nr. Moffat)
Newton. *G Man* 1D **84**
Newton. *Here* 2G **47** (nr. Ewyas Harold)
Newton. *Here* 5H **59** (nr. Leominster)
Newton. *High* 2B **158** (nr. Cromarty)
Newton. *High* 4B **158** (nr. Inverness)
Newton. *High* 5C **166** (nr. Kylestrome)
Newton. *High* 4F **169** (nr. Wick)
Newton. *Lanc* 2E **97** (nr. Carnforth)
Newton. *Lanc* 4F **97** (nr. Clitheroe)
Newton. *Lanc* 1C **90** (nr. Kirkham)
Newton. *Linc* 2H **75**
Newton. *Mers* 2E **83**
Newton. *Mor* 2F **159**
Newton. *Norf* 4H **77**
Newton. *Nptn* 2F **63**
Newton. *Nmbd* 3D **114**
Newton. *Notts* 1D **74**
Newton. *Bord* 2A **120**
Newton. *Shrp* 1B **60** (nr. Bridgnorth)
Newton. *Shrp* 2G **71** (nr. Wem)
Newton. *Som* 3E **20**
Newton. *S Lan* 3H **127** (nr. Glasgow)
Newton. *S Lan* 1B **118** (nr. Lanark)
Newton. *Staf* 3E **73**
Newton. *Suff* 1C **54**
Newton. *Swan* 4F **31**
Newton. *Warw* 3C **62**
Newton. *W Lot* 2D **129**
Newton. *Wilts* 4H **23**
Newton Abbot. *Devn* 5B **12**
Newtonairds. *Dum* 1F **111**
Newton Arlosh. *Cumb* 4D **112**
Newton Aycliffe. *Dur* 2F **105**
Newton Bewley. *Hart* 2B **106**
Newton Blossomville. *Mil* 5G **63**
Newton Bromswold. *Bed* 4G **63**
Newton Burgoland. *Leics* 5A **74**
Newton by Toft. *Linc* 2H **87**
Newton Ferrers. *Devn* 4B **8**
Newton Flotman. *Norf* 1E **66**
Newtongrange. *Midl* 3G **129**
Newton Green. *Mon* 2A **34**
Newton Hall. *Dur* 5F **115**
Newton Hall. *Nmbd* 3D **114**
Newton Harcourt. *Leics* 1D **62**
Newton Heath. *G Man* 4G **91**
Newtonhill. *Abers* 4G **153**
Newtonhill. *High* 4H **157**
Newton Hill. *W Yor* 2D **92**
Newton Ketton. *Darl* 2A **106**
Newton Kyme. *N Yor* 5G **99**
Newton-le-Willows. *Mers* 1H **83**
Newton-le-Willows. *N Yor* 1E **98**
Newton Longville. *Buck* 2G **51**
Newton Mearns. *E Ren* 4G **127**
Newtonmore. *High* 4B **150**
Newton Morrell. *N Yor* 4F **105**
Newton Mulgrave. *N Yor* 3E **107**
Newton of Ardtoe. *High* 1A **140**
Newton of Balcanquhal. *Per* 2D **136**
Newton of Beltrees. *Ren* 4E **127**
Newton of Falkland. *Fife* 3E **137**
Newton of Mountblairy. *Abers* 3E **160**
Newton of Pitcairns. *Per* 2C **136**
Newton-on-Ouse. *N Yor* 4H **99**
Newton-on-Rawcliffe. *N Yor* 5F **107**
Newton on the Hill. *Shrp* 3G **71**

Newton-on-the-Moor—Northstowe

Newton-on-the-Moor. *Nmbd* 4F 121
Newton on Trent. *Linc* 3F 87
Newton Poppleford. *Devn* 4D 12
Newton Purcell. *Oxon* 2E 51
Newton Regis. *Warw* 5G 73
Newton Reigny. *Cumb* 1F 103
Newton Rigg. *Cumb* 1F 103
Newton St Cyres. *Devn* 3B 12
Newton St Faith. *Norf* 4E 78
Newton St Loe. *Bath* 5C 34
Newton St Petrock. *Devn* 1E 11
Newton Solney. *Derbs* 3G 73
Newton Stacey. *Hants* 2C 24
Newton Stewart. *Dum* 3B 110
Newton Toney. *Wilts* 2H 23
Newton Tony. *Wilts* 2H 23
Newton Tracey. *Devn* 4F 19
Newton under Roseberry. *Red C* 3C 106
Newton Unthank. *Leics* 5B 74
Newton upon Ayr. *S Ayr* 2C 116
Newton upon Derwent. *E Yor* 5B 100
Newton Valence. *Hants* 3F 25
Newton-with-Scales. *Lanc* 1B 90
Newtown. *Abers* 2E 160
Newtown. *Cambs* 4H 63
Newtown. *Corn* 5C 10
Newtown. *Cumb* 5B 112 (nr. Aspatria)
Newtown. *Cumb* 3G 113 (nr. Brampton)
Newtown. *Cumb* 2G 103 (nr. Penrith)
Newtown. *Derbs* 2D 85
Newtown. *Devn* 4A 20
Newtown. *Dors* 2H 13 (nr. Beaminster)
New Town. *Dors* 1E 15 (nr. Sixpenny Handley)
New Town. *E Lot* 2H 129
Newtown. *Falk* 1C 128
Newtown. *Glos* 5B 48 (nr. Lydney)
Newtown. *Glos* 2E 49 (nr. Tewkesbury)
Newtown. *Hants* 1D 16 (nr. Bishop's Waltham)
Newtown. *Hants* 3G 25 (nr. Liphook)
Newtown. *Hants* 1A 16 (nr. Lyndhurst)
Newtown. *Hants* 5C 36 (nr. Newbury)
Newtown. *Hants* 4B 24 (nr. Romsey)
Newtown. *Hants* 2C 16 (nr. Warsash)
Newtown. *Hants* 1E 16 (nr. Wickham)
Newtown. *Here* 2A 48 (nr. Little Dewchurch)
Newtown. *Here* 1B 48 (nr. Stretton Grandison)
Newtown. *High* 3F 149
Newtown. *IOM* 4C 108
Newtown. *IOW* 3C 16
Newtown. *Lanc* 3D 90
New Town. *Lutn* 3A 52
Newtown. *Nmbd* 4E 121 (nr. Rothbury)
Newtown. *Nmbd* 2E 121 (nr. Wooler)
Newtown. *Pool* 3F 15
Newtown. *Powy* 1D 58
Newtown. *Rhon* 2D 32
Newtown. *Shrp* 2G 71
Newtown. *Som* 1F 13
Newtown. *Staf* 4D 84 (nr. Biddulph)
Newtown. *Staf* 5D 73 (nr. Cannock)
Newtown. *Staf* 4E 85 (nr. Longnor)
New Town. *W Yor* 2E 93
Newtown. *Wilts* 4E 23
Newtown-in-St Martin. *Corn* 4E 5
Newtown Linford. *Leics* 4C 74
Newtown St Boswells. *Bord* 1H 119
New Tredegar. *Cphy* 5E 47
Newtyle. *Ang* 4B 144
New Village. *E Yor* 1D 94
New Village. *S Yor* 4F 93
New Walsoken. *Cambs* 5D 76
New Waltham. *NE Lin* 4F 95
New Winton. *E Lot* 2H 129
New World. *Cambs* 1C 64
New Yatt. *Oxon* 4B 50
Newyears Green. *G Lon* 2B 38
New York. *Linc* 5B 88
New York. *Tyne* 2G 115
Nextend. *Here* 5F 59
Neyland. *Pemb* 4D 42
Nib Heath. *Shrp* 4G 71
Nicholashayne. *Devn* 1E 12
Nicholaston. *Swan* 4E 31
Nidd. *N Yor* 3F 99
Niddrie. *Edin* 2F 129
Niddry. *Edin* 2D 129
Nigg. *Aber* 3G 153
Nigg. *High* 1C 158
Nigg Ferry. *High* 2B 158
Nightcott. *Som* 4B 20
Nimmer. *Som* 1G 13
Nine Ashes. *Essx* 5F 53
Ninebanks. *Nmbd* 4A 114
Nine Elms. *Swin* 3G 35
Ninemile Bar. *Dum* 2F 111
Nine Mile Burn. *Midl* 4E 129
Ninfield. *E Sus* 4B 28
Ningwood. *IOW* 4C 16
Nisbet. *Bord* 2A 120
Nisbet Hill. *Bord* 4D 130
Niton. *IOW* 5D 16
Nitshill. *E Ren* 4G 127
Niwbwrch. *IOA* 4D 80
Noak Hill. *G Lon* 1G 39
Nobold. *Shrp* 4G 71
Nobottle. *Nptn* 4D 62
Nocton. *Linc* 4H 87
Nogdam End. *Norf* 5F 79
Noke. *Oxon* 4D 50
Nolton. *Pemb* 3C 42
Nolton Haven. *Pemb* 3C 42
No Man's Heath. *Ches W* 1H 71
No Man's Heath. *Warw* 5G 73
Nomansland. *Devn* 1B 12
Nomansland. *Wilts* 1A 16
Noneley. *Shrp* 3G 71
Nonikiln. *High* 1A 158
Nonington. *Kent* 5G 41
Nook. *Cumb* 2F 113 (nr. Longtown)
Nook. *Cumb* 1E 97 (nr. Milnthorpe)
Noranside. *Ang* 2D 144
Norbreck. *Bkpl* 5C 96
Norbridge. *Here* 1C 48
Norbury. *Ches E* 1H 71
Norbury. *Derbs* 1F 73
Norbury. *Shrp* 1F 59
Norbury. *Staf* 3B 72
Norby. *N Yor* 1G 99
Norby. *Shet* 6D 173
Norcross. *Lanc* 5C 96
Nordelph. *Norf* 5E 77
Norden. *G Man* 3G 91
Nordley. *Shrp* 1A 60
Norfolk Broads. *Norf* 5G 79
Norham. *Nmbd* 5F 131
Norland Town. *W Yor* 2A 92
Norley. *Ches W* 3H 83
Norleywood. *Hants* 3B 16
Normanby. *N Lin* 3B 94
Normanby. *N Yor* 1B 100
Normanby. *Red C* 3C 106
Normanby-by-Spital. *Linc* 2H 87
Normanby le Wold. *Linc* 1A 88
Norman Cross. *Cambs* 1A 64
Normandy. *Surr* 5A 38
Norman's Bay. *E Sus* 5A 28
Norman's Green. *Devn* 2D 12
Normanton. *Derb* 2H 73
Normanton. *Leics* 1F 75
Normanton. *Linc* 1G 75
Normanton. *Notts* 5E 86
Normanton. *W Yor* 2D 93
Normanton le Heath. *Leics* 4A 74
Normanton on Soar. *Notts* 3C 74
Normanton-on-the-Wolds. *Notts* 2D 74
Normanton on Trent. *Notts* 4E 87
Normoss. *Lanc* 1B 90
Norrington Common. *Wilts* 5D 35
Norris Green. *Mers* 1F 83
Norris Hill. *Leics* 4H 73
Norristhorpe. *W Yor* 2C 92
Northacre. *Norf* 1B 66
Northall. *Buck* 3H 51
Northallerton. *N Yor* 5A 106
Northam. *Devn* 4E 19
Northam. *Sotn* 1C 16
Northampton. *Nptn* 4E 63
North Anston. *S Yor* 2C 86
North Ascot. *Brac* 4A 38
North Aston. *Oxon* 3C 50
Northaw. *Herts* 5C 52
Northay. *Som* 1F 13
North Baddesley. *Hants* 4B 24
North Balfern. *Dum* 4B 110
North Ballachulish. *High* 2E 141
North Barrow. *Som* 4B 22
North Barsham. *Norf* 2B 78
Northbeck. *Linc* 1H 75
North Benfleet. *Essx* 2B 40
North Bersted. *W Sus* 5A 26
North Berwick. *E Lot* 1B 130
North Bitchburn. *Dur* 1E 105
North Blyth. *Nmbd* 1G 115
North Boarhunt. *Hants* 1E 16
North Bockhampton. *Dors* 3G 15
Northborough. *Pet* 5A 76
Northbourne. *Kent* 5H 41
Northbourne. *Oxon* 3D 36
North Bovey. *Devn* 4H 11
North Bowood. *Dors* 3H 13
North Bradley. *Wilts* 1D 22
North Brentor. *Devn* 4E 11
North Brewham. *Som* 3C 22
Northbrook. *Oxon* 3C 50
North Brook End. *Cambs* 1C 52
North Broomhill. *Nmbd* 4G 121
North Buckland. *Devn* 2E 19
North Burlingham. *Norf* 4F 79
North Cadbury. *Som* 4B 22
North Carlton. *Linc* 3G 87
North Cave. *E Yor* 1B 94
North Cerney. *Glos* 5F 49
North Chailey. *E Sus* 3E 27
Northchapel. *W Sus* 3A 26
North Charford. *Hants* 1G 15
North Charlton. *Nmbd* 2F 121
North Cheriton. *Som* 4B 22
North Chideock. *Dors* 3H 13
Northchurch. *Herts* 5H 51
North Cliffe. *E Yor* 1B 94
North Clifton. *Notts* 3F 87
North Close. *Dur* 1F 105
North Cockerington. *Linc* 1C 88
North Coker. *Som* 1A 14
North Collafirth. *Shet* 3E 173
North Common. *E Sus* 3E 27
North Commonty. *Abers* 4F 161
North Coombe. *Devn* 1B 12
North Cornelly. *B'end* 3B 32
North Cotes. *Linc* 4G 95
Northcott. *Devn* 3D 10 (nr. Boyton)
Northcott. *Devn* 1D 12 (nr. Culmstock)
Northcourt. *Oxon* 2D 36
North Cove. *Suff* 2G 67
North Cowton. *N Yor* 4F 105
North Craigo. *Ang* 2F 145
North Crawley. *Mil* 1H 51
North Cray. *G Lon* 3F 39
North Creake. *Norf* 2A 78
North Curry. *Som* 4G 21
North Dalton. *E Yor* 4D 100
North Deighton. *N Yor* 4F 99
North Dronley. *Ang* 5C 144
North Duffield. *N Yor* 1G 93
Northedge. *Derbs* 4A 86
North Elkington. *Linc* 1B 88
North Elmham. *Norf* 3B 78
North Elmsall. *W Yor* 3E 93
Northend. *Buck* 2F 37
North End. *E Yor* 1F 95
North End. *Essx* 4G 53 (nr. Great Dunmow)
North End. *Essx* 2A 54 (nr. Great Yeldham)
North End. *Hants* 5C 36
North End. *Leics* 4C 74
North End. *Linc* 1B 76
North End. *Norf* 1B 66
North End. *N Som* 5H 33
North End. *Port* 2E 17
Northend. *Warw* 5A 62
North End. *W Sus* 5C 26
North End. *Wilts* 2F 35
North Erradale. *High* 5B 162
North Evington. *Leic* 5D 74
North Fambridge. *Essx* 1C 40
North Fearns. *High* 5E 155
North Featherstone. *W Yor* 2E 93
North Feorline. *N Ayr* 3D 122
North Ferriby. *E Yor* 2C 94
Northfield. *Aber* 3F 153
Northfield. *Hull* 2D 94
Northfield. *Som* 3F 21
Northfield. *W Mid* 3E 61
Northfleet. *Kent* 3H 39
North Frodingham. *E Yor* 4F 101
Northgate. *Linc* 3A 76
North Gluss. *Shet* 4E 173
North Gorley. *Hants* 1G 15
North Green. *Norf* 2E 66
North Green. *Suff* 4F 67 (nr. Framlingham)
North Green. *Suff* 3F 67 (nr. Halesworth)
North Green. *Suff* 4F 67 (nr. Saxmundham)
North Greetwell. *Linc* 3H 87
North Grimston. *N Yor* 3C 100
North Halling. *Medw* 4B 40
North Hayling. *Hants* 2F 17
North Hazelrigg. *Nmbd* 1E 121
North Heasley. *Devn* 3H 19
North Heath. *W Sus* 3B 26
North Hill. *Corn* 5C 10
North Hinksey Village. *Oxon* 5C 50
North Holmwood. *Surr* 1C 26
North Huish. *Devn* 3D 8
North Hykeham. *Linc* 4G 87
Northiam. *E Sus* 3C 28
Northill. *C Beds* 1B 52
Northington. *Hants* 3D 24
North Kelsey. *Linc* 4D 94
North Kelsey Moor. *Linc* 4D 94
North Kessock. *High* 4A 158
North Killingholme. *N Lin* 3E 95
North Kilvington. *N Yor* 1G 99
North Kilworth. *Leics* 2D 62
North Kyme. *Linc* 5A 88
North Lancing. *W Sus* 5C 26
Northlands. *Linc* 5C 88
Northleach. *Glos* 4G 49
North Lee. *Buck* 5G 51
North Lees. *N Yor* 2E 99
Northleigh. *Devn* 3G 19 (nr. Barnstaple)
Northleigh. *Devn* 3E 13 (nr. Honiton)
North Leigh. *Kent* 1F 29
North Leigh. *Oxon* 4B 50
North Leverton. *Notts* 2E 87
Northlew. *Devn* 3F 11
North Littleton. *Worc* 1F 49
North Lopham. *Norf* 2C 66
North Luffenham. *Rut* 5G 75
North Marden. *W Sus* 1G 17
North Marston. *Buck* 3F 51
North Middleton. *Midl* 4G 129
North Middleton. *Nmbd* 2E 121
North Molton. *Devn* 4H 19
North Moor. *N Yor* 1D 100
Northmoor. *Oxon* 5C 50
Northmoor Green. *Som* 3G 21
North Moreton. *Oxon* 3D 36
Northmuir. *Ang* 3C 144
North Mundham. *W Sus* 2G 17
North Murie. *Per* 1E 137
North Muskham. *Notts* 5E 87
North Ness. *Orkn* 8C 172
North Newbald. *E Yor* 1C 94
North Newington. *Oxon* 2C 50
North Newnton. *Wilts* 1G 23
North Newton. *Som* 3F 21
Northney. *Hants* 2F 17
North Nibley. *Glos* 2C 34
North Oakley. *Hants* 1D 24
North Ockendon. *G Lon* 2G 39
Northolt. *G Lon* 2C 38
Northop. *Flin* 4E 83
Northop Hall. *Flin* 4E 83
North Ormesby. *Midd* 3C 106
North Ormsby. *Linc* 1B 88
Northorpe. *Linc* 4H 75 (nr. Bourne)
Northorpe. *Linc* 2B 76 (nr. Donington)
Northorpe. *Linc* 1F 87 (nr. Gainsborough)
North Otterington. *N Yor* 1F 99
Northover. *Som* 3H 21 (nr. Glastonbury)
Northover. *Som* 4A 22 (nr. Yeovil)
North Owersby. *Linc* 1H 87
Northowram. *W Yor* 2B 92
North Perrott. *Som* 2H 13
North Petherton. *Som* 3F 21
North Petherwin. *Corn* 4C 10
North Pickenham. *Norf* 5A 78
North Piddle. *Worc* 5D 60
North Poorton. *Dors* 3A 14
North Port. *Arg* 1H 133
Northport. *Dors* 4E 15
North Queensferry. *Fife* 1E 129
North Radworthy. *Devn* 3A 20
North Rauceby. *Linc* 1H 75
Northrepps. *Norf* 2E 79
North Rigton. *N Yor* 5E 99
North Rode. *Ches E* 4C 84
North Roe. *Shet* 3E 173
North Ronaldsay Airport. *Orkn* 2G 172
North Row. *Cumb* 1D 102
North Runcton. *Norf* 4F 77
North Sannox. *N Ayr* 5B 126
North Scale. *Cumb* 2A 96
North Scarle. *Linc* 4F 87
North Seaton. *Nmbd* 1F 115
North Seaton Colliery. *Nmbd* 1F 115
North Sheen. *G Lon* 3C 38
North Shian. *Arg* 4D 140
North Shields. *Tyne* 3G 115
North Shoebury. *S'end* 2D 40
North Shore. *Bkpl* 1B 90
North Side. *Cumb* 2B 102
North Skelton. *Red C* 3D 106
North Somercotes. *Linc* 1D 88
North Stainley. *N Yor* 2E 99
North Stainmore. *Cumb* 3B 104
North Stifford. *Thur* 2H 39
North Stoke. *Bath* 5C 34
North Stoke. *Oxon* 3E 36
North Stoke. *W Sus* 4B 26
Northstowe. *Cambs* 4D 64

North Street. Hants 3E 25
North Street. Kent 5E 40
North Street. Medw 3C 40
North Street. W Ber 4E 37
North Sunderland. Nmbd 1G 121
North Tamerton. Corn 3D 10
North Tawton. Devn 2G 11
North Thoresby. Linc 1B 88
North Town. Devn 2F 11
North Tuddenham. Norf 4C 78
North Walbottle. Tyne 3E 115
North Walney. Cumb 3A 96
North Walsham. Norf 2E 79
North Waltham. Hants 2D 24
North Warnborough. Hants 1F 25
North Water Bridge. Ang 2F 145
North Watten. High 3E 169
Northway. Glos 2E 49
Northway. Swan 4E 31
North Weald Bassett. Essx 5F 53
North Weston. N Som 4H 33
North Weston. Oxon 5E 51
North Wheatley. Notts 2E 87
North Whilborough. Devn 2E 9
Northwich. Ches W 3A 84
North Wick. Bath 5A 34
Northwick. Som 2G 21
Northwick. S Glo 3A 34
North Widcombe. Bath 1A 22
North Willingham. Linc 2A 88
North Wingfield. Derbs 4B 86
North Witham. Linc 3G 75
Northwold. Norf 1G 65
Northwood. Derbs 4G 85
Northwood. G Lon 1B 38
Northwood. IOW 3C 16
Northwood. Kent 4H 41
Northwood. Shrp 2G 71
Northwood. Stoke 1C 72
Northwood Green. Glos 4C 48
North Wootton. Dors 1B 14
North Wootton. Norf 3F 77
North Wootton. Som 2A 22
North Wraxall. Wilts 4D 34
North Wroughton. Swin 3G 35
North Yardhope. Nmbd 4D 120
North York Moors. N Yor 5D 107
Norton. Devn 3E 9
Norton. Glos 3D 48
Norton. Hal 2H 83
Norton. Herts 2C 52
Norton. IOW 4B 16
Norton. Mon 3H 47
Norton. Nptn 4D 62
Norton. Notts 3C 86
Norton. Powy 4F 59
Norton. Shrp 2G 59
(nr. Ludlow)
Norton. Shrp 5B 72
(nr. Madeley)
Norton. Shrp 5H 71
(nr. Shrewsbury)
Norton. S Yor 3F 93
(nr. Askern)
Norton. S Yor 2A 86
(nr. Sheffield)
Norton. Stoc T 2B 106
Norton. Suff 4B 66
Norton. Swan 4F 31
Norton. W Sus 5A 26
(nr. Arundel)
Norton. W Sus 3G 17
(nr. Selsey)
Norton. Wilts 3D 35
Norton. Worc 1F 49
(nr. Evesham)
Norton. Worc 5C 60
(nr. Worcester)
Norton Bavant. Wilts 2E 23
Norton Bridge. Staf 2C 72
Norton Canes. Staf 5E 73
Norton Canon. Here 1G 47
Norton Corner. Norf 3C 78
Norton Disney. Linc 5F 87

Norton East. Staf 5E 73
Norton Ferris. Wilts 3C 22
Norton Fitzwarren. Som 4F 21
Norton Green. IOW 4B 16
Norton Green. Stoke 5D 84
Norton Hawkfield. Bath 5A 34
Norton Heath. Essx 5G 53
Norton in Hales. Shrp 2B 72
Norton in the Moors. Stoke 5C 84
Norton-Juxta-Twycross. Leics 5H 73
Norton-le-Clay. N Yor 2G 99
Norton Lindsey. Warw 4G 61
Norton Little Green. Suff 4B 66
Norton Malreward. Bath 5B 34
Norton Mandeville. Essx 5F 53
Norton-on-Derwent. N Yor 2B 100
Norton St Philip. Som 1C 22
Norton Subcourse. Norf 1G 67
Norton sub Hamdon. Som 1H 13
Norton Woodseats. S Yor 2A 86
Norwell. Notts 4E 87
Norwell Woodhouse. Notts 4E 87
Norwich. Norf 5E 79
Norwich International Airport.
Norf 4E 79
Norwick. Shet 1H 173
Norwood. Derbs 2B 86
Norwood Green. W Yor 2B 92
Norwood Hill. Surr 1D 26
Norwood Park. Som 3A 22
Noseley. Leics 1E 63
Noss Mayo. Devn 4B 8
Nosterfield. N Yor 1E 98
Nostie. High 1A 148
Notgrove. Glos 3G 49
Nottage. B'end 4B 32
Nottingham. Nott 1C 74
Nottington. Dors 4B 14
Notton. Dors 3B 14
Notton. W Yor 3D 92
Notton. Wilts 5E 35
Nounsley. Essx 4A 54
Noutard's Green. Worc 4B 60
Nox. Shrp 4G 71
Noyadd Trefawr. Cdgn 1C 44
Nuffield. Oxon 3E 37
Nunburnholme. E Yor 5C 100
Nuncargate. Notts 5B 86
Nunclose. Cumb 5F 113
Nuneaton. Warw 1A 62
Nuneham Courtenay. Oxon 2D 36
Nun Monkton. N Yor 4H 99
Nunnerie. S Lan 3B 118
Nunney. Som 2C 22
Nunnington. N Yor 2A 100
Nunnykirk. Nmbd 5E 121
Nunsthorpe. NE Lin 4F 95
Nunthorpe. Red C 3C 106
Nunthorpe. York 5H 99
Nunton. Wilts 4G 23
Nunwick. Nmbd 2B 114
Nunwick. N Yor 2F 99
Nupend. Glos 5C 48
Nursling. Hants 1B 16
Nursted. W Sus 4F 25
Nursteed. Wilts 5F 35
Nurston. V Glam 5D 32
Nutbourne. W Sus 2F 17
(nr. Chichester)
Nutbourne. W Sus 4B 26
(nr. Pulborough)
Nutfield. Surr 5E 39
Nuthall. Notts 1C 74
Nuthampstead. Herts 2E 53
Nuthurst. Warw 3F 61
Nuthurst. W Sus 3C 26
Nutley. E Sus 3F 27
Nuttall. G Man 3F 91
Nutwell. S Yor 4G 93
Nybster. High 2F 169
Nyetimber. W Sus 3G 17
Nyewood. W Sus 4G 25
Nymet Rowland. Devn 2H 11

Nymet Tracey. Devn 2H 11
Nympsfield. Glos 5D 48
Nynehead. Som 4E 21
Nyton. W Sus 5A 26

O

Oadby. Leics 5D 74
Oad Street. Kent 4C 40
Oakamoor. Staf 1E 73
Oakbank. Arg 5B 140
Oakbank. W Lot 3D 129
Oakdale. Cphy 2E 33
Oakdale. Pool 3F 15
Oake. Som 4E 21
Oaken. Staf 5C 72
Oakenclough. Lanc 5E 97
Oakengates. Telf 4B 72
Oakenholt. Flin 3E 83
Oakenshaw. Dur 1F 105
Oakenshaw. W Yor 2B 92
Oakerthorpe. Derbs 5A 86
Oakford. Cdgn 5D 56
Oakford. Devn 4C 20
Oakfordbridge. Devn 4C 20
Oakgrove. Ches E 4D 84
Oakham. Rut 5F 75
Oakhanger. Ches E 5B 84
Oakhanger. Hants 3F 25
Oakhill. Som 2B 22
Oakington. Cambs 4D 64
Oaklands. Powy 5C 58
Oakle Street. Glos 4C 48
Oakley. Bed 5H 63
Oakley. Buck 4E 51
Oakley. Fife 1D 128
Oakley. Hants 1D 24
Oakley. Suff 3D 66
Oakley Green. Wind 3A 38
Oakley Park. Powy 2B 58
Oakmere. Ches W 4H 83
Oakridge. Glos 5E 49
Oaks. Shrp 5G 71
Oaksey. Wilts 2E 35
Oaks Green. Derbs 2F 73
Oakshaw Ford. Cumb 2G 113
Oakshott. Hants 4F 25
Oakthorpe. Leics 4H 73
Oak Tree. Darl 3A 106
Oakwood. Derb 2A 74
Oakwood. W Yor 1D 92
Oakwoodhill. Surr 2C 26
Oakworth. W Yor 1A 92
Oape. High 3B 164
Oare. Kent 4E 40
Oare. Som 2B 20
Oare. Wilts 5G 35
Oareford. Som 2B 20
Oasby. Linc 2H 75
Oath. Som 4G 21
Oathlaw. Ang 3D 145
Oatlands. N Yor 4F 99
Oban. Arg 1F 133
Oban. W Isl 7D 171
Oborne. Dors 1B 14
Obsdale. High 2A 158
Obthorpe. Linc 4H 75
Occlestone Green. Ches W 4A 84
Occold. Suff 3D 66
Ochiltree. E Ayr 2E 117
Ochtermuthill. Per 2H 135
Ochtertyre. Per 1H 135
Ockbrook. Derbs 2B 74
Ockeridge. Worc 4B 60
Ockham. Surr 5B 38
Ockle. High 1G 139
Ockley. Surr 1C 26
Ocle Pychard. Here 1A 48
Octofad. Arg 4A 124
Octomore. Arg 4A 124
Octon. E Yor 3E 101
Odcombe. Som 1A 14

Odd Down. Bath 5C 34
Oddingley. Worc 5D 60
Oddington. Oxon 4D 50
Oddsta. Shet 2G 173
Odell. Bed 5G 63
Odiham. Hants 1F 25
Odsey. Cambs 2C 52
Odstock. Wilts 4G 23
Odstone. Leics 5A 74
Offchurch. Warw 4A 62
Offenham. Worc 1F 49
Offenham Cross. Worc 1F 49
Offerton. G Man 2D 84
Offerton. Tyne 4G 115
Offham. E Sus 4F 27
Offham. Kent 5A 40
Offham. W Sus 5B 26
Offleyhay. Staf 3C 72
Offley Hoo. Herts 3B 52
Offleymarsh. Staf 3B 72
Offord Cluny. Cambs 4B 64
Offord D'Arcy. Cambs 4B 64
Offton. Suff 1D 54
Offwell. Devn 3E 13
Ogbourne Maizey. Wilts 4G 35
Ogbourne St Andrew. Wilts 4G 35
Ogbourne St George. Wilts 4H 35
Ogden. G Man 3H 91
Ogle. Nmbd 2E 115
Ogmore. V Glam 4B 32
Ogmore-by-Sea. V Glam 4B 32
Ogmore Vale. B'end 2C 32
Okeford Fitzpaine. Dors 1D 14
Okehampton. Devn 3F 11
Okehampton Camp. Devn 3F 11
Okus. Swin 3G 35
Old. Nptn 3E 63
Old Aberdeen. Aber 3G 153
Old Alresford. Hants 3D 24
Oldany. High 5B 166
Old Arley. Warw 1G 61
Old Basford. Nott 1C 74
Old Basing. Hants 1E 25
Oldberrow. Warw 4F 61
Old Bewick. Nmbd 2E 121
Old Bexley. G Lon 3F 39
Old Blair. Per 2F 143
Old Bolingbroke. Linc 4C 88
Oldborough. Devn 2A 12
Old Brampton. Derbs 3H 85
Old Bridge of Tilt. Per 2F 143
Old Bridge of Urr. Dum 3E 111
Old Buckenham. Norf 1C 66
Old Burghclere. Hants 1C 24
Oldbury. Shrp 1B 60
Oldbury. Warw 1H 61
Oldbury. W Mid 2D 61
Oldbury-on-Severn. S Glo 2B 34
Oldbury on the Hill. Glos 3D 34
Old Byland. N Yor 1H 99
Old Cassop. Dur 1A 106
Oldcastle. Mon 3G 47
Oldcastle Heath. Ches W 1G 71
Old Catton. Norf 4E 79
Old Clee. NE Lin 4F 95
Old Cleeve. Som 2D 20
Old Colwyn. Cnwy 3A 82
Oldcotes. Notts 2C 86
Old Coulsdon. G Lon 5E 39
Old Dailly. S Ayr 5B 116
Old Dalby. Leics 3D 74
Old Dam. Derbs 3F 85
Old Deer. Abers 4G 161
Old Dilton. Wilts 2D 22
Old Down. S Glo 3B 34
Oldeamere. Cambs 1C 64
Old Edlington. S Yor 1C 86
Old Eldon. Dur 2F 105
Old Ellerby. E Yor 1E 95
Old Fallings. W Mid 5D 72
Oldfallow. Staf 4D 72
Old Felixstowe. Suff 2G 55
Oldfield. Shrp 2A 60
Oldfield. Worc 4C 60

Old Fletton. Pet 1A 64
Oldford. Som 1C 22
Old Forge. Here 4A 48
Old Glossop. Derbs 1E 85
Old Goole. E Yor 2H 93
Old Gore. Here 3B 48
Old Graitney. Dum 3E 112
Old Grimsby. IOS 1A 4
Oldhall. High 3E 169
Old Hall Street. Norf 2F 79
Oldham. G Man 4H 91
Oldhamstocks. E Lot 2D 130
Old Heathfield. E Sus 3G 27
Old Hill. W Mid 2D 60
Old Hunstanton. Norf 1F 77
Old Hurst. Cambs 3B 64
Old Hutton. Cumb 1E 97
Old Kea. Corn 4C 6
Old Kilpatrick. W Dun 2F 127
Old Kinnernie. Abers 3E 152
Old Knebworth. Herts 3C 52
Oldland. S Glo 4B 34
Old Laxey. IOM 3D 108
Old Leake. Linc 5D 88
Old Lenton. Nott 2C 74
Old Llanberis. Gwyn 5F 81
Old Malton. N Yor 2B 100
Oldmeldrum. Abers 1F 153
Old Micklefield. W Yor 1E 93
Old Mill. Corn 5D 10
Oldmixon. N Som 1G 21
Old Monkland. N Lan 3A 128
Old Newton. Suff 4C 66
Old Park. Telf 5A 72
Old Pentland. Midl 3F 129
Old Philpstoun. W Lot 2D 128
Old Quarrington. Dur 1A 106
Old Radnor. Powy 5E 59
Old Rayne. Abers 1D 152
Oldridge. Devn 3B 12
Old Romney. Kent 3E 29
Old Scone. Per 1D 136
Oldshoremore. High 3C 166
Old Snydale. W Yor 2E 93
Old Sodbury. S Glo 3C 34
Old Somerby. Linc 2G 75
Old Spital. Dur 3C 104
Oldstead. N Yor 1H 99
Old Stratford. Nptn 1F 51
Old Swan. Mers 1F 83
Old Swarland. Nmbd 4F 121
Old Tebay. Cumb 4H 103
Old Town. Cumb 1G 97
Old Town. E Sus 5G 27
Oldtown. High 5C 164
Old Town. IOS 1B 4
Old Town. Nmbd 5C 120
Oldtown of Ord. Abers 3D 160
Old Trafford. G Man 1C 84
Old Tupton. Derbs 4A 86
Oldwall. Cumb 3F 113
Oldwalls. Swan 3D 31
Old Warden. C Beds 1B 52
Oldways End. Som 4B 20
Old Westhall. Abers 1D 152
Old Weston. Cambs 3H 63
Oldwhat. Abers 3F 161
Old Windsor. Wind 3A 38
Old Wives Lees. Kent 5E 41
Old Woking. Surr 5B 38
Oldwood Common. Worc 4H 59
Old Woodstock. Oxon 4C 50
Olgrinmore. High 3C 168
Oliver's Battery. Hants 4C 24
Ollaberry. Shet 3E 173
Ollerton. Ches E 3B 84
Ollerton. Notts 4D 86
Ollerton. Shrp 3A 72
Olmarch. Cdgn 5F 57
Olmstead Green. Cambs 1G 53
Olney. Mil 5F 63
Olrig. High 2D 169
Olton. W Mid 2F 61

Olveston. S Glo ... 3B 34
Ombersley. Worc ... 4C 60
Ompton. Notts ... 4D 86
Omunsgarth. Shet ... 7E 173
Onchan. IOM ... 4D 108
Onecote. Staf ... 5E 85
Onehouse. Suff ... 5C 66
Onen. Mon ... 4H 47
Ongar Hill. Norf ... 3E 77
Ongar Street. Here ... 4F 59
Onibury. Shrp ... 3G 59
Onich. High ... 2E 141
Onllwyn. Neat ... 4B 46
Onneley. Shrp ... 1B 72
Onslow Green. Essx ... 4G 53
Onslow Village. Surr ... 1A 26
Onthank. E Ayr ... 1D 116
Openwoodgate. Derbs ... 1A 74
Opinan. High ... 1G 155
(nr. Gairloch)
Opinan. High ... 4C 162
(nr. Laide)
Orasaigh. W Isl ... 6F 171
Orbost. High ... 4B 154
Orby. Linc ... 4D 89
Orchard Hill. Devn ... 4E 19
Orchard Portman. Som ... 4F 21
Orcheston. Wilts ... 2F 23
Orcop. Here ... 3H 47
Orcop Hill. Here ... 3H 47
Ord. High ... 2E 147
Ordhead. Abers ... 2D 152
Ordie. Abers ... 3B 152
Ordiquish. Mor ... 3H 159
Ordley. Nmbd ... 4C 114
Ordsall. Notts ... 3E 86
Ore. E Sus ... 4C 28
Oreham Common. W Sus ... 4D 26
Oreton. Shrp ... 2A 60
Orford. Suff ... 1H 55
Orford. Warr ... 1A 84
Organford. Dors ... 3E 15
Orgil. Orkn ... 7B 172
Orgreave. Staf ... 4F 73
Oridge Street. Glos ... 3C 48
Orlestone. Kent ... 2D 28
Orleton. Here ... 4G 59
Orleton. Worc ... 4A 60
Orleton Common. Here ... 4G 59
Orlingbury. Nptn ... 3F 63
Ormacleit. W Isl ... 5C 170
Ormathwaite. Cumb ... 2D 102
Ormesby. Midd ... 3C 106
Ormesby St Margaret. Norf ... 4G 79
Ormesby St Michael. Norf ... 4G 79
Ormiscaig. High ... 4C 162
Ormiston. E Lot ... 3H 129
Ormsaigbeg. High ... 2F 139
Ormsaigmore. High ... 2F 139
Ormsary. Arg ... 2F 125
Ormsgill. Cumb ... 2A 96
Ormskirk. Lanc ... 4C 90
Orphir. Orkn ... 7C 172
Orpington. G Lon ... 4F 39
Orrell. Lanc ... 4D 90
Orrell. Mers ... 1F 83
Orrisdale. IOM ... 2C 108
Orsett. Thur ... 2H 39
Orslow. Staf ... 4C 72
Orston. Notts ... 1E 75
Orthwaite. Cumb ... 1D 102
Orton. Cumb ... 4H 103
Orton. Mor ... 3H 159
Orton. Nptn ... 3F 63
Orton. Staf ... 1C 60
Orton Longueville. Pet ... 1A 64
Orton-on-the-Hill. Leics ... 5H 73
Orton Waterville. Pet ... 1A 64
Orton Wistow. Pet ... 1A 64
Orwell. Cambs ... 5C 64
Osbaldeston. Lanc ... 1E 91
Osbaldwick. York ... 4A 100
Osbaston. Leics ... 5B 74
Osbaston. Shrp ... 3F 71

Osbournby. Linc ... 2H 75
Osclay. High ... 5E 169
Oscroft. Ches W ... 4H 83
Ose. High ... 4C 154
Osgathorpe. Leics ... 4B 74
Osgodby. Linc ... 1H 87
Osgodby. N Yor ... 1E 101
(nr. Scarborough)
Osgodby. N Yor ... 1G 93
(nr. Selby)
Oskaig. High ... 5E 155
Oskamull. Arg ... 4F 139
Osleston. Derbs ... 2G 73
Osmaston. Derbs ... 2A 74
Osmaston. Derbs ... 1G 73
Osmington. Dors ... 4C 14
Osmington Mills. Dors ... 4C 14
Osmondthorpe. W Yor ... 1D 92
Osmotherley. N Yor ... 5B 106
Osnaburgh. Fife ... 2G 137
Ospisdale. High ... 5E 164
Ospringe. Kent ... 4E 40
Ossett. W Yor ... 2C 92
Ossington. Notts ... 4E 87
Ostend. Essx ... 1D 40
Ostend. Norf ... 2F 79
Osterley. G Lon ... 3C 38
Oswaldkirk. N Yor ... 2A 100
Oswaldtwistle. Lanc ... 2F 91
Oswestry. Shrp ... 3E 71
Otby. Linc ... 1A 88
Otford. Kent ... 5G 39
Otham. Kent ... 5B 40
Otherton. Staf ... 4D 72
Othery. Som ... 3G 21
Otley. Suff ... 5E 66
Otley. W Yor ... 5E 98
Otterbourne. Hants ... 4C 24
Otterburn. Nmbd ... 5C 120
Otterburn. N Yor ... 4A 98
Otterburn Camp. Nmbd ... 5C 120
Otterburn Hall. Nmbd ... 5C 120
Otter Ferry. Arg ... 1H 125
Otterford. Som ... 1F 13
Otterham. Corn ... 3B 10
Otterhampton. Som ... 2F 21
Otterham Quay. Kent ... 4C 40
Ottershaw. Surr ... 4B 38
Otterspool. Mers ... 2F 83
Otterswick. Shet ... 3G 173
Otterton. Devn ... 4D 12
Otterwood. Hants ... 2C 16
Ottery St Mary. Devn ... 3E 12
Ottinge. Kent ... 1F 29
Ottringham. E Yor ... 2F 95
Oughterby. Cumb ... 4D 112
Oughtershaw. N Yor ... 1A 98
Oughterside. Cumb ... 5C 112
Oughtibridge. S Yor ... 1H 85
Oughtrington. Warr ... 2A 84
Oulston. N Yor ... 2H 99
Oulton. Cumb ... 4D 112
Oulton. Norf ... 3D 78
Oulton. Staf ... 3B 72
(nr. Gnosall Heath)
Oulton. Staf ... 2D 72
(nr. Stone)
Oulton. Suff ... 1H 67
Oulton. W Yor ... 2D 92
Oulton Broad. Suff ... 1H 67
Oulton Street. Norf ... 3D 78
Oundle. Nptn ... 2H 63
Ousby. Cumb ... 1H 103
Ousdale. High ... 1H 165
Ousden. Suff ... 5G 65
Ousefleet. E Yor ... 2B 94
Ouston. Dur ... 4F 115
Ouston. Nmbd ... 2D 115
(nr. Bearsbridge)
Ouston. Nmbd ... 2D 114
(nr. Stamfordham)
Outer Hope. Devn ... 4C 8
Outertown. Orkn ... 7B 172
Outgate. Cumb ... 5E 103

Outhgill. Cumb ... 4A 104
Outlands. Staf ... 2B 72
Outlane. W Yor ... 3A 92
Out Newton. E Yor ... 2G 95
Out Rawcliffe. Lanc ... 5D 96
Outwell. Norf ... 5E 77
Outwick. Hants ... 1G 15
Outwood. Surr ... 1E 27
Outwood. W Yor ... 2D 92
Outwood. Worc ... 3D 60
Outwoods. Leics ... 4B 74
Outwoods. Staf ... 4B 72
Ouzlewell Green. W Yor ... 2D 92
Ovenden. W Yor ... 2A 92
Over. Cambs ... 3C 64
Over. Ches W ... 4A 84
Over. Glos ... 4D 48
Over. S Glo ... 3A 34
Over Burrows. Derbs ... 2G 73
Overbury. Worc ... 2E 49
Overcombe. Dors ... 4B 14
Over Compton. Dors ... 1A 14
Over End. Cambs ... 1H 63
Over Finlarg. Ang ... 4D 144
Overgreen. Derbs ... 3H 85
Over Green. W Mid ... 1F 61
Over Haddon. Derbs ... 4G 85
Over Hulton. G Man ... 4E 91
Over Kellet. Lanc ... 2E 97
Over Kiddington. Oxon ... 3C 50
Overleigh. Som ... 3H 21
Overley. Staf ... 4F 73
Over Monnow. Mon ... 4A 48
Over Norton. Oxon ... 3B 50
Over Peover. Ches E ... 3B 84
Overpool. Ches W ... 3F 83
Overscaig. High ... 1B 164
Overseal. Derbs ... 4G 73
Over Silton. N Yor ... 5B 106
Oversland. Kent ... 5E 41
Overstone. Nptn ... 4F 63
Over Stowey. Som ... 3E 21
Overstrand. Norf ... 1E 79
Over Stratton. Som ... 1H 13
Over Street. Wilts ... 3F 23
Overthorpe. Nptn ... 1C 50
Overton. Aber ... 2F 153
Overton. Ches W ... 3H 83
Overton. High ... 5E 169
Overton. Lanc ... 4D 96
Overton. N Yor ... 4H 99
Overton. Shrp ... 2A 60
(nr. Bridgnorth)
Overton. Shrp ... 3H 59
(nr. Ludlow)
Overton. Swan ... 4D 30
Overton. W Yor ... 3C 92
Overton. Wrex ... 1F 71
Overtown. Lanc ... 2F 97
Overtown. N Lan ... 4B 128
Overtown. Swin ... 4G 35
Over Wallop. Hants ... 3A 24
Over Whitacre. Warw ... 1G 61
Over Worton. Oxon ... 3C 50
Oving. Buck ... 3F 51
Oving. W Sus ... 5A 26
Ovingdean. Brig ... 5E 27
Ovingham. Nmbd ... 3D 115
Ovington. Dur ... 3E 105
Ovington. Essx ... 1A 54
Ovington. Hants ... 3D 24
Ovington. Norf ... 5B 78
Ovington. Nmbd ... 3D 114
Owen's Bank. Staf ... 3G 73
Ower. Hants ... 1A 16
(nr. Holbury)
Ower. Hants ... 1B 16
(nr. Totton)
Owermoigne. Dors ... 4C 14
Owlbury. Shrp ... 1F 59
Owler Bar. Derbs ... 3G 85
Owlerton. S Yor ... 2H 85
Owlsmoor. Brac ... 5G 37

Owlswick. Buck ... 5F 51
Owmby. Linc ... 4D 94
Owmby-by-Spital. Linc ... 2H 87
Ownham. W Ber ... 4C 36
Owrytn. Wrex ... 1F 71
Owslebury. Hants ... 4D 24
Owston. Leics ... 5E 75
Owston. S Yor ... 3F 93
Owston Ferry. N Lin ... 4B 94
Owstwick. E Yor ... 1F 95
Owthorne. E Yor ... 2G 95
Owthorpe. Notts ... 2D 74
Owton Manor. Hart ... 2B 106
Oxborough. Norf ... 5G 77
Oxbridge. Dors ... 3H 13
Oxcombe. Linc ... 3C 88
Oxen End. Essx ... 3G 53
Oxenhall. Glos ... 3C 48
Oxenholme. Cumb ... 5G 103
Oxenhope. W Yor ... 1A 92
Oxen Park. Cumb ... 1C 96
Oxenpill. Som ... 2H 21
Oxenton. Glos ... 2E 49
Oxenwood. Wilts ... 1B 24
Oxford. Oxon ... 5D 50
Oxgangs. Edin ... 3F 129
Oxhey. Herts ... 1C 38
Oxhill. Warw ... 1B 50
Oxley. W Mid ... 5C 72
Oxley Green. Essx ... 4C 54
Oxley's Green. E Sus ... 3A 28
Oxlode. Cambs ... 2D 65
Oxnam. Bord ... 3B 120
Oxshott. Surr ... 4C 38
Oxspring. S Yor ... 4C 92
Oxted. Surr ... 5E 39
Oxton. Mers ... 2E 83
Oxton. N Yor ... 5H 99
Oxton. Notts ... 5D 86
Oxton. Bord ... 4A 130
Oxwich. Swan ... 4D 31
Oxwich Green. Swan ... 4D 31
Oxwick. Norf ... 3B 78
Oykel Bridge. High ... 3A 164
Oyne. Abers ... 1D 152
Oystermouth. Swan ... 4F 31
Ozleworth. Glos ... 2C 34

P

Pabail Iarach. W Isl ... 4H 171
Pabail Uarach. W Isl ... 4H 171
Pachesham. Surr ... 5C 38
Packers Hill. Dors ... 1C 14
Packington. Leics ... 4A 74
Packmoor. Stoke ... 5C 84
Packmores. Warw ... 4G 61
Packwood. W Mid ... 3F 61
Packwood Gullett. W Mid ... 3F 61
Padanaram. Ang ... 3D 144
Padbury. Buck ... 2F 51
Paddington. G Lon ... 2D 38
Paddington. Warr ... 2A 84
Paddlesworth. Kent ... 2F 29
Paddock. Kent ... 5D 40
Paddockhole. Dum ... 1D 112
Paddock Wood. Kent ... 1A 28
Paddolgreen. Shrp ... 2H 71
Padeswood. Flin ... 4E 83
Padiham. Lanc ... 1F 91
Padside. N Yor ... 4D 98
Padson. Devn ... 3F 11
Padstow. Corn ... 1D 6
Padworth. W Ber ... 5E 36
Page Bank. Dur ... 1F 105
Pagham. W Sus ... 3G 17
Paglesham Churchend. Essx ... 1D 40
Paglesham Eastend. Essx ... 1D 40
Paibeil. W Isl ... 2C 170
(on North Uist)
Paibeil. W Isl ... 8C 171
(on Taransay)
Paignton. Torb ... 2E 9

Pailton. Warw ... 2B 62
Paine's Corner. E Sus ... 3H 27
Painleyhill. Staf ... 2E 73
Painscastle. Powy ... 1E 47
Painshawfield. Nmbd ... 3D 114
Painsthorpe. E Yor ... 4C 100
Painswick. Glos ... 5D 48
Painter's Forstal. Kent ... 5D 40
Painthorpe. W Yor ... 3D 92
Pairc Shiabost. W Isl ... 3E 171
Paisley. Ren ... 3F 127
Pakefield. Suff ... 1H 67
Pakenham. Suff ... 4B 66
Pale. Gwyn ... 2B 70
Palehouse Common. E Sus ... 4F 27
Palestine. Hants ... 2A 24
Paley Street. Wind ... 4G 37
Palgowan. Dum ... 1A 110
Palgrave. Suff ... 3D 66
Pallington. Dors ... 3C 14
Palmarsh. Kent ... 2F 29
Palmer Moor. Derbs ... 2F 73
Palmers Cross. W Mid ... 5C 72
Palmerstown. V Glam ... 5E 33
Palnackie. Dum ... 4A 112
Palnure. Dum ... 3B 110
Palterton. Derbs ... 4B 86
Pamber End. Hants ... 1E 24
Pamber Green. Hants ... 1E 24
Pamber Heath. Hants ... 5E 36
Pamington. Glos ... 2E 49
Pamphill. Dors ... 2E 15
Pampisford. Cambs ... 1E 53
Panborough. Som ... 2H 21
Panbride. Ang ... 5E 145
Pancakehill. Glos ... 4F 49
Pancrasweek. Devn ... 2C 10
Pandy. Gwyn ... 3A 70
(nr. Bala)
Pandy. Gwyn ... 5F 69
(nr. Tywyn)
Pandy. Mon ... 3G 47
Pandy. Powy ... 5C 70
Pandy. Wrex ... 2D 70
Pandy Tudur. Cnwy ... 4A 82
Panfield. Essx ... 3H 53
Pangbourne. W Ber ... 4E 37
Pannal. N Yor ... 4F 99
Pannal Ash. N Yor ... 4E 99
Pannanich. Abers ... 4A 152
Pant. Shrp ... 3E 71
Pant. Wrex ... 1F 71
Pantasaph. Flin ... 3D 82
Pant Glas. Gwyn ... 1D 68
Pant-glas. Shrp ... 2E 71
Pantgwyn. Carm ... 3F 45
Pantgwyn. Cdgn ... 1C 44
Pant-lasau. Swan ... 3F 31
Panton. Linc ... 3A 88
Pant-pastynog. Den ... 4C 82
Pantperthog. Gwyn ... 5G 69
Pant-teg. Carm ... 3E 45
Pant-y-Caws. Carm ... 2F 43
Pant-y-dwr. Powy ... 3B 58
Pant-y-ffridd. Powy ... 5D 70
Pantyffynnon. Carm ... 4G 45
Pantygasseg. Torf ... 5F 47
Pant-y-llyn. Carm ... 4G 45
Pant-yr-awel. B'end ... 3C 32
Pant y Wacco. Flin ... 3D 82
Panxworth. Norf ... 4F 79
Papa Stour Airport. Shet ... 6C 173
Papa Westray Airport. Orkn ... 2D 172
Papcastle. Cumb ... 1C 102
Papigoe. High ... 3F 169
Papil. Shet ... 8E 173
Papple. E Lot ... 2B 130
Papplewick. Notts ... 5C 86
Papworth Everard. Cambs ... 4B 64
Papworth St Agnes. Cambs ... 4B 64
Par. Corn ... 3E 7
Paramour Street. Kent ... 4G 41
Parbold. Lanc ... 3C 90
Parbrook. Som ... 3A 22

Parbrook. *W Sus* 3B **26**
Parc. *Gwyn* 2A **70**
Parcllyn. *Cdgn* 5B **56**
Parc-Seymour. *Newp* 2H **33**
Pardown. *Hants* 2D **24**
Pardshaw. *Cumb* 2B **102**
Parham. *Suff* 4F **67**
Park. *Abers* 4E **153**
Park. *Arg* 4D **140**
Park. *Dum* 5B **118**
Park Bottom. *Corn* 4A **6**
Parkburn. *Abers* 5E **161**
Park Corner. *E Sus* 2G **27**
Park Corner. *Oxon* 3E **37**
Parkend. *Glos* 5B **48**
Park End. *Nmbd* 2B **114**
Parkeston. *Essx* 2F **55**
Parkfield. *Corn* 2H **7**
Parkgate. *Ches W* 3E **83**
Parkgate. *Cumb* 5D **112**
Parkgate. *Dum* 1B **112**
Park Gate. *Hants* 2D **16**
Parkgate. *Surr* 1D **26**
Park Gate. *Worc* 3D **60**
Parkhall. *W Dun* 2F **127**
Parkham. *Devn* 4D **19**
Parkham Ash. *Devn* 4D **18**
Parkhead. *Cumb* 5E **113**
Parkhead. *Glas* 3H **127**
Park Hill. *Mers* 4C **90**
Parkhouse. *Mon* 5H **47**
Parkhurst. *IOW* 3C **16**
Park Lane. *G Man* 4F **91**
Park Lane. *Staf* 5C **72**
Parkmill. *Swan* 4E **31**
Park Mill. *W Yor* 3C **92**
Parkneuk. *Abers* 1G **145**
Parkside. *N Lan* 4B **128**
Parkstone. *Pool* 3F **15**
Park Street. *Herts* 5B **52**
Park Street. *W Sus* 2C **26**
Park Town. *Oxon* 5D **50**
Park Village. *Nmbd* 3H **113**
Parkway. *Here* 2C **48**
Parley Cross. *Dors* 3F **15**
Parmoor. *Buck* 3F **37**
Parr. *Mers* 1H **83**
Parracombe. *Devn* 2G **19**
Parrog. *Pemb* 1E **43**
Parsonage Green. *Essx* 4H **53**
Parsonby. *Cumb* 1C **102**
Parson Cross. *S Yor* 1A **86**
Parson Drove. *Cambs* 5C **76**
Partick. *Glas* 3G **127**
Partington. *G Man* 1B **84**
Partney. *Linc* 4D **88**
Parton. *Cumb* 2A **102**
(nr. Whitehaven)
Parton. *Cumb* 4D **112**
(nr. Wigton)
Parton. *Dum* 2D **111**
Partridge Green. *W Sus* 4C **26**
Parwich. *Derbs* 5F **85**
Passenham. *Nptn* 2F **51**
Passfield. *Hants* 3G **25**
Passingford Bridge. *Essx* 1G **39**
Paston. *Norf* 2F **79**
Pasturefields. *Staf* 3D **73**
Patchacott. *Devn* 3E **11**
Patcham. *Brig* 5E **27**
Patchetts Green. *Herts* 1C **38**
Patching. *W Sus* 5B **26**
Patchole. *Devn* 2G **19**
Patchway. *S Glo* 3B **34**
Pateley Bridge. *N Yor* 3D **98**
Pathe. *Som* 3G **21**
Pathfinder Village. *Devn* 3B **12**
Pathhead. *Abers* 2G **145**
Pathhead. *E Ayr* 3F **117**
Pathhead. *Fife* 4E **137**
Pathhead. *Midl* 3G **129**
Pathlow. *Warw* 5F **61**
Path of Condie. *Per* 2C **136**
Pathstruie. *Per* 2C **136**
Patmore Heath. *Herts* 3E **53**
Patna. *E Ayr* 3D **116**
Patney. *Wilts* 1F **23**
Patrick. *IOM* 3B **108**
Patrick Brompton. *N Yor* 5F **105**
Patrington. *E Yor* 2G **95**
Patrington Haven. *E Yor* 2G **95**
Patrixbourne. *Kent* 5F **41**
Patterdale. *Cumb* 3E **103**
Pattiesmuir. *Fife* 1D **129**
Pattingham. *Staf* 1C **60**
Pattishall. *Nptn* 5D **62**
Pattiswick. *Essx* 3B **54**
Patton Bridge. *Cumb* 5G **103**
Paul. *Corn* 4B **4**
Paulerspury. *Nptn* 1F **51**
Paull. *E Yor* 2E **95**
Paulton. *Bath* 1B **22**
Pauperhaugh. *Nmbd* 5F **121**
Pave Lane. *Telf* 4B **72**
Pavenham. *Bed* 5G **63**
Pawlett. *Som* 2G **21**
Pawston. *Nmbd* 1C **120**
Paxford. *Glos* 2G **49**
Paxton. *Bord* 4F **131**
Payhembury. *Devn* 2D **12**
Paythorne. *Lanc* 4H **97**
Payton. *Som* 4E **20**
Peacehaven. *E Sus* 5F **27**
Peak Dale. *Derbs* 3E **85**
Peak District. *Derbs* 2F **85**
Peak Forest. *Derbs* 3F **85**
Peak Hill. *Linc* 4B **76**
Peakirk. *Pet* 5A **76**
Pearsie. *Ang* 3C **144**
Peasedown St John. *Bath* 1C **22**
Peaseland Green. *Norf* 4C **78**
Peasemore. *W Ber* 4C **36**
Peasenhall. *Suff* 4F **67**
Pease Pottage. *W Sus* 2D **26**
Peaslake. *Surr* 1B **26**
Peasley Cross. *Mers* 1H **83**
Peasmarsh. *E Sus* 3C **28**
Peasmarsh. *Som* 1G **13**
Peasmarsh. *Surr* 1A **26**
Peaston. *E Lot* 3H **129**
Peastonbank. *E Lot* 3H **129**
Peathill. *Abers* 2G **161**
Peat Inn. *Fife* 3G **137**
Peatling Magna. *Leics* 1C **62**
Peatling Parva. *Leics* 2C **62**
Peaton. *Arg* 1D **126**
Peaton. *Shrp* 2H **59**
Peats Corner. *Suff* 4D **66**
Pebmarsh. *Essx* 2B **54**
Pebworth. *Worc* 1G **49**
Pecket Well. *W Yor* 2H **91**
Peckforton. *Ches E* 5H **83**
Peckham Bush. *Kent* 5A **40**
Peckleton. *Leics* 5B **74**
Pedair-ffordd. *Powy* 3D **70**
Pedham. *Norf* 4F **79**
Pedlinge. *Kent* 2F **29**
Pedmore. *W Mid* 2D **60**
Pedwell. *Som* 3H **21**
Peebles. *Bord* 5F **129**
Peel. *IOM* 3B **108**
Peel. *Bord* 1G **119**
Peel Common. *Hants* 2D **16**
Peening Quarter. *Kent* 3C **28**
Peggs Green. *Leics* 4B **74**
Pegsdon. *C Beds* 2B **52**
Pegswood. *Nmbd* 1F **115**
Peinchorran. *High* 5E **155**
Peinlich. *High* 3D **154**
Pelaw. *Tyne* 3G **115**
Pelcomb Bridge. *Pemb* 3D **42**
Pelcomb Cross. *Pemb* 3D **42**
Peldon. *Essx* 4C **54**
Pelsall. *W Mid* 5E **73**
Pelton. *Dur* 4F **115**
Pelutho. *Cumb* 5C **112**
Pelynt. *Corn* 3G **7**
Pemberton. *Carm* 5F **45**
Pembrey. *Carm* 5E **45**
Pembridge. *Here* 5F **59**
Pembroke. *Pemb* 4D **43**
Pembroke Dock. *Pemb* 4D **42**
Pembroke Ferry. *Pemb* 4D **43**
Pembury. *Kent* 1H **27**
Penallt. *Mon* 4A **48**
Penally. *Pemb* 5F **43**
Penalt. *Here* 3A **48**
Penalum. *Pemb* 5F **43**
Penare. *Corn* 4D **6**
Penarth. *V Glam* 4E **33**
Penbeagle. *Corn* 3C **4**
Penberth. *Corn* 4B **4**
Pen-bont Rhydybeddau. *Cdgn* 2F **57**
Penbryn. *Cdgn* 5B **56**
Pencader. *Carm* 2E **45**
Pen-cae. *Cdgn* 5D **56**
Pencaenewydd. *Gwyn* 1D **68**
Pencaerau. *Neat* 3G **31**
Pencaitland. *E Lot* 3H **129**
Pencarnisiog. *IOA* 3C **80**
Pencarreg. *Carm* 1F **45**
Pencarrow. *Corn* 4B **10**
Pencelli. *Powy* 3D **46**
Pen-clawdd. *Swan* 3E **31**
Pencoed. *B'end* 3C **32**
Pencombe. *Here* 5H **59**
Pencraig. *Here* 3A **48**
Pencraig. *Powy* 3C **70**
Pendeen. *Corn* 3A **4**
Pendeford. *W Mid* 5D **72**
Penderyn. *Rhon* 5C **46**
Pendine. *Carm* 4G **43**
Pendlebury. *G Man* 4F **91**
Pendleton. *G Man* 1C **84**
Pendleton. *Lanc* 1F **91**
Pendock. *Worc* 2C **48**
Pendoggett. *Corn* 5A **10**
Pendomer. *Som* 1A **14**
Pendoylan. *V Glam* 4D **32**
Pendre. *B'end* 3C **32**
Penegoes. *Powy* 5G **69**
Penelewey. *Corn* 4C **6**
Penffordd. *Pemb* 2E **43**
Penffordd-Lâs. *Powy* 1A **58**
Penfro. *Pemb* 4D **43**
Pengam. *Cphy* 2E **33**
Pengam. *Card* 4F **33**
Penge. *G Lon* 3E **39**
Pengelly. *Corn* 4A **10**
Pengenffordd. *Powy* 2E **47**
Pengorffwysfa. *IOA* 1D **80**
Pengover Green. *Corn* 2G **7**
Pengwern. *Den* 3C **82**
Penhale. *Corn* 5D **5**
(nr. Mullion)
Penhale. *Corn* 3D **6**
(nr. St Austell)
Penhale Camp. *Corn* 3B **6**
Penhallow. *Corn* 3B **6**
Penhalvean. *Corn* 5B **6**
Penhelig. *Gwyn* 1F **57**
Penhill. *Swin* 3G **35**
Penhow. *Newp* 2H **33**
Penhurst. *E Sus* 4A **28**
Peniarth. *Gwyn* 5F **69**
Penicuik. *Midl* 3F **129**
Peniel. *Carm* 3E **45**
Penifiler. *High* 4D **155**
Peninver. *Arg* 3B **122**
Penisa'r Waun. *Gwyn* 4E **81**
Penistone. *S Yor* 4C **92**
Penketh. *Warr* 2H **83**
Penkill. *S Ayr* 5B **116**
Penkridge. *Staf* 4D **72**
Penley. *Wrex* 2G **71**
Penllech. *Gwyn* 2B **68**
Penllergaer. *Swan* 3F **31**
Pen-llyn. *IOA* 2C **80**
Penmachno. *Cnwy* 5G **81**
Penmaen. *Swan* 4E **31**
Penmaenmawr. *Cnwy* 3G **81**
Penmaenpool. *Gwyn* 4F **69**
Penmaen Rhos. *Cnwy* 3A **82**
Pen-marc. *V Glam* 5D **32**
Penmark. *V Glam* 5D **32**
Penmarth. *Corn* 5B **6**
Penmon. *IOA* 2F **81**
Penmorfa. *Gwyn* 1E **69**
Penmyndd. *IOA* 3E **81**
Penn. *Buck* 1A **38**
Penn. *Dors* 3G **13**
Penn. *W Mid* 1C **60**
Pennal. *Gwyn* 5G **69**
Pennan. *Abers* 2F **161**
Pennant. *Cdgn* 4E **57**
Pennant. *Den* 2C **70**
Pennant. *Gwyn* 3B **70**
Pennant. *Powy* 1A **58**
Pennant Melangell. *Powy* 3C **70**
Pennar. *Pemb* 4D **42**
Pennard. *Swan* 4E **31**
Pennerley. *Shrp* 1F **59**
Pennington. *Cumb* 2B **96**
Pennington. *G Man* 1A **84**
Pennington. *Hants* 3B **16**
Pennorth. *Powy* 3E **46**
Penn Street. *Buck* 1A **38**
Pennsylvania. *Devn* 3C **12**
Pennsylvania. *S Glo* 4C **34**
Penny Bridge. *Cumb* 1C **96**
Pennycross. *Plym* 3A **8**
Pennygate. *Norf* 3F **79**
Pennyghael. *Arg* 1C **132**
Penny Hill. *Linc* 3C **76**
Pennylands. *Lanc* 4C **90**
Pennymoor. *Devn* 1B **12**
Pennyvenie. *E Ayr* 4D **117**
Pennywell. *Tyne* 4G **115**
Penparc. *Cdgn* 1C **44**
Penparcau. *Cdgn* 2E **57**
Penpedairheol. *Cphy* 2E **33**
Penperlleni. *Mon* 5G **47**
Penpillick. *Corn* 3E **7**
Penpol. *Corn* 5C **6**
Penpoll. *Corn* 3F **7**
Penponds. *Corn* 3D **4**
Penpont. *Corn* 5A **10**
Penpont. *Dum* 5H **117**
Penpont. *Powy* 3C **46**
Penprysg. *B'end* 3C **32**
Penquit. *Devn* 3C **8**
Penrherber. *Carm* 1G **43**
Penrhiw. *Pemb* 1C **44**
Penrhiwceiber. *Rhon* 2D **32**
Pen Rhiwfawr. *Neat* 4H **45**
Penrhiw-llan. *Cdgn* 1D **44**
Penrhiw-pal. *Cdgn* 1D **44**
Penrhos. *Gwyn* 2C **68**
Penrhos. *Here* 5F **59**
Penrhos. *IOA* 2B **80**
Penrhos. *Mon* 4H **47**
Penrhos. *Powy* 4A **46**
Penrhos Garnedd. *Gwyn* 3E **81**
Penrhyn. *IOA* 1C **80**
Penrhyn Bay. *Cnwy* 2H **81**
Penrhyn-coch. *Cdgn* 2F **57**
Penrhyndeudraeth. *Gwyn* 2F **69**
Penrhyn Side. *Cnwy* 2H **81**
Penrice. *Swan* 4D **31**
Penrith. *Cumb* 2G **103**
Penrose. *Corn* 1C **6**
Penruddock. *Cumb* 2F **103**
Penryn. *Corn* 5B **6**
Pensarn. *Carm* 4E **45**
Pen-sarn. *Gwyn* 3E **69**
Pensax. *Worc* 4B **60**
Pensby. *Mers* 2E **83**
Penselwood. *Som* 3C **22**
Pensford. *Bath* 5B **34**
Pensham. *Worc* 1E **49**
Penshaw. *Tyne* 4G **115**
Penshurst. *Kent* 1G **27**
Pensilva. *Corn* 2G **7**
Pensnett. *W Mid* 2D **60**
Penston. *E Lot* 2H **129**
Penstone. *Devn* 2A **12**
Pente-tafarn-y-fedw. *Cnwy* 4H **81**
Pentewan. *Corn* 4E **6**
Pentir. *Gwyn* 4E **81**
Pentire. *Corn* 2B **6**
Pentlepoir. *Pemb* 4F **43**
Pentlow. *Essx* 1B **54**
Pentney. *Norf* 4G **77**
Penton Mewsey. *Hants* 2B **24**
Pentraeth. *IOA* 3E **81**
Pentre. *Powy* 1E **59**
(nr. Church Stoke)
Pentre. *Powy* 2D **58**
(nr. Kerry)
Pentre. *Powy* 2C **58**
(nr. Mochdre)
Pentre. *Rhon* 2C **32**
Pentre. *Shrp* 4F **71**
Pentre. *Wrex* 2D **70**
(nr. Llanfyllin)
Pentre. *Wrex* 1E **71**
(nr. Rhosllanerchrugog)
Pentrebach. *Carm* 2B **46**
Pentre-bach. *Cdgn* 1F **45**
Pentrebach. *Mer T* 5D **46**
Pentre-bach. *Powy* 2C **46**
Pentrebach. *Swan* 5G **45**
Pentre Berw. *IOA* 3D **80**
Pentre-bont. *Cnwy* 5G **81**
Pentrecagal. *Carm* 1D **44**
Pentre-celyn. *Den* 5D **82**
Pentre-clawdd. *Shrp* 2E **71**
Pentreclwydau. *Neat* 5B **46**
Pentre-cwrt. *Carm* 2D **45**
Pentre Dolau Honddu. *Powy* 1C **46**
Pentre-dwr. *Swan* 3F **31**
Pentrefelin. *Carm* 3F **45**
Pentrefelin. *Cdgn* 1G **45**
Pentrefelin. *Cnwy* 3H **81**
Pentrefelin. *Gwyn* 2E **69**
Pentrefoelas. *Cnwy* 5A **82**
Pentre Galar. *Pemb* 1F **43**
Pentregat. *Cdgn* 5C **56**
Pentre Gwenlais. *Carm* 4G **45**
Pentre Gwynfryn. *Gwyn* 3E **69**
Pentre Halkyn. *Flin* 3E **82**
Pentre Hodre. *Shrp* 3F **59**
Pentre-Llanrhaeadr. *Den* 4C **82**
Pentre Llifior. *Powy* 1D **58**
Pentrellwyn. *IOA* 2E **81**
Pentre-llwyn-llwyd. *Powy* 5B **58**
Pentre-llyn-cymmer. *Cnwy* 5B **82**
Pentre Meyrick. *V Glam* 4C **32**
Pentre-piod. *Gwyn* 2A **70**
Pentre-poeth. *Newp* 3F **33**
Pentre'r Beirdd. *Powy* 4D **70**
Pentre'r-felin. *Powy* 2C **46**
Pentre-ty-gwyn. *Carm* 2B **46**
Pentre-uchaf. *Gwyn* 2C **68**
Pentrich. *Derbs* 5A **86**
Pentridge. *Dors* 1F **15**
Pen-twyn. *Cphy* 5F **47**
(nr. Oakdale)
Pentwyn. *Cphy* 5E **46**
(nr. Rhymney)
Pentwyn. *Card* 3F **33**
Pentyrch. *Card* 3E **32**
Pentywyn. *Carm* 4G **43**
Penuwch. *Cdgn* 4E **57**
Penwithick. *Corn* 3E **7**
Penwyllt. *Powy* 4B **46**
Penybanc. *Carm* 4G **45**
(nr. Ammanford)
Pen-y-banc. *Carm* 3G **45**
(nr. Llandeilo)
Pen-y-bont. *Carm* 2H **43**
Penybont. *Powy* 4D **58**
(nr. Llandrindod Wells)
Pen-y-bont. *Powy* 3E **70**
(nr. Llanfyllin)
Pen-y-Bont Ar Ogwr. *B'end* 3C **32**
Penybontfawr. *Powy* 3C **70**
Penybryn. *Cphy* 2E **33**
Pen-y-bryn. *Pemb* 1B **44**
Pen-y-bryn. *Wrex* 1E **71**

Pen-y-cae—Pontneddfechan

Pen-y-cae. *Powy* 4B **46**
Penycae. *Wrex* 1E **71**
Pen-y-cae-mawr. *Mon* 2H **33**
Penycaerau. *Gwyn* 3A **68**
Pen-y-cefn. *Flin* 3D **82**
Pen-y-clawdd. *Mon* 5H **47**
Pen-y-coedcae. *Rhon* 3D **32**
Penycwm. *Pemb* 2C **42**
Pen-y-Darren. *Mer T* 5D **46**
Pen-y-fai. *B'end* 3B **32**
Penyffordd. *Flin* 4F **83**
(nr. Mold)
Pen-y-ffordd. *Flin* 2D **82**
(nr. Prestatyn)
Penyffridd. *Gwyn* 5E **81**
Pen-y-garn. *Cdgn* 2F **57**
Pen-y-garnedd. *IOA* 3E **81**
Penygarnedd. *Powy* 3D **70**
Pen-y-graig. *Gwyn* 2B **68**
Penygraig. *Rhon* 2C **32**
Penygraigwen. *IOA* 2D **80**
Pen-y-groes. *Carm* 4F **45**
Penygroes. *Gwyn* 5D **80**
Penygroes. *Pemb* 1F **43**
Pen-y-Mynydd. *Carm* 5E **45**
Penymynydd. *Flin* 4F **83**
Penyrheol. *Cphy* 3E **33**
Pen-yr-heol. *Mon* 4H **47**
Penyrheol. *Swan* 3E **31**
Pen-yr-Heolgerrig. *Mer T* 5D **46**
Penysarn. *IOA* 1D **80**
Pen-y-stryt. *Den* 5E **82**
Penywaun. *Rhon* 5C **46**
Penzance. *Corn* 3B **4**
Peopleton. *Worc* 5D **60**
Peover Heath. *Ches E* 3B **84**
Peper Harow. *Surr* 1A **26**
Peplow. *Shrp* 3A **72**
Pepper Arden. *N Yor* 4F **105**
Perceton. *N Ayr* 5E **127**
Percyhorner. *Abers* 2G **161**
Perham Down. *Wilts* 2A **24**
Periton. *Som* 2C **20**
Perkinsville. *Dur* 4F **115**
Perlethorpe. *Notts* 3D **86**
Perranarworthal. *Corn* 5B **6**
Perranporth. *Corn* 3B **6**
Perranuthnoe. *Corn* 4C **4**
Perranwell. *Corn* 5B **6**
Perranzabuloe. *Corn* 3B **6**
Perrott's Brook. *Glos* 5F **49**
Perry. *W Mid* 1E **61**
Perry Barr. *W Mid* 1E **61**
Perry Crofts. *Staf* 5G **73**
Perry Green. *Essx* 3B **54**
Perry Green. *Herts* 4E **53**
Perry Green. *Wilts* 3E **35**
Perry Street. *Kent* 3H **39**
Perry Street. *Som* 2G **13**
Perrywood. *Kent* 5E **41**
Pershall. *Staf* 3C **72**
Pershore. *Worc* 1E **49**
Pertenhall. *Bed* 4H **63**
Perth. *Per* 1D **136**
Perthy. *Shrp* 2F **71**
Perton. *Staf* 1C **60**
Pertwood. *Wilts* 3D **23**
Peterborough. *Pet* 1A **64**
Peterburn. *High* 5B **162**
Peterchurch. *Here* 2G **47**
Peterculter. *Aber* 3F **153**
Peterhead. *Abers* 4H **161**
Peterlee. *Dur* 5H **115**
Petersfield. *Hants* 4F **25**
Petersfinger. *Wilts* 4G **23**
Peter's Green. *Herts* 4B **52**
Peters Marland. *Devn* 1E **11**
Peterstone Wentlooge. *Newp* 3F **33**
Peterston-super-Ely. *V Glam* 4D **32**
Peterstow. *Here* 3A **48**
Peter Tavy. *Devn* 5F **11**
Petham. *Kent* 5F **41**
Petherwin Gate. *Corn* 4C **10**
Petrockstowe. *Devn* 2F **11**
Petsoe End. *Mil* 1G **51**
Pett. *E Sus* 4C **28**
Pettaugh. *Suff* 5D **66**
Pett Bottom. *Kent* 5F **41**
Petteridge. *Kent* 1A **28**
Pettinain. *S Lan* 5C **128**
Pettistree. *Suff* 5E **67**
Petton. *Devn* 4D **20**
Petton. *Shrp* 3G **71**
Petts Wood. *G Lon* 4F **39**
Pettycur. *Fife* 1F **129**
Pettywell. *Norf* 3C **78**
Petworth. *W Sus* 3A **26**
Pevensey. *E Sus* 5A **28**
Pevensey Bay. *E Sus* 5A **28**
Pewsey. *Wilts* 5G **35**
Pheasants Hill. *Buck* 3F **37**
Philadelphia. *Tyne* 4G **115**
Philham. *Devn* 4C **18**
Philiphaugh. *Bord* 2G **119**
Phillack. *Corn* 3C **4**
Philleigh. *Corn* 5C **6**
Philpstoun. *W Lot* 2D **128**
Phocle Green. *Here* 3B **48**
Phoenix Green. *Hants* 1F **25**
Pibsbury. *Som* 4H **21**
Pibwrlwyd. *Carm* 4E **45**
Pica. *Cumb* 2B **102**
Piccadilly. *Warw* 1G **61**
Piccadilly Corner. *Norf* 2E **67**
Piccotts End. *Herts* 5A **52**
Pickering. *N Yor* 1B **100**
Picket Piece. *Hants* 2B **24**
Picket Post. *Hants* 2G **15**
Pickford. *W Mid* 2G **61**
Pickhill. *N Yor* 1F **99**
Picklenash. *Glos* 3C **48**
Picklescott. *Shrp* 1G **59**
Pickletillem. *Fife* 1G **137**
Pickmere. *Ches E* 3A **84**
Pickstock. *Telf* 3B **72**
Pickwell. *Devn* 2E **19**
Pickwell. *Leics* 4E **75**
Pickworth. *Linc* 2H **75**
Pickworth. *Rut* 4G **75**
Picton. *Ches W* 3G **83**
Picton. *Flin* 2D **82**
Picton. *N Yor* 4B **106**
Pict's Hill. *Som* 4H **21**
Piddinghoe. *E Sus* 5F **27**
Piddington. *Buck* 2G **37**
Piddington. *Nptn* 5F **63**
Piddington. *Oxon* 4E **51**
Piddlehinton. *Dors* 3C **14**
Piddletrenthide. *Dors* 2C **14**
Pidley. *Cambs* 3C **64**
Pidney. *Dors* 2C **14**
Pie Corner. *Here* 4A **60**
Piercebridge. *Darl* 3F **105**
Pierowall. *Orkn* 3D **172**
Pigdon. *Nmbd* 1E **115**
Pightley. *Som* 3F **21**
Pikehall. *Derbs* 5F **85**
Pikeshill. *Hants* 2A **16**
Pilford. *Dors* 2F **15**
Pilgrims Hatch. *Essx* 1G **39**
Pilham. *Linc* 1F **87**
Pill. *N Som* 4A **34**
Pillaton. *Corn* 2H **7**
Pillaton. *Staf* 4D **72**
Pillerton Hersey. *Warw* 1A **50**
Pillerton Priors. *Warw* 1A **50**
Pilleth. *Powy* 4E **59**
Pilley. *Hants* 3B **16**
Pilley. *S Yor* 4D **92**
Pillgwenlly. *Newp* 3G **33**
Pilling. *Lanc* 5D **96**
Pilling Lane. *Lanc* 5C **96**
Pillowell. *Glos* 5B **48**
Pill, The. *Mon* 3H **33**
Pillwell. *Dors* 1C **14**
Pilning. *S Glo* 3A **34**
Pilsbury. *Derbs* 4F **85**
Pilsdon. *Dors* 3H **13**
Pilsgate. *Pet* 5H **75**
Pilsley. *Derbs* 3G **85**
(nr. Bakewell)
Pilsley. *Derbs* 4B **86**
(nr. Clay Cross)
Pilson Green. *Norf* 4F **79**
Piltdown. *E Sus* 3F **27**
Pilton. *Edin* 2F **129**
Pilton. *Nptn* 2H **63**
Pilton. *Rut* 5G **75**
Pilton. *Som* 2A **22**
Pilton Green. *Swan* 4D **30**
Pimperne. *Dors* 2E **15**
Pinchbeck. *Linc* 3B **76**
Pinchbeck Bars. *Linc* 3A **76**
Pinchbeck West. *Linc* 3B **76**
Pinfold. *Lanc* 3B **90**
Pinford End. *Suff* 5H **65**
Pinged. *Carm* 5E **45**
Pinhoe. *Devn* 3C **12**
Pinkerton. *E Lot* 2D **130**
Pinkneys Green. *Wind* 3G **37**
Pinley. *W Mid* 3A **62**
Pinley Green. *Warw* 4G **61**
Pinmill. *Suff* 2F **55**
Pinmore. *S Ayr* 5B **116**
Pinner. *G Lon* 2C **38**
Pins Green. *Worc* 1C **48**
Pinsley Green. *Ches E* 1H **71**
Pinvin. *Worc* 1E **49**
Pinwherry. *S Ayr* 1G **109**
Pinxton. *Derbs* 5B **86**
Pipe and Lyde. *Here* 1A **48**
Pipe Aston. *Here* 3G **59**
Pipe Gate. *Shrp* 1B **72**
Pipehill. *Staf* 5E **73**
Piperhill. *High* 3C **158**
Pipe Ridware. *Staf* 4E **73**
Pipers Pool. *Corn* 4C **10**
Pipewell. *Nptn* 2F **63**
Pippacott. *Devn* 3F **19**
Pipton. *Powy* 2E **47**
Pirbright. *Surr* 5A **38**
Pirnmill. *N Ayr* 5G **125**
Pirton. *Herts* 2B **52**
Pirton. *Worc* 1D **49**
Pisgah. *Stir* 3G **135**
Pishill. *Oxon* 3F **37**
Pistyll. *Gwyn* 1C **68**
Pitagowan. *Per* 2F **143**
Pitcairn. *Per* 3F **143**
Pitcairngreen. *Per* 1C **136**
Pitcalnie. *High* 1C **158**
Pitcaple. *Abers* 1E **152**
Pitchcombe. *Glos* 5D **48**
Pitchcott. *Buck* 3F **51**
Pitchford. *Shrp* 5H **71**
Pitch Green. *Buck* 5F **51**
Pitch Place. *Surr* 5A **38**
Pitcombe. *Som* 3B **22**
Pitcox. *E Lot* 2C **130**
Pitcur. *Per* 5B **144**
Pitfichie. *Abers* 2D **152**
Pitgrudy. *High* 4E **165**
Pitkennedy. *Ang* 3E **145**
Pitlessie. *Fife* 3F **137**
Pitlochry. *Per* 3G **143**
Pitmachie. *Abers* 1D **152**
Pitmaduthy. *High* 1B **158**
Pitmedden. *Abers* 1F **153**
Pitminster. *Som* 1F **13**
Pitnacree. *Per* 3G **143**
Pitney. *Som* 4H **21**
Pitroddie. *Per* 1E **136**
Pitscottie. *Fife* 2G **137**
Pitsea. *Essx* 2B **40**
Pitsford. *Nptn* 4E **63**
Pitsford Hill. *Som* 3E **20**
Pitsmoor. *S Yor* 2A **86**
Pitstone. *Buck* 4H **51**
Pitt. *Hants* 4C **24**
Pitt Court. *Glos* 2C **34**
Pittentrail. *High* 3E **164**
Pittenweem. *Fife* 3H **137**
Pittington. *Dur* 5G **115**
Pitton. *Swan* 4D **30**
Pitton. *Wilts* 3H **23**
Pittswood. *Kent* 1H **27**
Pittulie. *Abers* 2G **161**
Pittville. *Glos* 3E **49**
Pitversie. *Per* 2D **136**
Pityme. *Corn* 1D **6**
Pity Me. *Dur* 5F **115**
Pixey Green. *Suff* 3E **67**
Pixley. *Here* 2B **48**
Place Newton. *N Yor* 2C **100**
Plaidy. *Abers* 3E **161**
Plaidy. *Corn* 3G **7**
Plain Dealings. *Pemb* 3E **43**
Plains. *N Lan* 3A **128**
Plainsfield. *Som* 3E **21**
Plaish. *Shrp* 1H **59**
Plaistow. *Here* 2B **48**
Plaistow. *W Sus* 2B **26**
Plaitford. *Wilts* 1A **16**
Plas Llwyd. *Cnwy* 3B **82**
Plastow Green. *Hants* 5D **36**
Plas yn Cefn. *Den* 3C **82**
Platt. *Kent* 5H **39**
Platt Bridge. *G Man* 4E **90**
Platt Lane. *Shrp* 2H **71**
Platts Common. *S Yor* 4D **92**
Platt's Heath. *Kent* 5C **40**
Platt, The. *E Sus* 2G **27**
Plawsworth. *Dur* 5F **115**
Plaxtol. *Kent* 5H **39**
Playden. *E Sus* 3D **28**
Playford. *Suff* 1F **55**
Play Hatch. *Oxon* 4F **37**
Playing Place. *Corn* 4C **6**
Playley Green. *Glos* 2C **48**
Plealey. *Shrp* 5G **71**
Plean. *Stir* 1B **128**
Pleasington. *Bkbn* 2E **91**
Pleasley. *Derbs* 4C **86**
Pledgdon Green. *Essx* 3F **53**
Plenmeller. *Nmbd* 3A **114**
Pleshey. *Essx* 4G **53**
Plockton. *High* 5H **155**
Plocrapol. *W Isl* 8D **171**
Ploughfield. *Here* 1G **47**
Plowden. *Shrp* 2F **59**
Ploxgreen. *Shrp* 5F **71**
Pluckley. *Kent* 1D **28**
Plucks Gutter. *Kent* 4G **41**
Plumbland. *Cumb* 1C **102**
Plumgarths. *Cumb* 5F **103**
Plumley. *Ches E* 3B **84**
Plummers Plain. *W Sus* 3D **26**
Plumpton. *Cumb* 1F **103**
Plumpton. *E Sus* 4E **27**
Plumpton. *Nptn* 1D **50**
Plumpton Foot. *Cumb* 1F **103**
Plumpton Green. *E Sus* 4E **27**
Plumpton Head. *Cumb* 1G **103**
Plumstead. *G Lon* 3F **39**
Plumstead. *Norf* 2D **78**
Plumtree. *Notts* 2D **74**
Plumtree Park. *Notts* 2D **74**
Plungar. *Leics* 2E **75**
Plush. *Dors* 2C **14**
Plushabridge. *Corn* 5D **10**
Plwmp. *Cdgn* 5C **56**
Plymouth. *Plym* 3A **8**
Plympton. *Plym* 3B **8**
Plymstock. *Plym* 3B **8**
Plymtree. *Devn* 2D **12**
Pockley. *N Yor* 1A **100**
Pocklington. *E Yor* 5C **100**
Pode Hole. *Linc* 3B **76**
Podimore. *Som* 4A **22**
Podington. *Bed* 4G **63**
Podmore. *Staf* 2B **72**
Poffley End. *Oxon* 4B **50**
Point Clear. *Essx* 4D **54**
Pointon. *Linc* 2A **76**
Pokesdown. *Bour* 3G **15**
Polbae. *Dum* 2H **109**
Polbain. *High* 3E **163**
Polbathic. *Corn* 3H **7**
Polbeth. *W Lot* 3D **128**
Polbrock. *Corn* 2E **6**
Polchar. *High* 3C **150**
Polebrook. *Nptn* 2H **63**
Pole Elm. *Worc* 1D **48**
Polegate. *E Sus* 5G **27**
Pole Moor. *W Yor* 3A **92**
Poles. *High* 4E **165**
Polesworth. *Warw* 5G **73**
Polglass. *High* 3E **163**
Polgooth. *Corn* 3D **6**
Poling. *W Sus* 5B **26**
Poling Corner. *W Sus* 5B **26**
Polio. *High* 1B **158**
Polkerris. *Corn* 3E **7**
Polla. *High* 3D **166**
Pollard Street. *Norf* 2F **79**
Pollicott. *Buck* 4F **51**
Pollington. *E Yor* 3G **93**
Polloch. *High* 2B **140**
Pollok. *Glas* 3G **127**
Pollokshaws. *Glas* 3G **127**
Pollokshields. *Glas* 3G **127**
Polmaily. *High* 5G **157**
Polmassick. *Corn* 4D **6**
Polmont. *Falk* 2C **128**
Polnessan. *E Ayr* 3D **116**
Polnish. *High* 5F **147**
Polperro. *Corn* 3G **7**
Polruan. *Corn* 3F **7**
Polscoe. *Corn* 2F **7**
Polsham. *Som* 2A **22**
Polskeoch. *Dum* 4F **117**
Polstead. *Suff* 2C **54**
Polstead Heath. *Suff* 1C **54**
Poltesco. *Corn* 5E **5**
Poltimore. *Devn* 3C **12**
Polton. *Midl* 3G **129**
Polwarth. *Bord* 4D **130**
Polyphant. *Corn* 4C **10**
Polzeath. *Corn* 1D **6**
Ponde. *Powy* 2E **46**
Pondersbridge. *Cambs* 1B **64**
Ponders End. *G Lon* 1E **39**
Pond Street. *Essx* 2E **53**
Pondtail. *Hants* 1G **25**
Ponsanooth. *Corn* 5B **6**
Ponsongath. *Corn* 5E **5**
Ponsworthy. *Devn* 5H **11**
Pontamman. *Carm* 4G **45**
Pontantwn. *Carm* 4E **45**
Pontardawe. *Neat* 5H **45**
Pontarddulais. *Swan* 5F **45**
Pontarfynach. *Cdgn* 3G **57**
Pont-ar-gothi. *Carm* 3F **45**
Pont ar Hydfer. *Powy* 3B **46**
Pontarllechau. *Carm* 3H **45**
Pontarsais. *Carm* 3E **45**
Pontblyddyn. *Flin* 4E **83**
Pontbren Llwyd. *Rhon* 5C **46**
Pont Cyfyng. *Cnwy* 5G **81**
Pontdolgoch. *Powy* 1C **58**
Pontefract. *W Yor* 2E **93**
Ponteland. *Nmbd* 2E **115**
Ponterwyd. *Cdgn* 2G **57**
Pontesbury. *Shrp* 5G **71**
Pontesford. *Shrp* 5G **71**
Pontfadog. *Wrex* 2E **71**
Pontfaen. *Pemb* 1E **43**
Pont-faen. *Powy* 2C **46**
Pont-Faen. *Shrp* 2E **71**
Pontgarreg. *Cdgn* 5C **56**
Pont-Henri. *Carm* 5E **45**
Ponthir. *Torf* 2G **33**
Ponthirwaun. *Cdgn* 1C **44**
Pont-iets. *Carm* 5E **45**
Pontllanfraith. *Cphy* 2E **33**
Pontlliw. *Swan* 5G **45**
Pont Llogel. *Powy* 4C **70**
Pontllyfni. *Gwyn* 5D **80**
Pontlottyn. *Cphy* 5E **46**
Pontneddfechan. *Neat* 5C **46**

Pont-newydd. *Carm* 5E **45**
Pont-newydd. *Flin* 4D **82**
Pontnewydd. *Torf* 2F **33**
Pont Pen-y-benglog. *Gwyn* 4F **81**
Pontrhydfendigaid. *Cdgn* 4G **57**
Pont Rhyd-y-cyff. *B'end* 3B **32**
Pontrhydyfen. *Neat* 2A **32**
Pont-rhyd-y-groes. *Cdgn* 3G **57**
Pontrhydyrun. *Torf* 2F **33**
Pont Rhythallt. *Gwyn* 4E **81**
Pontrilas. *Here* 3G **47**
Pontrilas Road. *Here* 3G **47**
Pontrobert. *Powy* 4D **70**
Pont-rug. *Gwyn* 4E **81**
Ponts Green. *E Sus* 4A **28**
Pontshill. *Here* 3B **48**
Pont-Sian. *Cdgn* 1E **45**
Pontsticill. *Mer T* 4D **46**
Pont-Walby. *Neat* 5B **46**
Pontwelly. *Carm* 2E **45**
Pontwgan. *Cnwy* 3G **81**
Pontyates. *Carm* 5E **45**
Pontyberem. *Carm* 4F **45**
Pontybodkin. *Flin* 5E **83**
Pontyclun. *Rhon* 3D **32**
Pontycymer. *B'end* 2C **32**
Pontyglazier. *Pemb* 1F **43**
Pontygwaith. *Rhon* 2D **32**
Pont-y-pant. *Cnwy* 5G **81**
Pontypool. *Torf* 2G **33**
Pontypridd. *Rhon* 2D **32**
Pontypwl. *Torf* 2G **33**
Pontywaun. *Cphy* 2F **33**
Pooksgreen. *Hants* 1B **16**
Pool. *Corn* 4A **6**
Pool. *W Yor* 5E **99**
Poole. *N Yor* 2E **93**
Poole. *Pool* 3F **15**
Poole. *Som* 4E **21**
Poole Keynes. *Glos* 2E **35**
Poolend. *Staf* 5D **84**
Poolewe. *High* 5C **162**
Pooley Bridge. *Cumb* 2F **103**
Poolfold. *Staf* 5C **84**
Pool Head. *Here* 5H **59**
Pool Hey. *Lanc* 3B **90**
Poolhill. *Glos* 3C **48**
Poolmill. *Here* 3A **48**
Pool o' Muckhart. *Clac* 3C **136**
Pool Quay. *Powy* 4E **71**
Poolsbrook. *Derbs* 3B **86**
Pool Street. *Essx* 2A **54**
Pootings. *Kent* 1F **27**
Pope Hill. *Pemb* 3D **42**
Pope's Hill. *Glos* 4B **48**
Popeswood. *Brac* 5G **37**
Popham. *Hants* 2D **24**
Poplar. *G Lon* 2E **39**
Popley. *Hants* 1E **25**
Porchfield. *IOW* 3C **16**
Porin. *High* 3F **157**
Poringland. *Norf* 5E **79**
Porkellis. *Corn* 5A **6**
Porlock. *Som* 2B **20**
Porlock Weir. *Som* 2B **20**
Portachoillan. *Arg* 4F **125**
Port Adhair Bheinn na Faoghla. *W Isl* 3C **170**
Port Adhair Thirlodh. *Arg* 4B **138**
Port Ann. *Arg* 1H **125**
Port Appin. *Arg* 4D **140**
Port Asgaig. *Arg* 3C **124**
Port Askaig. *Arg* 3C **124**
Portavadie. *Arg* 3H **125**
Port Bannatyne. *Arg* 3B **126**
Portbury. *N Som* 4A **34**
Port Carlisle. *Cumb* 3D **112**
Port Charlotte. *Arg* 4A **124**
Portchester. *Hants* 2E **16**
Port Clarence. *Stoc T* 2B **106**
Port Dinorwig. *Gwyn* 4E **81**
Port Driseach. *Arg* 2A **126**
Port Dundas. *Glas* 3H **127**
Port Ellen. *Arg* 5B **124**
Port Elphinstone. *Abers* 1E **153**
Portencalzie. *Dum* 2F **109**
Portencross. *N Ayr* 5C **126**
Port Erin. *IOM* 5A **108**
Port Erroll. *Abers* 5H **161**
Porter's Fen Corner. *Norf* 5E **77**
Portesham. *Dors* 4B **14**
Portessie. *Mor* 2B **160**
Port e Vullen. *IOM* 2D **108**
Port-Eynon. *Swan* 4D **30**
Portfield. *Som* 4H **21**
Portfield Gate. *Pemb* 3D **42**
Portgate. *Devn* 4E **11**
Port Gaverne. *Corn* 4A **10**
Port Glasgow. *Inv* 2E **127**
Portgordon. *Mor* 2A **160**
Portgower. *High* 2H **165**
Porth. *Corn* 2C **6**
Porth. *Rhon* 2D **32**
Porthaethwy. *IOA* 3E **81**
Porthallow. *Corn* 3G **7** (nr. Looe)
Porthallow. *Corn* 4E **5** (nr. St Keverne)
Porthalong. *High* 5C **154**
Porthcawl. *B'end* 4B **32**
Porthceri. *V Glam* 5D **32**
Porthcothan. *Corn* 1C **6**
Porthcurno. *Corn* 4A **4**
Port Henderson. *High* 1G **155**
Porthgain. *Pemb* 1C **42**
Porthgwarra. *Corn* 4A **4**
Porthill. *Shrp* 4G **71**
Porthkerry. *V Glam* 5D **32**
Porthleven. *Corn* 4D **4**
Porthllechog. *IOA* 1D **80**
Porthmadog. *Gwyn* 2E **69**
Porthmeirion. *Gwyn* 2E **69**
Porthmeor. *Corn* 3B **4**
Porth Navas. *Corn* 4E **5**
Portholland. *Corn* 4D **6**
Porthoustock. *Corn* 4F **5**
Porthtowan. *Corn* 4A **6**
Porth Tywyn. *Carm* 5E **45**
Porth-y-felin. *IOA* 2B **80**
Porthyrhyd. *Carm* 4F **45** (nr. Carmarthen)
Porthyrhyd. *Carm* 2H **45** (nr. Llandovery)
Porth-y-waen. *Shrp* 3E **71**
Portincaple. *Arg* 4B **134**
Portington. *E Yor* 1A **94**
Portinnisherrich. *Arg* 2G **133**
Portinscale. *Cumb* 2D **102**
Port Isaac. *Corn* 1D **6**
Portishead. *N Som* 4H **33**
Portknockie. *Mor* 2B **160**
Port Lamont. *Arg* 2B **126**
Portlethen. *Abers* 4G **153**
Portlethen Village. *Abers* 4G **153**
Portling. *Dum* 4F **111**
Port Lion. *Pemb* 4D **43**
Portloe. *Corn* 5D **6**
Port Logan. *Dum* 5F **109**
Portmahomack. *High* 5G **165**
Port Mead. *Swan* 3F **31**
Portmellon. *Corn* 4E **6**
Port Mholair. *W Isl* 4H **171**
Port Mor. *High* 1F **139**
Portmore. *Hants* 3B **16**
Port Mulgrave. *N Yor* 3E **107**
Portnacroish. *Arg* 4D **140**
Portnahaven. *Arg* 4A **124**
Portnalong. *High* 5C **154**
Portnaluchaig. *High* 5E **147**
Portnancon. *High* 2E **167**
Port Nan Giuran. *W Isl* 4H **171**
Port nan Long. *W Isl* 1D **170**
Port Nis. *W Isl* 1H **171**
Portobello. *Edin* 2G **129**
Portobello. *W Yor* 3D **92**
Port of Menteith. *Stir* 3E **135**
Porton. *Wilts* 3G **23**
Portormin. *High* 5D **168**
Portpatrick. *Dum* 4F **109**
Port Quin. *Corn* 1D **6**
Port Ramsay. *Arg* 4C **140**
Portreath. *Corn* 4A **6**
Portree. *High* 4D **155**
Port Righ. *High* 4D **155**
Port St Mary. *IOM* 5B **108**
Portscatho. *Corn* 5C **6**
Portsea. *Port* 2E **17**
Portskerra. *High* 2A **168**
Portskewett. *Mon* 3A **34**
Portslade-by-Sea. *Brig* 5D **26**
Portsmouth. *Port* 3E **17**
Portsmouth. *W Yor* 2H **91**
Port Soderick. *IOM* 4C **108**
Port Solent. *Port* 2E **17**
Portsonachan. *Arg* 1H **133**
Portsoy. *Abers* 2C **160**
Port Sunlight. *Mers* 2F **83**
Portswood. *Sotn* 1C **16**
Port Talbot. *Neat* 4G **31**
Porttannachy. *Mor* 2A **160**
Port Tennant. *Swan* 3F **31**
Portuairk. *High* 2F **139**
Portway. *Here* 1H **47**
Portway. *Worc* 3E **61**
Port Wemyss. *Arg* 4A **124**
Port William. *Dum* 5A **110**
Portwrinkle. *Corn* 3H **7**
Poslingford. *Suff* 1A **54**
Postbridge. *Devn* 5G **11**
Postcombe. *Oxon* 2F **37**
Post Green. *Dors* 3E **15**
Posthill. *Staf* 5G **73**
Postling. *Kent* 2F **29**
Postlip. *Glos* 3F **49**
Post-Mawr. *Cdgn* 5D **56**
Postwick. *Norf* 5E **79**
Potarch. *Abers* 4D **152**
Potsgrove. *C Beds* 3H **51**
Potten End. *Herts* 5A **52**
Potter Brompton. *N Yor* 2D **101**
Pottergate Street. *Norf* 1D **66**
Potterhanworth. *Linc* 4H **87**
Potterhanworth Booths. *Linc* 4H **87**
Potter Heigham. *Norf* 4G **79**
Potter Hill. *Leics* 3E **75**
Potteries, The. *Stoke* 1C **72**
Potterne. *Wilts* 1E **23**
Potterne Wick. *Wilts* 1E **23**
Potternewton. *W Yor* 1D **92**
Potters Bar. *Herts* 5C **52**
Potters Brook. *Lanc* 4D **97**
Potter's Cross. *Staf* 2C **60**
Potters Crouch. *Herts* 5B **52**
Potter Somersal. *Derbs* 2F **73**
Potterspury. *Nptn* 1F **51**
Potter Street. *Essx* 5E **53**
Potterton. *Abers* 2G **153**
Potthorpe. *Norf* 3B **78**
Pottle Street. *Wilts* 2D **22**
Potto. *N Yor* 4B **106**
Potton. *C Beds* 1C **52**
Pott Row. *Norf* 3G **77**
Pott Shrigley. *Ches E* 3D **84**
Poughill. *Corn* 2C **10**
Poughill. *Devn* 2B **12**
Poulner. *Hants* 2G **15**
Poulshot. *Wilts* 1E **23**
Poulton. *Glos* 5G **49**
Poulton-le-Fylde. *Lanc* 1B **90**
Pound Bank. *Worc* 3B **60**
Poundbury. *Dors* 3B **14**
Poundfield. *E Sus* 2G **27**
Poundgate. *E Sus* 3F **27**
Pound Green. *E Sus* 3G **27**
Pound Green. *Suff* 5G **65**
Pound Hill. *W Sus* 2D **27**
Poundland. *S Ayr* 1G **109**
Poundon. *Buck* 3E **51**
Poundsgate. *Devn* 5H **11**
Poundstock. *Corn* 3C **10**
Pound Street. *Hants* 5C **36**
Pounsley. *E Sus* 3G **27**
Powburn. *Nmbd* 3E **121**
Powderham. *Devn* 4C **12**
Powerstock. *Dors* 3A **14**
Powfoot. *Dum* 3C **112**
Powick. *Worc* 5C **60**
Powmill. *Per* 4C **136**
Poxwell. *Dors* 4C **14**
Poyle. *Slo* 3B **38**
Poynings. *W Sus* 4D **26**
Poyntington. *Dors* 4B **22**
Poynton. *Ches E* 2D **84**
Poynton. *Telf* 4H **71**
Poynton Green. *Telf* 4H **71**
Poystreet Green. *Suff* 5B **66**
Praa Sands. *Corn* 4C **4**
Pratt's Bottom. *G Lon* 4F **39**
Praze-an-Beeble. *Corn* 3D **4**
Prees. *Shrp* 2H **71**
Preesall. *Lanc* 5C **96**
Preesall Park. *Lanc* 5C **96**
Prees Green. *Shrp* 2H **71**
Prees Higher Heath. *Shrp* 2H **71**
Prendergast. *Pemb* 3D **42**
Prendwick. *Nmbd* 3E **121**
Pren-gwyn. *Cdgn* 1E **45**
Prenteg. *Gwyn* 1E **69**
Prenton. *Mers* 2F **83**
Prescot. *Mers* 1G **83**
Prescott. *Devn* 1D **12**
Prescott. *Shrp* 3G **71**
Preshute. *Wilts* 5G **35**
Pressen. *Nmbd* 1C **120**
Prestatyn. *Den* 2C **82**
Prestbury. *Ches E* 3D **84**
Prestbury. *Glos* 3E **49**
Presteigne. *Powy* 4F **59**
Presthope. *Shrp* 1H **59**
Prestleigh. *Som* 2B **22**
Preston. *Brig* 5E **27**
Preston. *Devn* 5B **12**
Preston. *Dors* 4C **14**
Preston. *E Lot* 2B **130** (nr. East Linton)
Preston. *E Lot* 2G **129** (nr. Prestonpans)
Preston. *E Yor* 1E **95**
Preston. *Glos* 5F **49**
Preston. *Herts* 3B **52**
Preston. *Kent* 4G **41** (nr. Canterbury)
Preston. *Kent* 4E **40** (nr. Faversham)
Preston. *Lanc* 2D **90**
Preston. *Nmbd* 2F **121**
Preston. *Rut* 5F **75**
Preston. *Bord* 4D **130**
Preston. *Shrp* 4H **71**
Preston. *Suff* 5B **66**
Preston. *Wilts* 4A **36** (nr. Aldbourne)
Preston. *Wilts* 4F **35** (nr. Lyneham)
Preston Bagot. *Warw* 4F **61**
Preston Bissett. *Buck* 3E **51**
Preston Bowyer. *Som* 4E **21**
Preston Brockhurst. *Shrp* 3H **71**
Preston Brook. *Hal* 3H **83**
Preston Candover. *Hants* 2E **24**
Preston Capes. *Nptn* 5C **62**
Preston Cross. *Glos* 2B **48**
Preston Gubbals. *Shrp* 4G **71**
Preston-le-Skerne. *Dur* 2A **106**
Preston Marsh. *Here* 1A **48**
Prestonmill. *Dum* 4A **112**
Preston on Stour. *Warw* 5G **61**
Preston on the Hill. *Hal* 2H **83**
Preston on Wye. *Here* 1G **47**
Prestonpans. *E Lot* 2G **129**
Preston Plucknett. *Som* 1A **14**
Preston-under-Scar. *N Yor* 5D **104**
Preston upon the Weald Moors. *Telf* 4A **72**
Preston Wynne. *Here* 1A **48**
Prestwich. *G Man* 4G **91**
Prestwick. *Nmbd* 2E **115**
Prestwick. *S Ayr* 2C **116**
Prestwold. *Leics* 3C **74**
Prestwood. *Buck* 5G **51**
Prestwood. *Staf* 1E **73**
Price Town. *B'end* 2C **32**
Prickwillow. *Cambs* 2E **65**
Priddy. *Som* 1A **22**
Priestcliffe. *Derbs* 3F **85**
Priesthill. *Glas* 3G **127**
Priest Hutton. *Lanc* 2E **97**
Priestland. *E Ayr* 1E **117**
Priest Weston. *Shrp* 1E **59**
Priestwood. *Brac* 4G **37**
Priestwood. *Kent* 4A **40**
Primethorpe. *Leics* 1C **62**
Primrose Green. *Norf* 4C **78**
Primrose Hill. *Derbs* 5B **86**
Primrose Hill. *Glos* 5B **48**
Primrose Hill. *Lanc* 4B **90**
Primrose Valley. *N Yor* 2F **101**
Primsidemill. *Bord* 2C **120**
Princes Gate. *Pemb* 3F **43**
Princes Risborough. *Buck* 5G **51**
Princethorpe. *Warw* 3B **62**
Princetown. *Devn* 5F **11**
Prinsted. *W Sus* 2F **17**
Prion. *Den* 4C **82**
Prior Muir. *Fife* 2H **137**
Prior's Frome. *Here* 2A **48**
Priors Halton. *Shrp* 3G **59**
Priors Hardwick. *Warw* 5B **62**
Priorslee. *Telf* 4B **72**
Priors Marston. *Warw* 5B **62**
Prior's Norton. *Glos* 3D **48**
Priory, The. *W Ber* 5B **36**
Priory Wood. *Here* 1F **47**
Priston. *Bath* 5B **34**
Pristow Green. *Norf* 2D **66**
Prittlewell. *S'end* 2C **40**
Privett. *Hants* 4E **25**
Prixford. *Devn* 3F **19**
Probus. *Corn* 4D **6**
Prospect. *Cumb* 5C **112**
Prospect Village. *Staf* 4E **73**
Provanmill. *Glas* 3H **127**
Prudhoe. *Nmbd* 3D **115**
Publow. *Bath* 5B **34**
Puckeridge. *Herts* 3D **53**
Puckington. *Som* 1G **13**
Pucklechurch. *S Glo* 4B **34**
Puckrup. *Glos* 2D **49**
Puddinglake. *Ches W* 4B **84**
Puddington. *Ches W* 3F **83**
Puddington. *Devn* 1B **12**
Puddlebrook. *Glos* 4B **48**
Puddledock. *Norf* 1C **66**
Puddletown. *Dors* 3C **14**
Pudleston. *Here* 5H **59**
Pudsey. *W Yor* 1C **92**
Pulborough. *W Sus* 4B **26**
Puleston. *Telf* 3B **72**
Pulford. *Ches W* 5F **83**
Pulham. *Dors* 2C **14**
Pulham Market. *Norf* 2D **66**
Pulham St Mary. *Norf* 2E **66**
Pulley. *Shrp* 5G **71**
Pulloxhill. *C Beds* 2A **52**
Pulpit Hill. *Arg* 1F **133**
Pulverbatch. *Shrp* 5G **71**
Pumpherston. *W Lot* 3D **128**
Pumsaint. *Carm* 1G **45**
Puncheston. *Pemb* 2E **43**
Puncknowle. *Dors* 4A **14**
Punnett's Town. *E Sus* 3H **27**
Purbrook. *Hants* 2E **17**
Purfleet. *Thur* 3G **39**
Puriton. *Som* 2G **21**
Purleigh. *Essx* 5B **54**
Purley. *G Lon* 4E **39**
Purley on Thames. *W Ber* 4E **37**
Purlogue. *Shrp* 3E **59**
Purl's Bridge. *Cambs* 2D **65**
Purse Caundle. *Dors* 1B **14**

Purslow. Shrp 2F 59
Purston Jaglin. W Yor 3E 93
Purtington. Som 2G 13
Purton. Glos 5B 48
(nr. Lydney)
Purton. Glos 5B 48
(nr. Sharpness)
Purton. Wilts 3F 35
Purton Stoke. Wilts 2F 35
Pury End. Nptn 1F 51
Pusey. Oxon 2B 36
Putley. Here 2B 48
Putney. G Lon 3D 38
Putsborough. Devn 2E 19
Puttenham. Herts 4G 51
Puttenham. Surr 1A 26
Puttock End. Essx 1B 54
Puttock's End. Essx 4F 53
Puxey. Dors 1C 14
Puxton. N Som 5H 33
Pwll. Carm 5E 45
Pwll. Powy 5D 70
Pwllcrochan. Pemb 4D 42
Pwll-glas. Den 5D 82
Pwllgloyw. Powy 2D 46
Pwllheli. Gwyn 2C 68
Pwllmeyric. Mon 2A 34
Pwlltrap. Carm 3G 43
Pwll-y-glaw. Neat 2A 32
Pyecombe. W Sus 4D 27
Pye Corner. Herts 4E 53
Pye Corner. Newp 3G 33
Pye Green. Staf 4D 73
Pyewipe. NE Lin 3F 95
Pyle. B'end 3B 32
Pyle. IOW 5C 16
Pylle. Som 3B 22
Pymoor. Cambs 2D 65
Pymoor. Dors 3H 13
Pyrford. Surr 5B 38
Pyrford Village. Surr 5B 38
Pyrton. Oxon 2E 37
Pytchley. Nptn 3F 63
Pyworthy. Devn 2D 10

Q

Quabbs. Shrp 2E 58
Quadring. Linc 2B 76
Quadring Eaudike. Linc 2B 76
Quainton. Buck 3F 51
Quaking Houses. Dur 4E 115
Quarley. Hants 2A 24
Quarndon. Derbs 1H 73
Quarrendon. Buck 4G 51
Quarrier's Village. Inv 3E 127
Quarrington. Linc 1H 75
Quarrington Hill. Dur 1A 106
Quarry Bank. W Mid 2D 60
Quarry, The. Glos 2C 34
Quarrywood. Mor 2F 159
Quartalehouse. Abers 4G 161
Quarter. N Ayr 3C 126
Quarter. S Lan 4A 128
Quatford. Shrp 1B 60
Quatt. Shrp 2B 60
Quebec. Dur 5E 115
Quedgeley. Glos 4D 48
Queen Adelaide. Cambs 2E 65
Queenborough. Kent 3D 40
Queen Camel. Som 4A 22
Queen Charlton. Bath 5B 34
Queen Dart. Devn 1B 12
Queenhill. Worc 2D 48
Queen Oak. Dors 3C 22
Queensbury. W Yor 2B 92
Queensferry. Flin 4F 83
Queenstown. Bkpl 1B 90
Queen Street. Kent 1A 28
Queenzieburn. N Lan 2H 127
Quemerford. Wilts 5F 35
Quendale. Shet 10E 173
Quendon. Essx 2F 53
Queniborough. Leics 4D 74
Quenington. Glos 5G 49
Quernmore. Lanc 3E 97
Quethiock. Corn 2H 7
Quick's Green. W Ber 4D 36
Quidenham. Norf 2C 66
Quidhampton. Hants 1D 24
Quidhampton. Wilts 3G 23
Quilquox. Abers 5G 161
Quina Brook. Shrp 2H 71
Quine's Hill. IOM 4C 108
Quinton. Nptn 5E 63
Quinton. W Mid 2D 61
Quintrell Downs. Corn 2C 6
Quixhill. Staf 1F 73
Quoditch. Devn 3E 11
Quorn. Leics 4C 74
Quorndon. Leics 4C 74
Quothquan. S Lan 1B 118
Quoyloo. Orkn 5B 172
Quoyness. Orkn 7B 172

R

Rableyheath. Herts 4C 52
Raby. Cumb 4C 112
Raby. Mers 3F 83
Rachan Mill. Bord 1D 118
Rachub. Gwyn 4F 81
Rack End. Oxon 5C 50
Rackenford. Devn 1B 12
Rackham. W Sus 4B 26
Rackheath. Norf 4E 79
Racks. Dum 2B 112
Rackwick. Orkn 8A 172
(on Hoy)
Rackwick. Orkn 3D 172
(on Westray)
Radbourne. Derbs 2G 73
Radcliffe. G Man 4F 91
Radcliffe. Nmbd 4G 121
Radcliffe on Trent. Notts 2D 74
Radclive. Buck 2E 51
Radernie. Fife 2G 137
Radfall. Kent 4F 41
Radford. Bath 1B 22
Radford. Nott 1C 74
Radford. Oxon 3C 50
Radford. W Mid 2H 61
Radford. Worc 5E 61
Radford Semele. Warw 4H 61
Radipole. Dors 4B 14
Radlett. Herts 1C 38
Radley. Oxon 2D 36
Radnage. Buck 2F 37
Radstock. Bath 1B 22
Radstone. Nptn 1D 50
Radway. Warw 1B 50
Radway Green. Ches E 5B 84
Radwell. Bed 5H 63
Radwell. Herts 2C 52
Radwinter. Essx 2G 53
Radyr. Card 3E 33
RAF Coltishall. Norf 3E 79
Rafford. Mor 3E 159
Ragdale. Leics 4D 74
Ragdon. Shrp 1G 59
Ragged Appleshaw. Hants 2B 24
Raggra. High 4F 169
Raglan. Mon 5H 47
Ragnall. Notts 3F 87
Raigbeg. High 1C 150
Rainford. Mers 4C 90
Rainford Junction. Mers 4C 90
Rainham. G Lon 2G 39
Rainham. Medw 4C 40
Rainhill. Mers 1G 83
Rainow. Ches E 3D 84
Rainton. N Yor 2F 99
Rainworth. Notts 5C 86
Raisbeck. Cumb 4H 103
Raise. Cumb 5A 114
Rait. Per 1E 137
Raithby. Linc 2C 88
Raithby by Spilsby. Linc 4C 88
Raithwaite. N Yor 3F 107
Rake. W Sus 4G 25
Rake End. Staf 4E 73
Rakeway. Staf 1E 73
Rakewood. G Man 3H 91
Ralia. High 4B 150
Ram Alley. Wilts 5H 35
Ramasaig. High 4A 154
Rame. Corn 4A 8
(nr. Millbrook)
Rame. Corn 5B 6
(nr. Penryn)
Ram Lane. Kent 1D 28
Ramnageo. Shet 2H 173
Rampisham. Dors 2A 14
Rampside. Cumb 3B 96
Rampton. Cambs 4D 64
Rampton. Notts 3E 87
Ramsbottom. G Man 3F 91
Ramsburn. Mor 3C 160
Ramsbury. Wilts 4A 36
Ramscraigs. High 1H 165
Ramsdean. Hants 4F 25
Ramsdell. Hants 1D 24
Ramsden. Oxon 4B 50
Ramsden. Worc 1E 49
Ramsden Bellhouse. Essx 1B 40
Ramsden Heath. Essx 1B 40
Ramsey. Cambs 2B 64
Ramsey. Essx 2F 55
Ramsey. IOM 2D 108
Ramsey Forty Foot. Cambs 2C 64
Ramsey Heights. Cambs 2B 64
Ramsey Island. Essx 5C 54
Ramsey Mereside. Cambs 2B 64
Ramsey St Mary's. Cambs 2B 64
Ramsgate. Kent 4H 41
Ramsgill. N Yor 2D 98
Ramshaw. Dur 5C 114
Ramshorn. Staf 1E 73
Ramsley. Devn 3G 11
Ramsnest Common. Surr 2A 26
Ramstone. Abers 2D 152
Ranais. W Isl 5G 171
Ranby. Linc 3B 88
Ranby. Notts 2D 86
Rand. Linc 3A 88
Randwick. Glos 5D 48
Ranfurly. Ren 3E 127
Rangag. High 4D 168
Rangemore. Staf 3F 73
Rangeworthy. S Glo 3B 34
Rankinston. E Ayr 3D 116
Rank's Green. Essx 4H 53
Ranmore Common. Surr 5C 38
Rannoch Station. Per 3B 142
Ranochan. High 5G 147
Ranskill. Notts 2D 86
Ranton. Staf 3C 72
Ranton Green. Staf 3C 72
Ranworth. Norf 4F 79
Raploch. Stir 4G 135
Rapness. Orkn 3E 172
Rapps. Som 1G 13
Rascal Moor. E Yor 1B 94
Rascarrel. Dum 5E 111
Rashfield. Arg 1C 126
Rashwood. Worc 4D 60
Raskelf. N Yor 2G 99
Rassau. Blae 4E 47
Rastrick. W Yor 2B 92
Ratagan. High 2B 148
Ratby. Leics 5C 74
Ratcliffe Culey. Leics 1H 61
Ratcliffe on Soar. Notts 3B 74
Ratcliffe on the Wreake. Leics 4D 74
Rathen. Abers 2H 161
Rathillet. Fife 1F 137
Rathmell. N Yor 4H 97
Ratho. Edin 2E 129
Ratho Station. Edin 2E 129
Rathven. Mor 2B 160
Ratley. Hants 4B 24
Ratley. Warw 1B 50
Ratlinghope. Shrp 1G 59
Rattar. High 1E 169
Ratten Row. Cumb 5E 113
Ratten Row. Lanc 5D 96
Rattery. Devn 2D 8
Rattlesden. Suff 5B 66
Ratton Village. E Sus 5G 27
Rattray. Abers 3H 161
Rattray. Per 4A 144
Raughton. Cumb 5E 113
Raughton Head. Cumb 5E 113
Raunds. Nptn 3G 63
Ravenfield. S Yor 1B 86
Ravenfield Common. S Yor 1B 86
Ravenglass. Cumb 5B 102
Ravenhills Green. Worc 5B 60
Raveningham. Norf 1F 67
Ravenscar. N Yor 4G 107
Ravensdale. IOM 2C 108
Ravensden. Bed 5H 63
Ravenseat. N Yor 4B 104
Ravenshead. Notts 5C 86
Ravensmoor. Ches E 5A 84
Ravensthorpe. Nptn 3D 62
Ravensthorpe. W Yor 2C 92
Ravenstone. Leics 4B 74
Ravenstonedale. Cumb 4A 104
Ravenstown. Cumb 2C 96
Ravenstruther. S Lan 5C 128
Ravensworth. N Yor 4E 105
Raw. N Yor 4G 107
Rawcliffe. E Yor 2G 93
Rawcliffe. York 4H 99
Rawcliffe Bridge. E Yor 2G 93
Rawdon. W Yor 1C 92
Rawgreen. Nmbd 4C 114
Rawmarsh. S Yor 1B 86
Rawnsley. Staf 4E 73
Rawreth. Essx 1B 40
Rawridge. Devn 2F 13
Rawson Green. Derbs 1A 74
Rawtenstall. Lanc 2F 91
Raydon. Suff 2D 54
Raylees. Nmbd 5D 120
Rayleigh. Essx 1C 40
Raymond's Hill. Devn 3G 13
Rayne. Essx 3H 53
Rayners Lane. G Lon 2C 38
Reach. Cambs 4E 65
Read. Lanc 1F 91
Reading. Read 4F 37
Reading Green. Suff 3D 66
Reading Street. Kent 2D 28
Readymoney. Corn 3F 7
Reagill. Cumb 3H 103
Rea Hill. Torb 3F 9
Rearquhar. High 4E 165
Rearsby. Leics 4D 74
Reasby. Linc 3H 87
Reaseheath. Ches E 5A 84
Reaster. High 2E 169
Reawick. Shet 7E 173
Reay. High 2B 168
Rechullin. High 3A 156
Reculver. Kent 4G 41
Redberth. Pemb 4E 43
Redbourn. Herts 4B 52
Redbourne. N Lin 4C 94
Redbrook. Glos 4A 48
Redbrook. Wrex 1H 71
Redburn. High 4D 158
Redburn. Nmbd 3A 114
Redcar. Red C 2D 106
Redcastle. High 4H 157
Redcliff Bay. N Som 4H 33
Red Dial. Cumb 5D 112
Redding. Falk 2C 128
Reddingmuirhead. Falk 2C 128
Reddings, The. Glos 3E 49
Reddish. G Man 1C 84
Redditch. Worc 4E 61
Rede. Suff 5H 65
Redenhall. Norf 2E 67
Redesdale Camp. Nmbd 5C 120
Redesmouth. Nmbd 1B 114
Redford. Ang 4E 145
Redford. Dur 1D 105
Redford. W Sus 4G 25
Redfordgreen. Bord 3F 119
Redgate. Corn 2G 7
Redgrave. Suff 3C 66
Redhill. Abers 3E 153
Redhill. Herts 2C 52
Redhill. N Som 5H 33
Redhill. Shrp 4B 72
Redhill. Surr 5D 39
Red Hill. Warw 5F 61
Red Hill. W Yor 2E 93
Redhouses. Arg 3B 124
Redisham. Suff 2G 67
Redland. Bris 4A 34
Redland. Orkn 5C 172
Redlingfield. Suff 3D 66
Red Lodge. Suff 3F 65
Redlynch. Som 3C 22
Redlynch. Wilts 4H 23
Redmain. Cumb 1C 102
Redmarley. Worc 4B 60
Redmarley D'Abitot. Glos 2C 48
Redmarshall. Stoc T 2A 106
Redmile. Leics 2E 75
Redmire. N Yor 5D 104
Rednal. Shrp 3F 71
Redpath. Bord 1H 119
Redpoint. High 2G 155
Red Post. Corn 2C 10
Red Rock. G Man 4D 90
Red Roses. Carm 3G 43
Red Row. Nmbd 5G 121
Redruth. Corn 4B 6
Red Street. Staf 5C 84
Redvales. G Man 4F 91
Red Wharf Bay. IOA 2E 81
Redwick. Newp 3H 33
Redwick. S Glo 3A 34
Redworth. Darl 2F 105
Reed. Herts 2D 52
Reed End. Herts 2D 52
Reedham. Linc 5B 88
Reedham. Norf 5G 79
Reedness. E Yor 2B 94
Reeds Beck. Linc 4B 88
Reemshill. Abers 4E 161
Reepham. Linc 3H 87
Reepham. Norf 3C 78
Reeth. N Yor 5D 104
Regaby. IOM 2D 108
Regil. N Som 5A 34
Regoul. High 3C 158
Reiff. High 2D 162
Reigate. Surr 5D 38
Reighton. N Yor 2F 101
Reilth. Shrp 2E 59
Reinigeadal. W Isl 7E 171
Reisque. Abers 1F 153
Reiss. High 3F 169
Rejerrah. Corn 3B 6
Releath. Corn 5A 6
Relubbus. Corn 3C 4
Relugas. Mor 4D 159
Remenham. Wok 3F 37
Remenham Hill. Wok 3F 37
Rempstone. Notts 3C 74
Rendcomb. Glos 5F 49
Rendham. Suff 4F 67
Rendlesham. Suff 5F 67
Renfrew. Ren 3G 127
Renhold. Bed 5H 63
Renishaw. Derbs 3B 86
Rennington. Nmbd 3G 121
Renton. W Dun 2E 127
Renwick. Cumb 5G 113
Repps. Norf 4G 79
Repton. Derbs 3H 73
Resaurie. High 4B 158
Rescassa. Corn 4D 6

Rescobie. *Ang* 3E **145**
Rescorla. *Corn* 3E **7** (nr. Rosevean)
Rescorla. *Corn* 4D **6** (nr. St Ewe)
Resipole. *High* 2B **140**
Resolfen. *Neat* 5B **46**
Resolis. *High* 2A **158**
Resolven. *Neat* 5B **46**
Rest and be thankful. *Arg* 3B **134**
Reston. *Bord* 3E **131**
Restrop. *Wilts* 3F **35**
Retford. *Notts* 2E **86**
Retire. *Corn* 2E **6**
Rettendon. *Essx* 1B **40**
Revesby. *Linc* 4C **88**
Rew. *Devn* 5D **8**
Rewe. *Devn* 3C **12**
Rew Street. *IOW* 3C **16**
Rexon. *Devn* 4E **11**
Reybridge. *Wilts* 5E **35**
Reydon. *Suff* 3H **67**
Reymerston. *Norf* 5C **78**
Reynalton. *Pemb* 4E **43**
Reynoldston. *Swan* 4D **31**
Rezare. *Corn* 5D **10**
Rhadyr. *Mon* 5G **47**
Rhaeadr Gwy. *Powy* 4B **58**
Rhandirmwyn. *Carm* 1A **46**
Rhayader. *Powy* 4B **58**
Rheindown. *High* 4H **157**
Rhemore. *High* 3G **139**
Rhenetra. *High* 3D **154**
Rhewl. *Den* 1D **70** (nr. Llangollen)
Rhewl. *Den* 4D **82** (nr. Ruthin)
Rhewl. *Shrp* 2F **71**
Rhewl-Mostyn. *Flin* 3D **82**
Rhian. *High* 2C **164**
Rhian Breck. *High* 3C **164**
Rhicarn. *High* 1E **163**
Rhiconich. *High* 3C **166**
Rhicullen. *High* 1A **158**
Rhidorroch. *High* 4F **163**
Rhifail. *High* 4H **167**
Rhigos. *Rhon* 5C **46**
Rhilochan. *High* 3E **165**
Rhiroy. *High* 5F **163**
Rhitongue. *High* 3G **167**
Rhiw. *Gwyn* 3B **68**
Rhiwabon. *Wrex* 1F **71**
Rhiwbina. *Card* 3E **33**
Rhiwbryfdir. *Gwyn* 1F **69**
Rhiwderin. *Newp* 3F **33**
Rhiwlas. *Gwyn* 2B **70** (nr. Bala)
Rhiwlas. *Gwyn* 4E **81** (nr. Bangor)
Rhiwlas. *Powy* 2D **70**
Rhodes. *G Man* 4G **91**
Rhodesia. *Notts* 2C **86**
Rhodes Minnis. *Kent* 1F **29**
Rhodiad-y-Brenin. *Pemb* 2B **42**
Rhondda. *Rhon* 2C **32**
Rhonehouse. *Dum* 4E **111**
Rhoose. *V Glam* 5D **32**
Rhos. *Carm* 2D **45**
Rhos. *Neat* 5H **45**
Rhosaman. *Carm* 4H **45**
Rhoscefnhir. *IOA* 3E **81**
Rhoscolyn. *IOA* 3B **80**
Rhos Common. *Powy* 4E **71**
Rhoscrowther. *Pemb* 4D **42**
Rhos-ddu. *Gwyn* 2B **68**
Rhosdylluan. *Gwyn* 3A **70**
Rhosesmor. *Flin* 4E **82**
Rhos-fawr. *Gwyn* 2C **68**
Rhosgadfan. *Gwyn* 5E **81**
Rhosgoch. *IOA* 2D **80**
Rhosgoch. *Powy* 1E **47**
Rhos Haminiog. *Cdgn* 4E **57**
Rhos-hill. *Pemb* 1B **44**
Rhoshirwaun. *Gwyn* 3A **68**
Rhoslan. *Gwyn* 1D **69**
Rhoslefain. *Gwyn* 5E **69**
Rhosllanerchrugog. *Wrex* 1E **71**
Rhos Lligwy. *IOA* 2D **81**
Rhosmaen. *Carm* 3G **45**
Rhosmeirch. *IOA* 3D **80**
Rhosneigr. *IOA* 3C **80**
Rhos-on-Sea. *Cnwy* 2H **81**
Rhossili. *Swan* 4D **30**
Rhosson. *Pemb* 2B **42**
Rhos, The. *Pemb* 3E **43**
Rhostrenwfa. *IOA* 3D **80**
Rhostryfan. *Gwyn* 5D **81**
Rhostyllen. *Wrex* 1F **71**
Rhoswiel. *Shrp* 2E **71**
Rhosybol. *IOA* 2D **80**
Rhos-y-brithdir. *Powy* 3D **70**
Rhos-y-garth. *Cdgn* 3F **57**
Rhos-y-gwaliau. *Gwyn* 2B **70**
Rhos-y-llan. *Gwyn* 2B **68**
Rhos-y-meirch. *Powy* 4E **59**
Rhu. *Arg* 1D **126**
Rhualt. *Den* 3C **82**
Rhubadach. *Arg* 2B **126**
Rhubha Stoer. *High* 1E **163**
Rhuddall Heath. *Ches W* 4H **83**
Rhuddlan. *Cdgn* 1E **45**
Rhuddlan. *Den* 3C **82**
Rhue. *High* 4E **163**
Rhulen. *Powy* 1E **47**
Rhunahaorine. *Arg* 5F **125**
Rhuthun. *Den* 5D **82**
Rhuvoult. *High* 3C **166**
Rhyd. *Gwyn* 1F **69**
Rhydaman. *Carm* 4G **45**
Rhydargaeau. *Carm* 3E **45**
Rhydcymerau. *Carm* 2F **45**
Rhydd. *Worc* 1D **48**
Rhyd-Ddu. *Gwyn* 5E **81**
Rhydding. *Neat* 3G **31**
Rhydfudr. *Cdgn* 4E **57**
Rhydlanfair. *Cnwy* 5H **81**
Rhydlewis. *Cdgn* 1D **44**
Rhydlios. *Gwyn* 2A **68**
Rhydlydan. *Cnwy* 5A **82**
Rhyd-meirionydd. *Cdgn* 2F **57**
Rhydowen. *Cdgn* 1E **45**
Rhyd-Rosser. *Cdgn* 4E **57**
Rhydspence. *Powy* 1F **47**
Rhydtalog. *Flin* 5E **83**
Rhyd-uchaf. *Gwyn* 2B **70**
Rhydwyn. *IOA* 2C **80**
Rhyd-y-clafdy. *Gwyn* 2C **68**
Rhydycroesau. *Shrp* 2E **71**
Rhydyfelin. *Cdgn* 3E **57**
Rhydyfelin. *Rhon* 3E **32**
Rhyd-y-foel. *Cnwy* 3B **82**
Rhyd-y-fro. *Neat* 5H **45**
Rhydymain. *Gwyn* 3H **69**
Rhyd-y-meirch. *Mon* 5G **47**
Rhyd-y-meudwy. *Den* 5D **82**
Rhydymwyn. *Flin* 4E **82**
Rhyd-yr-onen. *Gwyn* 5F **69**
Rhyd-y-sarn. *Gwyn* 1F **69**
Rhyl. *Den* 2C **82**
Rhymney. *Cphy* 5E **46**
Rhymni. *Cphy* 5E **46**
Rhynd. *Per* 1D **136**
Rhynie. *Abers* 1B **152**
Ribbesford. *Worc* 3B **60**
Ribbleton. *Lanc* 1D **90**
Ribby. *Lanc* 1C **90**
Ribchester. *Lanc* 1E **91**
Riber. *Derbs* 5H **85**
Ribigill. *High* 3F **167**
Riby. *Linc* 4E **95**
Riccall. *N Yor* 1G **93**
Riccarton. *E Ayr* 1D **116**
Richards Castle. *Here* 4G **59**
Richborough Port. *Kent* 4H **41**
Richings Park. *Buck* 3B **38**
Richmond. *G Lon* 3C **38**
Richmond. *N Yor* 4E **105**
Rickarton. *Abers* 5F **153**
Rickerby. *Cumb* 4F **113**
Rickerscote. *Staf* 3D **72**
Rickford. *N Som* 1H **21**
Rickham. *Devn* 5D **8**
Rickinghall. *Suff* 3C **66**
Rickleton. *Tyne* 4F **115**
Rickling. *Essx* 2E **53**
Rickling Green. *Essx* 3F **53**
Rickmansworth. *Herts* 1B **38**
Riddings. *Derbs* 5B **86**
Riddlecombe. *Devn* 1G **11**
Riddlesden. *W Yor* 5C **98**
Ridge. *Dors* 4E **15**
Ridge. *Herts* 5C **52**
Ridge. *Wilts* 3E **23**
Ridgebourne. *Powy* 4C **58**
Ridge Lane. *Warw* 1G **61**
Ridgeway. *Derbs* 5A **86** (nr. Alfreton)
Ridgeway. *Derbs* 2B **86** (nr. Sheffield)
Ridgeway. *Staf* 5C **84**
Ridgeway Cross. *Here* 1C **48**
Ridgeway Moor. *Derbs* 2B **86**
Ridgewell. *Essx* 1H **53**
Ridgewood. *E Sus* 3F **27**
Ridgmont. *C Beds* 2H **51**
Ridgwardine. *Shrp* 2A **72**
Riding Mill. *Nmbd* 3D **114**
Ridley. *Kent* 4H **39**
Ridley. *Nmbd* 3A **114**
Ridlington. *Norf* 2F **79**
Ridlington. *Rut* 5F **75**
Ridsdale. *Nmbd* 1C **114**
Riemore Lodge. *Per* 4H **143**
Rievaulx. *N Yor* 1H **99**
Rift House. *Hart* 1B **106**
Rigg. *Dum* 3D **112**
Riggend. *N Lan* 2A **128**
Rigsby. *Linc* 3D **88**
Rigside. *S Lan* 1A **118**
Riley Green. *Lanc* 2E **90**
Rileyhill. *Staf* 4F **73**
Rilla Mill. *Corn* 5C **10**
Rillington. *N Yor* 2C **100**
Rimington. *Lanc* 5H **97**
Rimpton. *Som* 4B **22**
Rimsdale. *High* 4H **167**
Rimswell. *E Yor* 2G **95**
Ringasta. *Shet* 10E **173**
Ringford. *Dum* 4D **111**
Ringing Hill. *Leics* 4B **74**
Ringinglow. *S Yor* 2G **85**
Ringland. *Norf* 4D **78**
Ringlestone. *Kent* 5C **40**
Ringmer. *E Sus* 4F **27**
Ringmore. *Devn* 4C **8** (nr. Kingsbridge)
Ringmore. *Devn* 5C **12** (nr. Teignmouth)
Ring o' Bells. *Lanc* 3C **90**
Ring's End. *Cambs* 5C **76**
Ringsfield. *Suff* 2G **67**
Ringsfield Corner. *Suff* 2G **67**
Ringshall. *Buck* 4H **51**
Ringshall. *Suff* 5C **66**
Ringshall Stocks. *Suff* 5C **66**
Ringstead. *Norf* 1G **77**
Ringstead. *Nptn* 3G **63**
Ringwood. *Hants* 2G **15**
Ringwould. *Kent* 1H **29**
Rinmore. *Abers* 2B **152**
Rinnigill. *Orkn* 8C **172**
Rinsey. *Corn* 4C **4**
Riof. *W Isl* 4D **171**
Ripe. *E Sus* 4G **27**
Ripley. *Derbs* 1B **74**
Ripley. *Hants* 3G **15**
Ripley. *N Yor* 3E **99**
Ripley. *Surr* 5B **38**
Riplingham. *E Yor* 1C **94**
Riplington. *Hants* 4E **25**
Ripon. *N Yor* 2F **99**
Rippingale. *Linc* 3H **75**
Ripple. *Kent* 1H **29**
Ripple. *Worc* 2D **48**
Ripponden. *W Yor* 3A **92**
Rireavach. *High* 4E **163**
Risabus. *Arg* 5B **124**
Risbury. *Here* 5H **59**
Risby. *E Yor* 1D **94**
Risby. *N Lin* 3C **94**
Risby. *Suff* 4G **65**
Risca. *Cphy* 2F **33**
Rise. *E Yor* 5F **101**
Riseden. *E Sus* 2H **27**
Riseden. *Kent* 2B **28**
Rise End. *Derbs* 5G **85**
Risegate. *Linc* 2B **76**
Riseholme. *Linc* 3G **87**
Riseley. *Bed* 4H **63**
Riseley. *Wok* 5F **37**
Rishangles. *Suff* 4D **66**
Rishton. *Lanc* 1F **91**
Rishworth. *W Yor* 3A **92**
Risley. *Derbs* 2B **74**
Risley. *Warr* 1A **84**
Risplith. *N Yor* 3E **99**
Rispond. *High* 2E **167**
Rivar. *Wilts* 5B **36**
Rivenhall. *Essx* 4B **54**
Rivenhall End. *Essx* 4B **54**
River. *Kent* 1G **29**
River. *W Sus* 3A **26**
River Bank. *Cambs* 4E **65**
Riverhead. *Kent* 5G **39**
Rivington. *Lanc* 3E **91**
Roach Bridge. *Lanc* 2D **90**
Roachill. *Devn* 4B **20**
Roade. *Nptn* 5E **63**
Road Green. *Norf* 1E **67**
Roadhead. *Cumb* 2G **113**
Roadmeetings. *S Lan* 5B **128**
Roadside. *High* 2D **168**
Roadside of Catterline. *Abers* 1H **145**
Roadside of Kinneff. *Abers* 1H **145**
Roadwater. *Som* 3D **20**
Road Weedon. *Nptn* 5D **62**
Roag. *High* 4B **154**
Roa Island. *Cumb* 3B **96**
Roath. *Card* 4E **33**
Roberton. *Bord* 3G **119**
Roberton. *S Lan* 2B **118**
Robertsbridge. *E Sus* 3B **28**
Robertstown. *Mor* 4G **159**
Robertstown. *Rhon* 5C **46**
Roberttown. *W Yor* 2B **92**
Robeston Back. *Pemb* 3E **43**
Robeston Wathen. *Pemb* 3E **43**
Robeston West. *Pemb* 4C **42**
Robin Hood. *Lanc* 3D **90**
Robin Hood. *W Yor* 2D **92**
Robin Hood Airport Doncaster Sheffield. *S Yor* 1D **86**
Robinhood End. *Essx* 2H **53**
Robin Hood's Bay. *N Yor* 4G **107**
Roborough. *Devn* 1F **11** (nr. Great Torrington)
Roborough. *Devn* 2B **8** (nr. Plymouth)
Rob Roy's House. *Arg* 2A **134**
Roby Mill. *Lanc* 4D **90**
Rocester. *Staf* 2F **73**
Roch. *Pemb* 2C **42**
Rochdale. *G Man* 3G **91**
Roche. *Corn* 2D **6**
Rochester. *Medw* 4B **40**
Rochester. *Nmbd* 5C **120**
Rochford. *Essx* 1C **40**
Rock. *Corn* 1D **6**
Rock. *Nmbd* 2G **121**
Rock. *W Sus* 4C **26**
Rock. *Worc* 3B **60**
Rockbeare. *Devn* 3D **12**
Rockbourne. *Hants* 1G **15**
Rockcliffe. *Cumb* 3E **113**
Rockcliffe. *Dum* 4F **111**
Rockcliffe Cross. *Cumb* 3E **113**
Rock Ferry. *Mers* 2F **83**
Rockfield. *High* 5G **165**
Rockfield. *Mon* 4H **47**
Rockford. *Hants* 2G **15**
Rockgreen. *Shrp* 3H **59**
Rockhampton. *S Glo* 2B **34**
Rockhead. *Corn* 4A **10**
Rockingham. *Nptn* 1F **63**
Rockland All Saints. *Norf* 1B **66**
Rockland St Mary. *Norf* 5F **79**
Rockland St Peter. *Norf* 1B **66**
Rockley. *Wilts* 4G **35**
Rockwell End. *Buck* 3F **37**
Rockwell Green. *Som* 1E **13**
Rodborough. *Glos* 5D **48**
Rodbourne. *Wilts* 3E **35**
Rodd. *Here* 4F **59**
Roddam. *Nmbd* 2E **121**
Rodden. *Dors* 4B **14**
Roddenloft. *E Ayr* 2D **117**
Roddymoor. *Dur* 1E **105**
Rode. *Som* 1D **22**
Rodeheath. *Ches E* 4C **84** (nr. Congleton)
Rode Heath. *Ches E* 5C **84** (nr. Kidsgrove)
Roden. *Telf* 4H **71**
Rodhuish. *Som* 3D **20**
Rodington. *Telf* 4H **71**
Rodington Heath. *Telf* 4H **71**
Rodley. *Glos* 4C **48**
Rodmarton. *Glos* 2E **35**
Rodmell. *E Sus* 5F **27**
Rodmersham. *Kent* 4D **40**
Rodmersham Green. *Kent* 4D **40**
Rodney Stoke. *Som* 2H **21**
Rodsley. *Derbs* 1G **73**
Rodway. *Som* 2F **21**
Rodway. *Telf* 4A **72**
Rodwell. *Dors* 5B **14**
Roecliffe. *N Yor* 3F **99**
Roe Green. *Herts* 2D **52**
Roehampton. *G Lon* 3D **38**
Roffey. *W Sus* 2C **26**
Rogart. *High* 3E **165**
Rogate. *W Sus* 4G **25**
Roger Ground. *Cumb* 5E **103**
Rogerstone. *Newp* 3F **33**
Roghadal. *W Isl* 9C **171**
Rogiet. *Mon* 3H **33**
Rogue's Alley. *Cambs* 5C **76**
Roke. *Oxon* 2E **37**
Rokemarsh. *Oxon* 2E **36**
Roker. *Tyne* 4H **115**
Rollesby. *Norf* 4G **79**
Rolleston. *Leics* 5E **75**
Rolleston. *Notts* 5E **87**
Rolleston on Dove. *Staf* 3G **73**
Rolston. *E Yor* 5G **101**
Rolvenden. *Kent* 2C **28**
Rolvenden Layne. *Kent* 2C **28**
Romaldkirk. *Dur* 2C **104**
Roman Bank. *Shrp* 1H **59**
Romanby. *N Yor* 5A **106**
Roman Camp. *W Lot* 2D **129**
Romannobridge. *Bord* 5E **129**
Romansleigh. *Devn* 4H **19**
Romers Common. *Worc* 4H **59**
Romesdal. *High* 3D **154**
Romford. *Dors* 2F **15**
Romford. *G Lon* 2G **39**
Romiley. *G Man* 1D **84**
Romsey. *Hants* 4B **24**
Romsley. *Shrp* 2B **60**
Romsley. *Worc* 3D **60**
Ronague. *IOM* 4B **108**
Rookby. *Cumb* 3B **104**
Rookhope. *Dur* 5C **114**
Rooking. *Cumb* 3F **103**
Rookley. *IOW* 4D **16**
Rooks Bridge. *Som* 1G **21**
Rooksey Green. *Suff* 5B **66**
Rook's Nest. *Som* 3D **20**
Rookwood. *W Sus* 3F **17**

Roos. *E Yor* 1F 95
Roosebeck. *Cumb* 3B 96
Roosecote. *Cumb* 3B 96
Rootfield. *High* 3H 157
Rootham's Green. *Bed* 5A 64
Rootpark. *S Lan* 4C 128
Ropley. *Hants* 3E 25
Ropley Dean. *Hants* 3E 25
Ropsley. *Linc* 2G 75
Rora. *Abers* 3H 161
Rorandle. *Abers* 2D 152
Rorrington. *Shrp* 5F 71
Rose. *Corn* 3B 6
Roseacre. *Lanc* 1C 90
Rose Ash. *Devn* 4A 20
Rosebank. *S Lan* 5B 128
Rosebush. *Pemb* 2E 43
Rosedale Abbey. *N Yor* 5E 107
Roseden. *Nmbd* 2E 121
Rose Green. *Essx* 3C 54
Rose Green. *Suff* 1C 54
Rosehall. *High* 3B 164
Rosehearty. *Abers* 2G 161
Rose Hill. *E Sus* 4F 27
Rose Hill. *Lanc* 1G 91
Rosehill. *Shrp* 2A 72
(nr. Market Drayton)
Rosehill. *Shrp* 4G 71
(nr. Shrewsbury)
Roseisle. *Mor* 2F 159
Rosemarket. *Pemb* 4D 42
Rosemarkie. *High* 3B 158
Rosemary Lane. *Devn* 1E 13
Rosemount. *Per* 4A 144
Rosenannon. *Corn* 2D 6
Roser's Cross. *E Sus* 3G 27
Rosevean. *Corn* 3E 6
Rosewell. *Midl* 3F 129
Roseworth. *Stoc T* 2B 106
Roseworthy. *Corn* 3D 4
Rosgill. *Cumb* 3G 103
Roshven. *High* 1B 140
Roskhill. *High* 4B 154
Roskorwell. *Corn* 4E 5
Rosley. *Cumb* 5E 112
Roslin. *Midl* 3F 129
Rosliston. *Derbs* 4G 73
Rosneath. *Arg* 1D 126
Ross. *Dum* 5D 110
Ross. *Nmbd* 1F 121
Ross. *Per* 1G 135
Ross. *Bord* 3F 131
Rossendale. *Lanc* 2F 91
Rossett. *Wrex* 5F 83
Rossington. *S Yor* 1D 86
Rosskeen. *High* 2A 158
Rossland. *Ren* 2F 127
Ross-on-Wye. *Here* 3B 48
Roster. *High* 4E 169
Rostherne. *Ches E* 2B 84
Rostholme. *S Yor* 4F 93
Rosthwaite. *Cumb* 3D 102
Roston. *Derbs* 1F 73
Rosudgeon. *Corn* 4C 4
Rosyth. *Fife* 1E 129
Rothbury. *Nmbd* 4E 121
Rotherby. *Leics* 4D 74
Rotherfield. *E Sus* 3G 27
Rotherfield Greys. *Oxon* 3F 37
Rotherfield Peppard. *Oxon* 3F 37
Rotherham. *S Yor* 1B 86
Rothersthorpe. *Nptn* 5E 62
Rotherwick. *Hants* 1F 25
Rothes. *Mor* 4G 159
Rothesay. *Arg* 3B 126
Rothienorman. *Abers* 5E 160
Rothiesholm. *Orkn* 5F 172
Rothley. *Leics* 4C 74
Rothley. *Nmbd* 1D 114
Rothwell. *Linc* 1A 88
Rothwell. *Nptn* 2F 63
Rothwell. *W Yor* 2D 92
Rothwell Haigh. *W Yor* 2D 92
Rotsea. *E Yor* 4E 101
Rottal. *Ang* 2C 144
Rotten End. *Suff* 4F 67
Rotten Row. *Norf* 4C 78
Rotten Row. *W Ber* 4D 36
Rotten Row. *W Mid* 3F 61
Rottingdean. *Brig* 5E 27
Rottington. *Cumb* 3A 102
Roud. *IOW* 4D 16
Rougham. *Norf* 3H 77
Rougham. *Suff* 4B 66
Rough Close. *Staf* 2D 72
Rough Common. *Kent* 5F 41
Roughcote. *Staf* 1D 72
Rough Haugh. *High* 4H 167
Rough Hay. *Staf* 3G 73
Roughlee. *Lanc* 5H 97
Roughley. *W Mid* 1F 61
Roughsike. *Cumb* 2G 113
Roughton. *Linc* 4B 88
Roughton. *Norf* 2E 78
Roughton. *Shrp* 1B 60
Roundbush Green. *Essx* 4F 53
Roundham. *Som* 2H 13
Roundhay. *W Yor* 1D 92
Round Hill. *Torb* 2F 9
Roundhurst. *W Sus* 2A 26
Round Maple. *Suff* 1C 54
Round Oak. *Shrp* 2F 59
Roundstreet Common. *W Sus* 3B 26
Roundthwaite. *Cumb* 4H 103
Roundway. *Wilts* 5F 35
Roundyhill. *Ang* 3C 144
Rousdon. *Devn* 3F 13
Rousham. *Oxon* 3C 50
Rous Lench. *Worc* 5E 61
Routh. *E Yor* 5E 101
Rout's Green. *Buck* 2F 37
Row. *Corn* 5A 10
Row. *Cumb* 1D 96
(nr. Kendal)
Row. *Cumb* 1H 103
(nr. Penrith)
Rowanburn. *Dum* 2F 113
Rowanhill. *Abers* 3H 161
Rowardennan. *Stir* 4C 134
Rowarth. *Derbs* 2E 85
Row Ash. *Hants* 1D 16
Rowberrow. *Som* 1H 21
Rowde. *Wilts* 5E 35
Rowden. *Devn* 3G 11
Rowden Hill. *Wilts* 4E 35
Rowen. *Cnwy* 3G 81
Rowfoot. *Nmbd* 3H 113
Row Green. *Essx* 3H 53
Row Heath. *Essx* 4E 55
Rowhedge. *Essx* 3D 54
Rowhook. *W Sus* 2C 26
Rowington. *Warw* 4G 61
Rowland. *Derbs* 3G 85
Rowland's Castle. *Hants* 1F 17
Rowlands Gill. *Tyne* 4E 115
Rowledge. *Surr* 2G 25
Rowley. *Dur* 5D 115
Rowley. *E Yor* 1C 94
Rowley. *Shrp* 5F 71
Rowley Hill. *W Yor* 3B 92
Rowley Regis. *W Mid* 2D 60
Rowlstone. *Here* 3G 47
Rowly. *Surr* 1B 26
Rowner. *Hants* 2D 16
Rowney Green. *Worc* 3E 61
Rownhams. *Hants* 1B 16
Rowrah. *Cumb* 3B 102
Rowsham. *Buck* 4G 51
Rowsley. *Derbs* 4G 85
Rowstock. *Oxon* 3C 36
Rowston. *Linc* 5H 87
Row, The. *Lanc* 2D 96
Rowthorne. *Derbs* 4B 86
Rowton. *Ches W* 4G 83
Rowton. *Shrp* 2G 59
(nr. Ludlow)
Rowton. *Shrp* 4F 71
(nr. Shrewsbury)
Rowton. *Telf* 4A 72
Row Town. *Surr* 4B 38
Roxburgh. *Bord* 1B 120
Roxby. *N Lin* 3C 94
Roxby. *N Yor* 3E 107
Roxton. *Bed* 5A 64
Roxwell. *Essx* 5G 53
Royal Leamington Spa. *Warw* 4H 61
Royal Oak. *Darl* 2F 105
Royal Oak. *Lanc* 4C 90
Royal Oak. *N Yor* 2F 101
Royal's Green. *Ches E* 1A 72
Royal Tunbridge Wells. *Kent* 2G 27
Royal Wootton Bassett. *Wilts* 3F 35
Roybridge. *High* 5E 149
Roydon. *Essx* 4E 53
Roydon. *Norf* 2C 66
(nr. Diss)
Roydon. *Norf* 3G 77
(nr. King's Lynn)
Roydon Hamlet. *Essx* 5E 53
Royston. *Herts* 1D 52
Royston. *S Yor* 3D 92
Royston Water. *Som* 1F 13
Royton. *G Man* 4H 91
Ruabon. *Wrex* 1F 71
Ruaig. *Arg* 4B 138
Ruan High Lanes. *Corn* 5D 6
Ruan Lanihorne. *Corn* 4C 6
Ruan Major. *Corn* 5E 5
Ruan Minor. *Corn* 5E 5
Ruarach. *High* 1B 148
Ruardean. *Glos* 4B 48
Ruardean Hill. *Glos* 4B 48
Ruardean Woodside. *Glos* 4B 48
Rubery. *W Mid* 3D 61
Ruchazie. *Glas* 3H 127
Ruckcroft. *Cumb* 5G 113
Ruckinge. *Kent* 2E 29
Ruckland. *Linc* 3C 88
Rucklers Lane. *Herts* 5A 52
Ruckley. *Shrp* 5H 71
Rudbaxton. *Pemb* 2D 42
Rudby. *N Yor* 4B 106
Ruddington. *Notts* 2C 74
Rudford. *Glos* 3C 48
Rudge. *Shrp* 1C 60
Rudge. *Wilts* 1D 22
Rudge Heath. *Shrp* 1B 60
Rudgeway. *S Glo* 3B 34
Rudgwick. *W Sus* 2B 26
Rudhall. *Here* 3B 48
Rudheath. *Ches W* 3A 84
Rudley Green. *Essx* 5B 54
Rudloe. *Wilts* 4D 34
Rudry. *Cphy* 3E 33
Rudston. *E Yor* 3E 101
Rudyard. *Staf* 5D 84
Rufford. *Lanc* 3C 90
Rufforth. *York* 4H 99
Rugby. *Warw* 3C 62
Rugeley. *Staf* 4E 73
Ruglen. *S Ayr* 4B 116
Ruilick. *High* 4H 157
Ruisaurie. *High* 4G 157
Ruishton. *Som* 4F 21
Ruisigearraidh. *W Isl* 1E 170
Ruislip. *G Lon* 2B 38
Ruislip Common. *G Lon* 2B 38
Rumbling Bridge. *Per* 4C 136
Rumburgh. *Suff* 2F 67
Rumford. *Corn* 1C 6
Rumford. *Falk* 2C 128
Rumney. *Card* 4F 33
Rumwell. *Som* 4E 21
Runcorn. *Hal* 2H 83
Runcton. *W Sus* 2G 17
Runcton Holme. *Norf* 5F 77
Rundlestone. *Devn* 5F 11
Runfold. *Surr* 2G 25
Runhall. *Norf* 5C 78
Runham. *Norf* 4G 79
Runnington. *Som* 4E 20
Runshaw Moor. *Lanc* 3D 90
Runswick. *N Yor* 3F 107
Runtaleave. *Ang* 2B 144
Runwell. *Essx* 1B 40
Ruscombe. *Wok* 4F 37
Rushall. *Here* 2B 48
Rushall. *Norf* 2D 66
Rushall. *W Mid* 5E 73
Rushall. *Wilts* 1G 23
Rushbrooke. *Suff* 4A 66
Rushbury. *Shrp* 1H 59
Rushden. *Herts* 2D 52
Rushden. *Nptn* 4G 63
Rushenden. *Kent* 3D 40
Rushford. *Devn* 5E 11
Rushford. *Suff* 2B 66
Rush Green. *Herts* 3C 52
Rushlake Green. *E Sus* 4H 27
Rushmere. *Suff* 2G 67
Rushmere St Andrew. *Suff* 1E 55
Rushmoor. *Surr* 2G 25
Rushock. *Worc* 3C 60
Rusholme. *G Man* 1C 84
Rushton. *Ches W* 4H 83
Rushton. *Nptn* 2F 63
Rushton. *Shrp* 5A 72
Rushton Spencer. *Staf* 4D 84
Rushwick. *Worc* 5C 60
Rushyford. *Dur* 2F 105
Ruskie. *Stir* 3F 135
Ruskington. *Linc* 5H 87
Rusland. *Cumb* 1C 96
Rusper. *W Sus* 2D 26
Ruspidge. *Glos* 4B 48
Russell's Water. *Oxon* 3F 37
Russel's Green. *Suff* 3E 67
Russ Hill. *Surr* 1D 26
Russland. *Orkn* 6C 172
Rusthall. *Kent* 2G 27
Rustington. *W Sus* 5B 26
Ruston. *N Yor* 1D 100
Ruston Parva. *E Yor* 3E 101
Ruswarp. *N Yor* 4F 107
Rutherglen. *S Lan* 3H 127
Ruthernbridge. *Corn* 2E 6
Ruthin. *Den* 5D 82
Ruthin. *V Glam* 4C 32
Ruthrieston. *Aber* 3G 153
Ruthven. *Abers* 4C 160
Ruthven. *Ang* 4B 144
Ruthven. *High* 5C 158
(nr. Inverness)
Ruthven. *High* 4B 150
(nr. Kingussie)
Ruthvoes. *Corn* 2D 6
Ruthwaite. *Cumb* 1D 102
Ruthwell. *Dum* 3C 112
Ruxton Green. *Here* 4A 48
Ruyton-XI-Towns. *Shrp* 3F 71
Ryal. *Nmbd* 2D 114
Ryall. *Dors* 3H 13
Ryall. *Worc* 1D 48
Ryarsh. *Kent* 5A 40
Rychraggan. *High* 5G 157
Rydal. *Cumb* 4E 103
Ryde. *IOW* 3D 16
Rye. *E Sus* 3D 28
Ryecroft Gate. *Staf* 4D 84
Ryeford. *Here* 3B 48
Rye Foreign. *E Sus* 3D 28
Rye Harbour. *E Sus* 4D 28
Ryehill. *E Yor* 2F 95
Rye Street. *Worc* 2C 48
Ryhall. *Rut* 4H 75
Ryhill. *W Yor* 3D 93
Ryhope. *Tyne* 4H 115
Ryhope Colliery. *Tyne* 4H 115
Rylands. *Notts* 2C 74
Rylstone. *N Yor* 4B 98
Ryme Intrinseca. *Dors* 1A 14
Ryther. *N Yor* 1F 93
Ryton. *Glos* 2C 48
Ryton. *N Yor* 2B 100
Ryton. *Shrp* 5B 72
Ryton. *Tyne* 3E 115
Ryton. *Warw* 2A 62
Ryton-on-Dunsmore. *Warw* 3A 62
Ryton Woodside. *Tyne* 3E 115

S

Saasaig. *High* 3E 147
Sabden. *Lanc* 1F 91
Sacombe. *Herts* 4D 52
Sacriston. *Dur* 5F 115
Sadberge. *Darl* 3A 106
Saddell. *Arg* 2B 122
Saddington. *Leics* 1D 62
Saddle Bow. *Norf* 4F 77
Saddlescombe. *W Sus* 4D 26
Saddleworth. *G Man* 4H 91
Sadgill. *Cumb* 4F 103
Saffron Walden. *Essx* 2F 53
Sageston. *Pemb* 4E 43
Saham Hills. *Norf* 5B 78
Saham Toney. *Norf* 5A 78
Saighdinis. *W Isl* 2D 170
Saighton. *Ches W* 4G 83
Sain Dunwyd. *V Glam* 5C 32
Sain Hilari. *V Glam* 4D 32
St Abbs. *Bord* 3F 131
St Agnes. *Corn* 3B 6
St Albans. *Herts* 5B 52
St Allen. *Corn* 3C 6
St Andrews. *Fife* 2H 137
St Andrews Major. *V Glam* 4E 33
St Anne's. *Lanc* 2B 90
St Ann's. *Dum* 5C 118
St Ann's Chapel. *Corn* 5E 11
St Ann's Chapel. *Devn* 4C 8
St Anthony. *Corn* 5C 6
St Anthony-in-Meneage. *Corn* 4E 5
St Arvans. *Mon* 2A 34
St Asaph. *Den* 3C 82
Sain Tathan. *V Glam* 5D 32
St Athan. *V Glam* 5D 32
St Austell. *Corn* 3E 6
St Bartholomew's Hill. *Wilts* 4E 23
St Bees. *Cumb* 3A 102
St Blazey. *Corn* 3E 7
St Blazey Gate. *Corn* 3E 7
St Boswells. *Bord* 1A 120
St Breock. *Corn* 1D 6
St Breward. *Corn* 5A 10
St Briavels. *Glos* 5A 48
St Brides. *Pemb* 3B 42
St Bride's Major. *V Glam* 4B 32
St Bride's Netherwent. *Mon* 3H 33
St Bride's-super-Ely. *V Glam* 4D 32
St Brides Wentlooge. *Newp* 3F 33
St Budeaux. *Plym* 3A 8
Saintbury. *Glos* 2G 49
St Buryan. *Corn* 4B 4
St Catherine. *Bath* 4C 34
St Catherines. *Arg* 3A 134
St Clears. *Carm* 3G 43
St Cleer. *Corn* 2G 7
St Clement. *Corn* 4C 6
St Clether. *Corn* 4C 10
St Colmac. *Arg* 3B 126
St Columb Major. *Corn* 2D 6
St Columb Minor. *Corn* 2C 6
St Columb Road. *Corn* 3D 6
St Combs. *Abers* 2H 161
St Cross. *Hants* 4C 24
St Cross South Elmham. *Suff* 2E 67
St Cyrus. *Abers* 2G 145
St David's. *Pemb* 2B 42
St David's. *Per* 1B 136
St Day. *Corn* 4B 6
St Dennis. *Corn* 3D 6
St Dogmaels. *Pemb* 1B 44
St Dominick. *Corn* 2H 7
St Donat's. *V Glam* 5C 32
St Edith's Marsh. *Wilts* 5E 35
St Endellion. *Corn* 1D 6
St Enoder. *Corn* 3C 6
St Erme. *Corn* 4C 6

St Erney. *Corn* 3H 7
St Erth. *Corn* 3C 4
St Erth Praze. *Corn* 3C 4
St Ervan. *Corn* 1C 6
St Eval. *Corn* 2C 6
St Ewe. *Corn* 4D 6
St Fagans. *Card* 4E 32
St Fergus. *Abers* 3H 161
St Fillans. *Per* 1F 135
St Florence. *Pemb* 4E 43
St Gennys. *Corn* 3B 10
St George. *Cnwy* 3B 82
St Georges. *N Som* 5G 33
St Georges. *V Glam* 4D 32
St George's Hill. *Surr* 4B 38
St Germans. *Corn* 3H 7
St Giles in the Wood. *Devn* 1F 11
St Giles on the Heath. *Devn* 3D 10
St Giles's Hill. *Hants* 4C 24
St Gluvias. *Corn* 5B 6
St Harmon. *Powy* 3B 58
St Helena. *Warw* 5G 73
St Helen Auckland. *Dur* 2E 105
St Helens. *Cumb* 1B 102
St Helens. *E Sus* 4C 28
St Helens. *IOW* 4E 17
St Helens. *Mers* 1G 83
St Hilary. *Corn* 3C 4
St Hilary. *V Glam* 4D 32
Saint Hill. *Devn* 2D 12
Saint Hill. *W Sus* 2E 27
St Illtyd. *Blae* 5F 47
St Ippolyts. *Herts* 3B 52
St Ishmael. *Carm* 5D 44
St Ishmael's. *Pemb* 4C 42
St Issey. *Corn* 1D 6
St Ive. *Corn* 2H 7
St Ives. *Cambs* 3C 64
St Ives. *Corn* 2C 4
St Ives. *Dors* 2G 15
St James' End. *Nptn* 4E 63
St James South Elmham. *Suff* 2F 67
St Jidgey. *Corn* 2D 6
St John. *Corn* 3A 8
St John's. *IOM* 3B 108
St Johns. *Worc* 5C 60
St John's Chapel. *Devn* 4F 19
St John's Chapel. *Dur* 1B 104
St John's Fen End. *Norf* 4E 77
St John's Hall. *Dur* 1D 104
St John's Town of Dalry. *Dum* 1D 110
St Judes. *IOM* 2C 108
St Just. *Corn* 5C 6
(nr. Falmouth)
St Just. *Corn* 3A 4
(nr. Penzance)
St Just in Roseland. *Corn* 5C 6
St Katherines. *Abers* 5E 161
St Keverne. *Corn* 4E 5
St Kew. *Corn* 5A 10
St Kew Highway. *Corn* 5A 10
St Keyne. *Corn* 2G 7
St Lawrence. *Corn* 2E 7
St Lawrence. *Essx* 5C 54
St Lawrence. *IOW* 5D 16
St Leonards. *Buck* 5H 51
St Leonards. *Dors* 2G 15
St Leonards. *E Sus* 5B 28
St Levan. *Corn* 4A 4
St Lythans. *V Glam* 4E 32
St Mabyn. *Corn* 5A 10
St Madoes. *Per* 1D 136
St Margarets. *Here* 2G 47
St Margaret's. *Herts* 4A 52
(nr. Hemel Hempstead)
St Margarets. *Herts* 4D 53
(nr. Hoddesdon)
St Margaret's. *Wilts* 5G 35
St Margaret's at Cliffe. *Kent* 1H 29
St Margaret's Hope. *Orkn* 8D 172
St Margaret South Elmham. *Suff* 2F 67
St Mark's. *IOM* 4B 108
St Martin. *Corn* 4E 5
(nr. Helston)
St Martin. *Corn* 3G 7
(nr. Looe)
St Martins. *Per* 5A 144
St Martin's. *Shrp* 2F 71
St Mary Bourne. *Hants* 1C 24
St Marychurch. *Torb* 2F 9
St Mary Church. *V Glam* 4D 32
St Mary Cray. *G Lon* 4F 39
St Mary Hill. *V Glam* 4C 32
St Mary Hoo. *Medw* 3C 40
St Mary in the Marsh. *Kent* 3E 29
St Mary's. *Orkn* 7D 172
St Mary's Bay. *Kent* 3E 29
St Maughan's Green. *Mon* 4H 47
St Mawes. *Corn* 5C 6
St Mawgan. *Corn* 2C 6
St Mellion. *Corn* 2H 7
St Mellons. *Card* 3F 33
St Merryn. *Corn* 1C 6
St Mewan. *Corn* 3D 6
St Michael Caerhays. *Corn* 4D 6
St Michael Penkevil. *Corn* 4C 6
St Michaels. *Kent* 2C 28
St Michaels. *Torb* 3E 9
St Michaels. *Worc* 4H 59
St Michael's on Wyre. *Lanc* 5D 96
St Michael South Elmham. *Suff* 2F 67
St Minver. *Corn* 1D 6
St Monans. *Fife* 3H 137
St Neot. *Corn* 2F 7
St Neots. *Cambs* 4A 64
St Newlyn East. *Corn* 3C 6
St Nicholas. *Pemb* 1D 42
St Nicholas. *V Glam* 4D 32
St Nicholas at Wade. *Kent* 4G 41
St Nicholas South Elmham. *Suff* 2F 67
St Ninians. *Stir* 4H 135
St Olaves. *Norf* 1G 67
St Osyth. *Essx* 4E 54
St Osyth Heath. *Essx* 4E 55
St Owen's Cross. *Here* 3A 48
St Paul's Cray. *G Lon* 4F 39
St Paul's Walden. *Herts* 3B 52
St Peter's. *Kent* 4H 41
St Peter The Great. *Worc* 5C 60
St Petrox. *Pemb* 5D 42
St Pinnock. *Corn* 2G 7
St Quivox. *S Ayr* 2C 116
St Ruan. *Corn* 5E 5
St Stephen. *Corn* 3D 6
St Stephens. *Corn* 4D 10
(nr. Launceston)
St Stephens. *Corn* 3A 8
(nr. Saltash)
St Teath. *Corn* 4A 10
St Thomas. *Devn* 3C 12
St Thomas. *Swan* 3F 31
St Tudy. *Corn* 5A 10
St Twynnells. *Pemb* 5D 42
St Veep. *Corn* 3F 7
St Vigeans. *Ang* 4F 145
St Wenn. *Corn* 2D 6
St Weonards. *Here* 3H 47
St Winnolls. *Corn* 3H 7
St Winnow. *Corn* 3F 7
Salcombe. *Devn* 5D 8
Salcombe Regis. *Devn* 4E 13
Salcott. *Essx* 4C 54
Sale. *G Man* 1B 84
Saleby. *Linc* 3D 88
Sale Green. *Worc* 5D 60
Salehurst. *E Sus* 3B 28
Salem. *Carm* 3G 45
Salem. *Cdgn* 2F 57
Salen. *Arg* 4G 139
Salen. *High* 2A 140
Salesbury. *Lanc* 1E 91
Saleway. *Worc* 5D 60
Salford. *C Beds* 2H 51
Salford. *G Man* 1C 84
Salford. *Oxon* 3A 50
Salford Priors. *Warw* 5E 61
Salfords. *Surr* 1D 27
Salhouse. *Norf* 4F 79
Saligo. *Arg* 3A 124
Saline. *Fife* 4C 136
Salisbury. *Wilts* 3G 23
Salkeld Dykes. *Cumb* 1G 103
Sallachan. *High* 2D 141
Sallachy. *High* 3C 164
(nr. Lairg)
Sallachy. *High* 5B 156
(nr. Stromeferry)
Salle. *Norf* 3D 78
Salmonby. *Linc* 3C 88
Salmond's Muir. *Ang* 5E 145
Salperton. *Glos* 3F 49
Salph End. *Bed* 5H 63
Salsburgh. *N Lan* 3B 128
Salt. *Staf* 3D 72
Salta. *Cumb* 5B 112
Saltaire. *W Yor* 1B 92
Saltash. *Corn* 3A 8
Saltburn. *High* 2B 158
Saltburn-by-the-Sea. *Red C* 2D 106
Saltby. *Leics* 3F 75
Saltcoats. *Cumb* 5B 102
Saltcoats. *N Ayr* 5D 126
Saltdean. *Brig* 5E 27
Salt End. *E Yor* 2E 95
Salter. *Lanc* 3F 97
Salterforth. *Lanc* 5A 98
Salters Lode. *Norf* 5E 77
Salterswall. *Ches W* 4A 84
Salterton. *Wilts* 3G 23
Saltfleet. *Linc* 1D 88
Saltfleetby All Saints. *Linc* 1D 88
Saltfleetby St Clements. *Linc* 1D 88
Saltfleetby St Peter. *Linc* 2D 88
Saltford. *Bath* 5B 34
Salthouse. *Norf* 1C 78
Saltmarshe. *E Yor* 2A 94
Saltmead. *Card* 4E 33
Saltney. *Flin* 4F 83
Salton. *N Yor* 2B 100
Saltrens. *Devn* 4E 19
Saltwick. *Nmbd* 2E 115
Saltwood. *Kent* 2F 29
Salum. *Arg* 4B 138
Salwarpe. *Worc* 4C 60
Salwayash. *Dors* 3H 13
Samalaman. *High* 1A 140
Sambourne. *Warw* 4E 61
Sambourne. *Wilts* 2D 22
Sambrook. *Telf* 3B 72
Samhia. *W Isl* 2C 170
Samlesbury. *Lanc* 1D 90
Samlesbury Bottoms. *Lanc* 2E 90
Sampford Arundel. *Som* 1E 12
Sampford Brett. *Som* 2D 20
Sampford Courtenay. *Devn* 2G 11
Sampford Peverell. *Devn* 1D 12
Sampford Spiney. *Devn* 5F 11
Samsonlane. *Orkn* 5F 172
Samuelston. *E Lot* 2A 130
Sanaigmore. *Arg* 2A 124
Sancreed. *Corn* 4B 4
Sancton. *E Yor* 1C 94
Sand. *High* 4D 162
Sand. *Som* 2H 21
Sandaig. *Arg* 4A 138
Sandaig. *High* 3F 147
Sandale. *Cumb* 5D 112
Sandal Magna. *W Yor* 3D 92
Sandavore. *High* 5C 146
Sanday Airport. *Orkn* 3F 172
Sandbach. *Ches E* 4B 84
Sandbank. *Arg* 1C 126
Sandbanks. *Pool* 4F 15
Sandend. *Abers* 2C 160
Sanderstead. *G Lon* 4E 39
Sandfields. *Neat* 3G 31
Sandford. *Cumb* 3A 104
Sandford. *Devn* 2B 12
Sandford. *Dors* 4E 15
Sandford. *Hants* 2G 15
Sandford. *IOW* 4D 16
Sandford. *N Som* 1H 21
Sandford. *Shrp* 3F 71
(nr. Oswestry)
Sandford. *Shrp* 2H 71
(nr. Whitchurch)
Sandford. *S Lan* 5A 128
Sandfordhill. *Abers* 4H 161
Sandford-on-Thames. *Oxon* 5D 50
Sandford Orcas. *Dors* 4B 22
Sandford St Martin. *Oxon* 3C 50
Sandgate. *Kent* 2F 29
Sandgreen. *Dum* 4C 110
Sandhaven. *Abers* 2G 161
Sandhead. *Dum* 4F 109
Sandhill. *Cambs* 2E 65
Sandhills. *Dors* 1B 14
Sandhills. *Oxon* 5D 50
Sandhills. *Surr* 2A 26
Sandhoe. *Nmbd* 3C 114
Sand Hole. *E Yor* 1B 94
Sandholme. *E Yor* 1B 94
Sandholme. *Linc* 2C 76
Sandhurst. *Brac* 5G 37
Sandhurst. *Glos* 3D 48
Sandhurst. *Kent* 3B 28
Sandhurst Cross. *Kent* 3B 28
Sandhutton. *N Yor* 1F 99
(nr. Thirsk)
Sand Hutton. *N Yor* 4A 100
(nr. York)
Sandiacre. *Derbs* 2B 74
Sandilands. *Linc* 2E 89
Sandiway. *Ches W* 3A 84
Sandleheath. *Hants* 1G 15
Sandling. *Kent* 5B 40
Sandlow Green. *Ches E* 4B 84
Sandness. *Shet* 6C 173
Sandon. *Essx* 5H 53
Sandon. *Herts* 2D 52
Sandon. *Staf* 3D 72
Sandonbank. *Staf* 3D 72
Sandown. *IOW* 4D 16
Sandplace. *Corn* 3G 7
Sandridge. *Herts* 4B 52
Sandridge. *Wilts* 5E 35
Sandringham. *Norf* 3F 77
Sandsend. *N Yor* 3F 107
Sandside. *Cumb* 2C 96
Sands, The. *Surr* 2G 25
Sandtoft. *N Lin* 4H 93
Sandway. *Kent* 5C 40
Sandwell Green. *Suff* 3D 66
Sandwich. *Kent* 5H 41
Sandwick. *Cumb* 3F 103
Sandwick. *Orkn* 6B 172
Sandwick. *Shet* 9F 173
Sandwith. *Cumb* 3A 102
Sandy. *Carm* 5E 45
Sandy. *C Beds* 1B 52
Sandy Bank. *Linc* 5B 88
Sandycroft. *Flin* 4F 83
Sandy Cross. *Here* 5A 60
Sandygate. *Devn* 5B 12
Sandygate. *IOM* 2C 108
Sandy Haven. *Pemb* 4C 42
Sandyhills. *Dum* 4F 111
Sandylands. *Lanc* 3D 96
Sandylane. *Swan* 4E 31
Sandy Lane. *Wilts* 5E 35
Sandystones. *Bord* 2H 119
Sandyway. *Here* 3H 47
Sangobeg. *High* 2E 167
Sangomore. *High* 2E 166
Sankyn's Green. *Worc* 4B 60
Sanna. *High* 2F 139
Sanndabhaig. *W Isl* 4G 171
(on Isle of Lewis)
Sanndabhaig. *W Isl* 4D 170
(on South Uist)
Sannox. *N Ayr* 5B 126
Sanquhar. *Dum* 3G 117
Santon. *Cumb* 4B 102
Santon Bridge. *Cumb* 4C 102
Santon Downham. *Suff* 2H 65
Sapcote. *Leics* 1B 62
Sapey Common. *Here* 4B 60
Sapiston. *Suff* 3B 66
Sapley. *Cambs* 3B 64
Sapperton. *Derbs* 2F 73
Sapperton. *Glos* 5E 49
Sapperton. *Linc* 2H 75
Saracen's Head. *Linc* 3C 76
Sarclet. *High* 4F 169
Sardis. *Carm* 5F 45
Sardis. *Pemb* 4D 42
(nr. Milford Haven)
Sardis. *Pemb* 4F 43
(nr. Tenby)
Sarisbury. *Hants* 2D 16
Sarn. *B'end* 3C 32
Sarn. *Powy* 1E 58
Sarnau. *Carm* 3E 45
Sarnau. *Cdgn* 5C 56
Sarnau. *Gwyn* 2B 70
Sarnau. *Powy* 2D 46
(nr. Brecon)
Sarnau. *Powy* 4E 71
(nr. Welshpool)
Sarn Bach. *Gwyn* 3C 68
Sarnesfield. *Here* 5F 59
Sarn Meyllteyrn. *Gwyn* 2B 68
Saron. *Carm* 4G 45
(nr. Ammanford)
Saron. *Carm* 2D 45
(nr. Newcastle Emlyn)
Saron. *Gwyn* 4E 81
(nr. Bethel)
Saron. *Gwyn* 5D 80
(nr. Bontnewydd)
Sarratt. *Herts* 1B 38
Sarre. *Kent* 4G 41
Sarsden. *Oxon* 3A 50
Satley. *Dur* 5E 115
Satron. *N Yor* 5C 104
Satterleigh. *Devn* 4G 19
Satterthwaite. *Cumb* 5E 103
Satwell. *Oxon* 3F 37
Sauchen. *Abers* 2D 152
Saucher. *Per* 5A 144
Saughall. *Ches W* 4F 83
Saughtree. *Bord* 5H 119
Saul. *Glos* 5C 48
Saundby. *Notts* 2E 87
Saundersfoot. *Pemb* 4F 43
Saunderton. *Buck* 5F 51
Saunderton Lee. *Buck* 2G 37
Saunton. *Devn* 3E 19
Sausthorpe. *Linc* 4C 88
Saval. *High* 3C 164
Saverley Green. *Staf* 2D 72
Sawbridge. *Warw* 4C 62
Sawbridgeworth. *Herts* 4E 53
Sawdon. *N Yor* 1D 100
Sawley. *Derbs* 2B 74
Sawley. *Lanc* 5G 97
Sawley. *N Yor* 3E 99
Sawston. *Cambs* 1E 53
Sawtry. *Cambs* 2A 64
Saxby. *Leics* 3F 75
Saxby. *Linc* 2H 87
Saxby All Saints. *N Lin* 3C 94
Saxelby. *Leics* 3D 74
Saxelbye. *Leics* 3D 74
Saxham Street. *Suff* 4C 66
Saxilby. *Linc* 3F 87
Saxlingham. *Norf* 2C 78
Saxlingham Green. *Norf* 1E 67
Saxlingham Nethergate. *Norf* 1E 67
Saxlingham Thorpe. *Norf* 1E 66
Saxmundham. *Suff* 4F 67
Saxondale. *Notts* 1D 74
Saxon Street. *Cambs* 5F 65
Saxtead. *Suff* 4E 67
Saxtead Green. *Suff* 4E 67
Saxthorpe. *Norf* 2D 78
Saxton. *N Yor* 1E 93

Sayers Common. W Sus 4D 26
Scackleton. N Yor 2A 100
Scadabhagh. W Isl 8D 171
Scaftworth. Notts 1D 86
Scagglethorpe. N Yor 2C 100
Scaitcliffe. Lanc 2F 91
Scaladal. W Isl 6D 171
Scalasaig. Arg 4A 132
Scalby. E Yor 2B 94
Scalby. N Yor 5H 107
Scalby Mills. N Yor 5H 107
Scaldwell. Nptn 3E 63
Scaleby. Cumb 3F 113
Scaleby Hill. Cumb 3F 113
Scale Houses. Cumb 5G 113
Scales. Cumb 2B 96
(nr. Barrow-in-Furness)
Scales. Cumb 2E 103
(nr. Keswick)
Scalford. Leics 3E 75
Scaling. Red C 3E 107
Scaling Dam. Red C 3E 107
Scalloway. Shet 8E 173
Scalpaigh. W Isl 8E 171
Scalpay House. High 1E 147
Scamblesby. Linc 3B 88
Scamodale. High 1C 140
Scampston. N Yor 2C 100
Scampton. Linc 3G 87
Scaniport. High 5A 158
Scapa. Orkn 7D 172
Scapegoat Hill. W Yor 3A 92
Scar. Orkn 3F 172
Scarasta. W Isl 8C 171
Scarborough. N Yor 1E 101
Scarcliffe. Derbs 4B 86
Scarcroft. W Yor 5F 99
Scardroy. High 3E 156
Scarfskerry. High 1E 169
Scargill. Dur 3D 104
Scarinish. Arg 4B 138
Scarisbrick. Lanc 3B 90
Scarning. Norf 4B 78
Scarrington. Notts 1E 75
Scarth Hill. Lanc 4C 90
Scartho. NE Lin 4F 95
Scarvister. Shet 7E 173
Scatwell. High 3F 157
Scaur. Dum 4F 111
Scawby. N Lin 4C 94
Scawby Brook. N Lin 4C 94
Scawsby. S Yor 4F 93
Scawton. N Yor 1H 99
Scayne's Hill. W Sus 3E 27
Scethrog. Powy 3E 46
Scholar Green. Ches E 5C 84
Scholes. G Man 4D 90
Scholes. W Yor 2B 92
(nr. Bradford)
Scholes. W Yor 4B 92
(nr. Holmfirth)
Scholes. W Yor 1D 93
(nr. Leeds)
Scholey Hill. W Yor 2D 93
School Aycliffe. Dur 2F 105
School Green. Ches W 4A 84
School Green. Essx 2H 53
Scissett. W Yor 3C 92
Scleddau. Pemb 1D 42
Scofton. Notts 2D 86
Scole. Norf 3D 66
Scolton. Pemb 2D 43
Scone. Per 1D 136
Sconser. High 5E 155
Scoonie. Fife 3F 137
Scopwick. Linc 5H 87
Scoraig. High 4E 163
Scorborough. E Yor 5E 101
Scorrier. Corn 4B 6
Scorriton. Devn 2D 8
Scorton. Lanc 5E 97
Scorton. N Yor 4F 105
Sco Ruston. Norf 3E 79
Scotbheinn. W Isl 3D 170

Scotby. Cumb 4F 113
Scotch Corner. N Yor 4F 105
Scotforth. Lanc 3D 97
Scot Hay. Staf 1C 72
Scothern. Linc 3H 87
Scotland End. Oxon 2B 50
Scotlandwell. Per 3D 136
Scot Lane End. G Man 4E 91
Scotsburn. High 1B 158
Scotsburn. Mor 2G 159
Scotsdike. Cumb 2E 113
Scots Gap. Nmbd 1D 114
Scotstoun. Glas 3G 127
Scotstown. High 2C 140
Scotswood. Tyne 3F 115
Scottas. High 3F 147
Scotter. Linc 4B 94
Scotterthorpe. Linc 4B 94
Scottlethorpe. Linc 3H 75
Scotton. Linc 1F 87
Scotton. N Yor 5E 105
(nr. Catterick Garrison)
Scotton. N Yor 4F 99
(nr. Harrogate)
Scottow. Norf 3E 79
Scoulton. Norf 5B 78
Scounslow Green. Staf 3E 73
Scourie. High 4B 166
Scourie More. High 4B 166
Scousburgh. Shet 10E 173
Scout Green. Cumb 4G 103
Scouthead. G Man 4H 91
Scrabster. High 1C 168
Scrafield. Linc 4C 88
Scrainwood. Nmbd 4D 121
Scrane End. Linc 1C 76
Scraptoft. Leic 5D 74
Scratby. Norf 4H 79
Scrayingham. N Yor 3B 100
Scredington. Linc 1H 75
Scremby. Linc 4D 88
Scremerston. Nmbd 5G 131
Screveton. Notts 1E 75
Scrivelsby. Linc 4B 88
Scriven. N Yor 4F 99
Scronkey. Lanc 5D 96
Scrooby. Notts 1D 86
Scropton. Derbs 2F 73
Scrub Hill. Linc 5B 88
Scruton. N Yor 5F 105
Scuggate. Cumb 2F 113
Sculamus. High 1E 147
Sculcoates. Hull 1D 94
Sculthorpe. Norf 2A 78
Scunthorpe. N Lin 3B 94
Scurlage. Swan 4D 30
Sea. Som 1G 13
Seaborough. Dors 2H 13
Seabridge. Staf 1C 72
Seabrook. Kent 2F 29
Seaburn. Tyne 3H 115
Seacombe. Mers 1F 83
Seacroft. Linc 4E 89
Seacroft. W Yor 1D 92
Seadyke. Linc 2C 76
Seafield. Midl 5G 165
Seafield. Midl 3F 129
Seafield. S Ayr 2C 116
Seafield. W Lot 3D 128
Seaford. E Sus 5F 27
Seaforth. Mers 1F 83
Seagrave. Leics 4D 74
Seaham. Dur 5H 115
Seahouses. Nmbd 1G 121
Seal. Kent 5G 39
Sealand. Flin 4F 83
Seale. Surr 2G 25
Seamer. N Yor 1E 101
(nr. Scarborough)
Seamer. N Yor 3B 106
(nr. Stokesley)
Seamill. N Ayr 5C 126
Sea Mills. Bris 4A 34
Sea Palling. Norf 3G 79

Searby. Linc 4D 94
Seasalter. Kent 4E 41
Seascale. Cumb 4B 102
Seaside. Per 1E 137
Seater. High 1F 169
Seathorne. Linc 4E 89
Seathwaite. Cumb 3D 102
(nr. Buttermere)
Seathwaite. Cumb 5D 102
(nr. Ulpha)
Seatle. Cumb 1C 96
Seatoller. Cumb 3D 102
Seaton. Corn 3H 7
Seaton. Cumb 1B 102
Seaton. Devn 3F 13
Seaton. Dur 4G 115
Seaton. E Yor 5F 101
Seaton. Nmbd 2G 115
Seaton. Rut 1G 63
Seaton Burn. Tyne 2F 115
Seaton Carew. Hart 2C 106
Seaton Delaval. Nmbd 2G 115
Seaton Junction. Devn 3F 13
Seaton Ross. E Yor 5B 100
Seaton Sluice. Nmbd 2G 115
Seatown. Abers 2C 160
Seatown. Dors 3H 13
Seatown. Mor 2C 160
(nr. Cullen)
Seatown. Mor 1G 159
(nr. Lossiemouth)
Seave Green. N Yor 4C 106
Seaview. IOW 3E 16
Seaville. Cumb 4C 112
Seavington St Mary. Som 1H 13
Seavington St Michael. Som . . .1H 13
Seawick. Essx 4E 55
Sebastopol. Torf 2F 33
Sebergham. Cumb 5E 113
Seckington. Warw 5G 73
Second Coast. High 4D 162
Sedbergh. Cumb 5H 103
Sedbury. Glos 2A 34
Sedbusk. N Yor 5B 104
Sedgeberrow. Worc 2F 49
Sedgebrook. Linc 2F 75
Sedgefield. Dur 2A 106
Sedgeford. Norf 2G 77
Sedgehill. Wilts 4D 22
Sedgley. W Mid 1D 60
Sedgwick. Cumb 1E 97
Sedlescombe. E Sus 4B 28
Seend. Wilts 5E 35
Seend Cleeve. Wilts 5E 35
Seer Green. Buck 1A 38
Seething. Norf 1F 67
Sefton. Mers 4B 90
Sefton Park. Mers 2F 83
Segensworth. Hants 2D 16
Seggat. Abers 4E 161
Seghill. Nmbd 2F 115
Seifton. Shrp 2G 59
Seighford. Staf 3C 72
Seilebost. W Isl 8C 171
Seisdon. Staf 1C 60
Seisiadar. W Isl 4H 171
Selattyn. Shrp 2E 71
Selborne. Hants 3F 25
Selby. N Yor 1G 93
Selham. W Sus 3A 26
Selkirk. Bord 2G 119
Sellack. Here 3A 48
Sellafirth. Shet 2G 173
Sellick's Green. Som 1F 13
Sellindge. Kent 2F 29
Selling. Kent 5E 41
Sells Green. Wilts 5E 35
Selly Oak. W Mid 2E 61
Selmeston. E Sus 5G 27
Selsdon. G Lon 4E 39
Selsey. W Sus 3G 17
Selsfield Common. W Sus 2E 27
Selside. Cumb 5G 103
Selside. N Yor 2G 97

Selsley. Glos 5D 48
Selsted. Kent 1G 29
Selston. Notts 5B 86
Selworthy. Som 2C 20
Semer. Suff 1D 54
Semington. Wilts 5D 35
Semley. Wilts 4D 23
Sempringham. Linc 2A 76
Send. Surr 5B 38
Send Marsh. Surr 5B 38
Senghenydd. Cphy 2E 32
Sennen. Corn 4A 4
Sennen Cove. Corn 4A 4
Sennicotts. W Sus 2G 17
Sennybridge. Powy 3C 46
Serlby. Notts 2D 86
Sessay. N Yor 2G 99
Setchey. Norf 4F 77
Setley. Hants 2B 16
Setter. Shet 3F 173
Settiscarth. Orkn 6C 172
Settle. N Yor 3H 97
Settrington. N Yor 2C 100
Seven Ash. Som 3E 21
Sevenhampton. Glos 3F 49
Sevenhampton. Swin 2H 35
Sevenoaks. Kent 5G 39
Sevenoaks Weald. Kent 5G 39
Seven Sisters. Neat 5B 46
Seven Springs. Glos 4E 49
Severn Beach. S Glo 3A 34
Severn Stoke. Worc 1D 48
Sevington. Kent 1E 29
Sewards End. Essx 2F 53
Sewardstone. Essx 1E 39
Sewell. C Beds 3H 51
Seworgan. Corn 5B 6
Sewstern. Leics 3F 75
Sgallairidh. W Isl 9B 170
Sgarasta Mhor. W Isl 8C 171
Sgiogarstaigh. W Isl 1H 171
Shabbington. Buck 5E 51
Shackerley. Shrp 5C 72
Shackerstone. Leics 5A 74
Shackleford. Surr 1A 26
Shadforth. Dur 5G 115
Shadingfield. Suff 2G 67
Shadoxhurst. Kent 2D 28
Shadsworth. Bkbn 2E 91
Shadwell. Norf 2B 66
Shadwell. W Yor 1D 92
Shaftesbury. Dors 4D 22
Shafton. S Yor 3D 93
Shafton Two Gates. S Yor 3D 93
Shaggs. Dors 4D 14
Shakesfield. Glos 2B 48
Shalbourne. Wilts 5B 36
Shalcombe. IOW 4B 16
Shalden. Hants 2E 25
Shaldon. Devn 5C 12
Shalfleet. IOW 4C 16
Shalford. Essx 3H 53
Shalford. Surr 1B 26
Shalford Green. Essx 3H 53
Shallowford. Devn 2H 19
Shallowford. Staf 3C 72
Shalmsford Street. Kent 5E 41
Shalstone. Buck 2E 51
Shamley Green. Surr 1B 26
Shandon. Arg 1D 126
Shandwick. High 1C 158
Shangton. Leics 1E 62
Shankhouse. Nmbd 2F 115
Shanklin. IOW 4D 16
Shannochie. N Ayr 3D 122
Shap. Cumb 3G 103
Shapwick. Dors 2E 15
Shapwick. Som 3H 21
Sharcott. Wilts 1G 23
Shardlow. Derbs 2B 74
Shareshill. Staf 5D 72
Sharlston. W Yor 3D 93

Sharlston Common. W Yor 3D 93
Sharnal Street. Medw 3B 40
Sharnbrook. Bed 5G 63
Sharneyford. Lanc 2G 91
Sharnford. Leics 1B 62
Sharnhill Green. Dors 2C 14
Sharow. N Yor 2F 99
Sharpe Green. Lanc 1D 90
Sharpenhoe. C Beds 2A 52
Sharperton. Nmbd 4D 120
Sharpness. Glos 5B 48
Sharp Street. Norf 3F 79
Sharpthorne. W Sus 2E 27
Sharrington. Norf 2C 78
Shatterford. Worc 2B 60
Shatton. Derbs 2G 85
Shaugh Prior. Devn 2B 8
Shavington. Ches E 5B 84
Shaw. G Man 4H 91
Shaw. W Ber 5C 36
Shaw. Wilts 5D 35
Shawbirch. Telf 4A 72
Shawbury. Shrp 3H 71
Shawdon Hall. Nmbd 3E 121
Shawell. Leics 2C 62
Shawford. Hants 4C 24
Shawforth. Lanc 2G 91
Shaw Green. Lanc 3D 90
Shawhead. Dum 2F 111
Shaw Mills. N Yor 3E 99
Shawwood. E Ayr 2E 117
Shearington. Dum 3B 112
Shearsby. Leics 1D 62
Shearston. Som 3F 21
Shebbear. Devn 2E 11
Shebdon. Staf 3B 72
Shebster. High 2C 168
Sheddocksley. Aber 3F 153
Shedfield. Hants 1D 16
Shedog. N Ayr 2D 122
Sheen. Staf 4F 85
Sheepbridge. Derbs 3A 86
Sheep Hill. Tyne 4E 115
Sheepscar. W Yor 1D 92
Sheepscombe. Glos 4D 49
Sheepstor. Devn 2B 8
Sheepwash. Devn 2E 11
Sheepwash. Nmbd 1F 115
Sheepway. N Som 4H 33
Sheepy Magna. Leics 5H 73
Sheepy Parva. Leics 5H 73
Sheering. Essx 4F 53
Sheerness. Kent 3D 40
Sheerwater. Surr 4B 38
Sheet. Hants 4F 25
Sheffield. S Yor 2H 85
Sheffield Bottom. W Ber 5E 37
Sheffield Green. E Sus 3F 27
Shefford. C Beds 2B 52
Shefford Woodlands. W Ber 4B 36
Sheigra. High 2B 166
Sheinton. Shrp 5A 72
Shelderton. Shrp 3G 59
Sheldon. Derbs 4F 85
Sheldon. Devn 2E 12
Sheldon. W Mid 2F 61
Sheldwich. Kent 5E 40
Sheldwich Lees. Kent 5E 40
Shelf. W Yor 2B 92
Shelfanger. Norf 2D 66
Shelfield. Warw 4F 61
Shelfield. W Mid 5E 73
Shelford. Notts 1D 74
Shelford. Warw 2B 62
Shell. Worc 5D 60
Shelley. Suff 2D 54
Shelley. W Yor 3C 92
Shell Green. Hal 2H 83
Shellingford. Oxon 2B 36
Shellow Bowells. Essx 5G 53
Shelsley Beauchamp. Worc 4B 60
Shelsley Walsh. Worc 4B 60
Shelthorpe. Leics 4C 74
Shelton. Bed 4H 63

Shelton. *Norf* 1E 67
Shelton. *Notts* 1E 75
Shelton. *Shrp* 4G 71
Shelton Green. *Norf* 1E 67
Shelton Lock. *Derb* 2A 74
Shelve. *Shrp* 1F 59
Shelwick. *Here* 1A 48
Shelwick Green. *Here* 1A 48
Shenfield. *Essx* 1H 39
Shenington. *Oxon* 1B 50
Shenley. *Herts* 5B 52
Shenley Brook End. *Mil* 2G 51
Shenleybury. *Herts* 5B 52
Shenley Church End. *Mil* 2G 51
Shenmore. *Here* 2G 47
Shennanton. *Dum* 3A 110
Shenstone. *Staf* 5F 73
Shenstone. *Worc* 3C 60
Shenstone Woodend. *Staf* 5F 73
Shenton. *Leics* 5A 74
Shenval. *Mor* 1G 151
Shepeau Stow. *Linc* 4C 76
Shephall. *Herts* 3C 52
Shepherd's Bush. *G Lon* 2D 38
Shepherd's Gate. *Norf* 4E 77
Shepherd's Green. *Oxon* 3F 37
Shepherd's Port. *Norf* 2F 77
Shepherdswell. *Kent* 1G 29
Shepley. *W Yor* 4B 92
Sheppardstown. *High* 4D 169
Shepperdine. *S Glo* 2B 34
Shepperton. *Surr* 4B 38
Shepreth. *Cambs* 1D 53
Shepshed. *Leics* 4B 74
Shepton Beauchamp. *Som* 1H 13
Shepton Mallet. *Som* 2B 22
Shepton Montague. *Som* 3B 22
Shepway. *Kent* 5B 40
Sheraton. *Dur* 1B 106
Sherborne. *Bath* 1A 22
Sherborne. *Dors* 1B 14
Sherborne. *Glos* 4G 49
Sherborne Causeway. *Dors* 4D 22
Sherborne St John. *Hants* 1E 24
Sherbourne. *Warw* 4G 61
Sherburn. *Dur* 5G 115
Sherburn. *N Yor* 2D 100
Sherburn Hill. *Dur* 5G 115
Sherburn in Elmet. *N Yor* 1E 93
Shere. *Surr* 1B 26
Shereford. *Norf* 3A 78
Sherfield English. *Hants* 4A 24
Sherfield on Loddon. *Hants* 1E 25
Sherford. *Devn* 4D 9
Sherford. *Dors* 3E 15
Sheriffhales. *Shrp* 4B 72
Sheriff Hutton. *N Yor* 3A 100
Sheriffston. *Mor* 2G 159
Sheringham. *Norf* 1D 78
Sherington. *Mil* 1G 51
Shermanbury. *W Sus* 4D 26
Shernal Green. *Worc* 4D 60
Shernborne. *Norf* 2G 77
Sherrington. *Wilts* 3E 23
Sherston. *Wilts* 3D 34
Sherwood. *Nott* 1C 74
Sherwood Green. *Devn* 4F 19
Shettleston. *Glas* 3H 127
Shevington. *G Man* 4D 90
Shevington Moor. *G Man* 3D 90
Shevington Vale. *G Man* 4D 90
Sheviock. *Corn* 3H 7
Shide. *IOW* 4D 16
Shiel Bridge. *High* 2B 148
Shieldaig. *High* 1H 155
(nr. Charlestown)
Shieldaig. *High* 3H 155
(nr. Torridon)
Shieldhill. *Dum* 1B 112
Shieldhill. *Falk* 2B 128
Shieldhill. *S Lan* 5D 128
Shieldmuir. *N Lan* 4A 128
Shielfoot. *High* 2A 140
Shielhill. *Abers* 3H 161
Shielhill. *Ang* 3D 144
Shifnal. *Shrp* 5B 72
Shilbottle. *Nmbd* 4F 121
Shilbottle Grange. *Nmbd* 4G 121
Shildon. *Dur* 2F 105
Shillford. *E Ren* 4F 127
Shillingford. *Devn* 4C 20
Shillingford. *Oxon* 2D 36
Shillingford St George. *Devn* 4C 12
Shillingstone. *Dors* 1D 14
Shillington. *C Beds* 2B 52
Shillmoor. *Nmbd* 4C 120
Shilton. *Oxon* 5A 50
Shilton. *Warw* 2B 62
Shilvinghampton. *Dors* 4B 14
Shilvington. *Nmbd* 1E 115
Shimpling. *Norf* 2D 66
Shimpling. *Suff* 5A 66
Shimpling Street. *Suff* 5A 66
Shincliffe. *Dur* 5F 115
Shiney Row. *Tyne* 4G 115
Shinfield. *Wok* 5F 37
Shingay. *Cambs* 1D 52
Shingham. *Norf* 5G 77
Shingle Street. *Suff* 1G 55
Shinner's Bridge. *Devn* 2D 9
Shinness. *High* 2C 164
Shipbourne. *Kent* 5G 39
Shipdham. *Norf* 5B 78
Shipham. *Som* 1H 21
Shiphay. *Torb* 2E 9
Shiplake. *Oxon* 4F 37
Shipley. *Derbs* 1B 74
Shipley. *Nmbd* 3F 121
Shipley. *Shrp* 1C 60
Shipley. *W Sus* 3C 26
Shipley. *W Yor* 1B 92
Shipley Bridge. *Surr* 1E 27
Shipmeadow. *Suff* 1F 67
Shippon. *Oxon* 2C 36
Shipston-on-Stour. *Warw* 1A 50
Shipton. *Buck* 3F 51
Shipton. *Glos* 4F 49
Shipton. *N Yor* 4H 99
Shipton. *Shrp* 1H 59
Shipton Bellinger. *Hants* 2H 23
Shipton Gorge. *Dors* 3H 13
Shipton Green. *W Sus* 3G 17
Shipton Moyne. *Glos* 3D 35
Shipton-on-Cherwell. *Oxon* 4C 50
Shiptonthorpe. *E Yor* 5C 100
Shipton-under-Wychwood. *Oxon* 4A 50
Shirburn. *Oxon* 2E 37
Shirdley Hill. *Lanc* 3B 90
Shire. *Cumb* 1H 103
Shirebrook. *Derbs* 4C 86
Shiregreen. *S Yor* 1A 86
Shirehampton. *Bris* 4A 34
Shiremoor. *Tyne* 2G 115
Shirenewton. *Mon* 2H 33
Shireoaks. *Notts* 2C 86
Shires Mill. *Fife* 1C 128
Shirkoak. *Kent* 2D 28
Shirland. *Derbs* 5A 86
Shirley. *Derbs* 1G 73
Shirley. *Sotn* 1C 16
Shirley. *W Mid* 3F 61
Shirleywich. *Staf* 3D 73
Shirl Heath. *Here* 5G 59
Shirrell Heath. *Hants* 1D 16
Shirwell. *Devn* 3F 19
Shiskine. *N Ayr* 3D 122
Shobdon. *Here* 4F 59
Shobnall. *Staf* 3G 73
Shobrooke. *Devn* 2B 12
Shoby. *Leics* 3D 74
Shocklach. *Ches W* 1G 71
Shoeburyness. *S'end* 2D 40
Sholden. *Kent* 5H 41
Sholing. *Sotn* 1C 16
Sholver. *G Man* 4H 91
Shoot Hill. *Shrp* 4G 71
Shop. *Corn* 1C 10
(nr. Bude)
Shop. *Corn* 1C 6
(nr. Padstow)
Shop. *Devn* 1D 11
Shopford. *Cumb* 2G 113
Shoreditch. *G Lon* 2E 39
Shoreditch. *Som* 4F 21
Shoregill. *Cumb* 4A 104
Shoreham. *Kent* 4G 39
Shoreham-by-Sea. *W Sus* 5D 26
Shoresdean. *Nmbd* 5F 131
Shoreswood. *Nmbd* 5F 131
Shore, The. *Fife* 2E 137
Shorncote. *Glos* 2F 35
Shorne. *Kent* 3A 40
Shorne Ridgeway. *Kent* 3A 40
Shortacombe. *Devn* 4F 11
Shortbridge. *E Sus* 3F 27
Shortgate. *E Sus* 4F 27
Short Green. *Norf* 2C 66
Shorthampton. *Oxon* 3B 50
Short Heath. *Leics* 4H 73
Short Heath. *W Mid* 1E 61
(nr. Erdington)
Short Heath. *W Mid* 5D 73
(nr. Wednesfield)
Shortlanesend. *Corn* 4C 6
Shorton. *Torb* 2E 9
Shortstown. *Bed* 1A 52
Shortwood. *S Glo* 4B 34
Shorwell. *IOW* 4C 16
Shoscombe. *Bath* 1C 22
Shotesham. *Norf* 1E 67
Shotgate. *Essx* 1B 40
Shotley. *Suff* 2F 55
Shotley Bridge. *Dur* 4D 115
Shotleyfield. *Nmbd* 4D 114
Shotley Gate. *Suff* 2F 55
Shottenden. *Kent* 5E 41
Shottermill. *Surr* 3G 25
Shottery. *Warw* 5F 61
Shotteswell. *Warw* 1C 50
Shottisham. *Suff* 1G 55
Shottle. *Derbs* 1H 73
Shotton. *Dur* 1B 106
(nr. Peterlee)
Shotton. *Dur* 2A 106
(nr. Sedgefield)
Shotton. *Flin* 4E 83
Shotton. *Nmbd* 2F 115
(nr. Morpeth)
Shotton. *Nmbd* 1C 120
(nr. Town Yetholm)
Shotton Colliery. *Dur* 5G 115
Shotts. *N Lan* 3B 128
Shotwick. *Ches W* 3F 83
Shouldham. *Norf* 5F 77
Shouldham Thorpe. *Norf* 5F 77
Shoulton. *Worc* 5C 60
Shrawardine. *Shrp* 4F 71
Shrawley. *Worc* 4C 60
Shreding Green. *Buck* 2B 38
Shrewley. *Warw* 4G 61
Shrewsbury. *Shrp* 4G 71
Shrewton. *Wilts* 2F 23
Shripney. *W Sus* 5A 26
Shrivenham. *Oxon* 3H 35
Shropham. *Norf* 1B 66
Shroton. *Dors* 1D 14
Shrub End. *Essx* 3C 54
Shucknall. *Here* 1A 48
Shudy Camps. *Cambs* 1G 53
Shulishadermor. *High* 4D 155
Shulista. *High* 1D 154
Shurdington. *Glos* 4E 49
Shurlock Row. *Wind* 4G 37
Shurrery. *High* 3C 168
Shurton. *Som* 2F 21
Shustoke. *Warw* 1G 61
Shute. *Devn* 3F 13
(nr. Axminster)
Shute. *Devn* 2B 12
(nr. Crediton)
Shutford. *Oxon* 1B 50
Shut Heath. *Staf* 3C 72
Shuthonger. *Glos* 2D 49
Shutlanehead. *Staf* 1C 72
Shutlanger. *Nptn* 1F 51
Shutt Green. *Staf* 5C 72
Shuttington. *Warw* 5G 73
Shuttlewood. *Derbs* 3B 86
Shuttleworth. *G Man* 3G 91
Siabost. *W Isl* 3E 171
Siabost bho Dheas. *W Isl* 3E 171
Siabost bho Thuath. *W Isl* 3E 171
Siadar. *W Isl* 2F 171
Sibbaldbie. *Dum* 1C 112
Sibbertoft. *Nptn* 2D 62
Sibdon Carwood. *Shrp* 2G 59
Sibertswold. *Kent* 1G 29
Sibford Ferris. *Oxon* 2B 50
Sibford Gower. *Oxon* 2B 50
Sible Hedingham. *Essx* 2A 54
Sibsey. *Linc* 5C 88
Sibsey Fen Side. *Linc* 5C 88
Sibson. *Cambs* 1H 63
Sibson. *Leics* 5A 74
Sibster. *High* 3F 169
Sibthorpe. *Notts* 1E 75
Sibton. *Suff* 4F 67
Sicklesmere. *Suff* 4A 66
Sicklinghall. *N Yor* 5F 99
Sid. *Devn* 4E 13
Sidbury. *Devn* 3E 13
Sidbury. *Shrp* 2A 60
Sidcot. *N Som* 1H 21
Sidcup. *G Lon* 3F 39
Siddick. *Cumb* 1B 102
Siddington. *Ches E* 3C 84
Siddington. *Glos* 2F 35
Side of the Moor. *G Man* 3F 91
Sidestrand. *Norf* 2E 79
Sidford. *Devn* 3E 13
Sidlesham. *W Sus* 3G 17
Sidley. *E Sus* 5B 28
Sidlow. *Surr* 1D 26
Sidmouth. *Devn* 4E 13
Sigford. *Devn* 5A 12
Sigglesthorne. *E Yor* 5F 101
Sighthill. *Edin* 2E 129
Sigingstone. *V Glam* 4C 32
Signet. *Oxon* 4H 49
Silchester. *Hants* 5E 37
Sileby. *Leics* 4D 74
Silecroft. *Cumb* 1A 96
Silfield. *Norf* 1D 66
Silian. *Cdgn* 5E 57
Silkstone. *S Yor* 4C 92
Silkstone Common. *S Yor* 4C 92
Silksworth. *Tyne* 4G 115
Silk Willoughby. *Linc* 1H 75
Silloth. *Cumb* 4C 112
Sills. *Nmbd* 4C 120
Sillyearn. *Mor* 3C 160
Silpho. *N Yor* 5G 107
Silsden. *W Yor* 5C 98
Silsoe. *C Beds* 2A 52
Silverbank. *Abers* 4E 152
Silverburn. *Midl* 3F 129
Silverdale. *Lanc* 2D 96
Silverdale. *Staf* 1C 72
Silverdale Green. *Lanc* 2D 96
Silver End. *Essx* 4B 54
Silver End. *W Mid* 2D 60
Silvergate. *Norf* 3D 78
Silver Green. *Norf* 1E 67
Silverhillocks. *Abers* 2E 161
Silverley's Green. *Suff* 3E 67
Silverstone. *Nptn* 1E 51
Silverton. *Devn* 2C 12
Silverton. *W Dun* 2F 127
Silvington. *Shrp* 3A 60
Simm's Cross. *Hal* 2H 83
Simm's Lane End. *Mers* 1H 83
Simonburn. *Nmbd* 2B 114
Simonsbath. *Som* 3A 20
Simonstone. *Lanc* 1F 91
Simprim. *Bord* 5E 131
Simpson. *Pemb* 3C 42
Simpson Cross. *Pemb* 3C 42
Sinclairston. *E Ayr* 3D 116
Sinclairtown. *Fife* 4E 137
Sinderby. *N Yor* 1F 99
Sinderhope. *Nmbd* 4B 114
Sindlesham. *Wok* 5F 37
Sinfin. *Derb* 2A 74
Singleborough. *Buck* 2F 51
Singleton. *Kent* 1D 28
Singleton. *Lanc* 1B 90
Singleton. *W Sus* 1G 17
Singlewell. *Kent* 3A 40
Sinkhurst Green. *Kent* 1C 28
Sinnahard. *Abers* 2B 152
Sinnington. *N Yor* 1B 100
Sinton Green. *Worc* 4C 60
Sipson. *G Lon* 3B 38
Sirhowy. *Blae* 4E 47
Sisland. *Norf* 1F 67
Sissinghurst. *Kent* 2B 28
Siston. *S Glo* 4B 34
Sithney. *Corn* 4D 4
Sittingbourne. *Kent* 4D 40
Six Ashes. *Staf* 2B 60
Six Bells. *Blae* 5F 47
Six Hills. *Leics* 3D 74
Sixhills. *Linc* 2A 88
Six Mile Bottom. *Cambs* 5E 65
Sixpenny Handley. *Dors* 1E 15
Sizewell. *Suff* 4G 67
Skail. *High* 4H 167
Skaills. *Orkn* 7E 172
Skares. *E Ayr* 3E 117
Skateraw. *E Lot* 2D 130
Skaw. *Shet* 5G 173
Skeabost. *High* 4D 154
Skeeby. *N Yor* 4E 105
Skeffington. *Leics* 5E 75
Skeffling. *E Yor* 3G 95
Skegby. *Notts* 4B 86
(nr. Mansfield)
Skegby. *Notts* 3E 87
(nr. Tuxford)
Skegness. *Linc* 4E 89
Skelberry. *Shet* 10E 173
(nr. Boddam)
Skelberry. *Shet* 3E 173
(nr. Housetter)
Skelbo. *High* 4E 165
Skelbo Street. *High* 4E 165
Skelbrooke. *S Yor* 3F 93
Skeldyke. *Linc* 2C 76
Skelfhill. *Bord* 4G 119
Skellingthorpe. *Linc* 3G 87
Skellister. *Shet* 6F 173
Skellorn Green. *Ches E* 2D 84
Skellow. *S Yor* 3F 93
Skelmanthorpe. *W Yor* 3C 92
Skelmersdale. *Lanc* 4C 90
Skelmorlie. *N Ayr* 3C 126
Skelpick. *High* 3H 167
Skelton. *Cumb* 1F 103
Skelton. *E Yor* 2A 94
Skelton. *N Yor* 4D 105
(nr. Richmond)
Skelton. *N Yor* 3F 99
(nr. Ripon)
Skelton. *Red C* 3D 106
Skelton. *York* 4H 99
Skelton Green. *Red C* 3D 106
Skelwick. *Orkn* 3D 172
Skelwith Bridge. *Cumb* 4E 103
Skendleby. *Linc* 4D 88
Skendleby Psalter. *Linc* 3D 88
Skenfrith. *Mon* 3H 47
Skerne. *E Yor* 4E 101
Skeroblingarry. *Arg* 3B 122
Skerray. *High* 2G 167
Skerricha. *High* 3C 166
Skerries Airport. *Shet* 4H 173
Skerton. *Lanc* 3D 97
Sketchley. *Leics* 1B 62

Sketty. *Swan* 3F 31
Skewen. *Neat* 3G 31
Skewsby. *N Yor* 2A 100
Skeyton. *Norf* 3E 79
Skeyton Corner. *Norf* 3E 79
Skiall. *High* 2C 168
Skidbrooke. *Linc* 1D 88
Skidbrooke North End. *Linc* 1D 88
Skidby. *E Yor* 1D 94
Skilgate. *Som* 4C 20
Skillington. *Linc* 3F 75
Skinburness. *Cumb* 4C 112
Skinflats. *Falk* 1C 128
Skinidin. *High* 4B 154
Skinnet. *High* 2F 167
Skinningrove. *Red C* 2E 107
Skipness. *Arg* 4G 125
Skippool. *Lanc* 5C 96
Skiprigg. *Cumb* 5E 113
Skipsea. *E Yor* 4F 101
Skipsea Brough. *E Yor* 4F 101
Skipton. *N Yor* 4B 98
Skipton-on-Swale. *N Yor* 2F 99
Skipwith. *N Yor* 1G 93
Skirbeck. *Linc* 1C 76
Skirbeck Quarter. *Linc* 1C 76
Skirlaugh. *E Yor* 1E 95
Skirling. *Bord* 1C 118
Skirmett. *Buck* 2F 37
Skirpenbeck. *E Yor* 4B 100
Skirwith. *Cumb* 1H 103
Skirwith. *N Yor* 2G 97
Skirza. *High* 2F 169
Skitby. *Cumb* 3F 113
Skitham. *Lanc* 5D 96
Skittle Green. *Buck* 5F 51
Skulamus. *High* 1E 147
Skullomie. *High* 2G 167
Skyborry Green. *Shrp* 3E 59
Skye Green. *Essx* 3B 54
Skye of Curr. *High* 1D 151
Slack. *W Yor* 2H 91
Slackhall. *Derbs* 2E 85
Slack Head. *Cumb* 2D 97
Slackhead. *Mor* 2B 160
Slackholme End. *Linc* 3E 89
Slacks of Cairnbanno. *Abers* 4F 161
Slack, The. *Dur* 2E 105
Slad. *Glos* 5D 48
Slade. *Swan* 4D 31
Slade End. *Oxon* 2D 36
Slade Field. *Cambs* 2C 64
Slade Green. *G Lon* 3G 39
Slade Heath. *Staf* 5D 72
Slade Hooton. *S Yor* 2C 86
Sladesbridge. *Corn* 5A 10
Slade, The. *W Ber* 5D 36
Slaggyford. *Nmbd* 4H 113
Slaidburn. *Lanc* 4G 97
Slaid Hill. *W Yor* 5F 99
Slaithwaite. *W Yor* 3A 92
Slaley. *Derbs* 5G 85
Slaley. *Nmbd* 4C 114
Slamannan. *Falk* 2B 128
Slapton. *Buck* 3H 51
Slapton. *Devn* 4E 9
Slapton. *Nptn* 1E 51
Slattock. *G Man* 4G 91
Slaugham. *W Sus* 3D 26
Slaughterbridge. *Corn* 4B 10
Slaughterford. *Wilts* 4D 34
Slawston. *Leics* 1E 63
Sleaford. *Hants* 3G 25
Sleaford. *Linc* 1H 75
Sleagill. *Cumb* 3G 103
Sleap. *Shrp* 3G 71
Sledmere. *E Yor* 3D 100
Sleightholme. *Dur* 3C 104
Sleights. *N Yor* 4F 107
Slepe. *Dors* 3E 15
Slickly. *High* 2E 169
Sliddery. *N Ayr* 3D 122
Sligachan. *High* 1C 146
Slimbridge. *Glos* 5C 48
Slindon. *Staf* 2C 72
Slindon. *W Sus* 5A 26
Slinfold. *W Sus* 2C 26
Slingsby. *N Yor* 2A 100
Slip End. *C Beds* 4A 52
Slipton. *Nptn* 3G 63
Slitting Mill. *Staf* 4E 73
Slochd. *High* 1C 150
Slockavullin. *Arg* 4F 133
Sloley. *Norf* 3E 79
Sloncombe. *Devn* 4H 11
Sloothby. *Linc* 3D 89
Slough. *Slo* 2A 38
Slough Green. *Som* 4F 21
Slough Green. *W Sus* 3D 27
Sluggan. *High* 1C 150
Slyne. *Lanc* 3D 97
Smailholm. *Bord* 1A 120
Smallbridge. *G Man* 3H 91
Smallbrook. *Devn* 3B 12
Smallburgh. *Norf* 3F 79
Smallburn. *E Ayr* 2F 117
Smalldale. *Derbs* 3E 85
Small Dole. *W Sus* 4D 26
Smalley. *Derbs* 1B 74
Smallfield. *Surr* 1E 27
Small Heath. *W Mid* 2E 61
Smallholm. *Dum* 2C 112
Small Hythe. *Kent* 2C 28
Smallrice. *Staf* 2D 72
Smallridge. *Devn* 2G 13
Smallwood Hey. *Lanc* 5C 96
Smallworth. *Norf* 2C 66
Smannell. *Hants* 2B 24
Smardale. *Cumb* 4A 104
Smarden. *Kent* 1C 28
Smarden Bell. *Kent* 1C 28
Smart's Hill. *Kent* 1G 27
Smeatharpe. *Devn* 1F 13
Smeeth. *Kent* 2E 29
Smeeth, The. *Norf* 4E 77
Smeeton Westerby. *Leics* 1D 62
Smeircleit. *W Isl* 7C 170
Smerral. *High* 5D 168
Smestow. *Staf* 1C 60
Smethwick. *W Mid* 2E 61
Smirisary. *High* 1A 140
Smisby. *Derbs* 4H 73
Smitham Hill. *Bath* 1A 22
Smith End Green. *Worc* 5B 60
Smithfield. *Cumb* 3F 113
Smith Green. *Lanc* 4D 97
Smithies, The. *Shrp* 1A 60
Smithincott. *Devn* 1D 12
Smith's Green. *Essx* 3F 53
Smithstown. *High* 1G 155
Smithton. *High* 4B 158
Smithwood Green. *Suff* 5B 66
Smithy Bridge. *G Man* 3H 91
Smithy Green. *Ches E* 3B 84
Smithy Lane Ends. *Lanc* 3C 90
Smockington. *Warw* 2B 62
Smyth's Green. *Essx* 4C 54
Snaigow House. *Per* 4H 143
Snailbeach. *Shrp* 5F 71
Snailwell. *Cambs* 4F 65
Snainton. *N Yor* 1D 100
Snaith. *E Yor* 2G 93
Snape. *N Yor* 1E 99
Snape. *Suff* 5F 67
Snape Green. *Lanc* 3B 90
Snapper. *Devn* 3F 19
Snarestone. *Leics* 5H 73
Snarford. *Linc* 2H 87
Snargate. *Kent* 3D 28
Snave. *Kent* 3E 28
Sneachill. *Worc* 5D 60
Snead. *Powy* 1F 59
Snead Common. *Worc* 4B 60
Sneaton. *N Yor* 4F 107
Sneatonthorpe. *N Yor* 4G 107
Snelland. *Linc* 2H 87
Snelston. *Derbs* 1F 73
Snetterton. *Norf* 1B 66
Snettisham. *Norf* 2F 77
Snibston. *Leics* 4B 74
Sniseabhal. *W Isl* 5C 170
Snitter. *Nmbd* 4E 121
Snitterby. *Linc* 1G 87
Snitterfield. *Warw* 5G 61
Snitton. *Shrp* 3H 59
Snodhill. *Here* 1G 47
Snodland. *Kent* 4A 40
Snods Edge. *Nmbd* 4D 114
Snowdonia. *Gwyn* 2G 69
Snowshill. *Glos* 2F 49
Snow Street. *Norf* 2C 66
Snydale. *W Yor* 3E 93
Soake. *Hants* 1E 17
Soar. *Carm* 3G 45
Soar. *Gwyn* 2F 69
Soar. *IOA* 3C 80
Soar. *Powy* 2C 46
Soberton. *Hants* 1E 16
Soberton Heath. *Hants* 1E 16
Sockbridge. *Cumb* 2F 103
Sockburn. *Darl* 4A 106
Sodom. *Den* 3C 82
Soham. *Cambs* 3E 65
Soham Cotes. *Cambs* 3E 65
Solas. *W Isl* 1D 170
Soldon Cross. *Devn* 1D 10
Soldridge. *Hants* 3E 25
Solent Breezes. *Hants* 2D 16
Sole Street. *Kent* 4A 40
(nr. Meopham)
Sole Street. *Kent* 1E 29
(nr. Waltham)
Solihull. *W Mid* 3F 61
Sollers Dilwyn. *Here* 5G 59
Sollers Hope. *Here* 2B 48
Sollom. *Lanc* 3C 90
Solva. *Pemb* 2B 42
Somerby. *Leics* 4E 75
Somerby. *Linc* 4D 94
Somercotes. *Derbs* 5B 86
Somerford. *Dors* 3G 15
Somerford. *Staf* 5C 72
Somerford Keynes. *Glos* 2F 35
Somerley. *W Sus* 3G 17
Somerleyton. *Suff* 1G 67
Somersal Herbert. *Derbs* 2F 73
Somersby. *Linc* 3C 88
Somersham. *Cambs* 3C 64
Somersham. *Suff* 1D 54
Somerton. *Oxon* 3C 50
Somerton. *Som* 4H 21
Somerton. *Suff* 5H 65
Sompting. *W Sus* 5C 26
Sonning. *Wok* 4F 37
Sonning Common. *Oxon* 3F 37
Sonning Eye. *Oxon* 4F 37
Sookholme. *Notts* 4C 86
Sopley. *Hants* 3G 15
Sopworth. *Wilts* 3D 34
Sorbie. *Dum* 5B 110
Sordale. *High* 2D 168
Sorisdale. *Arg* 2D 138
Sorn. *E Ayr* 2E 117
Sornhill. *E Ayr* 1E 117
Sortat. *High* 2E 169
Sotby. *Linc* 3B 88
Sots Hole. *Linc* 4A 88
Sotterley. *Suff* 2G 67
Soudley. *Shrp* 1G 59
(nr. Church Stretton)
Soudley. *Shrp* 3B 72
(nr. Market Drayton)
Soughton. *Flin* 4E 83
Soulbury. *Buck* 3G 51
Soulby. *Cumb* 3A 104
(nr. Appleby)
Soulby. *Cumb* 2F 103
(nr. Penrith)
Souldern. *Oxon* 2D 50
Souldrop. *Bed* 4G 63
Sound. *Ches E* 1A 72
Sound. *Shet* 7F 173
Soundwell. *Bris* 4B 34
Sourhope. *Bord* 2C 120
Sourin. *Orkn* 4D 172
Sour Nook. *Cumb* 5E 113
Sourton. *Devn* 3F 11
Soutergate. *Cumb* 1B 96
South Acre. *Norf* 4H 77
Southall. *G Lon* 3C 38
South Allington. *Devn* 5D 9
South Alloa. *Falk* 4A 136
Southam. *Glos* 3E 49
Southam. *Warw* 4B 62
South Ambersham. *W Sus* 3A 26
Southampton. *Sotn* 1C 16
Southampton International Airport.
Hants 1C 16
Southannan. *N Ayr* 4D 126
South Anston. *S Yor* 2C 86
South Ascot. *Wind* 4A 38
South Baddesley. *Hants* 3B 16
South Balfern. *Dum* 4B 110
South Ballachulish. *High* 3E 141
South Bank. *Red C* 2C 106
South Barrow. *Som* 4B 22
South Benfleet. *Essx* 2B 40
South Bents. *Tyne* 3H 115
South Bersted. *W Sus* 5A 26
Southborough. *Kent* 1G 27
Southbourne. *Bour* 3G 15
Southbourne. *W Sus* 2F 17
South Bowood. *Dors* 3H 13
South Brent. *Devn* 2D 8
South Brewham. *Som* 3C 22
South Broomage. *Falk* 1B 128
South Broomhill. *Nmbd* 4G 121
Southburgh. *Norf* 5B 78
South Burlingham. *Norf* 5F 79
Southburn. *E Yor* 4D 101
South Cadbury. *Som* 4B 22
South Carlton. *Linc* 3G 87
South Cave. *E Yor* 1C 94
South Cerney. *Glos* 2F 35
South Chard. *Som* 2G 13
South Charlton. *Nmbd* 2F 121
South Cheriton. *Som* 4B 22
South Church. *Dur* 2F 105
Southchurch. *S'end* 2D 40
South Cleatlam. *Dur* 3E 105
South Cliffe. *E Yor* 1B 94
South Clifton. *Notts* 3F 87
South Clunes. *High* 4H 157
South Cockerington. *Linc* 2C 88
South Common. *Devn* 2G 13
South Common. *E Sus* 4E 27
South Cornelly. *B'end* 3B 32
Southcott. *Devn* 1E 11
(nr. Great Torrington)
Southcott. *Devn* 3F 11
(nr. Okehampton)
Southcott. *Wilts* 1G 23
Southcourt. *Buck* 4G 51
South Cove. *Suff* 2G 67
South Creagan. *Arg* 4D 141
South Creake. *Norf* 2A 78
South Crosland. *W Yor* 3B 92
South Croxton. *Leics* 4D 74
South Dalton. *E Yor* 5D 100
South Darenth. *Kent* 4G 39
Southdean. *Bord* 4A 120
Southdown. *Bath* 5C 34
South Downs. *W Sus* 5D 26
South Duffield. *N Yor* 1G 93
Southease. *E Sus* 5F 27
South Elkington. *Linc* 2B 88
South Elmsall. *W Yor* 3E 93
Southend. *Arg* 5A 122
South End. *Cumb* 3B 96
Southend. *Glos* 2C 34
South End. *N Lin* 2E 94
South End. *W Ber* 4D 36
Southend (London) Airport.
Essx 2C 40
Southend-on-Sea. *S'end* 2C 40
Southerfield. *Cumb* 5C 112
Southerly. *Devn* 4F 11
Southernden. *Kent* 1C 28
Southerndown. *V Glam* 4B 32
Southerness. *Dum* 4A 112
South Erradale. *High* 1G 155
Southerton. *Devn* 3D 12
Southery. *Norf* 1F 65
Southey Green. *Essx* 2A 54
South Fambridge. *Essx* 1C 40
South Fawley. *W Ber* 3B 36
South Feorline. *N Ayr* 3D 122
South Ferriby. *N Lin* 2C 94
South Field. *E Yor* 2D 94
Southfleet. *Kent* 3H 39
South Garvan. *High* 1D 141
Southgate. *Cdgn* 2E 57
Southgate. *G Lon* 1E 39
Southgate. *Norf* 3D 78
(nr. Aylsham)
Southgate. *Norf* 2A 78
(nr. Fakenham)
Southgate. *Swan* 4E 31
South Godstone. *Surr* 1E 27
South Gorley. *Hants* 1G 15
South Green. *Essx* 1A 40
(nr. Billericay)
South Green. *Essx* 4D 54
(nr. Colchester)
South Green. *Kent* 4C 40
South Hanningfield. *Essx* 1B 40
South Harting. *W Sus* 1F 17
South Hayling. *Hants* 3F 17
South Hazelrigg. *Nmbd* 1E 121
South Heath. *Buck* 5H 51
South Heath. *Essx* 4E 54
South Heighton. *E Sus* 5F 27
South Hetton. *Dur* 5G 115
South Hiendley. *W Yor* 3D 93
South Hill. *Corn* 5D 10
South Hill. *Som* 4H 21
South Hinksey. *Oxon* 5D 50
South Hole. *Devn* 4C 18
South Holme. *N Yor* 2B 100
South Holmwood. *Surr* 1C 26
South Hornchurch. *G Lon* 2G 39
South Huish. *Devn* 4C 8
South Hykeham. *Linc* 4G 87
South Hylton. *Tyne* 4G 115
Southill. *C Beds* 1B 52
Southington. *Hants* 2D 24
South Kelsey. *Linc* 1H 87
South Kessock. *High* 4A 158
South Killingholme. *N Lin* 3E 95
South Kilvington. *N Yor* 1G 99
South Kilworth. *Leics* 2D 62
South Kirkby. *W Yor* 3E 93
South Kirton. *Abers* 3E 153
South Knighton. *Devn* 5B 12
South Kyme. *Linc* 1A 76
South Lancing. *W Sus* 5C 26
South Ledaig. *Arg* 5D 140
Southleigh. *Devn* 3F 13
South Leigh. *Oxon* 5B 50
South Leverton. *Notts* 2E 87
South Littleton. *Worc* 1F 49
South Lopham. *Norf* 2C 66
South Luffenham. *Rut* 5G 75
South Malling. *E Sus* 4F 27
South Marston. *Swin* 3G 35
South Middleton. *Nmbd* 2E 121
South Milford. *N Yor* 1E 93
South Milton. *Devn* 4D 8
South Mimms. *Herts* 5C 52
Southminster. *Essx* 1D 40
South Molton. *Devn* 4H 19
South Moor. *Dur* 4E 115
Southmoor. *Oxon* 2B 36
South Moreton. *Oxon* 3D 36
South Mundham. *W Sus* 2G 17
South Muskham. *Notts* 5E 87
South Newbald. *E Yor* 1C 94
South Newington. *Oxon* 2C 50
South Newsham. *Nmbd* 2G 115
South Newton. *N Ayr* 4H 125

South Newton. *Wilts* 3F 23
South Normanton. *Derbs* 5B 86
South Norwood. *G Lon* 4E 39
South Nutfield. *Surr* 1E 27
South Ockendon. *Thur* 2G 39
Southoe. *Cambs* 4A 64
Southolt. *Suff* 4D 66
South Ormsby. *Linc* 3C 88
Southorpe. *Pet* 5H 75
South Otterington. *N Yor* 1F 99
South Owersby. *Linc* 1H 87
Southowram. *W Yor* 2B 92
South Oxhey. *Herts* 1C 38
South Perrott. *Dors* 2H 13
South Petherton. *Som* 1H 13
South Petherwin. *Corn* 4D 10
South Pickenham. *Norf* 5A 78
South Pool. *Devn* 4D 9
South Poorton. *Dors* 3A 14
South Port. *Arg* 1H 133
Southport. *Mers* 3B 90
South Queensferry. *Edin* 2E 129
South Radworthy. *Devn* 3A 20
South Rauceby. *Linc* 1H 75
South Raynham. *Norf* 3A 78
Southrepps. *Norf* 2E 79
South Reston. *Linc* 2D 88
Southrey. *Linc* 4A 88
Southrop. *Glos* 5G 49
Southrope. *Hants* 2E 25
South Runcton. *Norf* 5F 77
South Scarle. *Notts* 4F 87
Southsea. *Port* 3E 17
South Shields. *Tyne* 3G 115
South Shore. *Bkpl* 1B 90
Southside. *Orkn* 5E 172
South Somercotes. *Linc* 1D 88
South Stainley. *N Yor* 3F 99
South Stainmore. *Cumb* 3B 104
South Stifford. *Thur* 3G 39
Southstoke. *Bath* 5C 34
South Stoke. *Oxon* 3D 36
South Stoke. *W Sus* 4B 26
South Street. *E Sus* 4E 27
South Street. *Kent* 5E 41
(nr. Faversham)
South Street. *Kent* 4F 41
(nr. Whitstable)
South Tawton. *Devn* 3G 11
South Thoresby. *Linc* 3D 88
South Tidworth. *Wilts* 2H 23
South Town. *Devn* 4C 12
South Town. *Hants* 3E 25
Southtown. *Norf* 5H 79
Southtown. *Orkn* 8D 172
Southwaite. *Cumb* 5F 113
South Walsham. *Norf* 4F 79
South Warnborough. *Hants* 2F 25
Southwater. *W Sus* 3C 26
Southwater Street. *W Sus* 3C 26
Southway. *Som* 2A 22
South Weald. *Essx* 1G 39
South Weirs. *Hants* 2A 16
Southwell. *Dors* 5B 14
Southwell. *Notts* 5D 86
South Weston. *Oxon* 2F 37
South Wheatley. *Corn* 3C 10
South Wheatley. *Notts* 2E 87
Southwick. *Hants* 2E 17
Southwick. *Nptn* 1H 63
Southwick. *Tyne* 4G 115
Southwick. *W Sus* 5D 26
Southwick. *Wilts* 1D 22
South Widcombe. *Bath* 1A 22
South Wigston. *Leics* 1C 62
South Willingham. *Linc* 2A 88
South Wingfield. *Derbs* 5A 86
South Witham. *Linc* 4G 75
Southwold. *Suff* 3H 67
South Wonston. *Hants* 3C 24
Southwood. *Norf* 5F 79
Southwood. *Som* 3A 22
South Woodham Ferrers. *Essx* 1C 40
South Wootton. *Norf* 3F 77
South Wraxall. *Wilts* 5D 34
South Zeal. *Devn* 3G 11
Sowerby. *N Yor* 1G 99
Sowerby. *W Yor* 2A 92
Sowerby Bridge. *W Yor* 2A 92
Sowerby Row. *Cumb* 5E 113
Sower Carr. *Lanc* 5C 96
Sowley Green. *Suff* 5G 65
Sowood. *W Yor* 3A 92
Sowton. *Devn* 3C 12
Soyal. *High* 4C 164
Soyland Town. *W Yor* 2A 92
Spacey Houses. *N Yor* 4F 99
Spa Common. *Norf* 2E 79
Spalding. *Linc* 3B 76
Spaldington. *E Yor* 1A 94
Spaldwick. *Cambs* 3A 64
Spalford. *Notts* 4F 87
Spanby. *Linc* 2H 75
Sparham. *Norf* 4C 78
Sparhamhill. *Norf* 4C 78
Spark Bridge. *Cumb* 1C 96
Sparket. *Cumb* 2F 103
Sparkford. *Som* 4B 22
Sparkwell. *Devn* 3B 8
Sparrow Green. *Norf* 4B 78
Sparrowpit. *Derbs* 2E 85
Sparrow's Green. *E Sus* 2H 27
Sparsholt. *Hants* 3C 24
Sparsholt. *Oxon* 3B 36
Spartylea. *Nmbd* 5B 114
Spath. *Staf* 2E 73
Spaunton. *N Yor* 1B 100
Spaxton. *Som* 3F 21
Spean Bridge. *High* 5E 149
Spear Hill. *W Sus* 4C 26
Speen. *Buck* 2G 37
Speen. *W Ber* 5C 36
Speeton. *N Yor* 2F 101
Speke. *Mers* 2G 83
Speldhurst. *Kent* 1G 27
Spellbrook. *Herts* 4E 53
Spelsbury. *Oxon* 3B 50
Spencers Wood. *Wok* 5F 37
Spennithorne. *N Yor* 1D 98
Spennymoor. *Dur* 1F 105
Spernall. *Warw* 4E 61
Spetchley. *Worc* 5C 60
Spetisbury. *Dors* 2E 15
Spexhall. *Suff* 2F 67
Speybank. *High* 3C 150
Spey Bay. *Mor* 2A 160
Speybridge. *High* 1E 151
Speyview. *Mor* 4G 159
Spilsby. *Linc* 4C 88
Spindlestone. *Nmbd* 1F 121
Spinkhill. *Derbs* 3B 86
Spinney Hills. *Leic* 5D 74
Spinningdale. *High* 5D 164
Spital. *Mers* 2F 83
Spitalhill. *Derbs* 1F 73
Spital in the Street. *Linc* 1G 87
Spithurst. *E Sus* 4F 27
Spittal. *Dum* 4A 110
Spittal. *E Lot* 2A 130
Spittal. *High* 3D 168
Spittal. *Nmbd* 4G 131
Spittal. *Pemb* 2D 43
Spittalfield. *Per* 4A 144
Spittal of Glenmuick. *Abers* 5H 151
Spittal of Glenshee. *Per* 1A 144
Spittal-on-Rule. *Bord* 3H 119
Spixworth. *Norf* 4E 79
Splatt. *Corn* 4C 10
Spofforth. *N Yor* 4F 99
Spondon. *Derb* 2B 74
Spon End. *W Mid* 3H 61
Spooner Row. *Norf* 1C 66
Sporle. *Norf* 4H 77
Spott. *E Lot* 2C 130
Spratton. *Nptn* 3E 62
Spreakley. *Surr* 2G 25
Spreyton. *Devn* 3H 11
Spridlington. *Linc* 2H 87
Springburn. *Glas* 3H 127
Springfield. *Dum* 3E 113
Springfield. *Fife* 2F 137
Springfield. *High* 2A 158
Springfield. *W Mid* 2E 61
Springhill. *Staf* 5D 73
Springholm. *Dum* 2F 111
Springside. *N Ayr* 1C 116
Springthorpe. *Linc* 2F 87
Spring Vale. *IOW* 3E 16
Spring Valley. *IOM* 4C 108
Springwell. *Tyne* 4F 115
Sproatley. *E Yor* 1E 95
Sproston Green. *Ches W* 4B 84
Sprotbrough. *S Yor* 4F 93
Sproughton. *Suff* 1E 55
Sprouston. *Bord* 1B 120
Sprowston. *Norf* 4E 79
Sproxton. *Leics* 3F 75
Sproxton. *N Yor* 1A 100
Sprunston. *Cumb* 5E 113
Spurstow. *Ches E* 5H 83
Squires Gate. *Bkpl* 1B 90
Sraid Ruadh. *Arg* 4A 138
Srannda. *W Isl* 9C 171
Sron an t-Sithein. *High* 2C 140
Sronphadruig Lodge. *Per* 1E 142
Sruth Mor. *W Isl* 2E 170
Stableford. *Shrp* 1B 60
Stackhouse. *N Yor* 3H 97
Stackpole. *Pemb* 5D 43
Stackpole Elidor. *Pemb* 5D 43
Stacksford. *Norf* 1C 66
Stacksteads. *Lanc* 2G 91
Staddiscombe. *Plym* 3B 8
Staddlethorpe. *E Yor* 2B 94
Staddon. *Devn* 2D 10
Staden. *Derbs* 3E 85
Stadhampton. *Oxon* 2E 36
Stadhlaigearraidh. *W Isl* 5C 170
Stafainn. *High* 2D 155
Staffield. *Cumb* 5G 113
Staffin. *High* 2D 155
Stafford. *Staf* 3D 72
Stafford Park. *Telf* 5B 72
Stagden Cross. *Essx* 4G 53
Stagsden. *Bed* 1H 51
Stag's Head. *Devn* 4G 19
Stainburn. *Cumb* 2B 102
Stainburn. *N Yor* 5E 99
Stainby. *Linc* 3G 75
Staincliffe. *W Yor* 2C 92
Staincross. *S Yor* 3D 92
Staindrop. *Dur* 2E 105
Staines-Upon-Thames. *Surr* 3B 38
Stainfield. *Linc* 3H 75
(nr. Bourne)
Stainfield. *Linc* 3A 88
(nr. Lincoln)
Stainforth. *N Yor* 3H 97
Stainforth. *S Yor* 3G 93
Staining. *Lanc* 1B 90
Stainland. *W Yor* 3A 92
Stainsacre. *N Yor* 4G 107
Stainton. *Cumb* 4E 113
(nr. Carlisle)
Stainton. *Cumb* 1E 97
(nr. Kendal)
Stainton. *Cumb* 2F 103
(nr. Penrith)
Stainton. *Dur* 3D 104
Stainton. *Midd* 3B 106
Stainton. *N Yor* 5E 105
Stainton. *S Yor* 1C 86
Stainton by Langworth. *Linc* 3H 87
Staintondale. *N Yor* 5G 107
Stainton le Vale. *Linc* 1A 88
Stainton with Adgarley. *Cumb* 2B 96
Stair. *Cumb* 2D 102
Stair. *E Ayr* 2D 116
Stairhaven. *Dum* 4H 109
Staithes. *N Yor* 3E 107
Stakeford. *Nmbd* 1F 115
Stake Pool. *Lanc* 5D 96
Stakes. *Hants* 2E 17
Stalbridge. *Dors* 1C 14
Stalbridge Weston. *Dors* 1C 14
Stalham. *Norf* 3F 79
Stalham Green. *Norf* 3F 79
Stalisfield Green. *Kent* 5D 40
Stallen. *Dors* 1B 14
Stallingborough. *NE Lin* 3F 95
Stalling Busk. *N Yor* 1B 98
Stallington. *Staf* 2D 72
Stalmine. *Lanc* 5C 96
Stalybridge. *G Man* 1D 84
Stambourne. *Essx* 2H 53
Stamford. *Linc* 5H 75
Stamford. *Nmbd* 3G 121
Stamford Bridge. *Ches W* 4G 83
Stamford Bridge. *E Yor* 4B 100
Stamfordham. *Nmbd* 2D 115
Stamperland. *E Ren* 4G 127
Stanah. *Lanc* 5C 96
Stanborough. *Herts* 4C 52
Stanbridge. *C Beds* 3H 51
Stanbridge. *Dors* 2F 15
Stanbury. *W Yor* 1A 92
Stand. *N Lan* 3A 128
Standburn. *Falk* 2C 128
Standeford. *Staf* 5D 72
Standen. *Kent* 1C 28
Standen Street. *Kent* 2C 28
Standerwick. *Som* 1D 22
Standford. *Hants* 3G 25
Standford Bridge. *Telf* 3B 72
Standingstone. *Cumb* 5D 112
Standish. *Glos* 5D 48
Standish. *G Man* 3D 90
Standish Lower Ground. *G Man* 4D 90
Standlake. *Oxon* 5B 50
Standon. *Hants* 4C 24
Standon. *Herts* 3D 53
Standon. *Staf* 2C 72
Standon Green End. *Herts* 4D 52
Stane. *N Lan* 4B 128
Stanecastle. *N Ayr* 1C 116
Stanfield. *Norf* 3B 78
Stanford. *C Beds* 1B 52
Stanford. *Kent* 2F 29
Stanford Bishop. *Here* 5A 60
Stanford Bridge. *Worc* 4B 60
Stanford Dingley. *W Ber* 4D 36
Stanford in the Vale. *Oxon* 2B 36
Stanford-le-Hope. *Thur* 2A 40
Stanford on Avon. *Nptn* 3C 62
Stanford on Soar. *Notts* 3C 74
Stanford on Teme. *Worc* 4B 60
Stanford Rivers. *Essx* 5F 53
Stanfree. *Derbs* 3B 86
Stanghow. *Red C* 3D 107
Stanground. *Pet* 1B 64
Stanhoe. *Norf* 2H 77
Stanhope. *Dur* 1C 104
Stanhope. *Bord* 1D 118
Stanion. *Nptn* 2G 63
Stanley. *Derbs* 1B 74
Stanley. *Dur* 4E 115
Stanley. *Per* 5A 144
Stanley. *Shrp* 2B 60
Stanley. *Staf* 5D 84
Stanley. *W Yor* 2D 92
Stanley Common. *Derbs* 1B 74
Stanley Crook. *Dur* 1E 105
Stanley Hill. *Here* 1B 48
Stanlow. *Ches W* 3G 83
Stanmer. *Brig* 5E 27
Stanmore. *G Lon* 1C 38
Stanmore. *Hants* 4C 24
Stanmore. *W Ber* 4C 36
Stannersburn. *Nmbd* 1A 114
Stanningfield. *Suff* 5A 66
Stannington. *Nmbd* 2F 115
Stannington. *S Yor* 2H 85
Stansbatch. *Here* 4F 59
Stansfield. *Suff* 5G 65
Stanshope. *Staf* 5F 85
Stanstead. *Suff* 1B 54
Stanstead Abbotts. *Herts* 4D 53
Stansted. *Kent* 4H 39
Stansted (London) Airport. *Essx* 3F 53
Stansted Mountfitchet. *Essx* 3F 53
Stanthorne. *Ches W* 4A 84
Stanton. *Derbs* 4G 73
Stanton. *Glos* 2F 49
Stanton. *Nmbd* 5F 121
Stanton. *Staf* 1F 73
Stanton. *Suff* 3B 66
Stanton by Bridge. *Derbs* 3A 74
Stanton by Dale. *Derbs* 2B 74
Stanton Chare. *Suff* 3B 66
Stanton Drew. *Bath* 5A 34
Stanton Fitzwarren. *Swin* 2G 35
Stanton Harcourt. *Oxon* 5C 50
Stanton Hill. *Notts* 4B 86
Stanton in Peak. *Derbs* 4G 85
Stanton Lacy. *Shrp* 3G 59
Stanton Long. *Shrp* 1H 59
Stanton-on-the-Wolds. *Notts* 2D 74
Stanton Prior. *Bath* 5B 34
Stanton St Bernard. *Wilts* 5F 35
Stanton St John. *Oxon* 5D 50
Stanton St Quintin. *Wilts* 4E 35
Stanton Street. *Suff* 4B 66
Stanton under Bardon. *Leics* 4B 74
Stanton upon Hine Heath. *Shrp* 3H 71
Stanton Wick. *Bath* 5B 34
Stanwardine in the Fields. *Shrp* 3G 71
Stanwardine in the Wood. *Shrp* 3G 71
Stanway. *Essx* 3C 54
Stanway. *Glos* 2F 49
Stanwell. *Surr* 3B 38
Stanwell Moor. *Surr* 3B 38
Stanwick. *Nptn* 3G 63
Staoinebrig. *W Isl* 5C 170
Stape. *N Yor* 5E 107
Stapehill. *Dors* 2F 15
Stapeley. *Ches E* 1A 72
Stapenhill. *Staf* 3G 73
Staple. *Kent* 5G 41
Staple Cross. *Devn* 4D 20
Staplecross. *E Sus* 3B 28
Staplefield. *W Sus* 3D 27
Staple Fitzpaine. *Som* 1F 13
Stapleford. *Cambs* 5D 64
Stapleford. *Herts* 4D 52
Stapleford. *Leics* 4F 75
Stapleford. *Linc* 5F 87
Stapleford. *Notts* 2B 74
Stapleford. *Wilts* 3F 23
Stapleford Abbotts. *Essx* 1G 39
Stapleford Tawney. *Essx* 1G 39
Staplegrove. *Som* 4F 21
Staplehay. *Som* 4F 21
Staple Hill. *S Glo* 4B 34
Staplehurst. *Kent* 1B 28
Staplers. *IOW* 4D 16
Stapleton. *Bris* 4B 34
Stapleton. *Cumb* 2G 113
Stapleton. *Here* 4F 59
Stapleton. *Leics* 1B 62
Stapleton. *N Yor* 3F 105
Stapleton. *Shrp* 5G 71
Stapleton. *Som* 4H 21
Stapley. *Som* 1E 13
Staploe. *Bed* 4A 64
Staplow. *Here* 1B 48
Star. *Fife* 3F 137
Star. *Pemb* 1G 43
Starbeck. *N Yor* 4F 99
Starbotton. *N Yor* 2B 98
Starcross. *Devn* 4C 12
Stareton. *Warw* 3H 61
Starkholmes. *Derbs* 5H 85
Starling. *G Man* 3F 91
Starling's Green. *Essx* 2E 53
Starston. *Norf* 2E 67

Start—Stratford sub Castle

Start. *Devn* 4E 9
Startforth. *Dur* 3D 104
Start Hill. *Essx* 3F 53
Startley. *Wilts* 3E 35
Stathe. *Som* 4G 21
Stathern. *Leics* 2E 75
Station Town. *Dur* 1B 106
Staughton Green. *Cambs* 4A 64
Staughton Highway. *Cambs* 4A 64
Staunton. *Glos* 3C 48
(nr. Cheltenham)
Staunton. *Glos* 4A 48
(nr. Monmouth)
Staunton in the Vale. *Notts* 1F 75
Staunton on Arrow. *Here* 4F 59
Staunton on Wye. *Here* 1G 47
Staveley. *Cumb* 5F 103
Staveley. *Derbs* 3B 86
Staveley. *N Yor* 3F 99
Staveley-in-Cartmel. *Cumb* 1C 96
Staverton. *Devn* 2D 9
Staverton. *Glos* 3D 49
Staverton. *Nptn* 4C 62
Staverton. *Wilts* 5D 34
Stawell. *Som* 3G 21
Stawley. *Som* 4D 20
Staxigoe. *High* 3F 169
Staxton. *N Yor* 2E 101
Staylittle. *Powy* 1A 58
Staynall. *Lanc* 5C 96
Staythorpe. *Notts* 5E 87
Stean. *N Yor* 2C 98
Stearsby. *N Yor* 2A 100
Steart. *Som* 2F 21
Stebbing. *Essx* 3G 53
Stebbing Green. *Essx* 3G 53
Stedham. *W Sus* 4G 25
Steel. *Nmbd* 4C 114
Steel Cross. *E Sus* 2G 27
Steelend. *Fife* 4C 136
Steele Road. *Bord* 5H 119
Steel Heath. *Shrp* 2H 71
Steen's Bridge. *Here* 5H 59
Steep. *Hants* 4F 25
Steep Lane. *W Yor* 2A 92
Steeple. *Dors* 4E 15
Steeple. *Essx* 5C 54
Steeple Ashton. *Wilts* 1E 23
Steeple Aston. *Oxon* 3C 50
Steeple Barton. *Oxon* 3C 50
Steeple Bumpstead. *Essx* 1G 53
Steeple Claydon. *Buck* 3E 51
Steeple Gidding. *Cambs* 2A 64
Steeple Langford. *Wilts* 3F 23
Steeple Morden. *Cambs* 1C 52
Steeton. *W Yor* 5C 98
Stein. *High* 3B 154
Steinmanhill. *Abers* 4E 161
Stelling Minnis. *Kent* 1F 29
Stembridge. *Som* 4H 21
Stemster. *High* 2D 169
(nr. Halkirk)
Stemster. *High* 2C 168
(nr. Westfield)
Stenalees. *Corn* 3E 6
Stenhill. *Devn* 1D 12
Stenhouse. *Edin* 2F 129
Stenhousemuir. *Falk* 1B 128
Stenigot. *Linc* 2B 88
Stenscholl. *High* 2D 155
Stenso. *Orkn* 5C 172
Stenson. *Derbs* 3H 73
Stenson Fields. *Derbs* 2H 73
Stenton. *E Lot* 2C 130
Stenwith. *Linc* 2F 75
Steòrnabhagh. *W Isl* 4G 171
Stepaside. *Pemb* 4F 43
Stepford. *Dum* 1F 111
Stepney. *G Lon* 2E 39
Steppingley. *C Beds* 2A 52
Stepps. *N Lan* 3H 127
Sterndale Moor. *Derbs* 4F 85
Sternfield. *Suff* 4F 67
Stert. *Wilts* 1F 23
Stetchworth. *Cambs* 5F 65
Stevenage. *Herts* 3C 52
Stevenston. *N Ayr* 5D 126
Stevenstone. *Devn* 1F 11
Steventon. *Hants* 2D 24
Steventon. *Oxon* 2C 36
Steventon End. *Cambs* 1G 53
Stevington. *Bed* 5G 63
Stewartby. *Bed* 1A 52
Stewarton. *Arg* 4A 122
Stewarton. *E Ayr* 5F 127
Stewkley. *Buck* 3G 51
Stewkley Dean. *Buck* 3G 51
Stewley. *Som* 1G 13
Stewton. *Linc* 2C 88
Steyning. *W Sus* 4C 26
Steynton. *Pemb* 4D 42
Stibb. *Corn* 1C 10
Stibbard. *Norf* 3B 78
Stibb Cross. *Devn* 1E 11
Stibb Green. *Wilts* 5H 35
Stibbington. *Cambs* 1H 63
Stichill. *Bord* 1B 120
Sticker. *Corn* 3D 6
Stickford. *Linc* 4C 88
Sticklepath. *Devn* 3G 11
Sticklinch. *Som* 3A 22
Stickling Green. *Essx* 2E 53
Stickney. *Linc* 5C 88
Stiffkey. *Norf* 1B 78
Stifford's Bridge. *Here* 1C 48
Stileway. *Som* 2H 21
Stillingfleet. *N Yor* 5H 99
Stillington. *N Yor* 3H 99
Stillington. *Stoc T* 2A 106
Stilton. *Cambs* 2A 64
Stinchcombe. *Glos* 2C 34
Stinsford. *Dors* 3C 14
Stiperstones. *Shrp* 5F 71
Stirchley. *Telf* 5B 72
Stirchley. *W Mid* 2E 61
Stirling. *Abers* 4H 161
Stirling. *Stir* 4G 135
Stirton. *N Yor* 4B 98
Stisted. *Essx* 3A 54
Stitchcombe. *Wilts* 5H 35
Stithians. *Corn* 5B 6
Stittenham. *High* 1A 158
Stivichall. *W Mid* 3H 61
Stixwould. *Linc* 4A 88
Stoak. *Ches W* 3G 83
Stobo. *Bord* 1D 118
Stobo Castle. *Bord* 1D 118
Stoborough. *Dors* 4E 15
Stoborough Green. *Dors* 4E 15
Stobs Castle. *Bord* 4H 119
Stobswood. *Nmbd* 5G 121
Stock. *Essx* 1A 40
Stockbridge. *Hants* 3B 24
Stockbridge. *W Yor* 5C 98
Stockbury. *Kent* 4C 40
Stockcross. *W Ber* 5C 36
Stockdalewath. *Cumb* 5E 113
Stocker's Head. *Kent* 5D 40
Stockerston. *Leics* 1F 63
Stock Green. *Worc* 5D 61
Stocking. *Here* 2B 48
Stockingford. *Warw* 1H 61
Stocking Green. *Essx* 2F 53
Stocking Pelham. *Herts* 3E 53
Stockland. *Devn* 2F 13
Stockland Bristol. *Som* 2F 21
Stockleigh English. *Devn* 2B 12
Stockleigh Pomeroy.
Devn 2B 12
Stockley. *Wilts* 5F 35
Stocklinch. *Som* 1G 13
Stockport. *G Man* 2D 84
Stocksbridge. *S Yor* 1G 85
Stocksfield. *Nmbd* 3D 114
Stocks, The. *Kent* 3D 28
Stockstreet. *Essx* 3B 54
Stockton. *Here* 4H 59
Stockton. *Norf* 1F 67
Stockton. *Shrp* 1B 60
(nr. Bridgnorth)
Stockton. *Shrp* 5E 71
(nr. Chirbury)
Stockton. *Telf* 4B 72
Stockton. *Warw* 4B 62
Stockton. *Wilts* 3E 23
Stockton Brook. *Staf* 5D 84
Stockton Cross. *Here* 4H 59
Stockton Heath. *Warr* 2A 84
Stockton-on-Tees. *Stoc T* 3B 106
Stockton on Teme. *Worc* 4B 60
Stockton-on-the-Forest. *York* 4A 100
Stockwell Heath. *Staf* 3E 73
Stockwood. *Bris* 5B 34
Stock Wood. *Worc* 5E 61
Stodmarsh. *Kent* 4G 41
Stody. *Norf* 2C 78
Stoer. *High* 1E 163
Stoford. *Som* 1A 14
Stoford. *Wilts* 3F 23
Stogumber. *Som* 3D 20
Stogursey. *Som* 2F 21
Stoke. *Devn* 4C 18
Stoke. *Hants* 1C 24
(nr. Andover)
Stoke. *Hants* 2F 17
(nr. South Hayling)
Stoke. *Medw* 3C 40
Stoke. *W Mid* 3A 62
Stoke Abbott. *Dors* 2H 13
Stoke Albany. *Nptn* 2F 63
Stoke Ash. *Suff* 3D 66
Stoke Bardolph. *Notts* 1D 74
Stoke Bliss. *Worc* 4A 60
Stoke Bruerne. *Nptn* 1F 51
Stoke by Clare. *Suff* 1H 53
Stoke-by-Nayland. *Suff* 2C 54
Stoke Canon. *Devn* 3C 12
Stoke Charity. *Hants* 3C 24
Stoke Climsland. *Corn* 5D 10
Stoke Cross. *Here* 5A 60
Stoke D'Abernon. *Surr* 5C 38
Stoke Doyle. *Nptn* 2H 63
Stoke Dry. *Rut* 1F 63
Stoke Edith. *Here* 1B 48
Stoke Farthing. *Wilts* 4F 23
Stoke Ferry. *Norf* 1G 65
Stoke Fleming. *Devn* 4E 9
Stokeford. *Dors* 4D 14
Stoke Gabriel. *Devn* 3E 9
Stoke Gifford. *S Glo* 4B 34
Stoke Golding. *Leics* 1A 62
Stoke Goldington. *Mil* 1G 51
Stokeham. *Notts* 3E 87
Stoke Hammond. *Buck* 3G 51
Stoke Heath. *Shrp* 3A 72
Stoke Holy Cross. *Norf* 5E 79
Stokeinteignhead. *Devn* 5C 12
Stoke Lacy. *Here* 1B 48
Stoke Lyne. *Oxon* 3D 50
Stoke Mandeville. *Buck* 4G 51
Stokenchurch. *Buck* 2F 37
Stoke Newington. *G Lon* 2E 39
Stokenham. *Devn* 4E 9
Stoke on Tern. *Shrp* 3A 72
Stoke-on-Trent. *Stoke* 1C 72
Stoke Orchard. *Glos* 3E 49
Stoke Pero. *Som* 2B 20
Stoke Poges. *Buck* 2A 38
Stoke Prior. *Here* 5H 59
Stoke Prior. *Worc* 4D 60
Stoke Rivers. *Devn* 3G 19
Stoke Rochford. *Linc* 3G 75
Stoke Row. *Oxon* 3E 37
Stoke St Gregory. *Som* 4G 21
Stoke St Mary. *Som* 4F 21
Stoke St Michael. *Som* 2B 22
Stoke St Milborough. *Shrp* 2H 59
Stokesay. *Shrp* 2G 59
Stokesby. *Norf* 4G 79
Stokesley. *N Yor* 4C 106
Stoke sub Hamdon. *Som* 1H 13
Stoke Talmage. *Oxon* 2E 37
Stoke Town. *Stoke* 1C 72
Stoke Trister. *Som* 4C 22
Stoke Wake. *Dors* 2C 14
Stolford. *Som* 2F 21
Stondon Massey. *Essx* 5F 53
Stone. *Buck* 4F 51
Stone. *Glos* 2B 34
Stone. *Kent* 3G 39
Stone. *Som* 3A 22
Stone. *Staf* 2D 72
Stone. *Worc* 3C 60
Stonea. *Cambs* 1D 64
Stoneacton. *Shrp* 1H 59
Stone Allerton. *Som* 1H 21
Ston Easton. *Som* 1B 22
Stonebridge. *N Som* 1G 21
Stonebridge. *Som* 2C 22
Stonebridge. *Surr* 1C 26
Stone Bridge Corner. *Pet* 5B 76
Stonebroom. *Derbs* 5B 86
Stonebyres. *S Lan* 5B 128
Stone Chair. *W Yor* 2B 92
Stone Cross. *E Sus* 5H 27
Stone Cross. *Kent* 2G 27
Stone-edge-Batch. *N Som* 4H 33
Stoneferry. *Hull* 1D 94
Stonefield. *Arg* 5D 140
Stonefield. *S Lan* 4H 127
Stonegate. *E Sus* 3A 28
Stonegate. *N Yor* 4E 107
Stonegrave. *N Yor* 2A 100
Stonehall. *Worc* 1D 49
Stonehaugh. *Nmbd* 2A 114
Stonehaven. *Abers* 5F 153
Stone Heath. *Staf* 2D 72
Stone Hill. *Kent* 2E 29
Stone House. *Cumb* 1G 97
Stonehouse. *Glos* 5D 48
Stonehouse. *Nmbd* 4H 113
Stonehouse. *S Lan* 5A 128
Stone in Oxney. *Kent* 3D 28
Stoneleigh. *Warw* 3H 61
Stoneley Green. *Ches E* 5A 84
Stonely. *Cambs* 4A 64
Stonepits. *Worc* 5E 61
Stoner Hill. *Hants* 4F 25
Stonesby. *Leics* 3F 75
Stonesfield. *Oxon* 4B 50
Stones Green. *Essx* 3E 55
Stone Street. *Kent* 5G 39
Stone Street. *Suff* 2C 54
(nr. Boxford)
Stone Street. *Suff* 2F 67
(nr. Halesworth)
Stonethwaite. *Cumb* 3D 102
Stoneyburn. *W Lot* 3C 128
Stoney Cross. *Hants* 1A 16
Stoneyford. *Devn* 2D 12
Stoneygate. *Leic* 5D 74
Stoneyhills. *Essx* 1D 40
Stoneykirk. *Dum* 4F 109
Stoney Middleton. *Derbs* 3G 85
Stoney Stanton. *Leics* 1B 62
Stoney Stoke. *Som* 3C 22
Stoney Stratton. *Som* 3B 22
Stoney Stretton. *Shrp* 5F 71
Stoneywood. *Aber* 2F 153
Stonham Aspal. *Suff* 5D 66
Stonnall. *Staf* 5E 73
Stonor. *Oxon* 3F 37
Stonton Wyville. *Leics* 1E 63
Stonybreck. *Shet* 1B 172
Stony Cross. *Devn* 4F 19
Stony Cross. *Here* 1C 48
(nr. Great Malvern)
Stony Cross. *Here* 4H 59
(nr. Leominster)
Stony Houghton. *Derbs* 4B 86
Stony Stratford. *Mil* 1F 51
Stoodleigh. *Devn* 3G 19
(nr. Barnstaple)
Stoodleigh. *Devn* 1C 12
(nr. Tiverton)
Stopham. *W Sus* 4B 26
Stopsley. *Lutn* 3B 52
Stoptide. *Corn* 1D 6
Storeton. *Mers* 2F 83
Stormontfield. *Per* 1D 136
Stornoway. *W Isl* 4G 171
Stornoway Airport. *W Isl* 4G 171
Storridge. *Here* 1C 48
Storrington. *W Sus* 4B 26
Storrs. *Cumb* 5E 103
Storth. *Cumb* 1D 97
Storwood. *E Yor* 5B 100
Stotfield. *Mor* 1G 159
Stotfold. *C Beds* 2C 52
Stottesdon. *Shrp* 2A 60
Stoughton. *Leics* 5D 74
Stoughton. *Surr* 5A 38
Stoughton. *W Sus* 1G 17
Stoul. *High* 4F 147
Stoulton. *Worc* 1E 49
Stourbridge. *W Mid* 2C 60
Stourpaine. *Dors* 2D 14
Stourport-on-Severn. *Worc* 3C 60
Stour Provost. *Dors* 4C 22
Stour Row. *Dors* 4D 22
Stourton. *Staf* 2C 60
Stourton. *Warw* 2A 50
Stourton. *W Yor* 1D 92
Stourton. *Wilts* 3C 22
Stourton Caundle. *Dors* 1C 14
Stoven. *Suff* 2G 67
Stow. *Linc* 2H 75
(nr. Billingborough)
Stow. *Linc* 2F 87
(nr. Gainsborough)
Stow. *Bord* 5A 130
Stow Bardolph. *Norf* 5F 77
Stow Bedon. *Norf* 1B 66
Stowbridge. *Norf* 5F 77
Stow cum Quy. *Cambs* 4E 65
Stowe. *Glos* 5A 48
Stowe. *Shrp* 3F 59
Stowe. *Staf* 4F 73
Stowe-by-Chartley. *Staf* 3E 73
Stowell. *Som* 4B 22
Stowey. *Bath* 1A 22
Stowford. *Devn* 2G 19
(nr. Combe Martin)
Stowford. *Devn* 4D 12
(nr. Exmouth)
Stowford. *Devn* 4E 11
(nr. Tavistock)
Stowlangtoft. *Suff* 4B 66
Stow Longa. *Cambs* 3A 64
Stow Maries. *Essx* 1C 40
Stowmarket. *Suff* 5C 66
Stow-on-the-Wold. *Glos* 3G 49
Stowting. *Kent* 1F 29
Stowupland. *Suff* 5C 66
Straad. *Arg* 3B 126
Strachan. *Abers* 4D 152
Stradbroke. *Suff* 3E 67
Stradbrook. *Wilts* 1E 23
Stradishall. *Suff* 5G 65
Stradsett. *Norf* 5F 77
Stragglethorpe. *Linc* 5G 87
Stragglethorpe. *Notts* 2D 74
Straid. *S Ayr* 5A 116
Straight Soley. *Wilts* 4B 36
Straiton. *Edin* 3F 129
Straiton. *S Ayr* 4C 116
Straloch. *Per* 2H 143
Stramshall. *Staf* 2E 73
Strang. *IOM* 4C 108
Strangford. *Here* 3A 48
Stranraer. *Dum* 3F 109
Strata Florida. *Cdgn* 4G 57
Stratfield Mortimer. *W Ber* 5E 37
Stratfield Saye. *Hants* 5E 37
Stratfield Turgis. *Hants* 1E 25
Stratford. *Glos* 2D 49
Stratford. *G Lon* 2E 39
Stratford St Andrew. *Suff* 4F 67
Stratford St Mary. *Suff* 2D 54
Stratford sub Castle. *Wilts* 3G 23

Stratford Tony. Wilts 4F 23
Stratford-upon-Avon. Warw 5G 61
Strath. High 1G 155
(nr. Gairloch)
Strath. High 3E 169
(nr. Wick)
Strathan. High 4B 148
(nr. Fort William)
Strathan. High 1E 163
(nr. Lochinver)
Strathan. High 2F 167
(nr. Tongue)
Strathan Skerray. High 2G 167
Strathaven. S Lan 5A 128
Strathblane. Stir 2G 127
Strathcanaird. High 3F 163
Strathcarron. High 4B 156
Strathcoil. Arg 5A 140
Strathdon. Abers 2A 152
Strathkinness. Fife 2G 137
Strathmashie House. High 4H 149
Strathmiglo. Fife 2E 136
Strathmore Lodge. High 4D 168
Strathpeffer. High 3G 157
Strathrannoch. High 1F 157
Strathtay. Per 3G 143
Strathvaich Lodge. High 1F 157
Strathwhillan. N Ayr 2E 123
Strathy. High 1A 158
(nr. Invergordon)
Strathy. High 2A 168
(nr. Melvich)
Strathyre. Stir 2E 135
Stratton. Corn 2C 10
Stratton. Dors 3B 14
Stratton. Glos 5F 49
Stratton Audley. Oxon 3E 50
Stratton-on-the-Fosse. Som 1B 22
Stratton St Margaret. Swin 3G 35
Stratton St Michael. Norf 1E 66
Stratton Strawless. Norf 3E 78
Stravithie. Fife 2H 137
Stream. Som 3D 20
Streat. E Sus 4E 27
Streatham. G Lon 3D 39
Streatley. C Beds 3A 52
Streatley. W Ber 3D 36
Street. Corn 3C 10
Street. Lanc 4E 97
Street. N Yor 4E 107
Street. Som 2G 13
(nr. Chard)
Street. Som 3H 21
(nr. Glastonbury)
Street Ash. Som 1F 13
Street Dinas. Shrp 2F 71
Street End. Kent 5F 41
Street End. W Sus 3G 17
Street Gate. Tyne 4F 115
Streethay. Staf 4F 73
Streethouse. W Yor 3D 93
Streetlam. N Yor 5A 106
Street Lane. Derbs 1A 74
Streetly. W Mid 1E 61
Streetly End. Cambs 1G 53
Street on the Fosse. Som 3B 22
Strefford. Shrp 2G 59
Strelley. Notts 1C 74
Strensall. York 3A 100
Strensall Camp. York 4A 100
Stretcholt. Som 2F 21
Strete. Devn 4E 9
Stretford. G Man 1C 84
Stretford. Here 5H 59
Strethall. Essx 2E 53
Stretham. Cambs 3E 65
Stretton. Ches W 5G 83
Stretton. Derbs 4A 86
Stretton. Rut 4G 75
Stretton. Staf 4C 72
(nr. Brewood)
Stretton. Staf 3G 73
(nr. Burton upon Trent)
Stretton. Warr 2A 84
Stretton en le Field. Leics 4H 73
Stretton Grandison. Here 1B 48
Stretton Heath. Shrp 4F 71
Stretton-on-Dunsmore. Warw 3B 62
Stretton-on-Fosse. Warw 2H 49
Stretton Sugwas. Here 1H 47
Stretton under Fosse. Warw 2B 62
Stretton Westwood. Shrp 1H 59
Strichen. Abers 3G 161
Strines. G Man 2D 84
Stringston. Som 2E 21
Strixton. Nptn 4G 63
Stroanfreggan. Dum 5F 117
Stroat. Glos 2A 34
Stromeferry. High 5A 156
Stromemore. High 5A 156
Stromness. Orkn 7B 172
Stronachie. Per 3C 136
Stronachlachar. Stir 2D 134
Stronchreggan. High 1E 141
Strone. Arg 1C 126
Strone. High 1H 149
(nr. Drumnadrochit)
Strone. High 3B 150
(nr. Kingussie)
Stronenaba. High 5E 148
Stronmilchan. Arg 1A 134
Stronsay Airport. Orkn 5F 172
Strontian. High 2C 140
Strood. Kent 2C 28
Strood. Medw 4B 40
Strood Green. Surr 1D 26
Strood Green. W Sus 3B 26
(nr. Billingshurst)
Strood Green. W Sus 2C 26
(nr. Horsham)
Strothers Dale. Nmbd 4C 114
Stroud. Glos 5D 48
Stroud. Hants 4F 25
Stroud Green. Essx 1C 40
Stroxton. Linc 2G 75
Struan. High 5C 154
Struan. Per 2F 143
Struanmore. High 5C 154
Strubby. Linc 2D 88
Strugg's Hill. Linc 2B 76
Strumpshaw. Norf 5F 79
Strutherhill. S Lan 4A 128
Struy. High 5F 157
Stryd. IOA 2B 80
Stryt-issa. Wrex 1E 71
Stuartfield. Abers 4G 161
Stubbington. Hants 2D 16
Stubbins. Lanc 3F 91
Stubble Green. Cumb 5B 102
Stubb's Cross. Kent 2D 28
Stubbs Green. Norf 1F 67
Stubhampton. Dors 1E 15
Stubton. Linc 1F 75
Stubwood. Staf 2E 73
Stuckton. Hants 1G 15
Studham. C Beds 4A 52
Studland. Dors 4F 15
Studley. Warw 4E 61
Studley. Wilts 4E 35
Studley Roger. N Yor 3E 99
Stuntney. Cambs 3E 65
Stunts Green. E Sus 4H 27
Sturbridge. Staf 2C 72
Sturgate. Linc 2F 87
Sturmer. Essx 1G 53
Sturminster Marshall. Dors 2E 15
Sturminster Newton. Dors 1C 14
Sturry. Kent 4F 41
Sturton. N Lin 4C 94
Sturton by Stow. Linc 2F 87
Sturton le Steeple. Notts 2E 87
Stuston. Suff 3D 66
Stutton. N Yor 5G 99
Stutton. Suff 2E 55
Styal. Ches E 2C 84
Stydd. Lanc 1E 91
Styrrup. Notts 1D 86
Suainebost. W Isl 1H 171
Suardail. W Isl 4G 171
Succoth. Abers 5B 160
Succoth. Arg 3B 134
Suckley. Worc 5B 60
Suckley Knowl. Worc 5B 60
Sudborough. Nptn 2G 63
Sudbourne. Suff 5G 67
Sudbrook. Linc 1G 75
Sudbrook. Mon 3A 34
Sudbrooke. Linc 3H 87
Sudbury. Derbs 2F 73
Sudbury. Suff 1B 54
Sudgrove. Glos 5E 49
Suffield. Norf 2E 79
Suffield. N Yor 5G 107
Sugnall. Staf 2B 72
Sugwas Pool. Here 1H 47
Suisnish. High 5E 155
Sulaisiadar. W Isl 4H 171
Sùlaisiadar Mòr. High 4D 155
Sulby. IOM 2C 108
Sulgrave. Nptn 1D 50
Sulham. W Ber 4E 37
Sulhamstead. W Ber 5E 37
Sullington. W Sus 4B 26
Sullom. Shet 4E 173
Sully. V Glam 5E 33
Sumburgh. Shet 10F 173
Sumburgh Airport. Shet 10E 173
Summer Bridge. N Yor 3E 98
Summercourt. Corn 3C 6
Summergangs. Hull 1E 95
Summerhill. Aber 3G 153
Summerhill. Pemb 4F 43
Summer Hill. W Mid 1D 60
Summerhouse. Darl 3F 105
Summersdale. W Sus 2G 17
Summerseat. G Man 3F 91
Summit. G Man 3H 91
Sunbury. Surr 4C 38
Sunderland. Cumb 1C 102
Sunderland. Lanc 4D 96
Sunderland. Tyne 4G 115
Sunderland Bridge. Dur 1F 105
Sundon Park. Lutn 3A 52
Sundridge. Kent 5F 39
Sunk Island. E Yor 3F 95
Sunningdale. Wind 4A 38
Sunninghill. Wind 4A 38
Sunningwell. Oxon 5C 50
Sunniside. Dur 1E 105
Sunniside. Tyne 4F 115
Sunny Bank. Cumb 5D 102
Sunny Hill. Derb 2H 73
Sunnyhurst. Bkbn 2E 91
Sunnylaw. Stir 4G 135
Sunnymead. Oxon 5D 50
Sunnyside. S Yor 1B 86
Sunnyside. W Sus 2E 27
Sunton. Wilts 1H 23
Surbiton. G Lon 4C 38
Surby. IOM 4B 108
Surfleet. Linc 3B 76
Surfleet Seas End. Linc 3B 76
Surlingham. Norf 5F 79
Surrex. Essx 3B 54
Sustead. Norf 2D 78
Susworth. Linc 4B 94
Sutcombe. Devn 1D 10
Suton. Norf 1C 66
Sutors of Cromarty. High 2C 158
Sutterby. Linc 3C 88
Sutterton. Linc 2B 76
Sutterton Dowdyke. Linc 2B 76
Sutton. Buck 3B 38
Sutton. Cambs 3D 64
Sutton. C Beds 1C 52
Sutton. E Sus 5F 27
Sutton. G Lon 4D 38
Sutton. Kent 1H 29
Sutton. Norf 3F 79
Sutton. Notts 2E 75
Sutton. Oxon 5C 50
Sutton. Pemb 3D 42
Sutton. Pet 1H 63
Sutton. Shrp 2B 60
(nr. Bridgnorth)
Sutton. Shrp 2A 72
(nr. Market Drayton)
Sutton. Shrp 3F 71
(nr. Oswestry)
Sutton. Shrp 4H 71
(nr. Shrewsbury)
Sutton. Som 3B 22
Sutton. S Yor 3F 93
Sutton. Staf 3B 72
Sutton. Suff 1G 55
Sutton. W Sus 4A 26
Sutton. Worc 4A 60
Sutton Abinger. Surr 1C 26
Sutton at Hone. Kent 4G 39
Sutton Bassett. Nptn 1E 63
Sutton Benger. Wilts 4E 35
Sutton Bingham. Som 1A 14
Sutton Bonington. Notts 3C 74
Sutton Bridge. Linc 3D 76
Sutton Cheney. Leics 5B 74
Sutton Coldfield. W Mid 1F 61
Sutton Corner. Linc 3D 76
Sutton Courtenay. Oxon 2D 36
Sutton Crosses. Linc 3D 76
Sutton cum Lound. Notts 2D 86
Sutton Gault. Cambs 3D 64
Sutton Grange. N Yor 2E 99
Sutton Green. Surr 5B 38
Sutton Howgrave. N Yor 2F 99
Sutton in Ashfield. Notts 5B 86
Sutton-in-Craven. N Yor 5C 98
Sutton Ings. Hull 1E 94
Sutton in the Elms. Leics 1C 62
Sutton Lane Ends. Ches E 3D 84
Sutton Leach. Mers 1H 83
Sutton Maddock. Shrp 5B 72
Sutton Mallet. Som 3G 21
Sutton Mandeville. Wilts 4E 23
Sutton Montis. Som 4B 22
Sutton-on-Hull. Hull 1E 94
Sutton on Sea. Linc 2E 89
Sutton-on-the-Forest. N Yor 3H 99
Sutton on the Hill. Derbs 2G 73
Sutton on Trent. Notts 4E 87
Sutton Poyntz. Dors 4C 14
Sutton St Edmund. Linc 4C 76
Sutton St Edmund's Common. Linc 5C 76
Sutton St James. Linc 4C 76
Sutton St Michael. Here 1A 48
Sutton St Nicholas. Here 1A 48
Sutton Scarsdale. Derbs 4B 86
Sutton Scotney. Hants 3C 24
Sutton-under-Brailes. Warw 2B 50
Sutton-under-Whitestonecliffe. N Yor 1G 99
Sutton upon Derwent. E Yor 5B 100
Sutton Valence. Kent 1C 28
Sutton Veny. Wilts 2E 23
Sutton Waldron. Dors 1D 14
Sutton Weaver. Ches W 3H 83
Swaby. Linc 3C 88
Swadlincote. Derbs 4G 73
Swaffham. Norf 5H 77
Swaffham Bulbeck. Cambs 4E 65
Swaffham Prior. Cambs 4E 65
Swafield. Norf 2E 79
Swainby. N Yor 4B 106
Swainshill. Here 1H 47
Swainsthorpe. Norf 5E 78
Swainswick. Bath 5C 34
Swalcliffe. Oxon 2B 50
Swalecliffe. Kent 4F 41
Swallow. Linc 4E 95
Swallow Beck. Linc 4G 87
Swallowcliffe. Wilts 4E 23
Swallowfield. Wok 5F 37
Swallownest. S Yor 2B 86
Swampton. Hants 1C 24
Swanage. Dors 5F 15
Swanbourne. Buck 3G 51
Swanbridge. V Glam 5E 33
Swan Green. Ches W 3B 84
Swanland. E Yor 2C 94
Swanley. Kent 4G 39
Swanmore. Hants 1D 16
Swannington. Leics 4B 74
Swannington. Norf 4D 78
Swanpool. Linc 3G 87
Swanscombe. Kent 3G 39
Swansea. Swan 3F 31
Swansmoor. Staf 3E 73
Swan Street. Essx 3B 54
Swanton Abbott. Norf 3E 79
Swanton Morley. Norf 4C 78
Swanton Novers. Norf 2C 78
Swanton Street. Kent 5C 40
Swanwick. Derbs 5B 86
Swanwick. Hants 2D 16
Swanwick Green. Ches E 1H 71
Swarby. Linc 1H 75
Swardeston. Norf 5E 78
Swarkestone. Derbs 3A 74
Swarland. Nmbd 4F 121
Swarraton. Hants 3D 24
Swartha. W Yor 5C 98
Swarthmoor. Cumb 2B 96
Swaton. Linc 2A 76
Swavesey. Cambs 4C 64
Sway. Hants 3A 16
Swayfield. Linc 3G 75
Swaythling. Sotn 1C 16
Sweet Green. Worc 4A 60
Sweetham. Devn 3B 12
Sweetholme. Cumb 3G 103
Sweets. Corn 3B 10
Sweetshouse. Corn 2E 7
Swefling. Suff 4F 67
Swell. Som 4G 21
Swepstone. Leics 4A 74
Swerford. Oxon 2B 50
Swettenham. Ches E 4C 84
Swetton. N Yor 2D 98
Swffyrd. Cphy 2F 33
Swiftsden. E Sus 3B 28
Swilland. Suff 5D 66
Swillington. W Yor 1D 93
Swimbridge. Devn 4G 19
Swimbridge Newland. Devn 3G 19
Swinbrook. Oxon 4A 50
Swincliffe. N Yor 4E 99
Swincliffe. W Yor 2C 92
Swinderby. Linc 4F 87
Swindon. Glos 3E 49
Swindon. Nmbd 5D 121
Swindon. Staf 1C 60
Swindon. Swin 3G 35
Swine. E Yor 1E 95
Swinefleet. E Yor 2A 94
Swineford. S Glo 5B 34
Swineshead. Bed 4H 63
Swineshead. Linc 1B 76
Swineshead Bridge. Linc 1B 76
Swiney. High 5E 169
Swinford. Leics 3C 62
Swinford. Oxon 5C 50
Swingate. Notts 1C 74
Swingbrow. Cambs 2C 64
Swingfield Minnis. Kent 1G 29
Swingfield Street. Kent 1G 29
Swingleton Green. Suff 1C 54
Swinhill. S Lan 5A 128
Swinhoe. Nmbd 2G 121
Swinhope. Linc 1B 88
Swinithwaite. N Yor 1C 98
Swinmore Common. Here 1B 48
Swinscoe. Staf 1F 73
Swinside Hall. Bord 3B 120
Swinstead. Linc 3H 75
Swinton. G Man 4F 91
Swinton. N Yor 2B 100
(nr. Malton)
Swinton. N Yor 2E 98
(nr. Masham)
Swinton. Bord 5E 131

Swinton. *S Yor* 1B **86**
Swithland. *Leics* 4C **74**
Swordale. *High* 2H **157**
Swordly. *High* 2H **167**
Sworton Heath. *Ches E* 2A **84**
Swyddffynnon. *Cdgn* 4F **57**
Swyffrd. *Cphy* 2F **33**
Swynnerton. *Staf* 2C **72**
Swyre. *Dors* 4A **14**
Sycharth. *Powy* 3E **70**
Sychdyn. *Flin* 4E **83**
Sychnant. *Powy* 3B **58**
Sychtyn. *Powy* 5B **70**
Syde. *Glos* 4E **49**
Sydenham. *G Lon* 3E **39**
Sydenham. *Oxon* 5F **51**
Sydenham. *Som* 3G **21**
Sydenham Damerel. *Devn* 5E **11**
Syderstone. *Norf* 2H **77**
Sydling St Nicholas. *Dors* 3B **14**
Sydmonton. *Hants* 1C **24**
Sydney. *Ches E* 5B **84**
Syerston. *Notts* 1E **75**
Syke. *G Man* 3G **91**
Sykehouse. *S Yor* 3G **93**
Sykes. *Lanc* 4F **97**
Syleham. *Suff* 3E **66**
Sylen. *Carm* 5F **45**
Sylfaen. *Powy* 5D **70**
Symbister. *Shet* 5G **173**
Symington. *S Ayr* 1C **116**
Symington. *S Lan* 1B **118**
Symondsbury. *Dors* 3H **13**
Symonds Yat. *Here* 4A **48**
Synod Inn. *Cdgn* 5D **56**
Syre. *High* 4G **167**
Syreford. *Glos* 3F **49**
Syresham. *Nptn* 1E **51**
Syston. *Leics* 4D **74**
Syston. *Linc* 1G **75**
Sytchampton. *Worc* 4C **60**
Sywell. *Nptn* 4F **63**

T

Tabost. *W Isl* 6F **171** (nr. Cearsiadar)
Tabost. *W Isl* 1H **171** (nr. Suainebost)
Tachbrook Mallory. *Warw* 4H **61**
Tackley. *Oxon* 3C **50**
Tacleit. *W Isl* 4D **171**
Tacolneston. *Norf* 1D **66**
Tadcaster. *N Yor* 5G **99**
Taddington. *Derbs* 3F **85**
Taddington. *Glos* 2F **49**
Taddiport. *Devn* 1E **11**
Tadley. *Hants* 5E **36**
Tadlow. *Cambs* 1C **52**
Tadmarton. *Oxon* 2B **50**
Tadwick. *Bath* 4C **34**
Tadworth. *Surr* 5D **38**
Tafarnaubach. *Blae* 4E **46**
Tafarn-y-bwlch. *Pemb* 1E **43**
Tafarn-y-Gelyn. *Den* 4D **82**
Taff's Well. *Rhon* 3E **33**
Tafolwern. *Powy* 5A **70**
Taibach. *Neat* 3A **32**
Tai-bach. *Powy* 3D **70**
Taigh a Ghearraidh. *W Isl* 1C **170**
Tain. *High* 5E **165** (nr. Invergordon)
Tain. *High* 2E **169** (nr. Thurso)
Tai-Nant. *Wrex* 1E **71**
Tai'n Lon. *Gwyn* 5D **80**
Tairbeart. *W Isl* 7D **171**
Tairgwaith. *Neat* 4H **45**
Takeley. *Essx* 3F **53**
Takeley Street. *Essx* 3F **53**
Talachddu. *Powy* 2D **46**
Talacre. *Flin* 2D **82**
Talardd. *Gwyn* 3A **70**
Talaton. *Devn* 3D **12**
Talbenny. *Pemb* 3C **42**
Talbot Green. *Rhon* 3D **32**
Taleford. *Devn* 3D **12**
Talerddig. *Powy* 5B **70**
Talgarreg. *Cdgn* 5D **56**
Talgarth. *Powy* 2E **47**
Talisker. *High* 5C **154**
Talke. *Staf* 5C **84**
Talkin. *Cumb* 4G **113**
Talladale. *High* 1B **156**
Talla Linnfoots. *Bord* 2D **118**
Tallaminnock. *S Ayr* 5D **116**
Tallarn Green. *Wrex* 1G **71**
Tallentire. *Cumb* 1C **102**
Talley. *Carm* 2G **45**
Tallington. *Linc* 5H **75**
Talmine. *High* 2F **167**
Talog. *Carm* 2H **43**
Talsarn. *Carm* 3A **46**
Talsarn. *Cdgn* 5E **57**
Talsarnau. *Gwyn* 2F **69**
Talskiddy. *Corn* 2D **6**
Talwrn. *IOA* 3D **81**
Talwrn. *Wrex* 1E **71**
Tal-y-bont. *Cdgn* 2F **57**
Tal-y-Bont. *Cnwy* 4G **81**
Tal-y-bont. *Gwyn* 3F **81** (nr. Bangor)
Tal-y-bont. *Gwyn* 3E **69** (nr. Barmouth)
Talybont-on-Usk. *Powy* 3E **46**
Tal-y-cafn. *Cnwy* 3G **81**
Tal-y-coed. *Mon* 4H **47**
Tal-y-llyn. *Gwyn* 5G **69**
Talyllyn. *Powy* 3E **46**
Talysarn. *Gwyn* 5D **81**
Tal-y-waenydd. *Gwyn* 1F **69**
Talywain. *Torf* 5F **47**
Talywern. *Powy* 5H **69**
Tamerton Foliot. *Plym* 2A **8**
Tamworth. *Staf* 5G **73**
Tamworth Green. *Linc* 1C **76**
Tandlehill. *Ren* 3F **127**
Tandridge. *Surr* 5E **39**
Tanerdy. *Carm* 3E **45**
Tanfield. *Dur* 4E **115**
Tanfield Lea. *Dur* 4E **115**
Tangasdale. *W Isl* 8B **170**
Tang Hall. *York* 4A **100**
Tangiers. *Pemb* 3D **42**
Tangley. *Hants* 1B **24**
Tangmere. *W Sus* 5A **26**
Tangwick. *Shet* 4D **173**
Tankerness. *Orkn* 7E **172**
Tankersley. *S Yor* 1H **85**
Tankerton. *Kent* 4F **41**
Tan-lan. *Cnwy* 4G **81**
Tan-lan. *Gwyn* 1F **69**
Tannach. *High* 4F **169**
Tannadice. *Ang* 3D **145**
Tanner's Green. *Worc* 3E **61**
Tannington. *Suff* 4E **67**
Tannochside. *N Lan* 3A **128**
Tan Office Green. *Suff* 5G **65**
Tansley. *Derbs* 5H **85**
Tansley Knoll. *Derbs* 4H **85**
Tansor. *Nptn* 1H **63**
Tantobie. *Dur* 4E **115**
Tanton. *N Yor* 3C **106**
Tanvats. *Linc* 4A **88**
Tanworth-in-Arden. *Warw* 3F **61**
Tan-y-bwlch. *Gwyn* 1F **69**
Tan-y-fron. *Cnwy* 4B **82**
Tanyfron. *Wrex* 5E **83**
Tan-y-goes. *Cdgn* 1C **44**
Tanygrisiau. *Gwyn* 1F **69**
Tan-y-pistyll. *Powy* 3C **70**
Tan-yr-allt. *Den* 2C **82**
Taobh a Chaolais. *W Isl* 7C **170**
Taobh a Deas Loch Aineort. *W Isl* 6C **170**
Taobh a Ghlinne. *W Isl* 6F **171**
Taobh a Tuath Loch Aineort. *W Isl* 6C **170**
Taplow. *Buck* 2A **38**
Tapton. *Derbs* 3A **86**
Tarbert. *Arg* 1E **125** (on Jura)
Tarbert. *Arg* 3G **125** (on Kintyre)
Tarbert. *W Isl* 7D **171**
Tarbet. *Arg* 3C **134**
Tarbet. *High* 4F **147** (nr. Mallaig)
Tarbet. *High* 4B **166** (nr. Scourie)
Tarbock Green. *Mers* 2G **83**
Tarbolton. *S Ayr* 2D **116**
Tarbrax. *S Lan* 4D **128**
Tardebigge. *Worc* 4E **61**
Tarfside. *Ang* 1D **145**
Tarland. *Abers* 3B **152**
Tarleton. *Lanc* 2C **90**
Tarlogie. *High* 5E **165**
Tarlscough. *Lanc* 3C **90**
Tarlton. *Glos* 2E **35**
Tarnbrook. *Lanc* 4E **97**
Tarnock. *Som* 1G **21**
Tarns. *Cumb* 5C **112**
Tarporley. *Ches W* 4H **83**
Tarpots. *Essx* 2B **40**
Tarr. *Som* 3E **20**
Tarrant Crawford. *Dors* 2E **15**
Tarrant Gunville. *Dors* 1E **15**
Tarrant Hinton. *Dors* 1E **15**
Tarrant Keyneston. *Dors* 2E **15**
Tarrant Launceston. *Dors* 2E **15**
Tarrant Monkton. *Dors* 2E **15**
Tarrant Rawston. *Dors* 2E **15**
Tarrant Rushton. *Dors* 2E **15**
Tarrel. *High* 5F **165**
Tarring Neville. *E Sus* 5F **27**
Tarrington. *Here* 1B **48**
Tarsappie. *Per* 1D **136**
Tarscabhaig. *High* 3D **147**
Tarskavaig. *High* 3D **147**
Tarves. *Abers* 5F **161**
Tarvie. *High* 3G **157**
Tarvin. *Ches W* 4G **83**
Tasburgh. *Norf* 1E **66**
Tasley. *Shrp* 1A **60**
Taston. *Oxon* 3B **50**
Tatenhill. *Staf* 3G **73**
Tathall End. *Mil* 1G **51**
Tatham. *Lanc* 3F **97**
Tathwell. *Linc* 2C **88**
Tatling End. *Buck* 2B **38**
Tatsfield. *Surr* 5F **39**
Tattenhall. *Ches W* 5G **83**
Tatterford. *Norf* 3A **78**
Tattersett. *Norf* 2H **77**
Tattershall. *Linc* 5B **88**
Tattershall Bridge. *Linc* 5A **88**
Tattershall Thorpe. *Linc* 5B **88**
Tattingstone. *Suff* 2E **55**
Tattingstone White Horse. *Suff* 2E **55**
Tattle Bank. *Warw* 4F **61**
Tatworth. *Som* 2G **13**
Taunton. *Som* 4F **21**
Taverham. *Norf* 4D **78**
Taverners Green. *Essx* 4F **53**
Tavernspite. *Pemb* 3F **43**
Tavistock. *Devn* 5E **11**
Tavool House. *Arg* 1B **132**
Taw Green. *Devn* 3G **11**
Tawstock. *Devn* 4F **19**
Taxal. *Derbs* 2E **85**
Tayinloan. *Arg* 5E **125**
Taynish. *Arg* 1F **125**
Taynton. *Glos* 3C **48**
Taynton. *Oxon* 4H **49**
Taynuilt. *Arg* 5E **141**
Tayport. *Fife* 1G **137**
Tay Road Bridge. *Fife* 1G **137**
Tayvallich. *Arg* 1F **125**
Tealby. *Linc* 1A **88**
Tealing. *Ang* 5D **144**
Teams. *Tyne* 3F **115**
Teangue. *High* 3E **147**
Tebay. *Cumb* 4H **103**
Tebworth. *C Beds* 3H **51**
Tedburn St Mary. *Devn* 3B **12**
Teddington. *Glos* 2E **49**
Teddington. *G Lon* 3C **38**
Tedsmore. *Shrp* 3F **71**
Tedstone Delamere. *Here* 5A **60**
Tedstone Wafer. *Here* 5A **60**
Teesport. *Red C* 2C **106**
Teesside. *Stoc T* 2C **106**
Teeton. *Nptn* 3D **62**
Teffont Evias. *Wilts* 3E **23**
Teffont Magna. *Wilts* 3E **23**
Tegryn. *Pemb* 1G **43**
Teigh. *Rut* 4F **75**
Teigncombe. *Devn* 4G **11**
Teigngrace. *Devn* 5B **12**
Teignmouth. *Devn* 5C **12**
Telford. *Telf* 4A **72**
Telham. *E Sus* 4B **28**
Tellisford. *Som* 1D **22**
Telscombe. *E Sus* 5F **27**
Telscombe Cliffs. *E Sus* 5E **27**
Tempar. *Per* 3D **142**
Templand. *Dum* 1B **112**
Temple. *Corn* 5B **10**
Temple. *Glas* 3G **127**
Temple. *Midl* 4G **129**
Temple Balsall. *W Mid* 3G **61**
Temple Bar. *Carm* 4F **45**
Temple Bar. *Cdgn* 5E **57**
Temple Cloud. *Bath* 1B **22**
Templecombe. *Som* 4C **22**
Temple Ewell. *Kent* 1G **29**
Temple Grafton. *Warw* 5F **61**
Temple Guiting. *Glos* 3F **49**
Templehall. *Fife* 4E **137**
Temple Hirst. *N Yor* 2G **93**
Temple Normanton. *Derbs* 4B **86**
Temple Sowerby. *Cumb* 2H **103**
Templeton. *Devn* 1B **12**
Templeton. *Pemb* 3F **43**
Templeton. *W Ber* 5B **36**
Templetown. *Dur* 5E **115**
Tempsford. *C Beds* 5A **64**
Tenandry. *Per* 2G **143**
Tenbury Wells. *Worc* 4H **59**
Tenby. *Pemb* 4F **43**
Tendring. *Essx* 3E **55**
Tendring Green. *Essx* 3E **55**
Tenga. *Arg* 4G **139**
Ten Mile Bank. *Norf* 1F **65**
Tenterden. *Kent* 2C **28**
Terfyn. *Cnwy* 3B **82**
Terhill. *Som* 3E **21**
Terling. *Essx* 4A **54**
Ternhill. *Shrp* 2A **72**
Terregles. *Dum* 2G **111**
Terrick. *Buck* 5G **51**
Terrington. *N Yor* 2A **100**
Terrington St Clement. *Norf* 3E **77**
Terrington St John. *Norf* 4E **77**
Terry's Green. *Warw* 3F **61**
Teston. *Kent* 5B **40**
Testwood. *Hants* 1B **16**
Tetbury. *Glos* 2D **35**
Tetbury Upton. *Glos* 2D **35**
Tetchill. *Shrp* 2F **71**
Tetcott. *Devn* 3D **10**
Tetford. *Linc* 3C **88**
Tetney. *Linc* 4G **95**
Tetney Lock. *Linc* 4G **95**
Tetsworth. *Oxon* 5E **51**
Tettenhall. *W Mid* 1C **60**
Teversal. *Notts* 4B **86**
Teversham. *Cambs* 5D **65**
Teviothead. *Bord* 4G **119**
Tewel. *Abers* 5F **153**
Tewin. *Herts* 4C **52**
Tewkesbury. *Glos* 2D **49**
Teynham. *Kent* 4D **40**
Teynham Street. *Kent* 4D **40**
Thackthwaite. *Cumb* 2F **103**
Thakeham. *W Sus* 4C **26**
Thame. *Oxon* 5F **51**
Thames Ditton. *Surr* 4C **38**
Thames Haven. *Thur* 2B **40**
Thamesmead. *G Lon* 2F **39**
Thamesport. *Medw* 3C **40**
Thanington Without. *Kent* 5F **41**
Thankerton. *S Lan* 1B **118**
Tharston. *Norf* 1D **66**
Thatcham. *W Ber* 5D **36**
Thatto Heath. *Mers* 1H **83**
Thaxted. *Essx* 2G **53**
Theakston. *N Yor* 1F **99**
Thealby. *N Lin* 3B **94**
Theale. *Som* 2H **21**
Theale. *W Ber* 4E **37**
Thearne. *E Yor* 1D **94**
Theberton. *Suff* 4G **67**
Theddingworth. *Leics* 2D **62**
Theddlethorpe All Saints. *Linc* 2D **88**
Theddlethorpe St Helen. *Linc* 2D **89**
Thelbridge Barton. *Devn* 1A **12**
Thelnetham. *Suff* 3C **66**
Thelveton. *Norf* 2D **66**
Thelwall. *Warr* 2A **84**
Themelthorpe. *Norf* 3C **78**
Thenford. *Nptn* 1D **50**
Therfield. *Herts* 2D **52**
Thetford. *Linc* 4A **76**
Thetford. *Norf* 2A **66**
Thethwaite. *Cumb* 5E **113**
Theydon Bois. *Essx* 1F **39**
Thick Hollins. *W Yor* 3B **92**
Thickwood. *Wilts* 4D **34**
Thimbleby. *Linc* 3B **88**
Thimbleby. *N Yor* 5B **106**
Thingwall. *Mers* 2E **83**
Thirlby. *N Yor* 1G **99**
Thirlestane. *Bord* 5B **130**
Thirn. *N Yor* 1E **98**
Thirsk. *N Yor* 1G **99**
Thirtleby. *E Yor* 1E **95**
Thistleton. *Lanc* 1C **90**
Thistleton. *Rut* 4G **75**
Thistley Green. *Suff* 3F **65**
Thixendale. *N Yor* 3C **100**
Thockrington. *Nmbd* 2C **114**
Tholomas Drove. *Cambs* 5D **76**
Tholthorpe. *N Yor* 3G **99**
Thomas Chapel. *Pemb* 4F **43**
Thomas Close. *Cumb* 5F **113**
Thomastown. *Abers* 4E **160**
Thomastown. *Rhon* 3D **32**
Thompson. *Norf* 1B **66**
Thomshill. *Mor* 3G **159**
Thong. *Kent* 3A **40**
Thongsbridge. *W Yor* 4B **92**
Thoralby. *N Yor* 1C **98**
Thoresby. *Notts* 3D **86**
Thoresway. *Linc* 1A **88**
Thorganby. *Linc* 1B **88**
Thorganby. *N Yor* 5A **100**
Thorgill. *N Yor* 5E **107**
Thorington. *Suff* 3G **67**
Thorington Street. *Suff* 2D **54**
Thorlby. *N Yor* 4B **98**
Thorley. *Herts* 4E **53**
Thorley Street. *Herts* 4E **53**
Thorley Street. *IOW* 4B **16**
Thormanby. *N Yor* 2G **99**
Thorn. *Powy* 4E **59**
Thornaby-on-Tees. *Stoc T* 3B **106**
Thornage. *Norf* 2C **78**
Thornborough. *Buck* 2F **51**
Thornborough. *N Yor* 2E **99**
Thornbury. *Devn* 2E **11**
Thornbury. *Here* 5A **60**
Thornbury. *S Glo* 3B **34**
Thornby. *Cumb* 4D **112**
Thornby. *Nptn* 3D **62**
Thorncliffe. *Staf* 5E **85**
Thorncombe. *Dors* 2G **13**

Thorncombe Street. Surr 1A 26
Thorncote Green. C Beds 1B 52
Thorndon. Suff 4D 66
Thorndon Cross. Devn 3F 11
Thorne. S Yor 3G 93
Thornehillhead. Devn 1E 11
Thorner. W Yor 5F 99
Thorne St Margaret. Som 4D 20
Thorney. Notts 3F 87
Thorney. Pet 5B 76
Thorney. Som 4H 21
Thorney Hill. Hants 3G 15
Thorney Toll. Cambs 5C 76
Thornfalcon. Som 4F 21
Thornford. Dors 1B 14
Thorngrafton. Nmbd 3A 114
Thorngrove. Som 3G 21
Thorngumbald. E Yor 2F 95
Thornham. Norf 1G 77
Thornham Magna. Suff 3D 66
Thornham Parva. Suff 3D 66
Thornhaugh. Pet 5H 75
Thornhill. Cphy 3E 33
Thornhill. Cumb 4B 102
Thornhill. Derbs 2G 85
Thornhill. Dum 5A 118
Thornhill. Sotn 1C 16
Thornhill. Stir 4F 135
Thornhill. W Yor 3C 92
Thornhill Lees. W Yor 3C 92
Thornhills. W Yor 2B 92
Thornholme. E Yor 3F 101
Thornicombe. Dors 2D 14
Thornington. Nmbd 1C 120
Thornley. Dur 1A 106
(nr. Durham)
Thornley. Dur 1E 105
(nr. Tow Law)
Thornley Gate. Nmbd 4B 114
Thornliebank. E Ren 4G 127
Thornroan. Abers 5F 161
Thorns. Suff 5G 65
Thornsett. Derbs 2E 85
Thornthwaite. Cumb 2D 102
Thornthwaite. N Yor 4D 98
Thornton. Ang 4C 144
Thornton. Buck 2F 51
Thornton. E Yor 5B 100
Thornton. Fife 4E 137
Thornton. Lanc 5C 96
Thornton. Leics 5B 74
Thornton. Linc 4B 88
Thornton. Mers 4B 90
Thornton. Midd 3B 106
Thornton. Nmbd 5F 131
Thornton. Pemb 4D 42
Thornton. W Yor 1A 92
Thornton Curtis. N Lin 3D 94
Thorntonhall. S Lan 4G 127
Thornton Heath. G Lon 4E 39
Thornton Hough. Mers 2F 83
Thornton in Craven. N Yor 5B 98
Thornton in Lonsdale. N Yor 2F 97
Thornton-le-Beans. N Yor 5A 106
Thornton-le-Clay. N Yor 3A 100
Thornton-le-Dale. N Yor 1C 100
Thornton le Moor. Linc 1H 87
Thornton-le-Moor. N Yor 1F 99
Thornton-le-Moors. Ches W 3G 83
Thornton-le-Street. N Yor 1G 99
Thorntonloch. E Lot 2D 130
Thornton Rust. N Yor 1B 98
Thornton Steward. N Yor 1D 98
Thornton Watlass. N Yor 1E 99
Thornwood Common. Essx 5E 53
Thornythwaite. Cumb 2E 103
Thoroton. Notts 1E 75
Thorp Arch. W Yor 5G 99
Thorpe. Derbs 5F 85
Thorpe. E Yor 5D 101
Thorpe. Linc 2D 89
Thorpe. Norf 1G 67
Thorpe. N Yor 3C 98
Thorpe. Notts 1E 75
Thorpe. Surr 4B 38
Thorpe Abbotts. Norf 3D 66
Thorpe Acre. Leics 3C 74
Thorpe Arnold. Leics 3E 75
Thorpe Audlin. W Yor 3E 93
Thorpe Bassett. N Yor 2C 100
Thorpe Bay. S'end 2D 40
Thorpe by Water. Rut 1F 63
Thorpe Common. S Yor 1A 86
Thorpe Common. Suff 2F 55
Thorpe Constantine. Staf 5G 73
Thorpe End. Norf 4E 79
Thorpe Fendike. Linc 4D 88
Thorpe Green. Essx 3E 55
Thorpe Green. Suff 5B 66
Thorpe Hall. N Yor 2H 99
Thorpe Hamlet. Norf 5E 79
Thorpe Hesley. S Yor 1A 86
Thorpe in Balne. S Yor 3F 93
Thorpe in the Fallows. Linc 2G 87
Thorpe Langton. Leics 1E 63
Thorpe Larches. Dur 2A 106
Thorpe Latimer. Linc 1A 76
Thorpe-le-Soken. Essx 3E 55
Thorpe le Street. E Yor 5C 100
Thorpe Malsor. Nptn 3F 63
Thorpe Mandeville. Nptn 1D 50
Thorpe Market. Norf 2E 79
Thorpe Marriott. Norf 4D 78
Thorpe Morieux. Suff 5B 66
Thorpeness. Suff 4G 67
Thorpe on the Hill. Linc 4G 87
Thorpe on the Hill. W Yor 2D 92
Thorpe St Andrew. Norf 5E 79
Thorpe St Peter. Linc 4D 89
Thorpe Salvin. S Yor 2C 86
Thorpe Satchville. Leics 4E 75
Thorpe Thewles. Stoc T 2B 106
Thorpe Tilney. Linc 5A 88
Thorpe Underwood. N Yor 4G 99
Thorpe Waterville. Nptn 2H 63
Thorpe Willoughby. N Yor 1F 93
Thorpland. Norf 5F 77
Thorrington. Essx 3D 54
Thorverton. Devn 2C 12
Thrandeston. Suff 3D 66
Thrapston. Nptn 3G 63
Thrashbush. N Lan 3A 128
Threapland. Cumb 1C 102
Threapland. N Yor 3B 98
Threapwood. Ches W 1G 71
Threapwood. Staf 1E 73
Three Ashes. Here 3A 48
Three Bridges. Linc 2D 88
Three Bridges. W Sus 2D 27
Three Burrows. Corn 4B 6
Three Chimneys. Kent 2C 28
Three Cocks. Powy 2E 47
Three Crosses. Swan 3E 31
Three Cups Corner. E Sus 3H 27
Threehammer Common. Norf 3F 79
Three Holes. Norf 5E 77
Threekingham. Linc 2H 75
Three Leg Cross. E Sus 2A 28
Three Legged Cross. Dors 2F 15
Three Mile Cross. Wok 5F 37
Threemilestone. Corn 4B 6
Three Oaks. E Sus 4C 28
Threlkeld. Cumb 2E 102
Threshfield. N Yor 3B 98
Thrigby. Norf 4G 79
Thringarth. Dur 2C 104
Thringstone. Leics 4B 74
Thrintoft. N Yor 5A 106
Thriplow. Cambs 1E 53
Throckenholt. Linc 5C 76
Throcking. Herts 2D 52
Throckley. Tyne 3E 115
Throckmorton. Worc 1E 49
Throop. Bour 3G 15
Throphill. Nmbd 1E 115
Thropton. Nmbd 4E 121
Throsk. Stir 4A 136
Througham. Glos 5E 49
Throughgate. Dum 1F 111
Throwleigh. Devn 3G 11
Throwley. Kent 5D 40
Throwley Forstal. Kent 5D 40
Throxenby. N Yor 1E 101
Thrumpton. Notts 2C 74
Thrumster. High 4F 169
Thrunton. Nmbd 3E 121
Thrupp. Glos 5D 48
Thrupp. Oxon 4C 50
Thrushelton. Devn 4E 11
Thrushgill. Lanc 3F 97
Thrussington. Leics 4D 74
Thruxton. Hants 2A 24
Thruxton. Here 2H 47
Thrybergh. S Yor 1B 86
Thulston. Derbs 2B 74
Thundergay. N Ayr 5G 125
Thundersley. Essx 2B 40
Thundridge. Herts 4D 52
Thurcaston. Leics 4C 74
Thurcroft. S Yor 2B 86
Thurdon. Corn 1C 10
Thurgarton. Norf 2D 78
Thurgarton. Notts 1D 74
Thurgoland. S Yor 4C 92
Thurlaston. Leics 1C 62
Thurlaston. Warw 3B 62
Thurlbear. Som 4F 21
Thurlby. Linc 3D 89
(nr. Alford)
Thurlby. Linc 4A 76
(nr. Baston)
Thurlby. Linc 4G 87
(nr. Lincoln)
Thurleigh. Bed 5H 63
Thurlestone. Devn 4C 8
Thurloxton. Som 3F 21
Thurlstone. S Yor 4C 92
Thurlton. Norf 1G 67
Thurmaston. Leics 5D 74
Thurnby. Leics 5D 74
Thurne. Norf 4G 79
Thurnham. Kent 5C 40
Thurning. Norf 3C 78
Thurning. Nptn 2H 63
Thurnscoe. S Yor 4E 93
Thursby. Cumb 4E 113
Thursford. Norf 2B 78
Thursford Green. Norf 2B 78
Thursley. Surr 2A 26
Thurso. High 2D 168
Thurso East. High 2D 168
Thurstaston. Mers 2E 83
Thurston. Suff 4B 66
Thurston End. Suff 5G 65
Thurstonfield. Cumb 4E 112
Thurstonland. W Yor 3B 92
Thurton. Norf 5F 79
Thurvaston. Derbs 2F 73
(nr. Ashbourne)
Thurvaston. Derbs 2G 73
(nr. Derby)
Thuxton. Norf 5C 78
Thwaite. Dur 3D 104
Thwaite. N Yor 5B 104
Thwaite. Suff 4D 66
Thwaite Head. Cumb 5E 103
Thwaites. W Yor 5C 98
Thwaite St Mary. Norf 1F 67
Thwing. E Yor 2E 101
Tibbermore. Per 1C 136
Tibberton. Glos 3C 48
Tibberton. Telf 3A 72
Tibberton. Worc 5D 60
Tibenham. Norf 2D 66
Tibshelf. Derbs 4B 86
Tibthorpe. E Yor 4D 100
Ticehurst. E Sus 2A 28
Tichborne. Hants 3D 24
Tickencote. Rut 5G 75
Tickenham. N Som 4H 33
Tickhill. S Yor 1C 86
Ticklerton. Shrp 1G 59
Ticknall. Derbs 3H 73
Tickton. E Yor 5E 101
Tidbury Green. W Mid 3F 61
Tidcombe. Wilts 1A 24
Tiddington. Oxon 5E 51
Tiddington. Warw 5G 61
Tiddleywink. Wilts 4D 34
Tidebrook. E Sus 3H 27
Tideford. Corn 3H 7
Tideford Cross. Corn 2H 7
Tidenham. Glos 2A 34
Tideswell. Derbs 3F 85
Tidmarsh. W Ber 4E 37
Tidmington. Warw 2A 50
Tidpit. Hants 1F 15
Tidworth. Wilts 2H 23
Tidworth Camp. Wilts 2H 23
Tiers Cross. Pemb 3D 42
Tiffield. Nptn 5D 62
Tifty. Abers 4E 161
Tigerton. Ang 2E 145
Tighnabruaich. Arg 2A 126
Tigley. Devn 2D 8
Tilbrook. Cambs 4H 63
Tilbury. Thur 3H 39
Tilbury Green. Essx 1H 53
Tilbury Juxta Clare. Essx 1A 54
Tile Hill. W Mid 3G 61
Tilehurst. Read 4E 37
Tilford. Surr 2G 25
Tilgate Forest Row. W Sus 2D 26
Tillathrowie. Abers 5B 160
Tillers Green. Glos 2B 48
Tillery. Abers 1G 153
Tilley. Shrp 3H 71
Tillicoultry. Clac 4B 136
Tillingham. Essx 5C 54
Tillington. Here 1H 47
Tillington. W Sus 3A 26
Tillington Common. Here 1H 47
Tillybirloch. Abers 3D 152
Tillyfourie. Abers 2D 152
Tilmanstone. Kent 5H 41
Tilney All Saints. Norf 4E 77
Tilney Fen End. Norf 4E 77
Tilney High End. Norf 4E 77
Tilney St Lawrence. Norf 4E 77
Tilshead. Wilts 2F 23
Tilstock. Shrp 2H 71
Tilston. Ches W 5G 83
Tilstone Fearnall. Ches W 4H 83
Tilsworth. C Beds 3H 51
Tilton on the Hill. Leics 5E 75
Tiltups End. Glos 2D 34
Timberland. Linc 5A 88
Timbersbrook. Ches E 4C 84
Timberscombe. Som 2C 20
Timble. N Yor 4D 98
Timperley. G Man 2B 84
Timsbury. Bath 1B 22
Timsbury. Hants 4B 24
Timsgearraidh. W Isl 4C 171
Timworth Green. Suff 4A 66
Tincleton. Dors 3C 14
Tindale. Cumb 4H 113
Tindale Crescent. Dur 2F 105
Tingewick. Buck 2E 51
Tingrith. C Beds 2A 52
Tingwall. Orkn 5D 172
Tinhay. Devn 4D 11
Tinshill. W Yor 1C 92
Tinsley. S Yor 1B 86
Tinsley Green. W Sus 2D 27
Tintagel. Corn 4A 10
Tintern. Mon 5A 48
Tintinhull. Som 1A 14
Tintwistle. Derbs 1E 85
Tinwald. Dum 1B 112
Tinwell. Rut 5H 75
Tippacott. Devn 2A 20
Tipperty. Abers 1G 153
Tipps End. Cambs 1E 65
Tiptoe. Hants 3A 16
Tipton. W Mid 1D 60
Tipton St John. Devn 3D 12
Tiptree. Essx 4B 54
Tiptree Heath. Essx 4B 54
Tirabad. Powy 1B 46
Tircoed. Swan 5G 45
Tiree Airport. Arg 4B 138
Tirinie. Per 2F 143
Tirley. Glos 3D 48
Tirnewydd. Flin 3D 82
Tiroran. Arg 1B 132
Tirphil. Cphy 5E 47
Tirril. Cumb 2G 103
Tirryside. High 2C 164
Tir-y-dail. Carm 4G 45
Tisbury. Wilts 4E 23
Tisman's Common. W Sus 2B 26
Tissington. Derbs 5F 85
Titchberry. Devn 4C 18
Titchfield. Hants 2D 16
Titchmarsh. Nptn 3H 63
Titchwell. Norf 1G 77
Tithby. Notts 2D 74
Titley. Here 5F 59
Titlington. Nmbd 3F 121
Titsey. Surr 5F 39
Titson. Corn 2C 10
Tittensor. Staf 2C 72
Tittleshall. Norf 3A 78
Titton. Worc 4C 60
Tiverton. Ches W 4H 83
Tiverton. Devn 1C 12
Tivetshall St Margaret. Norf 2D 66
Tivetshall St Mary. Norf 2D 66
Tivington. Som 2C 20
Tixall. Staf 3D 73
Tixover. Rut 5G 75
Toab. Orkn 7E 172
Toab. Shet 10E 173
Toadmoor. Derbs 5H 85
Tobermory. Arg 3G 139
Toberonochy. Arg 3E 133
Tobha-Beag. W Isl 1E 170
(on North Uist)
Tobha Beag. W Isl 5C 170
(on South Uist)
Tobha Mor. W Isl 5C 170
Tobson. W Isl 4D 171
Tocabhaig. High 2E 147
Tocher. Abers 5D 160
Tockenham. Wilts 4F 35
Tockenham Wick. Wilts 3F 35
Tockholes. Bkbn 2E 91
Tockington. S Glo 3B 34
Tockwith. N Yor 4G 99
Todber. Dors 4D 22
Todding. Here 3G 59
Toddington. C Beds 3A 52
Toddington. Glos 2F 49
Todenham. Glos 2H 49
Todhills. Cumb 3E 113
Todmorden. W Yor 2H 91
Todwick. S Yor 2B 86
Toft. Cambs 5C 64
Toft. Linc 4H 75
Toft Hill. Dur 2E 105
Toft Monks. Norf 1G 67
Toft next Newton. Linc 2H 87
Toftrees. Norf 3A 78
Tofts. High 2F 169
Toftwood. Norf 4B 78
Togston. Nmbd 4G 121
Tokavaig. High 2E 147
Tokers Green. Oxon 4F 37
Tolastadh a Chaolais. W Isl 4D 171
Tolladine. Worc 5C 60
Tolland. Som 3E 20
Tollard Farnham. Dors 1E 15
Tollard Royal. Wilts 1E 15
Toll Bar. S Yor 4F 93
Toller Fratrum. Dors 3A 14
Toller Porcorum. Dors 3A 14
Tollerton. N Yor 3H 99
Tollerton. Notts 2D 74
Toller Whelme. Dors 2A 14

Tollesbury—Trewen

Tollesbury. *Essx* 4C 54
Tolleshunt D'Arcy. *Essx* 4C 54
Tolleshunt Knights. *Essx* 4C 54
Tolleshunt Major. *Essx* 4C 54
Tollie. *High* 3H 157
Tollie Farm. *High* 1A 156
Tolm. *W Isl* 4G 171
Tolpuddle. *Dors* 3C 14
Tolstadh bho Thuath. *W Isl* 3H 171
Tolworth. *G Lon* 4C 38
Tomachlaggan. *Mor* 1F 151
Tomaknock. *Per* 1A 136
Tomatin. *High* 1C 150
Tombuidhe. *Arg* 3H 133
Tomdoun. *High* 3D 148
Tomich. *High* 1F 149
(nr. Cannich)
Tomich. *High* 1B 158
(nr. Invergordon)
Tomich. *High* 3D 164
(nr. Lairg)
Tomintoul. *Mor* 2F 151
Tomnavoulin. *Mor* 1G 151
Tomsleibhe. *Arg* 5A 140
Ton. *Mon* 2G 33
Tonbridge. *Kent* 1G 27
Tondu. *B'end* 3B 32
Tonedale. *Som* 4E 21
Tonfanau. *Gwyn* 5E 69
Tong. *Shrp* 5B 72
Tonge. *Leics* 3B 74
Tong Forge. *Shrp* 5B 72
Tongham. *Surr* 2G 25
Tongland. *Dum* 4D 111
Tong Norton. *Shrp* 5B 72
Tongue. *High* 3F 167
Tongue End. *Linc* 4A 76
Tongwynlais. *Card* 3E 33
Tonmawr. *Neat* 2B 32
Tonna. *Neat* 2A 32
Tonnau. *Neat* 2A 32
Ton-Pentre. *Rhon* 2C 32
Ton-Teg. *Rhon* 3D 32
Tonwell. *Herts* 4D 52
Tonypandy. *Rhon* 2C 32
Tonyrefail. *Rhon* 3D 32
Toot Baldon. *Oxon* 5D 50
Toot Hill. *Essx* 5F 53
Toot Hill. *Hants* 1B 16
Topcliffe. *N Yor* 2G 99
Topcliffe. *W Yor* 2C 92
Topcroft. *Norf* 1E 67
Topcroft Street. *Norf* 1E 67
Toppesfield. *Essx* 2H 53
Toppings. *G Man* 3F 91
Toprow. *Norf* 1D 66
Topsham. *Devn* 4C 12
Torbay. *Torb* 2F 9
Torbeg. *N Ayr* 3C 122
Torbothie. *N Lan* 3B 128
Torbryan. *Devn* 2E 9
Torcross. *Devn* 4E 9
Tore. *High* 3A 158
Torgyle. *High* 2F 149
Torinturk. *Arg* 3G 125
Torksey. *Linc* 3F 87
Torlum. *W Isl* 3C 170
Torlundy. *High* 1F 141
Tormarton. *S Glo* 4C 34
Tormitchell. *S Ayr* 5B 116
Tormore. *High* 3E 147
Tormore. *N Ayr* 2C 122
Tornagrain. *High* 4B 158
Tornaveen. *Abers* 3D 152
Torness. *High* 1H 149
Toronto. *Dur* 1E 105
Torpenhow. *Cumb* 1D 102
Torphichen. *W Lot* 2C 128
Torphins. *Abers* 3D 152
Torpoint. *Corn* 3A 8
Torquay. *Torb* 2F 9
Torr. *Devn* 3B 8
Torra. *Arg* 4B 124
Torran. *High* 4E 155
Torrance. *E Dun* 2H 127
Torrans. *Arg* 1B 132
Torranyard. *E Ayr* 5E 127
Torre. *Som* 3D 20
Torre. *Torb* 2E 9
Torridon. *High* 3B 156
Torrin. *High* 1D 147
Torrisdale. *Arg* 2B 122
Torrisdale. *High* 2G 167
Torrish. *High* 2G 165
Torrisholme. *Lanc* 3D 96
Torroble. *High* 3C 164
Torroy. *High* 4C 164
Torry. *Aber* 3G 153
Torryburn. *Fife* 1D 128
Torthorwald. *Dum* 2B 112
Tortington. *W Sus* 5B 26
Tortworth. *S Glo* 2C 34
Torvaig. *High* 4D 155
Torver. *Cumb* 5D 102
Torwood. *Falk* 1B 128
Torworth. *Notts* 2D 86
Toscaig. *High* 5G 155
Toseland. *Cambs* 4B 64
Tosside. *Lanc* 4G 97
Tostock. *Suff* 4B 66
Totaig. *High* 3B 154
Totardor. *High* 5C 154
Tote. *High* 4D 154
Totegan. *High* 2A 168
Tothill. *Linc* 2D 88
Totland. *IOW* 4B 16
Totley. *S Yor* 3H 85
Totnell. *Dors* 2B 14
Totnes. *Devn* 2E 9
Toton. *Derbs* 2B 74
Totronald. *Arg* 3C 138
Totscore. *High* 2C 154
Tottenham. *G Lon* 1E 39
Tottenhill. *Norf* 4F 77
Tottenhill Row. *Norf* 4F 77
Totteridge. *G Lon* 1D 38
Totternhoe. *C Beds* 3H 51
Tottington. *G Man* 3F 91
Totton. *Hants* 1B 16
Touchen-end. *Wind* 4G 37
Toulvaddie. *High* 5F 165
Towans, The. *Corn* 3C 4
Toward. *Arg* 3C 126
Towcester. *Nptn* 1E 51
Towednack. *Corn* 3B 4
Tower End. *Norf* 4F 77
Tower Hill. *Mers* 4C 90
Tower Hill. *W Sus* 3C 26
Towersey. *Oxon* 5F 51
Towie. *Abers* 2B 152
Towiemore. *Mor* 4A 160
Tow Law. *Dur* 1E 105
Town End. *Cambs* 1D 64
Town End. *Cumb* 4F 103
(nr. Ambleside)
Town End. *Cumb* 2H 103
(nr. Kirkby Thore)
Town End. *Cumb* 1D 96
(nr. Lindale)
Town End. *Cumb* 1C 96
(nr. Newby Bridge)
Town End. *Mers* 2G 83
Townend. *W Dun* 2F 127
Townfield. *Dur* 5C 114
Towngate. *Cumb* 5G 113
Towngate. *Linc* 4A 76
Town Green. *Lanc* 4B 90
Town Head. *Cumb* 4E 103
(nr. Grasmere)
Town Head. *Cumb* 3H 103
(nr. Great Asby)
Townhead. *Cumb* 1G 103
(nr. Lazonby)
Townhead. *Cumb* 1B 102
(nr. Maryport)
Townhead. *Cumb* 1H 103
(nr. Ousby)
Townhead. *Dum* 5D 111
Townhead of Greenlaw. *Dum* 3E 111
Townhill. *Fife* 1E 129
Townhill. *Swan* 3F 31
Town Kelloe. *Dur* 1A 106
Town Littleworth. *E Sus* 4F 27
Town Row. *E Sus* 2G 27
Towns End. *Hants* 1D 24
Townsend. *Herts* 5B 52
Townshend. *Corn* 3C 4
Town Street. *Suff* 2G 65
Town, The. *IOS* 1A 4
Town Yetholm. *Bord* 2C 120
Towthorpe. *E Yor* 3C 100
Towthorpe. *York* 4A 100
Towton. *N Yor* 1E 93
Towyn. *Cnwy* 3B 82
Toxteth. *Mers* 2F 83
Toynton All Saints. *Linc* 4C 88
Toynton Fen Side. *Linc* 4C 88
Toynton St Peter. *Linc* 4D 88
Toy's Hill. *Kent* 5F 39
Trabboch. *E Ayr* 2D 116
Traboe. *Corn* 4E 5
Tradespark. *High* 3C 158
Trafford Park. *G Man* 1B 84
Trallong. *Powy* 3C 46
Tranent. *E Lot* 2H 129
Tranmere. *Mers* 2F 83
Trantlebeg. *High* 3A 168
Trantlemore. *High* 3A 168
Tranwell. *Nmbd* 1E 115
Trapp. *Carm* 4G 45
Traquair. *Bord* 1F 119
Trash Green. *W Ber* 5E 37
Trawden. *Lanc* 1H 91
Trawscoed. *Powy* 2D 46
Trawsfynydd. *Gwyn* 2G 69
Trawsgoed. *Cdgn* 3F 57
Treaddow. *Here* 3A 48
Trealaw. *Rhon* 2D 32
Treales. *Lanc* 1C 90
Trearddur. *IOA* 3B 80
Treaslane. *High* 3C 154
Treator. *Corn* 1D 6
Trebanog. *Rhon* 2D 32
Trebanos. *Neat* 5H 45
Trebarber. *Corn* 2C 6
Trebartha. *Corn* 5C 10
Trebarwith. *Corn* 4A 10
Trebetherick. *Corn* 1D 6
Treborough. *Som* 3D 20
Trebudannon. *Corn* 2C 6
Trebullett. *Corn* 5D 10
Treburley. *Corn* 5D 10
Treburrick. *Corn* 1C 6
Trebyan. *Corn* 2E 7
Trecastle. *Powy* 3B 46
Trecenydd. *Cphy* 3E 33
Trecott. *Devn* 2G 11
Trecwn. *Pemb* 1D 42
Trecynon. *Rhon* 5C 46
Tredaule. *Corn* 4C 10
Tredavoe. *Corn* 4B 4
Tredegar. *Blae* 5E 47
Trederwen. *Powy* 4E 71
Tredington. *Glos* 3E 49
Tredington. *Warw* 1A 50
Tredinnick. *Corn* 2F 7
(nr. Bodmin)
Tredinnick. *Corn* 3G 7
(nr. Looe)
Tredinnick. *Corn* 1D 6
(nr. Padstow)
Tredogan. *V Glam* 5D 32
Tredomen. *Powy* 2E 46
Tredunnock. *Mon* 2G 33
Tredustan. *Powy* 2E 47
Treen. *Corn* 4A 4
(nr. Land's End)
Treen. *Corn* 3B 4
(nr. St Ives)
Treeton. *S Yor* 2B 86
Trefaldwyn. *Powy* 1E 58
Trefasser. *Pemb* 1C 42
Trefdraeth. *IOA* 3D 80
Trefdraeth. *Pemb* 1E 43
Trefecca. *Powy* 2E 47
Trefechan. *Mer T* 5D 46
Trefeglwys. *Powy* 1B 58
Trefeitha. *Powy* 2E 46
Trefenter. *Cdgn* 4F 57
Treffgarne. *Pemb* 2D 42
Treffynnon. *Flin* 3D 82
Treffynnon. *Pemb* 2C 42
Trefil. *Blae* 4E 46
Trefilan. *Cdgn* 5E 57
Trefin. *Pemb* 1C 42
Treflach. *Shrp* 3E 71
Trefnant. *Den* 3C 82
Trefonen. *Shrp* 3E 71
Trefor. *Gwyn* 1C 68
Trefor. *IOA* 2C 80
Treforest. *Rhon* 3D 32
Trefrew. *Corn* 4B 10
Trefriw. *Cnwy* 4G 81
Tref-y-Clawdd. *Powy* 3E 59
Trefynwy. *Mon* 4A 48
Tregada. *Corn* 4D 10
Tregadillett. *Corn* 4D 10
Tregare. *Mon* 4H 47
Tregarne. *Corn* 4E 5
Tregaron. *Cdgn* 5F 57
Tregarth. *Gwyn* 4F 81
Tregear. *Corn* 3C 6
Tregeare. *Corn* 4C 10
Tregeiriog. *Wrex* 2D 70
Tregele. *IOA* 1C 80
Tregeseal. *Corn* 3A 4
Tregiskey. *Corn* 4E 6
Tregole. *Corn* 3B 10
Tregolwyn. *V Glam* 4C 32
Tregonetha. *Corn* 2D 6
Tregonhawke. *Corn* 3A 8
Tregony. *Corn* 4D 6
Tregoodwell. *Corn* 4B 10
Tregorrick. *Corn* 3E 6
Tregoss. *Corn* 2D 6
Tregowris. *Corn* 4E 5
Tregoyd. *Powy* 2E 47
Tregrehan Mills. *Corn* 3E 7
Tre-groes. *Cdgn* 1E 45
Tregullon. *Corn* 2E 7
Tregurrian. *Corn* 2C 6
Tregynon. *Powy* 1C 58
Trehafod. *Rhon* 2D 32
Trehan. *Corn* 3A 8
Treharris. *Mer T* 2E 32
Treherbert. *Rhon* 2C 32
Trehunist. *Corn* 2H 7
Trekenner. *Corn* 5D 10
Trekenning. *Corn* 2D 6
Treknow. *Corn* 4A 10
Trelales. *B'end* 3B 32
Trelan. *Corn* 5E 5
Trelash. *Corn* 3B 10
Trelassick. *Corn* 3C 6
Trelawnyd. *Flin* 3C 82
Trelech. *Carm* 1G 43
Treleddyd-fawr. *Pemb* 2B 42
Trelewis. *Mer T* 2E 32
Treligga. *Corn* 4A 10
Trelights. *Corn* 1D 6
Trelill. *Corn* 5A 10
Trelissick. *Corn* 5C 6
Trellech. *Mon* 5A 48
Trelleck Grange. *Mon* 5H 47
Trelogan. *Flin* 2D 82
Trelystan. *Powy* 5E 71
Tremadog. *Gwyn* 1E 69
Tremail. *Corn* 4B 10
Tremain. *Cdgn* 1C 44
Tremaine. *Corn* 4C 10
Tremar. *Corn* 2G 7
Trematon. *Corn* 3H 7
Tremeirchion. *Den* 3C 82
Tremore. *Corn* 2E 6
Tremorfa. *Card* 4F 33
Trenance. *Corn* 2C 6
(nr. Newquay)
Trenance. *Corn* 1D 6
(nr. Padstow)
Trenarren. *Corn* 4E 7
Trench. *Telf* 4A 72
Trencreek. *Corn* 2C 6
Trendeal. *Corn* 3C 6
Trenear. *Corn* 5A 6
Treneglos. *Corn* 4C 10
Trenewan. *Corn* 3F 7
Trengune. *Corn* 3B 10
Trent. *Dors* 1A 14
Trentham. *Stoke* 1C 72
Trentishoe. *Devn* 2G 19
Trentlock. *Derbs* 2B 74
Treoes. *V Glam* 4C 32
Treorchy. *Rhon* 2C 32
Treorci. *Rhon* 2C 32
Tre'r-ddol. *Cdgn* 1F 57
Tre'r llai. *Powy* 5E 71
Trerulefoot. *Corn* 3H 7
Tresaith. *Cdgn* 5B 56
Trescott. *Staf* 1C 60
Trescowe. *Corn* 3C 4
Tresham. *Glos* 2C 34
Tresigin. *V Glam* 4C 32
Tresillian. *Corn* 4C 6
Tresimwn. *V Glam* 4D 32
Tresinney. *Corn* 4B 10
Treskillard. *Corn* 5A 6
Treskinnick Cross. *Corn* 3C 10
Tresmeer. *Corn* 4C 10
Tresparrett. *Corn* 3B 10
Tresparrett Posts. *Corn* 3B 10
Tressady. *High* 3D 164
Tressait. *Per* 2F 143
Tresta. *Shet* 6E 173
Treswell. *Notts* 3E 87
Treswithian. *Corn* 3D 4
Tre Taliesin. *Cdgn* 1F 57
Trethomas. *Cphy* 3E 33
Trethosa. *Corn* 3D 6
Trethurgy. *Corn* 3E 7
Tretio. *Pemb* 2B 42
Tretire. *Here* 3A 48
Tretower. *Powy* 3E 47
Treuddyn. *Flin* 5E 83
Trevadlock. *Corn* 5C 10
Trevalga. *Corn* 3A 10
Trevalyn. *Wrex* 5F 83
Trevance. *Corn* 1D 6
Trevanger. *Corn* 1D 6
Trevanson. *Corn* 1D 6
Trevarrack. *Corn* 3B 4
Trevarren. *Corn* 2D 6
Trevarrian. *Corn* 2C 6
Trevarrick. *Corn* 4D 6
Tre-vaughan. *Carm* 3E 45
(nr. Carmarthen)
Trevaughan. *Carm* 3F 43
(nr. Whitland)
Treveighan. *Corn* 5A 10
Trevellas. *Corn* 3B 6
Trevelmond. *Corn* 2G 7
Treverva. *Corn* 5B 6
Trevescan. *Corn* 4A 4
Trevethin. *Torf* 5F 47
Trevia. *Corn* 4A 10
Trevigro. *Corn* 2H 7
Trevilley. *Corn* 4A 4
Treviscoe. *Corn* 3D 6
Trevivian. *Corn* 4B 10
Trevone. *Corn* 1C 6
Trevor. *Wrex* 1E 71
Trevor Uchaf. *Den* 1E 71
Trew. *Corn* 4D 4
Trewalder. *Corn* 4A 10
Trewarlett. *Corn* 4D 10
Trewarmett. *Corn* 4A 10
Trewassa. *Corn* 4B 10
Treween. *Corn* 4C 10
Trewellard. *Corn* 3A 4
Trewen. *Corn* 4C 10

Trewennack. *Corn* 4D **5**
Trewern. *Powy* 4E **71**
Trewetha. *Corn* 5A **10**
Trewidland. *Corn* 2G **7**
Trewint. *Corn* 3B **10**
Trewithian. *Corn* 5C **6**
Trewoofe. *Corn* 4B **4**
Trewoon. *Corn* 3D **6**
Treworthal. *Corn* 5C **6**
Trewyddel. *Pemb* 1B **44**
Treyarnon. *Corn* 1C **6**
Treyford. *W Sus* 1G **17**
Triangle. *Staf* 5E **73**
Triangle. *W Yor* 2A **92**
Trickett's Cross. *Dors* 2F **15**
Trimdon. *Dur* 1A **106**
Trimdon Colliery. *Dur* 1A **106**
Trimdon Grange. *Dur* 1A **106**
Trimingham. *Norf* 2E **79**
Trimley Lower Street. *Suff* 2F **55**
Trimley St Martin. *Suff* 2F **55**
Trimley St Mary. *Suff* 2F **55**
Trimpley. *Worc* 3B **60**
Trimsaran. *Carm* 5E **45**
Trimstone. *Devn* 2F **19**
Trinafour. *Per* 2E **142**
Trinant. *Cphy* 2F **33**
Tring. *Herts* 4H **51**
Trinity. *Ang* 2F **145**
Trinity. *Edin* 2F **129**
Trisant. *Cdgn* 3G **57**
Triscombe. *Som* 3E **21**
Trislaig. *High* 1E **141**
Trispen. *Corn* 3C **6**
Tritlington. *Nmbd* 5G **121**
Trochry. *Per* 4G **143**
Troedrhiwdalar. *Powy* 5B **58**
Troedrhiwfuwch. *Cphy* 5E **47**
Troedrhiwgwair. *Blae* 5E **47**
Troedyraur. *Cdgn* 1D **44**
Troedyrhiw. *Mer T* 5D **46**
Trondavoe. *Shet* 4E **173**
Troon. *Corn* 5A **6**
Troon. *S Ayr* 1C **116**
Troqueer. *Dum* 2A **112**
Troston. *Suff* 3A **66**
Trottiscliffe. *Kent* 4H **39**
Trotton. *W Sus* 4G **25**
Troutbeck. *Cumb* 4F **103**
(nr. Ambleside)
Troutbeck. *Cumb* 2E **103**
(nr. Penrith)
Troutbeck Bridge. *Cumb* 4F **103**
Troway. *Derbs* 3A **86**
Trowbridge. *Wilts* 1D **22**
Trowell. *Notts* 2B **74**
Trowle Common. *Wilts* 1D **22**
Trowley Bottom. *Herts* 4A **52**
Trowse Newton. *Norf* 5E **79**
Trudoxhill. *Som* 2C **22**
Trull. *Som* 4F **21**
Trumaisgearraidh. *W Isl* 1D **170**
Trumpan. *High* 2B **154**
Trumpet. *Here* 2B **48**
Trumpington. *Cambs* 5D **64**
Trumps Green. *Surr* 4A **38**
Trunch. *Norf* 2E **79**
Trunnah. *Lanc* 5C **96**
Truro. *Corn* 4C **6**
Trusham. *Devn* 4B **12**
Trusley. *Derbs* 2G **73**
Trusthorpe. *Linc* 2E **89**
Tryfil. *IOA* 2D **80**
Trysull. *Staf* 1C **60**
Tubney. *Oxon* 2C **36**
Tuckenhay. *Devn* 3E **9**
Tuckhill. *Staf* 2B **60**
Tuckingmill. *Corn* 4A **6**
Tuckton. *Bour* 3G **15**
Tuddenham. *Suff* 3G **65**
Tuddenham St Martin. *Suff* 1E **55**
Tudeley. *Kent* 1H **27**
Tudhoe. *Dur* 1F **105**
Tudhoe Grange. *Dur* 1F **105**
Tudorville. *Here* 3A **48**
Tudweiliog. *Gwyn* 2B **68**
Tuesley. *Surr* 1A **26**
Tufton. *Hants* 2C **24**
Tufton. *Pemb* 2E **43**
Tugby. *Leics* 5E **75**
Tugford. *Shrp* 2H **59**
Tughall. *Nmbd* 2G **121**
Tulchan. *Per* 1B **136**
Tullibardine. *Per* 2B **136**
Tullibody. *Clac* 4A **136**
Tullich. *Arg* 2H **133**
Tullich. *High* 4B **156**
(nr. Lochcarron)
Tullich. *High* 1C **158**
(nr. Tain)
Tullich. *Mor* 4H **159**
Tullich Muir. *High* 1B **158**
Tulliemet. *Per* 3G **143**
Tulloch. *Abers* 5F **161**
Tulloch. *High* 4D **164**
(nr. Bonar Bridge)
Tulloch. *High* 5F **149**
(nr. Fort William)
Tulloch. *High* 2D **151**
(nr. Grantown-on-Spey)
Tulloch. *Per* 1C **136**
Tullochgorm. *Arg* 4G **133**
Tullybeagles Lodge. *Per* 5H **143**
Tullymurdoch. *Per* 3A **144**
Tullynessle. *Abers* 2C **152**
Tumble. *Carm* 4F **45**
Tumbler's Green. *Essx* 3B **54**
Tumby. *Linc* 4B **88**
Tumby Woodside. *Linc* 5B **88**
Tummel Bridge. *Per* 3E **143**
Tunbridge Wells, Royal. *Kent* 2G **27**
Tunga. *W Isl* 4G **171**
Tungate. *Norf* 3E **79**
Tunley. *Bath* 1B **22**
Tunstall. *E Yor* 1G **95**
Tunstall. *Kent* 4C **40**
Tunstall. *Lanc* 2F **97**
Tunstall. *Norf* 5G **79**
Tunstall. *N Yor* 5F **105**
Tunstall. *Staf* 3B **72**
Tunstall. *Stoke* 5C **84**
Tunstall. *Suff* 5F **67**
Tunstall. *Tyne* 4G **115**
Tunstead. *Derbs* 3F **85**
Tunstead. *Norf* 3E **79**
Tunstead Milton. *Derbs* 2E **85**
Tunworth. *Hants* 2E **25**
Tupsley. *Here* 1A **48**
Tupton. *Derbs* 4A **86**
Turfholm. *S Lan* 1H **117**
Turfmoor. *Devn* 2F **13**
Turgis Green. *Hants* 1E **25**
Turkdean. *Glos* 4G **49**
Turkey Island. *Hants* 1D **16**
Tur Langton. *Leics* 1E **62**
Turleigh. *Wilts* 5D **34**
Turlin Moor. *Pool* 3E **15**
Turnant. *Here* 3G **47**
Turnastone. *Here* 2G **47**
Turnberry. *S Ayr* 4B **116**
Turnchapel. *Plym* 3A **8**
Turnditch. *Derbs* 1G **73**
Turners Hill. *W Sus* 2E **27**
Turners Puddle. *Dors* 3D **14**
Turnford. *Herts* 5D **52**
Turnhouse. *Edin* 2E **129**
Turnworth. *Dors* 2D **14**
Turriff. *Abers* 4E **161**
Tursdale. *Dur* 1A **106**
Turton Bottoms. *Bkbn* 3F **91**
Turtory. *Mor* 4C **160**
Turves Green. *W Mid* 3E **61**
Turvey. *Bed* 5G **63**
Turville. *Buck* 2F **37**
Turville Heath. *Buck* 2F **37**
Turweston. *Buck* 2E **50**
Tushielaw. *Bord* 3F **119**
Tutbury. *Staf* 3G **73**
Tutnall. *Worc* 3D **61**
Tutsbill. *Glos* 2A **34**
Tuttington. *Norf* 3E **79**
Tutts Clump. *W Ber* 4D **36**
Tutwell. *Corn* 5D **11**
Tuxford. *Notts* 3E **87**
Twatt. *Orkn* 5B **172**
Twatt. *Shet* 6E **173**
Twechar. *E Dun* 2A **128**
Tweedale. *Telf* 5B **72**
Tweedmouth. *Nmbd* 4F **131**
Tweedsmuir. *Bord* 2C **118**
Twelveheads. *Corn* 4B **6**
Twemlow Green. *Ches E* 4B **84**
Twenty. *Linc* 3A **76**
Twerton. *Bath* 5C **34**
Twickenham. *G Lon* 3C **38**
Twigworth. *Glos* 3D **48**
Twineham. *W Sus* 3D **26**
Twinhoe. *Bath* 1C **22**
Twinstead. *Essx* 2B **54**
Twinstead Green. *Essx* 2B **54**
Twiss Green. *Warr* 1A **84**
Twiston. *Lanc* 5H **97**
Twitchen. *Devn* 3A **20**
Twitchen. *Shrp* 3F **59**
Two Bridges. *Devn* 5G **11**
Two Bridges. *Glos* 5B **48**
Two Dales. *Derbs* 4G **85**
Two Gates. *Staf* 5G **73**
Two Mile Oak. *Devn* 2E **9**
Twycross. *Leics* 5H **73**
Twyford. *Buck* 3E **51**
Twyford. *Derbs* 3H **73**
Twyford. *Dors* 1D **14**
Twyford. *Hants* 4C **24**
Twyford. *Leics* 4E **75**
Twyford. *Norf* 3C **78**
Twyford. *Wok* 4F **37**
Twyford Common. *Here* 2A **48**
Twyncarno. *Cphy* 5E **46**
Twynholm. *Dum* 4D **110**
Twyning. *Glos* 2D **49**
Twyning Green. *Glos* 2E **49**
Twynllanan. *Carm* 3A **46**
Twyn-y-Sheriff. *Mon* 5H **47**
Twywell. *Nptn* 3G **63**
Tyberton. *Here* 2G **47**
Tyburn. *W Mid* 1F **61**
Tyby. *Norf* 3C **78**
Tycroes. *Carm* 4G **45**
Tycrwyn. *Powy* 4D **70**
Tyddewi. *Pemb* 2B **42**
Tydd Gote. *Linc* 4D **76**
Tydd St Giles. *Cambs* 4D **76**
Tydd St Mary. *Linc* 4D **76**
Tye. *Hants* 2F **17**
Tye Green. *Essx* 3F **53**
(nr. Bishop's Stortford)
Tye Green. *Essx* 3A **54**
(nr. Braintree)
Tye Green. *Essx* 2F **53**
(nr. Saffron Walden)
Tyersal. *W Yor* 1B **92**
Ty Issa. *Powy* 3D **70**
Tyldesley. *G Man* 4E **91**
Tyle. *Carm* 3G **45**
Tyler Hill. *Kent* 4F **41**
Tylers Green. *Buck* 2G **37**
Tyler's Green. *Essx* 5F **53**
Tylorstown. *Rhon* 2D **32**
Tylwch. *Powy* 2B **58**
Ty-nant. *Cnwy* 1B **70**
Tyndrum. *Stir* 5H **141**
Tyneham. *Dors* 4D **15**
Tynehead. *Midl* 4G **129**
Tynemouth. *Tyne* 3G **115**
Tyneside. *Tyne* 3F **115**
Tyne Tunnel. *Tyne* 3G **115**
Tynewydd. *Rhon* 2C **32**
Tyninghame. *E Lot* 2C **130**
Tynron. *Dum* 5H **117**
Ty'n-y-bryn. *Rhon* 3D **32**
Tyn-y-celyn. *Wrex* 2D **70**
Tyn-y-cwm. *Swan* 5G **45**
Tyn-y-ffridd. *Powy* 2D **70**
Tynygongl. *IOA* 2E **81**
Tynygraig. *Cdgn* 4F **57**
Tyn-y-groes. *Cnwy* 3G **81**
Ty'n-yr-eithin. *Cdgn* 4F **57**
Tyn-y-rhyd. *Powy* 4C **70**
Tyn-y-wern. *Powy* 3C **70**
Tyrie. *Abers* 2G **161**
Tyringham. *Mil* 1G **51**
Tythecott. *Devn* 1E **11**
Tythegston. *B'end* 4B **32**
Tytherington. *Ches E* 3D **84**
Tytherington. *Som* 2C **22**
Tytherington. *S Glo* 3B **34**
Tytherington. *Wilts* 2E **23**
Tytherleigh. *Devn* 2G **13**
Tywardreath. *Corn* 3E **7**
Tywardreath Highway. *Corn* 3E **7**
Tywyn. *Cnwy* 3G **81**
Tywyn. *Gwyn* 5E **69**

U

Uags. *High* 5G **155**
Ubbeston Green. *Suff* 3F **67**
Ubley. *Bath* 1A **22**
Uckerby. *N Yor* 4F **105**
Uckfield. *E Sus* 3F **27**
Uckinghall. *Worc* 2D **48**
Uckington. *Glos* 3E **49**
Uckington. *Shrp* 5H **71**
Uddingston. *S Lan* 3H **127**
Uddington. *S Lan* 1A **118**
Udimore. *E Sus* 4C **28**
Udny Green. *Abers* 1F **153**
Udny Station. *Abers* 1G **153**
Udston. *S Lan* 4A **128**
Udstonhead. *S Lan* 5A **128**
Uffcott. *Wilts* 4G **35**
Uffculme. *Devn* 1D **12**
Uffington. *Linc* 5H **75**
Uffington. *Oxon* 3B **36**
Uffington. *Shrp* 4H **71**
Ufford. *Pet* 5H **75**
Ufford. *Suff* 5E **67**
Ufton. *Warw* 4A **62**
Ufton Nervet. *W Ber* 5E **37**
Ugadale. *Arg* 3B **122**
Ugborough. *Devn* 3C **8**
Ugford. *Wilts* 3F **23**
Uggeshall. *Suff* 2G **67**
Ugglebarnby. *N Yor* 4F **107**
Ugley. *Essx* 3F **53**
Ugley Green. *Essx* 3F **53**
Ugthorpe. *N Yor* 3E **107**
Uidh. *W Isl* 9B **170**
Uig. *Arg* 3C **138**
Uig. *High* 2C **154**
(nr. Balgown)
Uig. *High* 3A **154**
(nr. Dunvegan)
Uigshader. *High* 4D **154**
Uisken. *Arg* 2A **132**
Ulbster. *High* 4F **169**
Ulcat Row. *Cumb* 2F **103**
Ulceby. *Linc* 3D **88**
Ulceby. *N Lin* 3E **94**
Ulceby Skitter. *N Lin* 3E **94**
Ulcombe. *Kent* 1C **28**
Uldale. *Cumb* 1D **102**
Uley. *Glos* 2C **34**
Ulgham. *Nmbd* 5G **121**
Ullapool. *High* 4F **163**
Ullenhall. *Warw* 4F **61**
Ulleskelf. *N Yor* 1F **93**
Ullesthorpe. *Leics* 2C **62**
Ulley. *S Yor* 2B **86**
Ullingswick. *Here* 1A **48**
Ullinish. *High* 5C **154**
Ullock. *Cumb* 2B **102**
Ulpha. *Cumb* 5C **102**
Ulrome. *E Yor* 4F **101**
Ulsta. *Shet* 3F **173**
Ulting. *Essx* 5B **54**
Ulva House. *Arg* 5F **139**
Ulverston. *Cumb* 2B **96**
Ulwell. *Dors* 4F **15**
Umberleigh. *Devn* 4G **19**
Unapool. *High* 5C **166**
Underbarrow. *Cumb* 5F **103**
Undercliffe. *W Yor* 1B **92**
Underdale. *Shrp* 4H **71**
Underriver. *Kent* 5G **39**
Under Tofts. *S Yor* 2H **85**
Underton. *Shrp* 1A **60**
Underwood. *Newp* 3G **33**
Underwood. *Notts* 5B **86**
Underwood. *Plym* 3B **8**
Undley. *Suff* 2F **65**
Undy. *Mon* 3H **33**
Union Mills. *IOM* 4C **108**
Union Street. *E Sus* 2B **28**
Unstone. *Derbs* 3A **86**
Unstone Green. *Derbs* 3A **86**
Unthank. *Cumb* 5E **113**
(nr. Carlisle)
Unthank. *Cumb* 5H **113**
(nr. Gamblesby)
Unthank. *Cumb* 1F **103**
(nr. Penrith)
Unthank End. *Cumb* 1F **103**
Upavon. *Wilts* 1G **23**
Up Cerne. *Dors* 2B **14**
Upchurch. *Kent* 4C **40**
Upcott. *Devn* 2F **11**
Upcott. *Here* 5F **59**
Upend. *Cambs* 5G **65**
Up Exe. *Devn* 2C **12**
Upgate. *Norf* 4D **78**
Upgate Street. *Norf* 1C **66**
Uphall. *Dors* 2A **14**
Uphall. *W Lot* 2D **128**
Uphall Station. *W Lot* 2D **128**
Upham. *Devn* 2B **12**
Upham. *Hants* 4D **24**
Uphampton. *Here* 4F **59**
Uphampton. *Worc* 4C **60**
Up Hatherley. *Glos* 3E **49**
Uphill. *N Som* 1G **21**
Up Holland. *Lanc* 4D **90**
Uplawmoor. *E Ren* 4F **127**
Upleadon. *Glos* 3C **48**
Upleatham. *Red C* 3D **106**
Uplees. *Kent* 4D **40**
Uploders. *Dors* 3A **14**
Uplowman. *Devn* 1D **12**
Uplyme. *Devn* 3G **13**
Up Marden. *W Sus* 1F **17**
Upminster. *G Lon* 2G **39**
Up Nately. *Hants* 1E **25**
Upottery. *Devn* 2F **13**
Uppat. *High* 3F **165**
Upper Affcot. *Shrp* 2G **59**
Upper Arley. *Worc* 2B **60**
Upper Armley. *W Yor* 1C **92**
Upper Arncott. *Oxon* 4E **50**
Upper Astrop. *Nptn* 2D **50**
Upper Badcall. *High* 4B **166**
Upper Bangor. *Gwyn* 3E **81**
Upper Basildon. *W Ber* 4D **36**
Upper Batley. *W Yor* 2C **92**
Upper Beeding. *W Sus* 4C **26**
Upper Benefield. *Nptn* 2G **63**
Upper Bentley. *Worc* 4D **61**
Upper Bighouse. *High* 3A **168**
Upper Boddam. *Abers* 5D **160**
Upper Boddington. *Nptn* 5B **62**
Upper Bogside. *Mor* 3G **159**
Upper Booth. *Derbs* 2F **85**
Upper Borth. *Cdgn* 2F **57**
Upper Boyndlie. *Abers* 2G **161**
Upper Brailes. *Warw* 2B **50**
Upper Breinton. *Here* 1H **47**
Upper Broadheath. *Worc* 5C **60**
Upper Broughton. *Notts* 3D **74**
Upper Brynamman. *Carm* 4H **45**

Upper Bucklebury. *W Ber* 5D **36**
Upper Bullington. *Hants* 2C **24**
Upper Burgate. *Hants* 1G **15**
Upper Caldecote. *C Beds* 1B **52**
Upper Canterton. *Hants* 1A **16**
Upper Catesby. *Nptn* 5C **62**
Upper Chapel. *Powy* 1D **46**
Upper Cheddon. *Som* 4F **21**
Upper Chicksgrove. *Wilts* 4E **23**
Upper Church Village. *Rhon* 3D **32**
Upper Chute. *Wilts* 1A **24**
Upper Clatford. *Hants* 2B **24**
Upper Coberley. *Glos* 4E **49**
Upper Coedcae. *Torf* 5F **47**
Upper Cokeham. *W Sus* 5C **26**
Upper Common. *Hants* 2E **25**
Upper Cound. *Shrp* 5H **71**
Upper Cudworth. *S Yor* 4D **93**
Upper Cumberworth. *W Yor* 4C **92**
Upper Cuttlehill. *Abers* 4B **160**
Upper Cwmbran. *Torf* 2F **33**
Upper Dallachy. *Mor* 2A **160**
Upper Dean. *Bed* 4H **63**
Upper Dean. *Devn* 2D **8**
Upper Denby. *W Yor* 4C **92**
Upper Derraid. *High* 5E **159**
Upper Diabaig. *High* 2H **155**
Upper Dicker. *E Sus* 5G **27**
Upper Dinchope. *Shrp* 2G **59**
Upper Dochcarty. *High* 2H **157**
Upper Dounreay. *High* 2B **168**
Upper Dovercourt. *Essx* 2F **55**
Upper Dunsforth. *N Yor* 3G **99**
Upper Dunsley. *Herts* 4H **51**
Upper Eastern Green. *W Mid* 2G **61**
Upper Elkstone. *Staf* 5E **85**
Upper Ellastone. *Staf* 1F **73**
Upper End. *Derbs* 3E **85**
Upper Enham. *Hants* 2B **24**
Upper Farmcote. *Shrp* 1B **60**
Upper Farringdon. *Hants* 3F **25**
Upper Framilode. *Glos* 4C **48**
Upper Froyle. *Hants* 2F **25**
Upper Gills. *High* 1F **169**
Upper Glenfintaig. *High* 5E **149**
Upper Godney. *Som* 2H **21**
Upper Gravenhurst. *C Beds* 2B **52**
Upper Green. *Essx* 2E **53**
Upper Green. *W Ber* 5B **36**
Upper Green. *W Yor* 2C **92**
Upper Grove Common. *Here* 3A **48**
Upper Hackney. *Derbs* 4G **85**
Upper Hale. *Surr* 2G **25**
Upper Halliford. *Surr* 4B **38**
Upper Halling. *Medw* 4A **40**
Upper Hambleton. *Rut* 5G **75**
Upper Hardres Court. *Kent* 5F **41**
Upper Hardwick. *Here* 5G **59**
Upper Hartfield. *E Sus* 2F **27**
Upper Haugh. *S Yor* 1B **86**
Upper Hayton. *Shrp* 2H **59**
Upper Heath. *Shrp* 2H **59**
Upper Hellesdon. *Norf* 4E **79**
Upper Helmsley. *N Yor* 4A **100**
Upper Hengoed. *Shrp* 2E **71**
Upper Hergest. *Here* 5E **59**
Upper Heyford. *Nptn* 5D **62**
Upper Heyford. *Oxon* 3C **50**
Upper Hill. *Here* 5G **59**
Upper Hindhope. *Bord* 4B **120**
Upper Hopton. *W Yor* 3B **92**
Upper Howsell. *Worc* 1C **48**
Upper Hulme. *Staf* 4E **85**
Upper Inglesham. *Swin* 2H **35**
Upper Kilcott. *Glos* 3C **34**
Upper Killay. *Swan* 3E **31**
Upper Kirkton. *Abers* 5E **161**
Upper Kirkton. *N Ayr* 4C **126**
Upper Knockando. *Mor* 4F **159**
Upper Knockchoilum. *High* 2G **149**
Upper Lambourn. *W Ber* 3B **36**
Upper Langford. *N Som* 1H **21**
Upper Langwith. *Derbs* 4C **86**
Upper Largo. *Fife* 3G **137**
Upper Latheron. *High* 5D **169**
Upper Layham. *Suff* 1D **54**
Upper Leigh. *Staf* 2E **73**
Upper Lenie. *High* 1H **149**
Upper Lochton. *Abers* 4E **152**
Upper Longdon. *Staf* 4E **73**
Upper Longwood. *Shrp* 5A **72**
Upper Lybster. *High* 5E **169**
Upper Lydbrook. *Glos* 4B **48**
Upper Lye. *Here* 4F **59**
Upper Maes-coed. *Here* 2G **47**
Upper Midway. *Derbs* 3G **73**
Uppermill. *G Man* 4H **91**
Upper Millichope. *Shrp* 2H **59**
Upper Milovaig. *High* 4A **154**
Upper Minety. *Wilts* 2F **35**
Upper Mitton. *Worc* 3C **60**
Upper Nash. *Pemb* 4E **43**
Upper Netchwood. *Shrp* 1A **60**
Upper Nobut. *Staf* 2E **73**
Upper North Dean. *Buck* 2G **37**
Upper Norwood. *W Sus* 4A **26**
Upper Nyland. *Dors* 4C **22**
Upper Oddington. *Glos* 3H **49**
Upper Ollach. *High* 5E **155**
Upper Outwoods. *Staf* 3G **73**
Upper Padley. *Derbs* 3G **85**
Upper Pennington. *Hants* 3B **16**
Upper Poppleton. *York* 4H **99**
Upper Quinton. *Warw* 1G **49**
Upper Rochford. *Worc* 4A **60**
Upper Rusko. *Dum* 3C **110**
Upper Sandaig. *High* 2F **147**
Upper Sanday. *Orkn* 7E **172**
Upper Sapey. *Here* 4A **60**
Upper Seagry. *Wilts* 3E **35**
Upper Shelton. *C Beds* 1H **51**
Upper Sheringham. *Norf* 1D **78**
Upper Skelmorlie. *N Ayr* 3C **126**
Upper Slaughter. *Glos* 3G **49**
Upper Sonachan. *Arg* 1H **133**
Upper Soudley. *Glos* 4B **48**
Upper Staploe. *Bed* 5A **64**
Upper Stoke. *Norf* 5E **79**
Upper Stondon. *C Beds* 2B **52**
Upper Stowe. *Nptn* 5D **62**
Upper Street. *Hants* 1G **15**
Upper Street. *Norf* 4F **79**
(nr. Horning)
Upper Street. *Norf* 4F **79**
(nr. Hoveton)
Upper Street. *Suff* 2E **55**
Upper Strensham. *Worc* 2E **49**
Upper Studley. *Wilts* 1D **22**
Upper Sundon. *C Beds* 3A **52**
Upper Swell. *Glos* 3G **49**
Upper Tankersley. *S Yor* 1H **85**
Upper Tean. *Staf* 2E **73**
Upperthong. *W Yor* 4B **92**
Upperthorpe. *N Lin* 4A **94**
Upper Thurnham. *Lanc* 4D **96**
Upper Tillyrie. *Per* 3D **136**
Upperton. *W Sus* 3A **26**
Upper Tooting. *G Lon* 3D **38**
Uppertown. *Derbs* 4H **85**
(nr. Ashover)
Upper Town. *Derbs* 5G **85**
(nr. Bonsall)
Upper Town. *Derbs* 5G **85**
(nr. Hognaston)
Upper Town. *Here* 1A **48**
Uppertown. *High* 1F **169**
Upper Town. *N Som* 5A **34**
Uppertown. *Nmbd* 2B **114**
Uppertown. *Orkn* 8D **172**
Upper Tysoe. *Warw* 1B **50**
Upper Upham. *Wilts* 4H **35**
Upper Upnor. *Medw* 3B **40**
Upper Urquhart. *Fife* 3D **136**
Upper Wardington. *Oxon* 1C **50**
Upper Weald. *Mil* 2G **51**
Upper Weedon. *Nptn* 5D **62**
Upper Wellingham. *E Sus* 4F **27**
Upper Whiston. *S Yor* 2B **86**
Upper Wield. *Hants* 3E **25**
Upper Winchendon. *Buck* 4F **51**
Upperwood. *Derbs* 5G **85**
Upper Woodford. *Wilts* 3G **23**
Upper Wootton. *Hants* 1D **24**
Upper Wraxall. *Wilts* 4D **34**
Upper Wyche. *Here* 1C **48**
Uppincott. *Devn* 2B **12**
Uppingham. *Rut* 1F **63**
Uppington. *Shrp* 5H **71**
Upsall. *N Yor* 1G **99**
Upsettlington. *Bord* 5E **131**
Upshire. *Essx* 5E **53**
Up Somborne. *Hants* 3B **24**
Upstreet. *Kent* 4G **41**
Up Sydling. *Dors* 2B **14**
Upthorpe. *Suff* 3B **66**
Upton. *Buck* 4F **51**
Upton. *Cambs* 3A **64**
Upton. *Ches W* 4G **83**
Upton. *Corn* 2C **10**
(nr. Bude)
Upton. *Corn* 5C **10**
(nr. Liskeard)
Upton. *Cumb* 1E **102**
Upton. *Devn* 2D **12**
(nr. Honiton)
Upton. *Devn* 4D **8**
(nr. Kingsbridge)
Upton. *Dors* 3E **15**
(nr. Poole)
Upton. *Dors* 4C **14**
(nr. Weymouth)
Upton. *E Yor* 4F **101**
Upton. *Hants* 1B **24**
(nr. Andover)
Upton. *Hants* 1B **16**
(nr. Southampton)
Upton. *IOW* 3D **16**
Upton. *Leics* 1A **62**
Upton. *Linc* 2F **87**
Upton. *Mers* 2E **83**
Upton. *Norf* 4F **79**
Upton. *Nptn* 4E **62**
Upton. *Notts* 3E **87**
(nr. Retford)
Upton. *Notts* 5E **87**
(nr. Southwell)
Upton. *Oxon* 3D **36**
Upton. *Pemb* 4E **43**
Upton. *Pet* 5A **76**
Upton. *Slo* 3A **38**
Upton. *Som* 4H **21**
(nr. Somerton)
Upton. *Som* 4C **20**
(nr. Wiveliscombe)
Upton. *Warw* 5F **61**
Upton. *W Yor* 3E **93**
Upton. *Wilts* 3D **22**
Upton Bishop. *Here* 3B **48**
Upton Cheyney. *S Glo* 5B **34**
Upton Cressett. *Shrp* 1A **60**
Upton Crews. *Here* 3B **48**
Upton Cross. *Corn* 5C **10**
Upton End. *C Beds* 2B **52**
Upton Grey. *Hants* 2E **25**
Upton Heath. *Ches W* 4G **83**
Upton Hellions. *Devn* 2B **12**
Upton Lovell. *Wilts* 2E **23**
Upton Magna. *Shrp* 4H **71**
Upton Noble. *Som* 3C **22**
Upton Pyne. *Devn* 3C **12**
Upton St Leonards. *Glos* 4D **48**
Upton Scudamore. *Wilts* 2D **22**
Upton Snodsbury. *Worc* 5D **60**
Upton upon Severn. *Worc* 1D **48**
Upton Warren. *Worc* 4D **60**
Upwaltham. *W Sus* 4A **26**
Upware. *Cambs* 3E **65**
Upwell. *Cambs* 5D **77**
Upwey. *Dors* 4B **14**
Upwick Green. *Herts* 3E **53**
Upwood. *Cambs* 2B **64**
Urafirth. *Shet* 4E **173**
Uragaig. *Arg* 4A **132**
Urchany. *High* 4C **158**
Urchfont. *Wilts* 1F **23**
Urdimarsh. *Here* 1A **48**
Ure. *Shet* 4D **173**
Ure Bank. *N Yor* 2F **99**
Urgha. *W Isl* 8D **171**
Urlay Nook. *Stoc T* 3B **106**
Urmston. *G Man* 1B **84**
Urquhart. *Mor* 2G **159**
Urra. *N Yor* 4C **106**
Urray. *High* 3H **157**
Usan. *Ang* 3G **145**
Ushaw Moor. *Dur* 5F **115**
Usk. *Mon* 5G **47**
Usselby. *Linc* 1H **87**
Usworth. *Tyne* 4G **115**
Utkinton. *Ches W* 4H **83**
Uton. *Devn* 3B **12**
Utterby. *Linc* 1C **88**
Uttoxeter. *Staf* 2E **73**
Uwchmynydd. *Gwyn* 3A **68**
Uxbridge. *G Lon* 2B **38**
Uyeasound. *Shet* 1G **173**
Uzmaston. *Pemb* 3D **42**

V

Valley. *IOA* 3B **80**
Valley End. *Surr* 4A **38**
Valley Truckle. *Corn* 4B **10**
Valtos. *High* 2E **155**
Van. *Powy* 2B **58**
Vange. *Essx* 2B **40**
Varteg. *Torf* 5F **47**
Vatten. *High* 4B **154**
Vaul. *Arg* 4B **138**
Vauld, The. *Here* 1A **48**
Vaynol. *Gwyn* 3E **81**
Vaynor. *Mer T* 4D **46**
Veensgarth. *Shet* 7F **173**
Velindre. *Powy* 2E **47**
Vellow. *Som* 3D **20**
Velly. *Devn* 4C **18**
Venhay. *Devn* 1A **12**
Venn. *Devn* 4D **8**
Venngreen. *Devn* 1D **11**
Vennington. *Shrp* 5F **71**
Venn Ottery. *Devn* 3D **12**
Venn's Green. *Here* 1A **48**
Venny Tedburn. *Devn* 3B **12**
Venterdon. *Corn* 5D **10**
Ventnor. *IOW* 5D **16**
Vernham Dean. *Hants* 1B **24**
Vernham Street. *Hants* 1B **24**
Vernolds Common. *Shrp* 2G **59**
Verwood. *Dors* 2F **15**
Veryan. *Corn* 5D **6**
Veryan Green. *Corn* 4D **6**
Vicarage. *Devn* 4F **13**
Vickerstown. *Cumb* 3A **96**
Victoria. *Corn* 2D **6**
Vidlin. *Shet* 5F **173**
Viewpark. *N Lan* 3A **128**
Vigo. *W Mid* 5E **73**
Vigo Village. *Kent* 4H **39**
Village Bay. *High* 3B **154**
Vinehall Street. *E Sus* 3B **28**
Vine's Cross. *E Sus* 4G **27**
Viney Hill. *Glos* 5B **48**
Virginia Water. *Surr* 4A **38**
Virginstow. *Devn* 3D **11**
Vobster. *Som* 2C **22**
Voe. *Shet* 5E **173**
Vole. *Som* 2G **21**
Vowchurch. *Here* 2G **47**
Vulcan Village. *Warr* 1H **83**

W

Waberthwaite. *Cumb* 5C **102**
Wackerfield. *Dur* 2E **105**
Wacton. *Norf* 1D **66**
Wadborough. *Worc* 1E **49**
Wadbrook. *Devn* 2G **13**
Waddesdon. *Buck* 4F **51**
Waddeton. *Devn* 3E **9**
Waddicar. *Mers* 1F **83**
Waddingham. *Linc* 1G **87**
Waddington. *Lanc* 5G **97**
Waddington. *Linc* 4G **87**
Waddon. *Devn* 5B **12**
Wadebridge. *Corn* 1D **6**
Wadeford. *Som* 1G **13**
Wadenhoe. *Nptn* 2H **63**
Wadesmill. *Herts* 4D **52**
Wadhurst. *E Sus* 2H **27**
Wadshelf. *Derbs* 3H **85**
Wadsley. *S Yor* 1H **85**
Wadsley Bridge. *S Yor* 1H **85**
Wadswick. *Wilts* 5D **34**
Wadwick. *Hants* 1C **24**
Wadworth. *S Yor* 1C **86**
Waen. *Den* 4C **82**
(nr. Bodfari)
Waen. *Den* 4D **82**
(nr. Llandyrnog)
Waen. *Den* 4B **82**
(nr. Nantglyn)
Waen. *Powy* 1B **58**
Waen Fach. *Powy* 4E **70**
Waen Goleugoed. *Den* 3C **82**
Wag. *High* 1H **165**
Wainfleet All Saints. *Linc* 5D **89**
Wainfleet Bank. *Linc* 5D **88**
Wainfleet St Mary. *Linc* 5D **89**
Wainhouse Corner. *Corn* 3B **10**
Wainscott. *Medw* 3B **40**
Wainstalls. *W Yor* 2A **92**
Waitby. *Cumb* 4A **104**
Waithe. *Linc* 4F **95**
Wakefield. *W Yor* 2D **92**
Wakerley. *Nptn* 1G **63**
Wakes Colne. *Essx* 3B **54**
Walberswick. *Suff* 3G **67**
Walberton. *W Sus* 5A **26**
Walbottle. *Tyne* 3E **115**
Walby. *Cumb* 3F **113**
Walcombe. *Som* 2A **22**
Walcot. *Linc* 2H **75**
Walcot. *N Lin* 2B **94**
Walcot. *Swin* 3G **35**
Walcot. *Telf* 4H **71**
Walcot. *Warw* 5F **61**
Walcote. *Leics* 2C **62**
Walcot Green. *Norf* 2D **66**
Walcott. *Linc* 5A **88**
Walcott. *Norf* 2F **79**
Walden. *N Yor* 1C **98**
Walden Head. *N Yor* 1B **98**
Walden Stubbs. *N Yor* 3F **93**
Walderslade. *Medw* 4B **40**
Walderton. *W Sus* 1F **17**
Walditch. *Dors* 3H **13**
Waldley. *Derbs* 2F **73**
Waldridge. *Dur* 4F **115**
Waldringfield. *Suff* 1F **55**
Waldron. *E Sus* 4G **27**
Wales. *S Yor* 2B **86**
Walesby. *Linc* 1A **88**
Walesby. *Notts* 3D **86**
Walford. *Here* 3F **59**
(nr. Leintwardine)
Walford. *Here* 3A **48**
(nr. Ross-on-Wye)
Walford. *Shrp* 3G **71**
Walford. *Staf* 2C **72**
Walford Heath. *Shrp* 4G **71**
Walgherton. *Ches E* 1A **72**
Walgrave. *Nptn* 3F **63**
Walhampton. *Hants* 3B **16**
Walkden. *G Man* 4F **91**
Walker. *Tyne* 3F **115**
Walkerburn. *Bord* 1F **119**

Walker Fold. *Lanc* 5F 97
Walkeringham. *Notts* 1E 87
Walkerith. *Linc* 1E 87
Walkern. *Herts* 3C 52
Walker's Green. *Here* 1A 48
Walkerton. *Fife* 3E 137
Walkerville. *N Yor* 5F 105
Walkford. *Dors* 3H 15
Walkhampton. *Devn* 2B 8
Walkington. *E Yor* 1C 94
Walkley. *S Yor* 2H 85
Walk Mill. *Lanc* 1G 91
Wall. *Corn* 3D 4
Wall. *Nmbd* 3C 114
Wall. *Staf* 5F 73
Wallaceton. *Dum* 1F 111
Wallacetown. *S Ayr* 2C 116 (nr. Ayr)
Wallacetown. *S Ayr* 4B 116 (nr. Dailly)
Wallands Park. *E Sus* 4F 27
Wallasey. *Mers* 1F 83
Wallaston Green. *Pemb* 4D 42
Wallbrook. *W Mid* 1D 60
Wallcrouch. *E Sus* 2A 28
Wall End. *Cumb* 1B 96
Wallend. *Medw* 3C 40
Wall Heath. *W Mid* 2C 60
Wallingford. *Oxon* 3E 36
Wallington. *G Lon* 4D 39
Wallington. *Hants* 2D 16
Wallington. *Herts* 2C 52
Wallis. *Pemb* 2E 43
Wallisdown. *Pool* 3F 15
Walliswood. *Surr* 2C 26
Wall Nook. *Dur* 5F 115
Walls. *Shet* 7D 173
Wallsend. *Tyne* 3G 115
Wallsworth. *Glos* 3D 48
Wall under Heywood. *Shrp* 1H 59
Wallyford. *E Lot* 2G 129
Walmer. *Kent* 5H 41
Walmer Bridge. *Lanc* 2C 90
Walmersley. *G Man* 3G 91
Walmley. *W Mid* 1F 61
Walnut Grove. *Per* 1D 136
Walpole. *Suff* 3F 67
Walpole Cross Keys. *Norf* 4E 77
Walpole Gate. *Norf* 4E 77
Walpole Highway. *Norf* 4E 77
Walpole Marsh. *Norf* 4D 77
Walpole St Andrew. *Norf* 4E 77
Walpole St Peter. *Norf* 4E 77
Walsall. *W Mid* 1E 61
Walsall Wood. *W Mid* 5E 73
Walsden. *W Yor* 2H 91
Walsgrave on Sowe. *W Mid* 2A 62
Walsham le Willows. *Suff* 3C 66
Walshaw. *G Man* 3F 91
Walshford. *N Yor* 4G 99
Walsoken. *Cambs* 4D 76
Walston. *S Lan* 5D 128
Walsworth. *Herts* 2B 52
Walter's Ash. *Buck* 2G 37
Walterston. *V Glam* 4D 32
Walterstone. *Here* 3G 47
Waltham. *Kent* 1F 29
Waltham. *NE Lin* 4F 95
Waltham Abbey. *Essx* 5D 53
Waltham Chase. *Hants* 1D 16
Waltham Cross. *Herts* 5D 52
Waltham on the Wolds. *Leics* 3F 75
Waltham St Lawrence. *Wind* 4G 37
Waltham's Cross. *Essx* 2G 53
Walthamstow. *G Lon* 2E 39
Walton. *Cumb* 3G 113
Walton. *Derbs* 4A 86
Walton. *Leics* 2C 62
Walton. *Mers* 1F 83
Walton. *Mil* 2G 51
Walton. *Pet* 5A 76
Walton. *Powy* 5E 59
Walton. *Som* 3H 21
Walton. *Staf* 3C 72 (nr. Eccleshall)
Walton. *Staf* 2C 72 (nr. Stone)
Walton. *Suff* 2F 55
Walton. *Telf* 4H 71
Walton. *Warw* 5G 61
Walton. *W Yor* 3D 92 (nr. Wakefield)
Walton. *W Yor* 5G 99 (nr. Wetherby)
Walton Cardiff. *Glos* 2E 49
Walton East. *Pemb* 2E 43
Walton Elm. *Dors* 1C 14
Walton Highway. *Norf* 4D 77
Walton-in-Gordano. *N Som* 4H 33
Walton-le-Dale. *Lanc* 2D 90
Walton-on-Thames. *Surr* 4C 38
Walton-on-the-Hill. *Staf* 3D 72
Walton on the Hill. *Surr* 5D 38
Walton-on-the-Naze. *Essx* 3F 55
Walton on the Wolds. *Leics* 4C 74
Walton-on-Trent. *Derbs* 4G 73
Walton West. *Pemb* 3C 42
Walwick. *Nmbd* 2C 114
Walworth. *Darl* 3F 105
Walworth Gate. *Darl* 2F 105
Walwyn's Castle. *Pemb* 3C 42
Wambrook. *Som* 2F 13
Wampool. *Cumb* 4D 112
Wanborough. *Surr* 1A 26
Wanborough. *Swin* 3H 35
Wandel. *S Lan* 2B 118
Wandsworth. *G Lon* 3D 38
Wangford. *Suff* 2G 65 (nr. Lakenheath)
Wangford. *Suff* 3G 67 (nr. Southwold)
Wanlip. *Leics* 4D 74
Wanlockhead. *Dum* 3A 118
Wannock. *E Sus* 5G 27
Wansford. *E Yor* 4E 101
Wansford. *Pet* 1H 63
Wanshurst Green. *Kent* 1B 28
Wanstead. *G Lon* 2F 39
Wanstrow. *Som* 2C 22
Wanswell. *Glos* 5B 48
Wantage. *Oxon* 3C 36
Wapley. *S Glo* 4C 34
Wappenbury. *Warw* 4A 62
Wappenham. *Nptn* 1E 51
Warbleton. *E Sus* 4H 27
Warblington. *Hants* 2F 17
Warborough. *Oxon* 2D 36
Warboys. *Cambs* 2C 64
Warbreck. *Bkpl* 1B 90
Warbstow. *Corn* 3C 10
Warburton. *G Man* 2A 84
Warcop. *Cumb* 3A 104
Warden. *Kent* 3E 40
Warden. *Nmbd* 3C 114
Ward End. *W Mid* 2F 61
Ward Green. *Suff* 4C 66
Ward Green Cross. *Lanc* 1E 91
Wardhedges. *C Beds* 2A 52
Wardhouse. *Abers* 5C 160
Wardington. *Oxon* 1C 50
Wardle. *Ches E* 5A 84
Wardle. *G Man* 3H 91
Wardley. *Rut* 5F 75
Wardley. *W Sus* 4G 25
Wardlow. *Derbs* 3F 85
Wardsend. *Ches E* 2D 84
Wardy Hill. *Cambs* 2D 64
Ware. *Herts* 4D 52
Ware. *Kent* 4G 41
Wareham. *Dors* 4E 15
Warehorne. *Kent* 2D 28
Warenford. *Nmbd* 2F 121
Waren Mill. *Nmbd* 1F 121
Warenton. *Nmbd* 1F 121
Wareside. *Herts* 4D 53
Waresley. *Cambs* 5B 64
Waresley. *Worc* 4C 60
Warfield. *Brac* 4G 37
Warfleet. *Devn* 3E 9
Wargate. *Linc* 2B 76
Wargrave. *Wok* 4F 37
Warham. *Norf* 1B 78
Wark. *Nmbd* 1C 120 (nr. Coldstream)
Wark. *Nmbd* 2B 114 (nr. Hexham)
Warkleigh. *Devn* 4G 19
Warkton. *Nptn* 3F 63
Warkworth. *Nptn* 1C 50
Warkworth. *Nmbd* 4G 121
Warlaby. *N Yor* 5A 106
Warland. *W Yor* 2H 91
Warleggan. *Corn* 2F 7
Warlingham. *Surr* 5E 39
Warmanbie. *Dum* 3C 112
Warmfield. *W Yor* 2D 93
Warmingham. *Ches E* 4B 84
Warminghurst. *W Sus* 4C 26
Warmington. *Nptn* 1H 63
Warmington. *Warw* 1C 50
Warminster. *Wilts* 2D 23
Warmley. *S Glo* 4B 34
Warmsworth. *S Yor* 4F 93
Warmwell. *Dors* 4C 14
Warndon. *Worc* 5C 60
Warners End. *Herts* 5A 52
Warnford. *Hants* 4E 24
Warnham. *W Sus* 2C 26
Warningcamp. *W Sus* 5B 26
Warninglid. *W Sus* 3D 26
Warren. *Ches E* 3C 84
Warren. *Pemb* 5D 42
Warrenby. *Red C* 2C 106
Warren Corner. *Hants* 2G 25 (nr. Aldershot)
Warren Corner. *Hants* 4F 25 (nr. Petersfield)
Warren Row. *Wind* 3G 37
Warren Street. *Kent* 5D 40
Warrington. *Mil* 5F 63
Warrington. *Warr* 2A 84
Warsash. *Hants* 2C 16
Warse. *High* 1F 169
Warslow. *Staf* 5E 85
Warsop. *Notts* 4C 86
Warsop Vale. *Notts* 4C 86
Warter. *E Yor* 4C 100
Warthermarske. *N Yor* 2E 98
Warthill. *N Yor* 4A 100
Wartling. *E Sus* 5A 28
Wartnaby. *Leics* 3E 74
Warton. *Lanc* 2D 97 (nr. Carnforth)
Warton. *Lanc* 2C 90 (nr. Freckleton)
Warton. *Nmbd* 4E 121
Warton. *Warw* 5G 73
Warwick. *Warw* 4G 61
Warwick Bridge. *Cumb* 4F 113
Warwick-on-Eden. *Cumb* 4F 113
Warwick Wold. *Surr* 5E 39
Wasbister. *Orkn* 4D 172
Wasdale Head. *Cumb* 4C 102
Wash. *Derbs* 2E 85
Washaway. *Corn* 2E 7
Washbourne. *Devn* 3E 9
Washbrook. *Suff* 1E 54
Wash Common. *W Ber* 5C 36
Washerwall. *Staf* 1D 72
Washfield. *Devn* 1C 12
Washfold. *N Yor* 4D 104
Washford. *Som* 2D 20
Washford Pyne. *Devn* 1B 12
Washingborough. *Linc* 3H 87
Washington. *Tyne* 4G 115
Washington. *W Sus* 4C 26
Washington Village. *Tyne* 4G 115
Waskerley. *Dur* 5D 114
Wasperton. *Warw* 5G 61
Wasp Green. *Surr* 1E 27
Wasps Nest. *Linc* 4H 87
Wass. *N Yor* 2H 99
Watchet. *Som* 2D 20
Watchfield. *Oxon* 2H 35
Watchgate. *Cumb* 5G 103
Watchhill. *Cumb* 5C 112
Watcombe. *Torb* 2F 9
Watendlath. *Cumb* 3D 102
Water. *Devn* 4A 12
Water. *Lanc* 2G 91
Waterbeach. *Cambs* 4D 65
Waterbeach. *W Sus* 2G 17
Waterbeck. *Dum* 2D 112
Waterditch. *Hants* 3G 15
Water End. *C Beds* 2A 52
Water End. *E Yor* 1A 94
Water End. *Essx* 1F 53
Water End. *Herts* 5C 52 (nr. Hatfield)
Water End. *Herts* 4A 52 (nr. Hemel Hempstead)
Waterfall. *Staf* 5E 85
Waterfoot. *E Ren* 4G 127
Waterfoot. *Lanc* 2G 91
Waterford. *Herts* 4D 52
Water Fryston. *W Yor* 2E 93
Waterhead. *Cumb* 4E 103
Waterhead. *E Ayr* 3E 117
Waterhead. *S Ayr* 5C 116
Waterheads. *Bord* 4F 129
Waterhouses. *Dur* 5E 115
Waterhouses. *Staf* 5E 85
Wateringbury. *Kent* 5A 40
Waterlane. *Glos* 5E 49
Waterlip. *Som* 2B 22
Waterloo. *Cphy* 3E 33
Waterloo. *Corn* 5B 10
Waterloo. *Here* 1G 47
Waterloo. *High* 1E 147
Waterloo. *Mers* 1F 83
Waterloo. *Norf* 4E 78
Waterloo. *N Lan* 4B 128
Waterloo. *Pemb* 4D 42
Waterloo. *Per* 5H 143
Waterloo. *Pool* 3F 15
Waterloo. *Shrp* 2G 71
Waterlooville. *Hants* 2E 17
Watermead. *Buck* 4G 51
Watermillock. *Cumb* 2F 103
Water Newton. *Cambs* 1A 64
Water Orton. *Warw* 1F 61
Waterperry. *Oxon* 5E 51
Waterrow. *Som* 4D 20
Watersfield. *W Sus* 4B 26
Waterside. *Buck* 5H 51
Waterside. *Cambs* 3F 65
Waterside. *Cumb* 5D 112
Waterside. *E Ayr* 4D 116 (nr. Ayr)
Waterside. *E Ayr* 5F 127 (nr. Kilmarnock)
Waterside. *E Dun* 2H 127
Waterstein. *High* 4A 154
Waterstock. *Oxon* 5E 51
Waterston. *Pemb* 4D 42
Water Stratford. *Buck* 2E 51
Waters Upton. *Telf* 4A 72
Water Yeat. *Cumb* 1B 96
Watford. *Herts* 1B 38
Watford. *Nptn* 4D 62
Wath. *Cumb* 4H 103
Wath. *N Yor* 3D 98 (nr. Pateley Bridge)
Wath. *N Yor* 2F 99 (nr. Ripon)
Wath Brow. *Cumb* 3B 102
Wath upon Dearne. *S Yor* 1B 86
Watlington. *Norf* 4F 77
Watlington. *Oxon* 2E 37
Watten. *High* 3E 169
Wattisfield. *Suff* 3C 66
Wattisham. *Suff* 5C 66
Wattlesborough Heath. *Shrp* 4F 71
Watton. *Dors* 3H 13
Watton. *E Yor* 4E 101
Watton. *Norf* 5B 78
Watton at Stone. *Herts* 4C 52
Wattston. *N Lan* 2A 128
Wattstown. *Rhon* 2D 32
Wattsville. *Cphy* 2F 33
Wauldby. *E Yor* 2C 94
Waulkmill. *Abers* 4D 152
Waun. *Powy* 4E 71
Waunarlwydd. *Swan* 3F 31
Waun Fawr. *Cdgn* 2F 57
Waunfawr. *Gwyn* 5E 81
Waungilwen. *Carm* 1H 43
Waunlwyd. *Blae* 5E 47
Waun-y-Clyn. *Carm* 5E 45
Wavendon. *Mil* 2H 51
Waverbridge. *Cumb* 5D 112
Waverley. *Surr* 2G 25
Waverton. *Ches W* 4G 83
Waverton. *Cumb* 5D 112
Wavertree. *Mers* 2F 83
Wawne. *E Yor* 1D 94
Waxham. *Norf* 3G 79
Waxholme. *E Yor* 2G 95
Wayford. *Som* 2H 13
Way Head. *Cambs* 2D 65
Waytown. *Dors* 3H 13
Way Village. *Devn* 1B 12
Wdig. *Pemb* 1D 42
Wealdstone. *G Lon* 2C 38
Weardley. *W Yor* 5E 99
Weare. *Som* 1H 21
Weare Giffard. *Devn* 4E 19
Wearhead. *Dur* 1B 104
Wearne. *Som* 4H 21
Weasdale. *Cumb* 4H 103
Weasenham All Saints. *Norf* 3H 77
Weasenham St Peter. *Norf* 3A 78
Weaverham. *Ches W* 3A 84
Weaverthorpe. *N Yor* 2D 100
Webheath. *Worc* 4E 61
Webton. *Here* 2H 47
Wedderlairs. *Abers* 5F 161
Weddington. *Warw* 1A 62
Wedhampton. *Wilts* 1F 23
Wedmore. *Som* 2H 21
Wednesbury. *W Mid* 1D 61
Wednesfield. *W Mid* 5D 72
Weecar. *Notts* 4F 87
Weedon. *Buck* 4G 51
Weedon Bec. *Nptn* 5D 62
Weedon Lois. *Nptn* 1E 50
Weeford. *Staf* 5F 73
Week. *Devn* 4F 19 (nr. Barnstaple)
Week. *Devn* 2G 11 (nr. Okehampton)
Week. *Devn* 1H 11 (nr. South Molton)
Week. *Devn* 2D 9 (nr. Totnes)
Week. *Som* 3C 20
Weeke. *Devn* 2A 12
Weeke. *Hants* 3C 24
Week Green. *Corn* 3C 10
Weekley. *Nptn* 2F 63
Week St Mary. *Corn* 3C 10
Weel. *E Yor* 1D 94
Weeley. *Essx* 3E 55
Weeley Heath. *Essx* 3E 55
Weem. *Per* 4F 143
Weeping Cross. *Staf* 3D 72
Weethly. *Warw* 5E 61
Weeting. *Norf* 2G 65
Weeton. *E Yor* 2G 95
Weeton. *Lanc* 1B 90
Weeton. *N Yor* 5E 99
Weetwood Hall. *Nmbd* 2E 121
Weir. *Lanc* 2G 91
Welborne. *Norf* 4C 78
Welbourn. *Linc* 5G 87
Welburn. *N Yor* 1A 100 (nr. Kirkbymoorside)
Welburn. *N Yor* 3B 100 (nr. Malton)

Welbury. N Yor 4A 106
Welby. Linc 2G 75
Welches Dam. Cambs 2D 64
Welcombe. Devn 1C 10
Weld Bank. Lanc 3D 90
Weldon. Nptn 2G 63
Weldon. Nmbd 5F 121
Welford. Nptn 2D 62
Welford. W Ber 4C 36
Welford-on-Avon. Warw 5F 61
Welham. Leics 1E 63
Welham. Notts 2E 87
Welham Green. Herts 5C 52
Well. Hants 2F 25
Well. Linc 3D 88
Well. N Yor 1E 99
Welland. Worc 1C 48
Wellbank. Ang 5D 144
Well Bottom. Dors 1E 15
Welldale. Dum 3C 112
Wellesbourne. Warw 5G 61
Well Hill. Kent 4F 39
Wellhouse. W Ber 4D 36
Welling. G Lon 3F 39
Wellingborough. Nptn 4F 63
Wellingham. Norf 3A 78
Wellingore. Linc 5G 87
Wellington. Cumb 4B 102
Wellington. Here 1H 47
Wellington. Som 4E 21
Wellington. Telf 4A 72
Wellington Heath. Here 1C 48
Wellow. Bath 1C 22
Wellow. IOW 4B 16
Wellow. Notts 4D 86
Wellpond Green. Herts 3E 53
Wells. Som 2A 22
Wellsborough. Leics 5A 74
Wells Green. Ches E 5A 84
Wells-next-the-Sea. Norf 1B 78
Wells of Ythan. Abers 5D 160
Wellswood. Torb 2F 9
Wellwood. Fife 1D 129
Welney. Norf 1E 65
Welsford. Devn 4C 18
Welshampton. Shrp 2G 71
Welsh End. Shrp 2H 71
Welsh Frankton. Shrp 2F 71
Welsh Hook. Pemb 2D 42
Welsh Newton. Here 4H 47
Welsh Newton Common. Here 4A 48
Welshpool. Powy 5E 70
Welsh St Donats. V Glam 4D 32
Welton. Bath 1B 22
Welton. Cumb 5E 113
Welton. E Yor 2C 94
Welton. Linc 2H 87
Welton. Nptn 4C 62
Welton Hill. Linc 2H 87
Welton le Marsh. Linc 4D 88
Welton le Wold. Linc 2B 88
Welwick. E Yor 2G 95
Welwyn. Herts 4C 52
Welwyn Garden City. Herts 4C 52
Wem. Shrp 3H 71
Wembdon. Som 3F 21
Wembley. G Lon 2C 38
Wembury. Devn 4B 8
Wembworthy. Devn 2G 11
Wemyss Bay. Inv 2C 126
Wenallt. Cdgn 3F 57
Wenallt. Gwyn 1B 70
Wendens Ambo. Essx 2F 53
Wendlebury. Oxon 4D 50
Wendling. Norf 4B 78
Wendover. Buck 5G 51
Wendron. Corn 5A 6
Wendy. Cambs 1D 52
Wenfordbridge. Corn 5A 10
Wenhaston. Suff 3G 67
Wennington. Cambs 3B 64
Wennington. G Lon 2G 39
Wennington. Lanc 2F 97
Wensley. Derbs 4G 85
Wensley. N Yor 1C 98
Wentbridge. W Yor 3E 93
Wentnor. Shrp 1F 59
Wentworth. Cambs 3D 65
Wentworth. S Yor 1A 86
Wenvoe. V Glam 4E 32
Weobley. Here 5G 59
Weobley Marsh. Here 5G 59
Wepham. W Sus 5B 26
Wereham. Norf 5F 77
Wergs. W Mid 5C 72
Wern. Gwyn 1E 69
Wern. Powy 4E 46 (nr. Brecon)
Wern. Powy 4E 71 (nr. Guilsfield)
Wern. Powy 4B 70 (nr. Llangadfan)
Wern. Powy 3E 71 (nr. Llanymynech)
Wernffrwd. Swan 3E 31
Wernyrheolydd. Mon 4G 47
Werrington. Corn 4D 10
Werrington. Pet 5A 76
Werrington. Staf 1D 72
Wervin. Ches W 3G 83
Wesham. Lanc 1C 90
Wessington. Derbs 5A 86
West Aberthaw. V Glam 5D 32
West Acre. Norf 4G 77
West Allerdean. Nmbd 5F 131
West Alvington. Devn 4D 8
West Amesbury. Wilts 2G 23
West Anstey. Devn 4B 20
West Appleton. N Yor 5F 105
West Ardsley. W Yor 2C 92
West Arthurlie. E Ren 4F 127
West Ashby. Linc 3B 88
West Ashling. W Sus 2G 17
West Ashton. Wilts 1D 23
West Auckland. Dur 2E 105
West Ayton. N Yor 1D 101
West Bagborough. Som 3E 21
West Bank. Hal 2H 83
West Barkwith. Linc 2A 88
West Barnby. N Yor 3F 107
West Barns. E Lot 2C 130
West Barsham. Norf 2B 78
West Bay. Dors 3H 13
West Beckham. Norf 2D 78
West Bennan. N Ayr 3D 123
Westbere. Kent 4F 41
West Bergholt. Essx 3C 54
West Bexington. Dors 4A 14
West Bilney. Norf 4G 77
West Blackdene. Dur 1B 104
West Blatchington. Brig 5D 27
Westborough. Linc 1F 75
Westbourne. Bour 3F 15
Westbourne. W Sus 2F 17
West Bowling. W Yor 1B 92
West Brabourne. Kent 1E 29
West Bradford. Lanc 5G 97
West Bradley. Som 3A 22
West Bretton. W Yor 3C 92
West Bridgford. Notts 2C 74
West Briggs. Norf 4F 77
West Bromwich. W Mid 1D 61
Westbrook. Here 1F 47
Westbrook. Kent 3H 41
Westbrook. Wilts 5E 35
West Buckland. Devn 3G 19 (nr. Barnstaple)
West Buckland. Devn 4C 8 (nr. Thurlestone)
West Buckland. Som 4E 21
West Burnside. Abers 1G 145
West Burrafirth. Shet 6D 173
West Burton. N Yor 1C 98
West Burton. W Sus 4B 26
Westbury. Buck 2E 50
Westbury. Shrp 5F 71
Westbury. Wilts 1D 22
Westbury Leigh. Wilts 2D 22
Westbury-on-Severn. Glos 4C 48
Westbury on Trym. Bris 4A 34
Westbury-sub-Mendip. Som 2A 22
West Butsfield. Dur 5E 115
West Butterwick. N Lin 4B 94
Westby. Linc 3G 75
West Byfleet. Surr 4B 38
West Caister. Norf 4H 79
West Calder. W Lot 3D 128
West Camel. Som 4A 22
West Carr. N Lin 4H 93
West Chaldon. Dors 4C 14
West Challow. Oxon 3B 36
West Charleton. Devn 4D 8
West Chelborough. Dors 2A 14
West Chevington. Nmbd 5G 121
West Chiltington. W Sus 4B 26
West Chiltington Common. W Sus 4B 26
West Chinnock. Som 1H 13
West Chisenbury. Wilts 1G 23
West Clandon. Surr 5B 38
West Cliffe. Kent 1H 29
Westcliff-on-Sea. S'end 2C 40
West Clyne. High 3F 165
West Coker. Som 1A 14
Westcombe. Som 3B 22 (nr. Evercreech)
Westcombe. Som 4H 21 (nr. Somerton)
West Compton. Dors 3A 14
West Compton. Som 2A 22
West Cornforth. Dur 1A 106
Westcot. Oxon 3B 36
Westcott. Buck 4F 51
Westcott. Devn 2D 12
Westcott. Surr 1C 26
Westcott Barton. Oxon 3C 50
West Cowick. E Yor 2G 93
West Cranmore. Som 2B 22
West Croftmore. High 2D 150
West Cross. Swan 4F 31
West Cullerlie. Abers 3E 153
West Culvennan. Dum 3H 109
West Curry. Corn 3C 10
West Curthwaite. Cumb 5E 113
Westdean. E Sus 5G 27
West Dean. W Sus 1G 17
West Dean. Wilts 4A 24
West Deeping. Linc 5A 76
West Derby. Mers 1F 83
West Dereham. Norf 5F 77
West Down. Devn 2F 19
Westdowns. Corn 4A 10
West Drayton. G Lon 3B 38
West Drayton. Notts 3E 86
West Dunnet. High 1E 169
West Ella. E Yor 2D 94
West End. Bed 5G 63
West End. Cambs 1D 64
West End. Dors 2E 15
West End. E Yor 3E 101 (nr. Kilham)
West End. E Yor 1E 95 (nr. Preston)
West End. E Yor 1C 94 (nr. South Cove)
West End. E Yor 4F 101 (nr. Ulrome)
West End. G Lon 2D 39
West End. Hants 1C 16
West End. Herts 5C 52
West End. Kent 4F 41
West End. Lanc 3D 96
West End. Linc 1C 76
West End. Norf 4G 79
West End. N Som 5H 33
West End. N Yor 4D 98
West End. S Glo 3C 34
West End. S Lan 5C 128
West End. Surr 4A 38
West End. Wilts 4E 23
West End. Wind 4G 37
West End. Worc 2F 49
West End Green. Hants 5E 37
Westenhanger. Kent 2F 29
Wester Aberchalder. High 2H 149
Wester Balgedie. Per 3D 136
Wester Brae. High 2A 158
Wester Culbeuchly. Abers 2D 160
Westerdale. High 3D 168
Westerdale. N Yor 4D 106
Wester Dechmont. W Lot 2D 128
Wester Fearn. High 5D 164
Westerfield. Suff 1E 55
Wester Galcantray. High 4C 158
Westergate. W Sus 5A 26
Wester Gruinards. High 4C 164
Westerham. Kent 5F 39
Westerleigh. S Glo 4B 34
Westerloch. High 3F 169
Wester Mandally. High 3E 149
Wester Rarichie. High 1C 158
Wester Shian. Per 5F 143
Westerton. Ang 3F 145
Westerton. Dur 1F 105
Westerton. W Sus 2G 17
Westerwick. Shet 7D 173
West Farleigh. Kent 5B 40
West Farndon. Nptn 5C 62
West Felton. Shrp 3F 71
Westfield. Cumb 2A 102
Westfield. E Sus 4C 28
Westfield. High 2C 168
Westfield. Norf 5B 78
Westfield. N Lan 2A 128
Westfield. W Lot 2C 128
Westfields. Dors 2C 14
Westfields of Rattray. Per 4A 144
West Fleetham. Nmbd 2F 121
Westford. Som 1E 13
West Garforth. W Yor 1D 93
Westgate. Dur 1C 104
Westgate. Norf 1B 78
Westgate. N Lin 4A 94
Westgate on Sea. Kent 3H 41
West Ginge. Oxon 3C 36
West Grafton. Wilts 5H 35
West Green. Hants 1F 25
West Grimstead. Wilts 4H 23
West Grinstead. W Sus 3C 26
West Haddlesey. N Yor 2F 93
West Haddon. Nptn 3D 62
West Hagbourne. Oxon 3D 36
West Hagley. Worc 2C 60
West Hall. Cumb 3G 113
Westhall. Suff 2G 67
West Hallam. Derbs 1B 74
Westhall Terrace. Ang 5D 144
West Halton. N Lin 2C 94
Westham. Dors 5B 14
Westham. E Sus 5H 27
West Ham. G Lon 2E 39
Westham. Som 2H 21
Westhampnett. W Sus 2G 17
West Handley. Derbs 3A 86
West Hanney. Oxon 2C 36
West Hanningfield. Essx 1B 40
West Hardwick. W Yor 3E 93
West Harnham. Wilts 4G 23
West Harptree. Bath 1A 22
West Harting. W Sus 4F 25
West Harton. Tyne 3G 115
West Hatch. Som 4F 21
Westhay. Som 2H 21
Westhead. Lanc 4C 90
West Head. Norf 5E 77
West Heath. Hants 1D 24 (nr. Basingstoke)
West Heath. Hants 1G 25 (nr. Farnborough)
West Helmsdale. High 2H 165
West Hendred. Oxon 3C 36
West Heslerton. N Yor 2D 100
West Hewish. N Som 5G 33
Westhide. Here 1A 48
Westhill. Abers 3F 153
West Hill. Devn 3D 12
West Hill. E Yor 3F 101
Westhill. High 4B 158
West Hill. N Som 4H 33
West Hill. W Sus 2E 27
West Hoathly. W Sus 2E 27
West Holme. Dors 4D 15
Westhope. Here 5G 59
Westhope. Shrp 2G 59
West Horndon. Essx 2H 39
Westhorp. Nptn 5C 62
Westhorpe. Linc 2B 76
Westhorpe. Suff 4C 66
West Horrington. Som 2A 22
West Horsley. Surr 5B 38
West Horton. Nmbd 1E 121
West Hougham. Kent 1G 29
Westhoughton. G Man 4E 91
Westhouse. N Yor 2F 97
Westhouses. Derbs 5B 86
West Howe. Bour 3F 15
Westhumble. Surr 5C 38
West Huntspill. Som 2G 21
West Hyde. Herts 1B 38
West Hynish. Arg 5A 138
West Hythe. Kent 2F 29
West Ilsley. W Ber 3C 36
West Itchenor. W Sus 2G 17
West Keal. Linc 4C 88
West Kennett. Wilts 5G 35
West Kilbride. N Ayr 5D 126
West Kingsdown. Kent 4G 39
West Kington. Wilts 4D 34
West Kirby. Mers 2E 82
West Knapton. N Yor 2C 100
West Knighton. Dors 4C 14
West Knoyle. Wilts 3D 22
West Kyloe. Nmbd 5G 131
Westlake. Devn 3C 8
West Lambrook. Som 1H 13
West Langdon. Kent 1H 29
West Langwell. High 3D 164
West Lavington. W Sus 4G 25
West Lavington. Wilts 1F 23
West Layton. N Yor 4E 105
West Leake. Notts 3C 74
West Learmouth. Nmbd 1C 120
Westleigh. Devn 4E 19 (nr. Bideford)
Westleigh. Devn 1D 12 (nr. Tiverton)
West Leigh. Devn 2G 11 (nr. Winkleigh)
Westleigh. G Man 4E 91
West Leith. Buck 4H 51
Westleton. Suff 4G 67
West Lexham. Norf 4H 77
Westley. Shrp 5F 71
Westley. Suff 4H 65
Westley Waterless. Cambs 5F 65
West Lilling. N Yor 3A 100
West Lingo. Fife 3G 137
Westlington. Buck 4F 51
Westlinton. Cumb 3E 113
West Linton. Bord 4E 129
West Littleton. S Glo 4C 34
West Looe. Corn 3G 7
West Lulworth. Dors 4D 14
West Lutton. N Yor 3D 100
West Lydford. Som 3A 22
West Lyng. Som 4G 21
West Lynn. Norf 4F 77
West Mains. Per 2B 136
West Malling. Kent 5A 40
West Malvern. Worc 1C 48
Westmancote. Worc 2E 49
West Marden. W Sus 1F 17
West Markham. Notts 3E 86
Westmarsh. Kent 4G 41
West Marsh. NE Lin 4F 95
West Marton. N Yor 4A 98
West Meon. Hants 4E 25
West Mersea. Essx 4D 54
Westmeston. E Sus 4E 27

Westmill. Herts 3D 52
(nr. Buntingford)
Westmill. Herts 2B 52
(nr. Hitchin)
West Milton. Dors 3A 14
Westminster. G Lon 3D 39
West Molesey. Surr 4C 38
West Monkton. Som 4F 21
Westmoor End. Cumb 1B 102
West Moors. Dors 2F 15
West Morden. Dors 3E 15
West Muir. Ang 2E 145
(nr. Brechin)
Westmuir. Ang 3C 144
(nr. Forfar)
West Murkle. High 2D 168
West Ness. N Yor 2A 100
Westnewton. Cumb 5C 112
West Newton. E Yor 1E 95
West Newton. Norf 3F 77
Westnewton. Nmbd 1D 120
West Newton. Som 4F 21
West Norwood. G Lon 3E 39
Westoe. Tyne 3G 115
West Ogwell. Devn 2E 9
Weston. Bath 5C 34
Weston. Ches E 5B 84
(nr. Crewe)
Weston. Ches E 3D 84
(nr. Macclesfield)
Weston. Devn 2E 13
(nr. Honiton)
Weston. Devn 4E 13
(nr. Sidmouth)
Weston. Dors 5B 14
(nr. Weymouth)
Weston. Dors 2A 14
(nr. Yeovil)
Weston. Hal 2H 83
Weston. Hants 4F 25
Weston. Here 5F 59
Weston. Herts 2C 52
Weston. Linc 3B 76
Weston. Nptn 1D 50
Weston. Notts 4E 87
Weston. Shrp 1H 59
(nr. Bridgnorth)
Weston. Shrp 3F 59
(nr. Knighton)
Weston. Shrp 3H 71
(nr. Wem)
Weston. S Lan 5D 128
Weston. Staf 3D 73
Weston. Suff 2G 67
Weston. W Ber 4B 36
Weston Bampfylde. Som 4B 22
Weston Beggard. Here 1A 48
Westonbirt. Glos 3D 34
Weston by Welland. Nptn 1E 63
Weston Colville. Cambs 5F 65
Westoncommon. Shrp 3G 71
Weston Coyney. Stoke 1D 72
Weston Ditch. Suff 3F 65
Weston Favell. Nptn 4E 63
Weston Green. Cambs 5F 65
Weston Green. Norf 4D 78
Weston Heath. Shrp 4B 72
Weston Hills. Linc 4B 76
Weston in Arden. Warw 2A 62
Westoning. C Beds 2A 52
Weston-in-Gordano. N Som 4H 33
Weston Jones. Staf 3B 72
Weston Longville. Norf 4D 78
Weston Lullingfields. Shrp 3G 71
Weston-on-Avon. Warw 5F 61
Weston-on-the-Green. Oxon 4D 50
Weston-on-Trent. Derbs 3B 74
Weston Patrick. Hants 2E 25
Weston Rhyn. Shrp 2E 71
Weston-sub-Edge. Glos 1G 49
Weston-super-Mare. N Som 5G 33
Weston Town. Som 2C 22
Weston Turville. Buck 4G 51
Weston under Lizard. Staf 4C 72
Weston under Penyard. Here 3B 48
Weston under Wetherley.
Warw 4A 62
Weston Underwood. Derbs 1G 73
Weston Underwood. Mil 5F 63
Westonzoyland. Som 3G 21
West Orchard. Dors 1D 14
West Overton. Wilts 5G 35
Westow. N Yor 3B 100
Westown. Per 1E 137
West Panson. Devn 3D 10
West Park. Hart 1B 106
West Parley. Dors 3F 15
West Peckham. Kent 5H 39
West Pelton. Dur 4F 115
West Pennard. Som 3A 22
West Pentire. Corn 2B 6
West Perry. Cambs 4A 64
West Pitcorthie. Fife 3H 137
West Plean. Stir 1B 128
West Poringland. Norf 5E 79
West Porlock. Som 2B 20
Westport. Som 1G 13
West Putford. Devn 1D 10
West Quantoxhead. Som 2E 20
Westra. V Glam 4E 33
West Rainton. Dur 5G 115
West Rasen. Linc 2H 87
West Ravendale. NE Lin 1B 88
Westray Airport. Orkn 2D 172
West Raynham. Norf 3A 78
Westrigg. W Lot 3C 128
West Rounton. N Yor 4B 106
West Row. Suff 3F 65
West Rudham. Norf 3H 77
West Runton. Norf 1D 78
Westruther. Bord 4C 130
Westry. Cambs 1C 64
West Saltoun. E Lot 3A 130
West Sandford. Devn 2B 12
West Sandwick. Shet 3F 173
West Scrafton. N Yor 1C 98
Westside. Orkn 5C 172
West Sleekburn. Nmbd 1F 115
West Somerton. Norf 4G 79
West Stafford. Dors 4C 14
West Stockwith. Notts 1E 87
West Stoke. W Sus 2G 17
West Stonesdale. N Yor 4B 104
West Stoughton. Som 2H 21
West Stour. Dors 4C 22
West Stourmouth. Kent 4G 41
West Stow. Suff 3H 65
West Stowell. Wilts 5G 35
West Strathan. High 2F 167
West Stratton. Hants 2D 24
West Street. Kent 5D 40
West Tanfield. N Yor 2E 99
West Taphouse. Corn 2F 7
West Tarbert. Arg 3G 125
West Thirston. Nmbd 4F 121
West Thorney. W Sus 2F 17
West Thurrock. Thur 3G 39
West Tilbury. Thur 3A 40
West Tisted. Hants 4E 25
West Tofts. Norf 1H 65
West Torrington. Linc 2A 88
West Town. Bath 5A 34
West Town. Hants 3F 17
West Town. N Som 5H 33
West Tytherley. Hants 4A 24
West Tytherton. Wilts 4E 35
West View. Hart 1C 106
Westville. Notts 1C 74
West Walton. Norf 4D 76
Westward. Cumb 5D 112
Westward Ho!. Devn 4E 19
Westwell. Kent 1D 28
Westwell. Oxon 5H 49
Westwell Leacon. Kent 1D 28
West Wellow. Hants 1A 16
West Wemyss. Fife 4F 137
Westwick. Cambs 4D 64
Westwick. Dur 3D 104
Westwick. Norf 3E 79
West Wick. N Som 5G 33
West Wickham. Cambs 1G 53
West Wickham. G Lon 4E 39
West Williamston. Pemb 4E 43
West Willoughby. Linc 1G 75
West Winch. Norf 4F 77
West Winterslow. Wilts 3H 23
West Wittering. W Sus 3F 17
West Witton. N Yor 1C 98
Westwood. Devn 3D 12
Westwood. Kent 4H 41
Westwood. Pet 1A 64
Westwood. S Lan 4H 127
Westwood. Wilts 1D 22
West Woodburn. Nmbd 1B 114
West Woodhay. W Ber 5B 36
West Woodlands. Som 2C 22
West Woodside. Cumb 5E 112
Westwoodside. N Lin 4H 93
West Worldham. Hants 3F 25
West Worlington. Devn 1A 12
West Worthing. W Sus 5C 26
West Wratting. Cambs 5F 65
West Wycombe. Buck 2G 37
West Wylam. Nmbd 3E 115
West Yatton. Wilts 4D 34
West Yell. Shet 3F 173
West Youlstone. Corn 1C 10
Wetheral. Cumb 4F 113
Wetherby. W Yor 5G 99
Wetherden. Suff 4C 66
Wetheringsett. Suff 4D 66
Wethersfield. Essx 2H 53
Wethersta. Shet 5E 173
Wetherup Street. Suff 4D 66
Wetley Rocks. Staf 1D 72
Wettenhall. Ches E 4A 84
Wetton. Staf 5F 85
Wetwang. E Yor 4D 100
Wetwood. Staf 2B 72
Wexcombe. Wilts 1A 24
Wexham Street. Buck 2A 38
Weybourne. Norf 1D 78
Weybourne. Surr 2G 25
Weybread. Suff 2E 67
Weybridge. Surr 4B 38
Weycroft. Devn 3G 13
Weydale. High 2D 168
Weyhill. Hants 2B 24
Weymouth. Dors 5B 14
Weythel. Powy 5E 59
Whaddon. Buck 2G 51
Whaddon. Cambs 1D 52
Whaddon. Glos 4D 48
Whaddon. Wilts 4G 23
Whale. Cumb 2G 103
Whaley. Derbs 3C 86
Whaley Bridge. Derbs 2E 85
Whaley Thorns. Derbs 3C 86
Whalley. Lanc 1F 91
Whalton. Nmbd 1E 115
Wham. N Yor 3G 97
Whaplode. Linc 3C 76
Whaplode Drove. Linc 4C 76
Whaplode St Catherine. Linc 3C 76
Wharfe. N Yor 3G 97
Wharles. Lanc 1C 90
Wharley End. C Beds 1H 51
Wharncliffe Side. S Yor 1G 85
Wharram-le-Street. N Yor 3C 100
Wharton. Ches W 4A 84
Wharton. Here 5H 59
Whashton. N Yor 4E 105
Whasset. Cumb 1E 97
Whatcote. Warw 1A 50
Whateley. Warw 1G 61
Whatfield. Suff 1D 54
Whatley. Som 2G 13
(nr. Chard)
Whatley. Som 2C 22
(nr. Frome)
Whatlington. E Sus 4B 28
Whatmore. Shrp 3A 60
Whatstandwell. Derbs 5H 85
Whatton. Notts 2E 75
Whauphill. Dum 5B 110
Whaw. N Yor 4C 104
Wheatacre. Norf 1G 67
Wheatcroft. Derbs 5A 86
Wheathampstead. Herts 4B 52
Wheathill. Shrp 2A 60
Wheatley. Devn 3B 12
Wheatley. Hants 2F 25
Wheatley. Oxon 5D 50
Wheatley. S Yor 4F 93
Wheatley. W Yor 2A 92
Wheatley Hill. Dur 1A 106
Wheatley Lane. Lanc 1G 91
Wheatley Park. S Yor 4F 93
Wheaton Aston. Staf 4C 72
Wheatstone Park. Staf 5C 72
Wheddon Cross. Som 3C 20
Wheelerstreet. Surr 1A 26
Wheelock. Ches E 5B 84
Wheelock Heath. Ches E 5B 84
Wheelton. Lanc 2E 90
Wheldrake. York 5A 100
Whelford. Glos 2G 35
Whelpley Hill. Buck 5H 51
Whelpo. Cumb 1E 102
Whelston. Flin 3E 82
Whenby. N Yor 3A 100
Whepstead. Suff 5H 65
Wherstead. Suff 1E 55
Wherwell. Hants 2B 24
Wheston. Derbs 3F 85
Whetsted. Kent 1A 28
Whetstone. G Lon 1D 38
Whetstone. Leics 1C 62
Whicham. Cumb 1A 96
Whichford. Warw 2B 50
Whickham. Tyne 3F 115
Whiddon. Devn 2E 11
Whiddon Down. Devn 3G 11
Whigstreet. Ang 4D 145
Whilton. Nptn 4D 62
Whimble. Devn 2D 10
Whimple. Devn 3D 12
Whimpwell Green. Norf 3F 79
Whinburgh. Norf 5C 78
Whin Lane End. Lanc 5C 96
Whinnyfold. Abers 5H 161
Whinny Hill. Stoc T 3A 106
Whippingham. IOW 3D 16
Whipsnade. C Beds 4A 52
Whipton. Devn 3C 12
Whirlow. S Yor 2H 85
Whisby. Linc 4G 87
Whissendine. Rut 4F 75
Whissonsett. Norf 3B 78
Whisterfield. Ches E 3C 84
Whistley Green. Wok 4F 37
Whiston. Mers 1G 83
Whiston. Nptn 4F 63
Whiston. S Yor 1B 86
Whiston. Staf 1E 73
(nr. Cheadle)
Whiston. Staf 4C 72
(nr. Penkridge)
Whiston Cross. Shrp 5B 72
Whiston Eaves. Staf 1E 73
Whitacre Heath. Warw 1G 61
Whitbeck. Cumb 1A 96
Whitbourne. Here 5B 60
Whitburn. Tyne 3H 115
Whitburn. W Lot 3C 128
Whitburn Colliery. Tyne 3H 115
Whitby. Ches W 3F 83
Whitby. N Yor 3F 107
Whitbyheath. Ches W 3F 83
Whitchester. Bord 4D 130
Whitchurch. Bath 5B 34
Whitchurch. Buck 3G 51
Whitchurch. Card 4E 33
Whitchurch. Devn 5E 11
Whitchurch. Hants 2C 24
Whitchurch. Here 4A 48
Whitchurch. Pemb 2C 42
Whitchurch. Shrp 1H 71
Whitchurch Canonicorum.
Dors 3G 13
Whitchurch Hill. Oxon 4E 37
Whitchurch-on-Thames. Oxon 4E 37
Whitcombe. Dors 4C 14
Whitcot. Shrp 1F 59
Whitcott Keysett. Shrp 2E 59
Whiteash Green. Essx 2A 54
Whitebog. High 2B 158
Whitebridge. High 2G 149
Whitebrook. Mon 5A 48
Whitecairns. Abers 2G 153
White Chapel. Lanc 5E 97
Whitechurch. Pemb 1F 43
White Colne. Essx 3B 54
White Coppice. Lanc 3E 90
White Corries. High 3G 141
Whitecraig. E Lot 2G 129
Whitecroft. Glos 5B 48
White Cross. Corn 4D 5
(nr. Mullion)
Whitecross. Corn 1D 6
(nr. Wadebridge)
Whitecross. Falk 2C 128
White End. Worc 2C 48
Whiteface. High 5E 164
Whitefarland. N Ayr 5G 125
Whitefaulds. S Ayr 4B 116
Whitefield. Dors 3E 15
Whitefield. G Man 4G 91
Whitefield. Som 4D 20
Whiteford. Abers 1E 152
Whitegate. Ches W 4A 84
Whitehall. Devn 1E 13
Whitehall. Hants 1F 25
Whitehall. Orkn 5F 172
Whitehall. W Sus 3C 26
Whitehaven. Cumb 3A 102
Whitehaven. Shrp 3E 71
Whitehill. Hants 3F 25
Whitehill. N Ayr 4D 126
Whitehills. Abers 2D 160
Whitehills. Ang 3D 144
White Horse Common. Norf 3F 79
Whitehough. Derbs 2E 85
Whitehouse. Abers 2D 152
Whitehouse. Arg 3G 125
Whiteinch. Glas 3G 127
Whitekirk. E Lot 1B 130
White Kirkley. Dur 1D 104
White Lackington. Dors 3C 14
Whitelackington. Som 1G 13
White Ladies Aston. Worc 5D 60
White Lee. W Yor 2C 92
Whiteley. Hants 1D 16
Whiteley Bank. IOW 4D 16
Whiteley Village. Surr 4B 38
Whitemans Green. W Sus 3E 27
White Mill. Carm 3E 45
Whitemire. Mor 3D 159
Whitemoor. Corn 3D 6
Whitenap. Hants 4B 24
Whiteness. Shet 7F 173
White Notley. Essx 4A 54
Whiteoak Green. Oxon 4B 50
Whiteparish. Wilts 4H 23
White Pit. Linc 3C 88
Whiterashes. Abers 1F 153
White Rocks. Here 3H 47
White Roding. Essx 4F 53
Whiterow. High 4F 169
Whiterow. Mor 3E 159
Whiteshill. Glos 5D 48
Whiteside. Nmbd 3A 114
Whiteside. W Lot 3C 128
Whitesmith. E Sus 4G 27
Whitestaunton. Som 1F 13
Whitestone. Abers 4D 152
Whitestone. Devn 3B 12
White Stone. Here 1A 48
Whitestones. Abers 3F 161
Whitestreet Green. Suff 2C 54

Whitewall Corner. *N Yor* 2B **100**
White Waltham. *Wind* 4G **37**
Whiteway. *Glos* 4E **49**
Whitewell. *Lanc* 5F **97**
Whitewell Bottom. *Lanc* 2G **91**
Whiteworks. *Devn* 5G **11**
Whitewreath. *Mor* 3G **159**
Whitfield. *D'dee* 5D **144**
Whitfield. *Kent* 1H **29**
Whitfield. *Nptn* 2E **50**
Whitfield. *Nmbd* 4A **114**
Whitfield. *S Glo* 2B **34**
Whitford. *Devn* 3F **13**
Whitford. *Flin* 3D **82**
Whitgift. *E Yor* 2B **94**
Whitgreave. *Staf* 3C **72**
Whithorn. *Dum* 5B **110**
Whiting Bay. *N Ayr* 3E **123**
Whitington. *Norf* 1G **65**
Whitkirk. *W Yor* 1D **92**
Whitland. *Carm* 3G **43**
Whitleigh. *Plym* 3A **8**
Whitletts. *S Ayr* 2C **116**
Whitley. *N Yor* 2F **93**
Whitley. *Wilts* 5D **35**
Whitley Bay. *Tyne* 2G **115**
Whitley Chapel. *Nmbd* 4C **114**
Whitley Heath. *Staf* 3C **72**
Whitley Lower. *W Yor* 3C **92**
Whitley Thorpe. *N Yor* 2F **93**
Whitlock's End. *W Mid* 3F **61**
Whitminster. *Glos* 5C **48**
Whitmore. *Dors* 2F **15**
Whitmore. *Staf* 1C **72**
Whitnage. *Devn* 1D **12**
Whitnash. *Warw* 4H **61**
Whitney. *Here* 1F **47**
Whitrigg. *Cumb* 4D **112**
(nr. Kirkbride)
Whitrigg. *Cumb* 1D **102**
(nr. Torpenhow)
Whitsbury. *Hants* 1G **15**
Whitsome. *Bord* 4E **131**
Whitson. *Newp* 3G **33**
Whitstable. *Kent* 4F **41**
Whitstone. *Corn* 3C **10**
Whittingham. *Nmbd* 3E **121**
Whittingslow. *Shrp* 2G **59**
Whittington. *Derbs* 3B **86**
Whittington. *Glos* 3F **49**
Whittington. *Lanc* 2F **97**
Whittington. *Shrp* 2F **71**
Whittington. *Staf* 2C **60**
(nr. Kinver)
Whittington. *Staf* 5F **73**
(nr. Lichfield)
Whittington. *Warw* 1G **61**
Whittington. *Worc* 5C **60**
Whittington Barracks. *Staf* 5F **73**
Whittlebury. *Nptn* 1E **51**
Whittleford. *Warw* 1H **61**
Whittle-le-Woods. *Lanc* 2D **90**
Whittlesey. *Cambs* 1B **64**
Whittlesford. *Cambs* 1E **53**
Whittlestone Head. *Bkbn* 3F **91**
Whitton. *N Lin* 2C **94**
Whitton. *Nmbd* 4E **121**
Whitton. *Powy* 4E **59**
Whitton. *Bord* 2B **120**
Whitton. *Shrp* 3H **59**
Whitton. *Stoc T* 2A **106**
Whittonditch. *Wilts* 4A **36**
Whittonstall. *Nmbd* 4D **114**
Whitway. *Hants* 1C **24**
Whitwell. *Derbs* 3C **86**
Whitwell. *Herts* 3B **52**
Whitwell. *IOW* 5D **16**
Whitwell. *N Yor* 5F **105**
Whitwell. *Rut* 5G **75**
Whitwell-on-the-Hill. *N Yor* 3B **100**
Whitwick. *Leics* 4B **74**
Whitwood. *W Yor* 2E **93**
Whitworth. *Lanc* 3G **91**
Whixall. *Shrp* 2H **71**
Whixley. *N Yor* 4G **99**
Whoberley. *W Mid* 3G **61**
Whorlton. *Dur* 3E **105**
Whorlton. *N Yor* 4B **106**
Whygate. *Nmbd* 2A **114**
Whyle. *Here* 4H **59**
Whyteleafe. *Surr* 5E **39**
Wibdon. *Glos* 2A **34**
Wibtoft. *Warw* 2B **62**
Wichenford. *Worc* 4B **60**
Wichling. *Kent* 5D **40**
Wick. *Bour* 3G **15**
Wick. *Devn* 2E **13**
Wick. *High* 3F **169**
Wick. *Som* 2F **21**
(nr. Bridgwater)
Wick. *Som* 1G **21**
(nr. Burnham-on-Sea)
Wick. *Som* 4H **21**
(nr. Somerton)
Wick. *S Glo* 4C **34**
Wick. *V Glam* 4C **32**
Wick. *W Sus* 5B **26**
Wick. *Wilts* 4G **23**
Wick. *Worc* 1E **49**
Wick Airport. *High* 3F **169**
Wicken. *Cambs* 3E **65**
Wicken. *Nptn* 2F **51**
Wicken Bonhunt. *Essx* 2E **53**
Wickenby. *Linc* 2H **87**
Wicken Green Village. *Norf* 2H **77**
Wickersley. *S Yor* 1B **86**
Wicker Street Green. *Suff* 1C **54**
Wickford. *Essx* 1B **40**
Wickham. *Hants* 1D **16**
Wickham. *W Ber* 4B **36**
Wickham Bishops. *Essx* 4B **54**
Wickhambreaux. *Kent* 5G **41**
Wickhambrook. *Suff* 5G **65**
Wickhamford. *Worc* 1F **49**
Wickham Green. *Suff* 4C **66**
Wickham Heath. *W Ber* 5C **36**
Wickham Market. *Suff* 5F **67**
Wickhampton. *Norf* 5G **79**
Wickham St Paul. *Essx* 2B **54**
Wickham Skeith. *Suff* 4C **66**
Wickham Street. *Suff* 4C **66**
Wick Hill. *Wok* 5F **37**
Wicklewood. *Norf* 5C **78**
Wickmere. *Norf* 2D **78**
Wick St Lawrence. *N Som* 5G **33**
Wickwar. *S Glo* 3C **34**
Widdington. *Essx* 2F **53**
Widdrington. *Nmbd* 5G **121**
Widdrington Station. *Nmbd* 5G **121**
Widecombe in the Moor. *Devn* 5H **11**
Widegates. *Corn* 3G **7**
Widemouth Bay. *Corn* 2C **10**
Wide Open. *Tyne* 2F **115**
Widewall. *Orkn* 8D **172**
Widford. *Essx* 5G **53**
Widford. *Herts* 4E **53**
Widham. *Wilts* 3F **35**
Widmer End. *Buck* 2G **37**
Widmerpool. *Notts* 3D **74**
Widnes. *Hal* 2H **83**
Widworthy. *Devn* 3F **13**
Wigan. *G Man* 4D **90**
Wigbeth. *Dors* 2F **15**
Wigborough. *Som* 1H **13**
Wiggaton. *Devn* 3E **12**
Wiggenhall St Germans. *Norf* 4E **77**
Wiggenhall St Mary Magdalen. *Norf* 4E **77**
Wiggenhall St Mary the Virgin. *Norf* 4E **77**
Wiggenhall St Peter. *Norf* 4F **77**
Wiggens Green. *Essx* 1G **53**
Wigginton. *Herts* 4H **51**
Wigginton. *Oxon* 2B **50**
Wigginton. *Staf* 5G **73**
Wigginton. *York* 4H **99**
Wigglesworth. *N Yor* 4H **97**
Wiggonby. *Cumb* 4D **112**
Wiggonholt. *W Sus* 4B **26**
Wighill. *N Yor* 5G **99**
Wighton. *Norf* 1B **78**
Wightwick. *Staf* 1C **60**
Wigley. *Hants* 1B **16**
Wigmore. *Here* 4G **59**
Wigmore. *Medw* 4C **40**
Wigsley. *Notts* 3F **87**
Wigsthorpe. *Nptn* 2H **63**
Wigston. *Leics* 1D **62**
Wigtoft. *Linc* 2B **76**
Wigton. *Cumb* 5D **112**
Wigtown. *Dum* 4B **110**
Wigtwizzle. *S Yor* 1G **85**
Wike. *W Yor* 5F **99**
Wilbarston. *Nptn* 2F **63**
Wilberfoss. *E Yor* 4B **100**
Wilburton. *Cambs* 3D **65**
Wilby. *Norf* 2C **66**
Wilby. *Nptn* 4F **63**
Wilby. *Suff* 3E **67**
Wilcot. *Wilts* 5G **35**
Wilcott. *Shrp* 4F **71**
Wilcove. *Corn* 3A **8**
Wildboarclough. *Ches E* 4D **85**
Wilden. *Bed* 5H **63**
Wilden. *Worc* 3C **60**
Wildern. *Hants* 1C **16**
Wilderspool. *Warr* 2A **84**
Wilde Street. *Suff* 3G **65**
Wildhern. *Hants* 1B **24**
Wildmanbridge. *S Lan* 4B **128**
Wildmoor. *Worc* 3D **60**
Wildsworth. *Linc* 1F **87**
Wildwood. *Staf* 3D **72**
Wilford. *Nott* 2C **74**
Wilkesley. *Ches E* 1A **72**
Wilkhaven. *High* 5G **165**
Wilkieston. *W Lot* 3E **129**
Wilksby. *Linc* 4B **88**
Willand. *Devn* 1D **12**
Willaston. *Ches E* 5A **84**
Willaston. *Ches W* 3F **83**
Willaston. *IOM* 4C **108**
Willen. *Mil* 1G **51**
Willenhall. *W Mid* 3A **62**
(nr. Coventry)
Willenhall. *W Mid* 1D **60**
(nr. Wolverhampton)
Willerby. *E Yor* 1D **94**
Willerby. *N Yor* 2E **101**
Willersey. *Glos* 2G **49**
Willersley. *Here* 1G **47**
Willesborough. *Kent* 1E **28**
Willesborough Lees. *Kent* 1E **29**
Willesden. *G Lon* 2D **38**
Willesley. *Wilts* 3D **34**
Willett. *Som* 3E **20**
Willey. *Shrp* 1A **60**
Willey. *Warw* 2B **62**
Willey Green. *Surr* 5A **38**
Williamscot. *Oxon* 1C **50**
Willian. *Herts* 2C **52**
Willingale. *Essx* 5F **53**
Willingdon. *E Sus* 5G **27**
Willingham. *Cambs* 3D **64**
Willingham by Stow. *Linc* 2F **87**
Willingham Green. *Cambs* 5F **65**
Willington. *Bed* 1B **52**
Willington. *Derbs* 3G **73**
Willington. *Dur* 1E **105**
Willington. *Tyne* 3G **115**
Willington. *Warw* 2A **50**
Willington Corner. *Ches W* 4H **83**
Willisham Tye. *Suff* 5C **66**
Willitoft. *E Yor* 1H **93**
Williton. *Som* 2D **20**
Willoughbridge. *Staf* 1B **72**
Willoughby. *Linc* 3D **88**
Willoughby. *Warw* 4C **62**
Willoughby-on-the-Wolds. *Notts* 3D **74**
Willoughby Waterleys. *Leics* 1C **62**
Willoughton. *Linc* 1G **87**
Willow Green. *Worc* 5B **60**
Willows Green. *Essx* 4H **53**
Willsbridge. *S Glo* 4B **34**
Willslock. *Staf* 2E **73**
Wilmcote. *Warw* 5F **61**
Wilmington. *Bath* 5B **34**
Wilmington. *Devn* 3F **13**
Wilmington. *E Sus* 5G **27**
Wilmington. *Kent* 3G **39**
Wilmslow. *Ches E* 2C **84**
Wilnecote. *Staf* 5G **73**
Wilney Green. *Norf* 2C **66**
Wilpshire. *Lanc* 1E **91**
Wilsden. *W Yor* 1A **92**
Wilsford. *Linc* 1H **75**
Wilsford. *Wilts* 3G **23**
(nr. Amesbury)
Wilsford. *Wilts* 1G **23**
(nr. Devizes)
Wilsill. *N Yor* 3D **98**
Wilsley Green. *Kent* 2B **28**
Wilson. *Here* 3A **48**
Wilson. *Leics* 3B **74**
Wilsontown. *S Lan* 4C **128**
Wilstead. *Bed* 1A **52**
Wilsthorpe. *E Yor* 3F **101**
Wilsthorpe. *Linc* 4H **75**
Wilstone. *Herts* 4H **51**
Wilton. *Cumb* 3B **102**
Wilton. *N Yor* 1C **100**
Wilton. *Red C* 3C **106**
Wilton. *Bord* 3H **119**
Wilton. *Wilts* 5A **36**
(nr. Marlborough)
Wilton. *Wilts* 3F **23**
(nr. Salisbury)
Wimbish. *Essx* 2F **53**
Wimbish Green. *Essx* 2G **53**
Wimblebury. *Staf* 4E **73**
Wimbledon. *G Lon* 3D **38**
Wimblington. *Cambs* 1D **64**
Wimboldsley. *Ches W* 4A **84**
Wimborne Minster. *Dors* 2F **15**
Wimborne St Giles. *Dors* 1F **15**
Wimbotsham. *Norf* 5F **77**
Wimpole. *Cambs* 1D **52**
Wimpstone. *Warw* 1H **49**
Wincanton. *Som* 4C **22**
Winceby. *Linc* 4C **88**
Wincham. *Ches W* 3A **84**
Winchburgh. *W Lot* 2D **129**
Winchcombe. *Glos* 3F **49**
Winchelsea. *E Sus* 4D **28**
Winchelsea Beach. *E Sus* 4D **28**
Winchester. *Hants* 4C **24**
Winchet Hill. *Kent* 1B **28**
Winchfield. *Hants* 1F **25**
Winchmore Hill. *Buck* 1A **38**
Winchmore Hill. *G Lon* 1E **39**
Wincle. *Ches E* 4D **84**
Windermere. *Cumb* 5F **103**
Winderton. *Warw* 1B **50**
Windhill. *High* 4H **157**
Windle Hill. *Ches W* 3F **83**
Windlesham. *Surr* 4A **38**
Windley. *Derbs* 1H **73**
Windmill. *Derbs* 3F **85**
Windmill Hill. *E Sus* 4H **27**
Windmill Hill. *Som* 1G **13**
Windrush. *Glos* 4G **49**
Windsor. *Wind* 3A **38**
Windsor Green. *Suff* 5A **66**
Windyedge. *Abers* 4G **153**
Windygates. *Fife* 3F **137**
Windyharbour. *Ches E* 3C **84**
Windyknowe. *W Lot* 3C **128**
Wineham. *W Sus* 3D **26**
Winestead. *E Yor* 2G **95**
Winfarthing. *Norf* 2D **66**
Winford. *IOW* 4D **16**
Winford. *N Som* 5A **34**
Winforton. *Here* 1F **47**
Winfrith Newburgh. *Dors* 4D **14**
Wing. *Buck* 3G **51**
Wing. *Rut* 5F **75**
Wingate. *Dur* 1A **106**
Wingates. *G Man* 4E **91**
Wingates. *Nmbd* 5F **121**
Wingerworth. *Derbs* 4A **86**
Wingfield. *C Beds* 3A **52**
Wingfield. *Suff* 3E **67**
Wingfield. *Wilts* 1D **22**
Wingfield Park. *Derbs* 5A **86**
Wingham. *Kent* 5G **41**
Wingmore. *Kent* 1F **29**
Wingrave. *Buck* 4G **51**
Winkburn. *Notts* 5E **86**
Winkfield. *Brac* 3A **38**
Winkfield Row. *Brac* 4G **37**
Winkhill. *Staf* 5E **85**
Winklebury. *Hants* 1E **24**
Winkleigh. *Devn* 2G **11**
Winksley. *N Yor* 2E **99**
Winkton. *Dors* 3G **15**
Winlaton. *Tyne* 3E **115**
Winlaton Mill. *Tyne* 3E **115**
Winless. *High* 3F **169**
Winmarleigh. *Lanc* 5D **96**
Winnal Common. *Here* 2H **47**
Winnard's Perch. *Corn* 2D **6**
Winnersh. *Wok* 4F **37**
Winnington. *Ches W* 3A **84**
Winnington. *Staf* 2B **72**
Winnothdale. *Staf* 1E **73**
Winscales. *Cumb* 2B **102**
Winscombe. *N Som* 1H **21**
Winsford. *Ches W* 4A **84**
Winsford. *Som* 3C **20**
Winsham. *Devn* 3F **19**
Winsham. *Som* 2G **13**
Winshill. *Staf* 3G **73**
Winsh-wen. *Swan* 3F **31**
Winskill. *Cumb* 1G **103**
Winslade. *Hants* 2E **25**
Winsley. *Wilts* 5C **34**
Winslow. *Buck* 3F **51**
Winson. *Glos* 5F **49**
Winson Green. *W Mid* 2E **61**
Winsor. *Hants* 1B **16**
Winster. *Cumb* 5F **103**
Winster. *Derbs* 4G **85**
Winston. *Dur* 3E **105**
Winston. *Suff* 4D **66**
Winstone. *Glos* 5E **49**
Winswell. *Devn* 1E **11**
Winterborne Clenston. *Dors* 2D **14**
Winterborne Herringston. *Dors* 4B **14**
Winterborne Houghton. *Dors* 2D **14**
Winterborne Kingston. *Dors* 3D **14**
Winterborne Monkton. *Dors* 4B **14**
Winterborne St Martin. *Dors* 4B **14**
Winterborne Stickland. *Dors* 2D **14**
Winterborne Whitechurch. *Dors* 2D **14**
Winterborne Zelston. *Dors* 3E **15**
Winterbourne. *S Glo* 3B **34**
Winterbourne. *W Ber* 4C **36**
Winterbourne Abbas. *Dors* 3B **14**
Winterbourne Bassett. *Wilts* 4G **35**
Winterbourne Dauntsey. *Wilts* 3G **23**
Winterbourne Earls. *Wilts* 3G **23**
Winterbourne Gunner. *Wilts* 3G **23**
Winterbourne Monkton. *Wilts* 4F **35**
Winterbourne Steepleton. *Dors* 4B **14**
Winterbourne Stoke. *Wilts* 2F **23**
Winterbrook. *Oxon* 3E **36**
Winterburn. *N Yor* 4B **98**
Winter Gardens. *Essx* 2B **40**
Winterhay Green. *Som* 1G **13**
Winteringham. *N Lin* 2C **94**
Winterley. *Ches E* 5B **84**
Wintersett. *W Yor* 3D **93**
Winterton. *N Lin* 3C **94**
Winterton-on-Sea. *Norf* 4G **79**
Winthorpe. *Linc* 4E **89**
Winthorpe. *Notts* 5F **87**
Winton. *Bour* 3F **15**
Winton. *Cumb* 3A **104**

Winton. *E Sus* 5G **27**
Wintringham. *N Yor* 2C **100**
Winwick. *Cambs* 2A **64**
Winwick. *Nptn* 3D **62**
Winwick. *Warr* 1A **84**
Wirksworth. *Derbs* 5G **85**
Wirswall. *Ches E* 1H **71**
Wisbech. *Cambs* 4D **76**
Wisbech St Mary. *Cambs* 5D **76**
Wisborough Green. *W Sus* 3B **26**
Wiseton. *Notts* 2E **86**
Wishaw. *N Lan* 4B **128**
Wishaw. *Warw* 1F **61**
Wisley. *Surr* 5B **38**
Wispington. *Linc* 3B **88**
Wissenden. *Kent* 1D **28**
Wissett. *Suff* 3F **67**
Wistanstow. *Shrp* 2G **59**
Wistanswick. *Shrp* 3A **72**
Wistaston. *Ches E* 5A **84**
Wiston. *Pemb* 3E **43**
Wiston. *S Lan* 1B **118**
Wiston. *W Sus* 4C **26**
Wistow. *Cambs* 2B **64**
Wistow. *N Yor* 1F **93**
Wiswell. *Lanc* 1F **91**
Witcham. *Cambs* 2D **64**
Witchampton. *Dors* 2E **15**
Witchford. *Cambs* 3E **65**
Witham. *Essx* 4B **54**
Witham Friary. *Som* 2C **22**
Witham on the Hill. *Linc* 4H **75**
Witham St Hughs. *Linc* 4F **87**
Withcall. *Linc* 2B **88**
Witherenden Hill. *E Sus* 3H **27**
Withergate. *Norf* 3E **79**
Witheridge. *Devn* 1B **12**
Witheridge Hill. *Oxon* 3E **37**
Witherley. *Leics* 1H **61**
Withermarsh Green. *Suff* 2D **54**
Withern. *Linc* 2D **88**
Withernsea. *E Yor* 2G **95**
Withernwick. *E Yor* 5F **101**
Withersdale Street. *Suff* 2E **67**
Withersfield. *Suff* 1G **53**
Witherslack. *Cumb* 1D **96**
Withiel. *Corn* 2D **6**
Withiel Florey. *Som* 3C **20**
Withington. *Glos* 4F **49**
Withington. *G Man* 1C **84**
Withington. *Here* 1A **48**
Withington. *Shrp* 4H **71**
Withington. *Staf* 2E **73**
Withington Green. *Ches E* 3C **84**
Withington Marsh. *Here* 1A **48**
Withleigh. *Devn* 1C **12**
Withnell. *Lanc* 2E **91**
Withnell Fold. *Lanc* 2E **90**
Withybrook. *Warw* 2B **62**
Withycombe. *Som* 2D **20**
Withycombe Raleigh. *Devn* 4D **12**
Withyham. *E Sus* 2F **27**
Withypool. *Som* 3B **20**
Witley. *Surr* 1A **26**
Witnesham. *Suff* 5D **66**
Witney. *Oxon* 4B **50**
Wittering. *Pet* 5H **75**
Wittersham. *Kent* 3D **28**
Witton. *Norf* 5F **79**
Witton. *Worc* 4D **60**
Witton Bridge. *Norf* 2F **79**
Witton Gilbert. *Dur* 5F **115**
Witton-le-Wear. *Dur* 1E **105**
Witton Park. *Dur* 1E **105**
Wiveliscombe. *Som* 4D **20**
Wivelrod. *Hants* 3E **25**
Wivelsfield. *E Sus* 3E **27**
Wivelsfield Green. *E Sus* 4E **27**
Wivenhoe. *Essx* 3D **54**
Wiveton. *Norf* 1C **78**
Wix. *Essx* 3E **55**
Wixford. *Warw* 5E **61**
Wixhill. *Shrp* 3H **71**
Wixoe. *Suff* 1H **53**
Woburn. *C Beds* 2H **51**
Woburn Sands. *Mil* 2H **51**
Woking. *Surr* 5B **38**
Wokingham. *Wok* 5G **37**
Wolborough. *Devn* 5B **12**
Woldingham. *Surr* 5E **39**
Wold Newton. *E Yor* 2E **101**
Wold Newton. *NE Lin* 1B **88**
Wolferlow. *Here* 4A **60**
Wolferton. *Norf* 3F **77**
Wolfhill. *Per* 5A **144**
Wolf's Castle. *Pemb* 2D **42**
Wolfsdale. *Pemb* 2D **42**
Wolgarston. *Staf* 4D **72**
Wollaston. *Nptn* 4G **63**
Wollaston. *Shrp* 4F **71**
Wollaston. *W Mid* 2C **60**
Wollaton. *Nott* 1C **74**
Wollerton. *Shrp* 2A **72**
Wollescote. *W Mid* 2D **60**
Wolseley Bridge. *Staf* 3E **73**
Wolsingham. *Dur* 1D **105**
Wolstanton. *Staf* 1C **72**
Wolston. *Warw* 3B **62**
Wolsty. *Cumb* 4C **112**
Wolterton. *Norf* 2D **78**
Wolvercote. *Oxon* 5C **50**
Wolverhampton. *W Mid* 1D **60**
Wolverley. *Shrp* 2G **71**
Wolverley. *Worc* 3C **60**
Wolverton. *Hants* 1D **24**
Wolverton. *Mil* 1G **51**
Wolverton. *Warw* 4G **61**
Wolverton. *Wilts* 3C **22**
Wolverton Common. *Hants* 1D **24**
Wolvesnewton. *Mon* 2H **33**
Wolvey. *Warw* 2B **62**
Wolvey Heath. *Warw* 2B **62**
Wolviston. *Stoc T* 2B **106**
Womaston. *Powy* 4E **59**
Wombleton. *N Yor* 1A **100**
Wombourne. *Staf* 1C **60**
Wombwell. *S Yor* 4D **93**
Womenswold. *Kent* 5G **41**
Womersley. *N Yor* 3F **93**
Wonersh. *Surr* 1B **26**
Wonson. *Devn* 4G **11**
Wonston. *Dors* 2C **14**
Wonston. *Hants* 3C **24**
Wooburn. *Buck* 2A **38**
Wooburn Green. *Buck* 2A **38**
Wood. *Pemb* 2C **42**
Woodacott. *Devn* 2D **11**
Woodale. *N Yor* 2C **98**
Woodall. *S Yor* 2B **86**
Woodbank. *Ches W* 3F **83**
Woodbastwick. *Norf* 4F **79**
Woodbeck. *Notts* 3E **87**
Woodborough. *Notts* 1D **74**
Woodborough. *Wilts* 1G **23**
Woodbridge. *Devn* 3E **13**
Woodbridge. *Dors* 1C **14**
Woodbridge. *Suff* 1F **55**
Wood Burcote. *Nptn* 1E **51**
Woodbury. *Devn* 4D **12**
Woodbury Salterton. *Devn* 4D **12**
Woodchester. *Glos* 5D **48**
Woodchurch. *Kent* 2D **28**
Woodchurch. *Mers* 2E **83**
Woodcock Heath. *Staf* 3E **73**
Woodcombe. *Som* 2C **20**
Woodcote. *Oxon* 3E **37**
Woodcote Green. *Worc* 3D **60**
Woodcott. *Hants* 1C **24**
Woodcroft. *Glos* 2A **34**
Woodcutts. *Dors* 1E **15**
Wood Dalling. *Norf* 3C **78**
Woodditton. *Cambs* 5F **65**
Woodeaton. *Oxon* 4D **50**
Wood Eaton. *Staf* 4C **72**
Wood End. *Bed* 4H **63**
Woodend. *Cumb* 5C **102**
Wood End. *Herts* 3D **52**
Woodend. *Nptn* 1E **50**
Woodend. *Staf* 3F **73**
Wood End. *Warw* 2G **61** (nr. Bedworth)
Wood End. *Warw* 1G **61** (nr. Dordon)
Wood End. *Warw* 3F **61** (nr. Tanworth-in-Arden)
Woodend. *W Sus* 2G **17**
Wood Enderby. *Linc* 4B **88**
Woodend Green. *Essx* 3F **53**
Woodfalls. *Wilts* 4G **23**
Woodfield. *Oxon* 3D **50**
Woodfields. *Lanc* 1E **91**
Woodford. *Corn* 1C **10**
Woodford. *Devn* 3D **9**
Woodford. *Glos* 2B **34**
Woodford. *G Lon* 1E **39**
Woodford. *G Man* 2C **84**
Woodford. *Nptn* 3G **63**
Woodford. *Plym* 3B **8**
Woodford Green. *G Lon* 1F **39**
Woodford Halse. *Nptn* 5C **62**
Woodgate. *Norf* 4C **78**
Woodgate. *W Mid* 2D **61**
Woodgate. *W Sus* 5A **26**
Woodgate. *Worc* 4D **60**
Wood Green. *G Lon* 1D **39**
Woodgreen. *Hants* 1G **15**
Woodgreen. *Oxon* 4B **50**
Wood Hall. *E Yor* 1E **95**
Woodhall. *Inv* 2E **127**
Woodhall. *Linc* 4B **88**
Woodhall. *N Yor* 5C **104**
Woodhall Spa. *Linc* 4A **88**
Woodham. *Surr* 4B **38**
Woodham Ferrers. *Essx* 1B **40**
Woodham Mortimer. *Essx* 5B **54**
Woodham Walter. *Essx* 5B **54**
Woodhaven. *Fife* 1G **137**
Wood Hayes. *W Mid* 5D **72**
Woodhead. *Abers* 2G **161** (nr. Fraserburgh)
Woodhead. *Abers* 5E **161** (nr. Fyvie)
Woodhill. *N Som* 4H **33**
Woodhill. *Shrp* 2B **60**
Woodhill. *Som* 4G **21**
Woodhorn. *Nmbd* 1G **115**
Woodhouse. *Leics* 4C **74**
Woodhouse. *S Yor* 2B **86**
Woodhouse. *W Yor* 1C **92** (nr. Leeds)
Woodhouse. *W Yor* 2D **93** (nr. Normanton)
Woodhouse Eaves. *Leics* 4C **74**
Woodhouses. *Ches W* 3H **83**
Woodhouses. *G Man* 4H **91** (nr. Failsworth)
Woodhouses. *G Man* 1B **84** (nr. Sale)
Woodhouses. *Staf* 4F **73**
Woodhuish. *Devn* 3F **9**
Woodhurst. *Cambs* 3C **64**
Woodingdean. *Brig* 5E **27**
Woodland. *Devn* 2D **9**
Woodland. *Dur* 2D **104**
Woodland Head. *Devn* 3A **12**
Woodlands. *Abers* 4E **153**
Woodlands. *Dors* 2F **15**
Woodlands. *Hants* 1B **16**
Woodlands. *Kent* 4G **39**
Woodlands. *N Yor* 4F **99**
Woodlands. *S Yor* 4F **93**
Woodlands Park. *Wind* 4G **37**
Woodlands St Mary. *W Ber* 4B **36**
Woodlane. *Shrp* 3A **72**
Woodlane. *Staf* 3F **73**
Woodleigh. *Devn* 4D **8**
Woodlesford. *W Yor* 2D **92**
Woodley. *G Man* 1D **84**
Woodley. *Wok* 4F **37**
Woodmancote. *Glos* 3E **49** (nr. Cheltenham)
Woodmancote. *Glos* 5F **49** (nr. Cirencester)
Woodmancote. *W Sus* 2F **17** (nr. Chichester)
Woodmancote. *W Sus* 4D **26** (nr. Henfield)
Woodmancote. *Worc* 1E **49**
Woodmancott. *Hants* 2D **24**
Woodmansey. *E Yor* 1D **94**
Woodmansgreen. *W Sus* 4G **25**
Woodmansterne. *Surr* 5D **39**
Woodmanton. *Devn* 4D **12**
Woodmill. *Staf* 3F **73**
Woodminton. *Wilts* 4F **23**
Woodnesborough. *Kent* 5H **41**
Woodnewton. *Nptn* 1H **63**
Woodnook. *Linc* 2G **75**
Wood Norton. *Norf* 3C **78**
Woodplumpton. *Lanc* 1D **90**
Woodrising. *Norf* 5B **78**
Woodrow. *Cumb* 5D **112**
Woodrow. *Dors* 1C **14** (nr. Fifehead Neville)
Woodrow. *Dors* 2C **14** (nr. Hazelbury Bryan)
Wood Row. *W Yor* 2D **93**
Woods Eaves. *Here* 1F **47**
Woodseaves. *Shrp* 2A **72**
Woodseaves. *Staf* 3B **72**
Woodsend. *Wilts* 4H **35**
Woodsetts. *S Yor* 2C **86**
Woodsford. *Dors* 3C **14**
Wood's Green. *E Sus* 2H **27**
Woodshaw. *Wilts* 3F **35**
Woodside. *Aber* 3G **153**
Woodside. *Brac* 3A **38**
Woodside. *Derbs* 1A **74**
Woodside. *Dum* 2B **112**
Woodside. *Dur* 2E **105**
Woodside. *Fife* 3G **137**
Woodside. *Herts* 5C **52**
Woodside. *Per* 5B **144**
Wood Stanway. *Glos* 2F **49**
Woodstock. *Oxon* 4C **50**
Woodstock Slop. *Pemb* 2E **43**
Woodston. *Pet* 1A **64**
Wood Street. *Norf* 3F **79**
Wood Street Village. *Surr* 5A **38**
Woodthorpe. *Derbs* 3B **86**
Woodthorpe. *Leics* 4C **74**
Woodthorpe. *Linc* 2D **88**
Woodthorpe. *York* 5H **99**
Woodton. *Norf* 1E **67**
Woodtown. *Devn* 4E **19** (nr. Bideford)
Woodtown. *Devn* 4E **19** (nr. Littleham)
Woodvale. *Mers* 3B **90**
Woodville. *Derbs* 4H **73**
Woodwalton. *Cambs* 2B **64**
Woodyates. *Dors* 1F **15**
Woody Bay. *Devn* 2G **19**
Woofferton. *Shrp* 4H **59**
Wookey. *Som* 2A **22**
Wookey Hole. *Som* 2A **22**
Wool. *Dors* 4D **14**
Woolacombe. *Devn* 2E **19**
Woolage Green. *Kent* 1G **29**
Woolage Village. *Kent* 5G **41**
Woolaston. *Glos* 2A **34**
Woolavington. *Som* 2G **21**
Woolbeding. *W Sus* 4G **25**
Woolcotts. *Som* 3C **20**
Wooldale. *W Yor* 4B **92**
Wooler. *Nmbd* 2D **121**
Woolfardisworthy. *Devn* 4D **18** (nr. Bideford)
Woolfardisworthy. *Devn* 2B **12** (nr. Crediton)
Woolfords. *S Lan* 4D **128**
Woolgarston. *Dors* 4E **15**
Woolhampton. *W Ber* 5D **36**
Woolhope. *Here* 2B **48**
Woolland. *Dors* 2C **14**
Woollard. *Bath* 5B **34**
Woolley. *Bath* 5C **34**
Woolley. *Cambs* 3A **64**
Woolley. *Corn* 1C **10**
Woolley. *Derbs* 4A **86**
Woolley. *W Yor* 3D **92**
Woolley Green. *Wilts* 5D **34**
Woolmere Green. *Worc* 4D **60**
Woolmer Green. *Herts* 4C **52**
Woolminstone. *Som* 2H **13**
Woolpit. *Suff* 4B **66**
Woolridge. *Glos* 3D **48**
Woolscott. *Warw* 4B **62**
Woolsery. *Devn* 4D **18**
Woolsington. *Tyne* 3E **115**
Woolstaston. *Shrp* 1G **59**
Woolsthorpe By Belvoir. *Linc* 2F **75**
Woolsthorpe-by-Colsterworth. *Linc* 3G **75**
Woolston. *Devn* 4D **8**
Woolston. *Shrp* 2G **59** (nr. Church Stretton)
Woolston. *Shrp* 3F **71** (nr. Oswestry)
Woolston. *Som* 4B **22**
Woolston. *Sotn* 1C **16**
Woolston. *Warr* 1A **84**
Woolstone. *Glos* 2E **49**
Woolstone. *Oxon* 3A **36**
Woolston Green. *Devn* 2D **9**
Woolton. *Mers* 2G **83**
Woolton Hill. *Hants* 5C **36**
Woolverstone. *Suff* 2E **55**
Woolverton. *Som* 1C **22**
Woolwell. *Devn* 2B **8**
Woolwich. *G Lon* 3F **39**
Woonton. *Here* 5F **59** (nr. Kington)
Woonton. *Here* 4H **59** (nr. Leominster)
Wooperton. *Nmbd* 2E **121**
Woore. *Shrp* 1B **72**
Wooth. *Dors* 3H **13**
Wooton. *Shrp* 2B **60**
Wootton. *Bed* 1A **52**
Wootton. *Hants* 3H **15**
Wootton. *IOW* 3D **16**
Wootton. *Kent* 1G **29**
Wootton. *Nptn* 5E **63**
Wootton. *N Lin* 3D **94**
Wootton. *Oxon* 5C **50** (nr. Abingdon)
Wootton. *Oxon* 4C **50** (nr. Woodstock)
Wootton. *Shrp* 3G **59** (nr. Ludlow)
Wootton. *Shrp* 3F **71** (nr. Oswestry)
Wootton. *Staf* 3C **72** (nr. Eccleshall)
Wootton. *Staf* 1F **73** (nr. Ellastone)
Wootton Bridge. *IOW* 3D **16**
Wootton Common. *IOW* 3D **16**
Wootton Courtenay. *Som* 2C **20**
Wootton Fitzpaine. *Dors* 3G **13**
Wootton Rivers. *Wilts* 5G **35**
Wootton St Lawrence. *Hants* 1D **24**
Wootton Wawen. *Warw* 4F **61**
Worcester. *Worc* 5C **60**
Worcester Park. *G Lon* 4D **38**
Wordsley. *W Mid* 2C **60**
Worfield. *Shrp* 1B **60**
Workhouse Green. *Suff* 2C **54**
Workington. *Cumb* 2A **102**
Worksop. *Notts* 3C **86**
Worlaby. *N Lin* 3D **94**
Worlds End. *Hants* 1E **17**
Worldsend. *Shrp* 1G **59**
World's End. *W Ber* 4C **36**
Worlds End. *W Mid* 2F **61**
World's End. *W Sus* 4E **27**

Worle. *N Som* 5G **33**
Worleston. *Ches E* 5A **84**
Worley. *Glos* 2D **34**
Worlingham. *Suff* 1G **67**
Worlington. *Suff* 3F **65**
Worlingworth. *Suff* 4E **67**
Wormbridge. *Here* 2H **47**
Wormegay. *Norf* 4F **77**
Wormelow Tump. *Here* 2H **47**
Wormhill. *Derbs* 3F **85**
Wormingford. *Essx* 2C **54**
Worminghall. *Buck* 5E **51**
Wormington. *Glos* 2F **49**
Worminster. *Som* 2A **22**
Wormit. *Fife* 1F **137**
Wormleighton. *Warw* 5B **62**
Wormley. *Herts* 5D **52**
Wormley. *Surr* 2A **26**
Wormshill. *Kent* 5C **40**
Wormsley. *Here* 1H **47**
Worplesdon. *Surr* 5A **38**
Worrall. *S Yor* 1H **85**
Worsbrough. *S Yor* 4D **92**
Worsley. *G Man* 4F **91**
Worstead. *Norf* 3F **79**
Worsthorne. *Lanc* 1G **91**
Worston. *Lanc* 5G **97**
Worth. *Kent* 5H **41**
Worth. *W Sus* 2E **27**
Wortham. *Suff* 3C **66**
Worthen. *Shrp* 5F **71**
Worthenbury. *Wrex* 1G **71**
Worthing. *Norf* 4B **78**
Worthing. *W Sus* 5C **26**
Worthington. *Leics* 3B **74**
Worth Matravers. *Dors* 5E **15**
Worting. *Hants* 1E **24**
Wortley. *Glos* 2C **34**
Wortley. *S Yor* 1H **85**
Wortley. *W Yor* 1C **92**
Worton. *N Yor* 5C **104**
Worton. *Wilts* 1E **23**
Wortwell. *Norf* 2E **67**
Wotherton. *Shrp* 5E **71**
Wothorpe. *Nptn* 5H **75**
Wotter. *Devn* 2B **8**
Wotton. *Glos* 4D **48**
Wotton. *Surr* 1C **26**
Wotton-under-Edge. *Glos* 2C **34**
Wotton Underwood.
Buck 4E **51**
Wouldham. *Kent* 4B **40**
Wrabness. *Essx* 2E **55**
Wrafton. *Devn* 3E **19**
Wragby. *Linc* 3A **88**
Wragby. *W Yor* 3E **93**
Wramplingham. *Norf* 5D **78**
Wrangbrook. *W Yor* 3E **93**
Wrangle. *Linc* 5D **88**
Wrangle Lowgate. *Linc* 5D **88**
Wrangway. *Som* 1E **13**
Wrantage. *Som* 4G **21**
Wrawby. *N Lin* 4D **94**
Wraxall. *N Som* 4H **33**
Wraxall. *Som* 3B **22**
Wray. *Lanc* 3F **97**
Wraysbury. *Wind* 3B **38**
Wrayton. *Lanc* 2F **97**
Wrea Green. *Lanc* 1B **90**
Wreay. *Cumb* 5F **113**
(nr. Carlisle)
Wreay. *Cumb* 2F **103**
(nr. Penrith)
Wrecclesham. *Surr* 2G **25**
Wrecsam. *Wrex* 5F **83**
Wrekenton. *Tyne* 4F **115**
Wrelton. *N Yor* 1B **100**
Wrenbury. *Ches E* 1H **71**
Wreningham. *Norf* 1D **66**
Wrentham. *Suff* 2G **67**
Wrenthorpe. *W Yor* 2D **92**
Wrentnall. *Shrp* 5G **71**
Wressle. *E Yor* 1H **93**
Wressle. *N Lin* 4C **94**
Wrestlingworth. *C Beds* 1C **52**
Wretton. *Norf* 1F **65**
Wrexham. *Wrex* 5F **83**
Wrexham Industrial Estate.
Wrex 1F **71**
Wreyland. *Devn* 4A **12**
Wrickton. *Shrp* 2A **60**
Wrightlington Bar. *Lanc* 3D **90**
Wright's Green. *Essx* 4F **53**
Wrinehill. *Staf* 1B **72**
Wrington. *N Som* 5H **33**
Writtle. *Essx* 5G **53**
Wrockwardine. *Telf* 4A **72**
Wroot. *N Lin* 4H **93**
Wrotham. *Kent* 5H **39**
Wrotham Heath. *Kent* 5H **39**
Wroughton. *Swin* 3G **35**
Wroxall. *IOW* 4D **16**
Wroxall. *Warw* 3G **61**
Wroxeter. *Shrp* 5H **71**
Wroxham. *Norf* 4F **79**
Wroxton. *Oxon* 1C **50**
Wyaston. *Derbs* 1F **73**
Wyatt's Green. *Essx* 1G **39**
Wybers Wood. *NE Lin* 4F **95**
Wyberton. *Linc* 1C **76**
Wyboston. *Bed* 5A **64**
Wybunbury. *Ches E* 1A **72**
Wychbold. *Worc* 4D **60**
Wych Cross. *E Sus* 2F **27**
Wychnor. *Staf* 4F **73**
Wychnor Bridges. *Staf* 4F **73**
Wyck. *Hants* 3F **25**
Wyck Hill. *Glos* 3G **49**
Wyck Rissington. *Glos* 3G **49**
Wycliffe. *Dur* 3E **105**
Wycombe Marsh. *Buck* 2G **37**
Wyddial. *Herts* 2D **52**
Wye. *Kent* 1E **29**
Wyesham. *Mon* 4A **48**
Wyfold Grange. *Oxon* 3E **37**
Wyfordby. *Leics* 4E **75**
Wyke. *Devn* 3B **12**
Wyke. *Dors* 4C **22**
Wyke. *Shrp* 5A **72**
Wyke. *Surr* 5A **38**
Wyke. *W Yor* 2B **92**
Wyke Champflower. *Som* 3B **22**
Wykeham. *Linc* 3B **76**
Wykeham. *N Yor* 2C **100**
(nr. Malton)
Wykeham. *N Yor* 1D **100**
(nr. Scarborough)
Wyken. *Shrp* 1B **60**
Wyken. *W Mid* 2A **62**
Wyke Regis. *Dors* 5B **14**
Wyke, The. *Shrp* 5B **72**
Wykey. *Shrp* 3F **71**
Wykin. *Leics* 1B **62**
Wylam. *Nmbd* 3E **115**
Wylde Green. *W Mid* 1F **61**
Wylye. *Wilts* 3F **23**
Wymering. *Port* 2E **17**
Wymeswold. *Leics* 3D **74**
Wymington. *Bed* 4G **63**
Wymondham. *Leics* 4F **75**
Wymondham. *Norf* 5D **78**
Wyndham. *B'end* 2C **32**
Wynford Eagle. *Dors* 3A **14**
Wynyard Village. *Stoc T* 2B **106**
Wyre Piddle. *Worc* 1E **49**
Wysall. *Notts* 3D **74**
Wyson. *Here* 4H **59**
Wythall. *Worc* 3E **61**
Wytham. *Oxon* 5C **50**
Wythenshawe. *G Man* 2C **84**
Wythop Mill. *Cumb* 2C **102**
Wyton. *Cambs* 3B **64**
Wyton. *E Yor* 1E **95**
Wyverstone. *Suff* 4C **66**
Wyverstone Street. *Suff* 4C **66**
Wyville. *Linc* 3F **75**
Wyvis Lodge. *High* 1G **157**

Y

Yaddlethorpe. *N Lin* 4B **94**
Yafford. *IOW* 4C **16**
Yafforth. *N Yor* 5A **106**
Yalding. *Kent* 5A **40**
Yanley. *N Som* 5A **34**
Yanwath. *Cumb* 2G **103**
Yanworth. *Glos* 4F **49**
Yapham. *E Yor* 4B **100**
Yapton. *W Sus* 5A **26**
Yarburgh. *Linc* 1C **88**
Yarcombe. *Devn* 2F **13**
Yarde. *Som* 3D **20**
Yardley. *W Mid* 2F **61**
Yardley Gobion. *Nptn* 1F **51**
Yardley Hastings.
Nptn 5F **63**
Yardley Wood. *W Mid* 2F **61**
Yardro. *Powy* 5E **58**
Yarhampton. *Worc* 4B **60**
Yarkhill. *Here* 1B **48**
Yarlet. *Staf* 3D **72**
Yarley. *Som* 2A **22**
Yarlington. *Som* 4B **22**
Yarm. *Stoc T* 3B **106**
Yarmouth. *IOW* 4B **16**
Yarnbrook. *Wilts* 1D **22**
Yarnfield. *Staf* 2C **72**
Yarnscombe. *Devn* 4F **19**
Yarnton. *Oxon* 4C **50**
Yarpole. *Here* 4G **59**
Yarrow. *Nmbd* 1A **114**
Yarrow. *Bord* 2F **119**
Yarrow. *Som* 2G **21**
Yarrow Feus. *Bord* 2F **119**
Yarrow Ford. *Bord* 1G **119**
Yarsop. *Here* 1H **47**
Yarwell. *Nptn* 1H **63**
Yate. *S Glo* 3C **34**
Yateley. *Hants* 5G **37**
Yatesbury. *Wilts* 4F **35**
Yattendon. *W Ber* 4D **36**
Yatton. *Here* 4G **59**
(nr. Leominster)
Yatton. *Here* 2B **48**
(nr. Ross-on-Wye)
Yatton. *N Som* 5H **33**
Yatton Keynell. *Wilts* 4D **34**
Yaverland. *IOW* 4E **16**
Yawl. *Devn* 3G **13**
Yaxham. *Norf* 4C **78**
Yaxley. *Cambs* 1A **64**
Yaxley. *Suff* 3D **66**
Yazor. *Here* 1H **47**
Y Bala. *Gwyn* 2B **70**
Y Bont-Faen. *V Glam* 4C **32**
Y Clun. *Neat* 5B **46**
Y Dref. *Gwyn* 2D **69**
Y Drenewydd. *Powy* 1D **58**
Yeading. *G Lon* 2C **38**
Yeadon. *W Yor* 5E **98**
Yealand Conyers. *Lanc* 2E **97**
Yealand Redmayne. *Lanc* 2E **97**
Yealand Storrs. *Lanc* 2D **97**
Yealmpton. *Devn* 3B **8**
Yearby. *Red C* 2D **106**
Yearngill. *Cumb* 5C **112**
Yearsett. *Here* 5B **60**
Yearsley. *N Yor* 2H **99**
Yeaton. *Shrp* 4G **71**
Yeaveley. *Derbs* 1F **73**
Yeavering. *Nmbd* 1D **120**
Yedingham. *N Yor* 2C **100**
Yeldersley Hollies.
Derbs 1G **73**
Yelford. *Oxon* 5B **50**
Yelland. *Devn* 3E **19**
Yelling. *Cambs* 4B **64**
Yelsted. *Kent* 4C **40**
Yelvertoft. *Nptn* 3C **62**
Yelverton. *Devn* 2B **8**
Yelverton. *Norf* 5E **79**
Yenston. *Som* 4C **22**
Yeoford. *Devn* 3A **12**
Yeolmbridge. *Corn* 4D **10**
Yeo Mill. *Devn* 4B **20**
Yeovil. *Som* 1A **14**
Yeovil Marsh. *Som* 1A **14**
Yeovilton. *Som* 4A **22**
Yerbeston. *Pemb* 4E **43**
Yetlington. *Nmbd* 4E **121**
Yetminster. *Dors* 1A **14**
Yett. *N Lan* 4A **128**
Yett. *S Ayr* 2D **116**
Yettington. *Devn* 4D **12**
Yetts o' Muckhart. *Clac* 3C **136**
Y Fali. *IOA* 3B **80**
Y Felinheli. *Gwyn* 4E **81**
Y Fenni. *Mon* 4G **47**
Y Ferwig. *Cdgn* 1B **44**
Y Fflint. *Flin* 3E **83**
Y Ffor. *Gwyn* 2C **68**
Y Fron. *Gwyn* 5E **81**
Y Gelli Gandryll. *Powy* 1F **47**
Yielden. *Bed* 4H **63**
Yieldshields. *S Lan* 4B **128**
Yiewsley. *G Lon* 2B **38**
Yinstay. *Orkn* 6E **172**
Ynysboeth. *Rhon* 2D **32**
Ynysddu. *Cphy* 2E **33**
Ynysforgan. *Swan* 3F **31**
Ynyshir. *Rhon* 2D **32**
Ynyslas. *Cdgn* 1F **57**
Ynysmaerdy. *Rhon* 3D **32**
Ynysmeudwy. *Neat* 5H **45**
Ynystawe. *Swan* 5G **45**
Ynyswen. *Powy* 4B **46**
Ynys-wen. *Rhon* 2C **32**
Ynys y Barri. *V Glam* 5E **32**
Ynysybwl. *Rhon* 2D **32**
Ynysymaerdy. *Neat* 3G **31**
Yockenthwaite.
N Yor 2B **98**
Yockleton. *Shrp* 4G **71**
Yokefleet. *E Yor* 2B **94**
Yoker. *Glas* 3G **127**
Yonder Bognie. *Abers* 4C **160**
Yonderton. *Abers* 5G **161**
York. *York* 4A **100**
Yorkletts. *Kent* 4E **41**
Yorkley. *Glos* 5B **48**
Yorkshire Dales. *N Yor* 2H **97**
Yorton. *Shrp* 3H **71**
Yorton Heath. *Shrp* 3H **71**
Youlgreave. *Derbs* 4G **85**
Youlthorpe. *E Yor* 4B **100**
Youlton. *N Yor* 3G **99**
Young's End. *Essx* 4H **53**
Young Wood. *Linc* 3A **88**
Yoxall. *Staf* 4F **73**
Yoxford. *Suff* 4F **67**
Yr Hob. *Flin* 5F **83**
Y Rhws. *V Glam* 5D **32**
Yr Wyddgrug. *Flin* 4E **83**
Ysbyty Cynfyn. *Cdgn* 3G **57**
Ysbyty Ifan. *Cnwy* 1H **69**
Ysbyty Ystwyth. *Cdgn* 3G **57**
Ysceifiog. *Flin* 3D **82**
Yspitty. *Carm* 3E **31**
Ystalyfera. *Neat* 5A **46**
Ystrad. *Rhon* 2C **32**
Ystrad Aeron. *Cdgn* 5E **57**
Ystradfellte. *Powy* 4C **46**
Ystradffin. *Carm* 1A **46**
Ystradgynlais. *Powy* 4A **46**
Ystradmeurig. *Cdgn* 4G **57**
Ystrad Mynach.
Cphy 2E **33**
Ystradowen. *Carm* 4A **46**
Ystradowen. *V Glam* 4D **32**
Ystumtuen. *Cdgn* 3G **57**
Ythanbank. *Abers* 5G **161**
Ythanwells. *Abers* 5D **160**
Y Trallwng. *Powy* 5E **70**
Y Tymbl. *Carm* 4F **45**
Y Waun. *Wrex* 2E **71**

Z

Zeal Monachorum. *Devn* 2H **11**
Zeals. *Wilts* 3C **22**
Zelah. *Corn* 3C **6**
Zennor. *Corn* 3B **4**
Zouch. *Notts* 3C **74**